AA Lifestyle Guides

Caravan & Camping Europe 2005

This edition published 2005

Maps prepared by the Cartography Department of The Automobile Association from the Automaps database using electronic and computer technology

Typeset by: Keenes, Andover, Hampshire

Printed and bound by Printer Trento srl, Italy

Advertisement Sales: advertisingsales@theAA.com

Editorial: lifestyleguides@theAA.com

A CIP catalogue record for this book is available from the British Library

ISBN 10: 0-7495-4365-5
ISBN 13: 978-0-7495-4365-5

Published by AA Publishing, a trading name of Automobile Association Developments Limited, whose registered office is Southwood East, Apollo Rise, Farnborough, Hampshire GU14 0JW.

Registered number 1878835

A02211

Contents

How To Use this Guide	4
Symbols & Abbreviations	6
Preparing for Your Journey	8
Online Resources	13
Essential Information for Motoring	14
Principal Mountain Passes	37
Major Road & Rail Tunnels	47
Compulsory Equipment	50
Sample Booking Letters	52
Key to Country Regions	53
Directory of Caravan & Camping Sites	
Austria	55
Belgium	70
France	79
Germany	219
Italy	257
Luxembourg	298
Netherlands	302
Portugal	318
Spain	326
Andorra	329
Switzerland	360
Index	375
Country Maps	391
Reader's Report Form	407

How To Use this Guide

Each country in this guide is divided into regions, so that you can easily find all the sites in your chosen holiday area. Within the regions, place names are listed in alphabetical order, and details of site locations can be found on the country maps at the back of this book. If you need overnight stops on the way to your destination, the country maps should help you find something in the right place. Please remember that these maps are for town location purposes only and not for finding your way around. For route planning and use on the road, you should have a road atlas, such as the AA Big Road Atlas of Europe. Individual atlases of France, Germany and Italy are also available in the series.

BOOKING

Despite the carefree nature of a camping or caravanning holiday, it is best to book well in advance for peak holiday seasons, or for your first and last stop close to a ferry crossing point. However, we do find that some sites will not accept reservations. Although the AA cannot undertake to find sites or make reservations for you, we do include in this guide specimen booking letters in English, French, German, Italian and Spanish.

Please note that, although it is not common practice, some campsites may regard your deposit as a booking fee which is not deductible from the final account.

ARRIVAL

Look over the site if possible before you decide to stay. The information for any publication must be collected some time in advance, and ownership and standards may well have changed since our research was done. Even where standards are of the expected quality, the site may be very crowded and you may prefer to look elsewhere for more space and less noise. The descriptions in our guide are very brief, and are compiled from brochures provided by the sites. They are given only as a very loose guide.

The directions given to us by the campsites can also be very brief. If you have any difficulty locating a site, contact them directly for more comprehensive directions.

When you look over a site, consider the following:

- Pleasant general situation, clean and tidy with plenty of refuse bins, site fenced and guarded.
- Sufficient and clean lavatories, washing facilities and showers with hot water.
- Well defined roads on site, preferably lit at night.
- Pitches should not be cramped.
- If you have a tent, make sure the surface is suitable for pegs; if you have a caravan, make sure the ground is firm enough.
- In hot weather there should be suitable shade, and if the weather is damp the ground should appear well drained.
- A good supply of safe drinking water.
- If you need the following facilities, confirm that they exist on the site:
  electric point for razors, Camping Gaz, a well stocked shop, laundry facilities, restaurant serving reasonably priced food, ice for sale.

Although most of the sites in this guide have been selected for the high standards they maintain, we have included, at the request of AA members, a number of sites along touring routes and others near the Channel ports which are suitable for overnight stops. These transit sites tend to become crowded at the height of the season, but provide the necessary amenities.

If you require information on additional sites, lists are free from most national tourist offices. In the introductions for each country we give details of local organisations which either publish a camping guide or provide more detailed information.

CAMPSITE ENTRIES

In order to update our information we send out questionnaires each year to every campsite. Inevitably a number of the questionnaires are not returned to us in time for publication, and where this is the case the campsite name is printed in italics. Most of the sites listed here take both tents and caravans unless otherwise stated.

PRICES

Prices are given in local currencies and are detailed per night, per adult, car, caravan and tent. Most prices will be in Euros, which will make things a lot simpler for those travelling to more than one country. We do not give charges relating to children, as these vary, but generally a 50 per cent reduction is made for children aged 3-14. To determine the cost of one night, simply add up the prices that apply to your party.

Some campsites do have different ways of structuring their prices. Whatever the variations may be, these should be reflected in the entry. Exceptions are:

pp Campsite charges per person. The charge for the vehicle and caravan/tent is included in the price for each person. For a party of four people, multiply the pp price by four for the total cost per night.

pitch This is the price per pitch, regardless of whether it is a caravan or a tent. Where the word pitch follows the ✝ for adult price, you should multiply the ✝ price by the number of adults in the party, then add the pitch price to that total to obtain the cost per night for your party.

SAMPLE ENTRY

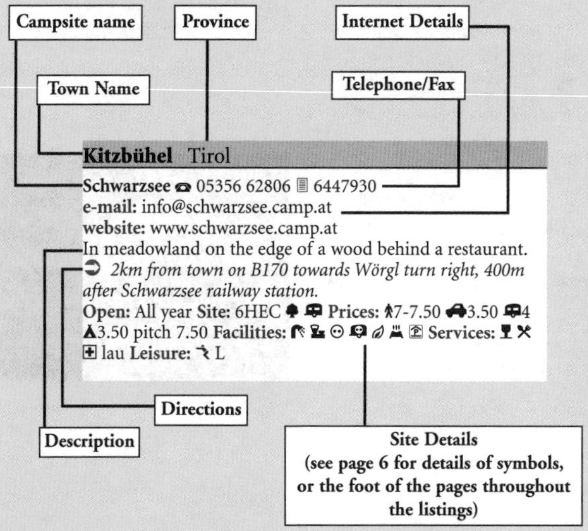
Campsite name
Province
Internet Details
Town Name
Telephone/Fax
Kitzbühel Tirol
Schwarzsee ☎ 05356 62806 6447930
e-mail: info@schwarzsee.camp.at
website: www.schwarzsee.camp.at
In meadowland on the edge of a wood behind a restaurant.
2km from town on B170 towards Wörgl turn right, 400m after Schwarzsee railway station.
Open: All year Site: 6HEC Prices: 7-7.50 3.50 4 3.50 pitch 7.50 Facilities: Services:
lau Leisure: L
Directions
Description
Site Details (see page 6 for details of symbols, or the foot of the pages throughout the listings)

OPENING TIMES

Dates shown are inclusive of opening dates. If the site is open all year, then 'All year' is written in the entry. All information was correct at the time of going to press, but we recommend you check with the site before arriving. Changes in opening times often occur because of demand and/or weather. Sometimes only restricted facilities are available between October and April.

COMPLAINTS

If you have any complaint about a site, do discuss the problem with the site proprietor immediately so that the matter can be dealt with promptly. If a personal approach fails, inform the AA when you return home. We regret, however, that the AA cannot act as intermediary in any dispute, or attempt to gain refunds or compensation. Your comments, however, help us to prepare new editions. Please use the form at the back of the guide.

WEBSITES

We including web addresses for the campsites where available. The AA cannot be held responsible for the content of any of these websites.

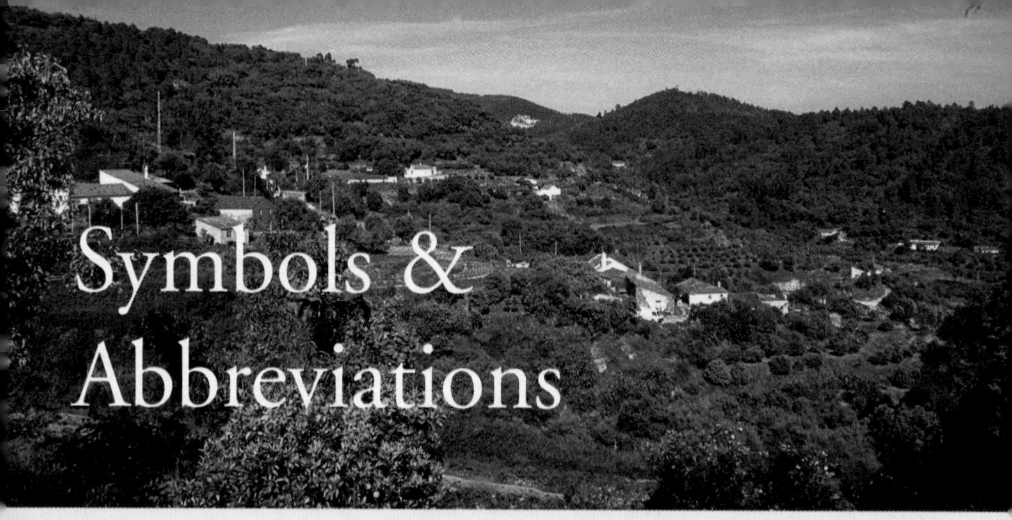

Symbols & Abbreviations

For ease of use, the following symbols and abbreviations can also be found at the foot of each page throughout the campsite directory.

- adult
- car
- pp per person
- caravan or motor caravan
- tent
- telephone
- HEC hectare(s)
- grass
- sand
- stone
- little shade
- partly shaded
- mainly shaded
- shower
- shop
- cafe/restaurant
- bar
- no dogs
- electric points for razors
- electric points for caravans
- Camping Gaz International
- gas other than Camping Gaz
- bungalows for hire
- (static) caravans for hire
- tents for hire
- swimming: L lake P pool R river S sea
- parking by tents permitted
- compulsory separate car park
- first-aid facilities
- site belongs to Castels & Camping Caravanning chain (France only)
- CM camping municipal, parque municipal de campismo, or parque de la camara municipal (local authority site)
- KC Kommunens Campingplads (local authority site)
- lau laundry
- pitch pitch charge per night for car with tent or caravan (there is usually a charge per adult in addition to this)

Off-site: facilities not on site, but within 2km

Entries that have the campsite name in italics indicate that particulars have not been confirmed by management.

Preparing for Your Journey

Please read this section before you set off on your journey, even if you are an experienced traveller, and also read the following section on Essential Motoring Information, and the appropriate country introductions.

Before setting off on your Continental holiday, there are certain preparations you should make and some regulations you should know about. Experienced campers and caravanners will, of course, be familiar with most of this, but we hope it will be a useful chapter for newcomers.

CARAVANS

Your caravan should of course be regularly serviced, but the following tips could be useful, especially for the first trip after winter storage.

Just before your trip give the caravan a good airing. If you have a water pump fitted, check the flow and, after sterilising the system, flush with clean water to get rid of any staleness. Make sure that there are no leaks and replace any doubtful washers. Examine all potential leak spots, especially around window rubbers, rear light clusters and roof lights, applying sealing compound as necessary. Test all window, cupboard and locker catches to make sure that they shut firmly. Outside, clean rain gutters and make sure down-spouts and window channel drainpipes are clear.

Brakes

Check that the caravan braking mechanism is correctly adjusted. If it has a breakaway safety mechanism, the cable between car and caravan must be firmly anchored so that the trailer brakes act immediately if the two part company.

Lights

Make sure that all the lights are working - rear lights, stop lights, number-plate lights, rear fog guard lamps and flashers (check that the flasher rate is correct - 60-120 times a minute).

Tyres

Both tyres on the caravan should be of the same size and type. Make sure that the tread depth is well above the legal minimum (see Tyres, page 27) and that there is no uneven wear. Look also for cuts and for cracks that might have developed during the winter. Replace any suspect tyres and any tyres over five years old, irrespective of the amount of tread remaining. Remember, caravan tyres rarely wear out but do deteriorate with age.

TENTS

Some weeks before your holiday, choose a fine day, spread the tent on the lawn or some other space so that you can make a close inspection of all potential stress points - where guylines attach, where the ground sheet meets tent walls, and where the frame poles come into contact with fabric. The fabric of the tent can be damaged by branches or sharp objects and by mildew if it has not been stored correctly. Additionally, it can lose its proofing through long exposure to the weather, as a result of being splashed by cooking fat or by washing-up water containing detergent. If your tent is damaged in this way, consult a specialist camping supplier. Patch kits of different colours and materials are available, as are proofing preparations and sprays.

Camping Equipment

Use this check list when planning what camping equipment to take:

- Air mattress and pump, or camp beds
- All-purpose knife
- Bucket
- Camp stove and fuel
- Clothes-line and pegs
- Cutlery, including cooking utensils
- Dishcloths, scouring pad, and tea towels
- First-aid kit
- Folding chairs or stools
- Folding table
- Food containers
- Ground sheet
- Icebox (portable)
- Kettle
- Mallet
- Matches
- Plastic bags or bags for litter
- Plates, cups and saucers, or mugs
- Rope
- Saucepans, frying pan
- Sleeping bags
- Small brush (useful when camping on sand)
- Teapot
- Tent, poles, tent pegs (spares), sand pegs and discs
- Tent-tidy (for scissors, string, needles, thread, etc.)
- Tin-opener, bottle-opener, and corkscrew
- Torch and batteries
- Washing powder
- Washing-up bowl and washing-up liquid
- Water and milk containers
- Water-purifying tablets
- Windshield

ROAD HANDLING

Before you load all your luggage and equipment into the caravan, check on the weight restrictions that apply to it and to the towing vehicle. The laden weight of the caravan should always be less than, and ideally no more than 85 per cent of the kerbside weight of the towing vehicle.

The kerbside weight is defined as the weight of the vehicle plus fuel and other necessary liquids (e.g. water, oil, brake fluid, etc.) but with no passengers and no load other than normal tools and equipment.

The weight of the caravan is normally specified in the purchase literature, and usually refers to the weight ex works or mass in running order (MIRO). This can be misleading because it is normally based on the standard model and may not take into account any fitted extras; one way to be certain is to take the caravan to your local public weighbridge. Once you have the accurate unladen weight, subtract that from the manufacturer's recommended gross weight (maximum technically permissable weight - MTPW), and the figure you arrive at will be the amount of equipment you can safely load into the caravan. Remember that, ideally, the gross weight of the caravan should not exceed 85 per cent of the kerbside weight of your car as given in the manufacturer's handbook. If in doubt, return the caravan to the weighbridge once fully loaded.

Loading can greatly affect the stability of the car-caravan combination on the road. Keep as much weight as possible near the trailer axle, and store heavy equipment on the caravan floor. Never store heavy items at the rear of the caravan in an attempt to counterbalance an excessive nose weight - this causes instability and can be very dangerous. Keep the roof lockers free of luggage if possible and ensure lockers, drawers and cupboards are securely closed so there are no loose items that could roll about.

After loading, check that the caravan, when coupled to the car, is level with the ground, or slightly nose down. If the nose is up, this can be corrected by a hitch height adjuster, available from caravan manufacturers or dealers. An adapter plate can be used to lower the tow-ball mounting, but it does put extra pressure on the bracket.

Check that the nose weight of the trailer complies with the car manufacturer's recommendations. As a guide, the nose weight should be heavier than the rear by about 40-50kg (90-119lbs). Check the nose weight of the laden caravan with bathroom scales and blocks of wood or a spring balance. A twin-axle trailer must be weighed when the coupling is at the exact towing height. Obtaining the ideal weight and weight distribution of the car-trailer combination helps prevent pitching and snaking. Pitching can also be prevented by

stiffening the towing car's rear suspension - either fit a supplementary rubber or air spring unit to the rear spring, or use heavier duty shock absorbers, (more expensive) but always ensure first that the car's front and rear shock absorbers are in good condition.

Excessive pitching and/or bad weight distribution can lead to snaking as the vertical movement sways the caravan sideways. This can be particularly dangerous, since the first instinct is to steer against the movement, which only makes matters worse. The best course is to steer straight and gently decelerate. Stabilisers are available, but it is far better to cure the cause.

When choosing a car with which you intend to tow a caravan or trailer, remember that the amount of overhang - the distance between the car's rear axle and the towing ball - has an effect on the handling. The greater the overhang the more difficult handling will be.

Final Checks

- corner steadies are fully wound up and the brace is handy for when you arrive on site;
- windows, vents and doors are firmly shut;
- any fires or flames are extinguished and the tap on the gas cylinder is turned off;
- the coupling is firmly in position and the breakaway cable is attached;
- the over-run brake is working correctly;
- both car mirrors give good visibility;
- all the car and caravan lights are working;
- the safety catch on the hitch is on;
- the jockey wheel is raised and secured, the handbrake is released, and the fire extinguishers are operational and close at hand.

Towing Tips

- Know your car well before attempting to tow.
- Stop before you get tired.
- Plan to use roads suitable for towing.
- Have the appropriate mirrors and use them.
- If traffic builds up behind you, pull up safely and let it pass.
- Keep a safe stopping distance between you and the vehicle in front.
- Switch on your headlights whenever visibility becomes poor.
- Make good use of the gears on hills.
- Allow plenty of time when overtaking or pulling across a main road.
- Never stop on narrow roads, bends, crests of hills, or anywhere that could be dangerous.
- In case of breakdown or accident, use hazard flashers and warning triangle(s).

Off-road Handling

On site you may encounter difficult ground. Try to avoid pitches liable to be waterlogged; sand that will not take the force of a driving wheel; and stone and shingle that provide no grip.

If you have to drive over difficult ground, keep moving slowly with a very light throttle. If you stop, do not accelerate hard or the wheels will spin and dig in. Move gently backwards and forwards to get out of a dip. If the driving wheels do dig in, put brushwood or sacks in front of and behind the wheels. To move the trailer manually, pull sideways on the drawbar and then work the trailer forwards by chocking alternate wheels.

CAMPING FUELS

(This information is intended as a guide only. Full safety regulations and legal information should be obtained from the suppliers or manufacturers of your equipment.)

Gas in cylinders or bottles, as used in caravans, is mainly of two types, butane and propane. Both are kept as liquid under pressure and become a combustible gas once the pressure is released. They are available on the Continent, but propane is more widely distributed in countries with low winter temperatures. Propane has a higher pressure than butane. See also the paragraph on Branded Gases, below.

Carriage of Gas by Car Ferries

Vehicles carrying unsealed cylinders of liquefied petroleum gas (LPG) must report at both United Kingdom and European ports for a leakage test at least 30 minutes before the published reporting time. A maximum of three Home Office approved cylinders, not exceeding 35lb net weight each, or up to 12 small expendable cartridges, sealed and packed in an outer container, are allowed for each caravan. Cylinders should be securely fixed in or on the caravan as intended by the caravan manufacturer.

New users of LPG particularly should follow safety instructions and experienced people sometimes need reminding of the safety rules:

- change cylinders with care
- provide fresh air for safe combustion
- don't improvise or tamper with equipment
- have regular maintenance carried out by qualified engineers

Gas Safety Rules

1 Always use the right type and length of hose for connections If in doubt, ask the dealer's advice.

2 Replace worn hose. Never try repairs.

3 When fitting the hose, where applicable use worm-drive clips and ensure they are tight.

4 Always use a spanner when fitting connections - finger tightness is not enough. Before fitting a regulator or other screwed connection to a butane cylinder, always ensure that the sealing washer is there and in good condition. When fitting to switch-on or clip-on valves, refer to the manufacturer's or supplier's instructions.

5 Check for leaks by applying soapy water. Any leaks will be shown by bubbles.

6 Never check for leaks with a naked flame.

7 Always keep containers away from excessive heat or naked flames.

8 When starting, open container valve slowly.

9 If the container is not to be used for a while close the valve, remove the pressure regulator and replace the valve cover if fitted.

10 When changing a cartridge or container, keep away from any naked light, flame or source of ignition. Ensure good ventilation. With cartridge appliances, check that the sealing washer, usually housed in the appliance inlet connection, is in position and in good condition. Make sure that the valve on the container, where fitted, and the tap on the regulator are fully closed. Never try to change a pierceable cartridge (such as the Camping Gaz type) until you are sure all the gas has been expended. You can usually hear any gas remaining by gently shaking.

11 Once the pressure regulators are set they should not be tampered with. Adjustments or repairs should be left to a dealer.

12 Containers must always stand upright, valves uppermost, whether in use or not. Carry them upright, but not by the valve.

13 Whether full or empty, never store the containers below ground or near drains, as all these gases are heavier than air and will collect at the lowest point in the event of a leak.

14 Good ventilation is essential where gas burning appliances are used. Un-flued appliances must not be installed in sleeping areas. Only room-sealed appliances should be installed in bath or shower rooms.

15 When moving, turn off all appliances and cylinder valves.

16 Do not sleep in a room where gas cylinders are in use.

17 Permanent storage must always be outdoors.

18 When fitting cylinders, always check that the cylinder valve is fully closed in a clockwise direction before removing the valve-sealing cap or plug.

Camping: Single-burner picnic set or double-burner camp stove with 4.5kg butane cylinder

Motor Caravan: Two-burner hotplate or two-burner hotplate grill with 4.5kg butane cylinder

Caravan: Two-burner hotplate or small cooker, with 4.5kg butane cylinder with screw-on connections or 15kg butane cylinder or 7kg butane cylinder which will both accept the switch-on regulator. Take two 4.5kg or two 7kg.

If you follow the instructions a 4.5kg cylinder will last a month on either single or double-burner units.

If you cannot take enough Calor Gas cylinders in your outfit, you are advised to buy a Camping Gaz connecting tap before leaving this country.

Paraffin

Paraffin (petrole or kerosene) is not easily obtainable in country districts in Europe and you are advised to get supplies on arrival in large towns. Methylated spirit (alcoöl à brûler) is easier to get.

Safety

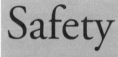

- Always make sure you have the right size and type of gas cartridge for the appliance.
- Never put a cartridge in a cartridge holder unless the upper part of the appliance has been unscrewed and completely removed.
- A cartridge with gas in it must never be removed from an appliance nor must the upper part of the appliance be unscrewed.

Online Resources

This selection of useful websites is provided for information only, the AA cannot be held responsible for their content.

CAMPING WEBSITES

www.calorgas.co.uk
Official site of Calor Gas

www.lpga.co.uk
Offical site of LP Gas, suppliers of Liquid Petroleum Gas

www.caravanclub.co.uk
Britain's major caravan club.

www.gear-zone.co.uk
Major suppliers of camping gear

www.campingeurope.com
The European Federation of Campingsite Organisations (EFCO)

UK GOVERNMENT WEBSITES

www.fco.gov.uk/travel
The Foreign and Commonwealth Office. Travellers' rights, Know Before You Go info.

www.hmce.gov.uk
HM Customs & Excise

www.passport.gov.uk
UK Passport Service

www.defra.gov.uk/animalh/quarantine/index.htm
Pet Travel Site of DEFRA and info on quarantine conditions

EU / EURO WEBSITES

europa.eu.int
The European Union

TOURIST WEBSITES

Austria: www.austria-tourism.at
The Austrian National Tourist Office

Belgium: www.belgium-tourism.net
OPT (Office for the Promotion of Tourism in Walloon + Brussels)

www.visitflanders.com
Toerisme Vlaanderen (Tourism Flanders)

France: www.franceguide.com
The French Government Tourist Board/Maison de la France

Germany: www.germany-tourism.de
The German National Tourist Board

Italy: www.enit.it
The Italian State Tourism Board

Luxembourg: www.luxembourg.co.uk
London's Luxembourg Tourist Office

Netherlands: www.holland.com
The Netherlands Board of Tourism

Portugal: www.portugal.org
and **www.portugalinsite.pt**
Official tourist sites

Spain: www.okspain.org
The Tourist Office of Spain

Andorra: www.turisme.ad
The Ministry of Tourism and Culture

Switzerland: www.myswitzerland.com
Switzerland Tourism

Essential Information for Motoring

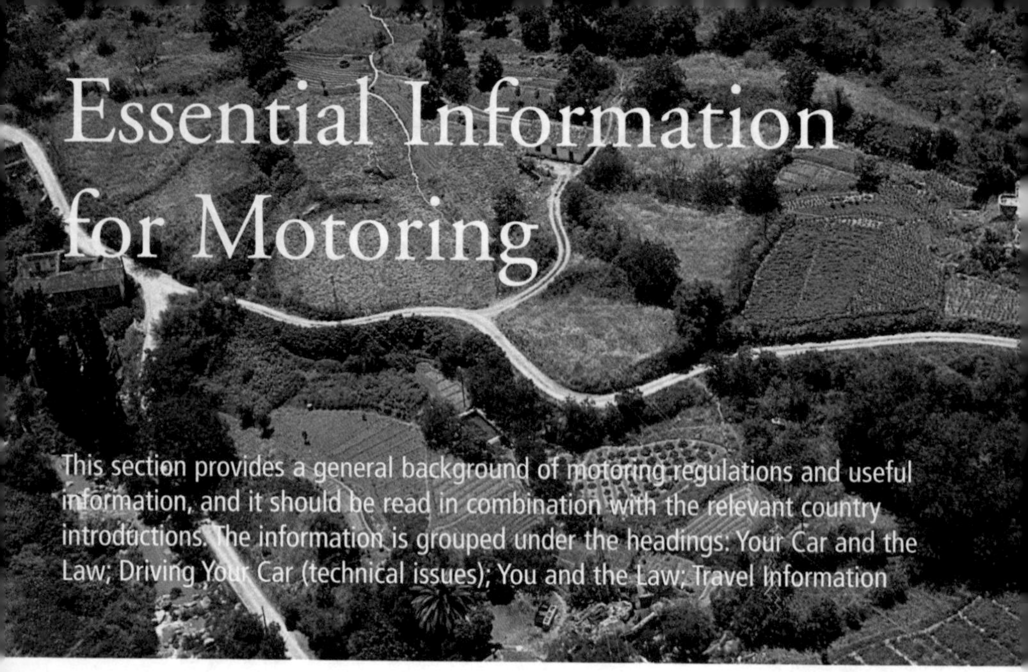

This section provides a general background of motoring regulations and useful information, and it should be read in combination with the relevant country introductions. The information is grouped under the headings: Your Car and the Law; Driving Your Car (technical issues); You and the Law; Travel Information

Motoring laws on the Continent should cause little difficulty to British motorists, but drivers should take more care and extend greater courtesy than they would normally do at home, and bear in mind the essentials of good motoring - avoiding any action likely to obstruct traffic, endanger persons or cause damage to property.

Road signs are mainly the familiar international ones, but in every country there are exceptions; watch especially for signs showing crossings and speed limits. Probably the most unfamiliar aspect of motoring abroad to British motorists is the rule giving priority to traffic coming from the right, and unless this priority is varied by signs, it must be strictly observed.

A tourist driving abroad should always carry a current passport, a full valid national driving licence (even when an International Driving Permit is held), the vehicle registration document and certificate of motor insurance. The proper international distinguishing sign should be displayed on the rear of the vehicle and any caravan or trailer. (See also International Distinguishing Sign, page 18.) The appropriate papers must be carried at all times. The practice of spot checks on foreign cars is widespread; to avoid a police fine and/or confiscation of your vehicle, be sure that your papers are in order and readily available for inspection.

Make sure that you have clear all-round vision. See that your seat belts are securely mounted and undamaged, and remember that in most Continental countries their use is compulsory. If you carry skis remember that their tips should point to the rear. You must be sure that your vehicle complies with the regulations concerning dimensions for all the countries you intend to pass through (see below and relevant country introductions). This is particularly necessary if you are towing a trailer of any sort.

Mechanical repairs and replacement parts can be very expensive abroad and many breakdowns occur because the vehicle has not been properly prepared before the journey, which may involve many miles of hard driving over unfamiliar roads.

We recommend a major service for your vehicle before you go abroad - to find your local AA Service Centre call 0845 609 1641. You should also carry out your own general check for any audible or visible defects.

Also consult your manufacturer's handbook.

AA members can arrange a thorough check of their car by one of the AA's experienced engineers who will submit a written report, complete with a list of repairs required. There is a fee for this service. For more information or, if you wish to book an inspection, please call 0845 750 0610.

Your Car and the Law

ACCIDENTS

The country introductions give telephone numbers for the fire, police and ambulance services. International regulations are similar to those in the UK; the following action is usually required or advisable:

If you are involved in an accident you must stop. A warning triangle should be placed on the road at a suitable distance to warn following traffic of the obstruction. The use of hazard warning lights in no way affects the regulations governing the use of warning triangles. Get medical assistance for anyone injured in the accident. If the accident necessitates calling the police, leave the vehicle in the position in which it came to rest. If it seriously obstructs other traffic, mark the position of the vehicle on the road and get the details confirmed by independent witnesses before moving it.

The accident must be reported to the police in the following circumstances: if it is required by law; if the accident has caused death or bodily injury; or if an unoccupied vehicle or property has been damaged and there is no one present to represent the interests of the party suffering damage.

Be sure to notify your insurance company (by letter if possible), within 24 hours of the accident (see the conditions of your policy). If a third party is injured, contact your insurers for advice or, if you have a Green Card, notify the company or bureau given on the back of your Green Card; this company or bureau will deal with any compensation claim from the injured party. AA policy holders should refer to the AA Policy Holders Driving Abroad statement. Make sure that all essential particulars are noted, especially details concerning third parties, and co-operate with police or other officials taking on-the-spot notes by supplying your name, address or other personal details as required. It is also a good idea to take photographs of the scene. Try to get good shots of other vehicles involved, their registration plates and any background which might help later enquiries. This record may be useful when completing the insurance company's accident form.

CLAIMS AGAINST THIRD PARTIES

The law and levels of damages in foreign countries are different to our own. Some types of claim present difficulties, the most common relating to recovery of car hire charges. Rarely are they fully recoverable, and in some countries they may be drastically reduced or not recoverable at all. General damages for pain and suffering will often be considerably less than awards made in the UK.

BREAKDOWN

If your car breaks down, try to move it to the side of the road, or to a position where it will obstruct the traffic flow as little as possible. Place a warning triangle at the appropriate distance on the road behind the obstruction. Bear in mind road conditions and, if near or on a bend, the triangle should be placed where it is clearly visible to following traffic. If the car is fitted with hazard warning lights these may only be effective on straight roads, and will have no effect at bends or rises in the road. If the fault is electrical, the lights may not operate, which is why they cannot take the place of a triangle.

Motorists are advised to take out AA European Breakdown Cover, the overseas motoring emergency service. You can purchase breakdown assistance cover and travel insurance from the AA. It is available to all motorists, but AA members receive 10% off standard non-member prices for breakdown assistance.

For further information and/or brochures call 0800 444500 (Republic of Ireland 01 617 9988).

The negotiation of claims against foreign insurers is extremely protracted and translation of documents slows the process. A delay of three months between sending a letter and getting a reply is not uncommon.

DRIVING LICENCE & INTERNATIONAL DRIVING PERMIT

You should always carry your national driving licence with you even when you hold an International Driving Permit (IDP). A driving licence issued in the UK or Republic of Ireland is generally acceptable, subject to the minimum age requirements of the country concerned, but see also the individual country introductions for Italy and Spain, under Driving Licence, if you hold a UK licence.

If you wish to drive a hired or borrowed car in the country you are visiting, make local enquiries. If your licence is due to expire before your return, renew it in good time prior to your departure. The Driver and Vehicle Licensing Agency (DVLA) will accept an application two months before the expiry of your old licence; Driver and Vehicle Licensing Northern Ireland (DVLNI) will accept an application for renewal two months before expiry of your old licence, but also offer "Optional Renewal", unique to Northern Ireland. Under this option the holder of a valid licence may apply for renewal at any stage during its validity; in the Republic of Ireland, one month before expiry.

The IDP, for which a statutory charge is made, is issued by the AA to an applicant who holds a valid full British driving licence and who is over 18. Call the AA on 0870 5500 600 for advice or to get an application form.

VEHICLE LICENCE

When taking a vehicle out of the UK for a temporary visit, remember that the vehicle licence (tax disc) needs to be valid throughout your journey and on your return*. If it expires while you are abroad, you can apply for a new one up to 42 days in advance of the expiry date on your present disc. Apply in writing to either a Post Office™ branch that deals with postal applications or to a DVLA Local Office. You should explain why you want the disk in advance, and ask for it to be posted to you before you leave, or to your address abroad. Your V10 application form must always be completed with your UK address, and due to new licensing rules you must enclose your registration document or certificate.

To find out which Post Office™ branch in your area offers this service, you should contact Post Office™ Customer Services Unit listed in your local telephone directory.

Residents of Northern Ireland must apply to Driver and Vehicle Licensing Northern Ireland, Vehicle Licensing Division, County Hall, Castlerock Road, Coleraine BT51 3TA. Residents of the Republic of Ireland should contact their Local Motor Tax Office.

**Agreement within the EU provides for the temporary use of foreign-registered vehicles within the member states. A vehicle which is properly registered and taxed in its home country should not be subject to the domestic taxation and registration laws of the host country during a temporary stay.*

REGISTRATION DOCUMENT OR CERTIFICATE

You must take the registration document/certificate with you. It should be in your name and kept with you. If you do not have one, apply to a DVLA Local Office (in Republic of Ireland, Motor Tax) for a temporary certificate of registration (V379) to cover the period away. The address of your nearest DVLA Local Office is in the local telephone directory or in leaflet V100, available from Post Office™ branches. You should apply well in advance of your journey, as it may take up to two weeks to issue the document if you are not already recorded as the vehicle keeper. Proof of identity (e.g. driving licence) and proof of ownership (e.g. bill of sale), should be produced for the DVLA Local Office.

In Northern Ireland contact Vehicle Licensing Division, County Hall, Castlerock Road, Coleraine BT51 3TA.
Tel 028 7034 1461 for further information.

If you plan to use a borrowed vehicle, the registration document/certificate must be accompanied by a letter of authority to use the vehicle from the registered keeper. If you plan to use a hired or leased vehicle, the registration document/certificate will not normally be available and you will need a Vehicle on Hire Certificate (VE103A). Generally the hiring/leasing operator or company transport manager will provide the certificate, but individual users may apply direct if necessary. For advice on the procedure to follow for personal or postal applications or for an application form, call the AA Information Centre on 0870 5500 600.

MOTOR INSURANCE

When driving abroad you must carry your certificate of motor insurance with you at all times. Third-party is the minimum legal requirement in most countries. Therefore, before taking a motor vehicle, caravan or trailer abroad, contact your motor insurer or broker to notify them of your intentions and ask their advice. Some insurers will extend your UK or Republic of Ireland motor policy to apply in the countries you plan to visit free of charge, others may charge an additional premium. It is most important to know the level of cover you will actually have and what documents you will need to prove it.

Of the countries covered by this guide, a Green Card is compulsory in Andorra. This document is issued by your motor insurer and provides instantly recognisable proof of insurance. The Green Card must be signed on receipt as it will not be accepted without the signature of the insured.

Motorists can obtain advice through AA Insurance Services for all types of insurance, including caravan. More information is available by contacting us on 0800 444 777 for a quotation; existing customers should contact 0870 533 6600, or visit our website **www.theAA.com.**

Finally, do check to make sure that you are covered against damage in transit (e.g. on the ferry) when the vehicle is not being driven.

CARAVAN & LUGGAGE TRAILERS

Take a list of contents, especially if any valuable or unusual equipment is being carried, as this may be required at a frontier. A towed vehicle should be readily identifiable by a plate in an accessible position showing the name of the maker of the vehicle and the production or serial number. (See Identification Plate, page 18, and also Principal Mountain Passes, page 37.)

CYCLE CARRIERS

If you intend taking your bicycles on a rear-mounted cycle rack, make sure that they do not obstruct rear lights and/or number plate, or you risk an on-the-spot fine. The AA recommends roof-mounted racks.

COMPULSORY EQUIPMENT

All countries have differing regulations as to how vehicles circulating on their roads should be equipped, but generally domestic laws are not enforced on visiting foreigners. However, where a country considers aspects of safety or other factors are involved, they will impose some regulations on visitors and these will be mentioned in the country introductions.

SAFETY HELMETS

All countries in this guide require visiting motorcyclists and their passengers to wear crash or safety helmets.

DIMENSIONS & WEIGHT RESTRICTIONS

For an ordinary private car, a height limit of 4 metres and a width limit of 2.50 metres are generally imposed. However, see country introductions for full details. Apart from a laden-weight limit imposed on commercial vehicles, every vehicle has an individual weight limit. (See Overloading, page 20, and also Major Road and Rail Tunnels, page 47, as some dimensions are restricted by the shape of the tunnels.)

DRINKING & DRIVING

There is only one safe rule: if you drink, don't drive. Laws are strict and the penalties severe.

HORN

In built-up areas, the general rule is that you should not use it unless safety demands it. In many large towns and resorts, and in areas indicated by the international sign (a horn inside a red circle, crossed through) use of the horn is totally banned.

IDENTIFICATION PLATE

If a boat trailer, caravan or trailer is taken abroad, it must have a unique chassis number for identification purposes. If yours does not have a number, you can buy an identification plate from the AA. Boats registered on the Small Ships Register have a unique number which must be permanently displayed on the boat (see Boats, page 31).

INTERNATIONAL DISTINGUISHING SIGN

An international distinguishing sign of the approved pattern, and size (oval with black letters on a white background; GB at least 6.9in by 4.5in), must be displayed on a vertical surface at the rear of your vehicle (and caravan or trailer if you are towing one). These signs indicate the country of registration of the vehicle. On the Continent, fines are imposed for failing to display a distinguishing sign, or for not displaying the correct distinguishing sign. (See also Police Fines, page 21.)

UK registration plates displaying the GB Euro-symbol (Euro Plates) became a legal option in March 2001, but must comply with the British standard (BS AU 145d). These plates make display of a conventional sticker unnecessary when circulating within the EU. The Euro-Plate is only legally recognised in the EU; it is still a requirement to display a GB sticker when travelling outside the EU.

A GB sign, or an AA Motoring Abroad Kit which includes one, may be purchased from the AA's Dover shop (Eastern Docks Terminal) or, if travelling via Eurotunnel, the AA's Folkestone shop (Eurotunnel Passenger Terminal).

MINIBUS

A minibus constructed and equipped to carry 10 or more persons (including the driver) and used outside the UK is subject to the regulations governing international bus and coach journeys, including controls on drivers' hours. Such vehicles must weigh no more than 3.5 tonnes (gross vehicle weight) or 4.25 tonnes including any specialist equipment for the carriage of disabled passengers. The vehicle must be fitted with a tachograph (except for journeys between UK and Republic of Ireland) and carry documentation

to show the type of journey being made. The documentation requirements are determined by whether the vehicle is owned or hired and countries to be visited, as follows:

a) **Outside EU** - hired minibus on an occasional service (EU documentation accepted in Norway and Switzerland, as well as the 25 Member States). An Interbus Waybill is required in Bulgaria and Romania. An ASOR Waybill is required in Belarus, Bosnia, Croatia, Moldova and Turkey. Operations of any other type, or to any other country, will require specific authorisation. Contact:

   The Dept for Transport,
   International Road Freight Office,
   Eastern Traffic Area,
   76 Marsham Street,
   1st Floor City House,
   126-130 Hills Road,
   Cambridge CB2 1NP
   Tel 01223 531030

b) **Inside EU** - own account certificate (owned vehicle); (new type) EU passenger waybills (hired vehicle).

For vehicles registered in and driven by holders of licences issued in UK (England, Scotland, Wales and Northern Ireland), contact:

a) Confederation of Passenger Transport

   UK, Imperial House,
   15-19 Kingsway,
   London WC2B 6UN
   Tel 020 7240 3131 for model control document and waybills.

b) Department for Transport, International Road Freight Office,
   Eastern Traffic Area,
   126-130 Hills Road,
   Cambridge CB2 1NP
   Tel 01223 531030 for own account certificate.

A person of 21 years or over and holding a car driving licence with D1 restricted entitlement (i.e. not for hire or reward) may drive a 17 seat (including the driver) minibus abroad, providing that it is not a hire or reward operation. See Section 1 (5) of the Public Passenger Vehicles Act 1981 for a definition of 'hire or reward'. As a result of subsequent court rulings, that definition has been further refined to encompass situations in which there is payment:

- of cash or kind
- whether paid directly or indirectly
- whether paid by the passenger or someone else on their behalf
- even when paid in the course of an arrangement which is a business activity or an activity which has a 'business-like' nature (i.e. is rather more than a 'one-off' social arrangement).

The effect of this is that most trips abroad by school or scout troops or similar organisations, running a minibus, could very likely be classed by the courts as 'hire or reward' operations for which full D1 driving licence entitlement is needed. In general, where an organisation is operating a minibus in the UK under a Section 19 'small bus' permit (as issued by the Traffic Area Offices) then this would almost certainly be regarded by the Courts as 'hire or reward'. Drivers involved in such operations are, therefore, advised to obtain a full D1 licence before taking the minibus abroad. To do this they will need to pass separate driving and theory tests for minibus at their local driving tests centre. Drivers or organisers are also advised in any event to check the position with their insurance company.

For vehicles registered in the Republic of Ireland, contact the Department of Transport, Road Haulage Section, Setanta Centre, South Frederick Street, Dublin 2 for details about tachographs, and the Government Publications Sales Office, Molesworth Street, Dublin 2 for information on documentation.

DISABLED PARKING

A standard blue parking badge for disabled people has been introduced throughout the EU. All EU Member States, with reciprocal arrangements in place, operate the Blue Badge Scheme. Badge holders across the participating EU states can enjoy the same parking concessions provided in the host country by displaying the badge issued under their own national scheme.

To obtain a booklet outlining details of these reciprocal arrangements, call the AA on 0800 262050 or contact Department for Transport, Mobility and Inclusion Unit, 1/18 Great Minster House, 76 Marsham Street, London SW1P 4DR. The information is also available on the DFT website **www.dft.gov.uk.**

However, the concessions do vary from country to country and badge holders should check local notices to ensure that they are parking within the law. As in the UK, these arrangements apply only to badge holders themselves and are not for the

benefit of non-disabled companions. Wrongful display of the badge may incur a penalty.

OVERLOADING

This can create risks, and in most countries the offence can involve on-the-spot fines (see Police Fines, page 21). You would also be made to reduce the load to an acceptable level before being allowed to continue your journey.

The maximum loaded weight, and its distribution between front and rear axles, is decided by the vehicle manufacturer, and if your owner's handbook does not give these facts, contact the manufacturer direct. There is a public weighbridge in all districts, and when the car is fully loaded (including driver and passengers) use this to check that the vehicle is within the limits.

Load your vehicle carefully so that no lights, reflectors, or number plates are masked, and the driver's view is not impaired. All luggage loaded on a roof-rack must be tightly secured, and should not exceed the manufacturer's recommended maximum limit. Any projections beyond the front, rear, or sides of a vehicle, that may not be noticed by other drivers, must be clearly marked. Limits apply to projections and may vary from country to country.

OVERTAKING

When overtaking on roads with two lanes or more in each direction, signal in good time, and also signal your return to the inside lane. Do not remain in any other lane. Failure to comply with this regulation, particularly in France, will incur an on-the-spot fine (immediate deposit in France; see Police fines, page 21). Always overtake on the left and use your horn to warn the driver (except where the use of a horn is banned). Do check the vehicles behind before overtaking. Do not overtake at level crossings, intersections, the crest of a hill or pedestrian crossings. When being overtaken, keep to the right and reduce speed if necessary.

PARKING

Parking is a problem everywhere in Europe, and the police are strict with offenders. Heavy fines are imposed and unaccompanied offending cars can be towed away. Heavy charges are imposed for the recovery of impounded vehicles. Find out about local parking regulations and make sure you understand all related signs. Always park on the right-hand side of the road or at an authorised place. If possible, park off the main carriageway, but not in cycle or bus lanes.

PASSENGERS

In many countries outside the UK, it is an offence to carry more passengers in a vehicle than the vehicle is constructed to seat, and some have regulations as to how the passengers should be seated. For information about regulations applied to visiting foreigners, see country introductions.

Special regulations (see Minibus, page 18) apply to passenger-carrying vehicles constructed and equipped to carry more than 10 passengers, including the driver.

POLICE FINES

Some countries impose on-the-spot fines for minor traffic offences. Others (e.g. France) impose an immediate deposit, and subsequently levy a fine which may be the same as, or greater or lesser than, this sum. Fines are normally paid in cash in the local currency, either to the police or at a Post Office™ branch against a ticket issued by the police. The amount can exceed the equivalent of £1000 for the most serious offences. The reason for the fines is to keep minor motoring offences out of the courts.

Disputing the fine usually leads to a court appearance, delays and expense. If the fine is not paid, legal proceedings will usually follow. Some countries immobilise vehicles until a fine is paid, and may sell it to pay the penalty.

Once paid, a fine cannot be recovered, but a receipt should always be obtained as proof of payment.

PRIORITY INCLUDING ROUNDABOUTS

(See also country introductions.) The general rule is to give way to traffic entering a junction from the right, but this is sometimes varied at roundabouts (see below). Road signs indicate priority or loss of priority, and tourists must be sure that they understand such signs.

Great care should be taken at intersections, and tourists should never rely on being ceded the right of way, particularly in small towns and villages where local, often slow moving, traffic - farm tractors etc., will assume right of way regardless of oncoming traffic. Always give way to public services and military vehicles, blind and disabled people, funerals and marching columns. Vehicles such as buses and coaches will expect, and should be allowed, priority.

Generally, priority at roundabouts is given to vehicles entering the roundabout unless signposted to the contrary (see France). This is a reversal of the UK and Republic of Ireland rule, and particular care should be exercised when circulating in an anti-clockwise direction on a roundabout. It is advisable to keep to the outside lane if possible, to make your exit easier.

RADIO TELEPHONE/ CITIZEN-BAND RADIOS, TRANSMITTERS & DETECTION DEVICES

Many countries control the temporary importation and use of radio telephones and radio transmitters.

The use or even possession of devices, whether inside or outside vehicles, to detect police radar speed traps is illegal in most countries. Penalties are severe, including confiscation of the equipment, payment of an immediate deposit to serve as collateral against any fine subsequently levied, and/or a driving ban. Finally, if the case is viewed sufficiently seriously, confiscation of vehicle and even imprisonment may result.

ROAD SIGNS

Most road signs throughout Europe conform to international standards and most will be familiar. Watch for road markings - do not cross a solid white or yellow line marked on the road centre. In Belgium there are three official languages, and signs will be in Dutch, French or German, see Belgian country information under Roads for further information. In the Basque and Catalonian areas of Spain local and national place names appear on signposts, see the country introduction for Spain for further information.

RULE OF THE ROAD

In all countries in this guide, drive on the right and overtake on the left.

SEAT BELTS

All countries in this guide require wearing of seat belts.

SPEED LIMITS

It is important to observe speed limits at all times. Remember that it can be an offence to travel so slowly as to obstruct traffic flow without good reason. Offenders may be fined, and driving licences confiscated on the spot, causing great inconvenience and possible expense.

The standard legal limits are given in the appropriate country introductions for private cars, for motor cycles and for car-caravan-trailer combinations, but these may be varied by road signs, and where such signs are displayed the lower limit applies. At certain times, limits may also be temporarily varied, so watch out for the appropriate signs.

TRAFFIC LIGHTS

In principal cities and towns, traffic lights operate in a way similar to those in the United Kingdom, although they are sometimes suspended over the roadway. The density of the light may be so poor that lights could be missed - especially those overhead. There is usually only one set on the right-hand side of the road some distance before the road junction, and if you stop too close to the corner the lights will not be visible. Look out for filter lights enabling you to turn right at a junction against the main lights. If you wish to go straight ahead, do not enter a lane leading to filter lights or you may obstruct traffic trying to turn right.

TRAMS

Trams take priority over other vehicles. Always give way to passengers boarding and alighting. Never position a vehicle so that it impedes the free passage of a tram. Trams must be overtaken on the right, except in one-way streets.

AUTOMATIC GEARBOXES

The fluid in an automatic gearbox does more work when it has to cope with the extra weight of a caravan. It becomes hotter and thinner, so there is more slip and more heat generated in the gearbox. Many manufacturers recommend the fitting of a gearbox oil cooler. Check with the manufacturer about what is suitable for your car.

AUTOMATIC TRANSMISSION FLUID

Automatic transmission fluid is not always readily available, especially in some of the more remote areas of Western Europe, so carry an emergency supply.

BRAKES

Car brakes must always be in peak condition. Check both the level in the brake fluid reservoir and the thickness of the brake lining/pad material. The brake fluid should be completely changed according to the manufacturer's instructions. It is always advisable to change the brake fluid before starting a Continental holiday, particularly if the journey includes travelling through a hilly or mountainous area.

COLD-WEATHER TOURING

If you are planning a winter tour, make sure that the strength of the antifreeze in your coolant is correct for low temperatures.

If travelling through snow-bound regions, it is important to remember that for many resorts and passes the authorities insist on wheel chains and/or winter tyres. However, chains should only be used when compulsory or necessary, prolonged use on hard surfaces may damage both the vehicle and the chains.

In fair weather, wheel chains are only necessary on the higher passes, but (as a rough guide) in severe weather you will probably need them at altitudes exceeding 610 metres (2000ft). Signposts usually indicate if wheelchains are compulsory.

Wheel or snow chains fit over the driving wheels to enable them to grip on snow or icy surfaces. Full-length chains which fit tightly round a tyre are the most satisfactory, but they must be fitted correctly. Check that they do not foul your vehicle bodywork; if your vehicle has front-wheel drive put the steering on full lock while checking. It is essential that you also check the vehicle's handbook for the manufacturer's recommendations. On some vehicles there is insufficient clearance between the tyre and bodywork and wheel chains cannot be used. Wheel or snow chains may be purchased from the AA's Dover and Eurotunnel shops. To check that the required size of chain is in stock, telephone Dover on 01304 208122 or Eurotunnel on 01303 273576. Winter or snow tyres are tyres with rugged treads which provide extra grip on snow and ice. Some are designed to take spikes or studs which require specialist fitting and removal limiting their use. In practice, although regulations exist, spikes or studs are seldom used in countries such as Austria and Switzerland. A vehicle equipped with winter tyres without spikes or studs may be used in all conditions. However, the use of winter tyres does not remove the need to carry chains; such tyres are generally more effective, reducing the need to fit chains. If you travel regularly to Alpine regions it may be worth considering a set of winter tyres. Contact your local tyre dealer for more information.

Note. *The above guidelines do not apply for extreme winter conditions. For extreme conditions the cost of preparing a car normally used in the UK may not be justified for a short period.*

WARM-CLIMATE TOURING

In hot weather and at high altitude, excessive heat in the engine compartment can cause problems. If towing a caravan, consult the manufacturers of your vehicle about the limitations of the cooling system, and the operating temperature of the gearbox fluid for automatics (see Automatic Gearboxes, page 23).

DIRECTION INDICATORS

All direction indicators should be working at between 60 and 120 flashes per minute. Most standard car-flasher units will be overloaded by the extra lamps of a caravan or trailer, and a special heavy duty unit or relay device should be fitted.

ENGINE & MECHANICAL SERVICING

Consult your vehicle handbook for servicing intervals. Unless the engine oil has been changed recently, drain and refill it with fresh oil and fit a new filter. Deal with any leaks.

Brands and grades of engine oil familiar to the British motorist are usually available in Western Europe, but may be difficult to find in remote country areas. When available, they will be much more expensive than in the UK and are generally packed in 2-litre cans (3.5 pints). Motorists are strongly advised to carry a sufficient supply of oil, especially for modern makes of car that require special oils.

If you suspect that there is anything wrong with the engine - even if it seems insignificant - it should be dealt with immediately. And do not neglect such common-sense precautions as checking all drive belts and under bonnet levels. Any obvious mechanical defects should be attended to at once. It is essential that all filters (fuel and air) should be cleaned or renewed.

The cooling system should be checked for leaks and the proportion of anti-freeze, and any perished hoses or suspect parts replaced.

Owners should seriously reconsider towing a caravan with a car that has already given appreciable service. Hard driving on motorways and in mountainous country puts an extra strain on ageing parts, and items such as a burnt-out clutch can be very expensive.

FIRE EXTINGUISHER

It is a wise precaution to take a fire extinguisher when motoring abroad. AA fire extinguishers may be purchased from the AA's Dover Shop (Eastern Docks Terminal) or, if travelling via Eurotunnel, the AA's Folkestone shop (Eurotunnel Passenger Terminal).

FIRST-AID KIT

It is a wise precaution (compulsory in Austria) to carry a first-aid kit when motoring abroad. An AA First-Aid Kit or an AA Motoring Abroad Kit, which includes a first-aid kit, can be purchased from the AA's Dover Shop (Eastern Docks Terminal) or, if travelling via Eurotunnel, the AA's Folkestone shop (Eurotunnel Passenger Terminal; see also Motoring Abroad Kit, page 25).

LIGHTS

(See also country introductions.) For driving abroad headlights should be adjusted so that the dipped beam does not dazzle oncoming drivers. For older vehicles this can be done using simple adhesive masks on the headlamp glass, but for newer vehicles with high intensity discharge (HID), xenon or many halogen headlamps things aren't so simple. Check out what you can do well before your intended departure by contacting your dealer.

Dipped headlights should also be used in fog, snowfall, heavy rain and in a tunnel, irrespective of its length and lighting. Police may wait at the end of a tunnel to check. Headlight flashing is used only to signal approach or as an overtaking signal at night. In other circumstances, it is taken as a sign of irritation, and may lead to misunderstandings.

Of the countries covered by the guide it is recommended (compulsory in Andorra and Spain) to carry a spare bulb kit. This will not avoid a fine if you are travelling with faulty lights, but being able to replace a bulb

on the spot may avoid the cost and inconvenience of a garage call-out. On some cars it is inadvisable or indeed impossible for anyone other than a qualified technician to change a headlamp bulb or lamp unit (eg. High intensity discharge (HID) lamps), and carrying spare bulbs is not an option. However, it is recommended that spare bulbs are carried for any lights which may be easily and/or safely replaced.

AA Headlamp Beam Converters and/or AA Bulb Kits or an AA Motoring Abroad Kit, which includes converters and bulbs, may be purchased from the AA's Dover shop (Eastern Docks Terminal) or, if travelling via Eurotunnel, the AA's Folkestone shop (Eurotunnel Passenger Terminal; see also Motoring Abroad Kit, this page).

LUGGAGE OR ROOF RACKS

Only use equipment suitable for your vehicle, i.e., approved by the vehicle manufacturer. Distribute the load evenly, taking care not to exceed the vehicle manufacturer's roof rack load limit. A roof rack laden with luggage increases fuel consumption, so remember this when calculating mileage per gallon, and it also reduces stability, especially when cornering.

MIRRORS

When driving or towing on the right, it is essential to have clear all-round vision. Ideally, external rear-view mirrors should be fitted to both sides of your vehicle, but certainly on the left, to allow for driving on the right.

When towing a caravan it is essential to fit mirror accessories for better rear vision. These include clip-on extensions, arms to extend wing mirrors, and long-arm wing or door mirrors. The longer the mirror arm, the more rigid its mounting has to be. Some have supporting legs or extra brackets to minimise vibration. A mirror mounted on the door pillar gives a wide field of vision because it is close to the driver, but it is at a greater angle to the forward line of sight. Convex mirrors give an even wider field of vision, but practice is needed in judging distance due to the diminished image.

MOTORING ABROAD KIT

An AA Motoring Abroad Kit has all the essential motoring accessories you require for the countries covered by this guide. Available from the AA's Dover shop (Eastern Docks Terminal) or, if travelling via Eurotunnel, the AA's Folkestone shop (Eurotunnel Passenger Terminal); the kit comprises a nylon holdall with bulb kit, first-aid kit, GB sticker, headlamp beam converters and warning triangle.

PETROL/DIESEL

You will find familiar brands and comparable grades of petrol along the main routes in most countries. However, remember that leaded petrol is no longer generally available in northern European countries. If a lead-replacement petrol (LRP) is not on sale, an anti-wear additive may be bought from a filling station shop; this should be used in accordance with the instructions if your car requires this protection. The sale of leaded petrol continues in some southern European countries, but not in Italy, Portugal and Spain.

You will normally have to buy a minimum of 5 litres (just over a gallon) but it is wise to keep the tank topped up, particularly in more remote areas. When

calculating mileage per gallon, don't forget that the extra weight of a caravan or roof rack increases petrol consumption. It is best to use a locking filler cap. Some garages may close 12.00-15.00, but petrol is generally available, with 24-hour service on motorways. Prices for petrol on motorways will normally be higher than elsewhere. Make sure you know the fuel requirement of the vehicle before you go (LRP, unleaded premium, unleaded super or diesel) and whether or not the car has an exhaust catalyst. Catalyst-equipped petrol cars will usually have a small fuel filler neck, to prevent the use of the larger sized nozzle dispensing LRP. If in doubt, check with a franchised dealer, or with the AA.

Some countries are supplying 97 octane unleaded petrol either in addition to, or instead of, 95 octane. The name may be 'super plus' or 'premium' but look for the octane rating 97. You should be careful to use the recommended type of fuel, particularly if your car has a catalytic converter, and the octane rating should be the same or higher. If you accidentally fill the tank of a catalyst-equipped car with LRP, it will do no harm; simply go back to normal petrol at the next fill. If your car requires LRP and you fill with unleaded, avoid hard use of the engine until about half the tank is used, then fill with an additised lead-substitute petrol or dose the fuel with an anti-wear additive.

Diesel fuel is generally known as 'diesel' or 'gas-oil'. Although readily available it is probably more inconvenient to run out of diesel, and it is wise to keep the tank topped up. If petrol is accidentally put into the tank of a diesel car (or vice versa), the action you need to take depends on the age and engine type of the vehicle. Some modern cars have no tolerance to such mis-fuelling and the tank must be drained and refilled with the correct fuel before the engine is started.

Note*. While you may wish to carry a reserve can of fuel, remember that all operators (e.g. ferry, motorail) will either forbid the carriage of fuel in spare cans or insist that spare cans must be empty. In Luxembourg motorists are forbidden to carry petrol in cans in the vehicle. If your vehicle has LPG or a dual fuel system - check. Eurotunnel and underground car parks in France don't allow LPG-fuelled vehicles.*

REFLECTIVE JACKET

Remember to carry a reflective jacket or waistcoat when visiting Italy or Spain (see relevant country introductions). The AA recommends that each vehicle has at least two jackets or waistcoats in the passenger compartment - one for the driver, and one for a paasenger who may need to assist, e.g. when changing a wheel. The jacket or waistcoat must conform to BS EN 471:1994, Class 1 or 2. They are available from the AA Dover and Folkestone shops, by mail order from Summit Accessories (tel 01295 220050), or from motor accessory stores.

SPARES

The spares you should carry depend on the vehicle and how long you are likely to be away. Useful items include a pair of windscreen wiper blades, spare fuses, bulbs (see Lights, page 24) and a torch.

Remember that when ordering spare parts for dispatch abroad, you must be able to identify them clearly - by the manufacturer's part numbers if known. Always quote your engine and vehicle identification (VIN).

TYRES

Inspect your tyres carefully. If you notice uneven wear, scuffed treads, or damaged walls, get expert advice on whether the tyres are suitable for further use.

The regulations in the UK governing tyres requires a minimum tread depth of 1.6mm over the central three-quarters of the tyre around the whole circumference. Most western European countries have similar or stricter requirements. However, the AA strongly advises against using tyres with 2mm or less of tread, ideally changing any tyres worn down to 3mm before you go. Tyres wear out quickly when down to 3mm and wet grip is markedly reduced.

Check the car handbook for recommended tyre pressures. Different tyre pressures will be recommended for a fully loaded car travelling at motorway speeds. Remember pressures can only be checked accurately when the tyres are cold, and don't forget the spare wheel.

If towing a caravan find out the recommended tyre pressures from the caravan manufacturer. These will vary with the type and size of tyre. For winter or snow tyres see Cold-weather Touring, page 23.

TOLLS

Tolls are payable on most motorways in France, Italy, Portugal, Spain and on sections in Austria. Over long distances, the toll charges can be quite considerable. Compare the cost against time and convenience (e.g. overnight stops), particularly as some of the all-purpose roads are often fast.

Always have some local currency ready to pay the tolls, as travellers cheques etc. are not acceptable at toll booths. Credit cards are accepted at toll booths in France and Spain.

In Austria and Switzerland authorities levy a tax for use of motorway netways.

See under Motorway tax in the respective country introduction for further information.

WARNING TRIANGLES & HAZARD WARNING LIGHTS

The use of a warning triangle is compulsory in most Continental countries. It should be placed on the road behind a stopped vehicle to warn traffic approaching from the rear. The triangle should be used when a vehicle has stopped for any reason - not just breakdowns. It should be clearly visible from up to 100m (109yds) by day and night, about 0.6m (2ft) from the edge of the road, but not in such a position as to be a danger to oncoming traffic. It should be set up about 30m (33yds) behind the obstruction, but this distance should be increased to 100m (109yds) on motorways.

A warning triangle is not required for two-wheeled vehicles.

An AA Warning Triangle, or an AA Motoring Abroad Kit, which includes a warning triangle, may be purchased from the AA's Dover shop (Eastern Docks Terminal) or, if travelling via Eurotunnel, the AA's Folkestone shop (Eurotunnel Passenger Terminal; see also Motoring Abroad Kit, page 25).

Although four flashing indicators are allowed in the countries covered by this guide, they do not affect the regulations governing warning triangles. Generally, hazard warning lights should not be used in place of a triangle, although they may complement it. See the country introductions for France, Netherlands and Switzerland. (See also Breakdown, page 14).

You and the Law

CUSTOMS REGULATIONS FOR CONTINENTAL COUNTRIES

Travelling within the EU

People travelling within the EU are free to take not only personal belongings but a motor vehicle, boat, caravan or trailer across the internal frontiers without being subject to Customs formalities. The EU countries are Austria, Belgium, Cyprus, Czech Republic, Denmark, Estonia, Finland, France, Germany, Greece, Hungary, Republic of Ireland, Italy, Latvia, Lithuania, Luxembourg, Malta, the Netherlands, Poland, Portugal, Slovakia, Slovenia, Spain (but not the Canaries), Sweden and the UK (but not the Channel Islands). Gibraltar is part of the EU, but Customs allowances for outside the EU apply.

When you return to the UK, use the blue exit reserved for EU travellers. You do not have to pay any tax or duty in the UK on goods you have bought in other EU countries for your own use, but you may be breaking the law if you sell alcohol or tobacco you have bought. If you are caught you face imprisonment, and/or confiscation of the goods and the vehicle in which they were transported. To help protect people in the UK, Customs carry out checks on some EU travellers to look for prohibited or restricted goods, including drugs, indecent or obscene material, firearms, ammunition, unlicensed animals and endangered species. This means they may ask you about your baggage. The law sets out guidelines for the amount of alcohol and tobacco you can bring into the UK. If you bring in more, you must be able to satisfy the Customs Officer that the goods are for your own use. If you cannot, the goods may be taken from you, and your vehicle may also be seized. The guidelines are; 3,200 cigarettes, 400 cigarillos, 200 cigars, 3kg smoking tobacco, 10 litres spirits, 20 litres fortified wine, 90 litres wine, 110 litres beer. People under 17 are not allowed to bring in alcohol or tobacco.

Travelling to the UK from outside the EU

When you enter the UK from a non-EU country, or from an EU country having travelled through a non-EU country, you must pass through Customs. If you have any goods over the allowance, or if you are not sure what to declare you must use the Red Channel or the phone provided at the Red Point. If you do not declare items on which you should pay duty you are breaking the law and Customs may prosecute you. Customs allowances for travellers from outside the EU are:

Tobacco: 200 cigarettes or 100 cigarillos or 50 cigars or 250gms tobacco

Wines & Spirits: 2 litres still table wine and 1 litre of spirits or strong liqueurs over 22% volume or 2 litres fortified wine, sparkling wine or other liqueurs.

Perfume: 60cc/ml of perfume and 250cc/ml of toilet water.

Other goods: £145 worth of all other goods including gifts and souvenirs.

All dutiable articles must be declared when you enter the UK from a non-EU country. Articles not properly declared may be forfeit, and if they are hidden in a vehicle that vehicle may also be forfeit. Customs Officers are legally entitled to examine your baggage and you are responsible for unpacking and repacking it. If you require further information, Customs Notice 1, A Customs Guide for Travellers entering the UK, is available at UK points of entry and exit or call 0845 010 9000. See also the HM Customs & Excise website **www.hmce.gov.uk**.

Travelling outside the EU

If, when leaving the UK, you take any items bought in the UK which are high value or look very new it is a good idea to carry the retailers' receipts with you as foreign Customs may wish to confirm where the goods were obtained.

Bona fide visitors to non-EU countries may generally assume that they may temporarily import personal articles duty free, providing the following conditions are met:

- that the articles are for personal use, and are not to be sold or otherwise disposed of;
- that they may be considered as being in use, and in keeping with the personal status of the importer;
- that they are taken out when the importer leaves the country;
- that the goods stay for no more than 6 months in any 12 month period, whichever is the earlier.

All dutiable articles must be declared when you enter a country, or you will be liable to penalties. If you will be taking a large number of personal effects with you, it would be wise to prepare an inventory to present to the Customs authorities on entry. Customs officers may withhold concessions at any time and ask travellers to deposit enough money to cover possible duty, especially on portable items of apparent high value such as television sets, radios, cassette recorders, portable computers, musical instruments, etc., all of which must be declared. Any deposit paid (for which a receipt must be obtained) is likely to be high; it is recoverable on leaving the country and exporting the item but only at the entry point at which it was paid. Alternatively the Customs may enter the item in the traveller's passport; if this happens it is important to get the entry cancelled when the item is exported. Duty and tax-free allowances may not apply if travellers enter the country more than once a month, or are under 17 years of age (other ages may apply in some countries). Residents of the Channel Islands and the Isle of Man do not benefit from EU allowances because of their fiscal policies.

A temporarily imported motor vehicle, boat, caravan, or any other type of trailer is subject to strict control on entering a country, attracting Customs duty and a variety of taxes. Much depends upon the circumstances

and the period of the import, and also upon the status of the importer. Non-residents entering a country with a private vehicle for holiday or recreational purposes who intend to export the vehicle within a short period enjoy special privileges, and minimal formalities in the interests of tourism.

A temporarily imported vehicle, etc, should not:

- be left in the country after the importer has left;
- be put at the disposal of a resident of the country;
- be retained in the country longer than the permitted period; or
- be lent, sold, hired, given away, exchanged or otherwise disposed of.

Generally, people entering a country with a motor vehicle to stay for a period of more than six months (see also Visas, page 30), or who intend to take up residence, employment, any commercial activity or who intend to dispose of the vehicle should seek advice concerning their position well in advance of their departure. The AA Information Centre can give advice to members; for assistance, telephone 0870 5500 600.

Additionally the importation of certain goods into the UK is prohibited or restricted.

PASSPORTS

Each person must hold, or be named on, a valid passport. Always carry your passport and, as an extra precaution, a separate note of the number, date and place of issue. The only type of passport now is the standard UK passport.

Standard UK passports are issued to British Nationals, i.e. British Citizens, British Overseas Territories Citizens, British Overseas Citizens, British Nationals (Overseas), British Subjects, and British Protected Persons. A standard UK passport is valid for travel to all countries in the world - but you must check whether a visa is also required. From 5 October 1998 it has been necessary for all children to have their own passports; children entered on the existing passport of a parent before 5 October 1998 may remain until the passport expires or until they reach 16. All passports issued to children under the age of 16 years are for 5 years only. After 5 years a new application must be made.

To obtain a passport application pack, including the application form, guidance notes and a fees leaflet, call 0901 4700 110 or fax 0901 4700 120 (calls cost 60p per minute, and the total cost should not exceed 90p), or visit the UK Passport Service website, **www.passport.gov.uk**. Otherwise obtain an application pack from one of the regional passport offices in Belfast, Durham, G;asgow, Liverpool, London, Newport (Wales), or a UKPS High Street Partner (selected Post Office™ branches and Worldchoice travel agents operating the Check & Send service). Allow 3 weeks for the processing of your application. Note. For personal callers who need a passport urgently (in less than 2 weeks), passport offices operate on an appointment only basis - call the UKPS 24-hour helpline, 0870 521 0410, to make an appointment.

Irish citizens who require an Irish Passport, and who are resident either in the Dublin metropolitan area or in Northern Ireland should apply to the Passport Office, Dublin; if, however, they are resident elsewhere in the Irish Republic, they should apply through the nearest Garda Station or Post Office. Irish citizens resident in Britain should apply to the Irish Embassy in London.

VISAS

EU citizens travelling within the EU do not require visas. A visa is not normally required by United Kingdom and Republic of Ireland passport holders when visiting non-EU countries within Western Europe for periods of three months or less. However, if you hold a passport of any other nationality, a UK passport not issued in this country, or if you are in any doubt at all, check with the embassies or consulates of the countries you intend to visit.

VISITOR'S REGISTRATION

In most countries registration formalities are to be undertaken by visitors spending up to three months. However, this formality is usually satisfied by completing a card or certificate when booking into a hotel, campsite or other accommodation. If you are staying with friends or relatives it is usually the responsibility of the host to seek advice from the police within 24 hours of the arrival of guests.

If you intend visiting a country for longer than three months and/or the circumstances are not as described above, then you should make the appropriate enquiries before your departure from the UK.

FOODSTUFFS

(See also country introductions.) Countries do have regulations governing the types and quantities of foodstuffs which may be imported. Although they are usually not strictly applied, visitors should know that they exist and only take reasonable quantities of food with them. See the country introductions for any specific regulations.

Tinned, frozen and dehydrated foods are useful for camping. It is best to take only as much as you need until you can shop locally. Good value for money will be found in supermarkets or in the open markets in towns.

Note. The importation of food products of animal origin (meat, meat products not heat treated, milk and dairy products) into any country may be prohibited due to the risk of foot and mouth disease.

BOATS

EU citizens may use their boats throughout the year in all EU countries provided VAT has been paid. However, the boats of non-EU citizens are still subject to temporary importation formalities.

All boats taken abroad by road should be registered in the UK. This is not a legal requirement but it is recommended. (See also Identification Plate, page 18.)

Registration is carried out by the Small Ships Register at the RSS. Currently the fee is £12 and provides registration for five years. The original Certificate of Registration is required - a photocopy is not acceptable. Application forms for Small Ships Registration, accompanied by notes on the purpose of the Register and eligibility for registration, are available from:

The Small Ships Register,
Maritime and Costguard Agency,
Anchor Court, Keen Rd,
Cardiff CF24 5JW
Tel 029 2044 8800

An online small-ships registration service is available at **www.mcga.gov.uk**. Application forms are also available from some yacht/boat clubs, marinas and shipyards.

Of the countries in this guide, an International Certificate of Competence (ICC) is required or recommended for Belgium, France, Germany, Italy, the Netherlands, Portugal and Spain. For further information, contact: The Royal Yachting Association, RYA House, Ensign Way,

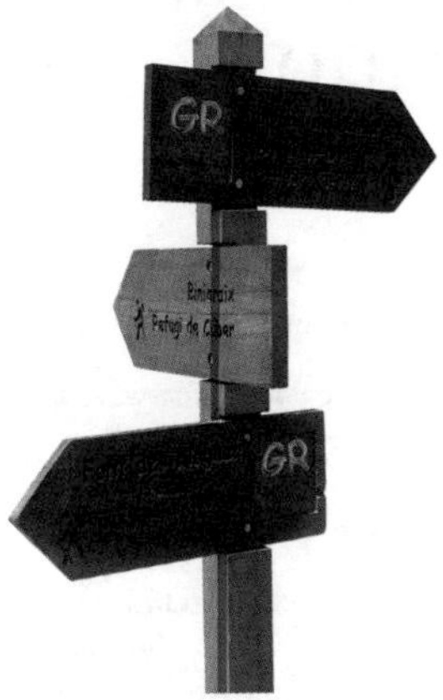

Hamble, Southampton,
Hampshire SO31 4YA,
tel 0845 345 0370,
www.rya.org.uk/cruising.

The UN agreement covering the ICC has been changed. Those renewing out-of-date certificates and wanting 'inland waters' endorsement must take a test on CEVNI rules. A rules booklet (G17) is obtainable from the RYA cost £6.50 plus postage.

The 1998 Recreational Craft Directive requires the CE mark on boats newly commissioned or imported into the EEA for the first time. Proof of use in EU waters before this date may become a useful document when visiting other EU countries.

The RYA recommends that all boats have marine insurance; it is compulsory in most countries. A translation of the insurance certificate is sometimes required, particularly in Greece, Italy and Spain. Check with your broker before you go.

OFF-SITE CAMPING

Off-site camping may contravene local regulations. You are strongly advised never to camp by the roadside and in isolated areas.

PET TRAVEL SCHEME

For information on how to bring pet cats and dogs back into the UK from certain countries without quarantine contact the Pets Helpline on 0870 2411710 or visit the Department for Environment, Food & Rural Affairs (DEFRA) website **www.defra.gov.uk/animalh/quarantine/index.htm.**

Local DEFRA Animal Health divisional offices can provide information on the requirements for taking pets from the UK to other countries.

Travel Information

BBC WORLD SERVICE

The international radio arm of the BBC broadcasts in 43 languages, including a 24-hour-a-day English Service. World news is on the hour every hour and there are regular bulletins of British news.

If you want to listen to World Service when you are abroad, write for information and a free programme guide to BBC World Service, Audience Relations, Bush House, London WC2B 4PH. Remember to state the country or countries you are visiting.

A monthly magazine, BBC On Air, provides details of all World Service programmes and frequencies, with background information about features and personalities. It costs £20.00 for an annual subscription. If you would like to receive details, please write to On Air at the above address, or browse their website **www.bbc.co.uk/worldservice/onair**.

If you are buying a new radio to listen to the BBC abroad, the World Service recommends digitally tuned radios as they make finding frequencies easier.

Make sure your short-wave set can receive some of the key European frequencies such as 9410 and 12095 kHz.

World Service programmes can also be heard on the Internet at **www.bbc.co.uk/worldservice**.

BRITISH EMBASSIES/CONSULATES

Many Continental countries have at least one British consulate in addition to the British embassy. British consulates (and consular sections in embassies) aim to help British travellers in distress overseas but there are limitations to what they can do. For example, they cannot pay your hotel, medical or any other bills, nor will they do the work of a travel agent, information bureau or the police.

Report any loss or theft of property to the local police in the first instance, not to the consular offices. If you need to obtain an emergency passport or guidance on how to transfer funds from the UK, contact the nearest British embassy or consulate; see the country introductions for details. Note that the hours and functions of honorary consuls are more restricted than full consular posts.

For up-to-date advice on travelling abroad, call 0870 606 0290 or visit **www.fco.gov.uk/knowbeforeyougo**.

CAMPING CARD INTERNATIONAL

A Camping Card International (CCI) is recognised at most campsites in Europe; in some cases it is essential and you will not be allowed to camp without it. At certain campsites a reduction to the advertised charge may be allowed on presentation of the camping card. The camping card, which is valid for 12 months, provides third-party insurance cover for up to 11 people camping away from home or staying in rented accommodation or at a hotel.

On arrival at the campsite, report to the campsite manager who will tell you where you may pitch your tent or caravan. You may be asked to pay in advance, or alternatively, to give into charge the camping card for the length of your stay. Some campsite managers may also insist upon retention of all passports.

The AA no longer sells the CCI. However, personal AA members wishing to purchase a CCI may obtain one from the Caravan Club. AA members requiring further information should call the Caravan Club on 01342

327410 (Mon-Fri 09.15-17.15), and be prepared to quote their AA membership number.

AA Ireland members who wish to obtain a CCI should call AA Dublin on 01 617 9988.

CURRENCY

See also country sections. There is no limit to the amount of sterling notes you may take abroad. Some countries do have curency import or export restrictions and you should check this with your bank or currency supplier. However, do not rely exclusively on any one payment method. A combination of a payment card, traveller's cheques and a small amount of local currency is suggested as the most practical arrangement.

Euro banknotes and coins were introduced on 1 January 2002 in the 12 countries of the Euro area* to replace national currencies. The banknotes have denominations of 5, 10, 20, 50, 100, 200 and 500 euros; the coins 1 and 2 euros, and 1, 2, 5, 10, 20 and 50 cents. The old European currencies have now been withdrawn. Arrangements for exchanging old currencies differ between countries, with many restricting exchange to Central Bank offices. It is possible that banks in Europe will make a charge to non-customers making this exchange.

**The 12 are Austria, Belgium, France, Germany, Italy, Luxembourg, Netherlands, Portugal, Spain (included in this guide) plus Finland, Greece and the Republic of Ireland.*

ELECTRICAL

The electricity supply in Europe is usually 220 volts (50 cycles) AC (alternating current), but can be as low as 110 volts. In some isolated areas, low voltage DC (direct current) is provided. Continental circular two-pin plugs and screw-type bulbs are usually the rule. Check for correct polarity when using a mains hook-up on a touring caravan.

Electrical adapters (not voltage transformers), which can be used in Continental power sockets, shaver points and light bulb sockets, are available in the UK from electrical retailers.

Check that all connections in the vehicle are sound, and wiring is in good condition. If problems arise with the charging system, you must consult a qualified auto-electrician.

EMERGENCY MESSAGES TO TOURISTS

In emergencies, the AA will assist in the passing on of messages to tourists when possible. Members wishing to use this service should telephone the AA Information Centre on 0870 5500 600.

The AA can arrange for messages to be published in overseas editions of the Daily Mail, and in an extreme emergency (death or serious illness of next-of-kin) pass on messages to the authorities so that they can be broadcast on overseas radio networks. Obviously the AA cannot guarantee that messages will be broadcast, nor can the AA or the Daily Mail accept responsibility for the authenticity of messages.

If you are expecting a message from home, it is best to contact the tourist office or motoring club of the country in which you're staying. They will advise you on radio frequencies, and at what time messages are normally broadcast. Before you leave home, make sure your relatives understand what to do if an emergency occurs.

Emergency 'SOS' messages about dangerous illness of a close relative may be broadcast on BBC Radio 4 LW 1515m/198Hz at the first opportunity before a news summary or bulletin. These should be arranged through the local police or hospital authorities.

EUROTUNNEL

Eurotunnel operates a fast frequent passenger service between Folkestone in Kent and Calais/Coquelles, for cars, motorcycles, camper vans, cars with caravans or trailers, cars with cycle racks, coaches and HGV trucks. Eurotunnel also participates in the PETS travel scheme. A specific cycle service operates during the summer months. Vehicles powered by LPG or dual fuel cars are not permitted to travel at the moment.

The crossing takes 35 minutes from platform to platform and is just over one hour from the M20 in Kent to A16 in France. To get to the Eurotunnel Terminal in Kent take the M20 and leave at Jct11a, signed Channel Tunnel, and arrive directly at Check-in. UK and French customs and immigration are cleared before travelling so there are no further checks on arrival in France.

Eurotunnel operates 24 hours a day, 365 days a year, with at least two departures an hour. For up-to-date travel information call 08705 35 35 35 or visit **www.eurotunnel.com**. Prices are per vehicle; all the passengers are included. It is possible to buy your ticket on arrival, however you might be subject to delay until there is space available.

Passengers stay with their vehicles for the crossing, although they can get out to stretch their legs or visit the cloakrooms on board. Visual display panels and onboard multilingual staff together with two in-car radio channels keep passengers up to date with information.

FERRY CROSSINGS

Before making ferry bookings, remember that the shortest sea crossing from a southern port to the Continent is not always the best choice; consider the roads and ease of travel from your home to a British port (an eastern British port might be easier if you are starting from the north of the country). Similarly consider the roads and travel from the Continental port to your final destination. Motorail services may be worth considering to save time.

LEVEL CROSSINGS

Almost all level crossings are indicated by international signs. Most guarded ones are the lifting barrier type, maybe with bells or flashing lights to warn of an approaching train.

MEDICAL TREATMENT

Travellers who normally take certain medicines should ensure they have a sufficient supply since they may be very difficult to get abroad.

Those with certain medical conditions (diabetes or coronary artery diseases, for example) should get a letter from their doctor giving treatment details. Some Continental doctors will understand a letter written in English, but it is better to have it translated into the language of the country you intend to visit. The AA cannot make translations.

Travellers who, for legitimate health reasons, carry drugs (see also Customs Regulations for the United Kingdom, page 28) or appliances (e.g. a hypodermic syringe), may have difficulty with Customs or other authorities. They should carry translations which describe their special condition and appropriate treatment in the language of the country they intend to visit to present to Customs. Similarly, people with special dietary requirements may find translations helpful in hotels and restaurants.

The National Health Service is available in the UK only, and medical expenses incurred overseas cannot be reimbursed by the UK Government. There are bilateral health agreements with most of the countries in this guide, but you should not rely exclusively on these arrangements, as the cover provided under the respective national schemes is not always comprehensive. (For instance, the cost of bringing a person back to the UK in the event of illness or death is never covered). The full costs of medical care must be paid in Andorra. Therefore, you are advised to take out adequate insurance cover before leaving the UK, such as the AA's Travel Insurance.

Necessary medical treatment in the event of an accident or unforeseen illness is available for most visitors at reduced costs, from the health care schemes of those countries with whom the UK has health-care arrangements. Details are in the Department of Health booklet Health Advice for Travellers, which also gives advice about precautions and vaccinations. Free copies are available from main Post Office™ branches or call the Health Literature Line 0800 555 777 (free of charge). In some of these countries, visitors can obtain urgently needed treatment by showing their UK passport, but in some an NHS medical card must be shown, and in most European Economic Area countries a certificate of entitlement (E111) is necessary. The E111 can be obtained at a Post Office™ branch on completion of the forms in booklet Health Advice for Travellers. The E111 must be stamped and signed by the Post Office™ clerk to be valid. Residents of the Republic of Ireland must apply to their Regional Health Board.

PAYMENT CARDS

Credit and debit cards are as easy to use abroad as they are at home. Their use is subject to the conditions set out by the issuing bank. Establishments display the symbols of cards that they accept. However, it is recommended that you don't rely exclusively on any one payment method. A combination of traveller's cheques, a payment card and a small amount of local currency is suggested as the most practical arrangement.

TRAVELLER'S CHEQUES

Local currency cheques can often be used like cash. Sterling cheques may be changed for local currency notes at banks, but charges can vary. Your bank will be able to recommend currency traveller's cheques for the countries you are visiting. However, it is recommended that you don't rely exclusively on any one payment method. A combination of a payment card, traveller's cheques and a small amount of local currency is the most practical arrangement.

POLLUTION

Pollution of seawater at certain Continental coastal resorts, including the Mediterranean, may still represent a health hazard, although the general situation is improving. Countries of the European Union publish detailed information on the quality of their bathing beaches, including maps, which are available from national authorities and the European Union. In most of the other Mediterranean countries, appropriate surveys regarding bathing water quality in populated beaches, are implemented every year. In many (though not all) popular resorts where the water quality may present risk, signs (generally small) forbid bathing:

FRENCH

No bathing
Défense de se baigner

Bathing prohibited
Il est défendu de se baigner

ITALIAN

No bathing
Vietato bagnarsi

Bathing prohibited
Evietato bagnarsi

SPANISH

No bathing
Prohibido bañarse

Bathing prohibited
Se prohibe bañarse

POSTE RESTANTE

If you are uncertain of having a precise address, you can be contacted through the local poste restante. Before leaving the UK notify family or friends of your approximate whereabouts abroad at given times. If you expect mail, call with your passport at the main post office of the town where you are staying. To ensure that the arrival of correspondence will coincide with your stay, your correspondent should check with the post office before posting, as delivery times differ throughout Europe. It is important that the recipient's name be written in full: Mr John Smith, Poste Restante, Sintra, Portugal. Do not use 'Esq'.

The Italian equivalent of 'Poste Restante' is 'Fermo in Posta' plus the name of the town or village and the province or region. The Spanish equivalent is 'Lista de Correos'.

Correspondence will be lodged at the main post office, and you will need proof of identity (e.g. a passport) to collect it.

TOURIST INFORMATION

National tourist offices are well equipped to deal with enquiries relating to their countries. They are particularly useful for information on current events, tourist attractions, car hire, equipment hire and specific

activities such as skin-diving, gliding, horse-riding, etc. The offices in London (see country introductions for addresses) are helpful, but the local offices overseas merit a visit when you arrive at your destination for information not available elsewhere.

WEATHER & TRAFFIC INFORMATION

The AA is one of Europe's largest traffic and travel information providers offering detailed and accurate reports for the whole of the UK.

Call 09003 401 100 (or 401 100* from your mobile phone) for a range of valuable traffic and travel services which include

- The latest traffic information for your local area or any other region of the UK
- A traffic report on a specific UK motorway or A road
- Local and national 5-day weather forecasts

For other weather information for the UK and the Continent (but not road conditions) call the Met Office on 0870 9000 100, or visit **www.metoffice.com** or contact:

The Met Office Customer Centre,
Fitzroy Road,
Exeter,
Devon EX1 3PB

* Calls to 09003 numbers are charged at 60p per minute at all times. Availablity and prices for mobile calls to 401 100 can vary - see your Service Provider for details.

Principal Mountain Passes

It is best not to attempt to cross mountain passes at night, and daily schedules should make allowances for the comparatively slow speeds inevitable in mountainous areas.

Gravel surfaces (such as dirt and stone chips) vary considerably; they are dusty when dry, slippery when wet. Where known to exist, this type of surface has been noted. Road repairs can be carried out only during the summer, and may interrupt traffic. Precipitous road sides are rarely, if ever, totally unguarded; on the older roads, stone pillars are placed at close intervals. Gradient figures take the mean figure on hairpin bends, and may be steeper on the inside of the curves, particularly on the older roads.

Gradients Conversion Table

All steep hill signs show the grade in percentage terms. The following conversion table may be used as a guide:

30% = 1 in 3	14% = 1 in 7
25% = 1 in 4	12% = 1 in 8
20% = 1 in 5	11% = 1 in 9
16% = 1 in 6	10% = 1 in 10

Before attempting late evening or early morning journeys across frontier passes, check the times of opening of the frontier controls. A number close at night; for example the Timmelsjoch border is closed between 20.00 and 07.00hrs and throughout the winter.

Always engage a low gear before either ascending or descending steep gradients, and keep well to the right-hand side of the road and avoid cutting corners. Avoid excessive use of brakes. If the engine overheats, pull off the road, making sure that you do not cause an obstruction, leave the engine idling, and put the heater controls (including the fan) into the maximum heat position. Under no circumstances should you remove the radiator cap until the engine has cooled down. Do not fill the coolant system of a hot engine with cold water.

Always engage a lower gear before taking a hairpin bend, give priority to vehicles ascending and remember that as your altitude increases, so your engine power decreases. Always give priority to postal coaches travelling in either direction. Their route is usually signposted.

Caravans

Passes suitable for caravans are indicated in the table on the following pages. Those shown to be negotiable by caravans are best used only by experienced drivers in cars with ample power; the rest are probably best avoided. A correct power-to-load ratio is always essential.

Winter Conditions

Winter conditions are given in italics in the last column. UO means usually open, although a severe fall of snow may temporarily obstruct the road for 24 to 48 hours, and wheel chains are often necessary; OC means occasionally closed, UC, usually closed, between the dates stated. Dates for opening and closing the passes are approximate only. Warning notices are usually posted at the foot of a pass if it is closed, or if chains or snow tyres should or must be used.

Wheel chains may be needed early and late in the season, and between short spells (a few hours) of obstruction. At these times, conditions are usually more difficult for caravans.

In fair weather, wheel chains or snow tyres are only necessary on the higher passes, but in severe weather you will probably need to use them (as a rough guide) at altitudes exceeding 610 metres (2000ft).

PRINCIPAL MOUNTAIN PASSES

Pass and height	From To	Distances from summit and max gradient	Min width of road	Conditions (see page 37 for key to abbreviations)
***Albula** 2312 metres (7585ft) Switzerland	Tiefencastel 851 metres (2792ft) La Punt 1687 metres (5535ft)	30km 1 in 10 18.6 miles 9km 1 in 10 5.6 miles	3.5 metres 11ft 6in	UC Nov - early Jun. An inferior alternative to the Julier; tar and gravel, fine scenery. Alternative rail tunnel.
Allos 2250 metres (7382ft) France	Barcelonnette 1132 metres (3714ft) Colmars 1235 metres (4052ft)	20km 1 in 10 12.4 miles 24km 1 in 12 14.9 miles	4.0 metres 13ft 1n	UC Early Nov - early Jun. Very winding, narrow mostly unguarded but not difficult otherwise; passing bays on southern slope, poor surface (maximum width vehicles 1.8 metres, 5ft 11in).
Aprica 1176 metres (3858ft) Italy	Tresenda 375 metres(1230ft) Edolo 699 metres (2293ft)	14km 1 in 11 8.7 miles 15km 1 in 16 9.3 miles	4.0 metres 13ft 1in	UO Fine scenery, good surface, well graded; suitable for caravans.
Aravis 1498 metres (4915ft) France	La Clusaz 1040 metres (3412ft) Flumet 917 metres (3009ft)	8km 1 in 11 5.0 miles 12km 1 in 11 7.4 miles	4.0 metres 13ft 1in	OC Dec - Mar. Outstanding scenery, and a fairly easy road.
Arlberg 1802 metres (5912ft) Austria	Bludenz 581 metres (1905ft) Landeck 816 metres (2677ft)	35km 1 in 8 21.7 miles 32km 1 in 7.5 20 miles	6 metres 19ft 8in	OC Dec - Apr. Modern road; short, steep stretch from west easing towards the summit; heavy traffic; parallel toll road tunnel. Suitable for caravans; using tunnel (see chapter on Major Road and Rail Tunnels). Pass road closed to vehicles towing trailers.
Aubisque 1710 metres (5610ft) France	Eaux Bonnes 750 metres (2461ft) Argelés-Gazost 463 metres (1519ft)	12km 1 in 10 7 miles 30km 1 in 10 19 miles	3.5 metres 11ft 6in	UC Mid Oct - Jun. A very winding road; continuous but easy ascent; the descent incorporates the Col de Soulor (1450 metres, 4757ft); 8km (5 miles) of very narrow, rough unguarded road, with a steep drop.
Ballon d'Alsace 1178 metres (3865ft) France	Giromagny 476metres (1562ft) St-Maurice-sur-Moselle 549 metres (1801ft)	17km 1 in 9 10.6 miles 9km 1 in 9 5.6 miles	4.0 metres 13ft 1in	OC Dec - Mar. A fairly straightforward ascent and descent, but numerous bends; negotiable by caravans.
Bayard 1248 metres (4094ft) France	Chauffayer 911 metres (2989ft) Gap 733 metres (2405ft)	18km 1 in 12 11.2 miles 8km 1 in 7 5.0 miles	6 metres 19ft 8in	UO Part of the Route Napoléon. Fairly easy, steepest on the southern side with several hairpin bends; negotiable by caravans from north to south.
***Bernina** 2330 metres (7644ft) Switzerland	Pontresina 1805 metres (5922ft) Poschiavo 1019 metres (3343ft)	15.5km 1 in 10 10.5 miles 18.5km 1 in 8 11.5 miles	5 metres 16ft 5in	OC Dec - Mar. A good road on both sides; negotiable by caravans.
Bonaigua 2072 metres (6797ft) Spain	Viella 974 metres (3195ft) Esterri d'Aneu 957 metres (3140ft)	23km 1 in 12 14 miles 23km 1 in 12 14 miles	4.3 metres 14ft 1in	UC Nov - Apr. A sinuous and narrow road with many hairpin bends and some precipitous drops; the alternative route to Lleida (Lérida) through the Viella tunnel is open in winter.
Bracco 613 metres (2011ft) Italy	Riva Trigoso 43 metres (141ft) Borghetto di Vara 104metres (341ft)	15km 1 in 7 9.3 miles 18km 1 in 7 11.2 miles	5 metres 16ft 5in	UO A two-lane road with continuous bends; passing usually difficult; negotiable by caravans; alternative toll motorway available.
Brenner 1374 metres (4508ft) Austria - Italy	Innsbruck 574 metres (1883ft) Vipiteno 948 metres (3110ft)	36km 1 in 12 22miles 15km 1 in 7 9.3 miles	6 metres 19ft 8in	UO Parallel toll motorway open; heavy traffic; suitable for caravans using toll motorway. Pass road closed to vehicles towing trailers.
+Brünig 1007 metres (3304ft) Switzerland	Brienzwiler Station 575 metres (1886ft) Giswil 485 metres (1591ft)	6km 1 in 12 3.7 miles 13km 1 in 12 8.1 miles	6 metres 19ft 8in	UO An easy but winding road, heavy traffic at weekends; suitable for caravans.

*** Permitted maximum width of vehicles 7ft 6in + Permitted maximum width of vehicles 8ft 2.5in ++ Maximum length of vehicle 30ft**

PRINCIPAL MOUNTAIN PASSES

Pass and height	From To	Distances from summit and max gradient	Min width of road	Conditions (see page 37 for key to abbreviations)
Bussang 721 metres (2365ft) France	Thann 340 metres (1115ft) St Maurice-sur-Moselle 549 metres (1801ft)	24km 1 in 14 15 miles 8km 1 in 14 5.0 miles	4 metres 13ft 1in	UO A very easy road over the Vosges; beautiful scenery; suitable for caravans.
Cabre 1180 metres (3871ft) France	Luc-en-Diois 580 metres (1903ft) Aspres sur Buëch 764 metres (2507ft)	24km 1 in 11 15 miles 17km 1 in 14 10.6 miles	5.5 metres 18ft	UO An easy pleasant road; suitable for caravans.
Campolongo 1875 metres (6152ft) Italy	Corvara in Badia 1568 metres (5144ft) Arabba 1602 metres (5256ft)	6km 1 in 8 3.7 miles 4km 1 in 8 2.5 miles	5 metres 16ft 5in	OC Dec - Mar. A winding but easy ascent; long level stretch on summit followed by easy descent; good surface; suitable for caravans.
Cayolle 2326 metres (7631ft) France	Barcelonnette 1132 metres (3714ft) Guillaumes 819 metres (2687ft)	30km 1 in 10 19 miles 33km 1 in 10 20.5 miles	4 metres 13ft 1in	UC early Nov - early Jun. Narrow and winding road with hairpin bends; poor surface and broken edges; steep drops. Long stretches of single-track road with passing places.
Costalunga (Karer) 1753 metres (5751ft) Italy	Cardano 282 metres (925ft) Pozza 1290 metres (4232ft)	24km 1 in 6 14.9 miles 11km 1 in 8 7 miles	5 metres 16ft 5in	OC Dec - Apr. A good well-engineered road but mostly winding; caravans prohibited.
Croix 1778 metres (5833ft) Switzerland	Villars-sur-Ollon 1253 metres (4111ft) Les Diablerets 1155 metres (3789ft)	8km 1 in 7.5 5.0 miles 9km 1 in 11 5.6 miles	3.5 metres 11ft 6in	UC Nov - May. A narrow and winding route but extremely picturesque.
Croix-Haute 1179 metres (3868ft) France	Monestier-de-Clermont 832 metres (2730ft) Aspres-sur-Buëch 764 metres (2507ft)	34km 1 in 14 21 miles 29km 1 in 14 18 miles	5.5 metres 18ft	UO Well engineered; several hairpin bends on the north side; suitable for caravans.
Envalira 2407 metres (7897ft) Andorra	Pas de la Casa 2091 metres (6860ft) Andorra 1029 metres (3376ft)	5km 1 in 10 3.1 miles 25km 1 in 8 16 miles	6 metres 19ft 8in	OC Nov - Apr. A good road with wide bends on ascent and descent; fine views; negotiable by caravans (maximum height vehicles 3.5 metres, 11ft 6in on northern approach near L'Hospitalet).
Falzárego 2117 metres (6945ft) Italy	Cortina d'Ampezzo 1224 metres (4016ft) Andraz 1428 metres (4685ft)	17km 1 in 12 10.6 miles 9km 1 in 12 5.6 miles	5 metres 16ft 5in	OC Dec - Apr. Well engineered bitumen surface; many hairpin bends on both sides; negotiable by caravans.
Faucille 1323 metres (4341ft) France	Gex 628 metres (2060ft) Morez 702 metres (2303ft)	11km 1 in 10 6.8 miles 27km 1 in 12 17miles	5 metres 16ft 5in	UO Fairly wide, winding road across the Jura mountains; negotiable by caravans, but it is probably better to follow La Cure-St-Cergue-Nyon.
Fern 1209 metres (3967ft) Austria	Nassereith 843 metres (2766ft) Lermoos 995 metres (3264ft)	10km 1 in 10 6 miles 10km 1 in 10 6 miles	6 metres 19ft 8in	UO An easy pass, but slippery when wet; heavy traffic at summer weekends; suitable for caravans.
Flexen 1784 metres (5853ft) Austria	Lech 1447 metres (4747ft) Rauzalpe (near Arlberg Pass) 1628 metres (5341ft)	6.5km 1 in 10 4 miles 3.5km 1 in 10 2.2 miles	5.5 metres 18ft	UO The magnificent 'Flexenstrasse', a well engineered mountain road with tunnels and galleries. The road from Lech to Warth, north of the pass, is usually closed between November and April due to danger of avalanches.

*** Permitted maximum width of vehicles 7ft 6in + Permitted maximum width of vehicles 8ft 2.5in ++ Maximum length of vehicle 30ft**

PRINCIPAL MOUNTAIN PASSES

Pass and height	From To	Distances from summit and max gradient	Min width of road	Conditions (see page 37 for key to abbreviations)
***Flüela** 2383 metres (7818ft) Switzerland	Davos-Dorf 1563 metres (5128ft) Susch 1438 metres (4718ft)	14km 1 in 10 9 miles 14km 1 in 8 9 miles	5metres 16ft 5in	OC Nov - May. Easy ascent from Davos; some acute hairpin bends on the eastern side; bitumen surface; negotiable by caravans.
+Forclaz 1527 metres (5010ft) Switzerland France	Martigny 476 metres (1562ft) Argentière 1253 metres (4111ft)	13km 1 in 12 8.1 miles 19km 1 in 12 11.8 miles	5 metres 16ft 5in	UO Forclaz; OC Montets Dec - early Apr. A good road over the pass and to the frontier; in France, narrow and rough over Col des Montets (1461 metres, 4793ft); negotiable by caravans.
Foscagno 2291 metres (7516ft) Italy	Bormio 1225 metres (4019ft) Livigno 1816 metres (5958ft)	24km 1 in 8 14.9 miles 14km 1 in 8 8.7 miles	3.3 metres 10ft 10in	OC Nov - May. Narrow and winding through lonely mountains, generally poor surface. Long winding ascent with many blind bends; not always well guarded. The descent includes winding rise and fall over the Passo d'Eira (2200 metres, 7218ft).
Fugazze 1159 metres (3802ft) Italy	Rovereto 201 metres (660ft) Valli del Pasubio 350 metres (1148ft)	27km 1 in 7 16.4 miles 12km 1 in 7 7.4 miles	3.5 metres 11ft 6in	UO Very winding with some narrow sections, particularly on northern side. The many blind bends and several hairpin bends call for extra care.
***Furka** 2431 metres (7976ft) Switzerland	Gletsch 1757 metres (5764ft) Realp 1538 metres (5046ft)	10km 1 in 9 6.2 miles 13km 1 in 10 8.1 miles	4 metres 13ft 1in	UC Oct - Jun. A well graded road, with narrow sections and several sharp hairpin bends on both ascent and descent. Fine views of the Rhône glacier. Alternative rail tunnel available.
Galibier 2645 metres (8678ft) France	Lautaret Pass 2058 metres (6752ft) St-Michel-de-Maurienne 712 metres (2336ft)	7km 1 in 9 4.4 miles 34km 1 in 8 21.1 miles	3 metres 9ft 10in	UC Oct - Jun. Mainly wide, well surfaced but unguarded. Ten hairpin bends on descent then 5km (3.1 miles) narrow and rough. Rise over the Col du Télégraphe (1600 metres, 5249ft), then 11 more hairpin bends. (The tunnel under the Galibier summit is closed.)
Gardena (Grödner-Joch) 2121 metres (6959ft) Italy	Val Gardena 1862 metres (6109ft) Corvara in Badia 1568 metres (5144ft)	6km 1 in 8 3.7 miles 10km 1 in 8 6.2 miles	5 metres 16ft 5in	OC Dec - Jun. A well engineered road, very winding on descent.
Gavia 2621 metres (8599ft) Italy	Bormio 1225 metres (4019ft) Ponte di Legno 1258 metres (4127ft)	25km 1 in 5.5 15.5 miles 18km 1 in 5.5 11 miles	3 metres 9ft 10in	UC Oct - Jul. Steep and narrow, but with frequent passing bays; many hairpin bends and a gravel surface; not for the faint-hearted; extra care necessary. (Maximum width for vehicles 1.8 metres, 5ft 11in.)
Gerlos 1628 metres (5341ft) Austria	Zell am Ziller 575 metres (1886ft) Wald 885 metres (2904ft)	29km 1 in 12 18 miles 15km 1 in 11 9.3 miles	4 metres 13ft 1in	UO Hairpin ascent out of Zell to modern toll road; the old, steep, narrow, and winding route with passing bays and 1-in-7 gradient is not recommended, but is negotiable with care; caravans prohibited.
+Grand St Bernard 2473 metres (8114ft) Switzerland - Italy	Martigny 476 metres (1562ft) Aosta 583 metres (1913ft)	46km 1 in 9 29 miles 34km 1 in 9 21 miles	4 metres 13ft 1in	UC Oct - Jun. Modern road to entrance of road tunnel (usually open; see chapter on Major Road and Rail Tunnels) then narrow over summit to frontier; also good surface in Italy; suitable for caravans using tunnel. Pass road closed to vehicles towing trailers.
***Grimsel** 2164 metres (7100ft) Switzerland	Innerkirchen 630 metres (2067ft) Gletsch 1757 metres (5764ft)	26km 1 in 10 16.1 miles 6km 1 in 10 3.7 miles	5 metres 16ft 5in	UC mid Oct - late Jun. A fairly easy road, but heavy traffic weekends. A long winding ascent, finally hairpin bends; then a terraced descent (six hairpins) into the Rhône valley. Negotiable by caravans.
Grossglockner 2503 metres (8212ft) Austria	Bruck an der Glocknerstrasse 755 metres (2477ft) Heiligenblut 1301 metres (4268ft)	34km 1 in 8 21 miles 15m 1 in 8 9.3 miles	5.5 metres 18ft	UC late Oct - early May. Numerous well engineered hairpin bends; moderate but very long ascent, toll road; very fine scenery; heavy tourist traffic; negotiable preferably from south to north, by caravans. Road closed 22.00-05.00.

*** Permitted maximum width of vehicles 7ft 6in + Permitted maximum width of vehicles 8ft 2.5in ++ Maximum length of vehicle 30ft**

PRINCIPAL MOUNTAIN PASSES

Pass and height	From To	Distances from summit and max gradient	Min width of road	Conditions (see page 37 for key to abbreviations)
Hochtannberg 1679 metres (5509ft) Austria	Schröcken 1269 metres(4163ft) Warth (near Lech) 1500 metres (4921ft)	5.5km 1 in 7 3.4 miles 4.5km 1 in 11 2.8 miles	4 metres 13ft 1in	OC Jan - Mar. A reconstructed modern road.
Ibañeta (Roncesvalles) 1057 metres (3468ft) France - Spain	St-Jean-Pied-de-Port 163 metres (535ft) Pamplona 415 metres (1362ft)	27km 1 in 10 17 miles 49km 1 in 10 30 miles	4 metres 13ft 1in	UO A slow and winding, scenic route; negotiable by caravans.
Iseran 2770 metres (9088ft) France	Bourg-St-Maurice 840 metres (2756ft) Lanslebourg 1399 metres (4590ft)	47km 1 in 12 29 miles 33km 1 in 9 20.5 miles	4 metres 13ft 1in	UC Mid Oct - late Jun. The second highest pass in the Alps. Well graded with reasonable bends, average surface; several unlit tunnels on northern approach.
Izoard 2360 metres (7743ft) France	Guillestre 1000 metres (3281ft) Briançon 1321 metres (4334ft)	32km 1 in 8 20 miles 22km 1 in 8 14 miles	5 metres 16ft 5in	UC Late Oct - mid Jun. A winding and sometimes narrow road with many hairpin bends. Care is required at several unlit tunnels near Guillestre.
***Jaun** 1509 metres (4951ft) Switzerland	Broc 718 metres (2356ft) Reidenbach 845 metres (2772ft)	25km 1 in 10 15.5 miles 8km 1 in 10 5 miles	4 metres 13ft 1in	UO A modernised but generally narrow road; some poor sections on ascent, and several hairpin bends on descent; negotiable by caravans.
+Julier 2284 metres (7493ft) Switzerland	Tiefencastel 851 metres (2792ft) Silvaplana 1815 metres (5955ft)	35km 1 in 10 22miles 7km 1 in 7.5 4.4 miles	4 metres 13ft 1in	UO Well engineered road, approached from Chur by Lenzerheide Pass (1549 metres, 5082ft); negotiable by caravans, preferably from north to south.
Katschberg 1641 metres (5384ft) Austria	Spittal 554 metres (1818ft) St Michael 1068 metres (3504ft)	37km 1 in 5 23 miles 6km 1 in 6 3.7 miles	6 metres 19ft 8in	UO Steep though not particularly difficult, parallel toll motorway, including tunnel available; negotiable by light caravans, using tunnel (see chapter on Major Road and Rail Tunnels, Tauern Autobahn)
***Klausen** 1948 metres (6391ft) Switzerland	Altdorf 458 metres (1503ft) Linthal 662 metres (2172ft)	25km 1 in 10 15.5 miles 23km 1 in 11 14.3 miles	5 metres 16ft 5in	UC Late Oct - early Jun. Narrow and winding in places, but generally easy, in spite of a number of sharp bends; no through route for caravans as they are prohibited from using the road between Unterschächen and Linthal.
Larche (della Maddalena) 1994 metres (6542ft) France - Italy	La Condamine-Châtelard 1308 metres (4291ft) Vinadio 910 metres (2986ft)	19km 1 in 12 11.8 miles 32km 1 in 12 19.8 miles	3.5 metres 11ft 6in	OC Dec - Mar. An easy, well graded road; narrow ascent, wider on descent; suitable for caravans.
Lautaret 2058 metres (6752ft) France	Le Bourg-d'Oisans 719 metres (2359ft) Briançon 1321 metres (4334ft)	38km 1 in 8 23.6 miles 28km 1 in 10 17.4 miles	4 metres 13ft 1in	OC Dec - Mar. Modern, evenly graded, but winding, and unguarded in places; very fine scenery; suitable for caravans.
Loibl (Ljubelj) 1067 metres (3500ft) Austria - Slovenia	Unterloibl 518 metres (1699ft) Kranj 385 metres (1263ft)	10km 1 in 5.5 6.2 miles 26km 1 in 8 16miles	6 metres 19ft 8in	UO Steep rise and fall over Little Loibl pass to tunnel (1.6km, 1 mile long) under summit. The old road over the summit is closed to through traffic.
***Lukmanier (Lucomagno)** 1916 metres (6286ft) Switzerland	Olivone 893 metres (2930ft) Disentis 1133 metres (3717ft)	20km 1 in 11 12 miles 20km 1 in 11 12 miles	5 metres 16ft 5in	UC early Nov - late May. Rebuilt, modern road; suitable for caravans.

*** Permitted maximum width of vehicles 7ft 6in + Permitted maximum width of vehicles 8ft 2.5in ++ Maximum length of vehicle 30ft**

PRINCIPAL MOUNTAIN PASSES

Pass and height	From To	Distances from summit and max gradient	Min width of road	Conditions (see page 37 for key to abbreviations)
+Maloja 1815 metres (5955ft) Switzerland	Silvaplana 1815 metres (5955ft) Chiavenna 333 metres (1093ft)	11km level 6.8 miles 32km 1 in 11 19.8 miles	4 metres 13ft 1in	UO Escarpment facing south; fairly easy, but many hairpin bends on descent; negotiable by caravans, possibly difficult on ascent.
Mauria 1298 metres (4258ft) Italy	Lozzo Cadore 753 metres (2470ft) Ampezzo 560 metres (1837ft)	13km 1 in 14 8 miles 31km 1 in 14 19.2 miles	5 metres 16ft 5in	UO A well designed road with easy, winding ascent and descent; suitable for caravans.
Mendola 1363 metres (4472ft) Italy	Appiano (Eppan) 411 metres (1348ft) Sarnonico 978 metres (3208ft)	15km 1 in 8 9.3 miles 9km 1 in 10 6 miles	5 metres 16ft 5in	UO A fairly straightforward but winding road, well guarded; suitable for caravans.
Mont Cenis 2083 metres (6834ft) France - Italy	Lanslebourg 1399 metres (4590ft) Susa 503 metres (1650ft)	11km 1 in 10 6.8 miles 28km 1 in 8 17.4 miles	5 metres 16ft 5in	UC Nov - May. Approach by industrial valley. An easy highway, with mostly very good surface; spectacular scenery; suitable for caravans. Alternative Fréjus road tunnel(see Major Road and Rail Tunnels).
Monte Croce di Comélico (Kreuzberg) 1636 metres (5368ft) Italy	San Candido 1174metres (3852ft) Santo Stefano di Cadore 908 metres (2979ft)	15km 1 in 12 9.3 miles 21km 1 in 12 13miles	5 metres 16ft 5in	UO A winding road with moderate gradients, beautiful scenery; suitable for caravans.
Montgenèvre 1850m (6070ft) France - Italy	Briançon 1321 metres (4334ft) Cesana Torinese 1344 metres (4409ft)	12km 1 in 14 7.4 miles 8km 1 in 11 5miles	5 metres 16ft 5in	UO An easy, modern road; suitable for caravans.
Monte Giovo (Jaufen) 2094 metres (6870ft) Italy	Merano 324 metres (1063ft) Vipiteno 948 metres (3110ft)	40km 1 in 8 24.8 miles 19km 1 in 11 11.8 miles	4 metres 13ft 1in	UC Nov - May. Many well engineered hairpin bends; caravans prohibited.
Montets (see Forclaz)				
Morgins 1369 metres (4491ft) France - Switzerland	Abondance 930 metres (3051ft) Monthey 424 metres (1391ft)	14km 1 in 11 8.7 miles 15km 1 in 7 9.3 miles	4 metres 13ft 1in	UO A lesser used route through pleasant, forested countryside crossing the French-Swiss border.
***Mosses** 1445m (4740ft) Switzerland	Aigle 417 metres (1368ft) Château d'Oex 958 metres (3143ft)	16km 1 in 12 10 miles 15km 1 in 12 9.3 miles	4 metres 13ft 1in	UO A modern road; suitable for caravans.
Nassfeld (Pramollo) 1530m (5020ft) Austria - Italy	Tröpolach 601 metres (1972ft) Pontebba 568 metres (1864ft)	10km 1 in 5 6.2 miles 10km 1 in 10 6.2 miles	4 metres 13ft 1in	OC Late Nov - Mar. The winding descent in Italy has been improved.
***Nufenen (Novena)** 2478 metres (8130ft) Switzerland	Ulrichen 1346 metres (4416ft) Airolo 1142 metres (3747ft)	13km 1 in 10 8.1 miles 24km 1 in 10 14.9 miles	4.0 metres 13ft 1in	UC Mid Oct - mid Jun. The approach roads are narrow, with tight bends, but the road over the pass is good; negotiable by caravans.
***Oberalp** 2044 metres (6706ft) Switzerland	Andermatt 1447 metres (4747ft) Disentis 1133 metres (3717ft)	10km 1 in 10 6.2 miles 21km 1 in 10 13miles	5 metres 16ft 5in	UC Nov - late May. A widened road with a modern surface; many hairpin bends, but long level stretch on summit; negotiable by caravans. Alternative rail tunnel for winter (see chapter on Major Road and Rail Tunnels).

*** Permitted maximum width of vehicles 7ft 6in + Permitted maximum width of vehicles 8ft 2.5in ++ Maximum length of vehicle 30ft**

PRINCIPAL MOUNTAIN PASSES

Pass and height	From To	Distances from summit and max gradient	Min width of road	Conditions (see page 37 for key to abbreviations)
***Ofen (Fuorn)** 2149 metres (7051ft) Switzerland	Zernez 1474 metres (4836ft) Santa Maria im Münstertal 1375 metres (4511ft)	22km 1 in 10 13.6 miles 14km 1 in 8 8.7 miles	4 metres 13ft 1in	UO Good, fairly easy road through the Swiss National Park; negotiable by caravans.
Petit St Bernard 2188 metres (7178ft) France - Italy	Bourg-St-Maurice 840 metres (2756ft) Pré St-Didier 1000 metres (3281ft)	30km 1 in 16 19 miles 23km 1 in 12 14.3 miles	5 metres 16ft 5in	UC Mid Oct - Jun. Outstanding scenery; a fairly easy approach, but poor surface and unguarded broken edges near the summit; good on the descent in Italy; negotiable by light caravans.
Peyresourde 1563 metres (5128ft) France	Arreau 704 metres (2310ft) Luchon 630 metres (2067ft)	18km 1 in 10 11.2 miles 14km 1 in 10 8.7 miles	4 metres 13ft 1in	UO Somewhat narrow with several hairpin bends, though not difficult.
***Pillon** 1546 metres (5072ft) Switzerland	Le Sépey 974 metres (3196ft) Gsteig 1184 metres (3885ft)	15km 1 in 11 9 miles 7km 1 in 11 4.4 miles	4 metres 13ft 1in	OC Jan - Feb. A comparatively easy modern road; suitable for caravans.
Plöcken (Monte Croce-Carnico) 1362 metres (4468ft) Austria - Italy	Kötschach 706 metres (2316ft) Paluzza 600 metres (1968ft)	16km 1 in 7 10 miles 16km 1 in 14 10 miles	5 metres 16ft 5in	OC Dec - Apr. A modern road with long, reconstructed sections; heavy traffic at summer weekends; delay likely at the frontier; negotiable by caravans, best used only by experienced drivers in cars with ample power.
Pordoi 2239 metres (7346ft) Italy	Arabba 1602 metres (5256ft) Canazei 1465 metres (4806ft)	9km 1 in 10 5.6 miles 12km 1 in 10 7.4 miles	5 metres 16ft 5in	OC Dec - Apr. An excellent modern road with numerous hairpin bends; negotiable by caravans.
Port 1249 metres (4098ft) France	Tarascon 474 metres (1555ft) Massat 650 metres (2133ft)	18km 1 in 10 11.2 miles 12km 1 in 10 7.4 miles	4 metres 13ft 1in	OC Nov - Mar. A fairly easy road, but narrow on some bends; negotiable by caravans.
Portet-d'Aspet 1069 metres (3507ft) France	Audressein 508 metres (1667ft) Fronsac 472 metres (1548ft)	18km 1 in 7 11.2 miles 29km 1 in 7 18miles	3.5 metres 11ft 6in	UO Approached from the west by the easy Col des Ares (797 metres, 2615ft) and Col de Buret (599 metres, 1965ft); well engineered road, but calls for particular care on hairpin bends; rather narrow.
Pötschen 982 metres (3222ft) Austria	Bad Ischl 469 metres (1539ft) Bad Aussee 659 metres (2162ft)	19km 1 in 11 11.8 miles 9 km 1 in 11 5.6 miles	7 metres 23ft	UO A modern road; suitable for caravans.
Pourtalet 1792 metres (5879ft) France - Spain	Eaux-Chaudes 656 metres (2152ft) Biescas 860 metres (2822ft)	23km 1 in 10 14.3 miles 32km 1 in 10 20 miles	3.5 metres 11ft 6in	UC late Oct - early Jun. A fairly easy, unguarded road, but narrow in places.
Puymorens 1915 metres (6283ft) France	Ax-les-Thermes 720 metres (2362ft) Bourg-Madame 1130 metres (3707ft)	28km 1 in 10 17.4 miles 27km 1 in 10 16.8 miles	5.5 metres 18ft	OC Nov - Apr. A generally easy, modern tarmac road, but narrow, winding and with a poor surface in places; not suitable for night driving; suitable for caravans (max height vehicles 3.5 metres, 11ft 6in). Parallel toll road tunnel available.
Quillane 1714 metres (5623ft) France	Quillan 291 metres (955ft) Mont-Louis 1600 metres (5249ft)	63km 1 in 12 39.1 miles 6 km 1 in 12 3.5 miles	5 metres 16ft 5in	OC Nov - Mar. An easy, straightforward ascent and descent; suitable for caravans.

*** Permitted maximum width of vehicles 7ft 6in + Permitted maximum width of vehicles 8ft 2.5in ++ Maximum length of vehicle 30ft**

Pass and height	From To	Distances from summit and max gradient	Min width of road	Conditions (see page 37 for key to abbreviations)
Radstädter-Tauern 1738 metres (5702ft) Austria	Radstadt 862 metres (2828ft) Mauterndorf 1122 metres (3681ft)	21km 1 in 6 13.0 miles 17km 1 in 7 10.6 miles	5 metres 16ft 5in	OC Jan - Mar. Northern ascent steep, but not difficult otherwise; parallel toll motorway including tunnel; negotiable by light caravans, using tunnel (see chapter on Major Road and Rail Tunnels).
Résia (Reschen) 1504 metres (4934ft) Italy - Austria	Spondigna 885 metres (2903ft) Pfunds 970 metres (3182ft)	29km 1 in 10 18 miles 21km 1 in 10 13miles	6 metres 19ft 8in	UO A good, straightforward alternative to the Brenner Pass; suitable for caravans.
Restefond (La Bonette) 2802 metres (9193ft) France	Jausiers (near Barcelonnette) 1220 metres (4003ft) St-Etienne-de-Tinée 1144 metres (3753ft)	23km 1 in 8 14.3 miles 27km 1 in 6 16.8 miles	3 metres 9ft 10in	UC Oct - Jun. The highest pass in the Alps, completed in 1962. Narrow, rough, unguarded ascent with many blind bends, and nine hairpins. Descent easier, winding with 12 hairpin bends. Not for the faint-hearted; extra care required.
Rolle 1970 metres (6463ft) Italy	Predazzo 1018 metres (3340ft) Mezzano 637 metres (2090ft)	21km 1 in 11 13.0 miles 27km 1 in 14 17 miles	5 metres 16ft 5in	OC Dec - Mar. A well engineered road with many hairpin bends on both sides; very beautiful scenery; good surface; negotiable by caravans.
Rombo (see Timmelsjoch)				
Routes des Crêtes 1283 metres (4210ft) France	St-Dié 343 metres (1125ft) Cernay 296 metres (971ft)	- 1 in 8 - 1 in 8	4 metres 13ft 1in	UC Nov - Apr. A renowned scenic route crossing seven ridges, with the highest point at 'Hôtel du Grand Ballon'.
+St Gotthard (San Gottardo) 2108 metres (6916ft) Switzerland	Göschenen 1106 metres (3629ft) Airolo 1142 metres (3747ft)	18km 1 in 10 11miles 15km 1 in 10 9.3 miles	6 metres 19ft 8in	UC Mid Oct - early Jun. Modern, fairly easy two to three-lane road. Heavy traffic; negotiable by caravans. Alternative road tunnel (see chapter on Major Road and Rail Tunnels).
***San Bernardino** 2066 metres (6778ft) Switzerland	Mesocco 790 metres (2592ft) Hinterrhein 1620 metres (5315ft)	21km 1 in 10 13miles 9.5km 1 in 10 5.9 miles	4 metres 13ft 1in	UC Oct - late Jun. Easy, modern roads on northern and southern approaches to tunnel(see chapter on Major Road and Rail Tunnels). Narrow and winding over summit, via tunnel suitable for caravans.
Schlucht 1139 metres (3737ft) France	Gérardmer 665 metres (2182ft) Munster 381 metres (1250ft)	15km 1 in 14 9.3 miles 18km 1 in 14 11miles	5 metres 16ft 5in	UO An extremely picturesque route crossing the Vosges mountains, with easy, wide bends on the descent; suitable for caravans.
Seeberg (Jezersko) 1218 metres (3996ft) Austria - Slovenia	Eisenkappel 555 metres (1821ft) Kranj 385 metres (1263ft)	14km 1 in 8 8.7 miles 33km 1 in 10 20.5 miles	5 metres 16ft 5in	UO An alternative to the steeper Loibl and Wurzen passes; moderate climb with winding, hairpin ascent and descent.
Sella 2240 metres (7349ft) Italy	Plan 1606 metres (5269ft) Canazei 1465 metres (4806ft)	9km 1 in 9 5.6 miles 12km 1 in 9 7 miles	5 metres 16ft 5in	OC Dec - Jun. A finely engineered, winding road; exceptional views of the Dolomites.
Semmering 985 metres (3232ft) Austria	Mürzzuschlag im Mürztal 672 metres (2205ft) Gloggnitz 457 metres (1499ft)	14km 1 in 16 8.7 miles 17km 1 in 16 10.6 miles	6 metres 19ft 8in	UO A fine, well engineered highway; suitable for caravans.
Sestriere 2033 metres (6670ft) Italy	Cesana Torinese 1344 metres (4409ft) Pinerolo 376 metres (1234ft)	12km 1 in 10 7.4 miles 55km 1 in 10 34.2 miles	6 metres 19ft 8in	UO Mostly bitumen surface; negotiable by caravans.

*** Permitted maximum width of vehicles 7ft 6in + Permitted maximum width of vehicles 8ft 2.5in ++ Maximum length of vehicle 30ft**

PRINCIPAL MOUNTAIN PASSES

Pass and height	From To	Distances from summit and max gradient	Min width of road	Conditions (see page 37 for key to abbreviations)
Silvretta (Bielerhöhe) 2032 metres (6666ft) Austria	Partenen 1051 metres (3448ft) Galtür 1584 metres (5197ft)	16km 1 in 9 9.9 miles 10km 1 in 9 6.2 miles	5 metres 16ft 5in	UC Late Oct - early Jun. For the most part reconstructed; 32 easy hairpin bends on western ascent; eastern side more straightforward. Toll road; caravans prohibited.
+Simplon 2005 metres (6578ft) Switzerland - Italy	Brig 681 metres (2234ft) Domodóssola 280 metres (919ft)	22km 1 in 9 13.6 miles 41km 1 in 11 25.5 miles	7 metres 23ft	OC Nov - Apr. An easy, reconstructed modern road, but 13 miles long, continuous ascent to summit; suitable for caravans.
Somport 1632 metres (5354ft) France - Spain	Bedous 416 metres (1365ft) Jaca 820 metres (2690ft)	31km 1 in 10 19.2 miles 32km 1 in 10 20miles	3.5 metres 11ft 6in	UO A favoured, old-established route; generally easy, but in parts narrow and unguarded; fairly well surfaced road; suitable for caravans.
***Splügen** 2113 metres (6932ft) Switzerland - Italy	Splügen 1457 metres (4780ft) Chiavenna 330 metres (1083ft)	9km 1 in 9 5.6 miles 30km 1 in 7.5 18.6 miles	3.5 metres 11ft 6in	UC Nov - Jun. Mostly narrow and winding, with many hairpin bends, and not well guarded; care is also required at many tunnels and galleries (max height vehicles 9ft 2in).
++Stelvio 2757 metres (9045ft) Italy	Bormio 1225 metres (4019ft) Spondigna 885 metres (2903ft)	22km 1 in 8 13.6 miles 28km 1 in 8 12.9 miles	4 metres 13ft 1in	UC Oct - late Jun. the third highest pass in the Alps; the number of acute hairpin bends, all well engineered, is exceptional - from 40 to 50 on either side; the surface is good, the traffic heavy. Hairpin bends are too acute for long vehicles.
+Susten 2224 metres (7297ft) Switzerland	Innertkirchen 630 metres (2067ft) Wassen 916 metres (3005ft)	28km 1 in 11 12.9 miles 19km 1 in 11 11.8 miles	6 metres 19ft 8in	UC Nov - Jun. A very scenic and well guarded mountain road; easy gradients and turns; heavy traffic at weekends; negotiable by caravans - extra care required. Not for the faint-hearted.
Tenda (Tende) 1321 metres (4334ft) Italy - France	Borgo S Dalmazzo 641 metres (2103ft) La Giandola 308 metres (1010ft)	24km 1 in 11 14.9 miles 29km 1 in 11 18miles	6 metres 19ft 8in	UO Well guarded, modern road with several hairpin bends; road tunnel at summit; suitable for caravans; but prohibited during the winter.
+Thurn 1274 metres (4180ft) Austria	Kitzbühel 762 metres (2500ft) Mittersill 789 metres (2588ft)	19km 1 in 12 11.8 miles 10km 1 in 16 6.2 miles	5 metres 16ft 5in	UO A good road with narrow stretches; northern approach rebuilt; suitable for caravans.
Timmelsjoch (Rombo) 2509 metres (8232ft) Austria - Italy	Obergurgl 1910 metres (6266ft) Moso 1007 metres (3304ft)	14km 1 in 7 8.7 miles 23km 1 in 8 14miles	3.5 metres 11ft 6in	UC mid Oct - late Jun. Pass open to private cars (without trailers) only as some tunnels on the Italian side are too narrow for larger vehicles; toll road. Border closed 20.00-07.00.
Tonale 1883 metres (6178ft) Italy	Edolo 699 metres (2293ft) Dimaro 766 metres (2513ft)	30km 1 in 12 18.6 miles 27km 1 in 10 16.7 miles	5 metres 16ft 5in	UO A relatively easy road; suitable for caravans.
Toses (Tosas) 1800 metres (5906ft) Spain	Puigcerdá 1152 metres (3780ft) Ribes de Freser 920 metres (3018ft)	26km 1 in 10 16miles 25km 1 in 10 15.5 miles	5 metres 16ft 5in	UO Now a fairly straightforward, but continuously winding, two-lane road with many sharp bends; negotiable by caravans.
Tourmalet 2114 metres (6936ft) France	Luz 711 metres (2333ft) Ste-Marie-de-Campan 857 metres (2812ft)	18km 1 in 8 11miles 17km 1 in 8 10.6 miles	4 metres 13ft 1in	UC Oct - mid Jun. The highest of the French Pyrenean routes; the approaches are good, though winding and exacting over summit; sufficiently guarded.
Tre Croci 1809 metres (5935ft) Italy	Cortina d'Ampezzo 1224 metres (4016ft) Auronzo di Cadore 864 metres (2835ft).	7km 1 in 9 4.4 miles 26 km 1 in 9 16 miles	6 metres 19ft 8in	OC Dec - Mar. An easy pass; very fine scenery; suitable for caravans.

*** Permitted maximum width of vehicles 7ft 6in + Permitted maximum width of vehicles 8ft 2.5in ++ Maximum length of vehicle 30ft**

Pass and height	From To	Distances from summit and max gradient	Min width of road	Conditions (see page 37 for key to abbreviations)
Turracher Höhe 1763 metres (5784ft) Austria	Predlitz 922 metres (3024ft) Ebene-Reichenau 1062 metres (3484ft)	20km 1 in 5.5 12.4 miles 8km 1 in 4.5 5miles	4 metres 13ft 1in	UO Formerly one of the steepest mountain roads in Austria; now much improved. A steep, fairly straightforward ascent is followed by a very steep descent; good surface and mainly two-lane width; fine scenery.
***Umbrail** 2501 metres (8205ft) Switzerland - Italy	Santa Maria im Münstertal 1375 metres (4511ft) Bormio 1225 metres (4019ft)	14km 1 in 11 9 miles 19km 1 in 11 11.8 miles	4.3 metres 14ft 1in	UC Early Nov - early Jun. Highest of the Swiss passes; narrow; mostly gravel surfaced with 34 hairpin bends, but not too difficult.
Vars 2109 metres (6919ft) France	St-Paul-sur-Ubaye 1470 metres (4823ft) Guillestre 1000 metres (3281ft)	8km 1 in 10 5miles 20km 1 in 10 12.4 miles	5 metres 16ft 5in	OC Dec - Mar. Easy winding ascent with seven hairpin bends; gradual winding descent with another seven hairpin bends; good surface; negotiable by caravans.
Wurzen (Koren) 1073 metres (3520ft) Austria - Slovenia	Riegersdorf 541 metres (1775ft) Kranjska Gora 810 metres (2657ft)	7km 1 in 5.5 4.5miles 6km 1 in 5.5 3.5 miles	4 metres 13ft 1in	UO A steep two-lane road, which otherwise is not particularly difficult; heavy traffic at summer weekends; delay likely at the frontier; caravans prohibited.
Zirler Berg 1009 metres (3310ft) Austria	Seefeld 1180 metres (3871ft) Zirl 622 metres (2041ft)	6km 1 in 7 3.5 miles 5km 1 in 6 3.1 miles	7 metres 23ft	UO An escarpment facing south, part of the route from Garmisch to Innsbruck; a good, modern road, but heavy tourist traffic and a long steep descent, with one hairpin bend, into the Inn Valley. Steepest section from the hairpin bend down to Zirl; caravans prohibited northbound.

*** Permitted maximum width of vehicles 7ft 6in + Permitted maximum width of vehicles 8ft 2.5in ++ Maximum length of vehicle 30ft**

Major Road & Rail Tunnels

ROAD TUNNELS

See Lights in the Essential Information for Motoring section. Minimum and maximum speed limits operate in the road tunnels.

During the winter wheel chains may occasionally be required on the approaches to some tunnels. However, you may not use them in tunnels. Use the laybys provided for removal and refitting. All charges listed below are one-way and should be used as a guide only.

BIELSA France-Spain

The trans-Pyrenean tunnel is 3km (2 miles) long, and runs nearly 1830 metres (6000ft) above sea level between Aragnouet and Bielsa.

SOMPORT France-Spain

The tunnel is over 1220 metres (4000ft) above sea level and runs between Les Forges d'Arbel and Canfranc. It is 4.5 metres (14ft 9in) high and the single carriageway is 10.15 metres (34ft 5in). No charges.

CADI Spain

The tunnel is 5km (3 miles) long and runs about 1220 metres (4000ft) above sea level under the Sierra del Cadi mountain range between the villages of Bellver de Cerdanya and Baga, and to the west of the Toses (Tosas) Pass.

Charges	(euros)
Motorcycle	8.84
Car	8.84
Car/caravan	18.75

FREJUS France-Italy

This tunnel is over 1220 metres (4000ft) above sea level and runs between Modane and Bardonecchia. It is 12.8km (8 miles) long, 4.3 metres (14ft 2in) high, and the single carriageway is 9 metres (29ft 6in) wide. Minimum speed is 60km/h (37mph) and the maximum 70km/h (43mph).

Charges	(euros)
Motorcycle	19.20
Vehicle/vehicle combinations (front axle up to 1.3 metres and total height up to 2 metres)	28.80
Vehicle/vehicle combinations (front axle more than 1.3 metres and total height up to 3 metres)	38.10

MONT BLANC Chamonix (France) - Courmayeur (Italy)

The tunnel is over 1220 metres (4000ft) above sea level and is 11.6km (7 miles) long. The single carriageway is 7 metres (23ft) wide. Permitted dimensions of vehicles are: height 4.30 metres (14ft 1in); length 20 metres (65ft 7in); width 2.80 metres (9ft 2in). Larger vehicles, up to 4.7 metres (15ft 5in) high, by special arrangement. Minimum speed is 50km/h (31mph); maximum 70km/h (43mph). When exiting the tunnel the maximum speed is 50km/h (31mph) (exiting in France) or 40km/h (24mph) exiting in Italy. Do not stop, overtake, sound your horn or make U-turns. Use only side/rear lights not headlights and keep 150 metres (164yds) distance between vehicles.

Make sure you have sufficient fuel for the journey, 30km (19 miles). There are breakdown bays with telephones. From November to March, wheel chains may be required on the approaches.

Charges	(euros)
Motorcycle	19.20
Vehicle/vehicle combinations (front axle up to 1.3 metres and total height up to 2 metres)	28.80
Vehicle/vehicle combinations (front axle more than 1.3 metres and total height up to 3 metres)	38.10

GRAND ST BERNARD Switzerland - Italy

The tunnel is over 1925 metres (7570ft) above sea level and runs between Bourg-St-Pierre and St Rhémy. Although there are covered approaches, wheel chains may be needed in winter. Customs, passport control and toll offices are at the entrance. It is 5.9km (3.6 miles) long. Permitted maximum dimensions of vehicles are: height 4 metres (13ft 1in), width 2.5 metres (8ft 2.5in). Minimum speed is 40km/h (24mph); maximum 80km/h (49mph). Do not stop or overtake. Breakdown bays have telephones.

Charges*	(Swiss francs)
Motorcycle	15
Car	27
Car/caravan	40
Minibus, camper van (2 axles)	40
Vehicles with three axles	100
Vehicles with four or more axles	150

*Motorway tax disc (see Switzerland section) must be displayed.

St Gotthard Switzerland

This tunnel is 1154 metres (3786 ft) above sea level. It is 16.9km (10.5 miles) long and runs under the St Gotthard Pass from Göschenen, on the northern side in the Alps, to Airolo in the Ticino. The tunnel is 4.5 metres (14ft 9in) high, and the single carriageway is 7.5 metres (25ft) wide. Maximum speed is 80km/h (49mph). Forming part of the Swiss motorway network, the tunnel is subject to motorway tax, and the tax disc must be displayed (see Switzerland section).

San Bernardino Switzerland

This tunnel is over 1644 metres (5396ft) above sea level. It is 6.6km (4 miles) long, 4.8 metres (15ft 9in) high; the carriageway is 7 metres (23ft) wide. Do not stop or overtake in the tunnel. Keep 100 metres (110yds) between vehicles. There are breakdown bays with telephones. As part of the Swiss motorway network, the tunnel is subject to motorway tax (see Switzerland section).

Arlberg Austria

This tunnel is 14km (8.75 miles) long and runs at about 1220 metres (4000ft) above sea level, to the south of and parallel to the Arlberg Pass.

Charges*	(euros)
Vehicles up to 3.5 tonnes (motorcycle, car, with or without caravan, minibus, van)	11.00

BOSRUCK Austria

This tunnel is 742 metres (2434ft) above sea level. It is 5.5km (3.4 miles) long and runs between Spital am Pyhrn and Selzthal, to the east of the Pyhrn Pass. Maximum speed is 80km/h (49mph). Do not overtake. Use of dipped headlights compulsory; occasional emergency laybys with telephones. With the Gleinalm Tunnel (see below) it forms part of the A9 Pyhrn Autobahn between Linz and Graz, being built in stages.

Charges*	(euros)
Vehicles up to 3.5 tonnes (motorcycle, car, with or without caravan, minibus, van)	6.00

*Motorway tax disc (see Austria section) must be displayed.

Felbertauern Austria

This tunnel, over 1650 metres (5415ft) above sea level, runs between Mittersill and Matrei, west of and parallel to the Grossglockner Pass. The tunnel is 5.2km (3.23 miles) long, 4.5 metres (14ft 9in) high, and the two-lane carriageway is 7 metres (23ft) wide. Wheel chains may be needed on the approach Nov-Apr.

Charges		(euros)
Motorcycle		8.00
Car, with or without caravan, minibus, van	summer	14.00
	winter	8.00

Gleinalm Austria

This tunnel, part of the A9 Pyhrn Autobahn, is 817 metres (2680ft) above sea level, 8.3km (5 miles) long and runs between St Michael and Friesach, near Graz.

Charges*	(euros)
Vehicles up to 3.5 tonnes (motorcycle, car, with or without caravan, minibus, van)	10.00

*Motorway tax disc (see Austria section) must be displayed.

Karawanken Austria-Slovenia

This motorway tunnel under the Karawanken mountains between Rosenbach in Austria and Jesenice in Slovenia is about 610 metres (2000ft) above sea level and nearly 8km (5 miles) long.

Charges*	(in Euros)
Vehicles up to 3.5 tonnes (motorcycle, car, with or without caravan, minibus, van)	7.00

*Motorway tax disc (see Austria section) must be displayed.

Tauern Autobahn (Katschberg and Radstädter) Austria

Two tunnels, the Katschberg and the Radstädter Tauern, form the key elements of the toll motorway between Salzburg and Carinthia. The Katschberg tunnel is 1110 metres (3642ft) above sea level. It is 5.4km (3.5 miles) long, 4.5 metres (14ft 9in) high, and the single carriageway is 7.5 metres (25ft) wide.

The Radstädter Tauern tunnel is 1340 metres (4396ft) above sea level and runs east of the Tauern railway tunnel (see below). The tunnel is 6.4km (4 miles) long, 4.5 metres (14ft 9in) high; the single carriageway is 7.5m (25ft) wide.

Charges* (toll section between Flachau and Rennweg)	(euros)
Vehicles up to 3.5 tonnes (motorcycle, car, with or without caravan, minibus, van)	13.60

*Motorway tax disc (see Austria section) must be displayed.

RAIL TUNNELS

Lotschberg Switzerland

This railway tunnel from Kandersteg to Goppenstein is 14km (8.7 miles) in length. Duration of the journey is 15 minutes, but loading and unloading formalities can take some time.

Services
Frequent with no booking necessary.

Charges	(Swiss francs)
Motorcycle	16
Car (including driver)	25
Car/caravan	50

A timetable and tariff is available from the Swiss National Tourist Office (see Switzerland section for address) or at most Swiss frontier crossings.

Albula Tunnel Switzerland

Thusis (723 metres, 2372ft) - Samedan (1722 metres, 5650ft). The railway tunnel is 5.9km (3.5 miles) long. It will accept vehicles, but you must give notice. Thusis telephone 081 6511113 and Samedan telephone 081 2886677. Journey time 90 minutes.

Services
9 trains daily southbound; 6 trains daily northbound.

Charges		(Swiss francs)
Motorcycle/car (up to 5.4 metres)	Mon-Thu	130
	Fri-Sun	145
Car/caravan (up to 10 metres)	Mon-Thu	260
	Fri-Sun	290
Driver/passengers (per person)	first class	38
	second class	23

Furka Tunnel Switzerland

Oberwald (1367 metres, 4482ft)-Realp (1539 metres, 5046ft). Railway tunnel is 15.4km (9.5 miles) long. Journey time 15 minutes.

Services
Hourly 06.50-21.00.

Charges		(Swiss francs)
Motorcycle		19
Car (including driver)	Jun-Sep	25
	Oct-May	30
Car/caravan	Jun-Sep	44
	Oct-May	49

Oberalp Railway Switzerland

Andermatt (1444 metres, 4737ft) - Sedrun (1441 metres, 4728ft). Journey duration 60 minutes.

Booking
Advance booking is necessary:
Andermatt tel 041 8887511
Sedrun tel 041 819204711.

Services
2-4 trains daily Oct-Apr.

Charges	(Swiss francs)
Car	68
Minibus	105
Driver/passengers (per person)	12

Tauern Tunnel Austria

Bockstein (1131 metres, 3711ft; near Badgastein)-Mallnitz, 8.5km (5.5 miles) long. Width 2 metres. Journey duration 13 minutes.

Booking
Advance booking unnecessary (except for request trains), but motorists must report at least 20 minutes before departure. Drivers must drive their vehicles on and off the wagon.

Services
Regular services available.

Charges	(euros)
Motorcycle	8.00
Car	15.00

Compulsory Equipment

What you should carry in the car when driving on the Continent

Here are some items of equipment that are compulsory or recommended when travelling within areas of Europe. Alternatively, download our guide to compulsory equipment when driving in Europe for easy reference. In addition follow these tips for stress-free driving:

- **Display the appropriate identification letters.**
- **In winter, remember that, authorities insist on wheel chains and/or winter tyres for many resorts and passes.**
- **Ideally, fit external rear view mirrors to both sides of your vehicle.**
- **Motorcyclists and passengers must wear crash helmets in all countries.**

Country	First Aid Kit[1]	Fire Extinguisher[3]	Warning Triangle[3]	Spare Bulbs[1&2]	Headlamp Adjustment[4]
Andorra	Recommended	Recommended	Compulsory	Compulsory	Compulsory
Austria	Compulsory	Recommended	Compulsory	Recommended	Recommended
Belgium	Recommended	Recommended	Compulsory	Recommended	Compulsory
France	Recommended	Recommended	Compulsory[5/6]	Recommended	Compulsory
Germany	Recommended	Recommended	Compulsory[7]	Recommended	Compulsory
Italy	Recommended	Recommended	Compulsory	Recommended	Recommended
Luxembourg	Recommended	Recommended	Compulsory[7]	Recommended	Recommended
Netherlands	Recommended	Recommended	Compulsory[5]	Recommended	Compulsory
Portugal	Recommended	Recommended	Compulsory[5]	Recommended	Recommended
Spain	Recommended	Recommended	Compulsory[8]	Compulsory	Compulsory
Switzerland	Recommended	Recommended	Compulsory	Recommended	Recommended

NOTES

1. Applies to all vehicles including motorcycles unless stated otherwise.
2. A spare bulb kit will not avoid a fine if you are travelling with faulty lights, but replacing a bulb on the spot may avoid the cost and inconvenience of a garage call out. On some cars, only a qualified technician to change a headlamp bulb or lamp unit eg high-intensity discharge (HID) headlamps, so carrying spare bulbs is not an option. However, carry spare bulbs for any lights which can be easily and/or safely changed.
3. Excludes motorcycles.
4. Regardless of local requirements, it is wise to adjust headlamp beams for driving on the right. For older vehicles this can be done using simple adhesive masks on the headlamp glass, but for newer vehicles with high-density discharge (HID), xenon or many halogen headlamps it's not so easy. Check out what you need to do well before your intended departure by contacting a dealer for your make of vehicle. Without adjustment, dipped beams will dazzle oncoming drivers, and you could be fined. This adjustment is not required for two-wheeled vehicles as the beam pattern is more symmetrical, but check that any extra loading has not affected the beam height.
5. Hazard warning lights or a warning triangle are compulsory in an accident or breakdown situation. However, a warning triangle should always be carried as hazard warning lights have no effect at bends or rises in the road and may, of course, become damaged or inoperative.
6. Warning triangle compulsory for trailers with total authorised laden weight exceeding 500kg.
7. Although visitors don't have to carry warning triangles, it is compulsory to use them in an accident or breakdown.
8. One warning triangle compulsory for non-Spanish registed vehicles; two for Spanish registered vehicles. NOTE: Drivers of non-Spanish registered vehicles should consider carrying two triangles as regardless of the regulations, local officials may impose on the spot fine if only one is available.

Sample Booking Letters

Please use block capitals and enclose an International Reply Coupon, obtainable from post offices. Be sure to fill in your own name and address, including the post code and the country.

English

Dear Sir,

I intend to stay at your site for ....days, arriving on............(date and month) and departing on...................(date and month).
We are a party of ....people, including....adults and ....children (aged..........) and would like a pitch for ....tent(s) and/or parking space for our car/caravan/caravan trailer.
We would like to hire a tent/caravan/bungalow.
Please quote full charges when replying and advise on the deposit required, which will beforwarded without delay.

French

Monsieur,
Je me propose de séjourner à votre terrain de camping pour ....jours, depuis le..... jusqu'au..........
Nous sommes.........personnes en tout, y compris ....adultes et ....enfants (âgés de......) et nous aurons besoin d'un emplacement pour ....tente(s), et/ou un parking pour notre voiture/caravane/remorque.
Nous voudrions louer une tente/caravane/bungalow.
Veuillez me donner dans votre réponse une idée de vos prix, m'indiquant en même temps le montant qu'il faut payer en avance, ce qui vous sera envoyé sans délai.

German

Sehr geehrter Herr!
Ich beabsichtige, mich auf Ihrem Campingplatz ....Tage aufzuhalten, und zwar vom.....bis zum......
Wir sind im ganzen ....Personen, ...Erwachsene und ....Kinder (in Alter von......), und benötigen Platz für Zelt(e) und/oder unseren Wagen/Wohnwagen/Wohnwagenanhänger.
Wir möchten ein Zelt/Wohnwagen/Bungalow mieten.
Bitte, geben Sie mir in Ihrem Antwortschreiben die vollen Preise bekannt, und ebenso die Höhe der von mir zu leistenden Anzahlung, die Ihnen alsdann unverzüglich überwiesen wird.

Italian

Egregio Signore,
Ho intenzione di remanere presso di voi per .....giorni. Arriverò il.....e partirò il......
Siamo un gruppo di.......persone in totale, compreso ......adulti e ......bambini (de età.....) e vorrremo un posto per ......tenda(tende) e/o spazio per parcheggiare la nostra vetture/carovana/roulette.
Desideriamo affittare una tenda/carovana/bungalow.
Vi preghiamo di quotare i prezzi completi quando ci risponderete, e darci informazioni sul deposito richiesto, che vi sarà rimesso senza ritardo.

Spanish

Muy señor mio,
Desearia me reservara espacio por ......dias, a partir del.......hasta el......
Nuestro grupo comprende .....personas todo comprendido, ...adultos y ....niños (.......de años de edad). Necesitarimos un espacio por......tienda(s) y/o espacio para apacar nuestro choche/caravana/remolque.
Deseariamos alquilar una tienda de campana/caravan/bungalow.
Le ruego nos comunique los precios y nos informe sobre el depósito que debemos remitirle.

Key to Country Regions

The country directories, with the exception of Andorra and Luxembourg, are divided into regions, each introduced by a brief description, to help you to plan your touring holidays. Below is a list of the regional headings used in each country directory, followed by a list of the departments , districts or administrative areas that may be included within each region. See also the country maps at the end of the book.

AUSTRIA

TIROL
CARINTHIA = Kärnten
STYRIA = Steiermark
LOWER AUSTRIA - Niederösterreich, Burgenland
UPPER AUSTRIA - Oberösterreich, Salzburg
VORARLBERG
VIENNA = Wien

BELGIUM

SOUTH-WEST/COAST - Hainaut, West-Vlaanderen
NORTH/CENTRAL - Brabant, Oost-Vlaanderen
NORTH-EAST - Antwerpen, Limburg
SOUTH-EAST - Liège, Luxembourg, Namur

FRANCE

ALPS/EAST - Ain, Doubs, Hautes-Alpes, Haute Saône, Haute Savoie, Jura, Isère, Savoie, Territoire-de-Belfort
ALSACE/LORRAINE - Bas-Rhin, Haut-Rhin, Meurthe-et-Moselle, Meuse, Moselle, Vosges
BURGUNDY/CHAMPAGNE - Aube, Ardennes, Côte-d'Or, Haute-Marne, Marne, Nièvre, Saône-et-Loire, Yonne
SOUTH-WEST/ PYRENEES - Ariège, Dordogne, Gers, Gironde, Haute-Garonne, Hautes-Pyrénées, Landes, Lot, Lot-et-Garonne, Pyrénées-Atlantiques, Tarn, Tarn-et-Garonne
LOIRE/CENTRAL - Charente, Charente-Maritime, Cher, Corrèze, Creuse, Deux-Sèvres, Eure-et-Loir, Haute-Vienne, Indre, Indre-et-Loire, Loire-Atlantique, Loiret, Loir-et-Cher, Maine-et-Loire, Mayenne, Sarthe, Vendée, Vienne
BRITTANY/NORMANDY - Calvados, Côtes-d'Armor, Eure, Finistère, Ille-et-Vilaine, Manche, Morbihan, Orne, Seine-Maritime
PARIS/NORTH - Aisne, Essonne, Hauts-de-Seine, Nord, Oise, Paris, Pas-de-Calais, Seine-et-Marne, Seine-St-Denis, Somme, Val-de-Marne, Val d'Oise, Yvelines
AUVERGNE - Allier, Aveyron, Cantal, Haute-Loire, Loire, Lozère, Puy-de-Dôme, Rhône
SOUTH COAST/RIVIERA - Alpes-Maritimes, Alpes-de-Haute-Provence, Ardèche, Aude, Bouches-du-Rhône, Drôme, Gard, Hérault, Monaco, Pyrénées-Orientales, Var, Vaucluse
CORSICA - Corse-du-Sud, Haute-Corse

GERMANY

SOUTH-EAST - Bayern
SOUTH-WEST - Baden-Württemberg
BERLIN & EASTERN PROVINCES - Brandenburg, Sachsen, Thüringen
CENTRAL - Hessen, Nordrhein-Westfalen, Rheinland-Pfalz, Saarland
NORTH - Bremen, Hamburg, Niedersachsen, Schleswig-Holstein

ITALY

NORTH-WEST/ALPS/LAKES - Aosta, Alessandria, Asti, Beramo, Bolzano, Brescia, Como, Cremona, Cuneo, Mantova, Milano, Novara, Pavia, Sondrio, Trento, Torino, Varese, Vercelli
VENICE/NORTH - Belluno, Gorizia, Padova, Pordenone, Rovigo, Treviso, Trieste, Udine, Venezia, Verona, Vicenza,
NORTH-WEST/MED COAST - Arezzo, Firenze, Genova, Grosseto, Imperia, Livorno, Lucca, Massa Carrara, Pisa, Pistoia, Savona, Siena, La Spezia
NORTH-EAST/ADRIATIC - Ancona, L'Aquila, Ascoli Piceno, Bologna, Campobasso, Chieti, Ferrara, Forli, Iserina, Macerata, Modena, Parma, Perugia, Pescara, Pesaro & Urbino, Piacenza, Ravenna, Reggio nell'Emilia, Teramo, Terni
ROME - Frosinone, Latina, Roma, Rieti, Viterbo

SOUTH - Avellino, Bari, Benevento, Brindisi, Caserta, Catanzaro, Cosenza, Foggia, Lecce, Matera, Napoli, Potenza, Reggio di Calabria, Salerno, Taranto
SARDINIA - Cagliari, Nuoro, Oristano, Sassari
SICILY - Agrigento, Caltanissetta, Catania, Enna, Messina, Palermo, Ragusa, Siracusa, Trapani

NETHERLANDS

NORTH - Ameland, Drenthe, Friesland, Groningen
CENTRAL - Flevoland, Gelderland, Noord-Holland, Overijssel, Utrecht
SOUTH - Limburg, Noord-Brabant, Zeeland, Zuid-Holland

PORTUGAL

SOUTH - Algarve, Baixo-Alentejo
NORTH - Costa Verde, Douro Litoral, Minho, Tras os Montes, Alto Douro
CENTRAL - Alto Alentejo, Beira Alta, Beira Baixo, Beira Litoral, Costa de Prata, Estremadura, Ribatejo

SPAIN

NORTH-EAST COAST - Barcelona, Girona
CENTRAL - Albacete, Avila, Badajoz, Cáceres, Ciudad Real, Cuenca, Guadalajara, Madrid, Salamanca, Segovia, Soria, Teruel, Toledo
SOUTH-EAST COAST - Alicante, Castellón, Tarragona, Valencia
NORTH COAST - Asturias, Cantabria, Guipúzcoa, La Coruña, Lugo, Vizcaya
NORTH-EAST - Alava, Burgos, Huesca, Lleida, La Rioja, Navarra, Zaragoza
NORTH-WEST - Léon, Logrono Orense, Palencia, Pontevedra, Valladolid, Zamora
SOUTH - Almeria, Cádiz, Cordoba, Granada, Huelva, Jaén, Málaga, Murcia, Sevilla
ISLANDS - Ibiza, Mallorca Menorca

SWITZERLAND

NORTH - Aargau, Basel, Solothurn
NORTH-EAST - Appenzell, Liechtenstein, St Gallen, Schaffhausen, Thurgau, Zürich
NORTH-WEST/CENTRAL - Bern, Jura, Luzern, Neuchâtel, Nidwalden, Obwalden, Schwyz, Uri, Zug
EAST - Glarus, Graubünden
SOUTH - Ticino
SOUTH-WEST - Fribourg, Genève, Valais, Vaud

AUSTRIA

Austria is a land of chalet villages, beautiful cities and majestic mountains. It is bordered by eight countries: the Czech Republic, Germany, Hungary, Italy, Liechtenstein, Switzerland, Slovakia and Slovenia.

FACTS AND FIGURES
Area: 83,858 sq km (32,378 sq miles)
Population: 8,169,929 (2002 est)
Capital: Wien (Vienna)
Language: German
IDD Code: 43
To call the UK, dial 00 44
Currency: Euro
Local time: GMT + 1 (summer GMT + 2)
Emergency services: Police 133; Fire 122; Ambulance 144. **Or** dial 112 and request service.
Banks: 08.00-12.30, 13.30-15.00 (to 17.30 Thu)
Shops: Mon-Fri 08.00-18.00, Sat 08.00-12.30
Average daily temperatures:
Jan -1°C Mar 3°C
May 15°C Jul 20°C
Sep 16°C Nov 5°C
Tourist information:
Austrian National Tourist Office
UK
PO Box 2363
London W1A 2QB
Tel (020) 7629 0461
USA
PO Box 1142,
New York NY 10108
Tel (212) 730 4568
Tourist info website:
www.austria-tourism.at

The Austrian scenery is predominantly Alpine, an inspiring mix of mountains, lakes and pine forests. There are splendid mountains in the imposing Dachstein region of upper Austria and among the Tyrolean peaks. The lakes of Burgenland and Salzkammergut, the River Danube, the forests and woods of Styria, and the world-famous city of Wien (Vienna) are outstanding features.

Most of the country has a moderate climate during the summer, although eastern areas are sometimes very hot. The heaviest rainfall occurs in midsummer. The language of Austria is German, and English is not widely spoken. The Austrians pride themselves on their informal and easy-going nature, a nature summed up by the word 'gemütlich', a word that defies simple translation.

Austria offers a variety of outdoor activities and there are numerous campsites throughout the country. Most are open from May to September, although a number remain open all year.

Off-site camping or caravanning is generally prohibited. In areas with no campsites contact local police to find out whether an overnight stay is possible. If permission is granted, no camping activity must be seen from outside, e.g. chairs, awnings etc. Open fires are generally prohibited in woodland areas. Campers not on an official site, e.g. private property, staying in Austria for more than three days should report to the police as soon as possible, and also inform them of subsequent changes of location. Within Wien and Tirol (Tyrol) any form of off-site camping or caravanning is prohibited.

HOW TO GET THERE

Apart from the Eurotunnel, the usual Continental Channel port for this journey is Calais. From Calais drive through eastern France to Strasbourg, then via Karlsruhe and Stuttgart, crossing into Austria at Füssen for **Innsbruck and the Tirol**, and beyond München (Munich) for **Salzburg and central Austria.**

As an alternative, you could cross to Dieppe, Le Havre, Caen (Ouistreham) or Cherbourg and drive through northern France via **Strasbourg** and **Stuttgart,** or via **Basel** and northern Switzerland. But see 'Motorway Tax' in this and the Swiss section.

DISTANCE

From the Continental Channel ports, Salzburg is about 1140km (708 miles) and Vienna is about 1310km (814 miles), and you will probably need one overnight stop on the way.

CAR SLEEPER TRAINS

All-year services go from **Düsseldorf** to Salzburg, Villach and Wien, and from **Hamburg** to Wien. Summer services go from **Dortmund** and **Hamburg** to Villach.

MOTORING & GENERAL

The information given here is specific to Austria. It must be read in conjunction with the Essential Information for Motoring section, which covers those regulations that are common to many countries.

British Embassy/Consulates*

The British Embassy is located at 1030 Wien, Jaurèsgasse 12 ☎ (01) 716130; consular section, Jaurèsgasse 10 ☎(01) 71613 5151. There are British consulates with Honorary Consuls, in Bregenz, Graz, Innsbruck and Salzburg.

Children in Cars

Children under 14 and under 1.5 metres in height are not permitted to travel as front or rear seat passengers unless using a suitable restraint system - see **Passengers** and **Seat Belts** in the Essential Information for Motoring section.

Currency

The **euro** is the currency of Austria. The Austrian schilling (ATS) ceased to be legal tender in 2002, though ATS coins and notes may still be exchanged at the Austrian Central Bank (Oesterreichische Nationalbank) for an unlimited period.

Dimension & Weight Restriction

Private **cars** and towed **trailers** or **caravans** are restricted to the following dimensions - height 4 metres, width 2.55 metres, length 12 metres. The maximum permitted overall length of vehicle/trailer or caravan combination is 18.75 metres.

Driving Licence*

A valid UK or Republic of Ireland licence is accepted in Austria. However, licences that do not incorporate a photograph are only accepted when accompanied by photographic proof of identity, e.g. a passport. The minimum age at which a visitor may use a temporarily imported motorcycle (exceeding 50cc) or car is 18 years.

First-Aid Kit*

In Austria all vehicles (including motorcycles) must be equipped with a first-aid kit by law and visitors are expected to comply. Spot checks are carried out by the police. Any motorist stopped at the scene of an accident must be able to produce a first-aid kit if this is requested by any competent authority; if this is not forthcoming the police may take action.

Foodstuffs*

If the imported foodstuffs are for personal use, there are no limits when travelling between EU countries. Visitors entering Austria from Andorra, Romania, San Marino and Switzerland may personally import: up to 5kg of meat and meat products, and milk and milk products; up to 1kg of other animal products (e.g. eggs, honey, fish and all sea animal products) and 250g of caviar; and up to 15kg of fruit and vegetables. Coffee (500g), coffee extract (200g), tea (100g), and tea extract (40g) are free of customs duties, but visitors under 15 cannot import coffee.

Lights*

It is compulsory for motorcyclists to use dipped headlights during the day.

Motoring Club

The **Österreichische Automobil-, Motorrad-und Touring Club** (ÖAMTC) has its headquarters at 1010 Wien, Schubertring 1-3 ☎ (01) 71199-0, and offices at the major frontier crossings. The Club is represented in most towns either directly or through provincial motoring clubs.

The offices are usually open 09.00-18.00 Mon-Fri, 09.00-12.00 Sat; closed Sun and public holidays.

Website: **www.oamtc.at**

Motorway Tax

All vehicles using Austrian motorways and expressways must display a tax sticker (Vignette). The stickers, valid for one year, two months or 10 days, may be purchased at many petrol stations located close to the border in neighbouring countries and in Austria, at the frontier or in ÖAMTC offices.

The cost of a 10-day sticker for vehicles up to 3.5 tonnes, with or without a trailer, is €7.60.

Roads

Austria has a network of well-engineered roads. The main traffic artery runs from Bregenz in the west to Wien in the east, via the Arlberg Tunnel (toll; see Major Road and Rail Tunnels), Innsbruck, Salzburg and Linz. Most of the major alpine roads are excellent, and a comprehensive tour can be made through the Tirol,

Salzkammergut and Carinthia without difficulty. Service stations are fairly frequent, even on mountain roads.

In July and August, several roads across the frontier become congested. The main points are on the Lindau-Bregenz road; at the Brenner Pass (possible alternative - the Résia (Reschen) Pass); at Kufstein; on the München (Munich)-Salzburg Autobahn and on the Villach-Tarvisio road. Additionally, because of increasing traffic from Germany, Klingenbach and Nickelsdorf on the Austro/Hungarian border are very busy. For details see Principal Mountain Passes .

Austria has over 1600km of motorway (*autobahn*) with additional tolls payable on the Brenner, Karawanken Tunnel, Tauern and Pyhrn (Gleinalm and Bosruck tunnels). Triangles marked on motorway posts indicate the nearest emergency telephone (every 2km). A flashing orange/yellow light at the top of telephone posts indicates danger ahead.

Speed Limits*

Car/motorcycle

Built-up areas	50km/h (31mph)
Other roads	100km/h (62mph)
Motorways	130km/h (80mph)

Car towing caravan not exceeding 750kg (1,650lb)†

Built-up areas	50km/h (31mph)
Other roads	100km/h (62mph)
Motorways	100km/h (62mph)

Car towing caravan exceeding 750kg (1,650lb)†

Built-up areas	50km/h (31mph)
Other roads	80km/h (49mph)
Motorways	100km/h (62mph)

† If the total weight of the two vehicles exceeds 3,500kg the following speed limits apply:

Built-up areas	50km/h (31mph)
Other roads	70km/h (43mph)
Motorways	80km/h (49mph)

Notes

i. To tow a caravan/trailer, the weight of any caravan/trailer equipped with over-run brakes must not exceed the maximum weight of towing vehicle.
ii. Driving licence must show entitlement to drive this kind of combination.

Warning Triangle*

It is compulsory for a vehicle to carry a warning triangle and to use it outside built-up areas in the event of an accident or breakdown. The triangle must be placed behind the vehicle at a distance that will allow the drivers of following vehicles sufficient time to react to the obstruction; it must be visible at a distance of 50 metres (55yds).

*** Additional information can be found in the Essential Information for Motoring section.**

Hallstatt

TIROL

ASCHAU TIROL

Aufenfeld Distelberg 1, 6274 05282 2916 05282 291611
e-mail: camping.fiegl@tirol.com
website: www.camping-zillertal.at
A well-equipped family site on meadowland backed by thickly wooded slopes.
Signed from the Aschau road.
Open: All year **Site:** 12HEC **Prices:** 4.50-7.50 6.60-9 pitch 6.60-11 **Facilities:** **Services:** lau **Leisure:** LP **Off-site:** R

EHRWALD TIROL

International Dr-Ing E Lauth Zugspitzstr 34, 6632
05673 2666 05673 26664
e-mail: camping-ehrwald@tirol.com
website: www.camping-ehrwald.at
On undulating grassland, surrounded by high conifers, below the Wetterstein mountain range. Cars may park by tents in winter.
To the right of the access road to the Zugspitz funicular.
Open: All year **Site:** 1HEC **Facilities:** **Services:** lau **Off-site:** P

Tiroler Zugspitzcamp Obermoos 1, 6632
05673 2309 05673 230951
e-mail: camping@zugspitze.com
website: www.ferienanlage-zugspitze.at
A well-equipped site on grassy terraces surrounded by woodland. Modern sanitary installations with bathrooms.
Near the Zugspitz funicular station.
Open: All year **Site:** 5HEC **Prices:** 11.25-13.25 pitch 6-8 **Facilities:** **Services:** **Leisure:** P

FIEBERBRUNN TIROL

Tirol-Camp 6391 05354 56666 05354 52516
e-mail: office@tirol-camp.at
website: www.tirol-camp.at
A summer and winter site in pleasant Alpine surroundings.
Open: All year **Site:** 4.7HEC **Facilities:** **Services:** lau **Leisure:** LP **Off-site:** L

FÜGEN TIROL

Hell Gagering 212b, 6263 05288 62203 05288 64615
e-mail: camping.hell@tirol.com
website: www.tirol.com/camping-hell
In a meadow surrounding a farm with fine views of the surrounding mountains.
1km N of Fügen on the B169.
Open: All year **Site:** 4HEC **Facilities:** **Services:** lau **Leisure:** P **Off-site:** L

HAIMING TIROL

Center Oberland Bundestr 9, 6425
05266 88294 05266 882949
e-mail: oberland@tirol.com
website: www.camping_oberland.at
On a sloping meadow in a picturesque mountain setting. A wide variety of sporting facilities are available.
Off B171 at Km485.
Open: All year **Site:** 4HEC **Prices:** 4.50 3.50 3.50 3.50 (static)203.50 **Facilities:** **Services:** lau **Leisure:** P **Off-site:** R

HEITERWANG TIROL

Heiterwangersee Hotel Fisher am See, 6611
05674 5116 05674 5260
e-mail: fischer.am.see@tirol.com
A quiet meadow location beside a lake behind the hotel.
By Hotel Fischer am See.
Open: All year **Site:** 1HEC **Facilities:** **Services:** lau **Leisure:** L

HOPFGARTEN TIROL

Schlossberg Itter 140, 6361 05335 2181 05335 2182
e-mail: info@camping-itter.at
website: www.camping-itter.at
A family site with good leisure facilities. In terraced meadowland below Schloss Itter on the Brixental Ache.
2km W on B170.
Open: Dec-Oct **Site:** 4HEC **Prices:** 4.20-5.60 pitch 5.85-7.80 **Facilities:** **Services:** lau **Leisure:** PR **Off-site:** L

HUBEN TIROL

Ötztaler Naturcamping 6444 05253 5855 05253 5538
e-mail: oetzt-naturcamp@utanet.at
website: www.oetztalernaturcamping.com
A well-kept site in a beautiful wooded location beside a mountain stream.
S of the town. Signed from Km27 on B186.
Open: All year **Site:** 0.5HEC **Prices:** 4.80-5 2.30-2.50 4.30-6 3.30-4.30 **Facilities:** **Services:** lau **Off-site:**

IMST TIROL

Imst-West Langgasse 62, 6460
05412 66293 05412 63364
e-mail: fink.franz@aon.at
website: www.imst-west.com
On open meadowland in the Langgasse area.
Off the bypass near the turn for the Pitztal.
Open: All year **Site:** 1HEC **Prices:** 4-5.50 pitch 5.50-7.50 **Facilities:** **Services:** lau **Off-site:** LPR

INNSBRUCK TIROL

Innsbruck-Kranebitten Kranebitter Allee 214, 6020
0512 284180 0512 284180
e-mail: campinnsbruck@hotmail.com
website: www.campinginnsbruck.com
A pleasant location close to the city. An Innsbruck Card giving reductions to many places of interest and some forms of public transport is available at the site.
Signed from A12/E60 Innsbruck-Arlberg.
Open: All year **Site:** 3HEC **Prices:** 5 3 3 3 (static)100-300 **Facilities:** **Services:** lau **Leisure:** R **Off-site:** P

KITZBÜHEL TIROL

Schwarzsee 6370 05356 62806 6447930
e-mail: office@bruggerhof-camping.at
website: www.bruggerhof-camping.at
In meadowland on the edge of a wood behind a large restaurant.
2km from town on B170 towards Wörgl turn right, 400m after Schwarzsee railway station.
Open: All year **Site:** 6HEC **Prices:** 7.80-8.50 4-5 3.70-3.70 pitch 7.70-8.30 **Facilities:** **Services:** lau **Leisure:** L

KÖSSEN TIROL

Wilder Kaiser Kranebittau 18, 6345
05375 6444 05375 2113
e-mail: info@eurocamp-koessen.com
website: www.eurocamp-koessen.com
A lovely position below Unterberg, this level site is adjoined on three sides by woodland.
For access follow road to Unterberg Lift, then turn right and continue for 200m.
Open: All year **Site:** 5HEC **Facilities:** **Services:** lau **Leisure:** P

KRAMSACH TIROL

Stadlerhof 6233 05337 63371 05337 65311
e-mail: camping.stadlerhof@chello.at
website: www.camping-stadlerhof.at
A pleasant, year-round site on the Reintaler See with well-defined pitches and good leisure facilities.
Access via A12.
Open: All year **Site:** 3HEC **Facilities:** **Services:** lau **Leisure:** LP **Off-site:** R

KUFSTEIN TIROL

Kufstein Salurner Str 36, 6330
05372 62229 05372 636894
e-mail: kufstein@hotelbaeren.at
website: www.hotelbaeren.at
A pleasant location with a good variety of sport facilities.
1km W of Kufstein between River Inn and B171.
Open: May-Oct **Site:** 1HEC **Prices:** 4.95 4 4 3 pitch 5.50 **Facilities:** **Services:** lau **Off-site:** LPR

LANDECK TIROL

Riffler 6500 05442 64898 05442 648984
e-mail: riffler@aon.at
website: www.camping-riffler.at
Site on meadowland between residential housing and the banks of the Sanna.
Open: Jan-Apr & Jun-Dec **Site:** 0.3HEC **Prices:** 4.40 2.30 7.10-8.30 4.50-7.10 **Facilities:** **Services:** lau **Leisure:** R **Off-site:** P

Sport Camp Tirol Mühlkanal 1, 6500
05442 64636 64037
e-mail: info@sportcamptirol.at
website: www.sportcamptirol.at
Meadowland site with many fruit trees.
On B316.
Open: All year **Site:** 1.5HEC **Facilities:** **Services:** lau **Leisure:** R **Off-site:** LP

LÄNGENFELD TIROL

Ötztal 6444 05253 5348 05253 5909
In meadowland with some tall trees on the edge of woodland.
Turn right off E186 at fire station.
Open: All year **Site:** 2.6HEC **Facilities:** **Services:** lau **Off-site:** P

LANGKAMPFEN TIROL

Hager Kufsteinerstrasse 38, 6336
05372 64170 05332 7296635
Site on level meadowland.
Open: All year **Site:** 0.5HEC **Facilities:** **Services:** lau **Off-site:** LR

LERMOOS TIROL

Happy Camp Hofherr Garmischer Str 21, 6631
05673 2980 05673 29805
e-mail: info@camping-lermoos.com
website: www.camping-lermoos.com
Well-equipped site in a wooded location with fine views of the surrounding mountains.
500m from the town, off B187 towards Ehrwald.
Open: 15 Dec-Apr & Jun-Oct **Site:** 0.8HEC **Prices:** 7-7.90 6.20-8.20 **Facilities:** **Services:** lau **Off-site:** PR

LEUTASCH TIROL

Holiday-Camping 6105 05214 65700 05214 657030
e-mail: info@holiday-camping.at
website: www.holiday-camping.at
A modern site on level grassland screened by trees on the Leutascher Ache.
Turn off B313 (Mittenwald-Scharnitz) towards Leutasch.
Open: 7 Dec-5 Nov **Site:** 2.6HEC **Prices:** 8.50 5 pitch 7-10.50 **Facilities:** **Services:** lau **Leisure:** PR

LIENZ TIROL

Falken Eichholz 7, 9900 04852 64022 04852 640226
e-mail: camping.falken@tirol.com
website: www.camping-falken.com
On open ground on the outskirts of the town with modern sanitary facilities.
S of Lienz. Signed from B100.
Open: 21 Dec-19 Oct **Site:** 2.5HEC **Facilities:** **Services:** lau **Off-site:** LPR

MAURACH TIROL

Karwendel 6212 05243 6116 05243 20036
e-mail: info@karwendel-camping.at
website: www.karwendel-camping.at
On a level meadow with fine views of the surrounding mountains.
In town turn off the B181 and follow the Pertisau road.
Open: All year **Site:** 1.8HEC **Prices:** 4.50 3 4.50 4 **Facilities:** **Services:** lau **Off-site:** LP

MAYRHOFEN TIROL

Mayrhofen Laubichl 125, 6290 05285 6258051 05285 6258060
e-mail: camping@alpenparadies.com
website: www.alpenparadies.com
A modern site with good facilities, a short walk from the village centre.
Near a farm at N entrance to village.
Open: Nov-20 Dec **Site:** 2HEC **Prices:** 4.90-6.50 2.50 3-4.50 2.90-4.50 **Facilities:** **Services:** **Leisure:** P **Off-site:** R

Natters Tirol

Natterer See Natterer See 1, 6161
0512 546732 0512 54673216
e-mail: info@natterersee.com
website: www.natterersee.com
A terraced site beautifully situated amid woodland and mountains on the shore of Natterersee. A wide variety of leisure facilities are available.
Approach via Brenner Motorway, exit Innsbruck Süd, via Natters, onto B182 and follow signs.
Open: 15 Dec-Oct **Site:** 7.5HEC
Prices: 5.70-7.60 pitch 7.80-10 (static)258.30-489.30
Facilities: **Services:** lau **Leisure:** L

Nauders Tirol

Alpencamping Nauders 6543
05473 87217 05473 8721750
e-mail: alpencamping@tirol.com
website: www.camping-nauders.at
A year-round family site in a delightful Alpine location with good recreational facilities.
Access via B315.
Open: 17 Dec-Oct **Site:** 3HEC **Facilities:** **Services:** lau **Off-site:** L

Pettneu am Arlberg Tirol

Arlberg 05448 22266 05448 2226630
e-mail: info@camping-arlberg.at
website: www.camping-arlberg.at
Site in the Tyrolean mountains, suitable for hiking and mountaineering in summer and close to winter sports resorts.
Open: 20 Nov-10 Oct **Site:** 4.8HEC **Prices:** pitch 11-20 **Facilities:** **Services:** lau
Leisure: PR

Pill Tirol

Plankenhof 6130 05242 641950 05242 72344
e-mail: m.khuen-belasi@tirol.com
Site in meadow.
On B171 near Gasthof Plankenhof.
Open: May-1 Oct **Site:** 0.6HEC **Prices:** 4.05 5 pitch 8 **Facilities:** **Services:** lau
Leisure: P **Off-site:** LR

Prutz Tirol

Aktiv-Camping Prutz 6522 05472 2648 05472 2652
e-mail: info@aktiv-camping.at
website: www.aktiv-camping.at
A pleasant site in a beautiful mountain setting with good modern facilities.
Open: All year **Site:** 1.5HEC **Prices:** 6.10-6.70 5.80-8.70 5.10-7.80 **Facilities:**
Services: lau **Leisure:** R **Off-site:** LP

Reutte Tirol

Seespitze A-6600 05672 78121 05672 63372
e-mail: agrar.breitenwang@aon.at
website: www.camping-plansee.at
Open: May-15 Oct **Site:** 2HEC **Prices:** 3.50 2 5 3-5 **Facilities:** **Services:** lau
Leisure: L **Off-site:**

Sennalpe 6600 05672 78115 05672 63372
e-mail: agrar.breitenwang@aon.at
website: www.camping-plansee.at
A quiet location next to a lake.
On Reutte-Oberammergau road 200m from the Hotel Forelle.
Open: 15 Dec-15 Oct **Site:** 4HEC **Prices:** 3.50 2 5 3-5 **Facilities:** **Services:** lau
Leisure: L **Off-site:**

Ried bei Landeck Tirol

Dreiländereck 6531 05472 6025 05472 60254
e-mail: camping-drellandereck@tirol.com
website: www.tirolcamping.at
Level site in centre of village beside a lake with spectacular views.
Open: All year **Site:** 1HEC **Facilities:** **Services:** lau **Off-site:** LPR

Rinn Tirol

Judenstein Judenstein 40, 6074 05223 78620 7887715
e-mail: kommunalgmbh@rinn.tirol.gv.at
website: www.tiscover.at/camping.judenstein
A wooded location with fine views.
Access via motorway exit Hall.
Open: May-Sep **Site:** 0.6HEC **Prices:** 3.50 2 3 3 **Facilities:** **Services:** lau **Off-site:**

St Johann Tirol

Michelnhof Weiberndorf 6, 6380
05352 62584 05352 625844
e-mail: camping@michelnhof.at
website: www.camping-michelnhof.at
1.5km S via B161 St-Johann-Kitzbühel.
Open: All year **Site:** 3HEC **Facilities:**
Services: lau **Off-site:** PR

Schwaz Tirol
at Weer (6km W)

Alpencamping Mark Maholmhof, 6114
05224 68146 05244 681466
e-mail: alpcamp.mark@aou.at
website: www.alpencampingmark.com
Situated on meadowland by a farm on the edge of a forest.
Off B171.
Open: Apr-Oct **Site:** 2HEC **Prices:** 4.30-5.50 6 pitch 4.50-6 **Facilities:** **Services:** lau
Leisure: P **Off-site:** L

Sölden Tirol

Sölden 6450 05254 26270 05254 26275
e-mail: info@camping-soelden.com
website: www.camping-soelden.com
Situated on meadowland on left bank of Ötztaler tributary. Beautiful views of the surrounding mountains.
By Grauer Bär Inn at Km36 on the B186.
Open: 11-18 Apr & 24 Jun-Dec **Site:** 1.3HEC
Prices: 6-9 6.70-11 pitch 6.70-11 **Facilities:** **Services:** lau **Off-site:** P

Stams Tirol

Eichenwald Schiessstand weg 10, 6422 05263 6159
Well-managed terraced site in an oak wood.
Turn off B171 at Esso filling station in direction of abbey, onto a steep, narrow access road.
Site: 2HEC **Facilities:**
Services: lau **Leisure:** P **Off-site:** R

Thiersee Tirol

Rueppenhof Seebauern 8, 6335 05376 5694
e-mail: atzl.barbara@tirol.com
website: www.rueppenhof-motinfo.com
Site made up of several meadows surrounding a farm on the banks of a lake.

Access via A12 exit Kufstein-Nord, then follow signs for Thiersee.
Open: Apr-Oct **Site:** 1.5HEC **Prices:** 4.20 2.20 2.70 1.50-2.20 **Facilities:** **Services:** **Leisure:** L **Off-site:**

Umhausen Tirol

Ötztal Arena Camp Krismer 6441
05255 5390 05255 5390
e-mail: info@oetztal-camping.at
website: www.oetztal-camping.at
Signed from B186.
Open: All year **Site:** 1HEC **Facilities:** **Services:** lau **Leisure:** LR

Unterperfuss Tirol

Farm 6175 05232 20097 06942094
e-mail: brangerbrau@aon.at
website: www.brangeralm.at
Modern site on a gently sloping meadow in a beautiful mountain setting.
W end of village near Amberg railway and main road.
Open: All year **Site:** 1.5HEC **Prices:** 5 pitch 8.90 **Facilities:** **Services:** **Off-site:**

Völs Tirol

Völs Bahnhofstr 10, 6176 0512 303533
Access via motorway exit Innsbruck-Kranebitten.
Open: Apr-Nov **Site:** 0.4HEC **Facilities:** **Services:** lau **Off-site:** LPR

Waidring Tirol

Steinplatte Unterwasser 43, 6384
05353 5345 05353 5406
e-mail: camping-steinplatte@aon.at
website: www.camping-steinplatte.at
A level meadow with panoramic views of the surrounding mountains.
Open: All year **Site:** 4HEC **Facilities:** **Services:** **Leisure:** L **Off-site:** PR

Walchsee Tirol

Seespitz Wassersportzentrum, 6344
05374 5359 05374 5845
e-mail: camping.seespitz@netway.at
website: www.camping-seespitz.at
In pleasant surroundings beside the Walchsee with good recreational facilities.
Between B172 and bank of lake.
Open: All year **Site:** 3HEC **Prices:** 5-5.50 5-5.50 **Facilities:** **Services:** lau **Leisure:** L

Terrassencamping Süd-See Seestr 76, 6344
05374 5339 05374 5529
e-mail: campingwalchsee@aon.at
website: www.camp-sud-see.com
A lakeside site in wooded surroundings with extensive terracing and fine mountain views.
500m W on B172 turn into 'no through road' and continue for 1.5km.
Open: All year **Site:** 11HEC **Facilities:** **Services:** lau **Leisure:** L

Westendorf Tirol

Panorama Mühltal 70, A-6363 05334 6166 05334 6843
e-mail: info@panorama.camping.at
website: www.panorama.camping.at
A beautiful Alpine setting with good modern facilities, including well-furnished studio apartments.
W towards Wörgl via B170.
Open: All year **Site:** 2.2HEC **Facilities:** **Services:** lau **Off-site:** P

Zell am Ziller Tirol

Hofer Gerlossasstr 33, 6280 05282 2248 05282 22488
e-mail: office@campinghofer.at
website: www.campinghofer.at
On meadowland with some fruit trees.
Site lies to the end of Zillertal off the road leading to the Gerlos Pass.
Open: All year **Site:** 1.5HEC **Prices:** 6 pitch 6.50 **Facilities:** **Services:** lau **Leisure:** P

Zirl Tirol

Alpenfrieden Eigenhofen 11, 6170 05238 53520
Terraced site with orchard surroundings.
Near the B171.
Open: May-Sep **Site:** 1HEC **Prices:** 5.60 6.30 (static)143.50 **Facilities:** **Services:** **Leisure:** P **Off-site:** R

Carinthia

Dellach Kärnten

Neubauer 9872 04766 2532 04766 25324
e-mail: info@camping-neubauer.at
website: www.camping-neubauer.at
A terraced site with direct access to the Millstättersee.
Access from B100, Leinz-Spittal road. The turn-off is well signed in the village.
Open: May-15 Oct **Site:** 1.5HEC **Prices:** 6.07-7.87 5.40-6.50 **Facilities:** **Services:** lau **Leisure:** L **Off-site:**

Dellach im Drautal Kärnten

Waldbad 9772 04714 288 & 234 04714 2343
e-mail: dellach-drau.info@ktn.gde.at
website: www.tiscover.com/dellach
A small site in a delightful wooded setting with two large swimming pools.
Leave A10 at Spittal & turn onto B100.
Open: May-Sep **Site:** 2HEC **Prices:** 4.50-7 pitch 14-23 (incl 2 persons) **Facilities:** **Services:** lau **Leisure:** P **Off-site:** R

Döbriach Kärnten

Brunner am See Glanzerstr 108, 9873
04246 7189 04246 7837
e-mail: camping.brunner@aon.at
website: www.camping-brunner.at
Tidily arranged with poplar trees. Private bathing area.
The access road is at the E end of Lake Millstatt.
Open: All year **Site:** 3.5HEC **Prices:** 5-7.50 pitch 6.60-10.90 **Facilities:** **Services:** lau **Leisure:** L

Burgstaller Seefeldstr 16, 9873
04246 7774 04246 77744
e-mail: info@burgsteller.co.at
website: www.burgstaller.co.at
A quiet site 100m from a lake, with good modern facilities.
At SE end of lake. From B98 continue towards Lake Millstatt for 1km.
Open: All year **Site:** 12HEC **Facilities:** **Services:** lau **Leisure:** LP

DÖLLACH KÄRNTEN

Zirknitzer 9843 04825 451 04825 45117
e-mail: camping.zirknitzer@utanet.at
website: web.utanet.at/zirknitp
Beside the River Möu.
Between Km8 and Km9 on the Glocknerstr (B107).
Open: 21 Dec-4 Nov **Site:** 0.6HEC
Prices: 3.20-4 1.80-2 1.80-2.50 1-2 **Facilities:** **Services:** lau **Leisure:** R **Off-site:** P

FELDKIRCHEN KÄRNTEN

Seewirt-Spiess Maltschach am See 2, 9560
04277 2637 04277 2637 - 4
e-mail: office@seewirl-spiess.com
website: www.seewirl-spiess.com
A pleasant wooded location on the shore of the Maltschacher See.
Access via B95 towards Klagenfurt.
Open: May-Sep **Site:** 1.2HEC **Prices:** 6 pitch 16-22 (incl 2 persons) (static)254-364 **Facilities:** **Services:** lau **Leisure:** L **Off-site:** P

HEILIGENBLUT KÄRNTEN

Grossglockner 9844 04824 2048 04824 24622
e-mail: nationalpark-camping@heiligenblut.at
website: www.heiligenblut.at/nationalpark-camping
On a meadow surrounded by woodland within the national park.
Signed.
Open: May-Oct & Dec-Apr **Site:** 2.5HEC
Prices: 5.90 2.20 2.20 **Facilities:**
Services: lau **Leisure:** R **Off-site:** P

HERMAGOR KÄRNTEN

Schluga 9620 04282 2051 04282 288120
e-mail: camping@schluga.com
website: www.schluga.com
Well-equipped family site in a rural setting 4km from Presseger See.
Open: All year **Site:** 5.5HEC **Prices:** 5-7.70 pitch 4-7.50 **Facilities:** **Services:** lau **Leisure:** LP

Schluga Seecamping 9620 04282 2051 04282 288120
e-mail: camping@schluga.com
website: www.schluga.com
A well-equipped family site 300m N of lake in meadowland with some terraces and fine views.
6km E of Hermagor.
Open: 20 May-20 Sep **Site:** 8.8HEC **Prices:** 5-7.70 pitch 4-7.50 **Facilities:** **Services:** lau **Leisure:** L **Off-site:** R

KEUTSCHACH KÄRNTEN

Strandcamping Süd 9074 04273 2773 04273 27734
In a pleasant setting among shrubs and trees on S side of the Keutschachersee.
Access via motorway exit Valden towards Kreutschacher-Seental.
Open: 20 Apr-Sep **Site:** 2HEC **Facilities:**
Services: lau **Leisure:** L

KLAGENFURT KÄRNTEN

Strandbad 9020 0463 21169 0463 21193
e-mail: camping@stw.at
website: www.tiscover.at/camping-klagenfurt
Large site divided into sections by trees and bushes.
From town centre take B83 towards Velden. Turn left just outside town in direction of bathing area.
Open: 15 Apr-5 Oct **Site:** 4HEC **Prices:** 4.20-7.30 pitch 8.40 **Facilities:** **Services:** lau
Leisure: L

KÖTSCHACH-MAUTHEN KÄRNTEN

Alpen 9640 04715 429 04715 429
e-mail: info@alpencamp.at
website: www.alpencamp.at
On meadowland beside the River Gail with good facilities for water sports.
Turn off B110 in the S part of the village on the road to the Plöcken Pass and drive 800m towards Lesachtal.
Open: 15 Dec-Oct **Site:** 1.5HEC **Prices:** 3.70-5.70 pitch 4-6.30 **Facilities:** **Services:** lau **Off-site:** PR

MALTA KÄRNTEN

Maltatal 9854 0043 4733 234 4733 23416
e-mail: info@maltacamp.at
website: www.maltacamp.at
On a gently rising alpine meadow with breathtaking views of the surrounding mountains.
In Gmünd turn off B99 and drive 5.5km through Malta valley.
Open: 03 Apr-Oct **Site:** 3.5HEC **Facilities:** **Services:** lau **Leisure:** PR

MÖLLBRÜCKE KÄRNTEN

Rheingold Mölltalstr 65, 9813 04769 2338
Site on main road from Spittal to Mallnitz, next to swimming pool.
Open: All year **Site:** 2HEC **Facilities:**
Services: **Leisure:** P **Off-site:**

OBERVELLACH KÄRNTEN

Sport Erlebnis 9821 04782 2727 04782 3183
e-mail: info@sporterlebnis.at
website: www.sporterlebnis.at
Open: May-Sep **Site:** 10HEC **Facilities:**
Services: lau **Leisure:** R **Off-site:** P

OSSIACH KÄRNTEN

Ossiach 9570 04243 436 04243 8171
e-mail: martinz@camping.at
website: www.terrassen.camping.at
Divided into pitches with generally well-situated terraces.
Off B94 on E bank of Kale Ossiacher.
Open: May-Sep **Site:** 10HEC **Facilities:** **Services:** lau **Leisure:** L

Parth 9570 04243 2744
e-mail: camping@parth.at
website: www.parth.at
On hilly ground on S shore of the lake. Steep, with some terraces.
Off B94 on S bank of Lake Ossiach.
Open: 20 Dec-30 Oct **Site:** 1.8HEC
Prices: 4.30-7.80 3.70-9.10 pitch 6.20-9.90 **Facilities:** **Services:** lau **Leisure:** L

AT HEILIGEN GESTADE (5KM SW)

Seecamping Berghof Ossiachersee-Süduferstr 241, 9523
04242 41133 04242 4113330
e-mail: office@camping-ertl.at
website: www.camping-ertl.at
Terraced meadowland in attractive setting. 800m promenade with bathing areas. Dogs not allowed in July and August

E shore of lake Ossiacher.
Open: Apr-Oct **Site:** 10HEC **Prices:** 5.20-7.80 pitch 7.50-12.50 **Facilities:** **Services:** lau **Leisure:** L

SACHSENBURG Kärnten

Markt Sachsenburg Marktpl 12, 9751
04769 292522 04769 292520
e-mail: sachsenburg@ktn.gde.at
website: www.draucamping.at
A modern family site with good facilities in a delightful mountain setting.
Access via A10 between Spittal and Lienz.
Open: May-Sep **Site:** 1.3HEC **Prices:** 11-15 **Facilities:** **Off-site:** P

ST PRIMUS Kärnten

Strandcamping Turnersee Breznik 9123
04239 2350 04239 235032
e-mail: info@breznik.at
website: www.breznik.at
A quiet site in a picturesque mountain setting with a variety of recreational facilities.
Access via B70 Klagenfurt-Graz towards Kopenersee.
Open: 16 Apr-1 Oct **Site:** 6HEC **Prices:** 4.50-7.50 pitch 6-9.20 (static)152.61-412.05 **Facilities:** **Services:** **Leisure:** L **Off-site:**

SEEBODEN Kärnten

Ferienpark Lieseregg Kras 27, 9871
04762 2723 04762 33857
e-mail: info@ferienpark-lieseregg.at
website: www.ferienpark-lieseregg.at
A family site on a large meadow with terraces and asphalt drives surrounded by woodland.
B99 from Spittal N to B98, then left for 1.5km.
Open: May-1 Oct **Site:** 3HEC **Prices:** 5.90-7.50 pitch 4-7.63 **Facilities:** **Services:** lau **Leisure:** P

SPITTAL AN DER DRAU Kärnten

Draufluss 9800 04762 2466 04762 2466
e-mail: drauwirt@aon.at
website: www.drauwirt.com
A long, narrow riverside site, partly surrounded by a hedge.
From town centre follow road to river towards Goldeckbahn.
Open: 15 Apr-15 Oct **Site:** 0.7HEC **Prices:** 4-4.50 2.50-3 2.50-3 2.50-3 pitch 5-6 **Facilities:** **Services:** lau **Leisure:** PR **Off-site:**

STOCKENBOI Kärnten

Ronacher Möse 6, 9714 04761 256 04761 2564
e-mail: terrassencamping.ronacher@net4you.at
website: www.campingronacher.at
Situated on meadow between forest slopes, gently sloping to the shore of lake Weissensee. Shop open in high season only.
Approach for caravans via Weissensee.
Open: May-10 Oct **Site:** 1.7HEC **Facilities:** **Services:** **Leisure:** L

VILLACH Kärnten

Gerli St Georgenerstr 140, 9500
04242 57402 04242 582909
e-mail: gerli.meidl@utanet.at
Quiet, isolated level site, with heated swimming pool annexed to it, which is open to the public.
From Spittal/Drau turn off B100, turn right just before Villach and continue for 2km.
Open: All year **Site:** 2.3HEC **Prices:** 3.90-4.50 pitch 3.90-4.50 **Facilities:** **Services:** lau **Off-site:** P

AT FAAK AM SEE (10KM SE)

Strandcamping Arneitz A-9583
04254 2137 04254 3044
On a wooded peninsula jutting into the Faakersee with good sporting facilities.
Open: 28 Apr-Sep **Site:** 6HEC **Facilities:** **Services:** lau **Leisure:** L

Strandcamping Florian Badeweg 3, 9583
04254 2261 04254 3943
e-mail: iris.effermann@eunet.at
website: www.camping-florian.at
A partially shaded site between the lake and the road.
Access from road by Hotel Fürst.
Open: May-25 Sep **Site:** 3.5HEC **Facilities:** **Services:** lau **Leisure:** L **Off-site:**

Strandcamping Gruber 9583
04254 2298 04254 2298-7
e-mail: gruber@strandcamping.at
website: www.strandcamping.at
On level ground beside the lake with fine views of the surrounding mountains.
Open: May-Sep **Site:** 2.5HEC **Prices:** 6.30 12-17.50 **Facilities:** **Services:** lau **Leisure:** L **Off-site:**

WERTSCHACH Kärnten

Alpenfreude 9612 04256 2708 04256 27084
e-mail: camping.alpenfreude@aon.at
website: www.alpenfreude.at
Open: May-Sep **Site:** 5HEC **Prices:** 3.10-4.80 pitch 4.50-6.60 (static)250-345 **Facilities:** **Services:** lau **Leisure:** P **Off-site:**

STYRIA

AUSSEE, BAD Steiermark

Traun Grundlseer Str 21, 8990
03622 54565 03622 52427
e-mail: gh.staudnwirt@aussee.at
website: www.aussee.at/staudnwirt
In pleasant wooded surroundings.
2.5km from Bad Aussee towards Grundlsee.
Open: All year **Site:** 0.4HEC **Prices:** 6.20 pitch 3 (static)140-245 **Facilities:** **Services:** lau **Leisure:** R **Off-site:** LP

GRAZ Steiermark

S C Central Martinhofstr 3, 8054
0316 281831 0316 697824
e-mail: Freizeir@netway.at
website: tiscover.com/campingcentral
A site with many lawns separated by asphalt paths and partly divided into pitches.
Turn off the B70 in Strassgang S of Graz and continue for 300m.
Open: Apr-Oct **Site:** 4HEC **Facilities:** **Services:** lau **Leisure:** P

Hirschegg Steiermark

Hirschegg 8584 03141 2201
e-mail: stoeklcamp@hotmail.com
website: www.camping-hirschegg.at
A delightful Alpine setting.
Access via A2 towards Klagenfurt, exit Modriach.
Open: All year **Site:** 2HEC **Facilities:** **Services:** lau **Off-site:** LPR

Langenwang-Mürtzal Steiermark

Europa Siglstr 5, 8665 03854 2950
e-mail: europa.camping.stmk@aon.at
website: www.campsite.at/europa.camping.langenwang
On a meadow with some trees, surrounded by hedges. The site has an attractive alpine setting.
The B306 (E7) by-passes the town, so be careful not to miss the exit 6km S of Mürzzuschlag.
Open: All year **Site:** 0.6HEC **Prices:** 4.15 3 3 3 **Facilities:** **Services:** lau **Off-site:** R

Leibnitz Steiermark

Leibnitz R-H-Bartsch-Gasse 33, 8430
03452 82463 03452 71491
e-mail: gde@leibnitz.steiermark.at
website: www.camping-steiermark.at
A well-equipped site in pleasant wooded surroundings with plenty of leisure facilities.
W of town. Signed.
Open: May-15 Sep **Site:** 0.7HEC **Facilities:** **Services:** lau **Leisure:** PR **Off-site:** L

Maria Lankowitz Steiermark

Piberstein Am See 1, 8591
03144 7095950 03144 7095974
e-mail: office@piberstein.at
website: www.piberstein.at
Large well-equipped site around a series of lakes. Plenty of sport facilities.
S of Maria Lankowitz towards Pack.
Open: May-15 Oct **Site:** 5.6HEC **Prices:** 6 9.50 7 pitch 9.50 **Facilities:** **Services:** lau **Leisure:** L **Off-site:**

Mitterndorf, Bad Steiermark

Grimmingsicht 8983 03623 2985
e-mail: camping@grimmingsicht.at
website: www.grimmingsicht.at
A modern site in a picturesque mountain setting with a variety of sport facilities.
Open: All year **Site:** 0.6HEC **Facilities:** **Services:** lau **Leisure:** R **Off-site:** P

Mühlen Steiermark

Badsee Hitzmannsdorf 2, 8822 03586 2418 03586 2204
e-mail: office@camping-am-badesee.at
website: www.camping-am-badesee.at
Family site with direct access to the lake.
N via B92. Signed.
Open: May-Sep **Site:** 1.5HEC **Prices:** 4 6 3-3.60 **Facilities:** **Services:** lau **Leisure:** L **Off-site:** P

Oberwölz Steiermark

Burg Rothenfels 8832 03581 8208 03581 82084
e-mail: rothenfels@aon.at
website: www.rothenfels.at
Picturesque Alpine surroundings in the grounds of a castle, with good recreational facilities.
On SE outskirts.
Open: Apr-Oct **Site:** 8HEC **Facilities:** **Services:** lau **Leisure:** L **Off-site:** PR

St Georgen Steiermark

Olachgut 8861 03532 2162 03532 2162
e-mail: olachgut@murau.at
website: www.murau.at/olachgut
On a meadow surrounded by beautiful mountain scenery.
Signed.
Open: All year **Site:** 10HEC **Facilities:** **Services:** lau **Leisure:** L **Off-site:** R

St Sebastian Steiermark

Erlaufsee Erlaufseestr 3, 8630
03882 4937 03882 214822
e-mail: gemeinde@st-sebastian.at
website: www.st-sebastian.at
A picturesque Alpine setting in woodland, 100m from the lake.
Signed.
Open: May-15 Sep **Site:** 1HEC **Prices:** 3.60 2.50 3 3 **Facilities:** **Off-site:** LR

Schladming Steiermark

Zirngast Linke Ennsau 633, 8970
03687 23195 03687 23495
e-mail: camping@zirngast.at
website: www.zirngast.at
Site in meadow on left bank of River Enns next to railway.
Turn off B308 towards town as far as the filling station.
Open: All year **Site:** 1.5HEC **Prices:** 6 6 4.50-17.50 **Facilities:** **Services:** lau **Leisure:** R **Off-site:** P

Ungersdorf bei Frohnleiten Steiermark

Lanzmaierhof Ungersdorf 16, 8130
03126 2360 03126 4174
e-mail: tourismus@frohnleiten.at
website: www.camping-steiermark.at
Signed 2km S of Frohnleiten on the Graz road.
Open: Apr-15 Oct **Site:** 0.5HEC **Prices:** 3.80 2.40 2.40 1.40-2.80 **Facilities:** **Services:** lau **Off-site:** P

Weisskirchen Steiermark

50Plus Campingpark Fisching Fisching 9, 8741
03577 82284 03577 8228846
e-mail: campingpark@fisching.at
website: www.camping50plus.at
A modern site with fine sanitary and sporting facilities, 6km from the Formula 1 circuit (A1-Ring) in Zeltweg.
Leave S36 at Zeltweg-Ost exit, head towards Obdach and follow signs for B78. Site well signed in centre of Fisching.
Open: Apr-15 Oct **Site:** 1.5HEC **Prices:** 4.10 pitch 5.80 **Facilities:** **Services:** lau **Leisure:** P **Off-site:**

Wildalpen Steiermark

Wildalpen 8924 03636 342 & 341 03636 313
e-mail: tourismus@wildalpen.at
website: www.wildalpen.at
Located in a nature reserve beside the River Salza with good canoeing facilities.
Open: Apr-Oct **Site:** 0.8HEC **Facilities:** **Services:** lau **Leisure:** R **Off-site:** P

LOWER AUSTRIA

BREITENBRUNN BURGENLAND

Seebad 7091 02683 5252 02683 5252
Open: May-Sep **Site:** 1HEC **Facilities:**
Services: lau **Leisure:** L **Off-site:** P

GMÜND NIEDERÖSTERREICH

Assangteich Albrechtser Str 10, 3950
02852 52506 02852 52506500
e-mail: stadtgemeinde@gmuend.at
website: www.gmuend.at
In a pleasant location with a good variety of recreational facilities.
Signed from B41.
Open: 5 Apr-6 Oct **Site:** 0.5HEC **Prices:** 4.06 pitch 6.20 **Facilities:** **Services:** lau **Off-site:** LP

HIRTENBERG NIEDERÖSTERREICH

Hirtenberg Leobersdorfefstr, 2552
02256 81111 02256 8111117
Take exit Leobersdorf on A2/E59 and continue W on B18 for 0.8km.
Open: 15 May-15 Sep **Site:** 1.5HEC **Facilities:** **Services:** lau **Off-site:** P

JENNERSDORF BURGENLAND

Jennersdorf Freizeitzentrum 3, 8380
03329 46133 03329 4626121
e-mail: post@jennersdorf.bgld.gv.at
website: www.jennersdorf.net
A pleasant site in wooded surroundings.
Access via A2 exit Fürstenfeld.
Open: 16 Mar-Oct **Site:** 1HEC **Prices:** 4.40 4.80 4.80 pitch 4.80 **Facilities:** **Services:** lau
Leisure: P **Off-site:** R

LAXENBURG NIEDERÖSTERREICH

Schlosspark Laxenburg Münchendorfer Str, 2361
02236 71333 02236 73966
e-mail: camping.laxenburg@verkehrsbuero.at
website: www.wiencamping.at
On level meadowland with surfaced roads. The site lies in a recreation centre within the grounds of the historic Laxenburg castle.
Access 600m S on the road leading to the B16.
Open: Apr-Oct **Site:** 2.4HEC **Facilities:** **Services:** lau **Leisure:** P **Off-site:**

MARBACH NIEDERÖSTERREICH

Marbacher 3671 0664 5581815 07413 703533
e-mail: info@marbach-freizeit.at
website: www.marbach-freizeit.at
In a pleasant situation beside the River Danube.
Access via A1 exit Ybbs.
Open: Apr-Oct **Site:** 0.4HEC **Prices:** 5.30 3.50 4.50 4 **Facilities:** **Services:** lau
Leisure: R **Off-site:** P

MARKT ST MARTIN BURGENLAND

Markt St Martin Mühlweg 2, 7341
0043 2618 02618 22394
e-mail: post@markt-st-martin.bgld.gv.at
On a level meadow with plenty of trees and bushes.
Access via A2 exit Krumbach/Schäffern.
Open: May-Sep **Site:** 0.5HEC **Prices:** 4.90 4 1.50 **Facilities:** **Services:** lau
Leisure: PR **Off-site:**

PODERSDORF BURGENLAND

Strandcamping Podersdorf am See Strandpl, 7141
02177 2279
Directly on the Neusiedler See next to the sportsground.
Open: Apr-Oct **Site:** 7HEC **Facilities:** **Services:** lau **Leisure:** L **Off-site:**

RAPPOLTENKIRCHEN NIEDERÖSTERREICH

Rappoltenkirchen Kreuthstr 5, 3443
02274 8425 02274 8422
Turn off B1 at Sieghartskirchen and continue S for 3km.
Site: 2.2HEC **Facilities:** **Services:** lau **Off-site:**

RECHNITZ BURGENLAND

GC Hauptpl 10, 7471 03363 79202 03363 7920222
e-mail: post@rechnitz.bgld.gv.at
website: www.rechnitz.com
On an artificial lake in the heart of the beautiful Faludi Valley.
Open: Jun-Aug **Site:** 1HEC **Prices:** 4.30 5.10 2.90 **Facilities:** **Services:** **Leisure:** L
Off-site:

RUST BURGENLAND

Rust 7071 02685 595 02685 595
e-mail: office@gmeiner.co.at
website: www.gmeiner.co.at
Situated on level meadowland with young trees.
From Rust follow the lake road.
Open: Apr-Oct **Site:** 56HEC **Prices:** 4.40-5.10 3.60-4 3.20-4 3.20-4 **Facilities:**
Services: lau **Leisure:** L **Off-site:** P

SCHÖNBÜHEL NIEDERÖSTERREICH

Stumpfer 3392 02752 8510 02752 851017
e-mail: office@stumpfer.com
website: www.stumpfer.com
A small site in a wooded location attached to a guesthouse close to the River Donau.
SW of town.
Open: Apr-Oct **Site:** 1.5HEC **Prices:** 4.40 5.50 2.50-5.50 **Facilities:** **Services:** lau
Leisure: R

TRAISEN NIEDERÖSTERREICH

Terrassen-Camping Traisen Kulmhof 1, 3160
02762 62900 02762 629004
e-mail: info@camping-traisen.at
website: www.camping-traisen.at
Set out in a circular formation around the main buildings with plenty of trees around the pitches.
0.6km W via B20.
Open: All year **Site:** 2.1HEC **Prices:** 5-5.50 pitch 5-5.50 **Facilities:** **Services:** lau
Leisure: P **Off-site:**

TULLN NIEDERÖSTERREICH

Donaupark-Camping Tulln Hafenstr, 3430
02272 65200 02272 65201
e-mail: camptulln@oeamtc.at
website: www.campingtulln.at
A modern site in a peaceful location with good facilities close to the River Danube with a high season bus service to Vienna.
Open: 25 Mar-Oct **Site:** 10HEC **Prices:** 6 4.50 7.50-11 2.50 **Facilities:**
Services: lau **Leisure:** L **Off-site:** PR

Facilities: -shop -shower -electric points for razors -electric points for caravans -parking by tents permitted -compulsory separate car park **Services:** -café/restaurant -bar -Camping Gaz International -gas other than Camping Gaz -first aid facilities lau-laundry **Leisure:** -swimming L-Lake P-Pool R-River S-Sea **Off-site:** All facilities within 2km

WAIDHOFEN AN DER THAYA NIEDERÖSTERREICH

Thayapark Badgasse, 3830 02842 50350 02842 50399
e-mail: info@waidhofen-thaya-stadt.at
website: www.waidhofen-thaya.at
A family site in wooded surroundings close to the River Thaya.
Signed from village.
Open: May-Sep **Site:** 10HEC **Facilities:** **Services:** lau **Leisure:** R **Off-site:** P

UPPER AUSTRIA/SALZBURG

ABERSEE SALZBURG

Wolfgangblick Seestr 24, A-5342
06227 3475 06227 3218
e-mail: camping@wolfgangblick.at
website: www.wolfgangblick.at
In a pleasant position directly on the Wolfgangsee.
Camping Card Compulsory.
Access via B1598 6km from St Gilgen. Signed from village.
Open: May-1 Oct **Site:** 2HEC **Prices:** 3.60-4.30 2.70-3.70 2.70-3.70 2.70-3.50 **Facilities:** **Services:** lau **Leisure:** LR **Off-site:**

ABTENAU SALZBURG

Oberwötzhof Erlfeld 37, 5441
06243 2698 06243 269855
e-mail: oberwoetzlhof@sbg.at
website: www.go.to/oberwoetzlhof-camp
A summer and winter site on a level meadow with panoramic views of the surrounding mountains.
NW of Abtenau.
Open: All year **Site:** 2HEC **Prices:** 5.50 3.20 5.50 5-5.50 **Facilities:** **Services:** **Leisure:** P **Off-site:** R

ALTMÜNSTER OBERÖSTERREICH

Schweizerhof Hauptstr 17, 4813
07612 89313 07612 872764
e-mail: office@schweizerhof.cc
website: www.schweizerhof.cc
A modern site on the shore of lake Traunsee with plenty of sporting facilities.
Signed from the motorway.
Open: May-Sep **Site:** 0.6HEC **Facilities:** **Services:** lau **Leisure:** L **Off-site:** P

BRUCK AN DER GROSSGLOCKNERSTRASSE SALZBURG

Woferlgut Kroessenbach 40, 5671
06545 73030 06545 73033
e-mail: info@sportcamp.at
website: www.sportcamp.at
In a beautiful valley beside a lake with good recreational facilities. Some noise from the main road which bisects the site.
Access via Bruck-Süd or Grossglockner on B311.
Open: All year **Site:** 17HEC **Prices:** 4.70-6.10 4.20-5.40 4.90-6.40 4.90-6.40 (static)385-532 **Facilities:** **Services:** **Leisure:** LP **Off-site:** R

ESTERNBERG OBERÖSTERREICH

Pyrawang 4092 07714 6504 07714 6504
At Km45.5 on B130 Passau-Linz.
Open: Apr-Oct **Site:** 3HEC **Prices:** 3 3 2.50 1.50 **Facilities:** **Services:** **Off-site:** R

GLEINKERAU OBERÖSTERREICH

Pyhrn Priel 4582 07562 7066 07562 7192
e-mail: pousek@pyhrn-priel.at
website: www.pyhrn-priel.at
A year-round site with a wide variety of facilities.
Signed from Windischgarsten towards Gleinkersee. 2.5km from town.
Open: May-Oct **Site:** 1HEC **Prices:** 5-5.80 2-2 5.50-10.90 4-5.50 **Facilities:** **Services:** lau **Off-site:** R

KAPRUN SALZBURG

Mühle N-Gassner Str 38, 5710
06547 8254 06547 825489
e-mail: muehle@kaprun.at
website: www.kaprun.at/muehle
A pleasant family site on long stretch of meadow by the Kapruner Ache.
S end of village towards cable lift.
Open: All year **Site:** 1.5HEC **Prices:** 5-5.90 3.60 2.90 2.90 pitch 6.50 **Facilities:** **Services:** lau **Leisure:** P

MAISHOFEN SALZBURG

Kammerlander Oberreit 18, 5751 06542 68755
On B168.
Open: May-15 Sep **Site:** **Facilities:** **Services:** **Off-site:** L

MITTERSILL SALZBURG

Mittersill Klausgasse 49, 5730
06562 4811 06562 4811-10
A modern, well-equipped site suitable for both summer and winter holidays.
0.5km from the centre of the town on the shores of the lake.
Open: All year **Site:** 1.7HEC **Facilities:** **Services:** lau

MONDSEE OBERÖSTERREICH

Mond-See-Land Punzau 21, 5310
06232 2600 06232 27218
e-mail: austria@campmondsee.at
website: www.campmondsee.at
In a picturesque, peaceful location between lake Mondsee and lake Irrsee with good facilities.
From Mondsee exit on A1/E55/E60 take B154 towards Strasswalden for 1.5km, then take Haider-Mühle road for 2km.
Open: Apr-Oct **Site:** 3HEC **Prices:** 4.90-5.50 3.20-3.40 pitch 6.50-7.50 (static)210-252 **Facilities:** **Services:** lau **Leisure:** P

NUSSDORF OBERÖSTERREICH

Gruber Dortstr 63, 4865 07666 80450 07666 80456
On fairly long meadow parallel to the promenade.
S of village, access is at Km19.7. Turn off B151 towards lake Attersee.
Open: 15 Apr-15 Oct **Site:** 2.6HEC **Facilities:** **Services:** lau **Leisure:** LP **Off-site:**

PERWANG AM GRABENSEE OBERÖSTERREICH

Perwang 5163 06217 8288 06217 824715
e-mail: gemeinde@perwang.ooe.gv.at
website: www.tiscover.com/perwang
Site beside lake.
Open: May-Oct **Site:** 1.5HEC **Facilities:** **Services:** lau **Leisure:** L **Off-site:**

PETTENBACH OBERÖSTERREICH

Almtal 4643 07586 86270
On a level meadow in the grounds of a former castle,with good, modern facilities.
Leave A1/E55/E60 at Sattledt exit and continue towards Graz.
Open: All year **Site:** 12HEC **Facilities:** **Services:** lau **Leisure:** P

RADSTADT SALZBURG

Forellencamp Gaismairallee 51, 5550
06452 7861 06452 5092
e-mail: forellencamp@aon.at
website: www.forellencamp.com
Flat meadowland near town
SW via B99.
Open: All year **Site:** 1HEC **Prices:** 4.50 2.40 4.50 2.20 **Facilities:** **Services:**
Off-site: PR

ST JOHANN IM PONGAU SALZBURG

Hirschenwirt Bundesstr 1, 5600
06412 6012 06412 60128
e-mail: hirschenwirt@aon.at
website: www.hirschenwirt.com
A small, pleasant site ideally placed for travelling on the Salzburg-Badgastein road or as a base for exploring this region of mountains and lakes. The flat open site has grass pitches on either side of gravel roads. There is a small pool for summer use. Being on a major road route there is traffic noise.
Site is behind Gasthof Hirschenwirt at St Johann im Pongau on B311.
Open: All year **Site:** 0.8HEC **Prices:** 4-5 pitch 6-9 **Facilities:** **Services:** **Leisure:** P
Off-site: R

Wieshof Wieshofgasse 8, 5600
06412 8519 06412 82929
On gently sloping meadow behind pension and farmhouse. Modern facilities. Big spa house with sauna, massage facilities and health bars, adjacent to site.
Off B311 towards Zell am Zee.
Open: All year **Site:** 1.6HEC **Prices:** 5.50 pitch 5.50
Facilities: **Services:** lau **Off-site:** LP

ST MARTIN BEI LOFER SALZBURG

Park Grubhof 5092 06588 8237 06588 82377
e-mail: camping@lofer.net
website: www.grubhof.com
Situated in meadowland on the banks of the River Saalach. Separate sections for dog owners, families, teenagers and groups.
1.5km S of Lofer turn left off B311.
Open: 25 Apr-5 Oct **Site:** 10HEC **Prices:** 5.20 2.20 3.20-4 2.20-3.20 **Facilities:**
Services: lau **Leisure:** R **Off-site:** P

ST WOLFGANG OBERÖSTERREICH

Appesbach Au 99, 5360 06138 2206 06138 220633
e-mail: camping@appesbach.at
website: www.appesbach.at
On sloping meadow facing lake with no shade at upper end.
0.8km E of St Wolfgang between lake and Strobl road.
Open: Mar-Oct **Site:** 2.2HEC **Prices:** 5-6.50 6-11 4-6 pitch 4-8 (static)315-420 **Facilities:**
Services: lau **Leisure:** L **Off-site:**

Berau Schwarzenbach 16, 5360
06138 2543 06138 254355
e-mail: camping@berau.at
website: www.berau.com
A family-run site in a picturesque setting on the edge of the Wolfgangsee. Spacious, level pitches and good, modern facilities.
From A1 exit Talgau, follow signs for Hof and Bad Ischl on N158 through Strobl village towards St Wolfgang and follow signs.
Open: All year **Site:** 2HEC **Prices:** 5.30-6.30 2-3.50 4-5 pitch 7.50-10 **Facilities:**
Services: lau **Leisure:** L

SALZBURG SALZBURG

Kasern C-Zuckmayerstr 26, 5101
0662 450576 0662 450576
e-mail: schwarzkopf@aon.at
website: www.camping-kasern-salzburg.com
Access via exit Salzburg-Nord on the A1.
Open: Apr-Oct **Site:** 0.9HEC **Facilities:**
Services: lau **Off-site:**

Nord Sam Samstr 22A, 5023 0662 660494 0662 660494
e-mail: office@camping-nord-sam.com
website: www.camping-nord-sam.com
Site divided into pitches.
400m from Salzburg Nord Autobahn Exit.
Open: May-Sep **Site:** 2HEC **Prices:** 4.50-6 pitch 7-8.50 **Facilities:** **Services:** lau
Leisure: P **Off-site:**

Schloss Aigen A5026 0662 622079 0662 622079
e-mail: camping.aigen@elsnet.at
Site divided into pitches in partial clearing on mountain slope.
From Salzburg-Süd motorway exit through Anif and Glasenbach.
Open: May-Sep **Site:** 25HEC **Facilities:**
Services: lau

Stadtblick Rauchenbichlerstr 21, 5020
0662 450652 0662 458018
e-mail: panorama.camping@utanet.at
website: www.panorama-camping
A terraced site affording spectacular views of the surrounding mountains.
Leave motorway at exit Salzburg-Nord and follow signs.
Open: 20 Mar-5 Nov **Site:** 0.8HEC
Facilities: **Services:** lau

SCHLÖGEN OBERÖSTERREICH

Terrassencamping Pension Schlögen A-4083
07279 8241 07279 8241-22
e-mail: schloegen.freizeit@netway.at
website: www.schloegen.at
On level ground beside the River Donau, backed by woods and mountains.
Open: Apr-20 Oct **Site:** 2.8HEC **Facilities:**
Services: lau **Leisure:** PR

SEEKIRCHEN SALZBURG

Strand Seestr 2, 5201 06212 4088 06212 4088
Beside the Wallersee in beautiful meadow.
Open: 15 Apr-15 Oct **Site:** 2HEC **Facilities:**
Services: lau **Leisure:** LP **Off-site:**

Zell am Wallersee 5201 06212 4080 06212 4080
e-mail: franz.klampfer@aon.at
Level meadowland separated from the lake by the Lido.

contd.

Facilities: -shop -shower -electric points for razors -electric points for caravans -parking by tents permitted -compulsory separate car park **Services:** -café/restaurant -bar -Camping Gaz International -gas other than Camping Gaz -first aid facilities lau-laundry **Leisure:** -swimming L-Lake P-Pool R-River S-Sea **Off-site:** All facilities within 2km

Access from A1 exit Wallersee then via Seekirchen to Zell.
Open: 11 May-19 Oct **Site:** 3HEC **Facilities:** **Services:** lau **Leisure:** LP

UNTERACH OBERÖSTERREICH

Insel 4866 07665 8311 07665 7255
e-mail: camping@inselcamp.at
website: www.inselcamp.at
Quiet site on shore of lake Attersee; divided into two sections by River Seeache. Family site.
Entrance below B152 towards Steinbach at Km24.5; about 300m from fork with B151.
Open: 15 May-15 Sep **Site:** 1.8HEC **Prices:** 4-4.73 2.30 3.50 2.60 **Facilities:** **Services:** lau **Leisure:** LR **Off-site:**

WALD SALZBURG

SNP Lahn 65, 5742 06565 8446-0 06565 8446-4
e-mail: info@snp-camping.at
website: www.snp-camping.at
A small family site in a beautiful Alpine setting.
W of town.
Open: All year **Site:** 0.7HEC **Prices:** 5.20-5.50 2-2.20 3.20-3.50 3-4 **Facilities:** **Services:** lau **Off-site:** LP

WESENUFER OBERÖSTERREICH

Nibelungen 4085 07718 7589 07718 7589
e-mail: nibelungen.camping@utanet.at
In a pleasant rural setting beside the River Donau.
500m from B130.
Open: Apr-Sep **Site:** 1.2HEC **Prices:** 3 2.30 pitch 4 **Facilities:** **Services:** lau **Leisure:** R **Off-site:** P

ZELL AM SEE SALZBURG

Seecamp Zell am See Thumersbacherstr 34, 5700 06542 72115 06542 72115
e-mail: zell@seecamp.at
website: www.seecamp.at
In a pleasant wooded location beside the lake with excellent site and recreational facilities.
Access via B311, N of lake towards Thumersbach. Signed.
Open: All year **Site:** 3HEC **Prices:** 6-7.50 2-2.50 3.30-4.10 pitch 6.80-10.90 **Facilities:** **Services:** lau **Leisure:** L **Off-site:** P

Süedufer Thumersbach, Seeuferstr 196, 5700 06542 56228 06542 562284
e-mail: zell@camping-suedufer.at
website: www.camping-suedufer.at
A family site on level ground in a picturesque spot on the southern bank of the Zeller See.
S via B311 towards Thumersbach.
Open: All year **Site:** 0.6HEC **Facilities:** **Services:** lau **Off-site:** LPR

VORARLBERG

BEZAU VORARLBERG

Bezau Ach 206, 6870 05514 2964
e-mail: camping.bezau@aon.at
website: www.campingfuehrer.at
Small family-owned site with modern sanitary facilities.
S via B200 Dornbirn-Warth.
Open: All year **Site:** 0.5HEC **Prices:** 4 6.55-7.30 5.80-7.30 pitch 5.80-7.30 **Facilities:** **Off-site:** PR

BLUDENZ VORARLBERG
AT BRAZ (7KM SE)

Traube 6751 05552 28103 05552 28103-40
e-mail: traube.braz@aon.at
website: www.traubebraz.at
On sloping grassland in the picturesque Klostertal valley with good, modern facilities.
7km SE of Bludenz via E17, S16 Bludenz-Arlberg-Innsbruck. Signed. Near railway.
Open: All year **Site:** 2HEC **Prices:** 4 pitch 16-27 (incl 2 persons) **Facilities:** **Services:** lau **Leisure:** P **Off-site:** R

DALAAS VORARLBERG

Erne 6752 05585 7223 05585 20049
e-mail: info@etpc.at
website: www.etpc.at
In the town, attached to a guesthouse and next to the swimming pool.
Access via S16, exit Dalass.
Open: All year **Site:** 0.6HEC **Prices:** pitch 18.50-20.50 (incl 2 persons) **Facilities:** **Leisure:** R **Off-site:** P

DORNBIRN VORARLBERG

In der Enz 6850 05572 29119
e-mail: camping@camping-enz.at
website: www.camping-enz.at
A municipal site beside a public park, in a wooded area some 100m beyond the Karren cable lift.
Access via autobahn exit Dornbirn-Süd.
Open: May-Sep **Site:** 10HEC **Prices:** 4.20 1.90 4.50 4.50 pitch 4.50 **Facilities:** **Services:** lau **Off-site:** PR

LINGENAU VORARLBERG

Feurstein Haidach 185, 6951 05513 6114 05513 61144
A small site located in a meadow adjacent to some farm buildings with sufficient facilities for a pleasant stay.
Open: All year **Site:** 1HEC **Prices:** 6 7.70 3.50 2-3.50 **Facilities:** **Services:** lau **Off-site:**

NENZING VORARLBERG

Alpencamping Nenzing 6710 05525 62491 05525 635676
e-mail: office@alpencamping.at
website: www.alpencamping.at
A well-appointed site in magnificent Alpine scenery. There are fine sporting facilities and modern sanitary blocks.
Signed from B190 from Nenzing, 2km towards Gurtis.
Open: Jan-11 Apr & 30 Apr-Dec **Site:** 3HEC **Prices:** 5.10-6.20 3.60 pitch 3.60-7 **Facilities:** **Services:** lau **Leisure:** P

AT NÜZIDERS (2.5KM NW)

Sonnenberg Hinterofers 12, 6714 05552 64035 05552 33900
e-mail: sonnencamp@aun.at
website: www.camping-sonnenberg.com
Clean site with modern facilities in gently sloping meadowland and splendid mountain scenery.
Access from Bludenz-Nüziders road, at first fork follow up hill.
Open: 30 Apr-3 Oct **Site:** 1.9HEC **Prices:** 5-5.20 6.50-10 6.50-10 pitch 6-10 **Facilities:** **Services:** lau **Off-site:** R

RAGGAL-PLAZERA VORARLBERG

Grosswalsertal 6741 05553 209 2094
e-mail: info@camping-grosswalsertal.at
website: www.camping-grosswalsertal.at
A family site in a quiet location on gently sloping terrain, with pleasant views.
On NE outskirts.
Open: 15 Apr-15 Nov **Site:** 0.8HEC **Prices:** 5 pitch 6.50-9 **Facilities:** **Services:** lau **Leisure:** P **Off-site:**

TSCHAGGUNS VORARLBERG

Zelfen 6774 0664 2002326
e-mail: dsandrell@sandrell.vol.at
website: www.camping-zelfen.at
Partly uneven, grassy site in a wooded location beside River Ill. Good recreational facilities.
Access via A14 to Bludenz, then B188 to Tschagguns.
Open: All year **Site:** 2HEC **Facilities:** **Services:** lau **Leisure:** R **Off-site:** P

VIENNA (WIEN)

WIEN (VIENNA) WIEN

Donaupark Klosterneuburg In der Au, 3400
02243 25877 02243 25878
e-mail: campklosterneuburg@oeamtc.at
website: www.campingklosterneuburg.at
A modern site in delightful wooded surroundings with fine recreational facilities and within easy reach of the city centre.
Signed from A1.
Open: 15 Mar-07 Nov **Site:** 2.2HEC **Prices:** 6 4.50 7.50-11 pitch 7.50-11 **Facilities:** **Services:** lau **Off-site:** PR

Neue Donau Am Kleehäufel, 1220
01 2024010 01 2024010
e-mail: camping.neuedonau@verkehrsbuero.at
website: www.campingwien.at
Situated in a meadow surrounded by trees on the banks of the Danube within a leisure park.
On E bank of the river with access to the A4 and A22.
Open: May-Sep **Site:** 3.3HEC **Prices:** 5.70-6.70 8-11 4.50-5.50 pitch 8-11 **Facilities:** **Services:** lau **Off-site:** LPR

Wien-West Hüttelbergstr 80, 1140
01 9142314 01 9113594
e-mail: camping.west@verkehrsbuero.at
website: www.campingwien.at
On slightly rising meadow with asphalt paths.
From end of A1/E5 (Linz-Wien) to Bräuhausbrücke, then turn left and across road to Linz, continue for 1.8km.
Open: Jan & Mar-Dec **Site:** 2.4HEC **Prices:** 5.70-6.70 8-9 4.50-5.50 pitch 8-9 **Facilities:** **Services:** lau

AT RODAUN (4KM SW)

Rodaun An der Au 2, 1230 01 8884154 01 8884154
Between An der Austr and Leising River dam. Access from Breitenfürter Str N492.
Open: 25 Mar-4 Nov **Site:** 0.8HEC **Facilities:** **Services:** lau **Off-site:**

BELGIUM

Belgium is a small, densely populated country bordered by France, Germany, Luxembourg and the Netherlands.

FACTS AND FIGURES
Area: 30,528 sq km (11,787 sq miles)
Population: 10,263,414 (2001)
Capital: Bruxelles (Brussel, Brussels)
Language: French, Dutch, German
IDD code: 32
To call the UK dial 00 44
Currency: Euro
Local time: GMT + 1 (summer GMT + 2)
Emergency Services: Police 101; Fire 100; Ambulance 100. From a mobile phone dial 112 and ask for the service required.
Banks: Mon-Fri 09.00-12.00, 14.00-16.00
Shops: Mon-Sat 09.00-18.00 (supermarkets 20.00)
Average daily temperatures: Bruxelles (Brussel, Brussels)

Jan 3°C	Mar 5°C
May 13°C	Jul 17°C
Sep14°C	Nov 5°C

Tourist Information:
UK
Belgian Tourist Office (Brussels & Wallonia)
217 Marsh Wall, London E14 9FJ
Tel 0906 302 0245 (premium rate info line)
Tourism Flanders Brussels
1a Cavendish Square, London W1G 0LD
Tel: 0906 550 8919 (premium rate info line)

USA
Belgian National Tourist Office
Suite 1501, 780 Third Ave,
New York NY10017
Tel (212) 758 8130
Tourist info website:
www.belgiumtheplaceto.be
www.visitflanders.co.uk

Despite being heavily industrialised, Belgium possesses some beautiful scenery. The rivers and gorges of the Ardennes contrast with the rolling plains that make up the rest of the countryside. The resorts in the Oostende (Ostend) area offer wide, safe, sandy beaches along 65km of coastline. Three main languages are spoken: French, Dutch and German (see Language below). The temperate climate is similar to that of Britain.

There are over 800 authorised campsites. They are normally open from April to October, but many are open throughout the year. Coastal sites can be very crowded in high season. **Off-site camping** (including sleeping) is prohibited beside public roads for more than 24 consecutive hours; on seashores; within a 100-metre radius of a main water point; or on a site classified for the conservation of monuments. Elsewhere, camping is permitted free of charge, as long as the stay does not exceed 24 hours and the camper has obtained authorisation from the landowner.

HOW TO GET THERE

The direct ferry service to Belgium operating to **Zeebrugge** from **Hull** takes 12 hrs 45 mins.

Alternatively, you could use Eurotunnel, or take a shorter crossing by ferry or catamaran to Calais, France, and drive along the coast road to Belgium.

MOTORING & GENERAL

The information given here is specific to Belgium. It **must** be read in conjunction with the Essential Information for Motoring section, which covers those regulations that are common to many countries.

ACCIDENTS

The police must be called if an unoccupied, stationary vehicle is damaged, or if injuries are caused to persons; in the latter case, the car must not be moved. See also the recommendations given under **Accidents** and also under **Warning Triangle** in the Essential Information for Motoring section.

BRITISH EMBASSY/CONSULATES*

The British Embassy is at B-1040 Bruxelles, rue d'Aarlenstraat 85 ☎ (02) 2876211. There are British consulates with Honorary Consuls in Antwerpen (Antwerp), Ghent and Liège.

CHILDREN IN CARS

Children 3 years or under must be in suitable restraint when travelling in the front and - if such a system is fitted - in the rear. Children over 3 and under 12 seated in front or rear must use the seat-belt or a child restraint appropriate to their size and weight. See Essential Information for Motoring section under **Passengers** and **Seat Belts**.

Currency*

The **euro** is the currency of Belgium. The Belgian franc (BEF) ceased to be legal tender in 2002, though BEF notes may still be exchanged at the Belgian Central Bank (**Nationale Bank van België/Banque National de Belgique**) and the Post Office for an unlimited period.

Dimensions & Weight Restrictions*

Private **cars** and towed **trailers** or **caravans** are restricted to the following dimensions: height 4 metres, width 2.55 metres, length 12 metres.The maximum length of vehicle and trailer/caravan combination is 18 metres. Trailers without brakes may have a total maximum weight of 750kg.

Driving Licence*

A valid UK or Republic of Ireland licence is accepted in Belgium. The minimum age at which visitors from the UK or Republic of Ireland may use a temporarily imported car or motorcycle is 18 years.

Foodstuffs*

If the imported foodstuffs are for personal use, there are no limits when travelling between EU countries. Visitors coming from other countries may import up to 1kg of meat for personal consumption. Coffee (500g), coffee extract (200g), tea (100g) and tea extract (40g) are free of customs duties, but visitors under 15 cannot import coffee.

Language

Dutch, **French** and **German** are the official languages of Belgium. Dutch is spoken in the north, French in the south, and German in the eastern provinces. Dutch and French are spoken in Brussels. The Dutch spoken in Belgium is different in many ways to the Dutch of the Netherlands. It is regarded by some as a seperate language (Flemish), but by most as a collection of Dutch dialects. Some of the town names in the directory are shown in both Dutch and French; that shown first is the one used locally.

Lights*

Motorcyclists must always use dipped headlights.

Motoring Club

The **Touring Club Royal de Belgique** (TCB) has its office at 1040 Bruxelles, 44 rue de la Loi ☎(02) 2332211. The Bruxelles (Brussels) office is open 09.00-17.00 Mon-Fri.

Website: **www.touring.be**

Petrol

See Essential Information for Motoring section under **Petrol/Diesel**.

Roads

Belgium has a comprehensive system of toll-free motorways. The route from Calais (France) through Belgium to Köln/Cologne (Germany) can be difficult due to the languages. In the Flemish part of Belgium place names are in Dutch; in Wallonia they are in French; and in the German part of Belgium they are in German and French or just in German. Only Brussels (Bruxelles-Brussel) has signs that show the two alternative spellings of place names. From the Flemish part of the country, Dunkirk (Dunkerque) in France is signed Duinkerke, Lille as Rijsel, and Paris as Parijs. Generally, motorway signs show foreign destination place names in the language of the country concerned.

Speed Limits*

Car/motorcycle/car towning caravan/trailer

Built-up areas	50km/h (31mph)
Other roads	90km/h (56mph)
Motorways and 4-lane roads separated by central reservation	120km/h (74mph)†

Minimum speed on motorways on straight level stretches is 70km/h (43mph). Vehicles being towed due to accident or breakdown are limited to 25km/h (15mph) on all roads and, if on a motorway, must leave at the first exit.

†On dual carriageways separated only by road markings the limit is 90km/h (55mph).

Warning Triangle*

Vehicles must carry a warning triangle, which must be used in the event of accident or breakdown. Place the triangle 30 metres behind the vehicle on ordinary roads and 100 metres on motorways to warn following traffic; it must be visible at a distance of 50 metres. In built-up areas the triangle may be placed close to or even on the vehicle if the 30-metre rule cannot be obeyed.

***Additional information can be found in the Essential Information for Motoring section.**

SOUTH-WEST/COAST

BLANKENBERGE WEST-VLAANDEREN

Bonanza I Zeebruggelaan 137, 8370
050 416658 050 427349
e-mail: bonanza1@kmonet.be
website: www.bonanza1.be
A family site in wooded surroundings 1km from both the village and the sea.
Open: 15Mar-15 Sep **Site:** 4.5HEC **Facilities:** **Services:** lau **Leisure:** P **Off-site:** LS

Dallas Ruzettelaan 191, 8370 050 418157 050 429479
Well equipped family site near a large department store 50m from the beach.
Open: 15 Mar-1 Oct **Site:** 2.6HEC **Prices:** 4.50 5 3.27-4 **Facilities:** **Services:** lau
Off-site: LPS

JABBEKE WEST-VLAANDEREN

Recreatiepark Klein Strand Varsenareweg 29, 8490
050 811440 050 814289
e-mail: kleinstrand@online.be
website: www.kleinstrand.be
A lakeside site with good modern facilities and offering a wide variety of leisure activities.
Off the main Oostende-Brugge road.
Open: All year **Site:** 20HEC **Prices:** 4 1.50 pitch 4-7.50 (static)300-399 **Facilities:** **Services:** lau **Leisure:** LP **Off-site:** R

KNOKKE-HEIST WEST-VLAANDEREN

De Vuurtoren Heistlaan 168, 8301 050 511782
e-mail: kampvuurtoren@attglobal.net
website: www.knokke-heist.be
On level meadow with tarred roads.
Turn S off Knokke-Oostende road 4km from Knokke and follow signposts.
Open: 15 Mar-15 Oct **Site:** 6.6HEC **Prices:** 3.40 7.80-17.20 6.45-14.60 **Facilities:**
Services: lau **Off-site:** PS

Zilvermeeuw Heistlaan 166, 8301
050 512726 050 512703
e-mail: info.campingzilvermeeuw@skynet.be
website: www.camping-zilvermeeuw.com
Level site in wooded surroundings.
SW via N300.
Open: Mar-15 Nov **Site:** 7HEC **Facilities:** **Services:** lau **Off-site:** LPS

AT WESTKAPELLE (3KM S)

Holiday Natienlaan 70-72, 8300
050 601203 050 613280
A quiet family site with good modern facilities within easy reach of the sea.
On S outskirts near the railway station.
Open: Apr-Sep **Site:** 1.5HEC **Facilities:** **Services:** lau **Off-site:** PS

KOKSIJDE WEST-VLAANDEREN

Blekker & Blekkerdal Jachtwakerstr 12, 8670
058 511633 058 511307
e-mail: camping.deblekker@belgacom.net
In a peaceful location, surrounded by trees, with good modern facilities.
Situated between Dunkerque and Oostende, 5km from the Belgian frontier. Leave motorway and head towards Veurne.
Open: All year **Site:** 3HEC **Facilities:**
Services: lau **Off-site:** S

LOMBARDSIJDE WEST-VLAANDEREN

Lombarde Elisabethlaan 4, 8434
058 236839 058 239908
e-mail: info@delombarde.be
website: www.delombarde.be
A well-equipped family site 400m from the sea and close to the centre of the village. Some facilities only available March to early November.
From E40 exit Nieuwpoort and follow signs.
Open: All year **Site:** 8.5HEC **Prices:** 14-25.90
Facilities: **Services:** lau
Leisure: L **Off-site:** PS

Zomerzon Elisabethlaan 1, 8434
058 237396 058 232817
In a quiet location, 800m from the sand dunes and beach with good facilities.
Open: 24 Mar-11 Nov **Site:** 10HEC
Facilities: **Services:** lau **Off-site:** PS

LOPPEM WEST-VLAANDEREN

Lac Loppem 8210 050 824262
Surrounded by fir trees on the edge of a lake.
Leave A10/E40 at Torhout exit and turn right by the Esso service station.
Open: All year **Site:** 14HEC **Prices:** 3.50-3 pitch 6-12 **Facilities:** **Services:** **Leisure:** L

Site: 6HEC-Site size -grass -sand -stone -little shade -partly shaded -mainly shaded -bungalows for hire -caravans for hire -tents for hire -no dogs **Prices:** -adult per night -car per night pp-per person per night -caravan per night -tent per night (static)-caravan hire per week

MIDDELKERKE West-Vlaanderen

Myn Plezier Duinenweg 489, 8430
059 300279 059 314503
In wooded surroundings close to the castle. The camp shop only operates during high season.
Open: Apr-10 Sep **Site:** 3HEC **Facilities:** **Services:** lau **Off-site:** S

MONS Hainaut

Waux-Hall av St-Pierre 17, 7000
065 337923 065 363848
In a secluded position 1km from the town centre, with direct access to the Parc du Waux-Hall.
From town ring road take exit for Beaumont/Binche, Charleroi. Turn right at lights, then take immediate right.
Open: All year **Site:** 1.4HEC **Prices:** 3.35 6.10 pitch 6.10 (incl 1 persons) **Facilities:** **Services:** lau **Off-site:** L

NIEUWPOORT West-Vlaanderen

Info Brugsesteenweg 49, 8620 058 236037 058 232682
e-mail: nieuwpoort@kompascamping.be
website: www.kompascamping.be
A family site in pleasant wooded surroundings. Plenty of recreational facilities including watersports.
From E40 exit 4 head towards Diksmuide and Nieuwpoort. Signed from St Joris.
Open: 26 Mar-8 Nov **Site:** 24HEC **Prices:** pitch 19-29.50 (incl 4 persons) (static)265-590 **Facilities:** **Services:** lau **Leisure:** P **Off-site:** LRS

OOSTENDE (OSTENDE) West-Vlaanderen

Asterix Duinenstr 200, 8450 059 331000 059 324202
A family site in wooded surroundings, 500m from the sea.
Camping Card Compulsory.
From Oostende follow N34 towards Knokke-Heist for 7km then right for Bredene-Dorp.
Open: All year **Site:** 3HEC **Prices:** 9 (static)280 **Facilities:** **Services:** lau **Off-site:** LPS

ST SAUVEUR Hainaut

Hauts r des Vertes Feuilles 13, 7912 069 768748
In a secluded, wooded situation within the Flemish Ardennes with fine facilities.
Signed from Renaix.
Open: All year **Site:** 1HEC **Facilities:** **Services:** lau **Off-site:**

TOURNAI Hainaut

Orient Vieux Chemin de Mons 8, 7500
069 222635 069 890229
e-mail: tourisme@tournai.be
website: www.tournai.be
A pleasant site in an area of woodland with good recreational facilities.
From motorway exit Tournai Est, head towards the town centre. Turn left at first crossroads and follow signs.
Open: All year **Site:** 20HEC **Prices:** 2.50 2.50 3 2.50 **Facilities:** **Services:** lau **Leisure:** LP **Off-site:**

WAREGEM West-Vlaanderen

Gemeentelijk Sportstadion Zuiderlaan 13, 8790
056 609532 056 621223
e-mail: toerisme@waregem.be
website: www.waregem.be
In a sports and leisure centre SE of the town centre.
Access via E17 Kortrijk-Gent.
Open: Apr-Sep **Site:** 1HEC **Facilities:** **Services:** **Off-site:** P

WESTENDE West-Vlaanderen

KACB Bassevillestr 81, 8434 058 237343 (058) 233505
e-mail: campingkacbwestende@pi.be
website: www.kacb.be
A well-appointed site close to the beach.
Camping Card Compulsory.
Situated between Westende and Lombardsijde towards the sea.
Open: All year **Site:** 6.5HEC **Facilities:** **Services:** lau **Off-site:** LPS

NORTH/CENTRAL

BACHTE-MARIA-LEERNE Oost-Vlaanderen

Groeneveld Groeneveldreef, 9800
09 3801014 09 3801760
e-mail: info@campinggroeneveld.be
website: www.campinggroeneveld.be
Well equipped site beside a lake.
Approach via E17 or E40.
Open: 24 Mar-12 Nov **Site:** 1.7HEC **Prices:** pitch 16-19 (incl 2 persons) **Facilities:** **Services:** **Leisure:** L **Off-site:** R

BEAUVECHAIN Brabant

Arpents Verts r Longue 115, 1320
010 866993 010 867457
e-mail: lesarpentsverts@msm.com
website: users.belgacombusiness.net/arpents.verts
Access via E411 exit 8 towards Louvain or E40 exit 23 towards Bevekom.
Open: May-Aug **Site:** 1HEC **Prices:** 3.50 3.50 3.50 pitch 12-40 **Facilities:** **Services:** lau

BEGYNENDYK Brabant

Roygaerden Betekomsesteenweg 75, 3130
016 531087 016531087
e-mail: immo.vdb@pi.be
Pitches are in wooded surroundings beside a lake.
Open: All year **Site:** 5HEC **Prices:** 3.75 8.70 3 **Facilities:** **Services:** lau **Off-site:** L

BEVERE Oost-Vlaanderen

Kompas Camping Oudenaarde Kortrijkstr 342, 9700
055 315473 055 300865
e-mail: oudenaarde@kompascamping.be
website: www.kompascamping.be
A family site with good recreational facilities.
Signed from N453.
Open: Apr-mid Nov **Site:** 24HEC **Prices:** pitch 17-25.50 (incl 6 persons) **Facilities:** **Services:** lau **Leisure:** LP

GENT (GAND) Oost-Vlaanderen

Blaarmeersen Zuiderlaan 12, 9000
+32 92668160 92668166
e-mail: camping.blaarmeersen@gent.be
website: www.gent.be/blaarmeersen
In pleasant wooded surroundings SW of Gent towards the railway station.
Open: Mar-15 Oct **Site:** 6HEC **Facilities:** **Services:** lau **Leisure:** L

Facilities: -shop -shower -electric points for razors -electric points for caravans -parking by tents permitted -compulsory separate car park **Services:** -café/restaurant -bar -Camping Gaz International -gas other than Camping Gaz -first aid facilities lau-laundry **Leisure:** -swimming L-Lake P-Pool R-River S-Sea **Off-site:** All facilities within 2km

GRIMBERGEN BRABANT

Grimbergen Veldkanstr 64, 1850
0479 760378 02 2701215
Access via exit 7 on Bruxelles ringroad.
Open: Apr-Oct **Site:** 1.5HEC **Prices:** 4 1.50 3 3 **Facilities:** **Services:** lau **Off-site:** P

HEVERLEE BRABANT

Ter Munck Sint Jansbergsesteenweg 152, 3001 016 228515
Access via E40 or E413.
Open: 18 Jun-9 Sep **Site:** 1.5HEC **Facilities:** **Services:** lau **Off-site:** P

ONKERZELE OOST-VLAANDEREN

Gavers Onkerzelestr 280, 9500 054 416324 054 410388
e-mail: gavers@oost-vlaanderen.be
A quiet, well-equipped site beside a lake between the Dendre valley and the foothills of the Ardennes. There are good sporting and sanitary facilities.
NE of town towards the river.
Open: All year **Site:** 15HEC **Prices:** pitch 18-18 (static)65-100 **Facilities:** **Services:** lau **Leisure:** LPR

STEKENE OOST-VLAANDEREN

Eurocamping Baudeloo Heirweg 183, 9190
03 7890663 03 7890663
Open: All year **Site:** 4.5HEC **Facilities:** **Services:** lau **Leisure:** P **Off-site:**

Reinaert Lunterbergstr 4, 9190
03 7798525
e-mail: peter.vandenbranden@skynet.be
Open: Apr-Oct **Site:** 5HEC **Prices:** 2 2 2 2 **Facilities:** **Services:** lau **Off-site:**

WACHTEBEKE OOST-VLAANDEREN

Puyenbroeck Puyenbrug 1A, 9185
09 3424231 09 3424258
website: www.puyenbroeck.be
Open: Apr-Sep **Site:** 500HEC **Prices:** pitch 14-18 **Facilities:** **Services:** lau **Off-site:** LP

NORTH-EAST

BRECHT ANTWERPEN

Floreal Het Veen Eekhoornlaan 1, St-Job In't Goor, 2960
03 6361327
A comfortable site in a pleasant wooded setting with residential and touring pitches.
Leave Autoroute E19 at exit St Job In't Goor.
Open: Mar-Oct **Site:** 7.5HEC **Facilities:** **Services:** lau **Leisure:** R **Off-site:**

EKSEL LIMBURG

Lage Kempen Kiefhoek str 19, B-3941
011 402243 011 348812
e-mail: info@lagekempen.be
website: www.lagekempen.be
Situated in the middle of a forest with a variety of recreational facilities.
From route 67 from Hasselt follow signs 'Lage Kampen' to the left.
Open: Etr-2 Nov **Site:** 3.8HEC **Prices:** 4 2.50 3.50 3.50 **Facilities:** **Services:** lau **Leisure:** P

GIERLE ANTWERPEN

Lilse Bergen Strandweg 6, 2275
014 557901 014 554454
e-mail: info@lilsebergen.be
website: www.lilsebergen.be
A very well-equipped family site surrounding a private lake.
E39 exit 22.
Open: All year **Site:** 60HEC **Prices:** pitch 17-23 **Facilities:** **Services:** lau **Leisure:** L

HOUTHALEN LIMBURG

Hengelhoef Hengelhoefdreef 1, 3530
089 844583 089 386940
e-mail: camp.hengelhoef@belgacom.net
A family site in pleasant wooded surroundings with good, modern facilities.
Access via E314 exit 30.
Open: All year **Site:** 15HEC **Facilities:** **Services:** lau **Off-site:**

MOL ANTWERPEN

Zilvermeer Zilvermeerlaan 2, 2400
014 829500 014 829501
e-mail: info@zilvermeer.provant.be
A pleasant lakeside site with good recreational facilities.
Site: 45HEC **Facilities:** **Services:** lau **Leisure:** L

OPGLABBEEK LIMBURG

Boseind Speeltuinstr 8, 3660 089 854347 089 854319
e-mail: info@hetlaer.be
website: www.hetlaer.be
A family site adjoining a wood. A wide variety of recreational facilities are available.
From town centre take N730 towards Bree and follow signs.
Open: Apr-Sep **Site:** 8HEC **Facilities:** **Services:** **Leisure:** P **Off-site:**

Wilhelm Tell Hoeverweg 87, 3660 089 854444 810010
e-mail: receptie@wilhelmtell.com
website: www.wilhelmtell.com
A family campsite situated in a vast nature reserve and offering opportunities for walks in a varied area of heathland, woodland and marshlands. A large variety of water attractions on site including a water chute and a swimming pool with a wave machine. Also an indoor family pool and bubble bath.
E313 exit 32 in direction of Opglabbeek.
Open: All year **Site:** 4HEC **Prices:** 4.20-6 pitch 8.40-12 (incl 2 persons) (static)210-590 **Facilities:** **Services:** lau **Leisure:** P

RETIE ANTWERPEN

Berkenstrand Brand 78, 2470 014 377590 014 375139
e-mail: info@berkenstrand.be **website:** www.berkenstrand.be
In wooded surroundings beside a lake.
3km NE on road to Postel.
Open: All year **Site:** 10HEC **Facilities:** **Services:** lau **Leisure:** L

TURNHOUT ANTWERPEN

Baalse Hei Roodhuisstr 10, B-2300
014 448470 014 448474
e-mail: info@baalsehei.be **website:** www.baalsehei.be
A family site in pleasant wooded surroundings with plenty of recreational facilities.
Open: 16 Jan-15 Dec **Site:** 30HEC **Prices:** pitch 15-22 (static)260-460 **Facilities:** **Services:** lau **Leisure:** L

VORST-LAAKDAL ANTWERPEN

Kasteel Meerlaer Verboekt 115, 2430
013 661420 013 667512
e-mail: camp.meerlaer@online.be
website: www.camping.be
E313 exit 24 towards Hosselt or exit 24 towards Antwerp.
Open: All year **Site:** 6HEC **Facilities:**
Services: lau **Off-site:**

ZONHOVEN LIMBURG

Berkenhof Teutseweg 33, 3520 011 814439 011 812736
Open: Apr-Oct **Site:** 3.5HEC **Facilities:** **Services:** **Off-site:**

Holsteenbron Hengelhoelseweg 9, 3520 011 817140
011 817140
e-mail: camping.holsteenbron@skynet.be
website: www.holsteenbron.be
A rural family site in a wooded location.
Access via E314 exit 29 towards Zondhoven.
Open: Apr-11 Nov **Site:** 4HEC **Prices:** 15-17 pitch 15-17 **Facilities:** **Services:** lau

SOUTH-EAST

AISCHE-EN-REFAIL NAMUR

Manoir de lá Bas rte de Gembloux 180, B-5310
081 655353
e-mail: europa-camping.sa@skynet.be
website: www.camping-manoirdelabas.be
In a beautiful situation within the wooded grounds of a former manor house.
5km W of Eghezée.
Open: Apr-Oct **Site:** 21HEC **Prices:** 3 4 4
Facilities: **Services:** lau **Leisure:** P
Off-site:

AMBERLOUP LUXEMBOURG

Tonny r Tonny 35-36, 6680 061 688285 061 688285
In a pleasant valley beside the River Ourthe with fine sporting facilities.
Access via E25 or A4 to Bastogne, then N826.
Open: 15 Feb-15 Nov **Site:** 3HEC **Facilities:** **Services:** lau **Leisure:** R

AMONINES LUXEMBOURG

Val de l'Aisne r de TTA, 6997 086 470067 086 470043
e-mail: info@levaldelaisne.be
website: www.levaldelaisne.br
Open: All year **Site:** 25HEC **Facilities:** **Services:** lau **Leisure:** LR

BARVAUX-SUR-OURTHE LUXEMBOURG

Hazalles Chainrue 77a, 6940 086 211642 086 211642
Situated in an orchard, this site is 600m from the village and sits beside a stream. Well maintained facilities.
Open: Apr-Sep & Nov-Mar **Site:** 0.4HEC
Prices: 1.75 2.50 pitch 3.75 **Facilities:**
Services: lau **Off-site:** PR

Rives de l'Ourthe r Inzespres 70, 6940 086 211730
A large site with plenty of touring pitches beside the River Ourthe.
200m from the village towards the river.
Open: Apr-Sep **Site:** 2HEC **Facilities:**
Services: **Leisure:** R **Off-site:** LP

BERTRIX LUXEMBOURG

Kompas rte de Mortehan, 6880
061 412281 061 412588
e-mail: bertrix@kompascamping.be
website: www.kompascamping.be
Well equipped family site in a pleasant wooded setting.
S of town beyond the church. Signed from N884.
Open: 30 Mar-11 Nov **Site:** 14HEC **Prices:** pitch 17.50-26.75 **Facilities:** **Services:** lau
Leisure: P

BÜLLINGEN (BULLANGE) LIÈGE

Hêtraie Rotheck 14, 4760 80 642413 80 642413
This site is situated on a sloping meadow near a fish pond and is surrounded by groups of beautiful beech trees and conifers.
Leave village in direction of Amel then left and continue for 2km. Signed.
Open: Apr-15 Nov **Site:** 3HEC **Prices:** 2 1 3.50 2.50 **Facilities:** **Services:** lau
Leisure: LP **Off-site:** R

BURE LUXEMBOURG

Parc la Clusure 30 chemin de la Clusure, 6927
084 360050 084 366777
e-mail: info@parclaclusure.be
website: www.parclaclusure.be
Pleasant site with good facilities in the centre of the Ardennes.
Access from E411 and N846 via Tellin.
Open: All year **Site:** 12HEC **Prices:** 3.20-4.50 3 pitch 15.20-24 (incl 2 persons) (static)210-763
Facilities: **Services:** lau **Leisure:** PR

BÜTGENBACH LIÈGE

Worriken Worriken Center 1, 4750
080 446358 080 447089
e-mail: camping.worriken@swing.be
website: www.tourist-info-butgenbach.be
Situated on the shores of a lake.
Open: All year **Site:** 8HEC **Prices:** 15.49 9.30 pitch 15.49 (incl 4 persons) **Facilities:** **Services:** lau **Leisure:** L **Off-site:** PR

CHEVETOGNE NAMUR

Domaine Provincial 5590 083 687211 083 688677
Located in the grounds of a castle and surrounded by fine ornamental gardens. There is a wide variety of leisure activities.
Open: All year **Site:** 0.5HEC **Facilities:** **Services:** lau **Leisure:** L **Off-site:** P

COO-STAVELOT LIÈGE

Cascade Chemin des Faravennes 5, 4970 080 684312
A small touring and holiday site beside the River Amblève.
3km from Trois-Ponts via motorway exit 10 or 11.
Open: Mar-Sep **Site:** 0.8HEC **Prices:** 2.75 3.75 3 3 pitch 6.75 **Facilities:** **Services:** lau
Leisure: R **Off-site:**

EUPEN LIÈGE

'An der Hill' Hutte 46, 4700 087 744617 087 557232
In wooded surroundings with well-defined pitches.
SW of town via N67 towards Monschau.
Open: All year **Site:** 0.6HEC **Facilities:** **Services:** lau **Off-site:** P

Facilities: -shop -shower -electric points for razors -electric points for caravans -parking by tents permitted -compulsory separate car park **Services:** -café/restaurant -bar -Camping Gaz International -gas other than Camping Gaz -first aid facilities lau-laundry **Leisure:** -swimming L-Lake P-Pool R-River S-Sea **Off-site:** All facilities within 2km

FLORENVILLE LUXEMBOURG

Rosière Rive Gauche de la Semois, 6820
061 311937 061 314873
e-mail: larosiere@pi.be **website:** www.larosiere.be
In wooded surroundings close to the town centre.
Access via E411 exit 26 for Verlaine/Nuefchâteau.
Open: Apr-10 Nov **Site:** 10HEC **Facilities:** **Services:** lau **Leisure:** PR

FORRIÈRES LUXEMBOURG

Pré du Blason r de la Ramée 30, 6953
084 212867 084 223650
e-mail: predublason@skynet.be
website: www.camping-predublason.be
This well-kept site lies on a meadow surrounded by wooded hills and is completely divided into pitches and crossed by rough gravel drives.
Off N49 Masbourg road.
Open: Apr-Oct **Site:** 3HEC **Prices:** 2 7.20 5.50 (static)185 **Facilities:** **Services:** lau **Leisure:** R

GEMMENICH LIÈGE

Kon Tiki Terstraeten 141, 4851 087 785973
Open: All year **Site:** 12HEC **Facilities:** **Services:** lau **Leisure:** PR

GOUVY LUXEMBOURG

Lac de Cherapont Cherapont 2, 6670
080 517082 080 517093
On an extensive lakeside tourist complex with a wide variety of recreational facilities.
Access via E25 exit 51 or E42 exit 15.
Open: Apr-Oct **Site:** 10HEC **Facilities:** **Services:** lau **Leisure:** LR **Off-site:**

GRAND-HALLEUX LUXEMBOURG

Neuf Prés av de la Résistance, 6698 080 216882
A family site in pleasant wooded surroundings beside a river.
Access via E42.
Open: Apr-Sep **Site:** 4HEC **Prices:** 2 1.20 3 2.30 **Facilities:** **Services:** lau **Leisure:** PR
Off-site:

HABAY-LA-NEUVE LUXEMBOURG

Portail de la Forêt r du Bon-Bois 3, 6720
063 422312 063 423410
e-mail: athiry@belgacom.net
Parklike, terraced site on a hill surrounded by woodland.
Access via E25/E411 exit 29.
Open: 15 Mar-15 Oct **Site:** 2.5HEC **Facilities:** **Off-site:** PR

HAMOIR-SUR-OURTHE LIÈGE

CM Dessous Hamoir r du Moulin, 4180 086 388925
A municipal site with well-equipped pitches and good facilities for children beside the River Ourthe.
From the Liège-Luxembourg motorway take exit Werbomont and continue for 15km.
Open: 15 Mar-15 Nov **Site:** 3.5HEC **Facilities:** **Services:** lau **Leisure:** R **Off-site:**

HOGNE NAMUR

Relais 16 r de Serinchamps, 5377
084 311580 084 312400
e-mail: info@campinglerelais.com
website: www.campinglerelais.com
A pleasant site in a wooded park beside a lake.
Take N4 from Courrière to Hogne via Marche.
Open: Mar-4 Jan **Site:** 12HEC **Prices:** 3 4 pitch 8 (static)180-400 **Facilities:** **Services:** lau **Leisure:** L

HOUFFALIZE LUXEMBOURG

Chasse et Pêche r de la Roche 63, 6660
061 288314 061 289660
e-mail: info@cpbuitensport.com
website: www.cpbuitensport.com
A pleasant site attached to a café-restaurant with good recreational facilities.
3km NW off E25.
Open: All year **Site:** 2HEC **Prices:** 4.50-4.50 3.50-3.50 4-41 3.50-3.50 **Facilities:** **Services:** lau **Leisure:** R

Moulin de Rensiwez Moulin de Rensiwez 1, 6663
061 289027 061 289027
A good transit site on a series of terraces beside the River Ourthe close to an old water-mill.
Open: All year **Site:** 5HEC **Prices:** pitch 17 (incl 4 persons) **Facilities:** **Services:** lau **Leisure:** R

LOUVEIGNÉ LIÈGE

Moulin du Rouge-Thier Rouge-Thier 8, 4141
04 3608341 04 3608341
A well-equipped site in a pleasant wooded location.
S of town towards Deigné.
Open: Apr-30 Oct **Site:** 8HEC **Prices:** pitch 13 (incl 4 persons) **Facilities:** **Services:** lau **Leisure:** P

MALONNE NAMUR

Trieux r des Tris 99, 5020 081 445583 081 44 5583
e-mail: camping.les.trieux@skynet.be
website: www.campinglestrieux.be
Open: Apr-30 Oct **Site:** 2.2HEC **Prices:** 2.50 2.50 8 3.75-4.50 pitch 3.75 (static)112-168
Facilities: **Services:** lau
Off-site: R

MARCHE-EN-FAMENNE LUXEMBOURG

Euro Camping Paola r du Panorama 10, 6900
084 311704 084 314722
e-mail: camping.paola@skynet.be
A long site on a hill with a beautiful view. The only noise comes from a railway line, which passes right by the site.
Take road towards Hotton, turn right after cemetery and continue 1km.
Open: All year **Site:** 13HEC **Prices:** 2.20 2.50 5 4-5 (static)200 **Facilities:** **Services:** **Off-site:** P

NEUFCHÂTEAU LUXEMBOURG

International Spineuse r de Malome 7, rte de Florenville, 6840
061 277320 061 277104
e-mail: info@camping-spineuse.be
website: www.camping-spineuse.be
Camp shop open July and August only.
Situated 2km from Florenville in the direction of Neufchâteau.
Open: All year **Site:** 2.5HEC **Prices:** 3.10 9-11.25 pitch 9-11.25 (static)225-350 **Facilities:** **Services:** lau **Leisure:** LPR

OLLOY-SUR-VIROIN NAMUR

Try des Baudets r de la Champagne, 5670
060 390108 060 390108
e-mail: masson_p@yahoo.fr
website: home.freegates.be/campingtrydesbaudets
In a peaceful situation on the edge of a forest.
Open: All year **Site:** 11HEC **Prices:** 0.50 12.25 7.15 (static)200 **Facilities:** **Services:** lau **Off-site:**

OTEPPE LIÈGE

Hirondelle r du Château 1, 4210
085 711131 085 711021
e-mail: hirondelle@skynet.be
Ideal family site with modern facilities in the picturesque Burdinale Valley.
N of town between E40 and E42. Signed.
Open: Etr-Sep **Site:** 65HEC **Facilities:** **Services:** lau **Leisure:** P

POLLEUR LIÈGE

Polleur r de Congrès 90, 4910 087 541033 087 542530
e-mail: info@campingpolleur.be
website: www.campingpolleur.be
A family site in a pleasant wooded location.
Signed from A27/E42.
Open: Apr-Oct **Site:** 3.7HEC **Facilities:** **Services:** lau **Leisure:** PR

PURNODE NAMUR

Camping du Bocq av de la Vallée, 5530
082 612269 082 646814
e-mail: campingdubocq@pi.be
website: www.camping-dubocq.be
In a beautiful wooded location beside the river.
Leave E411 at exit 19 (Spontin) towards Yvoir, exit Purnode.
Open: Apr-Oct **Site:** 3HEC **Prices:** 3.25 2.50 2.75 pitch 2.75 (static)150-300 **Facilities:** **Services:** lau **Leisure:** R **Off-site:**

REMOUCHAMPS LIÈGE

Eden r de Trois Ponts 92, 4920 04 3844165 3840055
e-mail: edencamping@swing.be
Open: Apr-Oct **Site:** 3.2HEC **Facilities:** **Services:** **Leisure:** R **Off-site:**

RENDEUX LUXEMBOURG

Festival rte de la Roche 89, 6987
084 477371 084 477364
website: www.lefestival.be
In unspoiled surroundings beside the River Ourthe.
Open: Etr-Sep **Site:** 12HEC **Prices:** 10-15 pitch 17-19 **Facilities:** **Services:** lau **Leisure:** R

ROBERTVILLE LIÈGE

Plage 33 rte des Bains, B-4950 080 446658 080 446178
Open: All year **Site:** 1.8HEC **Facilities:** **Services:** lau **Leisure:** LPR

ROCHE-EN-ARDENNE, LA LUXEMBOURG

Grillon r des Echarées, 6980 084 412062 084 412128
Well-equipped family site in a pleasant wooded setting.
Open: Etr-Oct **Site:** 3.5HEC **Facilities:** **Services:** lau **Leisure:** R **Off-site:** P

Lohan 20a rte de Houffalize, 6980 084 411545
In a park surrounded by woodland, on N bank of the River Ourthe.
3km E of La Roche towards Maboge and Houffalize.
Open: Apr-1 Nov **Site:** 4HEC **Prices:** 85-2.50 pitch 7-8 **Facilities:** **Services:** lau **Leisure:** R

Ourthe 6980 084 411459
e-mail: info@campingdelourthe.be
website: www.campingdelourthe.be
Well-kept site, beside the River Ourthe.
On SW bank of the Ourthe below the N34.
Open: 15 Mar-15 Oct **Site:** 2HEC **Prices:** 2 6 pitch 6 (static)200 **Facilities:** **Services:** lau **Leisure:** R **Off-site:** P

SART-LEZ-SPA LIÈGE

Touring Club Stockay 17, 4845 087 474400 087 475277
e-mail: spador@pophost.elinet.be
website: www.campingspador.be
Signed. The site lies to the E of Spa.
Open: All year **Site:** 6HEC **Prices:** pitch 18 (incl 2 persons) (static)700 **Facilities:** **Services:** lau **Leisure:** PR **Off-site:** L

Facilities: -shop -shower -electric points for razors -electric points for caravans -parking by tents permitted -compulsory separate car park **Services:** -café/restaurant -bar -Camping Gaz International -gas other than Camping Gaz -first aid facilities lau-laundry **Leisure:** -swimming L-Lake P-Pool R-River S-Sea **Off-site:** All facilities within 2km

SIPPENAEKEN LIÈGE

Vieux Moulin 114 Tebruggen, 4851 087 784255
A family site with good recreational facilities, set in a pleasant wooded location close to a nature reserve.
Access via E40 exit Battile towards Aubel-Hombourg-Sippenaeken.
Open: Apr-Sep **Site:** 6HEC **Prices:** 3 pitch 3.50 **Facilities:** **Services:** lau **Leisure:** PR

SPA LIÈGE

Parc des Sources r de la Sauvenière 141, 4900
087 772311 087 475965
e-mail: info@campingparcdessources.be
website: www.campingparcdessources.be
On the outskirts of the town close to the forest.
S of town centre on N32 towards Malmédy.
Open: All year **Site:** 2.5HEC **Prices:** pitch 15.60 (incl 2 persons) pp3.50 **Facilities:** **Services:** lau **Leisure:** P **Off-site:**

SPRIMONT LIÈGE

Tultay r de Tultay 22, 4140 04 3821162 04 3676397
e-mail: r3cb.tultay@teledismet.be
website: www.rcccb.com
A pleasant site in wooded surroundings on the edge of a nature reserve.
NE of Sprimont. Access via E9.
Open: All year **Site:** 1.5HEC **Prices:** 2.50 pitch 5 **Facilities:** **Services:** lau **Off-site:**

STAVELOT LIÈGE

Domaine de l'Eau Rouge Cheneux 25, 4970
080 863075
website: www.campingleaurouge.be
A pleasant riverside site with good sporting facilities.
Access via E42 to Francorchamps or Malmedy.
Open: All year **Site:** 4HEC **Facilities:** **Services:** lau **Leisure:** R **Off-site:** P

TENNEVILLE LUXEMBOURG

Pont de Berguème r Berguème 9, 6970
084 455443 084 456231
e-mail: info@pontbergueme.be
website: www.pontbergueme.be
In a peaceful, wooded setting in the beautiful Ardennes area with good, modern facilities.
Turn off E40/N4 towards Berguème then turn right.
Open: All year **Site:** 3HEC **Facilities:** **Services:** lau **Leisure:** R

THOMMEN-REULAND LIÈGE

Hohenbusch Grüfflingen 44, 4791 080 227523
e-mail: info@hohenbusch.be
website: www.hohenbusch.be
A well-appointed family site on a wooded meadow with plenty of recreational facilities.
Off N26 SW of St-Vith.
Open: Apr-Oct **Site:** 5HEC **Prices:** 4 pitch 8 **Facilities:** **Services:** lau **Leisure:** P

VIELSALM LUXEMBOURG

Salm chemin de la Vallée, B-6690
080 216241 080 217266
website: www.vielsham.be
Open: All year **Site:** 2.5HEC **Prices:** 1.20 1.20 7 6 **Facilities:** **Services:** lau **Leisure:** R **Off-site:** LP

VIRTON LUXEMBOURG

Vallée de Rabais r du Bonlieu, 6760
063 570144 063 583342
e-mail: info@campingvalleederabais.be
website: www.campingvaleederabais.be
A secluded family site in the heart of the Gaume region close to a lake with good recreational facilities.
NE of Virton between N87 and N82.
Open: All year **Site:** 8HEC **Facilities:** **Services:** lau **Leisure:** P **Off-site:** L

WAIMES LIÈGE

Anderegg Bruyères 4, 4950 080 679393 080 679396
e-mail: campinganderegg@skynet.be
website: www.campinganderegg.be
In a peaceful situation beside the Lac de Robertville.
Open: All year **Site:** 1.5HEC **Prices:** 3.50 4.75 4.75 **Facilities:** **Services:** lau

Site: 6HEC-Site size -grass -sand -stone -little shade -partly shaded -mainly shaded -bungalows for hire -caravans for hire -tents for hire -no dogs **Prices:** -adult per night -car per night pp-per person per night -caravan per night -tent per night (static)-caravan hire per week

FRANCE

France, rich in history and natural beauty, is Europe's most-popular camping destination. Its broad range of scenery offers something for everyone.

FACTS AND FIGURES
Area: 543,965 sq km (210,025 sq miles)
Population: 60,700,000 (2001)
Capital: Paris
Language: French
IDD code: 33
To call the UK, dial 00 44
Currency: Euro
Local time: GMT + 1 (summer GMT + 2)
Emergency services: Police 17; Fire 18; Ambulance 15. Or dial the European emergency call number 112, and request the service you require.
Banks: 10.00-13.00, 15.00-17.00 Mon-Fri (Paris area; Tue-Sat elsewhere).
Shops: 09.00-18.00 Mon-Sat (times may vary for food shops)
Average daily temperature: Paris

Jan 3°C	Mar 6°C
May 13°C	Jul 18°C
Sep15°C	Nov 6°C

Tourist information:
UK
French Government Tourist Office
178 Piccadilly
London W1J 9AL
Tel 09068 244123 (premium rate info line Mon-Fri 0900-1700)
Monaco Government Tourist Office
The Chambers, Chelsea Harbour
London SW10 0XF
Tel Freephone 0500 006 114 (Mon-Fri 9.30-17.30)

USA
French Government Tourist Office
16th Floor, 444 Madison Avenue
New York NY 10022
Tel (410) 286 8310
Tourist info website: www.franceguide.com

France's great variety of landscapes range from the mountain ranges of the Alps and the Pyrénées to the attractive river valleys of the Loire, Rhône and Dordogne. Add some 2,900km of coastline, which includes the golden sands of the Côte-d'Azur, and this is a country that can appeal to all tastes.

The climate of France is temperate but varies considerably. The Mediterranean coast enjoys a sub-tropical climate with hot summers, while along the coast of Brittany the climate is very similar to that of Devon and Cornwall. The language is, of course, French and this is spoken throughout the country, although there are many local dialects and variations, some of which may be impenetrable even to seasoned French speakers.

France has an enormous number of campsites, over 10,000 of them, under the auspices of the **French Federation of Camping and Caravanning.** During July and August, however, they are heavily booked, specially on the Mediterranean coast and other popular holiday destinations.

There are *castels et camping* caravanning sites in the grounds of châteaux (castles) and many are included in this guide. On sites in state forests, *forêts domaniales,* it is necessary to apply to the *garde forestier* for permission to camp and evidence of insurance must be produced (such as the *camping card*). Opening periods vary widely though some sites are open all year. Local information offices (see **Tourist information** above) can supply information about sites in their locality.

All graded sites must display their official classification, site regulations, capacity and current charges at the site entrance. Some sites have inclusive charges per pitch, others show basic prices per person, vehicle and space, with extra facilities like showers, swimming pools and ironing incurring additional charges. In practice, most campsites charge from midday to midday, with each part day being counted as a full day. Reductions for children are usually allowed up to 7 years of age; there is generally no charge for children under 3.

Off-site camping in the south of France is restricted because of the danger of fire. In other parts camping is possible, provided that permission has been obtained, although camping is seldom allowed near the water's edge, or at a large seaside resort. Casual camping is prohibited in state forests and national parks. Camping in an unauthorised place can lead to prosecution or confiscation of equipment, or both, especially in the south. However, an overnight stop on parking areas of some motorways is tolerated, but make sure you do not contravene local regulations; overnight stops in a lay-by are not permitted. Camping is not permitted in Monaco. Caravans in transit are allowed but it is forbidden to park them.

HOW TO GET THERE

Apart from the direct crossing by Eurotunnel (Folkestone-Calais, 35 mins platform to platform), the following services are available.

Short ferry crossings

From **Dover** to **Calais** takes 60mins (Seacat) or 75-90mins (ferry).

From **Dover** to **Boutogne** takes 50mins (catamaran).

Longer ferry crossings

From **Dover** to **Dunkerque** takes 2hrs by ferry.

From **Newhaven** to **Dieppe** takes 4hrs by ferry and 2hrs by Superseacat.

From **Portsmouth** to **Le Havre** takes 5hrs 30mins (day) - 7hrs 30mins (night); to **Caen (Ouistreham)** takes 6hrs (3hrs 25mins by catamaran, summer only); to **Cherbourg** takes 5hrs (day) - 7hrs (night) or 2hrs 45mins (fast ferry); to **St Malo** takes 8hrs 45mins (day) - 10hrs 30mins (night).

From **Poole** to **Cherbourg** takes 4hrs 15mins (day) - 5hrs 45mins (night) or 2hrs 15mins (fast ferry - summer only).

From **Plymouth** to **Roscoff** takes 6hrs; to **St Malo** (winter only) takes 8hrs.

CAR SLEEPER TRAINS

Summer services are available from **Calais** to Avignon, Brive, Narbonne, Nice and Toulouse.

MOTORING & GENERAL

The information given here is specific to France. It **must** be read in conjunction with the Essential Information for Motoring section, which covers regulations that are common to many countries.

BRITISH EMBASSY/CONSULATES*

The British Embassy is located at 35 rue du Faubourg St-Honoré, 75383 Paris Cedex 08 ☎ 0144513100; consular section 18bis rue d'Anjou, 75008 Paris; phone as for embassy. There are British consulates in Bordeaux, Lille, Lyon and Marseille.

There are British consulates with Honorary Consuls in Amiens, Biarritz, Boulogne-sur-Mer, Calais, Cherbourg, Clemont Ferrand, Dunkerque (Dunkirk), Le Havre, Lorient, Montpellier, Nantes, Nice, St Malo-Dinard, Saumur, Toulouse and Tours.

CHILDREN IN CARS

Children under 10 not permitted to travel as front-seat passenger, with the exception of a baby - up to 9 months and less than 9kg weight - in a rear-facing seat. Children under 10 in rear must use restraint system appropriate to their age and weight.

Under **no circumstances** fit a rearward facing child restraint in a seat with a frontal airbag. See Essential Information for Motoring section under **Passengers** and **Seat Belts**.

CURRENCY*

The **euro** is the currency of France. The French franc (FRF) ceased to be legal tender in 2002, though FRF coins and notes may still be exchanged at the French Central Bank (Banque de France) for 10 years (banknotes) and at least 3 years (coins).

DIMENSIONS & WEIGHT RESTRICTIONS*

Private cars and towed trailers or caravans are restricted to the following dimensions - height, no restrictions, but 4 metres is a recommended maximum; width 2.55 metres; length 12 metres (excluding tow-bar). The maximum permitted overall length of vehicle/trailer or caravan combination is 18.75 metres.

Trailers without brakes have a maximum authorised weight of 750kg or 50% of unladen weight of the towing vehicle, whichever is lower. If the weight of the trailer exceeds that of the towing vehicle, see Speed Limits below.

DRIVING LICENCE*

A valid UK or Republic of Ireland licence is accepted in France. The minimum age at which visitors from UK or Republic of Ireland may use a temporarily imported motorcycle (over 80cc) or car is 18. Visitors may use temporarily imported motorcycles of up to 80cc at 16. (See also Speed Limits below.)

FOODSTUFFS*

If the imported foodstuffs are for personal use, there are no limits when travelling between EU countries. Visitors entering France from Andorra should ensure that the following are not exceeded - 2.5kg milk powder, 3kg condensed milk, 6kg fresh

Café in Frejus

milk, 1kg butter, 4kg cheese, 5kg sugar/sweets, 5kg meat. Coffee (1kg), coffee extract (400g), tea (200g) and tea extract (80g) are free of customs duties. Visitors coming from other countries may import up to 1kg of meat, but meat and meat products from Africa are prohibited. Coffee (500g), coffee extract (200g), tea (100g) and tea extract (40g) are free of customs duties, but visitors under 15 cannot import coffee.

Lights*

Yellow tinted headlights are no longer necessary in France. It is compulsory for motorcyclists riding machines exceeding 125cc to use dipped headlights during the day.

Motoring Club

The AA is affiliated to the **Fédération Française des Automobile-Clubs et des Usagers de la Route** (FFAC), whose office is at 76 avenue Marceau, 75008 Paris ☎ 0156892070.

Website: **www.automobileclub.org**

Parking*

Parking restrictions are indicated by signs or yellow lines on the kerb. Stopping and parking is prohibited if the yellow line is continuous; parking if it is broken. In Paris parking is forbidden in many city-centre streets, and wheelclamps are in use. It is forbidden to stop or park on a *red route.*

The east-west route includes the left bank of the Seine and the Quai de la Megisserie; the north-south route includes the avenue du Général Leclerc, part of the boulevard St-Michel, the rue de Rivoli, the boulevards Sébastopol, Strasbourg, Barbès and Ornano, rue Lafayette and avenue Jean-Jaurès.

Priority Including Roundabouts*

In built-up areas, you must give way to traffic coming from the right - *priorité à droite.* However, at roundabouts with signs bearing the words *Vous n'avez pas la priorité* or *Cédez le passage* traffic **on the roundabout** has priority. Where no such sign exists, traffic **entering** the roundabout has priority.

Outside built-up areas, all main roads of any importance have right of way. This is indicated by a red-bordered triangle showing a black cross on a white background with the words *Passage Protégé* underneath; or a red-bordered triangle showing a pointed black upright with horizontal bar on a white background; or a yellow square within a white square with points vertical.

Petrol

See Essential Information for Motoring section under **Petrol/Diesel**.

Roads

France has more than 6,400km of motorway (*autoroute*). With the exception of a few sections into or around large cities, tolls are payable. Emergency telephones that connect the caller to the police are located about every 2km. There is also a comprehensive network of other roads, and surfaces are generally good; exceptions are usually signposted *Chauseé déformeé*. The camber is often severe and the edges rough.

During July and August, and specially at weekends, traffic on main roads can be very heavy. Special signs are erected to indicate alternative routes with the least congestion. Wherever they appear, it is usually advantageous to follow them, although you may not save time. The alternative routes are quiet, but they are not as wide as the main roads. They are not suitable for caravans.

A free road map showing the marked alternative routes, plus information centres and petrol stations open 24 hours, is available from service stations displaying the *Bison Futé* poster (a Red Indian chief in full war bonnet). These maps are also available from *Syndicats d'Initiative* and information offices.

Speed Limits*

Built-up areas	50km/h (31mph)
Other roads	90km/h (55mph)
Dual-carriageways	110km/h (69mph)
Motorways	130km/h (80mph)

The minimum speed in the outside lane on a level stretch of motorway during good daytime visibility is 80km/h (49mph), and drivers travelling below this speed are liable to a fine. The maximum speed on the Paris ring road is 80km/h (49mph), and, on other urban stretches of motorway 110km/h (69mph).

In fog, when visibility is reduced to 50 metres (55yds), the speed limit on all roads is 50km/h (31mph). In wet weather speed limits outside built-up areas are reduced to 80km/h (49mph), 100km/h (62mph) and 110km/h (69mph) on motorways.

The above limits apply to private cars, motorcycles (exceeding 80cc), and private cars towing a trailer/caravan if the latter's weight does not exceed that of the car and the total weight is less than 3.5 tonnes. However, if the weight of the trailer exceeds that of the car by less than 30%, the speed limit is 65km/h (40mph); if more than 30% the speed limit is 45km/h (28mph). Additionally these combinations must:

- Display a disc at the rear of the caravan/trailer showing the maximum speed
- Not be driven in the fast lane of a 3-lane motorway.

Motorists who have held a full driving licence for less than 2 years, must not exceed 80km/h (49mph) outside built-up areas, 100km/h (62mph) on dual carriageways, and 110km/h (69mph) on motorways.

Warning Triangle/Hazard-warning*

The use of a warning triangle or hazard-warning lights† is compulsory in the event of accident or breakdown. As hazard-warning lights may be damaged or inoperative, it is recommended that you carry a warning triangle in the vehicle. The triangle must be placed on the road 30 metres (33yds) behind the vehicle and clearly visible from 100 metres (109yds).

†If your vehicle is equipped with hazard warning lights, it is also complusory to use them if you are forced to drive temporarily at a greatly reduced speed. However, when traffic is slow moving in an uninterrupted lane or lanes, this only applies to the last vehicle in the lane(s).

***Additional information can be found in the Essential Information for Motoring section.**

ALPS/EAST

ABRETS, LES Isère

Coin Tranquille 38490 476321348 476374067
e-mail: contact@coin-tranquille.com
website: www.coin-tranquille.com
Completely divided into pitches with attractive flower beds in rural surroundings.
2 km E of village, 500m off N6.
Open: Apr-Oct **Site:** 7HEC **Prices:** 4-6.50 2.10-3 pitch 14.50-26.50 (incl 2 persons) **Facilities:** **Services:** lau **Leisure:** P

AILLON-LE-JEUNE Savoie

Jeanne et Georges Cher 73340 479546032
On a level meadow with heated sanitary installations. Situated close to the local ski station.
Open: All year **Site:** 2HEC **Facilities:** **Services:** lau **Off-site:**

ALBENS Savoie

Beauséjour rte de la Rippe, 73410 479541520
In a delightfully peaceful, wooded setting between Aix-les-Bains and Annecy.
SW via rte de la Chambotte. Signed.
Open: Jun-20 Sep **Site:** 2HEC **Prices:** 1.70 pitch 3.70 (static)160 **Facilities:** **Services:** lau **Off-site:** R

ALLEVARD Isère

Clair Matin rte de Pommiers, 38580
476975519 476458715
e-mail: jdavallet1@aol.com
website: www.ifrance.com/aucampingclairmatin
Gently sloping terraced area divided into pitches.
S of village, 300m off D525.
Open: 10 May-15 Oct **Site:** 5.5HEC **Prices:** 2.70 pitch 5.25-10.50 (static)113-265 **Facilities:** **Services:** lau **Leisure:** P **Off-site:** LR

ARBOIS Jura

CM Vignes av Gl-Leclerc, 39600 384661412 384661412
Terraced site. Shop open July and August only.
E on D107 Mesnay road at stadium.
Open: Apr-Sep **Site:** 5HEC **Facilities:** **Services:** lau **Off-site:** PR

ARGENTIÈRE Haute-Savoie

Glacier d'Argentière 161 chemin des Chosalets, 74400
450541736 450540373
Set on sloping meadowland in a beautiful situation at the foot of the Mont Blanc Massif.
Access is 1km S of Argentière, turn off N506 towards Cableway Lognan et de Grandes Montets, then a further 200m to site.
Open: 15 May-Sep **Site:** 1.5HEC **Prices:** 4.30 1.60 3.20 2.20 (static)175 **Facilities:** **Services:** lau **Off-site:**

ARS-SUR-FORMANS Ain

Bois de la Dame Chemin du Bois de la Dame, 1480
474007723
Compulsory separate car park for arrivals after 22.00hrs.
Access from A6, exit Villefranche and continue towards Jassans-Riottier.
Open: Apr-Sep **Site:** 1.5HEC **Prices:** 8 pitch 8 (incl 1 person) **Facilities:** **Services:** lau **Off-site:** P

AUTRANS Isère

Caravaneige du Vercors Les Gaillards, 38880
476953188 476953682
e-mail: camping.le.vercors@wanadoo.fr
website: www.camping-du-vercors.fr
Ideal for summer or winter holidays, situated in the heart of the Vercors with easy access to skiing.
0.6km S via D106 towards Méaudre.
Open: 20 May-20 Sep & Dec-Mar **Site:** 1HEC **Prices:** 3.90 12 pitch 12 (incl 2 persons) **Facilities:** **Services:** lau **Leisure:** P **Off-site:**

Joyeux Réveil 38880 476953344 476957298
e-mail: camping-au-joyeux-reveil@wanadoo.fr
website: camping-au-joyeux-reveil.fr
In a beautiful location surrounded by woodland, with fine mountain views.
NE of town via rte de Montaud.
Open: Dec-Mar & May-Sep **Site:** 1.5HEC **Prices:** pitch 16-25 (incl 2 persons) (static)290-670 **Facilities:** **Services:** lau **Leisure:** P **Off-site:**

BARATIER Hautes-Alpes

Verger 5200 492431587 4924981
e-mail: campingleverger@wanadoo.fr
website: www.campingleverger.fr
Terraced site in plantation of fruit trees with fine views of Alps. Divided into pitches.
From N94 drive 2.5km S of Embrun, 1.5km E on D40.
Open: Apr-Sep **Site:** 4HEC **Prices:** pitch 13.70 (incl 2 persons) (static)525 **Facilities:** **Services:** lau **Leisure:** P **Off-site:** LR

BELFORT Territoire-de-Belfort

Étang des Forges r du Général Béthouart, 90000
384225492 384227655
e-mail: contact@campings-belfort.com
website: www.campings-belfort.com
Situated by the side of the Malsaucy lake in the regional nature reserve of Ballons des Vosges. Ideal terrain for water and hiking activities.
A36/E54 exit 2, situated off D13 Richtung-Offemont road
Open: 10 Apr-Sep **Site:** 3.5HEC **Prices:** 3.50-3.80 pitch 7-8 (incl 2 persons) (static)220-390 **Facilities:** **Services:** lau **Leisure:** P **Off-site:** L

BELLEGARDE-SUR-VALSERINE AIN

Crêt d'Eau 2 av de Lattre-de-Tassigny, 01200
450566081 0450486209
In a pleasant mountain setting with good facilities.
3km N of town, 200m from N84.
Open: All year **Site:** 5HEC **Facilities:**
Services: lau **Leisure:** P **Off-site:** R

BOURG-D'OISANS, LE ISÈRE

Caravaneige le Vernis 38520 476800268
e-mail: camping.levernis@wanadoo.fr
website: www.oisans.com/levernis
Well-kept site at foot of mountain in summer skiing area.
2.5km of N91, rte de BrianÁon.
Open: Jun-10 Sep **Site:** 1.2HEC **Facilities:** **Services:** lau **Leisure:** P **Off-site:**

Cascade rte de l'Alpe-d'Huez, 38520
476800242 476802263
e-mail: lacascade@wanadoo.fr
website: www.pro.wanadoo.fr/camping.lacascade
Set at the foot of a mountain with a waterfall and modern, very well-kept sanitary arrangements. Television lounge with library, open fireplace. Booking essential.
From Grenoble follow signs 'Stations de l'Oisans' then from Bourg-d'Oisans continue towards Alpe-d'Huez.
Open: 15 Dec-Sep **Site:** 2.5HEC **Prices:** 14.80-22 **Facilities:** **Services:** lau **Leisure:** PR **Off-site:**

Colporteur le Mas du Plan, 38520
476791144 476791149
e-mail: info@camping-colporteur.com
website: www.camping-colporteur.com
Situated 200m from the centre of Bourg d'Oisans, a village situated in the centre of a plain surrounded by mountains.
Open: 14 May-18 Sep **Site:** 4HEC **Prices:** pitch 11.50-15.50 (incl 1 person) **Facilities:** **Services:** lau **Leisure:** R **Off-site:** P

Rencontre du Soleil rte de l'Alpe-d'Huez, 38520
476791222 476802637
e-mail: rencontre.soleil@wanadoo.fr
website: www.joliefrance.com/ais
Charming site in a lovely setting in the Dauphiny Alps at the foot of a mountain. Fine rustic common room with open fireplace. TV, playroom for children.
At the foot of the hairpin road to L'Alp-d'Huez, leave N91 (Grenoble-Briançon road) in Le Bourg d'Osians.
Open: 10 May-15 Sep **Site:** 1.6HEC **Prices:** pitch 14.30-22.85 (incl 2 persons) **Facilities:** **Services:** lau **Leisure:** P **Off-site:** R

AT VENOSC (10KM SE ON N91 AND D530)

Champ de Moulin 38520 476800738 476802444
website: www.champ-du-moulin.com
In a picturesque location with fine views of the surrounding mountains and a direct cablecar connection to local ski slopes. Separate car park for late arrivals.
Open: Jan-15 Sep & 15-31 Dec **Site:** 1HEC
Prices: pitch 13-18 (incl 2 persons) (static)280-340
Facilities: **Services:** lau **Leisure:** R **Off-site:** P

BOURG-EN-BRESSE AIN

CM de Challes 5 allée du Centre Nautique, 01000
474453721 474224032
e-mail: camping_municipal_bourgenbresse@wanadoo.fr
In football ground near swimming pool.
Well signed from outskirts of town.
Open: Apr-14 Oct **Site:** 2.7HEC **Prices:** 2.85 6.01 5.06 pitch 6.01 **Facilities:**
Services: lau **Leisure:** P **Off-site:** L

BOURGET-DU-LAC, LE SAVOIE

CM Ile aux Cygnes 73370 479250176 479253294
e-mail: camping@bourgetdulac.com
website: www.bourgetdulac.com
A family site on the shore of the Lac Bourdeau with plenty of recreational facilities.
Access via N514.
Open: 13 Apr-13 Oct & May-Sep **Site:** 4.5HEC
Facilities: **Services:** lau **Leisure:** LR
Off-site:

BOURG-ST-MAURICE SAVOIE

Versoyen rte des Arcs, 73700 479070345 479072541
e-mail: leversoyen@wanadoo.fr
website: www.leversoyen.com
Two communal sanitary blocks - one heated. Skiing facilities. Many secluded pitches in a wood.
On S outskirts of town. Access via N90.
Open: 28 May-2 Nov & 15 Dec-2 May **Site:** 4HEC **Prices:** 3.50-6.05 pitch 3.20-4.85 (static)160-340
Facilities: **Services:** lau **Off-site:** PR

BOUT-DU-LAC HAUTE-SAVOIE

International du Lac Bleu rte de la Plage, 74210
450443018 450448435
e-mail: lac-bleu@nwc.fr
website: www.camping-lac-bleu.com
Modern, well-kept site. Overflow area with own sanitary blocks.
On the southern shores of Lake Annecy via the N508, opposite ANTAR garage.
Open: 15 Apr-25 Sep **Site:** 3.3HEC
Prices: pitch 15.40-23.50 (incl 2 persons) (static)330-670
Facilities: **Services:** lau **Leisure:** LP
Off-site:

Nublière 74210 450443344 450443178
e-mail: nubliere@wanadoo.fr
website: www.campeoles.fr
Extensive site divided into pitches in attractive surroundings.
150m off N508 at S end of Lac d'Annecy.
Open: May-Sep **Site:** 9HEC **Prices:** pitch 11.85-18 (incl 2 persons) **Facilities:** **Services:** lau
Leisure: L **Off-site:** R

CHALEZEULE DOUBS

Plage 12 rte de Belfort, 25220 381880426 381505462
e-mail: laplage.besancon@ffcc.asso.fr
website: www.ffcc.asso.fr
A modern site with good facilities near the main roads and close to the River Doubs.
Access via N83 towards Belfort.
Open: Apr-Sep **Site:** 1.8HEC **Facilities:**
Services: lau **Leisure:** PR **Off-site:**

CHAMONIX-MONT-BLANC HAUTE-SAVOIE

Mer de Glace 200 Chemin de la Bagna, 74400
450534403 450536083
e-mail: campingmdg@tiscali.fr
website: www.chamonix_camping.com
In a forested setting with pitches divided by hedges. Enjoys fine mountain views.

2km NE to Les Praz. On approach to village (from Chamonix) turn right under railway bridge.
Open: 29 Apr-2 Oct **Site:** 2.2HEC **Prices:** 5.30-6.10 pitch 5-6.90 **Facilities:** **Services:** lau **Off-site:** P

Rosières 121 Clos des Rosières, 74400
450531042 450532955
e-mail: info@campinglesrosieres.com
website: www.campinglesrosieres.com
Picturesque site at the foot of the Mont Blanc range.
1.2km NE via N506.
Open: 27 May-18 Oct **Site:** 1.5HEC
Prices: 5.30-6.10 3 pitch 4.60-6 **Facilities:**
Services: lau **Off-site:** P

At **Bossons, Les** (3km W)

Cimes 28 rte des Tissieres, 74400 450535893
In a wooded meadow at the foot of Mont Blanc range. Ideal for hiking and mountain tours.
Open: 15 Jun-20 Sep **Site:** 1HEC **Facilities:** **Services:** lau **Leisure:** R **Off-site:** L

Deux Glaciers 80 rte des Tissières, 74400
450531584 450559081
e-mail: glaciers@clubinternet.fr
A glacial stream runs through the site. Pitches shaded by trees, very modern, well-kept sanitary installations. Rustic common room with open fires.
Leave N506 towards road underpass. 250m to site.
Open: All year **Site:** 16HEC **Facilities:**
Services: lau **Off-site:**

Champagnole Jura

CM Boyse r G-Vallery, 39300 384520032 384520116
e-mail: boyse@frce.fr
website: www.tourisme.champagnole.com
Clean and tidy site with asphalt drives and completely divided into pitches. In grounds of municipal swimming pool.
Turn onto D5 just before town and continue 1.3km to site.
Open: 2 Jun-17 Sep **Site:** 7HEC **Facilities:** **Services:** lau **Leisure:** PR

Châteauroux-les-Alpes Hautes-Alpes

Cariamas Fontmolines, 05380 492432263
e-mail: p.tim@free.fr
website: les.cariamas.free.fr
On a meadow in an attractive mountain setting beside the River Durance.
1.5km SE.
Open: Apr-Oct **Site:** 6HEC **Prices:** 4.50 5.25 5.25 pitch 5.25 (static)200-370 **Facilities:** **Services:** lau **Leisure:** P **Off-site:**

Choisy Haute-Savoie

Chez Langin 74330 450774165 450774101
e-mail: 352@wanadoo.fr
In pleasant wooded surroundings.
1.3km NE via D3.
Open: 14 Apr-Sep **Site:** 3HEC **Prices:** 18 1.60 pitch 18 (incl 2 persons) pp4.50 **Facilities:**
Services: lau **Leisure:** P

Choranche Isère

Gouffre de la Croix 38680 476360713 476360713
e-mail: camping.gouffre.croix@wanadoo.fr
website: camping-choranche.com
In a quiet location beside the River Bourne with fine views of the surrounding mountains and good, modern facilities.

Access via A49 exit St-Marcellin or Hostun.
Open: 15 Apr-15 Sep **Site:** 2.5HEC **Prices:** 3-4 1.50-2 pitch 3-4 **Facilities:** **Services:** lau **Leisure:** R

Clairvaux-les-Lacs Jura

Fayolan 39130 384252619 384252620
e-mail: relais.soleil.jura@wanadoo.fr
website: www.vacances-nature.com
In a wooded location beside the lake.
1.2km SE via D118.
Site: 17HEC **Facilities:**
Services: lau **Leisure:** LP **Off-site:** R

Grisière et Europe Vacances 39130
384258048 384252234
e-mail: la-grisiere.com
website: www.la-grisiere.com
Fenced in meadowland with some trees, sloping down to the Grand Lac. The site is guarded during July and August.
From village centre turn off N78, follow D118 towards Châtel-de-Joux for 800m to the site.
Open: May-Sep **Site:** 11HEC **Prices:** 3.30 pitch 7
Facilities: **Services:** lau **Leisure:** L

Clusaz, La Haute-Savoie

Plan du Fernuy route des Confins, 74220
450024475 450326702
e-mail: info@plandufernuy.com
website: www.plandufernuy.com
Airing rooms. 30 ski-lifts nearby. Several cable cars. Well-situated for skiing or walking.

contd.

At the road fork E of La Clusaz leave N50 the Col des Aravis road, and drive towards Les Confins from road fork 2km to site.
Open: 4 Jun-4 Sep & 18 Dec-24 Apr **Site:** 1.3HEC **Prices:** 5.50 16-18 pitch 16.50-20 (incl 2 persons) **Facilities:** **Services:** lau **Leisure:** P **Off-site:**

DIVONNE-LES-BAINS AIN

Fleutron Quartier Villard, 01220
450200195 450200035
e-mail: info@homair-vacances.fr
website: www.homair-vacances.fr
In wooded surroundings with large individual pitches.
3 km N.
Open: 26 Mar-23 Oct **Site:** 8HEC **Prices:** 4.50-7.50 2.50-3.50 pitch 5-9.50 (static)168-399 **Facilities:** **Services:** lau **Leisure:** P **Off-site:** LR

DOLE JURA

Pasquier 18 Chelin Theremot, 39100 384720261
Meadow site near River Doubs.
900m SE of town centre.
Open: 15 Mar-15 Oct **Site:** 2HEC **Facilities:** **Services:** lau **Off-site:** R

DOUCIER JURA

Domaine de Chalain 39130 384257878 384257006
e-mail: chalain@chalain.com
website: www.chalain.com
A large site beside Lake Chalain with a wide variety of recreational facilities.
3km NE.
Open: May-21 Sep **Site:** 20HEC **Prices:** 6.22-7.80 3 pitch 19.25-29.13 (incl 3 persons) (static)308-561 **Facilities:** **Services:** lau **Leisure:** LP

DOUSSARD HAUTE-SAVOIE

Ravoire rte de la Ravoire, 74210 450443780 45032960
e-mail: info@camping-la-ravoire.fr
website: www.camping-la-ravoire.fr
A well-appointed, modern site on level ground 800m from Lake Annecy. Spectacular mountain views.
Leave Autoroute at Annecy Sud exit towards Albertville and take N508 as far as Duingt to pick up signs.
Open: 15 May-15 Sep **Site:** 2HEC **Prices:** 5.85 pitch 27.80-31.80 (incl 2 persons) **Facilities:** **Services:** lau **Leisure:** P **Off-site:** L

Serraz r de la Poste, 74210 450443068 450448107
e-mail: info@campinglaserraz.com
website: www.campinglaserraz.com
Modern site divided into pitches. Cosy bar in rustic style.
At E end of village 500m from N508 on D181.
Open: 15 May-15 Sep **Site:** 4HEC **Prices:** 3-5.80 pitch 8-14 (static)269-602 **Facilities:** **Services:** lau **Leisure:** P **Off-site:** L

EMBRUN HAUTES-ALPES

CM Clapière av du Lac, 05200 492430183
Well-managed site with shaded pitches on stony ground, on N shore of lake. Site shop open during summer only.
2.5km SW on N94.
Open: May-Sep **Site:** 5.3HEC **Facilities:** **Services:** lau **Off-site:** LPR

ENTRE-DEUX-GUIERS ISÈRE

Arc en Ciel r des Berges, 38380 476660697 476668805
e-mail: info@camping-arc-en-ciel.com
website: www.camping-arc-en-ciel.com
In a wooded location on the river bank with well-shaded pitches.
On D520 300m from N6.
Open: Mar-15 Oct **Site:** 1.2HEC **Prices:** 3.60-4.20 1.30-1.80 pitch 2.60-3 **Facilities:** **Services:** lau **Leisure:** PR **Off-site:**

ÉVIAN-LES-BAINS HAUTE-SAVOIE

Clos Savoyard Maxilly sur Ciman, 74500
450752584 450753019
Attractive site with fine views of the lake and the mountains.
Turn onto D21 in town 1.2km after Hôtel le Maximillien and continue uphill.
Open: Jul-Aug **Site:** 2HEC **Facilities:** **Services:** lau **Off-site:** L

AT AMPHION-LES-BAINS (3.5KM W ON N5)

Plage 304 r de la Garenne, Amphion les Bains, 74500
450700046 450708445
e-mail: info@camping-dela-plage.com
website: www.camping-dela-plage.com
A pleasant site with direct access to the lake. There are good recreational facilities and modern, well-equipped bungalows and chalets are available for hire.
NW of town on N5, 150m from lake.
Open: All year **Site:** 1HEC **Prices:** 6-6.10 pitch 16-22 (incl 2 persons) **Facilities:** **Services:** lau **Leisure:** LP **Off-site:** R

FERRIÈRE-D'ALLEVARD ISÈRE

CM Neige et Nature chemin de Montarmand, 38580
476451984
e-mail: contact@neige-nature.fr
website: www.neige-nature.fr
In a beautiful situation with spectacular mountain views and good, modern facilities.
In Allevard take D525A towards Le Pleynet.
Open: 15 May-15 Sep **Site:** 1.2HEC **Prices:** 4.30 pitch 4.30 (static)275 **Facilities:** **Services:** lau **Leisure:** PR **Off-site:**

GRESSE-EN-VERCORS ISÈRE

4 Saisons 38650 0476343027 0476343952
e-mail: nieter.aalmoes@wanadoo.fr
website: www.camping-les4saisons.com
In a picturesque mountain setting with good facilities.
1.3km SW
Open: May-Sep & 20 Dec-15 Mar **Site:** 2.2HEC **Prices:** 4.75 3.50 pitch 13.40 (incl 2 persons) (static)227-423 **Facilities:** **Services:** lau **Leisure:** P **Off-site:** R

GUILLESTRE HAUTES-ALPES

Villard Le Villard, 5600 492450654 492450052
website: www.camping-levillard.com
In a magnificent location between the Ecrins national park and Queyras regional park. Good facilities, but bar and café operate July and August only.
2km W via D902A and N4, rte de Gap.
Open: All year **Site:** 3HEC **Prices:** 2.30-4.50 pitch 9.15-16.50 (incl 2 persons) **Facilities:** **Services:** lau **Leisure:** PR **Off-site:** L

HAUTECOURT-ROMANÈCHE AIN

Ile Chambod 01250 474372541 474372828
e-mail: camping.chambod@free.fr
website: www.campingilechambod.com
A well-equipped site close to the River Ain where swimming is supervised by lifeguards. Good sanitary and recreational facilities.
From Bourg-en-Bresse take D979 towards Geneva.
Open: May-Sep **Site:** 2.5HEC **Prices:** 4.50 2.50 pitch 3 **Facilities:** **Services:** lau **Leisure:** P **Off-site:** LR

HUANNE-MONTMARTIN DOUBS

Bois de Reveuge 25680 381843860 381844404
website: www.campingduboisdereveuge.com
A terraced site in a 20 hectare park surrounded by the Vosges and Jura mountains with good recreational facilities.
Access via A36 exit Baumes-les-Dames.
Open: 23 Apr-17 Sep **Site:** 24HEC **Prices:** pitch 17-29 (incl 2 persons) **Facilities:** **Services:** lau **Leisure:** LP

ISLE-SUR-LE-DOUBS, L' DOUBS

CM Lumes 10 r des Lumes, 25250
381927305 381927305
e-mail: jp-paillard@tiscali.fr
website: www.camping-Les-lumes.com
The site lies close to the town. Common room with TV.
Off N83. Entrance near bridge over the Doubs.
Open: 15 Apr-Sep **Site:** 1.5HEC **Prices:** 3 3.90 4.10 1.90 pitch 2.20 (static)150-180 **Facilities:** **Services:** lau **Leisure:** R **Off-site:**

LANDRY SAVOIE

Eden 73210 479076181 479076217
e-mail: info@camping-eden.net
website: www.camping-eden.net
A modern site with excellent sports and sanitary facilities, situated in the heart of the Savoie Olympic area.
Open: 18 Dec-8 May & Jun-15 Sep **Site:** 2.7HEC **Prices:** 3.42-5.70 pitch 3.60-10 (static)210-315 **Facilities:** **Services:** lau **Leisure:** PR **Off-site:**

LONS-LE-SAUNIER JURA

Majorie 640 bd de l'Europe, 39000
384242694 384240840
e-mail: info@camping-marjorie.com
website: www.camping-marjorie.com
Clean, tidy site with tent and caravan sections separated by a stream. Caravan pitches (80 sq m) are gravelled and surrounded by hedges. Heated common room with TV, reading area, kitchen.
Near swimming stadium on outskirts of town.
Open: Apr-15 Oct **Site:** 9HEC **Prices:** 1.70-4 pitch 10-16.50 (incl 2 persons) **Facilities:** **Services:** lau **Off-site:** P

LUGRIN HAUTE-SAVOIE

Myosotis 28 chemin du Grand Tronc, 74500 450760759
A terraced site with fine views over the lake and of the surrounding mountains.
W of town. Signed. 1km from Lac Leman
Open: 4May-25 Sep **Site:** 0.9HEC **Prices:** 2.20-2.60 pitch 5.10-5.80 **Facilities:** **Services:** lau **Off-site:** L

Rys Route le Rys, 74500 450760575 450760575
e-mail: jeanmichel.blanc@wanadoo.fr
Calm shady site with panoramic views of the lake and mountains. 10min walk from the beach
W of town. Signed.
Open: 30 Apr-1 Oct **Site:** 1.5HEC **Prices:** 3 1 pitch 11 (incl 2 persons) (static)245 **Facilities:** **Services:** lau **Off-site:** L

Vieille Église 74500 450760195 450761312
e-mail: campingvieilleeglise@wanadoo.fr
website: www.camping-vieille-eglise.com
On rising meadow between lake and mountains with good views. Close to lake Léman and its beaches.
D24 to Neuvecelle, then take D21, 1km after Maxilly on right.
Open: Apr-20 Oct **Site:** 1.5HEC **Prices:** 3.80-4.30 2.20-2.30 2.30-3.35 pitch 12-15 (incl 2 persons) pp3.80-4.30 (static)198-355 **Facilities:** **Services:** lau **Leisure:** P **Off-site:** L

MALBUISSON DOUBS

Fuvettes 25160 381693150 381697046
e-mail: les-fuvettes@wanadoo.fr
website: camping-fuvettes.com
Mainly level site with some terraces, gently sloping towards lake. At an altitude of 900m in the Jura mountains.
500m S on D437.
Open: Apr-Sep **Site:** 6HEC **Prices:** pitch 13-18.80 (incl 2 persons) pp3-4.40 (static)180-500 **Facilities:** **Services:** lau **Leisure:** LP

MARIGNY JURA

Sunelia la Pergola 39130 384257003 384257596
e-mail: contact@lapergola.com
website: www.lapergola.com
A well-equipped, terraced site with direct access to the lake.
S of Marigny off D27.
Open: 15 May-19 Sep **Site:** 12HEC **Prices:** 4.50-5.50 pitch 20-35 (incl 2 persons) (static)170-660 **Facilities:** **Services:** lau **Leisure:** LP **Off-site:** R

MATAFELON-GRANGES AIN

Gorges de l'Oignin r du Lac, 1580
474768097 474768097
e-mail: camping.lesgorgesdeloignin@wanadoo.fr
website: www.gorges-de-loignin.com
Campsite located in the heart of the countryside on the banks of a lake and surrounded by low mountains.
A404 exit 11, site signed after 1m.
Open: Apr-Sep **Site:** 2.6HEC **Prices:** 10.60-13.20 pitch 12.60-15.20 (incl 2 persons) **Facilities:** **Services:** lau **Leisure:** LP

MÉAUDRE ISÈRE

Buissonnets 38112 476952104
e-mail: camping-les-buissonnets@wanadoo.fr
website: www.camping-les-buissonets.com
A quiet, friendly site in the heart of the Vercors Regional Parc with modern sanitary blocks and a wide range of summer and winter recreational facilities.
200m from village centre.
Open: 15 Dec-Nov **Site:** 2.7HEC **Prices:** 4 8 pitch 12 (incl 2 persons) **Facilities:** **Services:** lau **Off-site:** PR

MESNOIS Jura

Beauregard 2 Grande Rue 384483251 384483251
Open: Apr-Sep **Site:** 6HEC **Facilities:** **Services:** lau **Leisure:** PR

MESSERY Haute-Savoie

Relais du Léman 74140 0450 450947111 450947766
e-mail: info@relaisduleman.com
website: www.relaisduleman.com
Well equipped site in a wooded location on the shore of Lac Léman.
1.5km SW via D25.
Open: Apr-Sep **Site:** 3.5HEC **Prices:** 5 5 5 5 **Facilities:** **Services:** lau **Leisure:** P **Off-site:** LP

MEYRIEU-LES-ÉTANGS Isère

Moulin 38440 474593034 474583612
e-mail: basedeloisirs.du.moulin@wanadoo.fr
In a quiet, rural setting with good recreational facilities.
On D552 between Vienne and Bourgoin-Jallieu.
Open: 15 Apr-Sep **Site:** 1.5HEC **Facilities:** **Services:** lau **Leisure:** L **Off-site:**

MIRIBEL-LES-ÉCHELLES Isère

Balcon de Chartreuse 950 chemin de la Foiet, 38380
476552853 476552582
e-mail: balcondechartreuse@wanadoo.fr
website: www.camping-balcondechartreuse.com
A peaceful site in the heart of the Parc Régional de Chartreuse, with fine views of the surrounding mountains.
400m from village centre.
Open: All year **Site:** 2.5HEC **Prices:** 4.20 pitch 12.50 (incl 2 persons) (static)258 **Facilities:** **Services:** lau **Leisure:** P **Off-site:**

MONTMAUR Hautes-Alpes

Mon Repos 5400 592580314
Generally well-kept site on wooded terrain with shaded pitches.
1km E on D937 and D994.
Open: May-Oct **Site:** 7HEC **Prices:** pitch 10 (incl 2 persons) (static)150 **Facilities:** **Services:** lau **Leisure:** LR **Off-site:**

MONTREVEL-EN-BRESSE Ain

Plaine Tonique Base de Plein Air, 01340
474308052 474308077
e-mail: plaine.tonique@wanadoo.fr
website: www.laplainetonique.com
A well-equipped site divided into a series of self contained sections beside the lake. Entrance closed 22.00-07.00. Booking advisable in July and August.
0.5km E on D28.
Open: 19 Apr-26 Sep **Site:** 17HEC **Facilities:** **Services:** lau **Leisure:** LP **Off-site:** R

MOUCHARD Jura

Halte Jurassienne Bel Air, 39330 384378392
Camping Card Compulsory.
NE, near the service station.
Open: 25 Mar-Oct **Site:** 0.8HEC **Facilities:** **Services:** lau **Off-site:**

MURS-ET-GELIGNIEUX Ain

Ile de la Comtesse rte des Abrets, 1300
479872333 479872333
e-mail: camping.comtesse@wanadoo.fr
website: www.ile-de-la-comtesse.com
Situated right next to lake Cuchet (part of the Rhone), with direct access to the water. In a stunning natural setting beneath the Alps.
From A43 Lyon to Chambery exit 10, take D592 to La Bruyere and site is off route to Belley.
Open: 30 Apr-3 Sep **Site:** 3HEC **Prices:** 5.60-6.90 pitch 18-23 (incl 2 persons) (static)250-580 **Facilities:** **Services:** lau **Leisure:** PR **Off-site:** L

NEYDENS Haute-Savoie

Colombière 74160 450351314 450351340
e-mail: la.colombiere@wanadoo.fr
website: www.camping-la-colombiere.com
A pleasant, friendly site with good recreational facilities.
Access via A40.
Open: Apr-Sep **Site:** 2.2HEC **Facilities:** **Services:** lau **Leisure:** P **Off-site:** R

NOVALAISE Savoie

Charmilles Lac d'Aiguebelette, 73470
479360467 479360467
e-mail: camping.les.charmilles@wanadoo.fr
website: www.marmotte.com/charmilles
A terraced site in a beautiful mountain setting, 150m from the lake.
On W shore of the lake on D941 towards St-Alban-de-Montbel.
Open: Jul-Aug **Site:** 2.3HEC **Facilities:** **Services:** lau **Off-site:** L

ORNANS Doubs

Chanet 9 chemin de Chanet, 25290
381622344 381621397
e-mail: contact@lechanet.com
website: www.lechanet.com
Comfortable site with good facilities in the peaceful Loue Valley.
1.5km SW on D241. Follow green signs.
Open: Mar-Oct **Site:** 2.2HEC **Prices:** (static)150-370 **Facilities:** **Services:** lau **Leisure:** P **Off-site:** R

ORPIERRE Hautes-Alpes

Princes d'Orange 05700 492662253 492663108
e-mail: campingorpierre@wanadoo.fr
website: www.campingorpierre.com
The site lies on a meadow with terraces.
Exit N75 at Eyguians and take D30.
Open: Apr-28 Oct **Site:** 20HEC **Prices:** 14-19 15-20.50 pitch 19 (incl 3 persons) (static)265-500 **Facilities:** **Services:** lau **Leisure:** P **Off-site:** R

OUNANS Jura

Plage Blanche 3 r de la Plage, 39380
384376963 384376021
e-mail: reservation@la-plage-blanche.com
website: www.la-plage-blanche.com
In a pleasant location beside the River Loue with good recreational facilities.
1.5km S via D71 (rte de Montbarcy).
Open: Apr-Sep **Site:** 7HEC **Prices:** 4.70 pitch 5.90 **Facilities:** **Services:** lau **Leisure:** PR **Off-site:**

PARCEY Jura

Bords de Loue Chemin du Val d'Amour, 39100
384710382 384710342
e-mail: contact@jura-camping.com
website: www.jura-camping.com
A quiet site on the River Loue.
1.5km from the centre of the village via N5. Signed.
Open: 20 Apr-15 Sep **Site:** 18HEC **Facilities:** **Services:** lau **Leisure:** PR **Off-site:**

PATORNAY Jura

Moulin 39130 384483121 384447121
e-mail: contact@camping-moulin.com
website: www.camping-moulin.com
A modern site on a level meadow in a peaceful, wooded location on the banks of the River Ain.
Access is NE via N78, rte de Clairvaux-les-Lacs.
Open: 31 May-14 Sep **Site:** 5HEC **Prices:** 3 **Facilities:** **Services:** lau **Leisure:** PR **Off-site:** L

PLAGNE-MONTCHAVIN Savoie

Montchavin les Coches 73210 479078323 479078018
e-mail: montchavin@wanadoo.fr
website: www.montchavin-lescoches.com
A summer and winter site overlooking the Tarentaise Valley with good, modern facilities.
Open: Nov-Sep **Site:** 1.3HEC **Prices:** pitch 11.30 (incl 2 persons) **Facilities:** **Services:** lau **Off-site:** P

PONTARLIER Doubs

Larmont r du Toulombief, 25300 381462333
A mountain site with good facilities in an area associated with winter sports.
Open: All year **Site:** **Facilities:** **Services:** lau **Off-site:** R

PONT-DE-VAUX Ain

Peupliers Port de Fleurville, 01190
385303365 385303365
e-mail: info@rivesdusoleil.com
website: www.rivesdusoleil.com
A family site beside the River Saône with good facilities.
3km from Pont-de-Vaux via N6.
Open: Apr-Sep **Site:** 7HEC **Prices:** 3.50-4.50 2.50 3.50-4.50 3.50-4.50 pitch 3.50-4.50 **Facilities:** **Services:** lau **Leisure:** PR

PORT-SUR-SAÔNE Haute-Saône

CM Maladière 70170 384915132 384781809
A quiet, comfortable site with modern facilities, close to the River Saône.
S on the D6, between the River Saône and the canal
Open: 15 May-15 Sep **Site:** 2HEC **Facilities:** **Services:** lau **Off-site:** PR

PRESLE Savoie

Combe Léat 73110 479255402
A quiet mountain site.
Access via A43 and D207.
Open: 15 Jun-5 Sep **Site:** 4HEC **Prices:** 2.50 2.50 pitch 2.50 (static)185-230 **Facilities:** **Services:** lau

RENAGE Isère

Verdon 185 av de la Piscine, 38140 476914802
5km N of Tullins on D45.
Open: Apr-15 Oct **Site:** 1.5HEC **Facilities:** **Services:** lau **Off-site:** PR

ROCHETTE, LA Savoie

Lac St-Clair 73110 479257355
At the foot of the Belledonne mountains, 1km from a lake with good fishing.
Access via D925B Grenoble-Albertville.
Open: Jun-Aug **Site:** 3HEC **Facilities:** **Services:** lau **Off-site:** P

ROSIÈRE-DE-MONTVALEZAN, LA Savoie

Forêt 73700 79068621 79401625
e-mail: campinglaforet@free.fr
A peaceful site in pleasant wooded surroundings, with good, modern facilities.
2km S via N90 towards Bourg-St-Maurice.
Open: 10 Jun-15 Sep & 15 Dec-1 May **Site:** 2.7HEC **Facilities:** **Services:** lau **Leisure:** P **Off-site:** R

ROUGEMONT Doubs

Val de Bonnal Bonnal, 25680 381869087 381860392
e-mail: val-de-bonnal@wanadoo.fr
Quiet woodland site beside the River Ognon. Supervised swimming in lake with beach.
Open: 8 May-5 Sep **Site:** 15HEC **Facilities:** **Services:** lau **Leisure:** LPR

ST-AVRE SAVOIE

Bois Joli St Martin-sur-la-Chambre, 73130
479562128 479562995
e-mail: camping-le-bois-joli@wanadoo.fr
website: www.campingleboisjoli.com
Well kept site with pitches and individual washing cabins.
1km N of St-Avre, off N6-E70 via La Chambre.
Open: Apr-15 Sep **Site:** 4HEC **Prices:** pitch 10-13 (incl 2 persons) **Facilities:** **Services:** lau **Leisure:** P **Off-site:**

ST-CLAIR-DU-RHÔNE ISÈRE

Daxia rte du Péage, 38370 474563920 474569346
A riverside site with good sanitary and recreational facilities.
Access via N7/A7.
Open: Apr-Sep **Site:** 7.5HEC **Facilities:** **Services:** lau **Leisure:** PR

ST-CLAUDE JURA

Martinet 39200 384450040
In a wooded location close to the Centre Nautique.
2km SE, beside the river
Open: May-Sep **Site:** 3HEC **Prices:** 2.30 1.10 1.70 1.25 **Facilities:** **Services:** lau **Leisure:** R **Off-site:** P

ST-GERVAIS-LES-BAINS HAUTE-SAVOIE

Dômes de Miage 197 rte des Contamines, 74170
450934596 450781075
e-mail: info@camping-mont-blanc.com
website: www.camping-mont-blanc.com
On a beautiful wooded plateau with fine views of the surrounding mountains.
2km S on D902.
Open: Jun-15 Sep **Site:** 2.5HEC **Prices:** pitch 14-19 (incl 2 persons) **Facilities:** **Services:** lau **Off-site:** P

ST-INNOCENT-BRISON SAVOIE

Rolande 24 chemin des Berthets, 73100 479543685
Situated on gently sloping terrain.
Signed from village centre.
Open: May-Sep **Site:** 1.5HEC **Facilities:** **Services:** lau **Off-site:** L

ST-JEAN-DE-COUZ SAVOIE

International la Bruyère 73160 479657911 479657427
e-mail: bearob@libertysurf.fr
website: www.camping-labruyere.com
In wooded surroundings close to the Grande Chartreuse range with a variety of sporting facilities.
2km S via N6, towards Côte-Barrier
Open: 25 Apr-10 Oct **Site:** 1HEC **Prices:** 2.90 pitch 2.80 (static)250 **Facilities:** **Services:** lau **Off-site:** R

ST-JEAN-ST-NICOLAS HAUTES-ALPES

CM le Châtelard Pont-du-Fossé, 5260 492559431
e-mail: comstjeanstnicolas@wanadoo.fr
Open: 15 Jun-15 Sep **Site:** 4HEC **Prices:** 3.25 4.40 3.60 **Facilities:** **Services:** lau **Leisure:** R **Off-site:** LP

ST-JORIOZ HAUTE-SAVOIE

Europa 1444 rte d'Albertville, 74410
450685101 450685520
e-mail: info@camping-europa.com
website: www.camping-europa.com
Well equipped site in picturesque surroundings close to lake Annecy.
1.4km SE
Open: 7 May-15 Sep **Site:** 3.7HEC
Prices: pitch 14.50-27 (incl 2 persons) (static)276-606
Facilities: **Services:** lau **Leisure:** P
Off-site: L

International du Lac d'Annecy 74410
450686793 450090122
e-mail: campannecy@wanadoo.fr
website: www.campannecy.com
N508 towards Albertville.
Open: 20 May-15 Sep **Site:** 2.5HEC **Prices:** pitch 14.50-17.50 (incl 2 persons) pp3.40-3.60 (static)230-540
Facilities: **Services:** lau **Leisure:** P
Off-site: L

ST-LAURENT-EN-BEAUMONT ISÈRE

Belvédère de l'Obiou rte Napoléon, Lieu-dit les Egats, 38350
476304080 476304486
e-mail: info@camping-obiou.com
website: www.camping-obiou.com
Terraced meadow site at the foot of mountains with hedge surrounds.
1m from Ortsteil Les Egats, on the N85, signed.
Open: Apr-15 Oct **Site:** 1HEC **Prices:** pitch 13.30-15.30 (static)280 **Facilities:**
Services: lau **Leisure:** P **Off-site:**

ST-PIERRE-DE-CHARTREUSE ISÈRE

Martinière rte du Col de Porte, 38380
476886036 476886910
e-mail: brice.gaude@wanadoo.fr
website: www.campingdemartiniere.com
In pleasant position surrounded by the Chartreuse mountains and close to the famous monastry.
2km SW off D512.
Site: 2.5HEC **Facilities:**
Services: lau **Leisure:** P **Off-site:**

SALLE-EN-BEAUMONT, LA ISÈRE

Champ-Long 38350 476304181 476304721
e-mail: champ.long@tiscali.fr
In a beautiful Alpine setting at the entrance to the Ecrins park at an altitude of 700m.
1.5km NW off N85.
Open: Apr-Oct **Site:** 5HEC **Prices:** 3.80-3.80 pitch 12.80-14.50 (static)150-230 **Facilities:** **Services:** lau **Leisure:** P **Off-site:** LR

SÉEZ SAVOIE

Reclus rte de Tignes, 73700 479410105 479410479
e-mail: campinglereclus@wanadoo.fr
website: www.campingsavoie.com
In a pleasant wooded location within easy reach of the ski slopes.
NW on N90.
Open: Dec-Oct **Site:** 1.8HEC **Facilities:**
Services: lau **Leisure:** R **Off-site:** P

SERRES Hautes-Alpes

Barillons 05700 492671735
e-mail: camping.les.barillons@wanadoo.fr
Well-laid out with terraces.
1km SE on N75.
Open: mid-May to mid-Sep **Site:** 3HEC
Prices: 3.50 pitch 13.10 (incl 2 persons) (static)150-200
Facilities: **Services:** lau **Leisure:** P
Off-site: LR

Domaine des 2 Soleils 05700 492670133 492670802
e-mail: dom.2.soleils@wanadoo.fr
website: perso.wanadoo.fr/2soleils
Well-kept terraced site in Buéch Valley.
S of town off N75. Signed.
Open: May-Sep **Site:** 12HEC **Prices:** 11.65-17.50 21.90 (static)175-290 **Facilities:** **Services:** lau **Leisure:** P **Off-site:** LR

SEYSSEL Ain

International de Seyssel chemin de la Barotte, 01420
450592847 450592847
e-mail: camp.inter@wanadoo.fr
A quiet site on steep, terraced meadowland, with individual washbasins and clean sanitary installations.
1km SW off Culoz road.
Open: 15 Jun-15 Sep **Site:** 1.5HEC **Facilities:** **Services:** lau **Leisure:** P **Off-site:** LR

TALLOIRES Haute-Savoie

Lanfonnet Angon, 74290
450607212 45060712 & 450233882
e-mail: camping.le.lanfonnet@wanadoo.fr
website: www.camping.lanfonnet.com
A well-equipped site 100m from the lake.
1.5km SE.
Open: May-Sep **Site:** 2.5HEC **Prices:** 6.50 pitch 23.35 (incl 2 persons) (static)210-525 **Facilities:** **Services:** lau **Leisure:** L

THOISSEY Ain

CM 01140 474040425
e-mail: mairie.thoissey@wanadoo.fr
Situated between two rivers, the Saône and the Chalaronne.
1km SW on D7.
Open: 20 Apr-20 Sep **Site:** 15HEC **Facilities:** **Services:** lau **Leisure:** PR **Off-site:**

THONON-LES-BAINS Haute-Savoie

Morcy 74200 450704487 450704487
In a quiet location close to Lac Léman and the thermal spa.
2.5km W of town.
Open: 15 Apr-15 Sep **Site:** 1.2HEC **Prices:** 3 pitch 11 (incl 2 persons) (static)250 **Facilities:** **Services:** lau **Off-site:** LR

TIGNES-LES-BRÉVIÈRES Savoie

Europeen dea Brevieres rte des Boisses, 73320
479063032 479061651
e-mail: diane.taxi@wanadoo.fr
website: campingbrevieres.free.fr
A well-equipped site 1km from the centre of the village.
Signed from D902.
Open: 15 Jun-29 Sep **Site:** 4.5HEC **Prices:** 3.20 1.60 2.20 2.20 pitch 2.20 **Facilities:**
Services: lau **Off-site:** LPR

TREPT Isère

3 Lac La Plaine, 38460 474929206 474929335
e-mail: leslacs@free.fr
Situated at the gateway to the Alps, an undulating woody area with small lakes.
On D517, 2.5km W.
Open: May-10 Sep **Site:** 4HEC **Facilities:** **Services:** lau **Leisure:** LP

VERNIOZ Isère

Bontemps 38150 474578352 474578370
e-mail: info@campinglebontemps.com
website: www.campinglebontemps.com
A pleasantly landscaped site beside the River Varèze.
Access via N7 and D131.
Open: Apr-Sep **Site:** 8HEC **Prices:** 5 2 6.50 6.50 pitch 6.50 **Facilities:** **Services:** lau **Leisure:** PR

VILLARD-DE-LANS Isere

L'Oursière 38250 04 476951477 476955811
e-mail: info@camping-oursiere.fr
website: www.camping-oursiere.fr
Peaceful site in the natural park region of Vercors. Summer and winter facilities.
N off D531 in direction of Grenoble.
Open: Dec-Sep **Site:** 4.2HEC **Prices:** 3.55-4.05 1.50 pitch 12.25-13.75 (incl 2 persons) **Facilities:** **Services:** lau **Off-site:** PR

VILLARS-LES-DOMBES Ain

CM Autières 164 av des Nations, 01330 474980021
e-mail: campingdesautieres@wanadoo.fr
Clean and tidy park-like site divided into plots and pitches. Part reserved for overnight campers. Clean, modern sanitary installations.
SW off N83.
Open: 29 Mar-21 Sep **Site:** 4.5HEC **Facilities:** **Services:** lau **Leisure:** PR **Off-site:**

VOIRON Isère

Porte de la Chartreuse 33 ave du 8 Mai 45, 38500
476051420
On level terrain with some trees, divided into pitches. Much traffic noise from nearby N75. Clean and modern sanitary installations.
Access is NW of town next to the Esso garage.
Open: All year **Site:** 1.5HEC **Facilities:** **Services:** **Off-site:** P

ALSACE/LORRAINE

ANOULD Vosges

Acacias 88650 329571106 329571106
e-mail: contact@accaciascamp.com
website: www.accaciascamp.com
In pleasant surroundings with well-defined pitches in the heart of the Hautes-Vosges region.
NE of town centre towards the ski slopes.
Open: Dec-10 Oct **Site:** 2.5HEC **Prices:** 3.50 1.80 1.80 1.80 pitch 1.80 **Facilities:** **Services:** lau **Leisure:** P **Off-site:** R

Facilities: -shop -shower -electric points for razors -electric points for caravans -parking by tents permitted -compulsory separate car park **Services:** -café/restaurant -bar -Camping Gaz International -gas other than Camping Gaz -first aid facilities lau-laundry **Leisure:** -swimming L-Lake P-Pool R-River S-Sea **Off-site:** All facilities within 2km

AUBURE Haut-Rhin

CM La Ménère 68150 389739299
e-mail: aubure@cc-ribeauville.fr
A peaceful site at an altitude of 800m.
Access via N415 or D416, then D11.
Open: 15 May-Sep **Site:** 1.8HEC **Prices:** 3.50 pitch 3 **Facilities:** **Services:** lau **Off-site:**

BAERENTHAL Moselle

Ramstein Plage Base de Baerenthal, Ramstein Plage, 57230
387065073 387066231
The River Zinsel runs through this rural wooded site close to the border with Germany.
W via r du Ramstein.
Open: Apr-Sep **Site:** 14HEC **Facilities:** **Services:** lau **Leisure:** LP **Off-site:** R

BIESHEIM Haut-Rhin

Ile du Rhin Zone Touristique, 68600
389725795 389721421
e-mail: camping@shn.fr
website: www.campingiledurhin.com
On the Ile du Rhin, between the Canal d'Alsace and the River Rhine in pleasant wooded surroundings.
From Colmar take N415 towards Germany as far as the Rhine bridge.
Open: 2 Jan-24 Dec & 27-31 Dec **Site:** 3HEC **Prices:** pitch 12.76 (incl 2 persons) pp3.90 **Facilities:** **Services:** lau **Off-site:** PR

BRESSE, LA Vosges

Belle Hutte Belle Hutte, 88250 329254975 329255263
e-mail: camping-belle-hutte@wanadoo.fr
website: www.camping-belle-hutte.com
Terraced site beside the River Moselotte.
Access via D34 towards Col de la Schlucht.
Open: All year **Site:** 3.2HEC **Prices:** 2.40-4.60 1.50-1.90 1.50-2.50 1.50-2.50 **Facilities:** **Services:** lau **Leisure:** PR **Off-site:** L

BURNHAUPT-LE-HAUT Haut-Rhin

Le Castor 4 rte de Guewenheim, 68520 389487858
389627466
e-mail: camping.les.castors@wanadoo.fr
A modern site in a rural setting close to a river and surrounded by woodland.
E of Burnhaupt towards Guewenheim on D466.
Open: 15 Feb-Dec **Site:** 2.5HEC **Facilities:** **Services:** lau **Leisure:** R **Off-site:**

BUSSANG Vosges

Domaine de Champé 14 Les Champs Navés, 88540
329858645 329615690
e-mail: info@domaine-de-champe.com
website: www.domaine-de-champe.com
In pleasant surroundings beside the River Moselle.
On N57.
Open: All year **Site:** 3.5HEC **Prices:** 3.80-4.90 **Facilities:** **Services:** lau
Off-site: L

CELLES-SUR-PLAINE Vosges

Lac Base de Loisirs, Les Lacs de Pierre-Percée, 88110
0329412800 0329411869
e-mail: camping@sma-lacs-pierre-percee.fr
website: www.sma-lacs-pierre-percee.fr
Set among wooded hills in an extensive natural leisure area around the lakes of Pierre-Percée.
Access via D392A.
Open: Apr-Sep **Site:** 3HEC **Facilities:** **Services:** lau **Leisure:** PR **Off-site:** L

CERNAY Haut-Rhin

CM Acacias 16 r Réne-Guibert, 68700
389755697 389397229
e-mail: lesacacias.cernay@ffcc.fr
Clean, quiet site on right bank of the River Thur.
Off N83 between Colmar and Belfort.
Open: Apr-10 Oct **Site:** 4HEC **Facilities:** **Services:** lau **Off-site:** P

COLMAR Haut-Rhin

Intercommunal de l'Ill 68180 389411594 389411594
e-mail: campingdelill@calixo.net
On a meadow beside the river with good, modern facilities. Separate sections for campers in transit.
2km E on N415.
Open: 21 Mar-21 Dec **Site:** 2.2HEC **Prices:** 3 3.30 1.80 **Facilities:** **Services:** lau
Off-site: P

CORCIEUX Vosges

Domaine des Bains r J-Wiese, 88430
329516467 0329516465
e-mail: les_bans@domaines_des_bans.com
On meadowland divided into pitches with a variety of recreational facilities.
E of village off D8.
Open: All year **Site:** 30HEC **Facilities:** **Services:** lau **Leisure:** LP **Off-site:**

DABO Moselle

Rocher CD 45, 57850 387074751 387074773
e-mail: info@ot-dabo.fr
website: www.ot-dabo.fr
In a beautiful position close to the historic town of Dabo in the Vosges mountains.
1.5km SW via D45.
Open: 9 Apr-Oct **Site:** 0.5HEC **Prices:** 2.50 1 2.30 1.50 **Facilities:** **Off-site:**

DAMBACH-LA-VILLE Bas-Rhin

CM rte d'Ebersheim, 67650 388924860
e-mail: otdambach-la-ville@tourisme-alsace.info
website: www.pays-de-barr.com/dambach-la-ville
In a wooded location close to the town centre. Booking recommended in July and August.

1km E via D120.
Open: Jun-Sep **Site:** 1.8HEC **Prices:** 2.60 1.65 2.10 1.65 **Facilities:** **Services:** lau **Off-site:**

EGUISHEIM HAUT-RHIN

CM Aux Trois Châteaux 10 r du Bassin, 68420
389231939 389241019
In a peaceful location at an altitude of 210m and surrounded by vineyards.
6km S of Colmar on N83.
Open: Apr-Sep **Site:** 1.8HEC **Prices:** 3.80 pitch 3.60 (static)250 **Facilities:** **Services:** lau **Off-site:**

FONTENOY-LE-CHÂTEAU VOSGES

Fontenoy rte de la Vierge, 88240
329363474 329363474
e-mail: marliesfontenoy@hotmail.com
website: www.campingfontenoy.com
Set on a hill in peaceful, wooded surroundings.
2.2km S via D40.
Open: 15 Apr-Sep **Site:** 1.2HEC **Prices:** 2.80 2.25 3 3 pitch 3 (static)250 **Facilities:** **Services:** lau **Leisure:** P **Off-site:** RS

GEMAINGOUTTE VOSGES

CM Le Violu 88520 329577070 329517260
e-mail: communedegemaingoutte@wanadoo.fr
W, beside the river, via N59.
Open: May-Sep **Site:** 0.9HEC **Prices:** 2.40 1.70 1.70 1.70 pitch 1.70 **Facilities:** **Services:** lau **Leisure:** R **Off-site:**

GÉRARDMER VOSGES

Ramberchamp 21 chemin du Tour du Lac, 88400
329630382 329632609
e-mail: boespflug.helene@wanadoo.fr
website: www.camping-de-ramberchamp.com/fra.html
On a level meadow on S side of Lac de Gérardmer.
2km from the village centre via N417 or 486.
Open: 20 Apr-20 Sep **Site:** 3.5HEC **Prices:** pitch 16 (incl 2 persons) (static)480 **Facilities:** **Services:** lau **Leisure:** L

GRANGES-SUR-VOLOGNE VOSGES

Château 2 Les Chappes, 88640 329575083
e-mail: camping-du-chateau@wanadoo.fr
A terraced site with good sports facilities 1km from the village,
Open: 15 Jun-15 Sep **Site:** 2HEC **Facilities:** **Services:** lau **Leisure:** P **Off-site:** R

Gina-Park 88460 329514195 329575952
website: www.ginapark.com
In a pleasant park at the foot of a wooded mountain. Streams cross the site and there is a lake and facilities for a variety of sports.
1km SE of town centre.
Open: All year **Site:** 4.5HEC **Facilities:** **Services:** lau **Leisure:** PR **Off-site:** L

HEIMSBRUNN HAUT-RHIN

Chaumière 62 r de la Galfingue, 68990
389819343 389819343
e-mail: infos@camping-lachaumiere.com
website: www.camping-lachaumiere.com
In a pleasant wooded location with good, modern facilities.
Signed from village centre.
Open: All year **Site:** 1HEC **Prices:** 3 3.50 pitch 3.50 **Facilities:** **Services:**
Leisure: P **Off-site:** R

HOHWALD, LE BAS-RHIN

CM 67140 388083090 388083090
A well-equipped terraced site in beautiful wooded surroundings.
W via D425
Open: All year **Site:** 2HEC **Facilities:**
Services: lau **Off-site:**

ISSENHEIM HAUT-RHIN

Florival rte de Soultz, 68500 389742047 389742047
e-mail: contact@camping-leflorival.com
website: www.camping-leflorival.com
Level meadowland site, situated in a Regional Park location and surrounded by forest.
Off N83 Colmar-Mulhouse, exit for Issenheim, site signed.
Open: Apr-Oct **Site:** 3.5HEC **Prices:** 3.20 6 6 pitch 12 (incl 2 persons) **Facilities:** **Services:** lau **Off-site:** P

KAYSERSBERG HAUT-RHIN

CM r des Acacias, 68240 389471447
Between a sports ground and the River Weiss. Subdivided by low hedges.
Camping Card Recommended.
200m from N415. Signed.
Open: Apr-Sep **Site:** 1.5HEC **Facilities:**
Services: lau **Leisure:** R **Off-site:** P

KRUTH HAUT-RHIN

Schlossberg r du Bourbach, 68820
389822676 389822017
e-mail: contact@schlossberg.fr
website: www.schlossberg.fr
In a quiet location in the heart of the Parc des Ballons with good, modern facilities.
2.3km NW via D13b.
Open: Etr-1 Oct **Site:** 5.2HEC **Prices:** 3.70 pitch 3.50 (static)190-270 **Facilities:**
Services: lau **Leisure:** R **Off-site:** L

LAUTERBOURG BAS-RHIN

CM des Mouettes chemin des Mouettes, 67630
388546860 388546860
e-mail: camping-lauterbourg@wanadoo.fr
A level site on the shores of a lake.
Access via D63 from Haguenau.
Open: 19 Apr-Nov **Site:** 3HEC **Prices:** 3.20 3 5.20 2-3.50 (static)220-250 **Facilities:** **Services:** lau **Leisure:** L **Off-site:** R

LUTTENBACH HAUT-RHIN

Amis de la Nature 4 r du Château, 68140
389773860 389772572
e-mail: camping.an@wanadoo.fr
Situated on a long strip of land, in the heart of Luttenbach countryside. Site is divided into pitches.
From Munster follow D10 for 1km.
Open: All year **Site:** 7HEC **Prices:** 2.55-3.25 1.35 pitch 1.65 **Facilities:** **Services:** lau
Leisure: R **Off-site:** P

MASEVAUX Haut-Rhin

Camping Municipal de Masevaux 3 r du Stade, 68290
389824229 389824229
e-mail: camping-masevaux@tv-com.tv
In wooded surroundings beside the River Doller.
Off the main road to Ballon-d'Alsace.
Open: Etr-Sep **Site:** 3.5HEC **Prices:** 2.60 pitch 2.60 **Facilities:** **Services:** lau **Off-site:** PR

METZERAL Haut-Rhin
At MITTLACH (3km SW)

CM 68380 389776377 0389777436
e-mail: mairiemittlach@wanadoo.fr
website: http://commune-de-mittlach.ifrance.com
Situated in forested area in small village, very quiet.
From Munster follow signs for Metzeral then Mittlach D10.
Open: May-Oct **Site:** 3HEC **Facilities:** **Services:** lau **Leisure:** R

MOOSCH Haut-Rhin

Mine d'Argent r de la Mine d'Argent, 68690 389823066
e-mail: serge.sorribas@free.fr
A well-established site in a peaceful wooded setting.
1.5km SW off N66.
Open: 15 Apr-15 Oct **Site:** 2.5HEC
Prices: 3.40 pitch 3.40 (static)125-200 **Facilities:** **Services:** lau **Leisure:** R **Off-site:** PR

MULHOUSE Haut-Rhin

CM Ill av P-de-Coubertin, 68100
0389062066 389611834
e-mail: campingdelill@aol.com
website: www.camping-de-lill.com
In park between the canal and the River Ill, a few minutes walk from the city centre.
From town centre follow signs for 'Fribourg & Allemagne'. At Ile Napoléon follow campsite signs.
Open: Apr-Oct **Site:** 6HEC **Prices:** 3.40 3.40 pitch 3.40 (static)100-150 **Facilities:** **Services:** lau **Off-site:** PR

MUNSTER Haut-Rhin

CM Parc de la Fecht rte de Gunsbach, 68140
389773108 389770455
e-mail: ville.munster@worldonline.fr
Well maintained site close to the town centre within a park-like area surrounded by high walls and trees.
Access on D417, 200m after entering Munster town centre, near the swimming pool.
Open: Apr-Sep **Site:** 4HEC **Facilities:** **Services:** lau **Leisure:** R **Off-site:** P

OBERBRONN Bas-Rhin

CM Eichelgarten r de Zinswiller, 67110
388097196 388099787
Follow signposts W from D28 Oberbronn-Zinswiller.
Open: 14 Mar-13 Nov **Site:** 4HEC
Prices: 3.32-3.50 1.61-1.70 pitch 2.18-2.30 **Facilities:** **Services:** lau **Leisure:** P **Off-site:**

OBERNAI Bas-Rhin

CM r de Berlin, 67210 388953848 388483147
e-mail: camping@obernai.fr
website: www.obernai.fr
Partly terraced site, situated in park.
W on D426 towards Ottrott.
Open: All year **Site:** 3HEC **Prices:** 3.30 pitch 4.40 **Facilities:** **Services:** lau **Off-site:** P

RIBEAUVILLE Haut-Rhin

Pierre de Coubertin 23 r de Landau, 68150
389736671 389736671
e-mail: camping.ribeauville@wanadoo.fr
website: www.camping-alsace.com
In a peaceful location. Shop open in summer only.
Access via D106.
Open: 15 Mar-14 Nov **Site:** 3.5HEC **Prices:** 3.80 pitch 4 **Facilities:** **Services:** lau **Off-site:** P

RIQUEWIHR Haut-Rhin

Inter Communal rte des Vins, 68340
389479008 389490563
e-mail: camping.riquewihr@tiscali.fr
Extensive site overlooking vineyards.
2km E on D16. Turn W off N83 Colmar-Strasbourg at Ostheim.
Open: Apr-Dec **Site:** 4HEC **Facilities:** **Services:** lau **Off-site:**

ST-MAURICE-SUR-MOSELLE Vosges

Deux Ballons 17 r du Stade, 88560 329251714
e-mail: vero@camping-deux-ballons.fr
website: www.camping-deux-ballons.fr
Well maintained site beside a stream and surrounded by woodland and mountains.
1km W on N66.
Open: 16 Apr-18 Sep **Site:** 4HEC **Prices:** 4.35-4.50 pitch 14.20-20.50 (incl 2 persons) **Facilities:** **Services:** lau **Leisure:** P **Off-site:** R

ST-PIERRE Bas-Rhin

Beau Séjour r de l'Église, F.67140
388085224 388085224
e-mail: commune.saintpierre@wanadoo.fr
website: www.pays-de-barr.com/beau-sejour/
Situated midway between Strasbourg and Colmar with good modern facilities.
Open: 15 May-1 Oct **Site:** 0.6HEC **Prices:** 3 pitch 10.50 (incl 2 persons) **Facilities:** **Services:** lau **Leisure:** R **Off-site:**

STE-CROIX-EN-PLAINE Haut-Rhin

Clair Vacances rte de Herrlisheim, 68127
389492728 389493137
e-mail: clairvacances@wanadoo.fr
website: www.clairvacances.com
In a pleasant woodland setting with good facilities for a family holiday.
On D1 towards Herrlisheim.
Open: Etr-17 Oct **Site:** 3.5HEC **Prices:** 12-16 **Facilities:** **Services:** lau **Leisure:** P **Off-site:**

SAVERNE Bas-Rhin

CM 67700 388913565 388913565
A pleasant tourist site at the foot of the Rocher du Haut Barr.
1.3km SW via D171
Open: Apr-Sep **Site:** 2.5HEC **Facilities:** **Services:** lau **Off-site:**

SÉLESTAT BAS-RHIN

CM Cigognes r de la 1-er DFL, 67600 388920398
In a rural setting at an altitude of 175m.
900m from the town centre.
Open: May-Sep **Site:** 0.7HEC **Prices:** 1.60-3.25 pitch 11.30-12.95 (incl 3 persons) **Facilities:** **Services:** lau **Off-site:** P

SEPPOIS-LE-BAS HAUT-RHIN

CM les Lupins r de l'Ancienne Gare, 68580
389256537 389256537
e-mail: leslupins@wanadoo.fr
website: www.campingalsace.com
Picturesque site close to the German and Swiss borders.
Access via A36, exit Burnhaupt and continue towards Dannemarie.
Open: Apr-Oct **Site:** 4HEC **Prices:** 3.50 3.50 pitch 3.50 **Facilities:** **Services:** lau
Leisure: P **Off-site:** R

SIVRY-SUR-MEUSE MEUSE

Brouzel 26 r du Moulin, 55110 0329858645
Open: Apr-1 Oct **Site:** 1.5HEC **Facilities:**
Services: lau **Off-site:** R

THOLY, LE VOSGES

Noir Rupt chemin de l'Étang de Noirrupt, 88530
329618127 329618305
e-mail: info@jpvacances.com
website: www.jpvacances.com
A peaceful site in a beautiful wooded location. Plenty of facilities.
2km SE on D417.
Open: 15 Apr-14 Oct **Site:** 3HEC **Prices:** 3.50-5 pitch 5.81-8.30 **Facilities:** **Services:** lau **Leisure:** P **Off-site:** R

TONNOY MEURTHE-ET-MOSELLE

Grande Vanné 54210 383266236 383266395
W via D74, beside the River Moselle
Open: 15 Jun-15 Sep **Site:** 7HEC **Facilities:** **Services:** lau **Leisure:** R **Off-site:**

TURCKHEIM HAUT-RHIN

Cigognes 7 quai de la Gare, 68230 389270200
Camping Card Compulsory.
From Colmar follow N417 to Wintzenheim, then to Turckheim. Before bridge turn left, continue past railway station and stadium.
Open: 15 Mar-Oct **Site:** 2.5HEC **Facilities:** **Services:** lau **Leisure:** R **Off-site:**

URBÈS HAUT-RHIN

CM Benelux Bale 68121 389827876
A well-maintained site with good facilities.
W of rte de Bussang.
Open: Apr-Oct **Site:** 2.4HEC **Facilities:**
Services: lau **Off-site:** R

VAGNEY VOSGES

CM du Mettey 88120 329248135
1.3km E on Gérardmer road.
Open: 15 Jun-15 Sep **Site:** 2HEC **Facilities:**
Services: lau **Off-site:**

VERDUN MEUSE

Breuils allée des Breuils, 55100 329861531 329867576
e-mail: contact@camping-lesbreuils.com
website: www.camping-lesbreuils.com
A family site in peaceful surroundings. Pitches are divided by trees and bushes and the sanitary facilities are well maintained.
SW via D34. Signed.
Open: Apr-Sep **Site:** 5.5HEC **Prices:** 4.20 pitch 4.20 **Facilities:** **Services:** lau
Leisure: P **Off-site:** LR

VILLERS-LÈS-NANCY MEURTHE-ET-MOSELLE

Campeole le Brabois av Paul Muller, 54600 383271828
383400643
e-mail: contact@campeoles.fr
website: www.campeoles.fr
In beautiful wooded surroundings with well-defined pitches and good recreational facilities.
SW in Brabois park.
Open: Apr-15 Oct **Site:** 6HEC **Facilities:** **Services:** lau **Off-site:**

WASSELONNE BAS-RHIN

CM rte de Romanswiller, 67310 388870008
On a level meadow adjoining the local sports complex.
1km W on D224.
Open: Apr-15 Oct **Site:** 2.5HEC **Prices:** 3-3.30 pitch 7.30 (incl 1 persons) **Facilities:**
Services: lau **Leisure:** P **Off-site:**

WATTWILLER HAUT-RHIN

Sources rte des Crêtes, 68700 389754494 389757198
e-mail: camping.les.sources@wanadoo.fr
website: www.camping-les-sources.com
A family site on the edge of the Vosges forest close to the Route du Vin.
Approach via N83 exit Cernay Nord.
Open: 9 Apr-Sep **Site:** 14HEC **Prices:** 5-7 2-3 pitch 5-8 (static)189-441 **Facilities:** **Services:** lau **Leisure:** P

WIHR-AU-VAL HAUT-RHIN

Route Verte 13 r de la Gare, 68230 389711010
e-mail: info@camping-routeverte.com
website: camping-routeverte.com
Near the centre of the village at an altitude of 320m.
Approach via D10.
Open: May-Sep **Site:** 1HEC **Prices:** 2.55 pitch 3.40
Facilities: **Services:** lau **Off-site:** R

XONRUPT/LONGEMER VOSGES

L'Eau-Vive rte de Colmar, 88400
329630737 329630737
e-mail: campingeauvive@wanadoo.fr
website: www.monsite.wanadoo.fr/camping_eau_vive
On a meadow surrounded by trees, close to the ski slopes.
2km SE on D67A next to Lac de Longemer.
Open: All year **Site:** 1HEC **Prices:** 3
Facilities: **Services:** lau **Leisure:** R
Off-site: L

Jonquilles rte du Lac, 88400 329633401 329600928
In a delightful wooded lakeside setting. Booking necessary in July and August.
2km SE on D67A beside Lac de Longemer.
Open: Apr-10 Oct **Site:** 4HEC **Prices:** pitch 6.50-11 (incl 2 persons) **Facilities:** **Services:**
lau **Leisure:** L **Off-site:**

BURGUNDY/CHAMPAGNE

ACCOLAY Yonne

Moulin Jacquot route de Bazarnes, 89460
386815687 386815687
A well-equipped site in a pleasant rural setting, close to the village.
W, beside the Canal du Nivernais.
Open: Apr-Sep **Site:** 0.8HEC **Facilities:** **Services:** lau **Off-site:** R

ANCY-LE-FRANC Yonne

CM rte de Cusy, 89160 386751321
In a sheltered position just beyond the village.
Access via Montbard road.
Open: Jun-15 Sep **Site:** 0.8HEC **Facilities:** **Services:** lau **Off-site:** R

ANDRYES Yonne

Bois Joli 89480 386817048 386817048
A small site in pleasant Burgundian countryside.
0.6km SW via N151.
Open: Apr-Sep **Site:** 5HEC **Prices:** 2.30-3.20 2.10-4.50 1.85-2.90 1.25-1.85 pitch 2-2.50 **Facilities:** **Services:** lau **Leisure:** P **Off-site:** R

ARNAY-LE-DUC Côte-D'Or

Fouché 21230 380900223 380901191
e-mail: info@campingfouche.com
website: www.campingfouche.com
In a quiet location beside a lake with good recreational facilities close to the medieval town of Arnay-le-Duc.
0.7km E on CD17.
Open: 15 Apr-15 Oct **Site:** 8HEC **Prices:** pitch 8.50-11.70 (incl 2 persons) **Facilities:** **Services:** lau **Leisure:** L **Off-site:**

AUXERRE Yonne

CM 8 rte de Vaux, 89000 386521115 386511754
e-mail: camping.mairie@auxerre.com
SE towards Vaux.
Open: Apr-Sep **Site:** 3HEC **Prices:** 2.32-2.90 pitch 2.55 **Facilities:** **Services:** lau **Off-site:** PR

AUXONNE Côte-D'Or

Arquebuse rte d'Athée, 21130 380310689 380311302
e-mail: camping.arquebuse@wanadoo.fr
website: www.campingarquebuse.com
Clean, well-equipped site on right bank of River Saône near bathing area.
From Auxonne travel W on N5 for 3km. Then turn N on D24 towards Athée and Pontailler-sur-Saône.
Open: All year **Site:** 4HEC **Prices:** 3.20 1 3.10 3.10 (static)300 **Facilities:** **Services:** lau **Off-site:** PR

AVALLON Yonne

CM Sous Roche 1 r Sous-Roche, 89200
386341039 386341039
e-mail: campingsousroches@ville-avallon.fr
2km SE by D944 and D427.
Open: 15 Mar-15 Oct **Site:** 2HEC **Prices:** 3 2 9.50 2 pitch 2-9.50 (incl 1 persons) **Facilities:** **Services:** lau **Leisure:** R **Off-site:** P

BANNES Haute-Marne

Hautoreille 52360 325848340 325848340
e-mail: campinghautoreille@free.fr
website: www.campinghautoreille.com
Small grassy site with modern facilities, offering large pitches, many in shaded positions. Separate car park for late arrivals.
Access via D74 towards Epinal.
Open: All year **Site:** 3.5HEC **Prices:** 3.50-4 pitch 5 (static)190-225 **Facilities:** **Services:** lau **Off-site:** LR

BAR-SUR-AUBE Aube

Gravière av du Parc, 10200 325271294 325271294
0.5km E of D13.
Open: 15 Mar-15 Oct **Site:** 2.8HEC **Prices:** 1.06 1.06 1.06 1.06 pitch 1.06 **Facilities:** **Services:** lau **Leisure:** PR **Off-site:** P

BAZOLLES Nièvre

Baye 58110 386389033
Open: Apr-Oct **Site:** 1.5HEC **Facilities:** **Services:** lau **Leisure:** L **Off-site:**

BEAUNE Côte-D'Or

CM Cent Vignes 10 r August-Dubois, 21200 380220391
On outskirts of town. Site divided into pitches, clean, well-looked after sanitary installations. From 20 Jun-Aug it is advisable to arrive before 16.00.
On N74 on Savigny-les-Beaune road.
Open: 15 Mar-Oct **Site:** 2HEC **Facilities:** **Services:** lau **Off-site:** LP

BOURBON-LANCY Saône-et-Loire

St-Prix r du St-Prix, 71140 385892098 385892098
website: www.camping-chalets-bourbon-lancy.com
A well-equipped family site close to an extensive water sports centre.
By the swimming pool off the D979a.
Open: Apr-Oct **Site:** 2.5HEC **Prices:** 2.60 2.60 2.60 pitch 2.15 (static)130-250 **Facilities:** **Services:** lau **Off-site:** LP

BOURBONNE-LES-BAINS Haute-Marne

Montmorency r du Stade, 52400 325900864
A well-equipped site in a pleasant natural setting.
Open: Apr-Oct **Site:** 2HEC **Prices:** 3 pitch 3 (static)140.70 **Facilities:** **Services:** lau **Leisure:** P **Off-site:** P

BOURG Haute-Marne

Croix d'Arles RN 74, 52200 325882402 325882402
e-mail: croix.arles@wanadoo.fr
website: perso.wanadoo.fr/escapecamping
A peaceful site in wooded surroundings close to Langres.
Access via N74 or A31.
Open: 15 Mar-1 Nov **Site:** 7HEC **Prices:** 2.50-4 pitch 5-6 (static)175-490 **Facilities:** **Services:** lau **Leisure:** P

BOURG-FIDÈLE Ardennes

Murée rte de Rocroi, 08230 324542445
e-mail: barbara.maire@wanadoo.fr
website: www.campinglamuree.com
A lakeside site in wooded surroundings.
1km N via D22.
Open: All year **Site:** 1.3HEC **Prices:** 3 1.60 pitch 4.60 (static)195 **Facilities:** **Services:** lau **Off-site:** P

Site: 6HEC-Site size -grass -sand -stone -little shade -partly shaded -mainly shaded -bungalows for hire -caravans for hire -tents for hire -no dogs **Prices:** -adult per night -car per night pp-per person per night -caravan per night -tent per night (static)-caravan hire per week

BUZANCY Ardennes

Samaritaine 8240 324300888 324302939
e-mail: info@campinglasamaritaine.com
website: www.campinglasamaritaine.com
Site set in a peaceful location in a small village in the heart of the Ardennes. The forests in the area are well suited for walking, horse-riding or cycling.
A203 from Charleville-Mezières, exit D977 at Sedan towards Vouziers. After 23km take D12 then D947 towards Buzancy for 17km.
Open: 28 Apr-25 Sep **Site:** 2.5HEC **Prices:** 3-4 pitch 7-10 (static)250-470 **Facilities:** **Services:** lau **Off-site:** L

CHAGNY Saône-et-Loire

Pâquier Fané 20 R de Paquier, 71150 385872142
e-mail: paquierfane@aol.eau
A clean site 600m W of the church.
Follow the D974 from town centre.
Open: 15 Apr-Oct **Site:** 1.8HEC **Prices:** 3.35-3.35 pitch 4.70-4.70 **Facilities:** **Services:** lau **Leisure:** R **Off-site:** P

CHÂLONS-EN-CHAMPAGNE Marne

CM r de Plaisance, 51000 326683800 326683800
In a pleasant wooded location with good recreational facilities.
Open: Apr-Oct **Site:** 7.5HEC **Prices:** 4.50 3 pitch 4.50 **Facilities:** **Services:** lau **Leisure:** L **Off-site:** P

CHAROLLES Saône-et-Loire

CM rte de Viny, 71120 385240490 385240490
In pleasant wooded surroundings with good, modern sanitary facilities.
NE of town via D33 towards Viry. Follow signs.
Open: Apr-05 Oct **Site:** 0.6HEC **Prices:** 2 1.50 2.50 2.50 **Facilities:** **Services:** lau **Leisure:** PR **Off-site:**

CHÂTILLON-SUR-SEINE Côte-D'Or

CM espl St-Vorles, 21400 380910305 380912146
e-mail: tourism-chatillon-sur-seine@wanadoo.fr
Hilly shaded site near the historic Renaissance church of St Vorles.
SE of town off rte de Langres (D928).
Open: Apr-Sep **Site:** 0.8HEC **Prices:** 3 1.20 pitch 3 **Facilities:** **Services:** lau **Off-site:** P

CHATONRUPT Haute-Marne

CM 52300 325948007 325948007
Open: May-Sep **Site:** 1.1HEC **Facilities:** **Services:** lau **Leisure:** R **Off-site:**

CHEVIGNY Nièvre

Hermitage de Chevigny 58230 386845097
A pleasant site with good facilities in wooded surroundings within the Morvan nature reserve. There is direct access to the lake and most watersports are available.
Open: Apr-Sep **Site:** 2.5HEC **Prices:** 4.50 3 pitch 2.50 **Facilities:** **Services:** lau **Leisure:** LR

CLAMECY Nièvre

Pont Picot rte de Chenoches, 58500 386270597
In a pleasant situation between the River Yonne and the Canal du Nivernais.
Open: May-Sep **Site:** 1.2HEC **Facilities:** **Services:** lau **Leisure:** R **Off-site:** P

COSNE-SUR-LOIRE Nièvre

Loire & Nohain Ile de Cosne, 18300 386282792 386281810
e-mail: campingile18@aol.com
Site borders River Loire.
Follow D955 W towards Sancerre.
Open: All year **Site:** 4HEC **Facilities:** **Services:** lau **Leisure:** PR **Off-site:** P

CRÊCHES-SUR-SAÔNE Saône-et-Loire

CM Le Port d'Arciat 71680 385371183 385365157
e-mail: camping-creches.sur.saone@wanadoo.fr
In a wooded location beside the River Saône.
1.5km E via D31
Open: 15 May-15 Sep **Site:** 6HEC **Prices:** 3.20 3.10 pitch 6.50 **Facilities:** **Services:** lau **Leisure:** LR **Off-site:**

DIGOIN Saône-et-Loire

CM Chevrette r de la Chevrette, 71160 385531149 385885970
e-mail: lachevrette@wanadoo.fr
website: www.lachevrette.com
W of village on N79.
Open: Mar-Oct **Site:** 1.5HEC **Prices:** 2.80-3.15 pitch 5.40-6 (static)105-105 **Facilities:** **Services:** lau **Leisure:** PR **Off-site:**

DIJON Côte-D'Or

Lac 3 bd Chanoine Kir, 21000 380435472 380435472
website: www.ville-dijon.fr
A well-maintained site in natural surroundings, an ideal base for exploring the historic town of Dijon.
1.5km W on N5.
Open: Apr-15 Oct **Site:** 2.5HEC **Facilities:** **Services:** lau **Off-site:** LP

DOMPIERRE-LES-ORMES Saône-et-Loire

Village des Meuniers 71520 385503660 385503661
e-mail: levillagedesmeuniers@wanadoo.fr
website: www.villagedesmeuniers.com
A well-equipped site in the heart of the southern Burgundy countryside. Booking advisable in July and August.
Access via N79. Signed.
Open: 15 May-Sep **Site:** 4HEC **Prices:** 4.30-6 pitch 5-7 **Facilities:** **Services:** lau **Leisure:** P

ÉCLARON-BRAUCOURT Haute-Marne

Presqu'Ile de Champaubert 52290 325041320 325943351
e-mail: info@lacduder.com
Situated on lake peninsula.
Open: Etr-Sep **Site:** 3.5HEC **Facilities:** **Services:** lau **Off-site:** L

Facilities: -shop -shower -electric points for razors -electric points for caravans -parking by tents permitted -compulsory separate car park **Services:** -café/restaurant -bar -Camping Gaz International -gas other than Camping Gaz -first aid facilities lau-laundry **Leisure:** -swimming L-Lake P-Pool R-River S-Sea **Off-site:** All facilities within 2km

EPINAC Saône-et-Loire

Pont Vert R de la Piscine, 71360
385820026 385821367
In a wooded location on the banks of the river. Modern facilities and motel within the site area.
S via D43 beside the River Drée.
Open: Apr-Sep **Site:** 4HEC **Prices:** 2.25 1.30 2 pitch 2.20 (static)235 **Facilities:** **Services:** lau **Leisure:** R **Off-site:**

FRONCLES Haute-Marne

Deux Ponts r des Ponts, 52320 325023121 325020980
In a peaceful location beside the River Marne.
Open: 15 Mar-15 Oct **Site:** 3HEC **Facilities:** **Off-site:** R

GIBLES Saône-et-Loire

Château de Montrouant Montrouant, 71800
385845113 385845430
A small site situated in the Charollais hill region with access to extensive parkland.
1.6km NE beside the lake.
Open: Jun-9 Sep **Site:** 1HEC **Facilities:** **Services:** lau **Leisure:** LPR **Off-site:**

GIFFAUMONT Marne

Plage Chemin de la Cachotte, Station Nautique, 51290
326726184
A well-maintained site situated at the Station Nautique.
2km from the village.
Open: May-10 Sep **Site:** 1.5HEC **Facilities:** **Services:** lau **Off-site:** L

GIGNY-SUR-SAÔNE Saône-et-Loire

Château de l'Epervière 71240 385441690 385941697
e-mail: domaine-de-leperviere@wanadoo.fr
website: www.domaine-eperviere.com
Quiet site in park surrounding 16th-century château. Close to the River Saône for fishing and sailing.
N6 to Sennecey-le-Grand, then follow signs.
Open: Apr-Sep **Site:** 10HEC **Prices:** 5.40-6.70 pitch 6.90-9.90 **Facilities:** **Services:** lau **Leisure:** P **Off-site:** R

GRANDPRÉ Ardennes

CM 8250 324305071
A peaceful riverside site.
150m from village centre on D6.
Open: Apr-Sep **Site:** 2HEC **Prices:** 1.60 0.80 1 1 pitch 1 **Facilities:** **Services:** lau **Leisure:** R **Off-site:**

ISSY-L'ÉVÊQUE Saône-et-Loire

CM de l'Étang Neuf 71760 385249605 385249605
e-mail: info@camping-etang-neuf.com
website: www.camping-etang-neuf.com
In a fine position beside the lake, overlooking the château.
Open: May-25 Sep **Site:** 4HEC **Prices:** pitch 17-20 (incl 2 persons) (static)300-499 **Facilities:** **Services:** lau **Leisure:** LP **Off-site:**

LAIVES Saône-et-Loire

Lacs 'La Heronnière' Les Bois de Laives, 71240
385449885 385449885
e-mail: camping.laives@wanadoo.fr
Compulsory separate car park for arrivals after 22.00.
Access via Chalon Sud autoroute exit towards Mâcon.
Open: May-15 Sep **Site:** 2HEC **Prices:** 4 2.50 8.20 pitch 4.50 **Facilities:** **Services:** lau **Leisure:** P **Off-site:** LR

MÂCON Saône-et-Loire

CM 71000 385381622 385381622
Divided into pitches. Water sports centre and pool nearby.
2km N on N6.
Open: 15 Mar-Oct **Site:** 5HEC **Facilities:** **Services:** lau **Leisure:** P **Off-site:** R

MARCENAY Côte-d'Or

Grebes Laignes, 21330 380816172 380816199
e-mail: marcenay@club-internet.fr
A peaceful site in unspoiled contryside with separate hedged pitches. Direct access to lake.
Open: 30 Mar-15 Sep **Site:** 2.4HEC **Prices:** 2.30 2 2 pitch 2.30 **Facilities:** **Services:** lau **Leisure:** L **Off-site:**

MATOUR Saône-et-Loire

CM Le Paluet Le Paluet, 71520 385597058 385597454
e-mail: contact@matour.com
website: www.matour.com
In pleasant countryside beside the river.
Open: May-Sep **Site:** 2HEC **Facilities:** **Services:** lau **Leisure:** P **Off-site:**

MESNIL-ST PÈRE Aube

Voie Colette 10140 325412715 325412715
e-mail: voiecolette@yahoo.fr
Grassland, with trees, ornamental shrubs and flower beds. Slightly sloping, with a man-made lake nearby.
About 2km from Mesnil-St-Père; signed from centre.
Open: Apr-10 Oct **Site:** 4HEC **Prices:** pitch 10.75-11.90 (incl 2 persons) (static)243-305 **Facilities:** **Services:** lau **Off-site:** L

MEURSAULT Côte-d'Or

Grappe d'Or 2 rte de Volnay, 21190
380212248 380216574
e-mail: camping.lagrappedor@wanadoo.fr
Clean terraced site on a meadow. Mountain bikes are available for hire.
700m NE on D11b.
Open: Apr-15 Oct **Site:** 5.5HEC **Prices:** 3-3.70 pitch 11.50-15.50 (incl 2 persons) (static)240-399 **Facilities:** **Services:** lau **Leisure:** P **Off-site:**

MONTAPAS Nièvre

CM La Chênaie La Chênaie, 58110
386583432 386582905
In a wooded location beside a lake with plenty of recreational facilities.
500m from town centre, beside the lake, via D259.
Open: Apr-Oct **Site:** 1HEC **Facilities:** **Services:** lau **Leisure:** L **Off-site:**

MONTBARD Côte-d'Or

CM r M-Servet, 21500 380922160 380922160
e-mail: mairie.montbard@wanadoo.fr
website: www.montbard.com
NW via rte de Laignes.
Open: Mar-28 Oct **Site:** 2.5HEC **Prices:** 2.70 4 pitch 8 **Facilities:** **Services:** lau **Off-site:** R

MONTHERMÉ ARDENNES

Base de Loisirs Départementale 8800
324328161 324323766
In a pleasant wooded situation.
0.8km NE beside the River Semoy.
Open: All year **Site:** 16HEC **Prices:** 2.60 1.40 1.40 1.40 pitch 1.35 **Facilities:** **Services:** lau **Leisure:** R

MONTSAUCHE NIÈVRE

Mesanges Lac des Settons, Rive Gauche, 58230
386845577 386845577
On the left bank of Lac des Settons.
Open: May-15 Sep **Site:** 5HEC **Prices:** 3.70 2.30 pitch 2.90 **Facilities:** **Services:** lau **Off-site:** LPR

Plage du Midi 58230 386845197 386845731
e-mail: plagedumidi@aol.com
website: www.settons-camping.com
In a wooded setting directly on the Lac des Settons with good facilities.
From Salieu (on N6) follow D977. From town centre follow D193 to Les Sultons, then to site.
Open: Etr-15 Oct **Site:** 4HEC **Facilities:** **Services:** lau **Leisure:** L **Off-site:**

PARAY-LE-MONIAL SAÔNE-ET-LOIRE

Mambré rte du Gué-Léger, 71600
385888920 385888781
On a level meadow with good, modern facilities.
Well signed from outskirts of town.
Open: Apr-Oct **Site:** 4HEC **Facilities:** **Services:** lau **Leisure:** P **Off-site:** R

PONT-SAINTE-MARIE AUBE

CM de Troyes 7 r Roger Salengro, 10150
325810264 325810264
Wooded site a short walk from the town of Troyes.
Open: Apr-15 Oct **Site:** 3.8HEC **Prices:** 4.10 pitch 5.60 **Facilities:** **Services:** lau **Off-site:**

POUGUES-LES-EAUX NIÈVRE

CM Chanternes av de Paris, 58320 386688618
On N7 7km N of Nevers.
Open: Jun-Oct **Site:** 1.4HEC **Prices:** 2.50 3 1.50 **Facilities:** **Services:** lau **Off-site:** P

PREMEAUX CÔTE-D'OR

Saule Guillaume 21700 380612799 380613519
Pleasant site beside a lake.
1.5km E via D109G.
Open: 15 Jun-5 Sep **Site:** 2.1HEC **Facilities:** **Services:** lau **Off-site:** P

RADONVILLIERS AUBE

Garillon R des Anciens Combattants, 10500
325922146 325922134
Beside the river, 250m from the lake.
Open: May-15 Sep **Site:** 1HEC **Prices:** 2.20 pitch 2.80 **Facilities:** **Services:** lau **Off-site:** LR

RIEL-LES-EAUX CÔTE-D'OR

Riel-les-Eaux 21570 380937276 380937276
A lakeside site with fishing and boating facilities.
2.2km W via D13.
Open: Apr-Oct **Site:** 0.2HEC **Facilities:** **Services:** lau **Leisure:** L **Off-site:**

ST-HILAIRE-SOUS-ROMILLY AUBE

Domaine de La Noue des Rois chemin des Brayes, 10100
325244160 325243418
e-mail: michele.desmont@wanadoo.fr
website: www.lanouedesrois.com
A quiet site in a pine forest on the Basin d'Arcachon. Booking recommended in July and August.
2km NE.
Open: All year **Site:** 30HEC **Prices:** 5 **Facilities:** **Services:** lau **Leisure:** LP

ST-HONORÉ NIÈVRE

Bains 15 av J-Mermoz, 58360 386307344 386306188
e-mail: camping-les-bains@wanadoo.fr
website: www.campinglesbains.com
A family site with good facilities close to the Morvan national park.
Access via A6 and D985.
Open: May-05 Oct **Site:** 4.5HEC **Prices:** 3.15-4.50 pitch 10.85-15.50 (incl 2 persons) **Facilities:** **Services:** lau **Leisure:** P **Off-site:**

ST-PÉREUSE NIÈVRE

Manoir de Bezolle 58110 386844255 386844377
e-mail: info@bezolle.com
website: www.bezolle.com
Situated in grounds of a manor house, at the edge of a national park. Well-kept site divided by hedges.
At x-roads of D11 and D978.
Open: May-15 Sep **Site:** 8HEC **Facilities:** **Services:** lau **Leisure:** P

STE-MENEHOULD MARNE

CM de la Grelette 51800 326607389
A well-equipped municipal site.
E of town towards Metz, beside the River Aisne
Open: May-Sep **Site:** 1HEC **Facilities:** **Services:** lau **Off-site:** PR

SAULIEU CÔTE-D'OR

CM Perron 21210 380641619 380641619
e-mail: saulieu.tourisme@wanadoo.fr
On level, open ground with good recreational facilities.
1 km NW on N6.
Open: Apr-Sep **Site:** 4.5HEC **Prices:** 3-3 3 pitch 11.50-12.50 (incl 2 persons) **Facilities:** **Services:** lau **Leisure:** P **Off-site:** P

SEDAN ARDENNES

CM de la Prairie bd Fabert, 08200
324271305 324271305
A well-equipped municipal site on the banks of the River Meuse, close to the centre of the village.
Open: Apr-Sep **Site:** 1.5HEC **Facilities:** **Services:** lau **Off-site:** LP

SELONGEY CÔTE-D'OR

CM Les Courvelles r H-Jevain, 21260
380757074 380755665
e-mail: info@selongey.com **website:** www.selongey.com
In a rural location close to the river.
Access via A31 and N74.
Open: May-Sep **Site:** 0.4HEC **Facilities:** **Services:** lau **Off-site:** LPR

SEURRE Côte-d'Or

Piscine 21250 380204922 0380203401
A well-equipped municipal site with direct access to the river.
From town centre follow N73 W for 600m in the direction of Beaune.
Open: 15 May-15 Sep **Site:** **Facilities:** **Services:** lau **Leisure:** PR **Off-site:**

SÉZANNE Marne

CM rte de Launat, 51120 0326805700
e-mail: campingdesezanne@wanadoo.fr
1.5km W on D239, rte de Launat.
Open: Apr-1 Oct **Site:** 1HEC **Facilities:** **Services:** lau **Leisure:** P **Off-site:**

SIGNY-LE-PETIT Ardennes

Pré Hugon Base de Loisirs, 08380
324535473 324535132
e-mail: tourisme@signy-le-petit.fr
website: www.signy-le-petit.com
A pleasant site in wooded surroundings.
Access via N43.
Open: 12 Apr-Sep **Site:** 0.8HEC **Facilities:** **Services:** lau **Leisure:** P **Off-site:** LR

SOULAINES-DHUYS Aube

CM La Croix Badeau 10200 0325927744
Open: May-Sep **Site:** 1.5HEC **Facilities:** **Services:** lau **Off-site:** R

TAZILLY Nièvre

Château de Chigy 58170 386301080 386309022
In a beautiful location within the extensive grounds of a magnificent chateau. Good sporting facilities and entertainment programme.
4km from Luzy on D973 Luzy-Moulins.
Open: Apr-Sep **Site:** 7HEC **Facilities:** **Services:** lau **Leisure:** LP

THONNANCE-LES-MOULINS Haute-Marne

Forge de Ste-Marie 52230
325944200 325944143
e-mail: la.forge.de.sainte.marie@wanadoo.fr
website: www.laforgedesaintemarie.com
Partially terraced, on the site of an 18th-century forge containing a lake.
Access via N67 and D427.
Open: May-Sep **Site:** 11HEC **Prices:** 3-6 pitch 15-25 (incl 2 persons) **Facilities:** **Services:** lau **Leisure:** PR

TOULON-SUR-ARROUX Saône-et-Loire

CM du Val d'Arroux rte d'Uxeau, 73120
385795122 385796217
e-mail: mairie.toulon@wanadoo.fr
On W outskirts beside the River Arroux.
Access via D985 then take Uxeau road.
Open: late Apr-late Oct **Site:** 0.6HEC **Prices:** 1.75 1.30 1.30 pitch 1.30 **Facilities:** **Services:** lau **Leisure:** R **Off-site:**

UCHIZY Saône-et-Loire

National 6 71700 385405390 385405390
Site surrounded by poplar trees on banks of river.
Turn off N6 towards Saône 6km S of Tournus and continue 0.8km.
Open: Apr-1 Oct **Site:** 6HEC **Prices:** 3.30-4.10 pitch 3.90-4.60 (static)260-325 **Facilities:** **Services:** lau **Leisure:** PR

VAL-DES-PRÉS Marne

Gentianes La Vachette, 5100 492212141 492212412
In a delightful wooded location backed by imposing mountains and bordered by a river.
On the edge of the village, 3km SE of Briançon.
Open: All year **Site:** 2HEC **Prices:** 4.70 pitch 4.70 pp2.10 (static)302-407 **Facilities:** **Services:** lau **Leisure:** PR **Off-site:**

VANDENESSE-EN-AUXOIS Côte-d'Or

Lac de Panthier 21320 380492194 380492580
e-mail: info@lac-de-panthier.com
website: www.lac-de-panthier.com
In a wooded location beside lake Panthier with a wide variety of sporting facilities.
5km SE from Pouilly-en-Auxois on A6.
Open: 18 Apr-27 Sep **Site:** 6HEC **Facilities:** **Services:** lau **Leisure:** LP

Voiliers 21320 380492194 380492580
e-mail: info@lac-de-panthier.com
website: www.lac-de-panthier.com
In a pleasant situation beside a lake with plenty of facilities for families.
2.5km NE via D977.
Open: 9 Apr-15 Oct **Site:** 7HEC **Prices:** 3.70-6.20 pitch 4.10-7 **Facilities:** **Services:** lau **Leisure:** LP

VENAREY-LES-LAUMES Côte-d'Or

Alésia r Dr-Roux, 21150 380960776 380960776
e-mail: mairie.vll@worldonline.fr
A peaceful site close to the lake and river.
Open: 19 Apr-15 Oct **Site:** 2HEC **Prices:** 2.50 4 1.60 pitch 1.60-4 **Facilities:** **Services:** lau **Off-site:** LR

VERMENTON Yonne

Coulemières 89270 386815302 386815302
website: www.vermenton.fr
A peaceful site with good facilities set amongst the meadows of Burgundy.
On the N6 S of Auxerre.
Open: 10 Apr-10 Oct **Site:** 1.5HEC **Facilities:** **Services:** lau **Leisure:** R **Off-site:**

VILLENEUVE-LES-GENÊTS Yonne

Bois Guillaume 89350 386454541 386454920
e-mail: camping@bois-guillaume.com
website: www.bois-guillaume.com
In wooded surroundings with good, modern facilities.
2.7km NE.
Open: All year **Site:** 8HEC **Prices:** 3.40-3.60 2.35 pitch 2.35 **Facilities:** **Services:** lau **Leisure:** P **Off-site:** R

VINCELLES Yonne

Ceriselles rte de Vincelottes, 89290
386423939 386423939
Rural situation beside the river Yonne, close to the local village.
Signed on exiting RN6 between Avallon and Auxerre.
Open: Apr-Sep **Site:** 21HEC **Facilities:** **Services:** lau **Off-site:** R

SOUTH-WEST/PYRÉNÉES

ABZAC GIRONDE

Paradis rte de Périgueux, 33230 557490510 557491888
e-mail: campingleparadis@free.fr
website: www.campingleparadis.free.fr
In a centre of gastronomic importance, this site stands on meadowland near an artificial lake. Pedal boats and fishing nearby.
Drive W on N89 from the direction of Périgueux. After St-Médard-de-Guizières turn onto D17E and follow signs.
Open: Feb-15 Nov **Site:** 5HEC **Facilities:** **Services:** lau **Leisure:** LR

AIGNAN GERS

Castex 32290 562092513 562092479
e-mail: gers.vacances@wanadoo.fr
Wooded site in peaceful surroundings.
800m from D48.
Open: 15 Mar-15 Oct **Site:** 3HEC **Facilities:** **Services:** lau **Leisure:** P **Off-site:** R

AIRE-SUR-L'ADOUR LANDES

Ombrages de l'Adour r des Graviers, 40800
558717510 558713259
e-mail: hetapsarl@yahoo.fr
A clean, tidy site next to a sports stadium beside the river. Clean sanitary installations.
Open: Mar-Nov **Site:** 2HEC **Prices:** 2.80-3.80 1.80-2.30 3-3.80 pitch 3-4 (static)150-320
Facilities: **Services:** lau **Leisure:** R
Off-site: P

ALBI TARN

Languedoc allée du Camping Caussels, 81000
563603706 563603706
The site is owned by the local automobile club. It lies on terraced land in a forest next to municipal swimming pools.
Camping Card Compulsory.
From village take N99 towards Millau, then turn left onto D100 and left again into site.
Open: Apr-Oct **Site:** 1.5HEC **Prices:** pitch 66 (incl 2 persons) **Facilities:** **Services:** lau
Off-site: P

ALLES-SUR-DORDOGNE DORDOGNE

Port de Limeuil 24480 553632976 553630419
e-mail: didierbonvallet@aol.com
website: www.leportdelimeuil.com
Situated in a conservation area at the confluence of the Dordogne and Vézère rivers, with a 400m beach.
Signed off D51.
Open: May-Sep **Site:** 7HEC **Prices:** 3.85-5.50 pitch 13.93-19.90 (incl 2 persons) **Facilities:**
Services: lau **Leisure:** PR

ANDERNOS-LES-BAINS GIRONDE

Fontaine-Vieille 4 bd du Colonel Wurtz, 33510
556820167 556820981
e-mail: fontaine-vieille-sa@wanadoo.fr
website: www.fontaine-vieille.com
On level ground in sparse forest.
S of village centre.
Open: Apr-Sep **Site:** 12.6HEC **Prices:** 3-5 2-3 pitch 16-24 (incl 2 persons) **Facilities:**
Services: lau **Leisure:** PS

Facilities: -shop -shower -electric points for razors -electric points for caravans -parking by tents permitted -compulsory separate car park **Services:** -café/restaurant -bar -Camping Gaz International -gas other than Camping Gaz -first aid facilities lau-laundry **Leisure:** -swimming L-Lake P-Pool R-River S-Sea **Off-site:** All facilities within 2km

Pleine Forêt 33510 556821718
Situated in a quiet location among pines.
Off D106E or D106 Andernos-les-Bains-Bordeaux road.
Open: All year **Site:** 6HEC **Facilities:** **Services:** lau **Leisure:** P **Off-site:** S

ANGLARS-JUILLAC LOT

Floiras 46140 565362739 565214100
e-mail: campingfloiras@aol.com
A quiet, level site beside the River Lot surrounded by vineyards in a hilly landscape dotted with villages, castles and caves. Good facilities for boating.
SW via D8.
Open: Apr-15 Oct **Site:** 1HEC **Prices:** 3.50-3.85 pitch 5.25-7 **Facilities:** **Services:** lau **Leisure:** R **Off-site:**

ANGLES TARN

Manoir de Boutaric rte de Lacabarede, 81260
563709606 563709605
e-mail: manoir@boutaric.com
website: www.boutaric.com
Site lies in the grounds of an old manor house in the heart of the Haute Languedoc region.
S of village, on D52 towards Lacabarède.
Open: Etr-Sep **Site:** 3.3HEC **Prices:** 3.10-5.50 1.60-4.50 1.60-4 pitch 13-25 **Facilities:** **Services:** lau **Leisure:** P **Off-site:** LR

ANGLET PYRÉNÉES-ATLANTIQUES

Parme Quartier Brindos, 64600
559230300 559412955
e-mail: campingdeparme@wanadoo.fr
website: campingdeparme.com
In a wooded area with good facilities on the outskirts of Biarritz.
3km SW off N10
Open: 15 Mar-30 Oct **Site:** 3.5HEC **Prices:** 4.20-6.50 pitch 15.94-23.44 (incl 2 persons) **Facilities:** **Services:** lau **Leisure:** P **Off-site:** LRS

ARCACHON GIRONDE

Camping Club d'Arcachon av de la Galaxie, Les Abatilles, 33120
556832415 557522851
e-mail: camparcachon@hotmail.com
In a delightful wooded position 800m from the town and 1km from the beaches.
1.5 km S.
Open: All year **Site:** 6HEC **Facilities:** **Services:** lau **Leisure:** P **Off-site:** S

ARCIZANS-AVANT HAUTES-PYRÉNÉES

Lac 65400 562970188 562970188
e-mail: campinglac@campinglac65.fr
website: www.campinglac65.fr
Set in delightful Pyrenean surroundings on outskirts of village. Lakeside site close to a château.
S on N21 take D13 through St-Savin.
Open: Jun-Sep **Site:** 3HEC **Prices:** 5.30 pitch 5.30 **Facilities:** **Services:** lau **Leisure:** P **Off-site:** L

ARÈS GIRONDE

Canadienne rte de Lège, 82 r du Gl-de-Gaulle, 33740
556602491 557704085
e-mail: camping-la-canadienne@wanadoo.fr
website: www.lacanadienne.com
A family site surrounded by pine and oak trees with good facilities.
1 km N off D106.
Open: Jan-Nov **Site:** 2HEC **Facilities:** **Services:** lau **Leisure:** P **Off-site:** L

Cigale rte de Lège, 33740 556602259 557704166
e-mail: campinglacigaleares@wanadoo.fr
website: www.camping-lacigale-ares.com
Clean tidy site with good recreational facilities amongst pine trees. Grassy pitches.
0.5 km N on D106 between the sea and the Arcachon basin.
Open: 29 Apr-2 Oct **Site:** 2.8HEC **Prices:** pitch 17-23 (incl 2 persons) **Facilities:** **Services:** lau **Leisure:** P **Off-site:**

Goëlands av de la Libération, 33740
556825564 556820751
e-mail: camping-les-goelands@wanadoo.fr
Situated among oak trees 200m from the beach with good facilities.
1.7km SE
Open: Apr-Oct **Site:** 10HEC **Facilities:** **Services:** lau **Off-site:** L

Pasteur 1 r du Pilote, 33704 556603333
website: www.atlantic-vacances.com
S of D3, 300m from the sea.
Open: Apr-Sep **Site:** 1HEC **Prices:** 4-23 pitch 12.50-23 (incl 2 persons) **Facilities:** **Services:** lau **Leisure:** P **Off-site:** S

ARGELÈS-GAZOST HAUTES-PYRÉNÉES AT AGOS-VIDALOS (5KM NE)

Soleil du Pibeste 65400 562975323
e-mail: info@campingpibeste.com
In a beautiful wooded setting in the heart of the Pyrénées.
S on N21.
Open: All year **Site:** 1.5HEC **Facilities:** **Services:** lau **Leisure:** P **Off-site:** R

ARREAU HAUTES-PYRÉNÉES

Refuge International route departemental 929, 65240
562986334 562986334
e-mail: camping.international.arreau@wanadoo.fr
website: perso.wanadoo.fr/camping.international.arreau
Enclosed terrace site.
2km N on D929.
Open: All year **Site:** 15HEC **Prices:** 3.10 pitch 4.20 (static)120-230 **Facilities:** **Services:** lau **Leisure:** PR **Off-site:** L

ASCAIN PYRÉNÉES-ATLANTIQUES

Nivelle 64310 ☎ 559540194 ℻ 559540194
e-mail: campinglanivelle@wanadoo.fr
website: www.camping-lanivelle.com
In a picturesque location beside the River Nivelle.
2km N of town on D918 to St-Jean-de-Luz.
Open: Apr-Oct **Site:** 2.8HEC **Prices:** 2.70-3.80 1.50-1.75 4.20-6 pitch 4.30-6.20 (static)164-330 **Facilities:** **Services:** lau **Leisure:** R **Off-site:**

ASCARAT PYRÉNÉES-ATLANTIQUES

Europ' Camping 64220 ☎ 559371278 ℻ 559372982
In rustic surroundings of mountains and vineyards, 300m from the River Nive.
1km W of St-Jean-Pied-de-Port on D918.
Open: Etr-Sep **Site:** 1.7HEC **Facilities:** **Services:** lau **Leisure:** P **Off-site:** R

ATUR DORDOGNE

Grand Dague 24750 ☎ 553042101 ℻ 553042201
e-mail: info@legranddague.fr
website: www.legranddague.fr
Well equipped family site in the heart of the Dordogne region with pitches divided by bushes and hedges.
NE of Atur via D2.
Open: Etr-Sep **Site:** 22HEC **Facilities:** **Services:** lau **Leisure:** P

AUREILHAN LANDES

Aurilandes Camping 1001 promenade de l'Étang, 40200
☎ 558091088 ℻ 558090189
e-mail: info@campingterreoceane.com
website: www.campingterreoceane.com
Quiet site separated by a small road on the banks of lake Aureilhan.
D626, 2km before Mimizan, on the right.
Open: Jun-Sep **Site:** 8HEC **Prices:** 3.20-4.20 pitch 19-25 **Facilities:** **Services:** lau **Leisure:** LP **Off-site:** PS

Parc St-James Eurolac Promenade de l'Étang, 40200
☎ 558090287 ℻ 558094189
e-mail: info@camping-parcstjames.com
website: www.camping-parcstjames.com
Well tended site under deciduous trees providing shade, partially on open meadow.
Turn right at Labouheyre off N10 on D626 to Aureilhan. Follow signs.
Open: end Mar-Sep **Site:** 13HEC **Facilities:** **Services:** lau **Leisure:** LP

AZUR LANDES

Camping Azu' Rivage 720 Route des Campings, Au bord du lac, 40140 ☎ 558483072 ℻ 558483072
e-mail: info@campingazurivage.com
website: www.campingazurivage.com
A family site in wooded surroundings close to the Lac de Soustons and 8km form the coast.
2 km S of Azur.
Open: 15 Jun-15 Sep **Site:** 7HEC **Prices:** 2.60-3.60 pitch 10.10-16.70 (incl 2 persons) **Facilities:** **Services:** lau **Leisure:** LPR

BAGNÈRES-DE-BIGORRE HAUTES-PYRÉNÉES

Bigourdan rte de Tarbes, 65200 ☎ 562951357
A level site recommended for caravans in a beautiful Pyrenean setting.
2.5km NW at Pouzac.
Open: 7 Apr-19 Oct **Site:** 1HEC **Prices:** 3.70 pitch 3.90 (static)150-390 **Facilities:** **Services:** lau **Leisure:** P **Off-site:** R

Tilleuls 12 av Maréchal Alan Brooke, 65200 ☎ 562952604
A well-equipped site at an altitude of 500m. There are good recreational facilities and a bakery operates during July and August.
Open: May-Sep **Site:** 2.6HEC **Facilities:** **Services:** lau **Off-site:** P

At TRÉBONS (4KM N ON D935)

Parc des Oiseaux RD26, 65200 ☎ 562953026
Clean, well-kept site with large pitches.
Open: All year **Site:** 2.8HEC **Prices:** 2.60-3 1-1 1-1 1-1 pitch 3.50-3.50 (static)180-200 **Facilities:** **Services:** lau **Leisure:** R **Off-site:** P

BASTIDE-DE-SEROU, LA ARIÈGE

Arize rte de Nescus, 9240 ☎ 561658151 ℻ 561658334
e-mail: camparize@aol.com **website:** www.camping-arize.com
A well-run site with a wide range of facilities in a peaceful, wooded location at the foot of the Pyrénées.
Open: Apr-Oct **Site:** 1.8HEC **Prices:** pitch 15.20-22.60 (incl 2 persons) (static)193-319 **Facilities:** **Services:** lau **Leisure:** PR **Off-site:**

BAYONNE PYRÉNÉES-ATLANTIQUES

Airotel la Chêneraie chemin de Cazenare, 64100
☎ 559550131 ℻ 559551117
On gently sloping field divided by hedges.
4km NE off N117 Pau road.
Open: Etr-1 Oct **Site:** 10HEC **Facilities:** **Services:** lau **Leisure:** LP **Off-site:**

BEAUCENS-LES-BAINS HAUTES-PYRÉNÉES

Viscos 65400 ☎ 562970545
In a secluded location at the foot of the Pyrénées.
1km N on D13, rte de Lourdes.
Open: 15 May-Sep **Site:** 2HEC **Prices:** 3.50 3 3 3 pitch 3 **Facilities:** **Services:** lau **Off-site:** R

BELVÈS DORDOGNE

Hauts de Ratebout 24170 ☎ 553290210 ℻ 553290828
e-mail: camping@hauts-ratebout.fr
website: www.hauts-ratebout.fr
A well-equipped site on an old Périgord farm, set in extensive grounds on top of a hill.
D710 to Fumel. After Vaurez-de-Belvès, take D54 to Casals.
Open: 24 Apr-4 Sep **Site:** 12HEC **Prices:** 4-6 pitch 19-31 (static)400-780 **Facilities:** **Services:** lau **Leisure:** P

Nauves Bos Rouge, 24170 ☎ 553291264 ℻ 553291264
e-mail: campinglesnauves@hotmail.com
Located on a site of 40 hectares surrounded by forest
4.5km SW via D53.
Open: Apr-Sep **Site:** 7HEC **Facilities:** **Services:** lau **Leisure:** P

RCN Le Moulin de la Pique 24170
☎ 553290115 ℻ 553282909
e-mail: info@rcn-lemoulindelapique,fr
website: www.rcn-campings.fr
A quiet well-equipped site set out around an imposing villa and a small lake. There are fine entertainment facilities and modern sanitary installations.

contd.

➲ *500m S on D710.*
Open: 16 Apr-2 Oct **Site:** 12HEC
Prices: pitch 17.50-45.50 (incl 2 persons) (static)250-740
Facilities: **Services:** lau
Leisure: LPR

BEYNAC-ET-CAZENAC DORDOGNE

Capeyrou 24220 553295495 553283627
e-mail: lecapeyrou@wanadoo.fr
website: www.camping-dordogne.com/lecapeyrou
Situated beside the River Dordogne close to the gates of the picturesque medieval town of Beynac.
➲ *Access via D703.*
Open: Etr-Sep **Site:** 5HEC **Prices:** 4.50 6 pitch 6
Facilities: **Services:** lau **Leisure:** P
Off-site: R

BEZ, LE TARN

Plô 81260 563740082
e-mail: info@leplo.com
website: www.leplo.com
A pleasant site in wooded surroundings.
➲ *0.9km W via D30.*
Open: Jun-Aug **Site:** 4.2HEC **Prices:** 2.30-2.80 1.10-1.40 pitch 11-13 (static)195 **Facilities:** **Services:** lau **Off-site:** R

BIARRITZ PYRÉNÉES-ATLANTIQUES

Biarritz 28 r d'Harcet, 64200 559230012 559437467
e-mail: biarritz.camping@wanadoo.fr
website: www.biarritz-camping.fr
A pleasant site with spacious pitches 200m from beach.
➲ *2km from town centre on N10, follow signs 'Espagne'.*
Open: 10 May-21 Sep **Site:** 2.6HEC
Facilities: **Services:** lau **Leisure:** P
Off-site: S

AT BIDART (4KM SW)

Jean Paris Quartier M-Pierre, 64210
559265558 559265558
600m from beaches.
➲ *S of town, cross railway line, site on S side of N10.*
Open: Jun-Sep **Site:** 1.1HEC **Facilities:**
Services: lau **Off-site:** S

Oyam Ferme Oyamburua, 64210 559549161
559549161
e-mail: accueil@camping-oyam.com
website: www.camping-oyam.com/
Level meadow site near farm. Views of the Pyrénées. Simple but pleasant site.
➲ *Turn off beyond the church in the direction of Arbonne, via N10, for 1km.*
Open: Jun-Sep **Site:** 6HEC **Prices:** 1.70-4.30 1-1.50 pitch 12-21 (incl 2 persons) **Facilities:**
Services: lau **Leisure:** P **Off-site:** S

Pavillon Royal av Prince de Galles, 64210 559230054
559234447
e-mail: info@pavillon-royal.com
website: www.pavillon-royal.com
Beautiful, well-kept site, divided into pitches, most of which have open view of sea. Beside rocky beach.
➲ *2 km N.*
Open: 15 May-25 Sep **Site:** 5HEC **Prices:** 24-36.50 17.50-28 pitch 15-33 **Facilities:**
Services: lau **Leisure:** P **Off-site:** S

Résidence des Pins rte de Biarritz, 64210
559230029 559412459
e-mail: contact@campingdespins.com
website: www.campingdespins.com
Terraced site with numbered pitches, 800m from sea.
➲ *2km N on N106 Biarritz road.*
Open: 15 May-25 Sep **Site:** 7HEC **Prices:** 15-23 pitch 15-23 **Facilities:** **Services:** lau
Leisure: P **Off-site:** LS

Ruisseau rte d'Arbonne, 64210
559419450 559419573
e-mail: francoise.dumont3@wanadoo.fr
website: www.camping-le-ruisseau.fr
A well-equipped site in wooded surroundings set out around two lakes.
➲ *2km E on D255.*
Open: 15 May-12 Sep **Site:** 15HEC **Prices:** 4.30-5.35 pitch 15-25 (incl 2 persons) **Facilities:**
Services: lau **Leisure:** LP

Sunelia Berrua rte Berrua, 64210
559549666 559547830
e-mail: contact@berrua.com
website: www.berrua.com
A well-equipped family site 1km from the beach and 500m from the village.
Open: 9 Apr-2 Oct **Site:** 5HEC **Prices:** 3.20-5.70 3.10 pitch 16.10-26.40 (incl 2 persons) (static)264-875
Facilities: **Services:** lau **Leisure:** P
Off-site: RS

Ur-Onéa r de la Chapelle, 64210 559265361 559265394
e-mail: uronea@wanadoo.fr
website: www.uronea.com
A well-equipped site lying at the foot of the Pyrénées with good recreational facilities.
➲ *0.6km E.*
Open: 3 Apr-17 Sep **Site:** 5HEC **Prices:** pitch 11.50-18.50 (incl 2 persons) **Facilities:**
Services: lau **Leisure:** P **Off-site:** RS

BIAS LANDES

CM Le Tatiou 40710 558090476 558824430
e-mail: campingletatiou@wanadoo.fr
website: www.campingletatiou.com
Well equipped family site in a forested setting 4km from the sea.
➲ *2km W towards Lespecier.*
Open: 4 Apr-14 Oct **Site:** 10HEC
Prices: pitch 12.60 (incl 2 persons) (static)300
Facilities: **Services:** lau **Leisure:** P
Off-site: S

BIRON DORDOGNE

Sunêlia le Moulinal 24540 553408460 553408149
e-mail: lemoulinal@perigord.com
website: www.lemoulinal.com
In a pleasant situation beside a lake close to the former mill of Biron Castle. This is a modern holiday village with a variety of recreational facilities.
➲ *2km S on the Lacapelle-Biron road.*
Open: 3 Apr-18 Sep **Site:** 18HEC **Prices:** 3-8.20 4-4 pitch 12-35 (incl 2 persons) **Facilities:**
Services: lau **Leisure:** LP

BISCARROSSE LANDES

Bimbo 176 chemin de Bimbo, 40600 558098233
558098014
e-mail: camping.bimbo@free.fr
website: campingbimbo.com
In delightful wooded surroundings 500m from the lake and 10 minutes from the sea. Reservations recommended.
3.5km N towards Sanguinet.
Open: All year **Site:** 6HEC **Prices:** 5.60-7 pitch 6.40-8 (static)250-759 **Facilities:** **Services:** lau **Leisure:** P **Off-site:** L

Ecureuils Port Navarrosse, 40600 558098000
e-mail: camping.les.ecureuils@wanadoo.fr
In a pleasant wooded location 200m from the lake shore. Plenty of recreational facilities.
Access via D652.
Open: Apr-Sep **Site:** 7HEC **Facilities:** **Services:** lau **Leisure:** P **Off-site:** L

Rive rte de Bordeaux, 40600 558781233 558781292
e-mail: info@camping-de-la-rive.fr
website: www.larive.fr
Level site in tall pine forest on E side of lake. Private port and beach.
N of town off D652 Sanguinet road.
Open: Apr-25 Sep **Site:** 15HEC **Prices:** pitch 20-36 (incl 2 persons) (static)266-973 **Facilities:** **Services:** lau **Leisure:** LP

BLAYE GIRONDE

AT MAZION (5.5KM NE ON N937)

Tilleuls 33390 557421813 557421301
5.5km NE on N937.
Open: May-Oct **Site:** 0.5HEC **Prices:** 3.50 pitch 2.50 **Facilities:** **Services:** lau **Off-site:**

BOURNEL LOT-ET-GARONNE

Ferme de Bourgade 47210 553366715
e-mail: bourgade47@libertysurf.fr
website: www.bourgade-holidays.co.uk
A small, tranquil site with good, clean facilities.
Signed from N21 between Castillonnès and Villeréal.
Open: 15 Jun-15 Sep **Site:** 1HEC **Prices:** 1.50 1.50 pitch 3 **Facilities:** **Services:** lau **Leisure:** L **Off-site:**

BRETENOUX LOT

Bourgnatelle 46130 565384407
e-mail: bourgnatel@aol.com
In a pleasant location beside the River Cére. Separate car park for arrivals after 22.30.
Access via D940 towards Rocamadour.
Open: May-Sep **Site:** 2HEC **Facilities:** **Services:** lau **Leisure:** R **Off-site:** P

BUGUE, LE DORDOGNE

Rocher de la Granelle rte du Buisson, 24260 53072432
Surrounded by woodland with pitches set out among trees and bushes on the banks of the Vézère with a wide variety of leisure facilities.
From Le Bugue centre cross the bridge and follow signs.
Open: Apr-Sep **Site:** 8HEC **Facilities:** **Services:** lau **Leisure:** PR

St-Avit Loisirs St-Avit-de-Vialard, 24260
553026400 553026439
e-mail: contact@saint-avit.loisirs.com
website: www.saint-avit-loisirs.com
A pleasant site in natural wooded surroundings.
W of town via C201.
Open: Apr-Sep **Site:** 7HEC **Prices:** 3.50-7.80 pitch 5.50-11.30 **Facilities:** **Services:** lau **Leisure:** P **Off-site:** R

CAHORS LOT

Rivière de Cabessut r de la Rivière, 46000
565300630 565239946
e-mail: camping/riviere/cabessut@wanadoo.fr
website: www.cabessut.com
N of town via the Cabessut Bridge over the River Lot.
Open: Apr-Sep **Site:** 3HEC **Prices:** 3 pitch 8 **Facilities:** **Services:** lau **Leisure:** PR **Off-site:**

AT ESCLAUZELS (18KM SE)

Pompit 46090 565315340 565317800
Situated in the heart of a large forest close to the magnificent Lot Valley.
5km NW of Esclauzels village.
Open: All year **Site:** 3.5HEC **Prices:** 3.40 3.60 3.60 pitch 3.60 **Facilities:** **Services:** lau **Leisure:** P

CALVIAC LOT

Chênes Verts rte de Sarlat, Souillac, 24370 553592107
In a beautiful wooded setting within the Périgord countryside. A wide variety of recreational facilities are available.
On D704A between Sarlat and Calviac.
Open: May-Sep **Site:** 6HEC **Facilities:** **Services:** lau **Leisure:** P **Off-site:** LR

Trois Sources Le Peyratel, 46190 565330301 565330645
e-mail: l3s@wanadoo.fr
website: www.les-trois-sources.com
Wooded location, family site with plenty of leisure facilities.
Access via D653, then D25 to Calviac.
Open: May-Sep **Site:** 6.4HEC **Facilities:** **Services:** lau **Leisure:** LPR

CAMBO-LES-BAINS PYRÉNÉES-ATLANTIQUES

Bixta Eder rte de St-Jean-de-Luz, 64250
5559299423 559292370
e-mail: camping.bixtaeden@wanadoo.fr
website: www.camping-bixtaeder.com
Modern site with good sports facilities.
Near the junction of D932 and D10.
Open: 15 Apr **Site:** 1HEC **Facilities:** **Services:** lau **Off-site:** LP

CAPBRETON LANDES

Pointe Quartier la Pointe, 40130
558721498 558723197
Family site in a wooded location on the banks of a river, 800m from the sea. Good recreational facilities.
2km S towards Labenne on N652.
Open: Apr-Oct **Site:** 13HEC **Facilities:** **Services:** lau **Leisure:** PRS

CAP FERRET GIRONDE

Truc Vert rte Forestière, 33970
556608955 556609947
e-mail: camping.truc-vert@worldonline.fr
website: www.trucvert.com
In a very pleasant location on a slope in a pine wood close to the beach.
On D106 in the direction of Cap Ferret to Petit Piquey. Turn right and follow signs.
Open: May-Sep **Site:** 11HEC **Prices:** 3-4.20 9.45 pitch 12-17.90 (incl 2 persons) **Facilities:** **Services:** lau **Off-site:** S

CARLUCET LOT

Château de Lacomté 46500 565387546 565331768
e-mail: chateaulacomte@wanadoo.fr
website: www.campingchateaulacomte.com
In wooded surroundings with good sized pitches and a variety of recreational facilities.
Follow signposts from D677/D32.
Open: 15 May-Sep **Site:** 12HEC
Prices: 3.77-5.80 3.70 pitch 4.80-7.40 (static)300-470
Facilities: **Services:** lau **Leisure:** P

CASTELJALOUX LOT-ET-GARONNE

Club de Clarens rte de Mont-de-Marsan, 47700
553930745 553939309
A large site with direct access to the 17-hectare Lac de Clarens and good recreational facilities.
Open: Jun-Sep **Site:** 2HEC **Facilities:** **Services:** lau **Leisure:** LR **Off-site:** P

CM de la Piscine rte de Marmande, 47700
553935468 553934807
NW on D933 Marmande road.
Open: Apr-Nov **Site:** 1HEC **Prices:** 2 2 pitch 2-3.35 **Facilities:** **Services:** lau **Off-site:** PR

CASTELNAUD-LA-CHAPELLE DORDOGNE

Maisonneuve 24250 553295129 553302706
e-mail: campmaison@aol.com
website: www.campingmaisonneuve.com
In picturesque surroundings, 800m from the village, close to the River Céou in the heart of the Périgord Noir region.
10kms S of Sarlat on D57.
Open: 29 Mar-Sep **Site:** 6HEC **Prices:** 3.40-4.80 pitch 4.40-6.30 **Facilities:** **Services:** lau **Leisure:** PR **Off-site:**

CAUTERETS HAUTES-PYRÉNÉES

Mamelon-Vert 32 av du Mamelon-Vert, 65110
562925156 562925156
e-mail: info@mamelon-vert.com
website: www.mamelon-vert.com
In a beautiful wooded mountain setting close to the local winter-sports facilities.
Open: Dec-23 Apr & 2 May-Sep **Site:** 2HEC
Prices: 3-3.80 1.30 1.20-1.40 pitch 9-10.50 (incl 2 persons) (static)165-255 **Facilities:**
Services: lau **Off-site:** PR

CLAOUEY GIRONDE

Airotel les Viviers rte du Cap Ferret, 33950
556607004 556607614
e-mail: lesviviers@wanadoo.fr
website: www.airotel.les.viviers.com
Beautiful, widespread site in a forest divided by seawater channels.
On the D106, 1km S of the town.
Open: Apr-Sep **Site:** 33HEC **Facilities:** **Services:** lau **Leisure:** LPS

CONTIS-PLAGE LANDES

Lous Seurrots 40170 558428582 558424911
e-mail: info@lous-seurrots.com
website: www.lous-seurrots.com
Well equipped site in a pine forest on outskirts of village between road and stream.
Access via D41.
Open: Apr-Sep **Site:** 15HEC **Facilities:** **Services:** lau **Leisure:** PRS

CORDES TARN

Moulin de Julien 81170 563561110 0563561110
website: www.cordes_sur_ciel.org
In a beautiful valley with good pitches for caravans and tents and plenty of modern facilities.
900m E on D600 and D922.
Open: 15 May-Sep **Site:** 6HEC **Prices:** 4.80-6 pitch 13.60-17 (incl 2 persons) (static)137-357
Facilities: **Services:** lau **Leisure:** LP
Off-site: R

COUX-ET-BIGAROQUE DORDOGNE

Clou Meynard, 24220 553316332 553316933
e-mail: info@camping-le-clou.com
website: www.camping-le-clou.com
Separate section for dog owners.
Access via D703 Le Bugue-Delve road.
Open: Etr-29 Sep **Site:** 3.5HEC **Prices:** 3.50-4.90 pitch 4-7.50 **Facilities:** **Services:** lau **Leisure:** P

Faval 24220 553316044 553283971
e-mail: camping.la.faval@libertysurf.fr
website: www.lafaval.com
In a wooded location 200m from River Dordogne. A family site with good recreational facilities.
1km E of village on D703, near junction with D710.
Open: Apr-Sep **Site:** 3HEC **Prices:** 4.90 6.40 4.80 (static)170-260 **Facilities:**
Services: lau **Leisure:** P **Off-site:** R

Valades Les Valades, 24220 553291427 553281928
e-mail: camping.valades@wanadoo.fr
website: perso.wanadoo.fr/les-valades
In wooded surroundings within a pleasant valley. Well-equipped pitches available.
5km N of town off N703.
Open: Apr-Sep **Site:** 11HEC **Prices:** 4.20 pitch 5.50 **Facilities:** **Services:** lau
Leisure: LP

CRÉON GIRONDE

Bel Air 33670 556230190 556230838
e-mail: info@camping-bel-air.com
website: www.camping-bel-air.com
A well-equipped, roomy site on a level meadow shaded by tall trees.
1.6km W of Créon on D671.
Open: All year **Site:** 2HEC **Prices:** 2.60 1.55 pitch 4.60 (static)72-270 **Facilities:**
Services:

Site: 6HEC-Site size -grass -sand -stone -little shade -partly shaded -mainly shaded -bungalows for hire -caravans for hire -tents for hire -no dogs Prices: -adult per night -car per night pp-per person per night -caravan per night -tent per night (static)-caravan hire per week

DAGLAN Dordogne

Moulin de Paulhiac 24250 553282088 553293345
e-mail: francis.armagnac@wanadoo.fr
website: www.moulin-de-paulhiac.com
In picturesque wooded surroundings with wide, well-marked pitches and good, modern facilities.
4km N via D57 beside the Céou.
Open: 15 May-15 Sep **Site:** 5HEC **Prices:** 6.20 pitch 9 (static)245-604 **Facilities:** **Services:** lau **Leisure:** PR

DAX Landes

Chênes Au Bois-de-Boulogne, 40100
558900553 558904243
e-mail: camping-chenes@wanadoo.fr
website: www.camping-les-chenes.fr
In a wooded park on the edge of the Bois-de-Boulogne with good facilities.
1.5km W of town beside River Adour.
Open: 26 Mar-Nov **Site:** 5HEC **Prices:** 10.50-13 pitch 13-18.20 (incl 2 persons) **Facilities:** **Services:** lau **Leisure:** P **Off-site:** R

DURAVEL Lot

Club de Vacances Port de Vire, 46700
565246506 565246496
e-mail: clubduravel@wanadoo.fr
website: www.clubdevaccances.fr
A pleasant site with good facilities beside the River Lot.
Camping Card Compulsory
2.3km S via D58.
Open: 25 Apr-Sep **Site:** 7HEC **Prices:** 4.30-6.75 pitch 6.85-9.75 (static)235-600 **Facilities:** **Services:** lau **Leisure:** PR

DURFORT Ariège

Bourdieu 09130 561673017 561672900
e-mail: lebourdieu@wanadoo.fr
website: www.lebourdieu.com
Well equipped site in a picturesque setting with fine views of the Pyrénées.
Off D14 Le Fossat-Saverdun.
Open: All year **Site:** 20HEC **Prices:** 2.10-3 6.30-9 4.90-7 pitch 4.90-7 (static)175-420 **Facilities:** **Services:** lau **Leisure:** PR

ESTAING Hautes-Pyrénées

Pyrénées Natura rte du Lac, 65400
562974544 562974581
e-mail: sarl.ruysschaert@wanadoo.fr
website: www.camping-pyrenees-natura.com
A well-run site at an altitude of 1000m, situated on the edge of the National Park with fine views of the surrounding mountains.
From Argèles-Gazost take road towards Arrens, then D13 for Lac d'Estaing.
Open: May-Sep **Site:** 2.5HEC **Prices:** pitch 14.50-22 (incl 2 persons) (static)280-570 **Facilities:** **Services:** lau **Leisure:** R **Off-site:**

ÉYZIES-DE-TAYAC, LES Dordogne

Pech Charmant 24620 553359708 553359709
e-mail: info@lepech.com
website: www.leplech.com
Located on the side of a wooded hill and contains a small farm with donkeys, goats, horses and chickens.
Open: Apr-Sep **Site:** 7HEC **Prices:** 3-4.50 pitch 5-8 (static)200-400 **Facilities:** **Services:** lau **Leisure:** P **Off-site:** R

Facilities: -shop -shower -electric points for razors -electric points for caravans -parking by tents permitted -compulsory separate car park **Services:** -café/restaurant -bar -Camping Gaz International -gas other than Camping Gaz -first aid facilities lau-laundry **Leisure:** -swimming L-Lake P-Pool R-River S-Sea **Off-site:** All facilities within 2km

FIGEAC LOT

Rives du Célé Domaine du Surgie, 46100 565345900
In a pleasant wooded location on the banks of the River Célé with plenty of leisure facilities, the site lies within a large recreation area. Separate carpark for late arrivals.
Open: Apr-Sep **Site:** 2HEC **Facilities:** **Services:** lau **Leisure:** LPR **Off-site:**

FOIX ARIÈGE

Lac RN 20, 09000 561651158 561651998
e-mail: camping-du-lac@wanadoo.fr
website: www.campingdulac.com
On well-kept meadow beside the Lac de Labarre.
3km N on N20.
Open: All year **Site:** 5HEC **Prices:** pitch 11-17 (incl 2 persons) **Facilities:** **Services:** lau **Leisure:** LP **Off-site:**

GASTES LANDES

Réserve 40160 0870 242 7777 0870 242 9999
website: www.haveneurope.com
A large, popular site situated in one of the largest forests in Europe. Plenty of sporting and entertainment facilities.
3km SW via D652
Open: 28 Apr-14 Sep **Site:** 32HEC **Facilities:** **Services:** lau **Leisure:** LP

See advertisement on page 107

GAUGEAC DORDOGNE

Moulin de David 24540 553226525 553239976
e-mail: info@moulin-de-david.com
website: www.moulin-de-david.com
Situated in a wooded valley alongside a small stream with well-defined pitches and good recreational facilities.
3km from town towards Villeréal.
Open: 14 May-10 Sep **Site:** 14HEC **Prices:** 3.75-6.60 5.15-9.60 (static)238-693 **Facilities:** **Services:** lau **Leisure:** LP

GOURDON LOT

Paradis La Peyrugue, 46300 565416501 565416501
e-mail: contact@campingparadis.com
website: www.campingleparadis.com
On a pleasant wooded meadow surrounded by hills.
1.6km SW off N673.
Open: 15 May-15 Sep **Site:** 2HEC **Prices:** 4.75 pitch 2.50 (static)250 **Facilities:** **Services:** lau **Leisure:** LP **Off-site:** LR

AT **GROLÉJAC** (15KM N ON D704)

Granges 24250 553281115 553285713
e-mail: lesueur.francine@wanadoo.fr
website: lesgranges-fr.com
Beautifully situated terraces on a hill with big pitches. The site has been constructed around a disused railway station, incorporating the old ticket office and the bridge into its modern design. Facilities for sports and entertainment.
Turn off D704 in village towards Domme.
Open: 2 May-14 Sep **Site:** 6.5HEC **Prices:** pitch 15-22.90 (incl 2 persons) pp6.20 **Facilities:** **Services:** lau **Leisure:** PR **Off-site:** L

AT **ST-MARTIAL-DE-NABIRAT** (6KM W)

Carbonnier 24250 553284253 553285131
Family site in a small, wooded valley with a variety of recreational facilities.
Off the D46.
Open: Etr-15 Sep **Site:** 8HEC **Facilities:** **Services:** lau **Leisure:** LP

GOURETTE PYRÉNÉES-ATLANTIQUES

Ley 64440 559051147 559051147
Terraced site with gravel and asphalt caravan pitches. TV, common room.
From Laruns drive E to Eaux-Bonnes and drive uphill to Gourette.
Open: Dec-Apr & Jul-Sep **Site:** 2HEC **Prices:** 6.10 pitch 10.70 (incl 2 persons) pp3.85 **Facilities:** **Services:** lau **Leisure:** R **Off-site:**

GRAULGES, LES DORDOGNE

Crozes les Graulges 24340 553607473
e-mail: info@lesgraulges.com
website: www.lesgraulges.com
In a picturesque setting in woodland beside a lake.
Off D939 between Angoulême and Périgueux.
Open: May-Oct **Site:** 8HEC **Prices:** 3.75-4.25 4.50-5.50 (static)195-275 **Facilities:** **Services:** **Leisure:** LPR

GRISOLLES TARN-ET-GARONNE

Aquitaine rte Nationalle 20, 82170 563673322
e-mail: campingaquitaine@aol.com
1.5km N off x-roads N20/N113. 28km N of Toulouse, 22km S of Montauban.
Open: All year **Site:** 3HEC **Facilities:** **Services:** lau **Leisure:** P **Off-site:** R

HASPARREN PYRÉNÉES-ATLANTIQUES

Chapital rte de Cambo, 64240 559296294 559296971
On level ground, surrounded by woodland. Good facilities for families.
0.5km W via D22. Access via A64 towards Hasparren.
Open: Etr-Oct **Site:** 2.6HEC **Facilities:** **Services:** lau **Off-site:** P

HAUTEFORT DORDOGNE

Moulin des Loisirs L'etang du Coucou, 24390 553504655
e-mail: moulin.des.loisirs@wanadoo.fr
website: www.moulin-des-loisirs.fr
2km SW via D72 & D71, 100m from Coucou lake.
Open: Etr-Sep **Site:** 4HEC **Prices:** 2.80 pitch 9.20-11.80 (incl 2 persons) (static)250 **Facilities:** **Services:** lau **Leisure:** LP **Off-site:** L

HENDAYE PYRÉNÉES-ATLANTIQUES

Acacias 64700 559207876 559207876
e-mail: campacacias@wanadoo.fr
website: www.les-campings.com/acacias
A pleasant family site in parkland, 5 minutes from the beach.
1.8km E (rte de la Glacière).
Open: Apr-Sep **Site:** 5HEC **Prices:** pitch 14-18 (incl 2 persons) **Facilities:** **Services:** lau **Leisure:** L **Off-site:** S

Airotel Eskualduna rte de la Corniche (D-912), 64700 559200464 559200464
website: www.camping-eskualduna.fr
On gently sloping meadow.
2km from village on N10c.
Open: 15 Jun-Sep **Site:** 10HEC **Facilities:** **Services:** lau **Leisure:** PR **Off-site:** S

HOURTIN GIRONDE

Acacia Ste-Hélène, 33990 556738080
e-mail: camping.lacacia@wanadoo.fr
website: www.camping-lacacia.com
Pleasant, quiet site on the edge of a forest with good sanitary facilities. Compulsory car park for arrivals after 23.30.
Off D3 towards the lake.
Open: 15 May-15 Oct **Site:** 5HEC **Prices:** 3.50 pitch 3.35 (static)190-280 **Facilities:** **Services:** lau **Off-site:** L

Mariflaude 33990 556091197 556092401
Level meadowland, shaded by pines, in rural setting 2km from one of the biggest lakes in the country.
Turn onto D4 at the chemist and continue E towards Pauillac.
Open: May-15 Sep **Site:** 7HEC **Facilities:** **Services:** lau **Leisure:** P **Off-site:** L

Ourmes av du Lac, 33990 556091276 556092390
e-mail: lesourmes@free.fr
website: www.lesourmes.com
In wooded surroundings close to the beach and 500m from the largest freshwater lake in France.
Follow D4 towards lake.
Open: Apr-Sep **Site:** 7HEC **Prices:** pitch 11-21.50 (incl 2 persons) (static)250-535 **Facilities:** **Services:** lau **Leisure:** P **Off-site:** LS

HOURTIN-PLAGE GIRONDE

Côte d'Argent 33990 556091025 556092496
e-mail: info@camping-cote-dargent.com
website: www.camping-cote-dargent.com
In a pine and oak forest 500m from beach with good facilities.
Access via D101 from Hourtin.
Open: mid-May to mid-Sep **Site:** 20HEC **Prices:** 19-30 pitch 15-25 (incl 2 persons) (static)210-469 **Facilities:** **Services:** lau **Leisure:** LPS

LABENNE LANDES

Pins Bleus av de l'Océan, 40530 559454113 559454470
e-mail: lespinsbleus@wanadoo.fr
website: www.lespinsbleus.com
On RN10.
Open: Apr-4 Nov **Site:** 6.5HEC **Prices:** 1.50-2 10.10-14.20 pitch 7.10-12.20 (incl 2 persons) **Facilities:** **Services:** lau **Off-site:** LPRS

LABENNE-OCÉAN LANDES

Boudigau 40530 559454207 559457776
e-mail: info@boudigau.com
website: www.boudigau.com
Situated in pine forest.
Turn right into site after bridge.
Open: 15 May-15 Sep **Site:** 6HEC **Prices:** pitch 12-26 (incl 2 persons) (static)400-590 **Facilities:** **Services:** lau **Leisure:** P **Off-site:** S

Côte d'Argent av de l'Océan, 40530 559454202 559457331
e-mail: info@camping-cotedargent.com
website: www.camping-cotedargent.com
Very well-managed modern site attached to holiday village.
3km W on D126.
Open: Apr-Oct **Site:** 4HEC **Prices:** 2.70-4.10 2.50 pitch 9.10-20.50 **Facilities:** **Services:** lau **Leisure:** P **Off-site:** RS

Mer rte de la Plage, 40530 559454209 559454307
e-mail: campinglamer@wanadoo.fr
website: www.campinglamer.com
In a pine forest 700m from the beach.
On D126 (rte de la Plage).
Open: Etr-Sep **Site:** 6.5HEC **Prices:** pitch 9.30-20.50 (incl 2 persons) (static)210-860 **Facilities:** **Services:** lau **Leisure:** PR **Off-site:** S

LACANAU-OCÉAN GIRONDE

Airotel de l'Océan 24 R du Répos, 33680 556032445 557700187
e-mail: airotel.lacanau@wanadoo.fr
website: www.airotel-ocean.com
On rising ground in pine forest. 800m from beach.
Open: 9 Apr-25 Sep **Site:** 9.5HEC **Prices:** 4.50-7.50 3-6 3-6 pitch 11-14 (static)195-469 **Facilities:** **Services:** lau **Leisure:** P **Off-site:** S

Grands Pins Plages Nord, 33680 556032077 557700389
e-mail: reception@lesgrandspins.com
website: www.lesgrandspins.com
On very hilly terrain in woodland. 350m from the beach, access to which is through dunes.
Approach via exit 7 on A10, then D6 to Lacanau.
Open: 24 Apr-25 Sep **Site:** 12HEC **Prices:** pitch 15-34 **Facilities:** **Services:** lau **Leisure:** P **Off-site:** S

AT MEDOC (8KM E)

Talaris rte de l'Océan, 33680 556030415 556262156
e-mail: talarisvacances@free.fr
website: www.talaris_vacances.fr
A family site in delightful wooded surroundings 1.2km from the lake. Separate car park for arrivals after 22.30.
2km E on rte de Lacanau.
Open: May-17 Sep **Site:** 8.2HEC **Prices:** 3.90 pitch 16.25-26.50 (incl 2 persons) (static)230-645 **Facilities:** **Services:** lau **Leisure:** P **Off-site:** L

AT MOUTCHIC (5KM E)

Lac 33680 556030026
On D6 rte de Lacanau, 60m from lake.
Open: Apr-15 Oct **Site:** 1HEC **Prices:** pitch 11.43-15.24 (incl 2 persons) (static)150-300 **Facilities:** **Services:** lau **Off-site:** L

Tedey rte de Longarisse, 33680 55603015 556030190
e-mail: campingletedey@wanadoo.fr
website: www.le-tedey.com
Quiet site in pine forest, on edge of lake Lacanau. Private bathing area.
Turn off D6 and continue along narrow track through forest for 0.5km.
Open: 30 Apr-17 Sep **Site:** 14HEC **Prices:** pitch 19.10-21.90 (incl 2 persons) (static)250-600 **Facilities:** **Services:** lau **Leisure:** L

Facilities: -shop -shower -electric points for razors -electric points for caravans -parking by tents permitted -compulsory separate car park **Services:** -café/restaurant -bar -Camping Gaz International -gas other than Camping Gaz -first aid facilities lau-laundry **Leisure:** -swimming L-Lake P-Pool R-River S-Sea **Off-site:** All facilities within 2km

LACAPELLE-MARIVAL LOT

CM Bois de Sophie Route d'Aymac, 46120
565408259 565408259
In a pleasant wooded location with a variety of sports facilities.
1km NW via D940.
Open: 15 May-Sep **Site:** 1HEC **Prices:** 2.20-3.25 3.20-4.25 2 pitch 3.20-4.25 (static)97-175 **Facilities:** **Services:** lau **Leisure:** P **Off-site:** LR

LANTON GIRONDE

Roumingue 33138 556829748 556829609
e-mail: info@roumingue.com
website: www.roumingue.com
Level terrain under a few deciduous trees partially in open meadow on the Bassin d'Arcachon.
1km NW of village towards sea.
Open: All year **Site:** 10HEC **Facilities:** **Services:** lau **Leisure:** PS **Off-site:**

LARNAGOL LOT

Ruisseau de Treil Le Ruisseau, 46160
565312339 565219970
e-mail: lotcamping@wanadoo
website: www.lotcamping.com
A quiet site situated within a small valley with well-defined pitches and good leisure facilities.
0.6km E via D662.
300m E of Larnagol off D662 in direction of Cajarc
Open: May-Sep **Site:** 3.2HEC **Prices:** 3.90-5.60 pitch 5-7.10 (static)170-280 **Facilities:** **Services:** lau **Leisure:** P **Off-site:** R

LARUNS PYRÉNÉES-ATLANTIQUES

Gaves 64440 559053237 559054714
e-mail: campingdesgaves@wanadoo.fr
website: www.camping-desgaves.com
On the bank of the Gave d'Ossan amid beautiful Pyrenean scenery. Some pitches reserved for caravans.
1km S.
Open: All year **Site:** 2.5HEC **Prices:** 2.90-3.51 5.64-8.38 pitch 7.32-9.15 **Facilities:** **Services:** lau **Leisure:** R **Off-site:** P

LARUSCADE GIRONDE

Relais du Chavan 33620 557686305
On well-kept meadow edged by a strip of forest. Some traffic noise.
6.5km NW on N10 near Km20.3.
Open: 15 May-15 Sep **Site:** 3.6HEC **Prices:** 3 pitch 3.50 **Facilities:** **Services:** lau **Leisure:** P

LECTOURE GERS

Lac des Trois Vallées 32700 562688233 562688882
e-mail: lac.des.trois.vallees@wanadoo.fr
website: lac-des-3-vallees.com
This rural site is part of a large park and lies next to a lake. It has spacious marked pitches.
3km SE on N21.
Open: 14 May-12 Sep **Site:** 40HEC **Prices:** pitch 15-40 (incl 2 persons) **Facilities:** **Services:** lau **Leisure:** LP

LÉON LANDES

Airotel Lou Puntaou av du Lac, 40550
558487430 558487042
e-mail: reception@loupuntaou.com
website: www.loupuntaou.com
In oak wood with separate sections for caravans.
Turn off N652 in village and continue towards lake for 1.5km on D142.
Open: 2 Apr-2 Oct **Site:** 8HEC **Prices:** 3-5 pitch 15-37 (incl 2 persons) **Facilities:** **Services:** lau **Leisure:** P **Off-site:** LRS

St-Antoine St-Michel-Escalus, 40500
558487850 558487190
e-mail: campingstantoine@wanadoo.fr
A pleasant, well-equipped site beside a river in peaceful wooded surroundings.
Open: Mar-Sep **Site:** 6HEC **Prices:** 3 pitch 5 (static)119-366 **Facilities:** **Services:** lau **Leisure:** R

LESCAR PYRÉNÉES-ATLANTIQUES

Terrier av du Vert Galant, 64230
559810182 559812683
e-mail: camping.terrier@wanadoo.fr
On meadowland split in two with pitches surrounded by hedges in foreground.
From Pau take N117 towards Bayonne for 6.5km, then turn left onto D501 towards Monein to site towards bridge.
Open: All year **Site:** 4HEC **Prices:** 3.80-3.80 1.60 pitch 5-5 **Facilities:** **Services:** lau **Leisure:** P **Off-site:**

LINXE Landes

CM Le Grandjean rte de Mixe, 40260 ☎ 558429000
A modern site situated on the edge of a forest. Ideal for family holidays.
From the Castets road, take the D42 towards Linxe.
Open: 29 Jun-Aug **Site:** 2.7HEC **Prices:** 2.75 0.67 5.52 3.22 pitch 3.22 **Facilities:** **Services:** lau **Off-site:**

LIT-ET-MIXE Landes

Vignes rte du Cap de l'Homy, 40170
☎ 558428560 558427436
e-mail: contact@les-vignes.com
website: www.les-vignes.com
In a pine forest with good sanitary and sports facilities.
3km S via D652 and D89.
Open: Jun-15 Sep **Site:** 15HEC **Prices:** pitch 14.50-35 (incl 2 persons) (static)235-497 **Facilities:** **Services:** lau **Leisure:** P

LIVERS-CAZELLES Tarn

Rédon 81170 ☎ 563561464 563561464
e-mail: campingcampredon@wanadoo.fr
website: www.campredon.com
A quiet site with fine views over the surrounding area and good modern facilities.
4km SE of Cordes on D600.
Open: 28 Mar-30 Oct **Site:** 4HEC **Prices:** pitch 13.50 (static)250 **Facilities:** **Services:** lau **Leisure:** P

LOUPIAC Lot

Hirondelles ☎ 565376625 565376665
In a natural setting, in the heart of the Quercy region with a variety of recreational facilities.
3km N via N20.
Open: Apr-15 Sep **Site:** 2.5HEC **Prices:** pitch 15 pp4 **Facilities:** **Services:** lau **Leisure:** P

LOURDES Hautes-Pyrénées

Arrouach 9 r des Trois Archanges, Quartier Biscaye, 65100
☎ 562421143 562420527
e-mail: camping.arrouach@wanadoo.fr
In pleasant wooded surroundings on N outskirts.
Situated on D947 Soumoulou road.
Open: All year **Site:** 13HEC **Prices:** 3.50 2.10 2.10 2.10 pitch 4.20 **Facilities:** **Services:** lau **Off-site:** LPR

Domec rte de Julos, 65100 ☎ 562940879 562940879
Off N21 Tarbes road N of town centre.
Open: Etr-Oct **Site:** 2HEC **Prices:** 2.30 pitch 2.40 (static)275 **Facilities:** **Services:** lau **Off-site:** PR

LUZ-ST-SAUVEUR Hautes-Pyrénées

Bergons rte de Barèges, 65120 ☎ 562929077
e-mail: abordenave@club-internet.fr
In a beautiful setting on a level meadow surrounded by woodland close to the main Pyreneean ski resorts.
600m E on D618 Barèges road.
Open: 15 Dec-15 Oct **Site:** 1HEC **Prices:** 3 2.70 2.70 pitch 2.70 **Facilities:** **Services:** lau **Off-site:** PR

Eliane & Jean-Paul Petit
Camping
★★★
Les Hirondelles
46350 LOUPIAC - LOT
Quercy Périgord Lot
CAMPING ★★★ LES HIRONDELLES
"Al Pech" 46350 LOUPIAC
Tél. 05 65 37 66 25 - Fax 05 65 37 66 65
Camp.les-hirondelles@wanadoo.fr - www.les-hirondelles.com
FRANCE

Pyrénées International rte de Lourdes, 65120
☎ 562928202 562929687
e-mail: camping.international.luz@wanadoo.fr
In a wooded valley at an altitude of 700m with panoramic views of the surrounding mountains.
1.3km NW on N21.
Open: 15 Dec-20 Apr & Jun-Sep **Site:** 4HEC **Facilities:** **Services:** lau **Leisure:** P **Off-site:** R

Pyrénévasion rte de Luz-Ardiden, Sazos, 65120
☎ 562929154 562929834
e-mail: camping-pyrenevasion@wanadoo.fr
website: www.campingpyrenevasion.com
A quiet site in an idyllic mountain setting close to the ski-runs. The pitches are well defined and all facilities are clean and modern.
2km from town on Luz-Ardiden road.
Open: All year **Site:** 2HEC **Prices:** pitch 14 **Facilities:** **Services:** lau **Leisure:** P **Off-site:** R

MARCILLAC-ST-QUENTIN Dordogne

Tailladis 24200 ☎ 553591095 553294756
e-mail: tailladis@aol.com
website: www.tailladis.com
Well maintained family site with good recreational facilities.
2km N near D48.
Open: All year **Site:** 4HEC **Prices:** 3.08-4.95 pitch 4.19-6.45 **Facilities:** **Services:** lau **Leisure:** LP

MARTRES-TOLOSANE Haute-Garonne

Moulin 31220 ☎ 561988640 561986690
e-mail: info@campinglemoulin.com
website: www.campinglemoulin.com
In a beautiful wooded location beside the River Garonne at the foot of the Pyrénées. Well maintained, with a wide variety of recreational facilities.
1.5km SE off N117.
Open: Etr-Sep **Site:** 7HEC **Prices:** 4-5 pitch 4.80-6 (static)160-325 **Facilities:** **Services:** lau **Leisure:** PR **Off-site:** L

MAULÉON-LICHARRE Pyrénées-Atlantiques

Saison rte de Libarrenx, 64130 ☎ 559281879 559280623
e-mail: camping.uhaitza@wanadoo.fr
website: www.camping-uhaitza.com
A peaceful site beside the river, near the town centre.
1.5km S on D918.
Open: Mar-Nov **Site:** 1.1HEC **Prices:** 3.50 1.40 pitch 3.80 (static)240-295 **Facilities:** **Services:** lau **Leisure:** R **Off-site:** P

MESSANGES LANDES

Acacias rte d'Azur, Quartier Delest
☎ 558480178 📠 558482312
e-mail: lesacacias@lesacacias.com
website: www.lesacacias.com
Facilities: **Services:**

Albret Plage 40660 ☎ 558480367 📠 558482191
e-mail: albertplage@wanadoo.fr **website:** www.albertplage.fr
Site with direct access to beach (300m).
➲ *1km from town of Vieux Boucau.*
Open: Apr-Oct **Site:** 6HEC **Prices:** 3.90 1.70 4.70 4.70 **Facilities:** **Services:** lau **Leisure:** S **Off-site:** L

Côte rte de Vieux Boucau, 40660
☎ 558489494 📠 558489444
e-mail: lacote@wanadoo.fr
website: www.campinglacote.com
In a picturesque wooded area 1km from the beach.
➲ *2.3km S via D652.*
Open: Apr-Sep **Site:** 4HEC **Prices:** 2.30-3.20 pitch 8.60-13.40 (incl 2 persons) **Facilities:** **Services:** lau **Off-site:** LS

Moïsan rte de la Plage, 40660 ☎ 558489206 📠 558489206
website: www.camping-moisan.com
In a pine forest, 800m from the sea with good modern facilities.
Open: 15 May-Sep **Site:** 7HEC **Facilities:** **Services:** lau **Off-site:** PS

Vieux Port Plage Sud, 40660 ☎ 558482200 📠 558480169
e-mail: contact@levieuxport.com
website: www.levieuxport.com
A family site in the heart of the Landes forest with direct access to the beach. Good recreational facilities.
➲ *2.5 km SW via D652.*
Open: Apr-Sep **Site:** 30HEC **Prices:** 3.50-6 pitch 12-33 (incl 2 persons) (static)230-550 **Facilities:** **Services:** lau **Leisure:** PS **Off-site:** LR

MÉZOS LANDES

Sen Yan 40170 ☎ 558426005 📠 558426456
e-mail: reception@sen-yan.com **website:** www.sen-yan.com
A pleasant site in exotic tropical gardens, surrounded by a pine wood.
➲ *1km E.*
Open: Jun-15 Sep **Site:** 8HEC **Prices:** 5 16.50-31 3.15 **Facilities:** **Services:** lau **Leisure:** P **Off-site:** R

MIERS LOT

Pigeonnier 46500 ☎ 565337195 📠 565337195
e-mail: veronique.bouny@wanadoo.fr
website: www.campinglepigeonnier.com
Peaceful, shady site close to the River Dordogne amid some of France's most spectacular scenery.
➲ *400m E via D91.*
Open: Apr-15 Oct **Site:** 1HEC **Prices:** 3.51-3.90 pitch 3.51-3.90 (static)150-300 **Facilities:** **Services:** lau **Leisure:** P **Off-site:**

Site: 6HEC-Site size -grass -sand -stone -little shade -partly shaded -mainly shaded -bungalows for hire -caravans for hire -tents for hire -no dogs **Prices:** -adult per night -car per night pp-per person per night -caravan per night -tent per night (static)-caravan hire per week

MIMIZAN LANDES
AT MIMIZAN-PLAGE (6KM E BY D626)

CM de la Plage bd de l'Atlantique, 40200
558090032 558094494
e-mail: contact@nimizan-camping.com
website: www.nimizan-camping.com
Open: 15 Apr-Oct **Site:** 16HEC **Prices:** pitch 13-18 (incl 2 persons) **Facilities:** **Services:** lau **Off-site:** S

See advertisement on page 112

Marina-Landes 40202 558091266 558091640
e-mail: contact@clubmarina.com
website: www.marinalandes.com
In a pine wood. 500m from beach.
Take D626 from Mimizan Plage.
Open: 14 May-19 Sep **Site:** 9HEC **Prices:** 14-34 pitch 17-37 (incl 3 persons) (static)220-790 **Facilities:** **Services:** lau
Leisure: P **Off-site:** LRS

MIRANDOL-BOURGNOUNAC TARN

Clots Les Clots, 81190 563769278 563769278
e-mail: campclots@wanadoo.fr
website: www.campinglesclots.info
In a wooded area within the Viaur valley with good facilities.
5.5km N via D905, rte de Rieupeyroux.
Open: May-Sep **Site:** 7HEC **Prices:** 3.70-4.60 1-1.50 pitch 3.40-4.70 (static)225-280 **Facilities:** **Services:** lau **Leisure:** PR

MOLIÈRES DORDOGNE

Grande Veyière 24480 553632584 553631825
e-mail: la_grande_veyiere@wanadoo.fr
Wooded site with good sporting facilities in the heart of Périgord's bastides country.
2.4km SE.
Open: Apr-5 Nov **Site:** 4HEC **Facilities:** **Services:** lau **Leisure:** P

MOLIÈRES TARN-ET-GARONNE

Lac du Malivert Centre de Loisirs du Malivert, 82220
563677637 563676216
e-mail: molieres.82@wanadoo.fr
website: www.cdg82.fr/molieres
In a pleasant lakeside setting.
Approaching Molières from the S, head towards Centre de Loisirs and Lac Malivert.
Open: 15 Jun-15 Sep **Site:** 0.7HEC
Prices: 2.20 pitch 2.50 **Facilities:** **Services:** lau **Leisure:** L **Off-site:**

MOLIETS-PLAGE LANDES

Airotel St-Martin av de l'Océan, 40660
558485230 558485073
e-mail: contact@camping-saint-martin.fr
website: www.camping-saint-martin.fr
Large site on the Atlantic coast with direct access to the largest sandy beach in the region.
Between the village and the beach.
Open: Etr-Oct **Site:** 18.5HEC **Prices:** pitch 17-27.50 (incl 2 persons) **Facilities:** **Services:** lau **Leisure:** P **Off-site:** S

Cigales av de l'Océan, 40660 558485118 558483527
e-mail: camping-les-cigales@wanadoo.fr
website: www.camping-les-cigales.fr
On undulating ground in pine trees.
300m from beach.
Open: Apr-Sep **Site:** 23HEC **Prices:** 3.70-5.30 pitch 12.50-15.50 **Facilities:**
Services: lau **Off-site:** LRS

MONCRABEAU LOT-ET-GARONNE

CM Mouliat Le Nouliat, 47600 553654328 553652178
A small site in a wooded location on the banks of the River La Baïse.
On D219, 200m from D930.
Open: 15 Jun-15 Sep **Site:** 1.3HEC **Facilities:** **Services:** lau **Off-site:** PR

MONTAUBAN-DE-LUCHON HAUTE-GARONNE

Lanette 31110 561790038
On gently sloping ground surrounded by pastures.
1.5km E of Luchon. Off D27.
Open: All year **Site:** 4.3HEC **Facilities:** **Services:** lau **Off-site:** PR

MONTESQUIOU GERS

Château le Haget 32320 562709580 562709483
e-mail: info@lehaget.com
website: www.lehaget.com
In grounds of Château.
Open: Apr-Oct **Site:** 12HEC **Facilities:** **Services:** lau **Leisure:** P **Off-site:** LR

MONTIGNAC DORDOGNE

Moulin du Bleufond av Aristide Briand, 24290
553518395 553511992
e-mail: le.moulin.du.bleufond@wanadoo.fr
website: www.bleufond.com
Situated beside a river in the grounds of an ancient 17th-century mill.
0.5km off D65 Montignac-Sergeac road.
Open: Apr-15 Oct **Site:** 1.3HEC **Prices:** 3.75-4.90 pitch 4.20-5.60 **Facilities:** **Services:** lau
Leisure: P **Off-site:** R

MUSSIDAN DORDOGNE

CM Le Port 24400 553812009
Open: 15 Jun-15 Sep **Site:** 0.5HEC **Facilities:** **Services:** lau **Off-site:** PR

NAGES TARN

Rieu Montagné Lac du Laouzas, 81320
563372471 563371542
e-mail: rieumontagne@camping-indigo.com
website: www.camping-indigo.com
In a wooded location beside the Laouzas lake with good recreational facilities.
4.5km S via D62.
Open: 11 Jun-18 Sep **Site:** 9HEC **Prices:** 4.50-4.80 4-10 (static)179-590 **Facilities:**
Services: lau **Leisure:** P **Off-site:** L

OLORON-STE-MARIE PYRÉNÉES-ATLANTIQUES

Val du Gave-d'Aspe rte du Somport, GurmenÁon, 64400
559360507 559360052
e-mail: chalet.aspe@wanadoo.fr
website: www.chalet-aspe.com
A pleasant site situated in the Aspe valley amid picturesque Pyrenean scenery.
Open: 5 Dec-21 Oct **Site:** 0.5HEC **Prices:** 3 pitch 12-15 **Facilities:** **Services:** lau **Leisure:** P
Off-site: R

Facilities: -shop -shower -electric points for razors -electric points for caravans -parking by tents permitted -compulsory separate car park **Services:** -café/restaurant -bar -Camping Gaz International -gas other than Camping Gaz -first aid facilities lau-laundry **Leisure:** -swimming L-Lake P-Pool R-River S-Sea **Off-site:** All facilities within 2km

ONESSE-ET-LAHARIE LANDES

CM Bienvenu 259 route de Mimizan, 40110
558073049 558073078
A family site situated within a forest.
500m from village centre on D38.
Open: 15 Jun-15 Sep **Site:** 1.2HEC **Prices:** 2.65 1.43 2.25 2.20 **Facilities:** **Services:** lau **Off-site:** R

OUSSE PYRÉNÉES-ATLANTIQUES

Sapins 64320 559817421
Access via N117, exit Pau or A64, exit Soumoulou.
Open: All year **Site:** 1HEC **Prices:** 3 pitch 3.50 (static)110 **Facilities:** **Services:** lau **Off-site:**

PADIRAC LOT

Chênes rte du Gouffre, 46500
565336554 0565337155
e-mail: les_chenes@hotmail.com
website: www.campingleschenes.com
In a fine position in the centre of the Haute-Quercy with good facilities.
1.5km NE via D90 towards Gouffre.
Open: May-14 Sep **Site:** 5HEC **Prices:** 3-6.50 pitch 4-8 **Facilities:** **Services:** lau **Leisure:** P

PAMIERS ARIÈGE

Ombrages rte d'Escosse, 9100 561671224 561601823
A pleasant site in wooded surroundings beside the River Ariège, 1.5km from the town centre.
NW on D119 beside river.
Open: All year **Site:** 2.5HEC **Facilities:** **Services:** lau **Off-site:** PR

PAUILLAC GIRONDE

CM Les Gabarreys rte de la Rivière, 33250
556591003 556733068
e-mail: camping.les.gabarreys@wanadoo.fr
website: www.pauillac-medoc.com
A municipal site with good sports facilities.
S of town. Follow signs.
Open: 25 Mar-Oct **Site:** 2HEC **Prices:** pitch 11-12 (incl 2 persons) pp7.50-8 **Facilities:** **Services:** lau **Off-site:** P

PAYRAC LOT

Panoramic rte de Loupiac, 46350
565379845 565379165
e-mail: camping.panoramic@wanadoo.fr
A peaceful family site 5km from the River Dordogne with good recreational facilities.
Off N20 N of Payrac.
Open: All year **Site:** 1.5HEC **Prices:** 2.50-2.80 pitch 3-4 (static)100-210 **Facilities:** **Services:** lau **Off-site:** P

Pins rte de Cahors, 46350 565379632 565379108
e-mail: info@les-pins-camping.com
website: www.les-pins-camping.com
A well-managed site, partly in forest, partly on meadowland. Sheltered from traffic noise.
S of village off N20. A20, *exit 55 from Paris.*
Open: Apr-Sep **Site:** 3.5HEC **Prices:** 2.75-5.50 4.20-8.40 pitch 7-11 (static)215-695 **Facilities:** **Services:** lau **Leisure:** P **Off-site:**

PÉRIGUEUX DORDOGNE

Barnabé 80 r des Bains, Boulazac, 24750
553534145 553541662
A well-appointed site in a wooded park-like location beside the river.
Signed from N89, 2km E of town centre.
Open: All year **Site:** 1.5HEC **Facilities:** **Services:** lau **Off-site:** P

PETIT-PALAIS GIRONDE

Pressoir Queyrai Petit-Palais, 33570
557697325 557697736
e-mail: camping.le.pressoir@wanadoo.fr
website: www.campinglepressoir.com
An old farm in the rolling countryside around St-Emilion.
On N89 Bordeaux-Périgeux road, exit at St-Médard de Guizières & follow signs.
Open: Apr-Sep **Site:** 2HEC **Prices:** pitch 6.90-9.90 pp6 (static)380 **Facilities:** **Services:** lau **Leisure:** P

PEZULS DORDOGNE

Forêt 24510 553227169 553237779
e-mail: camping.laforet@wanadoo.fr
website: www.camping-dordogne.com/la-foret
In extensive grounds on the edge of the forest with modern facilities.
600m off D703. 3km from the village centre.
Open: Apr-Oct **Site:** 9HEC **Prices:** 3.80-4.80 pitch 3.50-4.50 **Facilities:** **Services:** lau **Leisure:** P

PONT-ST-MAMET DORDOGNE

Lestaubière Pont-St-Mamet, 24140
553829815 553829017
e-mail: lestaubiere@cs.com
website: www.lestaubiere.com
Peaceful and secluded site in attractive part of the Dordogne, occupying the former outbuildings and wooded grounds of the adjacent château. Site commands fine views of the surrounding countryside.
Off N21. Between Perigueux and Bergerac on RN21, take exit Pont-St-Mamet, 500m N of Pont-St-Mamet is the campsite.
Open: 26 Apr-1 Oct **Site:** 22HEC **Prices:** 4.70-5.40 pitch 6.90-8 (static)360-420 **Facilities:** **Services:** lau **Leisure:** LP

PUYBRUN LOT

Sole 46130 565385237 565109109
e-mail: la-sole@wanadoo.fr
website: www.la-sole.com
A well-run site in pleasant wooded surroundings with good facilities.
On D703 leave village in the direction of Bretenoux and take the first turning after the garage.
Open: Apr-Sep **Site:** 3HEC **Facilities:** **Services:** lau **Leisure:** P **Off-site:** LR

PUY-L'ÉVÊQUE LOT
AT MONTCABRIER (7 KM NW)

Moulin de Laborde 46700 565246206 565365133
e-mail: moulindelaborde@wanadoo.fr
website: www.moulindelaborde.com
Well equipped site surrounded by woods and hills, in a picturesque valley on the River Thèze.

NW off D673.
Open: May-14 Sep **Site:** 9HEC **Prices:** 5.50 pitch 7.50 **Facilities:** **Services:** lau **Leisure:** LPR **Off-site:**

PYLA-SUR-MER GIRONDE

Dune rte de Biscarrosse, 33260 556227217 556227217
e-mail: campingdeladune@wanadoo.fr
website: www.campingdeladune.fr
A beautifully situated and quiet site partly on terraced sandy fields. Opposite a dune of over 100m in height, which separates the site from the sea.
Follow the road between Pilat-Plage.
Open: May-Sep **Site:** 6HEC **Prices:** pitch 15-26 (incl 2 persons) **Facilities:** **Services:** lau **Leisure:** P **Off-site:** S

Forêt rte de Biscarrosse, 33115 556227328 556227050
e-mail: camping.foret@wanadoo.fr
website: www.campinglaforet.fr
A well-equipped site surrounded by pine trees and with direct access to the fine sandy beaches at the mouth of the Arcachon Basin. There are good sporting facilities and evening entertainment is provided on a regular basis.
Access via N250 then D218.
Open: Apr-Oct **Site:** 12HEC **Facilities:** **Services:** lau **Leisure:** PS

Panorama rte de Biscarrosse, 33260
556221044 556221012
e-mail: mail@camping-panorama.com
website: www.camping-panorama.com
Partially terraced site amongst dunes, on the edge of the 100m high Dune de Pyla. Views of the sea from some pitches.
On the D218. Signed.
Open: 25 Apr-Oct **Site:** 15HEC
Prices: 3.50-8 pitch 8-17 (static)150-441 **Facilities:** **Services:** lau **Leisure:** PS

Pyla rte de Biscarrosse, 33115 556227456
e-mail: pylacamping@free.fr
website: www.pyla-camping.com
A well-equipped family site with good recreational facilities and direct access to the sea.
Open: May-Sep **Site:** 8HEC **Facilities:** **Services:** lau **Leisure:** PS

Sunêlia Petit Nice rte de Biscarrosse, 33115
556227403 556221431
e-mail: camping.petit.nice@wanadoo.fr
website: www.petitnice.com
Sandy terraced site, mainly suitable for tents; in parts sloping steeply in pine woodland. Paths and standings are strengthened with timber. 220 steps down to the beach.
6 km S on D218.
Open: Apr-Sep **Site:** 5.5HEC **Facilities:** **Services:** lau **Leisure:** PS

RAUZAN GIRONDE

Vieux Château Route Départementale 123, 33420
557841538 557841834
e-mail: hoekstra.camping@wanadoo.fr
website: www.vieux-chateau.com
A family site situated in a peaceful valley surrounded by vineyards and overlooked by the ruined 12th-century Rauzan castle.
200m N, 1.5km from N670.
Open: Apr-Oct **Site:** 2.5HEC **Prices:** pitch 11-15 **Facilities:** **Services:** lau **Leisure:** P **Off-site:**

Facilities: -shop -shower -electric points for razors -electric points for caravans -parking by tents permitted -compulsory separate car park **Services:** -café/restaurant -bar -Camping Gaz International -gas other than Camping Gaz -first aid facilities lau-laundry **Leisure:** -swimming L-Lake P-Pool R-River S-Sea **Off-site:** All facilities within 2km

Reyrevignes Lot

Papillon 46320 565401240 565401718
e-mail: info@domaine-papillon.com
website: www.domaine-papillon.com
In a wooded park in the heart of the Haut-Quercy region with good, modern facilities.
Access via N653.
Open: Apr-Oct **Site:** 3HEC **Prices:** 2.80-4 pitch 3.50-5 **Facilities:** **Services:** lau **Leisure:** P **Off-site:** LR

Rocamadour Lot

Cigales 46500 565336444 565336960
e-mail: camping.cigales@wanadoo.fr
website: www.camping-cigales.com
A peaceful, well-equipped site with shaded pitches and good, modern facilities. Fine views of Rocamadour.
Open: 21 Jun-Aug **Site:** 3HEC **Facilities:** **Services:** lau **Leisure:** P

Relais du Campeur l'Hospitalet 46500 565336328
Shady, level site with well-marked pitches and good facilities. Fine views of Rocamadour.
On D36.
Open: Apr-Sep **Site:** 1.7HEC **Facilities:** **Services:** lau **Leisure:** P **Off-site:**

Roche-Chalais, La Dordogne

Gerbes r de la Dronne, 24490 553914065 553903201
e-mail: camping.la.roche.chalais@wanadoo.fr
Well appointed family site on banks of River Dronne.
Off D674 in village centre. Signed.
Open: 15 Apr-Sep **Site:** 3.5HEC **Prices:** 2.10 pitch 2.60 (static)160 **Facilities:** **Services:** lau **Leisure:** R **Off-site:** P

Romieu, La Gers

Camp de Florence 32480 562281558 562282004
e-mail: info@campdeflorence.com
website: www.campdeflorence.com
Well equipped site in rural surroundings.
Take D931 in direction Agen-Condom. 3km before Condom turn left to La Romieu.
Open: Apr-9 Oct **Site:** 15HEC **Prices:** pitch 15-27.50 (incl 2 persons) (static)215-630 **Facilities:** **Services:** lau **Leisure:** P **Off-site:**

Roquefort Landes

CM de Nauton Cité Nauton, 40120
558455046 558455363
A small municipal site with good facilities.
1.6km N via D932 towards Bordeaux.
Open: Jun-Aug **Site:** 1.4HEC **Prices:** 2.31 3.36 2.63 pitch 2.63 **Facilities:** **Services:** **Off-site:** PR

Roquelaure Gers

Talouch 32810 562655243 562655368
e-mail: info@camping-talouch.com
website: www.camping-talouch.com
A family site in picturesque wooded surroundings, situated in the heart of Gascony. There are fine sports and entertainment facilities.
Access via N21 and D148.
Open: Apr-Sep **Site:** 9HEC **Prices:** pitch 13.30-21 (incl 2 persons) pp3.90-6.10 **Facilities:** **Services:** lau **Leisure:** P

Rouffignac Dordogne

Cantegrel 24580 553054830 553052787
e-mail: infos@camping-bleusoleil.com
website: www.camping-bleusoleil.com
In a peaceful location in the heart of the Périgord Noir, with good recreational facilities.
1.5km N via D31, rte de Thenon.
Open: Apr-1 Oct **Site:** 60HEC **Prices:** 2.20-3.70 pitch 5.20-6.80 (static)130-345 **Facilities:** **Services:** lau **Leisure:** P **Off-site:**

St-Antoine-de-Breuilh Dordogne

Riviere Fleurie St Aulaye, 24230
553248280 553248280
e-mail: info@la-riviere-fleurie.com
website: www.la-riviere-fleurie.com
Access via D936. Take a right turn before the village and travel 3kms in the direction of the Dordogne.
Open: Apr-Sep **Site:** 2.4HEC **Prices:** 4-5 pitch 12.80-16 (incl 2 persons) (static)140-330 **Facilities:** **Services:** lau **Leisure:** PR

St-Antonin-Noble-Val Tarn-et-Garonne

Trois Cantons 82140 563319857 563312593
e-mail: info@3cantons.fr
website: www.3cantons.fr
Divided into pitches, partly on sloping ground within an oak forest. Separate section for teenagers.
8.5km NW near D926. Signed.
Open: 15 Apr-Sep **Site:** 15HEC **Prices:** 4.10-5.35 pitch 4.80-6.70 (static)255-395 **Facilities:** **Services:** lau **Leisure:** P

St-Bertrand-de-Comminges Haute-Garonne

Es Pibous chemin de St-Just, 31510
561883142 561956383
A quiet, shaded site in an elevated position with good facilities.
Open: All year **Site:** 1.8HEC **Prices:** 3.66 pitch 3.50 (static)200 **Facilities:** **Services:** lau **Leisure:** P **Off-site:** LR

St-Céré Lot

CM de Soulhol quai A-Salesse, 46400
565381237 565381237
e-mail: info@campinglesoulhol.com
website: www.campingsoulhol.com
A family site bordered by two rivers with good recreational facilities.
200m SE on D940.
Open: May-Sep **Site:** 4HEC **Prices:** 3.80-4.20 pitch 4.10 **Facilities:** **Services:** lau **Leisure:** R **Off-site:** P

St-Cirq Dordogne

Brin d'Amour Saint Cirq, 24260
553072373 553072373
e-mail: brindamour2@wanadoo.fr
website: www.campings-dordogne.com/brindamour
In a fine location overlooking the Vézère valley with good facilities.
Open: Apr-10 Oct **Site:** 3.8HEC **Prices:** 3.40-4.20 4.20-5 pitch 4.20-5 (static)240-450 **Facilities:** **Services:** lau **Leisure:** P **Off-site:** LR

ST-CIRQ-LAPOPIE Lot

Plage 46330 ☎ 565302951 565302333
e-mail: camping-laplage@wanadoo.fr
website: www.la-plage-camping.com
In an ideal location beside the River Lot with well-defined pitches and good, modern facilities. Boat and bicycle hire available.
Access via D41 from N or D42 from S.
Open: All year **Site:** 3HEC **Prices:** 5 pitch 5-6 (static)305 **Facilities:** **Services:** lau **Leisure:** R **Off-site:**

ST-CRICQ Gers

Lac de Thoux 32440 ☎ 562657129 562657481
e-mail: lacdethoux@cacg.fr
A family site with good facilities situated on the edge of the lake, 50m from the beach.
On D654 between Cologne and L'Isle Jourdain.
Open: Apr-15 Oct **Site:** 3HEC **Facilities:** **Services:** lau **Leisure:** LP

ST-CYBRANET Dordogne

Bel Ombrage 24250 ☎ 553283414 553596464
e-mail: belombrage@wanadoo.fr
website: www.belombrage.com
Quiet holiday site in wooded valley.
Open: Jun-5 Sep **Site:** 6HEC **Facilities:** **Services:** lau **Leisure:** PR **Off-site:**

ST-CYPRIEN Dordogne

Ferme de Campagnac Castels, 24220
☎ 553292603 553292603
e-mail: maboureau@tiscali.fr
website: www.campagnac.fr.tc
A quiet site situated 200m from the farm in a sheltered position.
Access from town on D25. Signed.
Open: Apr-Oct **Site:** 0.8HEC **Prices:** 2 20 pitch 5 (static)140 **Facilities:** **Services:** lau **Off-site:**

CM Garrit 24220 ☎ 553292056 553292056
e-mail: pbecheau@aol.com
website: www.campingdugarritendordogneperigord.com
In a peaceful location beside the River Dordogne with safe bathing.
1.5km S on D48.
Open: May-15 Sep **Site:** 2HEC **Prices:** pitch 11-13.50 (incl 2 persons) (static)240-500 **Facilities:** **Services:** lau **Leisure:** PR **Off-site:** R

Plage Vezac, 24220 ☎ 553295083 553303163
Modest but attractive site in a pleasant riverside setting.
Access via D703 beyond La Roque Gageac.
Open: Apr-Sep **Site:** 3.5HEC **Prices:** 3.25-4.05 2-2.40 pitch 2-2.40 **Facilities:** **Services:** lau **Leisure:** PR **Off-site:**

ST-ÉMILION Gironde

Barbanne route de Montagne, 33330
☎ 57247580 57246968
e-mail: barbanne@wanadoo.fr
website: www.camping-saint-emilion.com
In a peaceful country setting among vineyards, close to a 5-hectare lake.
3km N via D122.
Open: Apr-19 Sep **Site:** 10HEC **Facilities:** **Services:** lau **Leisure:** LPR

BASQUE COAST
Le CAMPING ATLANTICA
SAINT-JEAN-DE-LUZ
The ideal place for family holidays that combine the pleasures of both the sea and the mountain.
You will find many kinds of entertainment, an aquatic park, quality services and catering.
F-64500 Saint-Jean-de-Luz / Phone: +33 (0)5 59 47 72 44

ST-GENIES Dordogne

Bouquerie 24590 ☎ 553289822 553291975
e-mail: labouquerie@wanadoo.fr
website: www.labouquerie.com
A family site in wooded surroundings with a good variety of facilities.
N of village on D704.
Open: 10 Apr-25 Sep **Site:** 8HEC **Facilities:** **Services:** lau **Leisure:** LP

ST-GIRONS Ariège

Pont du Nert rte de Lacourt (D33), 09200 ☎ 561665848
e-mail: dmmadre@aol.com
Grassy site between road and woodland.
3km SE at the junction of the D33 and the D3.
Open: Jun-15 Sep **Site:** 1.5HEC **Prices:** 3.50 2 2
Facilities: **Off-site:** R

ST-JEAN-DE-LUZ Pyrénées-Atlantiques

Atlantica Quartier Acotz, 64500 ☎ 559477244 559547227
e-mail: camping.atlantica@wanadoo.fr
website: www.campingatlantica.com
A family site with good facilities close to the Spanish border at the foot of the Pyrénées and only 500m from the beach.
Leave N10 at St-Jean-de-Luz Nord exit and continue towards Biarritz. Site 1km on left.
Open: 15 Mar-Sep **Site:** 3.5HEC **Prices:** pitch 14-23 (incl 2 persons) pp3-5 **Facilities:** **Services:** lau **Leisure:** P **Off-site:** S

Ferme d'Erromardie 64500
☎ 559263426 559512602
Site is situated by the sea and consists of several sections divided by roads and low hedges. Take away food.
If approached from N to N10, cross railway bridge and turn immediately right and follow signs.
Open: 15 Mar-15 Oct **Site:** 2HEC **Prices:** pitch 11-18.50 (incl 2 persons) **Facilities:** **Services:** lau **Leisure:** RS **Off-site:**

Iratzia ☎ 559261489 559266969
1km NE off N10. Leave autoroute, signed St-Jean-de-Luz Nord and follow directions for Plage d'Erromardie.
Open: May-Sep **Site:** 4HEC **Facilities:** **Services:** lau **Off-site:** S

Tamaris Plage quartier d'Acotz, 64500
☎ 559265590 559477015
e-mail: tamaris1@wanadoo.fr
website: www.tamaris-plage.com
Level family site with good facilities divided into sections by drives and hedges.

contd.

Signed from N10 towards the sea.
Open: Apr-Sep **Site:** 1.3HEC **Facilities:** **Services:** lau **Off-site:** S

AT SOCOA (3KM SW)

Juantcho rte de la Corniche, 64122
559471197 559471197
e-mail: camping@juantcho.com
website: www.juantcho.com
2km W on D912.
Open: 10 Apr-Sep & Oct-Mar **Site:** 6HEC
Facilities: **Services:** lau
Off-site: RS

ST-JEAN-PIED-DE-PORT PYRÉNÉES-ATLANTIQUES

Narbaïtz rte de Bayonne, Ascarat, 64220
559371013 559372142
e-mail: camping-narbaitz@wanadoo.fr
website: www.camping-narbaitz.com
A quiet, comfortable site beside the River Berroua.
2km NW towards Bayonne.
Open: 15 Mar-Sep **Site:** 2.5HEC **Facilities:** **Services:** lau **Leisure:** PR **Off-site:**

ST-JULIEN-EN-BORN LANDES

Lette Fleurie 40170 558427409 558424151
e-mail: mairie40170@wanadoo.fr
On undulating ground in a pine wood with good facilities, 5 minutes from the beach.
Open: Apr-Sep **Site:** 18HEC **Prices:** 3.45 1.30 3.50 3.50 **Facilities:**
Services: lau **Leisure:** P **Off-site:** R

ST-JUSTIN LANDES

Pin rte de Roquefort, 40240 558448891 358448891
e-mail: camping.lepin@wanadoo.fr
website: www.campinglepin.com
A quiet family site beside the lake. Bar and café open May to 15 September only.
2.3km N on D626.
Open: Apr-Sep **Site:** 3HEC **Prices:** 3-4.50 1.50 pitch 5-8 (static)175-380 **Facilities:**
Services: lau **Leisure:** P **Off-site:**

ST-LÉON-SUR-VÉZÈRE DORDOGNE

Paradis 24290 553507264 553507590
e-mail: le-paradis@perigord.com
website: www.le-paradis.com
Situated on the river bank in the picturesque Vézère valley.
S of village off D706 Les Éyzies road.
Open: 19 Mar-25 Oct **Site:** 7HEC **Prices:** 4.90-6.95 pitch 7.60-10.90 (static)205-755 **Facilities:** **Services:** lau **Leisure:** PR

AT TURSAC (7KM SW)

Pigeonnier 24620 553069690 553069690
e-mail: campinglepigeonnier@wanadoo.fr
website: www.campinglepigeonnier.fr.fm
A small, peaceful site in the heart of the Dordogne countryside.
Acces via D706 between Le Moustier and Les Éyzies.
Open: Jun-Sep **Site:** 1.1HEC **Prices:** 3.80 pitch 4.80 (static)270 **Facilities:** **Services:**
lau **Leisure:** P **Off-site:** R

Vézère Périgord route de Montignac, 24620
553069631 553067966
website: www.le-vezere-perigord.com
A well-equipped site in wooded surroundings close to the river.

0.8km NE on D706.
Open: Etr-Oct **Site:** 6HEC **Facilities:**
Services: lau **Leisure:** P **Off-site:** R

ST-MARTIN-DE-SEIGNANX LANDES

Lou P'tit Poun 40390 559565579 559565371
e-mail: ptitpoun@club-internet.fr
website: www.les-campings.com/lou-ptit-poun
A quiet site with well-defined pitches on terraces.
Access via A63 exit Bayonne Nord towards Pau.
Open: Jun-15 Sep **Site:** 7HEC **Prices:** 5-6.10 10-22.50 **Facilities:** **Services:**
lau **Leisure:** P

ST-MARTORY HAUTE-GARONNE

CM rte de St-Girons, 31360 561981465
e-mail: cccsm@wanadoo.fr
website: www.jetitespyrenees.com
Open: 15 Jun-15 Sep **Site:** **Prices:** 5.20 **Facilities:** **Services:** lau **Off-site:** R

ST-NICOLAS-DE-LA-GRAVE TARN-ET-GARONNE

Plan d'Eau Base de Plein Air, et de Loisirs, 82210
563955002 563955001
e-mail: basedeloisirs.stnicolas@cg82.fr
2.5km N via D15.
Open: 15 Jun-15 Sep **Site:** 1.5HEC **Prices:** pitch 9.10 (incl 2 persons) **Facilities:** **Services:** lau
Off-site: LPR

ST-PARDOUX-LA-RIVIÈRE DORDOGNE

Château le Verdoyer 24470 553569464 553563870
e-mail: chateau@verdoyer.fr
website: www.verdoyer.fr
A small, well-equipped site in the grounds of a restored castle.
3km N via D96.
Open: 23 Apr-15 Oct **Site:** 25HEC
Prices: 5-6 pitch 8-14.40 (static)300-600 **Facilities:** **Services:** lau **Leisure:** LP

ST-PAUL-LES-DAX LANDES

Pins du Soleil RD459, 40990 558913791 558910024
e-mail: pinsoleil@aol.com
website: www.pinsoleil.com
On a hotel complex with good modern facilities.
SW via D954.
Open: 2 Apr-29 Oct **Site:** 6HEC **Prices:** 3.50 pitch 15-23 (incl 2 persons) (static)265-671 **Facilities:** **Services:** lau **Leisure:** P **Off-site:** LRS

ST-PÉE-SUR-NIVELLE PYRÉNÉES-ATLANTIQUES

Goyetchea 64310 559541959
e-mail: c-goyetchea@wanadoo.fr
website: www.camping-goyetchea.com
Quiet, peaceful site in a wooded location at the foot of the Pyrénées.
0.8km N on rte d'Ahetze.
Open: Jun-17 Sep **Site:** 3HEC **Prices:** 3-4 pitch 12.70-17.70 (incl 2 persons) **Facilities:**
Services: lau **Leisure:** P **Off-site:** R

Ibarron 64310 559541043
e-mail: campingdibarron@wanadoo.fr
website: www.camping-ibarron.com
In a pleasant wooded location with level pitches and good, modern facilities.

2km W on D918.
Open: May-Sep **Site:** 2.9HEC **Prices:** 2.85-3.90 pitch 4.15-5.70 (static)160-330 **Facilities:** **Services:** lau **Leisure:** PR **Off-site:** LPR

ST-PIERRE-LAFEUILLE LOT

Graves 46090 565368312 565368312
e-mail: infos@camping-lesgraves.com
website: www.camping-lesgraves.com
On a small hill on the northern outskirts of the village providing fine views over the surrounding countryside.
10km N of Cahors.
Open: Apr-10 Oct **Site:** 1HEC **Prices:** 3-3.75 pitch 4-5 **Facilities:** **Services:** lau **Leisure:** P **Off-site:**

Quercy-Vacances Le Mas de Lacombe, 46090
565368715 565360239
e-mail: quercyvacances@wanadoo.fr
website: www.quercyvacances.com
A well-equipped site in pleasant wooded surroundings.
On N20. 12km N of Cahors.
Open: May-Sep **Site:** 3HEC **Facilities:** **Services:** lau **Leisure:** P **Off-site:** LR

ST-RÉMY-SUR-LIDOIRE DORDOGNE

Tuilière 24700 553824729 553824729
e-mail: la-tuiliere@wanadoo.fr
website: www.campinglatuiliere.com
In pleasant wooded surroundings beside a lake. Separate car park for arrivals after 22.00.
6km from Montpon on D708 towards Ste-Foy-la-Grande.
Open: May-15 Sep **Site:** 8HEC **Prices:** 2.50-3.10 pitch 3.60-4.50 (static)155-310 **Facilities:** **Services:** lau **Leisure:** LP

ST-SERNIN-DE-DURAS LOT-ET-GARONNE

Moulin de Borie Neuve 47120 553207073
e-mail: info@borieneuve.com
website: www.borieneuve.com
A pleasant site in the Dourdèze valley close to an old mill.
Access via D244 towards St-Astier-de-Duras.
Open: 15 May-15 Oct **Site:** 1HEC **Facilities:** **Services:** lau **Leisure:** PR **Off-site:** L

ST-SEURIN-DE-PRATS DORDOGNE

Plage 24230 553586107 553586107
In a peaceful, wooded setting beside the Dordogne with a variety of recreational facilities.
0.7kms on D11.
Open: May-Sep **Site:** 4.5HEC **Prices:** 4.50 pitch 15 (incl 2 persons) **Facilities:** **Services:** lau **Leisure:** PR **Off-site:**

STE-EULALIE-EN-BORN LANDES

Bruyères chemin Laffont, 40200 558097336 558097558
e-mail: bonjour@camping-les-bruyeres.com
website: www.camping-les-bruyeres.com
In the middle of the Landes forest close to the lakes and the sea.
2.5km N via D652.
Open: 14 May-29 Sep **Site:** 3HEC **Facilities:** **Services:** lau **Leisure:** P **Off-site:** LR

SALIGNAC DORDOGNE

Les Peneyrals Le Poujol, St-Crépin Carlucet, 24590
553288571 553288099
e-mail: camping.peneyrals@wanadoo.fr
website: www.peneyrals.com
Quiet site among trees between the Vézère and Dordogne rivers.
10 km N of Sarlat on D60.
Open: 14 May-10 Sep **Site:** 12HEC **Prices:** 4.30-6.90 pitch 6.10-9.90 (static)210-690 **Facilities:** **Services:** lau **Leisure:** P

SALLES GIRONDE

Val de l'Eyre 8 rte de Minoy, 33770
556884703 556884727
e-mail: levaldeleyre@free.fr
website: www.valdeleyre.com
A well-equipped family site in a pleasant wooded location between the Landes forests and the Bordeaux vineyards.
SW on D108, rte de Lugos.
Open: Apr-15 Oct **Site:** 13HEC **Prices:** 11-17 **Facilities:** **Services:** lau **Leisure:** PR **Off-site:** P

SALLES LOT-ET-GARONNE

Bastides 47150 553408309 553408176
e-mail: info@campingdesbastides.com
website: www.campingdesbastides.com
In peaceful wooded surroundings overlooking the Lède Valley with good sporting and entertainment facilities.
1km N via D150.
Open: Etr-Sep **Site:** 6HEC **Prices:** pitch 12-21 (incl 2 persons) pp4-5.25 **Facilities:** **Services:** lau **Leisure:** P

SARLAT-LA-CANÉDA DORDOGNE

Maillac Ste-Nathalène, 24200 553592212 553296017
e-mail: campingmaillac@wanadoo.fr
website: www.campingmaillac.fr
In wooded surroundings in the heart of the Périgord Noir region with good facilities for a family holiday. Separate car park for arrivals after 23.00.
7km NE on D47.
Open: 15 May-Oct **Site:** 6HEC **Prices:** 4.60 pitch 6.50 **Facilities:** **Services:** lau **Leisure:** P **Off-site:** LR

Moulin du Roch rte des Éyzies, Le Roch, 24200
553592027 553592095
e-mail: moulin.du.roch@wanadoo.fr
website: www.moulin-du-roch.com
In a picturesque location between the Dordogne and Vézère valleys.
10km NW via D704-D6-D47.
Open: 30 Apr-18 Sep **Site:** 8HEC **Prices:** 3-7.50 pitch 13.50-25 (incl 2 persons) **Facilities:** **Services:** lau **Leisure:** P

Périères 24203 553590584 553285751
e-mail: les-perieres@wanadoo.fr
website: www.lesperieres.com
Very well-kept terraced site situated in 5 hectares of parkland and woods in the heart of the Périgord Noir with fine views over the Sarlat valley. There are good recreational facilities and modern, well-equipped bungalows are available for hire.
1km N of town on D47.
Open: Etr-Sep **Site:** 11HEC **Prices:** 5.80 pitch 18.20-28.50 **Facilities:** **Services:** lau **Leisure:** P **Off-site:**

Val d'Ussel La Fond d'Ussel, 24200
☎ 553592873 📠 553293825
e-mail: valdussel@online.fr
website: www.valdussel.com
A well-equipped site in woodland in the heart of the Périgord Noir region. Separate car park for late arrivals.
➲ *Off D704 or D56.*
Open: 8 May-25 Sep **Site:** 7HEC ▥ ♣ ⌂ ▲ **Prices:** 🚶3.25-6.25 pitch 4.50-8.50 🚐 (static)135-620 **Facilities:** 🚿 🚾 ⊙ 🚐 ⧈ **Services:** 🍷 ✕ lau **Leisure:** 🏊P

AT CARSAC-AILLAC (7KM SE VIA D704A)

Aqua Viva 24200 ☎ 553314600 📠 553293637
e-mail: aqua-viva@perigord.com
website: www.aquaviva.fr
Site with numerous terraces in beautiful wooded surroundings in the heart of the Dordogne.
➲ *Along the main road Sarlat/Souillac D704A.*
Open: 16 Apr-24 Sep **Site:** 11HEC ▥ ⁙ ◔ ♣ ⌂
Prices: 🚶3.90-6.40 pitch 4.80-9.50 **Facilities:** 🚿 🚾 ⊙ 🚐 ⊘ ⧈
Services: 🍷 ✕ ⊞ lau **Leisure:** 🏊LP **Off-site:** 🏊R

Rocher de la Cave 24200 ☎ 553281426 📠 553282710
e-mail: rocher.de.la-cave@wanadoo.fr
website: www.rocherdelacave.com
Pleasant family site on level meadow beside the Dordogne, set in beautiful countryside.
➲ *Access via D703 & D704.*
Open: 15May-15 Sep **Site:** 4HEC ▥ ⁙ ♣ ⌂ 🚐 ▲
Prices: 🚶3.60-4.50 pitch 4.72-5.90 🚐 (static)160-260
Facilities: 🚿 🚾 ⊙ 🚐 ⊘ ⧈ **Services:** 🍷 ✕ ⊞ lau **Leisure:** 🏊PR

SAUVETERRE-DE-BÉARN PYRÉNÉES-ATLANTIQUES

CM Gave av de la Gare, 64390 ☎ 559385330
➲ *Turn left before bridge on St-Palais road.*
Open: Jun-Sep **Site:** 1.5HEC ▥ ◔ **Facilities:** 🚿 ⊙ 🚐 ⧈
Services: ⊞ lau **Leisure:** 🏊R **Off-site:** 🚾 🍷 ✕ ⊘ ⩝

SAUVETERRE-LA-LÉMANCE LOT-ET-GARONNE

Moulin du Périé rte de Loubejac, 47500 ☎ 553406726
In a wooded valley close to an 18th-century watermill with good, modern facilities.
➲ *3km E of town off D710. Follow signs from the entrance to the village and keep to the valley road.*
Open: Apr-Sep **Site:** 5HEC ▥ ♣ ⌂ 🚐 ▲ **Facilities:** 🚿 🚾 ⊙ 🚐 ⊘ ⩝ ⧈ **Services:** 🍷 ✕ ⊞ lau **Leisure:** 🏊PR **Off-site:** 🏊L

SEIGNOSSE LANDES

Chevreuils rte de Hossegor, 40510
☎ 558433280 📠 558433280
e-mail: chevreuils@wanadoo.fr
website: www.chevreuils.com
In a pine forest close to the sea with good recreational facilities.
➲ *On CD79 rte de Hossegor.*
Open: Jun-15 Sep **Site:** 8HEC ▥ ⁙ ♣ ⌂ 🚐
Prices: 🚶3.40-5 12-18 🚐 (static)168-434 **Facilities:** 🚿 🚾 ⊙ 🚐 ⊘ ⩝ ⧈ **Services:** 🍷 ✕ ⊞ lau **Leisure:** 🏊P **Off-site:** 🏊S

CM Hourn Naou av des Tucs, 40510
☎ 558433030 📠 558416421
e-mail: camping.municipal@ville-seignosse.fr
Very clean and tidy site situated in a pine forest 600m from the sea.
➲ *200m from Seignosse town centre.*
Open: 6 Apr-Sep **Site:** 16HEC ⁙ ◔ ⌂ **Facilities:** 🚿 🚾 ⊙ 🚐 ⊘ ⧈ 🅿 **Services:** 🍷 ✕ ⊞ lau **Off-site:** ⩝ 🏊LPS

Oyats rte de la Plage des Casenres, 40510
☎ 558433794 📠 0558432329
e-mail: cployats@atciat.com
website: www.campeoles.fr
Level site, subdivided into fields and surrounded by woodland. Separate section for young people. Children's play area.
➲ *Turn off D79 in N outskirts towards Plage des Casernes.*
Open: 11 May-15 Sep **Site:** 17HEC ⁙ ♣ ⌂ ▲ **Prices:** pitch 10.30-20.40 (incl 2 persons) **Facilities:** 🚿 🚾 ⊙ 🚐 ⊘ ⧈
Services: 🍷 ✕ ⊞ lau **Leisure:** 🏊P **Off-site:** 🏊S

AT SEIGNOSSE-LE-PENON (5KM W)

Forêt 40510 ☎ 558416850 📠 558432326
A pleasant, quiet site 300m from the sea.
Open: 29 Jun-2 Sep **Site:** 11HEC ⁙ ♣ ⌂ 🚫🐕 **Facilities:** 🚿 ⊙ 🚐 🅿 **Services:** 🍷 ✕ ⊞ lau **Leisure:** 🏊P **Off-site:** 🚾 ⊘ ⩝ 🏊LS

SEIX ARIÈGE

Haut Salat 09140 ☎ 561668178 📠 561669417
e-mail: camping.le-haut-salat@wanadoo.fr
website: www.ariege.com/campinglehautsalat
Very clean, well-kept site beside stream. Big gravel pitches for caravans. Common room with TV.
➲ *0.8km NE on D3.*
Open: All year **Site:** 2.5HEC ▥ ♣ 🚐 **Prices:** 🚶16 🚗14 🚐 (static)230-320 **Facilities:** 🚿 🚾 ⊙ 🚐 ⊘ ⩝ ⧈ **Services:** 🍷 ✕ ⊞ lau **Leisure:** 🏊PR **Off-site:** ✕

SÉRIGNAC-PÉBOUDOU LOT-ET-GARONNE

Vallée de Gardeleau 47410 ☎ 553369696 📠 553369696
e-mail: valleegardeleau@wanadoo.fr
In a shaded wooded position, offering peace and comfort in relaxing surroundings.
➲ *Situated between Lauzun and Castillonnès on RN21.*
Open: 28 May-17 Sep **Site:** 2HEC ▥ ♣ ⌂ ▲ **Prices:** 🚶2.50-3.90 pitch 3.80-6 **Facilities:** 🚿 ⊙ 🚐 ⧈ **Services:** 🍷 ✕ ⊞ lau **Leisure:** 🏊P

SOUILLAC LOT

♜Domaine de la Paille Basse 46200
☎ 565378548 📠 565370958
e-mail: paille.basse@wanadoo.fr
website: www.lapaillebasse.com
A family site in a picturesque wooded location in the grounds of a former château.
➲ *6.5km NW off D15 Salignac-Eyvignes road.*
Open: 14 May-15 Sep **Site:** 12HEC ▥ ◈ ◔ **Prices:** 🚶5.20-6.50 pitch 9.60-11.60 **Facilities:** 🚿 🚾 ⊙ 🚐 ⊘ ⧈ **Services:** 🍷 ✕ ⊞ lau **Leisure:** 🏊P

SOULAC-SUR-MER GIRONDE

Océan L'Amélié, 33780 ☎ 556097610 📠 556097475
A level site in a pine forest, 300m from the beach.
➲ *3.5km S.*
Open: Jun-15 Sep **Site:** 6HEC ▥ ⁙ ◔ 🚐 **Facilities:** 🚿 🚾 ⊙ 🚐 ⊘ ⧈ **Services:** 🍷 ✕ ⊞ lau **Off-site:** 🏊S

Sables d'Argent 33BD de l'Amèlie, 33780
☎ 556098287 📠 556099482
e-mail: camping.sables.d.argent@wanadoo.fr
website: www.sables-d-argent.com
In a pine forest, bordered by sand dunes with direct access to the beach.
➲ *1.5km SW of village.*
Open: Apr-Sep **Site:** 2.6HEC ▥ ⁙ ◔ ⌂ **Prices:** ▲1.80-2.65 pitch 14.50-18.60 **Facilities:** 🚿 🚾 ⊙ 🚐 ⊘ ⩝ ⧈
Services: 🍷 ✕ ⊞ lau **Leisure:** 🏊S **Off-site:** 🏊P

AT AMÉLIE-SUR-MER, L' (4.5KM S)

Amélie-Plage 33780 556098727 556736426
e-mail: camping.amelie.plage@wanadoo.fr
website: www.camping-amelie-plage.com
In hilly wooded terrain. Lovely sandy beach.
3km S on the Soulac road.
Open: Mar-Dec **Site:** 8.5HEC **Prices:** pitch 15-18 (incl 2 persons) **Facilities:** **Services:** lau **Leisure:** S

AT LILIAN (4.5KM S)

Pins 33780 556098252 5577365558
e-mail: contact@campingdispins.fr
website: www.campingdespins.fr
Situated in beautiful pine forest close to the beach with plenty of sports facilities.
S on D101.
Open: May-Oct **Site:** 3.2HEC
Facilities: **Services:** lau
Off-site: RS

SOUSTONS LANDES

CM Airial 40140 558411248 558415383
e-mail: contact@camping-airial.com
website: www.camping-airial.com
Situated in a shady park with plenty of recreational facilities and modern installations.
2km W on D652.
Open: Apr-15 Oct **Site:** 17HEC
Facilities: **Services:** lau **Leisure:** P

TARASCON-SUR-ARIÈGE ARIÈGE

Pré Lombard rte d'Ussat, 9400 561056194 561057893
e-mail: leprelombard@wanadoo.fr
website: www.prelombard.com
In beautiful wooded surroundings beside the River Ariège with good, modern facilities.
1.5km SE on D23.
Open: All year **Site:** 3.5HEC **Prices:** 4-8 pitch 15-25 (incl 2 persons) (static)220-740 **Facilities:** **Services:** lau **Leisure:** PR **Off-site:**

TEILLET TARN

Relais de l'Entre Deux Lacs 81120
563557445 563557565
e-mail: contact@campingdutarn.com
website: www.campingdutarn.com
Shady terraced site. Various activities arranged. Beautiful views.
Off D81 towards Lacaune.
Open: All year **Site:** 4HEC **Prices:** 4 pitch 13 (incl 2 persons) **Facilities:** **Services:** lau
Leisure: P **Off-site:** LR

THIVIERS DORDOGNE

CM Le Repaire 24800 553526975 553526975
In a wooded valley, this well-appointed family site lies in the Périgord Vert region of the Dordogne a short walk from the ancient village of Thiviers.
1.5km along D707 towards Lanouaille.
Open: May-Sep **Site:** 11HEC **Prices:** 3.40-4.20 pitch 4-6 **Facilities:** **Services:** lau
Leisure: P **Off-site:** LR

TONNEINS LOT-ET-GARONNE

CM Robinson 47400 553790228
500m from town centre on N113 Agen road.
Open: Jun-Sep **Site:** 0.7HEC **Facilities:**
Services: lau **Leisure:** R **Off-site:** P

TOUZAC LOT

Ch'Timi 46700 565365236 565365323
e-mail: info@campinglechtimi.com
website: www.campinglechtimi.com
A well-equipped site overlooking the River Lot. Entertainment available in high season.
800m from Touzac on D8.
Open: Apr-Sep **Site:** 3.5HEC **Prices:** 3.30-4.40 pitch 4.50-6 (static)110-280 **Facilities:**
Services: lau **Leisure:** PR

Clos Bouyssac 46700 565365221 565246851
e-mail: camping.leclosbouyssac@wanadoo.fr
website: monsite.wanadoo.fr/leclosbouyssac
On the fringe of a wooded hillside by the sandy shore of the River Lot. Good for walking.
S of Touzac on D65.
Open: Apr-Oct **Site:** 1.5HEC **Prices:** 4.90 1.20 (static)319 **Facilities:**
Services: lau **Leisure:** PR

URRUGNE PYRÉNÉES-ATLANTIQUES

Larrouleta 64122 559473784 559474254
e-mail: info@larrouleta.com **website:** www.larrouleta.com
Hilly meadow with young trees.
1.5 km N of Urrugne on N1 to Spain.
Open: All year **Site:** 10HEC **Prices:** 3.50-4.80 4-4.50 4-4.50 pitch 4-4.50 **Facilities:**
Services: lau **Leisure:** L **Off-site:** PS

URT PYRÉNÉES-ATLANTIQUES

Etche Zahar allée de Mesplès, 64240
559562736 559562962
e-mail: camping.etche-zahar@wanadoo.fr
website: www.etche-zahar.fr
A small, privately owned site in a wooded location and within easy reach of local tourist areas. Separate car parking for arrivals 22.00-07.00.
Access via exit 8 on A63 or exit 4 on A64.
Open: 15 Mar-15 Nov **Site:** 2.5HEC
Prices: 1.75-3.50 2 pitch 3.50-7 **Facilities:**
Services: lau **Leisure:** P **Off-site:** R

VALEUIL DORDOGNE

Bas Meygnaud D393 Brantome, 24310 553055844
e-mail: camping-du-bas-meygnaud@wanadoo.fr
website: www.basmeygnaud.com
A quiet, shady site in the Dronne Valley.
Access via D939, turning off at Lasserre.
Open: Apr-Sep **Site:** 1.7HEC **Prices:** 2.50 2 4.50 4.50 **Facilities:** **Services:** lau
Leisure: P **Off-site:** R

VARILHES ARIÈGE

CM Parc du Château av du 8 Mai 45, 9120
561674284 561605554
On the banks of the river and close to the town.
N on N20.
Open: All year **Site:** 1HEC **Prices:** 2.40-3.60 pitch 2.30-4 **Facilities:** **Services:** lau **Off-site:**
PR

VAYRAC LOT

Bourzolles Condat, 46110 565321632
e-mail: contact@camping-bourzolles.com
Off D20 between Condat and Vayrac.
Open: May-Oct **Site:** 4HEC **Prices:** 2.20 pitch 2.40 (static)200 **Facilities:** **Services:** lau
Leisure: P **Off-site:**

Facilities: -shop -shower -electric points for razors -electric points for caravans -parking by tents permitted -compulsory separate car park **Services:** -café/restaurant -bar -Camping Gaz International -gas other than Camping Gaz -first aid facilities lau-laundry **Leisure:** -swimming L-Lake P-Pool R-River S-Sea **Off-site:** All facilities within 2km

VENDAYS-MONTALIVET GIRONDE

Mayan 3 route de Mayan, 33930 556417651
A small site situated in a pine wood.
Access from Bordeaux direction via N215 and D102.
Open: Jul-Aug **Site:** 1HEC **Facilities:** **Services:** lau **Off-site:**

VERDON-SUR-MER, LE GIRONDE

Royannais 88 rte de Soulac, 33123
556096112 556737067
e-mail: camping.le.royannais@wanadoo.fr
website: www.royannais.com
Level, sandy terrain under high pine and deciduous trees.
S of Le Verdon-sur-Mer in Le Royannais district on D1.
Open: Apr-15 Oct **Site:** 3HEC **Prices:** pitch 13.54 (incl 2 persons) (static)200-305 **Facilities:** **Services:** lau **Off-site:** RS

VERGT-DE-BIRON DORDOGNE

Patrasses 24540 553630587 553248895
Situated in the heart of the Périgord Noir region with good facilities.
3.6km S via D2E.
Open: Jun-Sep **Site:** 4.7HEC **Facilities:** **Services:** lau **Leisure:** P

VEYRINES-DE-DOMME DORDOGNE

Pastourels Le Brouillet, 24250 553295249
A quiet site in a pleasant rural setting near the Château des Milandes.
3.6km N off D53 towards Belvès.
Open: Apr-Sep **Site:** 3.5HEC **Facilities:** **Services:** lau **Leisure:** P

VÉZAC DORDOGNE

Deux Vallées 24220 553295355 553310981
e-mail: les2v@perigord.com
website: www.les-2-vallees.com
A level site in a picturesque location in the Dordogne Valley. Good facilities for families.
Access via D57 from Sarlat or D703 from Bergerac.
Open: All year **Site:** 3.2HEC **Prices:** 3-5 3 2.60 pitch 4-6.50 (static)275-650 **Facilities:** **Services:** lau **Leisure:** P **Off-site:** R

VIELLE-ST-GIRONS LANDES

Eurosol rte de la Plage, 40560
558479014 & 558477674
e-mail: contact@camping-eurosol.com
website: www.camping-eurosol.com
Well maintained family site in a pine forest, 700m from one of the finest beaches in the country.
Access via A63 exit Castets.
Open: 7 May-17 Sep **Site:** 18HEC **Prices:** 4 pitch 2-18 (static)260-735 **Facilities:** **Services:** lau **Leisure:** P **Off-site:** S

Sunelia Col Vert Lac de Léon, 40560
558429406 558429188
e-mail: contact@colvert.com
website: www.colvert.com
Quiet site on lakeside in sparse pine woodland. Small natural harbour in the mouth of a stream.
Turn off D652 on N side of village and continue towards lake.
Open: Apr-Sep **Site:** 30HEC **Prices:** 2-6 1-4 pitch 6.50-16.50 **Facilities:** **Services:** lau **Leisure:** LP

VIEUX-BOUCAU-LES-BAINS LANDES

CM des Sablères bd du Marensin, 40480
558481229 558482070
e-mail: camping-lessableres@wanadoo.fr
website: www.lessableres.com
A family site with modern facilities and direct access to the beach.
Access via N10 and D652.
Open: Apr-15 Oct **Site:** 11HEC **Prices:** pitch 10.30-15.80 (incl 2 persons) **Facilities:** **Services:** lau **Off-site:** LS

VIGAN, LE LOT

Rêve Revers, 46300 565412520 565416852
e-mail: info@campinglereve.com
website: www.campinglereve.com
A modern family site in wooded surroundings.
From Payrac take D673 towards Le Vigan and follow signs.
Open: 26 Apr-15 Sep **Site:** 8HEC **Prices:** 2.80-4 pitch 4.20-6 **Facilities:** **Services:** lau **Leisure:** P

VILLEFRANCHE-DU-QUEYRAN LOT-ET-GARONNE

Moulin de Campech 47160 553887243 553880652
e-mail: campech@wanadoo.fr
website: www.moulindecampech.co.uk
A beautiful site in a peaceful location beside a small lake stocked with trout.
Access via D11 towards Casteljaloux.
Open: 24 Mar-23 Oct **Site:** 4HEC **Prices:** 3.60-5.10 pitch 18-22.75 (incl 2 persons) **Facilities:** **Services:** lau **Leisure:** LPR

VILLENAVE-D'ORNON GIRONDE

Gravières 35 ave Mirieu de Labarre, 33140 556870036
2km NE.
Open: All year **Site:** 3.5HEC **Facilities:** **Services:** lau **Leisure:** L **Off-site:**

VILLERÉAL LOT-ET-GARONNE

Château de Fonrives Rives, 47210
553366338 553360998
e-mail: chateau.de.fontives@wanadoo.fr
website: www.campingchateaufonrives.com
In a beautiful natural park in the grounds of a château with good facilities for all ages.
2.2km NW via D207.
Open: Apr-Sep **Site:** 20HEC **Prices:** pitch 16-23 (incl 2 persons) (static)185-599 **Facilities:** **Services:** lau **Leisure:** LP

VITRAC DORDOGNE

Bouysse Caudon, 24200 553283305 553303852
e-mail: la-bouysse.24@wanadoo.fr
website: www.labouysse.com
Well appointed site in a wooded valley beside the Dordogne.
2km E, near the River Dordogne.
Open: Apr-Sep **Site:** 3HEC **Prices:** 4.40-5.30 pitch 5.45-7 **Facilities:** **Services:** lau **Leisure:** PR **Off-site:**

Soleil Plage 24200 553283333 553283024
e-mail: info@soleilplage.com
website: www.soleilplage.com
Set out around an old farmhouse bordering the Dordogne with excellent facilities.

4km E on D703, turn by 'Camping Clos Bernard'.
Open: 10 May-20 Sep **Site:** 8HEC **Prices:** 4.20-6.60 pitch 6-11 (static)250-620 **Facilities:** **Services:** lau **Leisure:** PR

LOIRE/CENTRAL

AIGUILLON-SUR-MER, L' VENDÉE

Bel Air 85460 0251564405 0251971558
e-mail: camping.belair@wanadoo.fr
website: www.camping-belair.com
A long, level stretch of meadowland in rural surroundings.
1.5 km NW on D44 then turn left.
Open: Apr-Sep **Site:** 7HEC **Facilities:** **Services:** lau **Leisure:** P **Off-site:** LRS

AIRVAULT DEUX-SÈVRES

Courte Vallée Courte Vallée, 79600
549647065 549647065
e-mail: camping@caravanningfrance.com
website: www.caravanningfrance.com
A modern site, situated in a river valley, with large pitches and good facilities.
On the outskirts of the town, 0.5km NW towards Availles.
Open: 24 Mar-Sep **Site:** 12HEC **Prices:** 5.50-6.50 5-6 pitch 8-10 **Facilities:** **Services:** lau **Leisure:** P **Off-site:** P

ALLONNES MAINE-ET-LOIRE

Pô Doré Le Pô Doré, 49650 241387880 241387881
A family site in a pleasant rural setting in the heart of the Anjou region with good recreational facilities. Separate car park for arrivals after 22.00.
Access via D35 from Tours or N147 from Angers.
Open: Apr-Oct **Site:** 2HEC **Facilities:** **Services:** lau **Leisure:** P

ANCENIS LOIRE-ATLANTIQUE

Ile Mouchet La Charbonnière, 44150
240830843 240831619
e-mail: efberthelot@wanadoo.fr
Peaceful, wooded site located on the banks of the Loire.
Off N23 from Nantes-Ancenis.
Open: Apr-13 Oct **Site:** 3HEC **Facilities:** **Services:** lau **Leisure:** P **Off-site:**

ANDONVILLE LOIRET

Domaine de la Joullière rte de Richerelles, 45480
238395846 238396194
e-mail: domaine.joulliere@wanadoo.fr
website: www.domaine.joulliere.com
Spread over a series of small, wooded valleys with good sports and leisure facilities.
1km E on road to Richerelles.
Open: 15 Feb-15 Dec **Site:** 10HEC **Facilities:** **Services:** lau **Leisure:** P

ANGERS MAINE-ET-LOIRE

Lac de Maine av du Lac de Maine, 49000
241730503 241730220
e-mail: camping@lacdemaine.fr
website: www.lacdemaine.fr
In pleasant rural surroundings on the shore of the 100-hectare Lac de Maine. There are fine sporting and entertainment facilities and the historic town of Angers is within easy reach.

Access via A11 (Angers/Nantes) at Lac de Maine exit.
Open: 25 Mar-10 Oct **Site:** 4HEC
Prices: pitch 10-14 (incl 2 persons) (static)149-299
Facilities: **Services:** lau **Leisure:** P
Off-site: LR

ANGLES VENDÉE

Atlantique 5 bis R de Chemin de Fer
251270319 251276972
Open: 21 Apr-25 Sep **Site:** 6.9HEC
Prices: pitch 23 (incl 2 persons) **Facilities:**
Services: **Leisure:** P

Moncalm-Atlantique 85750 251560878 251563150
e-mail: camping-apv@wanadoo.fr
website: www.camping-apv.com
Two distinct sites, but sharing the same recreational facilities in a wooded setting close to the beach.
Open: 2 Apr-24 Sep **Site:** 3HEC **Prices:** 5 pitch 21-24 (static)145-565 **Facilities:** **Services:** lau **Leisure:** P **Off-site:** R

ANGOULINS-SUR-MER CHARENTE-MARITIME

Chirats rte de la Platère, 17690
546569416 546566595
website: camping.les.chirats.com
Modern site with good facilities 100m from a small sandy beach and providing panoramic views over the bay of Fouras. The more popular, larger beaches of the area are some 3km away. Reservations are strongly recommended.
7km S of La Rochelle.
Open: Apr-Sep **Site:** 4.5HEC **Prices:** 3.50-4.10 (static)213.50-330 **Facilities:**
Services: lau **Leisure:** PS

APREMONT VENDÉE

Prairies du Lac rte de Maché RD40, 85220
251557058 251557604
e-mail: infos@les-prairies-du-lac.com
website: www.camping-les-prairies-du-lac.com
Site located in a country setting but near the Vendée beaches and the lake of Apremont with its water slide.
D58 from Challans.
Open: May-Sep **Site:** 6HEC **Facilities:**
Services: lau **Leisure:** P **Off-site:** LR

Facilities: -shop -shower -electric points for razors -electric points for caravans -parking by tents permitted -compulsory separate car park **Services:** -café/restaurant -bar -Camping Gaz International -gas other than Camping Gaz -first aid facilities lau-laundry **Leisure:** -swimming L-Lake P-Pool R-River S-Sea **Off-site:** All facilities within 2km

ARCES Charente-Maritime

Chez Filleux 17120 546908433 546908433
e-mail: laferme.chezfilleux@wanadoo.fr
website: www.camping-chezfilleux.com
On a level meadow partly shaded by trees and bushes with good, modern facilities. 10 minutes from the local beaches.
Open: Apr-Sep **Site:** 3HEC **Prices:** pitch 12 (incl 3 persons) pp12 (static)290 **Facilities:** **Services:** lau **Leisure:** P

ARGENTAT Corrèze

Gibanel Le Gibanel, 19400 555281011 555288162
e-mail: contact@camping-gibanel.com
website: www.camping-gibanel.com
Pleasant site situated in grounds of a château next to a lake. Some facilities are only available in high season.
S from Tulle on N120.
Open: Jun-14 Sep **Site:** 6.5HEC **Facilities:** **Services:** lau **Leisure:** LP **Off-site:**

Saulou Vergnolles, 19400 555281233 555288067
e-mail: le.saulou@wanadoo.fr
website: www.saulou.com
A peaceful site in a wooded location beside the River Dordogne. Ideal for families.
6km S on D116.
Open: Apr-Sep **Site:** 7.5HEC **Prices:** pitch 11.40-18 (incl 2 persons) pp3.65-4.80 (static)164-545 **Facilities:** **Services:** lau **Leisure:** PR

AT MONCEAUX-SUR-DORDOGNE (3KM SW)

Vaurette 19400 555280967 555288114
e-mail: camping.le.vaurette@wanadoo.fr
website: www.vaurette.com
On the banks of the River Dordogne with a beach, swimming pool and tennis court.
On D12 between Argentat and Beaulieu.
Open: May-21 Sep **Site:** 4HEC **Prices:** pitch 13-19 (incl 2 persons) pp3-4.50 **Facilities:** **Services:** lau **Leisure:** PR

ARGENTON-CHÂTEAU Deux-Sèvres

CM du Lac d'Hautibus 79150 549659508 549657084
e-mail: marie-argenton-chateau@cegerel.net
0.4km S on D748.
Open: Apr-Oct **Site:** 16.2HEC **Prices:** 1.85 1.55 1.70 pitch 1.70 **Facilities:** **Services:** lau **Off-site:** LPR

AVRILLÉ Vendée

Forges Domaine Les Forges, 85440
251223885 251223885
e-mail: contact@domaine-des-forges.net
website: www.domaine-des-forges.net
In a pleasant position beside a lake, 300m from the town centre. Close to beach, the site has a variety of leisure facilities.
Open: Etr-Sep **Site:** 8HEC **Facilities:** **Services:** lau **Leisure:** LP **Off-site:**

Mancelières rte de Longeville-sur-Mer, 85440
251903597 251903931
e-mail: camping.mancellieres@tiscali.fr
website: www.lesmancellieres.com
A pleasant site in a wooded park 5km from the fine beaches of south Vendée. Separate car park for arrivals after 23.00.
1.7km S via D105 towards Longeville
Open: May-15 Sep **Site:** 2.6HEC **Prices:** 3.50 pitch 10.36-14.80 (incl 2 persons) (static)412 **Facilities:** **Services:** lau **Leisure:** P **Off-site:**

AZAY-LE-RIDEAU Indre-et-Loire

Parc du Sabot r du Stade, 37190
247454272 247454911
e-mail: mairie.azaylerideau@free.fr
Site lies in large meadow on bank of River Indre.
Near château in town centre.
Open: Apr-Oct **Site:** 9HEC **Prices:** pitch 11.70-12.70 (incl 2 persons) **Facilities:** **Services:** lau **Leisure:** R **Off-site:** P

BARRE-DE-MONTS, LA Vendée

Grande Côte 85550 251685189 251492557
website: www.campeoles.fr
In pine forest behind dunes with direct access to the beach. Plenty of recreational facilities.
3 km from village beside Noirmoutier toll bridge.
Open: 7 Apr-23 Sep **Site:** 22HEC **Facilities:** **Services:** lau **Leisure:** P **Off-site:** S

BATZ-SUR-MER Loire-Atlantique

Govelle rte de la Côte Sauvage, 44740 240239163
Direct access to the sea. Supervised beach and sea-fishing nearby.
On D45 between Le Pouliguen and Batz.
Open: 15 Jun-15 Sep **Site:** 6.8HEC **Facilities:** **Services:** lau **Leisure:** S

BAULE, LA Loire-Atlantique

Ajoncs d'Or chemin du Rocher, 44500
240603329 240244437
e-mail: contact@ajoncs.com
website: www.ajoncs.com
In a large wooded park, close to the beach with well-defined pitches.
Signed from the entrance to the town.
Open: Apr-Sep **Site:** 6HEC **Facilities:** **Services:** lau **Leisure:** P **Off-site:** S

CM av de Diane, 44505 240601740 240601148
e-mail: campi-boisamour@wanadoo.fr
website: www.campingdefrance.com/boisdamour/
Site consists of two sections, one for caravans, one for tents, each with separate entrance.
On NE outskirts near the railway.
Open: Feb-Oct **Site:** 5HEC **Prices:** pitch 10.30-14.10 (incl 2 persons) **Facilities:** **Services:** lau **Off-site:** PRS

Eden 1315 Route De Ker Rivaud, 44500
240600323 240119425
e-mail: eden-caravaning@wanadoo.fr
website: www.ledencaravaning.com
In pleasant rural surroundings with good sports and sanitary facilities.
1km NW via N171 exit La Baule-Escoublac.
Open: 9 Apr-15 Oct **Site:** 4.7HEC **Prices:** 3.70-5.50 2-3 pitch 13-19 (incl 2 persons) **Facilities:** **Services:** lau **Leisure:** LP **Off-site:** S

Site: 6HEC-Site size -grass -sand -stone -little shade -partly shaded -mainly shaded -bungalows for hire -caravans for hire -tents for hire -no dogs **Prices:** -adult per night -car per night pp-per person per night -caravan per night -tent per night (static)-caravan hire per week

Roseraie 20 av J-Sohier, 44500 240604666 240601184
e-mail: camping@laroserie.com
website: www.laroseraie.com
A well-planned site in wooded surroundings with good recreational facilities.
E of N171 towards the bay.
Open: Apr-Sep **Site:** 5HEC **Prices:** 4.50-7 pitch 8-13 **Facilities:** **Services:** lau **Leisure:** P **Off-site:** S

BAZOUGES-SUR-LE-LOIR SARTHE

CM rte de Cré-sur-Loir, 72200 243459580 243453826
On the bank of the River Loir with well-defined pitches.
Approach off A11 towards La Flèche.
Open: 15 May-Oct **Site:** 0.8HEC **Facilities:** **Services:** lau **Off-site:** RS

BEAULIEU-SUR-DORDOGNE CORRÈZE

Îles 19120 555910265 555910519
e-mail: jycastanet@aol.com
website: www.camping-des-iles.net
On an island in the River Dordogne, within easy reach of all facilities.
Open: 15 Apr-15 Oct **Site:** 4.5HEC **Facilities:** **Services:** lau **Leisure:** PR **Off-site:**

BESSINES-SUR-GARTEMPE HAUTE-VIENNE
AT MORTEROLLES-SUR-SEMME (4.5KM N ON N20)

CM 87250 555766018 555760124
e-mail: ot.bessines@wanadoo.fr
100m from N20; in town centre.
Open: All year **Site:** 8HEC **Prices:** pitch 6.50 (incl 2 persons) pp2 **Facilities:** **Services:** lau **Off-site:** R

BEYNAT CORRÈZE

Étang de Miel 19190 555855066 0555855796
e-mail: camping.lac.de.miel@wanadoo.fr
A family site in a picturesque wooded setting close to the lake within the 'Green Valley'.
4km E on N121 Argentat road.
Open: 15 Jun-15 Sep **Site:** 9HEC **Prices:** pitch 12-14 (static)220-320 **Facilities:** **Services:** lau **Leisure:** LR

BIGNAC CHARENTE

Marco de Bignac Lieudit "Les Sablons", 16170 545217841 545215237
e-mail: camping.marcodebignac@wanadoo.fr
website: www.camping-marco-bignac.com
In a beautiful wooded location set out around the shore of a 2-hectare lake with fine entertainment and sporting facilities.
N of Angoulême off N10. Take D11 W at La Touche through Vars to Basse then right onto D117 to Bignac. Site well signed close to the River Charente.
Open: 15 May-15 Sep **Site:** 8HEC **Prices:** 3-5 pitch 13-19 (incl 2 persons) (static)165-420 **Facilities:** **Services:** **Leisure:** P **Off-site:** R

BLÉRÉ INDRE-ET-LOIRE

CM r de la Gatine, 37150 247579260 247579260
e-mail: marie@blere-touraine.com
website: www.blere-touraine.com
Well-kept site beside River Cher. Two entrances.
Open: 7 Apr-15 Oct **Site:** 4HEC **Facilities:** **Services:** lau **Off-site:** P

BONNAC-LA-CÔTE HAUTE-VIENNE

Château de Leychoisier 87270 555399343 555399343
e-mail: contact@leychoisier.com
website: www.leychoisier.com
Well-managed site on ground sloping gently towards the woods. Divided into roomy pitches.
1km S off N20.
Open: 15 Apr-20 Sep **Site:** 4HEC **Prices:** 5.50-7 pitch 8-9 **Facilities:** **Services:** lau **Leisure:** LP

BONNES VIENNE

CM r de la Varenne, 86300 549564434 549564851
e-mail: camping-bonnes@hotmail.com
A quiet site with plenty of recreational facilities.
S beside the River Vienne.
Open: May-15 Sep **Site:** 1HEC **Facilities:** **Services:** lau **Leisure:** PR **Off-site:** L

BONNY-SUR-LOIRE LOIRET

Val 45420 238315771 238315771
e-mail: maisonpays-bonny@wanadoo.fr
Woodland site situated by the side of the Loire, near the town centre
At the junction of N7 and D965.
Open: mid May-30 Oct **Site:** 0.8HEC **Facilities:** **Services:** lau **Leisure:** R **Off-site:**

BOURGES CHER

CM de Bourges 26 bd de l'Industrie, 18000 248201685 248503239
e-mail: tourisme@wellbourges.fr
website: www.wellbourges.fr
In the town near Lake Auron.
Access via A71, N144 or N76.
Open: 15 Mar-15 Nov **Site:** 2.2HEC **Prices:** 3.30 4.60 3.30 **Facilities:** **Services:** lau **Off-site:** LPR

BOUSSAC-BOURG CREUSE

Château de Poinsouze rte de La Châtre - BP 12, 23600 555650221 555658649
e-mail: info.camping-de.poinsouze@wanadoo.fr
website: www.camping-de-poinsouze.com
In a picturesque location in the grounds of a château with good, modern facilities.
2km N via D917.
Open: 13 May-18 Sep **Site:** 22HEC **Prices:** pitch 18-26 (incl 2 persons) **Facilities:** **Services:** lau **Leisure:** P

BRACIEUX LOIR-ET-CHER

CM des Châteaux 11 r Roger-Brun, 41250 254464184 254464121
e-mail: campingdebracieux@wanadoo.fr
website: www.campingdeschateaux.com
In a pleasant, shady park close to the town centre and conveniently situated for visiting the chateaux of Chambord, Cheverny and Villesavin.
Open: 25 Mar-6 Nov **Site:** 8HEC **Prices:** 3.80-3.95 pitch 4.95-5.25 (static)250-420 **Facilities:** **Services:** lau **Leisure:** PR **Off-site:**

Facilities: -shop -shower -electric points for razors -electric points for caravans -parking by tents permitted -compulsory separate car park **Services:** -café/restaurant -bar -Camping Gaz International -gas other than Camping Gaz -first aid facilities lau-laundry **Leisure:** -swimming L-Lake P-Pool R-River S-Sea **Off-site:** All facilities within 2km

Brain-sur-l'Authion Maine-et-Loire

CM Caroline 49800 ☎ 241804218
A modern site in a pleasant wooded setting close to the river.
Open: 15 Mar-Oct **Site:** 3.5HEC ⬛ ♣ **Facilities:** ℝ ⊙ 🖴 🖾
Services: ⊞ lau **Off-site:** ⥥ ⛐ ✗ ⌀ ♨

Brétignolles-sur-Mer Vendée

Dunes Plage des Dunes, 85470 ☎ 251905532 251905485
e-mail: campinglesdunes@freesurf.fr
website: www.campinglesdunes.com
Direct access to the beach. All plots surrounded by hedges.
⮑ *2km S turn right off D38 and proceed for 1km across the dunes. 150m from beach.*
Open: Apr-11 Nov **Site:** 12HEC ⠶ ☀ **Facilities:** ℝ ⥥
⊙ 🖴 ⌀ ♨ 🖾 **Services:** ⛐ ✗ lau **Leisure:** ⥥P **Off-site:** ⥥S

Motine 4 r des Morinières, 85470
☎ 251900442 251338052
e-mail: campinglamotine@wanadoo.fr
website: www.lamotine.com
Pleasant site situated 350m from the town centre and 400m from the beach with good facilities.
Open: Apr-Sep **Site:** 1.8HEC ⬛ ☀ ♨ **Prices:** ⅄5.40 pitch 17-25.30 (incl 2 persons) **Facilities:** ℝ ⊙ 🖴 ♨ 🖾 **Services:** ⛐
✗ lau **Leisure:** ⥥P **Off-site:** ⥥ ⌀ ⥥LRS

Trevilliere rte de Bellevue, 85470
☎ 251900965 251900965
e-mail: camping-chadotel@wanadoo.fr
website: www.chadotel.com
⮑ *900m from the town centre and 2km from the beach.*
Open: 2 Apr-25 Sep **Site:** 3.5HEC ⬛ ♣ ☀ ♨ **Prices:** ⅄5.70 pitch 12-22.50 (incl 2 persons) ♨ (static)190-720
Facilities: ℝ ⥥ ⊙ 🖴 ⌀ ♨ 🖾 **Services:** ⛐ ✗ ⊞ lau **Leisure:** ⥥P
Off-site: ✗ ⥥S

Vagues 20 bd du Centre, 85470
☎ 251901948 240024988
e-mail: lesvagues@free.fr
website: www.campinglesvagues.fr
A family site situated on the Côte de Lumière in a delightful rural setting.
⮑ *N on D38 towards St-Gilles-Croix-de-Vie*
Open: Apr-Sep **Site:** 5HEC ⬛ ♣ ☀ ♨ **Prices:** ⅄3.29-4.70 ♨14-20 pitch 14-20 ♨ (static)244-335 **Facilities:** ℝ ⊙ 🖴 🖾
Services: ⛐ ✗ ⊞ lau **Leisure:** ⥥P **Off-site:** ⥥ ✗ ⌀ ⥥LRS

Brissac-Quincé Maine-et-Loire

L'Étang rte de St Mathurin, 49320
☎ 241917061 241917265
e-mail: info@campingetang.com
website: www.campingetang.com
A lakeside site in the heart of the Anjou countryside with good recreational facilities.
⮑ *Access via D748 towards Poitiers.*
Open: 14 May-10 Sep **Site:** 4HEC ⬛ ☀ ⛺ **Prices:** ⅄4.50-6 pitch 15-24 (incl 2 persons) **Facilities:** ℝ ⥥ ⊙ 🖴 ⌀ 🖾
Services: ⛐ ✗ ⊞ lau **Leisure:** ⥥P **Off-site:** ✗

Brûlon Sarthe

Brûlon-le-Lac 72350 ☎ 243956896 243926036
In attractive wooded surroundings beside a lake.
⮑ *Access via N157 towards Sable-sur-Sarthe.*
Open: 15 Apr-Sep **Site:** 3.5HEC ⬛ ♣ **Facilities:** ℝ ⥥ ⊙ ♨
⌀ ♨ 🖾 **Services:** ⛐ ✗ ⊞ lau **Leisure:** ⥥LPR

Candé-sur-Beuvron Loir-et-Cher

Grande Tortue 3 rte de Pontlevoy, 41120
☎ 254441520 254441945
e-mail: lagrandetortue@libertysurf.fr
website: www.la-grand-tortue.com
A family site in a peaceful wooded setting.
⮑ *D751, between Blois and Amboise, on the left bank of the river.*
Open: 9 Apr-26 Sep **Site:** 5.8HEC ⬛ ♣ ⛺ **Prices:** ⅄4.60-6 pitch 13.50-21.50 (incl 2 persons) ♨ (static)257-600
Facilities: ℝ ⥥ ⊙ 🖴 ⌀ ♨ 🖾 **Services:** ⛐ ✗ ⊞ lau **Leisure:** ⥥P

Chalard, Le Haute-Vienne

Vigères Les Vigères, 87500 ☎ 555093722 555099339
e-mail: lesvigeres@aol.com
website: www.lesvigeres.com
Generally level site in peaceful surroundings in an elevated position with fine views. English management.
⮑ *Between Châlus and Le Chalard on D901.*
Open: All year **Site:** 20HEC ⬛ ♣ ⛺ **Prices:** ⅄3-3.50 pitch 3-4 **Facilities:** ℝ ⊙ 🖴 ♨ 🖾 **Services:** ⊞ lau **Leisure:** ⥥LP
Off-site: ⥥ ⛐ ✗

Chalonnes-sur-Loire Maine-et-Loire

CM Candais rte de Rochefort, 49290
☎ 241780227 241780227
e-mail: info@campingteueoceane.com
website: www.campingteueoceane.com
On the banks of the River Loire at its confluence with the River Louet.
⮑ *NE off D751 towards Rochefort.*
Open: 15 May-Sep **Site:** 3HEC ⬛ ☀ ⛺ **Prices:** pitch 15-18 (incl 2 persons) **Facilities:** ℝ ⊙ 🖴 ♨ 🖾 **Services:** ⛐ ✗ ⊞ lau
Off-site: ⥥ ⛐ ✗ ⌀ ♨ ⥥P

Chapelle Hermier, La Vendée

Pin Parasol Lac du Jaunay, Chateaulong, 85220
☎ 251346472 251346462
e-mail: pinparasol@freesurf.fr
website: www.pinparasol.free.fr
In the heart of the Vendée countryside on the shore of Lac du Jaunay with good, modern facilities.
⮑ *Between D6 and D12.*
Open: May-25 Sep **Site:** 7HEC ⬛ ☀ ⛺ **Prices:** pitch 9.50-22 (incl 2 persons) **Facilities:** ℝ ⥥ ⊙ 🖴 ⌀ ♨ 🖾
Services: ⛐ ✗ ⊞ lau **Leisure:** ⥥PS

Chartres Eure-et-Loir

CM des Bords de l'Eure 9 r de Launay, 28000
☎ 237287943 237282943
e-mail: camping-rousell-chartres@wanadoo.fr
website: www.auxbordsdeleure.com
In wooded surroundings beside the river.
⮑ *Signed towards Orléans.*
Open: 10 Apr-10 Nov **Site:** 3.9HEC ⬛ ☀ ⛺ ♨
Prices: pitch 9-13 (incl 2 persons) ♨ (static)250 **Facilities:** ℝ
⥥ ⊙ 🖴 ♨ 🖾 **Services:** ⛐ ✗ ⊞ lau **Off-site:** ⌀ ♨ ⥥PR

Chartre-sur-le-Loir, La Sarthe

Vieux Moulin av des Déportés, 72340 ☎ 243444118
e-mail: campingvieuxmoulin@worldonline.fr
Open: 15 Apr-Sep **Site:** 2.4HEC ⬛ ☀ **Prices:** pitch 9-10 (incl 2 persons) **Facilities:** ℝ ⊙ 🖴 ♨ 🖾 **Services:** ⊞ lau
Leisure: ⥥PR **Off-site:** ⥥ ⛐ ✗ ⌀ ♨ ⥥LP

Site: 6HEC-Site size ⬛-grass ⠶-sand ♦-stone ☀-little shade ⊶-partly shaded ♣-mainly shaded
⛺-bungalows for hire ♨-caravans for hire ⛺-tents for hire ⌀-no dogs **Prices:** ⅄-adult per night ♨-car per night
pp-per person per night ♨-caravan per night ⛺-tent per night ♨ (static)-caravan per week

CHARTRIER-FERRIÈRE Corrèze

Magaudie La Magaudie Ouest, 19600
555852606 555852606
e-mail: camping@lamagaudie.com
website: www.lamagaudie.com
A peaceful site covering 8 hectares with half consisting of forest, 3km from Lac du Causse which has beaches and facilities for water sports. The 18th-century buildings on the site have been converted to give hygenic sanitary facilities.
A20 Limoges-Toulouse exit 53, take N20 in direction of Cahors. At roundabout take D19 in direction of Chasteaux and after railway viaduct 4th left for D154 in direction of Chartrier and remain on road towards Nadaillac. Third right for La Magaudie and then 1st right, site on left.
Open: All year **Site:** 8HEC **Prices:** 3.25 pitch 3.50-4.25 (static)150-260 **Facilities:** **Services:** lau **Leisure:** P

CHASSENEUIL-SUR-BONNIEURE Charente

CM Les Charmilles r des Écoles, 16260
545395536 545225245
e-mail: mairie.chasseneuil@wanadoo.fr
website: membres.lycos.fr/ville16260/
W of town via D27, beside the River Bonnieure.
Open: All year **Site:** 1.5HEC **Facilities:** **Services:** lau **Off-site:** P

CHÂTEAU D'OLONNE, LE Vendée

Pirons r des Marchais, La Pironnière, 85180
251952675 251239317
e-mail: contact@camping-les-pirons.com
website: www.camping-les-pirons.com
Site 300m from beach with three swimming pools and an aquatic chute.
Off D949.
Open: Apr-Oct **Site:** 7HEC **Facilities:** **Services:** lau **Leisure:** P **Off-site:** S

CHÂTEAU-DU-LOIR Sarthe

CM de Coemont 72500 243794463
Shady site on the bank of the Loir.
Open: Jun-Sep **Site:** 0.6HEC **Facilities:** **Services:** lau **Leisure:** R **Off-site:** LP

CHÂTELAILLON-PLAGE Charente-Maritime

Clos des Rivages av des Boucholeurs, 17340 546562609
Level, well-kept site with pitches divided by trees and bushes, 500m from the sea.
500m from the village. Signed.
Open: 15 Jun-5 Sep **Site:** 2.5HEC **Facilities:** **Services:** lau **Leisure:** P **Off-site:** S

Deux Plages 17340 546562753 546435118
e-mail: reception@2plages.com
website: www.2plages.com
In pleasant wooded surroundings 200m from the beach.
Open: May-Sep **Site:** 4.5HEC **Facilities:** **Services:** lau **Leisure:** P **Off-site:** S

CHÂTELLERAULT Vienne

Relais du Miel rte d'Antran, 86100 549020627
e-mail: camping@lerelaisdumiel.com
website: www.lerelaisdumiel.com
In the grounds of the Château de Valette, beside the River Vienne.
Access via A10 exit 26 Châtellerault Nord.
Open: 15 May-Aug **Site:** 7HEC **Prices:** pitch 19-24 (static)250-300 **Facilities:** **Services:** lau **Leisure:** PR **Off-site:**

CHÂTRES-SUR-CHER Loir-et-Cher

CM des Saules 41320 254980455
On N76 near bridge.
Open: May-Aug **Site:** 2HEC **Prices:** 4 **Facilities:** **Services:** lau **Off-site:** R

CHAUFFOUR-SUR-VELL Corrèze

Feneyrolles 19500 555253143
e-mail: feneyrolles@aol.com
In a quiet, wooded location with good facilities. Ideal for exploring the Dordogne Valley and surrounding area.
2.2km E.
Open: 15 Apr-15 Sep **Site:** 4HEC **Facilities:** **Services:** lau **Leisure:** P

CHEF-BOUTONNE Deux-Sèvres

Moulin Treneuillet, rte de Brioux, 79110
549297346 549297346
e-mail: campingchef@infonie.fr **website:** campingchef.com
Small, secluded family site in a rural setting.
1km NE via D740.
Open: All year **Site:** 2.5HEC **Prices:** 2-2.30 2 pitch 4.60-7 **Facilities:** **Services:** lau **Leisure:** PR **Off-site:**

CHENONCEAUX Indre-et-Loire

Moulin Fort 37150 247238622 247238093
e-mail: lemoulinfort@wanadoo.fr
website: www.lemoulinfort.com
2km SE.
Open: Etr-15 Oct **Site:** 3HEC **Facilities:** **Services:** lau **Leisure:** PR

CHÉVERNY Loir-et-Cher

Les Saules rte de Contres, 41700
254799001 254792834
e-mail: contact@camping-cheverny.com
website: www.camping-cheverny.com
In the heart of the Châteaux-du-Val-de-Loire, bordered by a golf course and the Cheverny forest.
1.5km from town towards Contres on D102.
Open: 27 Mar-16 Oct **Site:** 8HEC **Prices:** 4.50 pitch 15-23 (incl 2 persons) **Facilities:** **Services:** lau **Leisure:** P

CHOLET Maine-et-Loire

Lac de Ribou av L-Mandin, 49300
241497430 241582122
e-mail: village-vacances-cholet@wanadoo.fr
website: www.cholet-shorts-loisirs.fr
Well set out site bordering a lake, with fishing, boating, tennis and volleyball.
3km from town centre.
Open: Apr-Sep **Site:** 5HEC **Prices:** 2.90-4.50 pitch 9.05-18.55 (incl 2 persons) (static)236-515 **Facilities:** **Services:** lau **Leisure:** P **Off-site:** L

CLOYES-SUR-LE-LOIR Eure-et-Loir

Parc des Loisirs rte du Montigny, 28220
237985053 237983384
e-mail: info@parc-de-loisirs.com
website: www.parc-de-loisirs.com
On the bank of the River Loir. Extensive leisure facilities. Separate section for teenagers. Shop open in July and August only, bar and restaurant open May to September.

contd.

Access from Châteaudun S on N10 towards Cloyes, then right onto Montigny-le-Gamelon road.
Open: 15 Mar-15 Nov **Site:** 5HEC **Prices:** 4.50-5.25 pitch 6.50-8.40 **Facilities:** **Services:** lau **Leisure:** P **Off-site:**

COGNAC CHARENTE

Cognac rte de Ste-Sévère, bd de Chatenay, 16100
545321332 545321582
website: www.campingdecognac.fr
In wooded surroundings beside the River Charente with good, modern facilities.
2km N on D24.
Open: May-15 Oct **Site:** 1.6HEC **Prices:** pitch 11-13 (incl 2 persons) **Facilities:** **Services:** lau
Leisure: PR **Off-site:** P

CONDAT SUR GANAVEIX CORRÈZE

Moulin de la Geneste Moulin de la Geneste
555989008 555989008
e-mail: lageneste@lineone.net
website: www.lageneste.net
Situated in 6 hectares of undulating land with three small lakes and a small trout river. Part of the land and small wood have been left as a nature reserve with an abundance of wildlife.
From Limoges take autoroute A20, exit 44 (Uzerche) travelling S.
Open: May-15 Sep **Site:** 5.6HEC **Prices:** 3.20 pitch 2.70 **Facilities:** **Services:** lau

CONTRES LOIR-ET-CHER

Charmoise Sassay, 41700 254795515 254795515
On a level meadow with good facilities.
N956.
Open: Apr-Oct & Nov-Mar **Site:** 1HEC **Prices:** 2.30 1 **Facilities:** **Services:** lau **Off-site:**

COUHÉ-VERAC VIENNE

Peupliers 86700 549592116 549379209
e-mail: info@lespeupliers.fr
website: www.lespeupliers.fr
A family site in a forest beside the river.
N of village on N10 Poitiers road.
Open: 2 May-Sep **Site:** 16HEC **Prices:** 4.20-6 pitch 5.95-8.50 **Facilities:** **Services:** lau **Leisure:** PR **Off-site:**

COURÇON-D'AUNIS CHARENTE-MARITIME

Garenne 21 r du Stade, 17170 546016050 46016359
Open: Jun-Sep **Site:** **Prices:** 1.85-10 1.05 1.70 1.70 pitch 1.70-9 **Facilities:** **Services:** lau
Off-site: P

COUTURES MAINE-ET-LOIRE

Parc de Montsabert Montsabert, 49320
241579163 241579002
e-mail: camping@parcdemontsabert.com
website: www.parcdemontsabert.com
In a picturesque wooded park with mature trees.
Access via left bank of the River Loire (D751) between Angers and Saumur.
Open: 30 Apr-16 Sep **Site:** 10HEC
Prices: 4.60-4.60 pitch 14.90-21.10 (incl 2 persons)
Facilities: **Services:** lau **Leisure:** P
Off-site:

CROISIC, LE LOIRE-ATLANTIQUE

Océan 44490 240230769 240157063
e-mail: camping-ocean@wanadoo.fr
website: www.camping-ocean.fr
A quiet, well-appointed site situated 150m from the sea.
1.5km NW via D45.
Open: Apr-Sep **Site:** 7.5HEC **Facilities:** **Services:** lau **Leisure:** P **Off-site:** S

DISSAY VIENNE

CM du Parc 86130 549628429 549625872
Quiet, shady site at the foot of a 15th-century castle, with close proximity to Futuroscope, lake of St-Cyr and the forest of Mouliere.
Open: Jun-15 Sep **Site:** 1HEC **Facilities:**
Services: lau

DURTAL MAINE-ET-LOIRE

International 9 r du Camping, 49430
241763180 241763267
e-mail: mairie@ville-durtal.fr
website: www.ville-durtal.fr
A pleasant site beside the River Loire.
Near the centre of the town. Access via N23 or A11.
Open: Etr-Sep **Site:** 3HEC **Prices:** 2.90 pitch 9.20 (incl 2 persons) **Facilities:** **Services:** lau
Off-site: P

EGLETONS CORRÈZE

Egletons-Lac 19300 555931475
A lakeside site in wooded surroundings with a fine range of recreational facilities.

2km from Egletons towards Ussel.
Open: All year **Site:** 9HEC **Facilities:** **Services:** lau **Off-site:** LP

EYMOUTHIERS CHARENTE

Gorges du Chambon 16220 545707170 545708002
e-mail: gorges.chambon@wanadoo.fr
website: www.gorgesduchambon.fr
In a beautiful location on a wooded hilltop.
3km N via D163.
Open: 16 May-17 Sep **Site:** 7HEC
Prices: 3.50-6 pitch 12-20 (incl 2 persons) (static)252-570 **Facilities:** **Services:** lau
Leisure: PR

FAUTE-SUR-MER, LA VENDÉE

Fautais 18 rte de la Tranche, 85460 251564196
Situated in centre of village. Numbered pitches.
On D46.
Open: Apr-Sep **Site:** 1HEC **Facilities:**
Services: lau **Off-site:** LPRS

Flots Bleus av des Chardons, 85460
251271111 251294076
Family site only 100m from the sea.
In La Faute, cross Pont de l'Aiguillons-sur-Mer and follow Route de la Pointe d'ArÁay to site.
Open: 8 May-8 Sep **Site:** 1.5HEC
Facilities: **Services:** lau **Off-site:**
LRS

FENOUILLER, LE VENDÉE

SAS SHH Le Pas Opton rte de Nantes, 85800
251551198 251554494
website: www.springharvestholidays.com
Well-equipped family site a few minutes from the beach and close to the Des Vallées sailing centre.
2km N beside the River Vie on D754.
Open: May-Nov **Site:** **Facilities:**
Services: lau **Leisure:** PR

FOURAS CHARENTE-MARITIME

Charmilles St Laurent de la Pree, 17450
546840005 546840284
e-mail: charmilles17@wanadoo.fr
website: www.domainedescharmilles.com
Open: 2 Apr-Sep **Site:** 5HEC **Prices:** pitch 15-28 (incl 2 persons) pp5.50 **Facilities:** **Services:**
lau **Leisure:** P **Off-site:** S

FRESNAY-SUR-SARTHE SARTHE

CM Sans Souci r de Haut Ary, 72130 243973287
e-mail: camping-fresnay@wanadoo.fr
website: membres.tripod.fr/fresnay
A family site with good facilities and direct access to the river.
1km SE on D310.
Open: Apr-Sep **Site:** 2HEC **Prices:** 2.35 1.80 pitch 4.20 (incl 2 persons) **Facilities:**
Services: lau **Leisure:** PR **Off-site:**

FRIAUDOUR HAUTE-VIENNE

Freaudour 87250 555765722 555712393
website: www.lac-saint-pardoux.com
A well-equipped site beside Lac de St-Pardoux.
Access via A20 exit 25.
Open: 4 Jun-10 Sep **Site:** 3.5HEC
Prices: 11.20-17.30 (static)235-570 **Facilities:**
Services: lau **Leisure:** LP **Off-site:**

FROSSAY LOIRE-ATLANTIQUE

Migron Le Square de la Chaussée, 44320 240397783
In a pleasant location beside the canal.
Open: Jun-Sep **Site:** 2.5HEC **Facilities:**
Services: lau **Leisure:** R **Off-site:**

GENNES MAINE-ET-LOIRE

Au Bord de Loire av des Cadets de Saumur, 49350
241380467 241380712
e-mail: auborddeloire@free.fr
website: www.auborddeloire.free.fr
In a peaceful location on the river bank.
N beside the River Loire.
Open: May-Sep **Site:** 2.5HEC **Prices:** pitch 7.50 (incl 2 persons) (static)90-115 **Facilities:**
Services: lau **Leisure:** R **Off-site:** P

GIEN LOIRET

Bois du Bardelet rte de Bourges, Poilly, 45500
238674739 238382716
e-mail: contact@bardelet.com
website: www.bardelet.com
A family site with a good variety of sports facilities.
Access via D940 SW of Gien.
Open: 25 Mar-Sep **Site:** 12HEC **Prices:** 5.90 pitch 24-29.40 (incl 2 persons) **Facilities:**
Services: lau **Leisure:** P

GIVRAND VENDÉE

Europa Le Petit Bois, 85800 251553268 251558010
A pleasant family site with a wide variety of recreational facilities and modern sanitary blocks.
W from St-Gilles-Croix-de-Vie via D6 for 2.5km, then S for 0.2km.
Open: Apr-Sep **Site:** 4HEC **Facilities:**
Services: lau **Leisure:** P **Off-site:** LRS

GUÉMENÉ-PENFAO LOIRE-ATLANTIQUE

Hermitage 36 av du Paradis, 44290
240792348 240515 1187
e-mail: contact@campinglhermitage.com
website: www.campinglhermitage.com
In a beautiful setting overlooking the Don Valley with good, modern facilities.
1.5km E on rte de Châteaubriant.
Open: All year **Site:** 2.5HEC **Prices:** 2.90-2.90 pitch 8.15-9.60 (incl 2 persons) (static)183-290
Facilities: **Services:** lau **Leisure:** P
Off-site: R

GUÉRANDE LOIRE-ATLANTIQUE

Bréhadour 44350 240249312 240249277
e-mail: info@homair-vacances.fr
website: www.homair-vacances.fr
A well-equipped family site with good facilities, a few kilometres from the sea.
2km NE on D51, rte de St-Lyphard.
Open: 15 Apr-Sep **Site:** 7HEC **Facilities:**
Services: lau **Leisure:** P **Off-site:**

Domaine de Lévéno rte de l'Étang de Sandun, 44350
240247930 240620123
e-mail: domaine.leveno@wanadoo.fr
website: www.camping-leveno.com
In a pleasant location with good facilities.
3km E via rte de Sandun.
Open: 9 Apr-2 Oct **Site:** 12HEC **Prices:** 3-5 pitch 9-15 **Facilities:** **Services:** lau
Leisure: P **Off-site:** S

Pré du Château de Careil Careil, 44350
240602299 240602299
e-mail: chateau.careil@free.fr
website: www.pays-blanc.com/camping-careil
Divided into pitches. Caravans only. Booking recommended in July and August.
2km N of La Baule on D92.
Open: 22 May-12 Sep **Site:** 2HEC **Facilities:** **Services:** lau **Leisure:** P **Off-site:**

HÉRIC Loire-Atlantique

Pindière 44810 240576541 228022543
e-mail: patrick.ara@wanadoo.fr
website: www.camping-la-pindiere.com
A family site on a level meadow with good facilities.
1km from town on D16.
Open: All year **Site:** 3HEC **Prices:** 3.10-3.50 pitch 3.90-4.10 **Facilities:** **Services:** lau **Leisure:** P **Off-site:**

HOUMEAU, L' Charente-Maritime

Trépied au Plomb 17137 546509082 546500133
e-mail: info@aupetitport.com
website: www.aupetitport.com
NE via D106.
Open: Apr-Sep **Site:** 2HEC **Prices:** pitch 12-15 (incl 2 persons) (static)240-360 **Facilities:** **Services:** lau **Off-site:** S

INGRANDES Vienne
At St-Ustre (2km NE)

Petit Trianon de St-Ustre 86200
549026147 549026881
e-mail: chateau@petit-trianon.fr
website: www.petit-trianon.fr
In a beautiful park surrounding a small 18th-century castle, the site has good entertainment and recreational facilities.
Turn off N10 at sign N of Ingrandes and continue for 1km.
Open: 20 May-20 Sep **Site:** 7HEC **Prices:** 6-6.80 3.60-3.80 pitch 3.80-4 (static)260-360 **Facilities:** **Services:** lau **Leisure:** P **Off-site:**

JARD-SUR-MER Vendée

Écureuils rte des Goffineaux, 85520
251334274 251339114
e-mail: camping-ecureuils@wanadoo.fr
website: www.camping-ecureuils.com
Quiet woodland terrain 500m from the sea. Large pitches surrounded by hedges.
Signed.
Open: 15 May-15 Sep **Site:** 4.3HEC **Prices:** 5.85-6.50 pitch 13.95-15.50 pp1.80-4.50 (static)260-670 **Facilities:** **Services:** lau **Leisure:** P **Off-site:** S

Site: 6HEC-Site size -grass -sand -stone -little shade -partly shaded -mainly shaded -bungalows for hire -caravans for hire -tents for hire -no dogs **Prices:** -adult per night -car per night pp-per person per night -caravan per night -tent per night (static)-caravan hire per week

La Mouette Cendrée Les Malecots, St-Vincent-sur-Jard, 85520 251335904 251203139
e-mail: camping.mc@free.fr
website: www.mouettecendree.com
Open: Etr-Sep **Site:** 1.2HEC **Prices:** 2.30 pitch 10-16 (incl 2 persons) **Facilities:** **Services:** lau
Leisure: P **Off-site:** S

Océano d'Or r G-Clemenceau, 85520
251336508 251339404
e-mail: chadotel@wanadoo.fr
website: camping.chadotel.fr
A well-maintained site 1km from the beach and 500m from the town centre.
Access via D19.
Open: 2 Apr-25 Sep **Site:** 7.8HEC **Prices:** 5.70 pitch 14.50-23 (incl 2 persons) (static)200-730
Facilities: **Services:** lau **Leisure:** P
Off-site: S

Pomme de Pin r Vincent Auriol, 85520
251334385 251339404
e-mail: info@pommedepin.net
website: www.pommedepin.net
Situated in a pine forest.
300m from the town centre and 150m from the beach.
Open: 06 Apr-20 Sep **Site:** 3HEC **Facilities:** **Services:** lau **Leisure:** PS **Off-site:**

JARGEAU LOIRET

Isle aux Moulins r du 44ème RI, 45150
238597004 238591223
e-mail: kas@wanadoo.fr
In a wooded location on the bank of the Loire.
Open: Mar-15 Nov **Site:** 7HEC **Facilities:** **Services:** lau **Leisure:** R **Off-site:**

JAUNAY CLAN VIENNE

Croix du Sud rte de Neuville, 86130 549625814
e-mail: camping@la-croix-du-sud.fr
website: www.la-croix-du-sud.fr
Within easy reach of Futuroscope, the European Park of the Moving Image.
Access via A10 and D62.
Open: 29 Mar-13 Sep **Site:** 4HEC **Prices:** 1.90-3.40 pitch 6.30-6.80 **Facilities:** **Services:** lau **Leisure:** P

LAGORD CHARENTE-MARITIME

CM Parc r du Parc, 17140 546676154 546006201
e-mail: mairie.lagord@wanadoo.fr
Pleasant municipal site within easy reach of the coast.
Access via N137/D735.
Open: Jun-Sep **Site:** **Facilities:**
Services: lau **Off-site:** P

LANDEVIEILLE VENDÉE

Pong r du Stade, 85220 251229263 251229925
A family site with spacious pitches surrounded by trees and bushes. Good recreational facilities.
Open: Etr-Sep **Site:** 3HEC **Facilities:** **Services:** lau **Leisure:** P **Off-site:**

LESSAC CHARENTE

Roufferies 16500 545302126 545302126
Extremely rural situation; 8 hectares of grassland surrounded by trees hidden from the road with a large lake for swimming.
From Potiers take road to Confolens, through Preesac and take left turn for Leesac. Continue for 3m, signed on right.
Open: Apr-Sep **Site:** 20HEC **Facilities:**
Leisure: L **Off-site:**

LINDOIS, LE CHARENTE

Étang 16130 545650267 545650896
website: www.campingdeletang.com
Well shaded site with a natural lake, ideal for swimming and fishing with a small beach.
From Rochefoucauld take D13 towards Montemboeuf.
Open: Apr-1 Nov **Site:** 10HEC **Prices:** 2.75-3.65 pitch 5.50-6.90 **Facilities:** **Services:** lau
Leisure: L **Off-site:**

LION D'ANGERS, LE MAINE-ET-LOIRE

CM Frénes 49220 241953156
A municipal site on the banks of the River Oudon, 300m from the town centre.
NE on N162.
Open: May-Aug **Site:** 2HEC **Facilities:**
Services: lau **Off-site:** P

LONGEVILLE VENDÉE

Brunelles Le Bouil, 85560 251335075 251339821
e-mail: camping@les-brunelles.com
website: ww.camp-atlantique.com
A well-appointed site in a wooded location 700m from the beach.
On the coast between Longeville and Jard-sur-Mer.
Open: 9 Apr-17 Sep **Site:** 4.8HEC
Prices: pitch 14-20 (incl 2 persons) (static)100-530
Facilities: **Services:** lau
Leisure: P **Off-site:** S

Facilities: -shop -shower -electric points for razors -electric points for caravans -parking by tents permitted -compulsory separate car park **Services:** -café/restaurant -bar -Camping Gaz International -gas other than Camping Gaz -first aid facilities lau-laundry **Leisure:** -swimming L-Lake P-Pool R-River S-Sea **Off-site:** All facilities within 2km

Clos des Pins Les Conches, 85560
251903169 251903068
e-mail: philip.jones@freesbee.fr
website: campinginfrance.com
A family run site with good facilities, 250m from a sandy beach.
Between Longeville and La Tranche.
Open: Apr-2 Oct **Site:** 1.6HEC
Prices: 4.80-6 pitch 17.60-25 **Facilities:**
Services: lau **Leisure:** P **Off-site:** S

Jarny Océan Le Bouil, 85560 251334221 251339537
e-mail: jarny-ocean@wanadoo.fr
Subdivided well-tended meadow, with a holiday complex of the same name where shopping facilities are provided. 800m to sea via forest path.
Turn off D105 about 3km S of Longeville.
Open: May-Sep **Site:** 7.6HEC **Facilities:** **Services:** lau **Leisure:** P **Off-site:** S

AT CONCHES, LES (4KM S)

Dunes av de la Plage, 85560 251333293 251903861
e-mail: contact@camping-lesdunes.com
website: www.camping-lesdunes.com
Well-kept site amongst sand dunes in pine forest.
6km S of Longeville on D105.
Open: May-Sep **Site:** 5HEC **Facilities:** **Services:** lau **Leisure:** P **Off-site:** PRS

See advertisement on page 131

LUCHÉ-PRINGÉ SARTHE

CM de la Chabotière Place des Tilleuls, 72800
243451000 243451000
e-mail: lachabotiere@ville-luche-pringe.fr
website: www.ville-luche-pringe.fr
Site by a river just 100m from the village and a short drive from several Loire chateaux. Large marked sites are set on terraces above the river and most cars are kept in a private car park to ensure play areas are safe for children.
Open: Apr-15 Oct **Site:** 2HEC **Facilities:** **Services:** lau **Leisure:** PR **Off-site:**

LUSIGNAN VIENNE

CM Vauchiron Vauchiron, 86600
549433008 549436119
e-mail: lusignan@cg86.fr
In a quiet wooded location beside the River Vonne with good facilities.
500m NE on N11.
Open: 15 Apr-14 Oct **Site:** 4HEC **Prices:** 1.95 1.23 1.23 1.23 pitch 1.23 **Facilities:**
Services: lau **Leisure:** R **Off-site:**

LUYNES INDRE-ET-LOIRE

CM Granges Les Granges, 37230 247556085
Quiet site close to the village. Ideal for visiting historical sites, fishing, and wine tasting
S via D49.
Open: 8 May-15 Sep **Site:** 0.8HEC **Facilities:** **Services:** lau **Off-site:** P

MACHÉ VENDÉE

Val de Vie r du Stade, 85190 251602102 251602102
e-mail: campingvaldevie@aol.com
Open: Apr-Oct **Site:** 2.2HEC **Prices:** 3.20-4 1.60-2 pitch 5.60-7 **Facilities:** **Services:** lau
Leisure: P **Off-site:** LR

MAGNAC-BOURG HAUTE-VIENNE

Écureuils rte de Limoges, 87380 555008028 555004909
e-mail: mairie.magnac-bourg@wanadoo.fr
A grassy site close to the historic village.
25 kms S on N20.
Open: Apr-Sep **Site:** 1.3HEC **Prices:** 3 pitch 3
Facilities: **Services:** lau **Off-site:**

MANSIGNÉ SARTHE

CM de la Plage rte du Plessis, 72510
243461417 243461665
e-mail: campingmansigne@wanadoo.fr
A holiday complex set in extensive parkland around a 24-hectare lake with good recreational facilities.
On D13, 4km from D307 Le Mans-Le Lude.
Open: Etr-Oct **Site:** 3.4HEC **Facilities:**
Services: lau **Leisure:** LP **Off-site:**

MARANS CHARENTE-MARITIME

CM Le Bois Dinot rte de Nantes, 17230
546011051 546011051
e-mail: campingboisdinot.marans@wanadoo.fr
website: www.ville-marans.fr
Separate car park for arrivals after 22.00.
Access via N137 Nantes-Bordeaux.
Open: May-Sep **Site:** 6HEC **Prices:** 2.90 1.60 1.60 pitch 2 **Facilities:** **Services:** lau
Off-site: PR

MARÇON SARTHE

Lac des Varennes 72340 243441372 243445431
e-mail: camping.des.varennes.marcon@wanadoo.fr
An attractive site brodering the lake in the heart of the Loire Valley, with spacious pitches and well-maintained installations.
Open: 25 Mar-10 Oct **Site:** 7HEC **Prices:** 3-4.10 pitch 2.40-3.80 (static)122 **Facilities:**
Services: lau **Leisure:** LR **Off-site:**

MATHES, LES CHARENTE-MARITIME

Charmettes av de la Palmyre, 17570
546225096 546236970
website: www.camping-lescharmettes.com
Large site with plenty of organised activities. 5km from the beach.
1km SW via D141.
Open: 15 Apr-Sep **Site:** 34HEC
Facilities: **Services:** lau
Leisure: PS

Orée du Bois 225 rte de la Bouverie, La Fouasse, 17570
546224243 546225476
e-mail: info@camping-oree-du-bois.fr
website: www.oree-du-bois.fr/camping
A family site situated in a pine and oak forest, 5 minutes from the beach.
3.5km NW.
Open: 23 Apr-27 Sep **Site:** 6HEC **Prices:** pitch 15-30 (incl 2 persons) (static)208-520 **Facilities:** **Services:** lau **Leisure:** P **Off-site:** S

Pinède 2103 rte de la Fouasse, 17570
546224513 546225021
e-mail: campinglapinede@free.fr
website: www.campinglapinede.com
A modern family site in a wooded area around the large aquatic park. Excellent sporting facilities. Entertainment available in July and August.
3km NW.
Open: Apr-Sep **Site:** 7HEC
Prices: pitch 19-36.10 (incl 2 persons) (static)370-805
Facilities: **Services:** lau **Leisure:** P

MAYENNE MAYENNE

CM du Gue St Leonard r St-Léonard, 53100
243045714 243302110
e-mail: webmestre@mairie-mayenne.fr
website: www.mairie-mayenne.fr
In a wooded location on the banks of the River Mayenne.
800m from town centre near N12.
Open: 15 Mar-Sep **Site:** 1.8HEC **Facilities:** **Services:** lau **Leisure:** P **Off-site:**

MEMBROLLE-SUR-CHOISILLE, LA INDRE-ET-LOIRE

CM rte de Foudettes, 37390 247412040
On level meadow in sports ground beside River Choisille.
N on N138 Le Mans road.
Open: May-Sep **Site:** 1.5HEC **Facilities:** **Services:** lau **Leisure:** R **Off-site:** L

MERVENT VENDÉE

Chêne Tord 34 chemin du Chêne Tord, 85200
251002063 251002794
A well-appointed site 200m from a large artificial lake in the heart of the Mervent forest.
Access via D99.
Open: All year **Site:** 4HEC **Facilities:** **Services:** lau **Off-site:** LPR

MESLAND LOIR-ET-CHER

Parc du Val de Loire rte de Fleuray, 41150
254702718 254702171
In a sheltered position in the heart of the Touraine vineyards with good recreational facilities.
Camping Card Compulsory
1.5km W between the A10 and the N152.
Open: 28 Apr-15 Sep **Site:** 13.6HEC **Facilities:** **Services:** lau **Leisure:** P
Off-site: L

MESQUER LOIRE-ATLANTIQUE

Au Soir d'Été 44420 240425726 251739776
e-mail: nadine-houssais@wanadoo.fr
website: www.camping-soirdete.com
Open: 26 Mar-Oct **Site:** 1.5HEC **Prices:** 3.70-5.20 11.50-17 (incl 2 persons) **Facilities:** **Services:** lau **Leisure:** P **Off-site:** S

Beaupré rte de Kervarin, Kercabellec, 44420
240426748 2440426672
e-mail: camping.beaupre@wanadoo.fr
Well equipped site 500m from the beach.
On road between Mesquer and Quimiac. Entrance signed.
Open: 15 Jun-15 Aug **Site:** 0.6HEC
Facilities: **Services:** lau **Off-site:** S

CAMPING***
DE MAYENNE
53100 – (33) 243 04 57 14(33) 243 04 19 37
ON SITE

Château de Petit Bois 44420 240426877 240426558
e-mail: camping_du_petit_bois@wanadoo.fr
website: www.pays_blame.com/camping_du-Petit_bois
In the extensive grounds of an 18th-century castle with shaded, well-defined pitches.
Open: Apr-Sep **Site:** 10HEC **Facilities:** **Services:** lau **Leisure:** P **Off-site:** S

Praderoi alleé des Barges, Quimiac, 44420
240426672 240426672
e-mail: camping.praderoi@wanadoo.fr
website: perso.wanadoo.fr/mtger.debonne
On level ground 70m from Lanseria beach.
300m from Quimiac.
Open: 15 Jun-15 Sep **Site:** 0.5HEC **Prices:** pitch 12-14.90 (incl 2 persons) (static)200-290 **Facilities:** **Services:** lau **Off-site:** S

Welcome r de Bel-Air, 44420 240425085 251739984
e-mail: lewelcom@club-internet.fr
website: perso.club-internet.fr/lewelcom/
In pleasant wooded surroundings, 600m from the coast. Separate car park for arrivals after 22.30.
1.8km NW via D352
Open: Apr-Sep **Site:** 2HEC **Facilities:** **Services:** lau **Leisure:** P **Off-site:** S

Messe Deux-Sèvres

Grande Vigne 79120 ☎ 549059615
e-mail: admin@grande-vigne.com
website: www.grande-vigne.com
Flat orchard site bordered by fruit trees and set in rural countryside. No boundaries or marked pitches as only 5 pitches are let at any one time.
➲ *Off RN10 between Poitiers and Anguleme*
Open: All year **Site:** 0.5HEC **Prices:** pitch 10-15.50 **Facilities:** **Services:** lau **Leisure:** P

Missillac Loire-Atlantique

CM des Platanes 10 r du Château, 44780 ☎ 240883888
➲ *1km W via D2, 50m from the lake.*
Open: Jul-Aug **Site:** 2HEC **Facilities:** **Services:** lau **Off-site:**

Montargis Loiret

Forêt rte de Paucourt, 45200 ☎ 238980020
In the Forest of Montargis.
➲ *1.5km NE near the station and the stadium.*
Open: Feb-Nov **Site:** 5.5HEC **Prices:** 2.20 1.60 2.20 2.20 **Facilities:** **Services:** lau **Off-site:** LPR

Montgivray Indre

CM Solange Sand 2 r du Pont, 36400
☎ 254061036 254061039
e-mail: mairie.montgivray@wanadoo.fr
A pleasant, riverside site in the grounds of a château.
Open: 15 Mar-15 Oct **Site:** 1HEC **Prices:** 1.90 pitch 2.70 **Facilities:** **Services:** lau **Leisure:** R **Off-site:**

Montlouis-sur-Loire Indre-et-Loire

CM Peupliers 37270 ☎ 247458585 247451574
e-mail: mairie@ville-montlouis-loire.fr
website: www.ville-montlouis-loire.fr
On level meadow.
➲ *1.5km W on N751, next to swimming pool near railway bridge.*
Open: 15 Mar-15 Oct **Site:** 6HEC **Prices:** 2.40 pitch 7.95 (incl 2 persons) **Facilities:** **Services:** lau **Leisure:** P **Off-site:** R

Montmorillon Vienne

CM Allochon av F-Tribot, 86500
☎ 549910233 549915826
e-mail: montmorillon@cg86.fr
A well-equipped municipal site close to the river and 1.5km from the town centre.
➲ *SE via D54*
Open: Apr-Oct **Site:** 2HEC **Facilities:** **Services:** lau **Off-site:** PR

Montsoreau Maine-et-Loire

Isle Verte av de la Loire, 49730 ☎ 241517660 241510883
e-mail: isleverte@wanadoo.fr
website: www.cvtloisirs.com
In wooded surroundings beside the River Loire.
➲ *On D947 between road and river.*
Open: Apr-Sep **Site:** 2HEC **Prices:** pitch 13.50-16 (incl 2 persons) **Facilities:** **Services:** lau **Leisure:** P **Off-site:** R

Moutiers-en-Retz, Les Loire-Atlantique

Domaine du Collet 44760 ☎ 240214092 240214512
e-mail: info@domaine-du-collet.com
website: www.domaine-du-collet.com
Open: May-Sep **Site:** 12HEC **Prices:** pitch 14-22 (incl 2 persons) (static)230-520 **Facilities:** **Services:** lau **Leisure:** LPS

Village de la Mer 18 r de Prigny, 44760
☎ 240646590 251746317
e-mail: info@le-village-de-la-mer.com
website: www.village-mer.com
Quiet site close to a village and the beach.
➲ *On D97, 9kms S of Pornic.*
Open: 15 Jun-15 Sep **Site:** 7HEC **Prices:** pitch 16-26 (incl 2 persons) **Facilities:** **Services:** lau **Leisure:** P **Off-site:** S

Nantes Loire-Atlantique

Petit Port bd du Petit Port 21, 44300
☎ 240744794 240742306
e-mail: camping-petit-port@nge-nantes.fr
On modern well-kept park by a river.
➲ *In N part of town near Parc du Petit Port. From town centre follow Rennes road (N137) then signs to campsite.*
Open: All year **Site:** 6.5HEC **Prices:** 2.30-2.85 3.30-4.10 pitch 6.25-7.80 **Facilities:** **Services:** lau **Off-site:** PR

Neuville-sur-Sarthe Sarthe

Vieux Moulin 72190 ☎ 243253182 243253811
e-mail: christopher.dean@tiscali.fr
website: www.lemanscamping.net
A pleasant site with good recreational facilities, close to the village.
➲ *Access via N138 and D197.*
Open: Jul-Aug **Site:** 4.8HEC **Prices:** pitch 11 (incl 2 persons) pp3 **Facilities:** **Services:** lau **Leisure:** P **Off-site:** R

Nibelle Loiret

Nibelle rte de Boiscommun, 45340
☎ 238322355 238320387
website: www.parc-nibelle.com
Level site in the clearing of an oak woodland.
➲ *Access via D921 turning off to Nibelle in an E direction. Signed.*
Open: Mar-Nov **Site:** 12HEC **Prices:** 12 2-3 3.50-3 3 (static)206-258 **Facilities:** **Services:** lau **Leisure:** P **Off-site:**

Niort Deux-Sèvres

Niort-Noron 21 bd Salvador-Allendé, 79000
☎ 549790506 549790506
Shady site by a river.
Open: Apr-Sep **Site:** 3HEC **Prices:** 2.80 1.15 1.50 1.15 pitch 1.15 **Facilities:** **Services:** lau **Leisure:** R **Off-site:** P

Noirmoutier, Ile de Vendée

Barbâtre

Onchères 85630 ☎ 251398131 251397365
In quiet setting on sand dunes.
➲ *S of village on D95.*
Open: Apr-Sep **Site:** 10HEC **Facilities:** **Services:** lau **Leisure:** PS

Guerinière, La

Caravan'Ile BP N4, 85680 ☎ 251395029 ▤ 251358685
e-mail: contact@caravanile.com **website:** www.caravanile.com
Located near fine sand beaches. Swimming pool with aquatic toboggan.
Open: Mar-15 Nov **Site:** 9HEC ▬ ∴ ✵ ⌂ **Facilities:** 🚿 🏪 ⊖ 🔌 ⓟ **Services:** 🍷 ✕ lau **Leisure:** ≈PS

Noirmoutier-En-L'Ile

Vendette rte des Sableaux, 85330 ☎ 251390624
A well-equipped site in a pine wood close to the beach.
➲ *From town centre continue towards Plage des Sableaux.*
Open: 27 Mar-Sep **Site:** 12HEC ▬ ∴ ♣ **Facilities:** 🚿 ⊖ 🔌 ⓟ **Services:** 🍷 ✕ ⊞ lau **Leisure:** ≈S **Off-site:** 🏪 ⊘ ♜ ≈P

Notre-Dame-de-Monts Vendée

Beauséjour 85690 ☎ 251588388
➲ *2km NW on D38.*
Open: Etr-Sep **Site:** 1.3HEC ▬ ♠ 🚐 **Facilities:** 🚿 ⊖ 🔌 ⊘ ⓟ **Services:** ⊞ lau **Off-site:** 🏪 🍷 ≈S

Grand Jardin Le Grand Jardin, 50 r de la Barre, 85690
☎ 228112175
website: www.legrandjardin.net
A family site in a picturesque location facing the Ile d'Yeu. Modern sanitary installations and plenty of sports facilities. 1km from the beach.
➲ *0.6km N.*
Open: All year **Site:** 4HEC ▬ ♣ ⌂ 🚐 **Facilities:** 🚿 ⊖ 🔌 ♜ ⓟ ▣ **Services:** 🍷 ✕ ⊞ lau **Leisure:** ≈PR **Off-site:** 🏪 ⊘ ≈S

Nozay Loire-Atlantique

CM 'Henri Dubourg' rte de Rennes, 44170
☎ 240879433 ▤ 240793564
e-mail: marie@nozay.fr
A small site in a quiet location.
➲ *Access via N137 and N171.*
Open: 15 May-15 Sep **Site:** 1HEC ▬ ♠ **Prices:** 🚶2 🚗1.50 pitch 2 **Facilities:** 🚿 ⊖ 🔌 ⓟ **Services:** lau **Off-site:** 🏪 🍷 ✕ ⊘ ♜ ≈P ⊞

Oléron, Ile D' Charente-Maritime

Boyardville

Signol 17190 ☎ 546470122 ▤ 546472346
e-mail: contact@signol.com
website: www.signol.com
In attractive surroundings within a pine forest, close to the village centre and 800m from the beach.
➲ *W of town, leave D126 by the AVIA service station and follow signs for 0.6km.*
Open: Apr-Sep **Site:** 8HEC ∴ ♣ ⌂ 🚐 **Facilities:** 🚿 ⊖ 🔌 ⓟ **Services:** 🍷 ⊞ lau **Leisure:** ≈P **Off-site:** 🏪 ≈S

Château-D'Oléron, Le

Airotel d'Oléron Domaine de Montreavail, 17480
☎ 546476182 ▤ 546477967
e-mail: info@camping-airotel-oleron.com
website: www.camping-airotel-oleron.com
In a peaceful, parklike setting 1km from the beach and the town centre.
➲ *Signed from town centre.*
Open: Mar-1 Nov **Site:** 4HEC ▬ ♣ ⌂ **Prices:** pitch 13-21 (incl 2 persons) 🚐 (static)250-580 **Facilities:** 🚿 🏪 ⊖ 🔌 ⊘ ♜ ⓟ **Services:** 🍷 ✕ ⊞ lau **Leisure:** ≈LPS

Brande rte des Huîtres, 17480 ☎ 546476237 ▤ 546477170
e-mail: info@camping-labrande.com
website: www.camping-labrande.com
A family site with good facilities in beautiful surroundings.
➲ *2.5km NW, 250m from the sea.*
Open: 15 Mar-15 Nov **Site:** 5.5HEC ▬ ∴ ♠ ⌂
Prices: pitch 17-33 (incl 2 persons) **Facilities:** 🚿 🏪 ⊖ 🔌 ⊘ ♜ ⓟ **Services:** 🍷 ✕ ⊞ lau **Leisure:** ≈P **Off-site:** ≈S

Cotinière, La

Tamaris 72 av des Pins, 17310 ☎ 546471051 ▤ 546472796
About 150m from sea. Level site in pleasant olive grove.
➲ *W side of island. N of town.*
Open: 15 Mar-15 Nov **Site:** 5HEC ▬ ♠ ⌂ ▲ **Facilities:** 🚿 ⊖ 🔌 ♜ ⓟ **Services:** 🍷 ✕ ⊞ lau **Leisure:** ≈P
Off-site: 🏪 ⊘ ≈S

Dolus-D'Oléron

Ostréa rte des HuÓtres, 17550 ☎ 546476236 ▤ 546752001
A well-equipped site in wooded surroundings close to the beach.
➲ *3.5km NE.*
Open: 15 Mar-Sep **Site:** 2HEC ▬ ∴ ♠ ⌂ 🚐
Prices: 🚶3.50-5 pitch 12.95-18.50 (incl 2 persons) 🚐 (static)190-355 **Facilities:** 🚿 🏪 ⊖ 🔌 ⊘ ♜ ⓟ **Services:** 🍷 ✕ ⊞ lau **Leisure:** ≈PS

Domino

International Rex Domino, 17190
☎ 546765597 ▤ 546766788
Pleasant seaside site with good recreational facilities and access to the beach.
Open: May-14 Sep **Site:** 0.8HEC ∴ ♦ ♠ ⌂ **Facilities:** 🚿 🏪 ⊖ 🔌 ⊘ ⓟ **Services:** 🍷 ✕ ⊞ lau **Leisure:** ≈PS **Off-site:** ✕

St-Denis-D'Oléron

Phare Ouest 7 Impasse des Beaupins, 17650
☎ 251975550 ▤ 0251289109
e-mail: camping-apv@wanadoo.fr
website: www.camping-apv.com
On level ground with direct access to the beach.
➲ *1km NW towards the lighthouse.*
Open: Apr-Sep **Site:** 3.5HEC ▬ ♠ ⌂ 🚐 **Facilities:** 🚿 🏪 ⊖ 🔌 ⊘ ♜ ⓟ **Services:** 🍷 ✕ lau **Leisure:** ≈S **Off-site:** ⊞

St-Georges-D'Oléron

Gautrelle Plage des Saumonards, 17190 ☎ 546472157
In a pine wood close to the beach.
Open: 27 Mar-Sep **Site:** 6HEC ∴ ♠ **Facilities:** 🚿 ⊖ 🔌 ⓟ **Services:** ⊞ lau **Leisure:** ≈S

Gros Joncs 17190 ☎ 546765229 ▤ 546766774
e-mail: camping.gros.joncs@wanadoo.fr
website: www.les-gros-joncs.fr
Quiet location on undulating land in the midst of lovely pine woodland.
➲ *On tourist route from La Cotinière about 5km NW in the direction of Domino, 1km SW of St-Georges-d'Oléron.*
Open: End Mar-Oct **Site:** 5.2HEC ▬ ∴ ♠ ⌂ **Prices:** 🚶5-10 pitch 13.10-35.80 (incl 2 persons) **Facilities:** 🚿 🏪 ⊖ 🔌 ⓟ **Services:** 🍷 ✕ ⊞ lau **Leisure:** ≈PS **Off-site:** ⊘

Quatre Vents La Jousselinière, 17190
☎ 546756547 ▤ 546361566
e-mail: 4vents.oleron@wanado.fr
A peaceful site with good facilities.
➲ *3km E via N739.*
Open: Mar-Nov **Site:** 7.2HEC ▬ ✵ ⌂ **Facilities:** 🚿 🏪 ⊖ 🔌 ♜ ⓟ **Services:** 🍷 ✕ ⊞ lau **Leisure:** ≈P **Off-site:** ≈S

Facilities: 🏪-shop 🚿-shower ⊖-electric points for razors 🔌-electric points for caravans ⓟ-parking by tents permitted ▣-compulsory separate car park **Services:** ✕-café/restaurant 🍷-bar ⊘-Camping Gaz International ♜-gas other than Camping Gaz ⊞-first aid facilities lau-laundry **Leisure:** ≈-swimming L-Lake P-Pool R-River S-Sea **Off-site:** All facilities within 2km

Signol av de Albatros, Boyardville, 17190
546470122 546472346
e-mail: contact@signol.com
website: www.signol.com
Situated among pine and oak trees, 800m from a sandy beach.
Open: Apr-Sep **Site:** 8HEC **Facilities:** **Services:** **Leisure:** PS **Off-site:**

Suroît rte Touristique Côte Ouest, l'Ileau, 17190
546470725
e-mail: info@camping-lesuroit.com
website: www.camping-lesuroit.com
On level ground, sheltered by sand dunes with fine, modern facilities.
5km SW of town.
Open: Apr-Sep **Site:** 5HEC **Facilities:** **Services:** lau **Leisure:** PS **Off-site:**

Verébleu La Jousselinière, 17190
546765770
website: www.verebleu.tm.fr
1.7km SE via D273.
Open: 28 May-11 Sep **Site:** 7.5HEC
Prices: pitch 17-24 (incl 2 persons) **Facilities:** **Services:** lau **Leisure:** P **Off-site:**

St-Pierre-d'Oléron

Pierrière 18 rte de St-Georges, 17310
546470829 546751282
e-mail: camping-la-pierriere@wanadoo.fr
website: www.camping-la-pierriere.com
A pleasant site in wooded surroundings with well-defined pitches.
NW towards St-Georges-d'Oléron.
Open: 9 Apr-18 Sep **Site:** 4HEC **Prices:** 15.50-21.50 **Facilities:** **Services:** lau **Leisure:** P **Off-site:** S

Trois Masses Le Marais Doux, 17310
546472396 546751554
A well-equipped site in a picturesque location 2.5km from the beach.
Open: Etr-Sep **Site:** 3HEC **Facilities:** **Services:** lau **Leisure:** P **Off-site:** S

Olivet Loiret

CM Olivet r du Pont Bouchet, 45160
238635394 238635896
Site lies partly on shaded peninsula, partly on open lawns beside river.
2km E. Signed from village.
Open: Apr-Oct **Site:** 1HEC **Facilities:** **Services:** lau

Olonne-sur-Mer Vendée

Loubine 1 rte de la Mer, 85340
251331292 251331271
e-mail: camping.la.loubine@wanadoo.fr
Situated on the edge of a forest bordering the beach.
N via D87/D80.
Open: 2 Apr-24 Sep **Site:** 8HEC **Prices:** 3.80-5 pitch 16.40-25.70 (incl 2 persons) **Facilities:** **Services:** lau **Leisure:** P **Off-site:** S

Moulin de la Salle r.des Moulin de la salle, 85340
251959910 251969613
In pleasant surroundings close to the beach with good facilities.
2.7km W.
Open: Apr-Oct **Site:** 3.1HEC **Facilities:** **Services:** lau **Leisure:** P **Off-site:**

Oreé rte des Amis de la Nature, 85340
251331059 251331516
e-mail: loree@free.fr
website: www.l-oree.com
3km N.
Open: Apr-29Sep **Site:** 7HEC **Prices:** 3.40-5 pitch 12.80-23.70 **Facilities:** **Services:** lau **Leisure:** P **Off-site:** RS

Onzain Loir-et-Cher

Dugny rte de Chambon-sur-Cisse, 41150
254207066 254337169
e-mail: info@camping-de-dugny.fr
website: www.camping-de-dugny.fr
On a small lake, surrounded by farmland with well-marked pitches shaded by poplars.
From Onzain follow direction Chambon-sur-Cisse (CD45).
Open: All year **Site:** 10HEC **Prices:** 6-12 pitch 4-8 **Facilities:** **Services:** lau **Leisure:** P

Palmyre, La Charente-Maritime

Beausoleil 20 av de la Coubre, 17570
546223003 546223004
e-mail: camping.beausoleil@wanadoo.fr
website: www.campingbeausoleil.com
Situated in a pine forest, 400m from the beach.
Open: Apr-18 Sep **Site:** 4.4HEC **Prices:** pitch 12-22 (incl 3 persons) **Facilities:** **Services:** lau **Leisure:** P **Off-site:** S

Bonne Anse Plage 17570 546224090 546224230
e-mail: bonne.anse@wanadoo.fr
website: www.campingbonneanseplage.com
An extensive, gently undulating site in a pine wood, 400m from the beach.
1km from La Palmyre rdbt. Follow signs for Ronce-les-Bains.
Open: 21 May-5 Sep **Site:** 17HEC **Prices:** pitch 30 (incl 3 persons) **Facilities:** **Services:** lau **Leisure:** P **Off-site:** S

Palmyre Loisirs 28 des Mathes, 17570
546236766 546224881
Well equipped family site with plenty of recreational facilities and well-supervised activities for children.
From Les Mathes take the La Palmyre road.
Open: 16 May-12 Sep **Site:** 20HEC **Facilities:** **Services:** lau **Leisure:** P

Palmyr Océana 26 av des Mathes, 17570
546224035 546236476
e-mail: palmyr-oceana@wanadoo.fr
website: www.palmyr-oceana.fr
A well-equipped family site in a delightful wooded setting close to the beach. A wide variety of recreational facilities are available.
Open: 15 Jun-15 Sep **Site:** 17HEC **Prices:** 5 pitch 13-23 (incl 2 persons) (static)260-460 **Facilities:** **Services:** lau **Leisure:** P **Off-site:** RS

PERRIER, LE VENDÉE

CM de la Maison Blanche 85300
251493923 251493923
A family site on level ground, with pitches divided by trees. 6km from the coast.
Open: May-15 Sep **Site:** 3.2HEC **Prices:** 3.30 pitch 9.50-10.90 (incl 2 persons) **Facilities:** **Services:** lau **Leisure:** PR **Off-site:**

PEZOU LOIR-ET-CHER

CM Les Ilots rte de Renay, 41100
254234069 254236240
e-mail: commune.pezou@wanadoo.fr
A well-equipped site 400m from the town centre.
SE via D12, 50m from the River Loir.
Open: 4 May-5 Sep **Site:** 1HEC **Prices:** 2.50 pitch 2.50 **Facilities:** **Services:** lau **Off-site:**

PIRIAC-SUR-MER LOIRE-ATLANTIQUE

Parc du Guibel 44420 240235267 240155024
e-mail: camping@parcduguibel.com
website: www.parcduguibel.com
On level ground in a delightful wooded setting with good recreational facilities.
3.5km E via D52.
Open: 5 Apr-27 Sep **Site:** 14HEC **Facilities:** **Services:** lau **Leisure:** P **Off-site:** PS

PLAINE-SUR-MER, LA LOIRE-ATLANTIQUE

Tabardière 44770 603003417 240210268
e-mail: info@camping-la-tabardiere
website: www.camping-la-tabardiere.com
A wooded, terraced site 3km from the sea.

contd.

Facilities: shop shower electric points for razors electric points for caravans parking by tents permitted compulsory separate car park **Services:** café/restaurant bar Camping Gaz International gas other than Camping Gaz first aid facilities lau-laundry **Leisure:** swimming L-Lake P-Pool R-River S-Sea **Off-site:** All facilities within 2km

Situated between Pornic and La Plaine-sur-Mer off D13.
Open: Apr-Sep **Site:** 6HEC **Prices:** 3.30-5.50 (static)240-600 **Facilities:** **Services:** lau **Leisure:** P **Off-site:**

PONS CHARENTE-MARITIME

Chardon Chardon, 17800 546950125
e-mail: chardon2@wanadoo.fr
Quietly situated on the edge of a small village next to a farm.
From Pons take D732 W towards Royan. The site is 2.5km on left. Alternatively from exit 36 of Autoroute A10 turn towards Pons. Site is 800m on right.
Open: Apr-Oct **Site:** 1.6HEC **Facilities:** **Services:** lau **Off-site:** R

PONT-L'ABBÉ-D'ARNOULT CHARENTE-MARITIME

Parc de la Garenne 24 av Bernard Chambenoit, 17250 546970146
e-mail: info@lagarenne.net
website: www.lagarenne.net/gb
Peaceful site in a parkland setting. Shady individual pitches.
Access via A10, N137 and D18.
Open: 15 May-25 Sep **Site:** 2.8HEC **Prices:** 3.28-4.10 pitch 12-15 **Facilities:** **Services:** lau **Leisure:** P **Off-site:** R

PONTS-DE-CÉ, LES MAINE-ET-LOIRE

Ile du Château rte de Cholet, av de la Boire Salée, 49130 241446205 241446205
e-mail: ile-du-chateau@wanadoo.fr
website: www.camping-ileduchateau.com
Situated on a small island in the River Loire close to the Château des Ponts-de-Cé. Separate car park for arrivals after 9pm.
SW of Angers towards Cholet.
Open: Apr-Sep **Site:** 2.3HEC **Prices:** 2.40-2.70 pitch 9.90-11.60 (incl 2 persons) (static)145-340 **Facilities:** **Services:** lau **Leisure:** PR

PORNIC LOIRE-ATLANTIQUE

Boutinardière 44210 240820568 240824901
e-mail: info@boutinardiere.com
website: www.camping-boutinardaire.com
The site has three outdoor pools with water slides. Also a heated indoor pool.
Open: Apr-Sep **Site:** 7.5HEC **Prices:** pitch 12-28 (incl 2 persons) **Facilities:** **Services:** lau **Leisure:** P **Off-site:** S

See advertisement on page 137

Sunelia le Patisseau 29 r de Patisseau, 44210 240821039 240822281
e-mail: contact@lepatisseau.com
website: www.lepatisseau.com
In wooded surroundings close to the beach with fine recreational facilities.
3km E via D751.
Open: 26 Mar-13 Nov **Site:** 4.3HEC **Prices:** 4 pitch 20-30.50 (incl 2 persons) pp5-7 **Facilities:** **Services:** lau **Leisure:** P **Off-site:** S

PORNICHET LOIRE-ATLANTIQUE

Bel Air 150 av de Bonne Source, 44380 33240611078
website: www.belairpornichet.com
In a pleasant, wooded location 50m from the beach.
Open: 25 Mar-02 Oct **Site:** 6HEC **Prices:** pitch 11-26 (incl 2 persons) **Facilities:** **Services:** lau **Leisure:** P **Off-site:** S

Forges 98 rte de Villes Blais, 44380 240611884 240601184
e-mail: camping@campinglesforges.com
website: www.campinglesforges.com
In wooded surroundings with well-defined pitches and good recreational facilities.
Access via N171.
Open: All year **Site:** 2HEC **Prices:** 3-5.20 pitch 5-8.50 **Facilities:** **Services:** lau **Leisure:** P **Off-site:** L

PORT-DE-PILES VIENNE

Bec des Deux Eaux rte de Marigny, 86220 247650271
Wooded family site located close to the confluence of the Vienne and Creuse rivers with quite easy access to the Futuroscope.
E off N10.
Open: Apr-Sep **Site:** 3.5HEC **Facilities:** **Services:** lau **Leisure:** PR

PRAILLES DEUX-SÈVRES

Lambon Plan d'eau du Lambon, 78370 549799041 549797862
e-mail: comcanton.celles@wanadoo.fr
website: www.paysmellois.com/lambon
Peaceful rural site situated by a stretch of water with a beach for bathing.
Take D948 from Niort towards from Limoges. Follow signs for Celle-sur-Belle, site 6km N.
Open: Jun-Sep **Site:** 1HEC **Facilities:** **Services:** lau **Leisure:** L **Off-site:** R

RÉ, ILE DE CHARENTE-MARITIME

ARS-EN-RÉ

Cormoran rte de Radia, 17590 ☎ 546294604 ▤ 546292936
e-mail: info@cormoran.com
Situated on the edge of a forest, 500m from village of Ars.
Facilities: **Services:** **Leisure:** P

Soleil 57 r de la Plage, 17590 ☎ 546294062
On level, shaded meadow 150m from the beach and 500m from the village.
➲ *Signed from the N735 shortly before reaching Ars.*
Open: Mar-16 Nov **Site:** 2HEC **Facilities:** **Services:** lau **Off-site:** S

BOIS-PLAGE-EN-RÉ, LE

Antioche 17580 ☎ 546092386 ▤ 546094334
In quiet, wooded area among dunes with direct access to the beach.
➲ *3.5km SE of village towards the beach.*
Open: 27 Mar-Sep **Site:** 2.7HEC **Facilities:** **Services:** lau **Leisure:** S **Off-site:**

Camping Interlude-Gros-Jonc rte de Gros Jonc, 17580
☎ 546091822 ▤ 546092338
e-mail: infos@interlude.fr
website: www.interlude.fr
In a pleasant, wooded location 50m from the beach, this site has a fitness centre and can arrange guided tours of the area.
Open: 9 Apr-2 Nov **Site:** 7.5HEC **Prices:** pitch 21.50-39 (incl 2 persons) **Facilities:** **Services:** lau **Leisure:** P **Off-site:**

COUARDE-SUR-MER, LA

Océan 50 Route d'Ars, 17670 ☎ 546298770 ▤ 546299213
e-mail: campingdelocean@wanadoo.fr
website: www.campingocean.com
In a fine position facing the sea with good modern facilities.
➲ *3km NW on N735.*
Open: Apr-Sep **Site:** 8HEC **Prices:** pitch 14.50-36 **Facilities:** **Services:** lau **Leisure:** P **Off-site:** S

Tour des Prises rte d'Ars, B.P. 27 ☎ 546298482
e-mail: camping@lesprises.com
website: www.camping-la-tour-des-prises.com
Located in the heart of the island, next to a wood, in a peaceful and quiet location. The trees dotted throughout the campsite offer many shady areas.
Open: 23 Mar-Sep **Site:** 2.5HEC **Prices:** pitch 14-30 **Facilities:** **Services:** lau **Leisure:** P **Off-site:** S

FLOTTE, LA

Blanche Deviation de la Flotte, 17630
☎ 546095243 ▤ 546093694
website: www.ileblanche.com
A popular family site in a wooded location.
➲ *N on D735 towards St-Martin.*
Open: Apr-Sep **Site:** 4HEC **Facilities:** **Services:** lau **Leisure:** P **Off-site:** S

Facilities: -shop -shower -electric points for razors -electric points for caravans -parking by tents permitted -compulsory separate car park **Services:** -café/restaurant -bar -Camping Gaz International -gas other than Camping Gaz -first aid facilities lau-laundry **Leisure:** -swimming L-Lake P-Pool R-River S-Sea **Off-site:** All facilities within 2km

Peupliers 17630 0033 546096235 546095976
e-mail: contact@les-peupliers.com
website: www.camp-atlantique.com
Siutated in a large, wooded park 800m from the sea with good sporting facilities.
1.3km SE.
Open: 9 Apr-17 Sep **Site:** 4.4HEC **Prices:** pitch 15-28 (incl 2 persons) **Facilities:** **Services:** lau **Leisure:** P **Off-site:** S

LOIX

Ilates Le Petit Boucheau, rte du Grouin, 17111
546290543 546290679
e-mail: ilates@wanadoo.fr
Access E towards Pointe du Grouin, 500m from the sea.
Open: Apr-12 Nov **Site:** 4.5HEC **Facilities:** **Services:** lau **Leisure:** P **Off-site:** S

STE MARIE-DE-RE

Camping les Grenettes rte du Boise Plage, 17740
546302247 546302464
Open: All year **Site:** 7HEC **Prices:** 4.20 14
Facilities: **Services:** **Leisure:** PS

ST-MARTIN-DE-RÉ

CM r du Rempart, 17410 546092196 546099418
In pleasant wooded surroundings at the foot of the 17th-century ramparts.
N, beyond La Flotte.
Open: Mar-15 Oct **Site:** 4HEC **Prices:** 3.90 pitch 14-17 (incl 3 persons) **Facilities:**
Services: lau **Off-site:** S

île de Ré
les grenettes
domaine hôtelier
Direct access to the beach
Aquatic park, jet stream, water games, paddling pool, water slide.
Marked and shady pitches, restaurant, small supermarket, tennis, rental of bikes, many cycling paths (70 km) starting from the campsite.
Campsite and hotel open all year, swimming pool opened from 1.4. to 30.9., services all year.
Hotel booking recommended.
www.camping-les-grenettes.com
hotelier@club-internet.fr
RENTAL OF:
Mobile-homes, Caravans and Apartments
RD 201 - B.P. 9 F- 17740 STE-MARIE-DE-RÉ
Phone: 00 33 (0)5 46 30 22 47 - Fax: 00 33 (0)5 46 30 24

RILLE INDRE-ET-LOIRE

Huttopia Rille lac de Pincemaille
247246297 247246361
e-mail: rille@huttopia.com
website: www.huttopia.com
Site located at the edge of a lake surrounded by forest in the chateaux area of the Loire. Home to about 190 species of birds. Spacious shady piches.
Open: 25 Jun-30 Oct **Site:** 7HEC
Prices: 4.50-4.70 3.50-7.50 (static)390-690
Facilities: **Services:** lau **Leisure:** LP

RONCE-LES-BAINS CHARENTE-MARITIME

Pignade av des Monards, 17390 546361535 546855292
website: www.camping-lapignade.com
A family site with good recreational facilities.
1.5km S.
Open: 30 Apr-17 Sep **Site:** 16HEC
Prices: (static)693-1106 **Facilities:**
Services: lau **Leisure:** P **Off-site:** S

ROSIERS, LES MAINE-ET-LOIRE

Val de Loire 6 r Ste-Baudruche, 49350
241519433 241518913
A comfortable site partly on the banks of the River Loire with good recreational facilities.
N via D59.
Open: Apr-15 Oct **Site:** 4HEC **Facilities:** **Services:** lau **Leisure:** P **Off-site:** R

ROYAN CHARENTE-MARITIME
AT MÉDIS (4KM NE)

Chênes La Verdonneric, 17600 546067138
In a wooded location with good facilities. Separate late arrivals car park after 22.00.
2km from Royan on the Saintes-Royan road.
Open: All year **Site:** 6.5HEC **Facilities:** **Services:** lau **Leisure:** P

AT PONTAILLAC (2KM NE ON D25)

Clairfontaine allée des Peupliers, 17200
546390811 546381379
e-mail: camping.clairfontaine@wanadoo.fr
website: www.camping-clairfontaine.com
A well-equipped site in wooded surroundings 300m from the beach with a variety of recreational facilities.
Open: 20 May-15 Sep **Site:** 5HEC **Facilities:** **Services:** lau **Leisure:** PS

SABLES-D'OLONNE, LES VENDÉE

Dune des Sables La Paracou, 85100
251323121 251323121
e-mail: camping-chadotel@wanadoo.fr
website: www.chadotel.com
In a fine location facing the sea and close to the beach.
Open: Apr-Sep **Site:** 6HEC **Prices:** 5.70 pitch 14.50-23 (incl 2 persons) **Facilities:**
Services: lau **Leisure:** PS **Off-site:** S

Roses 1 r des Roses, 85100 251951042 251339404
e-mail: camping@chadotel.fr
website: www.chadotel.com
A level site, shaded by trees and bushes, 500m from the Remblai beach.
Close to the town centre off D949.
Open: Apr-3 Nov **Site:** 3.5HEC **Facilities:** **Services:** lau **Leisure:** P **Off-site:** S

Site: 6HEC-Site size -grass -sand -stone -little shade -partly shaded -mainly shaded -bungalows for hire -caravans for hire -tents for hire -no dogs **Prices:** -adult per night -car per night pp-per person per night -caravan per night -tent per night (static)-caravan hire per week

SABLÉ-SUR-SARTHE SARTHE

Hippodrome allée du Quebec, 77233
243954261 243927473
e-mail: camping-sable@wanadoo.fr
website: www.sable-sur-sarthe.com
In a peaceful wooded setting with a great variety of recreational facilities.
Situated 450m from the town.
Open: Apr-Oct **Site:** 3HEC **Prices:** 1.62-2.08 pitch 3.04-4.08 **Facilities:** **Services:** lau **Leisure:** P **Off-site:**

ST-AIGNAN-SUR-CHER LOIR-ET-CHER

CM Cochards 41110 254751559 254754472
e-mail: camping@lescochards.com
website: www.lescochards.com
On beautiful meadowland, completely surrounded by hedges.
1km from bridge on D17 towards Selles.
Open: 26 Mar-15 Oct **Site:** 4HEC **Prices:** 3-3.80 pitch 12.50-15.50 (incl 3 persons) (static)240-430
Facilities: **Services:** lau **Leisure:** P
Off-site: R

ST-AMAND-MONTROND CHER

CM Roche chemin de la Roche, 18200
248960936 248960936
e-mail: mairie-sam@wanadoo.fr
website: www.ville-saint-armond-montrond.fr
In a lovely wooded location between the River Cher and the Berry Canal with good modern facilities.
1.5km SW near river and canal.
Open: Apr-Sep **Site:** 4HEC **Prices:** 2.40 pitch 3.50
Facilities: **Services:** lau **Leisure:** R **Off-site:** P

ST-ANDRÉ-DES-EAUX LOIRE-ATLANTIQUE

CM Les Chalands Fleuris r du Stade, 44117
240012040 240915424
e-mail: chalfleu@club-internet.fr
website: www.chalandsfleuris.com
A peaceful site with good facilities in the middle of a natural park.
1km NE.
Open: Apr-15 Oct **Site:** 4HEC **Prices:** 16-18
Facilities: **Services:** lau **Leisure:** P
Off-site:

ST-AVERTIN INDRE-ET-LOIRE

CM Rives du Cher 61 r de Rochepinard, 37550
247272760 247258289
e-mail: contact@camping-lesrivesducher.com
website: www.camping-lesrivesducher.com
Municipal site on the banks of the River Cher. Only caravans weighing less than 1000kg accepted.
400m N of the town centre and 4km from Tours.
Open: Apr-15 Oct **Site:** 3HEC **Prices:** 3.15 2.10 5.78 3.15 pitch 3.15 (static)139.30-257.25
Facilities: **Services:** lau **Off-site:** LPR

Facilities: -shop -shower -electric points for razors -electric points for caravans -parking by tents permitted -compulsory separate car park **Services:** -café/restaurant -bar -Camping Gaz International -gas other than Camping Gaz -first aid facilities lau-laundry **Leisure:** -swimming L-Lake P-Pool R-River S-Sea **Off-site:** All facilities within 2km

St-Brévin-les-Pins Loire-Atlantique

CM Courance 100/110 av Ml-Foch, 44250
240272291 240272459
e-mail: francecamping@wanadoo.fr
In a pine forest with direct access to the beach.
S off D305.
Open: All year **Site:** 4HEC **Facilities:** **Services:** lau **Leisure:** S **Off-site:** P

Fief, Le 57 chemin du Fief, 44250
0033 240272386 240644619
website: www.lefief.com
A family site adjacent to a long sandy beach. The pitches are surrounded by trees and bushes and there are good modern facilities.
In town follow Route Bleue to Centre Leclerc then take 2nd on right to site.
Open: Apr-16 Oct **Site:** 7HEC **Prices:** 3.50-6.50 pitch 12-28 (incl 2 persons) **Facilities:** **Services:** lau **Leisure:** P **Off-site:** S

See advertisement on page 141

St-Brévin-l'Océan Loire-Atlantique

Pierres Couchées L'Ermitage, 44250
240278564 240849703
e-mail: contact@pierres-couchees.com
website: www.pierres-couchees.com
Extensive, well-screened terrain made up of 3 sites, 2 of which are open all year.
300m from the sea, 2km on D213 toward Pornic.
Open: Apr-15 Oct **Site:** 14HEC **Prices:** pitch 10-24 (incl 2 persons) pp3.50-5.50 (static)320-685 **Facilities:** **Services:** lau **Leisure:** P **Off-site:** S

St-Cyr Vienne

Parc de Loisirs 86130 549625722 549522858
e-mail: contact@parcdesaintcyr.com
website: www.parcdesaintcyr.com
In a delightful setting in a spacious park beside a lake. The Futuroscope is within easy reach via the A10.
1.5km NE via D4/D82.
Open: Apr-Sep **Site:** 5HEC **Facilities:** **Services:** lau **Leisure:** L

Saintes Charente-Maritime

Au Fill de l'Eau 6 r de Courbiac, 17100
546930800 546936188
On the banks of the River Charente, 900m from the town centre.

1km on D128.
Open: May-Sep **Site:** 7HEC **Prices:** 3.35-4.45 pitch 4.30-4.30 (static)300-500 **Facilities:** **Services:** lau **Leisure:** PR **Off-site:**

St-Florent-le-Vieil Maine-et-Loire

Ile Batailleuse 44370 240834501
e-mail: ilebatailleuse@wanadoo.fr
6km SE. N of Lac du Boudon.
Open: Apr-16 Nov **Site:** 2.5HEC **Facilities:** **Services:** lau **Leisure:** R **Off-site:** P

St-Gaultier Indre

Oasis du Berry r de la Pierre Plate, 36800 254471704
e-mail: campoasisduberry@aol.com
website: www.campoasisduberry.com
Open: All year **Site:** 2.5HEC **Prices:** 3.50 pitch 11.50 (incl 2 persons) (static)100-220 **Facilities:** **Services:** lau **Leisure:** P **Off-site:** R

St-Georges-de-Didonne Charente-Maritime

Bois Soleil 2 av de Suzac, 17110
546050594 546062743
e-mail: camping.bois.soleil@wanadoo.fr
website: www.bois-soleil.com
Pitches lie on different levels. Direct access to the beach.
2.5km S of town on D25 Meschers road.
Open: 3 Apr-1 Nov **Site:** 9HEC **Prices:** 3.50-6.50 pitch 17-32 (incl 2 persons) pp3.50-6 **Facilities:** **Services:** lau **Leisure:** PS

Ideal Camping No 1 av de Suzac, 17110
546052904 546063236
e-mail: info@ideal-camping.com
website: www.ideal-camping.com
A well-equipped, peaceful site in a pine forest 200m from Suzac beach.
W of St-Georges-de-Didonne via D25.
Open: 30 Apr-12 Sep **Site:** 8HEC **Prices:** pitch 14.40-18 (incl 3 persons) (static)280-383 **Facilities:** **Services:** lau **Leisure:** P **Off-site:** S

St-Georges-lès-Baillargeaux Vienne

Futuriste 86130 549524752 549524752
e-mail: camping-le-futuriste@wanadoo.fr
website: www.camping-le-futuriste.fr
In an elevated position offering fine views over the Parc du Furturoscope and the Clain valley. Advance booking is advisable from June to August.
Open: All year **Site:** 4HEC **Prices:** 1.70-2.40 pitch 13.10-18 (incl 3 persons) **Facilities:** **Services:** lau **Leisure:** LP **Off-site:**

St-Gilles-Croix-de-Vie Vendée

Bahamas Beach 168 rte des Sables, 85800
251546916 251546916
e-mail: camping-chadotel@wanadoo.fr
website: www.chadotel.com
2km from centre of town and 600m from the beach.
Open: Apr-Sep **Site:** 5HEC **Facilities:** **Services:** lau **Leisure:** PS **Off-site:** S

Domaine de Beaulieu Givrand, 85800 251555946
e-mail: info@camping.chadotel.com
website: www.chadotel.com

Site: 6HEC-Site size -grass -sand -stone -little shade -partly shaded -mainly shaded -bungalows for hire -caravans for hire -tents for hire -no dogs **Prices:** -adult per night -car per night pp-per person per night -caravan per night -tent per night (static)-caravan hire per week

4km from the town and 1km from the beach.
Open: 5 Apr-28 Sep **Site:** 7HEC **Facilities:** **Services:** lau **Leisure:** PS
Off-site: R

Pas Opton rte de Nantes, Le Fenouiller, 85800 251551198
Well tended garden-like site in rural surroundings.
On D754 Nantes Road.
Open: 20 May-10 Sep **Site:** 6.5HEC
Facilities: **Services:** lau **Leisure:** PR

St-Hilaire-de-Riez Vendée

Biches rte de Notre-Dame-de-Riez, 85270
251543882 251543074
e-mail: campingdesbiches@wanadoo.fr
website: www.campingdesbiches.com
A well-equipped site in a pine forest and close to the sea.
2km N.
Open: 15 May-15 Sep **Site:** 10HEC **Prices:** 10 pitch 25.90-37 (incl 3 persons) **Facilities:**
Services: lau **Leisure:** P

Bois Tordu 84 av de la Pège, 85270
251543378 251540829
e-mail: leboistordu@wanadoo.fr
website: www.leboistordu.fr
In a wooded location with good facilities.
5.3km NW.
Open: 15 May-15 Sep **Site:** 2HEC **Prices:** 5.60 pitch 24.80-31 (incl 3 persons) (static)300-660
Facilities: **Services:** lau **Leisure:** P
Off-site: S

Chouans 108 av de la Faye, 85270
251543490 251540592
e-mail: info@sunmarina.com
website: www.sunmarina.com
In a wooded location on the edge of the national forest.
2.5 km NW.
Open: 15 May-15 Sep **Site:** 5HEC **Facilities:** **Services:** lau **Leisure:** P **Off-site:** S

Ecureuils 100 av de la Pège, 85270
251543371 251556908
e-mail: info@camping-aux-ecureuils.com
In pleasant surroundings, 250m from a fine sandy beach, with good recreational facilities.
From A11 to Nantes, then via D178 and D753 to St-Hilaire-de-Riez.
Open: 15 May-15 Sep **Site:** 3HEC **Prices:** 4.35-5.35 pitch 23-31 (incl 2 persons) **Facilities:**
Services: lau **Leisure:** P **Off-site:** S

Padrelle 1 r Prévot, La Corniche de Sion/l'Océan, 85270
251553203
In a rural setting 50m from the beach and within 5 minutes of the town.
Open: May-Sep **Site:** 1.5HEC **Facilities:**
Services: lau **Off-site:** PS

Plage 106 av de la Pège, 85270 251543393 251559702
e-mail: campinglaplage@campingscollinet.com
website: www.campingscollinet.com
On a meadow with trees. Access to beach via dunes.
5.7km NW.
Open: 15 Apr-10 Sep **Site:** 5.5HEC
Prices: 4.32-4.80 pitch 18.45-20.50 (incl 2 persons) (static)310-425 **Facilities:** **Services:** lau **Leisure:** PS **Off-site:**

La Puerta del Sol
Hôtellerie de plein air
Grand confort ★★★★
Within the circle of our sunny site, surrounded by splendid pine and oak trees, in an ideal place for a holiday with your family in a quiet and peaceful setting, we offer: For your comfort: fully equipped, marked pitches of 100 m2; bar, self service, snacks, take-away meals, grocery, laundry, etc... For your relaxing and leisure time: heated swimming pool with 25 m waterslide, tennis, volleyball, table tennis, children's games, entertainment (in high season: karaoke and dancing evenings, games, etc.), mini club (in the morning), sports activities during the day.
85270 ST-HILAIRE-DE-RIEZ
Tel 02 51 49 10 10
Fax 02 51 49 84 84
info@campinglapuertadelsol.com
www.campinglapuertadelsol.com

Prairie chemin des Roselières, 85270
251540856 251559702
e-mail: campinglaprairie@campingscollinet.com
website: www.campingscollinet.com
A family site with pitches shaded by trees. Advance booking recommended in high season.
5.5km NW, 500m from the beach.
Open: 15 May-10 Sep **Site:** 4.7HEC
Prices: 3.96-4.40 pitch 21.15-23.50 (incl 2 persons) (static)350-430 **Facilities:** **Services:** lau
Leisure: P **Off-site:** S

Puerta del Sol Les Borderies - D59, 85270
251491010 251498484
e-mail: info@campinglapuertadelsol.com
website: campinglapuertadelsol.com
A peaceful site with well-defined pitches in a wooded location. Good facilities for family recreation.
4.5km N.
Open: Apr-Sep **Site:** 4HEC **Prices:** 8.50-13.50 pitch 8.50-13.50 **Facilities:**
Services: lau **Leisure:** P **Off-site:**

Sol-à-Gogo 61 av de la Pège, 85270
251542900 251548874
e-mail: solagogo@wanadoo.fr
website: www.solagogo.com
A family site with good recreational facilities, including an aquaslide, with direct access to the beach.
4.8km NW of St-Hilaire, 6km S of St-Jean-de-Monts.
Open: 15 May-15 Sep **Site:** 4HEC
Prices: pitch 24.80-32 (incl 3 persons) (static)330-660
Facilities: **Services:** lau **Leisure:** PS
Off-site:

Facilities: -shop -shower -electric points for razors -electric points for caravans -parking by tents permitted -compulsory separate car park **Services:** -café/restaurant -bar -Camping Gaz International -gas other than Camping Gaz -first aid facilities lau-laundry **Leisure:** -swimming L-Lake P-Pool R-River S-Sea **Off-site:** All facilities within 2km

ST-HILAIRE-LA-FORÊT VENDÉE

Batardières 85440 ☎ 251333385
In a pleasant location, surrounded by mature trees and shrubs with large individual pitches, separated by hedges.
➲ *W on D70.*
Open: Jul-Sep **Site:** 1.6HEC **Prices:** pitch 89 (incl 2 persons) **Facilities:** **Services:** lau **Off-site:**

Grand' Métairie 8 r de la Vineuse en Plaine, 85440
☎ 251333238 251332569
e-mail: grand-metairie@wanadoo.fr
website: www.la-grand-metairie.com
Site with flowers and trees with clearly marked sites. Entertainment for children and teenagers. Free shuttle available to nearby sandy beach.
Open: Apr-Sep **Site:** 3.8HEC **Prices:** pitch 18-26 (incl 2 persons) (static)210-710 **Facilities:** **Services:** lau **Leisure:** P **Off-site:** LS

ST-HILAIRE-PEYROUX CORRÈZE

Le Chazal 19560 ☎ 555257296
e-mail: camping.lechazal@wanadoo.fr
website: perso.wanadoo.fr/camping.lechazal/
A peaceful site on the edge of the Massif Central with fine views over the Couze valley.
➲ *N89 Brive to Tulle. At Malemort take D141 left off roundabout to Venarsal and then proceed 1.5m for St-Hilaire-Peyroux. Turn left onto C13 for campsite.*
Open: Apr-1 Nov **Site:** 1.5HEC **Prices:** 3.50 4 **Facilities:** **Services:** lau **Off-site:**

ST JEAN-D'ANGELY CHARENTE-MARITIME

Val de Boutonne ☎ 546322616
e-mail: info@valba.net **website:** www.valbanet
In a wooded location.
➲ *NE, near the river.*
Open: 16 May-Sep **Site:** 1.8HEC **Prices:** 2.40-3 pitch 9.20-11.50 **Facilities:** **Services:** lau **Leisure:** PR **Off-site:**

ST-JEAN-DE-MONTS VENDÉE

Abri des Pins rte de Notre-Dame-de-Monts, 85160
☎ 251588386 251593047
e-mail: abridespins@aol.com
website: www.abridespins.com
A family site on level grassland with pitches subdivided by hedges, bushes and trees. 10-minute walk from the beach.
➲ *4km N on D38 Notre-Dame-de-Monts road.*
Open: 3 May-12 Sep **Site:** 3HEC **Facilities:** **Services:** lau **Leisure:** P **Off-site:** S

Amiaux 223 rte de Notre-Dame de Monts, 85160
☎ 251582222 251582609
e-mail: accueil@amiaux.fr
website: www.amiaux.fr
A well-equipped site on the edge of a forest, 700m from the beach.
➲ *3.5km NW of D38.*
Open: Etr-Sep **Site:** 16HEC **Prices:** 3.70 pitch 11-22 **Facilities:** **Services:** lau **Leisure:** P **Off-site:** S

Avenhiriers de la Calypso rte de Notre-Dame-de-Monts, Les Tonnelles, 85160 ☎ 251597966 251597967
e-mail: camping_apv@wanadoo.fr
website: www.lesaventuriersdelacalypso.com
A holiday village with good, modern facilities, 700m from Tonnelles beach.
Open: Apr-Sep **Site:** 5HEC **Prices:** 5 pitch 21-24 (static)145-565 **Facilities:** **Services:** lau **Leisure:** P **Off-site:** S

Bois Dormant 168 r des Sables, 85160 ☎ UK Central Res 0870 242 7777 0870 242 9999 (Central Res)
website: www.haveneurope.com
Open: Apr-14 Sep **Site:** 11.5HEC
Facilities: **Services:** lau

Bois Joly 46 r de Notre-Dame-de-Monts, BP 507, 85165
☎ 251591163 251591106
e-mail: boisjoly@compuserve.com
website: www.camping-leboisjoly.com
A pleasantly landscaped, terraced site set among pine trees. Good facilities. Close to the beach and the town centre.
Open: Apr-26 Sep **Site:** 7.5HEC **Prices:** 2.20-4 pitch 15-24 (incl 2 persons) **Facilities:** **Services:** lau **Leisure:** PR **Off-site:** S

Bois Masson 149 r des Sables, 85160
☎ 251586262 251582997
e-mail: boismasson@haven.fr
website: www.haveneurope.com
A family site with a wide variety of facilities. In a wooded setting, just a few minutes from the beach. Aquatic complex includes covered and outdoor pools, water chutes, Jacuzzi and sauna.
➲ *2km SE.*
Open: 19 Mar-1 Oct **Site:** 7.5HEC
Prices: 3-6 pitch 13-34 (incl 2 persons) (static)210-749
Facilities: **Services:** lau **Leisure:** P
Off-site: S

Clarys Plage av des Epines, 85160
251581024 251595196
e-mail: leclarys@wanadoo.fr
website: www.leclarys.com
A family site with good facilities including an indoor swimming pool and an outdoor pool with a water slide.
S of town 300m from the beach.
Open: 15 May-15 Sep **Site:** 8HEC **Prices:** pitch 24.80-31 (incl 3 persons) (static)300-660 **Facilities:** **Services:** lau **Leisure:** P **Off-site:** S

Sirenes av des Demoiselles, 85160
251580131 251590367
In a forested location 500m from the beach with good facilities.
SE off D38.
Open: 27 Mar-Oct **Site:** 15HEC **Facilities:** **Services:** lau **Off-site:** PS

Forêt 190 chemin de la Rive, 85160
251588463 251588463
e-mail: camping-la-foret@wanadoo.fr
website: www.chez.com/campinglaforet
A well-equipped family site in a pleasant rural setting.
5.5km NW.
Open: 15 Apr-Sep **Site:** 1HEC **Prices:** 3-5 pitch 16-23.50 (incl 2 persons) **Facilities:** **Services:** lau **Leisure:** P **Off-site:** S

Zagarella rte des Sables, 85160 251581982 251593528
e-mail: zagarella@wanadoo.fr
website: www.zagarella.fr
Open: 15 May-15 Sep **Site:** 4.2HEC **Prices:** pitch 27.50 **Facilities:** **Services:** lau **Leisure:** P **Off-site:** S

At Orouet (6km SE)

Yole chemin des Bosses, 85160
251586717 251590535
e-mail: contact@la-yole.com
website: www.la-yole.com
In rural surroundings 1km from a fine sandy beach.
Signed from D38 in Orouet.
Open: 2 Apr-Sep **Site:** 6HEC **Prices:** pitch 17-28.20 (incl 2 persons) (static)304-612 **Facilities:** **Services:** lau **Leisure:** P **Off-site:** S

St-Julien-des-Landes Vendée

Fôret 85150 251466211 251466087
e-mail: camping@domainelaforet.com
website: www.domainelaforet.com
In a picturesque setting in the grounds of a château with well-defined pitches and modern facilities.
NE on D55, rte de Martinet.
Open: 15 May-15 Sep **Site:** 50HEC **Facilities:** **Services:** lau **Leisure:** P

Garangeoire 85150 251466539 251466985
e-mail: garangeoire@wanadoo.fr
website: www.camping-la-garangeoire.com
Family site set in 200-hectare estate. Pitches separated by hedges. A good variety of recreational facilities.
2km N of the village.
Open: 2 Apr-23 Sep **Site:** 15HEC **Prices:** 4.50 pitch 14-33.50 (incl 2 persons) **Facilities:** **Services:** lau **Leisure:** LP

Guyonnière La Guyonnière, 85150
251466259 251466289
e-mail: info@laguyonniere.com
website: www.laguyonniere.com
A pleasant site with pitches divided by hedges with good sanitary and recreational facilities.
2km from the town centre towards St-Gilles-Croix-de-Vie.
Open: May-Oct **Site:** 30HEC **Prices:** pitch 21 (incl 2 persons) **Facilities:** **Services:** lau **Leisure:** LP

St-Just-Luzac Charente-Maritime

Castel Camping Séquoia Parc La Josephtrie, 17320
546855555 546855556
e-mail: sequoia.parc@wanadoo.fr
website: www.sequoiaparc.com
Situated in a spacious park on the La Josephtrie estate containing an attractive château, some 5km from the coast.
Access via A10 exit Saintes then D728 towards Ile d'Oléron and follow signs from St-Just.
Open: 14 May-10 Sep **Site:** 45HEC **Prices:** 6-8 pitch 15-35 (incl 2 persons) **Facilities:** **Services:** lau **Leisure:** P

St-Laurent-Nouan Loir-et-Cher

Amitié r du Camping, 41220 254870152 254870993
On the shore of the River Loire between Blois and Orléans.
On D951.
Open: All year **Site:** 2HEC **Facilities:** **Services:** lau **Leisure:** R **Off-site:**

St-Léonard-de-Noblat Haute-Vienne

CM Beaufort 87400 555560279
e-mail: mairie-st-leonard-de-noblat@wanadoo.fr
website: www.ville-st-leonard.fr
In pleasant wooded surroundings with good facilities.
Access from the D39.
Open: 15 Jun-15 Sep **Site:** 2HEC **Prices:** 2.04 pitch 7.15-8.15 (incl 2 persons) **Facilities:** **Services:** lau **Off-site:**

St-Malô-du-Bois Vendée

La Vallee de Poupet 85590 251923145 251923865
e-mail: camping@valleedepoupet.com
website: www.valleedepoupet.com
In a picturesque location beside the River Sèvre Nantaise, surrounded by woodland.
From village take D72 for 1km, then take left fork and follow signs.
Open: 15 May-15 Sep **Site:** 3HEC **Prices:** 2.70-3 pitch 11.25-12.50 (incl 2 persons) **Facilities:** **Services:** lau **Leisure:** PR **Off-site:**

St-Palais-sur-Mer Charente-Maritime

Ormeaux 44 av de Bernezac, 17420
546390207 546385666
e-mail: campingormeaux@tiscali.fr
website: www.camping-ormeaux.com
Well equipped site in wooded surroundings, 500m from the beach.
1km N.
Open: Apr-Oct & Nov-Mar **Site:** 3.5HEC **Prices:** pitch 18.50-24.50 (incl 3 persons) (static)220-405 **Facilities:** **Services:** lau **Leisure:** P **Off-site:** LS

Facilities: -shop -shower -electric points for razors -electric points for caravans -parking by tents permitted -compulsory separate car park **Services:** -café/restaurant -bar -Camping Gaz International -gas other than Camping Gaz -first aid facilities lau-laundry **Leisure:** -swimming L-Lake P-Pool R-River S-Sea **Off-site:** All facilities within 2km

Puits de l'Auture La Grande Côte, 17420
546232031 546232638
e-mail: camping-lauture@wanadoo.fr
website: www.camping-puitsdelauture.com
A family site in a picturesque location at the edge of a forest facing the sea.
2km NW on D25 La Palmyre road.
Open: May-Sep **Site:** 5HEC **Prices:** pitch 15.50-31 (incl 2 persons) **Facilities:** **Services:** lau **Leisure:** P **Off-site:** S

SAINT-REVÉRÉND VENDÉE

Pont Rouge av Georges Clémenceau, 85220
251546850 251546850
e-mail: camping.pontrouge@wanadoo.fr
website: www.camping-lepontrouge.com
Quiet site situated in the Vendee countryside within easy reach of the sea.
From La Roche sur Yon, take D948 Noirmoutier-St Hilaire. Exit for Aizenay and take D6 towards Saint Gilles. Pass Coex and turn off at Saint Reverend.
Open: Apr-Oct **Site:** 1.6HEC **Prices:** pitch 11.82-13.90 (incl 2 persons) (static)160-312 **Facilities:** **Services:** lau **Leisure:** PR **Off-site:**

ST-VINCENT-SUR-JARD VENDÉE

'Bolée d'Air' rte du Bouil, 85520
251903605 251339404
e-mail: chadotel@wanadoo.fr
website: camping.chadotel.fr
A family site on level ground with pitches divided by hedges. Good recreational facilities, including a water slide, and 900m from Bouil beach.

2km E via D21.
Open: Apr-Sep **Site:** 6.5HEC **Prices:** 5.70 pitch 12-22.50 (incl 2 persons) **Facilities:** **Services:** lau **Leisure:** P **Off-site:** S

STE-CATHERINE-DE-FIERBOIS INDRE-ET-LOIRE

Parc de Fierbois 37800 247654335 247655375
e-mail: parc.fierbois@wanadoo.fr
website: www.fierbois.com
Beside artificial lake; good bathing area.
Follow D101 off N10, 1.5km SE.
Open: 15 May-14 Sep **Site:** 20HEC **Prices:** pitch 15-33 (incl 2 persons) (static)189-700 **Facilities:** **Services:** lau **Leisure:** LP

STE-GEMME CHARENTE-MARITIME

Jamica la Sablière Ferme de Magne, 17250 546229099
In a pleasant situation beside a lake within a country park.
Access via A10 exit 25 (Saintes) and D728 towards Ile d'Oléron.
Open: May-15 Oct **Site:** **Facilities:** **Services:** lau **Leisure:** L

STE-REINE-DE-BRETAGNE LOIRE-ATLANTIQUE

Château du Deffay BP 18, 44160
240880057 240016655
e-mail: campingdudeffay@wanadoo.fr
website: camping-le-deffay.com
Situated in the beautiful Parc de Brière providing fishing, walking and horse riding. Games and TV rooms.
4.5km W on D33 rte de Pontchâteau.
Open: 7 May-16 Sep **Site:** 12HEC **Prices:** 3-4.80 pitch 10.40-14.60 **Facilities:** **Services:** lau **Leisure:** LP

SANTROP HAUTE-VIENNE

Santrop 87640 555710808 555712393
e-mail: lacsaintpardoux@wanadoo.fr
website: www.lac-saint-pardoux.com
A well-equipped family site on the shore of Lac de St-Pardoux with good facilities for water sports.
Access via A20 exit 25.
Toboggen, Tennis **Open:** 8 May-20 Sep **Site:** 4.5HEC **Prices:** 3.10-4.10 pitch 9.70-15.80 (incl 2 persons) **Facilities:** **Services:** lau **Leisure:** L

SAUMUR MAINE-ET-LOIRE

Chantepie 49400 241679534 241679585
e-mail: info@campingchantepie.com
website: www.campingchantepie.com
A pleasant site with a fine view over the River Loire.
Access via D751 towards Gennes.
Open: 14 May-10 Sep **Site:** 10HEC **Prices:** 4.50-6 pitch 15-24 **Facilities:** **Services:** lau **Leisure:** P

Ile d'Offard av de Verden, 49400
241403000 241673781
e-mail: iledoffard@wanadoo.fr
website: www.cvtloisirs.com
On island in the Loire near municipal stadium. Some facilities are only available during the high season.
Open: Mar-Oct **Site:** 4.5HEC **Facilities:** **Services:** lau **Leisure:** P **Off-site:** R

SELLE CRAONNAISE, LA MAYENNE

Rincerie Base de Loisirs la Rincerie, 53800
243061752 243075020
website: www.la-rincerie.com
A modern site offering a good selection of sporting facilities. Separate carpark for arrivals after 22.00.
N of La Selle-Craonnaise towards Ballots.
Open: All year **Site:** 5HEC **Prices:** 5.80-9.50
Facilities: **Services:** lau

SILLÉ-LE-GUILLAUME SARTHE

Privé du Landereau 72140 243201269
1.5km NW via D304.
Open: Etr-15 Oct **Site:** 2.5HEC **Facilities:** **Services:** lau **Off-site:** LR

SILLÉ-LE-PHILIPPE SARTHE

Château de Chanteloup 72460
243275107 243890505
e-mail: chanteloup.souffront@wanadoo.fr
website: www.chateau-de-chanteloup.com
Set partly in wooded clearings and open ground within the park surrounding an old mansion. Good sanitary installations.
17km NE of Le Mans on D301.
Open: 28 May-3 Sep **Site:** 20HEC **Prices:** 5-6.50 pitch 7-11 **Facilities:** **Services:** lau
Leisure: P

SOUTERRAINE, LA CREUSE

Suisse Océan Le Cheix, 23300 555633332
1.8km E via D912 near the lake.
Open: All year **Site:** 2HEC **Facilities:**
Services: lau **Off-site:** L

SUÈVRES LOIR-ET-CHER

Château de la Grenouillère 41500
254878037 254878421
e-mail: la.grenouillere@wanadoo.fr
website: www.camping-loire.fr
Completely divided into pitches. Castle now hotel with common room for campers. Each pitch 150sq m. Separate area for overnight campers.
3km from village towards Orléans.
Open: May-5 Sep **Site:** 11HEC **Prices:** 5-7 19-29 **Facilities:** **Services:** lau
Leisure: P

SULLY-SUR-LOIRE LOIRET

CM chemin de la Salle Verte, 45600 238362393
Near Château, adjacent to River Loire.
100m from town.
Open: 26 Apr-29 Sep **Site:** 1.5HEC
Facilities: **Services:** lau **Off-site:** P

AT ST-PÉRE-SUR-LOIRE

St-Père rte d'Orléans, 45600 238363594
On a level meadow on the right bank of the River Loire.
W on D60 towards St-Benoît-sur-Loire.
Open: 4 Apr-Sep **Site:** 2.7HEC
Facilities: **Services:** lau **Off-site:** PR

TALMONT-ST-HILAIRE VENDÉE

Littoral Le Porteau, 85440 251220464 251220537
e-mail: info@campinglelittoral.fr
website: www.campinglelittoral.fr
Sitauted near Port Bourgenay, 80m from the sea. Good facilities and entertainment available during the season.
Open: Apr-Sep **Site:** 8.5HEC **Prices:** pitch 17-29 (incl 2 persons) pp4-5.60 **Facilities:**
Services: lau **Leisure:** P **Off-site:** S

TOURS INDRE-ET-LOIRE
AT BALLAN-MIRÉ (8.5KM W D751)

Mignardière 22 av des Aubepines, 37510
247733100 247733101
e-mail: info@mignardiere.com
website: www.mignardiere.com
A well-maintained site with a variety of sports facilities.
2.5km NE.
Open: 10 Apr-Sep **Site:** 3.5HEC **Facilities:**
Services: lau **Leisure:** P **Off-site:**

TRANCHE-SUR-MER, LA VENDÉE

Almadies rte de la Roche-sur-Yon, 85360
251303694 251303704
e-mail: le-repos-dupecheur@wanadoo.fr
website: www.lesalmadies.com
Situated on the banks of a canal 3km from the sea.
Open: Apr-Oct **Site:** 11HEC **Prices:** 4-6.50 pitch 12.50-23.85 (static)225-415 **Facilities:**
Services: lau **Leisure:** PR

Bale d'Aunis 10 r du Pertuis, 85360
251274736 251274454
e-mail: info@camping-baiedaunis.com
website: www.camping-baiedaunis.com
On level land on sea-shore, 50m from the beach and 400m from the town centre with a variety of leisure activities.
300m E on D46.
Open: May-18 Sep **Site:** 2.4HEC
Prices: pitch 22.20-25.80 (incl 2 persons) (static)310-620
Facilities: **Services:** lau **Leisure:** PS
Off-site:

Bel r du Bottereau, 85360 251304739 251277281
A quiet, family-run site 500m from a magnificent beach and a marine lake. Plenty of sports and entertainment facilities.
400m from town centre.
Open: 28 May-5 Sep **Site:** 3.5HEC
Prices: 24 24 pitch 24 (incl 2 persons) **Facilities:**
Services: lau **Leisure:** PS **Off-site:**

Cottage Fleuri La Grière-Plage, 85360
251303457 251277477
A level site with modern facilities.
2.5km E, 500m from the beach.
Open: Apr-15 Oct **Site:** 7.5HEC **Facilities:**
Services: lau **Leisure:** P **Off-site:** S

Jard 123 bd de Lattre-de-Tassigny, 85360
251274379 251274292
e-mail: info@camping-du-jard.fr
A family site on level ground with clearly defined pitches, 700m from the beach, with plenty of recreational facilities.
Access via D747.
Open: 23 May-15 Sep **Site:** 6HEC
Facilities: **Services:** lau **Leisure:** P
Off-site:

Savinière 85360 251274270 251274048
Set in a beautiful natural park with good, modern facilities.
1.5km NW via D105.
Open: Apr-Sep **Site:** 2.5HEC **Facilities:** **Services:** lau **Leisure:** P **Off-site:** S

TROCHE CORRÈZE

Domaine Vert Les Magnes 555735989 555735989
website: www.ledomainevert.nl
Peaceful farm site surrounded by grass and woodland where campers can select their own pitch. Simple facilities and the opportunity to try the organic produce from the farm.
A20 between Limoges and Brive take exit 45. Drive to Vigeois in the direction of Troche and shortly after Vigeois turn right. Take D50 in direction of Lubersac, campsite after 5km.
Open: 15 Apr-1 Oct **Site:** 3HEC **Prices:** 4 pitch 14 **Facilities:** **Services:** lau

TROGUES INDRE-ET-LOIRE

Château de la Rolandière 37220
247585371 247585371
e-mail: contact@larolandiere.com
website: www.larolandiere.com
Situated in the parkland surrounding a fine chateau. Ideal for visiting the chateaux of the Loire valley.
A10 exit 25, follow road for Chinon for 6km.
Open: 15 Apr-Sep **Site:** 4HEC **Prices:** 6 pitch 8.50 **Facilities:** **Services:** lau **Leisure:** P
Off-site: R

TURBALLE, LA LOIRE-ATLANTIQUE

Parc Ste-Brigitte Domaine de Bréhet, 44420
240248891 240156572
e-mail: saintebrigitte@wanadoo.fr
website: www.campingsaintebrigitte.com
Site in grounds of old Château. Parkland divided into pitches and surrounded by hedges.
E of village on D99 Guérande road.
Open: Apr-Sep **Site:** 6HEC **Prices:** 5.50 3 12 pitch 6 **Facilities:** **Services:** lau
Leisure: P

VALENÁAY INDRE

CM Chênes rte de Loches, 36600
254000392 254000392
A quiet site on level ground with well-defined pitches.
1km W on D960.
Open: 27 Apr-29 Sep **Site:** 5HEC **Facilities:** **Services:** lau **Leisure:** LP **Off-site:** R

VARENNES-SUR-LOIRE MAINE-ET-LOIRE

Étang de la Brèche 5 Impasse de la Brèche, 49730
241512292 241512724
e-mail: etang.breche@wanadoo.fr
website: www.etang-breche.com
Relaxing site in the heart of the Loire valley, ideal base for visiting sites of historical interest.
4.5km NW via N152.
Open: 15 May-15 Sep **Site:** 24HEC **Prices:** 4.50-6 pitch 17-28.50 (incl 2 persons) **Facilities:** **Services:** lau **Leisure:** P

VEILLON, LE VENDÉE

St-Hubert av de la Plage, Bourgenay Le Veillon, 85440
251222230 251222230
e-mail: campingsthubert@free.fr
website: www.campingsainthubert.com
In a wooded location with well-defined pitches, 300m from the sea.
From Talmont-St-Hilaire head towards Bourgenay and Veillon.
Open: Apr-Sep **Site:** 1HEC **Facilities:** **Services:** lau **Off-site:** LPS

VELLES INDRE

Grands Pins Les Maisons Neuves, 36330
254366193 254361009
e-mail: contact@les-grands-pins.fr
website: www.les-grands-pins.fr
The site has individual pitches and has easy access to the countryside. Swimming pool available July and August only.
7km S of Châteauroux on N20.
Open: All year **Site:** 5HEC **Prices:** 4.10 pitch 4.10 **Facilities:** **Services:** lau **Leisure:** P

VENDÔME LOIR-ET-CHER

Grand Prés r G-Martel, 41100
254770027 254834358
e-mail: camping.vendome@free.fr
Site lies on a meadow, next to a sports ground.
E of town on right bank of Loire.
Open: 10 Jun-Aug **Site:** 2.5HEC **Prices:** 2.71 pitch 7.15 (incl 2 persons) **Facilities:** **Services:** lau **Leisure:** PR **Off-site:**

VILLIERS-LE-MORHIER EURE-ET-LOIR

Ilots de St Val 237827130 237827767
e-mail: lesilots@campinglesilotsdestval.com
website: www.campinglesilotsdestval.com
In a peaceful and quiet rural setting between Maintenon and Nogent-le-Roi, nestling above the Eure river. A haven for wildlife.
On D983.
Open: All year **Site:** **Prices:** 4.70 4.70 (static)140-195 **Facilities:** **Services:** lau

VINEUIL LOIR-ET-CHER

Rives de Loire Lac de Loire, 41350
254788205 254786203
Level site on left bank of River Loire with modern buildings. Boating. Bathing not recommended.
From Blois drive towards St-Dye. After modern bridge continue towards Lac de Loire for 1.5km.
Open: Jun-15 Sep **Site:** 30HEC **Prices:** pitch 8-12 (incl 2 persons) **Facilities:** **Services:** lau
Leisure: PR

BRITTANY/NORMANDY

ALENÇON ORNE

CM de Guéramé 65 r de Guéramé, 61000 233263495
Situated in open country near a stream, 500m from town centre.
Access via the Boulevard Périphérique in the SW part of town.
Open: All year **Site:** 1.5HEC **Facilities:** **Services:** lau **Leisure:** R **Off-site:** P

Jacques Fould av H-Chanteloup, 61000 233292329
On N12.
Open: All year **Site:** 1HEC **Facilities:** **Services:** lau **Off-site:** PR

ALLINEUC CÔTES-D'ARMOR

Lac de Bosméléac Bosméléac, 22460
296288788 296288097
Wooded site situated by the sides of a lake with a beach.
Off RN 12 Brest-Paris road, exit for Loudéac.
Open: 14 Jun-15 Sep **Site:** 1.2HEC **Prices:** 2.30 2.80 2.80 pitch 2.80 **Facilities:** **Services:** lau **Leisure:** L **Off-site:** R

ARRADON MORBIHAN

Penboch 9 chemin de Penboch, 56610
297447129 297447910
e-mail: camping.penboch@wanadoo.fr
website: www.camping-penboch.fr
An exceptionally well-appointed site in a pleasant wooded location 200m from the beaches of the gulf of Morbihan.
Signed from N165.
Open: 9 Apr-24 Sep **Site:** 4HEC **Prices:** 3-4.70 pitch 3.95-18.70 (incl 2 persons) (static)215-720 **Facilities:** **Services:** lau **Leisure:** PS **Off-site:** S

ARZANO FINISTÈRE

Ty Nadan rte d'Arzano, 29310
298717547 298717731
e-mail: infos@camping-ty-nadan.fr
website: www.camping-ty-nadan.fr
A quiet riverside site in attractive parkland in the Ellé valley.
3km W. Leave N165 at Quimperlé exit and drive towards Arzano.
Open: 19 Mar-8 Sep **Site:** 12HEC **Prices:** 5-8 pitch 10-20 (static)322-770 **Facilities:** **Services:** lau **Leisure:** PR

AUDIERNE FINISTÈRE

Loquéran BP 55, 29770 298749506 298749114
e-mail: campgite.loqueran@free.fr
A terraced woodland site in calm and peaceful surroundings, a short distance from the sea.
Open: May-Sep **Site:** 1HEC **Prices:** 3 1.50 pitch 3 **Facilities:** **Services:** lau **Off-site:** S

AVRANCHES MANCHE
AT GENÊTS (10KM W ON D911)

Coques d'Or 14 rte du Bec d'Andaine, 50530
233708257 233708683
A well-equipped site 1km from the sea.
Open: Apr-Sep **Site:** 5HEC **Facilities:** **Services:** lau **Leisure:** P **Off-site:**

BADEN MORBIHAN

Mané Guernehué 56870 297570206 297571543
e-mail: mane-guernehue@wanadoo.fr
website: www.mane-guernehue.com
In a pleasant situation at the head of the gulf of Morbihan with good recreational facilities.
1km SW via Mériadec road.
Open: 9 Apr-Sep **Site:** 8HEC **Prices:** 3.10-6.40 pitch 10.50-18 **Facilities:** **Services:** lau **Leisure:** P **Off-site:** S

BAYEUX CALVADOS

CM Calvados bd d'Eindhoven, 14400
231920843 231920843
website: www.mairie-bayeaux.fr
Very clean and tidy site with tarmac drive and hardstanding for caravans. Adjoins football field.
N side of town on Boulevard Circulaire.
Open: May-Sep **Site:** 2.9HEC **Prices:** 3.04 3.75 3.75 pitch 3.75 **Facilities:** **Services:** lau **Off-site:** P

BEG-MEIL FINISTÈRE

Kervastard chemin de Kervastard, 29170
298949152 298949983
e-mail: camping.le.kervastard@wanadoo.fr
In a pleasant wooded area close to a fine sandy beach with plenty of leisure facilities.
Within the village, 250m from the beach.
Open: May-Sep **Site:** 2HEC **Prices:** 3.20-5.20 pitch 7.20-10 (static)228.67-548.81 **Facilities:** **Services:** lau **Leisure:** P **Off-site:** S

Roche Percée 29170 298949415 298944805
e-mail: contact@camping-larochepercée.com
website: www.camping-larochepercée.com
Wooded family site 400m from the Roche Percée beach.
1km from Beg Meil towards Fouesnant.
Open: 8 Apr-26 Sep **Site:** 2HEC **Prices:** 3-4.50 pitch 8.50-11.50 (static)229-520 **Facilities:** **Services:** lau **Leisure:** P **Off-site:** S

BÉNODET FINISTÈRE

Letty 29950 298570469 298662256
e-mail: reception@campingduletty.com
website: www.campingduletty.com
Site bordering beach, divided into sectors. Good sanitary installations, ironing rooms and games room. Good beach for children. Use of car park compulsory after 11pm.
By the sea 1km SE.
Open: 15 Jun-6 Sep **Site:** 10HEC **Prices:** 5 pitch 8 (static)310-420 **Facilities:** **Services:** lau **Leisure:** S

Pointe St-Gilles r du Poulmic, 29950
298570537 298572752
e-mail: information@camping-stgilles.fr
website: www.camping-stgilles.fr
Holiday site S of village, on fields by beach. Divided into several sectors; individual pitches. Well-equipped sanitary blocks.
Open: 19 Apr-20 Sep **Site:** 7HEC **Facilities:** **Services:** lau **Leisure:** PS **Off-site:**

Port de Plaisance 7 rte de Quimper, Prad Poullou, 29950
298570238 298572525
e-mail: info@camping-benodet.fr
website: www.camping-benodet.fr
A well-equipped family site on the outskirts of the town, 500m from the harbour.
NE off D34 at the entrance to the town.
Open: 15 Apr-Sep **Site:** 10HEC **Facilities:** **Services:** lau **Leisure:** P **Off-site:** RS

BÉNOUVILLE CALVADOS

Hautes Coutures rte de Ouistréham, 14970
231447308 231953080
e-mail: camping-hautes-coutures@wavadoo.fr
Pleasant site with good facilities near the Canal Maritîme and within easy reach of the Caen-Portsmouth ferry.
From Caen, driving toward Ouistréham on the dual carriageway, Camping Les Hautes Coutures has its own exit shortly after the Pegasus Bridge exit. On the R of the dual carriageway.
Open: Apr-Sep **Site:** 8HEC **Prices:** 6.50 pitch 7.50 **Facilities:** **Services:** lau **Leisure:** PR **Off-site:** S

BINIC CÔTES-D'ARMOR

Palmiers Kerviarc'h, 22520 296737259 296737259
e-mail: campingpalmiers.chantal@laposte.net
website: www.campingpalmiers.com
A well-equipped site within the Parc Tropical de Bretagne, just over 1km from the town centre.
Access via N12/D786.
Open: 15 Jul-Sep **Site:** 2HEC **Prices:** pitch 14 (incl 2 persons) pp4 **Facilities:** **Services:** lau **Leisure:** P **Off-site:** RS

BLAINVILLE-SUR-MER MANCHE

Senéquet 50910 233472311
A family site with plenty of recreational facilities.
2km NW on D651.
Open: Mar-early Dec **Site:** 13HEC **Facilities:** **Services:** lau **Leisure:** PS **Off-site:**

BLANGY-LE-CHÂTEAU CALVADOS

Brévedent 14130 231647288 231643341
e-mail: contact@campinglebrevedent.com
website: www.campinglebrevedent.com
Situated in the grounds of an 18th-century manor house with good facilities.
3km SE on D51 beside lake.
Open: May-25 Sep **Site:** 5.5HEC **Prices:** 4.10-5.50 pitch 6-8 **Facilities:** **Services:** lau **Leisure:** P **Off-site:**

Domaine du Lac 14130 231646200 231641591
Open: Apr-Oct **Site:** 4HEC **Facilities:** **Services:** lau **Leisure:** LR

BLANGY-SUR-BRESLE SEINE-MARITIME

CM r des Étangs, 76340 235945565 235940614
In the middle of the local Leisure Park comprising 80 hectares of woodland, lakes and streams.
300m on N28.
Open: 15 Mar-15 Oct **Site:** 8HEC **Prices:** 2.25 1.40 1.85 1.85 **Facilities:** **Services:** lau **Off-site:** R

BLONVILLE-SUR-MER CALVADOS

Village Club le Lieu Bill Le Lieu Bill, 14910
231879727 231814715
e-mail: info@villageclub.fr
website: www.villageclub.fr
A family site in a convenient location for Le Havre and other ferry ports.
Off D118 Villers-sur-Mer-Pont-l'Évêque.
Open: Apr-Sep **Site:** 7HEC **Prices:** 6-26 1 (static)227-855 **Facilities:** **Services:** lau **Leisure:** P **Off-site:** S

BOURG-ACHARD EURE

Clos Normand 235 rte de Pont-Audemer, 27310
232563484
In a peaceful location within an apple orchard.
1km from A13 exit Bourg-Achard.
Open: Apr-Sep **Site:** 1.5HEC **Prices:** 3.30-3.90 1.60 pitch 2.70-3 **Facilities:** **Services:** lau **Leisure:** P **Off-site:**

CALLAC CÔTES-D'ARMOR

CM Verte Vallée 22160 296455850
W via D28 towards Morlaix.
Open: 15 Jun-15 Sep **Site:** 1HEC **Facilities:** **Services:** lau **Off-site:**

CAMARET-SUR-MER FINISTÈRE

Grand Large Lambezen, 29570 298279141 298279372
Situated at the tip of the Armorique natural park, facing the sea.
On entering Camaret, at roundabout take right turn (D355), then right again after 2km.
Open: 29 Mar-Sep **Site:** 2.8HEC **Facilities:** **Services:** lau **Leisure:** P **Off-site:** S

Lambézen 29570 298277733 298273838
e-mail: contact@campingarmorique.com
website: www.campingarmorique.com
Situated beside the sea on the edge of the Armorique natural park with a wide variety of recreational facilities.
3km NE on rte de Roscanvel (D355).
Open: 29 Mar-Sep **Site:** 2.5HEC **Prices:** 3.40-4.90 pitch 5.50-9 **Facilities:** **Services:** lau **Leisure:** P **Off-site:** S

Plage de Trez Rouz 29570 298279396 298278454
e-mail: camping-plage-de-trez-rouz@wanadoo.fr
On level ground 50m from the beach.
3km from Camaret-sur-Mer via D355 towards Pointe-des-Espagnols.
Open: Etr-Sep **Site:** 3.1HEC **Facilities:** **Services:** lau **Off-site:** S

CANCALE ILLE-ET-VILAINE

Notre Dame du Verger 35260 299897284 299896011
Terraced site overlooking the sea with direct access to the beach.
2km from Pointe-du-Grouin on D201.
Open: 29 Mar-28 Sep **Site:** 2.2HEC **Prices:** 3.20-3.70 pitch 12.50-19 (incl 2 persons) **Facilities:** **Services:** lau **Off-site:** S

CARANTEC FINISTÈRE

Mouettes Grande Grève, 29660 298670246 298783146
e-mail: camping@lesmouettes.com
website: www.les-mouettes.com
Level site divided by low shrubs and trees.

Site: 6HEC-Site size -grass -sand -stone -little shade -partly shaded -mainly shaded -bungalows for hire -caravans for hire -tents for hire -no dogs **Prices:** -adult per night -car per night pp-per person per night -caravan per night -tent per night (static)-caravan hire per week

1.5km SW on rte de St-Pol-de-Léon, towards the sea.
Open: May-11 Sep **Site:** 12HEC **Prices:** 4-7 pitch 15-39.50 (incl 2 persons) **Facilities:** **Services:** lau **Leisure:** P **Off-site:** S

CARENTAN Manche

CM le Haut Dyck 30 chemin du Grand-Bas Pays, 50500
233421689 233421689
e-mail: lehautdick@aol.com
website: www.camping-municipal.com
A level site in wooded surroundings with well-defined pitches.
Take village road off N13 towards Le Port.
Open: 15 Jan-1 Nov **Site:** 2.5HEC **Prices:** 2.50 1.10 3.10 3.10 **Facilities:** **Services:** lau **Off-site:** PR

CARNAC Morbihan

Bruyères Kerogile, 56340 297523057 297523057
e-mail: camping.les.bruyeres@wanadoo.fr
Partly wooded site with modern facilities close to the local beaches.
N of Carnac on C4, 2km from Plouharnel.
Open: Apr-14 Oct **Site:** 2HEC **Prices:** 2.85-3.60 pitch 5.50-6.90 (static)150-500 **Facilities:** **Services:** lau **Off-site:**

Étang 67 rte de Kerlann, 56340 297521406 297522319
In a rural setting with pitches divided by hedges, 2.5km from the coast.
2km N at Kerlann on D119.
Open: Apr-15 Oct **Site:** 2.5HEC **Prices:** 3.10-4.50 pitch 4.80-6.50 (static)320 **Facilities:** **Services:** lau **Leisure:** P

Grande Métairie rte des Alignements, de Kermario, 56342
297522401 297528358
e-mail: info@lagrandemetairie.com
website: www.lagrandemetairie.com
Holiday site with modern amenities, completely divided into pitches.
2.5km NE on D196.
Open: 2 Apr-10 Sep **Site:** 15HEC **Prices:** 4.60-7.20 pitch 14.50-23.90 (static)315-765 **Facilities:** **Services:** lau **Leisure:** PS

Menhirs alleè St-Michel 297529467 297522538
Open: May-Sep **Site:** 6HEC **Prices:** 7.42 pitch 28.35 **Facilities:** **Services:** lau **Leisure:** P

Moulin de Kermaux 56340 297521590 297528385
e-mail: moulin-de-kermaux@wanadoo.fr
website: www.camping-moulinkermaux.com
In a quiet location, surrounded by trees and bushes, with good facilities. Within easy reach of the coast and local megaliths.
2.5km NE.
Open: 3 Apr-15 Sep **Site:** 3HEC **Prices:** 4 pitch 13.50 **Facilities:** **Services:** lau **Leisure:** P **Off-site:** RS

Moustoir rte du Moustoir, 56340
297521618 297528837
e-mail: info@lemoustoir.com
website: www.lemoustoir.com
Well equipped site in a rural setting close to the sea.
3 km NE of Carnac.
Open: 2 May-17 Sep **Site:** 5HEC **Prices:** 2.50-4.10 pitch 7.20-14 **Facilities:** **Services:** lau **Leisure:** P **Off-site:** R

Ombrages 56430 297521652
In a wooded location with shaded pitches divided by hedges.
Take rte Carnac to Auray and turn left at Shell filling station.
Open: 15 Jun-15 Sep **Site:** 1HEC **Prices:** 4 pitch 5.20 (static)300 **Facilities:** **Services:** lau **Off-site:** LS

Rosnual rte d'Auray, 56340 297521457
A pleasant site in a wooded rural setting with good recreational facilities.
1.5km from village, 2.5km from the sea.
Open: Apr-Sep **Site:** 4HEC **Facilities:** **Services:** lau **Leisure:** P **Off-site:**

Saules rte de Rosnual, 56340 297521498 297526584
Grassland family site with good facilities site between road and deciduous woodland, subdivided by hedges and shrubs.
2.5km N on D119.
Open: Apr-Sep **Site:** 2.5HEC **Facilities:** **Services:** lau **Leisure:** P **Off-site:**

AT CARNAC-PLAGE (1KM S)

Druides 55 chemin de Beaumer, 56340
297520818 297529613
e-mail: camping-les-druides@wanadoo.fr
website: www.camping-le-druides.com
Family site with well-defined pitches, 400m from a fine sandy beach.
SE of town centre. Approach via D781 or D119.
Open: 5 May-10 Sep **Site:** 2.5HEC **Prices:** pitch 16.50-27.30 (incl 2 persons) **Facilities:** **Services:** lau **Leisure:** P **Off-site:** S

Men Dü 22 bis Chemin de Beaumer, 56340 297520423
e-mail: mendu@wanadoo.fr
website: www.camping-mendu.fr
Peaceful site in a wooded setting close to the beach.
1km from Carnac Plage via D781 and D186.
Open: Apr-Sep **Site:** 1.5HEC **Prices:** 3-4 pitch 15-22 (incl 2 persons) (static)220-570 **Facilities:** **Services:** lau **Off-site:** PRS

Menhirs allée St-Michel, 56340 297529467 297522538
e-mail: campinglesmenhirs@free.fr
website: www.lesmenhirs.com
A family site near the beach and shops with good recreational facilities and modern sanitary blocks.
Open: 30 Apr-12 Sep **Site:** 6HEC **Facilities:** **Services:** lau **Leisure:** P **Off-site:** S

See advertisement on page 151

CAUREL CÔTES-D'ARMOR

Nautic International rte de Beau Rivage, 22530
296285794 296260200
e-mail: contact@campingnautic.fr.st
website: www.campingnautic.fr.st
A terraced site in woodland on the edge of lake Guerlédan with a variety of recreational facilities.
N164 towards Beau Rivage.
Open: 15 May-25 Sep **Site:** 3.6HEC **Prices:** 3.30-5 pitch 5.40-7 **Facilities:** **Services:** lau **Leisure:** LP **Off-site:**

CHAPELLE-AUX-FILZMÉENS, LA ILLE-ET-VILAINE

Camping du Logis 35190 299452545 299453040
e-mail: domainedeslogis@wanadoo.fr
A quiet, pleasant site in the wooded grounds of an 18th-century château.
NE of town towards Combourg.
Open: All year **Site:** 20HEC **Facilities:** **Services:** lau **Leisure:** P **Off-site:** R

CHÂTEAULIN FINISTÈRE

La Pointe Superbe rte St-Coulitz, 29150
298865153 298865153
e-mail: lapointecamping@aol.com
In a wooded valley close to the town with good modern facilities. Pitches divided by hedges. British owners.
From centre of Châteaulin take D770 S to Quimper for 1km, then left to St-Coulitz. Site 100m on right.
Open: 15 Mar-Oct **Site:** 2.5HEC **Prices:** pitch 7-13 (incl 2 persons) **Facilities:** **Off-site:** PRS

CLOÎTRE-ST-THEGONNEC, LE FINISTÈRE

Bruyères 29410 298797176
A small, secluded site in a picturesque setting within the Amorique nature park.
12km S of Morlaix via D769.
Open: Jul-Aug **Site:** 2.5HEC **Prices:** 4 2 pitch 3 pp3 **Facilities:** **Services:** lau **Off-site:**

COMBOURG ILLE-ET-VILAINE

Bois Coudrais Cuguen, 35270 299732745 299731308
e-mail: info@vacancebretagne.com
website: www.vacancebretagne.com
A small, level site with fine views.
Access via D83 Combourg-Mont-St-Michel.
Open: Apr-Oct **Site:** 2.2HEC **Prices:** 1.50-2.50 pitch 8 **Facilities:** **Services:** lau **Leisure:** P **Off-site:**

CONCARNEAU FINISTÈRE

Prés Verts Kernous Plage, 29900 298970974 298973206
e-mail: pres-verts-camp@wanadoo.fr
website: www.pres-verts.com
A landscaped site with good facilities overlooking Concarneau bay.
1.2km NW.
Open: May-22 Sep **Site:** 2.5HEC **Facilities:** **Services:** lau **Leisure:** PS **Off-site:** S

COUTERNE ORNE

Clos Normand rte de Bagnoles, 61410 233379243
A pleasant site in rural surroundings in a sheltered position close to the thermal spa of Bagnoles-de-l'Orne.
Approach D916.
Open: May-Sep **Site:** 1.3HEC **Prices:** 2.73 pitch 7.20 (incl 2 persons) (static)173-206 **Facilities:** **Services:** lau **Off-site:** LPR

CRACH MORBIHAN

Fort Espagnol rte de Fort Espagnol, 56950
297551488 297300104
e-mail: fort-espagnol@wanadoo.fr
website: www.fort-espagnol.com
In a secluded, wooded location, this is a family site with a wide variety of recreational facilities.
Due E of Crac'h towards the coast.
Open: May-10 Sep **Site:** 4.5HEC **Prices:** 4.20-5 pitch 8.30-10 **Facilities:** **Services:** lau **Leisure:** P **Off-site:** R

CRIEL-SUR-MER SEINE-MARITIME

Mouettes r de la Plage, 76910 235867073 235867073
website: camping-lesmouettes.com
Small grassy site overlooking the sea.
Open: Apr-2 Nov **Site:** 2HEC **Facilities:** **Services:** lau **Off-site:** RS

CROZON Finistère

Pen ar Menez bd de Pralognan, 29160 298271236
On fringe of a pinewood. Water-sport facilities 5km away. Cycles for hire.
Open: All year **Site:** 2.6HEC **Facilities:** **Services:** lau **Off-site:** S

Plage de Goulien Kernaveèno, 29160
298271710 298272195
e-mail: campingdelaplagedegoulien@presquile-crozon.com
website: www.presquile-crozon.com
Grassy site in wooded surroundings 150m from the sea.
5km W on D308.
Open: 10 Jun-15 Sep **Site:** 2.5HEC
Prices: 3.80 2.05 3.95 3.95 pitch 3.95 **Facilities:** **Services:** lau **Off-site:** S

DEAUVILLE Calvados
At St-Arnoult (3km S)

Vallée route de Beaumont, 14800
231885817 231881157
e-mail: loreca@free.fr
In a pleasant wooded setting with plenty of recreational facilities.
1km S via D27 and D275.
Open: Apr-3 Nov **Site:** 19HEC **Facilities:** **Services:** lau **Leisure:** LPR **Off-site:** S

At Touques (3km SE)

Haras chemin du Calvaire, 14800
231884484 231889708
e-mail: les.haras@wanadoo.fr
website: www.region_normandie.com/lesharas
A partially residential site in pleasant surroundings. Ideal for overnight stops, but booking recommended in July and August.
N on D62, to Honfleur.
Open: Feb-Nov **Site:** 4HEC **Facilities:** **Services:** lau **Off-site:** P

DÉVILLE-LÈS-ROUEN Seine-Maritime

CM r Jules-Ferry, 76250 235740759 235763521
Open: All year **Site:** 1.5HEC **Prices:** 4 2.80 1.55 **Facilities:** **Services:** lau **Off-site:** PR

DIEPPE Seine-Maritime
At Hautot-sur-Mer (6km SW)

Source Petit Appeville, 76550 235842704 235842704
Open: 15 Mar-15 Oct **Site:** 2.5HEC **Prices:** 4-5.40 1 7 5 **Facilities:** **Services:** lau **Leisure:** R **Off-site:** S

DINAN Côtes-d'Armor
At Taden (3.5km NE)

CM Hallerais 22100 296391593
Beautiful clean site with level pitches on gentle slope near a country estate. Asphalt drives. Good sanitary installations. Shop, bar and restaurant are open in July and August only.
SW of Taden off D12.
Open: 15 Mar-Oct **Site:** 6HEC **Facilities:** **Services:** lau **Leisure:** PR **Off-site:**

DINARD Ille-et-Vilaine

See also St-Lunaire

Mauny 35800 299469473
A family site in pleasant wooded surroundings with a variety of recreational facilities.
Off St-Briac road (CD603).
Open: 3 Mar-25 Sep **Site:** 5HEC **Facilities:** **Services:** lau **Leisure:** P **Off-site:** S

DOL-DE-BRETAGNE Ille-et-Vilaine

Château des Ormes 35120 299735300 299735355
e-mail: info@lesormes.com
website: www.lesormes.com
Site in grounds of château, within a large leisure complex with excellent facilities.
7km S on N795 Rennes road.
Open: 21 May-10 Sep **Site:** 160HEC **Prices:** 6.50-7.20 19-21 19-21 (static)306-847 **Facilities:** **Services:** lau **Leisure:** LP

CM Les Tendieres r des Tendieres, 35120 299481468
On level meadow.
SW on rte de Dinan 400m from town centre.
Open: 15 May-15 Sep **Site:** 1.7HEC **Facilities:** **Services:** lau **Leisure:** R **Off-site:** P

At Baguer-Pican (4km E on N176)

Camping du Vieux Chêne 35120
299480955 299481337
e-mail: vieux.chene@wanadoo.fr
website: www.camping-vieuxchene.fr
Spacious site in pleasant lakeside situation. Farm produce available.
5km E of Dol-de-Bretagne on D576.
Open: 26 Mar-2 Oct **Site:** 12HEC **Prices:** 4.20-5.70 pitch 6-16 **Facilities:** **Services:** lau **Leisure:** P

DOUARNENEZ Finistère

Kerleyou Tréboul, 29100 298741303 298740961
e-mail: camp-kerleyou@infonie.fr
website: www.camping-kerleyou.com
Family site in wooded surroundings near the beach. Separate car park for arrivals after 23.00.
1km W on r de Préfet-Collignon towards the sea.
Open: May-24 Sep **Site:** 3HEC **Prices:** 3.10-3.70 1-1.75 pitch 3.35-6.25 **Facilities:** **Services:** lau **Leisure:** P **Off-site:** S

At Poulan-sur-Mer (5km W on D765)

Pil Koad 29100 298742639 298745597
e-mail: camping.pil.koad@wanadoo.fr
website: www.pil-koad.com
In a natural wooded setting with a variety of recreational facilities.
E via D7 towards Douarnenez.
Open: Apr-Sep **Site:** 5.5HEC **Prices:** 3-4.50 pitch 6.20-13 (static)250-670 **Facilities:** **Services:** lau **Leisure:** P **Off-site:** S

Facilities: -shop -shower -electric points for razors -electric points for caravans -parking by tents permitted -compulsory separate car park **Services:** -café/restaurant -bar -Camping Gaz International -gas other than Camping Gaz -first aid facilities lau-laundry **Leisure:** -swimming L-Lake P-Pool R-River S-Sea **Off-site:** All facilities within 2km

ERDEVEN MORBIHAN

Ideal Route de la plage 297556766 297559312
Site: **Services:** lau **Leisure:** P

Sept Saints 56410 297555265 297552267
e-mail: campingseptsaints@wanadoo.fr
website: www.sept_saints.com
In wooded surroundings with good recreational facilities.
2km NW via D781 rte de Plouhinec.
Open: 15 May-15 Sep **Site:** 5HEC **Prices:** 4-6 pitch 10-17 **Facilities:** **Services:** lau **Leisure:** P **Off-site:** LRS

ERQUY CÔTES-D'ARMOR

Hautes Greés 123 r St-Michel, 22430
296723478 296723015
e-mail: hautesgrees@wanadoo.fr
website: www.camping-hautes-grees.com
Good family site, 2km from the town centre and 400m from the beach.
500m from the sea.
Open: Apr-Sep **Site:** 3HEC **Facilities:** **Services:** lau **Off-site:** S

Roches Caroual Village, 22430 296723290 296635784
e-mail: camping.les.roches@wanadoo.fr
website: www.camping-les-roches.com
In a rural setting with well-marked pitches, 800m from the beach.
3km SW.
Open: Apr-15 Sep **Site:** 3.1HEC **Prices:** 3.40 2.40 pitch 3.40 **Facilities:** **Services:** lau **Off-site:** S

St-Pabu 22430 296722465 296728717
e-mail: camping@saintpabu.com
website: www.saintpabu.com
On big open meadow with several terraces in beautiful, isolated situation by sea. Divided into pitches.
W on D786 then follow signposts from La Coutre.
Open: Apr-10 Oct **Site:** 5.5HEC **Prices:** 4.20 pitch 8 (static)275-550 **Facilities:** **Services:** lau **Leisure:** S

Vieux Moulin r des Moulins, 22430
296723423 296723663
e-mail: camp.vieux.moulin@wanadoo.fr
website: www.campingvieuxmoulin.com
Clean tidy site divided into pitches and surrounded by a pine forest. Suitable for children.
On D783.
Open: 30 Apr-10 Sep **Site:** 6.5HEC **Prices:** 4.50-5.50 pitch 10-13 **Facilities:** **Services:** lau **Leisure:** P **Off-site:** S

ÉTABLES-SUR-MER CÔTES-D'ARMOR

Abri Côtier 22680 296706157 296706523
e-mail: camping.abricotier@wanadoo.fr
website: perso.wanadoo.fr/abricotier
A pleasant family site in a wooded location close to the sea.
1km N of town centre on D786.
Open: 15 Apr-9 Sep **Site:** 2HEC **Facilities:** **Services:** lau **Leisure:** P **Off-site:** S

ETRÉHAM CALVADOS

Reine Mathilde 14400 231217655 231221833
e-mail: camping.reine_mathilde@wanadoo.fr
website: www.campingreinemathilde.com
In a quiet rural setting 4km from the sea.
1km W via D123.
Open: Apr-Sep **Site:** 6.5HEC **Prices:** 5.08-5.67 pitch 4.76-5.35 **Facilities:** **Services:** lau **Leisure:** P

FAOUËT, LE MORBIHAN

Beg Er Roch rte de Lorient, 56320
297231511 297231166
In pleasant surroundings on the banks of a river. A popular site with modern sanitary facilities and a wealth of opportunities for all kinds of sport.
Open: 10 Mar-Sep **Site:** 3.5HEC **Prices:** 2.55-3.55 1-2.05 pitch 2.05-3.10 **Facilities:** Services: lau **Leisure:** R **Off-site:**

FORÊT-FOUESNANT, LA FINISTÈRE

Kérantérec 29940 298569811 298568173
e-mail: info@camping-keranterec.com
website: www.camping-keranterec.com
Well-kept terraced site, divided into sections by hedges and extending to the sea.
3km SE.
Open: 10 Apr-19 Sep **Site:** 6.5HEC **Prices:** 5.25-7 pitch 6.75-9 (static)250-610 **Facilities:** **Services:** lau **Leisure:** PS **Off-site:**

Manoir de Pen Ar Steir 29940 298569775 298568049
e-mail: info@camping-penarsteir.com
website: www.camping-penarsteir.com
Well-tended site close to Port La Forêt, a major yachting arena.
NE off D44.
Open: Feb-15 Nov **Site:** 3HEC **Prices:** 3.80-4.80 pitch 6.25-7.80 **Facilities:** **Services:** lau **Off-site:** PS

Plage Plage de Kerleven, rte de Port la Forêt, 29940
298569625 298369625
e-mail: laplage.camp@wanadoo.fr
website: www.camping-en-finistere.com
2.5km SE on D783.
Open: May-Dec **Site:** 1HEC **Facilities:** **Services:** lau **Off-site:** S

Pontérec Pontérec, 29940 298569833 298569347
A modern site with well-defined pitches separated by hedges, 2.5km from the beach.
0.5km on D44 towards Bénodet.
Open: Apr-Sep **Site:** 3HEC **Facilities:** **Services:** lau **Off-site:**

St-Laurent Kerleven, 29940 298569765 298569251
e-mail: info@camping-du-saint-laurent.fr
website: www.camping-du-saint-laurent.fr
On rocky coast. Divided into pitches.
3.5km SE of village.
Open: 3 May-13 Sep **Site:** 5.2HEC **Facilities:** **Services:** lau **Leisure:** PS **Off-site:**

FOUESNANT Finistère

Atlantique rte de Mousterlin, 29170
298561444 298561867
e-mail: sunelia@latlantique.fr
website: www.latlantique.fr
Modern site with plenty of amenities 400m from the beach.
4.5km S on the road to Mousterlin.
Open: May-15 Sep **Site:** 9HEC **Prices:** pitch 21-38 (incl 2 persons) (static)300-875 **Facilities:** **Services:** lau **Leisure:** P **Off-site:** S

Grand Large Pointe de Mousterlin, 29170
298560406 298565826
e-mail: info@campingsbretagnesud.com
website: www.campingsbretagnesud.com
A family site in a wooded setting with direct access to the beach. Plenty of modern facilities.
S of Fouesnant via D145.
Open: 30 Apr-10 Sep **Site:** 6HEC **Prices:** 4-6 pitch 15-36 (incl 2 persons) **Facilities:** **Services:** lau **Leisure:** PR **Off-site:** S

Piscine 51 Hent Kerleya, 29170 298565606 298565764
e-mail: contact@campingdelapiscine.com
website: www.campingdelapiscine.com
In a beautiful location 1.5km from the beach.
4km NW towards Kerleya.
Open: 15 May-15 Sep **Site:** 5HEC **Prices:** 3.50-5.25 pitch 7-10.50 **Facilities:** **Services:** lau **Leisure:** PS

FOUGÈRES Ille-et-Vilaine

CM Paron rte de la Chapelle Janson, 35300
299994081 299942794
A well-managed site suitable for overnight stays.
1.5km E via D17.
Open: Apr-Oct **Site:** 2.5HEC **Prices:** 2.10 1.45 pitch 2-2.35 **Facilities:** **Services:** lau **Off-site:** PR

GUILLIGOMARC'H Finistère

Bois des Ecureuils 29300 298717098 298717098
e-mail: bois-des-ecureuils@tiscali.fr
website: www.bois-des-ecureuils.fr
Tranquil 1.6-hectare wooded site set among oak, chestnut and beech trees. An ideal base for walking, cycling, horse-riding and fishing.
2km W from D769 Roscoff-Lorient.
Open: 15 May-15 Sep **Site:** 2.5HEC **Prices:** 2.80 pitch 4.60 **Facilities:** **Services:** lau

GUILVINEC Finistère

Plage rte de Penmarc'h, 29730 298586190 298588906
e-mail: info@campingsbretagnesud.com
website: www.campingbretagnesud.com
On level meadow. Divided into pitches. Flat beach suitable for children.
2km W of village on the Corniche towards Penmarc'h.
Open: 30 Apr-10 Sep **Site:** 14HEC **Prices:** 4-6 pitch 15-36 **Facilities:** **Services:** lau **Leisure:** PS

HAYE-DU-PUITS, LA Manche

Étang des Haizes 50250 233460116 233472380
e-mail: etang.des.haizes@wanadoo.fr
website: www.etang-des-haizes.com
A well-equipped family site bordering a lake, shaded by apple trees.
Access via D903 from Carentan.
Open: 10 Apr-15 Oct **Site:** 5HEC **Prices:** 4-6 pitch 6-29 (incl 2 persons) **Facilities:** **Services:** lau **Leisure:** LP **Off-site:**

HOULGATE Calvados

Vallée 88 r de la Vallée, 14510 231244069 231244242
e-mail: camping.lavallee@wanadoo.fr
website: campinglavallee.com
Site with good recreational facilities, 900m from the beach.
1km S.
Open: Apr-Sep **Site:** 11HEC **Facilities:** **Services:** lau **Leisure:** P **Off-site:** S

IFFENDIC Ille-et-Vilaine

Domaine de Trémelin 35750 299097379 299097069
A lakeside site in beautiful wooded surroundings with good sports and entertainment facilities.
S of town towards Plélan-le-Grand.
Open: Apr-Sep **Site:** 2HEC **Facilities:** **Services:** **Leisure:** L

Facilities: -shop -shower -electric points for razors -electric points for caravans -parking by tents permitted -compulsory separate car park **Services:** -café/restaurant -bar -Camping Gaz International -gas other than Camping Gaz -first aid facilities lau-laundry **Leisure:** -swimming L-Lake P-Pool R-River S-Sea **Off-site:** All facilities within 2km

JULLOUVILLE Manche

Chaussée 1 av de la Libération, 50610
233618018 233614526
e-mail: jmb@campinglachaussee.com
website: www.campinglachaussee
On large meadow, completely divided into pitches. Separated from beach and coast road by row of houses.
Open: 8 Apr-18 Sep **Site:** 6HEC **Prices:** 4.50-5 pitch 20-20.60 (incl 2 persons) **Facilities:** **Services:** lau **Leisure:** P **Off-site:** S

AT ST-MICHEL-DES-LOUPS (4km SE)

Chaumière 50740 233488293
4km SE on D21 via Bouillon.
Site: 2HEC **Facilities:** **Services:** lau **Leisure:** LS

JUMIÈGES Seine-Maritime

Forêt r Mainberthe, 76480 235379343 235377648
e-mail: info@campinglaforet.com
website: www.campinglaforet.com
Located in the heart of the Brotonne regional natural park on the banks of the Seine.
10km from A13 Caen-Paris road, exit Bourg-Achard.
Open: 2 Apr-29 Oct **Site:** 2.5HEC
Prices: 3.60-4 pitch 14-16 (incl 2 persons) (static)260-450 **Facilities:** **Services:** lau **Leisure:** P
Off-site: R

KERLIN Finistère

Étangs de Trévignon Pointe de Trévignon, Kerlin, 29910
298500041 298500409
e-mail: camp.etangsdetrevignon@wanadoo.fr
website: www.camping-etangs.com
A family site with good, modern facilities 800m from the beach, reached by a short pathway.
Open: Jun-15 Sep **Site:** 3.5HEC **Prices:** 5.05 pitch 6.10 **Facilities:** **Services:** lau
Leisure: P **Off-site:** S

LANDAUL Morbihan

Le Pied-à-Terre Branzého, 56690
297245270 297245271
e-mail: jimrolland@wanadoo.fr
website: www.lepiedaterre.net
In a pleasant, quiet location, 15 minutes from the sea.
1km from N165. Signed from Landaul.
Open: Apr-Sep **Site:** 2.6HEC **Prices:** 4 2 3 3 pitch 3 **Facilities:** **Services:** lau **Off-site:**

LANDÉDA Finistère

Abers Dunes de Ste-Marguerite, 29870
298049335 298048435
e-mail: camping-des-abers@wanadoo.fr
website: www.camping-des-abers.com
Very quiet beautiful site among dunes. Ideal for children.
2.5km NW on a peninsula between bays of Aber-Wrac'h and Aber Bernoît.
Open: May-26 Sep **Site:** 4.5HEC **Facilities:** **Services:** lau **Leisure:** S **Off-site:** R

LESCONIL Finistère

Dunes 7 r P-Langevin, 29740 298878178 298822705
A family site on slightly sloping landscaped ground, 800m from the town centre and the harbour.
Access via D53, turning S in Plobannalac. Signed.
Open: end May-15 Sep **Site:** 2.8HEC **Prices:** 4.40 pitch 10.35 **Facilities:** **Services:** lau **Off-site:** RS

Grande Plage 71 r P-Langevin, 29740
298878827 298878827
Well equipped site on level ground, surrounded by woodland, 300m from the sea.
Open: Etr-Sep **Site:** 2.5HEC **Prices:** 3.30-4.10 pitch 4.85-6.05 (static)140-335 **Facilities:**
Services: lau **Off-site:** S

LOCUNOLE Finistère

Ty Nadan 29310 298717547 298717731
e-mail: ty-nadan@wanadoo.fr
Located in 24 hectares surrounding an old Breton village and situated in a riverside position.
off D22 Quimperle to Plouay, take W exit at Arzano and 3km to site.
Open: 19 Mar-8 Sep **Site:** 12HEC **Prices:** 8 pitch 20 **Facilities:** **Services:** lau
Leisure: PR **Off-site:** S

LOUVIERS Eure

Bel Air Hameau de St-Lubin, rte de la Haye Malherbe, 27400
232401077 232401077
e-mail: le.belain@wanadoo.fr
website: www.lebelair.fr.st
Small site on the edge of a forest with landscaped pitches and good facilities.

3km from the town centre via D81.
pen: 15 Mar-15 Oct **Site:** 2.5HEC **Prices:** 3.70-.90 pitch 4-4.80 **Facilities:** **Services:** lau **eisure:** P

LUC-SUR-MER CALVADOS

apricieuse 2 r Brummel, 14530
231973443 231968278
-mail: info@campinglacaprieuse.com
large family site 100m from the beach.
On W outskirts, access via A13 exit Douvres.
pen: Apr-Sep **Site:** 4.5HEC **Facilities:** **Services:** lau **Off-site:** PS

MARTIGNY SEINE-MARITIME

Rivières 76880 235856082 235859516
-mail: martigny.76@wanadoo.fr
ebsite: www.camping-2-rivieres.com
)n the shore of a lake in pleasant surroundings 8km from)ieppe.
Access via D154.
pen: 25 Mar-16 Oct **Site:** 6.8HEC **Prices:** pitch 13.45 (incl 3 persons) **Facilities:** **Services:** lau **Off-site:** P

MARTRAGNY CALVADOS

Château de Martragny 14740 231802140 231081491
-mail: chateau.martragny@wanadoo.fr
website: www.chateau-martragny.com
Family site in grounds of a château which also offers accommodation.
From N13 take exit for Martragny. Drive through St-Léger and campsite is on the right as you leave the village.
Open: May-15 Sep **Site:** 15HEC **Prices:** 4.20-4.70 pitch 9-10.60 **Facilities:** **Services:** lau **Leisure:** P **Off-site:** R

MAUPERTUS-SUR-MER MANCHE

Anse du Brick 50330 233543357 233544966
e-mail: welcome@anse-du-brick.com
website: www.anse-du-brick.com
Terraced site in a landscaped park between the sea and the forest.
200m from beach.
Open: Apr-Sep **Site:** 17HEC **Prices:** 4-6 pitch 8.70-12.50 **Facilities:** **Services:** lau **Leisure:** P **Off-site:** S

MERVILLE-FRANCEVILLE CALVADOS

Peupliers Allée des Pins, 14810 231240507 231240507
e-mail: asl-mondeville@wanadoo.fr
website: www.asl-mondeville.com
Situated in a rural setting, 300m from the beach. The sanitary arrangements include a bathroom for babies. Shop, bar and café available high season.
2km E from sign on D514.
Open: Apr-Oct **Site:** 3.6HEC **Prices:** 6.15 pitch 6.65 (static)140-325 **Facilities:** **Services:** lau **Leisure:** P **Off-site:** RS

MONTERBLANC MORBIHAN

Haras Aérodrome Vannes-Meucon, Vannes-Meucon, 56250
297446606 297444941
e-mail: campingvannes@free.fr
website: www.campingvannes.free.fr
Situated 4km from Vannes in the direction Aerodrome Vannes-Meucon.
Open: All year **Site:** 14HEC **Prices:** 3.50 1 3 3 pitch 1.50 (static)140-510 **Facilities:** **Services:** lau **Leisure:** P

MONT-ST-MICHEL, LE MANCHE

Gué de Beauvoir 5 rte du Mont-St-Michel, Beauvoir, 50170
233600923
A level site in an orchard close to the River Couesnon.
4km S of Abbey on D776 Pontorson road.
Open: Etr-Sep **Site:** 0.6HEC **Prices:** 2.50 1.20 2.50 2 **Facilities:** **Services:** lau **Off-site:**

MORGAT FINISTÈRE

Bruyeres Le Bouis, 29160 298261487
e-mail: camping.les.bruyeres@presquile-crozon.com
website: www.presquile-crozon.com
On a meadow surrounded by woodland with pitches divided by hedges on the extremity of the Parc Naturel Régional d'Armorique.
From Morgat follow D255 towards Cap de la Chèvre for 1.5km then right towards Bouis.
Open: May-Sep **Site:** 3HEC **Prices:** 3.50 1.80 pitch 3.70 **Facilities:** **Services:** lau **Off-site:** PS

MOYAUX CALVADOS

Colombier 14590 231636308 231631597
e-mail: chateau@camping-lecolombier.com
website: www.camping-lecolombier.com
Well-kept site in grounds of manor house.
Camping Card Compulsory
3km NE on D143.
Open: May-15 Sep **Site:** 10HEC **Facilities:** **Services:** lau **Leisure:** P

NÉVEZ FINISTÈRE

Deux Fontaine Raguènes, 29920
298068191 2980697180
e-mail: info@les2fontaines.fr
website: www.les2fontaines.fr
Mainly level site, subdivided into several fields surrounded by woodland with good recreational facilities including an aquaslide.
700m from Ragunès beach.
Open: 14 May-10 Sep **Site:** 7HEC **Prices:** 4-5.60 pitch 8.50-12 **Facilities:** **Services:** lau **Leisure:** P **Off-site:** RS

NOYAL-MUZILLAC MORBIHAN

Moulin de Cadillac Moulin de Cadillac, 56190
297670347 297670002
e-mail: infos@moulin-cadillac.com
website: www.camping-moulin-cadillac.com
A well-equipped family site in a pleasant wooded location with good facilities.
Access via N165, N through Muzillac.
Open: May-Sep **Site:** 3HEC **Prices:** 2.75-3.70 pitch 3.83-5.10 pp1.43-1.90 **Facilities:** **Services:** lau **Leisure:** P

Facilities: -shop -shower -electric points for razors -electric points for caravans -parking by tents permitted -compulsory separate car park **Services:** -café/restaurant -bar -Camping Gaz International -gas other than Camping Gaz -first aid facilities lau-laundry **Leisure:** -swimming L-Lake P-Pool R-River S-Sea **Off-site:** All facilities within 2km

OUISTREHAM CALVADOS

Prairies de la Mer rte de Lion, Riva-Bella, 14150 ☎ 231976161
A camping area attached to a larger static caravan site with good recreational facilities, 400m from the sea.
Access via D514.
Open: 13 Mar-17 Oct **Site:** 80HEC **Facilities:** **Services:** lau **Leisure:** P **Off-site:** S

PÉNESTIN-SUR-MER MORBIHAN

Airotel-Inly 56760 ☎ 299903509 299904093
e-mail: inly-info@wanadoo.fr
website: www.camping-inly.com
Situated in the centre of a nature reserve and close to the coast, with good recreational facilities.
2km SE via D201.
Open: 30 Apr-26 Sep **Site:** 30HEC **Prices:** 4-6 pitch 7-11 (incl 2 persons) (static)220-600 **Facilities:** **Services:** lau **Leisure:** LP **Off-site:** RS

Cénic 56760 ☎ 299904565 299904505
e-mail: info@lecenic.com
website: www.lecenic.com
In a forested area 2km from the sea. Spacious grassy pitches ideal for families.
Access via D34 from La Roche-Bernard.
Open: Apr-Sep **Site:** 7HEC **Prices:** 4.50-5.50 pitch 5-8.50 (static)170-460 **Facilities:** **Services:** lau **Leisure:** P **Off-site:** S

Iles La Pointe du Bile, 56760 ☎ 299903024 299904455
e-mail: contact@camping-des-iles.fr
website: www.camping-des-iles.fr
A family site with direct access to the beach and a separate residential section.
3km S on D201.
Open: 9 Apr-2 Oct **Site:** 4HEC **Prices:** 2.30-5 pitch 15-33 (incl 2 persons) (static)217-759 **Facilities:** **Services:** lau **Leisure:** PS

PENTREZ-PLAGE FINISTÈRE

Tamaris 29550 ☎ 298265395 298265248
e-mail: camping-kerys@wanadoo.fr
website: www.ker-ys.com
Level site divided into pitches 20m from the beach.
Access via D887.
Open: May-14 Sep **Site:** 3HEC **Facilities:** **Services:** lau **Off-site:** S

PERROS-GUIREC CÔTES-D'ARMOR

Claire Fontaine Toul ar Lann, 22700 ☎ 296230355 296490619
website: www.camping-claire-fontaine.com
Spacious, level site in a rural setting.
1.2km SW of town centre, 800m from Trestraou beach.
Open: Etr-Sep **Site:** 3HEC **Prices:** pitch 14-16 (incl 2 persons) **Facilities:** **Services:** lau **Off-site:** S

AT LOUANNEC (3KM SE)

CM Ernest Renan rte de Perros-Guirec, 22700 ☎ 296231178 293490447
e-mail: mairie-lovannec@wannadoo.com
Well situated site next to the sea. Take away food, games room.
1km W.
Open: May-Sep **Site:** 4.5HEC **Facilities:** **Services:** lau **Leisure:** LRS **Off-site:**

AT PLOUMANCH (2KM NW)

Ranolien 22700 ☎ 296916565 296914190
e-mail: leranolien@yellohvillage.com
website: www.leranolien.com
The site is divided into pitches by hedges; separate sections for caravans.
500m from the village.
Open: 2 Apr-17 Sep **Site:** 16HEC **Prices:** pitch 15-37 (incl 2 persons) **Facilities:** **Services:** lau **Leisure:** P **Off-site:** S

PIEUX, LES MANCHE

Grand Large 50340 ☎ 233524075 233525820
e-mail: Le-grand-Large@wanadoo.fr
website: www.legrandlarge.com
In an unspoiled location with direct access to the beach.
3km from the town centre on D117.
Open: 2 Apr-18 Sep **Site:** 4HEC **Prices:** pitch 17-25 (incl 2 persons) pp4-5.20 (static)300-690 **Facilities:** **Services:** lau **Leisure:** PS

PLÉRIN CÔTES-D'ARMOR

Mouettes Les Rosaires les Mouettes, 22190 ☎ 296745148
Open: Jul-30 Sep **Site:** 1HEC **Prices:** 3 pitch 10 (static)137.20 **Facilities:** **Services:** lau **Off-site:** PRS

PLEUBIAN CÔTES-D'ARMOR

Port la Chaîne 22610 ☎ 296229238 296228792
e-mail: info@portlachaine.com
website: www.portlachaine.com
A peaceful, terraced site on the 'Wild Peninsula', with direct access to the sea, with good facilities.
2km N via D20.
Open: May-Sep **Site:** 5HEC **Prices:** 4.20-5.20 pitch 7.20-9 **Facilities:** **Services:** lau **Leisure:** PS

PLOBANNALEC FINISTÈRE

Manoir de Kerlut 29740 ☎ 298822389 298822649
e-mail: info@campingsbretagnesud.com
website: www.campingsbretagnesud.com
A peaceful site located in the grounds of a manor house some 2km from the beach.
1.6km S via D102.
Open: 15 May-8 Aug **Site:** 12HEC **Facilities:** **Services:** lau **Leisure:** PS **Off-site:**

PLOËMEL MORBIHAN

Kergo 56400 ☎ 297568066
e-mail: camping.kergo@wanadoo.fr
website: www.members.lycos.fr/campingkergo
In pleasant wooded surroundings, close to the neighbouring beaches.
2km SE via D186.
Open: 15 Apr-Sep **Site:** 2.5HEC **Prices:** 3.30 1.70 3.70 3.70 pitch 3.70 (static)260-290 **Facilities:** **Services:** lau **Off-site:**

PLOEMEUR MORBIHAN

Ajoncs Beg Minio, 56270 ☎ 297863011 297863011
e-mail: secretariat@campingclub.200.fr
A rural site situated in an orchard.
From town centre continue towards Fort-Bloqué.
Open: 18 Mar-Sep **Site:** 2HEC **Facilities:**
Services: lau **Off-site:** LPS

PLOËRMEL Morbihan

ac Les Belles Rives, Taupont, 56800
297740122 297740122
-mail: camping.du-lac@wanadoo.fr
ebsite: www.le-camping-du-lac.com
lakeside family site with plenty of facilities for water sports.
2km from village centre, beside the lake.
pen: Apr-Oct **Site:** 3HEC **Prices:** 2.90 3.10
3 pitch 3.10 **Facilities:** **Services:**
au **Leisure:** L **Off-site:** P

allée du Ninian Le Rocher, 56800
297935301 297935727
-mail: info@camping-ninian.com
ebsite: www.camping-ninian.com
eaceful family site at the heart of Brittany which specialises
n homemade cider beside the River Ninian.
W of Taupont towards the river.
pen: May-Sep **Site:** 2.7HEC **Prices:** 2.50-
.10 4-5 (static)284-427 **Facilities:**
ervices: lau **Leisure:** PR **Off-site:**

PLOMEUR Finistère

orche Pointe de la Torche, Roz an Tremen, 29120
298586282 298588969
-mail: info@campingdelatorche.fr
ebsite: www.campingdelatorche.fr
family site with pitches surrounded by trees and bushes,
.5km from the beach.
3.5km W.
pen: 03 Apr-25 Sep **Site:** 4HEC
rices: 3.50-4.40 1.60-2 pitch 3.50-7 (static)185-300
acilities: **Services:** lau **Leisure:** P
ff-site: S

PLOMODIERN Finistère

roise Plage de Pors-ar-Vag, 29550
298815272 298812610
-mail: campingiroise@aol.com
website: www.camping-iroise.com
A family site with fine recreational facilities, providing
nagnificent views over the bay of Douarnenez.
5km SW, 150m from the beach.
Open: 10 Apr-20 Sep **Site:** 2.5HEC **Prices:** 4.35-
5.80 pitch 8.60-11.50 **Facilities:**
Services: lau **Leisure:** P **Off-site:** S

PLONÉVEZ-PORZAY Finistère

International de Kervel 29550 298925154 298925496
e-mail: camping.kervel@wanadoo.fr
website: www.kervel.com
One of the best sites in the region. Ideal for families. 800m from the sea.
SW of the village on the D107 Douarnenez road for 3km, then towards coast at x-roads.
Open: 30 Apr-10 Sep **Site:** 7HEC **Facilities:**
Prices: 4.30-5.50 pitch 9.15-11.50
Services: lau **Leisure:** P **Off-site:** S

Tréguer-Plage Ste-Anne-la-Palud, 29550
298925352 298925489
e-mail: camping-treguer-plage@wanadoo.fr
website: www.camping-treguer-plage.com
A level site with direct access to the beach.
1.3km N.
Open: 15 Jun-15 Sep **Site:** 6HEC
Prices: 3.60 2.60 pitch 3.60 (static)155-360
Facilities: **Services:** lau **Leisure:** S
Off-site: S

PLOUÉZEC Côtes-d'Armor

Cap Horn Port Lazo, 22470 296206428 296206388
e-mail: lecaphorn@hotmail.com **website:** lecaphorn.com
In an elevated position overlooking the Ile de Bréhat with direct access to the beach.
2.3km NE via D77 at Port-Lazo.
Open: Apr-10 Sep **Site:** 5HEC **Facilities:**
Services: lau **Leisure:** PS **Off-site:**

PLOUEZOCH Finistère

Baie de Térénez 29252 298672680 298672680
e-mail: camping@libertysurf.fr **website:** www.aucamping.com
A well-equipped site in a pleasant rural setting.
3.5km NW via D76.
Open: 5 Apr-Sep **Site:** 3HEC **Facilities:**
Services: lau **Leisure:** P **Off-site:** RS

PLOUGASNOU Finistère

Etangs de Mesqueau 26930 298673745 0298678279
e-mail: commune.de.plougasnou@wanadoo.fr
Large municipal site with good recreational facilities.
3.5km S via D46.
Open: Jul-Aug **Site:** 7HEC **Facilities:**
Services: lau **Leisure:** R **Off-site:** S

Trégor Kerjean, 29630 298673764
e-mail: bookings@campingdutregor.com
website: www.campingdutregor.com
A sheltered site with numbered, grassy pitches. Surrounded by hedges.
Off D46 towards Morlaix.
Open: Etr-Oct **Site:** 1HEC **Prices:** 2.40-2.90
1-1.20 1.80-2.10 1.80-2.10 (static)200-360
Facilities: **Services:** lau **Off-site:** S

PLOUHA CÔTES-D'ARMOR
AT TRINITÉ, LA (2KM NE)

Domaine de Keravel rte de Port Moguer, 22580
296224913
e-mail: keravel@wanadoo.fr
website: www.keravel.com
Forested site built around an elegant country mansion, 1km from the sea.
Open: 15 May-Sep **Site:** 5HEC **Prices:** 4.80-6 pitch 8-10 **Facilities:** **Services:** lau **Leisure:** P **Off-site:** S

PLOUHARNEL MORBIHAN

Étang de Loperhet 56340 297523468 297523468
e-mail: info@camping-loperhet.com
website: www.camping-loperhet.com
1km NW via D781.
Open: Apr-Sep **Site:** 6HEC **Prices:** 4.50 pitch 7.50 (static)155-360 **Facilities:** **Services:** lau **Leisure:** P **Off-site:** S

Kersily Ste-Barbe, 56340 297523965 & 297524476
Open: Apr-Oct **Site:** 3HEC **Prices:** 2.70-4.20 1.40-1.70 pitch 3.60-5.20 **Facilities:** **Services:** lau **Leisure:** P **Off-site:** S

Lande Kerzivienne, 56340 297523148 297523148
e-mail: campdelalande@aol.com
On partially shaded terrain, 600m from the beach.
Open: Jun-27 Sep **Site:** 1HEC **Prices:** 11.60 pitch 11.60 (incl 2 persons) (static)250-300 **Facilities:** **Services:** lau **Off-site:** S

PLOUHINEC MORBIHAN

Moténo rte du Magouer, 56680 297367663 297858184
e-mail: camping-moteno@wanadoo.fr
website: www.camping-le-moteno.com
On slightly sloping ground, subdivided into several fields in a wooded area 600m from the beach.
S beside the Mer d'Etel.
Site: 4HEC **Prices:** 2.60-4.20 pitch 4.50-9.50 (static)170-585 **Facilities:** **Services:** lau **Off-site:** PS

PLOZÉVET FINISTÈRE

Corniche rte de la Corniche, 29710
298913394 298914153
e-mail: info@campinglacorniche.com
website: www.campinglacorniche.com
Peaceful rural site 1.5km from the sea.
Open: Apr-Sep **Site:** 2HEC **Prices:** 4.30 pitch 5.80 **Facilities:** **Services:** lau **Leisure:** P **Off-site:** LRS

PONTAUBAULT MANCHE

Vallée de la Sélune 7 r Mal-Leclerc, 50220
233603900 233603900
e-mail: campselune@wanadoo.fr
This site is in a quiet village near the River Sélune. Ideal base for exploring the Normandy-Brittany area.
Access via N175 Portorson-Caen.
Open: Apr-20 Oct **Site:** 1.6HEC **Prices:** 2.50 2.50 2.50 1.50-2.50 (static)150-190 **Facilities:** **Services:** lau **Off-site:** R

PONT-AVEN FINISTÈRE

Domaine de Kerlann 29930
298060177 0870 242 9999
e-mail: kerlann@haven.fr
website: www.haveneurope.com
A wooded park with shady pitches featuring an indoor pool complex with waterslide and spa bath.
3m E of Pont Aven.
Open: 19 Mar-21 Oct **Site:** 26HEC **Prices:** 3-7 pitch 13-37 (incl 2 persons) (static)196-1183 **Facilities:** **Services:** lau **Leisure:** P **Off-site:**

PONT-L'ABBÉ FINISTÈRE

Bois Soleil 29120 298870339 298870339
website: www.camping-finistere.com
Shady site set in a wooded park with good recreational facilities.
3.5km NE onD44.
Open: May-Sep **Site:** 3HEC **Prices:** 2.80-3.50 1.50-1.80 pitch 3.50-4.40 (static)220-340 **Facilities:** **Services:** lau **Off-site:** P

PORDIC CÔTES-D'ARMOR

Madières rte de Vau Madec, 22590
296790248 296794667
e-mail: lesmadieres@wanadoo.fr
website: www.campinglesmadieres.com
A quiet coastal site in a well-shaded position.
1.5km from village on St-Brieuc road (D786).
Open: Apr-Oct **Site:** 2HEC **Prices:** 4.50 pitch 15 (incl 2 persons) (static)230-599 **Facilities:** **Services:** lau **Leisure:** P **Off-site:** S

PORT-EN-BESSIN Calvados

Port'land 14520 231510706 231517649
e-mail: campingportland@wanadoo.fr
website: www.camping-portland.com
Situated near Omaha beach in rural surroundings with an indoor heated swimming pool on site.
Open: 2 Apr-4 Nov **Site:** 8.6HEC
Prices: 4.80-7.30 pitch 19.20-27.30 **Facilities:**
Services: lau **Leisure:** LP **Off-site:** S

PORT-MANECH Finistère

St-Nicolas 29920 298068975 298067461
e-mail: info@campinglesaintnicolas.com
website: www.campinglesaintnicolas.com
Divided into hedge-lined pitches in beautiful surroundings close to the beach.
Open: May-Sep **Site:** 3.5HEC **Prices:** 4.70 pitch 8.50 **Facilities:** **Services:** lau **Leisure:** P
Off-site: S

POSES Eure

Ile Adeline 27740 232593581 232598895
A well-equipped site situated close to the Lery-Poses leisure centre.
Access via A13 exit 19 towards Val-de-Reuil.
Open: Apr-Sep **Site:** 2.5HEC **Facilities:**
Services: lau **Off-site:** LR

POULDU, LE Finistère

Embruns r du Philosophe Alain, 29360
298399107 298399787
e-mail: camping-les-embruns@wanadoo.fr
website: www.camping-les-embruns.com
A pleasant site with good facilities and easy access to the beach. Separate car park for arrivals after 22.00.
Open: 2 Apr-17 Sep **Site:** 5HEC **Prices:** 3.70-4.90 pitch 9.90-25.50 **Facilities:**
Services: lau **Leisure:** P **Off-site:** RS

QUETTEHOU Manche

Rivage rte de Morsalines, 50630 233541376
e-mail: camping.lerivage@wanadoo.fr
website: www.camping-lerivage.com
Quiet, sheltered site, 400m from the sea.
Access via D14.
Open: Apr-Sep **Site:** 2HEC **Prices:** 3.50-4.50 pitch 12.20-15.50 (incl 2 persons) (static)244-450
Facilities: **Services:** lau **Leisure:** P
Off-site: S

QUIBERON Morbihan

Bois d'Amour r St-Clement, 56170
297504267 297501352
e-mail: info@homair-vacances.fr
website: www.homair-vacances.fr
A family site with plenty of recreational facilities close to fine beaches.
1.5km SE at La Pointe de la Presqu'île, 100m from beach.
Open: Apr-Oct **Site:** 5.5HEC
Prices: 4.50-9 pitch 8-16.50 (static)175-525 **Facilities:**
Services: lau **Leisure:** P **Off-site:**
S

Conguel bd Teignouse, 56170 297501911
Directly on the beach, with fine recreational facilities.
Near the aerodrome towards Pointe de Conguel.
Open: Apr-Oct **Site:** 5HEC **Facilities:**
Services: lau **Leisure:** P **Off-site:** S

QUIMPER Finistère

Orangerie de Lanniron Chateau de Lanniron, 29336
298906202 298521556
e-mail: camping@lanniron.com
website: www.lanniron.com
In the grounds of the former residence of the Bishops of Quimper, beside the River Odet and surrounded by tropical vegetation.
2.5km from town centre via D34.
Open: 15 May-15 Sep **Site:** 27HEC
Prices: 4.20-6.20 pitch 14.70-22 **Facilities:**
Services: lau **Leisure:** PR

RAGUENÈS-PLAGE Finistère

Airotel International Raguenès-Plage 19 r des Iles, Raguenez, 29920 298068069 298068905
e-mail: info@camping-le-raguenes-plage.com
website: www.camping-le-raguenes-plage.com
Asphalt drives; 400m from beaches.
Leave Pont-Aven and take the road to Nevez. At Nevez follow directions to Raguenès.
Open: Apr-Sep **Site:** 7HEC **Prices:** 3.90-5.50 pitch 7.20-14 (static)247.50-720 **Facilities:**
Services: lau **Leisure:** PS

RAVENOVILLE-PLAGE Manche

Cormoran 50480 233413394 233951680
e-mail: lecormoran@wanadoo.fr
website: www.lecormoran.com
A pleasant family site with well-defined pitches, 20m from the sea.
300m from the town towards Utah Beach.
Open: Apr-25 Sep **Site:** 8.5HEC **Prices:** pitch 16.20-23 (incl 2 persons) (static)270-730 **Facilities:**
Services: lau **Leisure:** PS **Off-site:**

ROCHE-BERNARD, LA Morbihan

CM Patis 3 chemin du Patis, 56130
299906013 299908828
On banks of River Vilaine.
100m from village centre.
Open: Apr-Sep **Site:** 1HEC **Prices:** 3 2 2.50 pitch 4 **Facilities:** **Services:** lau **Leisure:** R
Off-site: P

ROCHEFORT-EN-TERRE Morbihan

Moulin Neuf 56220 297433752 297433545
A well-equipped site in wooded surroundings. The shop contains only basic items but there is a supermarket nearby.
Camping Card compulsory.
Signed from D744 in village.
Open: May-Sep **Site:** 2.5HEC **Prices:** 4.30-5 pitch 7-8 **Facilities:** **Services:** lau **Leisure:** P
Off-site: LR

Facilities: -shop -shower -electric points for razors -electric points for caravans -parking by tents permitted -compulsory separate car park **Services:** -café/restaurant -bar -Camping Gaz International -gas other than Camping Gaz -first aid facilities lau-laundry **Leisure:** -swimming L-Lake P-Pool R-River S-Sea **Off-site:** All facilities within 2km

ROSTRENEN CÔTES-D'ARMOR

Fleur de Bretagne Kerandouaron, 22110 ☎ 296291645
e-mail: aharrison@hotmail.com
A spacious site in a picturesque, sheltered valley with good, modern facilities.
➲ *1.5km from Rostrenen on D764 towards Pontivy.*
Open: Apr-Sep **Site:** 6HEC **Facilities:** **Services:** lau **Leisure:** P **Off-site:**

ST-ALBAN CÔTES-D'ARMOR

St-Vrêguet St-Vréguet, 22400 ☎ 296329021
e-mail: vreguet@wanadoo.fr
A peaceful site in a pleasant park with good sanitary and recreational facilities.
Open: Jun-Sep **Site:** 1HEC **Prices:** 2.70 1.40 pitch 1.70 (static)275 **Facilities:** **Services:** lau **Off-site:** R

ST-AUBIN-SUR-MER CALVADOS

Côte de Nacre 17 r du Major Moulton, 14750
☎ 231971445 231972211
A pleasant site with good recreational facilities. Reservations recommended in high season. Separate car park for arrivals after 22.00.
Open: Apr-Oct **Site:** 6HEC **Facilities:** **Services:** lau **Leisure:** P **Off-site:** S

CM Mesnil 76740 ☎ 235830283
A family site attached to a typical Norman farm.
➲ *2 km W on D68.*
Open: Apr-Oct **Site:** 2.3HEC **Facilities:** **Services:** lau **Off-site:** S

ST-BRIAC ILLE-ET-VILAINE

Emeraude 7 chemin de la Souris, 35800 ☎ 299883455
e-mail: camping.emeraude@wanadoo.fr
website: www.camping-emeraude.com
Well-kept site in pleasant quiet situation and divided into pitches.
➲ *Turn left off D786 and continue for 0.8 km.*
Open: Apr-Sep **Site:** 2HEC **Facilities:** **Services:** lau **Off-site:** S

ST-BRIEUC CÔTES-D'ARMOR

Vallées Parc de Brézillet, 22000 ☎ 296940505
e-mail: campingdesvallees@wanadoo.fr
Situated on the edge of the town in a plateau criss-crossed by wooded valleys. Restaurant open July and August only.
Open: Etr-15 Oct **Site:** 4.8HEC **Prices:** 3.75-4.10 pitch 8.40-10.50 (incl 1 persons) (static)305-360 **Facilities:** **Services:** lau **Leisure:** R **Off-site:** PS

ST-CAST-LE-GUILDO CÔTES-D'ARMOR

Château de Galinée 22380 ☎ 296411056 296410372
e-mail: contact@chateaudegalinee.com
website: www.chateaudegalinee.com
A family site in a 2-hectare wood incorporating the buildings of an old farm, 3km from beaches.
➲ *1km from CD786. Well signed.*
Open: 8 May-4 Sep **Site:** 14HEC **Prices:** 3.85-5.50 pitch 8.40-14 **Facilities:** **Services:** lau **Leisure:** P **Off-site:** LS

Châtelet r des Nouettes, 22380 ☎ 296419633 296419799
e-mail: chateletcp@aol.com
website: www.lachatelet.com
In superb landscaped surroundings overlooking the sea with good sporting facilities.
➲ *1km W, 250m from the beach*
Open: May-10 Sep **Site:** 8HEC **Prices:** 4-6 pitch 11.90-19.30 (static)320-690 **Facilities:** **Services:** lau **Leisure:** LPS **Off-site:**

Crique r de la Mare, 22380 ☎ 296418919
A tiered camp site with exceptional views across Fort Lalette and the sea. Direct access to the beach.
Open: 15 Mar-2 Jan **Site:** 2.8HEC **Facilities:** **Services:** lau **Off-site:** S

Mielles 22380 ☎ 296418760 296810477
Ideally positioned at the heart of the resort and within walking distance of the beach. Spacious defined pitches.
➲ *500 m NE on coast.*
Open: 15 Mar-2 Jan **Site:** 3.5HEC **Facilities:** **Services:** lau **Leisure:** P

ST-EFFLAM CÔTES-D'ARMOR

CM r de Ian-Carré, 22310 ☎ 296356215 296350975
e-mail: campingmunicipalplestin@wanadoo.fr
website: www.plestinlesgreves.com
On a level meadow with well-defined pitches 100m from a magnificent beach.
Open: Apr-Sep **Site:** 4HEC **Prices:** 2.21-2.60 1.30-1.60 pitch 2.86-3.40 **Facilities:** **Services:** lau **Off-site:** S

ST-GERMAIN-SUR-AY MANCHE

Aux Grands Espaces 50430 ☎ 233071014 233072259
website: www.aux-grand-espaces.com
On slightly sloping ground among dunes. Children's play area. Siesta 12.30-14.30. 500m from sea.

Leave D650 W of town and follow signs 'Plage' on D306.
Open: May-15 Sep **Site:** 15HEC **Prices:** 4.60 pitch 5.50 (static)550 **Facilities:** **Services:** lau **Leisure:** P **Off-site:** S

St-Gildas-de-Rhuys Morbihan

Menhir rte de Port Crouesty, 56730
297452288 297453718
e-mail: campingmenhir@aol.com
website: www.campingdumenhir.com
A family site with good facilities situated 1km from the beach.
3.5km N.
Open: 26 May-5 Sep **Site:** 3HEC **Prices:** 5.50 pitch 14.50 **Facilities:** **Services:** lau **Leisure:** PS **Off-site:** S

St-Jouan-des-Guérêts Ille-et-Vilaine

P'tit Bois 35430 299211430 299817414
e-mail: camping.ptitbois@wanadoo.fr
website: www.ptitbois.com
A pleasant family site in quiet wooded surroundings.
Access via N137.
Open: 16 Apr-10 Sep **Site:** 6HEC **Prices:** 6-8 10-20 pitch 10-20 **Facilities:** **Services:** lau **Leisure:** P **Off-site:** RS

St-Léger-du-Bourg-Denis Seine-Maritime

Aubette 23 r Vert Buisson, 76160
235084769 235084769
In a wooded valley, 3km E of Rouen.
Open: All year **Site:** 0.8HEC **Prices:** 2.50 pitch 2.60 **Facilities:** **Services:** lau **Off-site:** R

St-Lunaire Ille-et-Vilaine

Longchamp bd de St-Cast, 35800
299463398 299460271
In a beautiful wooded setting in the heart of the 'Emerald Coast' with a good range of facilities.
Turn off D786 towards St-Briac at end of village, site is on left. 100m from the sea.
Open: 15 May-10 Sep **Site:** 5HEC **Facilities:** **Services:** lau **Off-site:** S

Touesse 35800 299466113 299160258
e-mail: camping.la.touesse@wanadoo.fr
website: www.campinglatouesse.com
A well-equipped family site, 300m from the beach.
2km E via D786.
Open: Apr-Sep **Site:** 2.8HEC **Prices:** 3.70-4.80 pitch 4.80-6 (static)155-360 **Facilities:** **Services:** lau **Off-site:** PS

St-Malo Ille-et-Vilaine

CM le Nicet av de la Varde Rotheneuf, 35400 299402632
e-mail: camping@ville-saint-malo.fr
website: www.ville-saint-malo.fr/campings
100m from the beach; direct access via staircase. Water sports and other activities available.
Open: 15 Jun-1 Sep **Site:** 2.9HEC **Facilities:** **Services:** lau **Leisure:** S **Off-site:** S

Ville Huchet rte de la Passagère, 35400
299811183 299815189
e-mail: info@lavillehuchet.com
website: www.lavillehuchet.com

5km S via N137.
Open: 2 Apr-Sep **Site:** 6HEC **Prices:** 4.25-4.80 10.35-11.50 10.35-11.50 **Facilities:** **Services:** lau **Leisure:** P **Off-site:** R

St-Marcan Ille-et-Vilaine

Balcon de la Baie 35120 299802295 299802295
In a beautiful location overlooking the bay of Mont-St-Michel.
10km NW of Pontorson on D797.
Open: Apr-Oct **Site:** 2.7HEC **Prices:** 3.50 pitch 4.10 (static)460 **Facilities:** **Services:** lau **Leisure:** P **Off-site:**

St-Martin-des-Besaces Calvados

Puits 14350 231678002 231678002
e-mail: camping.le.puits@wanadoo.fr
website: www.lepuits.com
A small family run site surrounded by a pleasant garden and lush fields.
Access via N175 Caen/Mont-St-Michel.
Open: Mar-Oct **Site:** 3.6HEC **Prices:** 3 pitch 8 **Facilities:** **Services:** lau **Off-site:**

St-Martin-En-Campagne Seine-Maritime

Goelands r des Grèbes, Saint Martin Plage, 76370
235838290 235832179
e-mail: info@camping-les-goelands.com
website: www.camping-les-goelands.com
Site with good recreational facilities in an area of woodland, 100m from a small lake. Shop and bar open in high season only.

contd.

NE of Dieppe, 2km from D925.
Open: 30 Mar-30 Oct **Site:** 4HEC **Prices:** pitch 21-27 (incl 4 persons) **Facilities:**
Services: lau **Leisure:** S **Off-site:** P

ST-MICHEL-EN-GRÈVE CÔTES-D'ARMOR

Capucines Kervourdon, 22300
44 296357228 296357898
e-mail: les.capucines@wanadoo.fr
website: lescapucines.fr
In a peaceful setting near the beach with a large variety of facilities.
On D786 Lannion-Morlaix road.
Open: May-11 Sep **Site:** 4HEC **Facilities:** **Services:** lau **Leisure:** P **Off-site:** S

ST-PAIR-SUR-MER MANCHE

Ecutot 50380 233502629 233506494
e-mail: camping.ecutot@wanadoo.fr
website: www.ecutot.com
Situated in an orchard 1km from the sea.
On the main road between Granville and Avranches.
Open: Jun-15 Sep **Site:** 5HEC **Facilities:**
Services: lau **Leisure:** P **Off-site:** S

Lez-Eaux St-Aubin-des-Preaux, 50380
233516609 233519202
e-mail: lez.eaux@wanadoo.fr
website: www.lez-eaux.com
Situated in grounds of an old château. TV and reading room. Fishing available.
7km SE via D973 rte d'Avranches.
Open: May-15 Sep **Site:** 12HEC **Facilities:** **Services:** lau **Leisure:** P

Mariénée 50380 233906005
2km from sea; situated in grounds of an old farm.
2km S of town on D21.
Open: Avr-Sep **Site:** 1.2HEC **Facilities:**
Services: lau **Off-site:** PS

ST-PHILIBERT-SUR-MER MORBIHAN

Vieux Logis Kernivilit, 56470 297550117 297300391
e-mail: campvieuxlogis@aol.com
website: www.camping-au-vieux-logis.com
Beautiful, well-kept site divided by hedges.
2km W via D781.
Open: All year **Site:** 2.5HEC **Prices:** 3.60-4.50 pitch 6-7.90 (static)250-380 **Facilities:**
Services: lau **Leisure:** P **Off-site:** RS

ST-PIERRE-DU-VAUVRAY EURE

St-Pierre 1 r du Château, 27430
232610155 232610155
In wooded surroundings with pitches divided by hedges, 50m from the River Seine.
Access via A13/N15.
Open: 5 Jan-13 Dec **Site:** 3HEC **Prices:** 3.20 pitch 5 **Facilities:** **Services:** lau **Leisure:** P **Off-site:** R

ST-PIERRE-QUIBERON MORBIHAN

Park-er-Lann 56170 297502493 297502493
1.5km S on D768.
Open: Etr-Sep **Site:** 2.5HEC **Facilities:** **Services:** lau **Off-site:** S

ST-QUAY-PORTRIEUX CÔTES-D'ARMOR

Bellevue 68 bd du Littoral, 22410
296704184 269705546
e-mail: campingbellevue@free.fr
website: www.campingbellevue.net
A terraced site adjacent to the sea with numbered pitches.
800m from town centre off D786.
Open: May-15 Sep **Site:** 4HEC **Prices:** 3.60-4.50 pitch 5-6.40 **Facilities:** **Services:** lau **Leisure:** PS **Off-site:**

ST-VAAST-LA-HOUGUE MANCHE

Gallouette r de la Gallouette, 50550
233542057 233541671
e-mail: contact@camping-lagallouette.fr
website: www.camping-lagallouette.fr
A well-equipped site, 300m from the town centre and with direct access to the beach.
Open: Apr-Sep **Site:** 2.3HEC **Prices:** 4.40-5 pitch 6-9 (static)245-630 **Facilities:**
Services: lau **Leisure:** PS **Off-site:**

STE-MARIE-DU-MONT MANCHE

Utah Beach La Madeleine, 50480
233715369 233710711
e-mail: utah.beach@wanadoo.fr
website: www.campingutahbeach.com
On a level meadow 100m from the beach.
6km NE via D913 and D421.
Open: Apr-Sep **Site:** 3.5HEC **Prices:** 3.80-4.50 pitch 13.70-16.40 **Facilities:** **Services:** lau **Leisure:** P **Off-site:** S

STE-MARINE FINISTÈRE

Hellès 29120 298563146 298563146
e-mail: contact@le-helles.com
website: www.le-helles.com
400m from the beach.
Open: May-15 Sep **Site:** 3HEC **Prices:** 13.50-17.50 **Facilities:** **Services:** lau **Leisure:** P
Off-site: S

STE-MÈRE-ÉGLISE MANCHE

Cormoran Ravenoville-Plage, 50480
233413394 233951608
e-mail: lecormoran@wanadoo.fr
website: www.lecormoran.com
A quiet site with well-defined pitches, 20m from the sea.
Drive towards Ravenoville Plage, then take Utah Beach road for 500m.
Open: 30 Mar-22 Sep **Site:** 6.5HEC **Facilities:** **Services:** lau **Leisure:** P **Off-site:** S

SARZEAU Morbihan

Ferme de Lann Hoedic rte du Roaliguen, 56370
297480173 297417287
e-mail: contact@camping-lannhoedic.fr
website: www.camping-lannhoedic.fr
Quiet site 800m from a sheltered beach, accessible by foot or bike through a shady forest path. Pitches in sunny or shady locations, some surrounded by landscaped hedges.
From Vannes, take the exit for Sarzeau, continue in the direction for Arzon. Turn left at 1st roundabout, next to the Super U, after 2km take turning on left in direction for Lann Hoedic.
Open: Apr-Oct **Site:** 3.6HEC **Prices:** 4.10 pitch 7 (static)150-380 **Facilities:**
Services: lau **Off-site:** S

Treste rte de la Plage du Roaliguen, 56370
297417960 297413621
e-mail: letreste@campingletreste.com
website: www.campingletreste.com
A family site with good facilities 800m from the Roaliguen beach.
2.5km S.
Open: 11 Jun-11 Sep **Site:** 5HEC **Prices:** 4.95 pitch 8.90 (static)155-490 **Facilities:**
Services: lau **Leisure:** P **Off-site:** S

AT POINTE-ST-JACQUES (5.5KM S)

CM St-Jacques 56370 297417929 297480445
e-mail: camping-stjacques.com
website: www.camping-stjacques.com
On beach protected by dunes. Well kept site with asphalt drives in a pleasant wooded location.
Open: Apr-Sep **Site:** 7.6HEC **Facilities:** **Services:** lau **Leisure:** S **Off-site:**

SASSETOT-LE-MAUCONDUIT Seine-Maritime

Trois Plages 76540 235274011 235282320
Well equipped site 3km from the coast.
1.3km S near D925.
Open: 25 Apr-15 Sep **Site:** 4HEC **Facilities:** **Services:** lau **Off-site:**

SUBLIGNY Manche

Grand Chemin 50870 233513096
Small site in a rural setting with well-defined pitches within easy reach of the village.
Access via N175 towards Avranches, then D39 and follow signs.
Open: All year **Site:** **Facilities:**
Services: lau

TELGRUC-SUR-MER Finistère

Panoramic rte de la Plage, 29560
298277841 298273610
e-mail: info@camping-panoramic.com
website: www.camping-panoramic.com
Quiet terraced site with views across a wide sandy beach. Secluded pitches.
W on D887 and then S on D208.
Open: Jun-15 Sep **Site:** 4HEC **Prices:** 5 pitch 10 **Facilities:** **Services:** lau **Leisure:** P
Off-site: S

THEIX Morbihan

Rhuys Le Poteau Rouge, Atlantheix, 56450
297541477 297759854
Directly on the sea, with good modern facilities.

3.5km NW via N165.
Open: Apr-15 Oct **Site:** 2HEC **Facilities:** **Services:** lau **Leisure:** P **Off-site:**

THURY-HARCOURT Calvados

Vallée du Traspy 14220 231796180 231796180
Level meadow site near a small reservoir, 250m from Centre Aquatique de la Suisse Normande.
Open: 15 Apr-15 Sep **Site:** 1.5HEC
Prices: 4.10 pitch 4.10 (static)250-380 **Facilities:**
Services: lau **Leisure:** LPR **Off-site:**

TINTÉNIAC Ille-et-Vilaine

Peupliers La Besnelais, 35190 299454975
e-mail: camping.les.peupliers@wanadoo.fr
A peaceful site in a wooded location with good facilities.
2km SE via N137.
Open: Mar-Oct **Site:** 4.5HEC **Prices:** 4.60 pitch 6.35 **Facilities:** **Services:** lau
Leisure: P **Off-site:**

TOLLEVAST Manche

Village Vert 50470 233430078
e-mail: le.village.ver@wanadoo.fr
website: www.le-village-vert.com
A peaceful site situated in a pine grove within an extensive park.
From Cherbourg car ferry terminal follow N13 to the Auchan Hypermarket and then continue for 200m for site on left.
Open: All year **Site:** 5.5HEC **Prices:** 2.80-4 3-4.50 pitch 3-4.50 **Facilities:** **Services:** lau
Off-site:

TOURLAVILLE Manche

Espace Loisirs de Collignon 50110
233201688 233205303
e-mail: VPT50@wanadoo.fr
A pleasant site with good facilities, 1km from town centre.
Site: 2HEC **Facilities:** **Services:** lau **Leisure:** S **Off-site:** PS

TOURNIÈRES Calvados

Picard Holidays 14330 231228244 231517028
e-mail: paul.palmer@wanadoo.fr
website: www.camp-france.com
A quiet site with pleasant, sheltered pitches conveniently situated between Cherbourg and Caen.
Access via N13 and D15/D5.
Open: All year **Site:** 2HEC **Prices:** 5 pitch 5 (static)415-560 **Facilities:** **Services:** lau **Leisure:** LP **Off-site:** R

TRÉBEURDEN Côtes-D'Armor

Armor-Loisirs r de Kernevez-Lors-Mabo, 22560
296235231 296154036
e-mail: info@armorloisirs.com
website: www.armorloisirs.com
Modern site with individual pitches surrounded by hedges. Hardstandings for caravans.
500m S of the Kernévez road.
Open: Apr-Sep **Site:** 2.2HEC **Prices:** 3-5 pitch 5-7.50 **Facilities:** **Services:** lau **Leisure:** P **Off-site:** RS

★★★★
Camping de KERVILOR
E-mail : ebideau@camping-kervilor.com
Internet : www.camping-kervilor.com
F-56470 La Trinité sur Mer
Tel.: 00 33 (0)2 97 55 76 75 - Fax: 00 33 (0)2 97 55 87 26
Close to the harbour and the beaches, rental of mobile homes, heated swimming pools, waterslides, slide with several tracks, thermal waters, bar, animations, tennis, billiards, all services at the site.

TRÉGUNC Finistère

Pommeraie St-Philibert, 29910 298500273 298500791
e-mail: pommeraie@club-internet.fr
website: www.campingdelapommeraie.com
A well-equipped site with good facilities for children, 1.2km from the beach.
S via D1.
Open: May-5 Sep **Site:** 7HEC **Prices:** 3.50-5 5-9 **Facilities:** **Services:** lau **Leisure:** P **Off-site:** S

TRÉLÉVERN Côtes-D'Armor

Port l'Epine Pors-Garo, 22660 296237194 296237783
e-mail: camping-de-port-lepine@wanadoo.fr
website: www.camping-port-lepine.com
Well shaded site directly on the sea.
Open: Apr-Sep **Site:** 3HEC **Facilities:** **Services:** lau **Leisure:** PS

TRÉPORT, LE Seine-Maritime

CM les Boucaniers r Mendes-France, 76470 235863547
Well-kept site on flat meadow on E edge of village. Sports and games nearby.
Open: Etr-Sep **Site:** 5.5HEC **Prices:** 2.95 2.55 2.55-6.15 2.55-6.15 **Facilities:** **Services:** lau **Off-site:** PRS

Parc International du Golf rte de Dieppe, 76470
227280150 227280151
In a park on the cliffs.
1km W on D940.
Open: Apr-20 Sep **Site:** 5HEC **Prices:** 6-7
Facilities: **Services:** lau **Off-site:** PS

At MESNIL-VAL

Parc Val d'Albion 1 r de la Mer, 76910
235862142 235867851
Terraced site in wooded parkland next to the sea.
3km S from Le Tréport on D126.
Open: Jun-15 Sep **Site:** 3HEC **Prices:** 7.20
Facilities: **Services:** lau **Off-site:** S

TRÉVOU-TRÉGUIGNEC Côtes-D'Armor

Mât 38 r de Trestel, 22660 296237152
e-mail: camping-le-mat@wanadoo.fr
A family site on level ground, 50m from beach.
Access via D38.
Open: 15 Apr-15 Sep **Site:** 1.6HEC
Facilities: **Services:** lau **Leisure:** P
Off-site: LS

TRINITÉ-SUR-MER, LA Morbihan

Baie Plage de Kervilen, 56470 297557342 297558881
e-mail: camping@camping-la-baie-com
website: www.camping-la-baie.com
Several strips of land divided by tall trees on the edge of a fine sandy beach.
Signed towards Kerbihan.
Open: 15 May-15 Sep **Site:** 2.4HEC **Facilities:** **Services:** lau **Leisure:** P **Off-site:** S

Kervilor 56470 297557675 297558726
e-mail: ebideau@camping-kervilor.com
website: www.camping-kervilor.com
In a pleasant wooded location 1.5km from the port. Plenty of recreational facilities.
1.6km N.
Open: 5 May-11 Sep **Site:** 5HEC **Prices:** 3.60-4.80 pitch 8.63-11.50 **Facilities:** **Services:** lau **Leisure:** P **Off-site:**

Plage Plage de Kervilen, 56470 ☎ 297557328 ▤ 297558831
e-mail: camping@camping-plage.com
website: www.camping-plage.com
A family site divided into pitches and lying behind sand dunes which give direct access to the beach.
➲ *1km S towards Carnac-Plage.*
Open: 15 May-18 Sep **Site:** 3HEC **Prices:** 4 pitch 8.80-24.30 (static)239.40-716 **Facilities:** **Services:** lau **Leisure:** P **Off-site:** S

VEULES-LES-ROSES Seine-Maritime

Mouettes av J-Moulin, 76980 ☎ 235976198
Open: 15 Feb-Nov **Site:** 3.6HEC **Facilities:** **Services:** lau **Off-site:** S

Paradis chemin de Manneville, 76980 ☎ 235976142
A municipal site on the southern outskirts of the town.
Open: mid-May to mid-Sep **Site:** 0.9HEC
Facilities: **Services:** lau **Off-site:** PRS

VILLERS-SUR-MER Calvados

Ammonites rte de la Corniche, 14640
☎ 231870606 ▤ 231871800
e-mail: camping-lesammonites@wanadoo.fr
website: www.camping-les-ammonites.com
➲ *4km SW on rte de Cabourg and D163 towards Auberville.*
Open: Apr-Oct **Site:** 3HEC **Facilities:** **Services:** lau **Leisure:** P

PARIS/NORTH

ACY-EN-MULTIEN Oise

Ancien Moulin 60620 ☎ 344872128 ▤ 344872128
e-mail: secretariat@campingclub.2000.fr
website: www.campingclub.2000.fr
Situated beside a river and a small lake with good sports facilities.
Open: All year **Site:** 5HEC **Facilities:**
Services: lau **Leisure:** LR **Off-site:**

AMBLETEUSE Pas-de-Calais

Beaucamp 10 r de Ferquent, 62164
☎ 321326210 ▤ 321306377
A useful overnight stop between Boulogne and Calais.
Open: All year **Site:** 9HEC **Facilities:** **Services:** lau **Off-site:** RS

ARDRES Pas-de-Calais
At AUTINGUES (2km S)

St-Louis 223 r Leulène, 62610 ☎ 321354683 ▤ 321001978
website: www.campingstlouis.com
A well-equipped site in pleasant wooded surroundings.
➲ *Turn off N43 1km SE of Ardres onto D224 and follow signs.*
Open: Apr-Oct **Site:** 1.7HEC **Prices:** 2.50 pitch 6
Facilities: **Services:** lau
Off-site: L

AUDRUICQ Pas-de-Calais

CM Les Pyramides 62370 ☎ 321355917
A site with good sanitary and sports facilities beside the canal.
Open: Apr-Sep **Site:** **Facilities:**
Services: lau **Off-site:** P

BEAUVAIS Oise

Clos Normand 1 r de l'Abbaye, St-Paul, 60650 ☎ 344822730
A small site on a lake with facilities for fishing.
➲ *6km W via N31 towards Rouen.*
Open: Apr-Sep **Site:** 1.3HEC **Prices:** 4 pitch 15 (incl 2 persons) (static)100 **Facilities:**
Services: lau **Off-site:**

BERCK-SUR-MER Pas-de-Calais

Orée du Bois chemin Blanc 251, Rang-du-Fliers, 62180
☎ 321842851 ▤ 321842856
e-mail: oree.du.bois@wanadoo.fr
website: www.loreedubois.com
A modern site in wooded surroundings with good sports facilities.
➲ *2km NE.*
Open: 03 Apr-24 Oct **Site:** 18HEC **Facilities:** **Services:** lau **Off-site:**

BERNY-RIVIÈRE Aisne

Croix du Vieux Pont 2290 ☎ 323555002 ▤ 323550513
e-mail: lacroixduvieuxpont@wanadoo.fr
website: www.la-croix-du-vieux-pont.com
In wooded surroundings beside the River Aisne with ample facilities.
➲ *N of N31; cross River Aisne, site is 500m E of Vic-sur-Aisne on D91.*
Open: All year **Site:** 19HEC **Prices:** 9.50-11.50
Facilities: **Services:** lau **Leisure:** P
Off-site:

BERTANGLES Somme

Château r du Château, 80260 ☎ 322933773 ▤ 322936836
e-mail: camping.bertangles@wanadoo.fr
website: perso.wanadoo.fr/chateau.de.bertangles
Site in old orchard of château.
➲ *Signed off Amiens-Doullens road.*
Open: 22 Apr-12 Sep **Site:** 0.8HEC **Prices:** 3.10 2.10 3.20 3.20 **Facilities:** **Services:** lau
Off-site:

BEUVRY Pas-de-Calais

CM r Victor-Dutériez, 62660 ☎ 321650800
Open: 15 May-15 Sep **Site:** 1HEC **Prices:** 1.90 2.55 2.55 pitch 2.55 **Facilities:** **Services:** lau
Off-site: P

BLANDY-LES-TOURS Seine-et-Marne

Pre de L'Etang 34 r St Martin, 77115
☎ 160669634 ▤ 160669634
On the outskirts of the village, surrounded by fields in a calm and peaceful location and containing a large pond.
➲ *Take autoroute A5 exit 16 for Chatillon La Borde and follow directions for Blandy-Les-Tours. On reaching town, take direction for St Méry.*
Open: 15 Feb-15 Dec **Site:** 2HEC **Prices:** pitch 13.50 (static)206.50 **Facilities:** **Services:** lau
Off-site:

BOIRY-NOTRE-DAME Pas-de-Calais

Flandres Artois 1 r Verte, 62156 ☎ 321481540 ▤ 321220724
e-mail: campingflandresartois@wanadoo.fr
website: www.campingflandresartois.com
On a level meadow with a good variety of recreational facilities.
➲ *On D34. Access via A1 exit 15 towards Cambrai or A26 exit 8 towards Arras.*
Open: 26 Mar-Oct **Site:** 4.9HEC **Facilities:**
Services: lau **Leisure:** P **Off-site:**

BOISSY-LE-CUTTE ESSONNE

Boulinière La Boulinière, 91590 164576523 145448516
e-mail: secretariat@campingclub.asso.fr
website: www.campingclub.asso.fr
Situated in a wood 800m from the village.
Access via N20 and D148.
Open: All year **Site:** 4HEC **Prices:** pitch 12.20 (incl 2 persons) (static)75 **Facilities:** **Services:** lau **Off-site:** R

BOUBERS-SUR-CANCHE PAS-DE-CALAIS

Petit St Jean 27 r de Frevent, 62270
321048520 321048520
e-mail: arielle.triart@wanadoo.fr
website: perso.wanadoo.fr/camping.loisir/
In a peaceful, rural setting within easy reach of the village.
E via D340 towards Frévent.
Open: Apr-15 Oct **Site:** 1HEC **Facilities:** **Services:** lau **Off-site:** PR

BOULANCOURT SEINE-ET-MARNE

Ile de Boulancourt 6 allée des Marronniers, 77760
164241338 164241043
e-mail: camping-ile-de-boulancourt@wanadoo.fr
website: www.camping.paris.com
A peaceful site shaded by mature trees in a convenient situation in the Essonne valley.
Access via D410.
Open: All year **Site:** 5HEC **Prices:** 4 pitch 4.50 (static)108 **Facilities:** **Services:** lau **Leisure:** R **Off-site:**

BRAY-DUNES NORD

Perroquet-Plage 59123 328583737 328583701
e-mail: camping-perroquet@wanadoo.fr
website: www.campingduperroquet.com
An above average site situated among sand dunes with direct access to the beach.
3km NE towards La Panne.
Open: Apr-Sep **Site:** 28HEC **Prices:** 5 2 2.80 2 (static)250 **Facilities:** **Services:** lau **Leisure:** S

CAMIERS PAS-DE-CALAIS

Sables d'Or 62176 321849515
In a wooded location with good recreational facilities.
Open: All year **Site:** 10HEC **Facilities:** **Services:** lau **Leisure:** P

CAYEUX-SUR-MER SOMME

Voyeul rte des Canadiens, 80410
322266084 322266084
In pleasant surroundings, 400m from the sea, with pitches enclosed by hedges and flowerbeds.
1.5km S on D140.
Open: Apr-15 Oct **Site:** 1.7HEC **Prices:** 3.20 3.25 3.25 pitch 3.25 **Facilities:** **Services:** lau **Off-site:** S

CHAMOUILLE AISNE

Parc de l'Ailette Parc Nautique de l'Ailette, 02860
323246686 323246687
e-mail: ailette@wanadoo.fr **website:** perso.wanadoo.fr/ailette
On the shore of a lake within an extensive leisure park and nature reserve.
2km SE via D19.
Open: Apr-Sep **Site:** 6HEC **Prices:** 9-15 **Facilities:** **Services:** lau **Leisure:** L **Off-site:**

CONDETTE PAS-DE-CALAIS

Château 21 r Nouvelle, 62360 321875959 321875959
e-mail: campingduchateau@libertysurf.fr
website: camping-caravaning-du-chateau.com
On pleasant parkland, bordered by a forest, 500m from the town centre. Separate car park for arrivals after 23.00.
Access via D940 towards Hardelot.
Open: Apr-Oct **Site:** 1.2HEC **Prices:** 4.40-5.20 pitch 14.20-16.80 (static)220-270 **Facilities:** **Services:** lau **Off-site:** L

COUDEKERQUE NORD

Bois des Forts 59280 328610441
0.7km NW on D72.
Open: All year **Site:** 4HEC **Facilities:** **Services:** lau **Off-site:**

CROTOY, LE SOMME

Aubépines r de la Maye, Saint Firmin, 80550
322270134 322270134
e-mail: contact@camping-lesaubepines.com
website: www.camping-lesaubepines.com
Situated on the Picardy coast at the heart of the Somme estuary in a peaceful verdant location surrounded by hawthorn trees. The nearest beach, 1km away, is part of a nature reserve.
D940 from Abbeville.
Open: 25 Mar-6 Nov **Site:** 4HEC **Prices:** 3.33-3.70 pitch 13.50-15 **Facilities:** **Services:** lau **Leisure:** P **Off-site:** S

DUNKERQUE (DUNKIRK) NORD

CM bd de l'Europe, 59240 328692668 328695621
e-mail: campinglalicorne@wanadoo.fr
Open: Apr-Nov **Site:** 10HEC **Facilities:** **Services:** lau **Off-site:** PS

ÉPERLECQUES PAS-DE-CALAIS

Château de Gandspette 62910 321934393 321957498
e-mail: contact@chateau-gandspette.com
website: www.chateau-gandspette.com
A peaceful site, surrounded by woodland.
11.5km NW on N43 and D207.
Open: Apr-Sep **Site:** 11HEC **Prices:** 5-6 pitch 6-9 **Facilities:** **Services:** lau **Leisure:** P **Off-site:**

EQUIHEN-PLAGE PAS-DE-CALAIS

CM la Falaise r C-Cazin, 62224 321312261
e-mail: mairie.equinhen.plage@wanadoo.fr
website: www.ville-equinhen-plage.fr
150m between Boulogne and Le Touquet.
Open: 28 Mar-4 Nov **Site:** 8HEC **Facilities:** **Services:** lau **Off-site:** S

ÉTAMPES ESSONNE

Vauvert Ormoy La Rivière, 91150
164942139 169927259
In a pleasant woodland situation beside the river.
2km S via D49.
Open: 15 Jan-15 Dec **Site:** 11HEC **Prices:** 4.50 pitch 5 **Facilities:** **Services:** lau **Leisure:** R **Off-site:** LP

ÉTAPLES Pas-de-Calais

Pinède 62630 321943451
A well-equipped site situated amongst sand dunes and surrounded by pine trees close to the yacht basin and local shopping facilities.
Open: 15Feb-15Dec **Site:** 3HEC **Facilities:** **Services:** lau **Off-site:** R

FELLERIES Nord

CM La Boissellerie r de la Place, 59740
327590650 327590288
Open: 15 Apr-Sep **Site:** 1HEC **Prices:** 2.50 1.50 1.50 1.50 pitch 1.50 **Facilities:** **Off-site:**

FORT-MAHON-PLAGE Somme

Royon rte de Quend, 80790 322234030 322236515
e-mail: barbara.dutot@wanadoo.fr
website: www.campingleroyon.com
A family site with good facilities and well-marked pitches, 2.5km from the beach.
Open: 06 Mar-02 Nov **Site:** 5.5HEC **Facilities:** **Services:** lau **Leisure:** P **Off-site:** S

FRIAUCOURT Somme

CM Au Chant des Oiseaux Ruelle du Grand Patis, 80460
322264954
In pleasant surroundings with good sanitary and sporting facilities 2km from the sea. Separate car park for arrivals after 22.00.
NE via D63.
Open: Apr-15 Oct **Site:** 1.4HEC **Facilities:** **Services:** lau

GOUVIEUX Oise

César rte de Toutevoie 10, 60270 344571273
On a hill overlooking the River Oise.
Access via A1 to Gouvieux town centre, then towatds Creil.
Open: All year **Site:** 6HEC **Facilities:** **Services:** lau **Off-site:** P

GRAND-FORT-PHILIPPE Nord

CM de la Plage r Ml-Foch, 59153 328653195
On a level meadow separated from the beach (500m) by dunes.
On the seaward extremity of Grand-Fort Philippe.
Open: Apr-Oct **Site:** 1.5HEC **Prices:** 380 1.50 3 3 **Facilities:** **Services:** lau **Off-site:** S

GREZ-SUR-LOING Seine-et-Marne

CM Près chemin des Près, 77880
164457275 164457275
website: camping-grez@wanadoo.fr
NE towards Loing.
Open: end Mar-11 Nov **Site:** 6HEC **Prices:** 2.50 1.80 2.50 2.50 (static)157 **Facilities:** **Services:** lau **Off-site:** R

GUINES Pas-de-Calais

Bien Assise 62340 321352077 321367920
e-mail: castel@bien-assise.com
website: www.bien-assise.com
A nice site in the country near to a large forest and a charming little town.
Access via D231 towards Marquise.
Open: 19 Apr-21 Sep **Site:** 12HEC **Prices:** 4.60 pitch 11.50 **Facilities:** **Services:** lau **Leisure:** P

HIRSON Aisne

Cascade Site de Blangy, 2500 323581897 323587451
e-mail: tourisme.info.hirson@wanadoo.fr
In a picturesque woodland setting with good, modern facilities.
1.8km N via N43 towards La Capelle.
Open: 15 Apr-15 Sep **Site:** 1.6HEC **Prices:** 3 pitch 6-1.50 (static)150 **Facilities:** **Services:** lau **Leisure:** P **Off-site:**

ISQUES Pas-de-Calais

Cytises r de l'Église, 62360 321311110 321311110
In a pleasant rural setting beside the River Liane.
4km S of Boulogne-sur-Mer towards Abbeville, 100m from N1.
Open: Apr-15 Oct **Site:** 2.5HEC **Prices:** 2.90-3.20 2.85-3.10 pitch 2.65-3 (static)190-230 **Facilities:** **Services:** lau **Off-site:** R

JABLINES Seine-et-Marne

International 77450 160260937 160265333
e-mail: welcome@camping-jablines.com
website: www.camping-jablines.com
Only 9km from Disneyland Paris.
Access via A1 or A3 towards Marne-la-Vallée, then N3.
Open: 25 Mar-30 Oct **Site:** 3.5HEC **Prices:** 4.50-5.50 pitch 19-22 (incl 2 persons) (static)385-550 **Facilities:** **Services:** lau **Leisure:** L

LAON Aisne

CM La Chênaie allée de la Chênaie, 02000
323202556 323202556
A peaceful family site with good facilities close to the city centre.
W of the city centre towards N44.
Open: May-Sep **Site:** 3.3HEC **Facilities:** **Services:** lau **Off-site:** LPR

LICQUES Pas-de-Calais

Canchy r de Canchy, 62850 321826341 321826341
A quiet site on an open, level meadow well situated for access to the ferries and the Eurotunnel.
Open: 15 Mar-Oct **Site:** 1HEC **Prices:** 3.40 pitch 3.80 **Facilities:** **Services:** lau **Leisure:** R

LYNDE Nord

Becquerel 1396 r du Becquerelle, 59173 328432037
In a rural setting surrounded by woodland and hedges.
Open: Mar-Nov **Site:** 1.5HEC **Facilities:** **Services:** **Off-site:**

MAISONS-LAFFITTE YVELINES

International 1 r Johnson, 78600
139122191 139127050
e-mail: ci.mlaffitte@wanadoo.fr **website:** ww.campint.com
A well-kept site in a residential area on the banks of the Seine. Modern installations, heated in cold weather.
8 km N of St-Germain-en-Laye. Alternatively follow N308 from Porte Champerret or from Colombos-Ouest exit of Autoroute A86.
Open: Apr-Oct **Site:** 6.5HEC **Prices:** 5-5.60 pitch 21-24 (incl 2 persons) **Facilities:** **Services:** lau **Off-site:** PR

MARNE-LA-VALLÉE SEINE-ET-MARNE

Davy Crockett Ranch Disneyland Paris, 77777
160456900 160456933
A modern site in wooded surroundings on the Disneyland Paris complex.
Access via A4 Serris exit 13.
Open: Apr-Oct **Site:** 57HEC **Facilities:** **Services:** lau **Leisure:** P **Off-site:**

MAUBEUGE NORD

Camping Municipal de Clair de Lune rte de Mons, 59600
327622548 327622548
1.5km N via N2 Bruxelles road.
Open: All year **Site:** 2.1HEC **Facilities:** **Services:** lau **Off-site:**

MELUN SEINE-ET-MARNE

Belle Étoile Quai Joffre, 77000 164394812 164372555
e-mail: info@camplabelleetoile.com
website: www.camplabelleetoile.com
Pleasant grassy site with two central blocks.

At La Rochette, on left bank of River Seine 1km from the town.
Open: Apr-Oct **Site:** 3.5HEC **Prices:** 4.65-5.10 pitch 4.70-5.10 (static)200-492 **Facilities:** **Services:** lau **Leisure:** P **Off-site:** LPR

MERLIMONT PAS-DE-CALAIS

St-Hubert RD 940, 62155 321891010 321891012
e-mail: sthubert62@wanadoo.fr
website: www.sthubert62.com
In pleasant wooded surroundings with good recreational facilities.
3km S via D940, near Parc de Bagatelle.
Open: Apr-Oct **Site:** 16HEC **Facilities:** **Services:** lau **Leisure:** P

MILLY-LA-FORÊT ESSONNE

Musardière rte des Grandes Vallées, 91490
164989191 164989191
e-mail: lamusardiere@infonie.fr
In pleasant wooded surroundings.
4km SE via D948.
Open: 16 Feb-Nov **Site:** 12HEC
Prices: 5.50 3 5.50 3 pitch 3 (static)189-217
Facilities: **Services:** **Leisure:** P

MONNERVILLE ESSONNE

Bois de la Justice 91930 164950534 164951731
Pitches separated by trees and hedges in beautiful natural woodland with good facilities.
N20 Orléans to Étampes.
Open: Feb-Nov **Site:** 5.5HEC **Prices:** 6 2.50 5 5 **Facilities:** **Services:** lau **Leisure:** P

MONTIGNY-LE-BRETONNEUX YVELINES

Parc Étang Base de Loisirs-de-St Quentin, 78180
130585620 134600714
In beautiful rural surroundings within a leisure centre with easy access to Paris and Versailles.
SE of town centre towards the Centre de Volle.
Open: Mar-Oct **Site:** 12HEC **Facilities:** **Services:** lau **Off-site:** LP

MONTREUIL-SUR-MER PAS-DE-CALAIS

CM Fontaine des Clercs 1, r de l'Eglise, 62170
321060728
e-mail: freddy.monchaux@wanadoo.fr
N of town on N1.
Open: All year **Site:** 2HEC **Facilities:** **Services:** lau **Leisure:** R **Off-site:** P

MOUSSEAUX SUR SEINE YVELINES

Loisirs des Groux chemin de Vetheuil, 78270 134793382
e-mail: infos@loisirsdesgroux.com
website: www.loisirsdesgroux.com
Conveniently situated for visiting Paris, Giverny and Versailles.
Open: Mar-Nov **Site:** 3.5HEC **Prices:** 14.20 (static)140 **Facilities:** **Services:** lau **Leisure:** LR **Off-site:** L

MOYENNEVILLE SOMME

Val de Trie Bouillancourt-sous-Miannay, 80870
322314888 322313533
e-mail: raphael@camping-lavaldetrie.fr
website: www.camping-levaldetrie.fr
A small site in a picturesque wooded location with good facilities including a lake for fishing.

Site: 6HEC-Site size -grass -sand -stone -little shade -partly shaded -mainly shaded -bungalows for hire -caravans for hire -tents for hire -no dogs **Prices:** -adult per night -car per night pp-per person per night -caravan per night -tent per night (static)-caravan hire per week

1km from the D925 Abbeville-Le Tréport.
Open: 26 Mar-1 Nov **Site:** 3HEC **Prices:** 2.90-4.20 pitch 3.30-4.20 **Facilities:** **Services:** lau **Leisure:** P **Off-site:**

NESLES-LA-VALLÉE VAL-D'OISE

Parc de Séjour de l'Étang 10 Chemin des Belles Vues, 95690
134706289 134706289
e-mail: brehinier1@hotmail.com
website: www.campingparcset.com
Level site near a small lake.
A15 exit 10, then D927 & D79. From N1 exit for L'Isle Adam.
Open: Mar-15 Nov **Site:** 6HEC **Prices:** 3-4 pitch 3-4 **Facilities:** **Services:** lau **Off-site:**

NEUVILLE, LA NORD

Leu Pindu 2 r du Gl-de-Gaulle, 59239
320865087 320865177
N on D8.
Open: All year **Site:** 1.2HEC **Facilities:** **Services:** lau **Off-site:** L

ORVILLERS-SOREL OISE

Sorel 60490 344850274 355521165
Divided into pitches. Local tradesmen supply provisions.
Leave A1 at N17, turn right and continue 400m.
Open: Feb-15 Dec **Site:** 3HEC **Prices:** pitch 15 (incl 2 persons) **Facilities:** **Services:** lau

OYE-PLAGE PAS-DE-CALAIS

Oyats 272 Digue Vert, 62215 321851540 & 328603833
e-mail: bnilliet.nicolas@wanadoo.fr
4.5km NW directly on the beach.
Open: May-Sep **Site:** 5HEC **Facilities:** **Services:** lau **Leisure:** PS

PARIS

Bois de Boulogne 2 allée du Bord de l'Eau, 75016
145243000 142244295
Much of this site's popularity stems from its location close to the city centre and it can become crowded during high season as it is the only site in Paris.
Open: All year **Site:** 7HEC **Facilities:** **Services:** lau

PLESSIS-FEU-AUSSOUX SEINE-ET-MARNE

Château-de-Chambonnières 77540
164041585 0164041336
On D231 towards Provins, 23km from Disneyland Paris.
Open: All year **Site:** 5HEC **Facilities:** **Services:** lau

POIX-DE-PICARDIE SOMME

Bois des Pêcheurs rte de Forges-les-Eaux, 80290
322901171 322903291
e-mail: mairie.poix.de.picardie@wanadoo.fr
In a quiet riverside location with a high standard of sanitary facilities.
W via D919 towards Forges-les-Eaux.
Open: Apr-Sep **Site:** 2.4HEC **Facilities:** **Services:** lau **Off-site:** PR

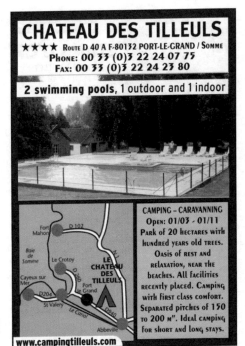

PORT-LE-GRAND SOMME

Chateau des Tilleuls rte D40 A, 80132
322240775 322242380
e-mail: contact@campingtilleuls.com
website: www.campingtilleuls.com
On gently sloping meadow surrounding a farm.
1km SE on D940A.
Open: Mar-Oct **Site:** 5HEC **Facilities:** **Services:** lau **Leisure:** P **Off-site:** R

PROYART SOMME

Loisir la Violette rte de Mericourt, 80340
322858136 322851737
Open: Mar-Oct **Site:** 1.8HEC **Prices:** 2.10 1 pitch 1.30 **Facilities:** **Services:** lau **Off-site:** P

QUEND-PLAGE-LES-PINS SOMME
AT MONCHAUX-LES-QUEND (3.5KM E VIA D102E)

Roses 80120 322277617 322239306
e-mail: sandrine.bruyelle@wanadoo.fr
website: www.campingdesroses.com
Well-kept site with trees and hedges surrounding individual pitches. Only recommended site in area.
Turn off D940 at Quend, site 500m on left of D102.
Open: 15 Mar-27 Oct **Site:** 9HEC **Prices:** pitch 25 (incl 2 persons) **Facilities:** **Services:** lau **Leisure:** P **Off-site:** S

Facilities: -shop -shower -electric points for razors -electric points for caravans -parking by tents permitted -compulsory separate car park **Services:** -café/restaurant -bar -Camping Gaz International -gas other than Camping Gaz -first aid facilities lau-laundry **Leisure:** -swimming L-Lake P-Pool R-River S-Sea **Off-site:** All facilities within 2km

RAMBOUILLET YVELINES

CM de l'Étang d'Or r du Château d'Eau, 78120
130410734 130410017
e-mail: ramboulillet.tourisme@wanadoo.fr
website: ot-rambouillet.fr
A pleasant location. Shop, bar only open Jun-Aug.
From railway station follow road SE for 1.3km passing Camping Pont Hardy.
Open: 31 Jan-18 Dec **Site:** 5HEC **Prices:** 3.90-4.30 pitch 4.30-4.90 **Facilities:** **Services:** lau **Off-site:** P

ST-AMAND-LES-EAUX NORD

Mont des Bruyères 806 r Basly, 59230
327485687 327485687
3.5km SE in the forest of St-Amand.
Open: Mar-Nov **Site:** 3.5HEC **Facilities:** **Services:** lau **Off-site:** LPR

ST-CHÉRON ESSONNE

Parc des Roches La Petite Beauce, 91530
164566550 164565450
e-mail: cantact@parcdesroches.com
website: www.parcdesroches.com
In a wooded park.
Open: 15 Apr-15 Sep **Site:** 23HEC **Prices:** 6.40 2.55 4.85 4.85 (static)420 **Facilities:** **Services:** lau **Leisure:** P **Off-site:**

ST-CYR-SUR-MORIN SEINE-ET-MARNE

Choisel Courcelles la Roue, 77750
160238493 160248174
e-mail: campingduchoisel@wanadoo.fr
In a pleasant location. Separate car park for arrivals after 22.00.
2km W via D31.
Open: Mar-Nov **Site:** 3.5HEC **Prices:** 4.50 6.90 3 (static)182.94 **Facilities:** **Services:** lau **Off-site:** LPR

ST-JANS-CAPPEL NORD

Domaine de la Sablière Le Mont Noir, 59270
328494634 328426290
A pleasant family site in a wooded location with large, well-defined pitches.
3.5km NE via D10 and D318.
Open: 15 Apr-15 Oct **Site:** 3.6HEC **Facilities:** **Services:** lau **Off-site:** LP

ST-LEU-D'ESSERENT OISE

Campix 44560848
In wooded surroundings, within easy reach of Chantilly.
3.5km NE via D12.
Open: 7 Mar-1 Dec **Site:** 6HEC **Facilities:** **Services:** lau **Off-site:** L

ST-QUENTIN AISNE

CM bd J-Bouin, 02100 323626866 &
A good site in pleasant wooded surroundings near the canal.
Open: Mar-Nov **Site:** 1.9HEC **Facilities:** **Off-site:** PR

ST-VALÉRY-SUR-SOMME SOMME

Domaine du Château de Drancourt 80230
322269345 322268587
e-mail: chateau.drancourt@wanadoo.fr
website: www.chateau-drancourt.com
In open countryside, surrounded by woods, fields and lakes, within the grounds of a former hunting lodge.
3.5km S via D48.
Open: 25 Mar-Oct **Site:** 15HEC **Prices:** pitch 19.90-29.80 (incl 2 persons) **Facilities:** **Services:** lau **Leisure:** P **Off-site:** L

SALENCY OISE

Étang du Moulin 54 r du Moulin, 60400 344099981
A small site opposite a trout fishing lake and recreational area under the ownership of the site proprietors.
3km from Noyon on the N32 towards Chauny.
Open: All year **Site:** 0.4HEC **Prices:** 1.90 2.30 3.85 3.85 **Facilities:** **Services:** **Off-site:** PR

SERAUCOURT-LE-GRAND AISNE

Pêche du Vivier aux Carpes 10 r Ch-Voyeux, 02790
323605010 323605169
e-mail: camping.du.vivier@wanadoo.fr
A peaceful site bordered by lakes. Separate car park for arrivals after 22.00.
A26 exit 11-left on D1 exit Essigny-D72.
Open: Mar-Oct **Site:** 3HEC **Prices:** 3.30 **Facilities:** **Services:** lau **Leisure:** L **Off-site:** R

SOISSONS AISNE

CM av du Mail, 02200 323745269 323596772
e-mail: officedetourisme@ville-soissons.fr
website: www.ville-soissons.fr
In pleasant surroundings with good, modern facilities.
Open: All year **Site:** 1.8HEC **Prices:** 3 3 3 3 pitch 3 **Facilities:** **Services:** lau **Off-site:** P

THIEMBRONNE PAS-DE-CALAIS

Pommiers rte de Desvres, 62560
321395019 321957920
A family site in pleasant wooded surroundings.
NW on D132.
Open: 15 Mar-15 Oct **Site:** 1.8HEC **Prices:** 3.40-4.10 1.65-2.70 3.40-4.10 pitch 3.40-4.10 (static)190-280 **Facilities:** **Services:** lau **Leisure:** P **Off-site:** R

TOLLENT PAS-DE-CALAIS

Val d'Authie CD 119 Rt de Berck, 62390
321471427 321471427
In a pleasant wooded location with wide, well-marked pitches.

SE via D119.
Open: Apr-Sep **Site:** 5.7HEC **Prices:** pitch 13 (incl 3 persons) (static)370 **Facilities:** ⊙ **Services:** lau **Leisure:** LP **Off-site:** R

TORCY Seine-et-Marne

Parc de la Colline rte de Lagny, 77200
160054232 164800517
e-mail: camping.parc.de.la.colline@wanadoo.fr
website: www.camping-de-la-colline.com
An ideal base for visiting Paris (30 minutes from the centre by Metro). Separate car park for arrivals after 22.00.
Access via exit 10 on the A104 and D10E.
Open: All year **Site:** 10HEC **Prices:** 6.70 pitch 10.70 **Facilities:** ⊙ **Services:** lau
Off-site: LP

TOUQUIN Seine-et-Marne

Étangs Fleuris rte de la Couture, 77131
164041636 164041228
e-mail: contact@etangs-fleuris.com
website: www.etangsfleuris.com
In wooded surroundings with well-defined pitches and modern facilities.
E of town towards Provins.
Open: Apr-15 Oct **Site:** 5.5HEC **Prices:** 8
Facilities: ⊙ **Services:** lau **Leisure:** P
Off-site:

TOURNEHEM Pas-de-Calais

Bal Parc 500 r du Vieux Château, 62890
321356590 321351857
e-mail: balparc@wanadoo.fr
A peaceful site in rural surroundings with good, modern facilities.
Access via D218 from village centre.
Open: All year **Site:** 1.6HEC **Facilities:** ⊙ **Services:** lau **Off-site:** R

VAILLY-SUR-AISNE Aisne

Domaine de la Nature chemin de Boufaud, Pont de Vailley, 02370 323547455 326883465
In a pleasant rural setting alongside the canal with well-defined pitches and modern sanitary facilities.
4km W via D144 near the canal and lake.
Open: All year **Site:** 3HEC **Prices:** pitch 11.50 (incl 2 persons) (static)150-320 **Facilities:** ⊙ **Services:** lau **Off-site:** R

VERNEUIL-SUR-SEINE Yvelines

Val de Seine chemin du Rouillard, 78480
139281620 139711860
website: www.valdeseine78.com
Situated on the outskirts of Paris in a pine forest.
Open: Apr-Sep 3.5 **Site:** 3.5HEC **Prices:** 3.50 2.50 4 pitch 4.50 **Facilities:** ⊙ **Services:** **Leisure:** L

VERSAILLES Yvelines

Huttopia Versailles 31 av Berthelot
139512361 139536829
e-mail: versailles@huttopia.com
website: www.camping-versailles.com
Site in forest location 2.5km from the palace of Versailles. Very convenient for Paris.
400m from RER C station at Porchefontaine.
Open: 26 Mar-30 Oct **Site:** 4.5HEC
Prices: 5.50-6 pitch 8-11 **Facilities:** ⊙
Services: lau **Leisure:** P **Off-site:**

VILLENNES-SUR-SEINE Yvelines

Club des Renardières rte de Vernouillet, 78670
139758897
Site for caravans only, in beautiful hilly park laid out with hedges, lawns and flower beds. Fully divided into completely separated pitches.
Follow D113 to Maison Blanche turn right and continue 3km.
Open: All year **Site:** 7HEC **Facilities:** ⊙
Services: lau **Off-site:** LPR

VILLERS-HÉLON Aisne

Castel des Biches Chateau Alexandre Dumas, 2600
323729393 323729333
e-mail: pacal.ginailhac@wanadoo.fr
website: www.castel-des-biches.com
Attractive site in grounds of an old castle.
Turn off N2 onto D2 between Soissons and Villers-Cotterêts and continue for 7km via Longport.
Open: All year **Site:** 10HEC **Facilities:** ⊙ **Services:** lau **Off-site:** LR

VILLERS-SUR-AUTHIE Somme

Val d'Authie 20 rte de Vercourt, 80120
322299247 322299330
e-mail: camping@valdauthie.fr **website:** www.valdauthie.fr
A well-designed site situated between the forest of Crécy and the sea. Bar and café open in high season only.
Access via N1.
Open: Apr-Oct **Site:** 7HEC **Prices:** 6 pitch 23 (incl 3 persons) **Facilities:** ⊙ **Services:** lau
Leisure: P **Off-site:** R

VIRONCHAUX Somme

Peupliers 221 r du Cornet, 80150
322235427 322290519
e-mail: les-peupliers2@wanadoo.fr
A peaceful site 3km form the forest of Crécy.
Approach via N1 and D938.
Open: Apr-Sep **Site:** 2.5HEC **Prices:** 3.30 2.80 3.80 3.80 pitch 3.80 **Facilities:** ⊙
Services: lau **Off-site:**

WACQUINGHEN Pas-de-Calais

Éscale 62250 321320069 321320069
In a pleasantly landscaped park with modern facilities 5 minutes from the coastal resorts.
Access via A16 and D231.
Open: 15 Mar-15 Oct **Site:** 11HEC **Prices:** 4 2 4 3 **Facilities:** ⊙ **Services:** lau
Off-site:

AUVERGNE

ALLANCHE Cantal

CM Pont Valat 15160 471204587 471204181
e-mail: mairie.allanche@wanadoo.fr
1km S on D679 towards St-Flour.
Open: 15 Jun-15 Sep **Site:** 3HEC **Prices:** 1.40 0.50 pitch 0.80 (static)200 **Facilities:** ⊙
Services: lau **Off-site:**

ALLEYRAS Haute-Loire

CM 43580 471575686
In pleasant surroundings on level ground beside the River Allier.
2.5km NW.
Open: May-Sep **Site:** 1HEC **Facilities:** ⊙
Services: lau **Off-site:** R

AMBERT PUY-DE-DÔME

Trois Chênes rte du Puy, 63600 473823468 473823468
e-mail: tourisme-ambert@wanadoo.fr
Open: May-Sep **Site:** **Facilities:**
Services: lau **Off-site:** LP

ANSE RHÔNE

Porte du Beaujolais chemin des Grandes Levées, 69480
474671287 474099097
e-mail: campingbeaujolais@wanadoo.fr
A pleasant, modern site in the heart of the Beaujolais country beside the River Saône.
Access via A6 or N6 then D39.
Open: 15 Mar-30 Oct **Site:** 7HEC **Facilities:** **Services:** lau **Leisure:** PR
Off-site:

ARNAC CANTAL

Gineste 15150 471629190 471629272
e-mail: lagineste@mairie-arnac.fr **website:** www.mairie-arnac.fr
Situated on a peninsula in lake Enchanet with good, modern facilities and access to local ski slopes.
NW of Arnac towards the lake.
Open: All year **Site:** 3HEC **Facilities:**
Services: lau **Leisure:** LP

ARPAJON-SUR-CÈRE CANTAL

Cère r F-Ramond, 15130 471645507
S towards Rodez via D920, beside the river.
Open: Jun-Sep **Site:** 2HEC **Facilities:**
Services: lau **Leisure:** R **Off-site:**

AUBIN AVEYRON

CM 12110 565630386
100m from the lake.
Open: 15 Apr-Sep **Site:** 4HEC **Facilities:** **Services:** lau **Off-site:** PR

AT BELLERIVE-SUR-ALLIER (3KM W)

Acacias r Claude-Decloître, 03700
470323622 470598852
e-mail: campingacacias@club-internet.fr
website: www.camping-acacias.com
Well-managed site, sub-divided into numbered pitches by hedges. Clean sanitary installations. Library, billiard room. Water sports are available nearby on lake.
From Vichy turn left after bridge beside Esso garage and follow river for 500m.
Open: 5 Apr-15 Oct **Site:** 3HEC **Facilities:** **Services:** lau **Leisure:** LPR **Off-site:**

Beau Rivage r Claude-Decloitre, 03700
470322685 470320394
e-mail: camping-beaurivage@wanadoo.fr
website: www.camping-beaurivage.com
Neat meadowland with marked out pitches. Well kept sanitary installations. TV.
Watch for turning over bridge onto left bank of River Allier.
Open: Apr-Sep **Site:** 1.5HEC **Prices:** 3.50-4.80 3.50-4.80 pitch 3.50-4.80 (static)161-230 **Facilities:** **Services:** lau **Leisure:** PR

BELMONT-SUR-RANCE AVEYRON

Val Fleuri 12370 565999513
A peaceful site beside the River Rance with good, modern facilities.
Access via N9 and D999.
Open: Jun-Aug **Site:** 1HEC **Facilities:** **Services:** lau **Leisure:** R **Off-site:** P

BOURBON-L'ARCHAMBAULT ALLIER

CM Parc Bignon Parc Jean Bignon, 03160
470670883 470673535
1km SW on N153, rte de Montluçon, turn right.
Open: Mar-Oct **Site:** 3HEC **Prices:** 2.10 0.80 1.20 1.20 pitch 1.20 **Facilities:** **Services:** lau
Off-site: LP

BOURG-ARGENTAL LOIRE

Astrée L'Allier, 42220 477397297 477397621
e-mail: prl@bourgargental.fr
In pleasant surroundings with good recreational facilities.
Access via N82.
Open: All year **Site:** 2HEC **Prices:** 2.50-3.50 1.25-1.75 5-7 2.50-3.50 **Facilities:**
Services: lau **Leisure:** R **Off-site:** P

BRAIZE ALLIER

Champ de la Chapelle 03360 470061545 470061545
e-mail: ccdlp@aol.com
A family site in the centre of the Tronçais forest with good recreational facilities.
7km SE via D28 and D978.
Open: 17 Apr-19 Sep **Site:** 5.6HEC **Prices:** pitch 9.90 (incl 1 persons) (static)150-270 **Facilities:**
Services: lau **Leisure:** P

BRUSQUE AVEYRON

VAL Camping Les Pibouls Domaine de Céras, 12360
565495066
Open: Jul-Aug **Site:** 1HEC **Facilities:**
Services: lau **Leisure:** L **Off-site:**

CANET-DE-SALARS AVEYRON

Caussanel Lac de Pareloup, 12290
565468519 565468985
e-mail: info@lecaussanel.com **website:** www.lecaussanel.com
Well equipped site on the shore of lake Pareloup.
Access via D911.
Open: 30 Apr-24 Sep **Site:** 10HEC **Prices:** 4.40-6 pitch 13.20-23.50 (incl 2 persons) **Facilities:**
Services: lau **Leisure:** LP

Soleil Levant Lac de Pareloup, 12290
565460365 565460362
e-mail: contact@camping-soleil-levant.com
website: www.camping-soleil-levant.com
A family site set on terraces on the shores of Lac de Pareloup with good recreational facilities.

S of Canet-de-Salars via D933 towards Salles-Curan.
Open: Apr-Sep **Site:** 11HEC **Prices:** 3.50-4.50 11-18 (static)530-580 **Facilities:** **Services:** lau **Leisure:** L

Capdenac-Gare Aveyron

Diège Vallée de la Diège, Sonnac, 12700 565646125
Level, sub-divided terrain located in a narrow valley of La Diège river.
From Figeac on N140 travel 7km, in the direction of Capdenac-Gare. Turn sharp right after the bridge and continue on D558 for about 7km in the direction of Naussac.
Open: May-1 Nov **Site:** 7HEC **Facilities:** **Services:** lau **Leisure:** R

CM Rives d'Olt bd Paul-Ramadier, 12700 565808887
A quiet site on level ground with pitches divided by hedges on the bank of a river.
7km from Figeac via N140 towards Rodez, then D35 to Capendac.
Open: Apr-Sep **Site:** 1.3HEC **Prices:** 2.60 1.70 2.70 1.90 **Facilities:** **Services:** lau **Leisure:** R **Off-site:** P

Champagnac-le-Vieux Haute-Loire

Chanterelle Le Plan d'Eau, 43440
471763400 471763400
e-mail: camping@es-conseil.fr
website: www.champagnac.com
Situated in the heart of the Auvergne beside a wooded lake.
1km N via D5.
Open: Apr-Oct **Site:** 4HEC **Prices:** 2.50 pitch 5 (static)305 **Facilities:** **Services:** lau **Leisure:** L **Off-site:** R

Champs-sur-Tarentaine Cantal

Tarentaine 15270 471787125
In an attractive location surrounded by lakes and woodland.
1km SW via D679 and D22 beside the River Tarentaine.
Open: 15 Jun-15 Sep **Site:** 4HEC **Facilities:** **Services:** lau **Off-site:** P

Châtel-de-Neuvre Allier

Deneuvre Les Graves, 03500
470420451 470420451
e-mail: campingdeneuvre@wanadoo.fr
website: www.deneuvre.com
In pleasant surroundings within a nature reserve beside the River Allier.
0.5km N via D9.
Open: Apr-Sep **Site:** 1HEC **Prices:** 3.10-3.85 pitch 3.10-3.85 (static)230-335 **Facilities:** **Services:** lau **Leisure:** R **Off-site:**

Châtel Guyon Puy-de-Dôme

Clos de Balanède r de la Piscine, 63140
473860247 473860564
e-mail: closde.pougheon@wauadoo.fr **website:** balanede.com
A pleasant site, situated in an orchard.
Access via A71 and D685.
Open: 14 Apr-Sep **Site:** 4HEC **Prices:** 3-4.20 1-1.40 pitch 2-2.70 **Facilities:** **Services:** lau **Leisure:** P **Off-site:** R

Châtel-Montagne Allier

Croix Cognat 03250 470593138
e-mail: campinglacroixcognat@wanadoo.fr
website: http://perso.wanadoo.fr/mairie-chatel-montagne
Well equipped site at an altitude of 540m.
0.5km NW via D25 towards Vichy.
Open: May-1 Oct **Site:** 1HEC **Prices:** pitch 10.50 (incl 2 persons) (static)360 **Facilities:** **Services:** lau **Leisure:** P **Off-site:** R

Chaudes-Aigues Cantal

CM du Couffour 15110 471235708 471235708
website: www.chaudesaigues.com
Tastefully sited around the town football pitch in the local leisure area.
2km S via D921.
Open: May-20 Oct **Site:** 2.5HEC **Prices:** 2.50 1 1 pitch 1 **Facilities:** **Services:** lau **Off-site:** PR

Condrieu Rhône

Belle Rive La Plaine, 69420 474595108
In wooded surroundings bordering the Rhône.
11km S of Vienne on N86.
Open: Apr-Sep **Site:** 5HEC **Prices:** 3.50 1.60 pitch 3.80 (static)140-490 **Facilities:** **Services:** lau **Leisure:** PR

Conques Aveyron

Beau Rivage 12320 565698223 565728929
Peaceful site beside the river with spacious, well-marked pitches.
On D901.
Open: Apr-Sep **Site:** 1HEC **Prices:** 3.50-4 2.50-3 pitch 4-5 **Facilities:** **Services:** lau **Leisure:** PR **Off-site:**

Cournon-d'Auvergne Puy-de-Dôme

CM Pré des Laveuses r de Laveuses, 63800 473848130 473846590
e-mail: camping@cournon-auvergne.fr
website: www.cournon-auvergne.fr/camping
In a rural setting on the shore of a 7-hectare lake, close to the River Allier.
1.5km E towards Billom.
Open: All year **Site:** 5HEC **Prices:** 2.95-3.25 pitch 4.10-4.45 **Facilities:** **Services:** lau **Leisure:** LR **Off-site:** P

Dallet Puy-de-Dôme

Ombrages rte de Pont-du-Château, 63111
473831097 473831097
e-mail: lesombrages@hotmail.com
website: www.lesombrages.nl
In a wooded location beside the River Allier.
Open: Jun-15 Sep **Site:** 3.5HEC **Prices:** 5 pitch 13 (incl 2 persons) **Facilities:** **Services:** lau **Leisure:** PR **Off-site:**

Dardilly Rhône

International de Lyon Porte de Lyon, 69570
478356455 472170426
e-mail: camping.lyon@mairie-lyon.fr
website: www.camping-lyon.com
Generously arranged and equipped site divided into pitches. Ideal for overnight stays near motorway. Concrete platforms for caravans.
9km N of Lyon La Garde exit off A6.
Open: All year **Site:** 6.5HEC **Prices:** 3.20 8.20 6.30 **Facilities:** **Services:** lau **Leisure:** P **Off-site:**

EBREUIL ALLIER

FilatHere de la Sioule Ile de Nieres, 3450
470907201 470907948
e-mail: camping.filature@libertysurf.fr
website: www.campingfilature.com
A peaceful, well equipped in an orchard beside the River Sioule.
Access signed from exit 12 on A71.
Open: 30 Mar-Sep **Site:** 3.6HEC **Prices:** 4 pitch 14 (incl 2 persons) **Facilities:** **Services:** lau **Leisure:** R **Off-site:**

FERRIÈRES-ST-MARY CANTAL

Vigeaires 15170 471206188
A level site surrounded by woodland close to the River Allagnon with good, modern facilities.
Access via A75 exit Massiac towards Aurillac.
Open: 15 Jun-Aug **Site:** 0.6HEC **Facilities:** **Services:** lau **Leisure:** R **Off-site:**

FLAGNAC AVEYRON

Port de Lacombe 12300 565601097 565601688
e-mail: info@campingportdelacombe.com
website: www.campingportdelarcombe.com
A shady site in the Lot valley. Water activities including fishing and canoeing on the river and an aquatic area incorporating a large water chute.
Follow A75 autoroute in the direction of Rodez, turn off for Decazeville/Flagnac.
Open: 15 May-15 Sep **Site:** 4HEC **Facilities:** **Services:** lau **Leisure:** R

FLEURIE RHÔNE

CM la Grappe Fleurie 69820 474698007 474698571
e-mail: info@fleurie.org
website: www.fleurie.org
A good quality municipal site in a picturesque setting in the heart of the Beaujolais region.
0.6km SE on D119 E.
Open: mid-Mar to mid-Oct **Site:** 2.5HEC
Prices: 3.50 10 pitch 10 (incl 2 persons) **Facilities:** **Services:** lau **Leisure:** P **Off-site:**

GOUDET HAUTE-LOIRE

Bord de l'Eau Plaine du Chambon, 43150
471571682 471571288
Well equipped site in wooded surroundings below the ruins of a castle.
W via D49, beside the River Loire.
Open: 15 Jun-5 Sep **Site:** 4HEC **Prices:** 4.50 4.50 4.50 **Facilities:** **Services:** lau **Leisure:** PR

ISLE-ET-BARDAIS ALLIER

Écossais 3360 470666257 470066399
In a peaceful location in the heart of the forest of Tronçais, beside the Pirot Lake.
Access via A71-E11.
Open: Apr-Sep **Site:** 25HEC **Prices:** 2.05-2.50 1.05-1.18 pitch 1.05-1.18 **Facilities:** **Services:** lau **Leisure:** L **Off-site:**

JASSAT PUY-DE-DÔME

Ribeyre 63790 473886429 473886841
e-mail: laribeyre@free.fr **website:** laribeyre.free.fr
Situated in the heart of the Auvergne amid lakes and mountains, a flat grassy site with access to a private beach with swimming.
Autoroute A71 exit 6, then take D978/D996 to Murol, then D5 S.
Open: May-15 Sep **Site:** 10HEC **Facilities:** **Services:** lau **Leisure:** LPR **Off-site:**

JENZAT ALLIER

Champ de Sioule rte de Chantelle, 03800
470568635 470568538
e-mail: mairie-jenzat@pays-allier.com
Open: 16 Apr-18 Sep **Site:** 1HEC **Prices:** 2.30 1 2.30 1.30 pitch 4 **Facilities:** **Services:** lau
Off-site: R

LACAPELLE-VIESCAMP CANTAL

Puech des Ouilhes 15150 471464238 0471464738
e-mail: campingpuech@infonie.fr
On a wooded peninsula on lake St-Étienne-Cantalès.
Open: 15 Jun-5 Sep **Site:** 2HEC **Facilities:** **Services:** lau **Leisure:** LP **Off-site:**

LANGEAC HAUTE-LOIRE

Gorges de l'Allier Domaine du Prad'Eau, 43300
471770501 471772734
e-mail: langeac@wanadoo.fr
In wooded surroundings within a natural park, 800m from the river. Good recreational facilities.
Access via N102.
Open: Apr-Oct **Site:** 14HEC **Prices:** pitch 10-12 (incl 2 persons) **Facilities:** **Services:** lau
Leisure: PR **Off-site:**

LAPEYROUSE PUY-DE-DÔME

CM Les Marins La Loge, 63700 473520273 473520389
e-mail: marie.lapeyrouse63@wanadoo.fr
website: 63lapeyrouse.free.fr
A modern, lakeside site with good facilities set among the rolling hills of the Combtaille.
2km E via D998.
Open: 15 Jun-1 Sep **Site:** 2HEC **Prices:** pitch 13
Facilities: **Services:** lau **Leisure:** L
Off-site:

LEMPDES HAUTE-LOIRE

Club A.Tou.Vert 43410 471765369 467363542
e-mail: a.tou.vert@net-up.com
Open: May-30 Oct **Site:** 2HEC **Facilities:** **Services:** lau **Leisure:** R **Off-site:** P

LOUBEYRAT PUY-DE-DÔME

Colombier 63410 473866694
1.5km S via D16.
Open: May-14 Oct **Site:** 1.3HEC **Prices:** 1.50-2.30 0.75-1.15 0.75-1.15 pitch 1.50-2.30 (static)153-351 **Facilities:** **Services:** lau **Leisure:** P
Off-site:

MALZIEU-VILLE, LE LOZÈRE

Piscine 48140 66314763
Peaceful shaded site on the banks of a river near to the municipal sports complex.
A75 Clermont-Ferrand-Millau road, exit for St Chély D'Apcher, at Malzieu turn right before the bridge over the river.
Open: May-Sep **Site:** 1HEC **Facilities:** **Services:** lau **Off-site:** PR

MARTRES-DE-VEYRE, LES PUY-DE-DÔME

Camping la Font de Bleix r des Roches, 63730
473392649 473392011
e-mail: ailes_libres@tiscali.fr
website: goeland03.chez.tiscali.fr/
A pleasant site beside the River Allier. A good centre for touring the surrounding area.
SE via D225 beside the River Allier.
Open: All year **Site:** 1.3HEC **Prices:** 2.65 1.60 pitch 1.60 **Facilities:** **Services:** lau **Leisure:** R **Off-site:**

MASSIAC CANTAL

CM Allagnon av de Courcelles, 15500 471230393
A riverside site with plenty of facilities.
0.8km W on N122.
Open: May-Sep **Site:** 2.5HEC **Facilities:** **Services:** lau **Leisure:** R **Off-site:** P

MAURS CANTAL
AT ST-CONSTANT (4.5KM SE VIA N663)

Moulin de Chaules rte de Calvinet, 15600
471491102 471491363
website: www.eurocampings.net
Terraced site in a valley by the stream of a former watermill with good, modern facilities.
3km E via D28.
Open: 20 Apr-Oct **Site:** 3HEC **Facilities:** **Services:** lau **Leisure:** PR

MENDE LOZÈRE

Tivoli av des Gorges-du-Tarn, 48000
466650038 466650038
e-mail: tivoli.camping@libertysurf.fr
website: www.campingtivoli.com
A level site in wooded surroundings beside the river.
2km from the town via A75 or N88.
Open: All year **Site:** 1.8HEC **Prices:** 4.20-4.20 2.70-2.70 2.30-2.30 2.30-2.30 pitch 2.30-2.30 **Facilities:** **Services:** lau **Leisure:** PR

MEYRUEIS LOZÈRE

Ayres rte de la Brèze, 48150 466456051 466456051
e-mail: campinglechampdayres@wanadoo.fr
website: www.campinglechampdayres.com
On a wooded meadow with well-defined pitches and modern sanitary installations within easy reach of the picturesque Gorges de la Jonte. Plenty of recreational facilities.
0.5km E via D57.
Open: 30 Apr-24 Sep **Site:** 1.5HEC **Prices:** 2.50-3.50 pitch 7-10 (incl 2 persons) **Facilities:** **Services:** lau **Leisure:** P **Off-site:** R

Capelan 48150 466456050 466456050
e-mail: camping.le.capelan@wanadoo.fr
website: www.campingcapelan.com
In picturesque surroundings alongside the Gorges de la Jonte with good sports facilities.
Access via D986 from Ste-Enimie.
Open: 30 Apr-17 Sep **Site:** 4HEC **Prices:** 2.70-3.90 pitch 12-17.50 (incl 2 persons) (static)230-610 **Facilities:** **Services:** lau **Leisure:** PR **Off-site:**

MILLAU AVEYRON

Millau Graufesenque av de L'Aigoual, 12100
565611883 565611883
1 km E on D591 next to River Dourbie.
Open: 15 Apr-Sep **Site:** 3.5HEC **Facilities:** **Services:** **Leisure:** PR

CM Millau Plage rte de Millau Plage, 12100
565601097 565601688
e-mail: info@campingmillauplage.com
website: www.campingmillauplage.com
Beside the River Tarn, flat shady parkland.
Access via D187.
Open: 30 Mar-Sep **Site:** 5HEC **Prices:** pitch 22 **Facilities:** **Services:** lau **Leisure:** PR

Rivages av de l'Aigoual, 12100 565610107 565590356
e-mail: campinglesriveages@wanadoo.fr
website: campinglesrivages.com
A family site with good facilities beside the River Dourbie.
1.7km E via D991.
Open: May-Sep **Site:** 7HEC **Facilities:** **Services:** lau **Leisure:** PR **Off-site:**

MIREMONT PUY-DE-DÔME

Confolant 63380 473799276
7km NE via D19 and D19E.
Open: Jun-10 Sep **Site:** 2.5HEC **Facilities:** **Services:** lau **Leisure:** L

MONTAIGUT-LE-BLANC PUY-DE-DÔME

CM Le Bourg, 63320 473967507
e-mail: montaigut-le-blanc@wanadoo.fr
website: www.ville-montaigut-le-blanc.fr
A quiet, level municipal site with good recreational facilities.
Open: May-Sep **Site:** 1.5HEC **Prices:** 2.20-3.50 pitch 3.10 **Facilities:** **Services:** lau **Leisure:** PR **Off-site:**

MONT-DORE, LE PUY-DE-DÔME

CM du L'Esquiladou rte des Cascades, 63240
473652374 473652374
e-mail: camping.esquiladou@wanadoo.fr
Mountainous situation in the heart of a national park region.
Open: 28 Apr-16 Oct **Site:** 2HEC **Prices:** 2.80 pitch 2.50 **Facilities:** **Services:** lau **Off-site:** R

MORNANT RHÔNE

CM de la Trillonière bd du Général-de-Gaulle, 69440
478441647 478449170
e-mail: mairiemornant@wanadoo.fr
website: www.ville-mornant.fr
In a rural setting on the southern outskirts of the town at an altitude of 333m.
Off D30 towards La Condamine.
Open: May-Sep **Site:** 1.6HEC **Prices:** 2.71-3.90 pitch 2.90 **Facilities:** **Services:** lau **Leisure:** R **Off-site:** LP

Facilities: -shop -shower -electric points for razors -electric points for caravans -parking by tents permitted -compulsory separate car park **Services:** -café/restaurant -bar -Camping Gaz International -gas other than Camping Gaz -first aid facilities lau-laundry **Leisure:** -swimming L-Lake P-Pool R-River S-Sea **Off-site:** All facilities within 2km

MUROL PUY-DE-DÔME

Europe 473886046 473886957
A family site in rural surroundings on the slopes of a forested valley close to the banks of Lake Chambon.
Access via A71/75 and D996.
Open: May-Sep **Site:** 5.5HEC **Facilities:** **Services:** lau **Leisure:** P **Off-site:** LR

Plage Plage du Lac Chambon, 63790
473886004 473888008
Busy site beside lake. Caravan section divided into pitches, terraced area for tents. Asphalt drive.
1.2km from centre of village. Turn off into allée de Plage before entering village & follow signs.
Open: May-Sep **Site:** 7HEC **Prices:** 25 10 10 6-10 **Facilities:** **Services:** lau **Leisure:** LR **Off-site:**

Pré-Bas Lac Chambon, 63790 473886304 473886593
e-mail: prebas@lac-chambon.com
website: www.campingauvergne.com
On the side of lake Chambon with direct access to the beach and windsurf beach.
SW off D996.
Open: May-Sep **Site:** 3.5HEC **Prices:** 3.50-4.50 pitch 8.30-13 **Facilities:** **Services:** lau **Leisure:** LP **Off-site:** LR

Ribeyre Jassat, 63790 473886429 473886841
e-mail: laribeyne@free.fr
website: www.laribeyne.free.fr
A modern site in a beautiful mountain location 1km from Lac Chambon.
1.2km S on rte de Jassat.
Open: May-15 Sep **Site:** 10HEC **Prices:** 3.75-5.10 9-12.50 (static)183-599 **Facilities:** **Services:** lau **Leisure:** LPR **Off-site:**

NANT AVEYRON

Val de Cantobre 12230 565584300 565621036
e-mail: info@valdecantbre.com
website: www.valdecantobre.com
Beside the river in the picturesque Gorges de la Dourbie with fine views from the terraced pitches.
4km N of Nant, towards Millau off D591.
Open: 15 May-13 Sep **Site:** 6.5HEC **Facilities:** **Services:** lau **Leisure:** PR

NAUCELLE AVEYRON

Lac de Bonnefon L'etang de Bonnefon, 12800
565593320 56693209
e-mail: campingdulac@hotmail.com
A peaceful site in a wooded location beside a lake with good modern facilities and well-marked pitches.
NW of N88. Signed.
Open: Apr-30 Oct **Site:** 2.6HEC **Facilities:** **Services:** lau **Leisure:** P **Off-site:**

NAUSSAC LOZÈRE

Terrasses du Lac Lac de Naussac, 48300
466692962 466692478
e-mail: naussac@club-internet.fr
website: www.naussac.com
Situated within a few metres of the lake at an altitude of 1000m with fine views.
Take Autoroute 75, exit 88 for Langogne.
Open: 15 Apr-Sep **Site:** 5.8HEC **Prices:** pitch 12.50 (incl 2 persons) pp3.50 **Facilities:** **Services:** lau **Leisure:** LP **Off-site:**

NÉBOUZAT PUY-DE-DÔME

Domes Les Quatre routes de Neébouzat, 63210
473871406 473871881
e-mail: camping.les-domes@wanadoo.fr
website: www.les-domes.com
A comfortable site with hard-standing for caravans. Advance reservations recommended.
On D216 towards Orcival.
Open: 15 May-15 Sep **Site:** 1HEC **Prices:** 9.50 6 3 pitch 4 (incl 2 persons) (static)216-360 **Facilities:** **Services:** lau **Leisure:** P **Off-site:** R

NÉRIS-LES-BAINS ALLIER

CM du Lac av Marx-Dormoy, 03310 470032470
470037999
website: www.ville-neris-les-bains.fr
Situated in a spa town, close to the town centre. Some of the pitches are close to a road with the remainder in the shaded hollow of a valley by the side of a stream.
Open: 04 Apr-24 Oct **Site:** 7HEC **Facilities:** **Services:** lau **Off-site:** P

NEUVÉGLISE CANTAL

Belvédère du Pont de Lanau 15260
471235050 471235893
e-mail: belvedere.cantal@wanadoo.fr
website: perso.wanadoo.fr/belvedere.cantal/
5km S on D921.
Open: Apr-15 Oct **Site:** 5HEC **Facilities:** **Services:** lau **Leisure:** P **Off-site:** LR

OLLIERGUES Puy-de-Dôme

Chelles 63880 473955434
e-mail: camping.les.chelles@wanadoo.fr
website: www.camping-les-chelles.com
A family site in wooded surroundings with good leisure facilities.
5km from town centre.
Open: May-Sep **Site:** 3.5HEC **Prices:** 3 pitch 10 (incl 2 persons) (static)150-300 **Facilities:** **Services:** lau **Leisure:** P

ORCET Puy-de-Dôme

Clos Auroy r de la Narse, 63670 473842697 473842697
e-mail: contact@campingclub.info
website: www.camping-le-clos-auroy.com
Terraced site in a green valley next to a small river.
From Clermont-Ferrand take A75 towards Montpellier, then exit 5 to Orcet (signed).
Open: All year **Site:** 2.5HEC **Prices:** 1.90-3.80 pitch 15 (incl 2 persons) (static)145-400 **Facilities:** **Services:** lau **Leisure:** PR **Off-site:**

PARAY-SOUS-BRIAILLES Allier

CM Le Moulin du Pré 3500 470450514 470456514
A small municipal site beside the river.
N via D142.
Open: Etr-Sep **Site:** 1.5HEC **Facilities:** **Services:** lau **Leisure:** R **Off-site:**

PEUX-ET-COUFFOULEUX Aveyron

Bouyssiére de Blanc 65495517
e-mail: vacances@labouyssiere.com
website: www.labouyssiere.com
Several shaded terraces in a peaceful wooded mountainside setting.
From Brusque cross the Dordou river & take D119 signed for Murat. Entrance on left 6km along road.
Open: 29 Apr-Sep **Site:** 2HEC **Prices:** 3.50-4 pitch 4-5 **Facilities:** **Services:** lau **Leisure:** P

POLLIONNAY Rhône

Col de la Luère Col de la Luere, 69290
478458111 478458947
e-mail: contact@camping-coldelaluere.com
website: camping-coldelaluere.com
Situated in the Monts du Lyonnais, 20 minutes from Lyon.
Open: All year **Site:** 5HEC **Prices:** 3.30 2.70 2.70 2.70 pitch 2.70 (static)230-380 **Facilities:** **Services:** lau **Leisure:** P

PONT-DE-SALARS Aveyron

Lac 12290 565468486 565743310
e-mail: camping.du.lac@wanadoo.fr
website: camping-du-lac.fr.st
A terraced site on the shore of a 200-hectare lake with good water-sports facilities.
1.5km N via D523.
Open: Jun-15 Sep **Site:** 4.8HEC **Facilities:** **Services:** lau **Leisure:** LP

Terrasses du Lac rte du Vibal, 12290
565468818 565468538
e-mail: terrasses12@aol.com
website: www.campinglesterrasses.com
Pleasant lake-side site with terraced pitches overlooking the Pont-de-Salars lake.
4km N via D523.
Open: Apr-Sep **Site:** 6HEC **Prices:** 3.50-4.50 pitch 11-19.90 (incl 2 persons) pp3.50-4.50 (static)170-430 **Facilities:** **Services:** lau **Leisure:** LP

PONTGIBAUD Puy-de-Dôme

CM rte de la Miouze, 63230 473889699 473887777
In a wooded area beside the River Sioule.
0.5km SW via D986 towards Rochefort-Montagne.
Open: Apr-15 Oct **Site:** 4.5HEC **Prices:** 2.40-2.80 pitch 2.90-3.10 (static)160-160 **Facilities:** **Services:** lau **Leisure:** R **Off-site:** L

PRADEAUX, LES Puy-de-Dôme

Châteaux la Grange Fort 63500 473710593 473710769
e-mail: chateau@grangefort.com
website: www.grangefort.com
Parklike area surrounding an old château on the bank of the River Allier.
From A75 take exit 13 for Parentignat, then take D999. Signed.
Open: Etr-15 Oct **Site:** 22HEC
Prices: 4-5.25 1.75 5-8 5-8 (static)575
Facilities: **Services:** lau **Leisure:** PR
Off-site:

PUY, LE Haute-Loire

Camping du Puy-en-Velay 43000 615082359 &
On a wooded meadow with a section reserved for motor caravans.
From the town centre follow sign for Clermont-Ferrand; at T-lights by church of St-Laurent, turn right following 'camping' sign, site is 500m on left of road.
Open: Etr-Sep **Site:** 1HEC **Prices:** 2.84 1.66 2.80 2.48 **Facilities:** **Services:** lau
Off-site: P

At BLAVOZY (9km E)

Moulin de Barette 43700 471030088 471030051
website: www.lepuyenvelay.com/lemoulindebarette
A pleasant site situated in woodland beside a picturesque stream.
Access via D156 off N88.
Open: Apr-15 Oct **Site:** 2HEC **Facilities:** **Services:** lau **Leisure:** PR

At BRIVES-CHARENSAC (4.5km E)

Audinet av des Sports, 43700 471091018 471091018
e-mail: camping.audinet@wanadoo.fr
website: www.brives-charensac.fr
A peaceful site in a wooded setting beside the River Loire with good recreational facilities.
E on N88.
Open: 14 Apr-15 Sep **Site:** 4.5HEC
Prices: 2.50 1.20 5.40 3.20 pitch 3.20 (static)124-180 **Facilities:** **Services:** lau **Off-site:** R

RIOM-ÈS-MONTAGNES Cantal

Sédour rte de Condat, 15400 471780571
In a pleasant situation beside the River Véronne.
Access via D678.
Open: May-Sep **Site:** 1.5HEC **Facilities:** **Services:** lau **Leisure:** R **Off-site:** LP

Facilities: -shop -shower -electric points for razors -electric points for caravans -parking by tents permitted -compulsory separate car park **Services:** -café/restaurant -bar -Camping Gaz International -gas other than Camping Gaz -first aid facilities lau-laundry **Leisure:** -swimming L-Lake P-Pool R-River S-Sea **Off-site:** All facilities within 2km

RIVIÈRE-SUR-TARN AVEYRON

Peyrelade rte des Gorges-du-Tarn, 12640
565626254 565626561
e-mail: campingpeyrelade@wanadoo.fr
website: www.campingpeyrelade.com
In wooded surroundings close to the Gorges du Tarn.
2km E via D907, beside the River Tarn.
Open: 15 May-15 Sep **Site:** 4HEC **Prices:** 3.50-5 pitch 14-21 (incl 2 persons) (static)210-650 **Facilities:** **Services:** lau **Leisure:** PR

RODEZ AVEYRON

CM Layoule 12000 565670952 565671143
Clean, tidy site in valley below town, completely divided into pitches.
NE of town centre. Well signed.
Open: Jun-Sep **Site:** 3HEC **Prices:** 2 4 pitch 12 (incl 3 persons) **Facilities:** **Services:** lau **Off-site:**

ROYAT PUY-DE-DÔME

Indigo Royat rte de Gravenoire, 63130
473359705 473356769
e-mail: royat@camping-indigo.com
website: www.camping-indigo.com
In a unique natural setting, at the foot of the Puy de Dome, and overlooking Clermont Ferrand, this site has high quality sites, comfortably shaded and laid out in terraces.
Off D941 SW of Royat.
Open: 26 Mar-29 Oct **Site:** 7HEC
Prices: 4-4.20 pitch 12.50-17.90 (incl 2 persons)
Facilities: **Services:** lau **Leisure:** P
Off-site: R

RUYNES-EN-MARGERIDE CANTAL

A Touvert le Petit Bois 15320 471234226 467363542
e-mail: a.tou.vert@net-up.com
A pleasant, well-equipped, parklike site on the bank of the River Charente.
0.5km SW on D13, rte de Garabit. Signed.
Open: Apr-15 Oct **Site:** 7HEC **Facilities:** **Services:** lau **Off-site:** P

SAIGNES CANTAL

Bellevue 15240 471406840 471406165
e-mail: saignes-mairie@wanadoo.fr
A pleasant rural site in the Sumène Valley.
Open: Jul-Aug **Site:** 0.9HEC **Facilities:**
Services: lau **Off-site:** P

ST-ALBAN-SUR-LIMAGNOLE LOZÈRE

Galier 48120 466315880 466314183
Well equipped site beside the river.
Access via A75 exit 34.
Open: Mar-15 Nov **Site:** 4HEC **Prices:** 7.70-9.60 pitch 10-12.40 (incl 2 persons) (static)272-340
Facilities: **Services:** lau **Leisure:** PR
Off-site:

ST-AMANT-ROCHE-SAVINE PUY-DE-DÔME

CM Saviloisirs 63890 73957360 73957360
Run by the local tourist authoriry with plenty of sports facilities within easy reach.
Open: May-Sep **Site:** 1.5HEC **Facilities:** **Services:** lau **Off-site:** R

ST-BONNET-TRONÇAIS ALLIER

Champ-Fossé 3360 470061130 470061501
In the forest of Tronçais beside a lake with plenty of recreational facilities.
Access via A71-E11.
Open: Apr-Sep **Site:** 35HEC **Prices:** 2.25-3 1-1 pitch 0.80 **Facilities:** **Services:** lau
Leisure: L **Off-site:**

ST-CLÉMENT-DE-VALORGUE PUY-DE-DÔME

Narcisses 63660 473954576
e-mail: nobilet.catherine@wanadoo.fr
website: www.campinglenarcisses.com
In a beautiful natural setting within the Livradois Forez national park area.
Open: May-Sep **Site:** 1.3HEC **Prices:** 2.40-3 1.28-1.60 2.70-3.40 2.70-3.40 pitch 2.70-3.40 (static)150-250 **Facilities:** **Services:** lau
Leisure: PR **Off-site:** L

ST-GAL-SUR-SIOULE PUY-DE-DÔME

Pont de St-Gal 63440 473974471
A pleasant site with well-defined, shaded pitches and access to the river for boating, fishing.
E via D16 towards Ebreuil, beside the River Sioule.
Open: May-Sep **Site:** 1HEC **Prices:** 2.20 1.95 1.95 pitch 1.95 (static)150-280 **Facilities:** **Services:** lau **Leisure:** R

ST-GENIEZ-D'OLT AVEYRON

Campéole La Boissière rte de la Cascade, 12130
565704043 565475639
website: www.campeoles.fr
A comfortable site in wooded surroundings with good facilities. Entertainment provided in July and August.
Access via A75 exit 41 towards St-Geniez-d'Olt.
Open: 20 Apr-Sep **Site:** 4.5HEC **Facilities:** **Services:** lau **Leisure:** PR **Off-site:**

Marmotel 12130 565704651 565474138
website: www.marmotel.com
Grassy family site on River Lot with a wide variety of recreational facilities.
On D19 about 1km NW of St Geniez-d'Olt.
Open: May-11 Sep **Site:** 5HEC **Prices:** 17-28.80 (static)220-655 **Facilities:** **Services:** lau
Leisure: PR **Off-site:**

ST-GERMAIN-DE-CALBERTE LOZÈRE

Garde 48370 466459482 466459518
e-mail: camping-lagarde@wanadoo.fr
In a pleasant situation on the edge of the Cevennes national park.
Access via A7 or A75.
Open: Jun-15 Sep **Site:** 2.4HEC **Facilities:** **Services:** lau **Leisure:** P **Off-site:** R

ST-GÉRONS CANTAL

Presqu'île d'Espinet 15150 471622890
e-mail: camping.despinet@wanadoo.fr
website: www.perso.wanadoo.fr/campingdespinet
On a wooded peninsula jutting into the lake with fine views of the Cantal mountains.
8.5km SE, 300m from lake St-Étienne-Cantalès.
Open: 15 Jun-Aug **Site:** 3HEC **Prices:** 3.50 pitch 12 (incl 2 persons) (static)250-450 **Facilities:** **Services:** lau **Leisure:** LP **Off-site:**

St-Gervais-d'Auvergne Puy-de-Dôme

CM de l'Étang Philippe rte de St-Eloy-les-Mines, 63390
473857484
e-mail: camping.stgervais-auvergne@wanadoo.com
website: www.ville-stgervais-auvergne.fr
A small municipal site beside a small lake.
Access via N987.
Open: Etr/Apr-Sep **Site:** 5HEC **Facilities:** **Services:** lau **Leisure:** L **Off-site:**

St-Hippolyte Aveyron

CM La Rivière 12140 565661450
A small site in wooded surroundings with good sporting facilities.
Access via D904.
Open: 15 Jun-15 Sep **Site:** 0.7HEC **Facilities:** **Services:** lau **Leisure:** PR **Off-site:**

St-Jacques-des-Blats Cantal

CM rte de la Gare, 15800 471470590 471470709
e-mail: i-tourisme-st-jacques@wanadoo.fr
A small site on the banks of the River Cère. A good centre for exploring the surrounding volcanic park area.
Open: May-Sep **Site:** 1HEC **Facilities:** **Services:** lau **Leisure:** R **Off-site:**

St-Jodard Loire

CM 42590 477634242 477634001
Open: May-Sep **Site:** 0.3HEC **Prices:** 1.30-1.80 0.65-0.90 17.50 pitch 0.65-0.90 **Facilities:** **Services:** lau **Off-site:** P

St-Just Cantal

CM Le Bourg, 15320 471737257 471737144
e-mail: commune.stjust@wanadoo.fr
website: www.saintjust.com
In the centre of the village beside the river.
Open: Etr-Sep **Site:** 2HEC **Prices:** 8-9 2 **Facilities:** **Services:** lau **Leisure:** P **Off-site:** R

St-Martin-Valmeroux Cantal

Moulin du Teinturier rte de Loupiac, 15140
471694312 4719692452
Wooded valley site close to medieval market town.
Off D922 Aurillac-Mauriac.
Open: May-Sep **Site:** 2.8HEC **Facilities:** **Services:** lau **Leisure:** R **Off-site:** P

St-Nectaire Puy-de-Dôme

Vallée Verte rte des Granges, 63710 473885268
e-mail: lavalleeverte@libertysurf.fr
website: www.campinglavalleeverte.com
In wooded surroundings by a river within the Auvergne natural volcanic Park.
On R146, 400m from R996.
Open: 15 Apr-Sep **Site:** 2.5HEC **Prices:** 8-11 pitch 8-10 (incl 2 persons) (static)340 **Facilities:** **Services:** lau **Leisure:** R **Off-site:** PR

St-Ours Puy-de-Dôme

Bel-Air 63230 473887214 173722044
e-mail: camping.belair@free.fr
website: http://camping.belair.free.fr
1km SW on D941.
Open: 15 May-15 Oct **Site:** 2HEC **Prices:** 3.75 1 pitch 3.50 (static)160-240 **Facilities:** **Services:** lau **Off-site:**

St-Pierre-Colamine Puy-de-Dôme

Ombrage 63610 473967787 473963040
e-mail: campombrage@infonie.fr
website: www.campombrage.com
A pleasant site in peaceful wooded surroundings at an altitude of 800m on the edge of the Auvergne natural volcanic park. All the usual services are provided and there are good recreational facilities.
300m from D978.
Open: All year **Site:** 2HEC **Prices:** 3.80 1.10 pitch 3.30 **Facilities:** **Services:** lau **Leisure:** P **Off-site:** R

St-Rémy-sur-Durolle Puy-de-Dôme

CM Chanterelles 63550 473943171 473943171
e-mail: mairie-saint-remy-sur-durolle@wanadoo.fr
website: www.saint-remy-sur-durolle.fr
In pleasant wooded surroundings close to the lake.
3km NE via D201
Open: May-Sep **Site:** 6HEC **Prices:** 2.65 1.40 1.70 1.40 **Facilities:** **Services:** lau **Off-site:** LP

St-Rome-de-Tarn Aveyron

Cascade 12490 565625659 565625862
e-mail: campingdelacascade@wanadoo.fr
Terraced site beside the River Tarn.
0.3km N via D993.
Open: All year **Site:** 4HEC **Prices:** pitch 13-18 pp5 (static)150-470 **Facilities:** **Services:** lau **Leisure:** LPR **Off-site:**

St-Salvadou Aveyron

Muret 12200 565818069 565818069
e-mail: campinglemuret@hotmail.com
website: www.campinglemuret.com
A modern site in peaceful, rural surroundings beside the lake.
3km SE.
Open: 15 Jun-Aug **Site:** 3HEC **Facilities:** **Services:** lau **Leisure:** L **Off-site:**

Ste-Catherine Rhône

CM du Châtelard 69440 478818060 478818773
e-mail: maizie-ste-catherine@wanadoo.fr
A quiet, well-equipped site providing magnificent views over the surrounding countryside.
2km S.
Open: Mar-Nov **Site:** 4HEC **Prices:** 1.95 2.25 **Facilities:** **Services:** lau **Off-site:** R

Ste-Sigolène Haute-Loire

Vaubarlet Vaubarlet, 43600 471666495 471661198
e-mail: camping@vaubarlet.com
website: www.vaubarlet.com
In a beautiful wooded valley beside the River Dunières with a variety of supervised family activities.
Exit for Ste-Sigolène on D44, then towards Grazac on D43.
Open: May-Sep **Site:** 3.5HEC **Prices:** pitch 13.60-16 (incl 2 persons) (static)160-470 **Facilities:** **Services:** lau **Leisure:** PR **Off-site:**

Facilities: -shop -shower -electric points for razors -electric points for caravans -parking by tents permitted -compulsory separate car park Services: -café/restaurant -bar -Camping Gaz International -gas other than Camping Gaz -first aid facilities lau-laundry Leisure: -swimming L-Lake P-Pool R-River S-Sea Off-site: All facilities within 2km

SALLES-CURAN AVEYRON

Beau Rivage Route des Vernhes, Lac de Pareloup, 12410
565463332 565463396
e-mail: camping-beau-rivage@wanadoo.fr
website: www.beau-rivage.fr
A terraced site located on the shore of Lac de Pareloup. There are facilities for all kinds of water sports and the site's popularity makes advance booking advisable.
3.5km N via D993n & D243.
Open: Apr-Oct **Site:** 2HEC **Prices:** pitch 11-23 (incl 2 persons) (static)198-395 **Facilities:** **Services:** lau **Leisure:** LP

Genêts 12410 565463534 565780072
e-mail: contact@camping-les-genets.fr
website: www.camping-les-genets.fr
On the edge of the Papeloup lake.
7 km W via D577.
Open: Jun-Sep **Site:** 3HEC **Facilities:** **Services:** lau **Leisure:** LP

SAZERET ALLIER

Petite Valette 03390 470076457 470072548
e-mail: la.petite.valette@wanadoo.fr
website: www.valette.nl
A well-equipped site attached to a farm with well-defined pitches and organised activities for children.
Access via A71 exit 11 & follow signs.
Site: 4HEC **Facilities:** **Services:** lau **Leisure:** LP

SEMBADEL-GARE HAUTE-LOIRE

Casses 43160 471009472
A family site in a rural setting at an altitude of 1000m, 2km from a lake.
1km W via D22.
Open: Jul-20 Sep **Site:** 2.4HEC **Prices:** 2.20 3.50 2.80 pitch 3.50 **Facilities:** **Services:** lau **Off-site:** LR

SÉNERGUES AVEYRON

Étang du Camp 12320 565796225 565728158
e-mail: conques@conques.com
website: www.conques.com
Well equipped site in a wooded setting beside the lake.
6km SW via D242.
Open: 15 Jun-15 Sep **Site:** 3HEC **Facilities:** **Services:** lau

SÉVÉRAC-LE-CHÂTEAU AVEYRON

CM av J-Moulin, 12150 565476482
A quiet, well-equipped municipal site close to the town centre. In a good location for visiting the Gorges du Tarn.
1.2km S via N9 towards Millau.
Open: Jun-Sep **Site:** 1.3HEC **Facilities:** **Services:** lau **Off-site:** PR

SÉVÉRAC-L'ÉGLISE AVEYRON

Grange de Monteillac Monteillac, 12310
565702100 565702101
e-mail: info@la-grange-de-monteillac.com
website: www.la-grange-de-monteillac.com
A family site in a quiet wooded location with good recreational facilities.
Access via A75 & N88.
Open: May-15 Sep **Site:** 4.5HEC **Prices:** pitch 21.50 (incl 2 persons) (static)221-297 **Facilities:** **Services:** lau **Leisure:** P **Off-site:**

SINGLES PUY-DE-DÔME

Moulin de Serre D 73 Vallee de la Burande, 63690
473211606 473211256
e-mail: moulin-de-serre@wanadoo.fr
website: www.moulindeserre.com
A well-equipped site beside the River Burande.
1.7km S of La Guinguette via D73.
Open: 15 Apr-18 Sep **Site:** 6.5HEC
Prices: pitch 10.95-14.60 (incl 2 persons) (static)145-370
Facilities: **Services:** lau
Leisure: PR

THÉRONDELS AVEYRON

Source Presqu'ile de Laussac, 12600
565660562 565662100
e-mail: campinglasource@:wanadoo.fr
website: camping-la-source.com
In a beautiful situation beside lake Sarrans.
Open: 24 Jun-2 Sep **Site:** 4.5HEC **Prices:** 3-4 pitch 11-18 (incl 2 persons) **Facilities:**
Services: lau **Leisure:** LP

TRIZAC CANTAL

Pioulat 15400 471786420 471786540
e-mail: mairie.trizac@wanadoo.fr
Open: 16 Jun-16 Sep **Site:** 4.7HEC **Facilities:** **Services:** lau **Leisure:** LR **Off-site:**

URÇAY ALLIER

CM r de la Gare, 3360 470069691 470069330
Open: 15 May-30 Aug **Site:** 0.7HEC **Prices:** 3.50
Facilities: **Services:** lau **Leisure:** R **Off-site:**

VARENNES-SUR-ALLIER ALLIER

Château de Chazeuil 03150
470450010 470450010
e-mail: camping-de-chazeuil@ifrance.com
website: www.camping-de-chazeuil.com
On well-kept meadow within the château park.
3km NW on N7.
Open: 15 Apr-15 Oct **Site:** 1.5HEC **Prices:** 4.50 2.75 pitch 4.50 **Facilities:** **Services:** lau
Leisure: P **Off-site:** R

VERRIÈRES-EN-FOREZ LOIRE

Ferme Le Soleillant Le Soleillant, 42600 477762273
e-mail: camille.rival@wanadoo.fr
website: www.lesoleillant.com
A small terraced site within the grounds of a farm.
Access via A47.
Open: All year **Site:** 3.2HEC **Prices:** 3 0.80 pitch 2.20 **Facilities:** **Services:** lau **Off-site:** R

VIC-SUR-CÈRE CANTAL

Pommeraie 15800 471475418 471496330
e-mail: pommeraie@wanadoo.fr
website: camping-la-pommeraie.com
A well-equipped family site in a peaceful situation with good recreational facilities.
2km SE.
Open: Apr-15 Sep **Site:** 4HEC
Facilities: **Services:** lau **Leisure:** P
Off-site: R

VIEILLE-BRIOUDE Haute-Loire

Dintillat Dintillat, 43100 471509336 471509336
e-mail: elie.sicard@wanadoo.fr
A terraced site with good modern facilities at an altitude of 500m.
Access via N102 & D16.
Open: May-Sep **Site:** 1HEC **Prices:** 3.20 2.50 2.50 (static)210 **Facilities:** **Services:** lau **Off-site:** R

VILLEFORT Lozère

Palhère rte du Mas de la Banque, 48800 466468063
A well-equipped, peaceful site on the edge of the Parc National des Cévennes.
4km SW via D66 beside the river.
Open: May-Sep **Site:** 2HEC **Facilities:** **Services:** lau **Leisure:** PR **Off-site:** L

VILLEFRANCHE-DE-PANAT Aveyron

Cantarelles Alrance, 12430 565464035 565464035
e-mail: cantarelles@wanadoo.fr
On level grassland by Lac de Villefranche-de-Panat.
On the D25 3km N.
Open: 15 Jun-15 Sep **Site:** 3.5HEC **Prices:** pitch 15 (incl 2 persons) (static)280-305 **Facilities:** **Services:** lau **Leisure:** L

VILLEFRANCHE-DE-ROUERGUE Aveyron

Rouergue 12202 565451624 565455558
e-mail: infos@villefranche.com
website: villefranche.com
A comfortable site in a pleasant, shady situation beside the River Aveyron.
1.5km SW via D47 rte de Monteils.
Open: 20 Apr-Sep **Site:** 1.8HEC **Facilities:** **Services:** lau **Off-site:** P

YSSINGEAUX Haute-Loire

CM Choumouroux 43200 471655344
800m S of town off rte de Puy.
Open: May-Sep **Site:** 0.8HEC **Facilities:** **Services:** lau **Off-site:** P

SOUTH COAST/RIVIERA

AGAY Var

Agay Soleil 1152 bd de la Plage, rte de Cannes RN 98, 83530 494820079 494828870
e-mail: camping-agay-soleil@wanadoo.fr
website: www.agaysoleil.com
A small site in a shady position directly on a sandy beach. The facilities are good and all kinds of water sports are available nearby.
Between N98 & the sea.
Open: 15 Mar-03 Nov **Site:** 0.7HEC **Prices:** 5.20-5.50 pitch 21-25 (incl 2 persons) **Facilities:** **Services:** lau **Leisure:** S **Off-site:**

Estérel rte de Valescure, 83530 494820328 494828737
e-mail: contact@esterel-caravaning.fr
website: www.esterel-caravaning.fr
A pleasant family-site of traditional buildings. There is plenty to entertain all age groups day and evening. Riding and cycling can be enjoyed in the nearby in the surrounding hills and woods.
3km from Agay-Plage towards Valescure. N of Agay near golf course.
Open: 19 Mar-Sep **Site:** 15HEC **Prices:** 8 pitch 22-40 (incl 2 persons) (static)650-999 **Facilities:** **Services:** lau **Leisure:** P **Off-site:** R

AGDE Hérault

Escale Rte de la Tamarissière, 34300 467212109 467211024
e-mail: camping.escale@wanadoo.fr
website: www.camping-lescale.com
A riverside site, 900m from the sea, with good recreational facilities.
Open: Apr-Sep **Site:** 3HEC **Prices:** pitch 15-27.20 (incl 2 persons) (static)255-610 **Facilities:** **Services:** lau **Leisure:** PR **Off-site:** S

International de l'Hérault rte de la Tamarissière, 34300 467941283
A grassy site on W bank of the River Hérault. There are fine sports and recreational facilities and free transport is provided to the beach 3km away.
Take the exit for Agde off autoroute A9, then continue via D13 & D32E.
Open: Etr-Sep **Site:** 11HEC **Facilities:** **Services:** lau **Leisure:** P **Off-site:** RS

Mer et Soliel rte de Rochelongue, 34300 467942114 467948194
e-mail: contact@camping-mer-soleil.com
website: www.camping-mer-soleil.com
A modern, well-equipped family site within easy reach of the beach.
Open: 8 Apr-15 Oct **Site:** 7.9HEC **Prices:** 3-6 3 3 3 pp15-33 (static)245-735 **Facilities:** **Services:** lau **Leisure:** P **Off-site:** RS

AT ROCHELONGUE-PLAGE (4KM S)

Champs Blancs rte de Rochelongue, 34300 467942342 467948781
e-mail: champs.blancs@wanadoo.fr
website: www.champs-blancs.fr
Quiet shady site with hedged pitches and surrounded by exotic vegetation. Good sports and entertainment facilities.
Situated between Agde & Cap d'Agde on route de Rochelongue.
Open: Apr-Sep **Site:** 4HEC **Facilities:** **Services:** lau **Leisure:** P **Off-site:** RS

AIGUES MORTES Gard

Camping Village La Petite Camargue Quartier du Mole, 30220 466539898 466539880
e-mail: info@yellohvillage-petite-camargue.com
website: www.yellohvillage-petite-camargue.com
A grassy site among vineyards on the D62. 3.5 km from the sea.
Access via autoroute exit Gallargues in direction of La Grande Motte.
Open: Apr-17 Sep **Site:** 10HEC **Prices:** 3-7.50 pitch 15-40 (incl 2 persons) **Facilities:** **Services:** lau **Leisure:** P **Off-site:** S

AIX-EN-PROVENCE BOUCHES-DU-RHÔNE

Arc en Ciel Pont de Trois Sautets, rte de Nice, 13100 442261428
website: campingarcenciel.free.fr
A pleasant terraced site on both sides of a stream.
Near motorway exit 3 Sautets on N7 towards Toulon. 3km SE near Pont des Trois Sautets.
Open: Apr-Sep **Site:** 3HEC **Prices:** 5.90 pitch 5.40 **Facilities:** **Services:** lau **Leisure:** PR **Off-site:**

Chantecler Val St Andre, 13100 442261298 442273353
Widespread, uneven site on hill. Terraced pitches.
Access off motorway exit Aix-Est on A8. 2.5 km SE of town.
Open: All year **Site:** 8HEC **Facilities:** **Services:** **Leisure:** P **Off-site:** S

ALET-LES-BAINS AUDE

Val d'Aleth chemin de la Paoulette, 11580
468699040 468699460
e-mail: camping@valdaleth.com
website: www.valdaleth.com
In picturesque surroundings beneath the ancient ramparts, on the banks of the River Aude. English owners.
From Carcassonne take D118 towards Quillan. Site 8km beyond Limoux.
Open: All year **Site:** 0.5HEC **Prices:** 2.75 pitch 10 (incl 2 persons) (static)135-195 **Facilities:** **Services:** lau **Leisure:** R **Off-site:** P

ANDUZE GARD

Arche 30140 0033 466617408 466618894
e-mail: resa@camping-arche.fr
website: www.camping-arche.fr
In a beautiful situation on the River Gard with fine views of the surrounding Cevennes scenery.
Access via A7 exit Bollène and D907.
Open: Apr-Sep **Site:** 10HEC **Prices:** 2.60-4.40 pitch 11.50-18.70 (incl 2 persons) **Facilities:** **Services:** lau **Leisure:** R

Brise des Pins rte de St-Félix de Pallières, 30140 466616339
A terraced site offering fine panoramic views over the surrounding countryside.
3km from Anduze.
Open: Jun-15 Sep **Site:** **Prices:** 8 pitch 11 (incl 2 persons) **Facilities:** **Services:** lau

Castel Rose 610 chemin de Recoulin, 30140 466618015
e-mail: castelrose@wanadoo.fr
website: www.castelrose.com
A well-equipped site on the banks of the River Gardon.
1 km NW on D907.
Open: 29 Mar-21 Sep **Site:** 7HEC **Prices:** pitch 9.90-15 (incl 2 persons) (static)200-500 **Facilities:** **Services:** lau **Leisure:** R **Off-site:**

Cévennes Provence 30140 466617310 466616074
e-mail: marais@camping-cevennes-provence.com
website: www.camping-cevennes-provence.com
Situated in a valley bordered by two rivers and offering a choice of pitches in varying levels of shade and terrain.
Near railway station.
Open: 20 Mar-2 Nov **Site:** 30HEC **Prices:** pitch 12-17.50 (incl 2 persons) **Facilities:** **Services:** lau **Leisure:** R

AT ATTUECH (5KM SE ON D907)

Fief 30140 466618171 466618171
On level meadow, divided by flowerbeds and shrubs.
Turn off D982 E of Attuech & continue for 400m on part rough track.
Open: Apr-Sep **Site:** 4.5HEC **Facilities:** **Services:** lau **Leisure:** P **Off-site:** LR

ANTHÉOR-PLAGE VAR

Azur Rivage RN 98, 83530 494448312 494448439
website: www.camping-azur-rivage.com
Well-equipped site only a few metres from a sandy beach.
Open: Etr-Sep **Site:** 1HEC **Prices:** 17-34 17-34 **Facilities:** **Services:** lau **Leisure:** P **Off-site:** S

Viaduc bd des Lucioles, 83530 494448231 494448231
website: www.campingduviaduc.com
A quiet site 150m from a sandy beach, with good facilities.
Access via N98.
Open: 15 May-15 Oct **Site:** 1.1HEC **Prices:** 3.50-4.50 pitch 23-29 (incl 2 persons) **Facilities:** **Services:** lau **Off-site:** S

ANTIBES ALPES-MARITIMES

Logis de la Brague 1221 rte de Nice, 06600 493335472
website: www.camping-logisbrague.com
On a level meadow beside a small river.
On N7.
Open: 2 May-Sep **Site:** 1.7HEC **Prices:** pitch 14.50-12 (incl 2 persons) (static)210-580 **Facilities:** **Services:** lau **Leisure:** RS **Off-site:**

AT **BIOT** (7KM N ON N7 AND A8)

Eden chemin du Val-de-Pome, 06410
☎ 493656370 ▮ 493655422
Site on level meadowland, no tents allowed.
➲ *On D4.*
Open: Apr-30 Oct **Site:** 2.5HEC ▥▥ ∴ ♠ ⚑ ⊞ ⚘
Prices: ♠3.80-5.40 pitch 15.50-19.30 (incl 2 persons)
Facilities: ℝ ⚎ ⊙ ⚑ ☎ **Services:** ♥ ✗ ⊞ lau **Leisure:** ⌇P
Off-site: ⌇S

AT **BRAGUE, LA** (4KM N ON N7)

Pylône av du Pylone, 06600 ☎ 493335286 ▮ 493333054
e-mail: contact@campingpylone.com
website: www.campingpylone.com
In an ideal location between Cannes and Nice, the Pylône is a
family site with good facilities.
➲ *From N7 take D4 for Biot. First turning on left.*
Open: All year **Site:** 16HEC ▥▥ ♠ ⚑ ⊞ ⚘ **Prices:** ♠5 pitch
18 **Facilities:** ℝ ⚎ ⊙ ⚑ ☎ **Services:** ♥ ✗ lau
Leisure: ⌇PR **Off-site:** ⌇S

ARGELÈS-SUR-MER PYRÉNÉES-ORIENTALES

Criques de Porteils La Corniche de Collioure, 66700
☎ 468811273 ▮ 468958576
e-mail: criques.costa@wanadoo.fr
website: www.lescriques.com
Terraced site with beautiful view of sea.
➲ *4km S on N114 turn left through railway underpass &*
continue for 0.3km.
Open: Mar-Oct/Nov **Site:** 5HEC ♠ ⚑ ⊞ **Facilities:** ℝ ⚎ ⊙
⚑ ⊘ ☎ **Services:** ♥ ✗ lau **Leisure:** ⌇S

Dauphin rte de Taxo d'Avall, 66701
☎ 468811754 ▮ 468958260
e-mail: camping.ledauphin6t6@wanadoo.fr
On a long stretch of grassland shaded by poplars, 1.5km
from sea.
➲ *3km N of town; at Taxo d'Avall turn right onto minor road.*
Open: May-Sep **Site:** 5.5HEC ▥▥ ♠ ⚑ **Prices:** pitch 20-
28.50 (incl 2 persons) ⚑ (static)210-710 **Facilities:** ℝ ⚎ ⊙
⚑ ⊘ ☎ ⊟ **Services:** ♥ ✗ ⊞ lau **Leisure:** ⌇P **Off-site:** ⌇LRS

Galets rte de Taxo a la Mer, 66700
☎ 468810812 ▮ 468816876
e-mail: lesgalets@campinglesgalets.fr
website: www.campmed.com
A well-equipped family site with trees, bushes and exotic
plants.
➲ *4km N.*
Open: 19 Mar-2 Oct **Site:** 5HEC ▥▥ ⚎ ⊞ **Prices:** ♠4.10-
6.80 pitch 19-30 (incl 2 persons) **Facilities:** ℝ ⚎ ⊙ ⚑ ⊘ ☎
Services: ♥ ✗ ⊞ lau **Leisure:** ⌇P **Off-site:** ⊘ ⌇RS

Marsouins chemin de la retirada, 66702
☎ 468811481 ▮ 468959358
e-mail: marsouins@campmed.com
website: www.campmed.com
A large family site with good facilities.
➲ *2km NE towards Plage Nord.*
Open: 9 Apr-Sep **Site:** 10HEC ▥▥ ♠ ⚑ **Prices:** pitch 12-
24.50 (incl 2 persons) **Facilities:** ℝ ⚎ ⊙ ⚑ ⊘ ♨ ☎
Services: ♥ ✗ ⊞ lau **Leisure:** ⌇P **Off-site:** ⌇S

Massane 66702 ☎ 468810685 ▮ 468815918
e-mail: camping.massane@infonic.fr
website: camping-massane.com
Well laid-out site in shady garden 1km from sea.

➲ *Beside D618 near the municipal sports field.*
Open: 15 Mar-15 Oct **Site:** 3HEC ▥▥ ∴ ♠ ⚑ ⊞ ⚑
Prices: pitch 11.50-23.50 (incl 2 persons) pp2.50-5 ⚑
(static)167-370 **Facilities:** ℝ ⚎ ⊙ ⚑ ⊘ ☎ **Services:** ♥ ⊞
lau **Leisure:** ⌇S

Neptune Plage Nord, 66702 ☎ 468810298 ▮ 468810041
e-mail: neptune@parcpemin.com
Flat site with both sunny and shady pitches 350m from the
northern beach. Modern sanitary facilities. Water slide.
Separate car park for arrivals after 23.00.
Open: May- 15 Sep **Site:** 4.5HEC ▥▥ ⚘ ⚎ ♠ **Prices:** ♠8
pitch 32 **Facilities:** ℝ ⚎ ⊙ ⚑ ⊘ ♨ ☎ ⊟ **Services:** ♥ ✗ ⊞ lau
Leisure: ⌇P **Off-site:** ⊘ ⌇LS

Ombrages av du Général-de-Gaulle, 66702
☎ 468812983 ▮ 468812983
e-mail: les-ombrages@freesurf.fr
website: www.les-ombrages.com
In a picturesque wooded setting, 300m from the beach. A
well-equipped site with good recreational facilities and
clearly defined pitches.
Open: Jun-Sep **Site:** 4HEC ▥▥ ♠ ⚑ **Prices:** ♠13.40-17.30
⚑12.90-17.50 ⚑18-22 **Facilities:** ℝ ⊙ ⚑ ⊘ ☎ **Services:** lau
Off-site: ⚎ ♥ ✗ ♨ ⌇LPRS ⊞

Pujol rte du Tamariguer, 66700 ☎ 468810025 ▮ 468812121
Set amid rich vegetation with a wide variety of recreational
facilities.
➲ *1km from the beach & 500m from the village.*
Open: Jun-Sep **Site:** 4.5HEC ▥▥ ♠ **Facilities:** ℝ ⚎ ⊙ ⚑ ⊘
♨ ☎ **Services:** ♥ ✗ ⊞ lau **Leisure:** ⌇P **Off-site:** ⌇S

CM Roussillonnais bd de la Mer
☎ 468811042 ▮ 468959611
On a long stretch of sandy terrain adjoining a fine sandy
beach.
➲ *In N part of town. Well signed.*
Open: mid Apr-mid Oct **Site:** 10HEC ▥▥ ∴ ⚎ ⚑ ⚑
Facilities: ℝ ⚎ ⊙ ⚑ ⊘ ☎ **Services:** ♥ ✗ ⊞ lau **Leisure:** ⌇S

Sirène rte de Taxo d'Avall, 66702
☎ 468810461 ▮ 468816974
e-mail: contact@camping.lasirene.fr
website: www.camping-lasirene.fr
A well-appointed family site with good facilities in a
delightful wooded setting.
➲ *4km NE.*
Open: 22 Apr-Sep **Site:** 17HEC ▥▥ ♠ ⚑ **Prices:** ♠6-9 pitch
23-40 (incl 3 persons) ⚑ (static)250-1270 **Facilities:** ℝ ⚎ ⊙
⚑ ⊘ ☎ **Services:** ♥ ✗ ⊞ lau **Leisure:** ⌇P **Off-site:** ♨ ⌇S

AT **ARGELÈS-PLAGE** (2.5KM E VIA D618)

Pins av du Tech, 66702 ☎ 468811046 ▮ 468813506
e-mail: cpglespins@frre.fr
website: www.les_pins.com
A peaceful family site situated on a narrow stretch of
grassland with some poplar trees.
Open: May-Sep **Site:** 4HEC ▥▥ ♠ ⚑ **Prices:** ♠3.60-4.50
pitch 16.40-22.40 (incl 2 persons) ⚑ (static)190-540
Facilities: ℝ ⊙ ⚑ ☎ **Services:** ✗ lau **Off-site:** ⚎ ⊘ ♨ ⌇PS

Soleil rte du Littoral, Plage Nord, 66702
☎ 468811448 ▮ 468814434
e-mail: camping.soleil@wanadoo.fr
website: campmed.com
Peaceful site in wide meadow surrounded by tall trees.
Private beach, natural harbour. Pitches must be booked in
advance.

contd.

Facilities: ⚎-shop ℝ-shower ⊙-electric points for razors ⚑-electric points for caravans ☎-parking by tents permitted
⊟-compulsory separate car park **Services:** ✗-café/restaurant ♥-bar ⊘-Camping Gaz International ♨-gas other than Camping
Gaz ⊞-first aid facilities lau-laundry **Leisure:** ⌇-swimming L-Lake P-Pool R-River S-Sea **Off-site:** All facilities within 2km

Follow rte du Littoral N out of town then 1.5km towards beach.
Open: 15 May-Sep **Site:** 16HEC **Prices:** 7 pitch 11 (static)245-574 **Facilities:** **Services:** lau **Leisure:** PRS

ARLES Bouches-du-Rhône

Rosiers Pont de Crau, 13200 490960212 490933672
e-mail: lesrosiers.arles@free.fr
website: www.arles-camping-club.com
On level ground, shaded by bushes.
Access via autoroute exit Arles Sud or N443.
Open: All year **Site:** 3.5HEC **Prices:** 3-3.50 pitch 12-15 (incl 2 persons) (static)160-350 **Facilities:** **Services:** lau **Leisure:** P
Off-site: R

ARLES-SUR-TECH Pyrénées-Orientales

Riuferrer 66150 468391106 468391209
e-mail: campingriuferrer@libertysurf.fr
website: www.campingduriuferrer.fr
Quiet holiday site on gently sloping ground in pleasant area. Clean sanitary installations. Separate area reserved for overnight stops. Bar, ice for ice boxes and nearby municipal swimming pool are available in summer only.
Signed from N115.
Open: All year **Site:** 4.5HEC **Prices:** 3-4 pitch 3.20-3.70 (static)170-300 **Facilities:** **Services:** lau **Leisure:** R **Off-site:** P

ARPAILLARGUES Gard

Mas de Rey rte d'Anduze, 30700 466221827 466221827
e-mail: info@campingmasderey.com
website: www.campingmasderey.com
In quiet wooded surroundings with pitches divided by trees and bushes. There are good facilities for sports and modern sanitary arrangements.
3km from Uzès towards Anduze.
Open: 10 Apr-10 Oct **Site:** 3HEC **Prices:** pitch 16 (incl 2 persons) **Facilities:** **Services:** lau **Leisure:** P **Off-site:**

AUBIGNAN Vaucluse

Intercommunal du Brégoux chemin du Vas, 84810
490626250 490626521
e-mail: camping-lebregoux@wanadoo.fr
A level site with good views of Mont Ventoux.
On southern outskirts of town turn off D7 onto D55 & continue towards Caromb for 0.5km.
Open: Mar-Oct **Site:** 3.5HEC **Prices:** 2.85 pitch 2.75 **Facilities:** **Services:** lau **Off-site:** PR

AUPS Var

International rte de Fox-Amphoux, 83630
494700680 494701051
e-mail: camping-aups@internationalcamping-aups.com
website: www.internationalcamping-aups.com
In wooded surroundings with well-defined pitches and good recreational facilities. An ideal centre for exploring the magnificent Gorges du Verdon.
0.5km W via D60 towards Fox-Amphoux.
Open: Apr-Sep **Site:** 4HEC **Prices:** 5.80 5 (static)457 **Facilities:** **Services:** lau
Leisure: P **Off-site:**

AURIBEAU Alpes-Maritimes

Parc des Monges 635 Chemin du Gabre, 06810
493609171 493609171
website: www.parcdesmonges.com
In a wooded setting on the banks of a fishing river, surrounded by mimosas fields.
Leave A8 at Mandelieu exit & head towards Grasse.
Open: 28 Mar-1 Oct **Site:** 1.4HEC
Prices: 3.50-4.50 pitch 14.50-21 (incl 2 persons) (static)230-390 **Facilities:** **Services:** lau
Leisure: PR **Off-site:**

AVIGNON Vaucluse

Bagatelle Ile de la Barthelasse, 84000
490863039 490271623
e-mail: camping.bagatelle@wanadoo.fr
Pleasant site with tall trees on the isle of Barthelasse. All pitches are numbered; on hard standing and divided by hedges. Separate section for young people.
Travel alongside the old town wall & the Rhône onto the Rhône bridge (Nîmes road). About halfway along turn right & follow signs.
Open: All year **Site:** 4HEC **Prices:** 11.30-16.50 9.60-16 **Facilities:** **Services:** lau
Off-site: P

CM Pont St-Bénézet Ile de la Barthelasse, 84000
490806350 490852212
e-mail: info@camping-avignon.com
website: www.camping-avignon.com
On island opposite bridge with fine views of town. Several tiled sanitary blocks with individual wash cabins. Individual pitches. Common room with TV, souvenir shop, car wash. Several playing fields for volleyball and basketball. Divisions for tents and caravans.
NW of the town on the right bank of the Rhône, 370m upstream from bridge on right (N100 leading to Nîmes).
Open: Mar-Oct **Site:** 7.5HEC **Facilities:** **Services:** lau **Leisure:** P

AXAT Aude

Crémade 11140 468205064
A shady, peaceful site, ideal for water sports.
Open: Etr-end Sep **Site:** 4HEC **Prices:** 3.20 pitch 3.80 **Facilities:** **Services:** lau
Off-site: PR

Moulin du Pont d'Alies 11140 468205327 468206277
e-mail: contact@alies.fr
website: www.alies.fr
In a picturesque location at the entrance to the Gorges de la Pierre.
Junction of D117 and D118, 800m from Axat.
Open: 15 Mar-11 Nov **Site:** 2HEC **Prices:** 4 pitch 6-10 **Facilities:** **Services:** lau
Leisure: PR

BANDOL VAR

Vallongue 83150 494294955 494294955
e-mail: camping.vallongue@wanadoo.fr
website: htp://site.viola.fr/camping_vallongue.
Terraced site, parts of which have lovely sea views.
Camping Card Compulsory
Open: Apr-Sep **Site:** 1.5HEC **Prices:** 4 pitch 12-15 **Facilities:** **Services:** lau **Leisure:** P **Off-site:**

BARCARÈS, LE PYRÉNÉES-ORIENTALES

Bousigues av des Corbières, 66420
468861619 468862844
e-mail: lasbousigues@wanadoo.fr
website: www.camping-barcares.com
Well equipped family site 1km from the sea. Bar and café open July and August only.
From D83 take exit 10.
Open: Apr-2 Oct **Site:** 3HEC **Prices:** 14-24.10 pitch 14-37 (incl 2 persons) (static)200-660 **Facilities:** **Services:** lau **Leisure:** P **Off-site:** RS

California rte de St-Laurent, 66423
468861608 468861820
e-mail: camping.calafornia@wanadoo.fr
website: www.camping-calafornia.fr
A friendly family site with regular organised entertainment in a pleasant wooded location close to the beach.
1.5km SW via D90.
Open: 3 Apr-18 Aug **Site:** 5.5HEC **Facilities:** **Services:** lau **Leisure:** P **Off-site:** RS

Europe rte de St-Laurent, 66420
468861536 468869788
e-mail: reception@europe-camping.com
website: www.europe-camping.com
A holiday village type of site with good recreational facilities, 500m from the beach.
Via D90 2km SW, 200m from Agly.
Open: All year **Site:** 6HEC **Prices:** pitch 16.50-33 (incl 2 persons) **Facilities:** **Services:** lau **Leisure:** P **Off-site:** RS

Presqu'île 66420 468861280 468862509
e-mail: contact@lapresquile.com
website: www.lapresquile.com
A well-equipped family site on the edge of the Leucate lake and close to the beach.
2km on rte de Leucate, turn right. Well-kept family site on strip of land between large inlet & the Mediterranean.
Open: 9 Apr-1 Nov **Site:** 3.5HEC
Prices: 3.60-5.70 pitch 12-22.20 (incl 2 persons)
Facilities: **Services:** lau
Leisure: LP **Off-site:** RS

Sable d'Or r des Palombes, 66420
468861841 466743730
A wooded site situated between the sea and the Lac Marin.
From Narbonne leave A9 at exit 40 & head towards Grand Plage.
Open: All year **Site:** 4HEC **Facilities:** **Services:** lau **Leisure:** PS **Off-site:** L

BAR-SUR-LOUP, LE ALPES-MARITIMES

Gorges du Loup 965 chemin des Vergers, 06620 493424506
Terraced site divided into pitches, in an olive grove. Very steep entrance.
Access from Grasse on D2085 towards Le Pré du Lac (NE), then turn left on D2210 towards Vence.
Open: Mar-Sep **Site:** 2HEC **Facilities:** **Services:** lau **Leisure:** P **Off-site:** R

BEAUCHASTEL ARDÈCHE

CM Voiliers 7800 475622404
In a wooded location beside the River Rhône with good recreational facilities.
1km E, 900m S of N86.
Open: Apr-Oct **Site:** 1.5HEC **Facilities:** **Services:** lau **Leisure:** P **Off-site:** R

BEYNES ALPES-DE-HAUTE-PROVENCE

Célestine rte de Moustiers (D907), 4270
492355254 492355007
e-mail: lacelestin@wanadoo.fr
website: www.camping-lacelestine.com
A quiet site on flat ground in the heart of the Haute Provence national park and surrounded by mountains.
Situated on D907, before climb to the village.
Open: May-Sep **Site:** 3HEC **Prices:** 4.50 4.50 pitch 4.50 **Facilities:** **Services:** **Leisure:** PR

BOISSET-ET-GAUJAC GARD

Domaine de Gaujac Boisset, 30140
466618065 466605390
e-mail: gravieres@clubinternet.fr
website: www.domaine-de-gaujac.com
A family site in wooded surroundings on the banks of a river.
Access via D910.
Open: Apr-Sep **Site:** 10HEC **Prices:** 3.50-4.50 pitch 6-9 (static)135-370 **Facilities:** **Services:** lau **Leisure:** PR

BOISSON GARD

Château de Boisson Boisson, 30500
466248561 466248014
e-mail: reception@chateaudeboisson.com
website: www.chateaudeboisson.com
A peaceful, well-equipped site in the beautiful Cevennes region. Painting, bridge and cookery courses are available.
Camping Card Compulsory
D7 in direction Fumades. Boisson is 10km on the right & the campsite is signed.
Open: 9 Apr-Sep **Site:** 7.8HEC **Prices:** 5.40-6.50 pitch 15-31 (static)189-749 **Facilities:** **Services:** lau **Leisure:** P

BOLLÈNE VAUCLUSE

Barry Lieu Dit St-Pierre, 84500 490301320 490404864
Well-kept site near ruins of Barry troglodite village.
Signed from Bollène via D26.
Open: All year **Site:** 3HEC **Facilities:** **Services:** lau **Leisure:** P **Off-site:** RS

Simioune Quartier Guffiage, 84500
490304462 490304477
e-mail: la-simioune@wanadoo.fr
website: www.la-simioune.fr
In pleasant wooded surroundings close to the River Rhône.
From A7 follow signs for Carpentras, at 3rd x-roads turn left towards Lambisque, then follow signs to site.
Open: All year **Site:** 2.5HEC **Prices:** 3.40 3.10 3 pitch 3.10 (static)300 **Facilities:** **Services:** lau **Leisure:** P **Off-site:** R

BORMES-LES-MIMOSAS VAR

Clau Mar Jo 895 chemin de Benat, 83230 ☎ 494715339
A well-shaded site 1.2km from the sea with good facilities.
➲ *Access via N98, then D298.*
Open: Apr-Sep **Site:** 1HEC ⏢ ♣ ♫ **A** **Facilities:** ℵ ⊙ ⊕ ☎
Services: ⊞ lau **Off-site:** ⊾ ⚊ ✗ ⊘ ⚌ ⇃S

Manjastre 150 Chemin des Girolles, 83230
☎ 494710328 ▦ 494716362
e-mail: manjastre@infonie.fr
A peaceful site 6km from the Mediterraneean beaches.
➲ *5km NW via N98 on road to La Môle/Cogolin.*
Open: All year **Site:** 8HEC ⏢ ♣ ⚞ **Facilities:** ℵ ⚊ ⊙ ⊕ ⊘
⚌ ☎ **Services:** ⚊ ✗ ⊞ lau **Leisure:** ⇃P

AT FAVIÈRE, LA (3KM S)

Domaine 83230 ☎ 494710312 ▦ 494151867
e-mail: mail@campdudomaine.com
website: www.campdudomaine.com
In a very attractive setting with a long sandy beach and
numbered pitches. Fine views of sea. Sports facilities.
➲ *0.5km E of Bormes-Cap Bénat road.*
Open: 18 Mar-Oct **Site:** 38HEC ⏢ ⁚⁚⁚ ♣ ♫ ⚞ **Prices:** ♠5-
6.50 pitch 17-30.50 **Facilities:** ℵ ⚊ ⊙ ⊕ ⊘ ⚌ ☎ **Services:**
✗ ⊞ lau **Leisure:** ⇃S

BOULOU, LE PYRÉNÉES-ORIENTALES

Mas Llinas 66165 ☎ 468832546
e-mail: info@camping-mas-llinas.com
website: www.camping-mas-llinas.com
A family site in wooded surroundings with a good variety of
leisure facilities.
➲ *3km N via N9.*
Open: Feb-Nov **Site:** 15HEC ⁚⁚⁚ ♣ ♫ ⚞ **Prices:** ♠4-4.70
pitch 4.50-5.70 **Facilities:** ℵ ⊙ ⊕ ☎ **Services:** ⚊ ✗ lau
Leisure: ⇃P **Off-site:** ⊾ ✗ ⊘ ⚌ ⊞

BOULOURIS-SUR-MER VAR

Ile d'Or, 83700
☎ 494955213 ▦ 494955213
In a quiet location, 50m from a private beach with well-
equipped pitches.
➲ *E off N98.*
Open: Mar-Oct **Site:** 10HEC ⏢ ♦ ♫ ⚞ **A Prices:** ♠5.40
pitch 24.90 (incl 2 persons) ⚞ (static)450 **Facilities:** ℵ ⊙
⊕ ⊘ ⚌ ☎ **Services:** ⚊ ✗ lau **Leisure:** ⇃S

Val Fleury RN 98, 83700 ☎ 494952152 ▦ 494190947
Terraced site with tarred drives set among pines and
mimosas close to the beach.
➲ *Off N98 at Km 93.1.*
Open: All year **Site:** 1HEC ♦ ♣ ♫ **Facilities:** ℵ ⊙ ⊕ ⚌ ☎ ⊡
Services: ⚊ ✗ lau **Off-site:** ⊾ ⊘ ⇃PS

BOURDEAUX DRÔME
AT POÀT-CÉLARD, LE (3KM NW)

Couspeau Quartier Bellevue, 26460
☎ 0033 475533014 ▦ 475533723
e-mail: info@couspeau.com
website: www.couspeau.com
In a beautiful natural setting with well-maintained facilities.
➲ *1.3km SE via D328A.*
Open: 19 Apr- 14 Sep **Site:** 3HEC ⏢ ♣ ♫ ⚞ **Prices:** ♠13-
23 ⚞ (static)168-505 **Facilities:** ℵ ⚊ ⊙ ⊕ ⊘ ☎ **Services:** ⚊
✗ ⊞ lau **Leisure:** ⇃P

BOURG-ST-ANDÉOL ARDÈCHE

Lion 07700 ☎ 475545320
Large well-shaped park in wooded terrain, beside River
Rhône.
➲ *N86 in direction of Viviers, through the centre of town.*
Open: Apr-15 Sep **Site:** 8HEC ⏢ ♣ ♫ **A Facilities:** ℵ ⊾ ⚊ ⊙
⊕ ☎ **Services:** ⚊ ✗ ⊞ lau **Leisure:** ⇃PR **Off-site:** ⊘ ⚌

BRISSAC HÉRAULT

Val d'Hérault St-Étienne d'Issensac, 34190
☎ 467737229 ▦ 467733081
A terraced site in a quiet location. Bar and restaurant open
July and August only.
➲ *4km S via D4.*
Open: 15 Mar-12 Nov **Site:** 3.4HEC ⁚⁚⁚ ♦ ♣ ♫ ⚞
Facilities: ℵ ⊾ ⚊ ⊙ ⊕ ⊘ ⚌ ☎ **Services:** ⚊ ✗ lau **Leisure:** ⇃PR
Off-site: ⊞

BROUSSES-ET-VILLARET AUDE

Martinet Rouge 11390 ☎ 468265198 ▦ 468265198
e-mail: martinet.bv@free.fr
website: camping-lemartinetrouge.com
A pleasant, well-equipped site on gently sloping terrain.
Terraced, with well-marked pitches.
➲ *Access via D48.*
Open: Apr-15 Oct **Site:** 2.8HEC ⏢ ♣ ♫ ⚞ **Prices:** pitch
10.50-12.50 (incl 2 persons) ⚞ (static)330 **Facilities:** ℵ ⊾ ⚊ ⊙
⊕ ⊘ ⚌ ☎ **Services:** ⚊ ✗ ⊞ lau **Leisure:** ⇃P **Off-site:** ⇃R

CADENET VAUCLUSE

Val de Durance Les Routes, 84160
☎ 33 490683775 ▦ 490681634
e-mail: info@homair-vacances.fr
website: www.homair-vacances.fr
A well-equipped family site on the shore of a lake and close
to the River Durance.
Open: 26 Mar-2 Oct **Site:** 11HEC ⏢ ♣ ♫ ⚞ **A**
Prices: ♠5.50-7.50 ⚞6.50-13 **A**6.50-13 ⚞ (static)156-495
Facilities: ℵ ⊾ ⚊ ⊙ ⊕ ☎ **Services:** ⚊ ✗ ⊞ lau **Leisure:** ⇃LP
Off-site: ⊾ ⚊ ✗ ⊘ ⚌ ⇃R

CAGNES-SUR-MER ALPES-MARITIMES

Colombier 35 chemin de Ste-Colombe, 06800
☎ 493731277 ▦ 493731277
e-mail: campinglecolombier06@wanadoo.fr
website: www.campinglecolombier.com
Well equipped site in a wooded location 2km from the sea.
Open: Apr-Sep **Site:** 0.6HEC ⏢ ⁚⁚⁚ ♣ ♫ ⚞ ⚞
Prices: pitch 15-22 (incl 2 persons) **Facilities:** ℵ ⊙ ⊕ ⊘ ☎ ⊡
Services: ⚊ ✗ ⊞ lau **Leisure:** ⇃P **Off-site:** ⊾ ✗ ⚌ ⇃S

Green Park 159 Vallon-des-Vaux, 06800
☎ 493070996 ▦ 493143655
e-mail: info@greenpark.fr
website: www.greenpark.fr
A modern site with well-defined pitches in pleasant wooded
surroundings with good recreational facilities.
➲ *From A8 exit Cagnes-sur-Mer take N7 towards Nice.*
Open: 26 Mar-19 Oct **Site:** 5.4HEC ⏢ ♣ ♫ **A**
Prices: ♠3.90-4.80 pitch 22-29 (incl 2 persons) ⚞
(static)269-612 **Facilities:** ℵ ⊾ ⚊ ⊙ ⊕ ☎ ⊡ **Services:** ⚊ ✗ ⊞
lau **Leisure:** ⇃P

Site: 6HEC-Site size ⏢-grass ⁚⁚⁚-sand ♦-stone ♫-little shade ♣-partly shaded ♠-mainly shaded
♫-bungalows for hire ⚞-caravans for hire **A**-tents for hire ⚞-no dogs **Prices:** ♠-adult per night ♣-car per night
pp-per person per night ⚞-caravan per night **A**-tent per night ⚞ (static)-caravan hire per week

La Rivière 168 chemin des Salles, 06800
493206227 493207253
In secluded wooded surroundings with good, modern facilities.
4km N beside River Cagne.
Open: All year **Site:** 1.2HEC **Prices:** 3.10 pitch 12.40 **Facilities:** **Services:** lau **Leisure:** P

Todos 159 Vallon des Vaux, 06800
493312005 492128166
e-mail: info@letodos.fr
website: www.letodos.fr
In a beautiful Mediterranean setting. Exceptionally shady with a mixture of flat and terraced sites. Evening entertainment. Use of car park compulsory after 23.00.
Access via N7 towards Nice.
Open: 27 Mar-24 Sep **Site:** 6HEC **Prices:** 3.90-4.80 pitch 22-29 (static)269-612 **Facilities:** **Services:** lau **Leisure:** P

AT CROS-DE-CAGNES (2KM S)

Panoramer 30 chemin des Gros-Buaux, 06800
493311615 493311615
Pleasant terraced site with sea view. Separate sections for tents and caravans.
2km N of town.
Open: Mar-Oct **Site:** 1.4HEC **Facilities:** **Services:** lau **Off-site:**

CAMURAC AUDE

Sapins 11340 468203811 468207475
e-mail: yvan.dabouis@libertysurf.fr
website: www.paysdesauft.com/sapins
In a picturesque, wooded location on the edge of a forest with excellent views of the surrounding mountains.
1.5km from village.
Open: May-Sep **Site:** 3HEC **Facilities:** **Services:** lau **Leisure:** P **Off-site:** L

CANET-PLAGE PYRÉNÉES-ORIENTALES

Domino r des Palmiers, 66140 468802725 468734741
e-mail: camping.domino@wanadoo.fr
website: www.campingdomino-canet.com
In a wooded location 150m from the sea.
Open: Apr-Sep **Site:** 0.7HEC **Prices:** 3-5 pitch 16-26 (incl 2 persons) **Facilities:** **Services:** lau **Off-site:** PRS

Mar Estang 1 rte de St-Cyprien, 66140
468803553 468733294
e-mail: marestang@wanadoo.fr
website: www.marestang.com
Open: 30 Apr-24 Sep **Site:** 15HEC **Prices:** pitch 15-29 (incl 2 persons) **Facilities:** **Services:** lau **Leisure:** PS **Off-site:**

AT CANET-VILLAGE (2KM W)

Brasilia Voie de la Crouste, Zone Technique du Port, 66140
468802382 468733297
e-mail: camping-le-brasilia@wanadoo.fr
website: www.brasilia.fr
Near beach. Divided into pitches which are surrounded by bushes and flowerbeds.
Turn off main road in village towards beach for 2km.
Open: 30 Apr-Sep **Site:** 15HEC **Prices:** pitch 15-42 (incl 2 persons) pp4.50-7.50 **Facilities:** **Services:** lau **Leisure:** PS **Off-site:**

Peupliers Voie de la Crouste, 66140
468803587 468733875
e-mail: camping.peupliers@clioz.net
Quiet, level site divided into pitches by hedges with a variety of leisure facilities. Booking recommended for July and August.
Open: Jun-Sep **Site:** 4HEC **Prices:** 4.60-5.80 pitch 10.80-15 (static)288-546 **Facilities:** **Services:** lau **Leisure:** PS

Ma Prairie av des Coteaux, 66140
468732617 468732882
e-mail: ma.prairie@wanadoo.fr
website: www.maprairie.com
Grassland site in a hollow surrounded by vineyards.

contd.

Facilities: -shop -shower -electric points for razors -electric points for caravans -parking by tents permitted -compulsory separate car park **Services:** -café/restaurant -bar -Camping Gaz International -gas other than Camping Gaz -first aid facilities lau-laundry **Leisure:** -swimming L-Lake P-Pool R-River S-Sea **Off-site:** All facilities within 2km

Access from D11 in the direction of Elne off N617 Perpignan-Canet-Plage road.
Open: 05 May-25 Sep **Site:** 4.5HEC **Prices:** 3-6 pitch 17-28 (incl 2 persons) (static)224-616 **Facilities:** **Services:** lau **Leisure:** P **Off-site:**

CANNES Alpes-Maritimes

Parc Bellevue 67 av M Chevalier, 6150
493472897 493486625
e-mail: contact@parcbellevue.com
website: www.parcbellevue.com
leave A41 at the exit for Cannes, at the first T-lights turn right.
Open: Apr-Sep **Site:** 4HEC **Prices:** 3-4 2 pitch 7-10 (static)170-350 **Facilities:** **Services:** lau **Leisure:** PS **Off-site:** S

AT CANNET, LE

Grand Saule 24 bd J-Moulin, 06110
493905510 493472455
e-mail: info@legrandsaule.com
website: www.legrandsaule.com
Separate sections for families and groups of young people. 5 minutes to the beach in peaceful surroundings with fine views and a variety of sports and leisure activities.
Access via A8 towards Ranguin.
Open: May-Sep **Site:** 1HEC **Facilities:** **Services:** lau **Leisure:** P **Off-site:** S

Ranch chemin St-Joseph, L'Aubarède, 6110
493460011 493464430
On a wooded hillside 2km from the local beaches with good facilities.
Access via A8 exit 41 & 42.
Open: 15 Apr-15 Oct **Site:** 2HEC **Prices:** 5-5 pitch 10-16 (static)250-510 **Facilities:** **Services:** lau **Leisure:** P **Off-site:** S

CARCASSONNE Aude

Breil d'Aude Le Breil d'Aude, rte de Limoux, Preixan, 11250
468268818 468268507
e-mail: air.hotel.grand.sud@wanadoo.fr
website: www.camping-grandsud.com
In a wooded location beside a private lake where free fishing is allowed.
1.5km N via D118.
Open: Mar-1 Oct **Site:** 11HEC
Prices: pitch 15-21 (incl 2 persons) **Facilities:** **Services:** lau **Leisure:** LPR **Off-site:**

Cité rte de St-Hilaire, 11000 468251177
website: www.campeoles.fr
In wooded surroundings beside the River Aude in a prime position for exploring the surrounding region.
Access via A61 or A9.
Open: 15 May-10 Oct **Site:** 7HEC **Prices:** pitch 13-19 **Facilities:** **Services:** lau **Leisure:** P **Off-site:** R

CARPENTRAS Vaucluse

Lou Comtadou rte de St-Didier, 881 av P-de-Coubertin, 84200 490670316 490866295
Near the Carpentras swimming pool in pleasant surroundings with good, modern facilities.
SE of town centre towards St-Didier.
Open: Apr-Oct **Site:** 2.5HEC **Facilities:** **Services:** lau **Off-site:** P

CARQUEIRANNE Var

Beau-Vezé rte de la Moutonne, 83320
494576530 494576530
e-mail: info@camping-beauveze.com
website: www.camping-beauveze.com
In a beautiful wooded park with good, modern facilities.
2.5km NW via N559 & D76 between Hyères & Toulon.
Open: 15 May-15 Sep **Site:** 7HEC **Prices:** 5.50-6.30 pitch 6-8.50 **Facilities:** **Services:** lau **Leisure:** P

CASTELLANE Alpes-de-Haute-Provence

International rte Napoléon, 04120 492836667
Family site at the foot of the Col des Lèques and close to the Gorges du Verdon.
1km from the centre of the village. Signed.
Open: Apr-Sep **Site:** 6HEC **Facilities:** **Services:** lau **Leisure:** P **Off-site:**

Nôtre Dame rte des Gorges du Verdon, 04120
492836302 492836302
website: www.castellane.org
200m W on D952.
Open: Apr-14 Oct **Site:** 0.6HEC **Prices:** pitch 11-15 (incl 2 persons) (static)240-490 **Facilities:** **Services:** lau **Off-site:** PR

Verdon Domaine du Verdon, 4120
492836129 492836937
e-mail: contact@camp-du-verdon.com
website: www.camp-du-verdon.com
Well-maintained site on meadowland on banks of River Verdon. Divided into pitches. Rooms in rustic style. Reservations recommended July and August.
Below the D952 towards the Gorges du Verdon.
Open: 15 May-15 Sep **Site:** 14HEC
Prices: pitch 14-25 (incl 2 persons) (static)238-455
Facilities: **Services:** lau **Leisure:** PR
Off-site:

AT CHASTEUIL (9KM W ON D952)

Gorges du Verdon Clos d'Arémus, 04120
492836364 492837472
e-mail: aremus@camping-gorgesduverdon.com
website: camping-gorgesduverdon.com
Situated on bank of the Verdon, surrounded by mountains and at an altitude of 660 metres. Fully divided into pitches split into two by road. Bathing in river not advised due to strong current.
0.5km S of village.
Open: May-15 Sep **Site:** 7HEC **Prices:** pitch 10.80-20.50 (incl 3 persons) pp3.50-4.30 **Facilities:** **Services:** lau **Leisure:** P

AT GARDE-CASTELLANE (7.5KM SE)

Collines de Castellane rte de Grasse Napoléon, 04120
492836896 492837540
e-mail: rcnlescollines@wanadoo.fr
Terraced site on wooded grassland with mountain views and fine recreational facilities.
On Grasse road beyond La Garde.
Open: 15 May-15 Sep **Site:** 10HEC **Facilities:** **Services:** lau **Leisure:** P

Site: 6HEC-Site size -grass -sand -stone -little shade -partly shaded -mainly shaded -bungalows for hire -caravans for hire -tents for hire -no dogs **Prices:** -adult per night -car per night pp-per person per night -caravan per night -tent per night (static)-caravan hire per week

CAVALAIRE-SUR-MER Var

Cros de Mouton 83240 ☎ 494641087 ▯ 494054638
e-mail: campingcrosdemouton@wanadoo.fr
website: www.crosdemouton.com
Terraced site with individual pitches, separated for caravans and tents. Good view of sea, 1.5km distance.
➲ *Turn off N559 in town centre & continue inland 1.5km.*
Open: 15 Mar-Oct **Site:** 5HEC **Prices:** 5.80-7.10 pitch 5.80-7.10 (static)350-655 **Facilities:**
Services: lau **Leisure:** P **Off-site:** S

Pinède Chemin des Mannes, 83240
☎ 494641114 ▯ 494641925
website: www.le-camping-la-pinede.com
A family site with well-defined pitches, 500m from the sea.
➲ *300m from the centre of the village.*
Open: 15 Mar-15 Oct **Site:** 2HEC **Prices:** 2.30 pitch 13.70-19 (incl 2 persons) **Facilities:**
Services: lau **Off-site:** S

CENDRAS Gard

Croix Clémentine rte de Mende, 30480
☎ 466865269 ▯ 466865484
e-mail: clementine@clementine.fr
website: www.clementine.fr
An extensive, partly terraced site, in wooded surroundings.
➲ *Signed W of town towards La Baume via D160.*
Open: 28 Mar-14 Sep **Site:** 12HEC **Facilities:** **Services:** lau **Leisure:** P **Off-site:** R

CHABEUIL Drôme

Grand Lierne 26120 ☎ 0033 475598314 ▯ 475598795
e-mail: contact@grandlierne.com
website: www.grandlierne.com
On the edge of the Vercors regional park.
➲ *Access via A7 exit Valence Sud towards Chabeuil, then follow signs for site.*
Open: 24 Apr-11 Sep **Site:** 4.8HEC
Facilities: **Services:** lau
Leisure: P **Off-site:** LR

CHAPELLE-EN-VERCORS, LA Drôme

Bruyères 26420 ☎ 475482146
e-mail: maine.levercos@wanadoo.fr
A well-appointed municipal site in the centre of the Parc Naturel Régional du Vercors.
Open: All year **Site:** 1HEC **Facilities:**
Services: lau **Off-site:** P

CHARLEVAL Bouches-du-Rhône

Orée des Bois av du Bois, 13350 ☎ 442284175 ▯ 442284748
e-mail: campingclub@wanadoo.fr
website: www.campoclub.com
Spacious, well-shaded pitches, 500m from the village.
➲ *Access via A7 exit Sémas. From Charleval follow road towards Cazan.*
Open: All year **Site:** 5HEC **Prices:** 3-4.30 pitch 4.50-9.40 (static)195-550 **Facilities:**
Services: lau **Off-site:** P

CHÂTEAU-ARNOUX Alpes-de-Haute-Provence

Salettes 04160 ☎ 492640240 ▯ 0492640240
e-mail: info@lessalettes.com
website: www.lessalettes.com
Some facilities (shop, café) available in summer only.
➲ *1km E beside the river.*
Open: All year **Site:** 4HEC **Facilities:**
Services: lau **Leisure:** P

CHAUZON Ardèche

Digue 07120 ☎ 475396357 ▯ 475397517
e-mail: info@camping-la-digue.fr
website: www.camping-la-digue.fr
In a beautiful wooded location with good recreational facilities.
➲ *1km E, 100m from the River Ardèche.*
Open: 20 Mar-Sep **Site:** 2.5HEC **Prices:** 7-14 pitch 13.90-19 (incl 2 persons) (static)250-582
Facilities: **Services:** lau **Leisure:** PR

CIOTAT, LA Bouches-du-Rhône

Oliviers rte du Bord de Mer, 13600
☎ 442831504 ▯ 442839443
website: www.camping_lesolivers.com
A terraced family site between the N559 and the railway line from Nice.
➲ *Turn inland off the N559 at Km34, some 5km E of the centre of the town & drive for 150m.*
Open: Mar-Sep **Site:** 10HEC **Prices:** 5 pitch 5.50 (static)206-237 **Facilities:**
Services: lau **Leisure:** P **Off-site:** S

St Jean 30 av de St-Jean, 13600
☎ 442831301 ▯ 442714641
e-mail: stjean@easyconnect.fr
website: www.asther.com/stjean
Site on the right side of the coast road in an excellent position with direct access to the beach.
➲ *Between D559 & sea behind the motel in NE part of town.*
Open: 21 Mar-Sep **Site:** 9.9HEC **Prices:** pitch 20-22 **Facilities:** **Services:** lau **Leisure:** S
Off-site:

Soleil 751 av Emile-Bodin, rte de Cassis, 13600
☎ 442715532 ▯ 442839581
e-mail: campingdusoleil@tiscali.fr
website: www.camping-du-soleil.com
A small site, divided into pitches, 1.5km from the beach.
➲ *Access via A50 exit 9 La Ciotat.*
Open: Apr-15 Oct **Site:** 0.5HEC **Prices:** 5 pitch 5-6 (static)200-260 **Facilities:** **Services:**
lau **Off-site:** PS

COGOLIN Var

Argentière chemin de l'Argentière, 83310
☎ 494546363 ▯ 494540615
e-mail: camping-largentiere@wanadoo.fr
website: www.camping-argentiere.com
Landscaped, partly terraced site.
➲ *1.5km NW along D48 rte de St-Maur.*
Open: Apr-Sep **Site:** 8HEC **Prices:** pitch 14-23 (incl 2 persons) (static)320-550 **Facilities:**
Services: lau **Leisure:** P

Facilities: -shop -shower -electric points for razors -electric points for caravans -parking by tents permitted -compulsory separate car park **Services:** -café/restaurant -bar -Camping Gaz International -gas other than Camping Gaz -first aid facilities lau-laundry **Leisure:** -swimming L-Lake P-Pool R-River S-Sea **Off-site:** All facilities within 2km

COLLE-SUR-LOUP, LA ALPES-MARITIMES

Castellas rte de Roquefort, 6480
493329705 493329705
e-mail: lecastellas.camping@wanadoo.fr
website: www.camping-le-castellas.com
In a wooded location with direct access to the river.
Open: All year **Site:** 1.2HEC **Facilities:** **Services:** lau **Leisure:** RS **Off-site:** P

Pinèdes rte du Pont de Pierre, 6480
493329894 493325020
e-mail: camplespinedes06@aol.com
website: www.lespinedes.com
Well-kept terraced site on steep slope with woodland providing shade, interesting walks and beautiful views.
By the motorway A8 exit Cagnes-sur-Mer turn right off D6 towards La Colle-sur-Loup.
Open: 15 Mar-Sep **Site:** 3.8HEC **Prices:** 3.80-4.70 2.10-3.10 6.10-10.30 4.20-8.60 (static)200-450 **Facilities:** **Services:** lau **Leisure:** P **Off-site:** R

Vallon Rouge rte Greolières, 06480
493328612 493328009
e-mail: auvallonrouge@aol.com
website: www.auvallonrouge.com
In a picturesque forested location, close to the river, with good facilities.
3km W of town, 100m to right of D6 towards Gréolières.
Open: 9 Apr-24 Sep **Site:** 3HEC **Prices:** 3-4.30 pitch 9-19 (static)240-630 **Facilities:** **Services:** lau **Leisure:** PR **Off-site:**

COURONNE, LA BOUCHES-DU-RHÔNE

Mas Plage de Ste-Croix, La Couronne, 13500
442807034
e-mail: camping.le-mas@wanadoo.fr
website: www.camping-le-mas.com
A well-equipped family site on a plateau with a fine view of the bay, and access to a sandy beach.
Access from A55, then D49.
Open: 15 Mar-15 Oct **Site:** 6HEC **Prices:** 4.50-6 pitch 4.50-6 **Facilities:** **Services:** lau **Leisure:** PS **Off-site:**

CRAU, LA VAR

Bois de Mont-Redon 480 chemin du Mont-Redon, 83260
494667408 494660966
e-mail: mont.redon@wanadoo.fr
website: www.mont-redon.com
Set among oak and pine trees with well-defined pitches and plenty of recreational facilities.
3km NE via D29.
Open: 15 Jun-15 Sep **Site:** 5HEC **Prices:** 5 22.50 **Facilities:** **Services:** lau **Leisure:** P

CRESPIAN GARD

Mas de Reilhe 30260 466778212 466802650
e-mail: info@camping-mas-de-reilhe.fr
website: www.camping-mas-de-reilhe.fr
In the grounds of a château, surrounded by pine trees with good recreational facilities.
On N110.
Open: 2 Apr-25 Sep **Site:** 3HEC **Prices:** pitch 12.50-19 (incl 2 persons) (static)150-645 **Facilities:** **Services:** lau **Leisure:** P **Off-site:** R

CROIX-VALMER, LA VAR

Selection 494551030
e-mail: camping-selection@pacwan.fr
Site in scattered pinewood; protected from wind. Many terraces, divided into pitches.
Turn off N559 at roundabout at Km78.5 and continue W for 300m along bd de Mer.
Open: Apr-mid Oct **Site:** 3.8HEC **Facilities:** **Services:** lau **Off-site:** S

DIE DRÔME

Pinède Quartier du Pont-Neuf, 26150
475221777 475222273
E-mail: info@camping-pinede.com
website: www.camping-pinede.com
In a picturesque mountain setting beside the River Drôme.
W via D93 then cross railway line & the river to site.
Open: 23 Apr-10 Sep **Site:** 5HEC
Prices: pitch 12-29 (incl 2 persons) (static)200-728
Facilities: **Services:** lau
Leisure: PR

DIEULEFIT DRÔME

Source du Jabron Jabron, 26220
475906130 475906130
website: www.campinglasource.com
A terraced site in a pleasant location beside the River Jabron.
N of town on D538.
Open: May-Sep **Site:** 5HEC **Facilities:** **Services:** lau **Leisure:** P

ENTRECHAUX VAUCLUSE

Bon Crouzet rte de St-Marcelin, 84340
490460162 490460162
On level ground with modern facilities beside the river.
From Vaison-la-Romaine exit follow road towards St-Marcelin-les-Vaison for 6km.
Open: Apr-Oct **Site:** 1.2HEC **Facilities:** **Services:** lau **Leisure:** R **Off-site:**

ESPARRON-DE-VERDON ALPES-DE-HAUTE-PROVENCE

Soleil rte de la Tuiliene, 4800 492771378 492771045
e-mail: campinglesoleil@wanadoo.fr
website: membres.lycos.fr/campinglesoleil
In wooded surroundings beside lake Esparron with well-defined pitches.
Open: Etr-Sep **Site:** 1.5HEC **Facilities:** **Services:** lau **Leisure:** L

FLEURY AUDE

Aux Hamacs Les Cabanes de Fleury, 11560
468332222 468332223
e-mail: info@campingauxhamacs.com
website: www.campingauxhamacs.com
A large site beside the River Aude and 1km from the coast.
Access via A9 exit Béziers, then 15km W.
Open: 15 Apr-17 Sep **Site:** 10HEC
Prices: 1.80-2.80 pitch 10.70-21.30 (incl 2 persons)
Facilities: **Services:** lau
Leisure: PR **Off-site:** S

FONTES HÉRAULT

Clairettes Route de Peret, Adissan, 34320
467250131 467253864
e-mail: camping-clairettes@wanadoo.fr
website: www.campinglesclairettes.com
D9 10km N of Pézenas, access via Adissan D128.
Open: All year **Site:** 2.2HEC **Prices:** pitch 17-20.50 (incl 2 persons) (static)325-495 **Facilities:** **Services:** lau **Leisure:** P **Off-site:**

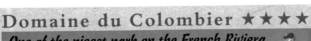

Facilities: -shop -shower -electric points for razors -electric points for caravans -parking by tents permitted -compulsory separate car park **Services:** -café/restaurant -bar -Camping Gaz International -gas other than Camping Gaz -first aid facilities lau-laundry **Leisure:** -swimming L-Lake P-Pool R-River S-Sea **Off-site:** All facilities within 2km

FONTVIEILLE BOUCHES-DU-RHÔNE

CM Pins r Michelet, 13990 ☎ 490547869 📠 490548125
In a pine wood close to the Moulin d'Alphonse Daudet.
➲ *1km from village via D17.*
Open: Apr-Sep **Site:** 3.5HEC **Prices:** 7 pitch 10 (incl 2 persons) **Facilities:** **Services:** lau **Off-site:** P

FORCALQUIER ALPES-DE-HAUTE-PROVENCE

Indigo Forcalquier rte de Sigonce, 4300
☎ 492752794 📠 492751810
e-mail: forcalquier@camping-indigo.com
website: www.camping-indigo.com
Open: 26 Mar-Oct **Site:** 3HEC **Prices:** 4.50-4.70 pitch 12.50-19 (incl 2 persons) **Facilities:** **Services:** lau **Leisure:** P **Off-site:**

FRÉJUS VAR

Domaine de Colombier D4 r des Anciens-Combattants d'Afrique du Nord, 83600
☎ 494515601 📠 494515557
e-mail: info@domaine-du-colombier.com
website: www.domaine-du-colombier.com
Widespread site on hill on some individual terraces under pine trees. Good recreational facilities.
➲ *Turn N off N7 onto D4 towards Bagnols & continue for 500m. Access also via A8 exit 38.*
Open: 19 Mar-1 Oct **Site:** 10HEC **Prices:** 5-8 21-36 pp4.80-6.50 **Facilities:** **Services:** lau **Leisure:** P **Off-site:**

See advertisement on page 193

Fréjus rte de Bagnols, 83600 ☎ 494199460 📠 494199469
e-mail: contact@lefrejus.com
website: www.lefrejus.com
Well equipped site in wooded surroundings.
➲ *Access via N7 & D4.*
Open: 15 Jan-15 Dec **Site:** 8HEC **Prices:** 4.30-6.30 pitch 16-27 **Facilities:** **Services:** lau **Leisure:** P

Holiday Green rte de Bagnols-en-Forêt, 83600
☎ 494198830 📠 494198831
e-mail: info@holiday-green.com
website: www.holiday-green.com
A family site in a beautiful wooded location, offering fine modern facilities and a wide variety of recreational and entertainment facilities.
➲ *6km N & D4.*
Open: 3 Apr-Sep **Site:** 15HEC **Facilities:** **Services:** lau **Leisure:** PS **Off-site:** L

Montourey Quartier Montourey, 83600
☎ 494532641 📠 494532675
e-mail: info@campingmontourey.com
website: www.campingmontourey.com
Comfortable, well-equipped site within 10 minutes of the beach.
➲ *2km N.*
Open: Apr-Sep **Site:** 5HEC **Prices:** 4-40 pitch 18-200 (incl 3 persons) pp4-40 **Facilities:** **Services:** lau **Leisure:** P

Pierre Verte rte de Bagnols, 83.6
☎ 494408830 📠 494407541
e-mail: info@campinglapierreverte.com
website: www.campinglapierreverte.com
A large family site in a pine forest 8km from the coast.
➲ *Access on A8 from Puget-sur-Argens.*
Open: Apr-Sep **Site:** 28HEC **Prices:** 5-6 pitch 17-25 (incl 2 persons) **Facilities:** **Services:** lau **Leisure:** P

Pins Parasols rte de Bagnols-en-Forêt, 83600
☎ 494408843 📠 494408199
e-mail: lespinsparasols@wanadoo.fr
website: lespinsparasols.com
A modern family site shaded by oaks and pines with spacious, well-defined pitches and good recreational facilities.
➲ *4km N via D4.*
Open: 2 Apr-24 Sep **Site:** 4.5HEC **Prices:** 4.40-6 pitch 17.40-25.50 (incl 2 persons) **Facilities:** **Services:** lau **Leisure:** P **Off-site:**

FRONTIGNAN HÉRAULT

Soleil ☎ 467430202 📠 467789002
Family site bordering the beach.
➲ *NE via D60.*
Open: May-Sep **Site:** 1.5HEC **Facilities:** **Services:** lau **Leisure:** PS

Tamaris av d'Ingril, 34110 ☎ 467434477 📠 467189790
e-mail: les-tamaris@wanadoo.fr **website:** www.les-tamaris.fr
A family site on level ground with direct access to the beach. Good recreational facilities.
➲ *From N112 take D129 & D60/D50 for 6km.*
Open: Apr-Sep **Site:** 4.5HEC **Prices:** pitch 20-32 (incl 2 persons) (static)140-390 **Facilities:** **Services:** lau **Leisure:** PS

GALLARGUES-LE-MONTUEUX GARD

Amandiers 30660 ☎ 466352802
e-mail: campamandiers@wanadoo.fr
A family site with good facilities in a beautiful wooded situation.
➲ *Along N113 heading from Lunel towards Nîmes.*
Open: May-10 Sep **Site:** 3HEC **Facilities:** **Services:** lau **Leisure:** P **Off-site:** R

GALLICIAN GARD

Mourgues 30600 ☎ 466733088 📠 466733088
e-mail: info@masdemourgues.com
website: www.masdemourgues.com
Situated in an old vineyard with some vines retained to separate pitches. Views overlooking the Camargue.
➲ *On the N572 between St-Gilles and Vauvert at the junction with the road to Gallician.*
Open: Apr-Sep **Site:** 2HEC **Prices:** pitch 10-12 (incl 2 persons) **Facilities:** **Services:** lau **Leisure:** P **Off-site:**

GASSIN VAR

Moulin de Verdagne 83580 ☎ 494797821 📠 494542265
e-mail: moulindeverdagne@aol.com
Flat grassy site with a family atmosphere, 4km from the beach.
➲ *SE of town towards the coast.*
Site: 5HEC **Facilities:** **Services:** lau **Leisure:** P

Parc St-James Gassin rte du Bourrian, 83580
☎ 494552020 📠 4945634877
Park-like site on slopes of a hill.
➲ *2.5km E of N559. Access from main road at Km84.5 & 84.9 on D89.*
Site: 32HEC **Facilities:** **Services:** lau **Leisure:** P

Les
TAMARIS
-34110 FRONTIGNAN PLAGE
RANCE
hone (00 33) 467.43.44.77 (26.03. - 18.09)
hone (00 33) 478.04.67.92 (19.09. - 25.03)
ax (00 33) 467.18.97.90
n the seafront. BOOKING RECOMMENDED.
PEN FROM 26/3 TILL 18/9
www.les-tamaris.fr • les-tamaris@wanadoo.fr
Rental of
mobile homes
and chalets

Facilities: -shop -shower -electric points for razors -electric points for caravans -parking by tents permitted -compulsory separate car park **Services:** -café/restaurant -bar -Camping Gaz International -gas other than Camping Gaz -first aid facilities lau-laundry **Leisure:** -swimming L-Lake P-Pool R-River S-Sea **Off-site:** All facilities within 2km

GIENS VAR

Mediterranée-Les Cigales Quartier du Pousset, bd Alsace-Lorraine, 83400
494582106 494589673
e-mail: aspicq@campinglemed.fr
website: www.campinglemed.fr
A well-kept site with numbered pitches. Special places for caravans.
0.3km E of D97.
Open: Apr-end Sep **Site:** 1.5HEC **Prices:** pitch 11.75-22.10 (incl 2 persons) pp3.25-4.05 (static)169-585
Facilities: **Services:** lau
Off-site: S

GRANDE-MOTTE, LA HÉRAULT

Lou Gardian 603 allée de la Petite Motte, 34280
467561414 467563103
A well-run site with well-defined pitches, 0.5km from the beach. Advisable to book in high season.
Open: 15 Apr-Sep **Site:** 2.6HEC **Facilities:** **Services:** lau **Off-site:** LPS

Lous Pibols 34280 467565008
Well-organised. Divided into level pitches.
W on D59, 0.4km from sea.
Open: Apr-Sep **Site:** 3HEC **Facilities:** **Services:** lau **Leisure:** P **Off-site:** S

GRASSE ALPES-MARITIMES

Paoute 160 rte de Cannes, 06130
493091142 493400640
A family site in a wooded location close to the town centre.
S of town centre, E of the Cannes road just beyond the Centre Commercial.
Site: 2.5HEC **Prices:** pitch 18 (incl 2 persons)
Facilities: **Services:** lau **Leisure:** P

AT OPIO (8KM E VIA D2085 & D3)

Caravan Inn 18 rte de Cannes, 6650
493773200 493777189
A well-equipped site in a wooded location between the sea and the mountains
1.5km S of Opio on D3.
Open: Jun-15 Sep **Site:** 5HEC **Facilities:** **Services:** lau **Leisure:** P **Off-site:**

GRAU-DU-ROI, LE GARD

Abri de Camargue rte du Phare de l'Espiguette, Port Camargue, 30240 466515483 466517642
e-mail: contact@abridecarmague.com
website: www.abridecamargue.com
A pleasant site near the beach on the edge of the Camargue with well-marked pitches and modern installations.
2.5km S on L'Espiguette road.
Open: Apr-Sep **Site:** 4HEC **Prices:** pitch 23-47 (static)273-742 **Facilities:** **Services:** lau **Leisure:** P **Off-site:** S

Eden Port-Camargue, 30240 466514981 466531320
e-mail: camping.eden@wanadoo.fr
website: www.campingleden.fr
Quiet site on both sides of access road. 300m from beach.
On D626 towards Espiguette.
Open: 4 Apr-3 Oct **Site:** 5.2HEC **Facilities:** **Services:** lau **Leisure:** P
Off-site: LS

Elysée Résidence 980 rte de l'Espiguette, 30240
466535400 466518512
e-mail: elysee.residence@elysee-residence.com
website: www.elysee-residence.com
Large family site on the edge of the Camargue with a good variety of sporting and entertainment facilities.
Access via A9.
Open: 15 May-12 Sep **Site:** 18HEC **Facilities:** **Services:** lau **Leisure:** LP
Off-site: S

Jardins de Tivoli rte de l'Éspiquette, 30240
466539700 466510981
A modern site with well-marked pitches in a wooded setting 600m from the beach. There are good recreational facilities including mountain bike hire.
Access via A9 continuing SE through Le Grau-du-Roi.
Open: Apr-Sep **Site:** 7HEC **Facilities:** **Services:** lau **Leisure:** P **Off-site:** S

Mouettes av Jean-Jaurès, 30240 466514400
On level ground, shaded by olive and poplar trees, this site is well equipped and the beach is only 500m away.
1.2km SE.
Open: Apr-Sep **Site:** 1HEC **Facilities:** **Services:** lau **Off-site:** S

Petits Camarguais rte de l'Espiguette, 30240
466511616 466511617
e-mail: info@yellohvillage-petits-camarguais.com
website: www.yellohvillage-petits-camarguais.com
A comfortable family site in woodland with a wide range of recreational facilities. Close to the beach.
Open: 9 Apr-17 Sep **Site:** 5HEC
Facilities: **Services:** lau **Leisure:** P
Off-site: S

GRIGNAN DRÔME

Truffières Lieu-dit Nachony, 26230 475469362
e-mail: info@lestruffieres.com
website: www.lestruffieres.com
A family site opposite the Château Grignan with good facilities.
Leave A7 at exit Montélimar Sud & follow N7 E.
Open: 20 Apr-Sep **Site:** 3HEC **Prices:** pitch 13-15.50 (incl 2 persons) **Facilities:** **Services:** lau **Leisure:** P **Off-site:**

HYÈRES VAR

AT AYGUARD-CEINTURON (4KM SE)

Ceinturon II 83400 494663966 494664730
e-mail: info@camping-ceinturon2.com
website: www.camping-ceinturon2.com
A popular site on level meadowland divided into pitches. 300m from the sea. Some individual washing cubicles.
4km SE of Hyères on D42.
Open: 15 Mar-15 Oct **Site:** 4.8HEC **Prices:** 3.80 pitch 19.45 (incl 2 persons) (static)387-738 **Facilities:** **Services:** lau **Off-site:** PRS

Ceinturon III L'Ayguade, 83400
494663265 494664843
e-mail: ceinturon3@securmail.net
website: www.provence-campings.com/azur/ceinturon3.htm
Well-kept site in wooded surroundings divided into numbered pitches. Individual washing cubicles.

Site: 6HEC-Site size -grass -sand -stone -little shade -partly shaded -mainly shaded -bungalows for hire -caravans for hire -tents for hire -no dogs **Prices:** -adult per night -car per night pp-per person per night -caravan per night -tent per night (static)-caravan hire per week

4km SE of Hyères on D42.
pen: Apr-Sep **Site:** 3HEC **Prices:** 4.90 pitch 20 **Facilities:** **Services:** lau
eisure: S **Off-site:** S

AT HYÈRES-PLAGE (4KM SE)

ins Maritimes 1633 bd de la Marine, 83400 494663357
ituated in a pine wood close to the beach.
Turn off D42 between Hyères-Plage & L'Ayguade & ntinue inland for 200m.
pen: Apr-Sep **Site:** 37HEC **Facilities:** **Services:** lau **Off-site:** S

ISLE-SUR-LA-SORGUE, L' VAUCLUSE

orguette rte d'Apt, 84800
490380571 490208461
-mail: sorguette@wanadoo.fr
ebsite: www.camping-sorguette.com
n tranquil wooded surroundings beside the River Sorguette ith good sports and entertainment facilities.
Access via N100 towards Apt.
pen: 15 Mar-15 Oct **Site:** 2.5HEC
rices: 4.90-6.30 pitch 4.90-5.70 (static)240-420
acilities: **Services:** lau
eisure: R **Off-site:** P

ISTRES BOUCHES-DU-RHÔNE

Vitou 31 rte de St-Chamas, 13800 442565157
n a wooded location with a large area for tents.
N of town on D16.
pen: All year **Site:** 6.5HEC **Facilities:** **Services:** **Leisure:** L **Off-site:**

LAROQUE-DES-ALBÈRES PYRÉNÉES-ORIENTALES

lanes 117 av du Vallespir, rte de Villelongue dels Monts, 6740 468892136 468890142
-mail: francois.camping.las.planes@libertysurf.fr
ebsite: www.camping66.com
n a picturesque setting surrounded by trees, bushes and lowers.
Approach via Laroque towards Villelongue-del-Monts.
pen: 15 Jun-Aug **Site:** 2.5HEC **Prices:** 3.60-4 pitch -8.30 **Facilities:** **Services:** lau **Leisure:** P
ff-site:

LÉZIGNAN-CORBIÈRES AUDE

CM Pinède av Gaston-Bonheur, 11200
468270508 468270508
ebsite: www.campinglapinede.fr
Well-kept terraced site with numbered pitches and tarred drives, decorated with bushes and flower beds. Shop open uly and August only.
Signed from N113.
pen: Mar-Oct **Site:** 3.5HEC **Prices:** 3.10-4.20 pitch 5.60-7.30 (static)280-470 **Facilities:** **Services:** lau **Leisure:** P **Off-site:**

LONDE-LES-MAURES, LA VAR

Moulières 83250 494015321 494015322
-mail: camping.les.moulieres@wanadoo.fr
Well tended level meadowland in quiet location. 1km from the sea.
Camping Card Compulsory
On western outskirts towards the coast.
Open: 14 Jun-6 Sep **Site:** 3HEC **Facilities:** **Services:** lau **Off-site:** S

Pansard 83250 494668322 494665612
e-mail: pansardcamping@aol.com
website: www.provence-campings.com/azur/pansard
Beautiful, wide piece of land in a pine forest beside the beach.
Turn off N98.
Open: Apr-Sep **Site:** 6HEC **Prices:** 6 pitch 23 (incl 3 persons) (static)315-710 **Facilities:** **Services:** lau **Leisure:** S

Val Rose 83250 494668136 494665267
e-mail: camping-valrose@wanadoo.fr
website: www.campingvalrose.com
In a rural setting at the foot of the Maures mountains, close to a golf course. Well defined pitches and good modern facilities.
4km NE on N98.
Open: Mar-Oct **Site:** 2.5HEC **Facilities:** **Services:** lau **Leisure:** P

LUNEL HÉRAULT

Bon Port rte de la Petite Camargue, 34400
467711565 467836027
e-mail: bonport@free.fr
website: www.bonport.free.fr
In a pleasant wooded location at the gateway to the Camargue.
Access via D24.
Open: Apr-Sep **Site:** 5HEC **Prices:** 3-4 pitch 13-16 **Facilities:** **Services:** lau
Leisure: P

Mas de l'Isle 85 chemin du Clapas, 34400
467832652 467711388
A pleasant site between the Cévennes mountains and the Mediterranean.
1.5km SE via D34 near junction with D61.
Open: Apr-Aug **Site:** 4HEC **Prices:** pitch 12-26 (incl 2 persons) **Facilities:** **Services:** lau
Leisure: P **Off-site:** R

MALLEMORT BOUCHES-DU-RHÔNE

Durance Luberon Domaine du Vergon, 13370
490591336 490574662
e-mail: duranceluberon@aol.com
website: www.campingduranceluberon.com
2.5 km on D23c, 200m from canal.
Open: Apr-15 Oct **Site:** 4.4HEC **Prices:** 3.40-4 pitch 3.60-6 **Facilities:** **Services:** lau
Leisure: P **Off-site:** R

MANDELIEU-LA-NAPOULE ALPES-MARITIMES

Cigales 505 av de la Mer, 06210 493492353 493493045
e-mail: campingcigales@wanadoo.fr
website: www.lescigales.com
A riverside site with well-defined pitches, 800m from the sea.
S on N7.
Open: All year **Site:** 2HEC **Prices:** 5.50 pitch 13.50-27 **Facilities:** **Services:** lau
Leisure: P **Off-site:** LRS

Plateau des Chasses r J-Monnet, 6210 493492593
Terraced land, on hill in a park.
Turn off N7 at Km 4.2 & continue uphill for 1.2km.
Open: Apr-Sep **Site:** 4HEC **Facilities:** **Services:** lau **Leisure:** P **Off-site:** RS

Facilities: -shop -shower -electric points for razors -electric points for caravans -parking by tents permitted -compulsory separate car park **Services:** -café/restaurant -bar -Camping Gaz International -gas other than Camping Gaz -first aid facilities lau-laundry **Leisure:** -swimming L-Lake P-Pool R-River S-Sea **Off-site:** All facilities within 2km

MANOSQUE ALPES-DE-HAUTE-PROVENCE

Ubacs av de la Repasse, 4100 492722808 492877529
e-mail: lesubacs.manosque@ffcc.asso.fr
A well-equipped site in the Durance valley, close to the town centre.
1.5 km W off D907, rte d'Apt.
Open: Apr-Sep **Site:** 4HEC **Facilities:** **Services:** lau **Leisure:** P **Off-site:**

MARSEILLAN-PLAGE HÉRAULT

Charlemagne av du Camping, 34340
467219249 467218611
e-mail: info@charlemagne-camping.com
website: www.charlemagne-camping.com
200m from the beach in quiet, wooded surroundings with good sanitary and sporting facilities.
Access via N112 at Marseillan Plage.
Open: 3 Apr-25 Sep **Site:** 6.6HEC **Facilities:** **Services:** lau **Leisure:** PS

Créole Chemin des campings 467219269 467265816

Languedoc-Camping 117 chemin du Pairollet, 34340
467219255 467016375
e-mail: languedoc.camping.fr@wanadoo.fr
A family site in wooded surroundings with direct access to the beach.
On the coast road between the Mediterranean and the Bassin de Thau.
Open: 15 Mar-Oct **Site:** 1.5HEC
Prices: pitch 25-32 (incl 3 persons) **Facilities:**
Services: lau **Leisure:** S **Off-site:** LPR

Plage 69 chemin du Pairollet, 34340
467219254 467016357
e-mail: laplagecamping@aol.com
A family site with direct access to a sandy beach.
Open: 15 Mar-Oct **Site:** 1.3HEC **Prices:** pitch 13.50-26 (incl 2 persons) pp3.50-4 **Facilities:**
Services: lau **Leisure:** S **Off-site:**

MAUREILLAS PYRÉNÉES-ORIENTALES

Val Roma Park Les Thermas du Boulou, 66480 468831972
2.5km NE on N9.
Open: All year **Site:** 3.5HEC **Facilities:** **Services:** lau **Leisure:** PR

MENTON ALPES-MARITIMES

Fleur de Mai 67 rte du Val de Gorbio, 06500
493572236 493572236
Terraced site in a peaceful situation by a stream in the heart of the Côte-d'Azur.
Exit from D23 at the Parc de la Madone.
Open: 23 Apr-22 May, 2 Jul-18 Sep **Site:** 1.3HEC
Prices: 4.75 3.70 13.50 11.50 **Facilities:**
Services: lau **Off-site:** PS

MÉOLANS-REVEL ALPES-DE-HAUTE-PROVENCE

Domaine de Loisirs de l'Ubaye 4340
492810196 492819253
e-mail: info@loisirsubaye.com
website: www.loisirsubaye.com
A large terraced site in a delightful wooded valley. There is a small lake and direct access to the river and good sporting and recreational facilities.
7km NW of Barcelonnette.
Site: 10HEC **Facilities:**
Services: lau **Leisure:** LPR

MIRABEL-ET-BLACONS DRÔME

Gervanne Camping 26400 475400020 475400397
e-mail: info@gervanne-camping.com
website: www.gervanne-camping.com
A pleasant site with scattered shade and plenty of facilities beside the River Drôme.
Access via D164 Crest-Die.
Open: Apr-Oct **Site:** 3.8HEC **Prices:** 3.30-4.90 2.20-2.50 3.10-4.30 **Facilities:**
Services: lau **Leisure:** LPR

MONTBLANC HÉRAULT

Rebau 34290 467985078 467986863
e-mail: gilbert@camping-lerebau.fr
website: www.camping-lerebau.fr
Divided into pitches and surrounded by vineyards.
From Pézenas follow N113. In La Bégude de Jordy turn onto D18 2km towards Montblanc.
Open: Mar-Oct **Site:** 3HEC **Prices:** pitch 18.50 (incl 2 persons) (static)290-365 **Facilities:**
Services: lau **Leisure:** P **Off-site:**

MONTCLAR AUDE

Au Pin d'Arnauteille Domaine d'Arnauteille, 11250
468268453 468269110
e-mail: arnauteille@mnet.fr
website: www.arnauteille.com
In a natural wooded park with fine views of the surrounding mountains.
2.2km SE via D43.
Open: Etr-26 Sep **Site:** 10HEC **Prices:** 4-6.80 2-4.50 3.50-6.90 3.50-6.90 pitch 3.50-6.90 (static)248-595 **Facilities:** **Services:** lau **Leisure:** P **Off-site:** R

MONTÉLIMAR DRÔME

Deux Saisons Chemin des Alexis, 26200 475018899
A well-equipped site on the bank of River Roubion.
From town centre follow D540 across Pont de la Libération; then first turning right onto chemin des Alexis.
Open: Mar-Nov **Site:** 1.5HEC **Facilities:** **Services:** lau **Leisure:** R **Off-site:** P

MONTPELLIER HÉRAULT

loréal rte de Palavas, 34970 467929305 467929305
·mail: info@camping-le-floreal
ebsite: www.camping-le-floreal.com
n level ground surrounded by vineyards.
500m off Autoroute A9, exit Montpellier-Sud. From town entre follow road for Palavas (D986).
pen: 15 Feb-Nov **Site:** 1.6HEC **Prices:** 3.50-.50 pitch 12-14.25 (incl 2 persons) (static)130-215
acilities: **Services:** lau **Off-site:** PRS

MONTPEZAT ALPES-DE-HAUTE-PROVENCE

oteau de la Marine 04500 492775333 492775934
pleasant wooded site, providing easy access to the Verdon orges. There are good facilities, especially for boating.
Access via D11 and D211.
pen: May-Sep **Site:** 10HEC **Facilities:** **Services:** lau **Leisure:** PR

MONTRÉAL ARDÈCHE

Ioulinage rte des Défilés de Ruoms, 7110
475368620 475369846
-**mail:** moulinage@aol.com
vebsite: www.ardeche-camping.com
Vell-equipped family site with a variety of bungalows, aravans and timber chalets. Close to the famous Gorges de 'Ardèche.
)pen: Apr-Sep **Site:** 3.5HEC **Prices:** 18-22 itch 15-19.50 (incl 2 persons) (static)244-627
acilities: **Services:** lau **Leisure:** PR

MORNAS VAUCLUSE

eauregard rte d'Uchaux 490370208 490370723
-**mail:** beaurega@wanadoo.fr
vebsite: www.camping-beauregard.com
ite: 15HEC **Facilities:** **Services:** lau

MOURIÈS BOUCHES-DU-RHÔNE

)evenson 13890 490475201 490476309
-**mail:** devenson@libertysurf.fr
'erraced site amongst pine and olive trees in Provençal ountryside.
Turn off N113 at La Samatane and continue N towards Aouriès. Site in N part of village.
)pen: 19 Mar-15 Sep **Site:** 3.5HEC **Prices:** 4.50 itch 5 (static)280 **Facilities:** **Services:** u **Leisure:** P **Off-site:**

MOUSTIERS-STE-MARIE ALPES-DE-HAUTE-PROVENCE

it-Jean rte de Riez, 04360 492746685 492746685
-**mail:** camping-st-jean@wanadoo.fr
vebsite: www.ville-moustiers-sainte-marie.fr
Quiet and relaxing site located at the gateway to the Gorges lu Verdon, 5 minutes from Ste-Croix Lake.
Access D952.
)pen: 24 Apr -27 Sep **Site:** 1.6HEC **Prices:** 3.90 itch 4 **Facilities:** **Services:** lau
eisure: R **Off-site:**

Vieux Colombier Quartier St-Michel, 04360
492746189 492746189
-**mail:** camping.vieux.colombier@wanadoo.fr
A family site near the entrance to the Gorges du Verdon at an ltitude of 630m.

0.8km S via D952 towards Castellane.
Open: Apr-Sep **Site:** 2.7HEC **Prices:** 3.90 pitch 4
Facilities: **Services:** lau
Off-site: R

MUY, LE VAR

Cigales 721 Chemin de Jas de la Paro, 83490
494451208 494458280
e-mail: contact@les-cigales.com
website: www.les-cigales.com
A family site set among Mediterranean vegetation with excellent facilities and organised entertainment during the high season.
Exit Draguignan off A8 onto N7. 0.8km to site. Well signed.
Open: Apr-Oct **Site:** 13.5HEC **Prices:** 3-5 2-3 pitch 4-8 **Facilities:** **Services:** lau
Leisure: P

Sellig 41 chemin des Valettes, 83490 494451171
A peaceful family site in a wooded location.
1.5km W on N7.
Open: Mar-15 Oct **Site:** 1.6HEC **Facilities:** **Services:** lau **Leisure:** P **Off-site:** LR

NAPOULE, LA ALPES-MARITIMES

Azur-Vacances bd du Bon Puits, 06120
493499216 493499112
Site with many long terraces, on edge of mountain slope in mixed woodland.
Turn inland 200m after fork at railway station & continue 600m.
Open: Apr-Sep **Site:** 6HEC **Facilities:** **Services:** lau **Off-site:** RS

NARBONNE AUDE

Nautique La Nautique, 11100 468904819 468907339
e-mail: info@campinglanautique.com
website: www.campinglanautique.com
Situated on the salt-water lake Étang de Bages et de Sigean, this site is particularly well appointed, each pitch having its own washing and toilet facilities. There are good recreational facilities and advance booking is recommended.
Access via Narbonne Sud exit on A9.
Open: Feb-25 Nov **Site:** 16HEC **Prices:** 4-5.50 pitch 8-19 (incl 2 persons) **Facilities:**
Services: lau **Leisure:** P **Off-site:** L

AT NARBONNE-PLAGE (15KM E D168)

CM de la Côte des Roses 11100 468498365 468494044
A modern site nestling at the foot of the massif of the Calpe close to the sea.
3 km SW.
Open: 25 May-1 Sep **Site:** 16HEC **Facilities:** **Services:** lau **Off-site:**

CM Falaise av des Vacances, 11100
468498077 468494044
On level ground at the foot of the massif of the Calpe with good modern facilities.
W of Narbonne Plage, 400m from beach.
Open: Apr-22 Sep **Site:** 8HEC **Facilities:** **Services:** lau **Off-site:** S

NÉBIAS AUDE

Fontaulié-Sud 11500 468201762
e-mail: lefontauliesud@free.fr
website: www.fontauliesud.com
In a beautiful setting in the heart of the Cathare region.
0.6km S via D117.
Open: May-15 Sep **Site:** 4HEC **Prices:** 4 pitch 6
Facilities: **Services:** lau
Leisure: P **Off-site:**

NÎMES GARD

Domaine de la Bastide Rte de Generac, 30900
466380921 466380921
In a rural setting with excellent facilities. Shop open summer only.
5km S of town centre on D13. Access via A9 exit Nîmes-Ouest.
Open: All year **Site:** 5HEC **Facilities:** **Services:** lau **Off-site:** L

NIOZELLES ALPES-DE-HAUTE-PROVENCE

Moulin de Ventre 4300 492786331 492798692
e-mail: moulindeventre@free.fr
website: www.moulindeventre.com
In a rural setting with good facilities.
2.5km E via N100.
Open: 25 Mar-Sep **Site:** 2.8HEC **Prices:** pitch 15-25 (incl 2 persons) **Facilities:** **Services:** lau **Leisure:** P

NYONS DRÔME

Domaine du Sagittaire Vinsobres, 26110
475270000 475270039
e-mail: camping.sagittaire@wanadoo.fr
website: www.le-sagittaire.com
Well-kept site divided by hedges in a beautiful Alpine setting.
S of town on D538 road to Vaison-la-Romaine.
Open: All year **Site:** 14HEC **Prices:** 6.40 pitch 25.50 (incl 3 persons) **Facilities:** **Services:** lau **Leisure:** LP **Off-site:** R

OLLIÈRES-SUR-EYRIEUX, LES ARDÈCHE

Domaine des Plantas 07360 475662153 47566236
e-mail: plantas.ardeche@wanadoo.fr
website: www.domainedesplantas.com
Games room, discotheque and other leisure activities.
Open: 8 May-18 Sep **Site:** 10HEC **Prices:** 4-7 pitch 18-28 (incl 2 persons) **Facilities:**
Services: lau **Leisure:** PR

ORANGE VAUCLUSE

Jonquier 1321 r Alexis-Carrel, 84100
490344948 490511697
e-mail: info@campinglejonquier.com
website: www.campinglejonquier.com
On the NW outskirts.
Open: Apr-Sep **Site:** 2HEC **Prices:** pitch 17.50-22.50 (incl 2 persons) (static)280-800 **Facilities:** **Services:** lau **Leisure:** P **Off-site:** R

PEYREMALE-SUR-CÈZE GARD

Drouilhédes 30160 466250480 466251095
In a beautiful location beside the River Cèze surrounded by pine and chestnut trees.
Access via A6 & D17.
Open: Mar-Sep **Site:** 2HEC **Facilities:** **Services:** lau **Leisure:** R **Off-site:**

PEYRUIS ALPES-DE-HAUTE-PROVENCE

Cigales chemin de la Digue du Bevon, 04310
492681604 492681604
website: www.lescigales.ifrance.com
A modern site in the heart of the Val de Durance.
Access via A51 & N96.
Open: Apr-Sep **Site:** 1HEC **Prices:** 3.85 pitch 3.85
Facilities: **Services:** lau **Off-site:** P

PONT-D'HÉRAULT GARD

Magnanarelles Le Rey, 30570 467824013 467825061
e-mail: info@maxfrance.com
website: www.maxfrance.fr
In a pleasant mountain setting with well-defined pitches.
0.3km W via D999, beside the river.
Open: All year **Site:** 2HEC **Facilities:** **Services:** lau **Leisure:** PR

PONT-DU-GARD GARD

International des Gorges du Gardon rte de Uzès, 30210
466228181 466229012
e-mail: camping.international@wanadoo.fr
website: www.le-camping-international.com
In a peaceful, wooded location beside the River Gardon.
1km from aqueduct on D981 Uzès road.
Open: 15 Mar-30 Oct **Site:** 4.2HEC
Prices: pitch 10.66-13 (incl 2 persons) **Facilities:** **Services:** lau **Leisure:** PR

Site: 6HEC-Site size -grass -sand -stone -little shade -partly shaded -mainly shaded -bungalows for hire -caravans for hire -tents for hire -no dogs **Prices:** -adult per night -car per night pp-per person per night -caravan per night -tent per night (static)-caravan hire per week

AT PORT-GRIMAUD (4KM E)

Club Holiday Marina RN 98 Le Ginestel, 83310
☎ 494560843 📠 494562388
e-mail: info@holiday-marina.com
website: www.holiday-marina.com
Located close to beaches with diving tuition available.
➲ *On N98.*
Open: Mar-3 Jan **Site:** 3.5HEC ▥ ♧ ⛟ **Prices:** pitch 15-45 (incl 2 persons) ⛟ (static)300-700 **Facilities:** ⛆ ⛾ ⊙ ⛟ ⛽ 🅿 **Services:** 🍷 ✕ ⊞ lau **Leisure:** ⛹PS

Domaine des Naiades St-Pons-les-M°res, 83310
☎ 494556780 📠 494556781
e-mail: naiades@lesnaiades.com
website: www.lesnaiades.com
Site on hilly land with terraces divided into pitches and with many modern facilities.
➲ *Access via N98 and D244, then turn right & continue uphill.*
Open: 26 Mar-Oct **Site:** 27HEC ▥ ♠ ⛺ **Prices:** pitch 27-44 (incl 3 persons) **Facilities:** ⛆ ⛾ ⊙ ⛟ ⛶ **Services:** 🍷 ✕ ⊞ lau **Leisure:** ⛹P **Off-site:** ✕ ⛹S

Plage RN 98, 83310 ☎ 494563115 📠 494564961
e-mail: campingplagegrimaud@wanadoo.fr
website: www.camping-de-la-plage.net
Wide area of land on both sides of road beside sea. Partly terraced and divided into pitches.
➲ *N on N98.*
Open: 4 Apr-9 Oct **Site:** 18HEC ▥ ∴ ♧ **Prices:** pitch 19 (incl 2 persons) **Facilities:** ⛆ ⛾ ⊙ ⛟ ⊘ ⛽ ⛶ **Services:** 🍷 ✕ ⊞ lau **Leisure:** ⛹S

Prairies de la Mer ☎ 494790909 📠 494790910
e-mail: praries@wanadoo.fr
Site: 20HEC ▥ ♧ **Facilities:** ⛾ ⊙ ⛟ **Services:** ✕ lau

See advertisement on page 202

PORTIRAGNES-PLAGE HÉRAULT

Mimosas 34420 ☎ 467909292 📠 467908539
e-mail: les.mimosas.portirgnes@wanadoo.fr
website: www.mimosas.com
A well-equipped family site located in a leisure park on the banks of the Canal du Midi, 1.3km from the sea.
➲ *Leave A9 at exit Béziers Est & continue towards coast via N112 & D37.*
Open: May-15 Sep **Site:** 7HEC ▥ ♧ ⛺ ⛟ ⛺ **Prices:** ⛹4.50-7 pitch 22-29 (incl 2 persons) pp4.50-7 ⛟ (static)310-670 **Facilities:** ⛆ ⛾ ⊙ ⛟ ⊘ ⛽ ⛶ **Services:** 🍷 ✕ ⊞ lau **Leisure:** ⛹PR **Off-site:** ⛹S

Facilities: ⛾-shop ⛆-shower ⊙-electric points for razors ⛟-electric points for caravans ⛶-parking by tents permitted 🅿-compulsory separate car park **Services:** ✕-café/restaurant 🍷-bar ⊘-Camping Gaz International ⛽-gas other than Camping Gaz ⊞-first aid facilities lau-laundry **Leisure:** ⛹-swimming L-Lake P-Pool R-River S-Sea **Off-site:** All facilities within 2km

Site: 6HEC-Site size ▥-grass ∴-sand -stone -little shade -partly shaded -mainly shaded -bungalows for hire -caravans for hire -tents for hire -no dogs **Prices:** -adult per night -car per night pp-per person per night -caravan per night -tent per night (static)-caravan hire per week

Sablons rte de Portiragnes, 34420
467909055 467908291
e-mail: les.sablons@wanadoo.fr.
website: les-sablons.com
Large site subdivided into fields by fences. Beside beach. Night club and disco.
0.5km N on D37.
Open: Apr-Sep **Site:** 15HEC **Prices:** 3 pitch 18 **Facilities:** **Services:** lau **Leisure:** PS

PRADET, LE VAR

Mauvallon chemin de la Gavaresse, 83220 494213173
A well-kept site amid young trees divided into pitches.
Turn off N559 in Le Pradet onto D86 for 2.5km towards sea.
Open: 15 Jun-15 Sep **Site:** 1.2HEC **Facilities:** **Services:** lau **Off-site:** S

PRAMOUSQUIER VAR

Pramousquier 83980 494058395 494057504
e-mail: camping-lavandou@wanadoo.fr
website: www.campingpramousquier.com
A terraced site set in a wooded park 400m from a fine sandy beach. Good recreational facilities.
2km E via D559.
Open: May-Sep **Site:** 3HEC **Prices:** 4.59-5.09 pitch 5.40-6.20 **Facilities:** **Services:** lau **Off-site:** S

PRIVAS ARDÈCHE

Ardeche rte de Montélimar, 07000
475640580 475645968
e-mail: jcray@wanadoo.fr
website: www.ardechecamping.fr
A comfortable municipal site with good facilities in the heart of the Ardèche region.
Open: Apr-Sep **Site:** 3.5HEC **Prices:** pitch 12-16 (incl 2 persons) (static)200-550 **Facilities:** **Services:** lau **Leisure:** R **Off-site:** P

PUGET-SUR-ARGENS VAR

Aubrèdes 408 chemin des Aubrédes, 83480
494455146 494452892
e-mail: campingaubredes@wanadoo.fr
website: www.campingaubredes.com
Situated on undulating meadowland surrounded by pine trees with good, modern facilities.
Leave autoroute A8 at exit Puget-sur-Argens, then site is 850m. From Fréjus on N7 turn left before Puget, cross motorway and follow road towards Lagourin.
Open: May-15 Sep **Site:** 3.8HEC **Facilities:** **Services:** lau **Leisure:** P

Bastiane 1056, chemin des Suvières, 83480
494555594 494555593
e-mail: info@labastiane.com **website:** www.labastiane.com
Hilly site divided into numbered pitches in pine and oak wood. Individual washing cubicles. Meals to take away. Separate car park for arrivals after 23.00.
Access from A8.
Open: 12 Mar-22 Oct **Site:** 3.1HEC **Prices:** 3.10-6.20 1.75-3.50 14.84-29.84 (static)115-475 **Facilities:** **Services:** lau **Leisure:** P **Off-site:** L

Parc St-James Oasis rte de la Bouverie, 83480
494454464 494454499
Open: 27 Mar-25 Sep **Site:** 42HEC **Facilities:** **Services:** **Leisure:** P

Facilities: -shop -shower -electric points for razors -electric points for caravans -parking by tents permitted -compulsory separate car park **Services:** -café/restaurant -bar -Camping Gaz International -gas other than Camping Gaz -first aid facilities lau-laundry **Leisure:** -swimming L-Lake P-Pool R-River S-Sea **Off-site:** All facilities within 2km

Quillan Aude

Sapinette 21r René Delpech, 11500
468201352 468202780
A comfortable site in a forest of fir trees with pitches separated by hedges.
Access W via D79, rte de Ginoles.
Open: Apr-Oct **Site:** 1.8HEC **Prices:** 3.30-3.60 pitch 3.15-3.45 **Facilities:** **Services:** lau **Leisure:** P **Off-site:** LPRS

Racou, le Pyrénées-Orientales

Bois de Valmarie 66 468810992 68958058
e-mail: contact@camping-lasirene.fr
website: www.camping-lasirene.fr
A family site with plentiful recreational facilities.
Leave N114 at Perpignan Sud exit.
Open: 22 Apr-Sep **Site:** 7HEC **Prices:** (static)250-890 **Facilities:** **Services:** lau **Leisure:** PS **Off-site:**

Ramatuelle Var

Cigale rte de L' Escalet, 83350 494792253 494791205
e-mail: campinglacigale@wanadoo.fr
website: www.camping-lacigale.fr
Site 800m from beach.
Off A8, exit Le Luc.
Open: Apr-15 Oct **Site:** 1.5HEC **Prices:** 5.50-7.50 pitch 18-30 (incl 2 persons) **Facilities:** **Services:** lau **Leisure:** P **Off-site:** S

Tournels rte de Camarat, 83350 494559090 494559099
e-mail: info@tournels.com **website:** www.tournels.com
Lovely views to Pampelonne Bay from part of this site. 1km to beach.
Access from D93 Croix-Valmer/St-Tropez road, follow signs to Cap Camarat.
Open: Mar-10 Jan **Site:** 20HEC **Prices:** 23-34 20-34 **Facilities:** **Services:** lau **Leisure:** P **Off-site:** S

See advertisement on page 203

Remoulins Gard

Soubeyranne rte de Beaucaire, 30210
466370321 466371465
e-mail: soubeyranne@wanadoo.fr
website: www.soubeyranne.com
In a picturesque location close to the River Gard with good, modern facilities.
S on D986.
Open: 3 Apr-13 Sep **Site:** 6HEC **Facilities:** **Services:** lau **Leisure:** P **Off-site:** R

Sousta av du Pont-du-Gard, 30210
466371280 466372369
e-mail: info@lasousta.fr
website: www.lasousta.com
Picturesque forest site a short distance from the Pont du Gard.
2km NW.
Open: Mar-Oct **Site:** 14HEC **Prices:** pitch 11-21 (incl 2 persons) (static)270-490 **Facilities:** **Services:** lau **Leisure:** PR

Revens Gard

Lou Triadou Le Bourg, 30750 467827358
e-mail: lou.triadou@wanadoo.fr
website: site.voila.fr/camping_lou_triadou
A well-equipped site in the heart of the Causse Noir.

Site: 6HEC-Site size [grass]-grass [sand]-sand [stone]-stone [little shade]-little shade [partly shaded]-partly shaded [mainly shaded]-mainly shaded [bungalows]-bungalows for hire [caravans]-caravans for hire [tents]-tents for hire [no dogs]-no dogs **Prices:** [adult]-adult per night [car]-car per night pp-per person per night [caravan]-caravan per night [tent]-tent per night [static caravan] (static)-caravan hire per week

Access via D159/D151.
Open: 20 Jun-1 Sep **Site:** 0.8HEC **Prices:** 3 pitch 4 (static)185 **Facilities:** **Services:** lau

RIA Pyrénées-Orientales

Bellevue 8 r Bellevue, 66500 468964896
Beautifully situated terraced site. Very well kept. Beside former vineyard.
2km S on N116, take road to Sirach, turn right & continue 600m up drive which is difficult for caravans.
Open: Apr-Sep **Site:** 2.2HEC **Prices:** 2.80 pitch 3.38 (static)175 **Facilities:** **Services:** lau **Off-site:** LPR

ROQUEBRUNE-SUR-ARGENS Var

Domaine de la Bergerie Valleé du Fournel, 83520
498114545 498114546
e-mail: info@domainelabergerie.com
website: www.domainelabergerie.com
A large, well-run family site set in pleasant Provençal countryside with fine recreational facilities.
Access via A8 exit Le Muy N7 & D7.
Open: 15 Feb-15 Nov **Site:** 60HEC **Prices:** 4-7 pitch 17.88-28.88 (incl 2 persons) (static)350-530 **Facilities:** **Services:** lau **Leisure:** LP

Domaine JJ Bousquet rte de la Bouverie, 83520 494454251 494816106
In a quiet, wooded location with good, modern facilities.
Access via N7 towards Le Muy.
Open: All year **Site:** 5HEC **Facilities:** **Services:** lau **Leisure:** P

Leï Suves Quartier du Blavet, 83520
494454395 494816313
e-mail: camping.lei.suves@wanadoo.fr
website: www.camping-lei-suves.com
In a picturesque forested area with good recreational facilities.
4km N via N7.
Open: Apr-15 Oct **Site:** 7.4HEC **Prices:** 4.50-6.60 pitch 19.50-31 (incl 2 persons) (static)250-450 **Facilities:** **Services:** lau **Leisure:** P

See advertisement on page 204

Moulin des Iscles Quartier La Valette, 83520
494457074 494454609
e-mail: moulin.iscles@wanadoo.fr
In a picturesque location beside the River Argens with good modern facilities.
Access via D7 towards St-Aygulf.
Open: Apr-Sep **Site:** 1.3HEC **Prices:** 3.20 pitch 19 (incl 3 persons) **Facilities:** **Services:** lau **Leisure:** R **Off-site:** L

Pêcheurs 83520 494457125 494816513
e-mail: info@camping-les-pecheurs.com
website: www.camping-les-pecheurs.com
A pleasant site with direct access to the river in a wooded location at the foot of the Roquebrune crag.
0.5km NW via D7, near the lake.
Open: 25 Mar-Sep **Site:** 5HEC **Prices:** 4-6 pitch 18-31 (incl 2 persons) (static)260-680 **Facilities:** **Services:** lau **Leisure:** LPR

ROQUE-D'ANTHÉRON, LA Bouches-du-Rhône

Domaine les Iscles 13640 442504425 442505629
e-mail: campoclub@wanadoo.com **website:** campoclub.com
1.8km N via D67c.
Open: 26 Mar-1 Oct **Site:** 10HEC **Prices:** 3.60-5.50 pitch 4.30-14 (static)195-760 **Facilities:** **Services:** lau **Leisure:** LPR

Silvacane av de la Libération, 13640
442504054 442504375
e-mail: campoclub@wanadoo.fr **website:** campoclub.com
Level gravelled ground with 100 sq m pitches. Heated common room with TV. Water-sports centre and stables nearby. Site in wood on slopes of hill.
Open: 14 May-17 Sep **Site:** 6HEC **Prices:** 3.20-4.50 pitch 9.80-13 **Facilities:** **Services:** lau **Leisure:** PR **Off-site:** LR

ROQUETTE-SUR-SIAGNE, LA Alpes-Maritimes

Panoramic 1630 av de la République, Quartier St-Jean, 06550
492190777 492190777
e-mail: campingpanoramic@wanadoo.fr
website: www.campingpanaramic.fr
A well-equipped, modern site in a wooded location affording magnificent views of the surrounding hills.
N of village off D9.
Open: All year **Site:** 1HEC **Prices:** 3.50 pitch 12.50-15 (incl 1 persons) **Facilities:** **Services:** lau **Leisure:** P **Off-site:** R

St-Louis av de la République, 6550
492192313 492192314
Well equipped site in a pleasant rural setting , backed by hills.
On D9, 800m from Pégomas towards La Bocca.
Open: Apr-1 Oct **Site:** 5HEC **Facilities:** **Services:** lau **Leisure:** P **Off-site:** R

RUOMS Ardèche

Bastide 7120 475396472 475397328
e-mail: info@rcn-labastideardeche.fr
website: www.rcn-campings.fr
Well equipped family site in a pleasant wooded location.
4km SW on the banks of the Ardèche.
Open: 16 Apr-8 Oct **Site:** 7HEC **Prices:** 6 pitch 19.50-42.50 (incl 2 persons) **Facilities:** **Services:** lau **Leisure:** PR

Ternis rte de Lagorce, 07120 475939315 475939090
e-mail: campternis@aol.com
website: www.camping.leternis.com
A terraced site in a delightful setting in the southern Ardèche region, with good recreational facilities. Separate car park for arrivals 22.00-08.00.
Access via D559 towards Lagorce.
Open: May-18 Sep **Site:** 6HEC **Prices:** 4.50 pitch 9 (static)200-600 **Facilities:** **Services:** lau **Leisure:** P **Off-site:** R

AT SAMPZON (6KM S)

Aloha-Plage 07120 608988503 475891026
e-mail: reception@camping-aloha-plage.fr
website: www.camping-aloha-plage.fr
In a fine situation beside the River Ardèche, midway between Ruoms and Vallon-Pont-d'Arc. The site has two private swimming pools.
50m from the river.
Open: Apr-20 Sep **Site:** 3HEC **Prices:** 3-4.50 pitch 16-25 (incl 2 persons) (static)170-390 **Facilities:** **Services:** lau **Leisure:** PR **Off-site:**

Soleil Vivarais 07120 475396756 475396469
e-mail: info@soleil-vivarais.com
website: www.soleil-vivarais.com
An exceptionally well-appointed, terraced site surrounded by the imposing scenery of the Gorges de l'Ardèche. An excellent canoeing centre with opportunities for all kinds of outdoor/water activities and regular organised entertainment.
From Vallon drive towards Ruoms on D579 for 5km & cross bridge over River Ardèche.
Open: 2 Mar-12 Sep **Site:** 14HEC **Prices:** 4.50-7.80 pitch 15-39 (incl 2 persons) **Facilities:** **Services:** lau **Leisure:** PR **Off-site:** S

Saillagouse Pyrénées-Orientales

Cerdan 11 Route d'Estavar, 66800
468047046 468040526
e-mail: lecerdan@lecerdan.com
website: www.lecerdan.com
Picturesque setting in meadow with some terraces. Hot meals served during peak season.
Access via N116.
Open: All year **Site:** 0.8HEC **Prices:** 3.70 11.50-12 11.50-12 **Facilities:**
Services: lau **Off-site:** PR

St-Alban-Auriolles Ardèche

Ranc Davaine 07120 475396055 475393850
e-mail: camping.ranc.davaine@wanadoo.fr
Well equipped, mainly level site with direct access to the River Chassezac and a variety of entertainment facilities.
2.3km SW via D58.
Open: 25 Mar-25 Sep **Site:** 13HEC
Prices: 6.20-9.30 pitch 25-39 (incl 2 persons) (static)308-868 **Facilities:** **Services:** lau **Leisure:** PR

St-Ambroix Gard

Beau-Rivage Le Moulinet, 30500
466241017 466242137
e-mail: mare@camping-beau-rivage.fr
website: www.camping-beau-rivage.fr
In a fine location between the sea and the Cevennes mountains beside the River Cèze.
3.5km SE on D37.
Open: Apr-Sep **Site:** 3.5HEC **Facilities:**
Services: lau **Leisure:** R **Off-site:**

Clos 30500 466241008 466602562
A quiet site in a pleasant setting beside the River Cèze with good, modern facilities.
Access to the right of the church square.
Open: Apr-Oct **Site:** 1.8HEC **Facilities:** **Services:** lau **Leisure:** PR **Off-site:**

St-Andiol Bouches-du-Rhône

St-Andiol 13670 490950113
e-mail: mendez11@viola.fr
Well situated on the edge of the village. Divided into pitches.
Access via A7.
Open: All year **Site:** 1HEC **Prices:** pitch 13 (incl 2 persons) **Facilities:** **Services:** lau **Leisure:** P
Off-site:

St-Aygulf Var

Étoile d'Argens chemin des Étangs, 83370
494810141 494812145
e-mail: info@etoiledargens.com
website: www.etoiledargens.com
In pleasant wooded surroundings 2km from the beach, which can be reached by a private boat service.
5km NW, beside the River Argens.
Open: Apr-Sep **Site:** 11HEC **Prices:** pitch 15-50 (incl 2 persons) **Facilities:** **Services:** lau **Leisure:** PR **Off-site:** L

Paradis des Campeurs La Gaillarde Plage, 83380
494969355 494496299
website: www.paradis-des-campeurs.com
A quiet family site in a picturesque location with direct access to the beach.
2.5km towards Gaillarde-Plage between St-Aygulf and Ste-Maxime.
Open: 29 Mar-3 Oct **Site:** 3.7HEC **Facilities:** **Services:** lau **Leisure:** S

Pont d'Argens RN98, 83370 494511497 494512944
website: www.provence-campings.com/esterel/pont-argens.htm
A pleasant site with good facilities beside the river.
Open: Apr-15 Oct **Site:** 7HEC **Prices:** 5-7 pitch 13.50-24 **Facilities:** **Services:** lau **Leisure:** PRS

St-Aygulf 270 av Salvarelli, 83370
494176249 494810316
e-mail: info@camping-cote-azur.com
A well-equipped family site in wooded surroundings with direct access to the beach.
Inland from N98 at Km881.3 N of town. Entrance on right of av Salvarelli.
Open: Apr-Oct **Site:** 22HEC **Facilities:** **Services:** lau **Leisure:** S

St-Chamas Bouches-du-Rhône

Canet Plage 13250 490509689 490509689 & 490508751
e-mail: canet-plage@wanadoo.fr
website: www.camping-lecanet.com
A well-equipped site beside the Étang de Berre with a wide range of recreational facilities.
On D10, S of Salon-de-Provence towards La Fare les Oliviers.
Open: All year **Site:** 3HEC **Prices:** 3.10-3.90 2-2.60 3.10-3.10 3.10-3.90 pitch 3.90-3.90 **Facilities:** **Services:** lau **Leisure:** LP **Off-site:**

ST-CYPRIEN PYRÉNÉES-ORIENTALES

Roussillon chemin de la Mer, 66750
468210645 468210645
e-mail: chadotel@wanadoo.fr
website: www.camping_le_roussilon.fr
Close to the Spanish border, flanked on one side by the Mediterrannean sea and on the other by the Pyrénées.
Open: Apr-Sep **Site:** 3HEC **Prices:** 5.70 pitch 14.50-23 (incl 2 persons) **Facilities:** **Services:** lau **Leisure:** P **Off-site:** S

ST-CYR-SUR-MER VAR

Clos Ste-Thérèse rte de Bandol, 83270 494321221
e-mail: camping@clos-therese.com
website: www.clos-therese.com
Located in the heart of the Bandol vinefields overlooking the sea. A well-shaded family camp site with well-defined pitches on terraces.
Open: Apr-Sep **Site:** 4HEC **Prices:** 3.10-4.60 pitch 12.30-18 (incl 2 persons) **Facilities:** **Services:** lau **Leisure:** P **Off-site:**

ST-JEAN-LE-CENTENIER ARDÈCHE

Arches Patrick Gaschet, 07580
475367545 475367545
e-mail: pgaschet@club-internet.fr
website: www.campinglesarches.htm
A family site in a wooded location with direct access to the river.

A7 exit Montélimar Nord then follow N102 to exit Mirabel & take D458 for 500m to site on right.
Open: Etr-Sep **Site:** 4HEC **Prices:** 3.20 2-3 1-2 1-2 pitch 2-3 pp1.20-2 (static)260 **Facilities:** **Services:** lau **Leisure:** R **Off-site:**

ST-JEAN-PLA-DE-CORTS PYRÉNÉES-ORIENTALES

Casteillets 66490 468832683 468833967
e-mail: je@campinglescasteillets.com
website: www.campinglescasteillets.com
A family site situated between the sea and the mountains close to the River Tech.
Access via A9 exit Le Boulu.
Open: All year **Site:** 5HEC **Facilities:** **Services:** lau **Leisure:** P **Off-site:** LR

Deux Rivières rte de Maureillas, 66490
468832320 468830794
website: www.2rivieres.com
Situated on the banks of the River Tech with large roomy pitches.
0.5km SE via D13, beside the River Tech.
Open: Apr-15 Oct **Site:** 11HEC **Facilities:** **Services:** lau **Leisure:** PR **Off-site:** L

ST-JULIEN-DE-LA-NEF GARD

Isis en Cevennes Domaine de St-Julien, 30440
467738028 467738848
e-mail: info@isisencevennes.com
website: www.isisencevennes.com
In wooded surroundings with direct access to the River Hérault. Plenty of sporting facilities.
5km from Ganges towards Le Vigan.
Open: Mar-Oct **Site:** 4HEC **Prices:** 3.50 2.11 pitch 0.39-4 **Facilities:** **Services:** lau **Leisure:** PR

ST-LAURENT-DU-VAR ALPES-MARITIMES

Magali 1814 rte de la Baronne, 06700
493315700 492120133
website: www.camping-magali.com
A family site on level meadowland, surrounded by trees and bushes at the foot of the southern Alps.
Leave A8 at St-Laurent-du-Var exit, cross industrial zone turn left for 100m, then right and continue for 2km.
Open: Feb-Oct **Site:** 1.2HEC **Prices:** 3.30-3.80 2.60-3.20 15.30-22.30 (static)182-320 **Facilities:** **Services:** lau **Leisure:** P **Off-site:**

ST-LAURENT-DU-VERDON ALPES-DE-HAUTE-PROVENCE

Farigoulette Lac de St Laurent, 4500
492744162 492740086
website: www.camping-la-farigoulette.com
1.5km NE near Verdon.
Open: 15 May-Sep **Site:** 14HEC **Facilities:** **Services:** lau **Leisure:** LP **Off-site:** S

ST-MAXIMIN-LA-STE-BAUME VAR

Provençal rte de Mazaugues, 83470
494781697 494780022
e-mail: camping.provencal@wanadoo.fr
A family site in wooded surroundings with plenty of recreational facilties. Bar, café and swimming pool are open in July and August only.
2.5km S via D64.
Open: Apr-Sep **Site:** 5HEC **Prices:** 4-4.50 pitch 4.20-4.80 (static)250-350 **Facilities:** **Services:** lau **Leisure:** P **Off-site:**

Facilities: -shop -shower -electric points for razors -electric points for caravans -parking by tents permitted -compulsory separate car park **Services:** -café/restaurant -bar -Camping Gaz International -gas other than Camping Gaz -first aid facilities lau-laundry **Leisure:** -swimming L-Lake P-Pool R-River S-Sea **Off-site:** All facilities within 2km

ST-PAUL-EN-FORÊT VAR

Parc 83440 494761535 494847184
e-mail: campingleparc@wanadoo.fr
website: www.campingleparc.com
Quiet, fairly isolated site surrounded by woodland.
3km N on D4.
Open: All year **Site:** 3.5HEC **Prices:** 11.50-19 pitch 10-17.50 (incl 2 persons) (static)197-311 **Facilities:** **Services:** lau **Leisure:** P

ST-PAUL-LES-ROMANS DRÔME

CM de Romans Les Chasses, 26100 475723527
Shady pitches separated by hedges.
Open: May-Sep **Site:** 1HEC **Facilities:** **Services:** lau **Off-site:** P

ST-RAPHAËL VAR

Douce Quiétude bd J-Baudino, 83700
494443000 494443030
e-mail: sunelia@douce-quietude.com
website: www.douce-quietude.com
Meadowland site in quiet location in attractively hilly countryside with good facilities.
Approach from Agay Plage past Esterel Camping towards Valescure.
Open: Apr-Sep **Site:** 10HEC **Facilities:** **Services:** lau **Leisure:** P

Dramont 83700 494820768 494827530
Located in a pine forest with direct access to the beach and good modern facilities.
Access via N98 at St-Raphaël. Between Boulouris & Agay.
Open: 15 Mar-15 Oct **Site:** 6.5HEC **Facilities:** **Services:** lau **Leisure:** S

Royal Camp Long, 83530 494820020
Level site divided by walls and hedges. Ideal bathing for children. Bar and hall next to site.
On N98 towards Cannes.
Open: 20 Jan-30 Oct **Site:** 0.6HEC **Facilities:** **Services:** lau **Leisure:** S **Off-site:**

ST-REMÈZE ARDÈCHE

Domaine de Briange rte de Gras, 07700 475041443
e-mail: briange07@aol.com
website: members.aol.com/briange07
In a wooded location close to the Gorges de l'Ardèche.
1.5km NE.
Open: May-Sep **Site:** 4HEC **Facilities:** **Services:** lau **Leisure:** P **Off-site:**

ST-RÉMY-DE-PROVENCE BOUCHES-DU-RHÔNE

Monplaisir chemin Monplaisir, 13210
490922270 490921857
e-mail: reception@camping-monplaisir.fr
website: www.camping-monplaisir.fr
Open: Mar-10 Nov **Site:** 2.8HEC **Prices:** pitch 12.50-16.80 **Facilities:** **Services:** lau **Leisure:** P

Pégomas av Jean-Moulin, 13210
490920121 490920121
e-mail: contact@campingpegomas.com
website: www.campingpegomas.com
Well-tended grassland with trees and bushes. Divided into several fields by high cedars providing shade.
500m E of village. Well signed.
Open: Mar-Oct **Site:** 2HEC **Prices:** 9-10.50 pitch 9-10.50 **Facilities:** **Services:** lau **Leisure:** P **Off-site:**

ST-ROMAIN-EN-VIENNOIS VAUCLUSE

Soleil de Provence rte de Nyons, 84110
490464600 490464037
e-mail: info@camping-soleil-de-provence.fr
website: www.camping-soleil-de-provence.fr
4km from Vaison-la-Romaine and 12km from the foot of Mont Ventoux, this peaceful site is located uphill on meadow with superb views of the surrounding mountains. Large swimming pool with an island and palm trees.
Open: 15 Mar-30 Oct **Site:** 5HEC **Prices:** 3.50-5.50 2.50-3 pitch 2.50-3 **Facilities:** **Services:** lau **Leisure:** P

ST-SAUVEUR-DE-MONTAGUT ARDÈCHE

Ardechois Le Chambon, Gluiras, 07190
475666187 475666367
e-mail: ardechois.camping@wanadoo.fr
website: www.ardechois-camping.fr
In the grounds of a restored 18th-century farm set in rolling countryside with fine views of the surrounding hills.
8.5km W on D102, beside the River Glueÿre.
Open: 18 Apr-Oct **Site:** 5.5HEC **Prices:** pitch 19-24 (incl 2 persons) (static)315-610 **Facilities:** **Services:** lau **Leisure:** PR

ST-SORLIN-EN-VALLOIRE DRÔME

Château de la Pérouze 26210 475317021 475316274
e-mail: campingchateaudelaperouz@libertysurf.fr
A well-appointed family site with a variety of recreational facilities.
2.5km SE via D1.
Open: 15 Jun-15 Sep **Site:** 14HEC **Prices:** 6 6 6 6 (static)457.35 **Facilities:** **Services:** lau **Leisure:** LP

ST-THIBÉRY HÉRAULT

Tane Le Causse, 34630 467778429
In pleasant wooded surroundings, 1km from the River Hérault.
Access via A9 exit Agde-Pézenas.
Open: Jun-Sep **Site:** 2.4HEC **Prices:** pitch 10-13 (incl 2 persons) **Facilities:** **Services:** lau **Leisure:** P **Off-site:** R

Site: 6HEC-Site size -grass -sand -stone -little shade -partly shaded -mainly shaded -bungalows for hire -caravans for hire -tents for hire -no dogs **Prices:** -adult per night -car per night pp-per person per night -caravan per night -tent per night (static)-caravan hire per week

ST-VALLIER-DE-THIEY ALPES-MARITIMES

Parc des Arboins 755 RN85, 06460
493426389 493096154
e-mail: reception@parc-des-arboins.com
website: www.parc-des-arboins.com
Pleasantly situated terraced site on hillside with some oak trees.
Entrance at KmV36 on N85.
Open: All year **Site:** 4HEC **Prices:** 3.30-3.70 7.70-11.60 7-10 (static)137-396 **Facilities:** **Services:** lau **Leisure:** P **Off-site:**

STE-MARIE PYRÉNÉES-ORIENTALES
AT TORREILLES (4KM NW ON D11)

Dunes de Torreilles 66440 468283829 468283257
e-mail: lesdunes@lesdunes.net **website:** www.lesdunes.net
A well-equipped site in wooded surroundings with direct access to the beach.
E of the village off D81.
Open: 15 Mar-15 Oct **Site:** 16HEC **Prices:** pitch 13.40-28.75 (incl 2 persons) **Facilities:** **Services:** lau **Leisure:** PS **Off-site:** R

Marisol Village Camping Resort Plage de Torreilles, 66440
468280407 468281823
e-mail: marisol@camping-marisol.com
website: www.camping-marisol.com
A family site with a wide variety of sports and entertainment facilities in a pleasant park-like setting 350m from the beach.
Off D81 towards the sea.
Open: Apr-Sep **Site:** 9HEC **Prices:** 5.30-6.80 pitch 12-34.30 (static)199-799 **Facilities:** **Services:** lau **Leisure:** PS **Off-site:** R

Trivoly bd des Plages, 66440 468282028 468281648
e-mail: chadotel@wanadoo.fr
website: camping-chadotel.fr
A modern site with excellent facilities and well-defined pitches, 800m from the beach.
Access via autoroute exit Perpignan Nord towards Le Barcarès.
Open: Apr-Sep **Site:** 4.7HEC **Prices:** 5.70 pitch 14.50-23 (incl 2 persons) (static)200-740 **Facilities:** **Services:** lau **Leisure:** P
Off-site: RS

STES-MARIES-DE-LA-MER BOUCHES-DU-RHÔNE

CM Brise 13460 490978467 490977201
e-mail: labrise@laposte.net
website: saintes-maries@enprovence.com
A well-equipped family site with direct access to the beach, situated in the heart of the Camargue. The sanitary blocks are modern and there are facilities for a wide variety of sports.
NE via D85A, towards the beach.
Open: 15 Dec-15 Nov **Site:** 22HEC
Prices: 4.20-6.90 pitch 11.40-18.90 (incl 2 persons) (static)245-592 **Facilities:** **Services:** lau
Leisure: P **Off-site:** RS

Clos-du-Rhône BP 74, 13460 490978599 490977885
e-mail: leclos@laposte.net
2km W via D38, near the beach.
Open: Apr-15 Nov **Site:** 7HEC **Facilities:** **Services:** lau **Leisure:** PRS

Facilities: -shop -shower -electric points for razors -electric points for caravans -parking by tents permitted -compulsory separate car park **Services:** -café/restaurant -bar -Camping Gaz International -gas other than Camping Gaz -first aid facilities lau-laundry **Leisure:** -swimming L-Lake P-Pool R-River S-Sea **Off-site:** All facilities within 2km

SALAVAS ARDÈCHE

Chauvieux 07150 ☎ 475880537 ▤ 475880537
e-mail: camping.chauvieux@wanadoo.fr
website: www.camping-le-chauvieux.com
A popular site in a wooded location close to the River
Ardèche with plenty of recreational facilities. Advance
booking recommended.
➲ NE off D579.
Open: 29 Apr-15 Sep **Site:** 2.3HEC ⚏ ∷ ♠ ☎ **Prices:** ⚌5
⚐2 pitch 13-19.50 (incl 2 persons) **Facilities:** ☏ ⚐ ⊙ ⚑ ∅ ☎
Services: ☟ ✗ ⊞ lau **Leisure:** ⇄PR

SALERNES VAR

Arnauds Quartier des Arnauds, 83690
☎ 494675195 ▤ 494707557
e-mail: lesarnauds@ville-salernes.fr
website: www.ville-salernes.fr
Level site situated alongside a river and a lake.
➲ Access via D560. Site entrance just beyond the village.
Open: 2 May-Sep **Site:** 3HEC ⚏ ♠ ☎ **Prices:** ⚌4.30-6 pitch
7.50-9.50 **Facilities:** ☏ ⊙ ⚑ ☎ **Services:** ☟ ✗ ⊞ lau
Leisure: ⇄R **Off-site:** ⚐ ✗ ∅ ⚏

SALINS-D'HYÈRES, LES VAR

Port Pothuau 101 chemin les Ourledes, 83400
☎ 494664117 ▤ 494663309
e-mail: pothuau@free.fr
website: www.campingportpothuau.com
A peaceful holiday village, completely divided into pitches
with good leisure facilities.
➲ 6km E of Hyères on N98 and D12.
Open: 04 Apr-19 Oct **Site:** 6HEC ⚏ ⚑ ☎ ⚐ **Prices:** ⚐30-
31.50 ⚐ (static)250-500 **Facilities:** ☏ ⚐ ⊙ ⚑ ∅ ⚏ ☎
Services: ☟ ✗ ⊞ lau **Leisure:** ⇄P **Off-site:** ⇄RS

SALON-DE-PROVENCE BOUCHES-DU-RHÔNE

Nostradamus rte d'Eyguières, 13300
☎ 490560836 ▤ 490566505
e-mail: gilles.nostra@wanadoo.fr
In pleasant, wooded surroundings with good sports facilities.
➲ 5km W on D17 towards Eyguières & Arles.
Open: Mar-Oct **Site:** 2.2HEC ⚏ ♠ ☎ **Prices:** ⚌4-4.50
⚐1.20-1.50 ⚐4-4.50 ⚌4-4.50 **Facilities:** ☏ ⚐ ⊙ ⚑ ☎
Services: ☟ ✗ ⊞ lau **Leisure:** ⇄PR

SALVETAT, LA HÉRAULT

Goudal rte de Lacaune, 34330 ☎ 467976044 ▤ 467976268
e-mail: info@goudal.com website: www.goudal.com
In a natural mountain setting within the Haut Lanquedoc
park.
➲ Access via D907.
Open: May-Sep **Site:** 5HEC ⚏ ⚑ ☎ ⚐ ⚌ **Prices:** ⚌2.20-
2.80 pitch 8-21.60 (incl 2 persons) **Facilities:** ☏ ⚐ ⊙ ⚑ ⚏ ☎
Services: ☟ ✗ ⊞ lau **Leisure:** ⇄L **Off-site:** ⇄R

SANARY-SUR-MER VAR

Girelles chemin de Beaucours, 83110
☎ 494741318 ▤ 494746004
website: www.lesgirelles.com
A modern family site with good facilities and direct access to
the sea.
Camping Card Compulsory
➲ 3km NW via D539, beside the sea.
Open: Etr-Sep **Site:** 2HEC ⚏ ♠ ☎ ⚐ **Prices:** ⚌5-6
⚐15.60-23 ⚌15.60-23 ⚐ (static)250-410 **Facilities:** ☏ ⚐ ⊙
⚑ ∅ ☎ **Services:** ☟ ✗ ⊞ lau **Leisure:** ⇄S

Mogador 83110 ☎ 494745316 ▤ 494741058
Situated 800m from the sea. The site, divided into pitches by
hedges, is well managed and very well kept.
➲ 2km NW on N559 turn off at Km15 and take next left.
Open: Etr-5 Oct **Site:** 2.7HEC ⚏ ♠ ☎ ⚘ **Facilities:** ☏ ⚐
⊙ ⚑ ∅ ⚏ ☎ ▣ **Services:** ☟ ✗ ⊞ lau **Leisure:** ⇄P **Off-site:** ⇄S

Pierredon 652 Chemin Raoul Coletta, 83110
☎ 494742502 ▤ 494746142
e-mail: campasun@free.fr website: www.campasun.fr
A well-equipped, wooded site providing a variety of family
entertainment, 3km from the sea.
➲ Access via A50 exit Bandol or Sanary.
Open: 15 Mar-Oct **Site:** 4HEC ⚏ ⚑ ☎ ⚌ **Prices:** ⚌4.50-
5.90 pitch 5.90-10.55 **Facilities:** ☏ ⚐ ⊙ ⚑ ⚏ ☎ **Services:** ☟
✗ lau **Leisure:** ⇄P **Off-site:** ⚐ ∅ ⊞

SAUVE GARD

Domaine de Bagard rte de Nîmes, 30610 ☎ 466775599
Shady site bordering the River Vidourle, surrounded by
hedges.
➲ 1.2km SE via D999.
Open: Apr-Sep **Site:** 16HEC ⚏ ♠ ☎ ⚐ **Facilities:** ☏ ⚐ ⊙
⚑ ∅ ☎ **Services:** ☟ ✗ lau **Leisure:** ⇄PR **Off-site:** ⊞

SAUVIAN HÉRAULT

Gabinelle 34410 ☎ 467395087
website: www.gabinelle.com
A modern site in pleasant wooded surroundings with good
facilities.
➲ Leave Sauvian in the direction of Valras Plage on D19.
Open: 15 Apr-10 Sep **Site:** 4HEC ⚏ ♠ ☎ ⚐ ⚌ **A**
Facilities: ☏ ⊙ ⚑ ⚏ ☎ **Services:** ☟ ✗ ⊞ lau **Leisure:** ⇄P
Off-site: ∅ ⇄R

SÉRIGNAN-PLAGE HÉRAULT

Clos Virgile 34410 ☎ 467322064 ▤ 467320542
e-mail: le.clos.virgile@wanadoo.fr website: leclosvirgile.com
Situated 400m from the beach, the site is on level
meadowland with large pitches and has two clean, well-kept
sanitary blocks.
Open: May-15 Sep **Site:** 5HEC ⚏ ♠ ☎ **Prices:** pitch 15-30
(incl 2 persons) **Facilities:** ☏ ⚐ ⊙ ⚑ ∅ ☎ **Services:** ☟ ✗ ⊞
lau **Leisure:** ⇄PS

Grand Large 34410 ☎ 467397130 ▤ 467325815
e-mail: legrandlarge@wanadoo.fr
website: www.camping-grandlarge.com
Situated by the sea with private access to the beach. Good
facilities. Entertainment during high season.
Open: 26 Apr-14 Sep **Site:** 7HEC ⚏ ∷ ⚑ ☎ **A**
Facilities: ☏ ⚐ ⊙ ⚑ ∅ ⚏ ☎ **Services:** ☟ ✗ ⊞ lau
Leisure: ⇄PS

Sérignan-Plage 34410 ☎ 467323533 ▤ 467322636
e-mail: info@leserignanplage.com
website: www.leserignanplage.com
On a fine sandy beach, this is a family site with good
recreational facilities.
➲ Access via A9 exit Béziers Est.
Open: 22 Apr-20 Sep **Site:** 16HEC ⚏ ♠ ☎ **Facilities:** ☏ ⚐
⊙ ⚑ ∅ ⚏ ☎ ▣ **Services:** ☟ ✗ ⊞ lau **Leisure:** ⇄PS

SEYNE-SUR-MER, LA VAR

Mimosas av M-Paul, 83500 ☎ 494947315 ▤ 494873613
e-mail: camping_des_mimosas@yahoo.fr
website: www.camping-mimosas.com
Situated among pine trees facing the fortress of Six-Fours.
Bar and café available during high season only.

Site: 6HEC-Site size ⚏-grass ∷-sand ♠-stone ⚘-little shade ⚑-partly shaded ♠-mainly shaded
☎-bungalows for hire ⚐-caravans for hire ⚌-tents for hire ⚘-no dogs **Prices:** ⚌-adult per night ⚐-car per night
pp-per person per night ⚐-caravan per night ⚌-tent per night ⚐ (static)-caravan hire per week

Access via A50 exit 13 towards La Seyne Centre, then towards Sanary-Bandol.
Open: All year **Site:** 1.1HEC **Prices:** pitch 10.50-13.50 (incl 3 persons) (static)155-437 **Facilities:** **Services:** lau **Off-site:** P

SILLANS-LA-CASCADE BOUCHES-DU-RHÔNE

Relais de la Bresque 15 chemin de la Piscine, 83690
494046489 494046489
e-mail: relaisdelabresque@aol.com
In a beautiful setting among pine trees with good sanitary and recreational facilities.
Open: All year **Site:** 3HEC **Facilities:** **Services:** lau **Off-site:** PR

SIX-FOURS-LES-PLAGES VAR

Héliosports La Font de Fillol, 83140 494256276
Between the town centre and the beach.
1km W.
Open: 25 Mar-15 Oct **Site:** 0.5HEC **Facilities:** **Services:** lau **Off-site:** PS

International St-Jean av de la Collégiale, 83140
494875151 494062823
e-mail: info@campingstjean.com
website: www.campingstjean.com
Site with pitches, separated by hedges and reeds. Well managed, and lies just below the Fort Six-Fours.
Access from N559 and D63 via chemin de St-Jean.
Open: All year **Site:** 3HEC **Prices:** 6 pitch 20-23 (incl 3 persons) **Facilities:** **Services:** lau **Leisure:** P **Off-site:**

Playes 419 r Grand, 83140 494255757 494071990
e-mail: campingplayes@wanadoo.fr
website: www.campingplayes.com
Terraced site on N side of town. Trees abound in this excellent location.
Access from N559 and D63 via chemin de St-Jean.
Open: All year **Site:** 1.5HEC **Prices:** 3.50-5 pitch 15-22 (static)150-395 **Facilities:** **Services:** lau **Off-site:** PS

SOSPEL ALPES-MARITIMES

Domaine St-Madeleine rte de Moulinet, 06380
493041048 493041837
e-mail: camp@camping-sainte-madeleine.com
website: camping-sainte-madeleine.com
A peaceful site in beautiful, unspoiled surroundings.
4.5km NW via D2566.
Open: 26 Mar-2 Oct **Site:** 3.5HEC **Prices:** pitch 13.60-17 (incl 2 persons) (static)210-410 **Facilities:** **Services:** lau **Leisure:** P

SOUBÈS HÉRAULT

Les Rials rte de Poujols, 34700 467441553
e-mail: mendez11@voila.fr
website: www.campinglesrials.site.voila.fr
A terraced site in wooded surroundings on the banks of the River Lergue.
4km from Lodève and 10km from Lac du Salagou.
Open: 25 Jun-Aug **Site:** 3.5HEC **Prices:** pitch 13 (incl 2 persons) **Facilities:** **Services:** lau **Leisure:** PR **Off-site:**

Sources Soubes, 34700 467443202 467443202
e-mail: jlsources@wanadoo.fr
website: www.campingdessources.cjb.net
A small, friendly site in a quiet location beside a river.

5km NE. Signed from N9.
Open: 15 May-15 Sep **Site:** 1.3HEC **Prices:** pitch 14 (incl 2 persons) **Facilities:** **Services:** lau **Leisure:** PR **Off-site:** L

TAIN-L'HERMITAGE DRÔME

CM Lucs 24 av Prés-Roosevelt, 26600
475083282 475083206
e-mail: camping.tainlhermitage@wanadoo.fr
Good overnight stopping place but some traffic noise.
S of town near N7. Turn towards River Rhône at Esso garage.
Open: 15 Mar-Oct **Site:** 1.5HEC **Prices:** pitch 13-15.70 (incl 2 persons) **Facilities:** **Services:** lau **Leisure:** P **Off-site:**

THOR, LE VAUCLUSE

Jantou Quartier le Bourdis, 84250
490339007 490337984
e-mail: accueil@lejantou.com **website:** www.lejantou.com
In wooded surroundings beside a river. Separate car park for arrivals after 22.00.
Access via N100.
Open: 15 Mar-Oct **Site:** 6HEC **Prices:** pitch 13 **Facilities:** **Services:** lau **Leisure:** PR **Off-site:**

TOURNON-SUR-RHÔNE ARDÈCHE

Manoir rte de Lamastre, 07300 475080250 475085710
e-mail: info@lemanoir-ardeche.com
website: www.lemanoir-ardeche.com
In picturesque wooded surroundings with good, modern facilities.
From N86 Lyon-Valence take Lamastre road for 3km.
Open: Apr-Sep **Site:** 2HEC **Prices:** pitch 10.50-13.50 (static)200-380 **Facilities:** **Services:** lau **Leisure:** PR

Tournon 1 Promenade Roche de France, 07300
475080528 475080528
e-mail: camping.tournon@wanadoo.fr
website: www.camping-tournon.com
Well laid-out site in town centre beside River Rhône.
NW on N86.
Open: All year **Site:** 1HEC **Facilities:** **Services:** lau **Leisure:** R **Off-site:** P

TOURRETTES-SUR-LOUP ALPES-MARITIMES

Camassade 523 rte de Pie Lombard, 06140
493593154 493593181
e-mail: camassade@aol.com **website:** www.camassade.com
Quiet site under oak trees and pines with several terraces.
From Vence turn left immediately beyond Tourette.
Open: All year **Site:** 2HEC **Facilities:** **Services:** lau **Leisure:** P

Rives du Loup rte de la Colle, 6140
493241565 493241565
e-mail: info@rivesduloup.com
website: www.rivesduloup.com
In a wooded riverside setting with good, modern facilities adjacent to a small hotel.
Between Vence and Grasse, 3km from Pont-du-Loup on the road to La Colle-sur-Loup.
Open: Apr-Sep **Site:** 2.2HEC **Prices:** 4 pitch 13.50-22.50 (incl 2 persons) (static)195-610 **Facilities:** **Services:** lau **Leisure:** PR

UCEL ARDÈCHE

Domaine de Gil rte de Vals, 07200
475946363 475940195
e-mail: info@domaine-de-gil.com
website: www.domaine-de-gil.com
Pleasantly situated on the banks of the River Ardèche. Surrounded by beautiful views of the countryside.
N of Aubenas off N104.
Open: 16 Apr-10 Sep **Site:** 4.5HEC **Prices:** 3.20-5.50 pitch 13.50-25 (incl 2 persons) **Facilities:** **Services:** lau **Leisure:** PR

UR PYRÉNÉES-ORIENTALES

Gare d'Ur rte d'Espagne, UR, 66760 468048095
website: www.cordgane.capcir.com
In a pleasant mountainous setting with well-defined pitches. 500m from the village.
Open: Nov-Sep **Site:** 1HEC **Prices:** 2.80 3.40 3.40 3.40 pitch 3.40 (static)200 **Facilities:** **Services:** lau **Off-site:** R

UZÈS GARD
AT ST-QUENTIN-LA-POTERIE (4KM NE)

Moulin Neuf 30700 466221721 466229182
e-mail: le.moulin.neuf@wanadoo.fr
website: www.le-moulin-neuf.com
Quiet site on extensive meadowland within an estate.
4 km NE on D982.
Open: Etr-Sep **Site:** 5HEC **Prices:** 3.50-4.50 pitch 12.50-18.50 pp3.50-4.50 **Facilities:** **Services:** lau **Leisure:** P

VAISON-LA-ROMAINE VAUCLUSE

International Carpe Diem rte de St-Marcellin, 84110
490360202 490363690
e-mail: contact@camping-carpe-diem.com
website: www.camping-carpe-diem.com
In wooded surroundings close to Mont Ventoux, with a wide variety of leisure facilities.
S of town towards Malaucène.
Open: 30 Mar-2 Nov **Site:** 10HEC **Prices:** 4-5.50 pitch 14.50-29 (incl 3 persons) (static)560-640 **Facilities:** **Services:** lau **Leisure:** P **Off-site:** R

Théâtre Romain Quartier des Arts, chemin du Brusquet, 84110 490287866 490287876
e-mail: info@camping-theatre.com
website: www.camping-theatre.com
500m from the town centre near the Roman theatre.
Open: 15 Mar-15 Nov **Site:** 1.5HEC **Prices:** 4.90-5.70 pitch 5-7.60 **Facilities:** **Services:** lau **Leisure:** P **Off-site:** R

VALENCE DRÔME

CM chemin de l'Epervière, 26000
475423200 475562067
e-mail: eperviere@vacanciel.com
A well-equipped site bordering the Rhône.
Access via exit Valence Sud off A7.
Open: Feb-15 Dec **Site:** 3.5HEC **Prices:** 3.20-4.70 pitch 10.60-15.80 (incl 2 persons) **Facilities:** **Services:** lau **Leisure:** P **Off-site:**

VALLABRÈGUES GARD

Lou Vincen 30300 466592129 466590741
e-mail: campinglouvincen@wanadoo.fr
In a pleasant shady location in the heart of a Provençal village.
Open: 24 Mar-15 Oct **Site:** 1.4HEC **Prices:** 3.50-4.40 pitch 11.20-16.50 (incl 2 persons) (static)297-493 **Facilities:** **Services:** lau **Leisure:** P **Off-site:** LR

VALLERAUGE GARD

Corconne Pont D'Hérault 467824682 467824682
e-mail: lacorconne@wanadoo.fr
website: www.lacorconne.com
Unspoiled campsite located in the Cevennes and blending well into the wooded landscape. Spacious terraced pitches. The River Herault is suitable for swimming.
Off A75 from Millau, 3km N of Pont d'Herault.
Open: Apr-Oct **Site:** 7HEC **Prices:** 4-4.20 4-4.20 4-4.20 pitch 4-4.20 **Facilities:** **Services:** lau **Leisure:** R

VALLON-PONT-D'ARC ARDÈCHE

Camping Nature Park L'Ardechois 07150
475880663 475371497
e-mail: ardecamp@bigfoot.com
website: www.ardechois-camping.com
In a pleasant situation in the Gorges de l'Ardèche. Good access for caravans and plentiful sporting facilities.
From Vallon take D290 towards St-Martin. Signed.
Open: 19 Mar-Sep **Site:** 6HEC **Prices:** 5.20-8 pitch 23-37 (incl 2 persons) **Facilities:** **Services:** lau **Leisure:** PR **Off-site:**

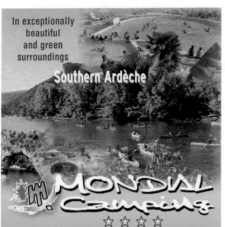

Mondial rte des Gorges de l'Ardèche, 7150
☎ 475880044 ▯ 475371373
Modernised site on the bank of the Ardèche with good sanitary arrangements.
➲ *Access from D290 Vallon-Pont-d'Arc. 800m towards Gorge d'Ardèche.*
Open: 20 Mar-Sep **Site:** 4.2HEC **Prices:** pitch 18-29 (incl 2 persons) **Facilities:** **Services:** lau **Leisure:** PR

Plage Fleurie Les Mazes, 7150 ☎ 475880115 ▯ 475881131
e-mail: info@laplagefleurie.com
website: www.laplagefleurie.com
Holiday site in unspoilt village beside river.
➲ *Take D579 towards Ruoms, turn left after 2.5km towards Les Mazes.*
Open: 29 Apr-15 Sep **Site:** 12HEC **Prices:** 4.60-5.25 pitch 13.50-21 **Facilities:** **Services:** lau **Leisure:** PR

VALRAS-PLAGE HÉRAULT

Lou Village chemin des Montilles, 34350
☎ 467373379 ▯ 467375356
e-mail: info@louvillage.com
website: www.louvillage.com
Situated along a sandy beach, bordered by sand dunes.
➲ *2km SW, 100m from the beach.*
Open: May-12 Sep **Site:** 8HEC **Facilities:** **Services:** lau **Leisure:** PS **Off-site:** R

Occitanie 34350 ☎ 467395906 ▯ 467325820
e-mail: campingoccitanie@wanadoo.fr
website: www.campingoccitanie.com
Family site on rising ground to the N of town, 1km from the beach.

➲ *Access from A9 exit Béziers-Est towards Valras.*
Open: 28 May-10 Sep **Site:** 6HEC **Prices:** 2-3.50 pitch 15.25-23.50 (incl 2 persons) (static)161-525 **Facilities:** **Services:** lau **Leisure:** P **Off-site:** RS

Plage & Bord du Mer rte de Vendres
☎ 467303637 ▯ 467315015
Open: 25 May-6 Sep **Site:** 10HEC **Facilities:** **Services:** lau

Vagues Vendres Plage, 34350 ☎ 467373312 ▯ 467375036
website: www.lesvagues.net
A well-organised family site 400m from the sea with a variety of sports and entertainment facilities.
Open: Apr-Sep **Site:** 7HEC **Facilities:** **Services:** lau **Leisure:** P **Off-site:** S

Yole 34350 ☎ 467373387 ▯ 467374489
e-mail: layole34@aol.com
website: www.campinglayole.com
Very comfortable site divided into pitches. Good sanitary installations with individual washing cubicles. Hot water tap. Sailing boats for hire. Riding stables in village. Booking recommended in July and August.
➲ *SW of D37E towards Vendres.*
Open: 30 Apr-17 Sep **Site:** 20HEC **Prices:** pitch 16.85-32.75 (incl 2 persons) (static)248.50-793.10 **Facilities:** **Services:** lau **Leisure:** P **Off-site:** S

See advertisement on page 214

VAUVERT GARD

Tourrades chemin des Canaux, 30600
☎ 466888020 ▯ 466883380
A modern family site with a wide range of recreational facilities.
➲ *3km W via N572 and D135.*
Open: All year **Site:** 7.5HEC **Facilities:** **Services:** lau **Leisure:** P **Off-site:**

VEDÈNE VAUCLUSE

Flory rte d'Entraigues, 84270 ☎ 490310051 ▯ 490234679
e-mail: campingflory@wanadoo.fr
website: www.campingflory.com
Well-kept site on a pine covered hill with good facilities.
➲ *From motorway, do not head for Vedène but follow D942 for 800m.*
Open: 15 Mar-Sep **Site:** 6.5HEC **Prices:** 4.50 pitch 5 (static)150-250 **Facilities:** **Services:** lau **Leisure:** P

Facilities: shop, shower, electric points for razors, electric points for caravans, parking by tents permitted, compulsory separate car park **Services:** café/restaurant, bar, Camping Gaz International, gas other than Camping Gaz, first aid facilities, lau-laundry **Leisure:** swimming L-Lake P-Pool R-River S-Sea **Off-site:** All facilities within 2km

VENCE ALPES-MARITIMES

Domaine de la Bergerie rte de la Sine, 06140
☎ 493580936 ▯ 493598044
Well-kept site on hilly land. Pitches near to a wood. Some facilities are only available in high season.
➲ *3km W on D2210.*
Open: 25 Mar-15 Oct **Site:** 13HEC **Prices:** 4.60 pitch 13.50-29 **Facilities:** **Services:** lau **Leisure:** P

VERCHENY DRÔME

Acacias 26340 ☎ 475217251 ▯ 475217398
e-mail: infos@campinglesacacias.com
website: campinglesacacias.com
Pleasant site beside the River Drôme.
Camping Card Compulsory
➲ *Access via D93.*
Open: Apr-Sep **Site:** 3.7HEC **Prices:** pitch 10-13.50 (incl 2 persons) (static)231-301 **Facilities:** **Services:** lau **Leisure:** R

VÉREILLES HÉRAULT

Sieste 34260 ☎ 467237296 ▯ 467237538
In a rural setting on the River Orb.
➲ *NE of Bédarieux, 10km from Lodève.*
Open: Jun-Aug **Site:** 2HEC **Prices:** 13 (static)100-200 **Facilities:** **Services:** lau **Leisure:** PR

VIAS HÉRAULT

Air Marin 34450 ☎ 467216490 ▯ 467217679
e-mail: info@camping-air-marin
website: www.camping-air-marin
A well-equipped family site in wooded surroundings, a 10-minute walk from the beach.
➲ *E of Vias Plage.*
Open: May-15 Sep **Site:** 7HEC **Prices:** 4.80-6 pitch 22.40-28 (incl 2 persons) (static)150-680 **Facilities:** **Services:** lau **Leisure:** P **Off-site:** RS

Carabasse rte de Farinette, 34450
☎ 467216401 ▯ 467217687
website: www.haveneurope.com
A lively camping park with a wide range of activites, especially for young families and teenagers, centred around a lagoon pool complex and entertainment terrace.
➲ *1.5m NE of Vias.*
Open: 15 Apr-15 Sep **Site:** **Facilities:** **Services:** lau **Leisure:** P **Off-site:** S

Cap Soleil Côte Ouest, 34450 ☎ 467216477 ▯ 467217066
website: www.capsoleil.fr
On level land near sea. Divided into pitches.
➲ *Cross Canal du Midi, S of town, then turn W.*
Open: All year **Site:** 5HEC **Facilities:** **Services:** lau **Leisure:** P **Off-site:** S

Hélios Vias-Plage, 34450 ☎ 467216366 ▯ 467216366
On level ground divided into pitches.
➲ *On D137 S of village signed Farinette.*
Open: May-Sep **Site:** 3HEC **Prices:** pitch 11-15.70 (incl 2 persons) (static)137-300 **Facilities:** **Services:** lau **Off-site:** RS

Mediterranee Plage 467909907 467909917
e-mail: camping.med@wanadoo.fr
website: www.mediterranee-plage.com
Direct access to a fine sandy beach.
Open: 3 Apr-20 Sep **Site:** 7HEC **Prices:** pitch 15.20-25.50 (incl 2 persons) **Facilities:** **Services:** lau **Leisure:** PS

Napoléon av de la Mediterranée, 34450
467010780 467010785
e-mail: reception@camping-napoleon.fr
website: www.camping-napoleon.fr
A well-equipped family site surrounded by tropical vegetation with direct access to the beach.
Access via A9 exit Agde-Vias.
Open: 25 Mar-26 Sep **Site:** 3HEC **Prices:** pitch 14-37 (incl 2 persons) pp4-6 **Facilities:** **Services:** lau **Leisure:** P **Off-site:** RS

Yelloh Village Farret 34450 467216445 467217049
e-mail: farret@wanadoo.fr
website: ww.farret.com
On level meadow beside flat sandy beach, ideal for children.
Access via A9 exit Agde-Vias.
Open: Apr-25 Sep **Site:** 7HEC **Facilities:** **Services:** lau **Leisure:** PS **Off-site:** R

VIC-LA-GARDIOLE HÉRAULT

Europe 34110 467781150 467784859
e-mail: campingdeleurope@wanadoo.fr
website: www.campingleurope.com
A pleasant site in peaceful surroundings.
1.5km W via D114.
Open: 19 Jun-05 Sep **Site:** 5HEC **Facilities:** **Services:** lau **Leisure:** P **Off-site:** LS

VIGAN, LE GARD

Val de l'Arre rte de Ganges, 30120
467810277 467817123
e-mail: valdelarre@wanadoo.fr
website: www.campingfrance.com/valdelarre
In wooded surroundings beside the River Arre. Compulsory separate car park for late arrivals.
2.5km E on D999.
Open: Apr-Sep **Site:** 4HEC **Prices:** pitch 11-14.50 (incl 2 persons) pp5.18-6.71 **Facilities:** **Services:** lau **Leisure:** PR **Off-site:**

VILLARS-COLMARS ALPES-DE-HAUTE-PROVENCE

Haut-Verdon 04370 492834009 492835661
e-mail: campinglehautverdon@wanadoo.fr
website: www.lehautverdon.com
A comfortable site in a picturesque wooded location beside the River Verdon.
N on D908.
Open: May-Sep **Site:** 3.5HEC **Prices:** 3-4 pitch 6-10 **Facilities:** **Services:** lau **Leisure:** PR **Off-site:**

VILLEMOUSTAUSSOU AUDE

Pinhiers chemin du Pont Neuf, 11620
468478190 468714349
e-mail: campingdaspinhiers@wanadoo.fr
website: bienvenuedanslaude.com
A61 in the direction of Mazamet.
Open: Apr-Sep **Site:** 2HEC **Prices:** 3-3.60 pitch 3.30-3.70 (static)190-304 **Facilities:** **Services:** lau **Leisure:** P **Off-site:**

VILLENEUVE-DE-BERG ARDÈCHE

Domaine de Pommier RN 102, 07170
475948281 475948390
Holiday site in beautiful setting with terraces divided into pitches.
On winding private road off N102, 2km from village.
Open: May-Sep **Site:** 30HEC **Facilities:** **Services:** **Leisure:** PR

VILLENEUVE-DE-LA-RAHO PYRÉNÉES-ORIENTALES

Rives-du-Lac chemin de la Serre, 66180
468558351 468558637
e-mail: camping.villeneuve@worldonline.fr
A quiet family site beside the lake.
7km from Perpignan.
Open: Mar-Nov **Site:** 2.5HEC **Prices:** pitch 10-13.30 (incl 2 persons) **Facilities:** **Services:** lau **Off-site:**

See advertisement on page 216

VILLENEUVE-LÈS-AVIGNON GARD

Île des Papes 30400 490151590 490151591
e-mail: ile.papes@wanadoo.fr
website: www.campeoles.fr
A well-equipped site situated on an island between the Rhône canal and the River Rhône.
Access via N7 and D228.
Open: 24 Mar-26 Oct **Site:** 20HEC **Prices:** 4.50-6.30 pitch 16-27 (incl 2 persons) (static)279-659 **Facilities:** **Services:** lau **Leisure:** P

Villeneuve-Loubet-Plage Alpes-Maritimes

Hippodrôme 5 av des Rives, 06270
493200200 492132007
e-mail: blsced@aol.com
website: meublecamping-hippodrome.com
In a spacious park with pitches divided by hedges with good facilities.
Turn right off the N7 at ATLAS furniture store.
Open: All year **Site:** 7.8HEC **Prices:** 3.70-4.70 pitch 11.50-25 (incl 2 persons) **Facilities:** **Services:** lau **Leisure:** P **Off-site:** S

Panorama 6270 493209153
Small terraced site mainly for tents 0.8km from the sea.
About 500m from the Nice-Cannes autoroute.
Open: All year **Site:** 1HEC **Facilities:** **Services:** lau **Off-site:** RS

Parc des Maurettes 730 av du Dr-Lefebvre, 06270
493209191 493737720
e-mail: info@parcdesmaurettes.com
website: www.parcsdesmaurettes.com
Terraced site in a pine forest with good, modern facilities.
Access via A8: from Cannes take exit Villeneuve-Loubet-Plage, then N7 towards Antibes for 1km; from Nice, take Villeneuve exit and A8 for 2km.
Open: 10 Jan-15 Nov **Site:** 2HEC **Prices:** 1-4.40 19.30-27.45 18.45-22.75 **Facilities:** **Services:** lau **Off-site:** S

Parc St-James Sourire rte de Grasse (D2085), 6270
493209611 493220752
website: www.camping-parcsaintjames.com
Parkland dominated by an 11th-century monastery.

2km W on D2085.
Open: end Mar-end Sep **Site:** 8HEC **Facilities:** **Services:** lau **Leisure:** P **Off-site:** R

Vieille Ferme 296 bd des Groules, 06270
493334144 493333728
e-mail: vieilleferme@bigfoot.com
website: www.vieilleferme.com
In a wooded park close to the sea. Shop and café open in summer only.
Access via A8/N7 from Antibes of Cagnes-sur-Mer.
Open: All year **Site:** 2.8HEC **Facilities:** **Services:** lau **Leisure:** P **Off-site:** S

Villerouge-la-Crémade Aude

Pinada 11200 468436182 468436861
e-mail: lepinada@libertysurf.fr **website:** camping_le_pinada.com
In pleasant rural surroundings on edge of forest.
600m NW on D106.
Open: Apr-15 Oct **Site:** 4.5HEC **Facilities:** **Services:** lau **Leisure:** P

Villes-sur-Auzon Vaucluse

Verguettes rte de Carpentras, 84570
490618818 490619787
e-mail: info@provence-camping.com
website: www.provence-camping.com
Lying at the foot of Mont Ventoux and Nesque gorges in a pine forest
W via D942.
Open: Apr-15 Oct **Site:** 2HEC **Prices:** 4.50-5 pitch 6.50-7.10 **Facilities:** **Services:** lau **Leisure:** P **Off-site:**

Vitrolles Bouches-du-Rhône

Marina Plage 13127 442893146 442795990
e-mail: information@marina-plage.com
website: www.marina-plage.com
A family site in pleasant wooded surroundings with good recreational facilities.
Access via N113 towards Rognac, then turn S at exit after Marignane Airport.
Open: All year **Site:** 11HEC **Facilities:** **Services:** lau **Leisure:** L

VIVIERS ARDÈCHE

Domaine d' Imbours 07220 475543950 475543920
e-mail: imbours@france.location.fr
website: www.domaine-imbours.com
In wooded surroundings with a variety of recreational facilities.
Access via N86 and D4.
Open: 26 Mar-Oct **Site:** 45HEC **Prices:** 4-5.50 pitch 23 (incl 3 persons) **Facilities:** **Services:** lau **Leisure:** P

Rochecondrie Loisirs 07220 475527466 475527466
e-mail: campingrochecondrie@wanadoo.fr
website: www.campingrochecondrie.com
A level site with good facilities beside the River L'Escoutay.
N of town on N86.
Open: Apr-15 Oct **Site:** 1.8HEC **Prices:** pitch 10-17.30 (incl 2 persons) (static)230-490 **Facilities:** **Services:** lau **Leisure:** PR **Off-site:**

VOGÜÉ ARDÈCHE

Domaine du Cros d'Auzon Hotellerie de Plein Air, 7200
475377586 475370102
e-mail: cros.d.auzon@wanadoo.fr
website: www.guideweb.com/ardeche/camping/cros-auzon
In wooded surroundings close to the Gorges de l'Ardèche with good recreational facilities.
2.5km via D579 bordering the river.
Open: 15 Apr-15 Sep **Site:** 20HEC **Facilities:** **Services:** lau **Leisure:** PR **Off-site:** LS

VOLONNE ALPES-DE-HAUTE-PROVENCE

Hippocampe rte Napoléon, 4290
492335000 492335049
e-mail: camping@l.hippocampe.com
website: www.l-hippocampe.com
Several strips of land, interspersed with trees, and running down the edge of lake. Surrounded by fields and gardens.
On S edge of town. 2km E of N85.
Open: 25 Mar-Sep **Site:** 8HEC **Prices:** pitch 13-39 (incl 2 persons) (static)203-889 **Facilities:** **Services:** lau **Leisure:** P

CORSICA

ALÉRIA HAUTE-CORSE

Marina d'Aléria rte de la Mer, 20270
495570142 495570429
e-mail: info@marina-aleria.com
website: www.marina-aleria.com
3km E of Cateraggio via RN200.
Open: 15 Apr-15 Oct **Site:** 10HEC
Prices: 5.40-7.60 2.40-3 2.50-3 1.90-2.40
Facilities: **Services:** lau **Leisure:** S

BONIFACIO CORSE-DU-SUD

Rondinara Suartone, 20169 495704315 495705679
e-mail: reception@rondinara.fr **website:** www.rondinara.fr
In a beautiful situation 300m from the beach with modern facilities and fine opportunities for water sports.
Midway between Porto-Vecchio and Bonifacio on N198 in the direction of Suartone-La Rondinara.
Open: 15 May-Sep **Site:** 6HEC **Prices:** 5-6.50 2.50-3 3-3.70 2.50-3 **Facilities:** **Services:** lau **Leisure:** PS

CALVI HAUTE-CORSE

Dolce Vita Ponte Bambino, 20260
495650599 0495653125
website: www.dolce-vita-org
In extensive woodland with well-defined pitches and good, modern facilities.
4km SW of Calvi between N197 to L'Ile Rousse & the sea.
Open: May-Sep **Site:** 6HEC **Prices:** 7.60 2.60 3.80 2.60 (static)406 **Facilities:** **Services:** lau **Leisure:** RS

CARGESE CORSE-DU-SUD

Torraccia Bagghiuccia, 20130 495264239 495264239
e-mail: contact@camping-torraccia.com
website: www.camping-torraccia.com
Terraced site close to the Chiuni and Pero beaches and backed by some fine mountain scenery.
4km N on N199.
Open: May-Sep **Site:** 3.5HEC **Prices:** 5-6 2-2.50 2.30-2.80 2-2.50 **Facilities:** **Services:** lau **Off-site:** S

CENTURI HAUTE-CORSE

Isulottu 20238 495356281
A peaceful, shady site, 200m from the beach.
1km from Centuri-Port towards Morsiglia.
Site: 3HEC **Facilities:** **Services:** lau **Off-site:** S

GALÉRIA HAUTE-CORSE

Deux Torrents 20245 495620067 495620332
e-mail: 2torrents@corsica-net.com
website: www.2torrents.corsica_net.com
A spacious, well-equipped site nestling between two torrents at the foot of the mountains.
5km E on D51 towards Calenzana.
Open: Jun-Sep **Site:** 6.3HEC **Prices:** 4.95 2.70 4.40 2.70 (static)280 **Facilities:** **Services:** lau **Off-site:** R

GHISONACCIA HAUTE-CORSE

Arinella-Bianca Arinella-Bianca, 20240
495560478 495561254
e-mail: arinella@arinellabianca.com
website: www.arinellabianca.com
In wooded surroundings, directly on the beach with good recreational facilities.
Open: 16 Apr-15 Oct **Site:** 9HEC **Prices:** pitch 19-33 (incl 2 persons) pp6.50-9 (static)240-770 **Facilities:** **Services:** lau **Leisure:** PRS

LOZARI HAUTE-CORSE

Clos des Chênes rte de Belgodère, 20226
495601513 495602116
e-mail: cdc.lozari@wanadoo.fr
website: www.closdeschenes.fr
In a delightful wooded setting, 1km from a fine sandy beach.
1.5km S via N197 towards Belgodère.
Open: Etr-end Sep **Site:** 5.5HEC **Facilities:** **Services:** lau **Leisure:** P **Off-site:** S

LUMIO HAUTE-CORSE

Panoramic rte de Lavataggio 1, 20260
495607313 493991932
Very clean and tidy site divided into pitches.
From Calvi, 12km on N197, 200m from main road.
Open: Jun-15 Sep **Site:** 6HEC **Facilities:** **Services:** lau **Leisure:** P **Off-site:** S

Facilities: -shop -shower -electric points for razors -electric points for caravans -parking by tents permitted -compulsory separate car park **Services:** -café/restaurant -bar -Camping Gaz International -gas other than Camping Gaz -first aid facilities lau-laundry **Leisure:** -swimming L-Lake P-Pool R-River S-Sea **Off-site:** All facilities within 2km

Olmeto-Plage Corse-du-Sud

Esplanade 20113 495760503 495761622
e-mail: campinglesplanada@clubinternet.fr
website: www.camping-esplanade.com
In a pleasant natural park, 100m from the sea.
Open: Apr-Oct **Site:** 4.8HEC **Prices:** 5-6.50 2-3 3-4 2.50-3.50 pitch 2.50-3.50 (static)200-455
Facilities: **Services:** lau
Leisure: PS **Off-site:** R

Pianottoli Corse-du-Sud

Kevano Plage Plage de Kevano, 20131
495718322 495718383
In a beautiful setting in the middle of woodland with modern facilities, 400m from the beach.
Open: May-Sep **Site:** 6HEC **Facilities:**
Services: lau **Off-site:** S

Pisciatello Corse-du-Sud

Benista 20166 495251930 495259370
e-mail: camping.benista@worldonline.fr
website: www.benista.com
In a beautiful wooded setting, 5 minutes from the local beaches. Pitches are divided by hedges and there are good sporting facilities.
Open: Apr-Oct **Site:** 5HEC **Prices:** pitch 18-22 (incl 2 persons) (static)210-390 **Facilities:** **Services:** lau **Leisure:** PR **Off-site:** S

Porto-Vecchio Corse-du-Sud

Pirellu rte de Palombaggia, 20137
495702344 495706022
e-mail: u-pirellu@wanadoo.fr
website: www.u-pirellu.com/camping.htm
A modern site situated in an oak grove 300m from the beach.
S of Porto-Vecchio, take road for Bonifacio. After Pont du Stabiacco take first road on the left.
Open: Apr-Sep **Site:** 2.5HEC **Prices:** 5.40-7.70 2.40-3.05 3.30-4 2.40-3.05 **Facilities:** **Services:** lau **Leisure:** P

Vetta rte de Bastia, 20137 495700986 495704321
e-mail: info@campinglavetta.com
website: www.campinglavetta.com
In natural parkland with good, modern facilities 3km from the sea.
5.5km N on N198.
Open: 15 May-15 Oct **Site:** 8HEC **Prices:** 6-7 2 2.50-3 2.50-3 pitch 2.50-3 **Facilities:** **Services:** lau **Leisure:** P **Off-site:** S

St-Florent Haute-Corse

U Pezzo chemin de la Plage, 20217
495370165 495370165
e-mail: contact@upezzo.com
website: www.upezzo.com
Pleasant site; partly level, partly terraced under eucalyptus trees. Private access to large beach.
S of town on road to beach.
Open: Apr-15 Oct **Site:** 2HEC **Prices:** 4.25-4.50 2.25-2.50 3.25-3.50 2.25-3.50 pitch 2.25-2.50
Facilities: **Services:** lau **Leisure:** S
Off-site: R

Sotta Corse-du-Sud

U Moru 20114 495712340 495712619
e-mail: u-moru@wanadoo.fr
A quiet family site 5 minutes from the beach.
4km SW via D859.
Open: 15 Jun-15 Sep **Site:** 6HEC **Prices:** 6.30 2.20 3.40 2.50 pitch 2.50 (static)360 **Facilities:** **Services:** lau **Leisure:** P

Tiuccia Corse-du-Sud

Couchants rte de Casaglione, 20111
495522660 495593177
e-mail: camping.les-couchants@wanadoo.fr
In a quiet location facing the vast Sagone bay and close to the River Liamone.
3km from the sea.
Open: All year **Site:** 5HEC **Prices:** 5.50-6 2.50-3.50 4-5 2.50-3.50 (static)228-280
Facilities: **Services:** lau **Off-site:** RS

GERMANY

Germany is a country of contrasts, an economic giant that offers a mix of fairytale castles, ancient towns, enormous forests and bustling modern cities.

FACTS AND FIGURES
Area: 357,022 sq km (137,846 sq miles)
Population: 83,251,851 (2002 est)
Capital: Berlin
Language: German
IDD code: 49
To call the UK, dial 00 44.
Currency: Euro
Local time: GMT + 1 (summer GMT + 2)
Emergency services: Fire and Ambulance 112; Police 110.
Banks: Mon-Wed, Fri 0830-1230, 1330-1530, Thu 0830-1230, 1330-1730. Approximate times - there are no uniform banking hours.
Shops: Mon-Fri 0900-2000, Sat 0900-1600 (city shops).
Average daily temperatures: Munich

Jan	2°C	Mar	4°C
May	13°C	Jul	18°C
Sep	15°C	Nov	3°C

Tourist information:
National Tourist Office
UK
PO Box 2695
London W1A 3TN
Tel (020) 7317 0908 (premium rate info line 09001 600100)
USA
52nd Floor, 122 East 42nd Street,
New York NY10168
Tel (212) 661-7174.
Tourist website:
www.germany-tourism.de

Germany is bordered by nine countries: Austria, Belgium, the Czech Republic, Denmark, France, Luxembourg, the Netherlands, Poland and Switzerland. The Rhine Valley has magnificent cliffs and woods, while the Black Forest has some fine scenery with countless waterfalls and gorges. The climate is temperate and variable but Germany has hotter summers than Britain.

Permission to camp off-site, away from an official campsite, must be obtained from the landowner or local police. Overnight parking at parking places is tolerated for one night, unless otherwise indicated, provided nearby campsites and hotels are fully booked. However, make sure you do not contravene local regulations.

HOW TO GET THERE

For western Germany use Eurotunnel or one of the short Channel crossings and travel via Belgium.

For northern Germany take a direct ferry from **Harwich** to **Cuxhaven** (minimum sailing time 16hrs 45mins) or one of the North Sea crossings to the Netherlands.

For southern Germany use Eurotunnel or one of the short Channel crossings and drive through northern France, entering Germany near **Strasbourg**. This is also the route if using the longer Channel crossings to Caen (Ouistreham), Cherbourg, Dieppe or Le Havre.

Distance

From the Continental Channel ports, Köln (Cologne) is about 414km (257 miles) and a comfortable 1-day drive; routes to southern and eastern Germany usually require one or two overnight stops.

MOTORING & GENERAL

The information given here is specific to Germany. It **must** be read in conjunction with the Essential Information for Motoring section, which covers regulations that are common to many countries.

British Embassy/Consulates*

The British Embassy, together with its consular section, is located at 10117 Berlin, Wilhelmstrasse 70 ☎ (030) 20457-0. There are British consulates in Düsseldorf, Frankfurt am Main, Hamburg, München (Munich) and Stuttgart; there are British consulates with Honorary Consuls in Bremen, Hanover, Kiel and Nürnberg (Nuremburg).

Children in Cars

Children under 12 and/or 1.5 metres in height are not permitted to travel as front- or rear-seat passengers unless using a suitable restraint system, if fitted. See Essential Information for Motoring section under **Passengers** and **Seat Belts**.

Currency*

The **euro** is the currency of Germany. The Deutsche Mark (DEM) ceased to be legal tender in 2002, though DEM coins and notes can be exchanged at the German Central Bank (Deutsche Bundesbank) for an unlimited period.

Dimensions & Weight Restrictions*

Private **cars** and **trailers** or **caravans** are restricted to the following dimensions - height 4 metres; width 2.55 metres; length 12 metres. The maximum permitted overall length of vehicle/trailer or caravan combinations is 18 metres. A fully laden trailer without brakes may have a total maximum weight of 750kg.

Driving Licence*

A valid UK or Republic of Ireland licence is accepted in Germany. The minimum age at which visitors from UK or Republic of Ireland may use a temporarily imported car or motorcycle is 17.

First-aid Kit*

The German authorities recommend that visiting motorists carry a first-aid kit in their vehicles.

Foodstuffs*

If the imported foodstuff are for personal use, there are no limits when travelling between EU countries. Visitors entering Germany from outside the EU may import up to 1kg of meat and meat products and up to 30kg of game and poultry.

The importation of meat products and sheep and goat's cheese from the CIS, Turkey and all African and Asian countries is prohibited. Coffee (500g) and coffee extract (200g) are free of customs duties, but visitors under 15 cannot import coffee.

Lights*

It is compulsory for motorcyclists to use dipped headlights during the day.

Motoring Club

The principal motoring club is the **Allgemeiner Deutscher Automobil Club e.V.** (ADAC) based at 81373 München, Am Westpark 8 ☎ (089) 7676-0. It has offices in the larger towns, and office hours are Mon-Fri 08.00-17.00. ADAC also has offices at major frontier crossings.

Website: **www.adac.de**

Roads

Germany has a comprehensive motorway (*Autobahn*) network, which takes most of the long-distance traffic. Emergency telephones are sited every 2km, the direction of the nearest telephone is indicated by the point of the black triangle on posts alongside the motorway.

The *Bundesstrassen*, or state roads, vary in quality. In the north and west, and in the touring Rhine Valley, Black Forest, and Bavaria, the roads are good and well-graded.

Traffic at weekends increases considerably during the school holidays from July to mid-

Castle at Schwerin

Konigssee at Berchtesgaden

September. In order to ease congestion, lorries of more than 7,500kg and lorries towing trailers are subject to restrictions. On all Saturdays from 1 July to 31 August such vehicles are not allowed on state roads or motorways from 07.00-20.00, and generally on all Sundays and public holidays from 00.01-22.00.

Speed limits*

Car/motorcycle

Built-up areas	50km/h (31mph)
Other roads	100km/h (62mph)
Motorways	130km/h (80mph)

Car/caravan/trailer

Built-up areas	50km/h (31mph)
Other roads	80km/h (49mph)
Motorways/ dual-carriageways	80km/h (49mph)

Outside built-up areas, vehicles to which a special speed limit applies, as well as vehicles with trailers with a combined length of more than 7 metres (23ft), must keep sufficient distance from the preceding vehicle so that an overtaking vehicle may pull in. Anyone driving so slowly that a line of vehicles has formed behind must permit the following vehicles to pass, by stopping at a suitable place if necessary.

Warning triangle*

Although it is not compulsory for visiting motorists to carry a warning triangle in their vehicles, its use is compulsory in the event of accident or breakdown. The triangle must be placed on the road behind the vehicle to warn following traffic of any obstruction: 100 metres (109yds) on ordinary roads and 150 metres (164yds) on motorways.

***Additional information can be found in the Essential Information for Motoring section.**

SOUTH-EAST

AACH BEI OBERSTAUFEN BAYERN

Aach 87534 08386 363 08386 961721
e-mail: camping-aach@t-online.de
website: www.camping-aach.de
A terraced site with beautiful views of the mountains. Sauna, solarium, games room.
From Oberstaufen follow B308 for 7km towards the Austrian border.
Open: All year **Site:** 2.5HEC **Facilities:** **Services:** lau **Leisure:** P **Off-site:** R

AITRANG BAYERN

Elbsee 3 Am Elbsee 3, 87648 08343 248 08343 929378
e-mail: info@elbsee.de
website: www.elbsee.de
On the E shore of the lake with good bathing facilities. Section reserved for campers with dogs.
Take B12 from Marktoberdorf travel for 11km then turn N to Aitrang.
Open: All year **Site:** 3.5HEC **Facilities:** **Services:** lau **Leisure:** L **Off-site:** P

ARLACHING BAYERN

Kupferschmiede Trostberger Str 4, 83339
08667 446 08667 16198
e-mail: campingkupfer@aol.com
website: campingkupferschmiede.de
On meadowland. Partially gravel.
On Seebruck-Traunstein road.
Open: Apr-Oct **Site:** 2.5HEC **Prices:** 4.95-5.50 1.50 4 3-4 **Facilities:** **Services:** lau **Leisure:** L **Off-site:** PR

AUGSBURG BAYERN

Augusta Mühlhauser Str 54B, 86169
0821 707575 0821 705883
e-mail: webmaster@campingplatzaugusta.de
website: www.campingplatz-augusta.de
Hard standings for caravans. Separate section for residential caravans.
Leave E11 by Augsburg-Ost exit. Continue N towards Neuburg & turn right after 400m.
Open: All year **Site:** 6.6HEC **Facilities:** **Services:** **Leisure:** L **Off-site:**

BAMBERG BAYERN
AT BUG (5KM S)

Insel 96049 0951 56320 0951 56321
e-mail: campinginsel@web.de
website: www.campinginsel.de
The site lies on the bank of the River Regnitz, S of Bamberg. Park and ride scheme into Bamberg.
Leave A73 at Bamberg S exit & follow B505/B4 towards Bamberg until camping signs leading off left.
Open: All year **Site:** 5HEC **Prices:** 4.20 pitch 6.70 **Facilities:** **Services:** lau **Leisure:** R

BERCHTESGADEN BAYERN

Allwegiehen 83471 08652 2396 08652 63503
e-mail: info@alpen-camping-allweg.de
website: www.alpen-camping-allweg.de
A terraced site at the foot of the Untersalzberg mountain surrounded by bushy woods. There is also a steep and narrow asphalt access road with passing places. A truck is available for towing caravans. The camp is closed 12.30-14.30, and from 21.00.
B305 3.5km towards Schellenberg.
Open: All year **Site:** 4HEC **Prices:** 5.40 pitch 8.50 **Facilities:** **Services:** lau **Leisure:** P **Off-site:** R

BERGEN BAYERN

Wagnerhof Campingstr 11, 83346 08662 8557
e-mail: info@camping-bergen.de
website: www.camping-bergen.de
Level site.
Camping Card Compulsory
Access from München-Salzburg motorway, Bergen exit. Turn right at sawmill just before entering town.
Open: All year **Site:** 2.8HEC **Facilities:** **Off-site:** LP

BRUNNEN FORGGENSEE BAYERN

Brunnen Seestr 81, 87645 08362 8273 08362 8630
e-mail: info@camping-brunnen.de
website: www.camping-brunnen.de
Situated on E shore of lake Forggensee.
From Füssen follow B17 to Schwangau, then N on minor road.
Open: 21 Dec-2 Nov **Site:** 6HEC **Prices:** 6-7 pitch 4-8 **Facilities:** **Services:** lau **Leisure:** L **Off-site:** P

CHIEMING BAYERN

Chieming Möwenplatz Haupstr 3, 83335 08664 361
Small site on shore of lake, with gravelly terrain.
Camping Card Compulsory
5km S of Chieming.
Open: Apr-Sep **Site:** 0.8HEC **Facilities:** **Services:** lau **Leisure:** L **Off-site:** P

DIESSEN BAYERN

St-Alban 86911 08807 7305 08807 1057
e-mail: ivan.pavic@t-online.de
website: www.camping-ammersee.de
Clean site next to St-Alban, lakeside with private bathing beach and reserved section for residential campers. Good sanitary installations also used by the public.
From München follow B12 towards Landsberg/Lech. Near Greifenberg turn left, proceed via Utting to St-Alban.
Open: Apr-Oct **Site:** 3.8HEC **Prices:** 6 pitch 9 **Facilities:** **Services:** **Leisure:** L **Off-site:**

DINKELSBÜHL BAYERN

Romantische Strasse 91550 09851 7817 09851 7848
e-mail: campdinkelsbuhl@aol.de
Terraced site with some hedges and trees. Separate field for young people. Good sporting facilities.
Signed.
Open: All year **Site:** 12HEC **Facilities:** **Services:** lau **Leisure:** L **Off-site:**

ENDORF, BAD BAYERN

Stein Hintersee 10, 83093 08053 9349 08053 798745
A family site in wooded surroundings on the shore of the Simsee.
Open: 15 May-15 Sep **Site:** 2.5HEC **Prices:** 4.50 2 4.50 4.50 **Facilities:** **Services:** lau **Leisure:** L **Off-site:**

ERLANGEN BAYERN

Rangau Campingstr 44, 91056
091351 8866 091351 724743
e-mail: info@camping-rangau.de
website: www.camping-rangau.de
Long stretch of land behind the sports ground and next to the Dechsendorfer Weiher lake in nature reserve.
Leave motorway (A3/E5 Nürnberg-Würzburg) at exit Erlangen-West.
Open: Apr-Sep **Site:** 18HEC **Prices:** 4.50 pitch 4.50 **Facilities:** **Services:** lau **Off-site:** L

ESCHERNDORF BAYERN

Escherndorf-Main 97332 09381 2889 09381 2889
e-mail: info@campingplatz-mainschleife.de
website: www.camplingplatz-escherndorf.de
Site lies on meadowland by the River Main, next to the ferry station (Northeim). Siesta 13.00-15.00.
From motorway A7/E70 exit Würzburg Estenfeld & follow road E towards Volkach.
Open: Apr-Oct **Site:** 1.5HEC **Prices:** 5.50 5 4 **Facilities:** **Services:** lau **Leisure:** PR

ESTENFELD BAYERN

Estenfeld Maidbronner Str 38, 97230
09305 228 09305 8006
e-mail: cplestenfeld@freenet.de
website: www.camping-estenfeld.de
On meadowland next to sports ground.
From motorway A7/E70 leave at exit Würzburg/Estenfeld & S on B19 for 1km.
Open: Mar-23 Dec **Site:** 0.5HEC **Prices:** 4.50 pitch 4 (static)130-380 **Facilities:** **Services:** lau **Off-site:**

FEILNBACH, BAD BAYERN

Tenda Reithof 2, 83075 08066 533 08066 8002
e-mail: info@tenda-camping.de
website: www.tenda-camping.de
Well organised site on level grassland with pitches laid out in circles and hardstandings for tourers near the entrance.
Camping Card Compulsory
Leave München-Salzburg motorway A8/E11 at Bad Aibling exit & S for 4km on minor road.
Open: All year **Site:** 14HEC **Prices:** 4.50-5.50 1.90-7 1.25-3.50 pitch 1.90-7 **Facilities:** **Services:** lau **Leisure:** P **Off-site:** L

FICHTELBERG BAYERN

Fichtelsee 95686 09272 801 09272 909045
e-mail: info@camping-fichtelsee.de
website: www.camping-fichtelsee.de
Gently sloping meadow amid pleasant woodland 100m from lake Fichtelsee.
From A9/E6 Bad Berneck exit, take B303 to the Fichtelsee Leisure Centre turning.
Open: 15 Dec-06 Nov **Site:** 2.6HEC **Prices:** 4.50-5.50 pitch 5-7 **Facilities:** **Services:** lau **Off-site:** LP

FINSTERAU BAYERN

Nationalpark-Ost 94151 08557 768 08557 1062
e-mail: 085571062@t-online.de
website: www.camping-nationalpark-ost.de
Terraced site on edge of extensive woodland area at entrance to national park.
N of Freyung towards the frontier.
Open: All year **Site:** 3HEC **Prices:** 4.60 pitch 5 **Facilities:** **Services:** lau **Off-site:**

FRICKENHAUSEN BAYERN

KNAUS Camping Park Frickenhausen Ochsenfurter Strabe 49, 97252 09331 3171 09331 5784
e-mail: knauscamp.frickenhausen@freenet.de
website: www.knauscamp.de
On level meadow in a small poplar wood beside River Main. Siesta 13.00-15.00.
On N bank of Main 0.5km E of Oshsenfurt.
Open: Jan-Oct & Dec **Site:** 3.4HEC **Prices:** 6 8 pitch 6-8 **Facilities:** **Services:** **Leisure:** PR **Off-site:**

FÜRTH IM WALD BAYERN

Einberg Daberger Str 33, 93437
09973 1811 09973 803220
e-mail: camping@stadtwerke-furth.de
website: www.stadtwerke-furth.de
Municipal site in Dabergerstr, near swimming pool.
NE of Cham on B20.
Open: Mar-Oct **Site:** 2HEC **Prices:** 3.90 2.60 3.10 2 **Facilities:** **Services:** lau **Leisure:** R **Off-site:** P

FÜSSEN BAYERN

Hopfensee 87629 08362 917710 08362 917720
e-mail: info@camping-hopfensee.com
website: www.camping-hopfensee.com
In quiet situation beside lake. Private beach. Skiing lessons.
4km N of Füssen.
Open: 18 Dec-6 Nov **Site:** 8HEC **Prices:** 7.80-8.90 pitch 11.55-12.80 **Facilities:** **Services:** lau **Leisure:** LP

FÜSSING, BAD BAYERN

Max I Falkenstr 12, Egglfing, 94072
08537 96170 08537 961710
e-mail: info@campingmax.de **website:** www.campingmax.de
On a level meadow with some trees. Good modern facilities.
Access via B12. Site S of Bad Füssing.
Open: All year **Site:** 3HEC **Prices:** 4.70 4 pitch 5.95 **Facilities:** **Services:** lau **Leisure:** P **Off-site:**

Max II 94072 08537 356 08537 356
e-mail: campingmax2@aol.com
website: www.camping-max2.de
On meadow divided into pitches and 1km from spa baths at Bad Füssing.
Turn at Passau end of Tutling on B12 to Kircham then follow signs to site on Egglfinger Strasse, 2km from Bad Füssing.
Open: All year **Site:** 1.5HEC **Prices:** 4.50 4 pitch 5.50 **Facilities:** **Services:** lau **Off-site:** PR

GADEN BAYERN

Schwanenplatz Schwanenpl 1, 83329
08681 281 08681 4276
e-mail: info@schwanenplatz.de
website: www.schwanenplatz.de
Site lies on a meadow, divided into sections beside one of Bavaria's warmest lakes, Waginger See.
Traunstein to Waging, then turn right towards Freilassing 2km, then left to lake.
Open: Apr-20 Oct **Site:** 4HEC **Prices:** 4.80-5.95 pitch 5.70-6 (static)280-280 **Facilities:** **Services:** lau **Leisure:** LR **Off-site:**

Facilities: -shop -shower -electric points for razors -electric points for caravans -parking by tents permitted -compulsory separate car park **Services:** -café/restaurant -bar -Camping Gaz International -gas other than Camping Gaz -first aid facilities lau-laundry **Leisure:** -swimming L-Lake P-Pool R-River S-Sea **Off-site:** All facilities within 2km

GARMISCH-PARTENKIRCHEN BAYERN

Zugspitze Griesener Str 4, 82491
08821 3180 08821 947594
In beautiful setting at the foot of the Zugspitze between the road and the Loisach.
On the B24 towards the Austrian frontier.
Open: All year **Site:** 2.9HEC **Facilities:** **Services:** lau **Leisure:** R **Off-site:** LP

GEMÜNDEN AM MAIN BAYERN

Saaleinsel Duivenallee 7, 97737 09351 8574
This municipal site lies a short distance off the main road bordering the River Fränkische Saale. It is in the grounds of a sports field and has a swimming pool. Individual washing cubicles with curtains for females.
Access signed off main B26 road.
Open: Apr-15 Oct **Site:** 5.1HEC **Facilities:** **Services:** **Leisure:** PR **Off-site:**

GEMÜNDEN-HOFSTETTEN BAYERN

Schönrain 97737 09351 8645 09351 8721
e-mail: info@spessart-camping.de
website: www.spessart-camping.de
Slightly sloping, partly terraced meadowland E of River Main. Siesta 13.00-15.00.
From Gemünden/Main along the left bank of the River Main about 3km downstream. Turn left of B26 through Hofstetten to site.
Open: 19 Apr-3 Oct **Site:** 7HEC **Prices:** 5-5.70 pitch 6.70-7.90 **Facilities:** **Services:** lau **Leisure:** P

GOTTSDORF BAYERN

DUG-Ferienzentrum Bayerwald Mitterweg 11, Untergriesbach, 94107
08593 880 08593 88111
Extensive terrain in quiet location.
Access via A3 Regensburg-Passau & B388.
Open: 27 Mar-30 Oct **Site:** 12HEC **Facilities:** **Services:** lau **Off-site:** LPR

GRIESBACH, BAD BAYERN

Kur-Und Feriencamping Dreiquellenbad 94086
08532 96130 08532 961350
e-mail: info@camping-bad-griesbach.de
website: www.camping-bad-griesbach.de
In pleasant wooded surroundings with good, modern facilities.
1km S of Griesbach Spa, on Karpfham-Schwaim road.
Open: All year **Site:** 3.7HEC **Prices:** 4.90 8.30-9.30 pp3.40 **Facilities:** **Services:** lau **Leisure:** P **Off-site:** RS

HASLACH BAYERN

Feriencenter Wertacher Hof 87466
08361 770 08361 9344
Well-kept site on lake Grüntensee.
Access road near the Wertach-Haslach railway station.
Open: All year **Site:** 3.5HEC **Prices:** 5.50 pitch 5 **Facilities:** **Services:** lau **Leisure:** L

HERSBRUCK BAYERN
AT HOHENSTADT (6KM E)

Pegnitz Eschenbacher Weg 4, 91224
09154 1500 09154 91200
A quiet holiday site in set among wooded hills near the River Pegnitz.
About 6km E of Hersbruck.
Open: Mar-Oct **Site:** 1.1HEC **Facilities:** **Services:** lau **Leisure:** R **Off-site:** LP

HOFHEIM BAYERN

Brugger am Riegsee 82418 08847 728 08847 228
e-mail: camping.brugger@t-online.de
A lakeside site in a rural setting with good, modern facilities.
Open: May-Sep **Site:** 6HEC **Prices:** 4.50 pitch 8-14 **Facilities:** **Services:** lau **Leisure:** L

HOHENWARTH BAYERN

Fritz-Berger-Comfort 93480 09946 367 477
e-mail: cpl.hohenwarth@fritz-berger.de
Meadowland in the valley of the Weissens Regens with views of the mountain range and town above.
Access from Cham on the B85 S to Miltach & continue via Kotzing to Hohenwarth.
Site: 12HEC **Facilities:** **Services:** **Leisure:** LP

INGOLSTADT BAYERN

AZUR Camping Auwaldsee 85053 0841 9611616 0841 9611617
Near to Auwaldsee, this site lies in a beautiful setting beside the München-Ingolstadt motorway.
Access via the Ingolstadt-Süd exit off the A9/E6 Mücher-Nürnberg motorway.
Open: All year **Site:** 10HEC **Facilities:** **Services:** lau **Leisure:** L **Off-site:** P

ISSIGAU BAYERN

Schloss Issigau Altes Schloss 3, 95188
09293 7173 09293 7050
e-mail: schloss_issigau@t.online.de
website: www.schloss-issigau.de
About 5km W off A9/E6 München-Berlin road via the Berg/Bad Steben exit.
Open: 15 Mar-Oct **Site:** 2HEC **Prices:** 4.50 6 5 pitch 6 (static)266 **Facilities:** **Services:** lau **Off-site:**

JODITZ BAYERN

Auensee 95189 09295 381 09281 1706666
e-mail: koeditz@landkreis-hof.de
website: www.gemeinde-koeditz.de
Municipal site on partly terraced meadowland above lake.
Leave München-Berlin motorway at Berg-Bad Steben exit & E for 4km.
Open: All year **Site:** 9HEC **Prices:** 4 2 8 3-5 **Facilities:** **Services:** lau **Leisure:** L **Off-site:** P

KIPFENBERG BAYERN

AZUR-Camping Altmühltal Campingstr, 85110
08465 905167 08465 3745
e-mail: kipfenberg@azur-camping.de
website: www.azur-camping.de/kipfenberg
Well equipped site in an unspoiled wooded location with good canoeing facilities.
Open: Apr-Oct **Site:** 5.5HEC **Facilities:** **Services:** lau **Leisure:** R **Off-site:** P

KIRCHZELL BAYERN

AZUR-Camping Odenwald 63931
09373 566 09373 7375
e-mail: kirchzell@azur-camping.de
website: www.azur-camping.de
In natural terraced meadowland in wooded hilly country. No admission after 21.30. Siesta 13.00-15.00.
From Amorbach follow Eberbach road for 5km. Site 1km from town.
Open: Apr-Oct **Site:** 7HEC **Prices:** person 5-6.50 4-4.70 pitch 6.50-7.50 **Facilities:** **Services:** lau
Leisure: P

KISSINGEN, BAD BAYERN

Bad Kissingen Euerdorfer Str 1, D-97688
0971 5211 0971 5211
e-mail: info@campingpark-badkissingen.de
website: www.campingpark-badkissingen.de
In park beside River Saale. Siesta 13.00-15.00hrs.
Access near the southern bridge over the Saale.
Open: Apr-15 Oct **Site:** 1.8HEC **Prices:** person 5 4.50 pitch 6.50 **Facilities:** **Services:** lau
Off-site: P

KITZINGEN BAYERN

Schiefer Turm Marktbreiter Str 20, 97318
09321 33125 09321 384795
e-mail: chr.schroeder@t-online.de
Access via A3 exit Biebelried/Kitzingen.
Open: Apr-15 Oct **Site:** 2.3HEC **Facilities:** **Services:** lau **Leisure:** R **Off-site:** P

KLINGENBRUNN BAYERN

NationalPark 94518 08553 727 08553 6930
website: www.camping-nationalpark.de
In pleasant wooded surroundings attractively set out around the restaurant building.
Leave the B85, which turns from Cham to Passau, 12km SE of Regen near Kirchdorf turn off E & drive 6km towards Klingenbrunn.
Open: All year **Site:** 5HEC **Prices:** person 3.60 3.30 pitch 4.10 **Facilities:** **Services:** lau
Off-site: LP

KÖNIGSDORF BAYERN

Königsdorf Am Bibisee, 82549
08171 81580 08171 81165
e-mail: mail@camping-koenigsdorf.de
website: www.camping-koenigsdorf.de
Unspoiled site in natural setting in meadowland. A number of individual pitches for tourers. Siesta 12.30-14.30.
Off B11, 2km N of town just beyond the edge of the forest.
Open: All year **Site:** 8.6HEC **Facilities:** **Services:** lau **Leisure:** L **Off-site:** PRS

KÖNIGSSEE BAYERN

Mühlleiten 83477 08652 4584 08652 69194
e-mail: buchung@camping-muehlleiten.de
website: www.camping-muehlleiten.de
A pleasant site in wooded surroundings adjacent to a small guesthouse. Beautiful views of the Berchtesgaden mountains.
N of Königsee towards Berchtesgaden.
Open: All year **Site:** 1.5HEC **Facilities:** **Services:** lau **Leisure:** R **Off-site:** LP

KRUN BAYERN

Tennsee 82493 08825 170 08825 17236
e-mail: info@camping-tennsee.de
website: www.camping-tennsee.de
A partially terraced site with fine views of the Karwendel and Zugspitz mountains.
From München-Garmisch-Partenkirchen motorway take B2 to Mittenwald and follow signs 'Tennsee'.
Open: 15 Dec-06 Nov **Site:** 5HEC **Prices:** person 9.50 pitch 17.50-20.50 (incl 2 persons) **Facilities:** **Services:** lau **Off-site:** L

KÜHNHAUSEN BAYERN

Stadler Strandbadstr 11, 83367
08686 8037 08685 919555
Level meadow on lake with private beach.
2m E shore of Lake Waginger.
Open: Apr-Sep **Site:** 0.8HEC **Facilities:** **Services:** lau **Leisure:** L **Off-site:**

LACKENHÄUSER BAYERN

KNAUS Lackenhäuser Lackenhauser 127, 94089
08583 311 08583 91079
e-mail: knaus-camping-lackenhaeuser@t-online.de
website: www.knauscamp.de
Extensive site with woodland parks, waterfalls. Siesta 13.00-15.00. Many health resort facilities. Garden chess. Curling.
Open: Dec-Oct **Site:** 14.5HEC **Prices:** person 6 8 pitch 4-8 **Facilities:** **Services:**
Leisure: LP **Off-site:**

LANGLAU BAYERN

Langlau Seestr 30, Kleiner Brombachsee, 91738
09834 96969 09834 96968
e-mail: mail@seecamping-langlau.de
website: www.seecamping-langlau.de
On the shores of the Kleiner Brombachsee.
From Gunzevhausen 10km in the direction of Pleinfield.
Open: Mar-15 Nov **Site:** 12.4HEC **Prices:** person 6 pitch 7 (static)180 **Facilities:** **Services:** lau
Off-site: L

LECHBRUCK BAYERN

DCC Stadt Essen Oberer Lechsee, 8923
08862 8426 08862 7570
Terraced site, very tidy and well maintained on Oberen Lech lake. Separate section for dog owners. Closed 13.00-15.00, 22.00-07.00.
Signed from town centre.
Open: All year **Site:** 20HEC **Facilities:**
Services: lau **Leisure:** L **Off-site:** P

LENGFURT BAYERN

Main-Spessart-Park 97855 09395 1079 09395 8295
e-mail: info@camping-main-spessart.de
website: www.camping-main-spessart.de
Site lies partly on terraced meadowland and partly on the E slopes of the Main valley. Siesta 13.00-15.00. Possibilities for water sports, nearby private mooring on the River Main.
From Frankfurt-Würzburg motorway A3/E5 leave at exit Markheidenfeld. N to Altfled then E for 6km to Lengfurt. Site at NW edge of village.
Open: All year **Site:** 10HEC **Prices:** person 5 car 2 caravan 3.50 3 **Facilities:** **Services:** lau
Off-site: PR

LINDAU IM BODENSEE BAYERN

Gitzenweiler Hof 88131 838294940 8382949415
e-mail: info@gitzenweiler-hof.de
website: www.gitzenweiler-hof.de
Located in hilly meadow ground near lake Constance surrounded with trees and hedges.
A96 Autobahn Memmingen-Bregenz, exit Weissensberg.
Open: All year **Site:** 14HEC **Prices:** 6.50 2 6-8 pitch 8 (static)600-800 **Facilities:** **Services:** lau **Leisure:** P

AT ZECH (4KM SE)

Lindau am See Fraunhoferstr 20, 88131
08382 72236 08382 976106
e-mail: info@park-camping.de
website: www.park-camping.de
Site lies on meadowland with trees, reaching down to the lake. Very large sanitary blocks. Common room, reading room, field for ball games and a separate common room for young people.
From Lindau, take the B31 towards Bregenz and turn right (signed) just before the level crossing. Site 500m down the road.
Open: All year **Site:** 5HEC **Prices:** 5-6 2.40-3 1.50-2.50 pitch 5-6 **Facilities:** **Services:** lau **Leisure:** L **Off-site:** P

MEMMINGEN BAYERN
AT BUXHEIM (5KM NW)

See International Am Weiherhaus 7, 87740
08331 71800 08331 63554
website: www.camping-buxheim.de
Terraced site beyond public bathing area.
Leave Um-Kempten motorway at Memminger Kreuz then right to Buxheim.
Open: May-Sep **Site:** 42HEC **Prices:** 4.20 3 7.50 2.50 pitch 7.50 **Facilities:** **Services:** lau **Leisure:** L **Off-site:** P

MITTENWALD BAYERN

Isarhorn 82481 08823 5216
In a loop of the River Isar with many pines. Siesta 13.00-15.00.
3km N to the W of B2 Garmisch-Partenkirchen Mittenwald road.
Open: All year **Site:** 7.5HEC **Facilities:** **Services:** **Leisure:** R **Off-site:** LP

MÖRSLINGEN BAYERN

Mörslingen 89435 09074 4024
Camping Card Compulsory
6km N of Dillengen.
Open: All year **Site:** 1HEC **Facilities:** **Services:** lau **Leisure:** L

MÜHLHAUSEN BEI AUGSBURG BAYERN

Lech Seeweg 6, 86444 08207 2200 08207 2202
e-mail: info@lech-camping.de
website: www.lech-camping.de
On level grassland with own swimming facilities on lakeside.
4km N in direction of Neuburg.
Open: Apr-15 Sep **Site:** 3HEC **Prices:** 5-5.50 1.50 7 5-7 (static)276.50-427 **Facilities:** **Services:** lau **Leisure:** L **Off-site:** P

Ludwigshof am See Augsburger Str 36, 86444
08207 96170 08207 961770
e-mail: info@bauer-caravan.de **website:** www.bauer-caravan.de
Clean site with small lake away from motorway, near restaurant of the same name. Separate section for residential pitches.
1.5km from Augsburg Ost exit towards Neuberg.
Open: Apr-Oct **Site:** 12HEC **Prices:** 4.50 5-9 **Facilities:** **Services:** lau **Leisure:** L **Off-site:** PR

MÜNCHEN (MUNICH) BAYERN
AT OBERMENZING

München-Obermenzing Lochhausener Str 59, 81247
089 8112235 089 8144807
e-mail: campingplatz-obermenzing@t-online.de
website: www.campingplatz-muenchen.de
Park-like site near motorway.
Camping Card or Identification Papers Compulsory
1km from the end of Stuttgart-München motorway.
Open: 15 Mar-Oct **Site:** 5.5HEC **Prices:** 4.35 6 6 3.85 **Facilities:** **Services:** lau **Off-site:** LPR

NEUBÄU BAYERN

Seecamping Seestr 4, 93426 09469 331
e-mail: seecamp-neubau@t-online.de
Meadowland site along lakeshore.
Access from Schwandorf on B85 towards Cham.
Site: 5HEC **Facilities:** **Services:** lau **Leisure:** L

NEUKIRCHEN VORM WALD BAYERN

Rotbrunn Pilling 22 08504 920260 08504 920265
e-mail: camping.rotbrunn@vr-web.de
Terraced and partially shaded site on edge of small town with shops and services.

Site: 6HEC-Site size -grass -sand -stone -little shade -partly shaded -mainly shaded -bungalows for hire -caravans for hire -tents for hire -no dogs **Prices:** -adult per night -car per night pp-per person per night -caravan per night -tent per night (static)-caravan hire per week

A3 Regensburg Deggendorf-München exit Aicha W, then 6km to Neukirchen
Open: All year **Site:** **Prices:** 4.50 3 6 3.50 pitch 6 **Facilities:** **Services:** lau **Leisure:** L **Off-site:**

Neustadt Bayern

Main-Spessart-Camping-International 97845
09393 639 09393 1607
Beautifully situated site along the River Main. Water sports, including water skiing. Siesta 12.00-14.00.
Access from Frankfurt-Würzburg motorway A3/E5, Marktheidenfeld exit & follow road towards Lohr.
Open: Apr-Sep **Site:** 5.6HEC **Prices:** 5 pitch 6 **Facilities:** **Services:** lau **Leisure:** PR **Off-site:**

Nürnberg (Nuremberg) Bayern

Knaus Campingpark Nürnberg Hans-Kalb-Str 56, 90471
0911 9812717 0911 9812718
e-mail: knaus.camp.nbg@freenet.de
website: www.knauscamp.de
Well-kept municipal site in beautiful situation in a forest between a stadium with a swimming pool and the trade fair centre.
Leave A9 München motorway at Nürnberg-Fischbach exit, continue towards the stadium.
Open: All year **Site:** 2.7HEC **Prices:** 6 8 pitch 10 **Facilities:** **Services:** **Off-site:** LP

Oberammergau Bayern

Oberammergau Ettaler Str 56, 82847
08822 94105 08822 94197
e-mail: campingpark-oberammergau@t-online.de
website: www.campingpark-oberammergau.de
A year-round site with good, modern facilities providing fine views of the Bavarian Alps.
Signed from the town.
Open: All year **Site:** 2.6HEC **Prices:** 7.50-12 7.50-12 7.50-12 pitch 7.50-12 **Facilities:** **Services:** lau **Leisure:** R **Off-site:** P

Oberstdorf Bayern

Oberstdorf 87561 08322 6525 08322 809760
e-mail: camping-oberstdorf@t-online.de
website: www.camping-oberstdorf.de/
Level grassland site with fine mountain views.
800m N of town centre near railway line.
Open: All year **Site:** 16HEC **Prices:** 4.60-5.10 2.60-2.60 4.60-5.10 2.60-4.60 **Facilities:** **Services:** lau **Off-site:** LPR

Oberwössen Bayern

Litzelau 83246 08640 8704 08640 5265
e-mail: camping-litzelau@t-online.de
website: www.camping-litzelau.de
Almost level meadowland surrounded by forested slopes.
Take B305 from Bernau exit on München-Salzburg motorway & continue through Marquartstein & Unterwössen.
Open: All year **Site:** 4.5HEC **Prices:** 4 6.50 3.50 **Facilities:** **Services:** lau **Leisure:** R **Off-site:** LP

Passau Bayern

Dreiflüsse 94113 08546 633 08546 2686
e-mail: dreifluessecamping@t-online.de
website: www.dreifluessecamping.privat.t-online.de
A well-equipped site in pleasant wooded surroundings.
From A3 exit Passau-Nord follow signs.
Open: Apr-Oct **Site:** 5HEC **Prices:** 4 pitch 5-9 **Facilities:** **Services:** lau **Leisure:** P

Pfraundorf Bayern

Kratzmühle 85125 08461 64170 08461 641717
e-mail: info@kratzmuehle.de
website: www.kratzmuehle.de
Terraced site, divided into pitches, on a wooded hillside overlooking the River Altmühl.
In village turn off to Kratzmühle.
Open: All year **Site:** 9.6HEC **Prices:** 5-5.50 pitch 5-7 **Facilities:** **Services:** lau **Leisure:** LR

Piding Bayern

Staufeneck 83451 08651 2134 08651 710450
e-mail: camping-staufeneck@t-online.de
website: www.camping-berchtesgadener-land.de
In beautiful and quiet situation beside River Saalach.
Leave motorway A8/E11 München-Salzburg via exit Bad Reichenall road for 2.5km & turn right.
Open: Apr-Oct **Site:** 2.7HEC **Prices:** 5.50 pitch 5 **Facilities:** **Services:** lau **Off-site:**

Pielenhofen Bayern

Naabtal 93188 09409 373 09409 723
e-mail: camping.pielenhofen@t-online.de
website: www.camping-pielenhofen.de
The site is well-situated beside the River Nab, and has a special section for overnight visitors.
Access from the Nittendorf turn off from A3/E5 Nürnberg-Regensburg N via Etterzhausen.
Open: All year **Site:** 6HEC **Prices:** 5.05 pitch 5.80 **Facilities:** **Services:** lau **Leisure:** R

Pottenstein Bayern

Bärenschlucht 91278 09243 206
The site lies on unspoilt meadowland in the narrow Püttlach valley and is surrounded by the rocky hills of the Fränkische Schweiz range.
From the München-Berlin motorway leave at the Pegnitz exit & W for 10km on the B470 towards Forchheim.
Open: All year **Site:** 5HEC **Facilities:** **Services:** lau **Leisure:** R

Prien am Chiemsee Bayern

Hofbauer Bernauerstrasse 110, 83209
08051 4136 08051 62657
e-mail: ferienhaus-campingpl.hofbauer@t-online.de
website: www.camping-prien-chiemsee.de
Situated in a peaceful location amid the Bavarian foothills of the Alps with fine views of the nearby mountains. Site divided into separate plots.
A8 motorway from Munich towards Salzburg, exit 106 for Bernau & right for Prien. Site 3km on left
Open: Apr-Oct **Site:** 2HEC **Prices:** 5.90-7 3 pitch 5.10 **Facilities:** **Services:** lau **Leisure:** P **Off-site:** L

ROSSHAUPTEN BAYERN

Warsitzka 87669 08367 406 08367 1256
e-mail: info@camping-warsitzka.de
website: www.camping-warsitzka.de
A well-kept site with good installations.
From Füssen follow road B16 for 10km towards Rosshaupten. About 2km before the village and before the bridge turn right.
Open: All year **Site:** 4.5HEC **Prices:** 5-5.50 6.70-7.70 6.70-7.70 pitch 6.70-7.70 **Facilities:** **Services:** lau **Leisure:** LR

ROTHENBURG OB DER TAUBER BAYERN

Tauber-Idyll Detwang 28A, 91541
09861 3177 09861 92848
e-mail: campingtauber-ldyll@t-online.de
website: www.rothenberg.de/tauber-idyll
The well-kept site lies on a meadow scattered with trees and bushes, on the outskirts of the N suburb of Detwang and next to the River Tauber.
Access from all main roads is well signed. The best route is from Nordinger Str (B25) W along the River Tauber towards Bad Mergentheim.
Open: 1 wk before Etr-Oct **Site:** 0.5HEC
Prices: 4.50 1.50 3.50 3 pitch 4.50-5 **Facilities:** **Services:** lau **Off-site:** R

Tauber-Romantik Detwang 39, 91541
09861 6191 09861 86899
e-mail: info@camping-tauberromantik.de
website: www.camping-tauberromantik.de
Open: 15 Mar-4 Nov **Site:** 1.2HEC
Prices: 4.50 1.50 6 4.50 pitch 6 (static)189
Facilities: **Services:** lau **Off-site:** R

ROTTENBUCH BAYERN

Terrassen-Camping am Richterbichl 82401
08867 1500 08867 8300
e-mail: christof.echtler@t-online.de
website: www.camping-rottenbuch.de
Several pleasant terraces with good views.
On S outskirts on B23.
Open: All year **Site:** 1.2HEC **Prices:** 4.20-4.80 pitch 4.80-5.40 (static)210-245 **Facilities:** **Services:** lau **Leisure:** L **Off-site:** PR

RUHPOLDING BAYERN

Ortnerhof Ort 5, 83324 08663 1764 08663 5073
e-mail: camping-ortnerhof@t-online.de
website: www.ruhpolding.de/camping
Well-kept site on a meadow at the foot of the Rauschberg mountain, opposite the cable-car station.
Off Deutsche Alpenstr.
Open: All year **Site:** 2.4HEC **Prices:** 4.50 1.50 3.50 3.50 pitch 5 **Facilities:** **Services:** lau **Off-site:**

SCHECHEN BAYERN

Erlensee Rosenheimer Str 63, 83135
08039 1695 08039 9416
The site lies on the shores of an artificial lake.
From Rosenheim take the B15 10km N of Rosenheim towards Wasserburg &turn right upon entering Schechen.
Open: All year **Site:** 6HEC **Prices:** 4.50-5 2 5 2.50 **Facilities:** **Services:** lau **Leisure:** L
Off-site:

SCHÖNAU AM KÖNIGSSEE BAYERN

Grafenlehen Königsseer Fussweg 71, 83471
08652 4140 08652 690768
e-mail: camping-grafenlehen@t-online.de
website: www.camping-grafenlehen.de
Terraced and well-drained site situated on the edge of the Berchtesgadener national park. A quiet, peaceful location near lake Königssee.
From Munich leave motorway at Reichenhall & take B20 to Berchtesgaden. Turn right at railway station onto B20 to Königssee, turn right before large car park, site 20m on right
Open: Jan-Oct & 11-31 Dec **Site:** 3HEC
Prices: 4.50 pitch 6 **Facilities:** **Services:** lau
Off-site: P

SEEFELD BAYERN

Strandbad Pilsensee Graf Toerringstr 11, 82229
08152 7232 08152 78473
e-mail: campingplatz@toerring-seefeld.de
website: www.toerring-seefeld.de
S towards Pilsensee.
Open: All year **Site:** 10HEC **Prices:** 4.20-5 1-1 6-7 5-6 (static)196 **Facilities:**
Services: lau **Leisure:** L

SOMMERACH AM MAIN BAYERN

Katzenkopf am See 97334 09381 9215 09381 6028
website: www.camping-katzenkopf.de
On level ground beside the river Main. Pitches divided by bushes and good recreational facilities.
Leave A3 Würzburg-Nürnberg at exit Kitzingen-Schwarzach-Volkach & continue towards Volkach for 7km.
Open: 23 Mar-Oct **Site:** 6HEC **Prices:** 4.80-5 pitch 5-6 **Facilities:** **Services:** lau
Leisure: LR **Off-site:** P

SONTHOFEN BAYERN

Iller Sinwagstr 2, 87527 ☎ 08321 2350 ℻ 08321 71561
Site lies on the shore of the River Iller (dangerous for swimming) near a swimming pool.
1km on the B19 towards Obersdorf, before the bridge over the River Iller.
Site: 2.1HEC **Facilities:** **Services:** lau **Off-site:** P

STADTSTEINACH BAYERN

Stadtsteinach 95346 ☎ 09225 800644 ℻ 09225 800645
e-mail: info@campingplatz-stadtsteinach.de
website: www.campingplatz-stadtsteinach.de
Terraced site on SE facing slope with a view over the town and surrounding hills. Siesta 13.00-15.00.
Access via Badstr.
Open: All year **Site:** 3.8HEC **Prices:** 6 7 4 pitch 7 **Facilities:** **Services:** lau **Off-site:** P

TETTENHAUSEN BAYERN

Gut Horn 83329 ☎ 08681 227 ℻ 08681 4282
e-mail: info@gut-horn.de
website: www.gut-horn.de
Quiet site, divided into pitches on lake shore, sheltered by forest. Siesta 13.00-14.00.
SE on Wagingersee.
Open: Mar-Nov **Site:** 5HEC **Prices:** 4.70-5.20 pitch 5.50-7 **Facilities:** **Services:** lau **Leisure:** L **Off-site:** PR

TITTMONING BAYERN

Seebauer 84529 ☎ 08683 1216 ℻ 08683 7175
e-mail: campinseebauer@t-online.de
website: www.camping-seebauer.de
On meadow with a few terraces. Near a farm, beside a lake.
3km NW towards Burghausen.
Open: All year **Site:** 2.3HEC **Facilities:** **Services:** lau **Leisure:** L **Off-site:** LP

TRAUSNITZ BAYERN

Trausnitz 92555 ☎ 09655 1304 ℻ 09655 1304
website: www.camping-trausnitz.de
In wooded surroundings on the shores of a lake with good, modern facilities.
Access via A93 exit Pfreimd.
Open: All year **Site:** 3.5HEC **Prices:** 4 5 3.50-8 **Facilities:** **Services:** lau **Leisure:** LR

TÜCHERSFELD BAYERN

Fränkische Schweiz Tüchersfeld, 91278
☎ 09242 1788 ℻ 09242 1040
e-mail: spaetling@t-online.de
website: www.campingplatz-fraenkishe-schweiz.info
Access from motorway A9/E6, leave at exit Pegnitz then 12km W on B470 towards Forchheim.
Open: 20 Mar-9 Oct **Site:** 2HEC **Prices:** 8.90-9.90 **Facilities:** **Services:** lau **Leisure:** R

VELBURG BAYERN

Hauenstein 92355 ☎ 09182 454 ℻ 902251
A well-appointed site, on several terraces divided into individual pitches, all with electric points.
From motorway A3 Nürnberg-Regensburg leave at exit Velberg, continue through village towards S following signs Naturbad.
Open: All year **Site:** 5HEC **Prices:** 5 2.80 3.80 3.20 **Facilities:** **Services:** lau **Off-site:** L

VIECHTACH BAYERN

KNAUS Viechtach Waldfrieden 22, 94234
☎ 09942 1095 ℻ 09942 902222
e-mail: knauscamp.viechtach@freenet.de
website: www.knauscamp.de
Site on slightly undulating meadow, divided by rows of trees. The site has modern installations.
For access, take the B85 which runs from the junction with the road towards Freibad Viechtach & follow signs.
Site: 5.7HEC **Prices:** 6 8 pitch 13-17 **Facilities:** **Services:** **Leisure:** P

WAGING BAYERN

Strandcamping Am See 1, 83329
☎ 08681 552 ℻ 08681 45010
e-mail: strandcamp@aol.com
website: www.strandcamp.de
Extensive, level grassland site divided in two by access road to neighbouring sailing club. The site lies near the Strandbad and Kurhaus bathing area and spa, and the Casino. There is a Kneipp (hydrotherapeutic) pool in the camp.
Follow signs to Strandbad bathing area.
Open: Apr-Sep **Site:** 30HEC **Facilities:** **Services:** lau **Leisure:** L

WALTENHOFEN BAYERN

Insel-Camping am See 87448 ☎ 08379 881 ℻ 08379 7308
e-mail: info@insel-camping.de
website: www.insel-camping.de
A well-equipped site situated on the lake shore with access to neighbouring ski slopes.
Off B19, S of Memhölz.
Open: All year **Site:** 1.5HEC **Prices:** 4 1 4-6.50 3-5 pitch 4-6.50 **Facilities:** **Services:** lau **Leisure:** L **Off-site:** PR

WEISSACH BAYERN

Wallberg Rainerweg 10, 83700
☎ 08022 5371 ℻ 08022 670274
e-mail: campingplatz-wallberg@web.de
The well-kept site lies on a level meadow with a few trees beside a stream.
B318 from Gmund to Tegernsee, drive through Bad Wiessee, onto Wiessach, 9km further on.
Open: All year **Site:** 3HEC **Facilities:** **Services:** **Leisure:** R **Off-site:** L

WEISSENSTADT BAYERN

Weissenstädter See Badstr 91, 8687
☎ 09253 288 ℻ 09253 8507
e-mail: st.weissenstadt@fichtelgebirge.org
website: www.weissenstadt.de
This municipal site is close to a swimming pool and a lake, so offering numerous sports facilities.
1km NW of the town.
Open: All year **Site:** 1.7HEC **Facilities:** **Services:** **Leisure:** LP **Off-site:**

WEMDING BAYERN

AZUR Waldsee Wemding 86650
09092 90101 09092 90100
e-mail: info@campingpark-waldsee.de
website: www.campingpark-waldsee.de
In a wooded lakeside setting with excellent recreational facilities.
Open: All year **Site:** 9HEC **Prices:** 4.50-6 3.50-4.50 pitch 5.50-7.50 **Facilities:** **Services:** lau **Leisure:** L **Off-site:** PR

WERTACH BAYERN

Grüntensee Grüntenseestr 41, 87497
08365 375 08365 1221
e-mail: info@gruentensee.de
website: www.gruentensee.de
A modern site beside lake Grünten.
From Kempten, turn right entering Nesselwerg & follow signs.
Open: All year **Site:** 5HEC **Prices:** 5.50-6.20 5.20-6.20 3.60-5.20 **Facilities:** **Services:** lau **Leisure:** L **Off-site:** P

WINKL BEI BISCHOFSWIESEN BAYERN

Winklandthal 83483 08652 8164 08652 979831
e-mail: camping-winkl@t-online.de
website: www.camping-winkl.de
In meadow between the B20 and edge of woodland.
From Bad Reichenhall to Berchtesgaden 8km.
Open: Dec-Oct **Site:** 2.5HEC **Prices:** 5.85 pitch 5.15 **Facilities:** **Services:** lau **Leisure:** R

ZWIESEL BAYERN

AZUR-Ferienzentrum Bayerischer Wald Waldesruhweg 34, 94227 09922 802595 09922 802594
e-mail: info@azur-camping.de
website: www.azur-camping.de
A modern site. Clean sanitary installations.
Open: All year **Site:** 16HEC **Prices:** 4.50-6.50 2.80-4.60 3.50-4.70 pitch 5.50-7.50 **Facilities:** **Services:** lau **Off-site:** PR

SOUTH-WEST

ABTSGMÜND BADEN-WÜRTTEMBERG
AT POMMERTSWEILER (6KM N)

Hammerschmiede-See Hammerschmiede 6, 73453
07963 1205 & 415
e-mail: camping.hammerschmiede@t-online.de
website: www.camping-hammerschmiede.de
A terraced site in a wooded setting beside the lake. Partly divided into pitches with concrete paths.
From Abtsgmünd travel 3km then turn N to Pommertsweiler, site signed.
Open: All year **Site:** 6HEC **Facilities:** **Services:** lau **Leisure:** L

ACHERN BADEN-WÜRTTEMBERG

Staedtischer Campingplatz am Achernsee Am Achernsee 8, 77855 07841 25253 07841 508835
e-mail: camping@achern.de
website: www.achern.de
Open: All year **Site:** 6.5HEC **Facilities:** **Services:** lau **Leisure:** L **Off-site:** P

ALPIRSBACH BADEN-WÜRTTEMBERG

Wolpert 72275 07444 6313
On level land beside the River Kinzig.
1km N of town below B294.
Open: All year **Site:** 1.2HEC **Facilities:** **Services:** lau **Leisure:** R **Off-site:**

ALTENSTEIG BADEN-WÜRTTEMBERG

Schwarzwald 72213 07453 8415
e-mail: info@schwarzwaldcamping.de
website: www.schwarzwaldcamping.de
Parkland site of motor sport club Altensteig beside the River Nagold. Separate section for dog owners.
On road to Garrweiler 1km from Altensteig.
Open: All year **Site:** 3.3HEC **Facilities:** **Services:** lau **Leisure:** R **Off-site:** P

ALTNEUDORF BADEN-WÜRTTEMBERG

Steinachperle Altneudorf, 69250
06228 467 06228 8568
e-mail: campingplatz-steinachperle@t-online.de
The site lies in the narrow shady valley of the River Steinach. Siesta 13.00-15.00.
The entrance to the camp lies next to the Gasthaus zum Pflug, on the outskirts of Altneudorf.
Open: Apr-Sep **Site:** 3.5HEC **Facilities:** **Services:** lau **Leisure:** R

BADENWEILER BADEN-WÜRTTEMBERG

Badenweiler Weilertalstr 73, 79410
07632 1550 07632 5268
e-mail: info@camping-badenweiler.de
website: www.camping-badenweiler.de
On a level meadow surrounded by beautiful Black Forest scenery. Good facilities for local walking.
Access via A5 exit Neuenburg.
Open: 16 Jan-14 Dec **Site:** 1.6HEC **Facilities:** **Services:** lau **Leisure:** P **Off-site:**

BUCHHORN BEI ÖHRINGEN BADEN-WÜRTTEMBERG

Seewiese Seestr 11, 74629 07941 61568 07941 38527
e-mail: campingseewiese@t-online.de
website: www.camping-seewiese.de
A well-equipped site on a meadow beside a lake with fine views of the surrounding mountains. Good recreational facilities.
7km S of Öhringen via Pfedelbach. Access via A6.
Open: All year **Site:** 5.5HEC **Prices:** 5 3 4 2-4 **Facilities:** **Services:** lau **Leisure:** LP

BÜHL BADEN-WÜRTTEMBERG

Adam Campingstr 1, 77185 07223 23194 07223 8982
e-mail: webmaster@campingplatz-adam.de
website: www.campingplatz-adam.de
On level grassland, by lake.
1km from the Bühl exit of the A5/E4-E11 Karlsruhe-Basel in direction of Lichtenau.
Open: All year **Site:** 15HEC **Facilities:** **Services:** lau **Leisure:** L **Off-site:** P

CREGLINGEN BADEN-WÜRTTEMBERG

Camping Romantische Strasse 97993
07933 20289 07933 990019
e-mail: camping.hausotter@web.de
website: www.camping-romantische-strasse.de
A site completely divided into pitches, lying on the S outskirts of Münster. Children's playground. Individual washing cubicles.

From Bad Mergentheim or Rothenburg/Tauber, take the Romantic road up to Creglingen. Then turn S 3km up to Münster.
Open: 15 Mar-15 Nov **Site:** 6HEC **Prices:** 4.50-5.50 3-3.50 pitch 6-7 **Facilities:** **Services:** lau **Leisure:** PR **Off-site:** L

DINGELSDORF BADEN-WÜRTTEMBERG

Fliesshorn 78465 07533 5262
At a farm, on meadowland with fine trees.
In town turn off Stadd-Dettingen road & follow signs to NW for 1.3km.
Open: Apr-Sep **Site:** 5HEC **Facilities:** **Services:** lau **Off-site:** LS

DONAUESCHINGEN BADEN-WÜRTTEMBERG

Riedsee 78166 0771 5511 0771 5511
e-mail: info@riedsee-camping.de
website: www.riedsee-camping.de
Level meadow on lakeside.
Turn off A81 exit Geisingen & continue 13km on B31 towards Pfohren, then turn left for 1km.
Open: All year **Site:** 8HEC **Prices:** 4.50 4-6 pitch 8 (static)56 **Facilities:** **Services:** lau **Leisure:** L

DÜRRHEIM, BAD BADEN-WÜRTTEMBERG

Sunthauersee 78073 07706 712 07706 922906
e-mail: kurcamping@web.de
website: www.kurcamping.net
Open: All year **Site:** 10HEC **Facilities:** **Services:** lau **Off-site:**

ELLWANGEN-JAGST BADEN-WÜRTTEMBERG

AZUR Ellwangen Rotenbacherstr 45, 73479
07961 7921 07961 562330
e-mail: ellwangen@azur-camping.de
website: www.azur.camping.de/ellwangen
A modern site with good facilities in a wooded loaction on the banks of the River Jagst.
Open: All year **Site:** 3.5HEC **Prices:** 4.50-6 3.50-4.50 pitch 5.50-7.50 **Facilities:** **Services:** lau **Leisure:** R **Off-site:** LPR

ERPFINGEN BADEN-WÜRTTEMBERG

AZUR Schwäbische Alb (Rosencamping) 72820
07128 466 07128 30137
e-mail: info@azur-camping.de
website: www.azur-camping.de
Extensive site on a hill.
Access from Reutlingen on B312 SE direction to Grooengstingen, then S on Schwabische Albstr (B313) for 3.5km to Haid, then right to Erpfingen. Site on W outskirts.
Open: All year **Site:** 9HEC **Facilities:** **Services:** lau **Leisure:** P **Off-site:** L

ETTENHEIM BADEN-WÜRTTEMBERG

Oase 77955 07822 4459 18 07822 445919
e-mail: info@campingpark-oase.de
website: www.campingpark-oase.de
In a wooded location with good, modern facilities.
Access via A5 exit Ettenheim.
Open: 2 Apr-4 Oct **Site:** 6HEC **Prices:** 6 pitch 6 **Facilities:** **Services:** lau **Off-site:** P

FREIBURG IM BREISGAU BADEN-WÜRTTEMBERG

Breisgau Seestr 20, 7801 07665 2346
Extensive level grassland site on outskirts of town. Section reserved for campers with dogs.
500m E of autobahn exit Freiburg Nord.
Open: All year **Site:** 6.5HEC **Facilities:** **Services:** lau **Leisure:** L

Ferien Freizeit Mösle-Park Waldseestr 77, 79117
0761 72938 0761 77578
e-mail: information@camping-freiburg.com
website: www.camping-freiburg.com
On outskirts of town near Busse's Waldschänke inn.
Turn right after town hall across railway & follow Waldseestr towards Littenweiler.
Open: 25 Mar-25 Oct **Site:** 0.7HEC **Prices:** 5 2.50 pitch 5 **Facilities:** **Services:** lau **Off-site:** P

FREUDENSTADT BADEN-WÜRTTEMBERG

Langenwald Strassburgerstr 167, 72250
07441 2862 07441 2893
e-mail: info@camping-langenwald.de
website: www.camping-langenwald.de
The site consists of several sections and lies next to a former mill beside the River Forbach.
4km W of Freudenstadt below the B28 Freudenstadt-Strasbourg.
Open: Apr-Nov **Site:** 2HEC **Facilities:** **Services:** lau **Leisure:** PR

HALLWANGEN BADEN-WÜRTTEMBERG

Königskanzel 72280 07443 6730 07443 4574
e-mail: info@camping-koenigskanzel.de
website: www.camping-koenigskanzel.de
In an elvated position in the centre of the Black Forest.
Follow B28 from Freudenstadt towards Altensteig past the Hallwangen junction to camping sign on left.
Open: All year **Site:** 6HEC **Prices:** 5-5.75 pitch 6.50 **Facilities:** **Services:** lau **Leisure:** P **Off-site:**

HAUSEN BADEN-WÜRTTEMBERG

Wagenburg 88637 07579 559
On meadowland between the railway bank and the Danube. Site has spectacular view of surrounding landscape. Entrance through subway.
Open: May-Sep **Site:** 1.2HEC **Prices:** 4.50 1 4.60 3.60-4.60 pitch 3.40-5.60 **Facilities:** **Services:** lau **Leisure:** R **Off-site:**

HEIDELBERG BADEN-WÜRTTEMBERG

Heidelberg-Neckartal Schlierbacher Landstr 151, 69118
06221 802506 06221 802506
e-mail: mail@camping-heidelberg.de
website: camping-heidelberg.de
Open: 15 Mar-15 Oct **Site:** 3HEC **Facilities:** **Services:** lau **Leisure:** R

HERBOLZHEIM BADEN-WÜRTTEMBERG

Herbolzheim Im Laue 1, 79336
07643 1460 07643 913382
e-mail: s.hugoschmidt@t-online.de **website:** www.laue-camp.de
In a pleasant rural setting with good facilities, a short distance from the Europa Park Rust amusement park.
On B3 between Freiburgh & Offenburg.
Open: 17 Mar-3 Oct **Site:** 8HEC **Prices:** 5 7 6 **Facilities:** **Services:** lau **Off-site:** LP

HÖFEN AN DER ENZ Baden-Württemberg

Quellgrund 75339 07081 6984 07081 6984
Well maintained municipal site on grassland between the B294 and the River Enz.
From Pforzheim on the B294 SW to the Quelle inn with entrance to Aral filling station at entrance to Höfen, then turn right.
Open: All year **Site:** 3.6HEC **Facilities:** **Services:** lau **Leisure:** R **Off-site:** P

HORB Baden-Württemberg

Schüttehof 72160 07451 3951 07451 1348
Situated on flat mountain top.
Access from Horb towards Freudenstadt. 1.5km beyond the town boundary turn towards stables & site for 1km.
Open: All year **Site:** 6HEC **Facilities:** **Services:** lau **Leisure:** P

ISNY Baden-Württemberg

Waldbad Isny Lohbauerstr.59-69, 88316
07562 2389 07562 2004
e-mail: info@isny-camping.de
website: www.isny-camping.de
In wooded surroundings beside a lake.
S of town on B12. Signed.
Open: Jan-Oct **Site:** 3HEC **Prices:** 5.50 5-8 pitch 8 (static)350 **Facilities:** **Services:** lau **Leisure:** LP

KARLSRUHE Baden-Württemberg
At DURLACH (8km SE)

AZUR Campingplatz Türmbergblick Tiengener Str 40, D-76227
0721 497236 0721 497237
e-mail: karlsruhe@azur-camping.de
website: www.azur-camping.de/karlsruhe
On level ground among orchards. Siesta 12.30-15.00.
Access via Karlsruhe-Dürlach exit on A5/E4. Signed.
Open: 15 Mar-Oct **Site:** 3.5HEC **Prices:** 4.50-6 3.50-4.50 pitch 5.50-7.50 **Facilities:** **Services:** lau **Off-site:** LP

KEHL Baden-Württemberg

Kehl-Strassburg 77694 07851 2603 07851 73076
Park-like site divided into separate sections for young campers, transit and holiday campers. Siesta 13.00-15.00.
Turn left at the Rhine dam on the outskirts of the town.
Open: 15 Mar-Oct **Site:** 2.3HEC **Prices:** 4 pitch 8-10 **Facilities:** **Services:** lau **Off-site:** PR

KIRCHBERG Baden-Württemberg

Christophorus 88486 07354 663 07354 91314
e-mail: info@camping-christophorus.de
website: www.camping-christophorus.de
Completely enclosed, clean site.
Leave motorway A7 Ulm-Memmingen at exit Illereichen Allenstadt to town centre, then towards the railway station.
Open: All year **Site:** 9.2HEC **Prices:** 5.50-8 pitch 6.50 **Facilities:** **Services:** lau **Leisure:** LP

KIRCHZARTEN Baden-Württemberg

Kirchzarten Diefenbacher Str 17, 79199
07661 9040910 07661 61624
e-mail: info@camping-kirchzarten.de
website: www.camping-kirchzarten.de
Extensive site with trees providing shade.
About 8km E of Freiburg im Breisgau off the B31.
Open: All year **Site:** 5.9HEC **Prices:** 5.20-8.20 pitch 5.50-6.80 **Facilities:** **Services:** lau **Leisure:** P

KRESSBRONN Baden-Württemberg

Gohren am See 88079 07543 60590 07543 605929
e-mail: info@campingplatz-gohren.de
website: www.campingplatz-gohren.de
A large site beside the lake. It has an older section divided by many hedges reserved for residential campers, and a newer section with fewer bushes.
3km from Kressbronn. Well signed from B31.
Open: 22 Mar-15 Oct **Site:** 38HEC **Facilities:** **Services:** lau **Leisure:** L **Off-site:** P

LAICHINGEN Baden-Württemberg

Heidehof Blaubeurer str 50, 89150
07333 6408 07333 21463
e-mail: heidehof.camping@t-online.de
Well-cared for site on hillside with some high firs. Asphalt roads. Separate section outside enclosure for overnight campers.
Leave Ulm-Stuttgart motorway at Merkingen exit, then continue S via Machtolsheim to camp 2km S.
Open: All year **Site:** 25HEC **Prices:** 5 6 **Facilities:** **Services:** lau **Leisure:** P

LAUTERBURG BADEN-WÜRTTEMBERG

Hirtenteich 73457 07365 296 07365 251
e-mail: campingplatz.hirtenteich@t-online.de
website: www.campingplatz-hirtenteich.de
This site lies on gently sloping terrain, near the Hirtenteich recreation area.
Turn off the B29 Aalen-Schwäbisch Gmünd in Essingen and drive S for 5km.
Open: All year **Site:** 4HEC **Prices:** 4 pitch 5-5.50 **Facilities:** **Services:** lau **Leisure:** P

LENZKIRCH BADEN-WÜRTTEMBERG

Kreuzhof Bonndorfer Str 65, 79853
07653 700 07653 6623
e-mail: info@brauerei-rogg.de
Grassland near former farm below the Rogg Brewery on the B315.
Access from Freiburg on B31 to Titisee, continue on B317 towards Schaffhausen junction then B315 via Lenzkirch, site is 2km from centre.
Open: All year **Site:** 2HEC **Facilities:** **Services:** lau **Leisure:** P

LIEBELSBERG BADEN-WÜRTTEMBERG

Erbenwald Neubulach 3, 75387
07053 7382 07053 3274
e-mail: info@camping-erbenwald.de
website: www.camping-erbenwald.de
Pleasant site on edge of wood.
Approach via Calw on the B463 for 6km travelling S, then turn right and shortly before Neubulach continue N about 2km.
Open: All year **Site:** 7.2HEC **Facilities:** **Services:** lau **Leisure:** P

LIEBENZELL, BAD BADEN-WÜRTTEMBERG

Bad-Liebenzell Pforzheimerstr.34, 75378
07052 935680 07052 935681
e-mail: campingpark@abelundneff.de
website: www.abelundneff.de/campingpark
Municipal site with trees near tennis courts. Divided by hedges and internal aspahlt roads.
Approach from Pforzheim on the B463 about 19km S. Turn left 500m before Bad Liebenzell to site on the banks of the Nagold.
Open: All year **Site:** 3HEC **Prices:** 5.50 4 pitch 6 (static)304.50-424.20 **Facilities:** **Services:** lau **Leisure:** PR **Off-site:**

LÖRRACH BADEN-WÜRTTEMBERG

Grütt Grüttweg 8, 79539 07621 82588 07621 165034
Level, grassy site near frontier.
From motorway exit Lörrach on B316 then via Freiburger Str & bridge over the Wiesse & turn left after 100m.
Open: 18 Mar-Oct **Site:** 2.4HEC **Facilities:** **Services:** lau **Off-site:** PR

LUDWIGSHAFEN AM BODENSEE BADEN-WÜRTTEMBERG

See Ende 78346 07773 5366 07773 7375
website: www.see-ende.de
Meadowland with tall trees W of town, between railway and lake.
Access via Stuttgart-Singen-Lindau motorway. In Ludwigshafen turn off towards Radolfzell.
Open: May-Sep **Site:** 2.6HEC **Facilities:** **Services:** lau **Leisure:** L

MANNHEIM BADEN-WÜRTTEMBERG
AT NECKARAU (5.5KM S)

Strandbad 68199 0621 856240
A municipal site in the grounds of a park beside the Rhine. At high water the site can flood.
From motorway exit Mannheim to Neckarau, via the Freudenheim Bridge, then drive through Morchfeldstr, Friedrichstr, Rheingoldstr, Franzosenweg and Strandbadweg to the camp.
Open: Mar-Oct **Site:** 0.9HEC **Facilities:** **Services:** lau **Leisure:** R **Off-site:** P

MARKDORF BADEN-WÜRTTEMBERG

Wirthshof 88677 07544 96270 07544 962727
e-mail: info@wirthshof.de
website: www.wirthshof.de
Open: 15 Mar-30 Oct **Site:** 10HEC **Facilities:** **Services:** lau **Leisure:** P **Off-site:** L

MERGENTHEIM, BAD BADEN-WÜRTTEMBERG

Willingertal 97980 07931 2177
Site lies on a meadow between high green bank and wooded hillside.
From Bad Mergentheim follow B19 S towards Stuttgart, then left towards Wachbach after 2km, then left to Gastätte.
Open: All year **Site:** 15HEC **Facilities:** **Services:** lau

MÖRTELSTEIN BADEN-WÜRTTEMBERG

Germania Mühlwiese 1, 6951 06261 1795 06261 37455
Site is in Mörtelstein, 5km W of Obrigheim. Site lies between the left bank of the River Neckar and a wooded hillside.
Follow road B292 W towards Sinsheim to just beyond Oberigheim, then N on a narrow, steep road into the Neckar valley.
Open: Apr-Oct **Site:** 0.8HEC **Facilities:** **Services:** lau **Leisure:** R **Off-site:**

MÜNSTERTAL BADEN-WÜRTTEMBERG

Münstertal Dietzelbachstr.6, 79244
07636 7080 07636 7448
e-mail: info@camping-muenstertal.de
website: www.camping-muenstertal.de
Level, grassy site in pleasant situation with fine views. Siesta 13.00-15.00.
Leave Karlsruhe-Basel motorway at Bad Kroningen exit & continue SE via Stauffen to W outskirts of Untermünstertal.
Open: All year **Site:** 7HEC **Prices:** 6.60-7.65 pitch 10.30-12.50 **Facilities:** **Services:** lau **Leisure:** P

MURRHARDT BADEN-WÜRTTEMBERG
AT FORNSBACH (6KM E)

Waldsee 71540 07192 6436 07192 5283
e-mail: waldsee@murrhardt.de
website: www.murrhardt.de
The site lies near lake Waldsee. Asphalt paths and pitches, with gravel surface.
Drive through Murrhardt towards Fornsbach and the camp, which is on E shore of the lake.
Open: All year **Site:** 2HEC **Prices:** 3.50-4 2.50-3.50 3-3.50 3-3.50 pitch 3-3.50 (static)168-210 **Facilities:** **Services:** lau
Leisure: L

Facilities: -shop -shower -electric points for razors -electric points for caravans -parking by tents permitted -compulsory separate car park **Services:** -café/restaurant -bar -Camping Gaz International -gas other than Camping Gaz -first aid facilities lau-laundry **Leisure:** -swimming L-Lake P-Pool R-River S-Sea **Off-site:** All facilities within 2km

NECKARGEMÜND Baden-Württemberg

Friedensbrücke 69151 06223 2178
Campsite lies on the left bank of the River Neckar below the Frieden's bridge.
Open: Mar-Sep **Site:** 2.5HEC **Facilities:** **Services:** lau **Leisure:** R **Off-site:** P

Haide 69151 06223 2111 06223 71959
e-mail: info@camping-haide.de
website: www.camping-haide.de
A well-appointed site in the picturesque Neckar valley, directly on the river on the outskirts of Heidelberg.
Follow the river towards the castle & Neckarsteinach.
Open: Apr-1 Nov **Site:** 3.6HEC **Facilities:** **Services:** lau **Leisure:** R **Off-site:** P

NECKARZIMMERN Baden-Württemberg

Cimbria 74865 06261 2562 06261 35716
Site lies on level meadowland on the bank of the River Neckar.
Signed from road B27.
Open: Apr-Oct **Site:** 3HEC **Facilities:** **Services:** lau **Leisure:** PR **Off-site:**

NEUENBURG Baden-Württemberg

Dreiländer Camping und Freizeitpark Oberer Wald, 79395
07631 7719 07635 3393
e-mail: info@camping-gugel.de
website: www.camping-gugel.de
An excellent site, very extensive, providing many separate pitches.
Access via Karlsruhe-Basel motorway A5/E4, take the Müllheim/Neuenburg exit, then 3km to site.
Open: All year **Site:** 12.8HEC **Prices:** 5.75 4 5.20 3.50-5.20 **Facilities:** **Services:** lau **Leisure:** P **Off-site:** L

NUSSDORF Baden-Württemberg

Nell Uberlinger See, 88662 07551 4254 07551 4254
e-mail: info@campingplatz-nell.de
website: www.camping-nell.de
Site within orchard between farm of same name and the lakeside promenade. Small private beach.
Under railway bridge, then turn right.
Open: 20 Mar-20 Oct **Site:** 0.6HEC **Prices:** 4.35-6 3 5 5 **Facilities:** **Services:** lau **Leisure:** L **Off-site:** P

ÖSTRINGEN Baden-Württemberg

Kraichgau Camping Wackerhof 76684
07259 361 07259 2431
website: www.wackerhof.de
A modern terraced site. Siesta 13.00-15.00 (except Saturday).
From motorway A5 exit Kronau/Bad Schönborn, follow road B292 to Östringen.
Open: 25 Mar-15 Oct **Site:** 3HEC **Prices:** 3 pitch 3 **Facilities:** **Services:** lau

PFORZHEIM Baden-Württemberg

International Schwarzwald Freibadweg 4, 75242
07234 6517 07234 5180
e-mail: fam.frech@t-online.de
website: www.camping-schwarzwald.de
Site on edge of wood with southerly aspect. Separate fields for residential, overnight and holiday campers.
S through Huchenfeld from Pforzheim to Schellbron (15km).
Open: All year **Site:** 4HEC **Prices:** 4.50 5.20 5.20 pitch 5.50 (static)252-490 **Facilities:** **Services:** lau **Leisure:** P **Off-site:** R

RHEINMÜNSTER Baden-Württemberg AT STOLLHOFEN

Freizeitcenter-Oberrhein 77836
07227 2500 07227 2400
e-mail: info@freizeitcenter-oberrhein.de
website: www.freizeitcenter-oberrhein.de
Modern leisure complex next to Rhine.
Open: All year **Site:** 36HEC **Prices:** 5-7.50 pitch 5-7.50 **Facilities:** **Services:** lau **Leisure:** L

ROSENBERG Baden-Württemberg

Hüttenhof Hüttenhof 1, 73494 07963 203 07963 203
website: www.ecamp.com
Flat meadow on incline in quiet woodland area, next to large farm.
From Ellwangen 3km N towards Crailsheim, turn W towards Adelmannsfelden 8km to turn N at Gaishardt.
Open: 18 Mar- 7 Nov **Site:** 4HEC **Prices:** 4 pitch 3.60 **Facilities:** **Services:** lau **Leisure:** L

ST PETER Baden-Württemberg

Steingrübenhof 79271 07660 210 07660 1604
e-mail: info@camping-steingrubenhof.de
website: www.camping-steingrubenhof.de
On a level plateau, surrounded by delightful mountain scenery.
Access via A5 and B294.
Open: All year **Site:** 2HEC **Prices:** 4 pitch 4.50 **Facilities:** **Services:** lau **Off-site:** P

SCHAPBACH Baden-Württemberg

Alisehof 77776 07839 203 07839 1263
e-mail: info@camping-online.de
website: www.camping-online.de
The site lies on well-kept ground with several terraces and is separated from the road by the River Wolfach.
In Wolfach turn off B924 at the Kinzighbrücke N for 8km to Schapbach. Site is 1km N of village.
Open: All year **Site:** 3HEC **Prices:** 5.90-6.30 4.90-5.40 4.90-5.40 4.90-5.40 pitch 4.90-5.40 (static)300 **Facilities:** **Services:** lau **Leisure:** R **Off-site:** LP

SCHILTACH Baden-Württemberg

Schiltach 77761 07836 7289 07836 7466
e-mail: info@campingplatz-schiltach.de
website: www.campingplatz-schiltach.de
The site lies on meadowland on the banks of the River Kinzig and is well placed for excursions.
Open: 24 Apr-03 Oct **Site:** 3.6HEC **Prices:** 2 3 pitch 3 pp3.50 **Facilities:** **Services:** lau **Leisure:** R **Off-site:** P

SCHÖMBERG Baden-Württemberg

Höhen-Camping-Langenbrand 75328
07084 6131 07084 931435
e-mail: eberhardt@hoehencamping.de
website: www.hoehencamping.de
Open: All year **Site:** 1.6HEC **Prices:** 4.50-5 5-6.50 5-6.50 5 pitch 5-6.50 **Facilities:** **Services:** lau **Off-site:** P

SCHUSSENRIED, BAD BADEN-WÜRTTEMBERG

Reiterhof von Steinhausen Reiterhof, 88427
07583 3060 07583 1004
e-mail: xschmid@t.online.de
website: www.campingplatz1.de
In a pleasant rural setting.
Access via B30 Ulm-Bad Waldsee.
Open: All year **Site:** 1HEC **Prices:** 2.50 9 5-7 pitch 9 (static)250 **Facilities:** **Services:** lau **Off-site:** LPR

SCHWÄBISCH GMÜND BADEN-WÜRTTEMBERG AT RECHBERG (6KM S)

Schurrenhof 73072 07165 8190 07165 1625
The site lies in a beautiful setting on the edge of a forest, and has a lovely view of the surrounding countryside.
Drive S on the B29 from Schwäbisch Gmünd, through Strassdorf & Rechberg towards Reichenbach on B10. Then turn towards Schurrenhof.
Open: All year **Site:** 3HEC **Facilities:** **Services:** lau **Leisure:** P

SCHWÄBISCH HALL BADEN-WÜRTTEMBERG

Steinbacher See Mühlsteige 26, 74523
0791 2984 0791 9462758
e-mail: camping@hohenlohe2000.de
website: camping.hohenlohe2000.de
A modern site situated in the beautiful Kocher Valley. There are good sporting facilities and many places of interest nearby in the medieval town.
Access via B14/19 to Steinbach.
Open: All year **Site:** 1.4HEC **Facilities:** **Services:** lau **Off-site:**

STAUFEN BADEN-WÜRTTEMBERG

Belchenblick Münstertaler Str 43, 79219
07633 7045 07633 7908
e-mail: camping.belchenblick@t-online.de
website: www.camping-belchenblick.de
Well kept site on level ground.
Access from motorway exit Bad Krozingen/Staufen & continue 4km SE.
Open: All year **Site:** 2.4HEC **Prices:** 6-7.50 pitch 8 **Facilities:** **Services:** lau **Leisure:** PR **Off-site:**

STEINACH BADEN-WÜRTTEMBERG

Kinzigtal 77790 07832 8122 07832 6619
e-mail: webmaster@campingplatz-kinzigtal.de
website: www.campingplatz-kinzigtal.de
Site on level meadowland with tall trees, situated next to the municipal heated swimming pool.
Signed from Steinach.
Open: All year **Site:** 2.6HEC **Prices:** 5 4-4.50 5 6.50 pitch 4.50-6.50 **Facilities:** **Services:** lau **Off-site:** PR

STUTTGART BADEN-WÜRTTEMBERG

Canstatter Wasen Mercedesstr 40, 70372
0711 556696 0711 557554
e-mail: info@campingplatz-stuttgart
website: www.campingplatz-stuttgart.de
Level site with tall poplar trees alongside the River Neckar. Siesta 12.30-14.00.
Access from Bad Cannstatt near sports stadium.
Open: All year **Site:** 1.7HEC **Prices:** 5 2.20 5.50 3.10-4.10 **Facilities:** **Services:** lau **Off-site:** P

TITISEE-NEUSTADT BADEN-WÜRTTEMBERG

Bankenhof Bruderhalde 31a, 79822
07652 1351 07652 5907
e-mail: info@bankenhof.de
website: www.bankenhof.de
A family site in a wooded location close to the lake.
From Titisee village follow signs 'Camping platz'. Access road to site closed 22.00-06.00.
Open: All year **Site:** 3.5HEC **Prices:** 5.70 pitch 6.90 (static)320 **Facilities:** **Services:** lau **Leisure:** R **Off-site:** L

Bühlhof Bühlhofweg 13, 79822 07652 1606 07652 1827
e-mail: hertha-jaeger@t-online.de
website: www.camping-buehlhof.de
In pleasant situation on hillside above lake. Siesta 13.00-14.30.
Well signed.
Site: 10HEC **Facilities:** **Services:** lau **Off-site:** LP

Sandbank 79822 07651 8243 & 8166 07651 8286 & 88444
e-mail: info@camping-sandbank.com
website: www.camping-sandbank.com
On terrain rising from lakeside, upper part terraced, landscaped with trees.
Access from Titisee, N bank of lake, turn onto old Feldbergstr. At SW end of lake turn left along narrow private road through Camping Bankenhof (closed 22.00-06.00) to the site 700m on SE bank of lake.
Open: Apr-20 Oct **Site:** 2HEC **Prices:** 3.40-4.40 pitch 5.10-6.70 **Facilities:** **Services:** lau **Leisure:** L **Off-site:** P

Weiherhof 79822 07652 1468 07652 1478
Mainly level site with trees, bordering on lake shore for about 400m.
Signed from Titisee.
Open: 15 May-Sep **Site:** 2HEC **Facilities:** **Services:** lau **Leisure:** L

TODTNAU BADEN-WÜRTTEMBERG

Hochschwarzwald D-79674 07671 1288 07671 95190
e-mail: camping.hochschwarzwald@web.de
website: www.camping-hochschwarzwald.de
Terraced site, partially grassland, by ski-lift.
6km NW of Todtnau.
Open: All year **Site:** 2.5HEC **Prices:** 4.10-4.60 5.10-5.60 4-5.60 pitch 5.10-5.60 **Facilities:** **Services:** lau **Leisure:** R

TÜBINGEN BADEN-WÜRTTEMBERG

Tübingen Fremdenverkehrsgesellschaft, Rappenberghalde 61, 72070 07071 43145 07071 793391
e-mail: mail@neckarcamping.de
website: www.neckarcamping.de
A quiet site, well situated on the left bank of the River Neckar.
From the town centre cross the Neckar bridge, then turn right S through Uhlandstr or Bahnhofstr to next bridge. Cross bridge & upstream to the Rappenberghalde hill.
Open: Apr-Oct **Site:** 1HEC **Facilities:** **Services:** lau **Leisure:** R **Off-site:** LP

ÜBERLINGEN BADEN-WÜRTTEMBERG

West Bahnhofstr 57, 88662 07551 64583 07551 945895
e-mail: info@campingpark-uberlingen.de
website: www.campingpark-uberlingen.de
The site lies on the western outskirts of the town, between the railway line and the road on one side, and the concrete shore wall on the other. It is divided into several sections by low wooden barriers and has a very small beach. No individual youths under 18.
Off B31 towards the lake.
Open: Apr-5 Oct **Site:** 3HEC **Prices:** 5.20-6 4 pitch 9-10 **Facilities:** **Services:** lau **Leisure:** L **Off-site:** P

UHLDINGEN BADEN-WÜRTTEMBERG
AT SEEFELDEN (1KM W)

Seeperle 88690 07556 5454 07556 966221
e-mail: info@camping-seeperle.de
website: www.camping-seeperle.de
This site has some large trees along the shore of the lake. 50m landing stage. It is one of the few camps that does not reserve its best pitches for residential campers.
Turn off B31 at Oberuhldingen towards Seefelden. Site 1km.
Open: Apr-3 Oct **Site:** 0.7HEC **Facilities:** **Services:** **Leisure:** L **Off-site:**

WALDKIRCH BADEN-WÜRTTEMBERG

Elztalblick 79183 07681 4212 07681 4213
e-mail: eltztalblick@t-online.de
website: www.camping-elztalblick.de
A small site with terraced pitches in the heart of the Black Forest.
Leave autobahn at Waldkirch/Ost exit & follow signs for 3km.
Open: 15 Mar-25Oct **Site:** 2HEC **Prices:** 5.50 5.50 5.50 pitch 5.50 **Facilities:** **Services:** lau **Off-site:** P

WALDSHUT BADEN-WÜRTTEMBERG

Rhein-Camping Jahnweg 22, 79761
07751 3152 07751 3252
e-mail: rheincamping@t-online.de
website: www.rheincamping.de
In wooded surroundings beside the River Rhein.
1km from Waldshut towards the Swiss border.
Open: All year **Site:** 8HEC **Facilities:** **Services:** lau **Leisure:** R **Off-site:** P

WERTHEIM BADEN-WÜRTTEMBERG

AZUR Wertheim An den Christwiesen 35, 97877
09342 83111 09342 83171
e-mail: wertheim@azur-camping.de
website: www.azur-camping.de
Site lies on a level, long stretch of meadowland on the banks of the River Main next to a swimming pool. Siesta 12.00-14.00.
Follow road towards Miltenberg, and in 1km turn right at the Aral filling station and head towards the site.
Open: Apr-Oct **Site:** 7HEC **Facilities:** **Services:** lau **Leisure:** R **Off-site:** P

AT BETTINGEN (5KM E)

Wertheim-Bettingen Geiselbrunnweg 31, 97877
09342 7077 09342-913077
In a peaceful wooded area on the bank of a river.
Motorway Frankfurt-Würzburg, exit Wertheim/Lengfurt, 1km.
Open: Apr-Oct **Site:** 7.5HEC **Prices:** 4 1.50 2.50 2.50 pitch 4 **Facilities:** **Services:** lau **Leisure:** R

WILDBAD IM SCHWARZWALD BADEN-WÜRTTEMBERG

AZUR-Camping Schwarzwald 75323
07055 1320 07055 929081
e-mail: info@azur-camping.de
website: www.azur-freizeit.de
Long narrow site with some terraces, set between the River Enz and the wooded hillside. Separate section for young campers.
Access is from Pforzheim along B294 via Calmbach southwards.
Open: All year **Site:** 2.5HEC **Facilities:** **Services:** lau **Leisure:** R

Kleinenzhof 75323 07081 3435 07081 3770
e-mail: info@kleinenzhof.de
website: www.kleinenzhof.de
A family site with good, modern facilities.
Access via B294 3km S of Calmbach.
Open: All year **Site:** 8HEC **Facilities:** **Services:** lau **Leisure:** PR

BERLIN & EASTERN PROVINCES

ALT SCHWERIN MEKLENBURG-VORPOMMERN

See An der Schaftannen Nr 1, 17214
039932 42073 039932 42072
e-mail: info@camping-alt-schwerin.de
website: www.camping-alt-schwerin.de
A pleasant lakeside site with good, modern facilities.
Access via B192.
Open: Apr-Oct **Site:** 3.6HEC **Facilities:** **Services:** lau **Leisure:** L

BERLIN

Dreilinden Albrechts-Teerofen, 14109 4930 8051201
A transit site close to the city.
Access via A115.
Open: Mar-Oct **Site:** 1HEC **Facilities:** **Services:**

Gatow Kladower Damm 213-217, 14089
4930 3654340 4930 36808492
-mail: info@lccberlin.de **website:** www.lccberlin.de
A good transit site close to the river.
Access via B5.
Open: All year **Site:** 2.7HEC **Facilities:** **Services:** lau **Off-site:** R

At Kladow

DCC Else-Eckert-Platz Krampnitzer Weg 111-117, 14089
030 3652797 030 3651245
-mail: info@dccberlin.de **website:** www.dccberlin.de
Large site in woodland close to the lake. Good, modern facilities.
Access via B5 and B2 exit Berlin Spandau.
Open: All year **Site:** 7HEC **Facilities:** **Services:** lau **Off-site:** L

At Schmöckwitz

Krosssinsee Wernsdorfer Str 45, 12527 4930 6758687
In pleasant wooded surroundings on the shore of the Krossinsee with plenty of recreational facilities.
Access via A10 exit Berlin Köpenick.
Open: All year **Site:** 7HEC **Facilities:** **Services:** lau **Leisure:** L

At Wannsee

Kohlhasenbrück Neue Kreisstr 36, 14109 4930 8051737
Very pleasantly situated site on shore of Lake Griebnitz, owned by Deutscher Camping Club. Bathing area.
From Wannsee railway station, through Königstr, past Rathaus, through Chausseestr, Kohlhasenbrückerstr & Kreisstr.
Open: Mar-Oct **Site:** 3.6HEC **Facilities:** **Services:** lau

Bodstedt Mecklenburg-Vorpommern

Bodstedt Damm 1, 18356 038231 4226 038231 4820
A pleasant site on the shore of the Saaler Bodden with good boating facilities.
Access via B105 exit Zingst/Barth.
Site: 3.5HEC **Facilities:** **Off-site:** LR

Caputh Brandenburg

Himmelreich Wentorfinsel, Geltow, 14542
033209 70475 033209 20100
e-mail: himmelreich@campingplatz-caputh.de
website: www.campingplatz-caputh.de
Open: All year **Site:** 7.5HEC **Facilities:** **Services:** lau **Leisure:** LR

Colditz Sachsen

Waldbad D-04680 034381 43122 034381 43122
In wooded surroundings with some shaded pitches.
Access via E176 exit Zschadras.
Open: 28 May-7 Oct **Site:** 2HEC **Facilities:** **Services:** lau **Leisure:** LPRS
Off-site: P

Dresden Sachsen

Wostra Trieskestr 100, 01259
0351 2013254 0351 2013254
Café open May to September only.
Access via B172 towards Heidenau. Signed.
Open: Apr-Oct **Site:** 1.8HEC **Facilities:** **Services:** **Off-site:** P

Falkenberg Brandenburg

Erholungsgebiet Kiebitz 04895
035365 2135 035365 38533
e-mail: info@kiebitz-eg-urlaub.de
website: www.kiebitz-eg-urlaub.de
Access via E55 Duben exit, then B87/B101 towards Herzberg.
Open: 28 Mar-2 Nov **Site:** 5.2HEC **Facilities:** **Services:** lau **Leisure:** L **Off-site:**

Freest Mecklenburg-Vorpommern

Waldcamp 17440 038370 20538 038370 20525
A modern site in wooded surroundings with good facilities.
300m from Freest centre.
Open: Apr-Oct **Site:** 2HEC **Facilities:** **Services:** lau **Off-site:** S

Georgenthal Thüringen

Georgenthal 99887 036253 41314 036253 25207
e-mail: campingplatz70@hotmail.com
website: www.campingplatz-georgenthal.de
Open: Apr-Oct **Site:** 1.2HEC **Prices:** 3.50 1.50 4.50 2.50-6 (static)105 **Facilities:** **Services:** lau **Leisure:** P **Off-site:** L

Gross-Leuthen Brandenburg

Spreewaldtor 15913 035471 303 035471 310
e-mail: eurocamp.spreewaldtor@t-online.de
website: www.eurocamp-spreewaldtor.de
On a level meadow beside the Gorss Leuthener See.
N of town off B179.
Open: All year **Site:** 9HEC **Facilities:** **Services:** lau **Off-site:** L

GROSS-QUASSOW Mecklenburg-Vorpommern

Havelberge am Wobiltzsee 17237
03981 24790 03981 247999
e-mail: info@haveltourist.de
website: www.haveltourist.de
In a rural setting beside the lake. Restricted facilities during March.
1.5km S of town. Signed.
Open: All year **Site:** 14HEC **Facilities:** **Services:** lau **Leisure:** L

See advertisement on page 237

KAMENZ Sachsen

AZUR Waldbad Deutschbaselitz Grobteichstr 30, 01917
03578 301489 03578 308316
e-mail: deutschbaselitz@azur.freizeit.de
website: www.azur-camping.de/deutschbaselitz
The site may close for a short time in the winter and the shop and café are open May to September only.
Open: 15 Mar-Oct **Site:** 5HEC **Facilities:** **Services:** **Leisure:** L

KELBRA Thüringen

Südharz Lange Str 150, 6537
034651 45290 & 45291 034651 45292
e-mail: info@seecampingharz.de
website: www.seecampingharz.de
Open: All year **Site:** 6.5HEC **Facilities:** **Services:** lau **Leisure:** LP **Off-site:**

KLEINMACHNOW Brandenburg

Yacht-Caravan-Club Bäkehang 9a, 14532
033203 79684 033203 77913
e-mail: citycamp-berlin@web.de
website: www.hettler-lange.de
A riverside site with an hotel SW of town off A115.
Open: All year **Site:** 2.2HEC **Facilities:** **Services:** lau **Leisure:** R

KLEINRÖHRSDORF Sachsen

LuxOase Arnsdorfer Str 1, 01900
035952 56666 035952 56024
e-mail: camping.luxoase@t-online.de
website: www.luxoase.de
In beautiful, peaceful surroundings bordering a lake among meadows and woods.
Access via A4 Dresden-Bautzen, exit Pulsnitz towards Radeberg & continue 4km through Leppersdorf then 1km after the village turn right for site.
Open: Mar-9 Nov **Site:** 7.2HEC **Facilities:** **Services:** lau **Leisure:** L

KLEINSAUBERNITZ Sachsen

Olbasee Olbaweg 16, 02694
035932 30232 035932 30886
e-mail: natur@campingplatz-olbasee.de
website: www.campingplatz-olbasee.de
In a rural location on the Olbasee.
Leave A4 at Bautzen Ost exit, B156 N to Kleinsaubernitz.
Open: 16 Apr- 24 Oct **Site:** 7HEC **Facilities:** **Services:** lau **Leisure:** L **Off-site:**

KÖNIGSTEIN Sachsen

Königstein Schandauer Str 25e, 01822
035021 68224 035021 60725
e-mail: camp.koenigstein@t-online.de
On level ground in a wooded location with fine views of the surrounding mountains.
Federal road B172 within Königstein near Dresden.
Site: 2.4HEC **Facilities:** **Services:** lau **Off-site:** PR

LASSAN Meklenburg-Vorpommern

Lassan Garthof 5-6, 17440
038374 80373 038374 80373
e-mail: naturcampingplatzlassan@gmx.de
website: www.campingplatz-lassan.de
A pleasant site on the Achterwasser.
Access via B110.
Open: Apr-Sep **Site:** 1.4HEC **Facilities:** **Services:** lau **Leisure:** LRS **Off-site:**

LEHNIN Brandenburg

Seeblick am Klostersee D-14797
03382 700274 03382 700274
website: www.campingplatz-lehnin.de
80km from Berlin on E30.
Open: Apr-15 Oct **Site:** 1.5HEC **Facilities:** **Services:** lau **Leisure:** L **Off-site:**

MÜHLBERG Thüringen

Drei Gleichen 99869 036256 22715 036256 86801
e-mail: service@campingplatz-muehlberg.de
website: www.campingplatz-muehlberg.de
In pleasant wooded surroundings.
Access via A4 exit Wandersleben, then follow signs for Mühlberg.
Open: All year **Site:** 2.8HEC **Prices:** 4.50 1.50 5 3 **Facilities:** **Services:** lau **Off-site:** L

NIESKY Sachsen

Tonschächte 02902 03588 205771 03588 205771
Open: May-Sep **Site:** 15HEC **Facilities:** **Services:** lau **Leisure:** L **Off-site:**

NIEWISCH Brandenburg

Schwielochsee-Camping Uferweg Nord 16, 15848
033676 5186 033676 5226
e-mail: fischer.camping@12move.de
website: www.fischer-camping.de
A family site in pleasant wooded surroundings on the banks of the Schwielochsee.
Open: All year **Site:** 4.2HEC **Facilities:** **Services:** lau **Leisure:** L

PLÖTZKY Sachsen

Ferienpark Plötzky Campingplatz Kleiner Waldsee, 39245
039200 50155 039200 77120
e-mail: info@ferienpark-ploetzky.de
In a wooded location beside a small lake with well-defined pitches.
20km S of Magdeburg. Access via A2 & B246.
Open: All year **Site:** 8HEC **Facilities:** **Services:** lau **Leisure:** L

POTSDAM BRANDENBURG

anssouci-Gaisberg An der Pirscheide, Templiner See 41, 4471 0331 9510988
mail: info@recra.de
ebsite: www.recra.de
wooded surroundings close to the Templiner See.
Signed from the B1.
pen: Apr-1 Nov **Site:** 6HEC **Facilities:** **Services:** **Leisure:** LR **Off-site:** P

REICHENBERG SACHSEN

onnenland Dresdner Str 115, 01468
0351 8305495 0351 8305494
mail: bad-sonnenland@t-online.de
ebsite: www.moritzburg.de
a pleasant location beside the lake with good modern cilities.
3km S of Moritzburg, access via A4 exit Wilder Mann.
pen: Apr-Oct **Site:** 18HEC **Facilities:** **Services:** lau **Leisure:** L **Off-site:** P

SUHRENDORF MECKLENBURG-VORPOMMERN

uhrendorf 18569 038305 82234 038305 8165
pen: All year **Site:** 90HEC **Facilities:** **Services:** lau **Leisure:** S

ZINNOWITZ MECKLENBURG-VORPOMMERN

ommernland Dr. Wachsmann-Strabe 40, 17454
038377 40348 038377 40349
-mail: camping-pommernland@m-vp.de
ebsite: www.camping-pommernland.m-vp.de
wooded surroundings on the coast.
Access via B111.
pen: All year **Site:** 7.7HEC **Facilities:** **Services:** lau **Leisure:** S **Off-site:** P

CENTRAL

ASBACHERHÜTTE RHEINLAND-PFALZ

Iarfenmühle 55758 06786 7076 06786 7570
-mail: camping-harfenmuehle@t-online.de
ebsite: www.camping-harfenmuehle.de
quiet site, beautifully situated in Fischbach valley. Level rassland, partly terraced.
3km NW of the B327 towards Kempfeld.
pen: All year **Site:** 6.2HEC **Facilities:** **Services:** lau **Leisure:** L

ATTENDORN NORDRHEIN-WESTFALEN

iggesee-Waldenburg 57439
02722 95500 02722 955099
-mail: camping-waldenburg@t-online.de
ebsite: www.camping-biggesee.de
enerously terraced recreational site on the northern shore f the Bigge reservoir, with adjoining public bathing area. rivate sunbathing area. Siesta 13.00-15.00.
From Attendorn follow road towards Heldren. Shortly after he railway turn right & follow the signs to the site 1.5km.
pen: All year **Site:** 6.5HEC **Prices:** 3.10-3.90 6.80-10 pitch 9.50-12.50 **Facilities:** **ervices:** lau **Leisure:** L **Off-site:** P

Hof Biggen Finnentroper Str 131, 57439
02722 95530 02722 9556366
e-mail: info@hof-biggen.de
website: www.hof-biggen.de
Well-equipped terraced site, surrounded by woodlands. Siesta 13.00-15.00.
Follow Atterdorn road to Ahauser Reservoir. Entrance near Haus am See inn.
Open: All year **Site:** 18HEC **Prices:** 3.50-5 1.75-2.50 3.50-5 3.50-5 **Facilities:** **Services:** lau **Off-site:** R

BACHARACH RHEINLAND-PFALZ

Sonnenstrand Strandbadweg 9, 55422
06743 1752 06743 3192
e-mail: info@camping-sonnenstrand.de
website: www.camping-sonnenstrand.de
On grassland beside the Rhine with some high trees. Close to a main road and two railway lines.
The turn off from B9 into the site can be difficult for caravans coming from the N, due to one-way traffic.
Open: 15 Mar-Oct **Site:** 1.4HEC **Facilities:** **Services:** lau **Leisure:** R

BALHORN HESSEN

Erzeberg 34308 05625 5274 05625 7116
website: www.campingplatz-erzeberg.de
Site lies on meadowland on slightly sloping ground above the village. Siesta 13.00-15.00.
On B450 between Istha & Fritzlar.
Open: All year **Site:** 5HEC **Facilities:** **Services:** lau **Leisure:** P **Off-site:**

BARNTRUP NORDRHEIN-WESTFALEN

Schwimmbad Fischteiche 4, 32683
05263 2221 05263 2221
This well-kept site lies next to an open-air swimming pool, which is covered over in autumn and winter.
Barntrup lies B66, near to junction with B1. Approach signed from Barntrup.
Open: All year **Site:** 2.4HEC **Facilities:** **Services:** lau **Leisure:** P **Off-site:**

BERNKASTEL-KUES RHEINLAND-PFALZ

Kueser Werth Am Hafen 2, 54470
06531 8200 06531 8282
website: www.camping-kueser-werth.de
Grassy site near Mosel and boating marina, with view of Castle Landshut.
On S outskirts of town.
Open: Apr-Oct **Site:** 2.2HEC **Facilities:** **Services:** lau

BIRKENFELD RHEINLAND-PFALZ

Waldwiesen D-55765 06782 5215 06782 5219
e-mail: info@waldwiesen.de
website: www.waldwiesen.de
In a wooded location close to the lake.
Leave the B41 E of Birkenfeld. Signed.
Open: 15 Apr-14 Oct **Site:** 9.5HEC
Prices: 5.75 5.75 pitch 6.75-8.25 **Facilities:** **Services:** lau **Leisure:** L **Off-site:** P

BÖMIGHAUSEN HESSEN

Barenberg 34508 05632 1044 05632 1044
Beautifully terraced site at Neerdar reservoir.
Access from B251 between Korbach & Brilon.
Open: All year **Site:** 1HEC **Facilities:** **Services:** lau **Leisure:** LR

BRAUNFELS HESSEN

Braunfels Am Weiherstieg 2, 35619
06442 4366 06442 6895
A terraced site surrounded by a forest of pine and deciduous trees. Separate meadow for touring campers. Siesta 12.30-14.30.
Access from Köln-Frankfurt motorway, exit Limburg, then B49 towards town.
Open: All year **Site:** 5.2HEC **Facilities:** **Services:** lau **Off-site:** P

BREISIG, BAD RHEINLAND-PFALZ

Rheineck 53498 02633 95645 02633 472008
e-mail: info@camping-rheineck.de
website: www.camping-rheineck.de
A quiet, well-kept site on a level meadow in Vinxtbach valley.
From Koblenz B9 NW to Bad Breisig, then turn left, cross railway & continue for 400m.
Open: All year **Site:** 5HEC **Facilities:** **Services:** lau **Off-site:** PR

BULLAY RHEINLAND-PFALZ

Bären-Camp Am Moselüfer 1/3, 56859
06542 900097 06542 900098
e-mail: info@baeren-camp.de
website: www.baren-camp.de
On level meadow on right bank of the Mosel, next to the football ground. Fine view.
Access via B49 Cochem-Alf, then over the bridge & through the village. Signed.
Open: 15 Mar-5 Nov **Site:** 1.8HEC **Prices:** 5.30 3.20 3.20 3.20 pitch 6.50-7 **Facilities:** **Services:** lau **Leisure:** R **Off-site:** P

COCHEM RHEINLAND-PFALZ

Freizeitzentrum Stadionstr, 56812
02671 4409 02671 910719
e-mail: info@campingplatz-cochem.de
website: www.campingplatz-cochem.de
Site lies on level meadowland with trees. On right bank of the Mosel, downstream from the swimming pool and sports ground.
From B49 in Cochem, follow 'Freizeitzentrum' signs, crossing the river on the downstream bridge. After swimming pool, turn left for site.
Open: end Mar-Oct **Site:** 2.8HEC **Prices:** 4.50 pitch 4.50-7.50 **Facilities:** **Services:** lau **Leisure:** R **Off-site:** P

AT LANDKERN (7KM N)

Altes Forsthaus Haupstr 2, 56814
02671 8701 02671 8722
e-mail: camping.stern@t-online.de
website: www.landkern.com
The partly terraced site lies near woodland in the valley below Landkern.
From motorway A48 (Eifel motorway) leave at exit Kaisersesch, S to Landkern, then follow signs to site.
Open: All year **Site:** 10HEC **Prices:** 3.25 1.75 5-7 5-7 **Facilities:** **Services:** lau **Off-site:** P

COLOGNE SEE KÖLN

DAHN RHEINLAND-PFALZ

Büttelwoog 66994 06391 5622 06391 5326
e-mail: buettelwoog@t-online.de
website: www.camping-buettelwoog.de
Site lies in a magnificent pine forest, partly surrounded by steep hills and rocks. Section reserved for young people with tents. Siesta 12.00-14.00.
From Pirmasens follow B10 up to Hinterweidenthal then S on B427 to Dahn.
Open: All year **Site:** 6HEC **Prices:** 5 6 pitch 6 (static)245 **Facilities:** **Services:** lau **Off-site:** P

DAUSENAU RHEINLAND-PFALZ

Lahn-Beach Hallgarten 16, 56132
02603 13964 02603 919935
e-mail: info@canutours.de **website:** www.canutours.de
A riverside site in a wooded setting.
Open: Apr-Oct **Site:** 3HEC **Prices:** 4-4.50 2 2.50-4 2.50-4 **Facilities:** **Services:** **Leisure:** R

DIEMELSEE-HERINGHAUSEN NORDRHEIN-WESTFALEN

AZUR-Camping Hohes Rad 34519
05633 99099 05633 99010
website: www.camping.diemelsee.de
A terraced site in the Sauerland hills overlooking Lake Diemel.
Access via B251 Korbach-Beilon.
Open: All year **Site:** 2.8HEC **Facilities:** **Services:** lau **Off-site:** LP

DIEZ RHEINLAND-PFALZ

Ochsenwiese 65582 06432 2122 06432 2122
e-mail: info@camping-diez.de **website:** www.camping-diez.de
On a meadow on the left bank of the River Lahn, below Schloss Oranienstein.
From N leave motorway A3 at Diez exit (from S at Limburg-Nord exit) then continue on B54 7km.
Open: Apr-Oct **Site:** 7HEC **Facilities:** **Services:** lau **Leisure:** R **Off-site:** L

DORSEL AN DER AHR RHEINLAND-PFALZ

Stahlhütte 53533 02693 438 02693 511
website: www.campingplatz-stahlhuette.de
Site with individual pitches, on meadowland with trees near River Ahr.
Off B258 Aachen-Koblenz road.
Open: All year **Site:** 7HEC **Facilities:** **Services:** lau **Leisure:** R

DORTMUND NORDRHEIN-WESTFALEN

Hohensyburg Syburger Dorfstr 69, 44265
0231 774374 0231 7749554
e-mail: info@camping-hohensyburg.de
website: www.camping-hohensyburg.de
Terraced site on hilly grassland near Weitkamp inn.
Access via B54.
Open: All year **Site:** 10HEC **Facilities:** **Services:** lau **Leisure:** LR

DREIEICH-OFFENTHAL HESSEN

Offenthal Bahnhofstr 77, 63303
06074 5629 06074 5629
e-mail: schoenweitz@t-online.de
website: www.t-online.de/home/schoenweitz/campa.htm
A well-equipped site in wooded surroundings.

Exit B486 at Dreieich-Offenthal towards Dietzenbach.
Open: All year **Site:** 3HEC **Prices:** 4 0.50-0.50 5 4 **Facilities:** **Services:** **Leisure:** P
Off-site:

DROLSHAGEN NORDRHEIN-WESTFALEN

Gut Kalberschnacke 57489 02763 7501 02763 7879
e-mail: camping-kalberschnacke@t-online.de
website: www.camping-kalberschnacke.de
Terraced site above Bigge-Lister Reservoir in wooded area.
Turn off A45 (E41) autobahn at Wegringhausen exit & continue NE for 4km.
Open: All year **Site:** 13.5HEC **Facilities:** **Services:** lau **Off-site:** L

DÜLMEN NORDRHEIN-WESTFALEN

Tannenwiese Borkenbergestr 217, 48249 02594 991759
The site lies on meadowland in a well-wooded country area, near the gliderdrome. Siesta 12.30-14.30.
Take the B51 from Recklinghausen towards Münster as far as Hausdülmen, then follow signs 'Segelflügplatz Borkenberge'.
Open: Mar-30 Oct **Site:** 3.7HEC **Facilities:** **Services:** lau **Off-site:**

DÜRKHEIM, BAD RHEINLAND-PFALZ

KNAUS Bad Dürkheim In den Almen 3, 67098
06322 61356 06322 8161
e-mail: knaus-camping-duerkheim@t-online.de
website: www.knauscamp.de
Lakeside site on level meadow between vineyards, adjoining a sports field. Siesta 12.00-15.00.
Access from E outskirts of town. Turn N at railway viaduct, near JET filling station.
Open: Jan-Oct & Dec **Site:** 16HEC
Prices: 6 8 pitch 6-10 **Facilities:**
Services: **Leisure:** L **Off-site:** P

DÜSSELDORF NORDRHEIN-WESTFALEN

Unterbacher See Kleiner Torfbruch 31, 40627
0211 8992038 0211 8929321
e-mail: service@uunterbachersee.de
website: www.unterbachersee.de
Site on sloping grassland.
From Düsseldorf B326 to Erkrath exit. Turn left by Unterbacher lake.
Open: 03 Apr-24 Oct **Site:** 6.5HEC
Facilities: **Services:** lau **Leisure:** LP
Off-site:

EMS, BAD RHEINLAND-PFALZ

Bad Ems 56130 02603 4679 02603 4487
Level grassy site with isolated trees by the River Lahn.
On E outskirts on B260.
Open: Apr-Oct **Site:** 16HEC **Facilities:**
Services: lau **Leisure:** PR

ESCHWEGE HESSEN

Knaus Campingpark Eschwege 37269
05651 338883 05651 338884
e-mail: knaus.camp.esw@freenet.de
website: www.knauscamp.de
Site situated by the Werratalsee
Leave A7 at exit for Eschwege, site signed.
Open: Jan-Oct & Dec **Site:** 6.8HEC
Prices: 6 8 pitch 4-8 **Facilities:**
Services: **Leisure:** LR **Off-site:** P

ESSEN NORDRHEIN-WESTFALEN AT WERDEN (10KM S)

Essen-Werden Im Löwental 67, 45239
0201 492978 0201 8496132
e-mail: stadtcamping@gmx.de
website: www.stadtcamping-essen.de
Several fields divided by bushes and surrounded by thick hedges. Siesta 13.00-15.00.
From centre of Essen towards Werden, then turn towards railway station & follow signs.
Open: All year **Site:** 6HEC **Facilities:**
Services: lau **Leisure:** R **Off-site:** P

FÜRTH IM ODENWALD HESSEN

Tiefertswinkel Am Schwimmbad, 64658
06253 5804 06253 3717
e-mail: info@camping-fuerth.de
website: www.camping-fuerth.de
Pleasantly landscaped site in beautiful setting next to the municipal open-air swimming pool. Siesta 13.00-15.00.
Open: Mar-Nov **Site:** 4.2HEC **Prices:** 3.30 5.50 3.50-5.50 **Facilities:** **Services:** lau **Off-site:** P

GAMMELSBACH HESSEN

Freienstein Neckartalstr 172, 64743
06068 1306 06068 912121
The site lies just off the B45 in a landscaped preservation area. It is terraced and divided into pitches. Siesta 13.00-15.00.
Open: Apr-Sep **Site:** 5HEC **Prices:** 3.50 pitch 4-5
Facilities: **Services:** lau

GEISENHEIM HESSEN

Geisenheim Postfach 1323, 65366
06722 75600 06722 75600
Level grassland site.
Between B42 road & River Rhine.
Open: Mar-Oct **Site:** 5HEC **Prices:** 3.95-4.30 4.50 pitch 4-7 (static)185 **Facilities:**
Services: lau **Leisure:** R **Off-site:** P

GERBACH RHEINLAND-PFALZ

AZUR-Camping Pfalz 67813 06361 8287 06361 22523
e-mail: gerbach@azur-camping.de
website: www.azur-camping.de/gerbach
Siesta 13.00-15.00.
Access from A8/E12 motorway at junction Enkenbach-Hochspeyer. Then N on B48 via Rockenhausen & at Dielkirchen continue E for 4.5km to Gerbach.
Open: Apr-Oct **Site:** 8.5HEC **Prices:** 4.50-6 pitch 5.50-7.50 **Facilities:** **Services:** lau
Leisure: P

GILLENFELD RHEINLAND-PFALZ

Feriedorf Pulvermaar 54558
06573 996500 06573 996500
Partly terraced municipal site on a slightly sloping meadow at Pulver Maar, surrounded by woods.
From motorway A48 (Eifel autobahn) leave at exit Mehren/Daun, continue S on B421 & take the first turning into Gillenfeld. On near side of village turn off towards Pulver Maar.
Open: All year **Site:** 3HEC **Facilities:**
Services: lau **Off-site:** LP

GRÜNBERG HESSEN

Spitzer Stein Alsfelderstr, 6310 ☎ 06401 804
Beautifully situated site at a forest swimming pool.
From the Frankfurt-Kassel motorway (A5) leave at Homberg junction. Campsite is 8km S.
Open: All year **Site:** 4HEC **Facilities:** **Services:** lau **Leisure:** P **Off-site:**

GRUNDMÜHLE BEI QUENTEL HESSEN

Grundmühle Quentel 37235 ☎ 05602 3659 05602 915811
A forest camp site with a sunny location. Siesta 13.00-15.00.
From Melsungen follow road B83 to Röhrenfurth. Turn right towards Furstenhagen & follow road via Eiterhagen to Quentel.
Open: All year **Site:** 1.8HEC **Facilities:** **Services:** lau **Leisure:** P **Off-site:**

GULDENTAL RHEINLAND-PFALZ

Guldental 55452 ☎ 06707 633 06707 18468
Site lies in a valley of the Guldenbach valley. Some terraces are reserved for tourers and there is a lake suitable for bathing.
From Bad Kreuznach N on B48 to Langenlonsheim, turn left to Guldental.
Open: All year **Site:** 8HEC **Facilities:**
Services:

HALDERN NORDRHEIN-WESTFALEN

Strandhaus Sonsfeld 46459 ☎ 02857 2247 02857 7171
On meadowland at the Hagener-Meer next to B8 and railway line.
Open: All year **Site:** 15HEC **Facilities:**
Services: lau **Leisure:** L

HAUSBAY RHEINLAND-PFALZ
AT PFALZFELD-HAUSBAY

Schinderhannes 56291 ☎ 06746 80280 06746 802814
e-mail: info@countrycamping.de
website: www.countrycamping.de
Terraced site on S facing slope, broken up by trees and shrubs beside a small lake. Separate section for young people. Siesta 13.00-15.00.
E of B327. 29km S of Koblenz.
Open: All year **Site:** 30HEC **Prices:** 5 pitch 8
Facilities: **Services:** lau **Leisure:** L
Off-site:

HEIDENBURG RHEINLAND-PFALZ

Moselhöhe 54426 ☎ 06509 99016 06509 99017
A small, well-appointed site on an open meadow.
Access via A1 exit Mehring towards Thalfang am Erbestopf.
Site: 3HEC **Facilities:** **Services:** lau
Off-site:

HEIMBACH NORDRHEIN-WESTFALEN

Rurthal 52396 ☎ 02446 3377 02446 911126
Site with individual pitches on meadowland beside the River Ruhr.
From Düren follow road S via Nideggen & Abenden to Blens, then cross bridge & turn left.
Site: 7HEC **Facilities:**
Services: lau **Leisure:** P **Off-site:** R

HEIMERTSHAUSEN HESSEN

Heimertshausen Ehringshauser Str, 36320
☎ 06635 206 06635 918359
e-mail: info@campingplatz-heimertshausen.de
website: www.campingplatz-heimertshausen.de
Near swimming pool in extensive grassy and wooded valley. Siesta 13.00-15.00.
From Kassel-Frankfurt motorway take Alsfeld-West exit, then continue via Romrod & Zell.
Open: Apr-Sep **Site:** 3.6HEC **Facilities:** **Services:** lau **Off-site:** P

HELLENTHAL NORDRHEIN-WESTFALEN

Hellenthal Platiss 1, 53940 ☎ 02482 1500 02482 2171
e-mail: info@camphellenthal.de
website: www.camphellenthal.de
On extensive meadowland.
0.5km S of town.
Open: All year **Site:** 6HEC **Facilities:**
Services: lau **Leisure:** P **Off-site:**

HERINGEN HESSEN

Werra 36266 ☎ 06624 919043 06624 915597
Municipal site on slightly sloping ground at the swimming pool. Siesta 13.00-15.00.
Open: All year **Site:** 4HEC **Facilities:**
Services: lau **Off-site:** PR

HIRSCHHORN AM NECKAR HESSEN

Odenwald Langenthalerstr 80, 69430
☎ 06272 809 06272 3658
e-mail: odenwald-camping-park@t-online.de
website: www.odenwald-camping-park.de
Extensive site in wooded valley. Divided by River Ülfenbach and hedges.
Turn off B37 towards Wald-Michelbach for 1.5km.
Open: Apr-1 Oct **Site:** 8HEC **Facilities:** **Services:** lau **Leisure:** PR

HOFGEISMAR HESSEN

Parkschwimmbad Schöneberger Str 16, 3520 ☎ 05671 1215
Municipal site, subdivided by hedges. Next to a swimming pool. Siesta 13.00-15.00. Mobile shop.
Open: All year **Site:** 1.5HEC **Facilities:**
Services: lau **Leisure:** P **Off-site:**

AT LIEBENAU-ZWERGEN (9KM W)

Ponyhof Camping Club Teichweg 1, 34396
☎ 05676 1509 05676 8880
e-mail: ponyhofcamping@t-online.de
website: www.ponyhofcamping.de
A terraced, south-facing site, with magnificent scenery. 300m from a swimming pool.
From B83 at Hofgeismar turn W towards Liebenau. From B7 turn N at Obemeiser towards Liebenau.
Site: 7HEC **Facilities:**
Services: **Leisure:** R **Off-site:** LP

HONNEF, BAD NORDRHEIN-WESTFALEN
AT HONNEF-HIMBERG, BAD (7KM E)

Jillieshof 53604 ☎ 02224 972066 02224 972067
e-mail: hpefferoth@t-online.de
Open: All year **Site:** 4HEC **Facilities:**
Services: lau **Off-site:**

HORN-BAD MEINBERG NORDRHEIN-WESTFALEN

Eggewald Kempener Str 33, 32805
05255 236 05255 1375
Site lies in well-wooded countryside.
Access via road B1. In Horn-Bad Meinberg turn off main road at the Waldschlosschen & follow Altenbeken road for 8km up to Kempen.
Open: All year **Site:** 2HEC **Facilities:**
Services: lau **Leisure:** P

IDSTEIN HESSEN

AZUR-Camping Idstein 65510
06126 91299 06126 990289
e-mail: idstein@azur-camping.de
website: www.azur-camping.de/idstein
In a peaceful rural setting close to the ancient town of Idstein.
Access via A3 Frankfurt-Limburg.
Open: All year **Site:** 2.6HEC **Facilities:**
Services: lau **Leisure:** P **Off-site:**

INGENHEIM RHEINLAND-PFALZ

SC Klingbachtal 76831 06349 6278
Municipal site lies on level meadowland at the edge of the village, next to the sports ground.
8km S of Landau via B38. Final approach well signed.
Open: Apr-Oct **Site:** 1.5HEC **Facilities:**
Services: **Off-site:** P

IRREL RHEINLAND-PFALZ

Nimseck 54666 06525 314 1299
e-mail: info@camping-nimseck.de
website: www.camping-nimseck.de
Site on long grassy strip in wooded valley on the bank of River Nims.
Approach from Bitburg via B257/E42 in SW direction. At the turn-off from the bypass to Irrel, turn left.
Open: 15 Mar-2Nov **Site:** 7HEC **Facilities:** **Services:** lau **Leisure:** PR **Off-site:**

KALLETAL-VARENHOLZ NORDRHEIN-WESTFALEN

Weser Freizeit-Zentrum 32689 05755 444 05755 723
e-mail: info@camping-wfz-kalletal.de
website: www.camping-wfz-kalletal.de
Extensive site in Weser recreation area near River Weser N of Schloss Varenholz. Separate field and common room for young campers.
Leave A2/E8 motorway at Exter exit then continue via Vlotho towards Rintein.
Open: Feb-Oct **Site:** 12HEC **Facilities:** **Services:** lau **Leisure:** L

KELL RHEINLAND-PFALZ

Freibad Hochwald 54427 06589 1695
On meadow on slightly sloping wooded hillside, near a public open-air swimming pool. Booking necessary in high season.
2km from B407 towards Trier.
Open: May-Sep **Site:** 2HEC **Facilities:**
Services: **Leisure:** P

KIRCHHEIM HESSEN

Seepark Kirchheim 36275 06628 1525 06628 8664
e-mail: info@campseepark.de
website: www.campseepark.de
This terraced site, with individual pitches, is part of an extensive and well-equipped leisure and recreation centre.
Open: All year **Site:** 10HEC **Facilities:** **Services:** lau **Leisure:** LP

KIRN RHEINLAND-PFALZ

Papiermühle Krebsweilererstr 8, 55606 06752 2267
Access via B41 exit Meisenheim
Open: All year **Site:** 6HEC **Facilities:**
Services: **Leisure:** R

KOBLENZ (COBLENCE) RHEINLAND-PFALZ AT WINNINGEN (9KM SW)

Ziehfurt Fährstr 35, 56333 02606 356 02606 2752
Site lies on level wooded meadowland.
From Koblenz follow road B416 for 11km towards Trièr. Access to site at the Schwimmbad (swimming pool).
Open: May-Sep **Site:** 7HEC **Prices:** 6 pitch 6
Facilities: **Services:** lau **Leisure:** R
Off-site: P

KÖLN (COLOGNE) NORDRHEIN-WESTFALEN

Berger Uferstr. 71, Rodenkirchen, 50996
0221 9355240 0221 9355246
e-mail: camping.berger@t-online.de
website: www.camping-berger-koeln.de
Situated on a meadow beside the River Rhine, the campsite has fine views of the beautiful surrounding area and good modern facilities.
Open: All year **Site:** 6HEC **Facilities:**
Services: lau **Leisure:** R

KÖNEN RHEINLAND-PFALZ

Horsch Könenerstr 36, 54329 06501 17571
Open: Apr-Oct **Site:** **Facilities:**
Services: **Leisure:** LPR

KÖNIGSTEIN IM TAUNUS HESSEN AT EPPSTEIN (8KM SW)

Hubertushof Bezirksstr 2, 65817
06198 7000 06198 7002
e-mail: info@taunuscamp.de
website: www.taunuscamp.de
In the Taunus landscape preservation area.
Follow B455 from Königstein.
Open: All year **Site:** 3HEC **Prices:** 6 pitch 6 (static)120-270 **Facilities:** **Services:**
Off-site: P

KRÖV RHEINLAND-PFALZ

Kröver-Berg 54636 06541 70040 06541 700444
website: www.kroverberg.de
Open: All year **Site:** 2HEC **Facilities:**
Services: lau **Off-site:** P

LADBERGEN NORDRHEIN-WESTFALEN

Waldsee Waldseestr 81, 49549 05485 1816 05485 3560
e-mail: info@waldsee-camping.de
website: www.waldsee-camping.de
Site lies at the inn, near the bathing area of the lake.
2km N. From motorway leave at Ladbergen exit following road towards Saerbeck/Emsdetten & 100m turn right.
Open: All year **Site:** 7HEC **Facilities:**
Services: lau **Leisure:** LP **Off-site:** R

LAHNSTEIN RHEINLAND-PFALZ

Burg Lahneck 56112 02621 2765 02621 18290
Level grassland site with sunny aspect and terraces which provide shade. Situated next to Lahneck castle. Pleasant view of the Rhine Valley.

contd.

From Koblenz (8km distance) follow road B42. In Lahnstein leave main road & follow signs 'Burg Lahneck' 1.5km to site.
Open: Apr-Oct **Site:** 1.8HEC **Prices:** 5.50 3.50 5.50 4.50-5.50 **Facilities:** **Services:** lau **Off-site:** P

LEIWEN Rheinland-Pfalz

AEGON-Ferienpark Sonnenberg 54340
06507 93690 06507 936936
e-mail: sonnenberg@landal.de
website: www.landal.de
Extensive terraced site in one of the largest wine growing areas of this district. Lies above the River Mosel.
Access from main B53 (Mosel valley road), cross the River Mosel at Thornich then via Leiwen to site.
Site: 25HEC **Facilities:** **Services:** lau **Leisure:** PR **Off-site:**

LEMGO Nordrhein-Westfalen

Alten Hansestadt Regenstorstr, 32657
05261 14858 05261-188324
e-mail: info@camping-lemgo.de
website: www.camping-lemgo.de
The site lies by the swimming pool directly on the river.
Open: All year **Site:** 15HEC **Facilities:** **Services:** lau **Leisure:** R **Off-site:** P

LIBLAR Nordrhein-Westfalen

Liblarer See 50374 02235 3899
This site lies at lake Liblar, with its own bathing area.
Camping Card Compulsory
Access SW from Cologne on the B265 (for 15km), 1km before Liblar turn left towards the lake.
Open: All year **Site:** 10HEC **Facilities:** **Services:** lau **Leisure:** L

LINDENFELS Hessen

Terrassencamping Schlierbach Am Zentbuckel 11, 64678
06255 630 06255 3526
e-mail: info@terrassencamping-schlierbach.de
website: www.terrassencamping-schlierbach.de
Site is fenced and lies on sloping terrain. Siesta 13.00-15.00.
From Bensheim-Michelstadt road B47 turn off in Lindenfels SW to Schlierbach.
Open: Apr-Oct **Site:** 3.2HEC **Prices:** 2.80-3.50 3-5.50 pitch 4.40-5.50 **Facilities:** **Services:** lau **Off-site:** P

LINGERHAHN Rheinland-Pfalz

Mühlenteich 56291 06746 533 6746 1566
e-mail: info@muehlenteich.de
website: www.muehlenteich.de
Site lies on slightly sloping meadowland, divided into sections by a group of trees. Isolated situation at the edge of woodland and adjoining the forest swimming pool (free entry for campers). Siesta 13.00-15.00. Trout fishing.
Access from Koblenz-Bingen motorway A61 via exit Pfalzfeld. For caravans, an easier approach is via exit Laudert.
Open: All year **Site:** 15HEC **Prices:** 4 4 4 4 pitch 8 **Facilities:** **Services:** **Leisure:** P **Off-site:** R

LORCH Hessen

Suleika 65382 06726 9464 06726 9440
website: suleika-camping.de
Well laid out terraced site in an ideal location for exploring the historic Rhine valley. Separate car park for users of the smaller pitches.
From Assmannshausen take B42 3km towards Lorch then turn right into the Bodental - access to site through railway underpass. Approach for larger caravans - turn right 1km before Lorch.
Open: 15 Mar-Oct **Site:** 4HEC **Prices:** 5 1.50 5 3-5 (static)210 **Facilities:** **Services:** lau **Off-site:** LR

LOSHEIM Saarland

AZUR-Camping Reiterhof Girtenmühle Girtenmuhle, 66679 06872 90240 06872 902411
e-mail: losheim@azur-camping.de
website: www.azur-camping.de/losheim
Access via B268 Trier-Losheim.
Open: All year **Site:** 5HEC **Prices:** 3-5.50 2.50-3.70 pitch 4-6.50 **Facilities:** **Services:** lau **Off-site:** LP

MAINZ-KOSTHEIM Hessen

Mainz-Wiesbaden Maarau 55246 06134 4383 06134 4383
e-mail: info@kakg.de
website: www.knkg.de
Shop closed in April.
Open: 15 Mar-Oct **Site:** 2HEC **Facilities:** **Services:** lau **Off-site:** PR

MARBURG AN DER LAHN Hessen

GC Lahnaue Tro je damm 47, 35037
06421 21331 06421 21331
e-mail: info@lahnaue.de **website:** www.lahnaue.de
Municipal site on level meadowland next to the Sommerbad (swimming pool) in the W part of the town.
Open: Apr-30 Oct **Site:** 1HEC **Facilities:** **Services:** lau **Leisure:** R **Off-site:** P

MEERBUSCH Nordrhein-Westfalen

AZUR-Camping Meerbusch Zur Rheinfähre 21, 40668
02150 911817 02150 912289
e-mail: info@azur-camping.de
website: www.azur-camping.de
In a peaceful location on the banks of the Rhine within easy reach of Dusseldorf.
Access via A57 Neuss-Krefeld.
Open: Apr-13 Oct **Site:** 3.8HEC **Facilities:** **Services:** lau **Leisure:** R

MEHLEM Nordrhein-Westfalen

Genienau 53179 0228 344949 0228 3294989
e-mail: genienau@freenet.de
The site lies opposite the Drachenfels.
Open: All year **Site:** 1.8HEC **Facilities:** **Services:** lau **Leisure:** R **Off-site:** P

MEINHARD Hessen

Werra-Meissner-Kreis 37276 05651 6200 05651 22272
e-mail: 0565113805-0001@t-online.de
website: www.eschwege.de/fez/index.htm
A lakeside site with facilities for water sports.
Access via B27 and B249.
Open: Apr-Oct **Site:** 7HEC **Facilities:** **Services:** lau **Leisure:** L **Off-site:** P

MESCHEDE NORDRHEIN-WESTFALEN

Knaus Campingpark Hennesee Mielinghausen 7
0291 7663 0291 7663
e-mail: knauscamp.hennesee@freenet.de
website: www.knauscamp.de
Terraced site on the eastern side of a lake in an attractive location of mountains and forests.
Open: Apr-Oct & Dec **Site:** 3HEC **Prices:** 6 8 pitch 6-10 **Facilities:** **Services:** **Leisure:** LP **Off-site:**

MESENICH RHEINLAND-PFALZ

Family Camping Club 56820
02673 4556 02673 9629829
e-mail: info@familycamping.de
website: www.familycamping.de
A family site with plenty of recreational facilities beside the River Moselle. Individual pitches are divided by trees and hedges.
Open: May-Sep **Site:** 3HEC **Prices:** 4-4.50 pitch 22-30 (incl 2 persons) **Facilities:** **Services:** lau **Leisure:** PR

MICHELSTADT HESSEN

Odenwaldparadies 6120 06061 74152 & 3256
Site is partly fenced in and lies next to the station and swimming pool in the NE part of town.
Well signed from the by-pass road of Michelstadt.
Open: May-Sep **Site:** 1.2HEC **Facilities:** **Services:** **Off-site:** P

MITTELHOF RHEINLAND-PFALZ

Eichenwald 57537
02742 931931 & 910643 02742 931931 & 910645
e-mail: k.kohieubeck@hatzfeldt.de
In an oak wood, mainly divided into pitches.
Camping Card Compulsory
From Siegen follow B62 towards Wissen. Turning to site 1km NE of Wissen.
Open: All year **Site:** 10HEC **Prices:** 3.50 4 4 3 pitch 4 **Facilities:** **Services:** lau **Off-site:** P

MONSCHAU NORDRHEIN-WESTFALEN

Perlenau Eifel, 52156 02472 4136 02472 4493
Open: Apr-Oct **Site:** 2HEC **Facilities:** **Services:** lau **Leisure:** PR **Off-site:**

MONTABAUR RHEINLAND-PFALZ
AT GIROD (4KM E)

Eisenbachtal 56412 06485 766 06485 4938
Situated in the Nassau nature park.
From motorway exit 40 Montabaur turn right, before Montabaur follow sign 5km towards Limburg. From motorway exit 41 Wallmerod/Diez, 5km towards Montabaur.
Open: All year **Site:** 3HEC **Prices:** 4 7 pitch 7 **Facilities:** **Services:** lau **Off-site:** P

MÖRFELDEN-WALLDORF HESSEN

Arndt Mörfelden Am Zeltplatz 5, 64546
06105 22289 06105 277459
e-mail: campingplatz.moerfelden@t-online.de
website: www.campingplatz-moerfelden.de
Well laid out site in two sections near motorway. Siesta 13.00-15.00.
Well signed 0.3km from Langen/Mörfelden exit on A5/E4 Frankfurt-Darmstadt motorway.
Open: All year **Site:** 6HEC **Prices:** 4.50 pitch 6-8 **Facilities:** **Services:** lau **Off-site:** LP

MÜLHEIM RHEINLAND-PFALZ

AZUR Camping Mülheim 54486
06534 940157 06534 940157
Near Mülheim-Lieser bridge over the Mosel.
Access from Bernkastel, 5.5km along B53 towards Trier.
Open: Est-Oct **Site:** 1.5HEC **Facilities:** **Services:** lau **Leisure:** R **Off-site:**

MÜLHEIM AN DER RUHR NORDRHEIN-WESTFALEN

Entenfangsee 45481 0203 760111 0203 765162
Extensive site near lake. Touring pitches near railway line. Adventure playground. Siesta 13.00-15.00.
From motorway exit Duisburg-Wedau, continue towards Bissingheim to lake.
Open: All year **Site:** 12.5HEC **Facilities:** **Services:** lau **Leisure:** L **Off-site:** P

MÜLLENBACH RHEINLAND-PFALZ

Nürburgring 53520 02692 224 02692 1020
e-mail: rezeption@camping-am-nuerburgring.de
website: www.camping-am-nuerburgring.de
A large, well-equipped site in a wooded location with direct access to the Nürburgring Grand Prix circuit.
Access via A61/A48 & B412.
Open: All year **Site:** 30HEC **Facilities:** **Services:** lau

NEHREN RHEINLAND-PFALZ

Nehren 56820 02673 4612 02671 910754
e-mail: campingnehren@aol.com
website: www.campingplatz-nehren.de
On level terrain beside the River Moselle. Separate section for teenagers. Siesta 13.00-15.00. Liable to flood at certain times of the year.
Turn off B49 Cochem-Alf road in Nehren.
Open: Apr-15 Oct **Site:** 5HEC **Prices:** 4 7 5 pitch 7 **Facilities:** **Services:** lau **Leisure:** R **Off-site:**

NIEDEREISENHAUSEN HESSEN

Hinterland Ouotshauser Weg 32, Steffenberg, 35329
06464 7564
e-mail: camphinterland01@aol.com
Siesta 13.00-14.30.
Follow signs to Schwimmbad.
Open: All year **Site:** 2HEC **Facilities:** **Services:** lau **Off-site:** PR

NIEDERKRÜCHTEN NORDRHEIN-WESTFALEN

Lelefeld Lelefeld 4, 41372 02163 81203 02163 81203
e-mail: gblut@aol.com
website: www.camping-lelefeld.com
A quiet, wooded location on the outskirts of the village.
Signed from Elmpt.
Open: All year **Site:** 1.5HEC **Facilities:** **Services:** lau **Off-site:** LPR

OBERSGEGEN RHEINLAND-PFALZ

Reles-Mühle Kapellenstr 3, 54675
06566 8741 06566 931064
e-mail: info@eifelcamping.com
website: www.eifelcamping.com
In rural surroundings next to a farmhouse, set on a level meadow at a brook with trees and bushes.
From Bitburg on B50 towards Vianden. Site near the Luxembourg frontier.
Open: All year **Site:** 2HEC **Facilities:** **Services:** lau **Leisure:** R **Off-site:** P

OBERWEIS RHEINLAND-PFALZ

Prümtal-Camping In der Klaus 5, 54636
06527 92920 06527 929232
e-mail: info@pruemtal.de
website: www.pruemtal.de
A family site in pleasant wooded surroundings with good sports facilities.
Access from Bitburg on B50 towards Luxembourg border.
Open: All year **Site:** 3HEC **Facilities:** **Services:** lau **Leisure:** PR **Off-site:**

OLPE NORDRHEIN-WESTFALEN
AT KESSENHAMMER

Biggesee-Kessenhammer Kessenhammer 3, 57462
02761 94420 02761 944299
e-mail: camping.kessenhammer@t-online.de
website: www.camping-biggesee.de
Long, narrow, partly terraced site in quiet woodland setting on E shore of Bigge reservoir. Siesta 13.00-15.00.
A45 exit Olpe continue B54 to Olpe eastwards on B55 and turn off at exit Rhode.
Open: All year **Site:** 5.7HEC **Facilities:** **Services:** lau **Leisure:** L **Off-site:**

AT SONDERN

Biggesee-Sondern Sonderner Kopf 3, 57462
02761 944111 02761 944141
e-mail: camping.sondern@t-online.de
website: www.camping-biggesee.de
A popular site in wooded surroundings on the shore of the Biggersee.
Exit Olpe A45 in direction Attendorn. In 6km turn off for Erholungsanlage Biggesee-Sondern.
Open: All year **Site:** 6HEC **Prices:** 3.10-3.90 pitch 10.50-13.10 **Facilities:** **Services:** lau **Leisure:** L **Off-site:**

PORTA WESTFALICA NORDRHEIN-WESTFALEN

Grosser Weserbogen 32457 05731 6188 05731 6601
e-mail: grosserweserbogen@t-online.de
website: www.grosserweserbogen.de
From A2 towards Dortmund take exit Porta Westfalica-Minden.
Open: All year **Site:** 7HEC **Facilities:** **Services:** lau **Leisure:** L **Off-site:** P

PRÜM RHEINLAND-PFALZ

Waldcampingplatz 54591 06551 2481 06551 6555
e-mail: info@waldcamping-pruem.de
website: www.waldcamping-pruem.de
Site lies on both side of the River Prüm and is surrounded by woods. Divided into three sections of level meadowland.
NW of Prüm.
Open: All year **Site:** 3.5HEC **Facilities:** **Services:** lau **Leisure:** R **Off-site:** P

REINSFELD RHEINLAND-PFALZ

AZUR Camping Hunsrück 54421
06503 95123 06503 95124
e-mail: reinsfeld@azur-camping.de
website: www.azur-camping.de/reinsfeld
In a peaceful location close to Trier on the Luxembourg border, surrounded by hills.
Access via the B52 or B407.
Open: All year **Site:** 20HEC **Facilities:** **Services:** lau **Leisure:** P

ROTHEMANN HESSEN

Rothemann Maulkuppenstr 17, 36124 06659 2285
A small, well-kept site surrounded by a hedge, lies next to the main Fulda road.
From Fulda follow B27 for 10km towards Bad Brükenau. Or from Kassel-Wüzburg motorway exit Fulda Süd, then 3km along B27 towards Bad Brükenau.
Open: Apr-Oct **Site:** 6.4HEC **Facilities:** **Services:** **Off-site:**

RÜDESHEIM HESSEN

Rhein 65385
06722 2528 & 2582 06722 941046 & 406783
website: www.campingplatz-ruedesheim.de
Near the open-air swimming pool and the River Rhine.
Open: May-3 Oct **Site:** 3HEC **Prices:** 4.40 3.40 4.40 4.20-4.60 **Facilities:** **Services:** lau **Off-site:** P

SAARBURG RHEINLAND-PFALZ

Landal Greenpark Warsberg 54439
06581 91460 06581 914646
website: www.landal.de
Open site in quiet situation on top of a hill. Chair-lift (700m leads down to the town.
At N end of the town leave the B51 Trier road & follow signs. 3km uphill on good road.
Open: 29 Mar-04 Nov **Site:** 11HEC **Facilities:** **Services:** lau **Leisure:** P

Leukbachtal 54439 06581 2228 06581 2228
e-mail: camping.leukbachtal@web.de
Municipal site on level meadows on both sides of the Leuk-Bach (brook).
Leave Saarburg on road B51 towards Trassen, then after x-roads, turn left off the B51.
Open: Apr-Oct **Site:** 3HEC **Facilities:** **Services:** lau **Off-site:** P

Waldfrieden Im Fichtenhain 4, 54439
06581 2255 06581 5809
e-mail: camping-waldfrieden@t-online.de
website: campingwaldfrieden.de
Site lies next to the Café Waldfrieden on unspoiled, slightly rising meadowland in woods.
S of town leave B51 or B407 & follow road towards Nennig (Luxembourg). 200m to site.
Open: Mar-3 Nov **Site:** 2HEC **Facilities:** **Services:** lau **Off-site:** PR

SAARLOUIS SAARLAND

AZUR-Camping Saarlouis Marschall-Ney-Weg 2, 66740
06831 3691 06831 122970
e-mail: campscs@aol.com
website: www.camping-saarlouis.de
A municipal site, divided into pitches, and set on level meadowland with tall trees. Siesta 13.00-14.30.

Turn off road B51 in suburb of Roden, cross new bridge ver the River Saar to site, beyond sports hall.
)pen: 15 Mar-Oct Site: 2HEC **Prices:** 4.50 5 3.50 **Facilities:** **Services:** lau **Off-site:** P

St Goar Rheinland-Pfalz

'riedenau Gruendelbach 103, 35629
06741 368 06741 368
)n level, narrow stretch of meadowland at Gasthaus riedenau.
Leave B9 in St Goar & continue through railway underpass owards Emmelshausen for 1km.
)pen: Mar-1 Dec Site: 2HEC **Facilities:** **Services:** lau **Leisure:** R **Off-site:** P

St Goarshausen Rheinland-Pfalz

oreleystadt 56346 06771 2592 02137 929641
Aunicipal site on level meadow beside the Rhine. Near a ports field and opposite Rheinfels castle.
Access via B42.
)pen: 15 Mar-Oct Site: 1.5HEC **Prices:** 4.80-5.40 2.20 3.50 2.60-4.50 **Facilities:** 'ervices: lau **Leisure:** R **Off-site:**

Schachen Hessen

Iochrhön 36129 06654 7836 06654 7836
-mail: campinghochrhoen@aol.com
vebsite: www.rhoenline.de/camping.hochrhon
ies 1.5km from the Kneipp (hydrotherapeutic) spa area of iersfeld.
2km N of Gersfeld.
)pen: All year Site: 3HEC **Facilities:** ervices: lau **Off-site:** P

Schalkenmehren Rheinland-Pfalz

'amp am Maar Maarstr 22, 54552
06592 95510 06592 955140
-mail: hotelschneider@t-online.de
vebsite: www.hotelschneider.de
'erraced lakeside site on meadowland at the chalkenmehrener Maar (water-filled crater). Towing help or caravans.
From A48 (Eifelautobahn) leave at Mehren/Daun exit & 42 to Mehren. Turn off to the SW.
)pen: All year Site: 1HEC **Facilities:** **Services:** lau **Leisure:** LP **Off-site:**

Schleiden Nordrhein-Westfalen

'chleiden Im Wiesengrund 39, 53937 02445 7030
ite lies on hilly, well-wooded country.
On the B258 to Monschau, 1km to site.
)pen: All year Site: 5HEC **Facilities:** **Services:** lau **Off-site:** P

Schlüchtern Hessen
At Hutten (8km E)

Iutten Heiligenborn Helga Herzog-Gericke, 36381
06661 2424 06661 917581
-mail: helga.herzog-gericke@online.de
ite lies at Heiligenborn and has a pleasant southerly aspect. iesta 13.00-15.00.
Approach from Fulda on B40 towards Frankfurt to Flieden or 19km, then turn left via Rückers to Hutten (8km).
)pen: All year Site: 3.5HEC **Facilities:** **Services:** lau **Off-site:** P

Schönenberg Saarland

Ohmbachsee 66901 06373 4001 06373 4002
Terraced site on sloping ground above E bank of the Ohmabachsee. Separate field for young people. Siesta 13.00-15.00.
Signed.
Open: All year **Site:** 7.8HEC **Facilities:** **Services:** lau **Leisure:** P **Off-site:** L

Schotten Hessen

Nidda-Stausee Vogelsbergstr 184, 63679
06044 1418 06044 987995
e-mail: campingplatz@schotten.de
website: www.schotten.de
A pleasant family site beside a lake.
Access via B455.
Open: All year **Site:** 3.2HEC **Facilities:** **Services:** lau **Off-site:** LP

Seck Rheinland-Pfalz

Weiherhof 56479 02664 8555 02664 6388
Site lies on level meadowland next to a small lake in a wooded nature reserve. Special section reserved for young people. Many bathers at weekends.
Take the B255 from Rennerod and drive to Hellenbahn-Schellenberg. Then turn S and continue for 2km.
Open: 15 Mar-15 Oct **Site:** 10HEC **Facilities:** **Services:** lau **Leisure:** L

Senheim Rheinland-Pfalz

Internationaler Holländischer Hof 56820
02673 4660 02673 4100
e-mail: holl.hof@t-online.de
website: www.moselcamping.com
On level meadowland, divided into pitches beside the River Mosel, which has mooring facilities.
Access from Cochem on the B49 in direction of Zell as far as Senhals, then over the bridge and turn left.
Open: 6 Apr-1 Nov **Site:** 4HEC **Prices:** 3.46-3.85 pitch 6.03-6.70 (static)205-435 **Facilities:** **Services:** lau **Leisure:** R

Sensweiler Mühle Rheinland-Pfalz

Sensweiler Mühle Bundestr 422, 55758
06786 2395 06781 35147
e-mail: info@sensweiler-muehle.de
website: www.sensweiler-muehle.de
On extensive grassland beside the Idar, partially terraced, in rural area near a farm. Views of wooded range of hills. Next to Camping Oberes Idartal. Separate section for young groups.
From Idar-Oberstein follow road B422 for 10km NW. Site between Katzenloch & Allenbach.
Open: 3 Oct-11-Feb **Site:** 4HEC **Facilities:** **Services:** lau **Leisure:** R **Off-site:** L

Oberes Idartal 55758 06786 2114 06786 2222
e-mail: cpoberesidartal@aol.com
website: www.oberes-idartal.de
Site lies on a farm by the Idar, set on several small meadows and partly on terraced terrain next to Camping Sensweiler Mühle. Blockhouse with facilities for spit-roasting.
From Idar-Oberstein follow B422 10km NW. Site between Katzenloch & Allenbach.
Open: All year **Site:** 2HEC **Facilities:** **Services:** lau **Leisure:** R **Off-site:**

SOLINGEN NORDRHEIN-WESTFALEN
AT GLÜDER

Waldcamping Glüder 42659 0212 242120 0212 2421234
Site on level terrain surrounded by woodland on banks of the River Wupper.
Access via Köln-Kamen autobahn exit Burscheid. Via Hilgen & Witzhelden to Glüder. From Solingen on B299/B224 towards Witzhelden via Burg Hohenscheid.
Open: All year **Site:** 2HEC **Facilities:** **Services:** lau **Off-site:** P

STADTKYLL RHEINLAND-PFALZ

Landal Greenparks Wirftt 54589
06597 92920 06597 929250
website: www.landal.de
Extensive, level grassland beside the upper of two small reservoirs, 1km outside the town.
S from Euskirchen on the A1, through Blankenheim towards Stadtkyll.
Open: All year **Site:** 6.4HEC **Facilities:** **Services:** lau **Leisure:** P

STEINEN RHEINLAND-PFALZ

Hofgut Schönerlen 56244 02666 207 02666 8429
e-mail: camping-kopper@t-online.de
website: www.camping-westerwald.de
Beautiful and quiet site at lake Hausweiher. Section reserved for residential campers. Campers under 18 years old not accepted unless with adults.
Take the B8 Limburg-Altenkirchen road. In Steinen turn left to the site.
Open: Dec-Oct **Site:** 15HEC **Prices:** 4.10-4.60 pitch 5.20-5.70 **Facilities:** **Services:** lau **Leisure:** L **Off-site:**

STUKENBROCK NORDRHEIN-WESTFALEN

Furlbach Am Furlbach 33, 33758
05257 3373 05257 940373
Extensive site, partly on level meadow and partly in woodland. Separate section for dog owners. Old barn is used as a common room for young campers. Siesta 12.30-14.30.
From the Dortmund-Hannover motorway (A2/E73) exit Bielefeld/Sennenstadt then follow B68 for 12km towards Paderborn. At Km44.2 turn off main road then 400m to site.
Open: Apr-1 Nov **Site:** 9HEC **Facilities:** **Services:** lau **Off-site:**

TANN HESSEN

Ulstertal Dippach 4, 36142 06682 8292 06682 10086
Terraced site on slightly sloping meadowland.
Leave the Bischofsheim-Tann road B278 in Wendershausen SE to Dippach.
Open: All year **Site:** 2.4HEC **Facilities:** **Services:** lau

TREIS-KARDEN RHEINLAND-PFALZ

Mosel-Islands 56253 02672 2613 02672 912102
e-mail: mosel-boating-center@t-online.de
An extensive, level site on a grassy island in the Mosel next to a yacht marina.
Turn off the B49 in Treis onto the southern coastal road.
Open: Apr-Oct **Site:** 4.5HEC **Prices:** 4 2.60 5.50 2.60 **Facilities:** **Services:** lau **Leisure:** R **Off-site:** P

TRENDELBURG HESSEN

Trendelburg 34388 05675 301 05675 5888
e-mail: conradi-camping@t-online.de
Site located at the foot of the castle, subdivided on the banks of the River Diemel. Covered tennis court.
Access from Kessel N via Hofgeismar (B83) to Trendelburg, cross the bridge & sharp left down to site.
Open: All year **Site:** 2.7HEC **Facilities:** **Services:** lau **Leisure:** R **Off-site:** P

TRIER RHEINLAND-PFALZ

Trier-City Luxemburger Str 81, 54294
0651 86921 0651 83079
Level site owned by the rowing club Treviris, on left bank of the Mosel 1.6km from the city centre.
Between the Romer bridge & Adenauer bridge on road towards Luxembourg.
Open: Apr-Oct **Site:** 1.5HEC **Facilities:** **Services:** **Leisure:** R **Off-site:** P

TRIPPSTADT RHEINLAND-PFALZ

Sägmühle Sägmühle 1, 67705 06306 92190 06306 200C
e-mail: info@saegmuehle.de
website: www.saegmuehle.de
The site lies in a wooded valley beside the Sagmühle lake. It consists of several unconnected sections, some of them terraced. Siesta 12.30-14.00.
14km S of Kaiserslautern.
Open: 16 Dec-Oct **Site:** 10HEC **Prices:** 5.70-6.90 pitch 6.30-8 **Facilities:** **Services:** lau
Leisure: L **Off-site:** P

UTSCHEID RHEINLAND-PFALZ

Michelbach 54675 06564 2097
A municipal site at the Michelbach, surrounded by meadows and woods, half individual pitches.
From the B50 Bittburg-Vianden road turn N in Sinspelt. Continue via Niederraden to Utscheid.
Open: All year **Site:** 1.5HEC **Facilities:** **Services:** lau **Off-site:**

VINKRATH BEI GREFRATH NORDRHEIN-WESTFALEN

SC Waldfrieden 47929 02158 3855 02158 3685
Site within nature reserve.
From Grefrath N towards Wankum after 3km. Turn right.
Site: 4.5HEC **Facilities:** **Services:** lau **Off-site:** LP

VLOTHO NORDRHEIN-WESTFALEN

Borlefzen Borlefzen 2, 32602
05733 80008 05733 89728
e-mail: info@borlefzen.de
website: www.borlefzen.de
Open: Apr-Oct **Site:** 40HEC **Facilities:** **Services:** lau **Leisure:** LR

WARBURG NORDRHEIN-WESTFALEN

Eversburg 34414 05641 8668
Site next to restaurant of the same name on the SE outskirts of the town.
Open: All year **Site:** 4.5HEC **Facilities:** **Services:** lau **Leisure:** R **Off-site:** P

WASSERFALL Nordrhein-Westfalen

Wasserfall Aurorastr 9, 59909 02905 332
Terraced site, surrounded by woodland, next to leisure centre Fort Fun. Little room for touring campers during the winter.
About 10km E of Meschedes, between Bestwig & Nuttlar, turn S off the B7. Pass Gevelinghausen up to Wasserfall.
Open: All year **Site:** 0.7HEC **Facilities:** **Services:** **Off-site:** PR

WAXWEILER Rheinland-Pfalz

AEGON-Ferienpark Im Prümtal 54649
06554 92000 06554 920029
e-mail: info@ferienpark-waxweiler.de
Site lies on level terrain and is divided into pitches, with a separate field on the opposite side of the River Prüm. Near swimming pool. Siesta 13.00-15.00.
From N end of Waxweiler turn off towards the River Prüm.
Open: 31 Mar-5 Nov **Site:** 3HEC **Facilities:** **Services:** lau **Leisure:** P **Off-site:** P

WEILBURG Hessen
AT ODERSBACH

Odersbach Runkler Str 5A, 35781
06471 7620 06471 379603
e-mail: camping-odersbach@t-online.de
website: www.camping-odersbach.de
Attractive setting beside the River Lahn, next to a public swimming pool. Siesta 12.00-14.00.
On S outskirts of town.
Open: Apr-Oct **Site:** 6HEC **Facilities:** **Services:** lau **Leisure:** PR **Off-site:**

WINTERBERG Nordrhein-Westfalen
AT NIEDERSFELD (8.5KM N)

Vossmecke 59955 02985 8418 02985 553
e-mail: info@camping-vossmecke.de
website: www.camping-vossmecke.de
A pleasant wooded location with facilities for winter camping.
Off B480 towards Winterberg.
Open: All year **Site:** 4HEC **Prices:** 10.95-11.95 pitch 13.90-16.90 (incl 2 persons) **Facilities:** **Services:** lau **Off-site:**

WISSEL Nordrhein-Westfalen

Wisseler See Zum Wisseler See 15, 47546
02824 96310 02824 963131
e-mail: wisseler-see@t-online.de **website:** www.wisseler-see.de
Well-kept municipal site with modern facilities beside Lake Wissel. There is a separate car park next to the open-air swimming pool. The pool belongs to the camp. The washrooms are closed lunchtimes and at night.
From Kieve take the B57 towards Xanten. After 9km, turn left 3km towards Wissel.
Open: All year **Site:** 40HEC **Facilities:** **Services:** lau **Leisure:** L **Off-site:** P

WITZENHAUSEN Hessen

Werratal Am Sande 11, 37213
05542 1465 05542 72418
website: www.campingplatz-werratal.de
The site lies on meadow between the outskirts of Witzenhausen and the banks of the Werra.
Leave Hannover-Kassel motorway at Werratal. 10km on B80 to Witzenhausen. From market place follow signs.
Open: All year **Site:** 3HEC **Facilities:** **Services:** lau **Leisure:** R **Off-site:** P

WOLFSTEIN Rheinland-Pfalz

AZUR Campingpark am Königsberg Am Schwimmbad 1, 67752 06304 4143 06304 7543
e-mail: benspruijt@gmx.de
website: www.camping-wolfstein.com
Municipal site, beside small River Lauter next to open air swimming pool.
At S end of Wolfstein to the right of B270 from Kaiserslautern.
Open: All year **Site:** 1.5HEC **Prices:** 4.50-6 2.10-2.10 pitch 5.50-7.50 **Facilities:** **Services:** lau **Off-site:** LPR

ZERF Rheinland-Pfalz

Rübezahl 54314 06587 814 06587 814
e-mail: seyffardt-zerf@t-online.de
Meadowland site on wooded hillside.
Leave Zerf S on B268 towards Saarbrücken then turn towards Oberzerf 2.5km to site. From Saarburg, follow B407 beyond Vierherrenhorn, turn right & follow track for 60m.
Open: Apr-Oct **Site:** 2.5HEC **Facilities:** **Services:** **Leisure:** P

ZWESTEN Hessen

Waldcamping Hinter dem Wasser, 34596
05626 379 06695 1320
e-mail: waldcamping@planet-interken.de
website: www.waldcamping.de
Site in bend of River Schwalm. Siesta 13.00-15.00. For touring campers there is an overflow site outside the campsite.
SW from Kassel via Fritzlar to Zwesten.
Open: All year **Site:** 5HEC **Facilities:** **Services:** lau **Leisure:** PR **Off-site:**

NORTH

ALTENAU Niedersachsen

Okertalsperre Kornhardtweg 1, 38707
05328 702 05328 911708
e-mail: okercamping@t.online.de
On a long stretch of grassland at the S end of the Oker reservoir. Siesta 13.00-15.00.
Signed from B498 Oker-Altenau.
Open: All year **Site:** 4HEC **Facilities:** **Services:** lau **Leisure:** L

BLECKEDE Niedersachsen

Alt-Garge (ADAC) Am Waldbad 23, 21354
05854 311 05854 1640
e-mail: adac-camping-altgarge@t-online.de
website: www.camping-urlaub.de
A modern site surrounded by tall trees, lying at the SE end of Alt-Garge next to a heated swimming pool in the woods. The camp has its own gas-filling station. Archery butts. Siesta 13.00-14.30.
5km SE of Bleckede.
Open: All year **Site:** 6.6HEC **Facilities:** **Services:** **Off-site:** LPR

Facilities: -shop -shower -electric points for razors -electric points for caravans -parking by tents permitted -compulsory separate car park **Services:** -café/restaurant -bar -Camping Gaz International -gas other than Camping Gaz -first aid facilities lau-laundry **Leisure:** -swimming L-Lake P-Pool R-River S-Sea **Off-site:** All facilities within 2km

BODENWERDER Niedersachsen

Himmelspforte Ziegeleiweg 1, 37619
05533 4938 05533 4432
Site on grassland, with a fruit orchard, next to the River Weser. Good possibilites for water sports. Separate section and common room for young campers.
Cross River Weser & turn right towards Rühle. Site 2km.
Open: All year **Site:** 8HEC **Facilities:** **Services:** **Leisure:** R **Off-site:** P

Rühler Schweiz 37619 05533 2827 05533 5882
e-mail: info@brader-ruehler-schweiz.de
website: www.brader-ruehler-schweiz.de
This site lies on well-kept meadowland by the River Weser.
From the Weser Bridge in Bodenwerder follow road for 4km towards Rühle.
Open: Mar-Oct **Site:** 50HEC **Facilities:** **Services:** lau **Leisure:** PR **Off-site:**

BOTHEL Niedersachsen

Hanseat 27384 04266 355
Open: All year **Site:** 20HEC **Facilities:** **Services:** lau **Off-site:** P

BRAUNLAGE Niedersachsen
At Zorge (14km S)

Harz Camping Im Waldwinkel 37449
05586 1048 05586 8113
A site on different levels, surrounded by high trees, 200m from an open-air woodland pool in the Kunzen valley.
Open: All year **Site:** 1.5HEC **Facilities:** **Services:** lau **Off-site:** P

BREMEN Bremen

Freie Hansestadt Bremen Am Stadtwaldsee 1, 28359
0421 212002 0421 219857
Situated in a nature reserve 700m from lake.
Access from autobahn A27 exit university Bremen.
Open: All year **Site:** 5.8HEC **Facilities:** **Services:** lau **Off-site:** LP

BRIETLINGEN-REIHERSEE Niedersachsen

Reihersee 1 Alte Salzstr 8, 21382
04133 3671 & 3577 04133 4391
Divided into pitches by hedges and pine trees. Private bathing area.
At car park, 2km beyond Brietlingen, turn E towards Reihersee for 800m.
Open: All year **Site:** 6.2HEC **Facilities:** **Services:** lau **Leisure:** LR **Off-site:**

BÜCHEN Schleswig-Holstein

Waldschwimmbad 21514 04155 5360 04155 499140
On gently sloping grassland. Siesta 13.00-15.00hrs.
From Lauenburg or Mölln follow road to Büchen then signs to site.
Open: All year **Site:** 1.6HEC **Facilities:** **Services:** lau **Off-site:** PR

BURG (ISLAND OF FEHMARN) Schleswig-Holstein
At Klausdorf (5km NW)

Klausdorfer Strand 23769 04371 2549 04371 2481
e-mail: info@camping-klausdorferstrand.de
website: www.camping-klausdorferstrand.de
A grassy site with sea views. Divided into pitches. Sandy beach. Siesta 12.30-14.30.
From Burg turn off the main road 2.5km before Klausdorf onto narrow asphalt road.
Open: Apr-15 Oct **Site:** 12HEC **Facilities:** **Services:** lau **Leisure:** PS **Off-site:** L

BURGWEDEL Niedersachsen

Erholungsgebiet Springhorstsee 30938
05139 3232 05139 27070
e-mail: springhorstsee@aol.com
On level ground on the shores of a lake with well-defined pitches and modern facilities.
25km N of Hannover, 2km from Grossburgwedel motorway exit.
Open: All year **Site:** 29HEC **Facilities:** **Services:** lau **Leisure:** LP **Off-site:**

CLAUSTHAL-ZELLERFELD Niedersachsen

Prahljust 38678 05323 1300 05323 78393
website: www.prahljust.de
The site lies on slightly sloping grassland in an area of woodland and lakes.
Follow road B242 SE from outskirts 2km towards Braunlage, then turn right to site in 1.5km.
Open: All year **Site:** 13HEC **Facilities:** **Services:** lau **Leisure:** LP **Off-site:**

Waldweben Spiegelthalerstr 31, 38678
05323 81712 05323 962134
website: www.campingplatz-waldweben.harz.de
Holiday village with individual pitches in open meadow and coniferous woodland by three small lakes.
Signed from B241 towards Goslar.
Open: All year **Site:** 4.5HEC **Facilities:** **Services:** lau **Off-site:** LP

DAHRENHORST Niedersachsen

Irenensee Dahrenhorst, 31311
05173 98120 05173 981213
e-mail: info@irenensee.de
website: www.irenensee.de
A lakeside site on meadowland, partly surrounded by woods, with separate sections for tourers, statics and residentials. Siesta 13.00-15.00.
From Burgdorf follow B188 for 15km towards Uetze.
Open: All year **Site:** 120HEC **Facilities:** **Services:** lau **Leisure:** L

DETERN Niedersachsen

Jümmesee 26847 04957 1808 04957 8112
e-mail: info@detern.com
website: www.detern.com
Access via B72 Aurich-Cloppenburg.
Open: Mar-Oct **Site:** 11.5HEC **Facilities:** **Services:** lau **Leisure:** LR **Off-site:** PS

DORUM SCHLESWIG-HOLSTEIN

AZUR Nordseecamp Dorumer Tief 27632
04741 5020 04741 914061
e-mail: dorum@azur-camping.de
website: www.azur-camping.deldorum
Next to a small harbour. Separated from the beach by a dyke.
Access via A27 Bremerhaven-Cuxhaven.
Open: Apr-Sep **Site:** 7HEC **Facilities:** **Services:** lau **Leisure:** PS

EGESTORF NIEDERSACHSEN

AZUR-Camping Lüneburger Heide 21272
04175 661 04175 8383
e-mail: egestorf@azur-camping.de
website: www.azurcamping.de/egestorf
Modern site on wooded heathland on the edge of the Lüneburger heath nature reserve, 2km S of town on slightly sloping terrain with asphalt internal roads.
Access via Hamburg-Hannover motorway A7/E4 Egestorf or Evendorf exits.
Open: All year **Site:** 22HEC **Facilities:** **Services:** lau **Leisure:** P **Off-site:**

EIMKE NIEDERSACHSEN

Eimke Im Extertal 32699 05262 3307 05262 992404
website: www.campingpark-eimke.de
Extensive, partly terraced site on slightly sloping meadowland with two ponds.
Camping Card Compulsory
From Dortmund-Hannover motorway (A2/E8) take Bad Eilsen exit & B238 S. 1km beyond Rinteln turn left for 18km along External-Barntrup road.
Open: All year **Site:** 20HEC **Facilities:** **Services:** lau **Leisure:** L **Off-site:** P

ELISABETH SOPHIENKOOG (ISLAND OF NORDSTRAND) SCHLESWIG-HOLSTEIN

Elisabeth-Sophienkoog 25845 04842 8534 04842 8306
e-mail: camping-nordstrand@t-online.de
On meadowland behind the North Sea dyke. Siesta 12.00-14.00.
Access via Husum to island of Nordstrand.
Open: Apr-Oct **Site:** 1.7HEC **Facilities:** **Services:** lau **Leisure:** S

ESENS-BENSERSIEL NIEDERSACHSEN

Bensersiel Am Strand, 26427
04971 917121 04971 917190
e-mail: campnig@bensersiel.de
website: www.bensersiel.de
Well-managed, extensive leisure centre with harbour, good fish restaurant and reading room. Swimming pools have sea water and artificial waves.
Take B210 NE from Aurich to Ogenbargenn then via Esens.
Open: Etr-15 Sep **Site:** 10HEC **Facilities:** **Services:** lau **Leisure:** S **Off-site:** P

EUTIN-FISSAU SCHLESWIG-HOLSTEIN

Prinzenholz Prinzenholzweg 20, 23701
04521 5281 04521 3601
e-mail: info@nc-prinzenholz.de
website: www.nc-prinzenholz.de
Terraced lakeside site divided by trees and bushes. Mobile shop.
N of town take Malente road & turn right after 2km.
Open: Apr-Oct **Site:** 2HEC **Facilities:** **Services:** lau **Leisure:** L **Off-site:** P

FALLINGBOSTEL NIEDERSACHSEN

Böhhmeschlucht Vierde 22, 29683
05162 5604 05162 5160
website: www.bohmeschlucht.de
Site located in a nature reserve beside the River Böhme.
A7/E45, exit 46/47. signed about 3km N
Open: All year **Site:** 4HEC **Facilities:** **Services:** lau **Leisure:** R

FEHMARN (ISLAND OF) FEHMARNSUND SCHLESWIG-HOLSTEIN

Miramar 23769 04371 3220 04371 868044
e-mail: campingmiramar@t-online.de
website: www.camping-miramar.de
A family site on meadowland situated at the southern end of the island.
Turn off the B207/E4 at the first turning after the Sundbrücke (bridge) towards Svendorf.
Open: All year **Site:** 13HEC **Facilities:** **Services:** lau **Leisure:** LS

GANDERSHEIM, BAD NIEDERSACHSEN

DCC Kur-Campingpark Braunschweiger Str 12, 37581
05382 1595 05382 1599
website: www.camping-bad-gandersheim.de
On level meadow, divided in two by a brook beside a public park. Good sports facilities. Separate section for young people.
From Hannover-Kassel motorway via exit Soesen.
Open: All year **Site:** 9HEC **Facilities:** **Services:** lau **Off-site:** P

GARTOW NIEDERSACHSEN

Gartow am See Am Helk, 29471
05846 8250 05846 2151
e-mail: campingpark@gartow.de
website: ww.campingpark-gartow.de
Situated in woodland with adjoining meadow.
Camping Card Compulsory
NE on A493 from Lüchow.
Open: All year **Site:** 14HEC **Facilities:** **Services:** lau **Leisure:** P **Off-site:** LR

GIFHORN NIEDERSACHSEN AT RÖTGESBÜTTEL (8KM S)

Glockenheide 38531 05304 1581 05304 1581
e-mail: camping-glockenheide@T-online.de
website: www.glockenheide.de
Tranquil site in heathland. Siesta 13.00-15.00.
Camping Card Compulsory
In Rötgesbüttel turn left, then left again after level crossing.
Open: All year **Site:** 5HEC **Facilities:** **Services:** lau **Off-site:**

GLÜCKSBURG-HOLNIS SCHLESWIG-HOLSTEIN

AZUR Ostseecamp Grenzblick Am Kurstrand 3, 24960
04631 622071 04631 622072
e-mail: info@azur-camping.de
website: www.azur-camping.de
Open: Apr-Oct **Site:** 6HEC **Facilities:** **Services:** lau **Off-site:**

GRUBE SCHLESWIG-HOLSTEIN

Rosenfelder Strand Textil 23749
04365 4112 04365 1494
e-mail: info@rosenfelder-strand.de
website: www.rosenfelder-strand.de
Excellently managed family site beside the sea with a 1km beach. Divided into separate fields by rows of bushes. Children's playground in woodland between site and sea. Strict observance of siesta 13.00-15.00.
Take the B207/E4 from Lübeck N to Lensahn, then E to Grube.
Open: Apr-Sep **Site:** 24HEC **Facilities:** **Services:** **Leisure:** S **Off-site:** S

HADDEBY SCHLESWIG-HOLSTEIN

Haithabu 24866 04621 32450 04621 33122
e-mail: camping@uumail.de
website: www.campingplatz-haithabu.de
Clean, tidy site beside River Schlei.
From Schleswig B76 towards Eckernförde.
Open: Apr-Sep **Site:** 5HEC **Facilities:** **Services:** lau **Leisure:** R

HADEMSTORF NIEDERSACHSEN

Waldhaus Allertal 29693 05071 1872 05071 1912516
In a picturesque wooded setting with pitches separated by hedges and bushes.
Access via A27/A7.
Open: Apr-Sep **Site:** 4HEC **Facilities:** **Services:** lau **Off-site:** R

HAHNENKLEE NIEDERSACHSEN

Kreuzeck 38644 05325 2570 05325 3392
e-mail: kreuzeck@aol.com
website: www.campingground.de
In the forest beside a lake. Terraces and a separate section for dog-owners.
Beside Café am Kreuzeck at the junction of the B241 & the Hahnenklee road.
Open: All year **Site:** 5HEC **Facilities:** **Services:** lau **Leisure:** LP **Off-site:**

HAMELN NIEDERSACHSEN

Waldbad Pfedeweg 2, 31787 05158 2774 05158 2774
A grassy terraced site on the edge of woodland beside a public swimming pool.
Camping Card Compulsory
Follow 'swimming pool' signs from Havelstorf.
Open: Apr-Oct **Site:** 2.8HEC **Facilities:** **Services:** lau **Off-site:** P

HANNOVER NIEDERSACHSEN
AT GARBSEN (10KM W)

Blauer See 30823 05137 89960 05137 899677
e-mail: info@camping-blauer-see.de
website: www.camping-blauer-see.de
On a small lake beside the Garbsen service area on Hannover-Bielefeld motorway A2/E8.
Open: All year **Site:** 22HEC **Facilities:** **Services:** lau **Leisure:** L

AT ISERNHAGEN (16KM NE)

Parksee Lohne Alter Postweg 12, 30916
05139 88260 05139 891665
e-mail: parksee-lohne@t-online.de
website: www.parksee-lohne.de
Recreation area by a lake. On the flight path for Hannover Langenhagen airport. Separate section for tourers.
From motorway exit Kirchorst follow Altwarmbüchen road to Isernhagen.
Open: All year **Site:** 16HEC **Facilities:** **Services:** lau **Leisure:** L

HARDEGSEN NIEDERSACHSEN

Ferienpark Solling 37181 05505 5585 05505 5585
Terraced site in forested area. Separate field for touring pitches. Siesta 13.00-15.00.
In town take Waldgebiet Gladeberg road.
Open: All year **Site:** 2.4HEC **Facilities:** **Services:** lau **Off-site:** P

HASSENDORF NIEDERSACHSEN

Stürberg 27367 04264 9124 04264 821440
e-mail: campingpark-stuerberg@gmx.de
website: www.stuerberg.de
In pleasant wooded surroundings beside a lake.
From Ab1 exit Stuckenborstel take B75 towards Rotenburg for 5km.
Open: Mar-Oct **Site:** 2HEC **Facilities:** **Services:** **Leisure:** L **Off-site:**

HATTEN NIEDERSACHSEN

Freizeitzentrum Hatten Kreyenweg 8, 26209
04482 677 04482 928027
e-mail: info@jzz.hatten.de
Open: All year **Site:** 2HEC **Facilities:** **Services:** lau **Leisure:** P **Off-site:**

HATTORF NIEDERSACHSEN

Oderbrücke 37197 05521 4359 05521 4360
e-mail: oderbruecke@t-online.de
website: www.oderbruecke.top.ms
In a pleasant wooded location with good recreational and sanitary facilities.
On B27 towards Herzberg.
Open: All year **Site:** 2.5HEC **Facilities:** **Services:** lau **Leisure:** R **Off-site:**

HEIKENDORF SCHLESWIG-HOLSTEIN

Möltenort 24226 0431 241316 0431 2379920
e-mail: gronau.heikendorf@freenet.de
website: www.camping-ostree-online.de
Terraced site by the Kieler Förde.
15km NE of Kiel to W of B502. Approach via a narrow winding road.
Open: Apr-1 Oct **Site:** 2HEC **Facilities:** **Services:** lau **Leisure:** S **Off-site:**

HELMSTEDT NIEDERSACHSEN

Waldwinkel Maschweg 46, 38350 05351 37161
In an orchard next to the Gasthaus Waldwinkel.
Signed from autobahn exit Helmstedt.
Open: All year **Site:** 10HEC **Facilities:** **Services:** lau **Off-site:** P

HEMELN NIEDERSACHSEN

Hemeln 34346 05544 1414 05544 1414
e-mail: camping-hemeln@gmx.de
website: www.weserecamping.de
Well-kept site on N outskirts of village, beside the River Weser.
From autobahn A7 take the Gothenburg exit & follow B3 to Dransfeld then follow signs.
Open: All year **Site:** 20HEC **Facilities:** **Services:** lau **Leisure:** R

HERMANNSBURG NIEDERSACHSEN

Örtzetal 29320 05052 3072 & 1555
website: www.campingplatz-oldendorf.de
Site lies on meadows on the E bank of the River Örtze, set in unspoiled woodlands of the Lüneburg heath. Boat landing stage. Siesta 13.00-15.00.
From B3 Celle-Soltau turn off in Bergen NE towards Hermannsburg, then continue towards Eschwege.
Open: 15 Mar-Oct **Site:** 6HEC **Facilities:** **Services:** lau **Leisure:** R **Off-site:** P

HOHEGEISS NIEDERSACHSEN

Bärenbache Barenbachweg 10, 38700
05583 1306 05583 1300
e-mail: info@campingplatz-hohegeiss.de
website: www.campingplatz-hohegeiss.de
Terraced site. Well-organised.
Open: All year **Site:** 2.8HEC **Facilities:** **Services:** **Off-site:** P

HOLLE NIEDERSACHSEN
AT DERNEBURG (2KM NW ON UNCLASS ROAD)

Seecamp-Derneburg An der B6, Derneburg, 31188
05062 565 05062 8785
e-mail: info@campingplatz-derneburg.de
website: www.campingplatz-derneburg.de
A terraced lakeside site on a hill slope with a southerly aspect. Separate touring field. Useful transit site near autobahn.
From the motorway exit Derneburg & continue to B6.
Open: Apr-15 Sep **Site:** 7.8HEC **Facilities:** **Services:** lau **Leisure:** L **Off-site:** R

KLEINWAABS SCHLESWIG-HOLSTEIN

Ostsee Heide 24369 04352 2530 04352 1398
e-mail: info@waabs.de
website: www.waabs.de
Divided into pitches and pleasantly landscaped. Large games room for teenagers. Siesta 13.00-14.30.
Open: Mar-Oct **Site:** 21.5HEC **Facilities:** **Services:** lau **Leisure:** PS

KLINT-BEI-HECHTHAUSEN NIEDERSACHSEN

Geesthof Am Ferienpark 1, 21755
04774 512 04774 9178
e-mail: ferienpark.geesthof@t-online.de
website: www.ferienpark-geesthof.de
On dry meadowland next to the River Oste, in quiet setting with trees. Siesta 13.00-15.00.
From Hechthausen B73 W towards Lamstedt for 3km.
Open: All year **Site:** 15HEC **Facilities:** **Services:** lau **Leisure:** P

LANGHOLZ ÜBER ECKERNFÖRDE SCHLESWIG-HOLSTEIN

Langholz Fischerstr 9, 24369 04352 2542
A holiday site surrounded by a belt of trees situated at a wide natural beach, at the mouth of the Eckernförde.
Camping Card Compulsory
From the Eckernförde take the B203 NE to the turn off for Langholz, then right & continue 3km to site.
Open: Apr-Sep **Site:** 20HEC **Facilities:** **Services:** lau **Leisure:** S **Off-site:**

LAUTERBERG, BAD NIEDERSACHSEN

Wiesenbeker Teich 37431 05524 2510 05524 932089
e-mail: info@campingwiesenbek.de
website: www.campingwiesenbek.de
In wooded surroundings on the Wiesenbeker Teich.
Approach via B243 SE of Bad Lauterberg.
Open: All year **Site:** 10HEC **Facilities:** **Services:** lau **Leisure:** L **Off-site:** P

LOOSE SCHLESWIG-HOLSTEIN

Gut Ludwigsburg 24369 04358 1068 04358 460370
This partly wooded holiday site lies between an inland lake and the sea. It is divided into pitches. 100m private beach.
From Eckernförde towards Klein-Wabbs up to Gut Ludwigsburg, then follow a dirt track for 2km.
Open: Apr-Sep **Site:** 10HEC **Facilities:** **Services:** lau **Leisure:** L **Off-site:** S

MALENTE-GREMSMÜHLEN SCHLESWIG-HOLSTEIN

Schwentine Wiesenweg 14, 23714
04523 4327 04523 202799
website: www.vcsh.de
A park-like setting with trees and bushes, at a river in the village of Malente.
A17 18km NW of Eutin.
Open: Apr-4 Oct **Site:** 2.5HEC **Facilities:** **Services:** lau **Leisure:** R **Off-site:** LP

MELBECK NIEDERSACHSEN

Melbeck 21406 04134 7311
Extensive site in woodland on the banks of the Ilmenau. Centre of site free of trees and reserved for tourers.
On B4, 9km Lüneburg.
Open: All year **Site:** 20HEC **Facilities:** **Services:** lau **Leisure:** R

NEUSTADT SCHLESWIG-HOLSTEIN

Strande Sandbergerweg, 23730 04561 4188 04361 7125
e-mail: am.strande@t-online.de
website: www.amstrande.de
The site is divided into small sections and slopes down to the sea. Narrow sandy beach.
From Neustadt towards Pelzerhaken, first site on the right after leaving Neustadt.
Open: Apr-Sep **Site:** 4.5HEC **Facilities:** **Services:** lau **Leisure:** S **Off-site:**

NORDSTRAND (ISLAND OF)

NORTHEIM NIEDERSACHSEN

Sultmer Berg Sultmerberg 3, 37154
05551 51559 05551 5656
e-mail: campingplatzmajora@web.de
Grassland site with views of surrounding hills. Siesta 13.00-15.00.
Follow B3 from town centre.
Open: All year **Site:** 5HEC **Facilities:** **Services:** lau **Leisure:** P **Off-site:** LR

OEHE-DRAECHT Schleswig-Holstein

Oehe-Draecht 24376 04642 6124 & 6029 04642 69159
e-mail: Gut-oehe@T-online.de
website: www.oehe-draecht.de
Grassy site divided into pitches, on sandy ground behind a sea dyke.
From Kappeln follow B199, turn towards Hasselberg and follow signs 'Strand'.
Open: 23 Mar-22 Sep **Site:** 6HEC
Facilities: **Services:** lau
Leisure: LS

At ORSTEIL GOTTINGERODE

Freizeit Oase Harz Camp Kreisstr 66, 38667 Bad Harzburg, 38667 05322 81215 05322 877533
e-mail: harz-camp@t-online.de
On outskirts of village next to main road. Terraced site with separate touring field. Siesta 13.00-15.00.
On the B6 between Bad Harzburg and Goslar.
Open: All year **Site:** 6.5HEC **Facilities:** **Services:** lau **Leisure:** P

OSNABRÜCK Niedersachsen

Niedersachsenhof Nordstr 109, 49084
0541 77226 0541 70627
e-mail: osnacamp@aol.com
The site lies on a gently sloping meadow bordering a forest, near a converted farmhouse with an inn.
5km from town centre NW on B51/65 towards Bremen, turn right and continue 300m.
Open: All year **Site:** 3HEC **Facilities:**
Services: lau **Off-site:** PRS

OSTERODE Niedersachsen

Sösestausee 37520 05522 3319 05522 72378
e-mail: harzcamp@t-online.de
website: www.harzcamp.de
Terraced site on edge of woodland and by a reservoir.
Follow road B498 from Osterode towards Altenau and after 3km turn right to the site.
Open: All year **Site:** 4HEC **Facilities:** **Services:** lau **Leisure:** LR **Off-site:**

OSTRHAUDERFEHN Niedersachsen

AZUR-Camping Idasee 26842
04952 994297 04952 994297
Situated beside a lake between Oldenburg and the Dutch border with good water-sports facilities.
Access via B27 (Cloppenburg-Aurich).
Open: 15 Mar-15 Nov **Site:** 5HEC **Facilities:** **Services:** lau **Leisure:** L

OTTERNDORF Niedersachsen

See Achtern Diek Deichstr 14, 21762
04751 2933 04751 3016
e-mail: campingplatz@otterndorf.de
website: www.otterndorf.de
A family site with good facilities close to the coast.
Access via B73 Cuxhaven-Hamburg.
Open: Apr-Oct **Site:** 13HEC **Facilities:**
Leisure: L **Off-site:** LPRS

PLÖN Schleswig-Holstein

Spitzenort Ascheberger Str 76, 24306
04522 2769 04522 4574
A pleasantly situated site with hedges on the shore of lake Plön. Surrounded by the lake on three sides, it is ideal for water sports.
Access from Plön on B430 towards Neumünster.
Open: Apr-15 Oct **Site:** 4.5HEC **Facilities:** **Services:** lau **Leisure:** L **Off-site:** P

PYRMONT, BAD Niedersachsen
At LÜGDE-ELBRINXEN (3km S)

Eichwald Obere Dorfstr 80, 32676
05283 335 05283 640
e-mail: campingeichwald@t-online.de
website: www.camping-eichwald.de
Pleasantly situated grassy site near woodland and pool.
S of Lüdge in direction of Rischenau to Elbrinxen.
Open: All year **Site:** 10HEC **Facilities:** **Services:** lau **Off-site:** P

RIESTE Niedersachsen

Alfsee Am Campingpark 10, 49597
05464 92120 05464 5837
e-mail: info@alfsee.de
website: www.alfsee.com
Open: All year **Site:** 15.5HEC **Facilities:** **Services:** lau **Leisure:** L

RINTELN Niedersachsen

Doktor-See Am Doktor-See, 31722
05751 964860 05751 964888
e-mail: info@doktorsee.de **website:** doktorsee.de
In a beautiful location by a recreation area and beside the Doktor See bathing beach. Section for touring campers. Siesta 13.00-15.00.
In town turn downstream at the River Weser bridge & continue along the left bank for 1.5km.
Open: All year **Site:** 152HEC **Facilities:** **Services:** lau **Leisure:** L **Off-site:** PR

ST ANDREASBERG Niedersachsen

Erikabrücke 37444 05582 1431 05582 923056
e-mail: camping@erikabruecke.de **website:** www.erikabruecke.de
Open site next to B27 NE of Oderstausee. Off B27 from Bad Lauterberg towards Braunlage.
Open: All year **Site:** 5.5HEC **Facilities:** **Services:** lau **Leisure:** LR

SCHOBÜLL Schleswig-Holstein

Seeblick 25875 04841 3321 04841 5773
e-mail: info@camping-seeblick.de
website: www.camping-seeblick.de
Beautifully situated beside the sea and divided into two sections.
Turn off the B5 on the N outskirts of Husum towards Insel Nordstrand for 4km up to Schobüll.
Open: Apr-15 Oct **Site:** 3.4HEC **Facilities:** **Services:** lau **Off-site:** PS

STELLE Niedersachsen

Steller See Zum Steller See 15, 28816
04206 6490 04206 6668
e-mail: steller.see@t-online **website:** www.steller-see.de
Delmenhorst-Ost eixt off motorway. Site 300m.
Open: Apr-Sep **Site:** 16HEC **Facilities:** **Services:** lau **Leisure:** L

Site: 6HEC-Site size -grass -sand -stone -little shade -partly shaded -mainly shaded
-bungalows for hire -caravans for hire -tents for hire -no dogs **Prices:** -adult per night -car per night
pp-per person per night -caravan per night -tent per night (static)-caravan hire per week

SUDERBURG NIEDERSACHSEN
AT HÖSSERINGEN (5KM SW)

Hardausee 29556 05826 7676 05826 8303
e-mail: info@camping-hardausse.de
website: www.camping-hardausse.de
Grassland site without firm internal roads. Statics have individual pitches and outbuildings. Separate fields for tourers.
Approach from Uelzen S on B4. In 9km turn right, continue via Suderburg to site on the right just before Hösseringen.
Open: All year **Site:** 12HEC **Facilities:** **Services:** lau **Off-site:** L

TARMSTEDT NIEDERSACHSEN

Rethbergsee 27412 04283 422 980139
e-mail: camping-rethbergsee@t-online.de
Level site on a grand scale. Siesta 13.00-15.00.
About halfway between Bremen-Lilienthal & Zeven.
Open: All year **Site:** 10HEC **Facilities:** **Services:** lau **Leisure:** L **Off-site:**

TELLINGSTEDT SCHLESWIG-HOLSTEIN

Tellingstedt Teichstr, 25789 04838 657 04838 786969
Divided by a row of high shrubs.
Off B203 towards the swimming pool.
Open: May-15 Sep **Site:** 1.2HEC **Facilities:** **Services:** lau **Leisure:** P **Off-site:**

TINNUM (ISLAND OF SYLT) SCHLESWIG-HOLSTEIN

Südhörn 25980 04651 3607 04651 3619
Well-kept site divided into pitches.
Well signed from railway unloading ramp. No vehicle connections between the island & the mainland - rail from Niebüll to Westerland.
Open: All year **Site:** 2HEC **Facilities:** **Services:** **Off-site:** PS

TÖNNING SCHLESWIG-HOLSTEIN

Lilienhof Katinger Landstr 5, 25832
04861 439 04861 439
e-mail: info@camping-lilienhof.de
website: www.camping-lilienhof.de
Well-maintained site in the woodland grounds of an old manor house next to a quiet country road.
Leave B202 at far end of Tönning, then 2km W towards Welt.
Open: All year **Site:** 2HEC **Facilities:** **Services:** lau **Off-site:** PR

USLAR NIEDERSACHSEN
AT DELLIEHAUSEN SOLLING (8KM NE)

Bergsee Bergsee-Camp-Solling, 37170
05573 1217 05573 1613
Well-kept site on meadow beside lake, in Solling nature reserve. Separate section for young campers. Siesta 13.00-15.00. Mobile shop.
Access from motorway exit Nörten-Hardenberg, take the B446 & B421 via Hardegsen to Volpriehausen, then right to Delliehausen (2.5km).
Open: Etr-Oct **Site:** 1HEC **Facilities:** **Services:** lau **Leisure:** L **Off-site:**

WALKENRIED NIEDERSACHSEN

KNAUS Walkenried Ellricher Str 7, 37445
05525 778 05525 2332
e-mail: knauscamp.walkenried@freenet.de
website: www.knauscamp.de
In an attractive location in the southern Harz area.
Access via A7 exit Seesen & B243 via Herzberg & Bad Sachsa.
Open: Dec-Oct **Site:** 5.4HEC **Prices:** 6 8 pitch 4-8 **Facilities:** **Services:** lau **Leisure:** P **Off-site:** LR

WEENER NIEDERSACHSEN

Weener Am Erholungsgebiet 4, 26826
04951 1740 04951 8613
e-mail: weener@t-online.de **website:** www.weener.de
A municpal site, pleasantly landscaped and set inside a leisure centre with swimming pool and harbour. Siesta 13.00-15.00.
B75 (E35) from Leer towards the Dutch frontier. Turn off in the centre of Weener & follow signs to site.
Open: 26 Mar-Oct **Site:** 3.2HEC **Facilities:** **Services:** lau **Leisure:** P **Off-site:** R

WIETZENDORF NIEDERSACHSEN

Südsee Soltau-Süd, 29649
05196 980116/7 05196 980299
e-mail: AA@sudseecamp.de
website: www.suedsee-camp.de
A beautiful location in a forest beside a lake.
Leave the Hannover-Hamburg motorway at the Soltau-Süd exit, take the B3 for 2km towards Bergen. At the underpass in Bokel turn left & drive 4km towards Wietzendorf.
Open: All year **Site:** 70HEC **Facilities:** **Services:** lau **Leisure:** LP

WILSUM NIEDERSACHSEN

AZUR-Ferienpark Wilsumer Berge 49849
05945 1029 05945 511
e-mail: wilsum@azur-camping.de
website: www.azur-camping.de/wilsum
Parts of the site adjoin a large lake. The separate section for touring campers has its own sanitary building.
From Nordhorn follow B403 via Uelsen to Wilsum. On nearside of Wilsum turn right.
Open: All year **Site:** 88HEC **Facilities:** **Services:** lau **Leisure:** L

WINGST NIEDERSACHSEN

Knaus Wingst Schwimmbadallee 13, 21789
04778 7604 04778 7608
e-mail: knauscamp.wingst@freenet.de
website: www.knauscamp.de
This modern comfortable site extends over several terraces, above a small artificial lake on the northern edge of an extensive forested area. Siesta 13.00-15.00. Municipal recreation centre across the road.
Turn off B73 between Stade & Cuxhaven, 3km S of Cadenberge.
Open: Mar-Oct **Site:** 8.7HEC **Prices:** 6 8 pitch 4-9 **Facilities:** **Services:** **Leisure:** LP **Off-site:** PS

WINSEN-ALLER NIEDERSACHSEN

Winsen 29308 05143 93199 05143 93144
e-mail: th-reiser@web.de **website:** www.camping-winsen.de
Site lies on meadowland at the River Aller. Water-sports available. Siesta 13.00-15.00.
From Celle go NW to Winsen.
Open: All year **Site:** 12HEC **Facilities:** **Services:** lau **Leisure:** R **Off-site:** P

WITTENBORN SCHLESWIG-HOLSTEIN

Weisser Brunnen 23829
04554 1757 & 1413 04554 4833
e-mail: gert.petzold@t-online.de
website: www.naturcamping-weisser-brunnen.de
A lakeside site consisting of several sections, hilly in parts, next to lake Mözen. A public road, leading to the lake, passes through part of the site.
Turn off B206 at Km23.6 towards lake.
Open: Apr-Oct **Site:** 7HEC **Facilities:** **Services:** lau **Leisure:** L

WULFEN (ISLAND OF FEHMARN) SCHLESWIG-HOLSTEIN

Wulfener Hals 23769 04371 8628-0 04371 3723
e-mail: camping@wulfenerhals.de **website:** www.wulfenerhals.de
Meadowland site beside the Baltic Sea and an inland lake (Burger Binnensee). 1.7km private beach.
Turn off B20/E4 (Vogelfluglinie) after the Sundbrücke towards Avendorf, then Wulfen and Wulfener Hals.
Open: All year **Site:** 34HEC **Facilities:** **Services:** lau **Leisure:** PS

ITALY

Italy, with its rich culture and architectural heritage, has mountain ranges, beautiful coastal areas and bustling cities.

FACTS AND FIGURES
Area: 301,338 sq km (116,346 sq miles)
Population: 57,844,017 (2001)
Capital: Roma (Rome)
Language: Italian
IDD code: 39
To call the UK, dial 00 44
Currency: Euro
Local time: GMT + 1 (summer GMT + 2)
Emergency Services: Police 113; Ambulance 113 or 118; Fire 115 (Carabinieri 112).
Banks: Mon-Fri 08.30-13.30, 15.30-16.30
Shops: Mon-Sat 08.30-13.30, 15.30-19.30
Average daily temperatures: Roma

Jan	8°C	Mar	11°C
May	18°C	Jul	25°C
Sep	21°C	Nov	12°C

Tourist information:
Italian State Tourist Office (ENIT)
UK
1 Princess Street
London W1R 8AY
Tel (020) 7408 1254
USA
630 Fifth Avenue, Suite 1565
New York NY 10111
Tel (212) 245 5618
Tourist info website:
www.enit.it

All approaches to Italy are dominated by mountains. The lakes of the north strikingly contrast with the sun-parched lands of the south, and there is beautiful countryside in the central Appenines. Both the Tyrrhenian and Adriatic coasts have fine, sandy beaches. Add the cities of Rome and Milan and there is truly something for everyone.

The north has a typically Continental climate while the south has a temperate Mediterranean climate with extremely hot summers. The language is Italian, a direct descendent of Latin. There are several dialect such as Sicilian and Sardinian, but the accepted standard derives from the vernacular spoken in Florence 700 years ago. German is spoken, to a small extent, near the Austrian frontier and French in Valle d'Aosta.

The International Reservation Centre in Calenzano (near Florence), *Federcampeggio*, provides a campsite information and reservation service ☎ 055-882391.

The *Assessorati Regionali per il Turismo* (ART) and the *Azienda Promozione Turistica* (APT) have regional and local information offices, and can provide details of campsites within their locality. In northern Italy, especially by the lakes and along the Adriatic coast, sites can be very crowded and it is advisable to book in advance during high season, which extends from May to the end of August.

Off-site camping is permitted provided the landowner's permission has been obtained, but is strictly prohibited in State forests and national parks. In built-up areas, if parking is allowed, the towing vehicle must remain connected to the trailer or caravan and the corner steadies must not be used.

HOW TO GET THERE

Although there are several ways of getting to Italy, most routes will probably be via France and Switzerland. Most major approaches are served by motorways and/or road or rail tunnels; it is seldom necessary to use the old Alpine passes, which are often closed. See Major Road and Rail Tunnels section.

DISTANCE

Milano (Milan) is about 1100km (684 miles) from the Channel ports, requiring one or two overnight stops. Roma (Rome) is about 580km (360 miles) further south.

CAR-SLEEPER TRAINS

A summer service is available from **'s-Hertogenbosch** (the Netherlands) to Bologna.

MOTORING & GENERAL

The information given here is specific to Italy. It **must** be read in conjunction with the Essential Information for Motoring section, which covers those regulations that are common to many countries.

Pariana - Alpi Apuane

British Embassy/Consulates*

The British Embassy together with its consular section is located at Via XX Settembre 80A, 00187 Roma ☎ 06-4220 0001. There are British consulates in Firenze (Florence), Milano (Milan), and Napoli (Naples); there are British consulates with honorary Consuls in Bari, Cagliari, Catania, Genova (Genoa), Palermo, Trieste, Torino (Turin) and Venezia (Venice).

Children in Cars

Children under 4 not permitted to travel as front- or rear-seat passenger unless using a suitable restraint system. Children between 4 and 12 travelling in the front seat must use a suitable restraint system. See the Essential Information for Motoring section under **Passengers** and **Seat Belts.**

Currency

The **euro** is the currency of Italy. The Italian lira (ITL) ceased to be legal tender in 2002, though ITL coins and notes may still be exchanged at the Italian Central Bank (Banca d'Italia) for 10 years.

Dimensions & Weight Restrictions*

Private cars and towed trailers or caravans are restricted to the following dimensions - car height 4 metres: width 2.55 metres: length (including tow-bar) 12 metres. Caravan/trailer height must not exceed 1.8 times the distance between the wheels of the vehicle; width 2.3 metres; length (including tow-bar) with one axle 6.5 metres, with two axles 8 metres. The maximum permitted overall length of vehicle/trailer or caravan combination is 18.75 metres. Trailers with an unladen weight of over 750kg or 50% of the weight of the towing vehicle must have service brakes on all wheels.

A load may only overhang at the rear, and must be indicated by a special reflectorised square panel. The load must not exceed 30% of the length of the vehicle, nor should the combined length of vehicle and overhanging load exceed the length restrictions given above.

Driving Licence*

All valid UK or Republic of Ireland licences should be accepted in Italy. This includes the older all-green style UK licences (for Northern Ireland the older paper style with photographic counterpart), though the European Commission appreciates that these may be difficult to understand, and that drivers may wish to voluntarily update them before travelling abroad, if time permits. Application form D1 (in Northern Ireland DL1) is available from most Post Office™ branches. Alternatively, older licences may be accompanied by an

International Driving Permit (IDP). The minimum age at which visitors from UK or Republic of Ireland may use a temporarily imported car is 18 years. The minimum age for using a temporarily imported motorcycle of up to 125cc, not transporting a passenger, is 16 years; to carry a passenger, or use a motorcycle over 125cc, the minimum age is 18 years.

Fiscal Receipt

In Italy, the law provides for the issue of a special numbered fiscal receipt (*ricevuta fiscale*) after paying for a wide range of goods and services, including meals and accommodation. This receipt indicates the cost of the various goods and services obtained, and the total charge after adding VAT. Tourists should ensure that this receipt is issued, as spot checks are made by the authorities, and both the proprietor and consumer are liable to an on-the-spot fine if the receipt cannot be produced.

Foodstuffs*

If the imported foodstuffs are for personal use, there are no limits when travelling between EU countries. Visitors entering Italy from outside the EU may import up to 1kg of meat or meat products. Coffee (500g), coffee extract (200g), tea (100g) and tea extract (40g) are free of customs duties, but visitors under 15 cannot import coffee.

Lights*

It is compulsory for all vehicles to use dipped headlights during the day on motorways and main highways; motorcyclists must also use them on all other roads during the day.

Motoring Clubs

There are two motoring organisations in Italy. The **Touring Club Italiano** (TCI), which has its head office at 10 Corso Italia, 20122 Milano ☎ 02-85261, and the **Automobile Club d'Italia** (ACI), whose head office is at 8 Via Marsala, 00185 Roma ☎ 06-49981. Both clubs have offices in most leading cities and towns.

Website: **www.touringclub.it** or **www.aci.it**

Reflective Jacket*

It is compulsory to wear a reflective jacket or waistcoat when getting out of an immobilised vehicle on the carriageway at night or in poor visibility. Fines for not wearing a reflective jacket or waistcoat range from €33.60 to €137.55.

Roads

Italy has over 4,000 miles of motorway (*autostrada*) with tolls payable on most sections. Emergency telephones are located every 2km on most motorways; there are two call buttons, one to call for technical assistance and one to alert the Red Cross services.

Main and secondary roads are generally good, and there are an exceptional number of by-passes. Mountain roads are usually well engineered; see **Principal Mountain Passes** section.

Speed Limits*

Built-up areas	50km/h (31mph)
Other roads	90km/h (55mph)
Dual-carriageways	110km/h (68mph)
Motorways	130km/h (80mph)

For cars towing a caravan or trailer the speed limits are 70km/h (43mph) outside built-up areas and 80km/h (49mph) on motorways.

Motorcycles under 150cc are not allowed on motorways.

Notes

i) These limits also apply to vehicles towing one axle (two-wheeled) luggage trailers.
ii) A speed limit of 150km/h (93mph) is to be introduced on some three-lane (plus emergency lane) motorways; the implementation date is not yet available.
iii) In wet weather speed limits on dual-carriageways and motorways are reduced to 90km/h (55mph) and 110km/h (68mph) respectively.

Warning Triangle*

It is compulsory to carry a warning triangle in a vehicle and to use it in the event of an accident or breakdown outside built-up areas. The triangle must be placed 50 metres (55yds) behind the vehicle on ordinary roads and 100 metres (109yds) on motorways. Motorists who fail to do this are liable to a fine from €33.60 to €137.55.

***Additional information can be found in the Essential Information for Motoring section.**

North-West/Alps & Lakes

Anfo Brescia

Palafitte via Calcaterra, 25070
0365 809051 0365 809051
Pleasant site divided into plots, sloping towards the lake where there are some trees.
Access as for Pilù, then turn right.
Open: 22 Apr-17 Sep **Site:** 20HEC **Facilities:** **Services:** lau **Leisure:** LP **Off-site:**

Pilù via Venturi 4, 25070 0365 809037 0365 809207
e-mail: info@pilu.it
website: www.pilu.it
Well-maintained, slightly sloping site subdivided by trees and rows of shrubs. By shingle beach from which it is separated by narrow public footpath.
On S outskirts, well signed.
Open: Apr-Sep **Site:** 2HEC **Prices:** 4.50-5.60 pitch 7.50-10.50 **Facilities:** **Services:** lau **Leisure:** LPR **Off-site:**

Angera Varese

Città di Angera via Bruschera 99, 21021
0331 930736 0331 960367
e-mail: info@campingcittadiangera.it
website: www.campingcittadiangera.it
Large family site with plenty of recreational facilities.
Signed.
Open: All year **Site:** 6.7HEC **Facilities:** **Services:** lau **Leisure:** LP

Arona Novara
At Dormelletto (5km S)

Lago Azzurro via E-Fermi 2, 28040
0322 497197 0322 497197
e-mail: info@campinglagoazzuro.it
website: www.campinglagoazzuro.it/
A lakeside site in beautiful surroundings with fine sports facilities.
S of Arona off SS Sempione 33.
Open: All year **Site:** 2.5HEC **Prices:** 5.50-6 pitch 7.50-8 (static)65-70 **Facilities:** **Services:** lau **Leisure:** LP

Lago Maggiore via L-da-Vinci 7, 28040
0322 497193 0322 497193
e-mail: info@lagomag.com
website: www.lagomag.com
Well-maintained site divided into plots, pleasantly landscaped by the lake.
Access from SS33, well signed.
Open: 19 Mar-Sep **Site:** 5HEC **Prices:** 4.50-6.50 pitch 7-12.50 (static)294-483 **Facilities:** **Services:** lau **Leisure:** LP

Lido Holiday Inn via M-Polo 1, 28040
0322 497047 0322 497047
e-mail: info@lidoholidayinn.com
website: www.lidoholidayinn.com
Site beside the lake, with some trees.
Turn off the SS33 at Km60/VII & IP filling station.
Open: Apr-29 Sep **Site:** 3.5HEC **Facilities:** **Services:** lau **Leisure:** LP **Off-site:**

Smeraldo via Cavour 131, 28040
0322 497031 0322 497031
e-mail: info@camping-smeraldo.com
website: www.camping-smeraldo.com
Well-landscaped site, divided into plots and situated in woodland by a lake.
Access from SS33.
Open: Mar-Oct **Site:** 24HEC **Facilities:** **Services:** lau **Leisure:** L **Off-site:** P

Arvier Aosta

Arvier via Chaussa 17, 11011 0165 99088 0165 99045
e-mail: campingarvier@yahoo.it
website: www.campingarvier.com
Quiet wooded site close to mountains and a peaceful village
Open: Jun-Aug **Site:** 1HEC **Prices:** 5.20-5.70 3.30-3.70 5-5.50 5-5.50 **Facilities:** **Services:** lau **Leisure:** P **Off-site:** R

Bastia Mondovi Cuneo

Cascina via Pieve 23, 12060 0174 60181 0174 60181
e-mail: camping.lacascina@libero.it
A peaceful site on level land surrounded by mountains.
Open: Jan-30 Aug & Oct-Dec **Site:** 4HEC **Prices:** 4.75-4.75 pitch 4.34-4.34 **Facilities:** **Services:** lau **Leisure:** PR **Off-site:**

Baveno Novara

Tranquilla via Cave 2, 28831
0323 923452 0323 923452
e-mail: info@tranquilla.com
website: www.tranquilla.com
In a peaceful location with fine panoramic views over the surrounding mountains and lake Maggiore. Good, modern facilities.
4 km from Stresa
Open: Mar-Oct **Site:** 1.8HEC **Prices:** 3.65-5 pitch 6-9 **Facilities:** **Services:** lau **Leisure:** P **Off-site:** LR

Bellagio Como

Azienda Agricola Clarke via Valassina 170/c, 22021
031 951325
e-mail: elizabethclarke@tin.it
A small, secluded site situated on a horsebreeding farm on the shores of lake Bellagio.
Open: Jun-Sep **Site:** 0.5HEC **Prices:** 6 pitch 10 **Facilities:** **Services:** **Off-site:** LP

Bolzano-Bozen Bolzano

Moosbauer Moritzingerweg 83, 39100
0471 918492 0471 204894
e-mail: info@moosbauer.com
website: www.moosbauer.com
Small site in attractive valley at the Gateway to the Dolomites.
Open: All year **Site:** 1.2HEC **Prices:** 5.50-7 pitch 12-15.50 **Facilities:** **Services:** lau **Leisure:** P **Off-site:**

Bréccia Como

International via Cecilio, 22100
031 521435 031 521435
e-mail: campingint@hotmail.com
website: www.camping-internationale.it
On a level meadow near the motorway. Siesta 13.00-15.30.
Off A9 Como-Milan motorway.
Open: 28 Mar-30 Oct **Site:** 1.8HEC **Prices:** 5 3 4 3.50 **Facilities:** **Services:** lau **Leisure:** P

Site: 6HEC-Site size -grass -sand -stone -little shade -partly shaded -mainly shaded -bungalows for hire -caravans for hire -tents for hire -no dogs Prices: -adult per night -car per night pp-per person per night -caravan per night -tent per night (static)-caravan hire per week

BRENTONICO TRENTO

Polsa Polsa, 38060 0464 867177 0464 421003
Situated at 1300m on mount Baldo with easy access and good, modern facilities.
Access via Brenner Autostrada exit Rovereto Sud & continue through Brentonico & Prada to Polsa.
Open: 15 Jun-15 Sep **Site:** 33HEC **Facilities:** **Services:** lau **Off-site:** P

BRESSANONE-BRIXEN BOLZANO

Löwenhof via Brennero 60, 39040
0472 836216 0472 801337
e-mail: info@loewenhof.it
website: www.loewenhof.it
Site offers rafting and canoeing school as well as sauna, pool which are avaliable in the Dolomiti resort 8km away.
Exit Bolzano/Brennero motorway at Varna. Site is just before Brixen.
Open: Apr-30 Oct **Site:** 0.5HEC **Prices:** 7-8 3.50-5 7-10 5-8 pitch 10-15 **Facilities:** **Services:** lau **Leisure:** PR **Off-site:** L

CALCERANICA TRENTO

Al Pescatore via dei Pescatori 1, 38050
0461 723062 0461 724212
e-mail: trentino@campingpescatore.it
website: www.campingpescatore.it
The site consists of several sections of meadowland, inland from the lakeside road to Lago di Caldonazzo. Well maintained with private beach.
Open: 22 May-15 Sep **Site:** 3.8HEC **Prices:** 7 pitch 9.20 **Facilities:** **Services:** lau **Leisure:** LP **Off-site:**

Fleiola via Trento 20, 38050 0461 723153 0461 724386
e-mail: info@campingfleiola.it
website: www.campingfleiola.com
Site is divided into sectors beside lake.
Exit the Verona/Brennero motorway at Trento, follow signs for Pergine & Caldonazzo.
Open: 24 Mar-5 Oct **Site:** 1.2HEC **Prices:** 5.50-7 pitch 6.50-13.50 **Facilities:** **Services:** lau **Leisure:** L **Off-site:**

Riviera viale Venezia 10, 38050
0461 724464 0461 718689
e-mail: riviera@dnet.it
website: www.campingriviera.net
Open: Etr-15 Sep **Site:** 1.5HEC **Prices:** 5-7.50 pitch 6-9 **Facilities:** **Services:** lau **Leisure:** L **Off-site:**

CAMPITELLO DI FASSA TRENTO

Miravalle vicolo camping 15, 38031
0462 750502 04621 751563
e-mail: info@campingmiravalle.it
website: www.campingmiravalle.it
In a wooded mountain setting beside the River Avisio and close to the town centre.
Signed.
Open: Jun-Sep & Dec-Apr **Site:** 3HEC **Prices:** 7.50-9.50 7.50-9.50 7.50 pitch 7.50-9.50 **Facilities:** **Services:** lau **Leisure:** R **Off-site:** P

CANAZEI TRENTO

Marmolada via Pareda 60, 38032
0462 601660 0462 601722
Grassland site extending to the river, part of it in spruce woods.
On S outskirts on the right of the road to Alba Penia.
Open: All year **Site:** 3HEC **Facilities:** **Services:** lau **Leisure:** R **Off-site:** P

CANNOBIO NOVARA

International Paradis via Casali Darbedo 12, 28052
0323 71227 0323 72591
e-mail: info@campingglagomaggiore.it
website: www.campingglagomaggiore.it
A level site on the bank of a lake.
Access from the SS34 at Km35/V.
Open: 20 Mar-15 Oct **Site:** 1.2HEC **Prices:** 4.50-5.50 4.50-6 4.50-6 4.50-6 pitch 9-12 (static)290.50-385 **Facilities:** **Services:** lau **Leisure:** L **Off-site:** R

Residence Campagna via Casali Darbedo 20/22, 28822
0323 70100 0323 72398
e-mail: info@campingcampagna.it
website: www.campingcampagna.it
A well-equipped site in a pleasant lakeside location.
Turn off SS34 to Locarno at Km35/V on N outskirts of village. W of lake on road 21.
Open: 20 Mar-4 Nov **Site:** 1.2HEC **Facilities:** **Services:** lau **Leisure:** L **Off-site:** R

Valle Romantica via Valle Cannobina, 28822
0323 71249 0323 71249
e-mail: valleromantico@riviera-valleromantica.com
website: www.riviera-valleromantica.com
A pleasant site with trees, shrubs and flowers. Internal roads are asphalted and a mountain stream provides bathing facilities.
1.5km w off road to Malesco.
Open: 20 Mar-Sep **Site:** 25HEC **Prices:** 5.50-7 pitch 9-12 (static)370-545 **Facilities:** **Services:** lau **Leisure:** PR **Off-site:** L

CASTELLETTO TICINO NOVARA

Italia Lido via Cicognola 88, 28053
0331 923032 0331 923032
e-mail: campingitalialido.campin@tin.it
website: www.campingitalialido.it
A large family site with its own private beach on lake Maggiore. The site is popular with families and there are good recreational facilities.
From A8 to Milan join A26 then signed.
Open: Mar-30 Oct **Site:** 3HEC **Prices:** 3.75-5 7-19.75 pitch 7-11.10 **Facilities:** **Services:** lau **Leisure:** L **Off-site:**

CHIUSA-KLAUSEN BOLZANO

Gamp Griesbruck 10, 39043 0472 847425 0472 845067
e-mail: info@camping-gamp.com
website: www.camping-gamp.com
The site lies next to the Gasthof Gamp, between the Brenner railway line and the motorway bridge, which passes high above the camp.
Access from the motorway exit & SS12 is well signed.
Open: All year **Site:** 0.6HEC **Prices:** 5.50-6.50 3.70-4.70 6.20-10 4.50-5.90 **Facilities:** **Services:** lau **Leisure:** P **Off-site:** P

COLFOSCO BOLZANO

Colfosco via Sorega 15, 39030
0471 836515 0471 830801
e-mail: info@campingcolfosco.it
website: www.campingcolfosco.it
In a beautiful setting at the foot of the Sella mountains.
Open: 8 Jun-30 Sep & 7 Dec-10 Apr **Site:** 2.5HEC **Prices:** 4.15-5.20 4.15-5.20 8-13 4-10.50 **Facilities:** **Services:** lau **Leisure:** PR **Off-site:** L

COLOMBARE BRESCIA

Sirmione via Sirmioncino 9, 25019
030 919045 030 919045
e-mail: www.camping-sirmione.com
website: info@camping-sirmione.com
A well-equipped site in a beautiful location on the Sirmione peninsula, with direct access to lake Garda.
From SS11 drive towards Sirmione & right after 0.4km.
Open: 25 Mar-5 Oct **Site:** 3.5HEC **Prices:** 6-9 pitch 9-14 **Facilities:** **Services:** lau **Leisure:** LP **Off-site:**

DESENZANO DEL GARDA BRESCIA

VÚ via VÚ 9, 25015 030 9121325 030 9120773
e-mail: vo@voit.it
website: www.voit.it
Situated on lake Garda, 2km from Desenzano, surrounded by meadows and woods.
2km from Desenzano, between Padenghe & Sirmione.
Open: Apr-Sep **Site:** 5HEC **Prices:** 5.50-7.50 pitch 9.50-11.50 **Facilities:** **Services:** lau **Leisure:** LP **Off-site:**

DIMARO TRENTO

Dolomiti di Brenta via Gole 105, 38025
0463 974332 0463 973200
e-mail: info@campingdolomiti.com
website: www.campingdolomiti.com
The campsite has large level plots surrounded by tall pine trees. The facilities for sports are excellent with special tuition for canoeing and white-water rafting.
Turn off SS42, at Km173.5.
Open: Jun-Sep & 6 Dec-15 Apr **Site:** 4HEC **Prices:** 6.40-8 pitch 8-11.50 **Facilities:** **Services:** lau **Leisure:** P **Off-site:** R

DOMASO COMO

Gardenia via Case Sparse 164, 22013
0344 96262 0344 83381
e-mail: campingardenia@interfree.it
website: www.campingardenia.it/
N at Case Sparse.
Open: Apr-29 Sep **Site:** 20HEC **Prices:** 4.40 pitch 7.90-9.80 **Facilities:** **Services:** lau **Leisure:** L **Off-site:** R

EDOLO BRESCIA

Adamello via Campeggio 10, 25048
0364 71694 0364 71694
e-mail: enrico.adamello@libero.it
A terraced site in wooded surroundings, 1km from the lake.

Site: 6HEC-Site size -grass -sand -stone -little shade -partly shaded -mainly shaded -bungalows for hire -caravans for hire -tents for hire -no dogs **Prices:** -adult per night -car per night pp-per person per night -caravan per night -tent per night (static)-caravan hire per week

1.5km W of SS39.
Open: All year **Site:** 1.2HEC **Prices:** 4.80 2 6.50 4.50-6.50 pitch 10.50 **Facilities:** **Services:** lau **Off-site:** LPR

FERIOLO Novara

Orchidea via Repubblica dell'Ossola, 28835
0323 28257 0323 28573
e-mail: info@campingorchidea.it
website: www.campingorchidea.it
A modern site on the extremity of lake Maggiore with good sports and entertainment facilities.
Access via SS33.
Open: 18 Mar-9 Oct **Site:** 4HEC **Prices:** 4.60-6.80 pitch 8-17 (static)266-357 **Facilities:** **Services:** lau **Leisure:** L

FONDOTOCE Novara

Continental Lido via 42 Martiri 156, 28924
0323 496300 0323 496218
e-mail: info@campingcontinental.com
website: www.campingcontinental.com
By lake Mergozzo and 1km from lake Maggiore.
On right side of road from Verbania Fondotoce to Gravellona.
Open: 5 Apr-20 Sep **Site:** 8HEC **Facilities:** **Services:** lau **Leisure:** L **Off-site:** R

Lido Toce via per Feriolo 41, 28924
0323 496298 0323 496220
e-mail: perucchinigiovanna@tiscalli.it
website: tiscali.it.lidotoce
In a beautiful location on the eastern shore of the lake offering spectacular views. Good recreational facilities.
Open: 20 Apr-Sep **Site:** 2HEC **Prices:** 3.80-5 pitch 7.50-10 **Facilities:** **Services:** lau **Leisure:** LR **Off-site:** P

Village Isolino via Per Feriolo 25, 28924
0323 496080 0323 496414
e-mail: info@isolino.com
website: www.isolino.it
Open: 18 Mar-19 Sep **Site:** 12HEC **Prices:** 4.10-6.75 3.05-6.15 pitch 17.55-24.05 (incl 2 persons) (static)213.85-559.30 **Facilities:** **Services:** lau **Leisure:** LP **Off-site:** R

FUCINE DI OSSANA Trento

Cevedale 38026 0463 751630 0463 751630
e-mail: info@campingcevedale.it
website: www.campingcevedale.it
A well-equipped site in a peaceful location at an altitude of 900m, close to ski resorts.
4km W of Savona.
Open: All year **Site:** 3HEC **Facilities:** **Services:** lau **Leisure:** LR **Off-site:**

GERMIGNAGA Varese

Il Boschetto via Mameli, 21010
0332 534740 0332 500791
e-mail: boshol@tin.it
website: www.boschhettoholiday.it
In a pleasant location beside lake Maggiore with a variety of facilities and opportunities for water sports.
Open: Apr-29 Sep **Site:** 1HEC **Facilities:** **Services:** lau **Leisure:** LPR **Off-site:**

IDRO Brescia

AZUR Idro Rio Vantone 25074
0365 83125 0365 823663
e-mail: idro@azur-freizeit.de
website: www.azur-camping.de/idro
The site lies at the mouth of the river of same name beside lake Idro. Subdivided into pitches (separate pitches for youths) on grass and woodland at the foot of unusual rock formations.
Approach from Idro direction of Vantone, well signed from there.
Open: 15 Mar-15 Nov **Site:** 4.5HEC **Prices:** 4.50-7 pitch 5-9.80 **Facilities:** **Services:** lau **Leisure:** LP

Vantone Pineta via Capovalle 11, 25074 0365 823385
e-mail: campingpineta@libero.it
website: www.vantonepineta.it
On E shore of lake. Grassland enclosed by rush and willow fencing. Part of site in a small wood on the bank of a stream.
Approach from Idro and follow signs for Camping Idro Rio Vantone.
Open: 31 Mar-Oct **Site:** 2HEC **Prices:** 4.50-5.60 pitch 7.50-10.20 **Facilities:** **Services:** lau **Leisure:** LP **Off-site:**

ISEO Brescia

Iseo via Antonioli 57, 25049 030 980213 030 980213
e-mail: campeggioiseo@intelligenza.it
In a picturesque location on the lake shore with well-shaded pitches and modern installations.
Access via A4 Brescia-Bergamo.
Open: Apr-Oct **Site:** 0.7HEC **Facilities:** **Services:** lau **Leisure:** L **Off-site:** P

Punta d'Oro via Antonioli 51/53, 25049
030 980084 030 980084
e-mail: info@camping-puntadoro.com
website: www.camping-puntadoro.com
A well set out campsite with roads and paths reaching every pitch.
From A4 exit at Rovato & follow signs Iseo.
Open: Apr-Oct **Site:** 0.6HEC **Prices:** 4.30-6.40 pitch 8.70-13.70 (static)231-455 **Facilities:** **Services:** lau **Leisure:** L **Off-site:** P

Quai via Antonioli 73, 25049 0309 821610
e-mail: info@campingquai.it
website: www.campingquai.it
Shady site close to the edge of lake Iseo.
W of town. Signed.
Open: 8 Apr-26 Sep **Site:** 1.3HEC **Prices:** 4.50 pitch 9.50-12 **Facilities:** **Services:** lau **Leisure:** L **Off-site:** P

Sassabanek via Colombera 2, 25049
030 980300 030 9821360
e-mail: sassabanek@sassabanek.it
website: www.sassabanek.it
In a pleasant wooded location on the shore of lake Iseo with good recreational facilities.
Open: Apr-Sep **Site:** 3.5HEC **Prices:** 4.20-7.50 2.30-5 pitch 8.20-15 **Facilities:** **Services:** lau **Leisure:** LP **Off-site:**

Facilities: -shop -shower -electric points for razors -electric points for caravans -parking by tents permitted -compulsory separate car park **Services:** -café/restaurant -bar -Camping Gaz International -gas other than Camping Gaz -first aid facilities lau-laundry **Leisure:** -swimming L-Lake P-Pool R-River S-Sea **Off-site:** All facilities within 2km

KALTERN BOLZANO

St Josef am Kalterer See Welnstr 75, 39052 0471 960170
e-mail: camping.st.josef@dnet.it
website: www.kalterersee.com/camping
On level ground surrounded by trees close to the lake.
Signed from Kalten-Tramin road.
Open: 15 Mar-10 Nov **Site:** 1.4HEC **Prices:** 4.50-5.50 pitch 5.80-11 **Facilities:** **Services:** lau **Leisure:** L

LAIVES-LEIFERS BOLZANO

Steiner Kennedystr 34, 39055
0471 950105 0471 951572
e-mail: campingsteiner@olmet.it
website: www.campingsteiner.com
The site lies behind the Gasthof Steiner, the AGIP filling station and a bungalow estate.
Off the SS12 on N outskirts of the village.
Open: Apr-5 Nov **Site:** 2.5HEC **Facilities:** **Services:** lau **Leisure:** P

LATSCH BOLZANO

Latsch an der Etsch Reichstr 4, 39021
0473 623217 0473 622333
e-mail: camping.latsch@dnet.it
website: www.camping-latsch.com
A terraced site beside the river.
Campsite is signed on SS38.
Open: All year **Site:** 1.6HEC **Prices:** 5.50-6.80 pitch 9.50-12.50 **Facilities:** **Services:** lau **Leisure:** PR

LECCO COMO

Rivabella via Alla Spiaggia 35, 23900 0341 421143
On a private, guarded beach on the shore of lake Como.
3km S towards Bergamo.
Site: 2HEC **Prices:** 5 pitch 9 **Facilities:** **Services:** lau **Leisure:** L **Off-site:**

LEVICO TERME TRENTO

Due Laghi Loc Costa 3, 38056
0461 706290 0461 707381
e-mail: info@campingclub.it
website: www.campingclub.it
Aimed mainly at families, this site offers 400 large flat grass pitches.
From Trento follow signs for Pergine & lake Caldonazza.
Open: 17 May- 13 Sep **Site:** 12HEC **Prices:** 6-8.50 pitch 11-14 **Facilities:** **Services:** lau **Leisure:** LP

Jolly Loc Pleina, 38056
0461 706934 & 701933 0461 700227 & 701933
The site is divided into plots and lies 200m from the lake with three inside swimming pools.
Open: Apr-1 Oct **Site:** 2HEC **Facilities:** **Services:** lau **Leisure:** P **Off-site:** LR

Levico 38056 0461 706491 0461 707735
e-mail: mail@campinglevico.com
website: www.campinglevico.com
Site is by a lake with a private beach.
Signed from the Levico/Caldonazzo exit on SS47.
Open: Apr-10 Oct **Site:** 4HEC **Facilities:** **Services:** lau **Leisure:** LR **Off-site:** P

LILLAZ AOSTA

Salasses 11012 0165 74252
Pleasant site surrounded by mountains, grassland and conifers. The site lies at the end of the Val di Cogne.
Entrance to site before Camping al Sole.
Open: All year **Site:** 1HEC **Facilities:** **Services:** **Leisure:** R **Off-site:**

LIMONE PIEMONTE CUNEO

Luis Matlas 12015 0171 927565 0171 927565
This tidy site offers winter facilities and skiing lessons are provided by the owner. Fishing is also available.
N of the town off the Limone-Nice road.
Open: All year **Site:** 1.5HEC **Prices:** 4.90 6 6 pitch 6 **Facilities:** **Services:** lau **Leisure:** R **Off-site:**

LIMONE SUL GARDA BRESCIA

Nanzel via 4 Novembre 3, 25010
0365 954155 0365 954468
e-mail: campingnanzel@cibero.it
website: www.limonesulgarde.it
Well-managed site, with low terraces in an olive grove.
Access from Km101.2 (Hotel Giorgiol).
Open: Apr-15 Oct **Site:** 0.7HEC **Prices:** 4.70-6 pitch 9-11.50 **Facilities:** **Services:** lau **Leisure:** L **Off-site:**

MACCAGNO VARESE

AZUR-Lago Maggiore 21010
0332 560203 0332 561263
e-mail: maccagno@azur-camping.de
website: www.azur-camping.de/maccagno
A popular site on the shore of the lake.
In village turn off SS394 at Km43/III towards lake & after 500m turn right.
Open: 15 Mar-15 Nov **Site:** 1.5HEC **Prices:** 4.90-7.20 pitch 5.60-10.80 **Facilities:** **Services:** lau **Leisure:** LR **Off-site:**

Brancheito via Pietraperzia 13, 21010 045 6784029
Open: All year **Site:** 1.6HEC **Facilities:** **Services:** lau **Off-site:**

Lido via 6 Pietraperzia 13, 21010
0332 560250 0332 560250
e-mail: campinglido@boschettoholiday.it
website: www.boschettoholiday.it
Lakeside site with good facilities, 200m from the river.
Open: Apr-Sep **Site:** 0.8HEC **Prices:** 5-6.50 pitch 8-9 **Facilities:** **Services:** lau **Leisure:** LR **Off-site:** R

Manerba Del Garda Brescia

Belvedere via Cavalle 5, 25080
0365 551175 0365 552350
e-mail: info@camping-belvedere.it
website: www.camping.belvedere.it
Terraced site by lake Garda.
Signed from SS572.
Open: 21 Mar-9 Oct **Site:** 2.1HEC
Prices: 3-6 pitch 7.80-14 (static)210-364 **Facilities:** **Services:** lau **Leisure:** LP **Off-site:**

Rio Feriengluck via del Rio 37, 25080
0365 551075 0365 551044
Follow SS572 Desenzano-Salo road, turn off between Km8 & Km9, site 4km N.
Open: Apr-Sep **Site:** 5HEC **Prices:** 4.50-6.50 4-6 5-6.50 4.50-6 **Facilities:**
Services: lau **Leisure:** LPR

Rocca via Cavalle 22, 25080 0365 551738 0365 552045
e-mail: info@laroccacamp.it **website:** www.laroccacamp.it
In a picturesque location with fine views over the gulf of Manerba.
Open: Apr-Sep **Site:** 5HEC **Prices:** 3.80-6.70 pitch 8.80-14 **Facilities:** **Services:** lau
Leisure: LP **Off-site:**

Zocco via del Zocco 43, 25080
0365 551605 0365 552053
e-mail: info@campingzocco.it
website: www.campingzocco.it
The site consists of several terraced sections. The section below the maintenance/supply building lies on a sloping olive grove and is somewhat obstructed by bungalows.
500m S of Gardonicino di Manerba.
Open: 23 Apr-25 Sep **Site:** 5HEC
Prices: 4.30-6.90 pitch 8.90-13.50 **Facilities:**
Services: lau **Leisure:** LP

Marone Brescia

Riva di San Pietro via Cristini 9, 25054
030 9827129 030 9827129
e-mail: rivasanpietro@hotmail.com
A good modern site on the E side of lake Iseo. Plenty of recreational facilities.
From Milano-Venezia road exit at Rovato or Palazzolo towards Iseo. Marone 10km N.
Open: May-Sep **Site:** 2HEC **Prices:** 5-6 10-12 7.50-10 **Facilities:** **Services:** lau
Leisure: LP **Off-site:**

Molina di Ledro Trento

International Camping Al Sole via Maffei, 38060
0464 508496 0464 508496
e-mail: info@campingalsole.it
website: www.campingalsole.it
A family site with good, modern facilities situated on the shore of lake Ledro at an altitude of 655m.
W of Molina beside the lake.
Open: 20 Apr-Sep **Site:** 3HEC **Prices:** 5.50-7 pitch 7-9.50 **Facilities:** **Services:** lau
Leisure: LP **Off-site:**

Molveno Trento

Spiaggia-Lago di Molveno via Lungolago 27, 38018
0461 586978 0461 586330
e-mail: camping@molveno.it
website: www.molveno.it/camping
In a picturesque setting on the lake shore, at the foot of the Brenta Dolomites.
Signed from SS421.
Open: All year **Site:** 4HEC **Prices:** 5-8.50 pitch 8-14
Facilities: **Services:** lau
Leisure: LP **Off-site:** P

Moniga Del Garda Brescia

Fontanelle via Magone 13, 25080
0365 502079 0365 503324 & 557449 (winter)
e-mail: info@campingfontanelle.it
website: www.campingfontanelle.it
Peaceful site on the shores of lake Garda shaded by olive trees. All staff speak English.
Open: 30 Apr-17 Sep **Site:** 45HEC **Prices:** 4.60-8.50 pitch 9.30-19 **Facilities:** **Services:**
lau **Leisure:** LP **Off-site:**

San Michele via San Michele 8, 25080
0365 502026 0365 503443
e-mail: gloriater@tiscalinet.it
A family site with good facilities and direct access to the lake via a private beach.
Exit A4 at Desenzano. Site is 8km from Desenzano towards Salo.
Open: 4Apr- 29Sep **Site:** 3HEC **Facilities:**
Services: lau **Leisure:** LP **Off-site:**

Naturno-Naturns Bolzano

Wald Dornsbergweg 8, 39025
0473 667298 0473 668072
e-mail: info@waldcamping.com
website: www.waldcamping.com
The site lies on gently rising ground, in a forest of pine and deciduous trees.
Turn off the SS38 near the Gasthof Alderwirt in the village & 0.8km S over the railway line.
Open: 15 Mar-5 Nov **Site:** 2.3HEC **Facilities:**
Services: lau **Leisure:** P **Off-site:** R

Novate Mezzola Sondrio

El Ranchero via Nazionale 3, 23025
0343 44169 0343 44169
Located on the edge of the Mezzola lake in front of a spectacular view of the mountains.
Open: May-15 Oct **Site:** 1HEC **Prices:** 5 4 5-7 5-7 **Facilities:** **Services:** lau
Leisure: L **Off-site:** PR

Orta San Giulio Novara

Cusio Lago d'Orta, 28016 0322 90290
website: www.orta.net/cusio
In a picturesque Alpine valley, surrounded by woodland on the bank of lake Orta. Good facilities.
S of Omegna towards Borgomanero.
Open: Apr-Nov **Site:** 2HEC **Facilities:**
Services: lau **Leisure:** P **Off-site:** L

Padenghe Brescia

Cá via S.Cassiano 12, 25080 030 9907006 030 9907693
e-mail: lacafab@tiscalinet.it
website: www.laca.it
The site has a park-like setting on terraced ground.
Turn off the road along lake Garda, 1.5km N turn for Padenghe & down a very steep road towards the lake.
Open: Mar-Oct **Site:** 2HEC **Prices:** 3.60-6.30 pitch 6-13 (static)196-339.50 **Facilities:**
Services: lau **Leisure:** LP

Facilities: -shop -shower -electric points for razors -electric points for caravans -parking by tents permitted -compulsory separate car park **Services:** -café/restaurant -bar -Camping Gaz International -gas other than Camping Gaz -first aid facilities lau-laundry **Leisure:** -swimming L-Lake P-Pool R-River S-Sea **Off-site:** All facilities within 2km

Villa Garuti via del Porto 5, 25080
030 9907134 030 9907817
e-mail: villagaruti@gardaleke.it
website: www.gardaleke.it/villagaruti
A campsite holiday village situated in the garden of the old Villa Garuti, directly on the lake with its own beach.
A4 from Brescia towards Verona, exit for Desenzano & SS572 to Padenghe.
Open: Mar-20 Oct **Site:** 1.5HEC **Prices:** 5-8 3-5 5-7.50 3-5.50 pitch 3-5.50 (static)120-280 **Facilities:** **Services:** lau **Leisure:** LP **Off-site:**

PEIO TRENTO

Val di Sole Loc Dossi di Cavia, 38020
0463 753177 0463 753176
e-mail: valdisole@camping.it
website: www.camping.it/trentino/valdisole
The site lies on terraced slopes at the foot of the Ortier mountain range.
400m off SP87.
Open: Jun-5 Nov & Dec-5 May **Site:** 2.3HEC **Prices:** 5-6.50 5-6 pitch 6-8 **Facilities:** **Services:** lau **Off-site:** P

PERA DI FASSA TRENTO

Soal via Dolomiti 32, 38030 0462 764519 0462 764609
e-mail: info@campingsoal.com
website: www.campingsoal.com
Breathtaking location among the Dolomites, ideal for skiing and walking.
Open: All year **Site:** 30HEC **Facilities:** **Services:** lau **Leisure:** R

PÉRGINE TRENTO

Punta Indiani Lago di Caldonazzo, 38058
0461 548062 0461 548607
e-mail: info@campingpuntaindiani.it
website: www.campingpuntaindiani.it
On level ground surrounded by trees with direct access to 400m of private beach on the banks of the lake.
A22 exit at Trento follow signs for Pergine, San Cristoforo & Caldonazzo.
Open: May-Sep **Site:** 1.5HEC **Prices:** 7 pitch 7-12 **Facilities:** **Services:** lau **Leisure:** L **Off-site:**

San Cristoforo via dei Pescatori, 38057
0461 512707 0461 707381
e-mail: info@campingclub.it
website: www.campingclub.it
A family-run site in a prime position on the sunniest side of lake. Owned and run by the Oss family with regular guests helping as staff.
Follow road 47 from Trento towards Venice for 14km. Site is in centre of San Cristoforo village.
Open: 17 May-14 Sep **Site:** 2.5HEC **Facilities:** **Services:** lau **Leisure:** LP

PETTENASCO NOVARA

Punta di Crabbia via Crabbia 2/A, 28028 0323 89117
A well-equipped site in a pleasant situation providing panoramic views over the surrounding area.
Open: Apr-Sep **Site:** 2HEC **Facilities:** **Services:** lau **Leisure:** L **Off-site:** L

PIEVE DI MANERBA BRESCIA

Faro via Repubblica 52, 25080
0365 651704 0365 651704
e-mail: campeggioilfaro@virgilio.it
Situated in a peaceful rural area close to the sea.
Leave A4 at Desenzano & take N572 to Manerba del Garda.
Open: 15 Apr-15 Sep **Site:** 1HEC **Prices:** 3.40-5.50 pitch 8-10.50 **Facilities:** **Leisure:** P **Off-site:** L

PISOGNE BRESCIA

Eden via Piangrande 3, 25055
0364 880500 0364 880500
The site lies on the E lake shore with tall trees and a level beach.
Turn off SS510 at Km37/VII, over railway line towards lake.
Open: 2 Apr-28 Sep **Site:** 2.5HEC **Prices:** 4.80-5.80 3.60-5.20 pitch 7.50-11.50 **Facilities:** **Services:** lau **Leisure:** L **Off-site:** PR

PONTE TRESA VARESE

Trelago via Trelago 20, 21030
0332 716583 0332 719650
e-mail: info@3lagocamping.com
website: www.3lagocamping.com
Lakeside campsite with grassy pitches shaded by tall trees.
Follow signs from Milan to Varese & Ghirla. Site 15km from Varese.
Open: Apr-15 Sep **Site:** 3.3HEC **Prices:** 4.50 pitch 6.50 (static)189 **Facilities:** **Services:** lau **Leisure:** LP **Off-site:**

PORLEZZA COMO

Paradiso Via Calbiga,30, 22018
0344 70393 0344 70715
e-mail: info@campingoklarivetta.com
website: www.campingoklarivetta.com
The site lies in meadowland on the NE lake shore.
S from SS340.
Open: 15 Mar-15 Nov **Site:** 5HEC **Prices:** 4-5 pitch 8-10 **Facilities:** **Services:** lau **Leisure:** LP **Off-site:** R

POZZA DI FASSA TRENTO

Caravan Garden Vidor Loc.Vidor,5, 38036
0462 763247 0462 764780
e-mail: info@campingvidor.it
website: www.campingvidor.it
This traditional family-run site is in a pine forest. Ideal for skiers, nature lovers and families all year round.
Signed from SS48.
Open: Jan-Apr, Jun-Dec **Site:** 2.5HEC **Prices:** 5.50-7.50 pitch 7-9.50 **Facilities:** **Services:** lau **Off-site:** R

Rosengarten via Avisio 15, Loc Puccia, 38036
0462 763305 0462 763501
e-mail: campingcatinacciorosen@tin.it
website: www.catinacciorosengarten.com
In the heart of the Dolomites, this well-tended site is an ideal base for a skiing or a walking holiday.
Signed from SS48.
Open: Jun-Sep & Nov-Apr **Site:** 3HEC **Prices:** 6.70-8.40 6-7 pitch 7.20-8.50 pp7-7.25 (static)280 **Facilities:** **Services:** lau **Leisure:** R **Off-site:** P

Site: 6HEC-Site size -grass -sand -stone -little shade -partly shaded -mainly shaded -bungalows for hire -caravans for hire -tents for hire -no dogs **Prices:** -adult per night -car per night pp-per person per night -caravan per night -tent per night (static)-caravan hire per week

RASUN Bolzano

Corones 39030 0474 496490 0474 498250
e-mail: info@corones.com
website: www.corones.com
A modern site in a mountain location with good sports facilities.
Exit Milan/Brenner motorway at Val Pusteria. Through Brunico & Valdaora to Rasun.
Open: All year **Site:** 2.7HEC **Facilities:** **Services:** lau **Leisure:** P

RIVA DEL GARDA Trento

Bavaria viale Rovereto 100, 38066
0464 552524 0464 559126
e-mail: camping@bavarianet.it
website: www.bavarianet.it
On SS240 towards Rovereto.
Open: Apr-Oct **Site:** 6HEC **Prices:** 6.80 pitch 9 **Facilities:** **Services:** **Leisure:** L
Off-site:

Monte Brione via Brione 32, 38066
0464 520885 0464 520890
e-mail: campingbrione@rivadelgarda.com
website: www.campingbrione.com
This site is at the foot of a hill covered with olive trees. Good sports facilities.
250m from San Nicolo' tourist centre.
Open: Etr-Sep **Site:** 3.3HEC **Prices:** 7.50 pitch 11
Facilities: **Services:** lau **Leisure:** P
Off-site: L

RIVOLTELLA Brescia

San Francesco strada Vicinale San Francesco, 25010
030 9110245 030 9119464
e-mail: info@campingsanfrancesco.it
website: www.campingsanfrancesco.it
This well-kept site is divided into many sections by drives, vineyards and orchards and has a private shingle beach.
At Km268 on SSN11.
Open: 21 Apr-Sep **Site:** 10.4HEC **Prices:** 5.40-8.80 pitch 11.30-28.80 **Facilities:**
Services: lau **Leisure:** LP

SAN ANTONIO DI MAVIGNOLA Trento

Faé 38084 0465 507178 0465 507178
e-mail: campingfae@campiglio.it
website: www.campiglio.it/campingfae
Situated in famous winter skiing region of Madonna di Campiglio. Good base for climbing in Brenta mountain range. On four gravel terraces, and Alpine meadow in hollow next to SS239.
Camping Card Compulsory
Open: Jun-Sep & Dec-Apr **Site:** 2.1HEC **Prices:** 6-7.50 pitch 7.50-9 **Facilities:** **Services:** lau **Off-site:**

SAN FELICE DEL BENACO Brescia

Camping Europa-Silvella via Silvella
0365 651095 0365 654395
e-mail: info@europasilvella.com
Site separated by the approach road. The beach is about 80m below.
Signed.
Open: Apr-Sep **Site:** 7.5HEC **Facilities:** **Services:** lau **Leisure:** LP

Facilities: -shop -shower -electric points for razors -electric points for caravans -parking by tents permitted -compulsory separate car park **Services:** -café/restaurant -bar -Camping Gaz International -gas other than Camping Gaz -first aid facilities lau-laundry **Leisure:** -swimming L-Lake P-Pool R-River S-Sea **Off-site:** All facilities within 2km

Fornella via Fornella 1, 25010
0365 62294 0365 559418
e-mail: fornella@fornella.it **website:** www.fornella.it
A quiet site in an ideal location on the shore of lake Garda.
Signed from SS572 Salo-Desenzano.
Open: 30 Apr-24 Sep **Site:** 9.2HEC
Prices: 4.60-8.80 pitch 9.30-16.50 (static)392-696
Facilities: **Services:** lau **Leisure:** LP

Gardiola via Gardiola 36, 25010
0365 559240 0365 557625
e-mail: info@lagardiola.com
website: www.baiaholiday.com
A terraced site with a variety of good facilities on the shore of lake Garda.
S of San Felice del Benaco off SS572.
Open: Apr-29 Sep **Site:** 0.4HEC **Prices:** 3.30-7.50 pitch 9-18.50 (static)210-476 **Facilities:** **Services:** lau **Leisure:** L **Off-site:** P

Ideal Molino 25010 0365 62023 0365 559395
e-mail: info@campingmolino.it
website: www.campingmolino.it
Situated right beside lake Garda amid beautiful scenery. Charming and quiet site 1km from San Felice. On the beach there is a pier and boat moorings. Pedal boats can be hired for lake trips.
Open: 23 Mar-Sep **Site:** 1.7HEC
Prices: 3.50-7.70 pitch 9.60-16 **Facilities:** **Services:** lau **Leisure:** L **Off-site:**

Weekend via Vallone della Selva 2, 25010
0365 43712 0365 42196
e-mail: info@weekend.it **website:** www.weekend.it
A quiet family site with modern facilities, situated in a olive grove overlooking lake Garda.
Exit A4 at Desenzano following road to Cisano. Signed San Felice D/B.
Open: 23 Apr-25 Sep **Site:** 9HEC **Prices:** 5.20-7.70 pitch 10.70-17.50 **Facilities:** **Services:** lau **Leisure:** P **Off-site:** L

San Martino di Castrozza Trento

Sass Maor via Laghetto 48, 38058
0439 68347 0439 68347
e-mail: info@campingsassmaor.it
website: www.campingsassmaor.it
A winter-sports site in a beautiful mountain setting.
From Trento travel to Ora, Cavalese & San Martino di Castrozza.
Open: All year **Site:** 0.2HEC **Prices:** 7-9 11-15 7-9 **Facilities:** **Services:** lau
Off-site: LPR

San Pietro di Corteno Golgi Brescia

Villaggio Aprica via Nazionale 507, 25040 0342 710001
e-mail: apricamp@apricaonline.com
website: www.apricaonline.com/camping
A small nature park ideal for winter skiing and summer walking.
On SS39 Aprica-Edolo.
Open: All year **Site:** 2.1HEC **Prices:** 4.55-6.50 pitch 4.90-11 (static)25-90 **Facilities:** **Services:** lau **Leisure:** R **Off-site:** LPS

San Vigilio di Marebbe Bolzano

Al Plan 39030 0474 501694 0474 506550
e-mail: camping.alplan@rolmail.net
website: www.campingalplan.com
In a wooded Alpine setting at an altitude of 1200m.
Access via A22 Brenner Autostrada.
Open: Dec-24 Apr & Jun-Nov **Site:** 1HEC
Facilities: **Services:** lau
Off-site: PR

Sarre Aosta

International Touring 11010
0165 257061 0165 363907
Flat, wooded site among the highest mountains in Europe.
4km W of Aosta on SS26.
Open: 15 May-15 Sep **Site:** 6HEC **Facilities:** **Services:** lau **Leisure:** PR

Monte Bianco Fraz St Maurice 15, 11010 0165 257523
In wooded surroundings close to the town centre.
Access via SS26 towards Aosta & Courmayer.
Open: Apr-Sep **Site:** 7.5HEC **Prices:** 4.40-4.70 2.40-2.60 3.80-4.10 3.80-4.10 **Facilities:**
Services: lau **Leisure:** R **Off-site:** P

Sexten Bolzano

Sexten St-Josefstr 54, 39030 0474 710444 0474 710053
e-mail: info@caravanparksexten.it
website: www.caravanparksexten.it
Open: 4 Dec-5 Nov **Site:** 6HEC **Prices:** 7-10 pitch 7.50-10 (static)364-714 **Facilities:**
Services: lau **Leisure:** PR

Sorico Como

Au Lac De Como via C-Battisti 18, 22010
0344 84035 0344 84802
The well-kept site lies on the right of the River Mera as it flows into lake Como.
Turn off the SS340d at Km25 near Total filling station & 200m towards the lake.
Open: All year **Site:** 17HEC **Prices:** 6.50 pitch 11 (static)476 **Facilities:** **Services:** lau **Leisure:** LR

Torbole Trento

Porto 38069 0464 505891 0464 505891
e-mail: alporto@torbole.com
website: www.torbole.com/alporto
A new site with modern facilities, situated in a quiet position near the lake. Ideal for sports and families.
At Torbole join SS240 then signed.
Open: 20 Mar-15 Oct **Site:** 1.1HEC **Prices:** 6.50-6.70 pitch 7.50-9.30 **Facilities:** **Services:** lau
Off-site: LR

TORRE DANIELE TORINO

Mombarone via Nazionale 54, 10010
0125 757907 0125 757396
website: www.campingmombarone.com
13km N of Ivrea on SS26. Very close to river.
Open: All year **Site:** 1.2HEC **Prices:** 3.50-4 2 3.50 3 **Facilities:** **Services:** lau
Leisure: PR **Off-site:**

TOSCOLANO MADERNO BRESCIA

Chiaro di Luna via Statale 218, 25088
0365 641179 0365 641179
website: www.chiarodiluna.org
Open: Apr-29 Sep **Site:** 9HEC **Prices:** 4.30-6 7-10 7-10 **Facilities:** **Services:** lau
Leisure: L **Off-site:**

VALNONTEY AOSTA

Lo Stambecco 11012 0165 74152 0165 749213
e-mail: campingstambecco@tiscali.it
website: www.campinglostambecco.com
Open: 15 May-Sep **Site:** 1.6HEC **Prices:** 4.50-5 2.50-3 3.50-4 2.50-4 (static)100-200 **Facilities:** **Services:** lau **Leisure:** R **Off-site:**

VIVERONE VERCELLI

Rocca via Lungo Lago 35, 13886
0161 98416 0161 98416
e-mail: Felicitaa@libero.it
website: www.la-rocca.org
Open: 15 Mar-15 Oct **Site:** 1HEC **Facilities:** **Services:** lau **Leisure:** P **Off-site:** L

VOLS BOLZANO

Seiseralm St Konstantin 16, 39050 0471 706459
The site is open all year round for skiers and climbers. Horse riding/trekking is a major activity.
From Bolzano motorway site is signed from Fie.
Open: All year **Site:** 2.5HEC **Facilities:** **Services:** lau **Off-site:** L

VENICE/NORTH

ARSIE BELLUNO

Gajole Loc Soravigo, 32030 0439 58505 0439 58505
website: www.campinggajole.it
In a delightful, peaceful setting on the shore of lake Corlo.
Access from SS50 bis.
Open: Apr-29 Sep **Site:** 1.5HEC **Prices:** 5 6 pitch 6
Facilities: **Services:** lau **Leisure:** L
Off-site:

ASIAGO VICENZA

Ekar Loc.Ta' Ekar, 36012 0424 455157 0424 455161
e-mail: campingasiago@keycomm.itg-ekar
website: www.altopiano-asiago.com/camping-ekar
On a level meadow in a striking setting among wooded hills in a popular skiing region.
Open: 18 May-30 Sep & 15 Nov-27 Apr **Site:** 3.5HEC
Facilities: **Services:** lau

AURISINA TRIESTE

Imperial Aurisina Cave 55, 34011
040 200459 040 200459
e-mail: campimperial@libero.it
website: www.campingimperialcarso.it
A well-maintained site in a secluded, wooded location.
Access via SS14 in Sistiana-Aurisina.
Open: Jun-29 Sep **Site:** 1.5HEC **Prices:** 3.70-6 4.50-7 3.50-5 3.50-5 pitch 8-12 (static)189-266
Facilities: **Services:** **Leisure:** P
Off-site:

BARDOLINO VERONA

Continental Localita Reboin, 37011
045 7210192 045 7211756
e-mail: continental@campingarda.it
website: www.campingarda.it
A pleasant site directly on the lake with good, modern facilities.
Open: Apr-5 Oct **Site:** 3.5HEC **Prices:** 4.50-6.80 pitch 9-14 **Facilities:** **Services:** lau
Leisure: L **Off-site:** L

Rocca S Pietro, 37011 045 7211111 045 7211300
e-mail: info@campinglarocca.com
website: www.campinglarocca.com
Subdivided site in slightly sloping grassland broken up by rows of trees. Separated from the lake by a public path (no cars). Part of site on the other side of the main road is terraced amongst vines and olives with lovely lake view.
Below the SS249 at Km40/IV.
Open: 23 Mar-2 Oct **Site:** 8HEC **Prices:** 4.50-6.80 **Facilities:** **Services:** lau
Leisure: LP **Off-site:**

BIBIONE VENEZIA

Villagio Turistico Internazionale via Colonie 2, 30020
0431 442611 0431 43231
e-mail: info@vti.it
website: www.vti.it
Mostly sandy terrain under pine trees. Some meadowland with a few deciduous trees. Wide sandy beach. Tennis court.
Well signed along approach.
Open: 12 Apr-23 Sep **Site:** 13HEC
Prices: 3.50-9.10 pitch 9-22.30 (static)290-720
Facilities: **Services:** lau
Leisure: PS

BRENZONE VERONA

Primavera via Benaco 5, 37010
045 7420421 045 7420421
e-mail: info@camping-primavera.com
website: www.camping-primavera.com
Small site on the shore of lake Garda.
Open: Apr-Oct **Site:** 0.8HEC **Prices:** 5 pitch 10
Facilities: **Services:** lau **Leisure:** L
Off-site:

CA'NOGHERA VENEZIA

Alba d'Oro via Triestina 214/B, 30030
041 5415102 041 5475971
e-mail: albadoro@tin.it
website: www.ecvacanze.it
On level ground directly on the lagoon with good, modern facilities including moorings for small boats. Regular bus service to Venice.
Access from SS14.
Open: Feb-Oct **Site:** 7HEC **Prices:** 7-8 pitch 13-14 **Facilities:** **Services:** lau
Leisure: PR **Off-site:** LS

Site: 6HEC-Site size -grass -sand -stone -little shade -partly shaded -mainly shaded -bungalows for hire -caravans for hire -tents for hire -no dogs **Prices:** -adult per night -car per night pp-per person per night -caravan per night -tent per night (static)-caravan hire per week

LAGO
DI
GARDA
è...
Consorzio di Promozione e
Commercializzazione Turistica
LAZISE
LAKE GARDA
REGIONE VENETO
PACENGO
LAKE GARDA

CAORLE VENEZIA

San Francesco via Selva Rosata, 25080
0421 2982 0421 299284
e-mail: info@villaggiosfrancesco.com
website: www.villaggiosfrancesco.com
This generously laid-out site, on level lawns with shady poplars, lies within a holiday village.
Follow signs from Caorle.
Open: 12 Apr-29 Sep **Site:** 32HEC
Facilities: **Services:** lau
Leisure: PS

CASSONE VERONA

Bellavista 37010 045 7420244
In a fine position in an olive grove overlooking lake Garda with modern sanitary installations. Access to the lake is by an underpass and water-sports facilities are available.
Open: All year **Site:** 27HEC **Facilities:** **Services:** lau **Leisure:** L **Off-site:** PR

CASTELLETTO DI BRENZONE VERONA

Maior VIA Croce N.10, 37010
045 7430333 045 7430333
A comfortable, modern site in a pleasant, quiet location.
Open: Etr-29 Sep **Site:** 8HEC **Prices:** 5.50-7 pitch 9-12.30 **Facilities:** **Services:** lau
Off-site: L

San Zeno via A-Vespucci 97, 37010
045 7430231 045 4430171
e-mail: info@campingsanzeno.it
Situated only a few metres from the lake surrounded by hundred-year old olive groves.
Exit the southbound motorway from Rovereto at Trento. The site is 10km S of Malcesine.
Open: May-Sep **Site:** 1.4HEC **Prices:** 4.50-6.50 pitch 7.50-10 **Facilities:** **Services:**
Off-site: L

CAVALLINO VENEZIA

Cavallino via delle Batterie 164, 30013
041 966133 041 5300827
e-mail: info@campingcavallino.com
website: www.baiaholiday.com
In a pine wood close to the sea with plenty of recreational facilities.
Open: 3 Apr-10 Oct **Site:** 11.4HEC
Facilities: **Services:** lau **Leisure:** PS

Europa via Fausta 332, 30013 041 968069 041 5370150
e-mail: info@campingeuropa.com
website: www.campingeuropa.com
On grassland reaching to the sea, with some poplars. Siesta 13.00-15.00.
Well signed on Punta Sabbioni road.
Open: 24 Mar-Sep **Site:** 11HEC
Prices: 4.20-7.50 pitch 8.20-19.40 **Facilities:** **Services:** lau **Leisure:** S **Off-site:**

Italy via Fausta 272, 30013 041 968090 041 5370076
e-mail: info@campingitaly.it
website: www.campingitaly.it
Small family campsite 6km from Lido di Jesolo on a peninsula. Venice can be reached by public ferry.
Brennero/Venezia motorway. Then follow signs for Jesolo-Cavallino.
Open: Etr-19 Sep **Site:** 3.9HEC
Prices: 4.45-6.70 pitch 7.40-18 (static)308-539
Facilities: **Services:** lau **Leisure:** PS
Off-site:

Joker via Fausta 318, 30013 041 5370766 041 968216
e-mail: jokercamping@iol.it
website: www.jokercamping.it
Between coastal road and the sandy beach with tall poplars. Partially subdivided.
Open: May-Sep **Site:** 4.4HEC
Facilities: **Services:** lau **Leisure:** PS

Residence via F-Baracca 47, 30013
041 968027 041 5370164
e-mail: info@campres.it
website: www.campres.it
Well laid out site on level, wooded grassland, by a sandy beach, between Jesolo and Cavallino. Siesta 13.00-15.00.
Signed.
Open: 24 Apr-21 Sep **Site:** 8HEC
Facilities: **Services:** lau
Leisure: PS **Off-site:** R

Sant' Angelo via F-Baracca 63, 30013
041 968882 041 5370242
e-mail: info@santangelo.it
website: www.santangelo.it
A large beach site with trees and flower beds. Good entertainment, sports and eating facilities.
Outside Venice follow signs for Caposile & Jesolo. Crossing the bridge just after Lido di Jesolo turn right & follow road round to coast.
Open: 30 Apr-18 Sep **Site:** 20HEC
Prices: 4.10-8.60 pitch 8.20-20.50 (static)282.10-684.60
Facilities: **Services:** lau **Leisure:** PS

Silva via F-Baracca 53, 30013 041 968087 041 968087
The site lies on sand and grassland and is located between road and beach, divided by a vineyard. The section of site near the beach is quiet.
Open: 10 May-15 Sep **Site:** 3.3HEC
Prices: 3-6 6.50-15 6-14 pitch 6.50-15 **Facilities:** **Services:** lau **Leisure:** S **Off-site:** R

Union-Lido via Fausta 258, 30013
041 2575111 041 5370355
e-mail: info@unionlido.com
website: www.unionlido.it
This large site lies on a long stretch of land next to a 1km beach. Separate section for tents and caravans. Minimum stay during peak period is one week. Ideal for families.
From Tarvisio follow motorway via Udine, San Dona di Piave then is signed to Jesolo & Cavallino.
Open: May-Sep **Site:** 60HEC **Prices:** 6-9 pitch 11.10-23.40 **Facilities:** **Services:**
lau **Leisure:** PS

Villa al Mare via del Faro 12, 30013
041 968066 041 5370576
e-mail: info@villaalmare.it
website: www.villaalmare.it
Level site divided into plots on a peninsula behind the lighthouse. Direct access to a long sandy beach.
Open: May-Sep **Site:** 2HEC **Prices:** 3.90-7.40 pitch 7.90-17.70 (static)311.60-796 **Facilities:** **Services:** lau **Leisure:** PRS

CHIOGGIA VENEZIA

Miramare via A-Barbarigo 103, 30019
041 490610 041 490610
e-mail: campmir@tin.it
website: www.miramarecamping.com
Long site reaching as far as the beach, clean and well maintained.

Site: 6HEC-Site size -grass -sand -stone -little shade -partly shaded -mainly shaded -bungalows for hire -caravans for hire -tents for hire -no dogs **Prices:** -adult per night -car per night pp-per person per night -caravan per night -tent per night (static)-caravan hire per week

➲ *Access from Strada Romeo (SS309) towards Chioggia Sottomarina, turn right on reaching beach & continue 500m.*
Open: 22 Apr-20 Sep **Site:** 5HEC ▥ ♣ ⌂ 🚫
Prices: 🚶4.50-7 🚐8.50-16 ▲7.50-10 **Facilities:** 🚿 🏪 ⊙ 🔌 ⌀ ⛽ ⓟ **Services:** 🍸 ✕ lau **Leisure:** 🏊PS **Off-site:** ⊞

Villaggio Turistico Isamar via Isamar 9, Isolaverde, 30015
☎ 041 5535811 📠 041 490440
e-mail: info@villaggioisamar.com
website: www.villaggioisamar.com
The site lies on level grassland at the mouth of the River Etsch. Shade is provided by high poplars. Good beach.
➲ *Access via the SS309. Caravans are advised to approach via Km84/VII near Brenta village.*
Open: 29 Apr-29 Sep **Site:** 33HEC ⁙ ♣ ⌂ 🚐 🚫
Prices: 🚶3.50-8.80 pitch 4-21.50 (incl 2 persons) **Facilities:** 🚿 🏪 ⊙ 🔌 ⌀ ⓟ **Services:** 🍸 ✕ ⊞ lau **Leisure:** 🏊PRS

CHIOGGIA SOTTOMARINA VENEZIA

Oasi via A-Barbarigo 147, 30019
☎ 041 490801 📠 041 490801
e-mail: info@campingoasi.com
website: www.campingoasi.com
A well-equipped site situated on a wooded peninsula near the mouth of the Brenta River with a wide private beach.
➲ *W of town centre towards the river and the beach.*
Open: Apr-Sep **Site:** 3HEC ▥ ♣ ⌂ **Facilities:** 🚿 🏪 ⊙ 🔌 ⌀ ⛽ ⓟ **Services:** 🍸 ✕ lau **Leisure:** 🏊PRS **Off-site:** ⊞

CISANO VERONA

Cisano via Peschiera, 37011 ☎ 045 6229098 📠 045 6229059
e-mail: cisano@camping-cisano.it
website: www.camping-cisano.it
Quiet, partly terraced site beside lake Garda with good water-sports facilities and entertainment.
➲ *AFFI exit on Brennero-Verona motorway, access 4km further.*
Open: 29 Mar-3 Oct **Site:** 14HEC ▥ ♣ ⌂ 🚐 🚫
Facilities: 🚿 🏪 ⊙ 🔌 ⌀ ⛽ ⓟ **Services:** 🍸 ✕ ⊞ lau
Leisure: 🏊LP

San Vito via Pralesi 3, 37010 ☎ 045 6229026 📠 045 6229059
e-mail: cisano@camping-cisano.it
website: www.camping-cisano.it
A tranquil and shady site with many modern facilities.
➲ *Off the Brennero motorway signed to the Sof Cisano.*
Open: 29 Mar-4 Oct **Site:** 5HEC ▥ ♣ ⌂ 🚐 🚫
Facilities: 🚿 🏪 ⊙ 🔌 ⌀ ⛽ ⓟ **Services:** 🍸 ✕ ⊞ lau
Leisure: 🏊LP

CORTINA D'AMPEZZO BELLUNO

Cortina via Campo 2, 32043 ☎ 0436 867575 📠 0436 867917
e-mail: campcortina@tin.it
This site lies among pine trees, several hundred metres from the edge of town, off the Dolomite road towards Belluno.
➲ *Turn off road and drive 1km to the campsite by a small river.*
Open: All year **Site:** 4.6HEC ▥ ⁙ ♣ **Prices:** 🚶4.50-7.50 pitch 7-9 **Facilities:** 🚿 🏪 ⊙ 🔌 ⌀ ⛽ ⓟ **Services:** 🍸 ✕ lau
Leisure: 🏊PR

Dolomiti via Campo di Sotto, 32043
☎ 0436 2485 📠 0436 5403
e-mail: campeggiodolomiti@tin.it
website: www.campeggiodolomiti.it
The site is beautifully situated on grassland with pine trees in a hollow, not far from the Olympic ski-jump.
➲ *Follow the directions for Camping Cortina. The camp is then 500m further on, 2.7km S of Cortina.*
Open: Jun-19 Sep **Site:** 5.4HEC ▥ ☂ **Prices:** 🚶4.50-7.50 pitch 7-9 **Facilities:** 🚿 🏪 ⊙ 🔌 ⌀ ⛽ ⓟ **Services:** 🍸 lau
Leisure: 🏊PR **Off-site:** ✕ 🏊L

Olympia Fiames 1, 32043 ☎ 0436 5057 📠 0436 5057
A very beautiful site in the centre of the magnificent Dolomite landscape.
➲ *It lies N of town off the SS51.*
Open: 5 Dec-5 Nov **Site:** 4HEC ▥ ☂ ⌂ 🚐 **Facilities:** 🚿 🏪 ⊙ 🔌 ⌀ ⓟ **Services:** 🍸 ✕ ⊞ lau **Leisure:** 🏊R **Off-site:** 🏊LP ⊞

Rocchetta via Campo 1, 32043 ☎ 0436 5063 📠 0436 5063
e-mail: camping@sunrise.it
website: www.campingrocchetta.it
In beautiful wooded surroundings.
➲ *Access S from Cortina via SS51.*
Open: Jun-20 Sep & Dec-15 Apr **Site:** 2.5HEC ▥ ☂
Prices: 🚶4.50-7.75 pitch 7-9 **Facilities:** 🚿 🏪 ⊙ 🔌 ⌀ ⛽ ⓟ
Services: 🍸 ✕ lau **Leisure:** 🏊R **Off-site:** ✕ 🏊LP

DUINO-AURISINA TRIESTE
AT SISTIANA

Marepinetá 34019 ☎ 040 299264 📠 040 299265
e-mail: info@marepineta.com
website: www.baiaholiday.com
A modern site in a pleasant wooded location with a wide range of recreational facilities. Free bus service to the beach.
➲ *On SS14 near the harbour & beach. Highway A4 Venice-Trieste, exit Duino, 1km on left.*
Open: Mar-Oct **Site:** 10.8HEC ♦ ♣ ⌂ 🚐 🚫 **Prices:** 🚶3.30-7.50 pitch 9-18 🚐 (static)210-567 **Facilities:** 🚿 🏪 ⊙ 🔌 ⌀ ⛽ ⓟ **Services:** 🍸 ✕ ⊞ lau **Leisure:** 🏊P **Off-site:** 🏊S

ERACLEA MARE VENEZIA

Portofelice viale dei Fiori 15, I-30010
☎ 0421 66411 📠 0421 66021
e-mail: info@portofelice.it
website: www.portofelice.it
A well-equipped family village site separated from the beach by a pine wood. A wide variety of recreational facilities are available.
➲ *Leave A4 at Venice/Mestre exit & follow signs for Carole & Eraclea Mare.*
Open: May-19 Sep **Site:** 19HEC ▥ ♣ ⌂ 🚫 **Prices:** 🚶3-8.40 pitch 6.70-18.80 **Facilities:** 🚿 🏪 ⊙ 🔌 ⌀ ⛽ ⓟ 🅿
Services: 🍸 ✕ ⊞ lau **Leisure:** 🏊PS **Off-site:** 🏊R

FUSINA VENEZIA VENEZIA

Fusina via Moranzani 79, 30030
☎ 041 5470055 📠 041 5470050
e-mail: info@camping-fusina.com
website: www.camping-fusina.com
This well-equipped site is ideal for visiting Venice and the Venetian lagoon.
Open: All year **Site:** 5.5HEC ▥ ♣ ⌂ 🚐 ▲ **Prices:** 🚶7 pitch 14 **Facilities:** 🚿 🏪 ⊙ 🔌 ⌀ ⛽ ⓟ **Services:** 🍸 ✕ ⊞ lau
Leisure: 🏊S

GEMONA DEL FRIÚLI UDINE

Ai Pioppi via del Bersaglio 118, 33013
☎ 0432 980358 📠 0432 980358
e-mail: bar-camping-taxi@aipioppi.it
website: www.aipioppi.it
Quiet, well-equipped site in a pleasant mountain setting.
➲ *1km from town centre via N13.*
Open: 15 Mar-30 Oct **Site:** 11HEC ▥ ☂ ⌂ 🚐
Facilities: 🚿 ⊙ 🔌 ⌀ ⛽ ⓟ **Services:** 🍸 ✕ lau
Off-site: 🏪 🏊R ⊞

GRADO GORIZIA

Europa 34073 0431 80877 0431 82284
e-mail: info@villaggioeuropa.com
website: www.villaggioeuropa.com
On level terrain under half grown poplars. Partially in shade in pine forest.
On road to Monfalcone, 20km from Palmanova via Aquileia.
Open: 23 Apr-25 Sep **Site:** 22HEC
Prices: 5.50-9.50 pitch 8-18.50 (static)385-490
Facilities: **Services:** lau
Leisure: PS

Tenuta Primero via Monfalcone 14, 34073
0431 896900 0431 896901
e-mail: info@tenutaprimero.com
website: www.tenutaprimero.com
The site lies in extensive level grassland between the road and the dam, which is 2m high along the narrow and level beach. Tennis court.
Access from Monfalcone road. Signed.
Open: 15 May-12 Sep **Site:** 20HEC **Prices:** 7-10 pitch 12-16 **Facilities:** **Services:** lau **Leisure:** PS

JÉSOLO, LIDO DI VENEZIA
AT JÉSOLO PINETA (6KM E)

Malibu Beach viale Oriente 78, 30017
0421 362212 0421 961338
e-mail: info@campingmalibubeach.com
In a pine wood facing the sea and a fine sandy beach.
From Venezia via Cavallino on coast road to Cortellazzo.
Open: 16 May-15 Sep **Site:** 10HEC
Prices: 4.55-7.25 pitch 12.80-19.90 (static)41-69.80
Facilities: **Services:** lau
Leisure: PS

Waikiki viale Oriente 144, 30017
0421 980186 0421 378040
e-mail: info@campingwaikiki.com
website: www.campingwaikiki.com
A family site in a pine wood with direct access to the beach. Regular bus service to Venice passes the campsite.
Open: 12 May-11 Sep **Site:** 5.2HEC
Prices: 3.50-6.50 pitch 8.40-17.70 **Facilities:**
Services: lau **Leisure:** PS **Off-site:** R

LAZISE VERONA

Parc Loc Sentieri, 37017 045 7580127 045 6470150
e-mail: info@campingduparc.com
website: www.campingduparc.com
Well-kept, lakeside site off main road.
From Garda, the site is on S side of Lazise just after turning for Verona.
Open: 15 Mar-30 Oct **Site:** 6HEC
Prices: 5.30-7.40 pitch 10.80-16.50 **Facilities:**
Services: lau **Leisure:** LP **Off-site:**

Camping La Quercia 045 6470577 045 6470243
The site is divided into many large sections by tarred drives and lies on terraced ground that slopes gently down to the lake. There is a large private beach.
For access, turn off the main road SS49 at Km31/8 for 400m.
Open: Apr-Sep **Site:** 20HEC **Facilities:**
Services: lau **Leisure:** LP

See advertisement on opposite page

LIGNANO SABBIADORO UDINE

Sabbiadoro via Sabbiadoro 8, 33054
0431 71455 0431 721355
e-mail: campsab@lignano.it
website: www.campingsabbiadoro.it
A peaceful site in a pine grove close to the beach.
Open: 19 Mar-25 Sep **Site:** 13HEC
Prices: 4.20-7.60 pitch 6.40-12 (static)252-686
Facilities: **Services:** lau
Leisure: P **Off-site:** S

MALCESINE VERONA

Claudia via Molini 2, 37018 045 7400786 045 7400786
e-mail: info@campingclaudia.it
website: www.campingclaudia.it
Flat grassy site only 30m from the lake. Excellent facilities available, especially for water sports.
From Rome-Brennero motorway continue via Trento, Arco, Torbole & site is on outskirts of Malcestine.
Open: Apr-20 Oct **Site:** 1HEC **Prices:** 5-5.70 pitch 9.40-11 **Facilities:** **Services:** lau **Off-site:** L

MALGA CIAPELA BELLUNO

Malga Ciapela Marmolada 32020
0437 722064 0437 722064
e-mail: camping.mc.marmolada@dolomiti.com
A terraced site in tranquil wooded surroundings at the foot of Marmolada.
Take the Bozen exit off the Brennero-Verona motorway. Follow signs for Canazei, Malga Ciapela & the site, Marmolada.
Open: Jun-18 Sep & Dec-25 Apr **Site:** 3HEC
Prices: 5.20-6.20 4.80-5.50 pitch 6-7 **Facilities:** **Services:** lau **Leisure:** R **Off-site:**

MARGHERA VENEZIA

Jolly delle Querce via A-de-Marchi 7, 30175
041 920312 041 920312
The site lies on meadowland scattered with poplars.
Turn off into the Autostrada in Venezia towards Chioggia on the SS309 for 200m.
Open: Apr-Oct **Site:** 1.2HEC **Facilities:** **Services:** lau **Off-site:** PRS

MASARÈ BELLUNO

Alleghe 32022 0437 723737 0437 723874
e-mail: alleghecamp@dolomites.com
website: www.camping.dolomites.com/alleghe
Several terraces on a wooded incline below a road.
Open: 14 Jun-29 Sep/6 Dec-30 Apr **Site:** 2HEC
Prices: 6-6.50 4-5 pitch 6-7.50 **Facilities:**
Services: lau **Off-site:** LP

MESTRE VENEZIA

Venezia via Orlanda 8, 30030 041 5312828
A well-equipped site on the shore of the lagoon close to the causeway with a regular bus service to Venice within easy reach.
Open: 15 Feb-Nov **Site:** 1.8HEC **Facilities:** **Services:** lau

Facilities: -shop -shower -electric points for razors -electric points for caravans -parking by tents permitted -compulsory separate car park **Services:** -café/restaurant -bar -Camping Gaz International -gas other than Camping Gaz -first aid facilities lau-laundry **Leisure:** -swimming L-Lake P-Pool R-River S-Sea **Off-site:** All facilities within 2km

Montegrotto Terme Padova

Sporting Center 35036 ☎ 049 793400 📠 049 8911551
e-mail: sporting@sportingcenter.it
website: www.sportingcenter.it
A peaceful site in a pleasant setting in the Euganean hills with good facilities including a thermal treatment centre.
Open: Mar-12 Nov **Site:** 6.5HEC **Prices:** 5.50-7.50 10-14 7.50-10.20 **Facilities:** **Services:** lau **Leisure:** P **Off-site:**

Oriago Venezia

Serenissima via Padana 334, 30030
☎ 041 920286 📠 041 920286
e-mail: campingserenissima@shineline.it
website: www.campingserenissima.com
A well looked after site with shade provided by woodland. Local bus service every 20 minutes to Venice.
➲ *A4 to Venice, SS11 at Oriago.*
Open: Etr-10 Nov **Site:** 2HEC **Prices:** 6-7 pitch 8-12 **Facilities:** **Services:** lau **Leisure:** R **Off-site:**

Pacengo Verona

Camping Lido via Peschiera 2, 37010
☎ 045 7590611 📠 045 7590030
e-mail: info@campinglido.it **website:** www.campinglido.it
Open: Apr-Oct **Site:** 10HEC **Facilities:** **Services:** lau **Leisure:** LP

Palafavera Belluno

Palafavera 32010 ☎ 0437 788506 📠 0437 788857
e-mail: palafavera@sunrise.it
website: www.camping.dolomiti.com/palafavera
A beautiful location in the heart of the Dolomites at an altitude of 1514m. Good, modern sanitary installations and plenty of recreational facilities.
Open: Jun-Sep **Site:** 5HEC **Prices:** 4.50-6 5.50-7.50 3.50-4.50 pitch 5.50-7.50 **Facilities:** **Services:** lau **Leisure:** LPR **Off-site:** P

Peschiera Del Garda Verona

Bella Italia via Bella Italia 2, 37019
☎ 045 6400688 📠 045 6401410
e-mail: bellaitalia@camping-bellaitalia.it
website: www.camping-bellaitalia.it
Extensive lakeside site. No animals or motorcycles allowed.
➲ *Turn off Brescia road between Km276.2 & Km275.8 & head towards lake.*
Open: 12 Mar-9 Oct **Site:** 30HEC **Prices:** 5-10 pitch 10-19 **Facilities:** **Services:** lau **Leisure:** P **Off-site:** LR

Bergamini via Bergamini 51, Porto Bergamini, 37010
☎ 045 7550283 📠 045 7550283
website: www.campingbergamini.it
Ideal for young families - site has two children's pools and extensive play areas.
➲ *Follow signs 'Porto Bergamini'.*
Open: May-20 Sep **Site:** 1.4HEC **Prices:** 7-8.50 pitch 12-15 **Facilities:** **Services:** lau **Leisure:** LP **Off-site:**

Garda via Marzan, 37019
☎ 045 7550540 & 7551899 📠 045 6400711
A quiet, pleasant site with beach access on the shore of lake Garda.
➲ *Near the town centre, 2km from Milan/Venice motorway exit.*
Open: Apr-Sep **Site:** 20.4HEC **Facilities:** **Services:** lau **Leisure:** LP **Off-site:** R

San Benedetto via Bergamini 14, 37010
☎ 045 7550544 📠 045 7551512
e-mail: info@campingsanbenedetto.it
website: www.campingsanbenedetto.it
A family site in a fine position overlooking the lake.
Open: Apr-Sep **Site:** 22HEC **Facilities:** **Services:** lau **Leisure:** LP **Off-site:**

Porto Santa Margherita Venezia

Pra'delle Torri Viale Altanea 201, 30021
☎ 0421 299063 📠 0421 299035
e-mail: torri@vacanze-natura.it
website: www.pradelletorri.it
Extensive site on level ground.
➲ *3km W at edge of beach.*
Open: 19 Mar-15 Oct **Site:** 92HEC **Prices:** 3.55-8.20 pitch 4.75-21 **Facilities:** **Services:** lau **Leisure:** PS

Punta Sabbioni Venezia

Marina di Venezia via Montello 6, 30010
☎ 041 5302511 📠 041 966036
e-mail: camping@marinadivenezia.it
website: www.marinadivenezia.it
Extensive, well-organised and well-maintained holiday centre, extremely well appointed, with ample shade by trees. A section of the site is designated for dog owners, caravans and tents.
➲ *Access from the coastal road, turn seawards about 500m before the end along narrow asphalt road. Well-signed approach.*
Open: 23 Apr-Sep **Site:** 70HEC **Prices:** 3.95-780 pitch 9.95-19 (static)54-91.50 **Facilities:** **Services:** lau **Leisure:** PS

Miramare Lungomare D-Alighieri 29, 30010
☎ 041 966150 📠 041 5301150
e-mail: info@camping-miramare.it
website: www.camping-miramare.it
In a magnificent location overlooking the lagoon.
Open: Apr-Nov **Site:** 1.8HEC **Facilities:** **Services:** lau **Off-site:** S

Rosolina Mare Rovigo

Margherita via Foci Adige 10, 45010 ☎ 0426 68212
A well-equipped family site sitauted between the sea and a pine wood in the Po delta park.
Open: May-Sep **Site:** 6.4HEC **Facilities:** **Services:** lau **Leisure:** PRS

Rosapineta Strada Nord 24, 45010
☎ 0426 68033 📠 0426 68105
e-mail: info@rosapineta.it
website: www.rosapineta.com
The site lies in the grounds of an extensive holiday camp. Pitches for caravans and tents are separate.
➲ *Take Strada Romea towards Ravenna & drive to bridge over the River Adige. Continue 800m then turn off, cross bridge & head towards Rosolina Mare & Rosapineta (8km).*
Open: 9 May-13 Sep **Site:** 47HEC **Facilities:** **Services:** lau **Leisure:** PS **Off-site:** R

Treporti Venezia

Ca' Pasquali Village via Poerio 33, 30010
☎ 041 966110 📠 041 5300797
e-mail: info@capasquali.it
website: www.capasquali.it
Sandy, meadowland site with poplar and pine trees.

Access from Cavallino-Punta Sabbioni coast road, along phalt road for 400m.
pen: 30 Apr-17 Sep **Site:** 9HEC **Prices:** 4.20-80 pitch 7.20-21.90 **Facilities:** **Services:** lau **Leisure:** PS **Off-site:**

á Savio via di Ca`Savio 77, 30010
041 966017 041 5300707
mail: info@casavio.it
ebsite: casavio.it
level site along the edge of the sea with private sandy each. Separate pitches for caravans and tents.
From Cá Savio at T-lights turn towards the sea & continue 00m to the beach.
pen: May-Sep **Site:** 26.8HEC
rices: 4.41-8.40 9.03-18.37 9.03-18.37 static)352.80-573.30 **Facilities:** **Services:**
Leisure: PS **Off-site:**

iori via Vettor Pisani 52, Ca`vio, 30010
041 966448 041 966724
-mail: fiori@vacanze-natura.it
ebsite: www.deifiori.it
he site stretches over a wide area of dunes and pine trees ith separate sections for caravans and tents.
From A4 at Venice follow coast road via Jesolo to Lido del avallino.
pen: 22 Apr-3 Oct **Site:** 11HEC
rices: 4.30-8.70 pitch 8.30-21.40 **Facilities:**
ervices: lau **Leisure:** PS **Off-site:**

1editerráneo via delle Batterie 38, Ca'Vio, 30010
041 966721 041 966944
-mail: mediterraneo@vacanze-natura.it
vebsite: campingmediterraneo.it
lightly hilly grassland site with trees and sunshade roofs.
iesta 13.00-15.00.
Well signed from Jesolo.
)pen: 22 Apr-25 Sep **Site:** 17HEC
rices: 3.90-8.40 pitch 6-20.90 **Facilities:**
ervices: lau **Leisure:** PS **Off-site:** R

carpiland via A-Poerio 14, 30010
041 966488 041 966488
-mail: info@scarpiland.com
vebsite: www.scarpiland.com
n a beautiful area surrounded by a pine wood with direct ccess to the beach and beautiful views of the sea.
)pen: 24 Apr-18 Sep **Site:** 4.5HEC
'rices: 3.70-6.90 pitch 6.70-15.50 **Facilities:**
Services: lau **Leisure:** S

VICENZA VICENZA

Vicenza Strada Pelosa 239, 36100
0444 582311 0444 582434
-mail: camping@.viest.it
vebsite: ascom.vi.it/camping
A modern, well-equipped site.
Access via A4 exit Vicenza-Est.
Open: Apr-30 Sep **Site:** 3HEC **Prices:** 5.30-7 5-6.90 10.50-13.70 5.50-7.70 **Facilities:**
Services: lau **Off-site:** R

ZOLDO ALTO BELLUNO

Pala Favera 32010 0437 788506 & 789161 0437 788857
e-mail: palafavera@sunrise.it
Site with some woodland, at the foot of Monte Pelmo.
Open: Dec-Apr & Jun-Sep **Site:** 5HEC
Facilities: **Services:** lau **Leisure:** R
Off-site: P

NORTH-WEST/MED COAST

ALBENGA SAVONA

Bella Vista Campochiesa, Reg Campore 23, 17031
0182 540213 0182 554925
e-mail: info@campingbellavista.it
website: www.campingbellavista.it
A friendly family site with good facilities. Pitches are divided by bushes and flowerbeds.
1km from Km613.5 on SS1.
Open: All year **Site:** 0.8HEC **Prices:** 3-6 2.50-5 4-7 2.50-4.50 pitch 4-7 (incl 2 persons) (static)196-364 **Facilities:** **Services:** lau
Leisure: P **Off-site:** S

Roma Regione Foce, 17031 0182 52317 0182 555075
e-mail: info@campingroma.com
website: www.campingroma.com
The site is divided into pitches and laid out with many flowerbeds.
N of bridge over Centa, turn left.
Open: Apr-29 Sep **Site:** 1HEC **Prices:** 4.50-6.50 pitch 11-18 **Facilities:** **Services:** lau
Leisure: RS **Off-site:** P

ALBINIA GROSSETO

Acapulco via Aurelia Km155, 58010
0564 870165 0564 870165
e-mail: campeggioacapulco@virgilio.it
website: campeggioacapulco.interfree.it
Set on hilly terrain in pine woodland.
Take coast road from via Aurelia at Km155.
Open: May-14 Sep **Site:** 2HEC **Prices:** 4.50-9 pitch 6-12 (static)224-525 **Facilities:**
Services: lau **Leisure:** S

Il Gabbiano 58010 0564 870202 0564 870470
Site in pine woodland and open meadowland with sunshade roofing.
Turn off SS at Km155.
Open: Apr-Sep **Site:** 2.5HEC **Facilities:** **Services:** lau **Leisure:** S

Hawaii 58010 0564 870164 0564 872952
e-mail: hawaiigr@libero.it **website:** www.campinghawaii.it
The site lies in a pine forest on rather hilly ground.
Turn off via Aurelia at Km154/V & drive towards the sea.
Open: 16 Apr-27 Sep **Site:** 4HEC
Facilities: **Services:** lau **Leisure:** S

BARBERINO VAL D'ELSA FIRENZE

Semifonte 50021 055 8075454 055 8075454
e-mail: semifonte@semifonte.it **website:** www.semifonte.it
Terraced site with pitches of varying sizes
Open: 15 Mar-20 Oct **Site:** 1.7HEC **Facilities:**
Services: lau **Leisure:** P **Off-site:**

BIBBONA, MARINA DI LIVORNO

Capanne via Aurelia KM.273, 57020
0586 600064 0586 600198
e-mail: info@campinglecapanne.it
website: www.campinglecapanne.it
A pleasant family site situated in a spacious wooded park amid magnificent Tuscan scenery. The pitches are well defined and there is a wide variety of recreational facilities.
Access from Km273 via Aurelia travelling inland.
Open: 22 Apr-Sep **Site:** 6HEC **Prices:** 4.80-8.60 pitch 8.20-14 **Facilities:** **Services:**
lau **Leisure:** P **Off-site:** S

Capannino via Cavalleggeri Sud 26, 57020
0586 600252 0586 600720
e-mail: capannino@capannino.it
website: www.capannino.it
Well-tended park site in pine woodland with private beach.
On via Aurelia by Km272/VII turn towards sea.
Open: May-15 Sep **Site:** 3HEC
Facilities: **Services:** lau
Leisure: S

Casa di Caccia via del Mare 40, La Calafornia, 57020
0586 600000 0586 600000
e-mail: info@campingcasadicaccia.com
website: www.campingcasadicaccia.com
A tranquil site by the sea with access to a private beach.
From the A12 exit Rosignano & join SS, follow signs for Cecina. 6km exit La California, site 3km south.
Open: 15 Mar-30 Oct **Site:** 3.5HEC
Facilities: **Services:** lau
Leisure: S

Forte via dei Platani 58, 57020
0586 600155 0586 600123
e-mail: campeggiodelforte@campeggiodelforte.it
website: www.campeggiodelforte.it
Level site, grassy, sandy terrain.
Open: 29 Mar-22 Sep **Site:** 8HEC
Prices: 4.10-7.50 2.20-3.20 7.10-11.40 7.10-11.40 (static)220-640 **Facilities:** **Services:**
lau **Leisure:** P **Off-site:** S

Free Beach via Cavalleggeri Nord 88, 57020
0586 600388 0586 602984
e-mail: umberto.free@tiscali.it
Situated 300m from the sea through pine woods.
From the SS206 at Cecina follow signs to San Guido.
Open: 8 Apr- 3 Oct **Site:** 9HEC **Prices:** 10 pitch 13 **Facilities:** **Services:** lau
Leisure: LP **Off-site:** S

Il Gineprino via dei Platani,56a, 57020
0586 600550 0586 636866
e-mail: ilgineprino@tiscalinet.it
website: www.ilgineprino.it
A modern site situated on the Tuscany coast and shaded by a pine wood. There are good recreational facilities and the beach is within 300m.
Access via motorway exit La California for Marina di Bibbona.
Site: 1.5HEC **Prices:** 6-10 pitch 7-13 (static)175-550 **Facilities:** **Services:** lau
Leisure: P **Off-site:** S

BOGLIASCO GENOVA

Genova Est via Marconi, Cassa, 16031
010 3472053 010 3472053
e-mail: camping@dada.it
website: www.camping-genova-est.it
Quiet and shady site 1km from the sea. A free bus service operates from the site to the railway station for links to Genoa and Portofino.
Exit A12 at Nervi, then 8km E.
Open: 10 Mar-30 Oct **Site:** 1.2HEC **Prices:** 5-5.45 2.90 5.40-5.90 4.60-7.20 (static)182
Facilities: **Services:** lau **Off-site:** PS

BORDIGHERA IMPERIA

Baia La Ruota via Madonna della Ruota 34, 18012
184 265222
A well-equipped holiday village with direct access to a private beach.
Access via A10.
Open: Apr-Oct **Site:** 1.5HEC **Facilities:** **Services:** **Leisure:** S

BOTTAI FIRENZE

Internationale Firenze via S Cristoforo 2, 50029
055 2374704 055 2373412
e-mail: internazionale@florencecamping.it
website: www.campingflorence.com
Situated on the welcoming Florentine hills this site offers a restful atmosphere close to many historic places.
Open: Apr-29 Oct **Site:** 6HEC **Facilities:** **Services:** lau **Leisure:** P
Off-site: LR

CALENZANO FIRENZE

Autosole via V-Emanuele 11, 50041
055 8827819 055 8827819
Motorway A1 exit Calenzano-Sesto Fiorentino at T-lights on left, 200m on left
Open: All year **Site:** 2.2HEC **Facilities:**
Services: lau **Leisure:** P **Off-site:**

CAPALBIO GROSSETO

Costa d'Argento Monte Alzato, 58010
0564 893007 0564 893107
e-mail: info@costadargento.it
website: www.costadargento.it
A camping village in the middle of a nature park, 1km from the Maremma coast.
Camping Card Compulsory
12km from Orbetello via SS Aurelia.
Open: Apr-Sep **Site:** 6HEC **Facilities:** **Services:** lau **Leisure:** P **Off-site:** S

CAPANNOLE AREZZO

Chiocciola via G-Cesare 14, 52020
055 995776 055 995776
e-mail: tourcountry@virgilio.it
website: www.campinglachiocciola.com
A modern site in a rural setting among chestnut trees at an altitude of 250m.
Open: Mar-1 Nov **Site:** 3HEC **Prices:** 7-8 2.50-3 9-10 8-9 **Facilities:**
Services: lau **Leisure:** P **Off-site:** LR

CASALE MARITTIMO PISA

Valle Gaia 56040 0586 681236 0586 683551
e-mail: info@vallegaia.it
website: www.vallegaia.it
Site among pines and olive trees in a quiet rural location.
In southern Cecina heading from Livorno take the autostrada/superstrada then take 2nd exit for Cecina (Casale Marittimo - ignore first sign for Cecina S Pietro). Camp is signed.
Open: 19 Mar-15 Oct **Site:** 4HEC **Prices:** 4.30-7.40 pitch 8.10-13.40 **Facilities:** **Services:** lau **Leisure:** P **Off-site:** S

CASTAGNETO CARDUCCI LIVORNO

Climatico Le Pianacce via Bolgherese, 57022
0565 763667 0565 766085
e-mail: info@campinglepiancce.it
website: www.campinglepianacce.it
Terraced site on slopes of mountain in Tuscan landscape, enhanced by site landscaping. Pleasant climate due to height.

Site: 6HEC-Site size -grass -sand -stone -little shade -partly shaded -mainly shaded -bungalows for hire -caravans for hire -tents for hire -no dogs **Prices:** -adult per night -car per night pp-per person per night -caravan per night -tent per night (static)-caravan hire per week

Turn off via Aurelia at Km344/VIII towards Castagneto arducci/Sassetta. In 3.2km left towards Bolgheri, in 500m rn right towards mountains.
pen: 22 Apr-Oct **Site:** 9HEC **Prices:** 4.80-60 pitch 8.20-14 **Facilities:** **Services:** lau **Leisure:** P

Castel Del Piano Grosseto

miata via Roma 15, 58033 0564 955107 0564 955107
mail: info@amiata.org
ebsite: www.amiata.org
grassland site with a separate section for dog owners.
On the outskirts of Castel del Piano, on SS323 towards rcidosso.
pen: All year **Site:** 4.2HEC **Prices:** 5-6.20 pitch 6.20 **Facilities:** **Services:** lau
ff-site: P

Castiglione Della Pescaia Grosseto

anta Pomata Strada della Rocchette, 58043
0564 941037 0564 941221
mail: info@campingsantapomata.it
ebsite: www.campingsantapomata.it
ite in hilly woodland terrain with some pitches among ushes. Flat clean sandy beach.
Turn off the SS322 at Km20, then towards Le Rocchette 5km NW & continue towards the sea for 1km to site on left.
pen: Apr-20 Oct **Site:** 6HEC **Prices:** 6-9 7-14 7-14 (static)280-525 **Facilities:**
ervices: lau **Leisure:** S

Ceriale Savona

aciccia via Torino 19, 17023
0182 990743 0182 993839
mail: info@campingbaciccia.it
ebsite: www.campingbaciccia.it
n orderly site lying inland off the via Aurelia, 500m from he sea.
Entrance 100m W of Km612/V.
pen: All year **Site:** 1.2HEC **Prices:** 4-8 pitch 1-20 (static)245-668.50 **Facilities:**
ervices: lau **Leisure:** P **Off-site:** S

Cervo Imperia

ino via N Sauro 4, 18010
0183 400087 0183 400089
mail: info@campinglino.it **website:** www.campinglino.it
seaside site shaded by vines, which is clean and well nanaged. There is a knee-deep lagoon suitable for children.

Turn off via Aurelia at Km637/V near the railway underpass & follow via Nazionale Sauro towards sea.
Open: 20 Mar-22 Oct **Site:** 1.1HEC **Prices:** pitch 19-43 (incl 2 persons) **Facilities:**
Services: lau **Off-site:** PS

Cutigliano Pistoia

Betulle via Cantamaggio 6, 51024 0573 68004
A pleasant year-round site with good facilities in a central location with access to three popular ski stations.
Open: All year **Site:** 4HEC **Facilities:**
Services: lau **Leisure:** LR

Deiva Marina La Spezia

La Sfinge Gea 5, 19013 0187 825464 0187 825464
e-mail: lasfinge@camping.it
website: www.camping.it/liguria/lasfinge
Partly terraced site in pleasant wooded surroundings. Ideal for both nature lovers and families.
Access via A12 Genova-La Spezia.
Open: All year **Site:** 1.8HEC **Prices:** 6-7 3-3.50 9-14 6-14 **Facilities:** **Services:**
lau **Leisure:** RS **Off-site:**

Villaggio Turistico Arenella Arenella, 19013
0187 825259 0187 815861 / 826884
e-mail: info@campingarenella.it
website: www.campingarenella.it
In a beautiful, quiet valley 1.5km from the sea with good facilities.
Access via A12 Genoa-La Spezia.
Open: Jan-Oct & Dec **Site:** 16.2HEC
Prices: 6.80-8 2 6.80-8 5.80-7 **Facilities:**
Services: lau **Off-site:** S

Elba, Isola D' Livorno

Lacona

Lacona Pineta Lacona CP 186, 57037
0565 964322 0565 964087
e-mail: info@campinglaconapineta.com
website: www.campinglaconapineta.com
In a picturesque location on a thickly wooded hillside sloping gently towards a sandy beach with plenty of recreational facilities.
Open: Apr-Oct **Site:** 4HEC **Facilities:**
Services: lau **Leisure:** S **Off-site:**

Facilities: -shop -shower -electric points for razors -electric points for caravans -parking by tents permitted -compulsory separate car park **Services:** -café/restaurant -bar -Camping Gaz International -gas other than Camping Gaz -first aid facilities lau-laundry **Leisure:** -swimming L-Lake P-Pool R-River S-Sea **Off-site:** All facilities within 2km

Nisporto

Sole e Mare 57039 0565 934907 0565 961180
e-mail: gschezzini@tiscalinet.it
A well-equipped modern site in pleasant wooded surroundings close to the beach. A wide variety of recreational facilities are available.
From Portoferraio take Porto Azzurro road, then turn towards Rio nell'Elba-Nisporto.
Open: Apr-15 Oct **Site:** 2HEC **Prices:** 4.50-12 pitch 20-50 (static)170-660 **Facilities:** **Services:** lau **Leisure:** S

Ortano

Canapai Loc Ortano, 57038 0565 939165
Camping Card Compulsory.
Open: Apr-Sep **Site:** 4HEC **Facilities:** **Services:** **Leisure:** P **Off-site:** S

Ottone

Rosselba le Palme Ottone 3, 57037
0565 933101 0565 933041
e-mail: info@rosselbalepalme.it
website: www.rosselbalepalme.it
Pitches are on varying levels up from the beach. Shade is provided by large palm trees.
8km from Portferraio around bay via Bivo Bagnaia.
Open: 25 Apr-Sep **Site:** 30HEC **Prices:** 6-13 2-4.70 9-17.50 5-12.60 **Facilities:** **Services:** lau **Leisure:** PS

Porto Azzurro

Reale 57036 0565 95678 0565 920127
e-mail: campingreale@tin.it
website: www.isolaelbacampingreale.com
A well-equipped site in a wooded location with direct access to the beach.
From Portoferraio take the Porto Azzurro road for 13km, then towards Rio Marina for 2km follow signs.
Open: Apr-5 Oct **Site:** 2.5HEC **Facilities:** **Services:** lau **Leisure:** S **Off-site:** P

Portoferraio

Acquaviva Acquaviva, 57037 0565 930674 0565 915592
e-mail: campingacquaviva@elbalink.it
website: www.campingacquaviva.it
This seafront site is surrounded by trees and has excellent facilities for scuba-diving, water-sports.
3km W of town.
Open: Etr-Oct **Site:** 1.7HEC **Prices:** 6-11.50 1.20-2.50 7.50-12.50 7-12.50 (static)189-602 **Facilities:** **Services:** lau **Leisure:** S

Enfola Enfola, Casella Postale 147, 57037
0565 939001 0565 918613
e-mail: info@campingenfola.it
website: www.campingenfola.it
Located on the isle of Elba, ideal for scuba-diving, sailing and sunshine.
Open: Etr-Oct **Site:** 0.8HEC **Facilities:** **Services:** lau **Off-site:** S

Scaglieri via Biodola 1, Casella Postale 158, 57037
0565 969940 0565 969834
e-mail: info@campingscaglieri.it
website: www.campingscaglieri.it
Sloping terraces 10m from the sea. Facilities such as tennis and golf are avaliable at the nearby Hotel Hermitage.
The island is accessable by plane & ferry. The site is on the N coast 7km from Portoferraio.
Open: 12 Apr-17 Oct **Site:** 1.7HEC **Prices:** 7.50-13 2-3.50 11-18 11-18 (static)38-170 **Facilities:** **Services:** lau **Leisure:** P **Off-site:** S

Fiésole Firenze

Panoramico via Peramonda 1, 50014
055 599069 055 59186
e-mail: panoramico@florencecamping.com
website: www.florencecamping.com
Site stretches over wide terraces on the Fiésole hillside surrounded by a variety of tall evergreens.
Exit A1 at Firenze Sud, follow signs through the city to Fiésole. Site is on SS Bolognese.
Open: All year **Site:** 5HEC **Facilities:** **Services:** lau **Leisure:** P **Off-site:**

Figline Valdarno Firenze

Norcenni Girasole via Norcenni 7, 50063
055 915141 055 9151402
e-mail: girasole@ecvacanze.it
website: www.ecvacanze.it
Terraced site on partial slope. Separate section for young people.
From Florence take Roma A1/E35 autostrada & exit Incisa Turn left on rd 69 towards Figline, turn right for Greve & look for Camping Girasole signs.
Open: 12 Mar-29 Oct **Site:** 15HEC
Prices: 6.80-9.70 3.90-5.40 pitch 10-13.80 **Facilities:** **Services:** lau **Leisure:** PR

Firenze (Florence) Firenze

See also Troghi

Semifonte via Ugo Foscolo 4, Barberino Val d'Elsa, 50021
055 8075454 055 8075454
e-mail: semifonte@semifonte.it **website:** www.semifonte.it
A peaceful, terraced site offering panoramic views over the Chianti hills. Regular bus services to Firenze and Siena.
25km S of Firenze & N of Barberino Val d'Elsa.
Open: 15 Mar-20 Oct **Site:** 1.6HEC **Prices:** 6-6.50 pitch 11-13 **Facilities:** **Services:** lau **Leisure:** P **Off-site:**

At Marcialla

Toscana Colliverdi via Marcialla 349, Certaldo, 50020
0571 669334 0571 669334
e-mail: toscolverdi@virgilio.it
website: www.toscanacolliverdi.it
A sloping, terraced site with good facilities, surrounded by vineyards and olive groves.
Access via Firenze-Certosa exit on Autostrada del Sole or Tavarnelle Valpesa exit on Autostrada del Palio.
Open: Apr-Sep **Site:** 2.2HEC **Facilities:** **Services:** lau **Leisure:** P **Off-site:**

Florence See Firenze

Grosseto, Marina di Grosseto

La Marze St Statale della Collacchie
0564 35501 0564 35534
e-mail: lemarze@ecvanze.it **website:** www.ecvacanze.it
Access via SS322.
Open: 23 Apr-3 Oct **Site:** 20HEC
Prices: 5.90-10.50 3.50-5.20 5.40-8.30 5.10-7.90
Facilities: **Services:** lau
Leisure: PS

Rosmarina via delle Colonie 37, 58046
0564 36319 0564 34758
e-mail: info@campingrosmarina.it
website: www.campingrosmarina.it
A modern site situated in a pine wood and close to the sea, with beautiful views. Various sports and entertainments for everyone.
Open: May-Sep **Site:** 1.4HEC **Prices:** 6-11 pitch 7-14 **Facilities:** **Services:** lau **Off-site:** S

LERICI LA SPEZIA

Maralunga via Carpanini 61, Maralunga, 19032
0187 966589 0187 966589
This terraced site is on the seafront and surrounded by olive groves.
Access from Sarzana-La Spezia motorway.
Open: Jun-29 Sep **Site:** 10HEC **Prices:** 7.30-9.60 6.60-8 12.40-14.30 8.60-13.60 **Facilities:** **Services:** **Leisure:** S **Off-site:**

LIMITE FIRENZE

San Giusto via Castra 71, 50050
055 8712304 055 8711856
A useful site on slightly sloping ground within easy reach of Florence by car or public transport.
Open: Etr-Oct **Site:** 2.5HEC **Facilities:** **Services:** **Off-site:** P

MASSA, MARINA DI MASSA CARRARA

Giardino viale delle Pinete 382, 54037
0585 869291 0585 240781
e-mail: cgiardono@tin.it
website: www.campinggiardino.com
Site in pine woodland and on two meadows, shade provided by roof matting.
On the island side of the SS328 to Pisa.
Open: Apr-Sep **Site:** 3.2HEC **Prices:** 4-6.50 pitch 13-21 **Facilities:** **Services:** lau **Leisure:** P **Off-site:** S

MONÉGLIA GENOVA

Villaggio Smeraldo Preata, 16030
0185 49375 0185 490484
e-mail: info@villaggiosmeraldo.it
website: www.villagiosmeraldo.it
A pleasant site in a pine wood overlooking the sea with good, modern facilities and direct access to the beach.
Access via A12/SS1.
Open: All year **Site:** 1.5HEC **Prices:** 5 pitch 12-28 **Facilities:** **Services:** lau **Leisure:** S **Off-site:**

MONTECATINI TERME PISTOIA

Belsito via delle Vigne 1/A, Vico, 51016
0572 67373 0572 67373
e-mail: cbelsito@tin.it
website: www.campingbelsito.it
A quiet site at an altitude of 250m with good-size pitches.
Open: 15 Feb-29 Nov **Site:** 3.5HEC **Prices:** 5-6.60 3-4 7-8.50 5.50-8.50 **Facilities:** **Services:** lau **Leisure:** P **Off-site:** L

MONTE DI FO FIRENZE

Sergente 50030 055 8423018 055 8423907
e-mail: info@campingilsergente.it
website: www.campingilsergente.it
The site is at 780m above sea level on a hill. The pitches are flat. Ideal for walkers.
Exit the SS65 at Barberino Mugollo & follow signs for Monte di Fo.
Open: All year **Site:** 3HEC **Facilities:** **Services:** lau

MONTERIGGIONI SIENA

Piscina Luxor Quies Loc. Trasqua, 53032
0577 743047 0577 743047
e-mail: info@luxorcamping.com
website: www.luxorcamping.com
Lies on a flat-topped hill, partly in an oak wood, partly in meadowland.
Turn off via Cassia (SS2) at Km239/II or Km238/IX & continue 2.5km, crossing railway line. Approach to site via very steep winding road.
Open: 17 May-7 Sep **Site:** 1.5HEC **Prices:** 6.90 3 3.80 3.70 **Facilities:** **Services:** lau **Leisure:** P

MONTESCUDÁIO LIVORNO

Montescudáio via del Poggetto, 56040
0586 683477 0586 630932
e-mail: info@camping-montescudaio.it
website: www.camping-montescudaio.it
This modern site is on a hill and is divided into individual pitches, some of which are naturally screened. Children under 2 years are not accepted.
From Cecinia (on SS1, via Aurelia) follow road to Guardistallo for 2.5km.
Open: 12 May-18 Sep **Site:** 25HEC **Prices:** 5.50-7.50 pitch 11.50-21 (static)238-941 **Facilities:** **Services:** lau **Leisure:** PS **Off-site:**

MONTICELLO AMIATA GROSSETO

Lucherino Lucherino, 58047 0564 992975 0564 992975
e-mail: meichu@tiscalinet.it
website: www.lucherino.nl
A peaceful site 735m above sea level on the slopes of mount Amiata. The shady but sloping site is ideal for walkers.
Access via SS223 to Paganico then follow signs to Monte Amiata.
Open: May-15 Oct **Site:** 2HEC **Prices:** 5.40-7 pitch 7-8.50 (static)210-315 **Facilities:** **Services:** lau **Leisure:** P **Off-site:**

PEGLI GENOVA

Villa Doria via al Campeggio 15n, 16156
010 6969600 010 6969600
e-mail: villadoria@camping.it
website: www.camping.it/liguria/villadoria
Quiet site in pleasant wooded surroundings.
Access via SS1. Signed.
Open: All year **Site:** 0.4HEC **Facilities:** **Services:** lau **Off-site:** S

PISA PISA

Torre Pendente viale della Cascine 86, 56122
050 561704 050 561734
e-mail: torrepen@campingtoscana.it
website: campingtoscana.it/torrependente
Pleasant, modern site on level ground in a rural setting. 1km walk to the Leaning Tower.
On the N outskirts of Pisa.
Open: 22 Mar-15 Oct **Site:** 2.5HEC **Prices:** 8 4.50 7 6.50 **Facilities:** **Services:** lau **Leisure:** P **Off-site:** PR

POPULÓNIA LIVORNO

Sant'Albínia via della Principessa, 57025
0565 29389 0565 221310
e-mail: arci.piobino@etruscan.li.it
A good overnight stopping place with plenty of facilities. Ideally placed for the ferry ports.
10km N of Piombino on San Vincenzo road.
Open: May-15 Sep **Site:** 3HEC **Facilities:** **Services:** lau **Leisure:** S

RIOTORTO LIVORNO

Orizzonte Perelli, 57020 0565 28007 0565 28033
A fine coastal position overlooking the island of Elba.
Open: All year **Site:** 10HEC **Facilities:** **Services:** lau **Leisure:** P **Off-site:** S

SAN BARONTO FIRENZE

Barco Reale via Nardini 11, 51030
0573 88332 0573 856003
e-mail: info@barcoreale.com
website: www.barcoreale.com
A well-equipped site in a hilly, wooded location.
Signed from Lamporecchio.
Open: Apr-Sep **Site:** 10HEC **Prices:** 6.70-9 3.70-5 6.20-8.20 5.50-7.30 **Facilities:** **Services:** lau **Leisure:** P

SAN GIMIGNANO SIENA

Boschetto di Piemma Santa Lucia, 53037
0577 940352 0577 907453
e-mail: info@boschettodipiemma.it
website: www.boschettodipiemma.it
This small grassy site is well equipped and has many facilities for both families and idividuals.
Open: Apr-15 Oct **Site:** 4HEC **Prices:** 6.40 2.80 6.80 6 **Facilities:** **Services:** **Leisure:** P

SAN PIERO A SIEVE FIRENZE

Village Mugello Verde via Massorondinaio 39, 50037
055 848511 055 8486910
e-mail: mugelloverde@florencecamping.com
website: www.florencecamping.com
Terraced site in wooded surroundings. Siesta 14.00-16.00.
Leave motorway at exit 18 & follow signs.
Open: All year **Site:** 12HEC **Prices:** 7.50-8 pitch 15-15.50 **Facilities:** **Services:** **Leisure:** P **Off-site:** R

SAN VINCENZO LIVORNO

Park Albatros Pineta di Torre Nuova, 57027
0565 701018 0565 703589
e-mail: info@parkalbatros.it
website: www.parkalbatros.it
The site lies among beautiful, tall pine trees. 1km from sea.
Turn off SP23 beyond San Vincenzo at Km7/III & continue 600m inland.
Open: 22 Apr-11 Sep **Site:** 11.4HEC **Prices:** 8-12 2 8.50-15 8.50-13 **Facilities:** **Services:** lau **Off-site:** S

SARTEANO SIENA

Bagno Santo via del Bagno Santo 29, 53047
0578 26971 0578 265889
e-mail: info@parcodellepiscine.it
website: www.parcodellepiscine.it
Open: 19 Mar-30 Sep **Site:** 15HEC **Prices:** 9.50-12.50 3.50-6 9.50-12.50 9.50-12.50 **Facilities:** **Services:** lau **Leisure:** P **Off-site:**

SARZANA LA SPEZIA

Iron Gate via XXV Aprile 54, 19038
0187 676370 0187 675014
A modern site with good facilities attached to the Iron Gate Marina.
Open: All year **Site:** 2HEC **Facilities:** **Services:** **Leisure:** PR **Off-site:**

SESTRI LEVANTE GENOVA

Fossa Lupara via Costa 31, 16039
0185 43992 0185 43992
Open: All year **Site:** 1.5HEC **Facilities:** **Services:** lau **Off-site:** S

SIENA SIENA

Montagnola Sovicille, 53018 0577 314473 0577 314473
e-mail: montagnolacamping@libero.it
Quiet site in an oak wood with individual plots separated by hedges. Facilities are modern and extensive.
From the A1 westbound, exit at Siena, campsite signed towards Sovicille.
Open: Etr-29 Sep **Site:** 2.5HEC **Prices:** 6 pitch 8 **Facilities:** **Services:** lau **Leisure:** R **Off-site:**

Siena Colleverde Strada di Scacciapensieri 47, 53100
0577 280044 0577 333298
e-mail: campingsiena@terresiena.it **website:** www.terresiena.it
The site offers both large areas for caravans and mobile homes and a large grassy area for tents. There is a local bus service to the centre of Siena.
The only campsite in Siena, situated just to the N.
Open: Etr-10 Nov **Site:** 4.5HEC **Prices:** 7.75 7.75
Facilities: **Services:** lau **Leisure:** P
Off-site:

Soline Casciano di Murlo, 53010
0577 817410 0577 817415
e-mail: camping@lesoline.it **website:** www.lesoline.it
Terraced hilly site surrounded by woodland. Wide variety of sports facilities and family entertainment.
Take the left turning at Fontazzi and ascend hill.
Open: All year **Site:** 6HEC **Prices:** 7 1.50 6.50 5-6 **Facilities:** **Services:** lau **Leisure:** P

STELLA SAN GIOVANNI SAVONA

Stella via Rio Basco 62, 17040 019 703269 019 703269
e-mail: campingdolcevita@libero.it
website: www.campingdolcevita.it
In wooded surroundings with well-defined pitches, 5.5km from the coast.
Access via SS334.
Open: Apr-Sep **Site:** 10HEC **Prices:** 4-5 pitch 10-17 (incl 2 persons) **Facilities:** **Services:** lau **Leisure:** PR **Off-site:**

TORRE DEL LAGO PUCCINI LUCCA

Burlamacco viale G-Marconi Int, 55048
0584 359544 0584 359387
e-mail: info@campingburlamacco.com
website: www.campingburlamacco.com
In a beautiful wooded location 1km from the sea on the Versilia Riviera and close to the former home of Puccini. Various facilities are available.
Open: Apr-29 Sep **Site:** 4.5HEC **Facilities:** **Services:** **Leisure:** P **Off-site:** LS

Europa Viale dei Tigli, 55048
0584 350707 0584 342592
e-mail: info@europacamp.it **website:** www.europacamp.it
Site in pine and poplar woodland.
On the land side of the viale dei Tigli, from Viareggio.
Open: 25 Mar-16 Oct **Site:** 60HEC
Prices: 4-8.50 8-12 6-10 **Facilities:**
Services: lau **Leisure:** P **Off-site:** LS

Italia 52 viale dei Tigli, 55048
0584 359828 0584 341504
e-mail: info@campingitalia.net **website:** www.campingitalia.net
This site is divided into pitches and lies in meadowland planted with poplar trees.
Inland from the Viareggio road (viale dei Tigli).
Open: 21 Apr-18 Sep **Site:** 9HEC
Prices: 5.50-8.50 11-11.50 8-11.50 **Facilities:** **Services:** lau **Off-site:** LS

Tigli Viale dei Tigli, 54, 55048 0584 341278 0584 341278
e-mail: info@campingdeitigli.com
website: www.campingdeitigli.com
Shady site close to a regional park, lake Massaciuccoli, and the villa where Puccini wrote much of his music.
Open: Apr-15 Sep **Site:** 9HEC **Prices:** 5-9 8-15 pitch 8-15 **Facilities:** **Services:** lau **Off-site:** LS

TROGHI FIRENZE

Il Poggetto via il Poggetto 143, 50010
055 8307323 055 8307323
e-mail: poggetto@tin.it
website: campingtoscana.it/ilpoggetto
A modern site with good facilities. Large, level, grassy pitches.
5km from exit Incisa Valdarno on the A1.
Open: 19 Mar-16 Oct **Site:** 4.5HEC
Prices: 7.50 pitch 13 (static)455-630 **Facilities:** **Services:** lau **Leisure:** P

VADA LIVORNO

Flori 57018 0586 770096 0586 770323
e-mail: campofiori@multinet.it
website: www.campingcampodeifiori.it
Level grassland surrounded by fields. Shade provided by roof matting.
Access from the SS1 S of Vada, after 1.5km turn right & continue 500m.
Open: 28 Mar-26 Sep **Site:** 15HEC **Prices:** 6-11 6-10 6-10 **Facilities:** **Services:** lau **Leisure:** P **Off-site:** S

VIAREGGIO LUCCA

Pineta via dei Lecci, 55049 0584 383397
e-mail: campinglapincta@interfree.it
website: www.campinglapineta.com
A well-organised site in a wooded location, 1km from a private beach.
Access via SSN1 between Km 354 & 355.
Open: Etr-19 Sep **Site:** 3.2HEC **Prices:** 5-9 pitch 10.50-16.50 **Facilities:** **Services:** lau **Leisure:** P **Off-site:** S

Viareggio via Comparini 1, 55049
0584 391012 0584 391012
e-mail: campingviareggio@tin.it
website: www.campingviareggio.it
The site lies in a poplar wood 700m from beach.
1.5km S of town. At Km354/V head towards coast.
Open: Apr-29 Sep **Site:** 2HEC **Prices:** 6-12 8-12 8-12 **Facilities:** **Services:** lau **Leisure:** P **Off-site:** LPS

ZINOLA SAVONA

Buggi International via N S del Monte 15, 17049
019 860120 019 804573
A well-equipped site with plenty of space for tents, 900m from the sea.
Open: All year **Site:** 2HEC **Prices:** 5 5 7 5 (static)400 **Facilities:** **Services:**
Off-site: S

NORTH-EAST/ADRIATIC

ALBA ADRIATICA TERAMO

AT TORTORETO, LIDO (4KM S)

Salinello c da Piane a Mare, 64019
0861 786306 0861 786451
e-mail: salinello@camping.it
website: www.camping.it/salinello
Well-tended meadowland site with numerous rows of poplars. Private beach. Siesta 13.30-16.00.
On S outskirts, signed from Km405 of the SS16.
Open: May-Sep **Site:** 15HEC **Facilities:** **Services:** lau **Leisure:** PS **Off-site:** R

ASSISI PERUGIA

Internationale Campiglione No. 110, 06081
075 813710 075 812335
e-mail: info@campingassisi.it
website: www.campingassisi.it
At the foot of the hill on which Assisi stands, this modern campsite is well equipped and a good touring centre.
W via SS147.
Open: 20 Mar-15 Oct **Site:** 3HEC **Prices:** 6-7 2-3 6-7 5-6 **Facilities:** **Services:** lau **Leisure:** P **Off-site:** R

BARREA L'AQUILA

Grenziana Parco Nazionale d'Abruzzo, Tre Croci, 67030
0864 88101 0864 88101
e-mail: pasettanet@tiscali.it
website: www.campinglagenzianapasetta.it
In picturesque wooded surroundings on the shore of a lake.
Open: All year **Site:** 2HEC **Prices:** 6.20 3 7 6.20-7 **Facilities:** **Services:**
Off-site: L

BELLARIA FORLI

Happy via Panzini 228, 47814
0541 346102 0541 346408
e-mail: happy@infotel.it
website: www.happycamping.it
The campsite is in a quiet position on the sea shore close to the centre of town.
A14, SS16, exit for Bellaria Cagnona San Mauro Mare, follow signs for Acquabell. Over level crossing & site is on right.
Open: All year **Site:** 4HEC **Facilities:** **Services:** lau **Leisure:** PS
Off-site: R

BEVAGNA PERUGIA

Pian di Boccio Pian di Boccio 10, 06031
0742 360164 0742 360391
e-mail: piandiboccio@tiscaliner.it
website: www.piandiboccio.com
In wooded surroundings in the centre of the Umbria region with good modern facilities. Popular with families.
Open: Apr-Sep **Site:** 8.5HEC **Prices:** 5.50-6.50 2-2.50 6-7 3.50-6.50 **Facilities:**
Services: lau **Leisure:** LP

BOLOGNA BOLOGNA

Citta di Bologna via Romita 12/IVA, 40127
051 325016 051 325318
e-mail: info@hotelcamping.com
website: www.hotelcamping.com
Located in the northern part of this ancient town, this site offers a cheap and convenient alternative to hotels.
Open: All year **Site:** 6.3HEC **Prices:** 5-7 pitch 8-12 **Facilities:** **Services:** lau **Leisure:** P
Off-site:

BORGHETTO PERUGIA

Badiaccia via Trasimenoi, no.91, 6061
075 9659097 075 9659019
e-mail: info@badiaccia.com **website:** www.badiaccia.com
A well-equipped site with large grassy pitches and direct access to the lake.
From the A1 exit at Valdichiana & join the road to Perugia & follow signs for lake Trasimeno.
Open: Apr-Sep **Site:** 5.5HEC **Prices:** 5-6.50 2 6-6.50 5-6 (static)245-350 **Facilities:**
Services: lau **Leisure:** LP **Off-site:**

CASAL BORSETTI RAVENNA

Adria via Spallazzi N30, 48010 0544 445217
The site lies in a field behind the Ristorante Lugo.
Turn off the motorway at Ravenna exit or take the SS309 (Romea) Km13 N of Ravenna.
Open: May-20 Sep **Site:** 5.5HEC **Facilities:** **Services:** lau **Leisure:** PS

Reno via Spallazzi 11, 48010 0544 445020 0544 442056
e-mail: info@campingreno.it
website: www.camping.it/emiliaromagna/reno
Meadowland in sparse pine woodland and separated from the sea by dunes.
Turn off SS309 at Km8 or 14.
Open: Apr-Oct **Site:** 3HEC **Prices:** 4-6 34.50-59 pitch 7.15-9.50 (incl 4 persons) (static)188-277 **Facilities:** **Services:** lau
Off-site: S

CASTIGLIONE DEL LAGO PERUGIA

Listro via Lungolago, 6061 075 951193 075 951193
e-mail: listro@listro.it **website:** www.listro.it
Attractive site on a peninsula in lake Trasimeno.
Open: Apr-29 Sep **Site:** 1HEC **Prices:** 3.80-4.50 1.30-1.80 3.80-4.50 3.80-4.50 pitch 3.50-4.20
Facilities: **Services:** lau **Leisure:** L
Off-site: P

CERVIA RAVENNA

Adriatico via Pinarella 90, 48015
0544 71537 0544 72346
e-mail: info@campingadriatico.net
website: www.campingadriatico.net
Level meadowland site with plenty of shade, pleasantly landscaped with olives, willows, elms and maples.
Located shortly before Pinarella di Cervia. Access by via Cadulti per le Liberta (SS16) 600m from sea.
Open: 23 Apr-5 Sep **Site:** 3.4HEC **Prices:** 4.60-7.30 pitch 9-12.70 **Facilities:** **Services:** lau **Leisure:** P **Off-site:** L

CESENATICO FORLI

Cesenatico via Mazzini 182, 47042
0547 81344 0547 672452
e-mail: info@campingcesenatico.com
website: www.campingcesenatico.com
The site stretches over an area of land belonging to the Azienda di Soggiomo e Turismo.
1.5km N at Km178 turn off the SS16 towards the sea.
Open: All year **Site:** 18HEC **Prices:** 5.30-9.70 pitch 13.50-21.60 **Facilities:** **Services:**
lau **Leisure:** PS **Off-site:**

Zadina via Mazzini 184, 47042
0547 82310 0547 672802
e-mail: info@campingzadina.it
Very pleasant terrain in dunes on two sides of a canal.
Open: 23 Apr-16 Sep **Site:** 11HEC **Facilities:** **Services:** lau **Leisure:** S

CITTA DI CASTELLO PERUGIA

La Montesca 06012 075 8521420 075 8520786
e-mail: villamontesca@sogepu.com
website: www.sogepu.com
In a large, wooded park with excellent facilities. An ideal base for exploring the surrounding area.
3km from the town, beside the River Tiber.
Open: May-Sep **Site:** 5HEC **Facilities:**
Services: lau **Leisure:** P

Site: 6HEC-Site size -grass -sand -stone -little shade -partly shaded -mainly shaded -bungalows for hire -caravans for hire -tents for hire -no dogs **Prices:** -adult per night -car per night pp-per person per night -caravan per night -tent per night (static)-caravan hire per week

CUPRA MARITTIMA ASCOLI PICENO

Calypso via Boccabianca 8, 63012
0735 778686 0735 778106
e-mail: calypso@camping.it
website: www.campingcalypso.it
Open: Apr-29 Sep **Site:** 26HEC **Prices:** 6-9 8.50-14 **Facilities:** **Services:** lau
Leisure: PS

DANTE, LIDO DI RAVENNA

Classe viale Catone, 48100 0544 492005 0544 492058
e-mail: info@campingclasse.it
website: www.campingclasse.it
Level meadowland in grounds of former farm.
Access from the SS16 turning towards the sea at Km154/V & continue 9km to site.
Open: 28 Mar-10 Oct **Site:** 7HEC **Prices:** 7.50 5 11-14 11-14 (static)350-490 **Facilities:** **Services:** lau **Leisure:** PS **Off-site:** LR

ESTENSI, LIDO DEGLI FERRARA

International Mare Pineta via delle Acacie 67, 44024
0533 330110 0533 330052
e-mail: info@campingmarepineta.com
website: www.campingmarepineta.com
Extensive site on slightly hilly ground, pines and decidous trees providing shade. Near the beach. Numerous mobile homes.
2km SE of Port Garibaldi.
Open: 16 Apr-20 Sep **Site:** 16HEC **Prices:** 3.70-7.95 2.60-4.20 pitch 6.90-13.25 (static)26-122 **Facilities:** **Services:** lau
Leisure: PS

FANO PESARO & URBINO

Mare Blu 61032 0721 884201 0721 884389
e-mail: mareblu@camping.it
website: www.camping.it/mareblu
The site is surrounded by tall poplars with direct access to a sandy beach. Facilities for most water-sports and entertainment for children and families.
Exit A14 at Fano & travel S for 3km.
Open: Apr-Sep **Site:** 2.5HEC **Prices:** 5-7.50 pitch 10-13 (static)300-400 **Facilities:** **Services:** lau **Leisure:** S **Off-site:** PR

FERRARA FERRARA

Estense via Gramicia 76, 44100
0532 752396 0532 752396
e-mail: camping.estense@freeinternet.it
A good overnight stop on the way S.
NE outskirts of Ferrara.
Open: 26 Feb-Dec **Site:** 3.3HEC **Prices:** 5 6.50 6.50 pitch 6.50 **Facilities:** **Off-site:** P

FIORENZUOLA DI FOCARA PESARO & URBINO

Panorama Strada Panoramica, 61010
0721 208145 0721 208145
e-mail: info@campingpanorama.it
website: www.campingpanorama.it
Located in a park 100m above sea level, this site welcomes families, animals, cyclists and anyone wishing to relax.
Signed off the SS16, 10km from Gabicce & 7km from Pesaro.
Open: May-Sep **Site:** 2.2HEC **Prices:** 5.50-7.75 2.50 7-10 7-10 (static)294-476 **Facilities:** **Services:** lau **Leisure:** PS

GATTEO MARE FORLI

Delle Rose via Adriatica 29, 47043
0547 86213 0547 87583
e-mail: info@villaggiorose.com
website: www.villaggiorose.com
A peaceful setting close to the sea and the town centre.
Turn off SS16 at Km186.
Open: 23 Apr-26 Sep **Site:** 4HEC
Prices: 4.20-8.20 pitch 9-16.60 (static)200-525
Facilities: **Services:** lau
Leisure: PS **Off-site:** R

GIULIANOVA LIDO TERAMO

Baviera Lungomare Zara, 64022
085 8000053 085 8004420
A family site in a wooded location with direct access to a private beach. Various sports and entertainment facilities are available, particularly in July and August, when all cars must use the designated car park.
Access via A14 and SS80.
Open: 31 May-15 Sep **Site:** 1.8HEC **Facilities:** **Services:** lau **Leisure:** PS

GUBBIO PERUGIA

Villa Ortoguidone Ortoguidone 214, 06024
075 9272037 075 9276620
e-mail: info@gubbiocamping.com
website: www.gubbiocamping.com
One of two well-equipped sites in the same location. Plenty of space for tents.
Access via SS298 Gubbio-Perugia.
Open: 23-29 Mar & 15 Apr-18 Sep **Site:** 0.5HEC **Prices:** 6.50-9 2.50 9-10.50 7-9 **Facilities:** **Services:** lau **Leisure:** P **Off-site:**

Facilities: shop shower electric points for razors electric points for caravans parking by tents permitted compulsory separate car park **Services:** café/restaurant bar Camping Gaz International gas other than Camping Gaz first aid facilities lau-laundry **Leisure:** swimming L-Lake P-Pool R-River S-Sea **Off-site:** All facilities within 2km

MARCELLI DI NUMANA ANCONA

Conero Azzurro via Litoranea, 60026
071 7390507 071 7390986
e-mail: coneroazzurro@camping.it
Well-equipped site situated between the Adriatic and mount Canero.
Open: Jun-15 Sep **Site:** 5HEC **Prices:** 7-10 pitch 9-13 **Facilities:** **Services:** lau **Leisure:** PS **Off-site:**

MAROTTA PESARO & URBINO

Gabbiano via Faa' di Bruno 95, 61035
0721 96691 0721 96691
e-mail: gabbiano.marche@camping.it
website: www.camping.it/marche/gabbiano
Quiet location surrounded by trees overlooking the sea.
Exit A14 at Marotta, join SS16 & site is 2.5km towards Fano.
Open: May-Sep **Site:** 1.9HEC **Prices:** 5-6.70 pitch 10.75-12.75 **Facilities:** **Services:** lau **Leisure:** PS

MARTINISCURO TERAMO

Duca Amedeo Lungomare Europa 158, 64014
0861 797376 0861 797264
e-mail: ducaamedeo@camping.it
In a pleasant location, surrounded by trees and lush vegetation. Close to the sea.
Access via A14 exit Martinsicuro.
Open: May-28 Sep **Site:** 1.5HEC **Prices:** 3.50-8 pitch 8-16 **Facilities:** **Services:** lau **Leisure:** PS **Off-site:**

MILANO MARITTIMA RAVENNA

Romagna viale Matteotti 190, 48016
0544 949326 0544 949345
Level site with young trees.
Access via the SS16 (Strada Adriatica), turn off beyond Milano Marittima & follow signs.
Open: 12 Apr-15 Sep **Site:** 40HEC **Prices:** 4.50-7.50 pitch 7-12.50 **Facilities:** **Services:** lau **Leisure:** S **Off-site:** P

MONTENERO, MARINA DI CAMPOBASSO

Costa Verde 86036 0873 803144 0873 362226
e-mail: info@costaverde.it **website:** www.costaverde.it
A level site with good facilities and direct access to the beach E of San Salvo Marino.
Leave the coast road SS16 at Km525/VII & continue by farm road 300m to the site.
Open: 15 May-15 Sep **Site:** 1HEC **Prices:** 4.30-7 pitch 5-10 **Facilities:** **Services:** lau **Leisure:** PRS **Off-site:**

NARNI TERNI

Monti del Sole strada di Borgheria 22
0744 796336 0744 796336
e-mail: info@campingmontidelsole.it
website: www.campingmontidelsole.it
A spacious wooded site, shaded and flat. All plots are grassed and easily reached by firm lanes.
Off autostrada A1 Florence-Rome, exit at Magliano Sabina & continue towards Terni, follow signs for Narni
Open: Apr-Sep **Site:** **Prices:** 5.50-6.70 1.50 5.20-6.20 4.50-5.70 **Facilities:** **Services:** lau **Leisure:** P

NAZIONI, LIDO DELLE FERRARA

Tahiti viale Libia 133, 44020 0533 379500 0533 37970
e-mail: info@campingtahiti.com
website: www.campingtahiti.com
Pleasantly laid out site 650m from sea. Private beach accessible via a miniature railway. Siesta 13.30-15.30.
Turn off SS309 near Km32.5 then 2km to site. Signed.
Open: 3 Apr-26 Sep **Site:** 12HEC **Facilities:** **Services:** lau **Leisure:** P **Off-site:** S

PERUGIA PERUGIA

Rocolo strada Fontana la Trinita, 6074
075 5178550 075 5177538
e-mail: ilrocolo@ilrocolo.it
website: www.ilrocolo.it
Open: 15 Apr-Sep **Site:** 2.4HEC **Prices:** 5-6 2-2.50 5-6 4.50-5 **Facilities:** **Services:** lau **Off-site:** P

PARMA PARMA

Cittadella parco Cittadella, 43100 0521 961434
Camping Card Compulsory
Open: Apr-Oct **Site:** 4HEC **Prices:** 7 5.50 5.50 5.50 **Facilities:** **Off-site:**

PASSIGNANO PERUGIA

Europa Loc San Donato, 06065 075 827405 075 827405
e-mail: info@camping-europa.it
website: www.camping-europa.it
Situated by lake Trasimeno with private beach.
From motorway exit Passignano Est & campsite signed.
Open: Etr-10 Oct **Site:** 3HEC **Prices:** 5.70-6.90 2.50-3.50 6-7 5.30-6.30 (static)290-434 **Facilities:** **Services:** lau **Leisure:** LP

Kursaal viale Europa 24, 06065
075 828085 075 827182
e-mail: kursaalcamp@libero.it
website: www.camping.it/umbria/kursaal
The site is between the road and the lake, near the villa of th same name.
Access from SS75, Arezzo to Perugia road, from Km35.2.
Open: Apr-29 Oct **Site:** 1HEC **Prices:** 6-7 pitch 10-11 **Facilities:** **Services:** lau **Leisure:** LP **Off-site:**

PIEVEPELAGO MODENA

Fra Dolcino 41027 0536 71229
Open: All year **Site:** 3.6HEC **Facilities:** **Services:** lau **Off-site:** PR

Rio Verde via M-de-Canossa 34, 41027
0536 72204 0536 72204
e-mail: info@abetour.it
website: www.abetour.it
In a wooded mountain setting close to the river with good, modern facilities.
Access via A1 from Firenze via Pistoia, La Lima & Abeton
Open: All year **Site:** 1.8HEC **Facilities:** **Services:** lau **Leisure:** R **Off-site:** LP

Site: 6HEC-Site size -grass -sand -stone -little shade -partly shaded -mainly shaded -bungalows for hire -caravans for hire -tents for hire -no dogs **Prices:** -adult per night -car per night pp-per person per night -caravan per night -tent per night (static)-caravan hire per week

PINARELLA RAVENNA

'inarella viale Abruzzi 52, 48015
0544 987408 0544 987408
-mail: campingpinarella@libero.it
vebsite: www.campingpinarella.com
ubdivided terrain surrounded by houses. Partially shaded, ome young poplars. Private beach. Management request eservations day before arrival.
ite: 1.8HEC **Facilities:** ⊙ **Services:** ✕ lau **Off-site:** ✕ S

afari viale Titano 130, 48015
0544 987356 0544 987356
-mail: csafari@cervia.com
vebsite: www.cervia.com
'he site is divided into several sections. Only families are ccepted.
)pen: May-15 Sep **Site:** 3.1HEC **Facilities:** **Services:** ✕ ⊞ lau **Off-site:** ✕ S

PINETO TERAMO

Ieliopolis Contrada Villa Fumosa, 64025
085 9492720 085 9492171
-mail: info@heliopolis.it
vebsite: www.heliopolis.it
ituated near a golden sandy beach. Various activies for all to njoy. Idyllic scenery for relaxing walks.
)pen: Apr-Sep **Site:** 12HEC **Facilities:** ⊙ **Services:** ✕ ⊞ lau **Leisure:** PS

nternational Loc Torre Cerrano, 64025
085 930639 085 930639
-mail: info@internationalcamping.it
vebsite: www.internationalcamping.it
ite on level terrain with young poplars. Sunshade roofing on ne beach.
Turn off SS16 at Km431.2 & continue under railway nderpass. Adjoining railway line.
)pen: May-Sep **Site:** 1.5HEC **Prices:** 4-8 itch 8-15 **Facilities:** ⊙ **Services:** ✕ ⊞ u **Leisure:** S

'ineto Beach S.s 16 km425, 64025
085 9492724 085 9492796
-mail: pinetobeach@camping.it
'ebsite: www.pinetobeach.it
well-equipped site in wooded surroundings with direct ccess to the beach.
At Km425 on SS16 Adriatica.
'pen: 15 May-29 Sep **Site:** 3HEC **Prices:** 6-8 1.50-2.50 9.50-14 7-14 **Facilities:** ⊙ ervices: ✕ ⊞ lau **Leisure:** PS

POMPOSA FERRARA

nternational Tre Moschettieri via Capanno Garibaldi 22, 4020 0533 380376 0533 380377
-mail: info@tremoschettieri.com
ebsite: www.tremoschettieri.com
ampsite set beneath pine trees next to sea.
Signed from SS309.
'pen: 23 Apr-23 Sep **Site:** 11HEC **Prices:** 4- pitch 9-15 **Facilities:** ⊙ **Services:** ✕ lau eisure: PS **Off-site:** L

PORTO SANT'ELPÍDIO ASCOLI PICENO

isacca via Gabbie 6, 63018 0734 991423 0734 997276
mail: info@larisacca.it
ebsite: www.larisacca.it
lean, well-kept site on level meadowland, with some trees ırrounded by fields.

Turn off SS16 N of village, follow road seawards under railway (narrow underpass maximum height 3m), then 1.2km along field paths to site. Caravan access is 400m further S along SS16, then under railway & along field paths to site.
Open: 21 May-10 Sep **Site:** 8HEC
Prices: 2.50-8 pitch 7-16 (static)140-364 **Facilities:** ⊙ **Services:** ✕ ⊞ lau **Leisure:** PS **Off-site:** R

PRECI PERUGIA

Il Collaccio Castelvecchio di Preci, 6047
0743 939005 0743 939094
e-mail: info@ilcollaccio.com **website:** www.ilcollaccio.com
In beautiful natural surroundings with plenty of roomy pitches and good recreational facilities.
Access via SS 209.
Open: Apr-Sep **Site:** 10HEC **Prices:** 5.50-7.50 2-3.50 6.50-9 5.50-7.50 **Facilities:** ⊙
Services: ✕ lau **Leisure:** P **Off-site:** R

PUNTA MARINA RAVENNA
AT ADRIANO, LIDO (4.5KM S)

Adriano via dei Campeggi 7, 48020
0544 437230 0544 438510
e-mail: info@campingadriano.com
website: www.campingadriano.com
300m from the sea. A pleasantly landscaped site amid the dunes of the Punta Marina.
On SS309 via Lido Adriano to Punta Marina.
Open: 17 Apr-21 Sep **Site:** 14HEC
Facilities: ⊙ **Services:** ✕ ⊞ lau
Leisure: PS

Coop 3 via dei Campeggi 8, 48020
0544 437353 0544 438144
e-mail: campingcoop3@libero.it
website: digilander.iol.it/campingcoop3
300m to the sea. Level site under isolated high pines and poplars. Across flat dunes to the beach.
Signed.
Open: 24 Apr-12 Sep **Site:** 7HEC **Prices:** 3.80-6.70 pitch 7.70-12 (static)149.20-262 **Facilities:** ⊙ **Services:** ✕ lau **Off-site:** PS ⊞

RAVENNA, MARINA DI RAVENNA

International Piomboni via Lungomare 421, 48023
0544 530230 0544 538618
e-mail: info@campingpiomboni.it
website: www.campingpiomboni.it
Site on slightly undulating, mainly grassy terrain with pines and poplars. Separate section for tents. Siesta 14.00-15.30.
Access is 1km S from town centre off coast road.
Open: 23 Apr-11 Sep **Site:** 5HEC **Prices:** 4-6.80 pitch 7.20-10.60 (static)182-315 **Facilities:** ⊙ **Services:** ✕ ⊞ lau **Leisure:** S

RICCIONE FORLI

Alberello via Torino 80, 47036
0541 615402 0541 615248
e-mail: direzione@alberello.it
website: www.alberello.it
On the seafront connected to the beach by a private subway. Popular with families, with a wide range of recreational facilities.
Access via A14 & SS16.
Open: 22 Apr-19 Sep **Site:** 4HEC **Prices:** 3.60-7.20 pitch 8-12.45 **Facilities:** ⊙ **Services:** ✕ lau **Off-site:** PRS ⊞

Facilities: -shop -shower ⊙-electric points for razors -electric points for caravans -parking by tents permitted -compulsory separate car park **Services:** ✕-café/restaurant -bar -Camping Gaz International -gas other than Camping Gaz ⊞-first aid facilities lau-laundry **Leisure:** -swimming L-Lake P-Pool R-River S-Sea **Off-site:** All facilities within 2km

Fontanelle via Torino 56, 47838
☎ 0541 615449 Fax 0541 610193
e-mail: info@campingfontanelle.com
website: www.campingfontanelle.com
On S outskirts separated from beach by coast road. Underpass to public beach.
Camping Card Compulsory
➲ *Turn off SS16 between Km216 & 217.*
Open: 21 Apr-22 Sep **Site:** 6HEC **Prices:** 3.60-7.20 pitch 8-12.45 **Facilities:** **Services:** lau **Leisure:** S

Riccione via Marsala N10, 47838
☎ 0541 690160 Fax 0541 690044
e-mail: info@campingriccione.it
website: www.campingriccione.it
About 300m from sea. Extensive flat meadowland, with poplars of medium height.
➲ *From SS16 turn seawards on the S outskirts of the town & continue 200m. Alternative access from coast road, turn inland on S outskirts at sign & continue 700m.*
Open: 18 Apr-20 Sep **Site:** 6.5HEC **Facilities:** **Services:** lau **Leisure:** P **Off-site:** S

ROSETO DEGLI ABRUZZI TERAMO

Eurcamping-Roseto Lungomare Trieste Sud 90, 64026
☎ 085 8993179 Fax 085 8930552
e-mail: eurcamping@campig.it
website: www.eurcamping.it
A meadow site at the S end of the beach road.
➲ *Leave the SS16 within the town, then continue 500m to the site.*
Open: Apr-Oct **Site:** 5HEC **Prices:** 3.50-7.50 pitch 6.50-13.50 **Facilities:** **Services:** lau **Leisure:** PS **Off-site:** R

Gilda viale Makarska, 64026 ☎ 085 8941023 Fax 085 8941023
e-mail: gilda@camping.it
In a picturesque wooded setting with direct access to the beach and good modern facilities.
Open: Jun-12 Sep **Site:** 1.5HEC **Prices:** 4.50-7.50 pitch 9.50-14.50 **Facilities:** **Services:** lau **Leisure:** S **Off-site:** P

SALSOMAGGIORE TERME PARMA

Arizona via Tabiano 42 A, 43030
☎ 0524 565648 Fax 0524 567589
e-mail: info@camping-arizona.it
website: www.camping-arizona.it
Family site with plenty of activities, and close to two thermal cure establishments.
Open: 26 Mar-15 Oct **Site:** 13HEC **Prices:** 6-7.50 8-12 6-12 **Facilities:** **Services:** lau **Leisure:** P **Off-site:**

S ARCANGELO SUL TRASIMENO PERUGIA

Polvese via Montivalle, 6060 ☎ 075 848078 Fax 075 848050
e-mail: cpolvese@interfree.iti
website: www.polvese.com
In a peaceful location beside lake Trasimeno with plenty of recreational facilities.
Open: Apr-Sep **Site:** 5HEC **Facilities:** **Services:** lau **Leisure:** LP

Villaggio Italgest via Martiri di Cefalonia, 06060
☎ 075 848238 Fax 075 848085
e-mail: camping@italgest.com
website: www.italgest.com
Situated by a lake and surrounded by woodland. There are good, modern facilities and various recreations are available.
Open: 24 Mar-Sep **Site:** 5.5HEC **Prices:** 5.70-8 1.80-2.50 6-8.30 6-8.30 **Facilities:** **Services:** lau **Leisure:** LP

SAN MARINO

Centro Turistico San Marino Strada San Michele 50, 47893
☎ 0549 903964 Fax 0549 907120
e-mail: info@centrovacanzesanmarino
website: www.centrovacanzesanmarino.com
In a quiet, wooded location close to the centre of the republi of San Marino.
➲ *Access via Rimini Sud exit on the A14.*
Open: All year **Site:** 100HEC **Prices:** 5-8 2-4 4-11 3-8 (static)224-252 **Facilities:** **Services:** lau **Leisure:** P **Off-site:** LRS

SAN PIERO IN BAGNO FORLI

Altosavio strada per Alfero 37c, 47026
☎ 0543 903409 Fax 0543 903409/917397
e-mail: i4std@libero.it
website: www.bagnodiromagnaturismo.it
On level ground at an altitude of 600m with good facilities.
➲ *Exit E45 at Bagno di Romagna for San Piero in Bagno*
Open: 24 Apr-Sep **Site:** 1.3HEC **Prices:** 4.40-5 pitch 7.80 **Facilities:** **Services:** lau **Off-site:** LR

SASSO MARCONI BOLOGNA

Piccolo Paradiso via Sirano, Marzabotto, 40037
☎ 051 842680 Fax 051 6756581
Pleasant site with plenty of trees. A new sports centre less than 100m from the site provides excellent facilities.
➲ *Leave A1 autostrada Milano-Roma at town exit & continu towards Vado for 2km. Signed.*
Open: All year **Site:** 6.5HEC **Facilities:** **Services:** lau **Off-site:** LPR

RELAX - SPORT - KULTUR
Camping Arizona
Tabiano - Salsomaggiore Terme
Tel. 0039/0524565648
Fax 0039/0524567589
e-mail: info@camping-arizona.com
www.camping-arizona.com
Imagine yourself in the wonderful countryside, with panoramic views.
Tennis – 4 free of charge swimming pools – Waterslide – Football pitch – Basketball – Volleyball – Hidromassage – Games for children. Restaurant with regional cooking.

Site: 6HEC-Site size -grass -sand -stone -little shade -partly shaded -mainly shaded -bungalows for hire -caravans for hire -tents for hire -no dogs **Prices:** -adult per night -car per night pp-per person per night -caravan per night -tent per night (static)-caravan hire per week

AT SAVIGNANO SUL RUBICONE

Rubicone via Matrice Destra 1, 47039
0541 346377 0541 346999
e-mail: info@campingrubicone.com
website: www.campingrubicone.com
An extensive, level site divided into two sections by a narrow canal. It extends to the beach.
Situated 0.8km from the road fork at Km187/0 off SS16 Strada Adriatica.
Open: 3 May-28 Sep **Site:** 13HEC
Prices: 4.90-8.75 pitch 10.50-15 **Facilities:**
Services: lau **Leisure:** PS

SCACCHI, LIDO DEGLI FERRARA

Florenz via alpi Centrali 199, 44020
0533 380193 0533 313166
e-mail: info@campingflorenz.com
website: www.campingflorenz.com
Site with dunes extending to the sea.
Turn off the Strada Romea towards Lido Degli Scacchi & continue along asphalt road to the sandy beach.
Open: 16 Apr-17 Sep **Site:** 8HEC **Prices:** 4-8 pitch 9.30-15.20 (static)203-483 **Facilities:**
Services: lau **Leisure:** PS

SENIGALLIA ANCONA

Summerland via Podesti 236, 60019
071 7926816 071 7927758
website: www.camping.it/marche/summerland
A pleasant site with good facilities, 150m from the sea.
3km from Senigallia exit on SS16.
Open: Jun-15 Sep **Site:** 4.5HEC **Prices:** 4-7 pitch 9-14.70 **Facilities:** **Services:** lau
Off-site: PS

SPINA, LIDO DI FERRARA

Spina via del Campeggio 99, 44024
0533 330179 0533 333566
e-mail: spina@clubdesole.com **website:** www.clubdesole.com
Widespread site on level meadowland and on slightly hilly dune terrain. Separate section for dog owners.
Off SS309. Signed.
Open: Mar-Oct **Site:** 24HEC **Facilities:**
Services: lau **Leisure:** PS **Off-site:**

SPOLETO PERUGIA

Girasole Loc. Petrognano, 6049
0743 51335 0743 51335
website: www.campingilgirasole.com
Site on high ground with terraces and thick tree coverage.
Camping Card required for 1-2 nights stay.
S via SS3 towards Montefalco.
Open: Apr-Sep **Site:** 2.5HEC **Prices:** 5.50-6.50 3 7-10 5-6 (static)105-175 **Facilities:**
Services: lau **Off-site:**

Monteluco S.Pietro, 06049 0743 220358 0743 207146
e-mail: campeggiomonteluco@libero.it
website: www.geocities.com/monteluco2002
A modern site on the slopes of Monteluco.
From the SS75 towards Foligno exit on to the SS3 towards Spoleto. The Monteluco road leads to the site.
Open: Apr-Sep **Site:** 6HEC **Prices:** 5-6 2-3 4-6 4-6 (static)140-200 **Facilities:**
Services: **Off-site:** P

TORINO DI SANGRO MARINA CHIETI

Belvedere 66020 0873 911381
Open: Jun-6 Sep **Site:** 1.5HEC **Prices:** 5.50-6 pitch 8-9 **Facilities:** **Services:** lau
Leisure: S **Off-site:** P

VALLICELLA DI MONZUNO BOLOGNA

Le Querce Rioveggio, 40036 051 6770248 051 6770394
A well-equipped site in a wooded mountain setting.
Access via Autostrada del Sole.
Open: May-Sep **Site:** 12HEC **Prices:** 5 7 6 (static)120 **Facilities:** **Services:**
lau **Leisure:** LPR

VASTO CHIETI

Europa 66055 0873 801988 0873 802553
Site on level terrain by the road with poplars.
At Km522 of road SS16.
Open: Apr-Sep **Site:** 2.3HEC **Prices:** 5-7.50 pitch 7.75-12.75 **Facilities:** **Services:** lau
Leisure: S **Off-site:**

Grotta del Saraceno via Osca 6, loc Vignola, 66054
0873 310213 0873 310295
e-mail: info@grottadelsaraceno.it
website: www.grottadelsaranceno.it
Site in an olive grove on steep coastal cliffs with lovely views. Steep path to beach. Siesta 14.00-16.00.
Turn off SS16 at Km512.200.
Open: 15 Jun-15 Sep **Site:** 12HEC **Facilities:**
Services: lau **Leisure:** S **Off-site:**

Pioppeto 66055 0873 801466 801466
Camping Card Compulsory.
Open: 15 May-14 Sep **Site:** 1.7HEC **Prices:** 5.50-7 pitch 10.50-14.50 **Facilities:** **Services:**
Leisure: S **Off-site:**

ZOCCA MODENA

Montequestiolo via Montequestiolo 184, 41059
059 985137 059 985137
e-mail: monteq@tin.it
Site: 1.8HEC **Facilities:**
Services: lau **Off-site:** P

ROME

BOLSENA VITERBO

Blu International via Cassia, 01023
0761 799197 0761 798855
e-mail: info@blucamping.it
website: www.blucamping.it
A modern site with good facilities in a wooded location on the shore of lake Bolsena. Compulsory separate car parking in July and August.
Access via A1 exit Orvieto, then Via Cassia at Km111.650.
Open: Apr-Sep **Site:** 3HEC **Prices:** pitch 17-22.50 (incl 2 persons) **Facilities:**
Services: lau **Leisure:** LP **Off-site:**

Lido via Cassia km111, 01023 0761 799258 0761 796105
e-mail: info@bolsencamping.it
website: www.bolsenacamping.it
A lakeside family site with good modern facilities.
Access via motorway exit Orvieto.
Open: Apr-Sep **Site:** 10HEC **Prices:** 4.50-6.10 1.70-2.60 pitch 8.50-10.50 (static)259-442.40
Facilities: **Services:** lau **Leisure:** LP

BRACCIANO ROMA

Porticciolo via Porticciolo, 00062
06 99803060 06 998803030
e-mail: info@porticciolo.it
website: www.porticciolo.it
A family site in a pleasant location on the shore of a lake.
Access via SS493 to Bracciano.
Open: Apr-Sep **Site:** 3HEC **Facilities:** **Services:** lau **Leisure:** L **Off-site:**

FIANO ROMANO ROMA

Bungalow Park I Pini via delle Sassete 1A, 00065
0765 453349 0765 453057
e-mail: ipini@camping.it
website: www.ecvacanze.it
A well-equipped, modern site within easy reach of the centre of Rome. An excellent base for excursions.
From A1 Firenze-Roma take exit Fiano Romana.
Open: 15 Mar-15 Nov **Site:** 5HEC **Facilities:** **Services:** lau **Leisure:** P

FORMIA LATINA

Gianola via delle Vigne, 04023 0771 720223
e-mail: gianolacamping@tiscalinet.it
Situated in a narrow grassland area near a stream and trees amid agricultural land. Pleasant sandy beach edged by rocks.
Access via Roma-Napoli road, from S Croce 800m.
Open: Apr-Sep **Site:** 4HEC **Facilities:** **Services:** **Leisure:** S

MINTURNO, MARINA DI LATINA

Golden Garden via Dunale 74, 04020
0771 681425 0771 614059
e-mail: servizio.clienti@goldengarden.it
website: www.goldengarden.it
Secluded quiet site within agricultural area by the sea.
Camping Card Compulsory
Access from the SS7 across river bridge (Garigliano) & continue 4.6km changing direction. Last 1km sandy field track.
Open: Apr-15 Oct **Site:** 2.3HEC **Facilities:** **Services:** lau **Leisure:** S **Off-site:** PR

MONTALTO DI CASTRO, MARINA DI VITERBO

California 01014 0766 802848 0766 801210
Situated on the coast below an ancient pine grove with good facilities for sports and leisure.
Open: May-Sep **Site:** 1.4HEC **Facilities:** **Services:** lau **Leisure:** S

Internazionale Pionier Etrusco via Vulsinia, 01014
0766 802199 0766 801214
e-mail: meleute@tin.it
website: www.campingpioneretrusco.com
Situated in a pine forest close to the beach. Various leisure and sports activities, and a relaxing aymosphere.
Camping Card Compulsory
Open: Mar-15 Oct **Site:** 3HEC **Prices:** 17-32 3.60-6.50 **Facilities:** **Services:** lau **Off-site:** RS

ROMA (ROME) ROMA

Flaminio Village via Flaminia Nuova 821, 00189
06 3332604 06 3330653
e-mail: info@villageflaminio.com
website: www.villageflaminio.com
An exstensive site with good facilities, in a quiet valley on narrow terraces.
From ring road follow via Flaminia, SS3, for 2.5km towards city centre.
Open: All year **Site:** 8.4HEC **Prices:** 8.90-10 4.20-4.70 6.70-7.80 4.90-6.40 **Facilities:** **Services:** lau **Leisure:** P **Off-site:** R

Happy via Prato della Corte 1915, 123
06 33626401 06 33613800
e-mail: info@happycamping.net
website: www.happycamping.net
Conveniently placed in northern area of city. Modern installations, electricity and hot water free throughout.
Exit 5 Grande Raccordo Anulare (ring road).
Open: Mar-6 Nov **Site:** 3.6HEC **Prices:** 7.90-9.50 3.90-4.20 5.90-6.90 4.20-5.30 **Facilities:** **Services:** lau **Leisure:** P

Roma via Aurelia 831, 00165 06 6623018 06 66418147
e-mail: campingroma@ecvacante.it
website: www.ecvacante.it
The site lies on terraces on a hill near the AGIP Motel. All kinds of excursions can be arranged.
From ring road follow SS1 (via Aurelia) 1.5km towards town centre, turn off to site at Km8/11.
Open: All year **Site:** 3HEC **Prices:** 8.50-9.50 4-4.50 7-7.80 4.20-4.60 **Facilities:** **Services:** lau **Leisure:** P **Off-site:**

Seven Hills via Cassia 1216, 00189
06 30310826 06 30310039
e-mail: seven-hills@camping.it
website: www.camping.it/lazio/seven-hills
A fine, partly terraced site in beautiful rural surroundings yet ideally situated for access to the city by bus or metro.

2.5km NE of the outer ring road via Exit 3.
Open: 15 Mar-30 Oct **Site:** 5HEC
Prices: 8.90-9.80 4-4.50 6.50-7.50 pp6-7 **Facilities:** **Services:** lau **Leisure:** P

Tiber via Tiberina Km1400, 188
06 33610733 06 33612314
e-mail: info@campingtiber.com
website: www.campingtiber.com
On level grassland, shaded by poplars beside the Tiber.
N of city. Signed from ringroad. Access from N via Exit 3 or from S follow signs 'Prima Porta'.
Open: 15 Mar-Oct **Site:** 5HEC **Facilities:** **Services:** lau **Leisure:** PR

SALTO DI FONDI LATINA

Fondi Holiday Camp via Flacca Km 6800, 04020
0771 555009
e-mail: info@holidayvillage.it
website: www.holidayvillage.it
Well-shaded and well-equipped site only a few metres from the Mediterranean.
Open: Apr-Sep **Site:** 4HEC
Prices: pitch 26-50 (incl 2 persons) **Facilities:** **Services:** lau **Leisure:** PS

TERRACINA LATINA

Badino Porto Badino, 04019 0773 764430 0773 764430
In wooded surroundings with direct access to the beach.
From the Roma-Napoli road head towards the canal (Porto Canale Badino) & the sea.
Open: Apr-15 Oct **Site:** 1.8HEC
Prices: 4.25-6.85 3.70-5 7.40-13.30 7.40-13.30 (static)266-409 **Facilities:** **Services:** lau **Leisure:** S **Off-site:**

SOUTH

BAIA DOMIZIA CASERTA

Baia Domizia Camping Villaggio Baia Domizia, 81030
0823 930164 0823 930375
e-mail: info@baiadomizia.it
website: www.baiadomizia.it
Part of this extensive seaside site is laid out with flowerbeds. Good sports and leisure facilities. Ideal for families. No radios allowed.
Turn off the SS7 (qtr) at Km6/V, then 3km seawards.
Open: 23 Apr-25 Sep **Site:** 30HEC
Prices: 4.40-10.20 2.80-5.70 7.70-15.10 7.70-15.10 (static)348-698 **Facilities:** **Services:** lau **Leisure:** PS

BATTIPAGLIA SALERNO

Lido Mediterraneo via Litoranea, Salerno Paestum, 84091
0828 624097 0828 624097
e-mail: mediterraneo.campania@camping.it
website: www.camping.it/campania/mediterraneo
In a pine wood with direct access to a private beach.
Open: 10 Mar-22 Sep **Site:** 1.2HEC
Facilities: **Services:** **Leisure:** S
Off-site: P

BRIATICO CATANZARO

Dolomiti 89817 0963 391355 0963 393009
e-mail: dolmar@tin.it
website: www.dolomitisulmare.com
The site is in a delightful setting on two terraces planted with olive trees. It lies by the road and 150m from the railway.
Turn off road 522 between Km17 & Km18 & head towards the sea.
Open: 24 Jun-27 Sep **Site:** 5HEC **Facilities:** **Services:** lau **Leisure:** PS **Off-site:** P

CAMEROTA, MARINA DI SALERNO

Risacca via delle Barche 11, Lentiscella, 84059
0974 932415 0974 932415
e-mail: larisacca@its2001.it
website: www.larisacca.com
On level ground shaded by olive trees, with direct access to a sandy beach.
Approach via SS18.
Open: 20 May-20 Sep **Site:** 2HEC **Prices:** 8.50-12 pitch 10-18 **Facilities:** **Services:**
Leisure: S **Off-site:**

CAPO VATICANO CATANZARO

Gabbiano San Nicolo di Ricadi, 89865
0963 663159 0963 663384
Open: Apr-Oct **Site:** **Facilities:** **Services:** lau **Leisure:** PS **Off-site:**

CAROVIGNO BRINDISI
AT SPECCHIOLLA, LIDO

Pineta al Mare Lido Specchiolla, 72012
0831 987821 0831 987826
e-mail: info@campingpinetamare.com
website: www.campingpinetamare.com
Site in pine woodland with a sandy beach and some rocks.
E of Bari-Brindisi road at Km21.5.
Open: All year **Site:** 5.5HEC **Prices:** 5.90-8.50 1.90-2.90 6.20-8.50 4.80-6.90 **Facilities:** **Services:** lau **Leisure:** PS

CIRÙ MARINA CATANZARO

Punta Alice 88811 0962 31160
The site lies on meadowland amid lush Mediterranean vegetation and borders a fine shingle beach, some 50m wide.
2km from town. From SS106 (Strada Ionica) turn off at Km290 seaward to Cira Marina. Pass through village & follow beach road 1.5km towards the lighthouse.
Open: Apr-Sep **Site:** 5.5HEC **Facilities:** **Services:** lau **Leisure:** PS

Villaggio Torrenova via Torrenova, 88811 0962 31482
Directly on sea, with on-site facilities for all the family.
Open: May-Sep **Site:** 1.2HEC **Facilities:** **Services:** lau **Leisure:** S

CORIGLIANO CÁLABRO COSENZA

Thurium Contrada Ricota Grande, 87060
0983 851101 0983 851955
e-mail: info@campingthurium.com
website: www.campingthurium.com
The site is close to the beach and has all the facilites needed for an enjoyable camping break. It is just a walk away from woodland and is ideal for peaceful walks.
Open: 15 May-18 Sep **Site:** 16HEC **Prices:** 2.50-9.60 0.50-4 2.80-11 2.80-11 **Facilities:** **Services:** lau **Leisure:** PS

EBOLI SALERNO

Paestum Foce Sele, 84020 0828 691003 0828 691003
e-mail: info@campingpaestum.com
website: www.campingpaestum.com
Sandy, meadowland site and tall poplar wood by river mouth. Steps and bus service to private beach, 600m from site.
Access from the Litoranea at Km20 from the road fork to Santa Cecilia & continue for 0.3km. Signed.
Open: 15 May-14 Sep **Site:** 8HEC **Prices:** 4-6 10.50-18 8-11 pitch 10.50-18 **Facilities:** **Services:** lau **Leisure:** P **Off-site:** RS

GALLIPOLI LECCE

Baia di Gallipoli 73014 0833 273210 0833 262760
e-mail: info@baiadigallipoli.com
website: www.baiadigallipoli.com
A holiday village set amid pine woods close to the sea with good facilities.
Camping Card Compulsory
5km SE of Gallipoli.
Open: All year **Site:** 11HEC **Facilities:** **Services:** lau **Leisure:** P **Off-site:** S

Vecchia Torre 73014 0833 209083
This well-kept and clean site lies amid dunes in a pine wood. Small size pitches.
5km N of Gallipoli & 200m S of Hotel Rivabella on seaward side of coast road.
Open: Jun-Sep **Site:** 8HEC **Facilities:** **Services:** lau **Leisure:** S

GIOVINAZZO BARI

Campofreddo Stada Statale 16, Focalita Ponte, 70054
080 3942112 080 3942290
e-mail: torraco@libero.it
website: www.campofreddo.com
Site on level terrain by the sea, mainly under sunshade roofing. Siesta 14.00-16.00.
Turn off the SS16, 20km N of Bari at Km784,300.
Open: 20 May-20 Sep **Site:** 34HEC **Prices:** 5.50 pitch 7.80-10.50 **Facilities:** **Services:** lau **Off-site:** S

GUARDAVALLE, MARINA DI CATANZARO

Dello Ionio via Nazionale, 88065
0967 86002 0967 86271
e-mail: calandrusa@yahoo.it
website: www.calalandrusa.it
Site is situated on the seafront and along 4km of sandy beach. All pitches are under the shade of tall trees and have large grassy areas.
Situated 2km from Santa Caterina dello Jonio on the SS106.
Open: Jun-15 Sep **Site:** 7HEC **Facilities:** **Services:** lau **Leisure:** PS

LÁURA SALERNO

Hera Argiva 84063 0828 851193
Site on sandy terrain in eucalyptus grove by the sea.
Signed from Km88/VII SS18.
Open: Apr-Sep **Site:** 40HEC **Prices:** 7-10 2-3 15-20 550-650 pitch 15-20 pp7-10 **Facilities:** **Services:** lau **Leisure:** S **Off-site:**

LEPORANO, MARINA DI TARANTO

Porto Pirrone Litoranea Salentina, 74020
099 5334844 099 5334844
e-mail: info@portopirrone.it
website: www.portopirrone.it
Set in a pine wood offering flat large plots for both tents and caravans. Good sports and entertainment. No Animals.
From A14 at Massafra towards Taranto & Leporano. Site is near marina.
Open: Jun-Sep **Site:** 3.2HEC **Facilities:** **Services:** **Leisure:** S **Off-site:**

MÁCCHIA FOGGIA

Monaco 71030 0884 530280
A pleasant situation with good facilities and direct access to the beach.
Open: Jun-Aug **Site:** 5.3HEC **Facilities:** **Services:** lau **Leisure:** S

MANFREDONIA FOGGIA

Ippocampo SS 159, 71043
0884 571121
e-mail: campingippocampo@email.it
website: www.campingippocampo.too.it
In the grounds of a holiday village.
Open: May-Sep **Site:** 8HEC
Prices: 3.30-5.70 2-3.60 3.50-8.10 2-5.60
Facilities: **Services:** **Leisure:** S
Off-site: P

MASSA LUBRENSE NAPOLI

Villa Lubrense via Partenope 31, 80061 081 5339781
website: www.villalubrense.it
Open: All year **Site:** 2.5HEC **Facilities:** **Services:** **Leisure:** PS

MATTINATA FOGGIA

Villaggio Turistico San Lorenzo 71030
0884 550152 0884 552042
e-mail: info@sanlorenzo.it
website: www.sanlorenzo.it
The site is situated above the coast road in direction of Viesta. Bungalows for hire.
Camping Card Compulsory
Open: All year **Site:** 3HEC **Facilities:** **Services:** lau **Leisure:** PS **Off-site:**

METAPONTO, LIDO DI MATERA

Camel Camping Club viale Magna Grecia, 75010
0835 741926
A modern, well-organised site. Sports and entertainment avaliable all season. Ideal for both relaxing and sightseeing.
Open: Jun-Sep **Site:** 3.5HEC **Facilities:** **Services:** **Leisure:** P **Off-site:** S

NICÓTERA MARINA CATANZARO

Sabbia d'Oro 88033 0963 886395
Lies on level ground amid farmland 100m from a beautiful lonely beach.
Turn off SS18 at Km453/VII & continue 15km.
Open: 15 Jun-10 Sep **Site:** 2.7HEC **Facilities:** **Services:** lau **Leisure:** S

OTRANTO LECCE

Mulino d'Acqua via S Stefano, 73028
0836 802191 0836 802196
e-mail: mulino.camping@anet.it
website: www.mulinodacqua.it
Shaded by olive trees, close to the beach and with plenty of organised activities.
Open: Jun-10 Sep **Site:** 10HEC **Prices:** 7-11 pitch 7-17 (incl 3 persons) (static)280-560 **Facilities:** **Services:** lau **Leisure:** PS **Off-site:**

PALMI REGGIO DI CALABRIA

San Fantino via S-Fantino, 89015
0966 479430 0966 479430
Site on several terraces with lovely views of the bay of Lido di Palmi. 200m to the beach. Siesta 13.00-16.00.
Turn off road SS18 seawards N of Palmi.
Open: All year **Site:** 4HEC **Facilities:** **Services:** lau **Off-site:** PS

PESCHICI FOGGIA

Centro Turistico San Nicola Loc San Nicola, 71010
0884 964024
Terraced site in lovely situation by the sea, in a bay enclosed by rocks. Can become overcrowded.
Turn off coast road Peschici-Vieste, follow signs along winding road to site in 1km.
Open: Apr-15 Oct **Site:** 14HEC **Prices:** 7-11 3.50-6 8.50-13.50 5.50-8.50 **Facilities:** **Services:** lau **Leisure:** S

Internazionale Manacore 71010
0884 911020 0884 911049
e-mail: manacore@grupposaccia.it
website: www.grupposaccia.it
Meadowland with a few terraces in attractive bay, surrounded by wooded hills.
Turn off the Peschici-Vieste coastal road towards the sea in a wide U bend.
Open: Apr-20 Oct **Site:** 22HEC **Prices:** 5.20-11 3.50-4.80 6.30-13 4-10 **Facilities:** **Services:** **Leisure:** S

PIZZO CATANZARO

Pinetamare 89812 0963 534871 0963 534871
A sandy site surrounded by tall pine trees. Most water sports are avaliable along the private beach and families are welcome.
From the Salerno/Reggio motorway take the Pizzo exit & site is N of town.
Open: Jun-Sep **Site:** 10HEC **Facilities:** **Services:** lau **Leisure:** PS **Off-site:** L

POMPEI NAPOLI

Spartacus via Plinio 127, 80045
081 8624078 081 8624078
e-mail: campingspartacus@tin.it
website: www.campingspartacus.it
Site is on a level meadow with orange trees.
Lies near the motorway exit, Pompei. Access from the main Napoli road, opposite Scavi di Pompei near an IP filling station.
Open: All year **Site:** 9HEC **Prices:** 5.50-6 2-3 5.50-6 pitch 2.50 (static)203-252 **Facilities:** **Services:** lau **Leisure:** P

POZZUOLI NAPOLI

Vulcano Solfatara via Solfatara 161, 80078
081 5267413 081 5263482
e-mail: info@solfatara.it
website: www.solfatara.it
Clean and orderly site situated in a deciduous forest near the crater of the extinct Solfatara volcano.
Leave Nuova via Domiziana (SS7 qtr) at Km60/1 (6km short of Napoli) & turn inland through stone gate.
Open: Apr-Oct & 24 Dec-8 Jan **Site:** 3HEC **Prices:** 7.20-9 5.20-6.50 6.60-8.20 4.80-6 (static)320.60-392 **Facilities:** **Services:** lau **Leisure:** P **Off-site:** S

AT VARCATURO, MARINA DI (12KM N)

Partenope 80014 081 5091076 081 5096767
Partially undulating terrain in woodland of medium height.
Camping Card Compulsory
Turn seawards for 300m at Km45/II of the SS7 (via Domiziana).
Open: Jun-8 Sep **Site:** 6HEC **Prices:** 6.70-7.80 pitch 7.80-11 **Facilities:** **Services:** **Leisure:** LRS

PRÁIA A MARE COSENZA

International Camping Village 87028
0985 72211 0985 72211
e-mail: reception@campinginternational.it
website: www.campinginternational.it
In a beautiful location on the gulf of Policastro with good recreational facilities.
Access via A3 to Falerna and then SS18.
Open: May-30Sep **Site:** 5.5HEC **Facilities:** **Services:** lau **Leisure:** PS

RODI GARGANICO FOGGIA

Ripa Contrada Ripa, 71012 0884 965367 0884 965695
e-mail: info@villaggioripa.it
website: www.villaggioripa.it
Well-equipped and attractive site close to the beach.
Open: 15 Jun-Aug **Site:** 6HEC **Prices:** 5-8 7 **Facilities:** **Services:** lau **Leisure:** PS **Off-site:**

ROSSANO SCALO COSENZA

Marina di Rossano Contrada Leuca, 87068
0983 516054 0983 512069
e-mail: marina.club@tiscalinet.it
website: web.tiscalinet.it/marinadirossano
In wooded surroundings close to the beach, with good modern facilities.
Access via N106.
Open: 15 May-29 Sep **Site:** 7HEC **Facilities:** **Services:** lau **Leisure:** PS **Off-site:**

San Menáio Foggia

Valle d'Oro via Degli Ulivi, 71010
0884 991580 & 991699 0884 991699 & 991580
e-mail: campingvalledoro@libero.it
Site in olive grove surrounded by wooded hills with some terraces.
Turn off SS89 onto SS528 to site at Km1.800. 2km from the sea.
Open: 15 Jun-15 Sep **Site:** 3HEC **Prices:** 3-5 pitch 4-6 **Facilities:** **Services:** **Off-site:** PS

Santa Cesárea Terme Lecce

Scogliera 73020 0836 949802 0836 949794
Attractive site close to the sea.
1km S on SS173.
Open: All year **Site:** 8HEC **Prices:** 4-8 2-3 4.50-7 4-7 pitch 4-6.50 **Facilities:** **Services:** **Leisure:** P **Off-site:** S

Santa Maria di Castellabate Salerno

Trezene 84072 0974 965027 0974 965013
e-mail: trezene@costacilento
website: www.trezene.it
The site is partly divided into pitches and consists of two sections lying either side of the access road. Pitches between road and fine sandy beach are reserved for touring campers.
Open: Apr-Oct **Site:** 2.5HEC **Facilities:** **Services:** lau **Leisure:** S **Off-site:**

Sorrento Napoli

Santa Fortunata Campogaio via Capo 39, 80067
081 8073579 081 8073590
e-mail: info@santafortunata.com
website: www.santafortunata.com
A well-appointed, terraced site shaded by olive trees and with direct access to the sea.
2km from town centre & 400m beyond the turning from the SS145 on road towards Massa Lubrense & 50m from sea.
Open: Apr-20 Oct **Site:** 20HEC **Prices:** 6-9 4-5 9-11 5-7 (static)270 **Facilities:** **Services:** lau **Leisure:** PS

Giardino delle Esperidi San Agnello, 80065
081 8783255 081 8785022
e-mail: info@esperidiresort.com
website: www.esperidiresort.com
In a pleasant park surrounded by lemon and orange trees, 2km from the centre of Sorrento and 250m from La Marinella beach. There are good facilities and modern bungalows for hire.
Open: Apr-Sep **Site:** 3HEC **Prices:** 6.50-7.50 3-3.50 5.50-6.50 4-6.50 **Facilities:** **Services:** **Off-site:** PS

International Camping Nube d'Argento via Capo 21, 80067
081 8781344 081 8073450
e-mail: info@nubedargento.com
website: www.nubedargento.com
The site lies on narrow terraces just off a steep concrete road between the beach and the outskirts of the town.
Access is rather difficult for caravans.
Open: Mar-Dec **Site:** 1.5HEC **Prices:** 7-9 4-5 8-9.50 5-6 (static)350-420 **Facilities:** **Services:** lau **Leisure:** PS

Santa Fortunata via Capo 081 8073579 081 8073590
Extensive site lying on terraces in a shady olive grove with many small secluded pitches.
Camping Card Compulsory
1km from town and 50m from sea.
Open: Apr-Sep **Site:** 12HEC **Facilities:** **Services:** lau **Leisure:** PS

Torre Rinalda Lecce

Torre Rinalda Litoranea Salentina, 73100
0832 382161 0832 382165
e-mail: info@torrerinalda.it **website:** www.torrerinalda.it
On an extensive level meadow, separated from the sea by dunes. Disco. Siesta 13.30-16.00.
Access via SS613 Brindisi-Lecce, exit Trepuzzi then coastal road for 1.5km.
Open: Jun-Sep **Site:** 15HEC **Prices:** pitch 18.50-35 (incl 3 persons) **Facilities:** **Services:** **Leisure:** PS

Ugento Lecce

Riva di Ugento Litoranea Gallipoli-SM diLeuca, 73059
0833 933600 0833 933601
e-mail: info@rivadiugeuto.it
website: www.rivadiugeuto.it
A well-equipped site in wooded surroundings close to the beach.
Open: 15 May-29 Sep **Site:** 32HEC **Prices:** pitch 16-35 (incl 3 persons) (static)31-62 **Facilities:** **Services:** lau **Leisure:** PS

Vico Equense Napoli

Sant' Antonio Marina d'Equa, 80069
081 8028570 081 8028570
e-mail: info@campingsantantonio.it
website: www.campingsantantonio.it
A modern site set among fruit trees, close to the beach with fine views over the bay of Naples.
Camping Card Compulsory
Open: 15 Mar-30 Oct **Site:** 1HEC **Prices:** 6.70-7.75 2.60-3.20 6.70-7.75 4-6 **Facilities:** **Services:** lau **Leisure:** S **Off-site:** PS

Seiano Spiaggia Marina Aequa, Via Murrano 15, 80069
081 8028560 081 8028560
e-mail: info@campingseiano.it
website: http://www.campingseiano.it
Set in a plantation of evergreen and orange trees only a few metres from the sea. There are good facilities and the site is ideally situated for excursions to Pompeii, Naples and Vesuvius.
Motorway A3 Naples-Pompeii-Salerno, exit at Castellammare di Stabia. Highway 145 after Seiano tunnel & bridge turn right to Marina Aequa.
Open: Apr-Sep **Site:** 1HEC **Prices:** 5.90-6.90 3-3.50 6.20-6.80 5-5.70 **Facilities:** **Services:** lau **Off-site:** PS

Villagio Turistico Azzurro via Murrano 9, 80069
081 8029984 081 8029176
e-mail: info@villaggioazzurro.net
website: www.villaggioazzurro.net
Shaded site among ancient olive groves, by the sea and in close proximity to the isle of Capri.
Take Autostrada A3 Napoli-Pompei-Salerno, exit Castellammare & follow directions for Vico Equense. After 3rd tunnel & one bridge turn right to Marina Aequa.
Open: Mar-1 Dec **Site:** **Prices:** 6.50-7.80 3.50-4.50 6-7.50 5-6.50 (static)352-396 **Facilities:** **Services:** lau **Leisure:** S **Off-site:**

VIESTE FOGGIA

Baia Turchese 71019 Lungomare Europa, 71019
0884 708587
A family site in wooded surroundings with direct access to the sea.
1km N of Vieste on Strada Panoramica towards Peschici.
Open: May-Sep **Site:** 3.6HEC **Facilities:** **Services:** **Leisure:** S

Capo Vieste 71019 0884 706326 0884 705993
e-mail: info@capovieste.it
website: www.capovieste.it
The site lies on a large area of unspoiled land, planted with a few rows of poplar and pine trees. It is by the sea and has a large bathing area.
Off coastal road to Peschici 7km beyond Vieste.
Open: 20 Mar-Oct **Site:** 6HEC **Prices:** 3-10 3-4.50 pitch 8-16 (static)273-310 **Facilities:** **Services:** lau **Leisure:** S

Umbramare Santa Maria di Merino, 706174
0884 706174 0884 706174
e-mail: umbramare@tiscali.it
website: www.umbramare.it
On A14 leave at Poggio Imperiale & take route via Rodi Gargánico & Peschici.
Open: Mar-Oct **Site:** 10.5HEC **Prices:** 3-8.50 pitch 6-14.50 **Facilities:** **Services:** **Leisure:** S **Off-site:**

Vieste Marina Litoranea Vieste, 71019
0884 706471 0884 706471
e-mail: viestemarina@tiscali.it
Tree-lined level site adjacent to the coast road in a quiet situation with good facilities.
5km N of Vieste, signed.
Open: Jun-Sep **Site:** 5HEC **Prices:** 4-9 pitch 20-42 (incl 4 persons) **Facilities:** **Services:** lau **Leisure:** PS **Off-site:** LS

Village Punta Lunga Defensola, CP 339, 71019
0884 706031 0884 706910
e-mail: puntalunga@puntalunga.com
website: www.puntalunga.it
A terraced site in wooded surroundings encompassing two sandy bathing bays and a rocky peninsula.
2km N of Vieste, signed from coast road.
Open: 23 Apr-16 Oct **Site:** 6HEC **Prices:** 3.50-10 pitch 7-15 **Facilities:** **Services:** lau **Leisure:** S

ISLANDS

SARDEGNA (SARDINIA)

AGLIENTU SASSARI

Baia Blu la Tortuga Pineta di Vignola Mare, 07020
079 602060 079 602040
e-mail: info@baiablu.com
website: www.baiaholiday.com
Site in pine forest by the sea.
Open: 22 Apr-30 Oct **Site:** 17HEC **Prices:** 3.30-9.90 pitch 9-22.90 (static)210-750 **Facilities:** **Services:** lau **Leisure:** S

ARBATAX NUORO

Telis Porto Frailis, 8041 0782 667261 0782 667140
e-mail: telisca@tiscalinet.it
website: www.campingtelis.com
Terraced site by the sea.
SS125 between Cagliari & Olbia.
Open: All year **Site:** 3HEC **Prices:** 6-9.50 pitch 7-9.50 (static)220-455 **Facilities:** **Services:** lau **Leisure:** S

CÁGLIARI
AT SANT'ANTIOCO

Tonnara Loc Calasapone, 09017
0781 809058 0781 809036
e-mail: tonnaracamping@tiscali.it
website: www.campine.it/italy/sardegna/cagliari
Situated in the centre of Calasapone bay with enclosed plots, good sports facilities and access to a sandy beach.
Access by road S of Carbonia to the small island of Sant'Antioco.
Open: Apr-Sep **Site:** 7HEC **Prices:** 7.10-9.70 pitch 16 (static)213-462 **Facilities:** **Services:** lau **Leisure:** S **Off-site:** P

CALASETTA CAGLIARI

Sardi Le Saline Le Saline, 9011 0781 88615 0781 88615
e-mail: info@campinglesaline.com
website: www.campinglesaline.com
In wooded surroundings close to the beach and 500m from the village with good recreational facilities.
Open: May-Oct **Site:** 6HEC **Prices:** 5.16-8.78 9.81-17.04 4.65-11.88 **Facilities:** **Services:** lau **Leisure:** S **Off-site:**

CANNIGIONE DI ARZACHENA SASSARI

Isuledda 07020 0789 86003 0789 86089
e-mail: informazioni@isuledda.it
website: www.isuledda.it
Near the sea on the beautiful Costa Smeralda with good, modern sanitary installations and plentiful sports and entertainment facilities.
Open: 24 Mar-15 Oct **Site:** 15HEC **Prices:** 5-10 2-4 7-16 7-16 **Facilities:** **Services:** lau **Leisure:** S

LOTZORAI NUORO

Cernie via Case Sparse 17, 08040
0782 669472 0782 669612
Close to the beach with beautiful views on all sides. Varied sports and leisure activities.
Open: All year **Site:** 1.5HEC **Facilities:** **Services:** lau **Leisure:** S **Off-site:**

PORTO ROTONDO SASSARI

Cugnana Loc Cugnana, 07026 0789 33184 0789 33398
e-mail: info@campingcugnana.it
website: www.campingcugnana.it
A well-appointed family site with good recreational facilities and free transport to the local beaches.
Open: 15 May-29 Sep **Site:** 5HEC **Facilities:** **Services:** lau **Leisure:** P **Off-site:** S

SANTA LUCIA NUORO

Cala-Pineta St Statale Orientale Sarde 125, 08029
0784 819184 0784 818128
e-mail: info@calapineta.it **website:** www.calipineta.it
Well-equipped site 1.5km from a white sand beach.
Open: 15 Jun-15 Sep **Site:** 10HEC
Prices: 5.80-10.90 4.70-8.80 4.70-8.80 (static)163-248.50 **Facilities:** **Services:** lau
Leisure: S

Selema 8029 079 953761 079 819068
e-mail: info@selemacamping.com
website: www.selemacamping.com
Wooded beach site on the island of Sardinia.
Open: May-Oct **Site:** 7.5HEC
Prices: 5.50-11 3 pitch 6-14.50 **Facilities:** **Services:** lau **Leisure:** RS **Off-site:**

SAN TEODORO NUORO

San Teodoro la Cinta via del Tirreno 89, 08020
0784 865777 0784 865777
e-mail: info@campingsanteodoro.com
website: www.campingsanteodoro.com
Situated in a large wooded park facing the sea. Ideal for families with small children.
25km from Olbia.
Open: 15 May-15 Oct **Site:** 3HEC
Facilities: **Services:** lau
Leisure: S **Off-site:** R

TEULADA CAGLIARI

Porto Tramatzu 09019 070 9283027 070 9283028
e-mail: coop.proturismo@libero.it
website: www.italiaabc.it/camping/sardegna/cagliari/camping/cagliari2/portutramatzu
Extensive facilities and large individual plots. The site is less than 100m from the beautiful Port Tramatzu.
SS195 from Cagliari.
Open: Etr-Oct **Site:** 3.5HEC **Facilities:**
Services: lau **Leisure:** S

TORRE SALINAS CAGLIARI

Torre Salinas 09043 070 999032 070 999001
e-mail: information@camping-torre-salinas.de
website: www.camping-torre-salinas.de
Open: Apr-14 Oct **Site:** 1.5HEC
Prices: 4.80-9.50 pitch 7-11.50 (static)28-41 **Facilities:** **Services:** lau **Leisure:** S

VALLEDORIA SASSARI

Foce via Ampurias 1 CS, 07039 079 582109 079 582191
e-mail: info@foce.it **website:** www.foce.it
A delightful wooded setting separated from the main beach by the River Coghinas, which can be crossed by ferry. Modern sanitary installations and plenty of recreational facilities.
Open: May-Sep **Site:** 20HEC **Prices:** 6-14 1.50-3.50 (static)210-420 **Facilities:** **Services:** lau **Leisure:** PRS **Off-site:**

Valledoria 07039 079 584070 079 584058
e-mail: info@campingvalledoria.com
website: www.campingvalledoria.com
Located in a pine wood, this site has both white sand beaches and rocky cliffs.
Open: 15 May-29 Sep **Site:** 10HEC
Prices: 6.50-11 1.80-3 (static)252-364 **Facilities:** **Services:** lau **Leisure:** S **Off-site:**

SICILIA (SICILY)

AVOLA SIRACUSA

Pantanello Lungomare di Avola, 96012 0931 823275
Open: All year **Site:** 7.5HEC **Facilities:**
Services: **Off-site:** S

Sabbia d'Oro 96012
0931 822415 0931 822415 & 833233
e-mail: info@campeggiosabbiadoro.com
website: www.campeggiosabbiadoro.com
Situated close to the beach in a picturesque area surrounded by trees with magnificient views.
Open: All year **Site:** 2.2HEC **Prices:** 5.50 3 9 7.50-9 (static)150-300 **Facilities:**
Services: lau **Leisure:** S **Off-site:** R

CASTEL DI TUSA MESSINA

Scoglio S.S. 113-KM 164, 98070
0921 334345 0921 334303
e-mail: loscoglio@loscoglio.net
website: www.loscoglio.net
A terraced site. No shade on the shingle beach.
Turn off SS113 st Km164, 2km W of Castel di Tusa.
Open: All year **Site:** 1.5HEC **Prices:** 5-9 3-3 6-7 6-7 (static)350-490 **Facilities:** **Services:** lau **Leisure:** S

CATÁNIA CATÁNIA

Ionio via Villini a Mare 2, 95126
095 491139 095 492277
e-mail: jonio@camping.it
website: camping.it/sicilia/jonio
On a clifftop plateau. Access to beach via steps. Siesta 14.00-17.00.
Turn off SS14 N of town towards sea.
Open: All year **Site:** 1.2HEC **Facilities:** **Services:** lau **Leisure:** S

CEFALÙ PALERMO

Plaja degli Uccelli 90010 0921 999068 0921 999068
In wooded surroundings with good, modern equipment, close to a fine sandy beach.
Open: Apr-10 Oct **Site:** 1.8HEC **Facilities:** **Services:** lau **Leisure:** S

FINALE DI POLLINA PALERMO

Rais Gerbi S.S.113KM 172,900, 90010
0921 426570 0921 426577
e-mail: camping@raisgerbi.it
website: www.raisgerbi.it
A well-equipped modern site with a private beach in picturesque wooded surroundings.
Take the SS113 Messina-Palermo road to Km172.9.
Open: All year **Site:** 5HEC **Facilities:** **Services:** lau **Leisure:** PS **Off-site:**

FONDACHELLO CATANIA

Mokambo 95016 095 938731
Level terrain, thickly wooded in parts not directly next to the sea.
Leave A18 Messina-Catania at Giarre exit, through Giarre & via Máscali to Fondachello on coast.
Open: Apr-Sep **Site:** 2.8HEC **Facilities:** **Services:** lau **Leisure:** S

FÚRNARI MARINA — MESSINA

Village Bazia Contrada Bazia, 98054
0941 800130 0941 81006
e-mail: info@bazia.it
website: www.bazia.it
A pleasant seaside site with plenty of recreational facilities.
Open: Jun-14 Sep **Site:** 4HEC **Prices:** 7.20 2.80 7.60 7.60 **Facilities:** **Services:** **Leisure:** PS

ÕSOLA DELLE FÉMMINE — PALERMO

La Playa viale Marino 55, 90040
091 8677001 091 8677001
e-mail: campinglaplaya@virglio.it
website: www.campinglaplaya.net
A ideal site for a relaxing holiday with beautiful views and quiet woodland walks. Direct access to the beach.
A29 Palermo to Trapini & SS113.
Open: Mar-10 Oct **Site:** 2.2HEC **Prices:** 3.90-5.20 pitch 6.20-12.40 **Facilities:** **Services:** lau **Leisure:** S **Off-site:** S

MENFI — AGRIGENTO

Palma via delle Palme n 29, 92013
0925 78392 0925 78392
e-mail: campinglapalma@li bero.it
website: www.camping-lapalma.com
Camping Card Compulsory.
6km S.
Open: All year **Site:** 1HEC **Prices:** 5.50 3 7.50 5.50 pitch 5.50 (static)300 **Facilities:** **Services:** lau **Leisure:** S

NICOLOSI — CATANIA

Etna via Goethe, 95030 095 914309 095 914309
e-mail: camping.etna@tiscalimet.it
Open: All year **Site:** 2.9HEC **Facilities:** **Services:** **Leisure:** P **Off-site:**

OLIVERI — MESSINA

Marinello Contrada Marinello, 98060
0941 313000 0941 313702
e-mail: marinello@camping.it
website: www.camping.it/sicilia/marinello
Small pitches set in a woodland area 100m from the sea. Dogs not allowed in July and August.
A20 motorway exit at Falcone.
Open: Apr-Oct **Site:** 3.2HEC **Facilities:** **Services:** lau **Leisure:** S **Off-site:**

PACHINO
AT PORTOPALO (6.6KM SE)

Capo Palssero 96010 0931 842333
Site slightly sloping towards the sea with view of fishing harbour of Portopalo. Disco.
Turn S on 115 in Noto or Iolspica towards Pachino.
Open: 10 Mar-30 Oct **Site:** 3.5HEC **Facilities:** **Services:** **Off-site:** S

PALAZZOLO ACREIDE — SIRACUSA

Torre Torre Tudica, 96010 0931 32694
Open: All year **Site:** 2HEC **Facilities:** **Services:** **Leisure:** P **Off-site:**

PUNTA BRACCETTO — RAGUSA

Rocca dei Tramonti 97017 0932 918054 0932 918054
e-mail: info@roccadeitramonti.com
website: www.roccadeitramonti.com
The site lies in a quiet setting on rather barren land near a beautiful sandy bay surrounded by cliffs.
From Marina di Ragusa 10km W on coast road to Punta Braccetto.
Open: Etr-29 Sep **Site:** 3HEC
Prices: 2.50-4.50 3-4 5-6 5-6 **Facilities:** **Services:** **Leisure:** S **Off-site:**

RAGUSA, MARINA DI — RAGUSA

Baia del Sole Lungomare A-Doria, 97010
0932 239844 0932 230341
e-mail: infobaiadelsole.it
website: www.baiadelsole.it
Well-tended level site. Pitches provided with roofs of straw matting.
Open: All year **Site:** 3.5HEC **Facilities:** **Services:** **Leisure:** PS **Off-site:**

SANT' ALESSIO SICULO — MESSINA

Focetta Sicula via Torrente AgrÚ, 98030
0942 751657 0942 756708
e-mail: lafocetta@camping.it
website: http://www.lafocetta.it
A well-equipped site with a private beach in a quiet location.
From Messina take autostrada to Roccalumera exit, then SS114 towards Sant' Alessio & follow signs.
Open: All year **Site:** 1.2HEC **Prices:** 4-6 2.50-3.50 5-8 5-8 (static)161-234 **Facilities:** **Services:** lau **Leisure:** S **Off-site:**

SANT' ANTONIO DI BARCELLONA — MESSINA

Centro Vacanze Cantoni 98050
090 9710165 090 9710165
e-mail: c.cantoni@hotmail.com
website: www.centrovacanzecantoni.it
Open: Jun-15 Sep **Site:** 1HEC **Prices:** 5.50-6.50 pitch 12.50-14.50 **Facilities:** **Services:** lau **Leisure:** PS

SECCAGRANDE — AGRIGENTO

Kamemi Camping Village 92016
0925 69212 0925 69212
e-mail: info@kamemicamping.it
website: www.kamemicamping.it
In wooded surroundings close to the beach with good recreational facilities.
Open: All year **Site:** 5HEC **Facilities:** **Services:** lau **Leisure:** PS **Off-site:**

LUXEMBOURG

Luxembourg, the tiny Grand Duchy only 2,586 square kilometres in size, offers a wide range of facilities to the visitor.

FACTS AND FIGURES
Area: 2,586 sq km (999 sq miles)
Population: 439,764 (2001)
Capital: Luxembourg City
Language: Luxembourgeois, French and German
IDD code: 352
To call the UK dial 00 44
Currency: Euro
Local time: GMT + 1 (summer GMT + 2)
Emergency Services: Fire and Ambulance 112; Police 113.
Banks: Mon-Fri 09.00-12.00, 13.30-16.30
Shops: Mon-Sat 09.00-18.00
Average daily temperatures:
Luxembourg City
Jan 1°C Mar 6°C
May 13°C Jul 19°C
Sep 15°C Nov 5°C
Tourist information:
Luxembourg National Tourist Office
UK
122 Regent Street
London W1B 5SA
Tel (020) 7434 2800
USA
17 Beekman Place
New York NY 10022
Tel (212) 935 8888
Tourist info website:
www.luxembourg.co.uk

Luxembourg is entirely landlocked by France, Belgium and Germany. One-third of the country is covered by the hills and forests of the Ardennes, while the rest is mostly wooded farmland or the rich wine-growing area around the Moselle. The climate is temperate, with summer often extending from May to late October. Luxembourgeois is the everyday language but the official languages are French and German. English is widely spoken and understood.

There are over 100 officially recognised campsites throughout the country. Most open from April to October, some throughout the year. A booklet containing details of campsites is obtainable from the National Tourist Office (PO Box 1001, L-1010 Luxembourg. ☎ 42 82 82 1) or visit the website **www.ont.lu**. All campsites open to the public are authorised by the Minister of Tourism.

Caravans can only be parked on campsites. Non-coupled caravans cannot be parked on the public highway or used as living accommodation. **Casual camping** with a tent is permitted, but permission must be obtained from the landowner. The owner is not allowed to give permission for more than two tents to be erected on his/her land. Casual camping is not allowed on the banks of Esch-sur-Sure.

HOW TO GET THERE

Luxembourg is easily approached through either Belgium or France. Apart from crossing by Eurotunnel, the usual Continental Channel ports for this journey are Dunkerque or Calais in France, and Zeebrugge in Belgium.

DISTANCE

Luxembourg City is just over 330km (205 miles) from the Belgian ports, or about 420km (260 miles) from the French ports, and is, therefore within a 1-day drive from the Channel coast.

MOTORING & GENERAL

The information given here is specific to Luxembourg. It **must** be read in conjunction with the Essential Information for Motoring section, which covers regulations that are common to many countries.

BRITISH EMBASSY/CONSULATE*

The British Embassy together with its consular section is located at 14 Boulevard Roosevelt, L-2450 Luxembourg ☎ 229864/65/66

Children in Cars

Children under 12 and/or 1.5 metres in height are not permitted to travel as front-seat passengers unless using a suitable restraint system. Children under 3 in the rear must be seated in a suitable restraint system. See Essential Information for Motoring section under **Passengers** and **Seat Belts**.

Currency*

The **euro** is the currency of Luxembourg. The Luxembourg Franc (LUF) ceased to be legal tender in 2002, though LUF notes may still be exchanged at the Luxembourg Central Bank (Banque Central du Luxembourg) for an unlimited period.

Dimensions & Weight Restrictions*

Private cars and towed trailers or caravans are restricted to the following dimensions - height 4 metres; width 2.5 metres; length 12 metres. The maximum permitted overall length of vehicle/trailer or caravan combination is 25 metres.

The weight of a caravan must not exceed 75% of the weight of the towing vehicle.

Driving Licence*

A valid UK or Republic of Ireland licence is accepted in Luxembourg. The minimum age at which visitors from UK or Republic of Ireland may use a temporarily imported car or motorcycle is 17 years.

Foodstuffs*

The importation of meat is limited to 1kg, but there are no limits on other foodstuffs imported for personal use when travelling between EU countries.

Lights*

It is compulsory for motorcyclists to use dipped headlights during the day.

Motoring Club

The **Automobile Club du Grand-Duché de Luxembourg** (ACL) has its office at 54 route de Longwy, 8007 Bertrange ☎ 450045-1. Office hours are Mon-Fri 08.30-12.00, 13.30-18.00.

Website: **www.acl.lu**

Roads

There is a comprehensive system of good main and secondary roads. Luxembourg has 109km (68 miles) of toll-free motorway.

Speed Limits*

Car/motorcycle

Built-up areas	50km/h (31mph)
Other roads	90km/h (55mph)
Motorways	130km/h (80mph) 110km/h (68mph) in wet weather

Motorists who have held a full driving licence for **less than one year:**

Built-up areas	50km/h (31mph)
Other roads	75km/h (46mph)
Motorways	90km/h (55mph)

Car/caravan/trailer

Built-up areas	50km/h (31mph)
Other roads	75km/h (46mph)
Motorways	90km/h (56mph)

Warning Triangle*

Although it is not compulsory for visiting motorists to carry a warning triangle in their vehicles, its use is compulsory in the event of accident or breakdown. The triangle must be placed on the road about 100 metres (109yds) behind the vehicle on ordinary roads and 200-300 metres (219-328 yds) on motorways to warn following traffic of any obstruction.

***Additional information can be found in the International Motoring Information section.**

LUXEMBOURG

BERDORF

Parc Martbusch 3 Baim Maartbesch, 6552 ☎ 790545
A comfortable, modern site in picturesque wooded surroundings.
➲ *NW of town centre.*
Open: All year **Site:** 3HEC **Facilities:** **Services:** lau **Leisure:** P **Off-site:**

BOULAIDE

Haute-Sûre 34 r J-de-Busleyden, 9639
☎ 993061 993604
e-mail: info@campinghautesure.com
website: www.campinghautsure.com
Open: 15 Apr-15 Sep **Site:** 2HEC **Prices:** pitch 23.60 (incl 2 persons) pp2.50 **Facilities:** **Services:** lau **Leisure:** P

CLERVAUX

Official de Clervaux 33 r Klatzewee, 9714
☎ 920042 929728
e-mail: campingclervaux@internet.lu
website: www.camping-clervaux.lu
Situated next to the sports stadium, between the La Clervé stream and the railway in a forested area. Trains only run during the day and there is little noise. Separate field for tents.
➲ *0.5km SW from the village.*
Open: 15 Mar-30 Oct **Site:** 3HEC **Prices:** 4.30 pitch 4.30 **Facilities:** **Services:** lau **Leisure:** PR **Off-site:**

CONSDORF

Bel Air Burgkapp 15 r Burgkapp, 6211 ☎ 790353
The site is divided into pitches and lies on level meadowland in the forest area of Petite Suisse Luxembourgeoise.
➲ *On W outskirts of village. Turn right off E42. 6km S of Echternach.*
Open: May-Aug **Site:** 2HEC **Facilities:** **Services:** lau **Off-site:**

DIEKIRCH

Bleesbruck 9359 ☎ 803134
e-mail: info@camping-bleesbruck.lu
website: www.camping-bleesbruck.lu
A modern site in tranquil wooded surroundings.
Open: Apr-Oct **Site:** 5HEC **Facilities:** **Services:** lau **Leisure:** R **Off-site:** P

Op der Sauer rte de Gilsdorf, 9201
☎ 808590 809470
e-mail: camsauer@pt.lu
website: www.campsauer.lu
➲ *500m from town centre on Gilsdorf road near the sports stadium.*
Open: All year **Site:** 5HEC **Facilities:** **Services:** lau **Leisure:** P

DILLINGEN

Wies-Neu 12 r de la Sûre, 6350 ☎ 836110 26876438
A comfortable family site on the bank of the River Sûre.
➲ *Between Diekirch & Echternacht.*
Open: Apr-30 Oct **Site:** 45HEC **Facilities:** **Services:** lau **Leisure:** R **Off-site:**

ECHTERNACH

Official 5 rte de Diekirch, 6430 ☎ 720272 26720847
e-mail: info@camping_echternach.lu
website: www.mullerthal.lu
➲ *Take E42 to Echternach.*
Open: 15 Mar-1 Nov **Site:** 7HEC
Prices: 4.80 5 5 (static)200-250 **Facilities:** **Services:** lau **Leisure:** P **Off-site:** LPR

ENSCHERANGE

Val d'Or L-9747 ☎ 920691 929725
e-mail: valdor@pt.lu
website: www.valdor.lu
Quiet family site in a beautiful natural setting beside the River Clervé.
➲ *8km S of Clervaux between Drauffelt & Wilwerwiltz.*
Open: All year **Site:** 4HEC **Prices:** 5 pitch 6 (static)175-460 **Facilities:** **Services:** **Leisure:** R **Off-site:** LPS

ESCH-SUR-ALZETTE

Gaalgebierg L-4001 ☎ 541069 549630
e-mail: gaalcamp@pt.lu
A level park-like site with lovely trees on a hillock.
➲ *SE along N6 from the town centre towards Dudelange as far as the motorway underpass. Then turn right & follow the steep climb uphill.*
Open: All year **Site:** 2.5HEC **Facilities:** **Services:** lau

HEIDERSCHEID

Fuussekaul 4 Fussekaul, 9156 ☎ 268888-1 268888-28
e-mail: info@fuussekaul.lu
website: www.fuussekaul.lu
A level grassland family site adjoining a woodland area. Good recreational facilities.

Turn off the N15 Ettelbruck-Wiltz/Bastogne S of Heiderscheid in W direction.
Open: All year **Site:** 18HEC **Prices:** pitch 16.50-26.50 (incl 2 persons) pp2 (static)40-90 **Facilities:** **Services:** lau **Leisure:** P **Off-site:** L

Ingledorf

Gritt r du Pont, 9161 802018 802019
On S bank of River Sûre between Ettelbruck and Diekirch. A beautiful country setting ideal for fishing.
Open: Apr-Oct **Site:** 5HEC **Prices:** 4 4 pitch 4 **Facilities:** **Services:** lau **Leisure:** R **Off-site:** LP

Kockelscheuer

Kockelscheuer 22 rte de Bettembourg, 1899 471815 401243
e-mail: mail@camp-kockelscheuer.lu
website: www.camp-kockelscheuer.lu
A modern site on the edge of a forest.
4km from Luxembourg off N31.
Open: Etr-Oct **Site:** 3.8HEC **Prices:** 3.75 pitch 4.50 **Facilities:** **Services:** lau **Off-site:**

Larochette

Kengert L-7633 837186 878323
e-mail: info@kengert.lu **website:** www.kengert.lu
On gently sloping meadow in a pleasant rural location.
Take the N8 towards Mersch, then the CR119 towards Nommern & turn right after 2km.
Open: Mar-7 Nov **Site:** 4HEC **Prices:** 11-14 (static)325-475 **Facilities:** **Services:** lau **Leisure:** P

Maulusmühle

Woltzdal Maison 12, 9974 998938 979739
e-mail: info@camping-woltzdal.lu
website: www.campingwoltzdal.com
Quiet family site situated in the deep valley of the River Woltz.
From Liege take N30 to Bastogne, then N874 to Clervaux & take N12.
Open: Apr-Oct **Site:** 1.5HEC **Prices:** 5.50 2.75 2.75 2.75 (static)400 **Facilities:** **Services:** lau **Leisure:** R

Mersch

Krounebierg r du camping, 7572 329756 327987
e-mail: contact@campingkrounebeirg.lu
website: www.campingkrounebierg.lu
A clean, well-kept site on five terraces, split into sections by hedges.
0.5km W of village church.
Open: 15 Mar-Oct **Site:** 5.5HEC **Prices:** pitch 21.50-27.20 (incl 2 persons) (static)315-455 **Facilities:** **Services:** lau **Leisure:** P

Mondorf-les-Bains

Risette 4 rte de Burmerange, 5659 660746 660758
e-mail: info@belhorizon.lu
website: www.belhorizon.lu
In pleasant wooded surroundings near the French and German borders.
1km from Mondorf-les-Bains.
Open: Mar-Oct **Site:** 5HEC **Facilities:** **Services:** lau **Off-site:** LPR

Nommern

Europe Nommerlayen r Nommerlayen, 7465 878078 879678
e-mail: nommerlayen@vo.lu
website: www.nommerlayen-ec.lu
A terraced site in wooded surroundings with plenty of recreational facilities.
Open: 16 Jan-15 Dec **Site:** 15HEC **Prices:** 4.40 pitch 18-36 (static)270-645 **Facilities:** **Services:** lau **Leisure:** P

Obereisenbach

Kohnenhof 1 Maison, 9838 929464 929690
e-mail: kohnenho@pt.lu
website: www.campingkohnenhof.lu
Quiet site in a rural setting in the Our valley.
Open: 20 Mar-1 Nov **Site:** 6HEC **Prices:** 3.50-4.60 pitch 7-9.60 (static)225-650 **Facilities:** **Services:** lau **Leisure:** R

Rosport

Barrage rte d'Echternach, 6580 730160 735155
e-mail: campingrosport@pt.lu
website: www.campingrosport.com
Situated by lake Sûre on the German border at the entrance to Petite Suisse Luxembourgeoise.
Main road from Echternach to Wasserbillig.
Open: 15 Mar-Oct **Site:** 3.2HEC **Prices:** 2.80-3.50 pitch 3.20-4 **Facilities:** **Services:** lau **Leisure:** LR **Off-site:**

Steinfort

Steinfort 72 rte de Luxembourg, 8440 398827 397410
e-mail: campstei@pt.lu
website: www.camping-steinfort.lu
A small family site with good recreational and entertainment facilities, well situated for exploring the Seven Castles area.
Access via E25 Steinfort exit.
Open: All year **Site:** 3.5HEC **Prices:** 2.40-4 2.40-4 pitch 4.50-7.50 **Facilities:** **Services:** lau **Leisure:** P

Vianden
At Walsdorf (2km SW)

Romantique Tandelerbaach, L-9465 834464 834440
A terraced grassland site in picturesque wooded surroundings.
W of Diekirch-Vianden road, access from the N17 & CR354.
Open: 3 Mar-1 Nov **Site:** 6HEC **Facilities:** **Services:** lau **Leisure:** R **Off-site:** LP

Weiler-la-Tour

Ma Campagne 9 rte de Thionville, 5771 369497 366912
Camp shop and bar available in August only.
Access via Luxembourg-Thionville road.
Open: All year **Site:** 0.5HEC **Facilities:** **Services:** lau **Off-site:**

NETHERLANDS

Much more than Edam, tulips and windmills, the Netherlands has a rich history, stunning scenery and a vibrant capital city.

FACTS AND FIGURES
Area: 41,528 sq km (16,034 sq miles)
Population: 16,255,000 (2004)
Capital: Amsterdam
Language: Dutch, English
IDD code: 31
To call the UK, dial 00 44
Currency: Euro
Local time: GMT + 1 (summer GMT + 2)

Emergency Services: Fire, Police and Ambulance 112.
Banks: Mon-Fri 09.00-17.00
Shops: Mon-Fri 09.00-18.00, supermarkets 08.00-20.00, Sat 08.00-17.00, Sun (Amsterdam and Rotterdam) 12.00-17.00.

Average daily temperature:
Amsterdam

Jan 2°C	Mar 5°C
May 13°C	Jul 18°C
Sep15°C	Nov 7°C

Tourist information:
Netherlands Board of Tourism (postal/telephone enquiries only)
UK
PO Box 30783, London WC2B 6DH
Tel: (020) 7539 7950 (Mon-Fri 09.30-17.30) or 09068 717777 (premium rate info line)
USA
355 Lexington Avenue, 19th Floor, New York NY 10017
Tel (212) 370 7360
Tourist info website:
www.holland.com/uk

A fifth of this level country lies below sea-level. The areas reclaimed from the sea, the *polders,* are extremely fertile. The landscape is broken up by the forests of Arnhem, the bulb fields in the west, the lakes in the central and northern areas, and the impressive coastal dunes.

The climate is generally mild and tends to be damp. The summers are moderate with changeable weather and are seldom excessively hot. The language, Netherlandish (better known as Dutch), is fairly guttural and closely allied to the low German dialect. Other dialects exist throughout the Netherlands.

There are some 900 officially recognised and classifed campsites throughout the Netherlands. It is not generally possible to book sites in advance. Coastal sites can be crowded in June, July and August when the locals take their holidays. Tourist information offices (VVV) can provide detailed information about sites in their area. The camping season is mainly from April to September, but some sites are open all year. **Off-site camping** is not possible and overnight stops are not permitted.

HOW TO GET THERE

There are direct ferry services to the Netherlands. The services and minimum sailing times are **Harwich to Hoek van Holland**, (6hrs 30mins or 3hrs 40mins by catamaran); **Hull to Rotterdam** (Europoort; 12hrs 30mins); **Newcastle to Amsterdam** (terminal at Ijmuiden, 29km from Amsterdam; 15hrs).

Alternatively, use the Eurotunnel or one of the short Channel crossings and drive through France and Belgium.

DISTANCE

Calais to Den Haag (The Hague) is just over 340km (211 miles; within a 1-day drive).

MOTORING & GENERAL

The information given here is specific to the Netherlands. It **must** be read in conjunction with the Essential Information for Motoring section, which covers regulations that are common to many countries.

BRITISH EMBASSY/CONSULATE*

The British Embassy is located at Lange Voorhout 10, 2514 ED Den Haag ☎ (070) 4270427, but the embassy has no consular section. The British Consulate-General is located at Koningslaan 44, 1075 AE Amsterdam ☎ (020) 6764343.

CHILDREN IN CARS

Children under 12 and/or 1.5 metres in height cannot travel as a front-seat passenger unless using a suitable restraint. (A child of 10, for example, 1.6 metres in height may sit in the front wearing normal seat belts.) A child under 3 in the rear does not have to wear a seat belt but must use child seat or restraint if fitted; children over 3 and under 12 must wear a seat belt in the absence of such equipment. See Essential Information for Motoring section under **Passengers** and **Seat Belts**.

Currency*

The **euro** is currency of the Netherlands. The Netherlands guilder (NLG) ceased to be legal tender in 2002, though NLG coins and notes may still be exchanged at the Netherlands Central Bank (**De Nederlandsche Bank**) until 1 January 2032 (banknotes) and 1 January 2007 (coins).

Dimensions & Weight Restrictions*

Private cars and towed trailers or caravans are restricted to the following dimensions - height 4 metres; width 2.55 metres†; length, car 12 metres, caravan 12 metres. The maximum permitted overall length of a vehicle/trailer or caravan combination is 18 metres. The maximum weight of caravan/luggage trailers will be determined by the instructions of the manufacturer of the towing vehicle and/or the manufacturer of the caravan/luggage trailer.

†Some very small roads have a maximum width restriction of 2.2 metres.

Driving Licence*

A valid UK or Republic of Ireland licence is accepted in the Netherlands. The minimum age at which visitors from UK or Republic of Ireland may use an imported car or motorcycle is 18 years.

Firearms

Dutch laws concerning the possession of firearms are the most stringent in Europe. Any person crossing the frontier with any type of firearm will be arrested. The law applies also to any object which, on superficial inspection, shows any resemblance to real firearms (e.g. plastic imitations). If you wish to carry firearms, real or imitation, of any description into the Netherlands, then contact the Netherlands Consulate.

Foodstuffs*

If the imported foodstuffs are for personal use, there are no limits when travelling between EU countries. However, importation of unpreserved meat products is forbidden and any other unpreserved foodstuffs must be declared.

Motoring Club*

The **Koninklijke Nederlandse Toeristenbond ANWB** has its headquarters at Wassenaarseweg 220, 2596 EC 's-Gravenhage ☎ (070) 31 47 14 7, and has offices in numerous provincial towns. They will assist motoring tourists generally, and supply road and touring information. Offices are open Mon-Fri 09.00-17.30, Sat 09.00-14.00.

Website: **www.anwb.nl**

Roads

The Netherlands has a dense network of motorways (*autosnelweg*) carrying most inter-city and long distance traffic. Yellow ANWB telephone pillars are located every 2km along highways.

Main roads usually have only two lanes, but are well-surfaced. The best way to see the countryside is to use minor roads, often by canals.

However, non-motorway roads have numerous traffic signal-controlled junctions, all of which give priority to cyclists and hence often result in rather slow journeys.

Speed Limits*

Car/motorcycle	
Built-up areas	50km/h (31mph)
Other roads	80km/h (49mph)
	or 100km/h (62mph)
Motorways	120km/h (74mph)
Car/caravan/trailer	
Built-up areas	50km/h (31mph)
Other roads	80km/h (49mph)
Motorways	80km/h (49mph)

Warning Triangle/Hazard Warning*

In the event of an accident or breakdown a motorist must use either a warning triangle or hazard-warning lights to warn approaching traffic of any obstruction. However, a warning triangle is recommended as hazard-warning lights may be damaged or inoperative. The triangle must be placed 30 metres (33yds) behind the vehicle on ordinary roads and 100 metres 109yds) on motorways: it must be visible at a distance of 100 metres (109yds).

***Additional information can be found in the Essential Information for Motoring section.**

NORTH

AMEN DRENTHE

Reservaat Diana Heide 53 Amen, 9446
0592 389297 0592 389432
e-mail: info@dianaheide.nl **website:** www.dianaheide.nl
An ideal site for relaxation, which lies away from the traffic among forest and heathland.
Approaching from Assen along the E35, drive through Amen towards Hooghalen.
Open: Apr-1 Oct **Site:** 30HEC
Prices: 3 pitch 9.50-11.50 **Facilities:**
Services: lau **Leisure:** P **Off-site:** R

ANNEN DRENTHE

Hondsrug Annerweg 3, 9463 0592 271292 0592 271440
e-mail: info@hondsrug.nl **website:** www.hondsrug.nl
A family site in a pleasant rural setting with good recreational facilities.
Access via N34 to site SE of Annen.
Open: Apr-1 Oct **Site:** 18HEC
Facilities: **Services:** lau **Leisure:** P

ASSEN DRENTHE

Witterzomer Witterzomer 7, 9405
0592 393535 0592 393530
e-mail: info@witterzomer.nl **website:** www.witterzomer.nl
A large site with asphalt internal roads, lying in mixed woodland near nature reserve. Separate sections for dog owners.
Turn off the E35 at Assen W exit into Europaweg Zuid & continue 100m, then turn right. Continue through Witten & follow signs.
Open: All year **Site:** 75HEC **Prices:** 3.50 pitch 29 (static)190-525 **Facilities:**
Services: lau **Leisure:** LP

BERGUM FRIESLAND

Bergumermeer Solcamastr 30, 9262
0511 461385 0511 463955
e-mail: info@bergumermeer.nl **website:** www.bergumermeer.nl
In pleasant wooded surroundings close to the marina on the Bergumermeer with good recreational facilities.
From N355 Groningen-Leeuwarden turn S via Bergum on N356 then exit E to Sumar towards Oostermeer.
Open: 27 Mar-16 Oct **Site:** 29HEC
Facilities: **Services:** lau **Leisure:** LP

BORGER DRENTHE

Hunzedal De Drift 3, 9531 0599 234698 0599 235183
e-mail: info@hunzedal.nl **website:** www.hunzedal.nl
The site is clean, well-kept and lies NE of the village.
For access, turn off the road towards Buinen, drive 200m E of the bridge over the Buinen-Schoondoord canal, then head S for 1km.
Open: 4 Apr-Oct **Site:** 30HEC **Facilities:**
Services: lau **Leisure:** LP **Off-site:**

DIEVER DRENTHE

Hoeve AAn den Weg Bosweg 12, 8439 SN
521 387269 521 387326
e-mail: camping@hoeveAAndenweg.nl
website: www.hoeveAAndenweg.nl
In pleasant wooded surroundings with good recreational facilities.
Camping Card Compulsory
Open: Apr-Oct **Site:** 5HEC **Facilities:**
Services: lau **Leisure:** P

DWINGELOO DRENTHE

Noordster Noordster 105, 7991
0521 597238 0521 597589
e-mail: noordster@rcn-centra.nl **website:** www.rcn-centra.nl
A large family site with static and touring pitches, surrounded by woodland.
3km S on E35.
Open: All year **Site:** 42HEC **Prices:** pitch 17-28 (incl 6 persons) **Facilities:** **Services:**
lau **Leisure:** P

FRANEKER FRIESLAND

Bloemketerp Burg J Dykstraweg 3, 8801
0517 395099 0517 395150
e-mail: bloemketerp@wxs.nl **website:** www.bloemketerp.nl
In a well-equipped leisure centre near the historic city of Franeker.
Open: All year **Site:** **Facilities:**
Services: lau **Leisure:** P **Off-site:** P

GRONINGEN GRONINGEN

Stadspark Campinglaan 6, 9727
050 5251624 050 5250099
e-mail: camping_stadspark@planet.nl
website: www.grunopark.nl
A well-kept site on patches of grass between rows of bushes and groups of pine and deciduous trees. Some of its pitches are naturally screened.
For access from the SW outskirts of the town, take the road towards Peize and Roden.
Open: 15 Mar-15 Oct **Site:** 6HEC **Facilities:**
Services: lau **Off-site:** LP

HARKSTEDE GRONINGEN

Grunopark Hoofdweg 163, 9617
050 416371 050 424521
website: www.grunopark.nl
Situated within a large waterpark with a great variety of sports facilities available.
Open: All year **Site:** 23HEC **Facilities:**
Services: lau **Leisure:** L

HARLINGEN FRIESLAND

Zeehoeve 8862 517 413465 517 416971
e-mail: info@zeehoeve.nl **website:** www.zeehoeve.nl
A well-kept meadow site which is divided into large sections by rows of bushes.
1km S of Harlingen near a dyke.
Open: Apr-Sep **Site:** 10HEC **Prices:** 3.50
2 3.50 3.50 (static)360 **Facilities:**
Services: lau **Leisure:** S **Off-site:**

HEE (ISLAND OF TERSCHELLING) FRIESLAND

Kooi Hee 9, 8882 562 442743 562 442835
website: www.campingdekooi.nl
5km from the harbour.
Open: 15 Apr-15 Sep **Site:** 8.5HEC **Facilities:**
Services: lau **Off-site:** L

HINDELOOPEN FRIESLAND

Hindeloopen Westerdijk 9, 8713
0514 521452 0514 523221
e-mail: info@campinghindeloopen.nl
website: www.campinghindeloopen.nl
A peaceful site on the Ysselmeer with fishing and water-sports facilities.
1km S.
Open: Apr-Nov **Site:** 16HEC **Facilities:**
Services: lau **Leisure:** L

Site: 6HEC-Site size -grass -sand -stone -little shade -partly shaded -mainly shaded
-bungalows for hire -caravans for hire -tents for hire -no dogs **Prices:** -adult per night -car per night
pp-per person per night -caravan per night -tent per night (static)-caravan hire per week

KOUDUM FRIESLAND

De Kuilart Kuilart 1, 8723 0514 522221 0514 523010
e-mail: info@kuilart.nl **website:** www.kuilart.nl
A camping and water-sports centre on the shores of De Fluessen lake.
Access via N359.
Open: All year **Site:** 30HEC **Facilities:** **Services:** lau **Leisure:** LP **Off-site:** S

LAUWERSOOG GRONINGEN

Lauwersoog Strandweg 5, 9976
0159 349133 0519 349195
e-mail: info@lauwersoog.nl **website:** www.lauwersoog.nl
In a pleasant situation on the shores of Lauwersmeer. A good excursion centre with fine water sports facilities.
Camping Card Compulsory
Open: All year **Site:** 15HEC **Prices:** pitch 20-23 (incl 2 persons) (static)200-500 **Facilities:** **Services:** lau **Leisure:** L **Off-site:** S

MAKKUM FRIESLAND

Holle Poarte Holle Poarte 2, 8754
0515 231344 0515 231339
A modern site with fine water sports facilities on the Ijsselmeer.
Open: All year **Site:** 32HEC **Facilities:** **Services:** lau **Leisure:** L

ONNEN GRONINGEN

Fruitberg Dorpsweg 67, 9755 050 4061282
A peaceful site situated in an orchard.
S of the village, and right of the Haren-Zuidlaren road.
Open: 15 Mar-1 Nov **Site:** 5.5HEC **Facilities:** **Services:** lau **Leisure:** P
Off-site: L

OPENDE FRIESLAND

't Strandheem Parkweg 2, 9865
0594 659555 0594 658592
e-mail: info@strandheem.nl **website:** www.strandheem.nl
A family site with modern sanitary blocks and a wide variety of recreational facilities.
Access from A7 (Groningen-Afsluitdijk) exit 31.
Open: Apr-1 Oct **Site:** 15HEC **Facilities:** **Services:** lau **Leisure:** LP

RUINEN DRENTHE

Engeland Oude Benderseweg 11, 7963 0522 471770
A family site in pleasant wooded surroundings with well-sheltered pitches on the edge of a national park.
Access via A28 exit Ruinen-Pesse.
Open: Apr-24 Oct **Site:** 25HEC **Facilities:** **Services:** lau **Leisure:** P **Off-site:**

Wiltzangh Witteveen 2, 7963
0522 471227 0522 472178
e-mail: wiltzangh@dwingelderveld.com
website: www.dwingelderveld.com/wiltzangh
N of the village in the middle of a coniferous and deciduous forest, and within the grounds of a big holiday village. Advance booking is necessary for the peak season.
From Ruinen towards Ansen for 3km, then turn N.
Open: Apr-Oct **Site:** 13HEC **Facilities:** **Services:** lau **Leisure:** P

SONDEL FRIESLAND

Sondel Beuckenswijkstr 26, 8565
0514 602300 0514 605026
e-mail: e.landman@zonnet.nl
website: www.campingsondel.nl
In a dense wood.
Just off the Sondel-Rijs road.
Open: Apr-Oct **Site:** 3HEC **Prices:** 7.85 pitch 11.30 (incl 2 persons) pp3.80 **Facilities:** **Services:** lau **Leisure:** LPRS **Off-site:**

TERMUNTERZIJL GRONINGEN

Zeestrand Eems-Dollard Schepperbuurt 4a
0596 601443 0596 601209
e-mail: campingzeestrand@wanadoo.nl
website: www.campingzeestrand.nl
Situated on a tongue of land in the Wadden sea with views of Germany and close proximity to a beach.
A7 exit 45 for Delfzijl, campsite signed.
Open: 25 Mar-1 Nov **Site:** 6.5HEC
Prices: 3.15-3.50 1.45-1.60 3.30-3.70 3.30-3.70 (static)100 **Facilities:** **Services:** lau
Leisure: LPRS **Off-site:**

TERSCHELLING (ISLAND OF)

WEDDE GRONINGEN

Wedderbergen Molenweg 2, 9698
0597 561673 0597 562595
e-mail: info@wedderbergen.nl
website: www.wedderbergen.nl
On meadowland divided by deciduous trees and bush hedges.
On the E outskirts of the village take a narrow asphalt road N for 3.2km. Then take Spanjaardsweg & Molenweg to the camp.
Open: Apr-1 Nov **Site:** 40HEC **Facilities:** **Services:** lau **Leisure:** LR

WEST TERSCHELLING ISLAND OF TERSCHELLING) FRIESLAND

Cnossen Hoofdweg 8, 8881 HA 0562 442321
Several patches of meadowland, left of the road towards Formerum, and right of the forest.
Ferry from Harlingen.
Open: Apr-1 Nov **Site:** 2.5HEC **Facilities:** **Services:** **Off-site:** LP

CENTRAL

AALSMEER NOORD-HOLLAND

Amsterdamse Bos Kleine Noorddijk 1, 1432
020 6416868 020 6402378
e-mail: camping@dab.amsterdam.nl
website: www.campingamsterdamsebos.nl
The site is in a park-like setting in the Amsterdam wood. The camp is near the Airport flight path and is subject to noise depending on the wind direction.
From The Hague along the motorway, turn at the northern edge of the airport towards Amstelveen. Then follow directions for Aalsmeer. From Utrecht, leave the motorway at Amstelveen exit towards Aalsmeer, passing through Bovenkerk.
Open: Apr-14 Oct **Site:** 6.8HEC **Prices:** 5 3 3.50 3 **Facilities:** **Services:** lau
Off-site: LRS

Facilities: -shop -shower -electric points for razors -electric points for caravans -parking by tents permitted -compulsory separate car park **Services:** -café/restaurant -bar -Camping Gaz International -gas other than Camping Gaz -first aid facilities lau-laundry **Leisure:** -swimming L-Lake P-Pool R-River S-Sea **Off-site:** All facilities within 2km

ALKMAAR Noord-Holland

Alkmaar Bergerweg 201, 1817 072 5116924
e-mail: campingalkmaar@planet.nl
website: www.campingalkmaar.nl
The site is well kept and divided into many sections by rows of trees and bushes.
Camping Card Compulsory
On the NW outskirts of the town, off the Bergen road.
Open: Apr-Oct **Site:** 3HEC **Prices:** 5 2.30 4.50 3.40 **Facilities:** **Services:** lau **Off-site:** LPS

AMSTERDAM Noord-Holland

See also Aalsmeer

Gaasper Loosdrechtdreef 7, 1108
020 6967326 020 6969369
website: www.gaaspercamping.nl
Situated on the edge the beautiful Gaasperpark within easy reach of Amsterdam.
Camping Card Compulsory
From A9 take Gaasperplas exit before city centre and follow camping signs.
Open: 15 Mar-1 Nov **Site:** 5.5HEC **Prices:** 4.50 4 6 5.25-6.25 **Facilities:** **Services:** lau **Off-site:** L

Vliegenbos Meeuwenlaan 138, 1022 020 6368855
A tent site for young people.
From main railway station through tunnel, then right & right again at traffic lights, then follow signs.
Open: Apr-Sep **Site:** 25HEC **Facilities:** **Services:** lau **Off-site:** P

Zeeburg Zuider Ijdijk 20, 1095
020 6944430 020 6946238
e-mail: info@campingzeeburg.nl
website: www.campingzeeburg.nl
On an island in the Ijmeer, 15 minutes from the city centre, with good facilities. Popular with backpackers and holidaymakers alike.
Access via A10 exit S114 by 2nd set of T-lights.
(Exit A10 at junct 114, follow signs for central station)
Open: All year **Site:** 3.8HEC **Prices:** 4.50 4 5 3.50 pitch 3.50 **Facilities:** **Services:** lau **Off-site:** P

ANDIJK Noord-Holland

Vakantiedorp Het Grootslag Proefpolder 4, 1619
0228 592944 0228 592457
e-mail: info@andijkvakanties.nl
website: www.andijkvakanties.nl
One of the most well-equipped sites in the area, situated on the IJsselmeer. Individual bathrooms are allocated to each pitch and a wide range of recreational facilities are available.
From A7 exit Hoorn-Noord/Enkhuizen/Lelystad turn left for Andijk, then follow signs for Het Grootslag and Dijkweg.
Open: 25 Mar-30 Oct **Site:** 40HEC **Prices:** 3 pitch 18-29 (incl 4 persons) **Facilities:** **Services:** lau **Leisure:** LP

APPELTERN Gelderland

Het Groene Eiland Lutenkampstr 2, 6629
0487 562130 0487 561540
e-mail: info@hetgroeneeiland.nl
website: www.hetgroeneeiland.nl
In a 'water recreation' park with plenty of sports facilities.
From A15 take Leeuwen turn & follow signs.
Open: 15 Mar-Oct 31 **Site:** 16HEC **Prices:** 2.30 2.60 10.50 10.50 (static)415 **Facilities:** **Services:** lau **Leisure:** LR **Off-site:**

ARNHEM Gelderland

Arnhem Kemperbergerweg 771, 6816
026 4431600 026 4457705
e-mail: arnhem@holiday.nl
website: www.campingarnhem.nl
The site lies on grassland and is surrounded by trees.
NW of town and S of E36.
Open: Apr-Oct **Site:** 36HEC **Prices:** pitch 15.75-24 (incl 2 persons) **Facilities:** **Services:** lau **Leisure:** P

Hooge Veluwe Koningsweg 14, 6816
026 4432272 026 4436809
e-mail: info@dehoogeveluwe.nl
website: www.dehoogeveluwe.nl
Situated in a pleasant natural park with good facilities.
From Apeldoorn exit on E36 NW towards Hooge Veluwe.
Open: 31 Mar-28 Oct **Site:** 18HEC **Facilities:** **Services:** lau **Leisure:** P

Warnsborn Bakenbergseweg 257, 6816
026 4423469 026 4421095
e-mail: info@campingwarnsborn.nl
website: www.campingwarnsborn.nl
The site is surrounded by woodland and lies on slightly sloping meadowland. Near zoo and open-air museum.
Near the E36 motorway NW of town towards Utrecht. 200m S of Shell filling station, continue W 0.7km.
Open: Apr-Oct **Site:** 3.5HEC **Facilities:** **Services:** lau **Off-site:** P

BABBERICH Gelderland

Rivo Torto Beekseweg 8, 6909
0316 247332 0316 246628
e-mail: info@rivotorto.nl **website:** www.rivotorto.nl
A riverside site with good recreational facilities.
3km W on E36.
Open: 15 Mar-Oct **Site:** 8.5HEC **Prices:** 1.80 2.35 6 3.65 pitch 3.65 **Facilities:** **Services:** lau **Off-site:** L

BEEKBERGEN GELDERLAND

Bosgraaf Kanaal Zuid 444, 7364 055 5051359
Situated on hilly grassland and woodland, but the woodland pitches are mainly used by residential caravans.
From the N50 Arnhem-Apeldoorn road, turn N in West Hoeve onto the Loenen road, then follow signs for 2km.
Site: 22HEC **Facilities:**
Services: lau **Leisure:** P

BERKHOUT NOORD-HOLLAND

Westerkogge Kerkebuurt 202, 1647
0229 551208 0229 551390
e-mail: info@camping-westerkogge.nl
website: www.camping-westerkogge.nl
A fine situation with well-sheltered pitches and a good range of recreational facilities.
Access via A7 Amsterdam-Leeuwarden, exit Hoorn-Berkhout or Berkhout-Avenhorn.
Open: Apr-Oct **Site:** 11HEC **Prices:** 2.90-3.15 2.30-2.65 7.75-8.70 4.30 (static)233-399 **Facilities:** **Services:** lau **Leisure:** P

BILTHOVEN UTRECHT

Bospark Bilthoven Burg v.d Borchlaan 7, 3722
030 2286777 030 2293888
e-mail: bosparkbilthoven@wanadoo.nl
Family site in wooded surroundings with asphalt drives.
Signed from town centre.
Open: Apr-Oct **Site:** 20HEC **Prices:** 2.50 13-18.50 **Facilities:** **Services:** lau **Leisure:** P **Off-site:**

BLOKZIJL OVERIJSSEL

Tussen de Diepen Duinigermeerweg 1A, 8356
0527 291565 0527 292203
e-mail: camping@tussendediepen.nl
website: www.tussendediepen.nl
Secluded site surrounded by water. Fishing, water sports and sailing.
Open: Apr-Oct **Site:** 5.2HEC **Prices:** 4.05-4.50 1.55-1.70 4.05-4.50 4.50-4.50 pitch 1.55-1.70 (static)370-450 **Facilities:** **Services:** lau **Leisure:** R **Off-site:** P

BUURSE OVERIJSSEL

't Hazenbos Oude Buurserdijk 1, 7481 053 5696338
e-mail: info@hazenbos.nl **website:** www.hazenbos.nl
On several meadows, partially surrounded by trees.
7km from the German border.
Open: All year **Site:** 6HEC **Prices:** 2.60 1.75 2.65 2.05-2.65 **Facilities:** **Services:** lau **Off-site:** LP

CALLANTSOOG NOORD-HOLLAND

Recreatiecentrum de Nollen Westerweg 8, 1759
0224 581281 0224 582098
e-mail: info@denollen.nl **website:** www.denollen.nl
A modern family site with plenty of facilities. Less than 1.6km from the beach.
E of town towards N9.
Open: Apr-1 Nov **Site:** 9HEC **Prices:** pitch 19-26 **Facilities:** **Services:** lau **Off-site:** PS

Tempelhof Westerweg 2, 1759
0224 581522 0224 582133
e-mail: tempelhof@planet.nl **website:** www.tempelhof.nl
Well equipped site on level meadowland.
Open: All year **Site:** 12.7HEC **Prices:** 3.73 pitch 25.06-29.06 (incl 2 persons) **Facilities:** **Services:** lau **Leisure:** P **Off-site:** LS

DALFSEN OVERIJSSEL

Buitenplaats Gerner Haersolteweg 9-17, 7722
0529 439191 0529 439199
e-mail: info@gerner.nl **website:** www.gerner.nl
Turn off at Dalfsen & 2nd road on the left.
Open: All year **Site:** 12HEC **Facilities:** **Services:** lau **Leisure:** P

DENEKAMP OVERIJSSEL

Papillon Kanaalweg 30, 7591
05413 51670 05413 55217
website: www.depapillon.nl
Predominantly a chalet site on meadowland in a tall coniferous and deciduous forest, about 2km N of Denekamp. It has a few naturally screened pitches.
Turn off the E72 towards Nordhorn (Germany), about 0.3km N of the signs for Almelo-Nordhorn canal, continue NE for 1.5km.
Open: Apr-1 Oct **Site:** 11HEC **Facilities:** **Services:** lau **Leisure:** LP

DIEPENHEIM OVERIJSSEL

Molnhofte Nyhofweg 5, 7478
0547 351514 0547 351641
e-mail: molnhofte@planet.nl **website:** www.molnhofte.nl
A family site in a rural setting with modern bungalows for hire.
E of town.
Open: All year **Site:** 6HEC **Prices:** 3 2.50 3 3 pitch 2.50 **Facilities:** **Services:** lau **Leisure:** P

DOESBURG GELDERLAND

Ijsselstrand Eekstr 18, 6984 0313 472797 0313 473376
e-mail: ijsselstrand@planet.nl
website: www.ijsselstrand.nl
On level meadow with trees and hedges beside the River Ijssel. Separate field for young people. Water sports.
NE across river. Signed.
Open: All year **Site:** 45HEC **Prices:** 3.05 1.95 3.45 2.70 (static)150-300 **Facilities:** **Services:** lau **Leisure:** LR

DOETINCHEM GELDERLAND

Wrange Rekhemseweg 144, 7004 0314 324852
e-mail: info@dewrange.nl **website:** www.dewrange.nl
On the E outskirts of the town. It is set in meadowland and surrounded by bushes and deciduous trees.
200m E of link road between roads to Varsseveld & Terborg.
Open: 25 Mar-1 Oct **Site:** 10HEC
Prices: pitch 14-15 (incl 2 persons) **Facilities:** **Services:** lau **Leisure:** P

DOORN UTRECHT

Bonte Vlucht Leersumsestraatweg 23, 3941
0343 473232 0343 414517
e-mail: info@bontevlucht.nl **website:** www.bontevlucht.nl
3km E.
Open: Apr-Oct **Site:** 17HEC **Facilities:** **Services:** **Off-site:** P

Het Grote Bos Hydeparklaan 24, 3941
0343 513644 0343 512324
Well-layed out site on wooded grassland. Varied leisure activities for children and adults.
About 1km NW of Doorn.
Open: All year **Site:** 80HEC **Facilities:** **Services:** lau **Leisure:** P

DRONTEN GELDERLAND
AT BIDDINGHUIZEN (9KM S)

Riviera Park Spijkweg 15, 8256
0321 331344 0321 331402
e-mail: info@riviera.nl **website:** www.riviera.nl
Situated on grassland near a forest of deciduous trees and surrounded by shrubs.
On the Polder beside the Veluwemeer, 5km S of Biddinghuizen turn left.
Open: 10 Mar-30 Oct **Site:** 60HEC **Prices:** pitch 23-30 (incl 4 persons) (static)205-575 **Facilities:** **Services:** lau **Leisure:** LP

EDAM NOORD-HOLLAND

Strandbad Zeevangszeedijk 7a, 1135
0299 371994 0299 371510
e-mail: info@campingstrandbad.nl
website: www.campingstrandbad.nl
A friendly family site on the Ijssel lake with plenty of facilities and close to the historic town of Edam.
Open: Apr-Sep **Site:** 5HEC **Prices:** 3.05 3.20 4.45 4.45 **Facilities:** **Services:** lau **Leisure:** L **Off-site:** P

EERBEEK GELDERLAND

Landal Greenparks Coldenhove Boshoffweg 6, 6961
0313 659101 0313 654776
website: www.landal.nl
In woodland.
From Apeldoorn-Dieren road, drive 2km SW, then NW for 1km.
Open: All year **Site:** 74HEC **Facilities:** **Services:** lau **Leisure:** P **Off-site:**

Robertsoord Doonweg 4, 6961
0313 651346 0313 655751
e-mail: info@robertsoord.nl **website:** www.robertsoord.nl
In a wooded location with good recreational facilities.
1km SE.
Open: Apr-Oct **Site:** 2.5HEC **Facilities:** **Services:** lau **Off-site:** P

EGMOND AAN ZEE NOORD-HOLLAND

Camping Egmond ann Zee Nollenweg 1, 1931 AV
072 5061702 072 5067147
website: www.euroase.com
Part of a chain of family sites with excellent facilities. In a wooded location 1.5km from the beach.
Open: Apr-Oct **Site:** 11HEC **Facilities:** **Services:** lau **Leisure:** PS **Off-site:** P

ENSCHEDE OVERIJSSEL

De Twentse Es Keppelerdijk 200, 7534
053 4611372 053 4618558
e-mail: info@twentse-es.nl **website:** www.twentse-es.nl
In a wooded location with good recreational facilities.
E towards Glanerbrug.
Open: All year **Site:** 10HEC **Prices:** pitch 20.40 (incl 5 persons) **Facilities:** **Services:** lau **Leisure:** P

EPE GELDERLAND

Euroase Parc Epe Centrumweg 5, 8162 PT
05780 616204 05780 627775
On level ground, surrounded by mature woodland, with recreational facilities.
SW of village.
Open: Apr-1 Nov **Site:** 15HEC **Facilities:** **Services:** lau **Leisure:** P

ERMELO GELDERLAND

Haeghehorst Fazantlaan 4, 3852
0341 553185 0341 562751
e-mail: haeghehorst@vvc.nl **website:** www.haeghehorst.nl
Well equipped site in pleasant wooded surroundings.
Camping Card Compulsory
Access via A28/E35 towards Amersfoort, then N303.
Open: All year **Site:** 10HEC **Prices:** 14-25 15.25-30 pitch 15.25-30 (incl 2 persons) **Facilities:** **Services:** lau **Leisure:** P

GROET NOORD-HOLLAND

Groede Hargerweg 8, 1871 72 5091555 5092862
e-mail: campinggroede@planet.nl
website: www.camping-groede.nl
The site consists of a meadow enclosed by hedges.
Open: 15 Apr-15 Sep **Site:** 3HEC **Facilities:** **Services:** lau **Off-site:**

GROOTE KEETEN NOORD-HOLLAND

Callassande Voorweg 5A, 1759
0224 581663 0224 582588
e-mail: info@callassande.nl **website:** www.callassande.nl
A large tourist site with fine facilities close to the sea.
Open: Apr-Oct **Site:** 12HEC **Prices:** 3.80 11.90 8-11.90 pitch 11.90 **Facilities:** **Services:** lau **Leisure:** P **Off-site:** S

HAAKSBERGEN OVERIJSSEL

't Stien'nboer Scholtenhagenweg 42, 7481
053 5722610 053 5729394
e-mail: info@stien-nboer.nl **website:** www.stien-nboer.nl
A family site with good recreational facilities S of the town.
Open: 15 Mar-Nov **Site:** 10.5HEC **Facilities:** **Services:** lau **Leisure:** P **Off-site:**

HALFWEG NOORD-HOLLAND

Houtrak Zuiderweg 2, 1165 NA
020 4972796 020 4975887
e-mail: info@campinghoutrak.nl
website: www.campinghoutrak.nl
Grassy site on several levels subdivided by trees, hedges and shrubs. Separate section for young campers.
Signed from Spaarwonde exit on A5.
Open: Apr-Sep **Site:** 13HEC **Prices:** 3 2.40 4.60 3.60 **Facilities:** **Services:** lau **Leisure:** L **Off-site:** P

HATTEM GELDERLAND

Leemkule Leemkuilen 6, 8051 PN
038 4441945 038 4446280
e-mail: info@leemkule.nl **website:** www.leemkule.nl
A holiday centre situated in one of the largest nature reserves in the country.
2.5km SW.
Open: Apr-Oct **Site:** 16HEC **Prices:** 3.50 19-25 pitch 19-25 (incl 2 persons) **Facilities:** **Services:** lau **Leisure:** P **Off-site:**

HEILOO Noord-Holland

Heiloo De Omloop 24, 1852 072 5355555 072 5355551
e-mail: info@campingheiloo.nl
website: www.campingheiloo.nl
One of the best sites in the area. It is divided into many large squares by hedges.
Open: Apr-Oct **Site:** 4HEC **Prices:** pitch 14.50-23 (incl 2 persons) (static)175-410 **Facilities:** ⊙ **Services:** ✕ lau **Off-site:** LP

Klein Varnebroek De Omloop 22, 1852
072 5331627 072 5331620
e-mail: info@kleinvarnebroek.nl
website: www.kleinvarnebroek.nl
A grassy family campsite surrounded by trees.
Off the Alkmaar road towards the swimming pool.
Open: 25 Mar-1 Nov **Site:** 4.9HEC **Facilities:** ⊙ **Services:** ✕ lau **Off-site:** LPS

HELDER, DEN Noord-Holland

Donkere Duinen Jan Verfailleweg 616, 1783
0223 614731 0223 615077
e-mail: info@donkereduinen.nl
website: www.donkereduinen.nl
A quiet, pleasant site with good facilities.
800m towards the beach. Follow signs 'Nieuw-Den Helder' Strand.
Open: 9 Apr-28 Aug **Site:** 7HEC **Facilities:** ⊙ **Services:** lau **Leisure:** S **Off-site:** ✕ PS

Noorder Sandt Noorder Sandt 2, Julianadorp aan Zee, 1787
0223 641266 0233 645600
e-mail: info@noordersandt.com
website: www.noordersandt.com
A flat, well-maintained site on meadowland, with good sanitary blocks.
Access from the Den Helder to Callantsoog coastal road.
Open: Etr-15 Sep **Site:** 10HEC **Facilities:** ⊙ **Services:** ✕ lau **Leisure:** P **Off-site:** S

HENGELO Gelderland

Kom-Es-An Handwijzersdijk 4, 7255 0575 467242
A family site in wooded surroundings on the outskirts of the village.
NE of village in wooded area towards Ruurlo.
Open: Apr-Oct **Site:** 10.5HEC **Facilities:** ⊙ **Services:** ✕ lau **Leisure:** P

HENGELO Overijssel

Zwaaikom Kettingbrugweg 60, 7552
074 2916560 074 2916785
A family site with good facilities situated on the Twente canal.
SE towards Enschede between canal & road.
Open: 15 Apr-15 Sep **Site:** 4HEC **Prices:** 3.50 3.05 3.05 3.05 **Facilities:** ⊙ **Services:** ✕ **Leisure:** P

HEUMEN Gelderland

Heumens Bos Vosseneindseweg 46, 6582
024 3581481 024 3583862
e-mail: info@heumensbos.nl **website:** www.heumensbos.nl
One of the best sites in the area with good, modern facilities and spacious pitches.
NW of village, 100m N of the Wijchen road.
Open: All year **Site:** 16HEC **Prices:** 4 pitch 15.50-24 (incl 2 persons) **Facilities:** ⊙ **Services:** ✕ lau **Leisure:** P

HOENDERLOO Gelderland

Pampel Woeste Hoefweg 35, 7351 TN
055 3781760 055 3781992
e-mail: info@pampel.nl **website:** www.pampel.nl
A most attractive site in pleasant wooded surroundings with good facilities for families.
Open: All year **Site:** 14.5HEC **Prices:** pitch 19.20-23.50 (incl 2 persons) **Facilities:** ⊙ **Services:** ✕ lau **Leisure:** P

't Veluws Hof Krimweg 154, 7351 055 3781777
Comfortable site with good, modern facilities.
W of N93.
Open: All year **Site:** 31HEC **Facilities:** ⊙ **Services:** ✕ lau **Leisure:** P

HOORN, DEN (ISLAND OF TEXEL) Noord-Holland

Kogerstrand Badweg 33 0222 317208 0222 317018
e-mail: info@rsttexel.nl **website:** www.rsttexel.nl
Site is part of the Duinen van Texel national park, close to the sand dunes and the sea. A separate part of the site is reserved for the 16-25 age group and there is a restricted-traffic policy. Cars may only enter the site on arrival and departure - at other times the car park must be used.
From ferry proceed to De Koog & continue along road (Nikadel). Pass Catholic church & continue along Badweg. Drive to end of road.
Open: 19 Mar-30 Oct **Site:** 52HEC **Prices:** 2.25 pitch 11.65-19.45 **Facilities:** ⊙ **Services:** ✕ lau **Leisure:** S **Off-site:** P

Loodsmansduin Rommelpot 19, 1797 0222 317208
e-mail: info@rsttexel.nl **website:** www.rsttexel.nl
Extensive site, numerous large and small hollows between dunes, connected by paved paths. Several sanitary blocks. At the highest part there is a bungalow village among a shopping and administrative complex. A section is reserved for naturists and there is a naturists beach 2km away.
From the ferry drive N towards Den Burg, then turn left at x-roads towards Den Hoorn.
Open: 18 Mar-30 Oct **Site:** 38HEC **Prices:** 2.25 pitch 9-19.45 **Facilities:** ⊙ **Services:** ✕ lau **Leisure:** PS **Off-site:** S

KESTEREN Gelderland

Lede en Oudewaard Hogedijkseweg 40, 4041
0488 481477 0488 482599
On level meadowland surrounded by bushy hedges and divided into individual pitches. 100m from private beach and pool.
2km N of village, turn W off main Rhenen-Kesteren road for 2.7km.
Open: All year **Site:** 30HEC **Prices:** 3 pitch 14 (incl 2 persons) **Facilities:** ⊙ **Services:** ✕ lau **Leisure:** L

KOOG, DE (ISLAND OF TEXEL) Noord-Holland

Om de Noord Boodtlaan 80 0222 317208 0222 317018
e-mail: info@rsttexel.nl **website:** www.rsttexel.nl
Site with spacious pitches located close to woodlands, dunes and the beach.
From ferry proceed to De Koog & continue along road (Nikadel) passing Catholic church on right. Turn right at junction with Boodtlaan. Proceed to football pitch, driveway to campsite on left.
Open: 19 Mar-30 Oct **Site:** 3.3HEC **Prices:** 2.25 pitch 11-18.50 **Facilities:** ⊙ **Services:** lau **Leisure:** S **Off-site:** ✕ P

Shelter Boodtlaan 43, 1796 0222 317208 0222 317018
e-mail: info@rsttexel.nl
website: www.rsttexel.nl
Small family site a short distance from the sea.
Open: All year **Site:** 1.1HEC **Prices:** 1.50-2.50 15.50-26 pitch 15.50-26 **Facilities:** **Services:** lau **Off-site:** S

Kootwijk Gelderland

Kerkendel Kerkendelweg 49, 3775
0577 456224 0577 456545
e-mail: kerkendel@kerkendel.nl **website:** www.kerkendel.nl
A family site with good facilities situated in the heart of the Veluwe national park.
Open: 27 Mar-Oct **Site:** 7.5HEC **Facilities:** **Services:** lau **Leisure:** P **Off-site:** LR

Laag-Soeren Gelderland

Jutberg Jutberg 78, 6957 0313 619220 0313 619760
A well-equipped site in the woods of the south-east Veluwezoom near Arnhem.
Access via A12 (Arnhem) towards Zulfa, then follow signs.
Open: All year **Site:** **Facilities:** **Services:** lau **Leisure:** P

Lathum Gelderland

Mars Marsweg 6, 6988 0313 631131 0313 631435
website: www.campingdemars.nl
Divided into pitches on level meadowland beside a dammed tributary of River Ijssel.
Turn off Arnhem-Doesberg road N of village & continue W for 1.7km.
Open: Apr-Oct **Site:** 10HEC **Prices:** 3.60 1.75 3.25 3.25 **Facilities:** **Services:** lau **Leisure:** L

Luttenberg Overijssel

Luttenberg Heuvelweg 9, 8105
0572 301405 0572 301757
e-mail: info@luttenberg.nl **website:** www.luttenberg.nl
A large holiday park with spacious, well-defined pitches separated by bushes. Wide variety of recreational facilities.
Camping Card Compulsory
Open: Apr-Sep **Site:** 12HEC **Prices:** pitch 20-23 (incl 2 persons) **Facilities:** **Services:** lau **Leisure:** P

Maarn Utrecht

Laag-Kanje Laan van Laag-Kanje 1, 3951
0343 441348 0343 443295
e-mail: info@laagkanje.nl **website:** www.laagkanje.nl
Situated 500m from the lake.
2km NE.
Open: Apr-Sep **Site:** 28HEC **Prices:** pitch 12.20 (incl 2 persons) **Facilities:** **Services:** lau **Off-site:** L

Markelo Overijssel

Hessenheem Potdijk 8, 7475 0547 361200 0547 363647
Situated near a swimming pool.
3km NE.
Open: All year **Site:** 30HEC **Facilities:** **Services:** lau **Leisure:** P

Mijnden Utrecht

Mijnden Bloklaan 22a, 1231 AZ
0294 233165 0294 233402
e-mail: info@mijnden.nl **website:** www.mijnden.nl
Situated directly on the Loosdrechtse Plassen lake with good sporting facilities.
Take A2 from Utrecht to Amsterdam. Exit at Hilversum, after bridge turn right, drive through Loenen & turn left.
Open: 25 Mar-3 Oct **Site:** 25HEC **Prices:** 4 3 3-12 3-12 pitch 3.50-5.50 (incl 2 persons) **Facilities:** **Services:** lau **Leisure:** P **Off-site:** L

Neede Gelderland

Eversman Bliksteeg 1, 7161 0545 291906
Situated in a quiet position, surrounded by trees.
W of town.
Open: Apr-Sep **Site:** 3.8HEC **Facilities:** **Services:** lau **Leisure:** P

Noord Scharwoude Noord-Holland

Molengroet Molengroet 1, 1723
0226 393444 0226 391426
e-mail: info@molengroet.nl **website:** www.molengroet.nl
Site with modern facilities within easy reach of the beach and the Geestmerambacht water park.
Signed on N245.
Open: Apr-Oct **Site:** 11HEC **Prices:** pitch 21.50-24.50 (incl 2 persons) **Facilities:** **Services:** lau **Off-site:** LPS

Nunspeet Gelderland

Vossenberg Groenlaantje 25, 8071 0341 252458
Open: Apr-1 Nov **Site:** 3.6HEC **Facilities:** **Services:** lau **Off-site:** LP

Putten Gelderland

Strand Nulde Strandboulevard 27, 3882
0341 361304 0341 361210
Open: Apr-Oct **Site:** 8HEC **Facilities:** **Services:** lau **Leisure:** L **Off-site:** P

Reutum Overijssel

De Molenhof Kleijsenweg 7, 7667
0541 661165 0541 662032
e-mail: molenhof@wxs.nl **website:** www.demolenhof.nl
A large family site in wooded surroundings with plenty of modern facilities.
S of Reutum off N343 towards Weerselo.
Open: Apr 3-Oct 3 **Site:** 16HEC **Facilities:** **Services:** lau **Leisure:** P

Rhenen Utrecht

Thymse Berg Nieuwe Veenendaalseweg 229, 3911
0317 612384 0317 618119
e-mail: thymseberg@planet.nl
website: www.thymseberg.nl
N of town.
Open: Apr-Sep **Site:** 10HEC **Prices:** 4 1.20 pitch 5.50-9.50 **Facilities:** **Services:** lau **Leisure:** P **Off-site:** LR

Ruurlo Gelderland

't Sikkeler Sikkelerweg 8, 7261
0573 461221 0573 461586
e-mail: info@sikkeler.nl **website:** www.sikkeler.nl
In a beautiful wooded location with good, modern facilities. Popular with walkers.

4km SW. N315 Ruurlo-Doetinchem.
Open: All year **Site:** 7HEC **Facilities:** **Services:** lau **Off-site:** LP

ST MAARTENSZEE NOORD-HOLLAND

St Maartenszee Westerduinweg 30, 1753
0224 561401 0224 561901
e-mail: info@campingsintmaartenszee.nl
website: www.campingsintmaartenszee.nl
Completely surrounded and divided into pitches by hedges, meadowland on the edge of a wide belt of dunes.
Turn off the Alkmaar to Den Helder road at St Maartensvlotburg towards the sea. Take the road over the dunes for 1.5km then turn right for 300m.
Open: 26Mar-26Sep **Site:** 5HEC **Facilities:** **Services:** lau **Off-site:** LPS

SOEST UTRECHT

King's Home Birkstr 136, 3768
033 4619118 033 4610808
e-mail: camping@kingshome.nl **website:** www.kingshome.nl
Well maintained site with modern facilities in a natural setting on the edge of woodland.
On N221 between Amersfoort & Soest.
Open: All year **Site:** 5HEC **Facilities:** **Services:** lau **Off-site:** P

STEENWIJK OVERIJSSEL

Kom Bultweg 25, 8346 0521 513736 0521 518736
e-mail: info@campingdekom.nl
website: www.campingdekom.nl
Split into two sections, lying near a country house, and surrounded by a beautiful oak forest.
The access road off the Steenwijk-Frederiksoord road is easy to miss.
Open: Apr-Sep **Site:** 12.5HEC
Prices: pitch 16.10-19.20 (incl 2 persons) **Facilities:** **Services:** lau **Leisure:** P

TEXEL (ISLAND OF)

UITDAM NOORD-HOLLAND

Uitdam Zeedijk 2, 1154 020 4031433 020 4033692
e-mail: info@campinguitdam.nl
website: www.campinguitdam.nl
A well-maintained site on the Markermeer adjoining the marina.
Access via N247 Amsterdam-Monnickendam.
Open: Mar-Oct **Site:** 21HEC **Prices:** 4.60 pitch 17.20-21.80 (incl 2 persons) **Facilities:** **Services:** lau **Leisure:** L

URK FLEVOLAND

Hazevreugd Vormtweg 9, 8321
0527 681785 0527 686298
e-mail: info@hazevreugd.nl **website:** www.hazevreugd.nl
A modern family site in wooded surroundings with a wide variety of recreational facilities.
Access via A6.
Open: Apr-Oct **Site:** 12HEC **Prices:** pitch 23-29 (incl 4 persons) **Facilities:** **Services:** lau **Leisure:** P **Off-site:** S

UTRECHT UTRECHT

Berekuil Arienslaan 5, 3573 030 713870 030 721436
In a wooded location beside a lake with well-defined pitches and good facilities.
On N outskirts near motorway to Hilversum.
Open: All year **Site:** 4.5HEC **Facilities:** **Services:** lau **Leisure:** P

VOGELENZANG NOORD-HOLLAND

Vogelenzang Doodweg Tweede 17, 2114 AP
023 5847014 023 5849249
e-mail: camping@vogelenzang.nl
website: www.vogelenzang.nl
1km W.
Open: Etr-15 Sep **Site:** 22HEC **Prices:** 2.90 pitch 13.10 **Facilities:** **Services:** lau **Leisure:** P

WAGENINGEN GELDERLAND

Wielerbaan Zoomweg 7-9, 6705 0317 413964
A friendly family site on the edge of a forest.
Access via A12, then follow signs.
Open: All year **Site:** 7.5HEC **Facilities:** **Services:** lau **Leisure:** P

WEZEP GELDERLAND

Heidehoek Heidehoeksweg 7, 8091
038 3761382 038 3765571
e-mail: heidehoek@info.nl **website:** www.heidehoek.nl
0.5km W of railway station.
Open: Apr-Oct **Site:** 16HEC **Prices:** pitch 27-48 (incl 2 persons) (static)235-485 **Facilities:** **Services:** lau **Leisure:** LP

WIJDENES NOORD-HOLLAND

Het Hof Zuideruitweg 64, 1608
0229 501435 0229 503244
e-mail: info@campinghefhof.nl
website: www.campinghethof.nl
A series of fields in a sheltered position on the shore of the Ijsselmeer.
From A7 exit 8 (Hoorn) follow N506 towards Enkhuizen, then right to Wijdenes & follow camping signs.
Open: 28 Mar-26 Oct **Site:** 3.9HEC **Facilities:** **Services:** lau **Leisure:** LP

WINTERSWIJK GELDERLAND

Twoe Bruggen Meenkmolenweg 11, 7109
0543 565366 0543 565222
e-mail: info@detweebruggen.nl
website: www.detweebruggen.nl
A family site in pleasant wooded surroundings with good, modern facilities.
Open: All year **Site:** 34HEC **Prices:** pitch 9.50-20 (incl 2 persons) **Facilities:** **Services:** lau **Leisure:** LP

SOUTH

AFFERDEN LIMBURG

Klein Canada Dorpsstr 1, 5851
0485 531223 0485 532218
e-mail: info@kleincanada.nl
website: www.kleincanada.nl
Situated among heath and woodland close to the River Meuse.
Open: All year **Site:** 12.5HEC **Prices:** 3.60 pitch 11.70-17.10 (incl 2 persons) (static)197.50-450
Facilities: **Services:** lau
Leisure: P

ARCEN LIMBURG

Maasvallei Dorperheideweg 34, 5944 077 473 1564
In wooded surroundings near the beach, this family site has varied sports facilities and play areas for children.
Off the N271.
Open: All year **Site:** 11HEC **Facilities:** **Services:** **Leisure:** LP **Off-site:** R

ARNEMUIDEN ZEELAND

Witte Raaf Muidenweg 3, 4341
0118 601212 0118 603650
A modern well-maintained site in meadowland, divided into sections by rows of shrubs, ideal for sailing and motor-boat enthusiasts with yacht marina.
Situated on the Veersmeer, N of the Goes-Vlissingen motorway, from Arnemuiden exit follow signs for 5km.
Open: Apr-Sep **Site:** 20HEC **Facilities:** **Services:** lau **Leisure:** L

BAARLAND ZEELAND

Comfort Camping Scheldeoord Landingsweg 1, 4435
0113 639900 0113 639500
e-mail: info@scheldeoord.nl
website: www.scheldeoord.nl
A popular family site in a beautiful location by the Scheldt River.
S of town on the coast.
Open: Apr-Oct **Site:** 16HEC **Facilities:** **Services:** lau **Leisure:** PS

BAARLE NASSAU NOORD-BRABANT

Heimolen Heimolen 6, 5111 EH 0507 9425 0507 7885
e-mail: info@deheimolen.nl
website: www.deheimolen.nl
In a wooded location with good, modern facilities.
1.5km SW.
Open: All year **Site:** 15HEC **Facilities:** **Services:** lau **Off-site:** P

BAARLO LIMBURG

Euroase Parc Napoleonsbaan Ned 4, 5991 NV 077 4771547
Part of a chain of family sites with excellent facilities.
SW of Venlo.
Open: 15 Mar-1 Nov **Site:** 32HEC **Facilities:** **Services:** lau **Leisure:** P

BARENDRECHT ZUID-HOLLAND

Jachthaven de Oude Maas Achterzeedijk 1a, 2991
078 6772445 078 076773013
e-mail: info@deoudemaas.com
website: www.deoudemaas.com
On the banks of the Oude Maas, the site is particularly suitable for families and hikers.
Open: Apr-15 Oct **Site:** 12HEC **Prices:** 3.45 3.45 3.45 3.45 pitch 3.45 (static)252.75 **Facilities:** **Services:** lau **Off-site:**

BERG EN TERBLIJT LIMBURG

Oriëntal Rijksweg 6, 6325 043 6040075 043 6042912
e-mail: info@campingoriental.nl
website: www.campingoriental.nl
On Maastricht-Valkenburg road 3km from Maastricht.
Open: 08 Apr-24 Oct **Site:** 5.5HEC **Prices:** 2.25 pitch 15-19.50 (incl 2 persons) (static)220-505 **Facilities:** **Services:** lau **Leisure:** P **Off-site:**

BERGEYK NOORD-BRABANT

Paal De Paaldreef 14, 5571 0497 571977 0497 577164
e-mail: info@depaal.nl **website:** www.depaal.nl
Campsite especially catering for families with children.
Camping Card Compulsory
Signed.
Open: Mar-Oct **Site:** 41HEC **Prices:** pitch 24-35.50 (incl 2 persons) **Facilities:** **Services:** lau **Leisure:** P **Off-site:** L

BOSSCHENHOOFD NOORD-BRABANT

Langoed de Wildert Pagnevaartdreef 3
0165 312582 0165 310941
website: www.landgoeddewildert.nl
Peaceful location in woodland.
Take A16 towards Breda, exit 16 towards Etten-Leur on A58. Take exit 21 to Bosschenhoofd, pass church on right & campsite is 500m on left.
Open: Apr-Sep **Site:** 15HEC **Prices:** 3.75 pitch 19 **Facilities:** **Services:** lau **Off-site:** P

BOXTEL NOORD-BRABANT

Dennenoord Dennendreef 5, 5282
0411 601280 0411 601393
e-mail: info@dennenoord.nl
website: www.dennenoord.nl
Level, grassy site with hedging and groups of trees. Leisure activities organised for adults and young people. Soundproof disco.
Turn off the N2 at Esch in direction of Osterwijk. Follow signs.
Open: Apr-1 Oct **Site:** 7HEC **Facilities:** **Services:** lau **Leisure:** P

BRESKENS ZEELAND

Napoleon Hoeve Zandertje 30, 4511
0117 383838 0117 383550
e-mail: info@napoleonhoeve.nl
website: www.napoleonhoeve.nl
A family site with access to the beach.
Open: All year **Site:** 13HEC **Facilities:** **Services:** lau **Leisure:** PS

Schoneveld Schoneveld 1, 4511 HR
0117 383220 0117 383650
e-mail: schoneveld@zeelandnet.nl
website: www.zeelandnet.nl/schoneveld
Camping Card Compulsory
3km S at the beach.
Open: All year **Site:** 14HEC **Prices:** pitch 20-35 (incl 4 persons) **Facilities:** **Services:** lau **Leisure:** PS

BRIELLE ZUID-HOLLAND

Krabbeplaat Oude Veerdam 4, 3231
0181 412363 0181 412093
e-mail: info@krabbeplaat.nl
website: www.krabbeplaat.com
On level ground scattered with trees and groups of bushes. It has asphalt drives. Nearest campsite to the coast and ferries.
Signed.
Open: Apr-Oct **Site:** 18HEC **Prices:** pitch 13 (incl 2 persons) **Facilities:** **Services:**

BROEKHUIZENVORST LIMBURG

Kasteel Ooyen Blitterswijkseweg 2, 5871
077 4631307 077 4632765
e-mail: info@kasteelooijen.nl **website:** www.kasteelooijen.nl
Open: Apr-Oct **Site:** 16HEC **Prices:** pitch 15.15-21.60 (incl 2 persons) **Facilities:** **Services:** lau **Leisure:** P

BROUWERSHAVEN ZEELAND

Osse Blankersweg 4, 4318 0111 691513 0111 691058
e-mail: denosse@zeelandnet.nl **website:** ww.campingdenosse.nl
An attractive site with good water-sports facilities.
Open: Apr-Oct **Site:** 8.3HEC **Facilities:** **Services:** lau **Leisure:** P **Off-site:** L

BURGH-HAAMSTEDE ZEELAND

Zeeland Camping Ginsterveld J J Boeijesweg 45, 4328 HA
0111 651590 0111 653040
e-mail: ginsterveld@zeelandcamping.nl
website: www.zeelandcamping.nl/ginsterveld
A family holiday centre with well-defined pitches on level ground and plenty of recreational facilities.
NW of town, signed from R107.
Open: Apr-Sep **Site:** 14HEC **Prices:** pitch 18-29 (incl 2 persons) **Facilities:** **Services:** lau **Leisure:** P **Off-site:** S

DELFT ZUID-HOLLAND

Delftse Hout Korftlaan 5, 2616
015 2130040 015 2131293
e-mail: info@delftsehout.nl **website:** www.delftsehout.nl
On a level meadow surrounded by woodland close to the lake.
Camping Card Compulsory
1.6km E of A13. Signed.
Open: All year **Site:** 5.5HEC **Prices:** pitch 17.80-24 (incl 2 persons) (static)260-460 **Facilities:** **Services:** lau **Leisure:** P **Off-site:** L

ECHT LIMBURG

Marisheem Brugweg 89, 6102
04754 481458 04754 488018
e-mail: info@marisheem.nl **website:** www.marisheem.nl
The site is well-kept and lies E of the village.
From town 2.2km towards Echterbosch & border, then turn left.
Open: Apr-Oct **Site:** 12HEC **Prices:** 7.85 8 8 **Facilities:** **Services:** lau **Leisure:** P

EERSEL NOORD-BRABANT

Ter Spegelt Postelseweg 88, 5521
0497 512016 0497 514162
e-mail: info@terspegelt.nl **website:** www.terspegelt.nl
A large family-orientated site with good recreational facilities.
Open: Mar-Nov **Site:** 63HEC **Facilities:** **Services:** lau **Leisure:** LP

'S-GRAVENZANDE ZUID-HOLLAND

Jagtveld Nieuwlandsedijk 41, 2691
0174 413479 0174 422127
e-mail: info@jagtveld.nl **website:** www.jagtveld.nl
A quiet family site on level meadowland with good facilities.
Access via N220.
Open: Apr-Sep **Site:** 3.3HEC **Prices:** 3.25 3.25 8 8 **Facilities:** **Services:** lau **Off-site:** S

GROEDE ZEELAND

Groede Zeeweg 1, 4503
0117 371384 0117 372277
e-mail: info@campinggroede.nl
website: www.campinggroede.nl
A large family site with a wide variety of leisure facilities and close to the beach.
Open: Apr-Oct **Site:** 20HEC **Prices:** pitch 14-26.25 **Facilities:** **Services:** lau **Leisure:** S

HAAG, DEN (THE HAGUE) ZUID-HOLLAND

Kijkduinpark Machiel Vrijenhoeklaan 450, 2555 NW
070 4482100 070 3232457
e-mail: info@kijkduinpark.nl **website:** www.kijkduinpark.nl
A modern chalet and camp site in an extensive leisure park close to the beach with excellent recreational facilities
Open: All year **Site:** 40HEC **Prices:** pitch 17-38 (incl 6 persons) **Facilities:** **Services:** lau **Leisure:** P **Off-site:** S

HELLEVOETSLUIS ZUID-HOLLAND

't Weergors Zuiddyk 2, 3221
0181 312430 0181 311010
e-mail: weergors@publishnet.nl **website:** www.weergors.nl
A pleasant, peaceful site on a level meadow close to the beach. A good overnight stopping place or holiday site.
Open: Apr-Oct **Site:** 9.7HEC **Prices:** 3.50 2.50 6 6 (static)200-400 **Facilities:** **Services:** lau **Leisure:** S

HENGSTDIJK ZEELAND

Vogel Vogelweg 4, 4585 0114 681625 0114 682527
e-mail: info@de-vogel.nl **website:** www.de-vogel.nl
Open: All year **Site:** 33HEC **Facilities:** **Services:** lau **Leisure:** LP

HERPEN NOORD-BRABANT

Herperduin Schaykseweg 12, NL-5373
0486 411383 0486 416171
e-mail: info@herperduin.nl **website:** www.herperduin.nl
Situated in extensive woodland.
Access from the 's-Hertogenbosch-Nijmegen motorway. Take the Ravenstein exit towards Herpen, then towards Bergheim/Oss.
Open: Apr-20 Oct **Site:** 7HEC **Facilities:** **Services:** lau **Leisure:** P

HILVARENBEEK NOORD-BRABANT

Beekse Bergen Beekse Bergen 1, 5081 NJ
031 5360032 031 5366716
e-mail: beeksebergen@libema.nl
website: www.beeksebergen.com
Situated in a holiday centre in the Brabant forest on the edge of a safari park. Lake suitable for swimming. Various facilities.
10km S of Tilburg.
Open: 30 Mar-4 Nov **Site:** 400HEC **Facilities:** **Services:** lau **Leisure:** LP

HOEK ZEELAND

Braakman Holiday Park Middenweg 1, 4542 PN
0115 481730 0115 482077
e-mail: info@braakman.co.uk **website:** www.braakman.co.uk
A large family site situated on the edge of extensive nature reserves. The pitches are shaded by woodland and there is direct access to the Braakman lake. Plenty of recreational facilities.

contd.

4km W of town. Signed from N61.
Open: All year **Site:** 80HEC **Prices:** pitch 25-65 (incl 5 persons) **Facilities:** **Services:** lau **Leisure:** LP

HOEK VAN HOLLAND ZUID-HOLLAND

Hoek van Holland Wierstraat 100, 3151
0174 382550 0174 310210
e-mail: camping.hvh@hetnet.nl
website: www.campinghoekvanholland.nl
On grass, surrounded by bushes and paved drives.
Approaching from the N, turn off the E36 to the beach.
Open: 15 Mar-12 Oct **Site:** 5.5HEC **Facilities:** **Services:** lau **Off-site:** S

HOEVEN NOORD-BRABANT

Bosbad Hoeven Oude Antwerpse Postbaan 81b, 4741
0165 502570 0165 504254
e-mail: info@bosbadhoeven.nl
website: www.bosbadhoeven.nl
Extensive site with good, modern facilities.
Between Breda and Roosendaal W of Etten-Leur.
Open: 23 Mar-4 Sep **Site:** 35HEC **Prices:** pitch 16-22.50 (incl 2 persons) **Facilities:** **Services:** lau **Leisure:** P

HOOGERHEIDE NOORD-BRABANT

FamilyLand Groene Papegaai 19, 4631
0164 613155 0164 615216
In pleasant wooded surroundings, the site, as its name suggests has fine facilities for both adults and children with all kinds of sports and entertainments available.
2km from junction of A30 and A58.
Open: All year **Site:** 25HEC **Facilities:** **Services:** lau **Leisure:** P

KAMPERLAND ZEELAND

Roompot Mariapolderseweg 1, 4493
0113 374000 0113 374170
e-mail: info@roompot.nl **website:** www.roompot.nl
A level, well-maintained site with a private beach.
Turn off Kamperland-Wissenkerke road N for 0.5km.
Open: All year **Site:** 33HEC **Prices:** pitch 22-35 (incl 5 persons) **Facilities:** **Services:** lau **Leisure:** PS

KATWIJK AAN ZEE ZUID-HOLLAND

Noordduinen Campingweg 1, 2221
071 4025295 071 4033977
Family site set among dunes close to the sea.
Access via Hoorneslaan.
Open: mid Mar-Oct **Site:** 11HEC **Facilities:** **Services:** lau **Leisure:** S

KORTGENE ZEELAND

Zeeland Camping de Paardekreek Havenweg 1, 4484
0113 302051 0113 302280
e-mail: paardekreek@zeelandcamping.nl
website: www.zeelandcamping.nl/paardekreek
A municipal site next to the Veerse Meer canal.
Turn off the Zierikzee-Goes trunk road at the Chevron filling station towards Kortgene, continue through the village & continue SW.
Open: Apr-Oct **Site:** 10HEC **Prices:** pitch 16.80-30.90 (static)245-560 **Facilities:** **Services:** lau **Leisure:** LP

KOUDEKERKE ZEELAND

Dishoek Dishoek 2, 4371 0118 551348 0118 552990
e-mail: info@campingdishoek.nl **website:** www.roompct.nl
W on Vlissingen-Dibhoek road.
Open: 18 Mar-23 Oct **Site:** 6HEC **Prices:** pitch 22-36 (static)245-695 **Facilities:** **Services:** lau **Off-site:** S

Duinzicht Strandweg 7, 4371 PK
0118 551397 0118 553222
e-mail: info@campingduinzicht.nl
website: www.campingduinzicht.nl
A small family site with good facilities.
1.5km SW of Koudekerke.
Open: Apr-Oct **Site:** 6.5HEC **Prices:** pitch 15.30-16.35 (incl 2 persons) **Facilities:** **Services:** lau **Off-site:** S

LAGE MIERDE NOORD-BRABANT

Vakantlecentrum de Hertenwei Wellenseind 7-9, 5094
013 5091295
website: www.hertenwei.nl
Pleasant wooded site with modern facilities.
Camping Card Compulsory
2km N on N269 Tilburg-Reusel.
Open: All year **Site:** 20HEC **Prices:** pitch 19.15-32.75 (incl 2 persons) **Facilities:** **Services:** lau **Leisure:** P

LANDGRAAF LIMBURG

Bousberg Boomweg 10, 6370
045 5311213 045 5323143
NW towards Kakert.
Open: Apr-Oct **Site:** 7.5HEC **Facilities:** **Services:** lau **Leisure:** P

LUYKSGESTEL NOORD-BRABANT

Zwarte Bergen Zwarte Bergen Dreef 1, 5575
0497 541373 0497 542673
e-mail: info@zwartebergen.nl **website:** www.zwartebergen.nl
The site is isolated and very quiet, in a pine forest.
From Eindhoven through Valkenswaard & Bergiejkl. Signed.
Open: All year **Site:** 25.5HEC **Facilities:** **Services:** lau **Leisure:** P **Off-site:** L

MAASBREE LIMBURG

BroeBronne Lange Heide 9, 5993PB
077 4652360 077 4652095
e-mail: info@breebronne.nl
website: www.breebronne.nl
A family site in quiet surroundings with good facilities.
On the E3 just before Venlo, on the border with Germany.
Open: All year **Site:** 23HEC **Facilities:** **Services:** lau **Leisure:** LP

MAASTRICHT LIMBURG

Dousberg Dousbergweg 102, 6216
043 3432171 043 3430556
e-mail: dousbergcamping@dousberg.nl
website: www.dousberg.nl
A modern site with good facilities.
From the Eindhoven-Liège motorway follow sings for Hasselt, then signs to the site.
Open: Apr-Oct **Site:** 10HEC **Facilities:** **Services:** lau **Off-site:** P

MIDDELBURG Zeeland

Middelburg Koninginnelaan 55, 4335
0118 625395 0118 625395
e-mail: campingmiddelburg@komnaarons.nl
website: www.campingmiddelburg.nl
On meadowlands surrounded by trees and bushes.
On W outskirts of town.
Open: Etr-15 Oct **Site:** 3.4HEC **Prices:** 3.90 3.70 4.65 3-4.65 (static)165-370 **Facilities:** **Services:** lau **Off-site:** PS

MIERLO Noord-Brabant

Wolfsven Patrijslaan 4, 5731 0492 661661
Large campsite with wooded areas and several lakes. Asphalt drives.
Open: All year **Site:** 70HEC **Facilities:** **Services:** lau **Leisure:** LP

NIEUWVLIET Zeeland

Pannenschuur Zeedijk 19, 4504
0117 372300 0117 371415
e-mail: info@pannenschuur.nl
website: www.pannenschuur.nl
A modern site with good facilities. Close to the beach.
NW of town. Signed.
Open: All year **Site:** 14HEC **Facilities:** **Services:** lau **Leisure:** PS

NOORDWIJK AAN ZEE Zuid-Holland

Club Soleil Kraaierslaan 7, 2204
0252 374225 0252 376450
e-mail: info@clubsoleil.nl **website:** www.clubsoleil.nl
In a pleasant situation near bulb fields and the sea.
Signed.
Open: Apr-Nov **Site:** 5.5HEC **Prices:** pitch 39 **Facilities:** **Services:** lau **Leisure:** P **Off-site:** LS

Jan de Wit Kapelleboslaan 10, 2204
0252 372485 0252 340140
e-mail: camjam@xs4all.nl
website: www.campingjandewit.nl
A well-equipped family site in a wooded location 2km from the beach.
Open: 15 Mar-Sep **Site:** 6HEC **Facilities:** **Services:** lau **Off-site:** LS

OISTERWIJK Noord-Brabant

Reebok Duinenweg 4, 5062 013 5282309 013 5217592
e-mail: info@dereebok.nl
website: www.dereebok.nl
Situated in a large pine forest, hardly fenced off and impossible to overlook. In attractive surroundings with numerous small lakes.
SE of town.
Open: 15 Mar-Oct **Site:** 8HEC **Facilities:** **Services:** lau **Off-site:** LP

OOSTERHOUT Noord-Brabant

Katjeskelder Katjeskelder 1, 4904
0162 453539 0162 454090
e-mail: kkinfo@katjeskelder.nl
website: www.katjeskelder.nl
A large, modern family site with good sanitary and recreational facilities.
Access via A27 Breda-Utrecht, exit 17 & follow signs.
Open: All year **Site:** 25HEC **Prices:** 24.50-38 **Facilities:** **Services:** lau **Leisure:** P **Off-site:**

OOSTKAPELLE Zeeland

Dennenbos Duinweg 64, 4356
0118 581310 0118 583773
e-mail: dennenbos@zeelandnet.nl
website: www.dennenbos.nl
A well-maintained family site in a wooded loaction, 500m from the beach.
Open: Mar-Nov **Site:** 3HEC **Facilities:** **Services:** lau **Leisure:** PS **Off-site:**

In de Bongerd Brouwerijstr 13, 4356
0118 581510 0118 581510
e-mail: info@campingindebongerd.nl
website: www.campingindebongerd.nl
A well-kept family campsite, set in a meadow with hedges and apple trees. There are fine recreational facilities and the beach is within easy reach.
500m S.
Open: 30Mar-28Oct **Site:** 7.4HEC **Prices:** 3.50 pitch 14.50-23 (incl 2 persons) (static)140-360 **Facilities:** **Services:** lau **Leisure:** PS

Ons Buiten Aagtekerkeseweg 2a, 4356
0118 581813 0118 583771
e-mail: onsbuiten@zeelandcamping.nl
website: www.zeelandcamping.nl/onsbuiten
In a beautiful location with a wide choice of recreational activities.
From church S towards Grijpskerke, turn W & continue 400m.
Open: 18 Mar-Oct **Site:** 11.5HEC **Prices:** 3.75-4 pitch 16.75-35.25 (incl 2 persons) pp4 **Facilities:** **Services:** lau **Leisure:** PS

Pekelinge Landmetersweg 1, 4356
0118 582820 0118 583782
e-mail: depekelinge@zeelandcamping.nl
website: www.zeelandcamping.nl/depekelinge
The on-site facilities are open in high season.
Open: Apr-Oct **Site:** 15HEC **Facilities:** **Services:** lau **Leisure:** P **Off-site:** S

OOSTVOORNE Zuid-Holland

Kruininger Gors Gorspl 2, 3233
0181 482711 0181 485957
e-mail: info@kruiningergors.nl
website: www.kruiningergors.nl
A small site, divided by hedges, close to the lake.
Access via N15.
Open: Apr-Sep **Site:** 108HEC **Prices:** 2.70 pitch 14.90-16.90 (incl 2 persons) **Facilities:** **Services:** lau **Leisure:** LS

OUDDORP Zuid-Holland

Klepperstee Vrijheidsweg 1, 3253
0187 681511 0187 683060
e-mail: info@klepperstee.com
website: www.klepperstee.com
On level meadow divided by hedges and trees.
Access via N57 Rotterdam-Vlissingen exit Ouddorp.
Open: Apr-Oct **Site:** 40HEC **Prices:** pitch 28-33 (incl 4 persons) **Facilities:** **Services:** lau **Leisure:** P **Off-site:** LPS

PLASMOLEN LIMBURG

Eldorado Witteweg 18, 6586 024 6961914 024 6963017
e-mail: info@eldorado-mook.nl
Well equipped site in wooded surroundings on the Mooker See.
S of N271.
Open: Apr-1 Oct **Site:** 6HEC **Facilities:** **Services:** lau **Leisure:** L

RENESSE ZEELAND

International Scharendijkseweg 8, 4325
0111 461391 0111 462571
e-mail: info@camping-international.net
website: www.camping-international.net
On grassland, between rows of tall shrubs and trees. Between dyke road and main road to Scharendijk on E outskirts of village.
Open: Mar-Nov **Site:** 3HEC **Prices:** 4.25 2.50 4 4 **Facilities:** **Services:** lau
Off-site: S

Wyde Blick Hogezoom 112, 4325
0111 468888 0111 468889
e-mail: dewijdeblick@zeelandcamping.nl
website: www.zeelandcamping.nl/dewijdeblick
A family site with good facilities.
Well signed.
Open: All year **Site:** 10HEC **Prices:** pitch 17-27.50 (incl 2 persons) (static)280-495 **Facilities:** **Services:** lau **Leisure:** P **Off-site:** S

RETRANCHEMENT ZEELAND

De Zwinhoeve Duinweg 1, 4525
0117 392120 0117 392248
e-mail: info@zwinhoeve.net
website: www.zwinhoeve.net
In a beautiful position backed by dunes with easy access to the fine beaches of the Zeeuws-Vlaanderen coast.
Open: All year **Site:** 9HEC **Facilities:** **Services:** lau **Leisure:** S **Off-site:** P

RIJNSBURG ZUID-HOLLAND

Koningshof Elsgeesterweg 8, 2231
071 4026051 071 4021336
e-mail: info@koningshofholland.nl
website: www.koningshofholland.nl
Modern site on level meadow near the flower fields.
1km N. Signed.
(A44 exit 7 to Rijnsburg) **Open:** All year **Site:** 7.5HEC **Prices:** pitch 19.50-29.50 (incl 2 persons)
Facilities: **Services:** lau
Leisure: P **Off-site:** S

ROCKANJE ZUID-HOLLAND

Waterboscamping Duinrand 11, 3235
0181 401900 0181 404233
e-mail: info@waterboscamping.nl
website: www.waterboscamping.nl
A small, pleasant site near the beach. **Motor caravans and tents only.**
Access via N15.
Open: Apr-Sep **Site:** 7HEC **Prices:** 2.05 pitch 17.10-21.10 (incl 2 persons) **Facilities:**
Services: lau **Off-site:** S

ROERMOND LIMBURG

Hatenboer Hatenboer 51, 6041
0475 336727 0475 310113
Situated in a water park with access to all water sports.
Camping Card Compulsory
Leave A68 Roermond-Eindhoven at Hatenboer exit.
Open: Apr-1 Nov **Site:** 15HEC **Facilities:** **Services:** lau **Leisure:** LR **Off-site:** P

Marina Oolderhuuske Oolderhuuske 1, 6041
0475 588686 0475 582652
e-mail: info@oolderhuuske.nl **website:** www.oolderhuuske.nl
A well-equipped site within the marina area on the Maasplassen.
Open: 28 Mar-1 Nov **Site:** 6HEC
Prices: 2.50 pitch 18-23 (static)250-400 **Facilities:** **Services:** lau **Leisure:** LPR

ROOSENDAAL NOORD-BRABANT

Zonneland Tufvaartsestr 6, 4709 01656 365429
e-mail: info@zonneland.nl **website:** www.zonneland.nl
S of town towards the Belgian border.
Open: Mar-15 Oct **Site:** 14HEC **Prices:** 3 2 5 5 **Facilities:** **Services:** lau **Leisure:** P

ST ANTHONIS NOORD-BRABANT

Ullingse Bergen Bosweg 36, 5845
0485 388566 0485 388569
e-mail: info@ullingsebergen.nl **website:** www.ullingsebergen.nl
A family site in natural wooded surroundings with good facilities for children.
W of town.
Open: Apr-Oct **Site:** 11HEC **Facilities:** **Services:** lau **Leisure:** P

ST OEDENRODE NOORD-BRABANT

Kienehoef Zwembadweg 35-37, 5491
0413 472877 0413 477033
e-mail: info@kienehoef.nl **website:** www.kienehoef.nl
An exceptionally well-appointed site in a peaceful rural setting.
NW towards Boxtel.
Open: All year **Site:** 4HEC **Facilities:** **Services:** lau **Leisure:** P **Off-site:**

SEVENUM LIMBURG

Schatberg Midden Peelweg 5, 5975
077 4677777 077 4677799
e-mail: receptie@schatberg.nl **website:** www.schatberg.nl
A well-appointed family site in wooded surroundings with plenty of leisure facilities.
SW towards Eindhoven. A67 exit at junct 38 & follow signs for Schatberg.
Open: All year **Site:** 86HEC **Prices:** 10.75-32 pitch 10.75-32 (incl 4 persons) pp4.65 **Facilities:** **Services:** lau **Leisure:** LP

SLUIS ZEELAND

Meldoorn Hoogstr 68, 4524 0117 461662 0117 461662
website: www.campingdemeidoorn.nl
In a meadow surrounded by rows of deciduous trees.
N on the road to Zuidzande.
Open: 26 Mar-15 Oct **Site:** 6.5HEC **Facilities:** **Services:** lau **Off-site:**

VALKENBURG LIMBURG

Europa Couberg 29, 6301 043 6013097 043 6013525
A quiet family site within easy reach of the town.

SW of town.
)pen: Apr-Oct **Site:** 10HEC **Facilities:** **Services:** lau **Leisure:** P

VENRAY LIMBURG

le Oude Barrier Maasheseweg 93, 5802 0478 582305
ebsite: www.de-oude-barrier.nl
quiet site recommended for young children.
NE of town.
)pen: Apr-Sep **Site:** 14HEC **Facilities:**
ervices: lau **Leisure:** P **Off-site:**

VROUWENPOLDER ZEELAND

)ranjezon Koningin Emmaweg 16a, 4354
0118 591549 0118 591920
-mail: oranjezon@oranjezon.nl **website:** www.oranjezon.nl
Vell-kept between tall, thick hedges and bushes. SW of the
illage.
Camping Card Compulsory
Drive towards Oostkapelle for 2.5km, then turn N for 300m.
)pen: Apr-Oct **Site:** 9.8HEC **Prices:** 31 pitch
31 (incl 4 persons) **Facilities:**
Services: lau **Leisure:** PS

Zandput Vroondijk 9, 4354 0118 597210 0118 591954
-mail: info@roompot.nl **website:** www.roompot.nl
On level ground behind dunes and close to the beach.
2km N.
Open: 18 Mar-23 Oct **Site:** 12HEC **Prices:** 4
pitch 19-44 (static)265-730 **Facilities:**
Services: lau **Off-site:** LS

WASSENAAR ZUID-HOLLAND

Duinhorst Buurtweg 135, 2244
070 3242270 070 3246053
e-mail: info@duinhorst.nl **website:** www.duinhorst.nl
A peaceful site in wooded surroundings with modern facilities and opportunities for sports and entertainment.
Open: Apr-1 Oct **Site:** 11HEC **Prices:** 4
2.50 3.50 3-3.50 **Facilities:**
Services: lau **Leisure:** P

Duinrell Duinrell 1, 2242 070 5155255 070 5155371
website: www.duinrell.nl
Very well-maintained site with additional recreation centre which is free for campers. NW in area of same name. Some noise from aircraft. Area restricted to cars. Naturist beach nearby.
Turn off A44 Den Haag-Leiden at T-lights in Wassenaar dorp' & camping signs.
Open: All year **Site:** 110HEC **Prices:** 9.15
pitch 8.25-12 **Facilities:** **Services:**
lau **Leisure:** P **Off-site:** LS

WEERT LIMBURG

Yzeren Man Herenvennenweg 60, 6006
0495 533202 0495 546812
e-mail: info@deyzerenman.nl
website: www.deyzerenman.nl
Well-kept with asphalt drives, in a big nature reserve with zoo, heath and forest.
Off E9.
Open: Apr-1 Nov **Site:** 8.5HEC **Prices:** pitch 19-26 (incl 2 persons) **Facilities:** **Services:**
lau **Leisure:** P **Off-site:** L

WELL LIMBURG

Leukermeer De Kamp 5, 5855 EG
0478 502444 0478 501260
e-mail: info@leukermeer.nl **website:** www.leukermeer.nl
In beautiful surroundings on lake Leukermeer with good modern installations and plenty of leisure facilities.
Signed from N271.
Open: 27 Mar-Oct **Site:** 12HEC **Facilities:**
Services: lau **Leisure:** LP

WEMELDINGE ZEELAND

Linda Oostkanaalweg 4, 4424
0113 621259 0113 622638
e-mail: info@campinglinda.nl **website:** www.campinglinda.nl
On meadowland surrounded by rows of tall shrubs.
Turn opposite bridge in town & continue 100m, over bridge to campsite.
Open: Apr-Nov **Site:** 8HEC **Prices:** 4.50
3.50 6.50 3 (static)4.25 **Facilities:**
Services: lau **Leisure:** S

WESTKAPELLE ZEELAND

Boomgaard Domineeshofweg 1, 4361
0118 571377 0118 572383
A flat grassy site.
Turn off the Middleburg road on the S outskirts of the town, then follow signs.
Open: 27 Mar-24 Oct **Site:** 8HEC **Facilities:**
Services: lau **Leisure:** P **Off-site:** S

ZOUTELANDE ZEELAND

Meerpaal Duinweg 133, 5375 0118 561300
On meadowland hidden behind bushy hedges at the end of a cul-de-sac.
1km SE.
Open: 27 Mar-1 Nov **Site:** 2HEC **Facilities:**
Services: lau **Leisure:** S **Off-site:**

Facilities: -shop -shower -electric points for razors -electric points for caravans -parking by tents permitted -compulsory separate car park **Services:** -café/restaurant -bar -Camping Gaz International -gas other than Camping Gaz -first aid facilities lau-laundry **Leisure:** -swimming L-Lake P-Pool R-River S-Sea **Off-site:** All facilities within 2km

PORTUGAL

This relatively small but once-powerful country lies in the south-western corner of the Iberian peninsula. Portugal's only land frontier is the Spanish border in the east and north.

FACTS AND FIGURES
Area: 92,345 sq km 35,655 sq miles
Population: 10,102,022 (2003)
Capital: Lisbon
Language: Portuguese
IDD code: 351
To call the UK, dial 00 44
Currency: Euro
Local time: GMT (summer GMT+1)
Emergency Services: Police, Fire and Ambulance 112
Banks: Mon-Fri 08.30-15.00
Shops: Mon-Fri 09.00-13.00, 15.00-19.00, Sat 09.00-13.00 (and 15.00-19.00 Dec); shopping centres Mon-Sun 10.00-24.00
Average daily temperature: Lisbon
Jan 11°C Mar 13°C
May 17°C Jul 21°C
Sep20°C Nov14°C
Tourist information:
ICEP/Portuguese Trade and Tourism Office
UK
22-25A Sackville Street, London W1S 3LY
Tel 09063 640610 (premium rate info line)
USA
590 Fifth Avenue, 4th Floor,
New York NY 10036
Tel (212) 719 3985
Tourist info website:
www.portugal.org/tourism

The country is perhaps best known for its 800km (500 miles) of coastline. The Algarve in the south is one of the finest stretches of coastline in Europe, with unique caves and a remoteness that has been preserved despite the development of the area. Inland, the cool valleys and pastures of the Tagus contrast with the wooded mountain slopes of the Minho area in the north.

Generally, the country has a mild climate with the Algarve being very hot in the summer. The language is Portuguese, which developed from Latin and closely resembles Spanish, though English is often spoken in the Algarve.

Mainland Portugal has 198 campsites, most of which are on the coast. A campoing guide is available from Roteiro Campista, Rua do Giestal 5 1ºfte, 1300-274 Lisboa ☎ 213642370 (fax 213619284, e-mail info@roteiro-campista.pt). There are about 22 Orbitur parks in the country, which are privately owned and of a high standard, as indeed are the municipal parks. Orbitur parks are open all year and most of them offer fully equipped bungalows that can accommodate four people. A booklet with details of officially classified parks is produced by the Direcção Geral de Turismo, Palácio Foz, Praça dos Restauradores, Lisboa ☎ 213466307 or 213463624. The Oporto office is at Praça D João I, 25-4 L 222005805 and the Coimbra office is at Largo da Portagem. Otherwise ask for Comissao Municipal de Turismo, Junta de Turismo or Câmara Municipal.

Off-site camping is prohibited You must stay on an organised site. However, when stopping in a motorway rest or service area with a caravan, it is permissible to cook a meal.

HOW TO GET THERE

You can use one of the direct ferry services to Spain and then continue by road. The services and minimum sailing times are **Plymouth to Santander** (24hrs); and **Portsmouth to Bilbao** (27hrs).

DISTANCE

From Santander to Lisboa (Lisbon) is about 920km (570 miles), normally requiring one or two overnight stops. Using the Channel ports, or the Eurotunnel, drive through France and Spain. Enter Spain on the Biarritz-San Sebastian (Donostia) road at the western end of the Pyrénées.

From the Channel ports to Lisboa (Lisbon) is about 2,157km (1,340 miles), which will require three or four overnight stops.

CAR-SLEEPER TRAINS

Summer services are available from **Calais** to Avignon, Brive, Narbonne, Nice and Toulouse, and from **'s-Hertogenbosch** (the Netherlands) to Avignon.

MOTORING & GENERAL

The information given here is specific to Portugal. It **must** be read in conjunction with the Essential Information for Motoring section, which covers regulations that are common to many countries.

Portuguese law requires that everyone carries **photographic** proof of identity at all times.

British Embassy/Consulates*

The British Embassy is located at rua de São Bernardo 33, 1249-082 Lisboa ☎ 213924000; consular section ☎ 213924188. There is a British Consulate in Porto (Oporto) and one with an Honorary Consul in Portimão.

Children in Cars

Children under 12 cannot travel as front-seat passenger unless seated in an approved child seat or if the car is a two-seater; children under 3 must use an approved restraint system. See Essential Information for Motoring section under **Passengers** and **Seat Belts**.

Currency

The **euro** is the currency of Portugal. The Portuguese escudo (PTE) ceased to be legal tender in 2002, though PTE banknotes may still be exchanged at the Portuguese Central Bank (Banco de Portugal) for 20 years.

Dimensions & Weight Restrictions*

Private cars and towed trailers or caravans are restricted to the following dimensions - height 4 metres; width 2.55 metres; length 12 metres. The maximum permitted overall length of vehicle/ trailer or caravan combination is 18.75 metres.

Portuguese traffic regulations stipulate that the total permitted weight of a trailer or caravan cannot exceed one and a half times the total permitted weight of the towing vehicle. For example, a car of 1000kg must not tow a trailer or caravan with a total laden weight of more than 1500kg.

Driving licence*

A valid UK or Republic of Ireland licence is accepted in Portugal. The minimum age at which a visitor may use a temporarily imported motorcycle (over 50cc) or car is 18 years. See also Speed Limits below.

Fiscal Receipt

Visiting motorists should ensure that they can provide proof of ownership (e.g. fiscal receipts) of any goods and electrical equipment (such as computers, cameras, quantities of wine, cigarettes and groceries) carried in the vehicle when entering Portugal.

Both the Brigada de Trânsito (traffic police) and the Brigada Fiscal (fiscal police), part of the Guarda Nacional Republicana (GNR), have the authority to make spot checks on all roads within Portugal and at the frontier with Spain.

Foodstuffs*

If the imported foodstuffs are for personal use, there are no limits when travelling between EU countries.

Lights*

It is compulsory for motorcyclists to use dipped headlights during the day.

Motoring Club

The **Automóvel Club de Portugal** (ACP) has its headquarters at rua Rosa Araüjo 24, Lisboa 1250-195 ☎ 213180100, and has offices in a number of provincial towns. ACP offices are normally open Mon-Fri 09.00-17.00 (to 17.30 Ap-Sep); English and French are spoken.

Website: **www.acp.pt**

Roads

Main roads and most of the important secondary roads are good, as are the mountain roads to the north-east.

Portugal has about 1,125km (700 miles) of motorway (*auto-estrada*) with tolls payable on most sections. Emergency telephones are located every 2km on most motorways.

Speed Limits*

Car/motorcycle	
Built-up areas	50km/h (31mph)
Other roads	90km/h (55mph)
	or 100km/h (62mph)
Motorways	min† 40km/h (24mph)
	max 120km/h (74mph)

continued

Car/caravan/trailer

Built-up areas	50km/h (31mph)
Other roads	70km/h (43mph)
	or 80km/h (49mph)
Motorways	min† 40km/h (24mph)
	max 100km/h (62mph)

†Minimum speeds on motorways apply, except where otherwise signposted.

Both Portuguese residents and visitors to Portugal, who have held a full driving licence for less than one year, must not exceed 90km/h (50mph) when driving on any road or motorway outside built-up areas.

Warning triangle*

The use of a warning triangle is compulsory at all times in the event of an accident or breakdown. Hazard warning lights must also be used but they do not substitute the warning triangle. The triangle must be placed on the road 30 metres (33yds) behind the vehicle and must be clearly visible from 100 metres (109yds).

***Additional information canl be found in the Essential Information for Motoring section.**

Praia da Dona Ana beach

SOUTH

ALBUFEIRA ALGARVE

Albufeira 8200-55 289587629 289587633
e-mail: campingalbufeira@mail.telepac.pt
A modern, purpose-built site with excellent sanitary blocks and a wide variety of sports and entertainment facilities.
1.5km from Albufeira. Signed from N125
Open: All year **Site:** 19HEC **Prices:** 4.85 4.35 485 4.60 **Facilities:** **Services:** lau **Leisure:** P **Off-site:** S

ALVITO BAIXO ALENTEJO

Markádia Barragem de Odivelas, 7920-999
284763141 284763102
website: www.roteiro-campista.pt/Beja/ing/markadia-info-uk.htm
Savannah terrain beside a lake with good, modern facilities.
Leave N121 (Beja-Lisboa) at Ferrera do Alentejo and continue N towards Torrão. From Odivelas follow signs.
Open: All year **Site:** 10HEC **Prices:** 2.30-4.60 2.30-4.60 2.30-4.60 2.30-4.60 **Facilities:** **Services:** lau **Leisure:** L **Off-site:** P

BEJA BAIXO ALENTEJO

CM de Beja Vasco da Gama, 7800-397
284311911 284311911
website: http://www.cmbeja.pt/culturadesporto/parque.htm
Open: All year **Site:** 1HEC **Prices:** 1.07-2.13 0.79-1.57 1.09-3.13 0.79-1.57 **Facilities:** **Services:** lau **Off-site:** LPRS

OLHÃO ARGARVE

Olhão Pinheiros de Marim, 8703
289700300 289700390
e-mail: sbsicamping@mail.telepac.pt
Open: All year **Site:** 10HEC **Prices:** 150-350 120-285 185-425 110-350 **Facilities:** **Services:** **Leisure:** P **Off-site:** S

PORTIMÃO ALGARVE

Da Dourada Alvor, 8500 282459178 282459178
In a parklike area close to the beach with good facilities.
N off Portimão-Lagos road.
Open: All year **Site:** 4HEC **Prices:** 1.75-3.50 1.50-3 2.25-4.50 2.25-4.50 (static)1140-225 **Facilities:** **Services:** lau **Leisure:** LRS **Off-site:** P

PRAIA DA LUZ ALGARVE AT VALVERDE

Orbitur Estrada da Praia da Luz, 8600
282789211 282789213
e-mail: info@orbitur.pt
website: www.orbitur.pt
Well-equipped site with children's playground and tennis courts.
Off N125 Lagos-Cape St Vincent road. 4km from Lagos.
Open: All year **Site:** 9.1HEC **Prices:** 2.70-5.15 2.30-4.65 3.90-6.80 3.20-5.50 **Facilities:** **Services:** lau **Leisure:** P **Off-site:** S

QUARTEIRA ALGARVE

Orbitur Estrada da Forte Santa, 8125
289302826 289302822
e-mail: info@orbitur.pt **website:** www.orbitur.pt
A terraced site at the top of a hill.

Off M125 in Almoncil & follow signs to Quarteira. About 500m before reaching the sea turn left into the camp.
Open: All year **Site:** 9.7HEC **Prices:** 2.70-5.15 2.30-4.65 3.90-6.80 3.20-5.20 **Facilities:** **Services:** lau **Leisure:** P **Off-site:** S

SAGRES ALGARVE

Orbitur Cerro Das Moitas, 8650
282624371 282624445
e-mail: info@orbitur.pt
website: www.orbitur.pt
Site situated in dune and forest area.
1.5km W of N268.
Open: All year **Site:** 6.7HEC **Prices:** 2.30-4.30 1.90-3.80 2.80-5.50 2.50-4.60 **Facilities:** **Services:** lau **Off-site:** S

Facilities: shop shower electric points for razors electric points for caravans parking by tents permitted compulsory separate car park **Services:** café/restaurant bar Camping Gaz International gas other than Camping Gaz first aid facilities lau-laundry **Leisure:** swimming L-Lake P-Pool R-River S-Sea **Off-site:** All facilities within 2km

SANTO ANDRE Baixo Alentejo

Lagoa de Santo Andre 7500 269708550 269708559
e-mail: info@fpcampismo.pt
website: www.fpcampismo.pt
In wooded surroundings with good facilities.
Signed.
Open: 18 Jan-30 Oct **Site:** 15HEC **Facilities:** **Services:** lau **Off-site:** LS

SINES Baixo Alentejo

S Tonnes S Tonnes, 7520 269632105 269862430
In a pine wood on the Cabo de Sines peninsula, to the N of the town.
Follow signs for Algarve/S Tonnes.
Open: All year **Site:** 7.5HEC **Facilities:** **Services:** lau **Off-site:** S

VILA DO BISPO Algarve
At PRAIA DE SALEMA (7.5km SE)

Quinta dos Carriços 8650 282695201 28265122
e-mail: quintacarrico@oninet.pt
A well-equipped site with good facilities. There is a naturist section in a separate valley with its own facilities.
Open: All year **Site:** 20HEC **Prices:** 4.20 4.20 5.90 4.20-5.20 **Facilities:** **Services:** lau **Off-site:** S

VILA NOVA DE MILFONTES Baixo Alentejo

Parque de Campismo de Milfontes 7645
283996104 283996104
e-mail: parquemilfontes@netc.pt
website: www.roteiro-campista.pt/beja/milfontes.htm
Open: All year **Site:** 6.5HEC **Facilities:** **Services:** lau **Off-site:** RS

NORTH

CAMINHA Minho

Orbitur Mata do Camarido, 4910
258921295 258921473
e-mail: info@orbitur.pt
website: http://www.orbitur.pt
On undulating sandy ground with trees.
Turn off N13 at Km89.7 W along the Rio Minho for 800m, then turn left.
Open: 16 Jan-30 Nov **Site:** 2.1HEC **Prices:** 2.20-3.90 1.80-3.60 2.70-4.95 2.30-4.05 **Facilities:** **Services:** lau **Leisure:** S **Off-site:** S

CAMPO DO GERES Minho

Cerdeira 4840 253351005 253353315
e-mail: parque.cerdeira@portugalmail.pt
In a picturesque wooded location with mature oak trees surrounding the pitches.
Camping Card Compulsory
Open: All year **Site:** 5.1HEC **Facilities:** **Services:** lau **Off-site:** LR

MATOSINHOS Douro Litoral
At ANGEIRAS (12km N)

Orbitur Angeiras, 4455-039 229270571 229271178
e-mail: info@orbitur.pt
website: www.orbitur.pt
A modern, well-kept site in a pine wood on a hill overlooking the sea.
W of the N13 at x-roads at Km12.1, E of Vila do Pinheiro & towards the sea for 5km.
Open: All year **Site:** 7HEC **Prices:** 2.40-4.40 2.10-3.95 3.30-5.70 2.80-4.75 **Facilities:** **Services:** lau **Leisure:** P **Off-site:** S

MONDIM DE BASTO Minho

Mondim de Basto 4880-187 255381650 255381650
e-mail: ccporto@sapo.pt **website:** www.ccporto.pt
In wooded surroundings beside the River Olo.
Signed.
Open: Feb-Nov **Site:** 3HEC **Facilities:** **Services:** lau **Leisure:** R **Off-site:**

PÓVOA DE VARZIM Douro Litoral

Rio Alto Estela-Rio Alto, 4570-275
252615699 252615599
e-mail: info@orbitur.pt
website: www.orbitur.pt
Situated near dunes 150m from the sea.
Off NX111 towards Viana.
Open: All year **Site:** 7.9HEC **Prices:** 2.50-4.65 2.30-4.55 3.90-6.40 3.20-5.05 **Facilities:** **Services:** lau **Leisure:** PS **Off-site:** S

VIANA DO CASTELO Minho

Orbitur Cabedelo, 4900-161
258322167 258321946
e-mail: info@orbitur.pt
website: www.orbitur.pt
A well-equipped site with direct access to a sandy beach.
Approach via N13 Porto-Viana do Castelo.
Open: All year **Site:** 3HEC **Prices:** 2.40-4.40 1.20-3.95 3.30-5.70 2.80-4.75 **Facilities:** **Services:** lau **Leisure:** PS

VILA NOVA DE GAIA Douro Litoral

Orbitur Madalena, 4405-736 227122520 227122534
e-mail: info@orbitur.pt
website: www.orbitur.pt
Well equipped site in a pine wood 500m from Madalena beach.
Open: All year **Site:** 24HEC **Prices:** 2.40-4.40 2.10-3.95 3.30-5.70 2.80-4.75 **Facilities:** **Services:** lau **Leisure:** P **Off-site:** S

VILA REAL Tras-Os-Montes Alto Douro

Parque Campismo de Vila Real r Dr-Manuel Cardona, 5000
259324724
In the E part of town off N2 by Galp filling station. Site in 300m near new school.
Open: 16 Jan-15 Dec **Site:** 4HEC **Facilities:** **Services:** lau **Off-site:** PR

CENTRAL

ABRANTES Ribatejo

Castelo do Bode Martinchel, 2200
241849262 241849244
e-mail: castelo.bode@fcmportugal.com
website: www.fcmportugal.com
In natural wooded surroundings.
Signed.
Open: 15 Jan-Oct **Site:** 2.5HEC **Prices:** 2.24-2.80 0.88-1.10 3-3.75 1.56-3.35 **Facilities:** **Services:** lau **Leisure:** R **Off-site:**

ALENQUER ESTREMADURA

Alenquer Estrada Nacional No.9-KM94, 2580-330
☎ 263710375 263710375
e-mail: camping@:dosdin.pt **website:** www.dosdin.pt/agirdin
A modern well-equipped terraced site surrounded by walnut trees. **Reductions available to campers presenting this publication.**
Open: All year **Site:** 1.5HEC **Prices:** 3.20-3.50 pitch 20-25 (static)245-285 **Facilities:** **Services:** lau **Leisure:** P **Off-site:** RS

ARGANIL BEIRA LITORAL

Arganil Sarzedo, 3300 ☎ 035 205706 035 25423
e-mail: campingma@hotmail.com
website: www.cm-arganil.pt
A pleasant situation among pine trees, close to the River Alva.
On N342-4.
Open: All year **Site:** 2.5HEC **Facilities:** **Services:** lau **Leisure:** R **Off-site:**

CALDAS DA RAINHA ESTREMADURA

Orbitur Foz do Arelho Foz Do Arelho, 2500
☎ 262978683 262978685
e-mail: info@orbitur.pt
website: www.orbitur.pt
Situated in a fine lagoon on the estuary of the Arelho.
3kms SE of Foz do Arelho.
Open: All year **Site:** 6HEC **Prices:** 2.30-4.30 1.90-3.80 2.80-5.50 2.50-4.60 **Facilities:** **Services:** lau **Leisure:** P **Off-site:** S

CASFREIRES BEIRA LITORAL

Quinta Chava Grande 3560-043
☎ 232665552 232665552
e-mail: bert@mail.telepac.pt
website: www.chave-grande.com
A terraced site overlooking a beautiful valley. There are modern installations and leisure facilities.
Open: Apr-15 Oct **Site:** 10HEC **Prices:** 4 3.60 4 4 **Facilities:** **Services:** lau
Leisure: P **Off-site:**

COJA BEIRA LITORAL

Coja 3305 ☎ 235729666 235728945
e-mail: coja@fpcampismo.pt
website: www.fpcampismo.pt
In a wooded location beside the River Alva.
Signed.
Open: 15 Mar-30 Oct **Site:** 3HEC **Facilities:** **Services:** lau **Leisure:** R **Off-site:** R

COSTA DA CAPARICA ESTREMADURA

Orbitur 2825 ☎ 212909710 212919715
e-mail: info@orbitur.pt
website: http://www.orbitur.pt
This site has a small touring section and is 200m from a fine sandy beach.
After crossing the Ponte Sul on the road to Caparica, turn right at 1st T-lights. Campsite 1km on left.
Open: All year **Site:** 5.7HEC **Prices:** 2.50-4.65 2.30-4.55 3.90-6.40 3.20-5.05 **Facilities:** **Services:** lau **Off-site:** S

Facilities: -shop -shower -electric points for razors -electric points for caravans -parking by tents permitted -compulsory separate car park **Services:** -café/restaurant -bar -Camping Gaz International -gas other than Camping Gaz -first aid facilities lau-laundry **Leisure:** -swimming L-Lake P-Pool R-River S-Sea **Off-site:** All facilities within 2km

ÉVORA Alto Alentejo

Orbitur Estrada de Alcacovas, 7000-703
☎ 266705190 ▯ 266709830
e-mail: info@orbitur.pt
website: www.orbitur.pt
In wooded surroundings with good, modern facilities.
➲ *2km S right of road near Km94.5.*
Open: All year **Site:** 3.3HEC **Prices:** 2.40-4.40 2.10-3.95 2.80-5.70 2.80-4.75 **Facilities:** **Services:** lau **Leisure:** P **Off-site:**

ÉVORA DE ALCOBAÇA Estremadura

Rural de Silveira Capuchos, 2460-479 ☎ 262509573
e-mail: silveira.capuchos@clix.pt
In a wooded, rural location.
➲ *3km from Alcobaça on N86.*
Open: May-Sep **Site:** 0.5HEC **Prices:** 3 2 3-4 2-3 **Facilities:** **Services:** lau
Off-site:

FIGUEIRA DA FOZ Beira Litoral

Foz do Mondego Cabedelo, Gala, 3080
☎ 233402740 ▯ 233402749
e-mail: info@fpcampismo.pt
website: www.fpcampismo.pt
Open: 19 Jan- 30 Oct **Site:** 4HEC **Facilities:** **Services:** lau **Leisure:** RS **Off-site:**

Orbitur Gala, 3080 ☎ 233431492 ▯ 233431231
e-mail: info@orbitur.pt
website: www.orbitur.pt
In an enclosed area within a municipal park on top of Guarda hill.
➲ *At Km177, on the NW outskirts of the town, turn left off the N16 Porto road uphill for 500m.*
Open: All year **Site:** 6HEC **Prices:** 2.30-4.30 1.90-3.80 2.80-5.50 2.50-4.60 **Facilities:** **Services:** lau **Leisure:** S **Off-site:** S

GOUVEIA Beira Litoral

Curral do Negro 6290 ☎ 238491008
e-mail: info@fpcampismo.pt
website: www.fpcampismo.pt
In a mountain setting, surrounded by woodland.
➲ *Signed.*
Open: 18 Jan- 30 Oct **Site:** 2HEC **Facilities:** **Services:** lau **Leisure:** P

GUARDA Beira Alta

Orbitur 6300 ☎ 271211264
A well-equipped site in a pleasant location.
➲ *Access via N18 Guarda-Castelo Branco.*
Open: Mar-Oct **Site:** 2HEC **Facilities:**
Services: lau

GUINCHO Estremadura

Orbitur Areia-Guincho, 2750-053
☎ 214870450 ▯ 214872167
e-mail: info@orbitur.pt
website: www.orbitur.pt
On hilly ground amidst a pine wood in the Parque du Guincho, near the Boca do Inferno.
➲ *4km W of Cascais at Km98, turn right & follow road 247-6 for 1km.*
Open: All year **Site:** 7.7HEC **Prices:** 2.50-4.65 2.30-4.55 3.90-6.40 3.20-5.05 **Facilities:** **Services:** lau **Off-site:** S

LOURIÇAL Beira Litoral

De Klomp 11 Casas Brancas, 3100-231
☎ 236952551 ▯ 236952551
e-mail: campismo.o.tamanco@mail.telepac.pt
website: www.campismo-o-tamanco.com
In pleasant wooded surroundings.
➲ *Access via N109 or A1.*
Open: Feb-Oct **Site:** 1.5HEC **Prices:** 3.15 2.35 3.40 2.35-3.05 **Facilities:** **Services:** lau **Leisure:** P **Off-site:**

LUSO Beira Litoral

Orbitur E.N 336, Pampilhosa, Quinta Do Vale Do Jorge, 3050-246 ☎ 231930916 ▯ 231930917
e-mail: info@orbitur.pt
website: www.orbitur.pt
Open: All year **Site:** 3HEC **Prices:** 2.10-3.60 1.80-3.50 2.60-4.85 2.20-3.70 **Facilities:** **Services:** lau **Off-site:** P

MONTARGIL Alto Alentejo

Orbitur Montargil, 7425-017 ☎ 242901207 ▯ 242901220
e-mail: info@orbitur.pt
website: www.orbitur.pt
In a beautiful wooded location with good recreational facilities close to the River Alva.
➲ *N off N2.*
Open: All year **Site:** 6HEC **Prices:** 2.30-4.30 1.90-3.80 2.80-5.50 2.50-4.60 **Facilities:** **Services:** lau **Off-site:** L

NAZARÉ Estremadura

Orbitur Valado Valado, 2450-148
☎ 262561609 ▯ 262561137
e-mail: info@orbitur.pt
website: www.orbitur.pt
In a pine wood 2km from the village with good facilities.
➲ *300m E of village, S of road 8-4 Nazaré-Alcobaça.*
Open: Feb-Nov **Site:** 6.3HEC **Prices:** 2.10-3.60 1.80-3.50 2.60-4.85 2.20-4.05 **Facilities:** **Services:** lau **Off-site:** S

Vale Paraiso Estrada Nacional 242, 2450-138
☎ 262561800 ▯ 262561900
e-mail: info@valeparaiso.com
website: www.valeparaiso.com
Situated in a beautiful natural park amid tall pine trees, this site is exceptionally well appointed with very high standards of hygiene and various recreational facilities.
Open: All year **Site:** 8.3HEC **Prices:** 2.90-3.80 2.50-3 3.50-4.20 2.50-4.70 (static)114-350 **Facilities:** **Services:** lau **Leisure:** P **Off-site:** S

PALHEIROS DE MIRA Beira Litoral

Orbitur 3070-792 ☎ 231471234 ▯ 231472047
e-mail: info@orbitur.pt
website: www.orbitur.pt
Site lies in a dense forest.
➲ *N off the N334 at KM2, towards Videira, opposite road fork.*
Open: Feb-Nov **Site:** 3HEC **Prices:** 2.20-3.90 1.80-3.60 2.70-4.95 2.30-4.05 **Facilities:** **Services:** lau **Leisure:** S **Off-site:** LS

PENACOVA BEIRA LITORAL

Penacova est da Carvoeira, 3360
239477464 239477464
e-mail: info@fpcampismo.pt
website: www.fpcampismo.pt
A pleasant riverside site in wooded surroundings.
Signed.
Open: 18Jan- 30Dec **Site:** 1HEC **Facilities:** **Services:** lau **Leisure:** R **Off-site:**

PENICHE ESTREMADURA

CM Av. Monsenhor Bastos, 2520
262789529 262789529
website: www.cm-peniche.pt
On a sandy hillock, partly wooded 0.5km from sea.
2km E.
Open: All year **Site:** 12.6HEC **Prices:** 1.05-2.10 0.88-1.75 1.23-4.50 0.88-4.25 **Facilities:** **Services:** lau **Off-site:** PS

Peniche Praia 2520 262783460 262789447
e-mail: penichepraia@hotmail.com
website: www.roteiro-campista.pt
On level ground 500m from the sea.
N towards Cabo Carudeiro.
Open: All year **Site:** 1.5HEC **Facilities:** **Services:** lau **Off-site:** PS

PORTALEGRE ALTO ALENTEJO

Orbitur Quinta da Saude, 7300-435
245308384 245308385
e-mail: info@orbitur.pt
website: www.orbitur.pt
A hilltop site commanding magnificent views.
Access via N18 Estremoz-Castelo Branco.
Open: Apr-Sep **Site:** 2HEC **Prices:** 2.10-3.60 1.80-3.50 2.60-4.85 2.20-3.70 **Facilities:** **Services:** lau **Off-site:**

SALVATERRA DE MAGOS RIBATEJO

Parque de Campismo de Escaroupim Mata Florestal de Escaroupim, 2120 263595484 263595484
e-mail: info@fpcampismo.pt
website: www.fpcampismo.pt
Open: 18 Jan- 30 Oct **Site:** 3HEC **Facilities:** **Services:** lau **Leisure:** P **Off-site:** R

SÃO JACINTO BEIRA LITORAL

Orbitur 3800-901 234838284 234838122
e-mail: info@orbitur.pt
website: www.orbitur.pt
In a dense pine wood seawards from the uneven paved road from Ovar that runs alongside the lagoon.
1.5km from the sea.
Open: Feb-Nov **Site:** 2.2HEC **Prices:** 2.10-3.60 1.80-3.50 2.60-4.85 2.20-3.70 **Facilities:** **Services:** lau **Leisure:** R **Off-site:** RS

SÃO PEDRO DE MOEL ESTREMADURA

Orbitur 2430 244599168 244599148
e-mail: info@orbitur.pt **website:** www.orbitur.pt
On a hill amid pine trees.
Off road 242-2 from Marinha Grande at rdbt near the Shell filling station on the E outskirts of the village. Drive N for 100m.
Open: All year **Site:** 7HEC **Prices:** 2.40-4.40 2.10-5.70 3.30-5.70 2.80-4.75 **Facilities:** **Services:** lau **Leisure:** P **Off-site:** PS

VISEU BEIRA ALTA

Orbitur Fontelo, 3500 232436146 232432076
e-mail: info@orbitur.pt **website:** www.orbitur.pt
A pleasant, quiet site in a rural location.
Access via N2.
Open: Apr-Sep **Site:** 3HEC **Prices:** 2.10-3.60 1.80-3.50 2.60-4.85 2.20-3.70 **Facilities:** **Services:** lau **Off-site:**

Facilities: -shop -shower -electric points for razors -electric points for caravans -parking by tents permitted -compulsory separate car park **Services:** -café/restaurant -bar -Camping Gaz International -gas other than Camping Gaz -first aid facilities lau-laundry **Leisure:** -swimming L-Lake P-Pool R-River S-Sea **Off-site:** All facilities within 2km

SPAIN

Rich in history and natural beauty, Spain is bordered by Andorra and France in the north and by Portugal in the west.

FACTS AND FIGURES
Area: 504,782 sq km (194,897 sq miles)
Population: 40,217,413 (2003)
Capital: Madrid
Language: Spanish (Castilian), Catalan, Galician, Basque
IDD code: 34
To call the UK, dial 00 44
Currency: Euro
Local time: GMT + 1 (summer GMT + 2)
Emergency Services: Police, Fire and Ambulance 112.
Banks: Mon-Fri 08.30-14.30
Shops: Mon-Sat 09.00-13.00, 16.30-19.30.
Average daily temperatures: Madrid
Jan 4°C Mar 9°C
May 16°C Jul 24°C
Sep19°C Nov 8°C
Tourist information:
Spanish National Tourist Office
UK
22-23 Manchester Square,
London W1U 3PX
Tel (020) 7486 8077
USA
666 Fifth Avenue, 35th Floor,
New York NY 10103
Tel (212) 265 8822
Tourist info website:
www.okspain.org

Central Spain is mountainous and barren while the coastline can be extremely rocky. Some of the most popular holiday areas in Europe are in Spain, such as the Costa Brava, the Costa Blanca, the Costa Dorada and the Costa del Sol. More recently, the island of Ibiza has become a very popular destination for young clubbers. All these regions offer fine, sandy and safe beaches.

Spain has a varied climate: temperate in the north, dry and hot in the south and in the Balearic Islands. Languages spoken are Spanish, Catalan, Basque and Galician. Spanish developed from Castilian and there are many local dialects spoken thoughout the provinces.

Campsites are numerous on the Costa Brava and elsewhere along the coast, but there are not many inland. They are officially classified according to the facilities and services provided, and their classification should be displayed at the site entrance and on any literature. If you intend to visit sites at popular resorts along the coast between late spring and mid-October, it is not generally possible to book in advance. It is best to arrive before midday when the new charge begins. Late spring is recommended, avoiding the intense heat of mid-summer, and sites and roads are less congested. Opening dates vary considerably and some sites are open all year. Information about campsites and a detailed guide book are available from the Spanish National Tourist Office (address above) and local tourist information offices.

Hire of equipment is not generally possible, but some sites have bungalow accommodation.

Off-site camping is generally prohibited. Permission to camp off-site must be obtained from the landowner or local police. **Camp fires are absolutely forbidden.** Free camping near to beaches, rivers, towns or established campsites is forbidden too.

HOW TO GET THERE

There are direct ferry services to Spain. The services and minimum sailing times are **Plymouth** to **Santander** (24hrs) and **Portsmouth** to **Bilbao** (27hrs).

Alternatively, using Eurotunnel or the Channel ports, approach Spain by passing either end of the Pyrénées. For **central and southern Spain** take the Biarritz to San Sebastian (Donostia) road or motorway at the western end. For the **Costa Brava** and beyond, take the Perpignan to Barcelona road, or motorway, at the eastern end of the mountains.

For **Andorra** from France, go via Pas de la Casa (6,860ft) then over the Envalira Pass (7,897ft). Roads through the central Pyrénées may sometimes close November to April. From Spain, the approach via La Seu d'Urgell is always open.

DISTANCE

From Calais to Madrid is about 1,600km (994 miles), usually requiring two or three overnight stops.

Palau March Museum

Car-sleeper Trains

Summer services go from **Calais** to Avignon, Brive, Narbonne, Nice and Toulouse, and from **'s-Hertogenbosch** (the Netherlands) to Avignon.

MOTORING & GENERAL

The information given here is specific to Spain and/or Andorra. It **must** be read in conjunction with the Essential Information for Motoring section, which covers regulations that are common to many countries.

British Embassy/Consulates*

The British Embassy is located at Calle de Fernando el Santo 16, Madrid 28010 ☎ 917008200; consular section, Paseo de Recoletos 7-9, 4a, 28004 Madrid ☎ 915249700. There are British consulates in Alicante, Barcelona, Bilbao, Málaga and Palma (Majorca), and British consulates with Honorary Consuls in Santander and Vigo. There is a British Vice-Consulate in Ibiza and a British Vice-Consulate with Honorary Vice-Consul in Menorca.

Children in Cars

Children under 12 not permitted to travel as a front-seat passenger unless using a suitable restraint system. See Essential Information for Motoring section under **Passengers** and **Seat Belts.**

Currency

The **euro** is the currency of Spain. The Spanish peseta (ESP) ceased to be legal tender in 2002, though ESP coins and notes may still be exchanged at the Spanish Central Bank (Banco de España) for an unlimited period.

Dimensions & Weight Restrictions*

Private cars and towed trailers or caravans are restricted to the following dimensions - height 4 metres; width 2.5 metres; length 12 metres. The maximum permitted overall length of private vehicle/trailer or caravan combinations is 18.75 metres.

Trailers with an unladen weight exceeding 750kg must have an independent braking system.

Driving Licence*

All valid UK or Republic of Ireland licences should be accepted in Spain. This includes the older all-green style UK licences (in Northern Ireland the older paper style with photographic counterpart), though the European Commision appreciates that these may be more difficult to understand and that drivers may wish to voluntarily update them before travelling abroad, if time permits. Application form D1 (in Northern Ireland DL1) is available from most Post Office™ branches.

Alternatively, older licences may be accompanied by an International Driving Permit (IDP).The minimum age at which visitors from UK or Republic of Ireland may use a temporarily imported motorcycle (over 75cc) or car is 18 years.

Foodstuffs*

If the imported foodstuffs are for personal use there are no limits when travelling between EU countries.

Lights*

Visitors must equip their vehicle with a spare set of bulbs. It is compulsory for motorcyclists to use dipped headlights during the day.

Motoring Club

The **Real Automóvil Club de España** (RACE) has its headquarters at 28760 Tres Cantos, Isaac Newton 4, Parque Technologico de Madrid ☎ 915947275. It is associated with local clubs in a number of provincial towns. RACE has three offices in Madrid - 28013 Calle Elroy Gonzalo, 32; 28020 Calle General Peron, 32; 28045 Calle Mendez Alvaro, 33. These offices are open Jun-Sep, Mon-Thu 08.30-17.30, Fri 8.30-14.30; Oct-May, Mon-Fri 08.30-17.30.

Website: **www.race.net**

Reflective Jacket*

It is compulsory to wear a reflective jacket or waistcoat when getting out of an immobilised vehicle on the carriageways of motorways and main or busy roads. Fines for not wearing a a reflective jacket or waistcoat may be up to €90.

Roads & Holiday Traffic

Spain has an excellent network of motorways (mostly toll) and dual-carriageways (*autovías*). Emergency telephones are located every 2km on both. The surfaces of the other main roads vary, but on the whole are good. The main roads are winding in many places, and at times it is not advisable to exceed 50km/h. Secondary roads are often rough and winding.

Holiday traffic, particularly on the coast road to Barcelona and Tarragona and in the San Sebastian-Donostia area, can be heavy and congested at weekends.

In the Basque and Catalan areas some place names appear on signposts as alternative spellings, e.g. San Sebastian-Donostia and Gerona-Girona. The current AA directories and maps show both names.

Speed Limits*

Car/motorcycle

Built-up areas	50km/h (31mph)
Other roads	†90km/h (55mph) ††100km/h (62mph)
Motorways	120km/h (74mph)

Car/caravan/trailer

Built-up areas	50km/h (31mph)
Other roads	†70km/h (43mph) or ††80km/h (49mph)
Motorways	80km/h (49mph)

†On ordinary roads.
††On roads with more than one lane in each direction, a special lane for slow-moving vehicles or wide lanes.

Warning Triangles*

It is compulsory for non-Spanish registered vehicles to carry a warning triangle (two for Spanish registered vehicles). The use of a warning triangle is compulsory outside built-up areas when the vehicle (or trailer) is stationary in an area where standing is prohibited. Drivers of **non-Spanish registered vehicles** should consider carrying **two** triangles, regardless of the regulations, as local officials may impose on-the-spot fines if only one is available.

***Additional information can be found in the Essential Information for Motoring section.**

ANDORRA

Andorra is an independent principality located high in the Pyrénées between France and Spain.

FACTS AND FIGURES
Area: 468 sq km (180 sq miles)
Population: 69,150 (2003)
Capital: Andorra la Vella
Language: Catalan, Spanish and French
IDD Code: 376
To call the UK, dial 0044

Currency: Euro
Local time: GMT + 1 (summer GMT + 2)
Emergency services: Fire and Ambulance 118; Police 110; Rescue in Mountains 112.

Banks: Mon-Fri 09.00-13.00, 15.00-17.00, Sat 09.00-12.00
Shops: Daily 09.00-20.00
Average daily temperatures:

Jan 3°C	Mar 9°C
May 11°C	Jul 19°C
Sep16°C	Nov 6°C

Tourist information: UK
Andorran Delegation
63 Westover Road
London SW18 2RF
Tel (020) 8874 4806 (am if telephoning; personal visit by appointment only)
Tourist info website:
www.turisme.ad/index.html

Andorra is administered by its own government and independent Legislative Assembly. The constitutional heads of state are its traditional co-princes: the president of France and the bishop of Seu d'Urgell. Catalan is the official language, but French and Spanish are widely spoken. General regulations for France and Spain apply to Andorra with the following exceptions.

British Consulate*

The British Consulate with Honorary Consul is located at Casa Jacint Pons 3/2, La Massana, Principality of Andorra ☎ 83 98 40.

Children in Cars

Child under 10 not permitted as a front-seat passenger. See Essential Information for Motoring section under **Passengers** and **Seat Belts**.

Currency*

The **euro** is the currency of Andorra.

Dimensions

The maximum height for vehicles going through tunnels is 3.5 metres.

Driving Licence*

A valid UK or Republic of Ireland driving licence is accepted. The minimum age at which a visitor may use a temporarily imported car or motorcycle is 18.

Lights*

Visitors must carry a spare set of bulbs in their vehicle. It is compulsory for motorcyclists to use dipped headlights during the day.

Motoring Club*

The **Automobil Club d'Andorra** (ACA) is the official motoring club, and has its head office at rue Babot-Camp 13, Andorra La Vella ☎ 803400.
Website: **www.aca.ad**

Roads

The three main roads in Andorra are prefixed 'N' and numbered; side roads are prefixed 'C'. Andorra has no motorways.

Speed Limits*

Car/motorcycle/car towing caravan/trailer

Some villages	20km/h (12mph).
Built-up areas	50km/h (31mph)
Other roads	90km/h (55mph)

Warning Triangle*

It is compulsory for a vehicle to carry a warning triangle and to use it in the event of an accident or breakdown.

***Additional information can be found in the Essential Information for Motoring section.**

NORTH-EAST COAST

BEGUR GIRONA

Begur CTRA. D'Esclanya Km2, 17255
☎ 972 623201　▤ 972 624566
e-mail: info@campingbegur.com
website: www.campingbegur.com
A terraced site in a wooded valley.
➭ *1.4km SE of town and right of the road to Palafrugell, 400m after the turn towards Fornells and Aiguablava.*
Open: 29 Apr-25 Sep　**Site:** 8HEC ⚏ ⁘ ♣ ⊞ **Prices:** ⋔3-5.24 ⊞3.20-6.31 ▲2.57-5.13 pitch 8.13-15.51 **Facilities:** ⋔ ⊛ ⊙ ⊟ ⚏ ⛺ **Services:** ⬤ ✗ ⊞ lau **Leisure:** ⋩P **Off-site:** ⛿ ∅ ⋩S

Maset Playa de sa Riera, 17255 ☎ 972 623023　▤ 972 623901
e-mail: info@campingelmaset.com
website: www.campingelmaset.com
A well-kept terraced site, divided into pitches in a beautiful valley, 300m from the sea.
➭ *2km N of Begur. From the W turn left just before the town.*
Open: 21 Mar-24 Sep　**Site:** 1.2HEC ⁘ ♣ ⊞ ⛺ ⊘
Prices: ⋔4.30-6 ⊛4-5.30 ⊞5.40-7.60 ▲4.70-7 **Facilities:** ⋔ ⛿ ⊙ ⊟ ∅ 🅿 **Services:** ⬤ ✗ ⊞ lau **Leisure:** ⋩P **Off-site:** ⋩S

BLANES GIRONA

Bella Terra av Villa de Madrid, 17300
☎ 972 348017　▤ 972 348275
e-mail: cbellaterra@cbellaterra.com
website: www.cbellaterra.com
A large family site in a luxuriant pine wood beside the beach with good, modern facilities.
➭ *Access via main N11.*
Open: Apr-Sep　**Site:** 10.5HEC ⚏ ⁘ ♣ ⊞ ⛺ **Facilities:** ⋔ ⛿ ⊙ ⊟ ∅ ⛺ **Services:** ⬤ ✗ ⊞ lau **Leisure:** ⋩PS

Blanes Avenida Villa de Madrid 33, 17300
☎ 972 331591　▤ 972 337063
e-mail: info@campingblanes.com
website: www.campingblanes.com
In a pine forest bordering the beach, 1km from the town centre.
➭ *On left of the Paseo Villa de Madrid coast road towards town.*
Open: All year　**Site:** 2HEC ⁘ ♣ **Prices:** ⋔4.50-5.89 pitch 13.22-17.07 **Facilities:** ⋔ ⛿ ⊙ ⊟ ∅ ⛺ **Services:** ⬤ ✗ ⊞ lau **Leisure:** ⋩PS **Off-site:** ⋩R

Masia c Colon 44, Los Pinos, 17300
☎ 972 331013　▤ 972 333128
e-mail: info@campinglamasia.com
website: www.campinglamasia.com
A pleasant family site on level ground with shady pitches, 150m from the sea.
➭ *50m inland from Paseo Villa de Madrid coast road.*
Open: May-Sep　**Site:** 9HEC ⚏ ⊛ ♣ ⊞ **Prices:** ⋔4.60-6.20 pitch 13.37-22.30 **Facilities:** ⋔ ⛿ ⊙ ⊟ ∅ ⛺ **Services:** ⬤ ✗ ⊞ lau **Leisure:** ⋩PRS **Off-site:** ⛿ ⬤ ✗ ∅ ⋩P

Pinar av Villa de Madrid, 17300 ☎ 972 331083
e-mail: camping@elpinarbeach.com
website: www.elpinarbeach.com
Divided into two by the coastal road. Partially meadow with poplars.
➭ *1km on Paseo Villa de Madrid coast road.*
Open: Apr-Sep　**Site:** 5HEC ⚏ ⁘ ♣ ⊞ **Prices:** ⋔5 ⊛5 pitch 15.80 **Facilities:** ⋔ ⛿ ⊙ ⊟ ∅ ⛺ **Services:** ⬤ ✗ ⊞ lau **Leisure:** ⋩PS

S'Abanell av Villa Madrid 7-9, 17300
☎ 972 331809　▤ 972 350506
e-mail: info@sabanell.com website: www.sabanell.com
Within a pine wood, a section of which is inland and open to the public.
➭ *On either side of the Avenida Villa de Madrid road. Off coast road S of Blanes.*
Open: 8 Jan-23 Dec　**Site:** 3.3HEC ⁘ ♣ ⊞ ⛺ **Facilities:** ⋔ ⛿ ⊙ ⊟ ∅ ⛺ **Services:** ⬤ ✗ ⊞ lau **Leisure:** ⋩S

CALELLA DE LA COSTA BARCELONA

Botanic Bona Vista Ctra. N2 KM 665, 08370
☎ 93 7692488　▤ 93 7695804
e-mail: info@botanic-bonavista.net
website: www.botanic-bonavista.net
Subdivided and well-tended terraced site on a hillside, beautifully landscaped. Internal roads steep. Access to beach via pedestrian underpass.
Camping Card Compulsory
➭ *Turn off the N11 at Km665. Site immediately round a blind corner*
Open: All year　**Site:** 2.8HEC ⁘ ⊛ ♣ **Prices:** ⋔5.51 ⊛5.51 ⊞5.51 ▲5.51 **Facilities:** ⋔ ⛿ ⊙ ⊟ ∅ ⛺ **Services:** ⬤ ✗ ⊞ lau **Leisure:** ⋩PS **Off-site:** ⋩P

Far 08370 ☎ 93 7690967　▤ 93 7690967
e-mail: elfar@reset.es
Terraced site on a hillock under deciduous trees with lovely view of Calella and out to sea. Steep internal roads.
➭ *For access, travel S before reaching a major left hand bend at Km666 to the right of the N11.*
Open: Apr-Sep　**Site:** 2.5HEC ⁘ ⊛ ⊞ ⛺ ∅ ⛺ **Services:** ⬤ ✗ ⊞ lau **Off-site:** ⛺ ⋩PS

CASTELL D'ARO GIRONA

Castell d'Aro crta S'Agaro, 17249
☎ 972 819699　▤ 972 819699
e-mail: campingcastelldaro@yahoo.es
website: www.campingsonline.com/campingcastelldaro
A quiet family site, 2km from the beach, with good recreational facilities.
➭ *Access at Km1 on S'Agaro road.*
Open: Feb-8 Dec　**Site:** 8HEC ⚏ ♣ ⊞ **Prices:** ⋔3.90-5.20 pitch 14.35-17.95 **Facilities:** ⋔ ⛿ ⊙ ⊟ ∅ ⛺ **Services:** ⬤ ✗ ⊞ lau **Leisure:** ⋩P **Off-site:** ⋩S

CASTELLÓ D'EMPURIES GIRONA

Castell-Mar Platja de la Rubina, 17486
☎ 972 450822　▤ 972 452330
e-mail: cmar@campingparks.com
website: www.campingparks.com
A modern family site close to the beach on the edge of a national park.
➭ *From A7 exit 3 or 4 (Figueres) follow C260 through Castello d'Empuries towards Roses.*
Open: 14 May-25 Sep　**Site:** 4HEC ⚏ ⁘ ⊛ ⊞ ▲
Prices: ⋔3 pitch 32 **Facilities:** ⋔ ⛿ ⊙ ⊟ ∅ ⛺ **Services:** ⬤ ✗ ⊞ lau **Leisure:** ⋩PS

Mas-Nou Crta. Figueres a Roses, km38, 17486
☎ 972 454175　▤ 972 454358
e-mail: info@masnou.com
website: www.campingmasnou.com
A family site with good recreational facilities, 2.5km from the coast.
➭ *Exit from the Figueres-Roses road at Km38.*
Open: 19 Mar-25 Sep　**Site:** 9.8HEC ⚏ ⊛ ⊞ **Prices:** ⋔2.35-3.74 pitch 13.91-21.40 ⛺ (static)44.40-90.63 **Facilities:** ⋔ ⛿ ⊟ ⛺ **Services:** ⬤ ✗ ⊞ lau **Leisure:** ⋩P **Off-site:** ⛿ ∅ ⋩RS

Site: 6HEC-Site size ⚏-grass ⁘-sand ⊛-stone ⋇-little shade ⊛-partly shaded ♣-mainly shaded
⊞-bungalows for hire ⛺-caravans for hire ▲-tents for hire ⊘-no dogs **Prices:** ⋔-adult per night ⊛-car per night
pp-per person per night ⛺-caravan per night ▲-tent per night ⛺ (static)-caravan hire per week

Nautic Almanta 17486 ☎ 972 454477 📠 972 454686
e-mail: info@almata.com
website: www.almata.com
Level meadowland, no shade, good facilities, reaching as far as the sea. Alongside the River Fluvia which has been made into a canal. Boating is possible in the canal which flows into the sea.
➲ *Turn S at Km11 on C260, halfway along the road & turn E along the track for 2.2km.*
Open: 14 May-18 Sep **Site:** 22HEC **Prices:** 1.65-3.30 pitch 18-36 **Facilities:** **Services:** lau **Leisure:** PRS

CUBELLES BARCELONA

La Rueda Ctra.C-31 KM146,2, 8880
☎ 938 950207 📠 938 950347
e-mail: larueda@la-rueda.com
website: www.la-rueda.com
Level terrain between road and railway. Access to beach by means of an underpass.
➲ *The site lies about 1km N of Cunit near C-31, km 146.2*
Open: 19 Mar-11 Sep **Site:** 6HEC **Prices:** 3.36-5.60 pitch 10.07-16.79 **Facilities:** **Services:** lau **Leisure:** PS

ESCALA, L' GIRONA

Maite Playa Riells, 17310 ☎ 972 770544 📠 972 770599
e-mail: maite@campings.net
website: www.campings.net/moite
An extensive site, lying inland, but near the sea, at a small lake. Partly on a hillock under pine trees.
➲ *The access is well signed from the outskirts of L'Escala on road towards Cala Montgo.*
Site: 6HEC **Facilities:** **Services:** **Leisure:** LS

Neus Cala Montgó, 17130 ☎ 972 770403 📠 972 772751
e-mail: info@campingneus.com
website: www.campingneus.com
Peaceful situation among pine trees, 800m from the beach.
Open: 30 Apr-18 Sep **Site:** 4HEC **Facilities:** **Services:** lau **Leisure:** P **Off-site:** S

ESTARTIT, L' GIRONA

Castell Montgri 17258 ☎ 972 751630 📠 972 750906
e-mail: c.montgri@campingparks.com
website: www.campingparks.com
On a large terraced meadow in pine woodlands.
➲ *100m N of GE road from Torroella de Montgri & 0.5km before L'Estartit on a hillock.*
Open: 14 Mar-9 Oct **Site:** 25HEC **Facilities:** **Services:** lau **Leisure:** P **Off-site:** S

See advertisement on page 332

Estartit Cap Villa Primavera 12, 17258
☎ 972 751909 📠 972 750991
In a valley on sloping ground which is rather steep in places. Some terraces, shaded by pine trees.
➲ *200m from the church & the road from Torroella de Montgri.*
Open: Apr-Sep **Site:** 2.5HEC **Facilities:** **Services:** lau **Leisure:** LPRS **Off-site:**

Medes 17258 ☎ 972 751805 📠 972 750413
e-mail: info@campinglesmedes.com
website: www.campinglesmedes.com
Quiet holiday site in rural surroundings with clearly marked pitches and good modern facilities.

➲ *Turn right off GE641 from Torroella di Montgri by Km5 for 1.5km.*
Open: Dec-Oct **Site:** 2.6HEC **Prices:** 3.30-6 pitch 7.30-13.50 **Facilities:** **Services:** lau **Leisure:** P **Off-site:** S

Molino 17258 ☎ 972 750629 📠 972 750629
e-mail: branders@teleline.es
Divided into several sections of open meadowland near the beach on grassland with young poplars. The reconstructed mill is a landmark.
➲ *Approaching from Torroella de Montgri turn right on entering L'Estartit & follow signs.*
Open: Apr-Sep **Site:** 10HEC **Facilities:** **Services:** lau **Leisure:** S **Off-site:** R

GUARDIOLA DE BERGUEDA BARCELONA

El Bergueda 8694 ☎ 93 8227432 📠 93 8227432
e-mail: campingbergueda@worldonline.es
website: www.campingbergueda.com
A peaceful site in the middle of a forest at an altitude of 900m with a wide variety of sports facilities.
➲ *On B400.*
Open: 24 Jun-1 Sep **Site:** 3HEC **Prices:** 4.28 4.28 4.28 4.28 (static)283.50 **Facilities:** **Services:** lau **Leisure:** P **Off-site:** R

GUILS DE CERDANYA GIRONA

Pirineus ctra Guils de Cerdanya, 17528
☎ 972 881062 📠 972 882471
e-mail: guils@stel.es
website: www.stel.es
In a fine, level location at an altitude of 1200m with fine views over the Cerdanya valley.

contd.

Facilities: shop, shower, electric points for razors, electric points for caravans, parking by tents permitted, compulsory separate car park **Services:** café/restaurant, bar, Camping Gaz International, gas other than Camping Gaz, first aid facilities, lau-laundry **Leisure:** swimming L-Lake P-Pool R-River S-Sea **Off-site:** All facilities within 2km

Site: 6HEC-Site size -grass -sand -stone -little shade -partly shaded -mainly shaded -bungalows for hire -caravans for hire -tents for hire -no dogs **Prices:** -adult per night -car per night pp-per person per night -caravan per night -tent per night (static)-caravan hire per week

On the main Puigcerda-Guils de Cerdanya road.
Open: 18 Jun-12 Sep **Site:** 5HEC **Facilities:** **Services:** lau **Leisure:** P

Lloret de Mar Girona

Tucan Ctra. de Lloret a Blanes,S/N, 17310
972 369965 972 360079
e-mail: info@campingtucan.com
website: www.campingtucan.com
A modern, family site, close to the sea with plenty of recreational facilities.
Access via A7 exit 9 to Lloret de Mar.
Open: May-Sep **Site:** 4HEC **Facilities:** **Services:** lau **Leisure:** P **Off-site:** S

Malgrat de Mar Barcelona

Naciones 08380 93 7654153
Level site divided by a small stream. Partially dusty, another part in meadow under high poplars.
Approach road passes through Camping Malgrat de Mar.
Site: 9.7HEC **Facilities:** **Services:** lau **Leisure:** PS

Masnou, El Barcelona

Masnou ctra Nac 2, 8320 93 5551503 93 5551503
e-mail: campingmasnou@hotmail.com
A well-equipped site in wooded surroundings, 150m from the beach on the Costa del Maresme.
Inland from the N11 at Km633.
Open: Jun-Sep **Site:** 2HEC **Facilities:** **Services:** lau **Leisure:** PS

Palafrugell Girona
At Llafranc

Kim's Font d'En Xeco 1, 17211 972 301156 972 610894
e-mail: info@campingkims.com
website: www.campingkims.com/
Terraced site with winding drives, lying on the wooded slopes of a narrow valley leading to the sea.
Turn right off the Palafrugell-Tamariu road, follow a wide tarred road for 1km past the El Paranso Hotel towards Llafranc. 0.4km from sea.
Open: Etr-Sep **Site:** 5.8HEC **Prices:** 2.50-6 pitch 12-25 **Facilities:** **Services:** lau **Leisure:** P **Off-site:** S

At Montrás (3km SW)

Relax-Ge 17253 972 301549 972 601100
e-mail: campingpal@grn.es
website: www.campingrelaxge.com
Level meadow under poplars and olive trees.
Turn off the C255 at Km38.7. 4km to the sea.
Open: Jun-Aug **Site:** 3HEC **Prices:** 5 pitch 10-16 **Facilities:** **Services:** lau **Leisure:** P **Off-site:** S

At Playa de ensueños

Tamariu 17212 972 620422 972 620592
e-mail: info@campingtamariu.com
website: www.campingtamariu.com
Terraced site with mixture of high young pines. Direct access to the beach.
Turn towards site at beach parking area & continue 300m.
Open: May-Sep **Site:** 2HEC **Prices:** 3.50-5 3-4.30 3.50-5 3-4.30 (static)200-300 **Facilities:** **Services:** lau **Leisure:** PS **Off-site:**

Palamós Girona

Castell Park 17230 972 315263 972 315263
Level and gently sloping meadow with poplars and pine woodland on a hill.
At Km40 100m to the right of C255 to Palamós & 3km S of Montras.
Open: 19 Mar-18 Sep **Site:** 4.5HEC **Prices:** 2.70-4.40 pitch 10-18 **Facilities:** **Services:** lau **Leisure:** P **Off-site:** S

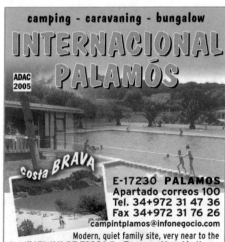

Coma Ronda Est, 17230 972 314638 972 315470
e-mail: lacoma@campinglacoma.com
website: www.campinglacoma.com
Sloping terraced terrain with young deciduous trees and isolated pines, 0.8km from the sea.
In N outskirts turn seawards off C255 near Renault garage.
Open: Apr-Sep **Site:** 5.2HEC **Facilities:** **Services:** lau **Leisure:** P **Off-site:** S

Internacional Palamós Playa de la Fosca, 17230
☎ 972 314736 ▤ 972 317626
A family site in a picturesque wooded location close to the beach.
➲ *Signed.*
Open: 19 Mar-Sep **Site:** 5.2HEC **Facilities:** **Services:** lau **Leisure:** PS **Off-site:**
See advertisement on page 333

Palamós ctra la Fosca 12, 17230
☎ 972 314296 ▤ 972 601100
e-mail: campingpal@grn.es
website: www.campingpalamos.com
A picturesque situation on a wooded headland overlooking the sea.
Open: 19 Mar-Sep **Site:** 5.5HEC
Prices: 4.80-5.50 pitch 10-19 (static)210-490
Facilities: **Services:** lau **Leisure:** PS
Off-site:

Vilarromá calle del Mar-Avda catalunya, 17230
☎ 972 314375 ▤ 972 314375
e-mail: camping@vilarroma.com
website: www.campingvilarroma.com
Clean and tidy site, mostly divided into pitches.
➲ *Turn off on the E outskirts of Palamós near big filling station.*
Open: Apr-25 Sep **Site:** 1.8HEC **Facilities:** **Services:** lau **Off-site:** LPS

AT CALONGE (5KM W)

Cala Gogo 17251 ☎ 972 651564 ▤ 972 650553
e-mail: calagogo@calagogo.es
website: www.calagogo.es
Terraced site in tall pine woodland and poplars with some good views of the sea. Underpass across to section of site with private beach. Some internal dusty roads

➲ *From Palamós 4 km S on coastal road C253, entrance on right shortly after Km47.*
Open: 12Apr-28 Sep **Site:** 16HEC
Facilities: **Services:** lau **Leisure:** PS

Internacional de Calonge 17250
☎ 972 651233 ▤ 972 652507
e-mail: info@intercalonge.com
website: www.intercalonge.com
Set on a pine covered hill overlooking the sea within easy reach of a sandy beach.
➲ *On the coast road between Platja d'Aro & Palamós.*
Open: All year **Site:** 13HEC **Prices:** 3.40-6.25 pitch 12.20-22.80 pp11.10-21.80 (static)255.15-544.60
Facilities: **Services:** lau **Leisure:** PS

PALS GIRONA

Cypsela 17256 ☎ 972 667696 ▤ 972 667300
e-mail: info@cypsela.com
website: www.cypsela.com
Well-kept grassy site in a pine wood.
➲ *Turn towards the sea N of Pals towards Playa de Pals, then turn left after Km3.*
Open: 14 May-25 Sep **Site:** 20HEC
Prices: 5.67 pitch 17.62-30.55 (static)449.40-898.80
Facilities: **Services:** lau
Leisure: P **Off-site:** S

Mas Patoxas 17256 ☎ 972 636928 ▤ 972 667349
e-mail: info@campingmaspatoxas.com
website: www.campingmaspatoxas.com
A family site in a quiet location close to the sea. Good, modern sanitary blocks and plenty of recreational facilities.
➲ *At Km5 on Palafrugell to Torroella.*
Open: 19 Mar-Sep **Site:** 5.5HEC
Prices: 3.85-5.35 pitch 20.33-27.82 (static)381.99-674.10
Facilities: **Services:** lau **Leisure:** P

AT PLAYA DE PALS

Playa Brava 17256 ☎ 972 636894 ▤ 972 636952
e-mail: info@playabrava.com
website: www.playabrava.com
On level terrain adjoining pine woodlands, golf course, rivers and sea.
➲ *From N end of village of Pals turn towards sea & Playa de Pals.*
Open: 14 May-18 Sep **Site:** 11HEC
Prices: 1.87-2.67 pitch 23.54-33.70 **Facilities:**
Services: lau **Leisure:** LPRS **Off-site:**

PINEDA DE MAR BARCELONA

Camell Ada de los Naranjos 12, 08397
☎ 93 7671520 ▤ 93 7670270
e-mail: campingcamell@teleline.es
Surrounded by deciduous trees next to a small wood owned by the Taurus Hotel.
➲ *Turn off the N11 at Km670 along av de los Naranjos towards sea.*
Open: May-Sep **Site:** 2.2HEC **Facilities:** **Services:** lau **Leisure:** PS **Off-site:**

PLATJA D'ARO, LA GIRONA

Valldaro ctra Santa Cristina 113, 17250
☎ 972 817515 ▤ 972 816662
e-mail: info@valldaro.com **website:** www.valldaro.com
Extensive level meadowland under poplars, pines and eucalyptus trees. Some large pitches without shade.

On the left of the GE662 towards Castell & Santa Cristinia d 'Aro at Km4.
Open: 18 Mar-2 Oct **Site:** 20HEC
Prices: 3.25-5.20 pitch 15-25.75 **Facilities:**
Services: lau **Leisure:** P **Off-site:** S

PUIGCERDÀ GIRONA

Stel ctra Llivia, 17520 972 882361 972 140419
e-mail: puigcerda@stel.es **website:** www.stel.es
Modern campsite in the Pyrénées on level land. Wonderful views of the mountains and surrounding area. Good sanitary installations.
Access via N340 between Comarruga & Tarragona.
Open: 28 May-26 Sep **Site:** 7HEC **Facilities:** **Services:** lau **Leisure:** P

RIPOLL GIRONA

Solana del Ter 17500 972 701062 972 714343
e-mail: hotel@solanadelter.com
website: www.solanadelter.com
In a peaceful location close to the local ski resorts at the foot of the Pyrénées. Part of a small hotel-restaurant complex.
Open: May-Oct **Site:** 8.5HEC **Prices:** 5.80
Facilities: **Services:** lau **Leisure:** P
Off-site:

SALDES BARCELONA

Repos del Pedraforca 08697 93 8258044 93 8258061
e-mail: pedra@campingpedraforca.com
website: www.campingpedraforca.com
A well-equipped site sitauted in an area of natural beauty.
Open: All year **Site:** 4HEC **Prices:** 4.15-5.19 pitch 10.44-13.05 **Facilities:** **Services:** lau **Leisure:** P **Off-site:** LR

SANTA CRISTINA D'ARO GIRONA

Mas St Josep 17246 Santa Cristina d'Aro, Costa Brava, 17246
972 835108 972 837018
e-mail: info@campingmassantjosep.com
website: www.campingmassantjosep.com
A family site with plenty of recreational facilities.
At Km2 on the main Sta Cristina d'Aro road.
Open: 18 Feb-12 Dec **Site:** 35HEC **Prices:** 5.50-7 pitch 14.40-19 **Facilities:** **Services:** lau **Leisure:** P

SANT ANTONI DE CALONGE GIRONA

Eurocamping ctra. Palamós-Platja d'Aro, 17252
972 650879 972 661987
e-mail: info@euro-camping.com
website: www.euro-camping.com
A family site in a peaceful location close to the sea with fine recreational facilities.
Access via A7 exit 9.
Open: 19-28 Mar, 30 Apr-25 Sep **Site:** 13HEC
Prices: 2.30-5.67 pitch 16.21-26.59 (static)368.51-804.43
Facilities: **Services:** lau **Leisure:** P
Off-site: S

Treumal Apartado de Correos 348, 17251
972 651095 972 651671
e-mail: info@campingtreumal.com
website: www.campingtreumal.com
A peaceful family site in a beautiful location between a pine wood and the beach.
Entrance on Sant Feliú-Platja d'Aro-Palamós road.
Open: Mar-Sep **Site:** 7HEC **Prices:** 3.85-7.06 14.44-25.68 13.91-24.61 **Facilities:** **Services:** lau **Leisure:** PS

SANTA SUSANA BARCELONA

Bon Répos 08398 93 7678475 93 7678526
e-mail: info@campingbonrepos.com
website: www.campingbonrepos.com
In pine woodland between railway and the beach with some sunshade roofing.
Turn off the N11 at Km681 & approach via the underpass (height 2.5m) just before the beach.
Open: All year **Site:** 6HEC **Facilities:** **Services:** lau **Leisure:** PS **Off-site:** S

SANT CEBRIÁ DE VALLALTA BARCELONA

Verneda av Maresme, 08396 93 7631185 93 7631185
e-mail: verneda@teleline.es
Inland among tall trees.
Leave the N11 Girona-Barcelona road at end of Sant Pol de Mar, turn inland at Km670. Continue 2km to edge of the village & before bridge over River Vallala turn right.
Open: Apr-Sep **Site:** 1.6HEC **Prices:** 4.20 4.20 4.20 4.20 **Facilities:** **Services:** lau
Leisure: P

SANT FELIU DE GUIXOLS GIRONA

Sant Pol Doctor Fleming, 17220
972 327269 972 327211
e-mail: info@campingsantpol.com
website: www.campingsantpol.com
In wooded surroundings near the beach with good facilities.
800m from the town centre towards Palamós.
Open: 12 Mar-30 Nov **Site:** 1.2HEC **Facilities:** **Services:** lau **Leisure:** P **Off-site:** S

LAS
Dunas
CAMPING
CARAVANING
The Holiday-Park
for all the family
SANT PERE PESCADOR
COSTA BRAVA ~ SPAIN
Special off-season offers
• Generously-sized pitches (up to 100 sqm)
• Luxurious sanitary facilities
• Family entertainment • Club Mini Duni
• Diving Centre• 2 swimming pools • Large shopping centre
• Advanced booking possible • English is spoken • Discotheque
Information and reservation:
Camping Las Dunas . Apdo. Correos 23 . E-17130 L'Escala (Girona)
Tel.: +34 972 52 17 17 . Fax: +34 972 55 00 46
Your contact person: Family Callaway. Tel. 01205366856
How to find us: A-7 exit (sortida) nr. 5.
to L'Escala. 2 km before L'Escala turn direction Sant Martí d'Empúries.
Then another 4,5 km.
www.campinglasdunas.com ~ info@campinglasdunas.com

Sant Pere Pescador Girona

Amfora av J-Terradellas 2, 17470
972 520540 972 520539
e-mail: info@campingamfora.com
website: www.campingamfora.com
A pleasant site directly on the beach, with good modern sanitary facilities. There are many leisure facilities and English is spoken.
Open: 19 Apr-Sep **Site:** 12HEC **Prices:** 3.22-4.28 pitch 19.26-33.17 **Facilities:** **Services:** lau **Leisure:** PRS **Off-site:** L

Aquarius 17470 972 520003 972 550216
e-mail: camping@aquarius.es
website: www.aquarius.es
Level meadowland. Partially in shade, quiet well-organised site by the lovely sandy beach of Bahia de Rosas.
Towards L'Escala & turn towards the beach following signs.
Open: 15 Mar-10 Jan **Site:** 6HEC **Prices:** 2.94-3.53 pitch 11.24-29.96 **Facilities:** **Services:** lau **Leisure:** S

Ballena Alegre 2 17470 902 510520 902 510521
e-mail: infb2@ballena-alegre.com
website: www.ballena-alegre.com
Extensive site near wide sandy beach with dunes. Large shopping complex. Washing and sanitary facilities have undergone extensive modernisation.
Access from L'Escala to San Martin de Ampurias, then to site in 2km .
Open: 15 May-28 Sep **Site:** 24HEC **Prices:** 3.53 pitch 15.94-37.45 **Facilities:** **Services:** lau **Leisure:** PS

Dunas 17470 972 520400
Level extensive grassland site with young poplars, some of medium height, on the beach, totally subdivided.
5km SE of village. Approaching from L'Escala follow asphalt road to San Martin, then dusty earth track for 2.5km.
Open: 9 May-25 Sep **Site:** 30HEC **Facilities:** **Services:** lau **Leisure:** PS

Palmeras ctra de la Platja, 17470 972 520506 972 550285
e-mail: info@campinglaspalmeras.com
website: www.campinglasplmeras.com
On level grassland with plenty of shade. Modern sanitary blocks and heated swimming pool.
Off the road from Sant Pere Pescador to the beach 200m from the sea.
Open: 19 Mar-15 Oct **Site:** 5HEC **Prices:** 2.14-3.42 pitch 12.62-31.13 **Facilities:** **Services:** lau **Leisure:** PS **Off-site:** R

Sitges Barcelona

El Garrofer Ctra C-31-Km. 3g, 8870
93 8941780 93 8110623
e-mail: info@garroferpark.com
website: www.garroferpark.com
An 8-hectare site with many pine trees. Surrounded by a golf course and the Garraf natural park. Close to the beach
Open: 24 Jan-9 Dec **Site:** 8HEC
Prices: 2.77-4.87 4.32-6.54 14.84-19.16 4.65-7.03 pitch 14.84-19.16 **Facilities:** **Services:** lau **Leisure:** P **Off-site:** S

Taradell Barcelona

Vall Cami de la Vallmitjana, 08552 93 8126336 93 8126027
website: www.campinglavall.com
In the mountains near the Guilleries-Montseny, with good recreational facilities.
Open: 25 & 26 Dec **Site:** 8HEC **Prices:** 4.12-4.65 pitch 10.11-11.93 **Facilities:** **Services:** lau **Leisure:** P

Torroella de Montgri Girona

Delfin Verde 17257 972 758450 972 760070
e-mail: info@eldelfinverde.com
website: www.eldelfinverde.com
On undulating ground with some pine trees, and an open meadow beside the long sandy beach.
Turn left off the road to Begur 2km S of Torroella de Montgri towards Maspinell, following a wide asphalt road 4.8km towards the sea.
Site: 35HEC **Prices:** 3.50 pitch 13-38 **Facilities:** **Services:** lau **Leisure:** PRS

See advertisement on page 338

Tossa de Mar Girona

Cala Llevadó 17320 972 340314 972 341187
e-mail: info@calallevado.com
website: www.calallevado.com
Magnificent terraced site with hairpin roads overlooking three bays, all suitable for bathing. Narrow, winding drives are quite steep in parts. Separate section for caravans.
Take the coast road for 4km towards Lloret de Mar & turn towards the sea.
Open: May-Sep **Site:** 17HEC **Prices:** 5.19-7.81 5.19-7.81 5.99-8.35 5.19-7.81 (static)323.94-456.89
Facilities: **Services:** lau
Leisure: PS

Facilities: -shop -shower -electric points for razors -electric points for caravans -parking by tents permitted -compulsory separate car park **Services:** -café/restaurant -bar -Camping Gaz International -gas other than Camping Gaz -first aid facilities lau-laundry **Leisure:** -swimming L-Lake P-Pool R-River S-Sea **Off-site:** All facilities within 2km

el delfin verde
bungalows and apartments for hire
One of the best and most beautiful holiday sites on the COSTA BRAVA
In quiet surroundings, by a magnificent wide and miles-long sandy beach and with the largest fresh-water swimming pool of the Costa Brava. By the way, we also have the most generously-sized pitches of the region. Many green areas and groups of trees. Commercial centre. Fresh water plants.
GASTRONOMY: 3 bars, 2 restaurants, 2 grills, pizzeria, 2 snackbars and beach bar. SPORTS: large sports area for hand-, volley-, basket- and football and badminton. 8 tennis courts, mini-golf (3000 m2 - 18 holes), windsurfing school. ACTIVITIES: Organised 'fiestas', disco 'light', dancing. Excursions, organised sports competitions and movie/video shows. 8 Modern ablution blocks with hot water everywhere, money exchange, safe, medical service, tel.
OPEN: 19.03 - 16.10
Tel. (34) 972 758 454 . Fax (34) 972 760 070
www.eldelfinverde.com . info@eldelfinverde.com
Apartat de correus 43 . E-17257 TORROELLA DE MONTGRI

Site: 6HEC-Site size -grass -sand -stone -little shade -partly shaded -mainly shaded -bungalows for hire -caravans for hire -tents for hire -no dogs **Prices:** -adult per night -car per night pp-per person per night -caravan per night -tent per night (static)-caravan hire per week

Can Marti 17320 ☎ 972 340851 ▤ 972 342461
website: www.campingsgi.com
Pleasant, unspoiled site in a partly wooded location. Good modern facilities. English spoken.
➲ *1km from the sea.*
Open: 29 May-11 Sep **Site:** 10HEC **Prices:** 6-8 6-8 6-8 **Facilities:** ⊙ **Services:** ✕ lau **Leisure:** PRS

Tossa ctra Llagostera, 17320 ☎ 972 340547 ▤ 972 341531
On a meadow in a quiet, isolated valley, in a deciduous forest. 3km from the sea.
➲ *3km SW near the GE681 Tossa de Mar-Llagostera, in 600m to site along an unmade road.*
Open: Apr-Sep **Site:** 9.5HEC **Facilities:** ⊙ **Services:** ✕ lau **Leisure:** PS

VALLROMANES BARCELONA

El Vedado 08188 ☎ 93 5729026 ▤ 93 5729621
e-mail: vedado@campingsonline.com
website: www.campingsonline.com/vedado
Surrounded by wooded mountains in a valley location with the beach only a short drive away. Ideal for visiting Barcelona. Many facilities.
➲ *A17 exit 13 towards Masnou. C32 exit 8 in direction of Granollers.*
Open: Mar-15 Nov **Site:** 100HEC **Prices:** 5.75 5.75 5.75 (static)420 **Facilities:** ⊙ **Services:** ✕ lau **Leisure:** P **Off-site:** S

VILALLONGA DE TER GIRONA

Conca de Ter ctra Camprodon-Setcases s/n, 17869
☎ 972 740629 ▤ 972 130171
e-mail: concater@concater.com
website: www.concater.com
A pleasant family site in wooded surroundings with a variety of recreational facilities.
➲ *Between Camprodón and Setcases, 20km from the French border.*
Open: All year **Site:** 3.2HEC **Prices:** 5 pitch 12 **Facilities:** ⊙ **Services:** ✕ lau **Leisure:** PR **Off-site:** ✕ R

VILANOVA I LA GELTRÚ BARCELONA

Vilanova Park 08800 ☎ 93 8933402 ▤ 93 8935528
e-mail: info@vilanovapark.es
website: www.vilanovapark.es
A well-equipped family site on the edge of a densely wooded area close to the coast in the heart Catalonian wine region. Modern sanitary block recently added.
➲ *Access via A7 exit 29.*
Open: All year **Site:** 51HEC **Prices:** 4.75-6.90 4.15-6.90 pitch 12.30-18.12 **Facilities:** ⊙ **Services:** ✕ lau **Leisure:** P **Off-site:** LS

CENTRAL

ALBA DE TORMES SALAMANCA

Tormes av Dehesa Boyal, 37800 ☎ 923 160998
In a rural setting close to the River Tormes.
Camping Card Compulsory
20km from Salamanca.
Open: All year **Site:** 2.2HEC **Facilities:** **Services:** lau **Leisure:** R **Off-site:** P

ALBARRACIN TERUEL

Ciudad de Albarracin Camino de Gea, Arrabal, 44100
☎ 978 710197 978 710107
website: www.campingalbarracin.arrakis.es
A modern site on mainly level ground with good facilities.
Signed from A1512.
Open: Apr-Oct **Site:** 1.4HEC **Prices:** 3.21 3.21 3.32 3.21 **Facilities:** **Services:** lau **Off-site:** LPR

ARANJUEZ MADRID

Soto del Castillo Soto Del Rebollo S/N, 28300
☎ 91 8911395 91 8911395
Site in two parts with trees and lawns in large castle park.
Turn off NIV at Km46. In the village 200m beyond Firestone filling station turn sharp NE for 1km.
Open: All year **Site:** 33HEC **Facilities:** **Services:** lau **Leisure:** PR

CABRERA, LA MADRID

Pico de la Miel 28751 ☎ 91 8688082 91 8688541
e-mail: info@picodelamiel.com
website: www.picodelamiel.com
Open: All year **Site:** 10HEC **Facilities:** **Services:** lau **Leisure:** P **Off-site:**

CUENCA CUENCA

Cuenca Carretera Cuenca-Tragacete KM7, 16147
☎ 969 231656 969 231656
e-mail: info@campingcuenca.com
website: www.campingcuenca.com
A modern site in a peaceful wooded location.
N towards Mariana.
Open: 18 Mar-12 Oct **Site:** 23HEC **Prices:** 4.40 4 5.40 4.40 **Facilities:** **Services:** lau **Leisure:** P **Off-site:** LR

ESCORIAL, EL MADRID

El Escorial ctra Guadarrama, Km3500, 28280
☎ 91 8902412 91 8961062
e-mail: info@campingelescorial.com
website: www.campingescorial.com
In pleasant wooded surroundings with good recreational facilities.
Open: All year **Site:** 40HEC **Facilities:** **Services:** lau **Leisure:** P

FUENTE DE SAN ESTEBAN, LA SALAMANCA

Cruce 37200 ☎ 923 440130
e-mail: campingelcruce@yahoo.es
Useful transit site in quiet Castillian countryside.
50m from N620 at Km291.
Open: Jul-Sep **Site:** 0.5HEC **Prices:** 3.50 3 4 3 (static)105 **Facilities:** **Services:** lau **Leisure:** P **Off-site:** R

GARGANTILLA DE LOZOYA MADRID

Monte Holiday 28739 ☎ 91 8695278 91 8695278
e-mail: camp.m.holiday@teleline.es
website: www.vayacamping.net
A terraced site with good modern facilities in a beautiful mountain setting.
Turn off N1 Burgos-Madrid at Km69 towards Cotos for 10km.
Open: All year **Site:** 30HEC **Prices:** 4.80 4.80 4.80 **Facilities:** **Services:** lau **Leisure:** P **Off-site:** LR

GETAFE MADRID

Alpha Ctra. N-4, Km12,400, 28906
☎ 91 6958069 91 6831659
e-mail: info@campingalpha.com
website: www.campingalpha.com
Surrounded by pine woods at about the geographical centre of Spain, with well-defined pitches and modern facilities. Direct bus service to Madrid.
Access via NIV at Km12,400.
Open: All year **Site:** 4.8HEC **Prices:** 5.40 5.80 5.80 **Facilities:** **Services:** lau **Leisure:** P

MADRID MADRID

Arco Iris 28670 ☎ 91 6160387 91 6160059
e-mail: madrid@bungalowsarcoiris.com
website: www.bungalowsarcoiris.com
A family site in a peaceful location, yet with easy access to Madrid.
From M40 (Madrid ring road) take exit 36 to Boadilla del Monte towards Villaviciosa to Km12.
Open: All year **Site:** 4HEC **Prices:** 5.15 5.15 5.15 5.15 pitch 13.65 **Facilities:** **Services:** lau **Leisure:** P

Osuna av de Logrono, 28042 ☎ 91 7410510 91 3206365
On long stretch of land, shade being provided by pines, acacias and maple. Some noise from airfield, road and railway.
From the town centre take N11 road towards Barajas for about 7.5km. At Km1 in 300m after railway underpass turn right.
Open: All year **Site:** 23HEC **Facilities:** **Services:** lau **Off-site:** LP

Site: 6HEC-Site size -grass -sand -stone -little shade -partly shaded -mainly shaded -bungalows for hire -caravans for hire -tents for hire -no dogs **Prices:** -adult per night -car per night pp-per person per night -caravan per night -tent per night (static)-caravan hire per week

MALPARTIDA DE PLASENCIA CÁCERES

Parque Natural de Monfrague Ctra Plasencia-Trujillo Km10, 10680
927 459220 927 459233
website: www.campingmonfrague.com
A modern site with well-defined pitches and good facilities.
10km from Plasencia on C524.
Open: All year **Site:** 7HEC **Prices:** 3.30 3 3.30 3.30 **Facilities:** **Services:** lau **Leisure:** P **Off-site:**

MÉRIDA BADAJOZ

Lago de Proserpina Apdo 121, 06800
924 123055 924 317555
e-mail: campingproserpina@estudiarte.com
website: www.campingproserpina.com
Open: May-Dec **Site:** 5.5HEC **Facilities:** **Services:** lau **Leisure:** LP **Off-site:** P

MIRANDA DEL CASTAÑAR SALAMANCA

El Burro Blanco 37660 923 161100 923 161100
e-mail: elburroblanco@internet-rural.com
website: www.elburroblanco.internet-rural.com
A well-equipped site in an area of woodland overlooking the village.
1km from the village centre.
Open: Apr-Sep **Site:** 3.5HEC **Prices:** 4 pitch 9 **Facilities:** **Services:** lau **Off-site:** PR

NAVALAFUENTE MADRID

Camping Piscis 28729 91 8432268 91 8471341
e-mail: campiscis@campiscis.com
website: www.campiscis.com
Spacious pitches surrounded by oak trees.
Turn off N1/E5 Madrid-Burgos at exit 50 towards Guadalix de la Sierra.
Open: All year **Site:** 23HEC **Prices:** 4.80 4.80 4.80 4.80 **Facilities:** **Services:** lau **Leisure:** P

SALAMANCA SALAMANCA

Don Quijote Carrta. Aldealengua Km4, Cabrerizos, 37193
923 209052 923 209052
e-mail: info@campingdonquijote.com
website: www.campingdonquijote.com
NE of the town towards Aldealengua.
Open: All year **Site:** 6.5HEC **Prices:** 3.15-3.30 2.80-2.95 3.15-3.30 3.15-3.30 (static)210-245 **Facilities:** **Services:** lau **Leisure:** PR

Facilities: -shop -shower -electric points for razors -electric points for caravans -parking by tents permitted -compulsory separate car park **Services:** -café/restaurant -bar -Camping Gaz International -gas other than Camping Gaz -first aid facilities lau-laundry **Leisure:** -swimming L-Lake P-Pool R-River S-Sea **Off-site:** All facilities within 2km

SANTA MARTA DE TORMES SALAMANCA

Regio ctra Salamanca/Madrid Km4, 37900
923 138888 923 138044
e-mail: recepcion@campingregio.com
website: www.campingregio.com
A pleasant site, divided into several fields, with good modern facilities.
100m from the N501 Salamanca-Avila behind Hotel Jardin-Regio.
Open: All year **Site:** 3HEC **Prices:** 2.88-3.42 2.88-3.42 2.88-3.42 **Facilities:** **Services:** lau **Leisure:** PR

SEGOVIA SEGOVIA

Acueducto 40004 921 425000 921 425000
e-mail: campingsg@navegalia.com
website: www.campingacueducto.com
SE next to N601 at Km112.
Open: Apr-Sep **Site:** 3HEC **Prices:** 4.50-5 pitch 14-15.50 **Facilities:** **Services:** lau **Leisure:** P **Off-site:** L

TOLEDO TOLEDO

Greco 45004 925 220090 925 220090
e-mail: elgreco@retemail.es
website: www.accom.nct/elgreco
Few shady terraces on slope leading down to the River Tajo. On SW outskirts of town.
From the town centre take the C401, Carretera Comarcal SW for 2km. Turn right at Km28 & continue 300m towards Puebla de Montalban.
Open: All year **Site:** 2.5HEC **Prices:** 5.35 5.24 5.24 5.24 **Facilities:** **Services:** lau **Leisure:** PR **Off-site:**

VALDEMAQUEDA MADRID

El Canto la Gallina 28295 091 8984820 091 8984823
e-mail: camping@elcantolagallina.com
website: www.elcantolagallino.com
In a wooded location at the foot of a mountain.
Open: All year **Site:** 12.5HEC
Prices: 5.35-6.42 4.28-4.28 5.35-6.42 4.82-5.35 pitch 3.85 **Facilities:** **Services:** lau **Leisure:** LP **Off-site:** R

VILLAMAYOR SALAMANCA

Ruta de la Plata Camino Alto de Villamayor, 37184
923 289574 923 289574
e-mail: reception@campingrutadelaplata.com
website: www.campingrutadelaplata.com
Open: All year **Site:** 1.2HEC **Prices:** 3.20 3.20 3.20 3.20 **Facilities:** **Services:** lau **Leisure:** P **Off-site:**

SOUTH-EAST COAST

ALCOCEBER CASTELLÓN

Playa Tropicana 12579 964 412463 964 412805
e-mail: info@playatropicana.com
website: www.playatropicana.com
On a 500m sandy beach 3km from the village.
Leave motorway at exit 44, 3km N on CN340 & turn towards the sea at Km1018.
Open: All year **Site:** 3HEC **Facilities:** **Services:** lau **Leisure:** PS

Ribamar Partida Ribamar s/n, 12579
964 761163 964 761163
Quiet wooded site between sea and mountains. Individual pitches.
Open: 19 Mar-25 Sep **Site:** 2.2HEC **Prices:** 3.32-4.07 3.21-3.91 4.23-5.19 4.23-5.19 **Facilities:** **Services:** lau **Leisure:** PS **Off-site:** S

ALFAZ DEL PI ALICANTE

Excalibur Camino, Viejo del Albir s/n, 03580
96 6867139 96 6866928
e-mail: c-m@camping-medieval.com
website: www.camping-medieval.com
Open: All year **Site:** 12HEC **Facilities:** **Services:** lau **Leisure:** P **Off-site:** S
See advertisement on opposite page

ALTEA ALICANTE

Cap Blanch Playa del Cap-Blanch, 3590 96 5845946
A well-equipped site on Albir beach backed by imposing mountains. Good sports and recreational facilities.
Access via A7 exit 65 Benidorm-Callosa.
Open: All year **Site:** 4HEC **Prices:** 5.50 pitch 24 **Facilities:** **Services:** lau **Leisure:** S **Off-site:**

AMETLLA DE MAR, L' TARRAGONA

L'Ametlla Village Platja Paratge Santes Creus, 43860
977 267784 977 267868
e-mail: info@campingametlla.com
website: www.campingametlla.com
A modern site with first-class equipment. Direct access to two beaches. Substantial improvements have been made to the access road.
2km W, S of A7.
Open: Apr-Oct **Site:** 8HEC **Prices:** 400-700 450-750 450-750 450-750 **Facilities:** **Services:** lau **Leisure:** PS

BENICARLÓ CASTELLÓN

Alegria del Mar Playa Norte, 12580
964 470871 964 470871
Open: All year **Site:** 10HEC **Prices:** 4.25 4.25 4.25 **Facilities:** **Services:** lau **Leisure:** PS

BENICASIM CASTELLÓN

Bonterra Park av Barcelona 47, 12560
964 300007 964 300008
e-mail: info@campingbonterra.com
website: www.campingbonterra.com
Between the railway line and avenida de Barcelona with a number of deciduous trees.
300m N towards Las Villas de Benicasim.
Open: All year **Site:** 5HEC **Prices:** 3.32-4.39 pitch 12.15-34.13 **Facilities:** **Services:** lau **Leisure:** P **Off-site:** PS

BENIDORM ALICANTE

Arena Blanca av Dr Severo Ochoa 44, 03500
96 5861889 96 5861107
e-mail: arenablanca@ctv.es
website: www.camping-arenablanca.es
A modern site with good facilities.
Access via N332 Benidorm-Altea.
Open: All year **Site:** 2.2HEC **Prices:** 5.50 pitch 16 **Facilities:** **Services:** lau **Leisure:** PS

Armanello av Comunidad, 03500
96 5853190 96 5853100
e-mail: armanello@camping-arenablanca.es
website: www.camping-arenablanca.es
Divided by bushes with large pitches on terraces under olive and palm trees next to a small orange grove.
Turn off the N332 at Km123.1 N of the town.
Open: All year **Site:** 1.6HEC **Prices:** 2-5.50 4.40-5.50 pitch 7-22 (incl 2 persons) **Facilities:** **Services:** lau **Leisure:** PS

Benisol av Comunidad Valenciana S/N, 3503
96 5851673 96 5860895
A modern family site with plenty of facilities. The large pitches are separated by hedges and the centre of Benidorm is within easy reach.
NE of Benidorm off N332 towards Altea.
Open: All year **Site:** 7HEC **Facilities:** **Services:** lau **Leisure:** P

BENISA ALICANTE

Fanadix ctra Calpe-Moraira Km 5, 03720
96 5747307 96 5747307
e-mail: campingfanadix@campingfanadix.com
website: www.campingfanadix.com
Terraced site completely divided into pitches.
10km E, 400m from the sea. Access off AV-1445.
Site: 1.6HEC **Prices:** 4.15 4.90 4.90 pitch 12.90 **Facilities:** **Services:** lau **Leisure:** P **Off-site:** S

CAMBRILS TARRAGONA

Playa Cambrils-Don Camilo av Diputación 42, 43850
977 361490 977 364988
e-mail: camping@playacambrils.com
website: www.playacambrils.com
Divided into pitches, lying on both sides of the coast road in a wooded location.
2km N of the town towards Salou & W of the bridge over the river.
Open: 15 Mar-12 Oct **Site:** 9HEC **Prices:** 2.14-4.28 pitch 10.70-24.61 **Facilities:** **Services:** lau **Leisure:** P **Off-site:** S

CAMPELLO ALICANTE

Costa Blanca c Convento 143, 03560
965 630670 965 630670
e-mail: info@campingcostablanca.com
website: www.campingcostablanca.com
On most level ground scattered with old olive and eucalyptus trees. The Alicante-Denia railway line runs behind the camp.
Turn off the N332 at Km94.2 next to the big filling station along a narrow gravel track towards the sea for 0.5km.
Open: All year **Site:** 1.1HEC **Prices:** 4.50 pitch 13.65 **Facilities:** **Services:** lau **Leisure:** P **Off-site:** S

CUNIT TARRAGONA

Mar de Cunit Playa Cunit, 43881
977 674058 977 675006
e-mail: mardecunit@seker.es
website: www.mardecunit.com
A friendly site on level ground overlooking the beach.
Open: 15 May-1 Oct **Site:** 1.2HEC **Facilities:** **Services:** lau **Leisure:** LS **Off-site:**

Facilities: -shop -shower -electric points for razors -electric points for caravans -parking by tents permitted -compulsory separate car park **Services:** -café/restaurant -bar -Camping Gaz International -gas other than Camping Gaz -first aid facilities lau-laundry **Leisure:** -swimming L-Lake P-Pool R-River S-Sea **Off-site:** All facilities within 2km

Site: 6HEC-Site size -grass -sand -stone -little shade -partly shaded -mainly shaded -bungalows for hire -caravans for hire -tents for hire -no dogs **Prices:** -adult per night -car per night pp-per person per night -caravan per night -tent per night (static)-caravan hire per week

Facilities: shop, shower, electric points for razors, electric points for caravans, parking by tents permitted, compulsory separate car park **Services:** café/restaurant, bar, Camping Gaz International, gas other than Camping Gaz, first aid facilities lau-laundry **Leisure:** swimming L-Lake P-Pool R-River S-Sea **Off-site:** All facilities within 2km

Daimus Valencia

Aventura ctra Playa Daimus, 46710 96 2818330
Picturesque setting in wooded surroundings on a safe, sandy beach.
Access via N332 Alicante-Valencia.
Site: 1.8HEC **Facilities:**
Services: lau **Leisure:** PS

Guardamar Del Segura Alicante

Mare Nostrum 3140 96 5728073 96 5728073
e-mail: cmarenostrum@wanadoo.es
website: www.costablanca.org/marenstrum.asp
Partially terraced meadow with some shade from roofing.
Turn towards the sea off the N332 Alicante-Cartagena road at about Km38.5.
Open: 15 Apr-15 Sep **Site:** 20HEC **Prices:** 4 4 pitch 12 **Facilities:** **Services:** lau
Leisure: PS **Off-site:** LRS

Marjal Cartagena-Alicante Rd (N 332), 03140
966 725022 966 726695
e-mail: camping@marjal.com
website: www.marjal.com
Located in Dunas de Guardamar national park next to the estuary of the River Segura, alongside pine and eucalyptus forests with access to fine sandy beaches.
Open: All year **Site:** 3.5HEC **Prices:** 4-6 pitch 16-28 **Facilities:** **Services:** lau
Leisure: P **Off-site:** S

See advertisement on page 344

Palm Mar E -03140 96 5728856 96 5728856
Open: Jun-Sep **Site:** 2HEC **Facilities:**
Services: lau **Leisure:** S **Off-site:** P

Hospitalet de l'Infant, l' Tarragona

El Templo del Sol Platja del Torn, 43890
977 810486 977 811306
A new site with modern sanitary installations and good recreational facilities on a 1.5km long beach. **This is a naturist site and only families or holders of an International Naturism Carnet are allowed.**
Access via A3 Barcelona-Valencia, 4km from exit 38 towards the sea.
Open: 20 Mar-20 Oct **Site:** **Facilities:** **Services:** lau **Leisure:** PS

Jaraco Valencia

San Vincente Playa Xeraco, 46770
96 2888188 96 2888147
website: www.campingsanvincente.com
Level subdivided site with some trees.
On leaving Jaraco at Km332 turn off at Km304 Valencia-Alicante towards Playa to the site in 3.5km.
Open: All year **Site:** 5HEC **Prices:** 3.73-4.25 5.11-5.95 3.73-4.25 **Facilities:** **Services:** lau **Leisure:** S **Off-site:** PR

Marina, la Alicante

La Marina ctra N-332 Km76, 03194
96 5419200 96 5419110
e-mail: info@campinglamarina.com
website: www.campinglamarina.com
A modern site in a wooded setting, 500m from a sandy beach.
At Km79 on Alicante-Cartagena road.
Open: All year **Site:** 6.3HEC **Prices:** 1.45-7.20 pitch 37.20 **Facilities:** **Services:** lau
Leisure: P **Off-site:** S

See advertisement on page 345

Miramar Playa Valencia

Coelius av del Mar, 46711 96 2819574 96 2818733
e-mail: camping@coelius.com
website: www.coelius.com
A fine campsite 500m from the Miramar beach with good modern facilities.
Access via N430.
Open: All year **Site:** 2HEC **Prices:** 2.89-4.39 pitch 10.22-15.51 **Facilities:** **Services:** lau
Leisure: P **Off-site:** S

Mont-Roig Del Camp Tarragona

Marius 43892 977 810684 977 179658
e-mail: schmid@teleline.es
website: www.campingmarius.com
Pitches are planted with flowers and shrubs. Separate section for dog owners.
Leave the N340 Tarragona-Valencia road at Km1137 & continue through a 4.9m-wide railway underpass with a clearance of 3.65m towards the beach.
Site: 4.5HEC **Prices:** 5-7 pitch 12-18
Facilities: **Services:** lau **Leisure:** S

Playa Montroig 43300 977 810637 977 811411
e-mail: info@playamontroig.com
website: www.playamontroig.com
An ideal holiday centre for the whole family with sanitary installations of the highest quality. Situated on a fine sandy beach and surrounded by tropical gardens, this site offers a wide range of sports and recreational facilities and is noted for its helpful and friendly staff.
Turn left off the N340 at Km1136. Use motorway exit 37 or 38.
Open: 15 Mar-Oct **Site:** 35HEC **Facilities:** **Services:** lau **Leisure:** PS

Torre Del Sol 43892 977 810486 977 811306
e-mail: info@latorredelsol.com
website: www.latorredelsol.com
A level tidy grassland site on two levels, with young popolars and some of medium height between a long stretch of beach and the railway.
Turn off the N340 Tarragona-Valencia road at Km224.1 then follow the road towards the sea.
Open: 15 Mar-23 Oct **Site:** 24HEC
Prices: 3-7.50 3-8 **Facilities:** **Services:** lau **Leisure:** PS

Navajas Castellón

Altomira 12470 964 713211 964 713512
e-mail: reservas@campingaltomira.com
website: www.campingaltomira.com
Situated in the valley of the River Palancia. Terraced campsite with touring pitches on the higher levels.
500m W of Navajas. From N234 take exit for Sagunto.
Open: All year **Site:** 2.5HEC **Prices:** 4.20 2.81 4.12-4.80 3.50 **Facilities:** **Services:**
lau **Leisure:** P **Off-site:** LR

Oliva Valencia

Azul Apartado de Correos 96, 46780
96 2854106 96 2854096
e-mail: campingazul@ctv.es **website:** www.campingazul.com
A well-equipped site with direct access to the beach.
Open: All year **Site:** 2.5HEC **Prices:** 4 pitch 12-14
Facilities: **Services:** lau
Leisure: S **Off-site:** R

Facilities: shop, shower, electric points for razors, electric points for caravans, parking by tents permitted, compulsory separate car park **Services:** café/restaurant, bar, Camping Gaz International, gas other than Camping Gaz, first aid facilities, lau-laundry **Leisure:** swimming L-Lake P-Pool R-River S-Sea **Off-site:** All facilities within 2km

Euro Camping 46780 ☎ 96 2854098 Fax 96 2851753
e-mail: info@eurocamping-es.com
website: www.eurocamping-es.com
On a wide sandy beach between orange groves and well-shaded with poplar and eucalyptus trees.
➲ *Turn off the N332 at Km184.9, 600m from Oliva. Follow signs for campsite towards the sea for 3.3km. The access road has narrow stretches and some blind corners so beware of oncoming traffic.*
Open: All year **Site:** 4.5HEC **Prices:** 2.08-4.17 pitch 8.11-28.46 **Facilities:** **Services:** lau **Leisure:** S **Off-site:** R

Ferienplatz Olé 46780 ☎ 96 2857517 Fax 96 2857517
e-mail: camping-ole@hotmail.com
website: www.camping-ole.com
An extensive site with some pitches amongst dunes.
➲ *Turn off the N332 at Km209.9 about 5km S of Oliva. In 3km continue to site on access road partially asphalt, through an orchard.*
Open: Apr-Sep **Site:** 46HEC **Prices:** 4.74 6.93 4.74 **Facilities:** **Services:** lau **Leisure:** S **Off-site:**

Kiko Playa de Oliva, 46780 ☎ 96 2850905 Fax 96 2854320
e-mail: kikooark@kikopark.com
website: www.kikopark.com
Family holiday camp, divided into pitches, lying between marshland and vineyard. The sea can be reached by crossing a dyke and there are sunshade roofs.
➲ *From motorway A7 exit 61 continue via CN332 towards Oliva.*
Open: All year **Site:** 4HEC **Prices:** 2.78-5.88 pitch 9.95-31.05 **Facilities:** **Services:** lau **Leisure:** PS **Off-site:** P

OROPESA DEL MAR CASTELLÓN

Didota av de la Didota, 12594 ☎ 964 319551 Fax 964 319557
e-mail: fenollosa@infonegocio.com
Open: 16 Mar-14 Oct **Site:** 1.7HEC **Facilities:** **Services:** lau **Leisure:** P **Off-site:** S

PEÑISCOLA CASTELLÓN

Camping Eden Avda. Papa Luna, KM.6, 12598
☎ 964 480562 Fax 964 489828
e-mail: camping@camping-eden.com
website: www.camping-eden.com
A modern, well-appointed site on level ground close to the seafront.
➲ *Access via A7, then head for Peñiscola & turn towards Benicarlo.*
Open: All year **Site:** 4HEC **Prices:** 1.61-6.15 pitch 4.87-38.52 **Facilities:** **Services:** lau **Leisure:** PS **Off-site:**

PUEBLA DE FARNALS VALENCIA

Brasa 46137 ☎ 96 1460388
Level meadowland site with poplars near village centre.
➲ *Leave motorway Barcelona-Valencia at exit 3 towards Playa Puebla de Farnals.*
Open: All year **Site:** 3.9HEC **Prices:** 3.60 5 5 **Facilities:** **Services:** lau **Leisure:** P **Off-site:** S

SALOU TARRAGONA

Pineda de Salou Playa de la Pineda, 43840
☎ 977 373080 Fax 977 373081
e-mail: info@campingglapineda.com
website: www.campingglapineda.com
A well-equipped site close to the sea.
➲ *At Km5 on the Tarragona-Salou road.*
Open: All year **Site:** 4HEC **Facilities:** **Services:** lau **Leisure:** P **Off-site:** S

Sangulí Salou 43840 ☎ 977 381641 Fax 977 384616
e-mail: mail@sanguli.es **website:** www.sanguli.es
A large, family site in pleasant wooded surroundings, 50m from the beach, with extensive sports and entertainment facilities.
➲ *3km from Port Aventura on SW outskirts, 50m inland from coast road to Cambrils.*
Open: 11 Mar-1 Nov
Site: 23HEC **Prices:** 5.35-5.35 pitch 12.84-37.45 **Facilities:** **Services:** lau **Leisure:** PS

See advertisement opposite

Siesta 43840 977 380852
Divided into pitches and planted with young deciduous trees and old olive trees. Sunshade roofs.
From Tarragona turn right off the main road on outskirts of Salou 150m to the camp. The site is between railway & road 0.4km from the sea.
Open: 16 Mar-3 Nov **Site:** 6HEC **Facilities:** **Services:** lau **Leisure:** P **Off-site:** S

Union c Pompeu Fabra 37, 43840
977 384816 977 351444
e-mail: launion@campings.net
A well-equipped site in wooded surroundings, 350m from the sea.
On S outskirts, 1km from the Port Aventura theme park.
Open: Apr-Sep **Site:** 3.8HEC **Prices:** 4-5.30 4-7 5-8 4-5.30 (static)280-350 **Facilities:** **Services:** lau **Leisure:** PS

SANTA OLIVA TARRAGONA

Santa Oliva Jaume Balmes 122, 43710
977 679546 977 679228
At Km3 on Vendrell-Santa Oliva road.
Open: All year **Site:** 2HEC **Prices:** 4 4 4 4 **Facilities:** **Services:** lau **Leisure:** P **Off-site:** S

TAMARIT TARRAGONA

Caledonia 43008 977 650098 977 652867
e-mail: caledonia@camping-caledoia.com
website: www.camping-caledonia.com
A well-appointed site in wooded surroundings, 800m from the sea.
At Km1172 on N340.
Open: 18 Jun-20 Sep **Site:** 3.5HEC **Prices:** 2.62-5.25 2.62-5.25 **Facilities:** **Services:** lau **Leisure:** P **Off-site:** S

Trillas Platja Tamarit 43008 977 650249 977 650926
e-mail: info@campingtrillas.com
website: www.campingtrillas.com
About 50m from the sea. On several terraces planted with olive trees next to a farm.
Turn off N340 at Km1.172 8km N of Tarragona. Follow road across narrow railway bridge (beware of oncoming traffic).
Open: Apr-17 Oct **Site:** 4HEC **Facilities:** **Services:** lau **Leisure:** PRS

TARRAGONA TARRAGONA

Tamarit-Park Platja Tamarit, 43008
977 650128 977 650451
e-mail: tamaritpark@tamarit.com
website: www.tamarit.com
Well-kept site at the sea beneath Tamarit castle. One section lies under tall shady trees, and a new section lies in a meadow with some trees.
Turn off N340 at Km1171.5 towards the beach, turn left at end of road.
Open: All year **Site:** 17HEC **Prices:** 4.55 pitch 16.05-48.15 **Facilities:** **Services:** lau **Leisure:** PRS

Site: 6HEC-Site size -grass -sand -stone -little shade -partly shaded -mainly shaded -bungalows for hire -caravans for hire -tents for hire -no dogs **Prices:** -adult per night -car per night pp-per person per night -caravan per night -tent per night (static)-caravan hire per week

TORREBLANCA Castellón

Mon Rossi Carrasa Mon Rossi, Torrenostra, 12596
964 425096 964 420296
e-mail: campingmonrossi@hotmail.com
Open: All year **Site:** 0.8HEC **Prices:** 4 5 4
Facilities: **Services:** lau **Leisure:** P
Off-site: S

VALENCIA Valencia

Saler 46012 96 1830023 96 1830024
Among pines providing shade with its own entrance to sandy beach in 300m. The site has undergone many improvements and has modern sanitary and recreational facilities.
Access from Valencia via coastal road towards Cullera as far as El Saler, then turn left at SE end of village & turn right.
Open: All year **Site:** 80HEC **Facilities:**
Services: lau **Leisure:** P **Off-site:** LS

VENDRELL, EL Tarragona

San Salvador av Palfuriana 68, 43880
977 680804 977 680804
e-mail: campingsantsalvador@trx.com
website: www.campingsantsalvador.com
On two large grassy terraces with some sunshade roofs. Near the sea in the centre of the town.
Access via A7 exit 31 Barcelona-Tarragona. Site in centre of Comarruga-Sant Salvador.
Open: 6 Apr-Sep **Site:** 2.9HEC **Facilities:**
Services: lau **Off-site:** PS

Vendrell Platja 43820 977 694009 977 694106
e-mail: vendrell@camping-vendrellplatja.com
website: www.camping-vendrellplatja.com
A large family site in a pleasant wooded location close to the beach.
Open: 18 Mar-16 Oct **Site:** 7.3HEC **Prices:** 2.54-6.64 3.75-6.64 3.75-6.64 3.75-6.64 **Facilities:**
Services: lau **Leisure:** P **Off-site:** S

VILANOVA DE PRADES Tarragona

Serra de Prades Sant Antoni, 43439
977 869050 977 869050
e-mail: info@serradeprades.com
website: www.serradeprades.com
A fine site close to the beach and within easy reach of Barcelona and the Port Aventura theme park.
Open: All year **Site:** 5HEC **Facilities:**
Services: lau **Leisure:** P **Off-site:**
LR

VINAROZ Castellón

Garoa-Sol de Riu Playa 12500 964 496356 964 496368
In wooded surroundings close to the sea with good, modern facilities.
Open: All year **Site:** 5.5HEC **Facilities:**
Services: lau **Leisure:** PRS **Off-site:** R

NORTH COAST

AJO-BAREYO Cantabria

Cabo de Ajo ctra al Faro, 39170
942 670624 942 630725
e-mail: losmolinos@ceoecant.es
On level ground 2km from the coast.
Access via A8/E70 exit beranga Km185.
Open: Jun-Sep **Site:** **Prices:** 3.40 7.50 3.65 pitch 7.50 **Facilities:** **Services:** lau **Leisure:** P
Off-site: S

BAREYO Cantabria

Los Molinos de Bareyo ctra Bareyo-Güemes, 39190
942 670569 942 630725
e-mail: losmolinosdebareyo@ceoecant.es
website: www.campinglosmolinosdebareyo.com
In a quiet location with fine views.
Open: Jun-Sep **Site:** 12HEC **Prices:** 3.45-4.50 6.50-7.40 4.10-5.50 pitch 6.70-8 **Facilities:**
Services: lau **Leisure:** P **Off-site:** S

BARREIROS Lugo

Gaivota Playa de Barreiros, 27793
982 124451 982 124451
Site leads down to a sandy beach with windsurfing. The main buildings have been designed and built by the owner, who is a painter.
Open: 10 Jun-Sep **Site:** 1HEC **Prices:** 3.50 3.50 4 3.50 **Facilities:** **Services:**
lau **Leisure:** S **Off-site:** PR

BERGONDO La Coruña

Santa Marta-Coruña 15166 981 795826
e-mail: info@campingsantamarta.com
website: www.campingsantamarta.com
Open: 15 May-15 Sep **Site:** 2.8HEC
Facilities: **Services:** lau
Leisure: PS

CADAVEDO Asturias

Regalina ctra de la Playa, 33788
98 5645056 98 5645014
e-mail: laregalina@la-regalina.com
website: www.laregalina.com
A modern site with good facilities, noted for its mountain and sea views.
On N632 between Luarca & Avilés.
Open: All year **Site:** 1HEC **Facilities:**
Services: lau **Leisure:** P
Off-site: S

CASTRO-URDIALES Cantabria

Castro Barrio Campijo s/n, 39700
942 867423 630725
e-mail: losmolinos@ceoecant.es
In a quiet location with terraces.
Access via A8 exit Castro-Urdiales Km151.
Open: Jun-Sep **Site:** 3HEC **Prices:** 4.50 9 pitch 9 **Facilities:** **Services:** lau
Leisure: P **Off-site:** S

CÓBRECES Cantabria

Cóbreces Playa de Cóbreces, 39320 942 725120
A peaceful site on level ground with modern facilities.
50m from Luaña beach.
Open: 15 Jun-15 Sep **Site:** 1.5HEC **Facilities:**
Services: lau **Leisure:** S

COMILLAS Cantabria

Comillas ctra M-Noriga, 39520
942 720074 942 720074
e-mail: campingcomillas@hotmail.com
Level grassland site to the right of the road to the beach.
E on C6316 at Km23.
Open: Jun-Sep **Site:** 3HEC **Prices:** 4.16 pitch 10.65
Facilities: **Services:** lau **Leisure:** S
Off-site: P

Facilities: -shop -shower -electric points for razors -electric points for caravans -parking by tents permitted -compulsory separate car park **Services:** -café/restaurant -bar -Camping Gaz International -gas other than Camping Gaz -first aid facilities lau-laundry **Leisure:** -swimming L-Lake P-Pool R-River S-Sea **Off-site:** All facilities within 2km

CUDILLERO Asturias

Amuravela El Pito, 33150 985 590995 985 590995
e-mail: www.camping@lamuravela.com
website: www.lamuravela.com
Open: Jun-15 Sep **Site:** 2.5HEC **Facilities:** **Services:** lau **Leisure:** P **Off-site:** RS

FOZ Lugo

San Rafael Playa de Peizas, 27789 982 132218 982 132218
e-mail: info@campingsanrafael.com
website: www.campingsanrafael.com
A small site on open, level ground 50m from the beach.
2km from the town centre.
Open: May-Sep **Site:** 1.2HEC **Prices:** 2.97-3.18 2.97-3.18 3.97-4.25 3.37-3.61 **Facilities:** **Services:** lau **Off-site:** LPRS

FRANCA, LA Asturias

Las Hortensias Playa de la Franca, 33590
98 5412442 98 5412153
e-mail: lashortensias@campinglashortensias.com
website: www.campinglashortensias.com
A well-maintained site with good facilities beside La Franca beach.
Open: Jun-Sep **Site:** 2.8HEC **Prices:** 3.74-4.35 3.42-3.95 4.90-5.75 3.69-4.30 **Facilities:** **Services:** lau **Leisure:** RS **Off-site:**

ISLARES Cantabria

Playa Arenillas 39798 942 863152 942 863152
e-mail: cueva@mundivia.es
website: www.campingplayaarenillas.com
Well equipped site in meadowland with some pine trees, 100m from the beach.
On N634 at Km155.8 turn N & continue 100m. The entrance is rather steep.
Open: Apr-Sep **Site:** 2.5HEC **Prices:** 4.37 pitch 11.22 **Facilities:** **Services:** lau **Leisure:** S

LAREDO Cantabria

Carlos V pl de Carlos V, 39770 942 605593
Camp surrounded by walls and buildings on W outskirts of Laredo.
Turn off N634 at Km171.6 onto an avenue towards the sea. Turn left before the beach & around rdbt on plaza de Carlos V.
Open: Apr-Oct **Site:** 10HEC **Facilities:** **Services:** lau **Off-site:** LPRS

LLANES Asturias

Barcenas Antigua CN 634, 33500
98 5402887 98 5400175
100m from the town centre and beaches beside the River Carrocedo.
SW of town beyond the hospital.
Open: Etr & Jun-Sep **Site:** 2.2HEC **Facilities:** **Services:** lau **Off-site:** S

Palacio de Garaña 33591 98 5410075 98 5410298
e-mail: info@campingpalacio.com
website: www.campingpalacio.com
Situated in the grounds of the former palace of the Marquis of Argüelles, the site is enclosed by stone walls and has good facilities.
Open: May-15 Sep **Site:** 2.8HEC **Facilities:** **Services:** lau **Leisure:** PRS
Off-site: L

LUARCA Asturias

Cantiles 33700 98 5640938 98 5640938
e-mail: cantiles@conectia.net
website: www.conectica.es/cantiles
Meadowland situated high above the cliffs with little shade from bushes. Footpath to bay 70m below.
At Km308.5 turn off the N634 from Oviedo, turn towards Faro de Luarca beyond the Firestone filling station. In Villar de Luarca turn right & 1km to site.
Open: All year **Site:** 2.3HEC **Prices:** 3.90 3.90 4.50 3.90 **Facilities:** **Services:** lau
Off-site: PRS

MOTRICO (MUTRIKU) Guipúzcoa

Aitzeta 20830 943 603356
On two sloping meadows, partially terraced. Lovely view of the sea 1km away.
0.5km NE on C6212 turn at KmSS56.1.
Open: All year **Site:** 1.5HEC **Facilities:** **Services:** lau **Leisure:** S **Off-site:**

NOJA Cantabria

Los Molinos c la Ria S/N, 39180 942 630426 942 630725
e-mail: losmolinos@ceoecant.es
website: www.campinglosmolinos.com
In pleasant surroundings close to the Esmerald Coast with its fine beaches. Various leisure and sports activities.
Open: Etr & Jun-Sep, **Site:** 18HEC **Facilities:** **Services:** lau **Leisure:** P **Off-site:** S

Playa Joyel Playa de Ris, 39180 942 630081 942 631294
e-mail: playajoyel@telefonica.net
website: www.playajoyel.com
On a level meadow on a peninsula with direct access to the beach.
Between Laredo & Solares.
Open: 19 Mar-Sep **Site:** 24HEC
Prices: 3.70-5.50 4-5 pitch 10.70-16.40 **Facilities:** **Services:** lau **Leisure:** PS

ORIO Guipúzcoa

CM Playa de Orio 20810 943 834801 943 133433
e-mail: kanpina@terra.es **website:** www.oriora.com
On two flat terraces along cliffs and surrounded by hedges.
Turn off the N634 San Sebastian-Bilbao road at about Km12.5 in Orio. Shortly before the bridge over the River Orio turn towards the sea & continue for 1.5km.
Open: Mar-1 Nov **Site:** 5.4HEC **Prices:** 2.60-4 pitch 14-28 **Facilities:** **Services:** lau
Leisure: P **Off-site:** RS

PECHÓN Cantabria

Arenas 39594 942 717188 942 717188
e-mail: lasarenas@ctv.es
website: www.ctv.es/users/lasarenas
On terraces between rocks, reaching down to the sea.
Turn off N634 E of Unquera at Km74 towards sea & take road S.
Open: Jun-Sep **Site:** 12HEC **Facilities:** **Services:** lau **Leisure:** PRS

PERLORA-CANDAS Asturias

Perlora 33491 98 5870048
On top of a large hill on a peninsula with a few terraced pitches.
Access 7km W of Gijon, turn off N632 towards Luanco for 5km.
Open: All year **Site:** 1.4HEC **Facilities:** **Services:** lau **Leisure:** S **Off-site:**

REINANTE Lugo

Reinante 27279 982 134005 982 134005
Longish site beyond a range of dunes on lovely sandy beach.
On N634 at Km391.7.
Open: All year **Site:** **Prices:** 3.50 3.50
Facilities: **Services:** lau
Leisure: LRS

SAN SEBASTIÁN (DONOSTIA) Guipúzcoa
At Igueldo

Garoa Camping Igueldo Aita Orkolaga Pasealekua 69, 20008
943 280490 943 217841
e-mail: info@campingigueldo.com
website: www.campingigueldo.com
Terraced site on Monte Igualdo divided by hedges.
Follow signs Monte Igualdo from town & beach road, about 4.5km.
Open: All year **Site:** 5HEC **Prices:** 2.80-3.90 2.20-3.20 pitch 13.10-24.90 (incl 2 persons) **Facilities:** **Services:** lau

SANTIAGO DE COMPOSTELA La Coruña

As Cancelas r do 25 de Xulls 35, 15704
981 580266 981 575553
Open: All year **Site:** 1.8HEC **Facilities:** **Services:** lau **Leisure:** P

SANTILLANA DEL MAR Cantabria

Santillana 39330 942 818250 942 840183
e-mail: campingsantillana@ceocatnt.es
Slightly sloping meadow with bushes on a hillock, within the area of a restaurant adjoining a swimming pool.
Access from Santander via C6316 turn off shortly after Santillana sign & continue up the hill.
Open: All year **Site:** 70HEC **Prices:** 4.80-5.20 4.80-5.20 4.65-5.05 (static)40.33-85.99 **Facilities:** **Services:** lau **Leisure:** P

VALDOVIÑO La Coruña

Valdoviño ctra de la Playa, 15552
981 487076 981 486131
Six gently sloping fields partly in shade. Located behind Cafeteria Andy and block of flats with several villas beyond.
Turn off the C646 seawards towards Cedeira & 700m to site.
Open: All year **Site:** 2HEC **Prices:** 4.60-4.80 pitch 12.40-12.80 **Facilities:** **Services:** lau
Off-site: LPRS

VIVEIRO Lugo

Vivero 27850 982 560004
In tall woodland near beach road and sea.
Turn off the C642 Barreois-Ortueire road at Km443.1 & follow signs.
Open: Jun-Sep **Site:** 1.2HEC **Facilities:** **Services:** lau **Off-site:** RS

ZARAUZ (ZARAUTZ) Guipúzcoa

Talai Mendi 20800 943 830042
In meadowland on hillside divided by interior roads without shade. 0.5km from the sea.
On outskirts of town at Firestone filling station at Km17.5 on N634 turn towards the sea for 350m along narrow asphalt road.
Open: Jul-10 Sep **Site:** 3.8HEC **Facilities:** **Services:** lau **Leisure:** S **Off-site:** PR

Zarauz Monte Talai-Mendi, 20800
943 831238 943 132486
Site with terraces separated by hedges.
1.8km from the N634 San Sebastian-Bilbao road. Asphalt access road from Km15.5.
Open: All year **Site:** 5HEC **Prices:** 4.10 4.10 pitch 17.20 **Facilities:** **Services:** lau
Off-site: RS

NORTH-EAST

ARANDA DE DUERO Burgos

Costajàn 9400 947 502070
In a wooded setting with good facilities.
Turn off N1 Burgos-Madrid at Km162.1 N of town.
Open: All year **Site:** 1.8HEC **Facilities:** **Services:** lau **Leisure:** P **Off-site:** LR

BELLVER DE CERDANYA Lleida

Solana del Segre Ctra N-260 Km198, 25720
973 510310 973 510698
e-mail: info@solanadelsegre.com
website: www.solanadelsegre.com
A well-equipped site on the River Segre, known for its trout fishing.
Off N260.
Open: All year **Site:** 6.5HEC **Facilities:** **Services:** lau **Leisure:** PR **Off-site:** L

BIESCAS Huesca

Edelweiss 22630 974 485084
In meadow with deciduous trees on a hill in a pleasant situation.
Turn right off C138 at Km97.
Open: 15 Jun-15 Sep **Site:** 50HEC **Facilities:** **Services:** lau **Off-site:** PR

BONANSA Huesca

Baliera Cruce ctra Castejon de Sos, 22486
974 554016 974 554099
e-mail: info@baliera.com
website: www.baliera.com
A well-equipped site in a beautiful Pyrenean location on the bank of a river.
At Km365.5 on N260.
Open: All year **Site:** 5HEC **Prices:** 3.76-4.70 pitch 11 **Facilities:** **Services:** lau
Leisure: LPR **Off-site:**

BORDETA, LA Lleida

Prado Verde 25551 973 647172 973 647172
e-mail: foseluisperise@hotmail.com
Level meadowland on River Garona with sparse trees and sheltered by high hedges from traffic noise.
On the N230 Puente de Rey-Lleida road French border, at Km199 behind Pirelli filling station.
Open: All year **Site:** 1.7HEC **Prices:** 4.40 4.40 4.40 4.40 **Facilities:** **Services:** lau
Leisure: LPR

BOSSOST LLEIDA

Bedurá-Park 25551 73 648293 73 648293
e-mail: bedurapark@ibercom.com
website: www.bedurapark.com
A terraced site in the Aran valley offering spectacular views over the surrounding mountains. The site, in wooded surroundings, offers all modern facilities and a wide variety of sports opportunities.
Access via N230 Km174.4.
Open: Apr-15 Sep **Site:** 5HEC **Prices:** 4.60 pitch 8-16 **Facilities:** **Services:** lau **Leisure:** PR **Off-site:** L

CALATAYUD ZARAGOZA

Calatayud ctra Madrid-Barcelona KM239, 50300
976 880592 976 880592
Open: 15 Mar-15 Oct **Site:** 1.7HEC **Facilities:** **Services:** lau **Leisure:** P **Off-site:**

ESPOT LLEIDA

Sol I Neu ctra d'Espot, 25597 973 624001 973 624107
e-mail: camping@solineu.com
A peaceful site in a beautiful mountain setting with good, modern facilities. Organised all-terrain excursions available.
Open: Jun-15 Sep **Site:** 1.5HEC **Prices:** 4.40-4.60 pitch 8.80-12.50 **Facilities:** **Services:** lau **Leisure:** PR **Off-site:** L

ESTELLA NAVARRA

Lizarra Paraje de Ordoiz, 31200
948 551733 948 554755
Open: All year **Site:** 4HEC **Prices:** 4.28 4.28 pitch 11.66 **Facilities:** **Services:** lau **Leisure:** P

GUINGUETA, LA LLEIDA

Vall d'Aneu 25597 973 626390
In meadowland on rising ground on both sides of the road, partially in shade. No shade on terrace between road and lake.
On outskirts of town near the by-pass C147.
Open: May-Sep **Site:** 0.5HEC **Facilities:** **Services:** lau **Leisure:** P **Off-site:** LR

HUESCA HUESCA

San Jorge Ricardo del Arco, 22004 974 227416
website: www.camping-sanjorge.com
Site with sports field surrounded by high walls. Subdivided by hedges, sparse woodland.
From town centre 1.5km along M123 towards Zaragoza & follow signs.
Open: Apr-15 Oct **Site:** 0.7HEC **Prices:** 3.75 3.75 3.75 **Facilities:** **Services:** lau **Leisure:** P **Off-site:**

JACA HUESCA
AT GUASA

Peña Oroel ctra Jaca-Sabiñanigo, 22700 974 360215
Grassland site with rows of high poplars.
At Km13.8 of C134 Jaca-Sabiñanigo road.
Open: 15 Jun-15 Sep **Site:** 50HEC **Facilities:** **Services:** lau **Leisure:** P

LABUERDA HUESCA

Peña Montañesa ctra Aínsa-Francia, Km2, 22360
974 500032 974 500991
e-mail: info@penamontanesa.com
website: www.penamontanesa.com
A well-equipped family site in a wooded location near the entrance to the Ordesa and Monte Perdido national park.
Open: All year **Site:** 10HEC **Prices:** 5.75 pitch 16.50 **Facilities:** **Services:** lau **Leisure:** P **Off-site:** LR

MENDIGORRIA NAVARRA

El Molino ctra N111, 31150 948 340604 948 340082
e-mail: molino@cmn.navaua.net
website: www.navaua.net/molino
Open: All year **Site:** 15HEC **Facilities:** **Services:** lau **Leisure:** PR **Off-site:** R

NÁJERA LA RIOJA

Ruedo ps San Julian 24, 26300 941 360102
Among poplars and the area of the bullring, almost no shade.
Turn off the N120 Logroño-Burgos road in Nájera & continue along the river bank, just before the stone bridge across the River Majerilla turn left.
Open: Etr-10 Sep **Site:** 0.5HEC **Prices:** 3.75 3.50 3.75 3.75 **Facilities:** **Services:** lau **Off-site:** PR

NUEVALOS ZARAGOZA

Lago Park ctra Alhama de Aragón-Nuevalos, 50210
976 849038 976 849038
e-mail: info@campingpark.com
website: www.campingpark.com
In a pleasant location, 100m from the Laguna de la Tranquera.
NE towards Alhama de Aragon.
Open: Apr-Sep **Site:** 3HEC **Prices:** 4.90 5.20 4.90 **Facilities:** **Services:** lau **Leisure:** LPR

ORICAIN NAVARRA

Ezcaba ctra Francia-Irun Km7, 31194
948 330315 948 331316
e-mail: info@campingezcaba.com
website: www.campingezcaba.com
Gently sloping meadowland and a few terraces on a flat topped hill.
N of Pamplona. Turn off N121 at Km7.3 towards Berriosuso. Turn right uphill after crossing the bridge over the River Ulzama.
Open: All year **Site:** 2HEC **Prices:** 3.96 3.96 6.64 4.90 **Facilities:** **Services:** lau **Leisure:** PR **Off-site:** R

PANCORBO BURGOS

Desfiladero 9280 947 354027
A well-appointed site close to the river.
Off N1 at Km305.2.
Open: All year **Site:** 13HEC **Facilities:** **Services:** lau **Leisure:** L **Off-site:** PR

Puebla de Castro, La Huesca

Lago Barasona crta Nacional 123 A Km25, 22435
974 545148 974 545228
e-mail: info@lagobarasona.com
website: www.lagbarasona.com
A well-equipped, terraced site in a beautiful setting beside the lake and backed by mountains.
Open: Apr-Sep **Site:** 5HEC **Prices:** 3.95-5.19 3.95-5.56 3.95-5.56 3.95-5.56 (static)214-389.48 **Facilities:** **Services:** lau **Leisure:** P **Off-site:** LR

Ribera de Cardós Lleida

Cardós 25570 973 623112 973 623183
website: www.campingdelcardos.com
Long stretch of meadowland divided by four rows of poplars.
Camping Card Compulsory
Near the electricity plant in Llavorsi turn NE onto the Ribera road for 9km. Entrance near hostel Soly Neu.
Open: Apr-29 Sep **Site:** 3HEC **Facilities:** **Services:** lau **Leisure:** PR

Santo Domingo de la Calzada La Rioja

Bañares 26250 941 342804 941 340131
Open: All year **Site:** 12HEC **Facilities:** **Services:** lau **Leisure:** P

Solsona Lleida

Solsonès 25280 973 482861 973 481300
e-mail: info@campingsolsones.com
website: www.campingsolsones.com
A well-equipped site in a picturesque mountain setting with facilities for summer and winter holidays.
Open: All year **Site:** 6.3HEC **Prices:** 4.92 4.92 4.92 4.92 (static)32.10-38.50 **Facilities:** **Services:** lau **Leisure:** P

Tiermas Zaragoza

Mar del Pirineo 50682 948 398073 948 887177
e-mail: aytosigues@teleline.es
On broad terraces sloping down to the banks of the Embalse de Yese. Roofing provides shade for tents and cars.
On the N240 Huesca-Pamplona road at Km317.7.
Open: May-Sep **Site:** 2.9HEC **Facilities:** **Services:** lau **Leisure:** LP

Torla Huesca

Ordesa ctra de Ordesa, 22376 974 486146 974 486381
e-mail: hotelordesa@wanadoo.es **website:** www.hotelordesa.com
On three terraces between well-kept hedges.
2km N of the village at Km96 & N of the C138.
Open: Etr-Oct **Site:** 3.5HEC **Prices:** 4.10 4.10 4.70 4.10 **Facilities:** **Services:** lau **Leisure:** P **Off-site:** R

Villoslada de Cameros La Rioja

Los Cameros ctra La Virgen, 26125
941 747021 941 742091
e-mail: info@camping-loscameros.com
website: www.camping-loscameros.com
Situated in the national park of the Sierra Cebollera in the Iberian mountain range.
Access via N111, turn off 50km before Logroño towards Soria & on to Villoslada.
Open: All year **Site:** 4HEC **Facilities:** **Services:** lau **Leisure:** R

North-West

Baiona Pontevedra

Baiona Playa ctra Vigo-Baiona (km 19.4), 36393
986 350035 986 352952
e-mail: campingbayona@campingbayona.com
website: www.campingbayona.com
On a long sandy peninsula on the Galicia coast with direct access to the beach. The site has good, modern facilities and a variety of water-sports are available.
Open: All year **Site:** 4HEC **Prices:** 3.44-5.30 3.64-5.60 3.44-5.30 3.44-5.30 **Facilities:** **Services:** lau **Leisure:** PRS

Cubillas de Santa Marta Valladolid

Cubillas 47290 983 585002 983 585016
e-mail: campingcubillas@verial.es
website: www.varial.es/valladolid/campingcubillas.htm
Meadowland with young trees, subdivided by hedges.
Entrance on the right of the N620 from Burgos between Km100 & 101.
Open: All year **Site:** 4HEC **Facilities:** **Services:** lau **Leisure:** P **Off-site:** R

Nigrán Pontevedra

Playa America 36350 986 365404 986 365404
e-mail: oficina@campingplayaamerica.com
website: www.campingplayaamerica.com
Modern site in a poplar wood, 300m from a magnificent beach.
Access at Km 9.250 on Vigo-Bayona road.
Open: 15 Jun-15 Sep **Site:** 4HEC **Facilities:** **Services:** lau **Leisure:** PS **Off-site:** R

Portonovo Pontevedra

Paxariñas 36970 986 72 723055
website: www.sauxenxotur/paxarinas.com
Slightly sloping towards a bay, in among dunes, with tall pines and young deciduous trees. Lovely beach.
Camping Card Compulsory
Open: All year **Site:** 3HEC **Facilities:** **Services:** lau **Leisure:** S

Santa Marina de Valdeon Léon

El Cares 24915 987 742676 987 742676
e-mail: cares@elcares.com **website:** elcares.com
In a wooded mountain setting with good facilities.
N off N621 from Portilla de la Reina.
Open: Apr-Sep **Site:** 15HEC **Prices:** 3.75 3.75 4.28 4.28 **Facilities:** **Services:** lau **Leisure:** R **Off-site:** L

San Vicente Do Mar Pontevedra

Siglo XXI 36988 986 738100 986 738113
e-mail: info@campingsiglo21.com
website: www.campingsiglo21.com
A popular modern site with individual sanitary facilities attached to each pitch.
Open: Jun-Sep **Site:** 1.5HEC **Facilities:** **Services:** lau **Leisure:** PS **Off-site:** S

Simancas Valladolid

Plantió 47130 983 590082
In a poplar wood, on the river bank.
On outskirts turn off N620 at Km132.2 & continue 500m on narrow asphalt road & long single-track stone bridge over the River Pisverga.
Open: 15 Jun-25 Sep **Site:** 1HEC **Facilities:** **Services:** lau **Leisure:** PR **Off-site:**

Facilities: -shop -shower -electric points for razors -electric points for caravans -parking by tents permitted -compulsory separate car park **Services:** -café/restaurant -bar -Camping Gaz International -gas other than Camping Gaz -first aid facilities lau-laundry **Leisure:** -swimming L-Lake P-Pool R-River S-Sea **Off-site:** All facilities within 2km

TORDESILLAS VALLADOLID

Astral Camino de Pollos 8, 47100
983 770953 983 770953
e-mail: info@campingelastral.com
website: www.campingelastral.com
A well-equipped site in a pleasant rural location close to the River Duero.
Leave motorway at Tordesillas exit & follow signs.
Open: 19 Mar-Sep **Site:** 3HEC **Prices:** 3.85-5.20 3.30-4.40 3.85-5.20 3.85-5.20 **Facilities:** **Services:** lau **Leisure:** P **Off-site:** R

VALENCIA DE DON JUAN LÉON

Pico Verde Ctra C-621 Mayorga-Astorga, 24200
987 750525 987 750525
e-mail: campingpicoverde@terra.es
Turn E off N630 Léon-Madrid at Km32.2 and continue for 4km.
Open: 17 Jun-11 Sep **Site:** 2.7HEC **Prices:** 3.88 3.88 3.88 3.88 **Facilities:** **Services:** lau **Leisure:** P **Off-site:** R

VILLAMEJIL LÉON

Rio Tuerto 24711 987 605076
Open: Jul-Aug **Site:** 0.6HEC **Prices:** 2.70 2.70 3.10 2.70 **Facilities:** **Services:** lau **Leisure:** R **Off-site:**

SOUTH

ADRA ALMERIA

Habana 4770 950 522127
A quiet site with good facilities and direct access to the sea.
2km W at Km58.3 on N340 Almeria-Málaga.
Open: All year **Site:** 1.5HEC **Facilities:** **Services:** lau **Leisure:** S

AGUILAS MURCIA

Calarreona ctra de Aguilas a Vera, 30880
968 413704 968 413704
e-mail: info@campingcalarreona.com
website: www.campingcalarreona.com
A quiet site, 50m from the sea.
Near Km4 on N332 Aguilas-Murcia.
Open: All year **Site:** 3.6HEC **Prices:** 3.52 3.92 3.52 (static)262.51 **Facilities:** **Services:** lau **Leisure:** S

ALCAZARES, LOS MURCIA

Cartagonova 30710 968 575100 968 575225
On CN332 between Los Alcazares & La Union.
Open: All year **Site:** 30HEC **Facilities:** **Services:** lau **Leisure:** PS **Off-site:**

ALMAYATE MÁLAGA

Almayate Costa 29749 952 556289 952 556310
e-mail: almayatecosta@campings.net
website: www.campings.net/almayatacosta
Open: 5 May-Sep **Site:** 3HEC **Prices:** 5.35 5.35 7 6.40 **Facilities:** **Services:** lau **Leisure:** P **Off-site:** S

BAÑOS DE FORTUNA MURCIA

Fuente 30326 968 685017 968 685125
e-mail: campingfuente@terra.es
website: www.campingfuente.com
A camping ground within a hotel complex with individual bathroom facilities attached to each pitch and good recreational facilities.
Take C3223 from Fortuna à Pinoso to Balncario de Fortuna. Signed.
Open: All year **Site:** 1.9HEC **Prices:** 3.25 pitch 8-10 **Facilities:** **Services:** lau **Leisure:** LP

BOLNUEVO MURCIA

Garoa Camping Playa de Mazarrón 30877
968 150660 968 150837
On level ground divided by a footpath and partly bordered by palm trees.
Turn W off N332 in Puerto de Mazarrón at about Km111 towards Bolnuevo. Then take the MU road 4.6km to site entrance, 1km E of Punta Bela.
Open: All year **Site:** 8.5HEC **Facilities:** **Services:** lau **Leisure:** PS

CABO DE GATA ALMERIA

Cabo de Gata 04150 950 160443 950 160443
e-mail: info@campingcabodegata.com
website: www.campingcabodegata.com
In a natural parkland location with separate pitches and within 1km of the beach.
N340 (E15), exit 467/471.
Open: All year **Site:** 3.6HEC **Prices:** 3.90 3.70 3.70 pitch 7.40 **Facilities:** **Services:** lau **Leisure:** PS

CARCHUNA GRANADA

Don Cactus Carchuna-Motril, 18730
958 623109 958 624294
e-mail: info@campingcastillo.com
website: www.campingcstillo.com
Modern site adjoining the beach. Dogs not allowed in July and August.
At Km343 on N340 Carchuna-Motril.
Open: All year **Site:** 4HEC **Facilities:** **Services:** lau **Leisure:** PS

CARLOTA, LA CORDOBA

Carlos III ctra N-4 Km430, 14100
957 300697 957 3000697
e-mail: camping@campingcarlosIII.com
website: www.campingcarlosIII.com
In wooded surroundings with modern facilities.
Access via La Carlota exit on NIV.
Open: All year **Site:** 7HEC **Prices:** 4.50 4.10 4.50 4.30 **Facilities:** **Services:** lau **Leisure:** P **Off-site:** PS

CASTILLO DE BAÑOS GRANADA

Castillo de Baños Castillo de Baños, La Mamola, 18750
☎ 958 829528 ▊ 958 829768
e-mail: castillo@doucactus.com
website: www.doucactus.com
Well equipped site next to the beach.
➲ At Km360 on N340 Castillo de Baños-La Mamola.
Open: All year Site: 3HEC ∷∷ ♠ Facilities: ℕ 🚿 ⊙ 🔌 ⌀ 🅿
Services: 🍽 ✕ ⊞ lau Leisure: ⟲PS

CONIL DE LA FRONTERA CÁDIZ

Fuente del Gallo Fuente del Gallo, 11140
☎ 956 440137 ▊ 956 442036
e-mail: camping@campingfuentedelgallo.com
website: www.campingfuentedelgallo.com
A well-equipped site in a wooded location 300m from the
beach.
➲ Signed from N340, Km21.6.
Open: Mar-Oct Site: 3HEC ▙▙▙ ♠ 🏠 ▲ Prices: ♙4.50 ▲4
pitch 21 Facilities: ℕ 🚿 ⊙ 🔌 ⌀ 🅿 Services: 🍽 ✕ ⊞ lau
Leisure: ⟲P Off-site: ⟲S

Roche Pago del Zorro, 11149 ☎ 956 442216 ▊ 956 232319
e-mail: info@campingroche.com
website: www.campingroche.com
Spread among pine groves with well-defined pitches close to
the beach.
Open: All year Site: 3.3HEC ▙▙▙ ∷∷ ♠ 🏠 Facilities: ℕ 🚿 ⊙
🔌 ⌀ 🅿 Services: 🍽 ✕ ⊞ lau Leisure: ⟲P Off-site: ⟲S ⊞

ESTEPONA MÁLAGA

Parque Tropical 29680 ☎ 95 2793618 ▊ 95 2793618
A modern site situated at the foot of the Sierra Bermeja
mountains, a 5-minute walk from the sea.
➲ Access via N340 at Km162.
Open: All year Site: 12.4HEC ♦ 🔌 🏠 Prices: ♙3.53-5.46
♠2.25-4.28 🚐4.49-8.35 ▲4.49-8.35 Facilities: ℕ 🚿 ⊙ 🔌 ⌀
🅿 Services: 🍽 ✕ ⊞ lau Leisure: ⟲PS Off-site: ⟲S

FUENTE DE PIEDRA MÁLAGA

Espacious Rurales Camino de la Rábita s/n
☎ 952 735294 ▊ 952 735461
e-mail: info@camping-rural.com
website: www.camping-rural.com
Site situated within a wild life reserve on the shores of a lagoon.
Open: All year Site: ▙▙▙ ∷∷ 🔌 🏠 Prices: ♙4.12-4.51
♠2.64-2.94 🚐3.79-4.12 ▲2.64-2.97 Facilities: ℕ 🚿 ⊙ 🔌 🏗
🅿 Services: 🍽 ✕ ⊞ lau Leisure: ⟲LP Off-site: ⌀ ⊞

GALLARDOS, LOS ALMERIA

Gallardos 04280 ☎ 950 528324 ▊ 950 469596
e-mail: campinglosgallardos@hotmail.com
website: www.campinglosgallardos.com
Level site with individual pitches, 11km from the sea and
10km from the old Moorish village of Mojacar. English
management.
➲ 500m from Km525 on CN340.
Open: All year Site: 3.5HEC ∷∷ 🔌 Prices: ♙3.95 ♠3.95
🚐3.95 ▲3.95 Facilities: ℕ 🚿 ⊙ 🔌 ⌀ 🅿 Services: 🍽 ✕ ⊞ lau
Leisure: ⟲P

GRANADA GRANADA

Sierra Nevada ctra de Jaen 107, 18014
☎ 958 150062 ▊ 958 150954
e-mail: campingmotel@terra.es
website: www.campingsierranevada.com
Almost level grassy site, in numerous sections, within motel
complex.
Open: Mar-1 Nov Site: 3HEC ▙▙▙ ♠ 🏠 Prices: ♙480 pitch
10.90 Facilities: ℕ 🚿 ⊙ 🔌 ⌀ 🅿 Services: 🍽 ✕ ⊞ lau
Leisure: ⟲P Off-site: ⟲LRS

GUIJARROSA, LA CORDOBA

Campiña 14547 ☎ 957 315303 ▊ 957 315158
e-mail: info@campinglacampina.com
website: www.campinglacampina.com
In a quiet location in a rural setting surrounded by olive trees
and elms with good, modern facilities.
➲ Access via N4 turn off at Km424 or Km441 & follow signs
to Santaella & campsite.
Open: All year Site: 0.7HEC ∷∷ 🔌 🏠 ▲ Prices: ♙3.96
♠3.96 🚐4.12 ▲3.75 Facilities: ℕ 🚿 ⊙ 🔌 ⌀ 🅿 Services: 🍽 ✕
⊞ lau Leisure: ⟲P

ISLA CRISTINA HUELVA

Giralda 21410 ☎ 959 343318 ▊ 959 343318
e-mail: campinggiralda@infonegocio.com
website: www.campinggiralda.com
On level ground dotted with trees within easy reach of the
beach. Good, modern facilities and plenty of entertainment.
➲ On Isla Cristina-La Antilla road.
Open: All year Site: 15HEC ∷∷ ♠ 🏠 Prices: ♙3.89-5.19
♠3.21-4.28 🚐4.21-5.62 ▲3.65 Facilities: ℕ 🚿 ⊙ 🔌 ⌀ 🅿
Services: 🍽 ✕ ⊞ lau Leisure: ⟲PR Off-site: ✕ ⟲S

ISLA PLANA MURCIA

Madrilles ctra de la Azohia Km45, 30868
☎ 968 152151 ▊ 968 152092
A large family site with a wide variety of recreational
facilities.
➲ Access via Mazarron-Cartagena road.
Open: All year Site: 5.5HEC ▙▙▙ 🔌 🏠 🎿 Prices: ♙4-5 pitch
12-15 Facilities: ℕ 🚿 ⊙ 🔌 ⌀ 🏗 🅿 Services: 🍽 ✕ ⊞ lau
Leisure: ⟲PS Off-site: ✕

MANGA DEL MAR MENOR, LA MURCIA

La Manga 30370 ☎ 968 563014 ▊ 968 563426
e-mail: lamanga@caravaning.es
website: caravaning.es
A large, family site on the Mar Menor lagoon. Pitches
separated by hedges or trees. Good recreational facilities.
➲ Off the Cartagena motorway.
Open: All year Site: 32HEC ♦ 🔌 🏠 🚐 Prices: pitch 15.50-23
(incl 2 persons) Facilities: ℕ 🚿 ⊙ 🔌 ⌀ 🏗 🅿 Services: 🍽 ✕ ⊞
lau Leisure: ⟲PS

MARBELLA MÁLAGA

Buganvilla 29600 ☎ 95 2831973 ▊ 95 2831974
A well-equipped site in a pine forest close to the beach.
Camping Card Compulsory
➲ E of Marbella off the N340 coast road towards Mijas.
Open: All year Site: 4HEC ▙▙▙ ∷∷ 🔌 🏠 🚐 Facilities: ℕ 🚿
⊙ 🔌 ⌀ 🏗 🅿 Services: 🍽 ✕ ⊞ lau Leisure: ⟲PS

Facilities: 🚿-shop ℕ-shower ⊙-electric points for razors 🔌-electric points for caravans 🅿-parking by tents permitted
🅿-compulsory separate car park Services: ✕-café/restaurant 🍽-bar ⌀-Camping Gaz International 🏗-gas other than Camping
Gaz ⊞-first aid facilities lau-laundry Leisure: ⟲-swimming L-Lake P-Pool R-River S-Sea Off-site: All facilities within 2km

MAZAGÓN HUELVA

Mazagón cuesta de la Barca s/n, 21130
959 376208 959 536256
e-mail: info@campingplayamazagon.com
website: www.campingplayamazagon.com
Undulating terrain among dunes in sparse pine forest. Long sandy beach.
Turn off the N431 Sevilla-Huelva road just before San Juan del Puerto towards Moguer & continue S via Palso de la Frontera.
Open: All year **Site:** 8HEC **Prices:** 4.60 pitch 16 **Facilities:** **Services:** lau **Leisure:** P **Off-site:** S

MOJÁCAR ALMERIA

Sopalmo Sopalmo, 04637 950 478413
Open: All year **Site:** 1.7HEC **Facilities:** **Services:** lau **Off-site:** S

MORATALLA MURCIA

La Puerta Carpetera del Canal, Paraje La Puerta Km8
968 730008 968 706365
e-mail: lapuenta@forodigital.es
website: www.campinglapuerta.com
Wooded site alongside the river Al-aharabe with big pitches and pleasant views.
A30 from Albacete to Murcia & C415 to Moratalla
Open: All year **Site:** 10HEC **Prices:** 3.45 3.80 3.60 **Facilities:** **Services:** lau **Leisure:** PR **Off-site:**

MOTRIL GRANADA

Playa de Poniente 18613 958 820303 958 604191
e-mail: camplapo@infogocio.com
website: www.infonegocio.com/camplapo
Open: All year **Site:** 2.4HEC **Prices:** 4.30 pitch 9.20 **Facilities:** **Services:** lau **Leisure:** P **Off-site:** S

OTURA GRANADA

Suspiro del Moro 18630 958 555105 958 555105
A modern site with good facilities, 5 minutes from the town centre.
10km S of Granada via N323.
Open: All year **Site:** 1HEC **Facilities:** **Services:** lau **Leisure:** P **Off-site:** R

PELIGROS GRANADA

Granada Cerro de la Cruz, 18210
958 340548 958 340548
In a wooded location with panoramic views.
Access via N323 Jaen-Granada exit 123 towards Peligros.
Open: 15 Mar-15 Oct **Site:** 2.2HEC **Prices:** 4.71 pitch 10.38 **Facilities:** **Services:** lau **Leisure:** P

PUERTO DE SANTA MARÍA, EL CÁDIZ

Playa Las Dunas de San Anton ps Maritimo de la Puntilla, 11500 956 872210 956 860117
e-mail: info@lasdunascamping.com
website: lasdunascamping.com
Large site with good recreational facilities close to the beach.
Open: All year **Site:** 13.2HEC **Prices:** 3.68-4.08 4-4.45 3.68-4.08 **Facilities:** **Services:** lau **Leisure:** PS **Off-site:** RS

RONDA MÁLAGA

El Sur ctra de Algeciras, 29400 95 2875939 95 2877054
e-mail: info@campingelsur.com
website: www.campingelsur.com
In a beautiful location in the heart of the Serrania of Ronda.
Open: All year **Site:** 4HEC **Facilities:** **Services:** lau **Leisure:** P

ROQUETAS-DE-MAR ALMERIA

Roquetas Los Parrales, 04740 950 343809 950 342525
e-mail: info@campingroquetas.com
website: www.campingsroquetas.com
Access by road No 340. 1.7km from Km428.6.
Open: All year **Site:** 8HEC **Prices:** 3.80 3.80 3.80 3.80 **Facilities:** **Services:** lau **Leisure:** LPS

SANTA ELENA JAÉN

Despeñaperros 23213 953 664192 953 664192
e-mail: campingdesp@navegalia.com
website: www.campingdespenaperros.com
A clean, restful site, in a nature reserve with fine views of the surrounding mountains.
At Km257 on NIV-E5.
Open: All year **Site:** 5HEC **Prices:** 3.30 3.30 3.30 3.50 **Facilities:** **Services:** lau **Leisure:** P

SEVILLA (SEVILLE) SEVILLA

Sevilla 41008 954 514379 954 514379
e-mail: campingsevilla@turinet.net
website: es.turinet.net/empresa/campingsevilla
Level site near airfield, road and railway.
About 2km from airfield, 100m from the NIV Madrid-Sevilla at Km533.8.
Open: All year **Site:** 2HEC **Prices:** 3.25 pitch 8 **Facilities:** **Services:** lau **Leisure:** P

TARIFA CÁDIZ

Paloma 11380 956 684203 956 681880
A modern site in a secluded situation 400m from the beach and next to the prehistoric Necrolopis de los Algarbes. Fine views of the African coast across the Straits of Gibraltar.
Access via N340 Cádiz-Málaga at Km74.
Open: All year **Site:** 4.9HEC **Facilities:** **Services:** lau **Leisure:** P **Off-site:** RS

Rió Jara 11380 956 680570 956 680570
e-mail: campingriojara@terra.es
Extensive site on meadowland with good tree coverage. Long sandy beach.
On the N340 Málaga-Cádiz road at Km79.7 turn towards the sea.
Open: All year **Site:** 3HEC **Prices:** 6 5 2.50 pitch 5 **Facilities:** **Services:** lau **Leisure:** RS

Tarifa 11380 956 684778 956 684778
e-mail: camping-tarifa@camping-tarifa.com
website: www.camping-tarifa.com
A terraced site in wooded surroundings, 100m from the sea.
At Km78 on Málaga-Cádiz road.
Open: All year **Site:** 3.2HEC **Facilities:** **Services:** lau **Leisure:** P **Off-site:** RS

At Torre de la Peña (7km NW)

Torre de la Peña 11380 ☎ 956 684903 ▤ 956 681473
e-mail: info@campingtp.com
website: www.campingtp.com
Terraced, on both sides of through road. Upper terraces are considerably quieter. Roofing provides shade. View of the sea, Tarifa and on clear days North Africa (Tangier).
➲ *Entrance on the N340 Cádiz-Málaga, at Km76.5 turn inland by old square tower.*
Open: All year **Site:** 3HEC **Facilities:** **Services:** lau **Leisure:** PS

Torre Del Mar Málaga

Torre del Mar 29740 ☎ 952 540224
A fine site on a beautiful beach, with good facilities. Shop open June to September only.
➲ *SW of town. Access via N340 Almeria-Málaga.*
Open: All year **Site:** 2.4HEC **Facilities:** **Services:** lau **Leisure:** P **Off-site:** S

Vejer de la Frontera Cádiz

Vejer ctra National (N340), 11150
☎ 956 450098 ▤ 956 450098
e-mail: info@campingvejer.com
website: www.campingvejer.com
A quiet family site in a pleasant shady location.
➲ *At Km39.5 on N340 Cádiz-Málaga.*
Open: Etr-end Sep **Site:** 0.8HEC **Prices:** 6-10
Facilities: **Services:** lau **Leisure:** P

Andorra

Sant Julià de Lória

Huguet ctra de Fontaneda ☎ 843718 ▤ 843718
e-mail: campinghuguet@hotmail.com
On level strip of meadowland with rows of fruit and deciduous trees.
➲ *Off La Seu d'Urgell road N1, S of village & W across river.*
Open: All year **Site:** 1.5HEC **Prices:** 4-4.50 4-4.50 4-4.50 **Facilities:** **Services:** lau
Leisure: R **Off-site:** LP

Facilities: -shop -shower -electric points for razors -electric points for caravans -parking by tents permitted -compulsory separate car park **Services:** -café/restaurant -bar -Camping Gaz International -gas other than Camping Gaz -first aid facilities lau-laundry **Leisure:** -swimming L-Lake P-Pool R-River S-Sea **Off-site:** All facilities within 2km

SWITZERLAND

Bordered by France in the west, Germany in the north, Austria in the east, and Italy in the south, Switzerland is considered by many to be one of the most-beautiful countries in Europe.

FACTS AND FIGURES
Area: 41,285 sq km (15,940 sq miles)
Population: 7,318,638 (2003)
Capital: Bern (Berne)
Language: German, French, Italian, Romansh
IDD code: 41
To call the UK, dial 00 44
Currency: Swiss Franc (CHF)
Local time: GMT + 1 (summer GMT + 2)
Emergency Services: Police 117; Fire 118; Ambulance 144.
Banks: Mon-Fri 08.30-16.30 (in towns)
Shops: Mon-Fri 08.00/08.30-12.00, 13.30-18.30/19.00 (no lunchtime closure in large cities; Sat to 16.00/17.00)
Average daily temperatures: Zurich

Jan 0°C	Mar 5°C
May 9°C	Jul 19°C
Sep15°C	Nov 5°C

Tourist information:
Switzerland Travel Centre
UK
Swiss Centre
10 Wardour Street,
London W1D 6QF
Tel 00800 100 200 30 (freephone)
USA
608 Fifth Avenue
New York NY 10020
Tel (212) 757 5944
Tourist info website:
www.myswitzerland.com

Switzerland has the highest mountains in Europe and some of the most awe-inspiring waterfalls and lakes. These features are offset by picturesque villages set amid green pastures, and an abundance of Alpine flowers covering the valleys and lower mountain slopes during the spring. The highest peaks are Monte Rosa (15,217ft) on the Italian border, the Matterhorn (14,782ft) and the Jungfrau (13,669ft). Some of the most beautiful areas are the Via Mala Gorge, the Falls of the Rhine near Schaffhausen, the Rhône Glacier, and the lakes of Luzern and Thun.

The Alps cause many climatic variations throughout Switzerland, but generally the climate is said to be the healthiest in the world. In the higher Alpine regions temperatures tend to be low, whereas the lower land of the north has higher temperatures and hot summers. French is spoken in the western cantons (regions), Swiss-German dialects (although German is understood) in the central and northern cantons, and Italian in Ticino. Romansh is spoken in Grisons.

Switzerland has some 340 campsites, 43 of which are run by the Touring Club Suisse (TCS) who publish details of classified sites annually. Information can also be obtained from tourist offices, which are found in most provincial towns and resorts. High season extends from April or May to September or October, though some sites are open all year, particularly at winter-sports resorts.

Off-site camping regulations differ from canton to canton. However, permission to camp off-site must be obtained from the landowner or local police. Overnight parking may be tolerated in rest areas of some motorways, but at all times the high standard of hygiene regulations must be observed. Make sure you do not contravene local laws.

HOW TO GET THERE

From Britain, Switzerland is usually approached via France.

DISTANCE

From the Channel ports to Bern is approximately 810km (503 miles), a distance that normally requires an overnight stop.

If you intend to use Swiss motorways, you will be liable for a tax of CHF40 - see Motorway Tax below.

CAR SLEEPER TRAINS

Summer services are available from Auray, Nantes and Paris (France) to Genève (Geneva).

MOTORING & GENERAL

The information given here is specific to Switzerland. It **must** be read in conjunction with the Essential Information for Motoring section, which covers regulations that are common to many countries.

British Embassy/Consulates*

The British Embassy together with its consular section is located at Thunstrasse 50, 3005 Berne ☎ 031 359 77 41. There is a British Consulate in Genève, and a British Consulate with Honorary Consul in St Légier (above Vevey/Montreux) and Vice-Consulates with Honorary Consuls in Allschwil (Basel), Lugano, Mollens (Valais) and Zurich.

Children in Cars

Children between 7 and 12 must use seat belts or a restraint system appropriate to their size when travelling as a front- or rear-seat passenger. A child under 7 should use a restraint sysytem appropriate to their size. See Essential Information for Motoring section under **Passengers** and **Seat Belts**.

Currency

The currency is the **Swiss franc** (CHF), which is divided into 100 centimes. Banknotes have denominations of CHF 10, 20, 50, 100, 200, and 1000; the coins are CHF 1, 2, and 5, and centimes 5, 10, 20 and 50.

There are no restrictions on the import or export of foreign or Swiss currency. In addition to banks there are exchange offices at the border, railway stations in large towns, airports and in travel agencies and hotels, which are usually open 08.00-20.00.

Although the **euro** is not the Swiss currency, many sites may quote prices in euros, rather than Swiss francs. Please contact such sites directly to check prices.

Dimensions & Weight Restrictions*

Private **cars** are restricted to the following dimensions: height 4 metres; width 2.55 metres; length 12 metres. **Trailers or caravans** are restricted to the following dimensions: height 4 metres; width 2.55 metres; length 12 metres (including tow bar). The maximum permitted overall length of a vehicle/trailer or caravan combination is 18.75 metres.

It is dangerous or forbidden to use a vehicle towing a trailer or caravan on some mountain roads; motorists should ensure that roads on which they are about to travel are suitable for their vehicle/trailer or caravan combinations.

The fully-laden weight of trailers which do not have an independent braking system should not exceed 50% of the unladen weight of the towing vehicle. Trailers that do have an independent braking system can weigh up to 100% of the unladen weight of the towing vehicle.

Driving Licence*

A valid UK or Republic of Ireland licence is accepted in Switzerland. The minimum age at which visitors from UK or Republic of Ireland may use a temporarily imported car is 18 years and a temporarily imported motorcycle of between 50-125cc (not exceeding 40km/h) 16 years, exceeding 125cc 18 years.

Foodstuffs*

Visitors may import foodstuffs and non-alcoholic drinks duty-free, for private use up to the value of CHF300 per person per day. Subject to certain prohibitions and restrictions, meat and meat products may be imported duty free up to 500g per person per day (e.g. beef, veal) and up to 3.5kg per person per day (e.g. chicken).

Lights*

It is recommended that motorcyclists use dipped headlights during the day.

Motoring Club

The **Touring Club Suisse** (TCS) has branch offices in all important towns, and has its head office at Chemin de Blandonnet 4, 1214 Vernier/Genève ☎ 022 417 27 27. The TCS will extend a courtesy service to all motorists but their major services will have to be paid for. The opening hours of TCS offices vary according to location and time of year, but generally they are Mon-Fri 08.00/09.00-11.45/12.30, 13.30/14.00-17.00/18.30hrs, Sat (summer only) 08.00/09.00-11.45/12.00.

Motorway Tax

The Swiss authorities levy an annual motorway tax and substantial fines are imposed for non-payment (CHF100 plus cost of *vignette*). A vehicle sticker, costing CHF40 for vehicles up to 3.5 tonnes maximum total weight and known as a *vignette*, must be displayed by vehicles using Swiss motorways including motorcycles, trailers and caravans. Motorists can purchase the stickers in the UK from Switzerland Tourism, Swiss Centre, 10 Wardour Street, London W1D 6QF; in Switzerland from customs offices, post offices, service stations and garages.

Vehicles over 3.5 tonnes maximum total weight are taxed on all roads in Switzerland. For coaches and caravans a licence for one day, 10 days, one month and one year periods is available. For lorries the tax depends on weight and distance. There are no stickers, and the tax must be paid at the Swiss frontier.

PETROL*

See Essential Information for Motoring section under **Petrol/Diesel**.

ROADS

Switzerland has about 1,600 km (1,000 miles) of motorway (*Autobahn* or *autoroute*). Tolls are not payable but see Motorway Tax above. Emergency telephones, which connect you to the motorway control police, are located every 2km.

The road surfaces are generally good, but some main roads are narrow in places. Traffic congestion can be severe at the beginning and end of the German school holidays.

On any stretch of mountain road, the driver of a private car may be asked by the driver of a postal bus which is painted yellow, to reverse, or otherwise manoeuvre to allow the postal bus to pass. Postal bus drivers often sound a distinctive three-note horn; no other vehicles can use this type of horn in Switzerland.

SPEED LIMITS*

Car/motorcycle	
Built-up areas	50km/h (31mph)
Other roads	80km/h (49mph)
Semi-motorways	100km/h (62mph)
Motorways	120km/h (74mph)
Car/caravan/trailer	
Built-up areas	50km/h (31mph)
Other roads	80km/h (49mph)
Semi-motorways	80km/h (49mph)
Motorways	80km/h (49mph)

These limits do not apply if another limit is indicated by signs, or if the vehicle is subject to a lower general speed limit.

WARNING TRIANGLE/HAZARD WARNING

It is compulsory to carry a warning triangle in a vehicle and to use it in the event of an accident or breakdown. The triangle must be placed on the road at least 50 metres (55yds) behind the vehicle on ordinary roads, and at least 100 metres (109yds) on faster roads. If in an emergency lane, the triangle must be placed on the right. Hazard-warning lights may be used in conjunction with the triangle or when traffic slows due to accident or traffic jam.

***Additional information can be found in the Essential Information for Motoring section.**

Appenzell

North

Künten Aargau

Sulz 5444 ☎ 079 6607426 Fax 056 4964879
e-mail: info@camping-sulz.ch **website:** www.camping-sulz.ch
Situated by a river.
From motorway A1 turn off at Baden towards Bremgarten.
Open: 15 Mar-Oct **Site:** 3HEC **Prices:** 6 2 10-15 6-15 (static)200 **Facilities:** **Services:** lau **Leisure:** PR

Läufelfingen Basel

Läufelfingen 4448 ☎ 062 2991189
On road from Basel to Olten.
Open: Apr-Oct **Site:** 0.5HEC **Prices:** 4 3 5-6 3-4 **Facilities:** **Services:**

Möhlin Aargau

Bachtalen (TCS) 4313 ☎ 061 815095 Fax 061 8539494
e-mail: camping.moehlin@bluewin.ch
website: www.campingtcs.ch
A pleasant site in a wooded rural setting.
2km N towards the River Rhine.
Open: Apr-Sep **Site:** 1HEC **Facilities:** **Services:** lau **Off-site:** PR

Reinach Basel

Waldhort Heideweg 16, 4153 ☎ 061 7116429 Fax 061 7139835
e-mail: camp.waldhort@gmx.ch
website: camping-waldhort.ch
In pleasant wooded surroundings close to the Basle-Delémont road.
Open: Mar-29 Oct **Site:** 3.3HEC **Prices:** 8 18 11 **Facilities:** **Services:** lau **Leisure:** P
Off-site:

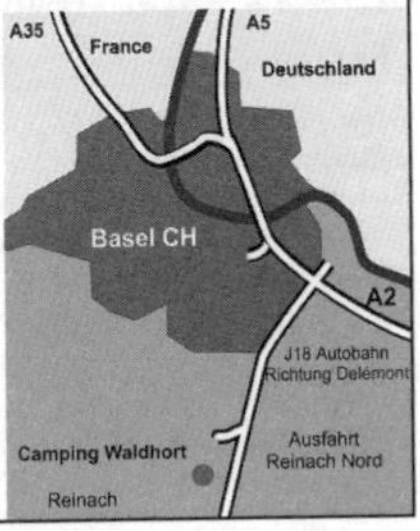

Zurzach Aargau

Oberfeld 5330 ☎ 56 2492575 Fax 56 2492579
e-mail: oberfield@camping-zurzach.ch
website: www.camping-zurzach.ch
Open: 19 Mar-29 Oct **Site:** 2HEC **Prices:** 6 9-12 4.50-7 pitch 9-12 (static)350 **Facilities:** **Services:** **Leisure:** PR

North-East

Altnau Thurgau

Ruderbaum 8595 ☎ 071 6952965
e-mail: camping@ruderbaum.ch
website: www.ruderbaum.ch
A small tourist site with ample facilities.
Close to the railway station by lake Bodensee between Constance & Romanshorn.
Open: Apr-Oct **Site:** 7.5HEC **Facilities:** **Services:** lau **Leisure:** L **Off-site:**

Appenzell Appenzell

Kau Appenzell 9050 ☎ 071 7875030
A woodland site with good modern installations.
Camping Card Compulsory
S of Appenzell towards Wattwil.
Open: All year **Site:** 2HEC **Facilities:** **Services:** lau

Eschenz Thurgau

Hüttenberg Hüttenberg, 8264
☎ 052 7412337 Fax 052 7415671
e-mail: info@huettenberg.ch
website: www.huettenberg.ch
Terraced site lying above village.
1km SW.
Open: All year **Site:** 6HEC **Prices:** 6.70-7.50 2.70-3 9.90-11 5.40-9 (static)385-490 **Facilities:** **Services:** **Leisure:** P
Off-site: LR

Goldingen St-Gallen

Atzmännig 8638 ☎ 055 2846434 Fax 055 2846435
e-mail: info@atzmaennig.ch
website: www.atzmaennig.ch
Suitable for summer and winter holidays, the site is close to the main cable-car and ski-lift stations and the giant mountainside slide.
Open: All year **Site:** 1.5HEC **Prices:** 6-6 7-7 7-7 **Facilities:** **Services:** lau

Krummenau St-Gallen

Adler 9643 ☎ 071 9941030
On edge of village.
Open: All year **Site:** 0.8HEC **Facilities:**
Services: lau

Leutswil Bei Bischoffzell Thurgau

Sitterbrücke 9220 ☎ 071 4226398
Signed from Bischoffzell on Konstanz-St Gallen road.
Open: Apr-15 Oct **Site:** 1HEC **Facilities:** **Services:** lau **Leisure:** R

Mammern Thurgau

Guldifuss Guldifusstr 1, 8265 ☎ 052 7411320
A terraced site directly on the Untersee.
Open: All year **Site:** 1.6HEC **Facilities:** **Services:** lau **Leisure:** L **Off-site:**

Facilities: shop, shower, electric points for razors, electric points for caravans, parking by tents permitted, compulsory separate car park **Services:** café/restaurant, bar, Camping Gaz International, gas other than Camping Gaz, first aid facilities, lau-laundry **Leisure:** swimming L-Lake P-Pool R-River S-Sea **Off-site:** All facilities within 2km

OTTENBACH Zürich

Reussbrücke (TCS) Muristr 32, 8913
01 7612022 01 7612042
e-mail: reussbruecke@tcs-ccz.ch
website: www.tcs-ccz.ch
By river of same name.
Access from Zürich via road 126 in SW direction, via Affoltern to Ottenbach.
Open: Apr-Oct **Site:** 1.5HEC **Prices:** 5.50-6.60 11-16 10-14 8-11 **Facilities:** **Services:** lau **Leisure:** R **Off-site:**

SCHÖNENGRUND Appenzell

Kronenfeld 9105 071 3611268 071 3611166
e-mail: hotel.krone.schoenengrund@bluewin.ch
website: www.gasthaus-krone.ch.tf
A comfortable, partly residential site with well-defined touring pitches.
Open: All year **Site:** 1HEC **Prices:** 3.70-5.50 2-3 3-4.50 3-4.50 **Facilities:** **Services:** lau **Off-site:** P

WAGENHAUSEN Schaffhausen

Wagenhausen Hauptstr 82, 8259
052 7414271 052 7414157
e-mail: campingwagenhausen@bluewin.ch
website: www.campingwagenhausen.ch
In a delightful wooded location beside the River Rhein.
Open: Apr-Oct **Site:** 4.5HEC **Prices:** 7 4 14 7 pitch 11 **Facilities:** **Services:** lau **Leisure:** PR

WALENSTADT St-Gallen

See-Camping 8880 081 7351212 081 7351841
e-mail: see-camping@bluewin.ch
A well-equipped family site with direct access to the the Walensee.
Accvess via Zürich-Chur motorway
Open: May-Sep **Site:** 1.2HEC **Prices:** 8 4 8-12 6-12 **Facilities:** **Services:** lau **Leisure:** L **Off-site:**

WILDBERG Zürich

Weid 8321 052 3853388 052 3853477
e-mail: seiler.camping@bluewin.ch
On a terraced meadow in a very peaceful situation surrounded by woods.
In Winterthur follow Tösstal signs, then turn right after spinning-mill in Turbenthal.
Open: All year **Site:** 6.1HEC **Facilities:** **Services:** lau **Off-site:** PR

WINTERTHUR Zürich

Schützenweiher Eichliwaldstr 4, 8400
052 2125260 052 2125260
e-mail: campingplatz@win.ch
To the left of the Schaffhausen road, near the Schützenhaus restaurant.
Open: All year **Site:** 1HEC **Prices:** 7.50 4 7.50 4.50 **Facilities:** **Services:** lau **Off-site:** P

NORTH-WEST & CENTRAL

AESCHI Bern

Panorama 3703 033 2233615 033 2233656
e-mail: postmaster@camping-aeschi.ch
website: www.camping-aeschi.ch
400m SE of Camping Club Bern.
Open: 15 May-Sep **Site:** 1HEC **Prices:** 5.60 3 10-12 8-12 **Facilities:** **Services:** lau **Off-site:**

ALTDORF Uri

Moosbad Flülerstr, 6460 041 8708541
A delightful mountain setting.
Access via Altdorf exit on A2.
Open: All year **Site:** 0.9HEC **Facilities:** **Services:** lau

BERN (BERNE) Bern
At WABERN

SC Eichholz Strandweg 49, 3084
031 9612602 031 9613526
e-mail: info@campingeichholz.ch
website: www.campingeicholz.ch
In municipal parkland. Separate section for caravans.
Approach via Gossetstr & track beside river.
Open: 20 Apr-Sep **Site:** 2HEC **Facilities:** **Services:** lau **Leisure:** R **Off-site:** P

BRENZIKOFEN Bern

Wydeli (TCS) Wydeli 60, 3671 031 7711141
e-mail: info@camping-brenzikofen.ch
website: www.camping-brenzikofen.ch
8km N of Thun.
Open: Jul-Aug **Site:** 1.3HEC **Facilities:** **Services:** lau **Leisure:** P **Off-site:**

BRUNNEN Schwyz

Hopfreben 6440 041 8201873
website: www.camping-brunnen.ch
On the right bank of the Muotta stream 100m before it flows into the lake.
1km W.
Open: May-29 Sep **Site:** 1.5HEC **Facilities:** **Services:** lau **Leisure:** LRS

COLOMBIER Neuchâtel

Paradis-Plage 2013 032 8412446 032 8414305
e-mail: paradisplage@freesurf.ch
website: www.paradisplage.ch
In a delightful setting beside lake Neuchâtel with good, modern facilities.
Open: Mar-Oct **Site:** 4HEC **Prices:** 8-9 2-3 8-15 8-15 (static)420-476 **Facilities:** **Services:** lau **Leisure:** L

ERLACH Bern

Mon Plaisir 3235 032 3381358 032 3381305
e-mail: info@camping24.ch
website: www.camping24.ch
Well equipped site beside the lake.
Open: All year **Site:** 0.6HEC **Facilities:** **Services:** lau **Leisure:** L **Off-site:** PR

EUTHAL Schwyz

Euthal 8844 055 4122718 055 4127673
e-mail: info@hotelposteuthal.ch
website: www.hotelposteuthal.ch
On the shore of the Sihlsee in a beautiful mountain setting.
The site is reserved for tents only.
Open: Apr-Oct **Site:** 1HEC **Prices:** 7.50 2.50 6-8 **Facilities:** **Services:** **Leisure:** L **Off-site:**

FLÜELEN Uri

Urnersee 6454 041 8709222 041 8709216
e-mail: info@windsurfing-urnersee.ch
website: www.windsurfing-urnersee.ch
On level ground on the shore of the Vierwaldstättersee with plenty of sports facilities.
Open: 15 Apr-Oct **Site:** 4.5HEC **Facilities:** **Services:** **Leisure:** LR **Off-site:** P

FRUTIGEN Bern

Grassi 3714 033 6711149 033 6711380
e-mail: campinggrassi@bluewin.ch
website: www.campinggrassi.ch
Scattered with fruit trees beside a farm on the right bank of the River Engstilgern.
From the Haupstr, turn right at the Simplon Hotel.
Open: All year **Site:** 1.5HEC **Prices:** 6.40 pitch 8-14 **Facilities:** **Services:** lau **Off-site:** P

GAMPELEN Bern

Fanel (TCS) 3236 032 3132333 032 3131407
e-mail: camping.gampelen@tcs.ch
website: www.campingtcs.ch
A level site on the shore of lake Neuchâtel protected by trees and bushes.
Access via A5 towards Gampelen.
Open: 2 Apr-3 Oct **Site:** 11.3HEC **Facilities:** **Services:** lau **Leisure:** L **Off-site:** R

GISWIL Obwalden

Giswil 6074 041 6752355
Open: Apr-20 Oct **Site:** 1.9HEC **Facilities:** **Services:** lau **Leisure:** L

GOLDAU Schwyz

Bernerhöhe 6410 041 8551887 041 8555970
On the edge of a forest with a beautiful view of lake Lauerz. Separate field for tents.
1.5km SE & turn left.
Open: All year **Site:** 2.5HEC **Prices:** 5.30 1 3 3 **Facilities:** **Services:** lau

GRINDELWALD Bern

Aspen 3818 033 8531124 033 534157
Sunny hill terraces.
Open: Jun-15 Oct **Site:** 2.5HEC **Facilities:** **Services:** lau **Off-site:**

GSTAAD Bern

Bellerive 3780 033 7446330 033 7446345
e-mail: bellerive.camping@bluewin.ch
Open: All year **Site:** 0.8HEC **Facilities:** **Services:** lau **Leisure:** R **Off-site:** P

INNERTKIRCHEN Bern

Aareschlucht Hauptstr 6/11, 3862
0339715532 033 9715344
e-mail: campaareschlucht@bluewin.ch
website: www.swisscamps.ch
A beautiful Alpine location with superb mountain views.
Open: May-Oct **Site:** 0.5HEC **Facilities:** **Services:** lau **Off-site:** R

Grund 3862 033 9714409 033 9714767
e-mail: info@camping-grund.ch
website: www.camping-grund.ch
Next to a farm on S outskirts of village.
Turn S off main road in centre of village at hotel Urweider. Continue 300m, turn right.
Open: All year **Site:** 120HEC **Prices:** 3.90-4.50 15-19 10-15 **Facilities:** **Services:** lau **Off-site:** R

INTERLAKEN Bern

Hobby 3 Lehnweg 16, 3800
033 8229652 & 033 8229657
e-mail: info@campinghobby.ch
website: www.campinghobby.ch
Family site with excellent sanitary facilities, quietly situated with fine views of the surrounding mountains and within easy walking distance of Interlaken.
Access via A8 Spiez-Interlaken towards Gunten/Beatenberg. Exit A3 at Unterseen, follow campsign number 3.
Open: Apr-Sep **Site:** 1.5HEC **Prices:** 5.50-6.90 pitch 15-30 **Facilities:** **Services:** lau **Off-site:** LPRS

Jungfrau Steindlerstr 50, 3800
033 8227107 033 8225730
e-mail: info@jungfraucamp.ch
website: www.jungfraucamp.ch
Beautiful views of the Eiger, the Mönch and the Jungfrau.
Turn right at Unterseen, drive through the Schulhaus and Steinler Str to site.
Open: May-Sep **Site:** 2.5HEC **Facilities:** **Services:** lau **Leisure:** P **Off-site:** LR

Jungfraublick Gsteigstr 80, 3800
033 8224414 033 8221619
e-mail: info@jungfraublick.ch
website: www.jungfraublick.ch
A family site with clean, modern facilities in a fine central location.

contd.

➲ *Take Autobahn A8 through tunnel, leave at Lauterbrunnen-Grindelwald exit, site on left 300m.*
Open: May-20 Sep **Site:** 1.3HEC **Prices:** 7.40-8.40 pitch 16-30 **Facilities:** **Services:** lau **Leisure:** P **Off-site:** R

Lazy Rancho 4 3800 ☎ 033 8228716 033 8231920
e-mail: info@lazyrancho.ch
website: www.lazyrancho.ch
A family campsite in a magnificent position with views of the Eiger, Mönch and Jungfrau with fine facilities.
➲ *Motorway A8 exit Unterseen, turn toward Gunten. After 2km turn right, then at Landhotel Golf turn left.*
Open: May-15 Oct **Site:** 16HEC **Prices:** 6-7.50 pitch 10-28 **Facilities:** **Services:** lau **Leisure:** P **Off-site:** LR

Manor Farm 3800 ☎ 033 8222264 033 8222279
e-mail: manorfarm@swisscamps.ch
website: www.manorfarm.ch
A well-equipped site in a beautiful mountain setting.
➲ *From motorway A8 (Bern-Speiz-Interlaken-Brienz) exit Gunten/Beatenberg; follow signs.*
Open: All year **Site:** 7.5HEC **Facilities:** **Services:** lau **Leisure:** LR

KANDERSTEG BERN

Rendez-Vous 3718 ☎ 033 6751534 033 6751737
e-mail: rendez-vous.camping@bluewin.ch
website: www.camping-kandersteg.ch
In a delightful mountain setting with good modern facilities.
➲ *750m E of town.*
Open: All year **Site:** 1HEC **Prices:** 7.50 3 8-16 6-12 **Facilities:** **Services:** lau **Off-site:** P

LANDERON, LE NEUCHÂTEL

Peches 2525 ☎ 032 7512900 032 7516354
e-mail: info@camping-lelanderon.ch
website: www.camping-lelanderon.ch
A small site at the meeting point of the River Thielle and Lac de Bienne.
Open: Apr-15 Oct **Site:** 2.1HEC **Prices:** 8 4 9-10.50 7.50-9.50 **Facilities:** **Services:** lau **Leisure:** L **Off-site:** PR

LAUTERBRUNNEN BERN

Schützenbach (TCS) 3822 ☎ 033 8551268 033 8551275
e-mail: www.schutzenbach.ch
In an fine Alpine location close to the main skiing areas and about 300m from the lake.

S of village to the left of road leading to Stechelberg opposite 350. 0.8km SE towards Stechelberg.
Open: All year **Site:** 3HEC **Facilities:** **Services:** lau **Off-site:** P

Lignières Neuchâtel

Fraso-Ranch 2523 032 7514616 032 7514614
e-mail: camping.fraso-ranch@bluewin.ch
website: mypage.bluewin.ch/camping_lignieres
A modern family site with good recreational facilities and a separate section for tourers.
NE of Lignières on Nods road. Signed.
Open: All year **Site:** 8.7HEC **Prices:** 6-8 pitch 11-15 **Facilities:** **Services:** lau **Leisure:** P

Locle, le Neuchâtel

Communal (TCS) 2400 032 9317493 032 9317408
e-mail: camping.lelode@tcs.ch
website: www.campingtcs.ch
On a level meadow surrounded by woodland. Good recreational facilities.
S of town off the La Sagne road.
Open: 29 Apr-16 Oct **Site:** 1.2HEC **Prices:** 5.20-6.20 10-16 7-8 **Facilities:** **Services:** lau **Leisure:** P **Off-site:**

Lungern Obwalden

Obsee 6078 041 6781463 041 6782163
e-mail: camping@obsee.ch
website: www.obsee.ch
In a beautiful setting between the lake and the mountains with good facilities for watersports.
1km W.
Open: All year **Site:** 1.5HEC **Prices:** 6 13 13 **Facilities:** **Services:** lau **Leisure:** LPR **Off-site:**

Luzern (Lucerne) Luzern

Steinibachried (TCS) Horw, 6048
041 3403558 041 3403556
e-mail: camping.horw@tcs.ch
website: www.campingtcs.ch
In gently sloping meadow next to the football ground and the beach, separated from the lake by a wide belt of reeds.
3.2km S of Luzern.
Open: 2 Apr-3 Oct **Site:** 2HEC **Prices:** 5.60-7.80 pitch 14-19.60 (static)525-735 **Facilities:** **Services:** lau **Off-site:** L

Meiringen Bern

Balmweid Balmweidstrasse 22, 3860
033 9715115 033 9715117
e-mail: camping.balmweid@popnet.ch
Mainly flat meadowland site with mountain views.
Open: All year **Site:** 2.2HEC **Facilities:** **Services:** lau

Mosen Luzern

Seeblick 6295 041 9171666 041 9171666
e-mail: mptrunz@gmx.ch
website: www.camping-seeblick.ch
In two strips of land on edge of lake, divided by paths into several squares.
N on the A26.
Open: Apr-Oct **Site:** 3HEC **Prices:** 4 2 4 2.70-3.40 **Facilities:** **Services:** lau **Leisure:** L **Off-site:**

Nottwil Luzern

St Margrethen 6207 041 9371404 041 9371865
e-mail: st.margrethen@swisscamps.ch
website: www.swisscamps.ch
Natural meadowland under fruit trees, with own access to lakeside.
Turn off road to Sursee 400m NW of Nottwil towards lake for 100m.
Open: Apr-Oct **Site:** 1HEC **Prices:** 6.50-7 4 4-4.50 3-5 **Facilities:** **Services:** lau **Leisure:** L **Off-site:** LP

Prêles Bern

Prêles 2515 032 3151716 032 3155160
e-mail: info@camping-jura.ch
website: www.camping-jura.ch
On a wooded plateau overlooking lake Biel.
Turn off the main Biel-Neuchâtel road at Twann & follow signs for Prêles. Through village, site on left.
Open: All year **Site:** 6HEC **Prices:** 8 2.50 13-15 7-10 **Facilities:** **Services:** lau **Leisure:** P

Saanen Bern

Beim Kappeli (TCS) 3792 033 7446191 033 7446184
e-mail: camping.saaren@tcs.ch
website: www.campingtcs.ch
In a long meadow between railway and River Saane.
1km SE.
Open: Jan-Oct & 11-31 Dec **Site:** 0.8HEC **Facilities:** **Services:** lau **Leisure:** R **Off-site:** P

SACHSELN OBWALDEN

Ewil CH-6072 041 6663270 041 6663279
e-mail: m.k.berlinger@pop.agri.ch
website: www.camping.ch
On a level meadow on the SW shore of the Sarnersee.
W of the main Sachseln-Ewil road towards the lake.
Open: Apr-Sep **Site:** 1.5HEC **Prices:** 5.80-6.50 3 8 4-8 **Facilities:** **Services:** lau **Leisure:** LS **Off-site:** R

SEMPACH LUZERN

Seeland (TCS) 6204 041 4601466 041 4604766
e-mail: camping.sempach@tcs.ch
website: www.campingtcs.ch
Rectangular, level site on SW shore of lake.
700m S on Luzern road by lake.
Open: Apr-Nov **Site:** 5.2HEC **Prices:** 6-7.80 3 16-29 6-9 **Facilities:** **Services:** lau **Leisure:** L

STECHELBERG BERN

Breithorn 3824 033 8551225 033 8553561
e-mail: breithorn@stechelberg.ch
In a beautiful location in the Lauterbrunnen valley.
3km S of Lauterbrunnen.
Open: All year **Site:** 1HEC **Prices:** 6.70 **Facilities:** **Services:** lau

SURSEE LUZERN

Sursee Waldheim, 6216 041 9211161 041 9211160
e-mail: campingsursee@bluewin.ch
website: www.camping-sursee.ch
Next to Waldheim country estate.
0.8km W of Sursee, 100m from Sursee-Basel road.
Open: Apr-Sep **Site:** 1.7HEC **Facilities:** **Services:** lau **Off-site:** L

VITZNAU LUZERN

Vitznau 6354 041 3971280 041 3972457
e-mail: camping-vitznau@bluewin.ch
website: www.camping-vitznau.ch
Well tended terraced site, in lovely countryside with fine views of lake.
From N, turn towards mountain at church & follow signs.
Open: Dec-24 Oct **Site:** 1.8HEC **Prices:** 8-9.50 pitch 14-22 **Facilities:** **Services:** lau **Leisure:** P **Off-site:** L

WILDERSWIL BERN

Oberei 3812 033 8221335 033 8221335
e-mail: oberei8@swisscamps.ch
website: www.campingwilderwil.ch
A peaceful site in a picturesque village with fine views of the Jungfrau and surrounding mountains. There are good facilities and booking is recommended in July and August.
Open: 15 Apr-15 Oct **Site:** 0.6HEC **Prices:** 5-5.90 pitch 10-18 **Facilities:** **Services:** lau **Off-site:** LPR

ZUG ZUG

Innere Lorzenallmend (TCS) Chamer Fussweg 36, 6300 041 7418422 041 7418130
e-mail: tcscamping.zug@tcs.ch
website: www.campingtcs.ch
Pleasantly situated with beautiful view of lake Zug and surrounding mountains. Much traffic on railway which passes the site.
1km NW by lake.
Open: 2 Apr-3 Oct **Site:** 1.1HEC **Facilities:** **Services:** lau **Leisure:** LRS **Off-site:**

EAST

ANDEER GRAUBÜNDEN

Sut Baselgia (TCS) 7440
041 816611453 041 816611080
e-mail: camping.andeer@bluewin.ch
website: www.viamalaferien.ch
In a pleasant, peaceful setting N towards Chur.
Open: Dec-Oct **Site:** 1.2HEC **Prices:** 6.50 3 13 8-13 **Facilities:** **Services:** lau **Off-site:** PR

AROSA GRAUBÜNDEN

Arosa Tourismus 7050 081 3771745 081 3773005
Open: All year **Site:** 0.6HEC **Facilities:** **Off-site:** LP

CHUR (COIRE) GRAUBÜNDEN

Camp Au Felsenaustr 61, 7000
081 2842283 081 2845683
e-mail: info@camping-chur.ch
website: www.camping-chur.ch
A summer and winter site on level ground with fine views of the surrounding mountains. Good recreational facilities.
Take exit Chur-Süd from A13. 2km NW of town centre on bank of Rhein. Access is via outskirts of town.
Open: All year **Site:** 2.6HEC **Facilities:** **Services:** lau **Off-site:** P

CHURWALDEN GRAUBÜNDEN

Pradafenz 7075 081 3821921 081 3821921
e-mail: camping@pradafenz.ch
website: www.pradafenz.ch
A year round site in a beautiful mountain area close to the local ski slopes.
Open: Jan-22 Apr & 28 May-Oct **Site:** 1.5HEC **Facilities:** **Services:** lau **Off-site:** PR

LENZ GRAUBÜNDEN

St Cassian 7083 081 3842472 081 3842489
e-mail: camping.st.cassian@bluwin.ch
A level, shady site in a beautiful location at an altitude of 1415m. There are good facilities and the site is 1km from the town.
Leave motorway at Chur-Süd exit & follow signs for Lenzerheide/St Moritz up a well-constructed mountain road.
Open: All year **Site:** 25HEC **Prices:** 8 2.50 9.50 9.50 **Facilities:** **Services:** lau **Off-site:**

MÜSTAIR GRAUBÜNDEN

Clenga 7537 081 8585410 081 8585422
e-mail: clenga@campclenga.ch **website:** www.campclenga.ch
Next to small river near the Italian frontier.
Open: 15 May-20 Oct **Site:** 1.5HEC **Prices:** 6-6.50 pitch 10-12 (static)490 **Facilities:** **Services:** lau **Leisure:** R

PONTRESINA Graubünden

Plauns (TCS) 7504 081 8426285 081 8345136
e-mail: a.brueli@bluewin.ch
website: www.pontresina.ch
Beautiful situation at foot of Pit Palü.
Access from road towards Bernina pass 4.5km beyond Pontresina. Turn off main road 29 towards Hotel Morteratsch then 0.5km to site.
Open: Jun-15 Oct & 15 Dec-15 Apr **Site:** 4HEC **Facilities:** **Services:** lau

POSCHIAVO Graubünden

Boomerang 7745 081 8440713 081 8441575
e-mail: camping.boomerang@bluewin.ch
A quiet setting.
2km SE.
Open: All year **Site:** 1.5HEC **Prices:** 9-12 2 8 **Facilities:** **Services:** lau
Off-site: LP

SAMEDAN Graubünden

Punt Muragl (TCS) 7503 081 8428197 081 8428197
e-mail: camping.samedan@tcs.ch
website: www.campingtcs.ch
A summer and winter site in a pleasant alpine setting.
Near Bernina railway halt, to the right of the fork of the two roads Samedan & Celerina/Schlarigna to Pontresina.
Open: Jun-3 Oct & Dec-15 Apr **Site:** 2HEC
Prices: 6.75-8.35 13-18 6-8 (static)385-630
Facilities: **Services:** lau
Off-site: L

SPLÜGEN Graubünden

Sand 7435 081 6641476 081 6641460
e-mail: camping@splugen.ch
website: www.campingsplugen.ch
On left bank of River Hinterrhein.
Turn off the main road in the village and follow signs.
Open: All year **Site:** 0.8HEC **Facilities:** **Services:** lau **Leisure:** R **Off-site:**

SUSCH Graubünden

Muglinas 7542 081 0797875689
200m W.
Open: Jun-15 Sep **Site:** 1HEC **Facilities:** **Services:** lau **Leisure:** R **Off-site:**

THUSIS Graubünden

Viamala 7430 081 6512472
In pleasant wooded surroundings near the River Hinterrhein and close to the beautiful Viamala gorge.
NE towards Chur.
Open: May-Sep **Site:** 4.5HEC **Facilities:** **Services:** lau **Off-site:** PR

TSCHIERV Graubünden

Sternen (TCS) Chasa Maruya, 7532 081 8585628
e-mail: maruya@tiscalinet.ch
website: www.muenstertal.ch
In village behind the Sternen Hotel.
Between Ofen Pass & Santa Maria.
Open: All year **Site:** 1HEC **Prices:** 6 3 5 3
Facilities: **Services:** lau **Leisure:** PR

ZERNEZ Graubünden

Cul 7530 081 8561456 081 8561462
e-mail: a.filli@camping-cul.ch **website:** www.camping-cul.ch
In a delightful mountain setting close to the Swiss national park.
Off road 27 W of Zernez.
Open: May-15 Oct **Site:** 3.6HEC **Facilities:** **Services:** lau **Leisure:** R **Off-site:** P

SOUTH

ACQUACALDA Ticino

Ai Cembri Lukmanierstr, 6718 091 8722610
In a beautiful mountain location with good hiking facilities.
Open: Apr-Oct **Site:** 5HEC **Facilities:** **Services:** lau **Leisure:** R

AGNO Ticino

Eurocampo 6982 091 6052114 091 6053187
website: mypage.bluewin.ch/eurocampo
Part of site is near its own sandy beach and is divided by groups of trees.
600m E on road from Lugano to Ponte Tresa. Entrance opposite Aeroport sign & Alfa Romeo building.
Open: 20 Mar-Oct **Site:** 6HEC **Prices:** 9 pitch 8
Facilities: **Services:** lau
Leisure: LR **Off-site:**

Golfo del Sole via Rivera 8, 6982
091 6054802 091 6052319
e-mail: info@golfodelsole.ch **website:** www.golfodelsole.ch
By lake. Separate play area for children.
Open: Apr-15 Oct **Site:** 6HEC **Prices:** 8-9 2 10-13 8-10 **Facilities:** **Services:**
Leisure: L **Off-site:** P

CUGNASCO Ticino

Park-Camping Riarena 6516
091 8591688 091 8592885
e-mail: camping.riarena@bluewin.ch
website: www.camping-riarena.ch
Beautiful park-like, family site in level, natural woodland. All facilities are well maintained and lake Maggiore is within easy reach.
1.5km NW. Turn off road 13 at BP filling station 9km NE of Locarno & continue 0.5km.
Open: Mar-26 Oct **Site:** 3.2HEC
Facilities: **Services:** lau
Leisure: P **Off-site:** R

GORDEVIO Ticino

Bellariva 6672 091 7531444 091 7531764
e-mail: camping.gerdevio@tcs.ch **website:** www.campingtcs.ch
In quiet location between the road and the left bank of the River Maggia.
Open: Apr-Oct **Site:** 2.5HEC **Facilities:** **Services:** lau **Leisure:** PR

LOCARNO Ticino

Delta via Respini 7, 6600 091 7516081 091 7512243
e-mail: info@campingdelta.com
website: www.campingdelta.com
A beautiful, well-equipped and well-organised site at lake Maggiore.
2km from the city.
Open: Mar-Oct **Site:** 6.5HEC **Prices:** 11-18 pitch 21-57 (static)392-700 **Facilities:**
Services: lau **Leisure:** LR **Off-site:** P

AT LOSONE (4KM W)

Zandone 6616 091 7916563 091 7910047
A quiet, picturesque location beside the River Melezza with fine views of the Tessin mountains.
Between the Losone-Golino road & river.
Open: Etr-Oct **Site:** 2.1HEC **Facilities:** **Services:** **Leisure:** R **Off-site:**

MOLINAZZO DI MONTEGGIO TICINO

Tresiana 6995 091 6083342 091 6083142
e-mail: mail@camping-tresiana
website: www.camping-tresiana.ch
A family site on meadowland with trees on riverbank.
Turn right after bridge in Ponte Tresa, then 5km to site.
Site: 1.5HEC **Prices:** 6.50-8.50 3-5 13-21 7-21 (static)350-770 **Facilities:** **Services:** lau **Leisure:** PR **Off-site:**

TENERO TICINO

Campofelice Lago Maggiore, 6598
091 7451417 091 7451888
e-mail: camping@campofelice.ch
website: www.campofelice.ch
Beautifully situated and extensive site completely divided into pitches, and crossed by asphalt drives.
1.9km S. Signed.
Open: 18 Mar-22 Oct **Site:** 15HEC **Prices:** pitch 38-84 (incl 2 persons) **Facilities:** **Services:** lau **Leisure:** LR

Lido Mappo Via Mappo, 6598 091 7451437 091 7454808
e-mail: camping@lidomappo.ch
website: www.lidomappo.ch
Beautifully situated, well-appointed site on lakeside. Teenagers not accepted on their own. Minimum stay 1 week in July and August.
700m SW. Signed.
Open: 18 Mar- 23 Oct **Site:** 6.5HEC **Prices:** pitch 32-49 (incl 2 persons) **Facilities:** **Services:** lau **Leisure:** L **Off-site:** PR

Tamaro via Mappo, 6598 091 7452161 091 7456636
e-mail: info@campingtamaro.ch
website: www.campingtamaro.ch
Well-equipped site with direct access to the lake. Groups of young persons must be accompanied by adults.
4km from Locano. Signed from motorway.
Open: 18 Mar-23 Oct **Site:** 6HEC **Prices:** pitch 33-62 (incl 2 persons) **Facilities:** **Services:** lau **Leisure:** L **Off-site:** P

SOUTH-WEST

AGARN VALAIS

Gemmi Briannenstr, 3952 027 4731154 027 4734295
e-mail: info@campgemmi.ch
website: www.campgemmi.ch
In a very pleasant location on the outskirts of the town, providing outstanding views of the surrounding mountains. There are clean, modern facilities and individual bathrooms are available for weekly hire.
Exit from A9 at Agarn. Signed.
Open: 24 Apr-16 Oct **Site:** 0.9HEC **Prices:** 7-8 pitch 11-19 **Facilities:** **Services:** lau **Off-site:** P

AIGLE VAUD

Glariers (TCS) 1860 024 4662660 024 4662660
e-mail: camping.aigle@tcs.ch
website: www.campingtcs.ch
On level ground with trees and bushes near railway line and the avenue des Glariers. Fine mountain views.
800m NE off the A9 near Shell Migrol filling station.
Open: 02 Apr-03 Oct **Site:** 1HEC **Prices:** 6.20-8.20 14-18 7-10 **Facilities:** **Services:** lau **Leisure:** PR **Off-site:**

AROLLA VALAIS

Petit Praz 1986 027 2832295
e-mail: camping@arolla.com
An imposing mountain setting.
Open: Jun-20 Sep **Site:** 1HEC **Prices:** 6 3 7 5-7 **Facilities:** **Services:** lau

BALLENS VAUD

Bois Gentil 1144 021 8095120
200m S of station.
Open: Apr-Sep **Site:** 2.5HEC **Prices:** 6.50 2 6.50 5 **Facilities:** **Services:** **Leisure:** P

BOURG-ST-PIERRE VALAIS

Grand St-Bernard 1946 027 7871411 027 7871411
e-mail: grand-st-bernard@swisscamps.ch
website: www.campinggrand-st-bernard.ch
In beautiful mountain scenery with easy access to winter-sports areas.
Near the Italian border, between Martigny and Aosta.
Open: May-Sep **Site:** 1HEC **Facilities:** **Services:** lau **Leisure:** P **Off-site:** R

BOUVERET, LE VALAIS

Rive Bleue 1897 024 4812161
e-mail: info@camping-rive-bleue.ch
website: www.camping-rive-bleue.ch
Beside lake with a natural sandy beach and good, modern facilities.
Turn off A37 to Monthey in the SW district of Bouveret & NE for about 0.8km.
Open: Apr-Sep **Site:** 3HEC **Prices:** 7.60-9.30 1.90 8.30-11.40 6.50-10.30 (static)365-460 **Facilities:** **Services:** lau **Leisure:** LP **Off-site:** R

BULLET VAUD

Cluds 1453 024 4541440 024 4541440
e-mail: vd28@campings-ccyverdon.ch
website: www.campings-ccyverdon.ch
In beautiful mountain setting among pine trees.
1.5km NE.
Open: All year **Site:** 1.2HEC **Prices:** 7 3 7-11 5-11 **Facilities:** **Services:** lau **Off-site:**

CHÂTEAU-D'OEX VAUD

Berceau (TCS) 1837
026 9246234 026 9246234/ 026 9242526
e-mail: info@chateaudoex.ch
website: www.chateau-doex.ch
On level strip of grass between the mountain and the river bank.
1km SE at junction of roads 77 & 76.
Open: All year **Site:** 1HEC **Facilities:** **Services:** lau **Leisure:** PR **Off-site:**

CHÂTEL-ST-DENIS FRIBOURG

Bivouac rte des Paccots, 1618 021 9487849 021 9487849
e-mail: bivouac@swissonline.ch
website: www.le-bivouac.ch
Beautiful views of the rolling Swiss countryside. Various sports and leisure activities.
Turn E in Chatel-St Denis and continue for 2km.
Open: Apr-Sep **Site:** 2HEC **Prices:** 5-6 pitch 10-15 **Facilities:** **Services:** lau **Leisure:** PR **Off-site:**

CHESSEL VAUD

Grands Bois 1846 024 4814225 024 4815113
e-mail: au.grand-bois@bluewin.ch
website: www.augrandebois.ch
On a level meadow close to a canal and only a few kilometres from lake Geneva.
N of town towards the lake.
Open: All year **Site:** 4HEC **Prices:** 4.50-6 2.50-3 6.50-9 3.50-9 (static)250-380 **Facilities:** **Services:** lau **Leisure:** PR

CUDREFIN VAUD

Chablais 1588 037 773277
500m from the town centre, directly by the lake.
Open: 15 Mar-Oct **Site:** 228HEC **Facilities:** **Services:** lau **Leisure:** L **Off-site:** R

DÜDINGEN FRIBOURG

Schiffenensee 3186 026 493486
Leave the A12 (Bern-Fribourg) at Düdingen & N towards Murten.
Open: Apr-Oct **Site:** 9HEC **Facilities:** **Services:** lau **Leisure:** LP **Off-site:**

EVOLÈNE VALAIS

Evolène 1983 027 2831144 027 2833255
e-mail: evolene@swisscamps.ch
website: www.camping-evolene.ch
On a level meadow with fine views of the surrounding mountains.
200m from town.
Open: All year **Site:** 10HEC **Prices:** 6.50 3 7-10 5-10 (static)300 **Facilities:** **Services:** lau **Leisure:** P **Off-site:** R

FOREL VAUD

Forel 1606 021 7811464 021 7813126
A family site in a pleasant rural setting with good recreational facilities.
Leave the A9 at Chexbres towards Forel and take left turning to Savigny.
Open: All year **Site:** 4HEC **Facilities:** **Services:** lau **Leisure:** P

FOULY, LA VALAIS

Glaciers 1944 027 7831735 027 7833605
e-mail: camping.glaciers@st-bernard.ch
website: www.camping-glaciers.ch
At end of village in a beautiful Alpine location with fine views of the surrounding mountains.
Open: 15 May-Sep **Site:** 8HEC **Prices:** 6.50 pitch 14-16 **Facilities:** **Services:** lau **Off-site:** R

GENÈVE (GENEVA) GENÈVE
AT SATIGNY (6KM SW)

Bois-de-Bay 1242 022 3410505 022 3410606
Leave A1 at Bernex and follow campsite signs.
Open: All year **Site:** 2.8HEC **Facilities:** **Services:**

AT VÉSENAZ (6KM NE)

Pointe á la Bise (TCS) 12223
022 7521296 022 7523767
e-mail: camping.geneve@tcs.ch
In a pleasant wooded setting on the shore of lake Léman.
NE between Vésenaz & Collonge-Bellerive.
Open: Etr-mid Oct **Site:** 3.2HEC **Prices:** 6.40-6.60 3 pitch 14-23.60 **Facilities:** **Services:** **Leisure:** L

GRANDSON VAUD

Pécos VD24, 1422 024 4454969 024 4462904
e-mail: vd24@campings-ccyverdon.ch
website: www.campings-ccyverdon.ch
400m SW of railway station between railway & lake.
Open: Apr-Sep **Site:** 2HEC **Prices:** 7.90 3 7-9 6-12 (static)560 **Facilities:** **Services:** lau **Leisure:** L

GUMEFENS FRIBOURG

Lac 1643 026 9152162 026 9152162
e-mail: campingdulac@planet.ch
On the borders of the lake.
Open: 15 May-15 Sep **Site:** 1.5HEC **Facilities:** **Services:** lau **Leisure:** L

LAUSANNE VAUD

Vioy chemin du Camping 3, 1007
021 6225000 021 6225001
e-mail: info@campinglausannevidy.ch
website: www.campinglausannevidy.ch
In a delightful location amid trees and flowerbeds overlooking Lac Léman. Shop and restaurant open May to September only.
Open: All year **Site:** 4.5HEC **Facilities:** **Services:** lau **Leisure:** L

LEYSIN VAUD

Sémiramis 1854 024 4943939 024 4942121
e-mail: info@camping-leysin.ch
website: camping-leysin.ch
In a picturesque Alpine setting.
After entering the village turn left at Shell filling station & continue for 400m.
Open: All year **Site:** 1.1HEC **Prices:** 5-6.50 3-5 6-7.20 2-4 **Facilities:** **Services:** lau **Off-site:** P

MORGINS VALAIS

Morgins (TCS) 1875 024 4772361 024 4773708
e-mail: touristoffice@morgins.ch
website: www.morgins.ch
A terraced site below pine forest.
Turn left at end of village towards Pas de Morgins near Swiss customs.
Open: All year **Site:** 1.3HEC **Prices:** 6.70 pitch 10 **Facilities:** **Services:** lau **Off-site:** PR

PAYERNE VAUD

Piscine de Payerne 1530 037 614322
Camping Card compulsory
Open: Apr-Sep **Site:** 8HEC **Facilities:**
Services: lau **Leisure:** P

RARON VALAIS

Camping Simplonblick 3942 027 9341274 027 9342600
e-mail: simplon-blick@bluewin.ch
website: www.camping-simplonblick.ch
300m W of Turtig.
Open: All year **Site:** 6HEC **Facilities:** **Services:** lau **Leisure:** P **Off-site:**

Santa Monica 3942 027 9342424 027 9342450
e-mail: info@santa-monica.ch
website: www.santa-monica.ch
Open: All year **Site:** 4HEC **Prices:** 5-6 pitch 9.50-12 **Facilities:** **Services:** lau **Leisure:** P **Off-site:** LR

RECKINGEN VALAIS

Ellbogen (TCS) CH-3998 027 9731395 027 9732677
e-mail: info@campingaugenstern.ch
website: www.campingaugenstern.ch
On an alpine meadow close to the River Rhône.
400m S on bank of Rhône.
Open: 10 Dec-Apr & 10 May-24 Oct **Site:** 3HEC **Prices:** 8.30 8.50 7.50 pitch 8.50 **Facilities:** **Services:** lau **Off-site:** PR

RIED-BRIG VALAIS

Tropic 3911 027 9232537
To the left of Simplon road near entrance to village. 3km above Brig.
Open: May-15 Sep **Site:** 1.5HEC **Prices:** 5.50 4 6-7 4-7 pitch 4 **Facilities:**
Services: lau **Off-site:** P

SAAS-GRUND VALAIS

Kapellenweg 3910 027 9574997 027 9573316
e-mail: camping@kapellenweg.ch
website: www.kapellenweg.ch
On a level meadow in a picruresque mountain setting in the Saas Valley. Good, modern facilities.
Turn right over bridge towards Saas-Almagell.
Open: May-Oct **Site:** 1.5HEC **Prices:** 4.80-6 3.60-4.50 3.60-4.50 3.60-4.50 **Facilities:** **Services:** lau **Off-site:**

SALGESCH VALAIS

Swiss Plage 3970 027 4816023 027 4556608
e-mail: info@swissplage.ch
website: http://swissplage.ch
Situated beside a small lake and surrounded by vineyards. Good recreational facilities.
Open: Etr-1 Nov **Site:** 10HEC
Prices: 7.40 pitch 10-16 (static)595 **Facilities:** **Services:** lau **Leisure:** LR

SEMBRANCHER VALAIS

Prairie (TCS) 1933 027 7852206 027 7852131
e-mail: prairie01@bluewin.ch
12km from Martigny and 500m from town.
Open: Jun-Sep **Site:** 50HEC **Facilities:** **Services:** lau **Off-site:** R

SIERRE (SIDERS) VALAIS

Bois de Finges (TCS) 3960 027 4550284 027 4553351
e-mail: camping.sierre@tcs.ch
website: www.campingtcs.ch
Situated in a pine forest with well-defined pitches set on terraces.
Access via motorway exit Sierre-Ouest towards Sierre.
Open: 28 Apr-03 Oct **Site:** 5HEC
Facilities: **Services:** lau
Leisure: P **Off-site:** LR

SORENS FRIBOURG

Forêt 1642 026 9151882 026 9150363
e-mail: camping.laforet@caramail.com
A pleasant site on a level meadow surrounded by woodland and with pleant of vegetation.
Turn off the A12 in Gumefens to the village.
Open: All year **Site:** 4HEC **Prices:** 6 2.50 5 5 pitch 4 (static)330 **Facilities:**
Services: lau **Leisure:** P

SUSTEN VALAIS

Bella Tola (TCS) Waldstrosse 57, CH 3952
027 4731491 027 4733641
e-mail: info@bella-tola.ch
website: www.bella-tola.ch
A peaceful, terraced site at an altitude of 750m, sheilded by a belt of woodland. Good, clean modern facilities.
2km from village.
Open: 4 May-2 Oct **Site:** 3.6HEC **Prices:** 9.80 pitch 15-26 **Facilities:** **Services:** lau
Leisure: P

Rhodania Kantonstr, 3952 027 4731312
Open: May-Oct **Site:** 0.2HEC **Facilities:**
Services: **Off-site:** PR

ULRICHEN VALAIS

Nufenen 3988 027 9731437 027 9731437
e-mail: camping-nufenen@rhone.ch
website: www.rhone.ch/camping-nufenen
1km SE to right of road to Nufenen Pass.
Open: Jun-Sep **Site:** 8HEC **Prices:** 7 3 7-8 5-5.50 **Facilities:** **Services:** lau **Leisure:** R
Off-site:

VALLORBE VAUD

Pré sous Ville (TCS) 1337 021 8432309
In a wooded riverside location. Neighbouring swimming pool available to campers free of charge.
On left bank of River Orbe.
Open: mid-Apr to mid-Oct **Site:** 1HEC **Prices:** 6-7 8.50-9.50 4-9.50 **Facilities:** **Services:**
lau **Leisure:** P **Off-site:** R

VERS-L'ÉGLISE VAUD

Murée (TCS) 1864 021 6345284 021 6345284
e-mail: dagonch@bluewinch.
website: www.camping-caravaningvd.com
Partially terraced site by a stream.
Signed on the right at the entry to village.
Open: All year **Site:** 1.1HEC **Prices:** 4.80-5.30 6-9 pitch 9-10 **Facilities:** **Services:** lau
Leisure: R **Off-site:**

VÉTROZ Valais

Botza (TCS) 1963 ☎ 027 3461940 ▤ 027 3462535
e-mail: info@botza.ch
website: www.botza.ch
On a level meadow with pitches divided by hedges. Fine panoramic views and good leisure facilities.
Open: All year **Site:** 3HEC **Prices:** 5.20-8.40 pitch 7.50-20.50 **Facilities:** **Services:** lau **Leisure:** P

YVONAND Vaud

VD 8 Pointe D'Yvonard 1462
☎ 024 4301655 ▤ 024 4302463
e-mail: vd8@campings-ccyverdon.ch
website: www.campings-ccyverdon.ch
6km NE of Yverdon bordering lake Neuchâtel with private beach 1km away, boat moorings, private jetty and boat hire.
3km W. Signed.
Open: Apr-Sep **Site:** 5HEC **Prices:** 6.90-8.90 3.50 7-15 7-15 **Facilities:** **Services:** lau **Leisure:** L

Facilities: -shop -shower -electric points for razors -electric points for caravans -parking by tents permitted -compulsory separate car park **Services:** -café/restaurant -bar -Camping Gaz International -gas other than Camping Gaz -first aid facilities lau-laundry **Leisure:** -swimming L-Lake P-Pool R-River S-Sea **Off-site:** All facilities within 2km

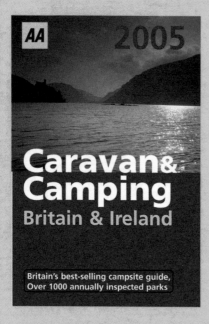

INDEX

AUSTRIA

Abersee, Salzburg 66
Abtenau, Salzburg 66
Altmünster, Oberösterreich 66
Aschau, Tirol 58
Aussee, Bad, Steiermark 63
Bezau, Vorarlberg 68
Bludenz, Vorarlberg 68
Breitenbrunn, Burgenland 65
Bruck an Der Grossglocknerstrasse, Salzburg 66
Dalaas, Vorarlberg 68
Dellach, Kärnten 61
Dellach Im Drautal, Kärnten 61
Döbriach, Kärnten 61
Döllach, Kärnten 62
Dornbirn, Vorarlberg 68
Ehrwald, Tirol 58
Esternberg, Oberösterreich 66
Feldkirchen, Kärnten 62
Fieberbrunn, Tirol 58
Fügen, Tirol 58
Gleinkerau, Oberösterreich 66
Gmünd, Niederösterreich 65
Graz, Steiermark 63
Haiming, Tirol 58
Heiligenblut, Kärnten 62
Heiterwang, Tirol 58
Hermagor, Kärnten 62
Hirschegg, Steiermark 64
Hirtenberg, Niederösterreich 65
Hopfgarten, Tirol 58
Huben, Tirol 58
Imst, Tirol 58
Innsbruck, Tirol 58
Jennersdorf, Burgenland 65
Kaprun, Salzburg 66
Keutschach, Kärnten 62
Kitzbühel, Tirol 59
Klagenfurt, Kärnten 62
Kössen, Tirol 59
Kötschach-Mauthen, Kärnten 62
Kramsach, Tirol 59
Kufstein, Tirol 59
Landeck, Tirol 59
Längenfeld, Tirol 59
Langenwang-Mürtzal, Steiermark 64
Langkampfen, Tirol 59
Laxenburg, Niederösterreich 65
Leibnitz, Steiermark 64
Lermoos, Tirol 59
Leutasch, Tirol 59
Lienz, Tirol 59
Lingenau, Vorarlberg 68
Maishofen, Salzburg 66
Malta, Kärnten 62
Marbach, Niederösterreich 65
Maria Lankowitz, Steiermark 64
Markt St Martin, Burgenland 65
Maurach, Tirol 59
Mayrhofen, Tirol 59
Mitterndorf, Bad, Steiermark 64
Mittersill, Salzburg 66
Möllbrücke, Kärnten 62
Mondsee, Oberösterreich 66
Mühlen, Steiermark 64
Natters, Tirol 60
Nauders, Tirol 60
Nenzing, Vorarlberg 68
Nussdorf, Oberösterreich 66
Obervellach, Kärnten 62
Oberwölz, Steiermark 64
Ossiach, Kärnten 62
Perwang Am Grabensee, Oberösterreich 66
Pettenbach, Oberösterreich 67
Pettneu Am Arlberg, Tirol 60
Pill, Tirol 60
Podersdorf, Burgenland 65
Prutz, Tirol 60
Radstadt, Salzburg 67
Raggal-Plazera, Vorarlberg 69
Rappoltenkirchen, Niederösterreich 65
Rechnitz, Burgenland 65
Reutte, Tirol 60
Ried Bei Landeck, Tirol 60
Rinn, Tirol 60
Rust, Burgenland 65
Sachsenburg, Kärnten 63
Salzburg, Salzburg 67
Schladming, Steiermark 64
Schlögen, Oberösterreich 67
Schönbühel, Niederösterreich 65
Schwaz, Tirol 60
Seeboden, Kärnten 63
Seekirchen, Salzburg 67
Sölden, Tirol 60
Spittal an Der Drau, Kärnten 63
St Georgen, Steiermark 64
St Johann, Tirol 60
St Johann Im Pongau, Salzburg 67
St Martin Bei Lofer, Salzburg 67
St Primus, Kärnten 63
St Sebastian, Steiermark 64
St Wolfgang, Oberösterreich 67
Stams, Tirol 60
Stockenboi, Kärnten 63
Thiersee, Tirol 60
Traisen, Niederösterreich 65
Tschagguns, Vorarlberg 69
Tulln, Niederösterreich 65
Umhausen, Tirol 61
Ungersdorf Bei Frohnleiten, Steiermark 64
Unterach, Oberösterreich 68
Unterperfuss, Tirol 61
Villach, Kärnten 63
Völs, Tirol 61
Waidhofen an Der Thaya, Niederösterreich 66
Waidring, Tirol 61
Walchsee, Tirol 61
Wald, Salzburg 68
Weisskirchen, Steiermark 64
Wertschach, Kärnten 63
Wesenufer, Oberösterreich 68
Westendorf, Tirol 61
Wien (Vienna), Wien 69
Wildalpen, Steiermark 64
Zell Am See, Salzburg 68
Zell Am Ziller, Tirol 61
Zirl, Tirol 61

BELGIUM

Aische-En-Refail, Namur 75
Amberloup, Luxembourg 75
Amonines, Luxembourg 75
Bachte-Maria-Leerne, Oost-Vlaanderen 73
Barvaux-sur-Ourthe, Luxembourg 75
Beauvechain, Brabant 73
Begynendyk, Brabant 73
Bertrix, Luxembourg 75
Bevere, Oost-Vlaanderen 73
Blankenberge, West-Vlaanderen 72
Brecht, Antwerpen 74
Büllingen (Bullange), Liège 75
Bure, Luxembourg 75
Bütgenbach, Liège 75
Chevetogne, Namur 75
Coo-Stavelot, Liège 75
Eksel, Limburg 74
Eupen, Liège 75
Florenville, Luxembourg 76
Forrières, Luxembourg 76
Gemmenich, Liège 76
Gent (Gand), Oost-Vlaanderen 73
Gierle, Antwerpen 74
Gouvy, Luxembourg 76
Grand-Halleux, Luxembourg 76
Grimbergen, Brabant 74
Habay-la-Neuve, Luxembourg 76
Hamoir-sur-Ourthe, Liège 76
Heverlee, Brabant 74
Hogne, Namur 76
Houffalize, Luxembourg 76
Houthalen, Limburg 74
Jabbeke, West-Vlaanderen 72
Knokke-Heist, West-Vlaanderen 72
Koksijde, West-Vlaanderen 72
Lombardsijde, West-Vlaanderen 72
Loppem, West-Vlaanderen 72
Louveigné, Liège 76
Malonne, Namur 76
Marche-En-Famenne, Luxembourg 76
Middelkerke, West-Vlaanderen 73

Mol, Antwerpen 74
Mons, Hainaut 73
Neufchâteau, Luxembourg 76
Nieuwpoort, West-Vlaanderen 73
Olloy-sur-Viroin, Namur 77
Onkerzele, Oost-Vlaanderen 74
Oostende (Ostende), West-Vlaanderen 73
Opglabbeek, Limburg 74
Oteppe, Liège 77
Polleur, Liège 77
Purnode, Namur 77
Remouchamps, Liège 77
Rendeux, Luxembourg 77
Retie, Antwerpen 74
Robertville, Liège 77
Roche-En-Ardenne, la, Luxembourg 77
Sart-Lez-Spa, Liège 77
Sippenaeken, Liège 78
Spa, Liège 78
Sprimont, Liège 78
St Sauveur, Hainaut 73
Stavelot, Liège 78
Stekene, Oost-Vlaanderen 74
Tenneville, Luxembourg 78
Thommen-Reuland, Liège 78
Tournai, Hainaut 73
Turnhout, Antwerpen 74
Vielsalm, Luxembourg 78
Virton, Luxembourg 78
Vorst-Laakdal, Antwerpen 75
Wachtebeke, Oost-Vlaanderen 74
Waimes, Liège 78
Waregem, West-Vlaanderen 73
Westende, West-Vlaanderen 73
Zonhoven, Limburg 75

FRANCE

Abrets, les, Isère 83
Abzac, Gironde 101
Accolay, Yonne 96
Acy-En-Multien, Oise 167
Agay, Var 183
Agde, Hérault 183
Aignan, Gers 101
Aigues Mortes, Gard 183
Aiguillon-sur-Mer, l', Vendée 123
Aillon-le-Jeune, Savoie 83
Aire-sur-l'Adour, Landes 101
Airvault, Deux-Sèvres 123
Aix-En-Provence, Bouches-du-Rhône 184
Albens, Savoie 83
Albi, Tarn 101
Alençon, Orne 149
Aléria, Haute-Corse 217
Alet-les-Bains, Aude 184
Allanche, Cantal 173
Alles-sur-Dordogne, Dordogne 101
Allevard, Isère 83
Alleyras, Haute-Loire 173
Allineuc, Côtes-D'Armor 149
Allonnes, Maine-et-Loire 123
Ambert, Puy-de-Dôme 174
Ambleteuse, Pas-de-Calais 167
Ancenis, Loire-Atlantique 123
Ancy-le-Franc, Yonne 96
Andernos-les-Bains, Gironde 101
Andonville, Loiret 123
Andryes, Yonne 96
Anduze, Gard 184
Angers, Maine-et-Loire 123
Anglars-Juillac, Lot 102
Angles, Tarn 102
Angles, Vendée 123
Anglet, Pyrénées-Atlantiques 102
Angoulins-sur-Mer, Charente-Maritime 123
Anould, Vosges 91
Anse, Rhône 174
Anthéor-Plage, Var 184
Antibes, Alpes-Maritimes 184
Apremont, Vendée 123
Arbois, Jura 83
Arcachon, Gironde 102
Arces, Charente-Maritime 124
Arcizans-Avant, Hautes-Pyrénées 102
Ardres, Pas-de-Calais 167
Arès, Gironde 102
Argelès-Gazost, Hautes-Pyrénées 102
Argelès-sur-Mer, Pyrénées-Orientales 185
Argentat, Corrèze 124
Argentière, Haute-Savoie 83
Argenton-Château, Deux-Sèvres 124
Arles, Bouches-du-Rhône 186
Arles-sur-Tech, Pyrénées-Orientales 186
Arnac, Cantal 174
Arnay-le-Duc, Côte-D'Or 96
Arpaillargues, Gard 186
Arpajon-sur-Cère, Cantal 174
Arradon, Morbihan 149
Arreau, Hautes-Pyrénées 102
Ars-En-Ré, Charente-Maritime 139
Ars-sur-Formans, Ain 83
Arzano, Finistère 149
Ascain, Pyrénées-Atlantiques 103
Ascarat, Pyrénées-Atlantiques 103
Atur, Dordogne 103
Aubignan, Vaucluse 186
Aubin, Aveyron 174
Aubure, Haut-Rhin 92
Audierne, Finistère 149
Audruicq, Pas-de-Calais 167
Aups, Var 186
Aureilhan, Landes 103
Auribeau, Alpes-Maritimes 186
Autrans, Isère 83
Auxerre, Yonne 96
Auxonne, Côte-D'Or 96
Avallon, Yonne 96
Avignon, Vaucluse 186
Avranches, Manche 149
Avrillé, Vendée 124
Axat, Aude 186
Azay-le-Rideau, Indre-et-Loire 124
Azur, Landes 103
Baden, Morbihan 149
Baerenthal, Moselle 92
Bagnères-de-Bigorre, Hautes-Pyrénées 103
Bandol, Var 187
Bannes, Haute-Marne 96
Baratier, Hautes-Alpes 83
Barbâtre, Vendée 134
Barcarès, le, Pyrénées-Orientales 187
Barre-de-Monts, la, Vendée 124
Bar-sur-Aube, Aube 96
Bar-sur-Loup, le, Alpes-Maritimes 187
Bastide-de-Serou, la, Ariège 103
Batz-sur-Mer, Loire-Atlantique 124
Baule, la, Loire-Atlantique 124
Bayeux, Calvados 149
Bayonne, Pyrénées-Atlantiques 103
Bazolles, Nièvre 96
Bazouges-sur-le-Loir, Sarthe 125
Beaucens-les-Bains, Hautes-Pyrénées 103
Beauchastel, Ardèche 187
Beaulieu-sur-Dordogne, Corrèze 125
Beaune, Côte-D'Or 96
Beauvais, Oise 167
Beg-Meil, Finistère 149
Belfort, Territoire-de-Belfort 83
Bellegarde-sur-Valserine, Ain 84
Belmont-sur-Rance, Aveyron 174
Belvès, Dordogne 103
Bénodet, Finistère 149
Bénouville, Calvados 150
Berck-sur-Mer, Pas-de-Calais 167
Berny-Rivière, Aisne 167
Bertangles, Somme 167
Bessines-sur-Gartempe, Haute-Vienne 125
Beuvry, Pas-de-Calais 167
Beynac-et-Cazenac, Dordogne 104
Beynat, Corrèze 125
Beynes, Alpes-de-Haute-Provence 187
Bez, le, Tarn 104
Biarritz, Pyrénées-Atlantiques 104
Bias, Landes 104
Biesheim, Haut-Rhin 92
Bignac, Charente 125
Binic, Côtes-D'Armor 150
Biron, Dordogne 104
Biscarrosse, Landes 105
Blainville-sur-Mer, Manche 150
Blandy-les-Tours, Seine-et-Marne 167
Blangy-le-Château, Calvados 150

Blangy-sur-Bresle, Seine-Maritime 150
Blaye, Gironde 105
Bléré, Indre-et-Loire 125
Blonville-sur-Mer, Calvados 150
Boiry-Notre-Dame, Pas-de-Calais 167
Bois-Plage-En-Ré, le, 139
Boisset-et-Gaujac, Gard 187
Boisson, Gard 187
Boissy-le-Cutte, Essonne 168
Bollène, Vaucluse 187
Bonifacio, Corse-du-Sud 217
Bonnac-la-Côte, Haute-Vienne 125
Bonnes, Vienne 125
Bonny-sur-Loire, Loiret 125
Bormes-les-Mimosas, Var 188
Boubers-sur-Canche, Pas-de-Calais 168
Boulancourt, Seine-et-Marne 168
Boulou, le, Pyrénées-Orientales 188
Boulouris-sur-Mer, Var 188
Bourbon-l'Archambault, Allier 174
Bourbon-Lancy, Saône-et-Loire 96
Bourbonne-les-Bains, Haute-Marne 96
Bourdeaux, Drôme 188
Bourg, Haute-Marne 96
Bourg-Achard, Eure 150
Bourg-Argental, Loire 174
Bourg-D'Oisans, le, Isère 84
Bourg-En-Bresse, Ain 84
Bourges, Cher 125
Bourget-du-Lac, le, Savoie 84
Bourg-Fidèle, Ardennes 96
Bourg-St-Andéol, Ardèche 188
Bourg-St-Maurice, Savoie 84
Bournel, Lot-et-Garonne 105
Boussac-Bourg, Creuse 125
Bout-du-Lac, Haute-Savoie 84
Boyardville, Charente-Maritime 135
Bracieux, Loir-et-Cher 125
Brain-sur-l'Authion,
Maine-et-Loire 126
Braize, Allier 174
Bray-Dunes, Nord 168
Bresse, la, Vosges 92
Bretenoux, Lot 105
Brétignolles-sur-Mer, Vendée 126
Brissac, Hérault 188
Brissac-Quincé, Maine-et-Loire 126
Brousses-et-Villaret, Aude 188
Brûlon, Sarthe 126
Brusque, Aveyron 174
Bugue, le, Dordogne 105
Burnhaupt-le-Haut, Haut-Rhin 92
Bussang, Vosges 92
Buzancy, Ardennes 97
Cadenet, Vaucluse 188
Cagnes-sur-Mer, Alpes-Maritimes 188
Cahors, Lot 105
Callac, Côtes-D'Armor 150
Calvi, Haute-Corse 217
Calviac, Lot 105
Camaret-sur-Mer, Finistère 150
Cambo-les-Bains,
Pyrénées-Atlantiques 105
Camiers, Pas-de-Calais 168
Camurac, Aude 189
Cancale, Ille-et-Vilaine 150
Candé-sur-Beuvron, Loir-et-Cher 126
Canet-de-Salars, Aveyron 174
Canet-Plage, Pyrénées-Orientales 189
Cannes, Alpes-Maritimes 190
Cap Ferret, Gironde 106
Capbreton, Landes 105
Capdenac-Gare, Aveyron 175
Carantec, Finistère 150
Carcassonne, Aude 190
Carentan, Manche 151
Cargese, Corse-du-Sud 217
Carlucet, Lot 106
Carnac, Morbihan 151
Carpentras, Vaucluse 190
Carqueiranne, Var 190
Casteljaloux, Lot-et-Garonne 106
Castellane,
Alpes-de-Haute-Provence 190
Castelnaud-la-Chapelle, Dordogne 106
Caurel, Côtes-D'Armor 152
Cauterets, Hautes-Pyrénées 106
Cavalaire-sur-Mer, Var 191
Cayeux-sur-Mer, Somme 168
Celles-sur-Plaine, Vosges 92
Cendras, Gard 191
Centuri, Haute-Corse 217
Cernay, Haut-Rhin 92
Chabeuil, Drôme 191
Chagny, Saône-et-Loire 97
Chalard, le, Haute-Vienne 126
Chalezeule, Doubs 84
Chalonnes-sur-Loire,
Maine-et-Loire 126
Châlons-En-Champagne, Marne 97
Chamonix-Mont-Blanc,
Haute-Savoie 84
Chamouille, Aisne 168
Champagnac-le-Vieux,
Haute-Loire 175
Champagnole, Jura 85
Champs-sur-Tarentaine, Cantal 175
Chapelle Hermier, la, Vendée 126
Chapelle-Aux-Filzméens, la, Ille-et-Vilaine 152
Chapelle-En-Vercors, la, Drôme 191
Charleval, Bouches-du-Rhône 191
Charolles, Saône-et-Loire 97
Chartres, Eure-et-Loir 126
Chartre-sur-le-Loir, la, Sarthe 126
Chartrier-Ferrière, Corrèze 127
Chasseneuil-sur-Bonnieure,
Charente 127
Château D'Olonne, le, Vendée 127
Château-Arnoux, Alpes-de-Haute-Provence 191
Château-D'Oléron, le, 135
Château-du-Loir, Sarthe 127
Châteaulin, Finistère 152
Châteauroux-les-Alpes,
Hautes-Alpes 85
Châtel Guyon, Puy-de-Dôme 175
Châtelaillon-Plage,
Charente-Maritime 127
Châtel-de-Neuvre, Allier 175
Châtellerault, Vienne 127
Châtel-Montagne, Allier 175
Châtillon-sur-Seine, Côte-D'Or 97
Chatonrupt, Haute-Marne 97
Châtres-sur-Cher, Loir-et-Cher 127
Chaudes-Aigues, Cantal 175
Chauffour-sur-Vell, Corrèze 127
Chauzon, Ardèche 191
Chef-Boutonne, Deux-Sèvres 127
Chenonceaux, Indre-et-Loire 127
Chéverny, Loir-et-Cher 127
Chevigny, Nièvre 97
Choisy, Haute-Savoie 85
Cholet, Maine-et-Loire 127
Choranche, Isère 85
Ciotat, la, Bouches-du-Rhône 191
Clairvaux-les-Lacs, Jura 85
Clamecy, Nièvre 97
Claouey, Gironde 106
Cloître-St-Thegonnec, le, Finistère 152
Cloyes-sur-le-Loir, Eure-et-Loir 127
Clusaz, la, Haute-Savoie 85
Cognac, Charente 128
Cogolin, Var 191
Colle-sur-Loup, la,
Alpes-Maritimes 192
Colmar, Haut-Rhin 92
Combourg, Ille-et-Vilaine 152
Concarneau, Finistère 152
Condat sur Ganaveix, Corrèze 128
Condette, Pas-de-Calais 168
Condrieu, Rhône 175
Conques, Aveyron 175
Contis-Plage, Landes 106
Contres, Loir-et-Cher 128
Corcieux, Vosges 92
Cordes, Tarn 106
Cosne-sur-Loire, Nièvre 97
Cotinière, la, 135
Couarde-sur-Mer, la, 139
Coudekerque, Nord 168
Couhé-Verac, Vienne 128
Courçon-D'Aunis,
Charente-Maritime 128
Cournon-D'Auvergne,
Puy-de-Dôme 175
Couronne, la, Bouches-du-Rhône 192
Couterne, Orne 152
Coutures, Maine-et-Loire 128
Coux-et-Bigaroque, Dordogne 106

Crach, Morbihan 152
Crau, la, Var 192
Crêches-sur-Saône, Saône-et-Loire 97
Créon, Gironde 106
Crespian, Gard 192
Criel-sur-Mer, Seine-Maritime 152
Croisic, le, Loire-Atlantique 128
Croix-Valmer, la, Var 192
Crotoy, le, Somme 168
Crozon, Finistère 153
Dabo, Moselle 92
Daglan, Dordogne 107
Dallet, Puy-de-Dôme 175
Dambach-la-Ville, Bas-Rhin 92
Dardilly, Rhône 175
Dax, Landes 107
Deauville, Calvados 153
Déville-Lès-Rouen, Seine-Maritime 153
Die, Drôme 193
Dieppe, Seine-Maritime 153
Dieulefit, Drôme 193
Digoin, Saône-et-Loire 97
Dijon, Côte-D'Or 97
Dinan, Côtes-D'Armor 153
Dinard, Ille-et-Vilaine 153
Dissay, Vienne 128
Divonne-les-Bains, Ain 86
Dol-de-Bretagne, Ille-et-Vilaine 153
Dole, Jura 86
Dolus-D'Oléron, 135
Domino, 135
Dompierre-les-Ormes, Saône-et-Loire 97
Douarnenez, Finistère 153
Doucier, Jura 86
Doussard, Haute-Savoie 86
Dunkerque (Dunkirk), Nord 168
Duravel, Lot 107
Durfort, Ariège 107
Durtal, Maine-et-Loire 128
Ebreuil, Allier 176
Éclaron-Braucourt, Haute-Marne 97
Egletons, Corrèze 128
Eguisheim, Haut-Rhin 93
Embrun, Hautes-Alpes 86
Entrechaux, Vaucluse 193
Entre-Deux-Guiers, Isère 86
Éperlecques, Pas-de-Calais 168
Epinac, Saône-et-Loire 98
Equihen-Plage, Pas-de-Calais 168
Erdeven, Morbihan 154
Erquy, Côtes-D'Armor 154
Esparron-de-Verdon, Alpes-de-Haute-Provence 193
Estaing, Hautes-Pyrénées 107
Étables-sur-Mer, Côtes-D'Armor 154
Étampes, Essonne 168
Étaples, Pas-de-Calais 169
Etréham, Calvados 154
Évian-les-Bains, Haute-Savoie 86
Eymouthiers, Charente 129
Éyzies-de-Tayac, les, Dordogne 107
Faouët, le, Morbihan 154
Faute-sur-Mer, la, Vendée 129
Felleries, Nord 169
Fenouiller, le, Vendée 129
Ferrière-D'Allevard, Isère 86
Ferrières-St-Mary, Cantal 176
Figeac, Lot 108
Flagnac, Aveyron 176
Fleurie, Rhône 176
Fleury, Aude 193
Flotte, la, 139
Foix, Ariège 108
Fontenoy-le-Château, Vosges 93
Fontes, Hérault 193
Fontvieille, Bouches-du-Rhône 194
Forcalquier, Alpes-de-Haute-Provence 194
Forêt-Fouesnant, la, Finistère 154
Fort-Mahon-Plage, Somme 169
Fouesnant, Finistère 155
Fougères, Ille-et-Vilaine 155
Fouras, Charente-Maritime 129
Fréjus, Var 194
Fresnay-sur-Sarthe, Sarthe 129
Friaucourt, Somme 169
Friaudour, Haute-Vienne 129
Froncles, Haute-Marne 98
Frontignan, Hérault 194
Frossay, Loire-Atlantique 129
Galéria, Haute-Corse 217
Gallargues-le-Montueux, Gard 194
Gallician, Gard 194
Gassin, Var 194
Gastes, Landes 108
Gaugeac, Dordogne 108
Gemaingoutte, Vosges 93
Gennes, Maine-et-Loire 129
Gérardmer, Vosges 93
Ghisonaccia, Haute-Corse 217
Gibles, Saône-et-Loire 98
Gien, Loiret 129
Giens, Var 196
Giffaumont, Marne 98
Gigny-sur-Saône, Saône-et-Loire 98
Givrand, Vendée 129
Goudet, Haute-Loire 176
Gourdon, Lot 108
Gourette, Pyrénées-Atlantiques 108
Gouvieux, Oise 169
Grande-Motte, la, Hérault 196
Grand-Fort-Philippe, Nord 169
Grandpré, Ardennes 98
Granges-sur-Vologne, Vosges 93
Grasse, Alpes-Maritimes 196
Grau-du-Roi, le, Gard 196
Graulges, les, Dordogne 108
Gresse-En-Vercors, Isère 86
Grez-sur-Loing, Seine-et-Marne 169
Grignan, Drôme 196
Grisolles, Tarn-et-Garonne 108
Guémené-Penfao, Loire-Atlantique 129
Guérande, Loire-Atlantique 129
Gueriniere, la, 135
Guillestre, Hautes-Alpes 86
Guilligomarc'H, Finistère 155
Guilvinec, Finistère 155
Guines, Pas-de-Calais 169
Hasparren, Pyrénées-Atlantiques 108
Hautecourt-Romanèche, Ain 87
Hautefort, Dordogne 108
Haye-du-Puits, la, Manche 155
Heimsbrunn, Haut-Rhin 93
Hendaye, Pyrénées-Atlantiques 108
Héric, Loire-Atlantique 130
Hirson, Aisne 169
Hohwald, le, Bas-Rhin 93
Houlgate, Calvados 155
Houmeau, l', Charente-Maritime 130
Hourtin, Gironde 109
Hourtin-Plage, Gironde 109
Huanne-Montmartin, Doubs 87
Hyères, Var 196
Iffendic, Ille-et-Vilaine 155
Ingrandes, Vienne 130
Isle-et-Bardais, Allier 176
Isle-sur-la-Sorgue, l', Vaucluse 197
Isle-sur-le-Doubs, l', Doubs 87
Isques, Pas-de-Calais 169
Issenheim, Haut-Rhin 93
Issy-l'Évêque, Saône-et-Loire 98
Istres, Bouches-du-Rhône 197
Jablines, Seine-et-Marne 169
Jard-sur-Mer, Vendée 130
Jargeau, Loiret 131
Jassat, Puy-de-Dôme 176
Jaunay Clan, Vienne 131
Jenzat, Allier 176
Jullouville, Manche 156
Jumièges, Seine-Maritime 156
Kaysersberg, Haut-Rhin 93
Kerlin, Finistère 156
Kruth, Haut-Rhin 93
Labenne, Landes 109
Labenne-Océan, Landes 109
Lacanau-Océan, Gironde 109
Lacapelle-Marival, Lot 110
Lacapelle-Viescamp, Cantal 176
Lagord, Charente-Maritime 131
Laives, Saône-et-Loire 98
Landaul, Morbihan 156
Landéda, Finistère 156
Landevieille, Vendée 131
Landry, Savoie 87
Langeac, Haute-Loire 176
Lanton, Gironde 110
Laon, Aisne 169
Lapeyrouse, Puy-de-Dôme 176

Larnagol, Lot 110
Laroque-des-Albères,
Pyrénées-Orientales 197
Laruns, Pyrénées-Atlantiques 110
Laruscade, Gironde 110
Lauterbourg, Bas-Rhin 93
Lectoure, Gers 110
Lempdes, Haute-Loire 176
Léon, Landes 110
Lescar, Pyrénées-Atlantiques 110
Lesconil, Finistère 156
Lessac, Charente 131
Lézignan-Corbières, Aude 197
Licques, Pas-de-Calais 169
Lindois, le, Charente 131
Linxe, Landes 111
Lion D'Angers, le, Maine-et-Loire 131
Lit-et-Mixe, Landes 111
Livers-Cazelles, Tarn 111
Locunole, Finistère 156
Loix, 140
Londe-les-Maures, la, Var 197
Longeville, Vendée 131
Lons-le-Saunier, Jura 87
Loubeyrat, Puy-de-Dôme 176
Loupiac, Lot 111
Lourdes, Hautes-Pyrénées 111
Louviers, Eure 156
Lozari, Haute-Corse 217
Luché-Pringé, Sarthe 132
Luc-sur-Mer, Calvados 157
Lugrin, Haute-Savoie 87
Lumio, Haute-Corse 217
Lunel, Hérault 197
Lusignan, Vienne 132
Luttenbach, Haut-Rhin 93
Luynes, Indre-et-Loire 132
Luz-St-Sauveur, Hautes-Pyrénées 111
Lynde, Nord 169
Maché, Vendée 132
Mâcon, Saône-et-Loire 98
Magnac-Bourg, Haute-Vienne 132
Maisons-Laffitte, Yvelines 170
Malbuisson, Doubs 87
Mallemort, Bouches-du-Rhône 197
Malzieu-Ville, le, Lozère 176
Mandelieu-la-Napoule,
Alpes-Maritimes 197
Manosque,
Alpes-de-Haute-Provence 198
Mansigné, Sarthe 132
Marans, Charente-Maritime 132
Marcenay, Côte-D'Or 98
Marcillac-St-Quentin, Dordogne 111
Marçon, Sarthe 132
Marigny, Jura 87
Marne-la-Vallée, Seine-et-Marne 170
Marseillan-Plage, Hérault 198
Martigny, Seine-Maritime 157
Martragny, Calvados 157
Martres-de-Veyre, les,
Puy-de-Dôme 177
Martres-Tolosane, Haute-Garonne 111
Masevaux, Haut-Rhin 94
Massiac, Cantal 177
Matafelon-Granges, Ain 87
Mathes, les, Charente-Maritime 132
Matour, Saône-et-Loire 98
Maubeuge, Nord 170
Mauléon-Licharre,
Pyrénées-Atlantiques 111
Maupertus-sur-Mer, Manche 157
Maureillas, Pyrénées-Orientales 198
Maurs, Cantal 177
Mayenne, Mayenne 133
Méaudre, Isère 87
Melun, Seine-et-Marne 170
Membrolle-sur-Choisille, la,
Indre-et-Loire 133
Mende, Lozère 177
Menton, Alpes-Maritimes 198
Méolans-Revel,
Alpes-de-Haute-Provence 198
Merlimont, Pas-de-Calais 170
Mervent, Vendée 133
Merville-Franceville, Calvados 157
Mesland, Loir-et-Cher 133
Mesnil-St Père, Aube 98
Mesnois, Jura 88
Mesquer, Loire-Atlantique 133
Messanges, Landes 112
Messe, Deux-Sèvres 134
Messery, Haute-Savoie 88
Metzeral, Haut-Rhin 94
Meursault, Côte-D'Or 98
Meyrieu-les-Étangs, Isère 88
Meyrueis, Lozère 177
Mézos, Landes 112
Miers, Lot 112
Millau, Aveyron 177
Milly-la-Forêt, Essonne 170
Mimizan, Landes 113
Mirabel-et-Blacons, Drôme 198
Mirandol-Bourgnounac, Tarn 113
Miremont, Puy-de-Dôme 177
Miribel-les-Échelles, Isère 88
Missillac, Loire-Atlantique 134
Molières, Dordogne 113
Molières, Tarn-et-Garonne 113
Moliets-Plage, Landes 113
Moncrabeau, Lot-et-Garonne 113
Monnerville, Essonne 170
Montaigut-le-Blanc, Puy-de-Dôme 177
Montapas, Nièvre 98
Montargis, Loiret 134
Montauban-de-Luchon,
Haute-Garonne 113
Montbard, Côte-D'Or 98
Montblanc, Hérault 198
Montclar, Aude 198
Mont-Dore, le, Puy-de-Dôme 177
Montélimar, Drôme 198
Monterblanc, Morbihan 157
Montesquiou, Gers 113
Montgivray, Indre 134
Monthermé, Ardennes 99
Montignac, Dordogne 113
Montigny-le-Bretonneux, Yvelines 170
Montlouis-sur-Loire,
Indre-et-Loire 134
Montmaur, Hautes-Alpes 88
Montmorillon, Vienne 134
Montpellier, Hérault 199
Montpezat,
Alpes-de-Haute-Provence 199
Montréal, Ardèche 199
Montreuil-sur-Mer, Pas-de-Calais 170
Montrevel-En-Bresse, Ain 88
Montsauche, Nièvre 99
Montsoreau, Maine-et-Loire 134
Mont-St-Michel, le, Manche 157
Moosch, Haut-Rhin 94
Morgat, Finistère 157
Mornant, Rhône 177
Mornas, Vaucluse 199
Mouchard, Jura 88
Mouriès, Bouches-du-Rhône 199
Mousseaux sur Seine, Yvelines 170
Moustiers-Ste-Marie,
Alpes-de-Haute-Provence 199
Moutiers-En-Retz, les,
Loire-Atlantique 134
Moyaux, Calvados 157
Moyenneville, Somme 170
Mulhouse, Haut-Rhin 94
Munster, Haut-Rhin 94
Murol, Puy-de-Dôme 178
Murs-et-Gelignieux, Ain 88
Mussidan, Dordogne 113
Muy, le, Var 199
Nages, Tarn 113
Nant, Aveyron 178
Nantes, Loire-Atlantique 134
Napoule, la, Alpes-Maritimes 199
Narbonne, Aude 199
Naucelle, Aveyron 178
Naussac, Lozère 178
Nébias, Aude 200
Nébouzat, Puy-de-Dôme 178
Néris-les-Bains, Allier 178
Nesles-la-Vallée, Val-D'Oise 171
Neuvéglise, Cantal 178
Neuville, la, Nord 171
Neuville-sur-Sarthe, Sarthe 134
Névez, Finistère 157
Neydens, Haute-Savoie 88
Nibelle, Loiret 134
Nîmes, Gard 200
Niort, Deux-Sèvres 134
Niozelles,

Alpes-de-Haute-Provence 200
Noirmoutier, Ile de, Vendée 134
Noirmoutier-En-l'Ile, 135
Notre-Dame-de-Monts, Vendée 135
Novalaise, Savoie 88
Noyal-Muzillac, Morbihan 157
Nozay, Loire-Atlantique 135
Nyons, Drôme 200
Oberbronn, Bas-Rhin 94
Obernai, Bas-Rhin 94
Oléron, Ile D', Charente-Maritime 135
Olivet, Loiret 136
Ollières-sur-Eyrieux, les, Ardèche 200
Olliergues, Puy-de-Dôme 179
Olmeto-Plage, Corse-du-Sud 218
Olonne-sur-Mer, Vendée 136
Oloron-Ste-Marie,
Pyrénées-Atlantiques 113
Onesse-et-Laharie, Landes 114
Onzain, Loir-et-Cher 136
Orange, Vaucluse 200
Orcet, Puy-de-Dôme 179
Ornans, Doubs 89
Orpierre, Hautes-Alpes 89
Orvillers-Sorel, Oise 171
Ouistreham, Calvados 158
Ounans, Jura 89
Ousse, Pyrénées-Atlantiques 114
Oye-Plage, Pas-de-Calais 171
Padirac, Lot 114
Palmyre, la, Charente-Maritime 136
Pamiers, Ariège 114
Paray-le-Monial, Saône-et-Loire 99
Paray-Sous-Briailles, Allier 179
Parcey, Jura 89
Paris, 171
Patornay, Jura 89
Pauillac, Gironde 114
Payrac, Lot 114
Pénestin-sur-Mer, Morbihan 158
Pentrez-Plage, Finistère 158
Périgueux, Dordogne 114
Perrier, le, Vendée 137
Perros-Guirec, Côtes-D'Armor 158
Petit-Palais, Gironde 114
Peux-et-Couffouleux, Aveyron 179
Peyremale-sur-Cèze, Gard 200
Peyruis, Alpes-de-Haute-Provence 200
Pezou, Loir-et-Cher 137
Pezuls, Dordogne 114
Pianottoli, Corse-du-Sud 218
Pieux, les, Manche 158
Piriac-sur-Mer, Loire-Atlantique 137
Pisciatello, Corse-du-Sud 218
Plagne-Montchavin, Savoie 89
Plaine-sur-Mer, la,
Loire-Atlantique 137
Plérin, Côtes-D'Armor 158
Plessis-Feu-Aussoux,
Seine-et-Marne 171
Pleubian, Côtes-D'Armor 158
Plobannalec, Finistère 158
Ploëmel, Morbihan 158
Ploemeur, Morbihan 158
Ploërmel, Morbihan 159
Plomeur, Finistère 159
Plomodiern, Finistère 159
Plonévez-Porzay, Finistère 159
Plouézec, Côtes-D'Armor 159
Plouezoch, Finistère 159
Plougasnou, Finistère 159
Plouha, Côtes-D'Armor 160
Plouharnel, Morbihan 160
Plouhinec, Morbihan 160
Plozévet, Finistère 160
Poix-de-Picardie, Somme 171
Pollionnay, Rhône 179
Pons, Charente-Maritime 138
Pontarlier, Doubs 89
Pontaubault, Manche 160
Pont-Aven, Finistère 160
Pont-D'Hérault, Gard 200
Pont-de-Salars, Aveyron 179
Pont-de-Vaux, Ain 89
Pont-du-Gard, Gard 200
Pontgibaud, Puy-de-Dôme 179
Pont-l'Abbé, Finistère 160
Pont-l'Abbé-D'Arnoult,
Charente-Maritime 138
Pont-Sainte-Marie, Aube 99
Ponts-de-Cé, les, Maine-et-Loire 138
Pont-St-Mamet, Dordogne 114
Pordic, Côtes-D'Armor 160
Pornic, Loire-Atlantique 138
Pornichet, Loire-Atlantique 138
Port-de-Piles, Vienne 138
Port-En-Bessin, Calvados 161
Portiragnes-Plage, Hérault 201
Port-le-Grand, Somme 171
Port-Manech, Finistère 161
Porto-Vecchio, Corse-du-Sud 218
Port-sur-Saône, Haute-Saône 89
Poses, Eure 161
Pougues-les-Eaux, Nièvre 99
Pouldu, le, Finistère 161
Pradeaux, les, Puy-de-Dôme 179
Pradet, le, Var 203
Prailles, Deux-Sèvres 138
Pramousquier, Var 203
Premeaux, Côte-D'Or 99
Presle, Savoie 89
Privas, Ardèche 203
Proyart, Somme 171
Puget-sur-Argens, Var 203
Puy, le, Haute-Loire 179
Puybrun, Lot 114
Puy-l'Évêque, Lot 114
Pyla-sur-Mer, Gironde 115
Quend-Plage-les-Pins, Somme 171
Quettehou, Manche 161
Quiberon, Morbihan 161
Quillan, Aude 204
Quimper, Finistère 161
Racou, le, Pyrénées-Orientales 204
Radonvilliers, Aube 99
Raguenès-Plage, Finistère 161
Ramatuelle, Var 204
Rambouillet, Yvelines 172
Rauzan, Gironde 115
Ravenoville-Plage, Manche 161
Ré, Ile de, Charente-Maritime 139
Remoulins, Gard 204
Renage, Isère 89
Revens, Gard 204
Reyrevignes, Lot 116
Ria, Pyrénées-Orientales 205
Ribeauville, Haut-Rhin 94
Riel-les-Eaux, Côte-D'Or 99
Rille, Indre-et-Loire 140
Riom-Ès-Montagnes, Cantal 179
Riquewihr, Haut-Rhin 94
Rivière-sur-Tarn, Aveyron 180
Rocamadour, Lot 116
Roche-Bernard, la, Morbihan 161
Roche-Chalais, la, Dordogne 116
Rochefort-En-Terre, Morbihan 161
Rochette, la, Savoie 89
Rodez, Aveyron 180
Romieu, la, Gers 116
Ronce-les-Bains,
Charente-Maritime 140
Roquebrune-sur-Argens, Var 205
Roque-D'Anthéron, la,
Bouches-du-Rhône 205
Roquefort, Landes 116
Roquelaure, Gers 116
Roquette-sur-Siagne, la,
Alpes-Maritimes 205
Rosière-de-Montvalezan, la, Savoie 89
Rosiers, les, Maine-et-Loire 140
Rostrenen, Côtes-D'Armor 162
Rouffignac, Dordogne 116
Rougemont, Doubs 89
Royan, Charente-Maritime 140
Royat, Puy-de-Dôme 180
Ruoms, Ardèche 205
Ruynes-En-Margeride, Cantal 180
Sables-D'Olonne, les, Vendée 140
Sablé-sur-Sarthe, Sarthe 141
Saignes, Cantal 180
Saillagouse, Pyrénées-Orientales 206
Saintes, Charente-Maritime 142
Saint-Revérénd, Vendée 146
Salavas, Ardèche 210
Salency, Oise 172
Salernes, Var 210
Salignac, Dordogne 119
Salins-D'Hyères, les, Var 210
Salle-En-Beaumont, la, Isère 90
Salles, Gironde 119

Salles, Lot-et-Garonne 119
Salles-Curan, Aveyron 182
Salon-de-Provence,
Bouches-du-Rhône 210
Salvetat, la, Hérault 210
Sanary-sur-Mer, Var 210
Santrop, Haute-Vienne 146
Sarlat-la-Canéda, Dordogne 119
Sarzeau, Morbihan 165
Sassetot-le-Mauconduit,
Seine-Maritime 165
Saulieu, Côte-D'Or 99
Saumur, Maine-et-Loire 146
Sauve, Gard 210
Sauveterre-de-Béarn,
Pyrénées-Atlantiques 120
Sauveterre-la-Lémance,
Lot-et-Garonne 120
Sauvian, Hérault 210
Saverne, Bas-Rhin 94
Sazeret, Allier 182
Sedan, Ardennes 99
Séez, Savoie 90
Seignosse, Landes 120
Seix, Ariège 120
Sélestat, Bas-Rhin 95
Selle Craonnaise, la, Mayenne 147
Selongey, Côte-D'Or 99
Sembadel-Gare, Haute-Loire 182
Sénergues, Aveyron 182
Seppois-le-Bas, Haut-Rhin 95
Seraucourt-le-Grand, Aisne 172
Sérignac-Péboudou,
Lot-et-Garonne 120
Sérignan-Plage, Hérault 210
Serres, Hautes-Alpes 91
Seurre, Côte-D'Or 100
Sévérac-l'Église, Aveyron 182
Sévérac-le-Château, Aveyron 182
Seyne-sur-Mer, la, Var 210
Seyssel, Ain 91
Sézanne, Marne 100
Signy-le-Petit, Ardennes 100
Sillans-la-Cascade,
Bouches-du-Rhône 211
Sillé-le-Guillaume, Sarthe 147
Sillé-le-Philippe, Sarthe 147
Singles, Puy-de-Dôme 182
Sivry-sur-Meuse, Meuse 95
Six-Fours-les-Plages, Var 211
Soissons, Aisne 172
Sospel, Alpes-Maritimes 211
Sotta, Corse-du-Sud 218
Soubès, Hérault 211
Souillac, Lot 120
Soulac-sur-Mer, Gironde 120
Soulaines-Dhuys, Aube 100
Soustons, Landes 121
Souterraine, la, Creuse 147
St Jean-D'Angely,
Charente-Maritime 144
St-Aignan-sur-Cher, Loir-et-Cher 141
St-Alban, Côtes-D'Armor 162
St-Alban-Auriolles, Ardèche 206
St-Alban-sur-Limagnole, Lozère 180
St-Amand-les-Eaux, Nord 172
St-Amand-Montrond, Cher 141
St-Amant-Roche-Savine,
Puy-de-Dôme 180
St-Ambroix, Gard 206
St-Andiol, Bouches-du-Rhône 206
St-André-des-Eaux,
Loire-Atlantique 141
St-Antoine-de-Breuilh, Dordogne 116
St-Antonin-Noble-Val,
Tarn-et-Garonne 116
St-Aubin-sur-Mer, Calvados 162
St-Avertin, Indre-et-Loire 141
St-Avre, Savoie 90
St-Aygulf, Var 206
St-Bertrand-de-Comminges,
Haute-Garonne 116
St-Bonnet-Tronçais, Allier 180
St-Brévin-l'Océan,
Loire-Atlantique 142
St-Brévin-les-Pins,
Loire-Atlantique 142
St-Briac, Ille-et-Vilaine 162
St-Brieuc, Côtes-D'Armor 162
St-Cast-le-Guildo, Côtes-D'Armor 162
St-Céré, Lot 116
St-Chamas, Bouches-du-Rhône 206
St-Chéron, Essonne 172
St-Cirq, Dordogne 116
St-Cirq-Lapopie, Lot 117
St-Clair-du-Rhône, Isère 90
St-Claude, Jura 90
St-Clément-de-Valorgue,
Puy-de-Dôme 180
St-Cricq, Gers 117
St-Cybranet, Dordogne 117
St-Cyprien, Dordogne 117
St-Cyprien, Pyrénées-Orientales 207
St-Cyr, Vienne 142
St-Cyr-sur-Mer, Var 207
St-Cyr-sur-Morin, Seine-et-Marne 172
St-Denis-D'Oléron, 135
Ste Marie-de-Re, 140
Ste-Catherine, Rhône 181
Ste-Catherine-de-Fierbois,
Indre-et-Loire 146
Ste-Croix-En-Plaine, Haut-Rhin 94
Ste-Eulalie-En-Born, Landes 119
St-Efflam, Côtes-D'Armor 162
Ste-Gemme, Charente-Maritime 146
Ste-Marie, Pyrénées-Orientales 209
Ste-Marie-du-Mont, Manche 164
Ste-Marine, Finistère 164
Ste-Menehould, Marne 99
Ste-Mère-Église, Manche 164
St-Émilion, Gironde 117
Ste-Reine-de-Bretagne,
Loire-Atlantique 146
Ste-Sigolène, Haute-Loire 181
Stes-Maries-de-la-Mer,
Bouches-du-Rhône 209
St-Florent, Haute-Corse 218
St-Florent-le-Vieil, Maine-et-Loire 142
St-Gal-sur-Sioule, Puy-de-Dôme 180
St-Gaultier, Indre 142
St-Genies, Dordogne 117
St-Geniez-D'Olt, Aveyron 180
St-Georges-D'Oléron, 135
St-Georges-de-Didonne,
Charente-Maritime 142
St-Georges-Lès-Baillargeaux,
Vienne 142
St-Germain-de-Calberte, Lozère 180
St-Germain-sur-Ay, Manche 162
St-Gérons, Cantal 180
St-Gervais-D'Auvergne,
Puy-de-Dôme 181
St-Gervais-les-Bains, Haute-Savoie 90
St-Gildas-de-Rhuys, Morbihan 163
St-Gilles-Croix-de-Vie, Vendée 142
St-Girons, Ariège 117
St-Hilaire-de-Riez, Vendée 143
St-Hilaire-la-Forêt, Vendée 144
St-Hilaire-Peyroux, Corrèze 144
St-Hilaire-Sous-Romilly, Aube 99
St-Hippolyte, Aveyron 181
St-Honoré, Nièvre 99
St-Innocent-Brison, Savoie 90
St-Jacques-des-Blats, Cantal 181
St-Jans-Cappel, Nord 172
St-Jean-de-Couz, Savoie 90
St-Jean-de-Luz,
Pyrénées-Atlantiques 117
St-Jean-de-Monts, Vendée 144
St-Jean-le-Centenier, Ardèche 207
St-Jean-Pied-de-Port,
Pyrénées-Atlantiques 118
St-Jean-Pla-de-Corts,
Pyrénées-Orientales 207
St-Jean-St-Nicolas, Hautes-Alpes 90
St-Jodard, Loire 181
St-Jorioz, Haute-Savoie 90
St-Jouan-des-Guérêts,
Ille-et-Vilaine 163
St-Julien-de-la-Nef, Gard 207
St-Julien-des-Landes, Vendée 145
St-Julien-En-Born, Landes 118
St-Just, Cantal 181
St-Justin, Landes 118
St-Just-Luzac, Charente-Maritime 145
St-Laurent-du-Var,
Alpes-Maritimes 207
St-Laurent-du-Verdon,
Alpes-de-Haute-Provence 207
St-Laurent-En-Beaumont, Isère 90

St-Laurent-Nouan, Loir-et-Cher 145
St-Léger-du-Bourg-Denis, Seine-Maritime 163
St-Léonard-de-Noblat, Haute-Vienne 145
St-Léon-sur-Vézère, Dordogne 118
St-Leu-D'Esserent, Oise 172
St-Lunaire, Ille-et-Vilaine 163
St-Malo, Ille-et-Vilaine 163
St-Malô-du-Bois, Vendée 145
St-Marcan, Ille-et-Vilaine 163
St-Martin-de-Ré, 140
St-Martin-des-Besaces, Calvados 163
St-Martin-de-Seignanx, Landes 118
St-Martin-En-Campagne, Seine-Maritime 163
St-Martin-Valmeroux, Cantal 181
St-Martory, Haute-Garonne 118
St-Maurice-sur-Moselle, Vosges 94
St-Maximin-la-Ste-Baume, Var 207
St-Michel-En-Grève, Côtes-D'Armor 164
St-Nectaire, Puy-de-Dôme 181
St-Nicolas-de-la-Grave, Tarn-et-Garonne 118
St-Ours, Puy-de-Dôme 181
St-Pair-sur-Mer, Manche 164
St-Palais-sur-Mer, Charente-Maritime 145
St-Pardoux-la-Rivière, Dordogne 118
St-Paul-En-Forêt, Var 208
St-Paul-les-Dax, Landes 118
St-Paul-les-Romans, Drôme 208
St-Pée-sur-Nivelle, Pyrénées-Atlantiques 118
St-Péreuse, Nièvre 99
St-Philibert-sur-Mer, Morbihan 164
St-Pierre, Bas-Rhin 94
St-Pierre-Colamine, Puy-de-Dôme 181
St-Pierre-D'Oléron, 136
St-Pierre-de-Chartreuse, Isère 90
St-Pierre-du-Vauvray, Eure 164
St-Pierre-Lafeuille, Lot 119
St-Pierre-Quiberon, Morbihan 164
St-Quay-Portrieux, Côtes-D'Armor 164
St-Quentin, Aisne 172
St-Raphaël, Var 208
St-Remèze, Ardèche 208
St-Rémy-de-Provence, Bouches-du-Rhône 208
St-Rémy-sur-Durolle, Puy-de-Dôme 181
St-Rémy-sur-Lidoire, Dordogne 119
St-Romain-En-Viennois, Vaucluse 208
St-Rome-de-Tarn, Aveyron 181
St-Salvadou, Aveyron 181
St-Sauveur-de-Montagut, Ardèche 208
St-Sernin-de-Duras, Lot-et-Garonne 119
St-Seurin-de-Prats, Dordogne 119
St-Sorlin-En-Valloire, Drôme 208
St-Thibéry, Hérault 208
St-Vaast-la-Hougue, Manche 164
St-Valéry-sur-Somme, Somme 172
St-Vallier-de-Thiey, Alpes-Maritimes 209
St-Vincent-sur-Jard, Vendée 146
Subligny, Manche 165
Suèvres, Loir-et-Cher 147
Sully-sur-Loire, Loiret 147
Tain-l'Hermitage, Drôme 211
Talloires, Haute-Savoie 91
Talmont-St-Hilaire, Vendée 147
Tarascon-sur-Ariège, Ariège 121
Tazilly, Nièvre 100
Teillet, Tarn 121
Telgruc-sur-Mer, Finistère 165
Theix, Morbihan 165
Thérondels, Aveyron 182
Thiembronne, Pas-de-Calais 172
Thiviers, Dordogne 121
Thoissey, Ain 91
Tholy, le, Vosges 95
Thonnance-les-Moulins, Haute-Marne 100
Thonon-les-Bains, Haute-Savoie 91
Thor, le, Vaucluse 211
Thury-Harcourt, Calvados 165
Tignes-les-Brévières, Savoie 91
Tinténiac, Ille-et-Vilaine 165
Tiuccia, Corse-du-Sud 218
Tollent, Pas-de-Calais 172
Tollevast, Manche 165
Tonneins, Lot-et-Garonne 121
Tonnoy, Meurthe-et-Moselle 95
Torcy, Seine-et-Marne 173
Toulon-sur-Arroux, Saône-et-Loire 100
Touquin, Seine-et-Marne 173
Tourlaville, Manche 166
Tournehem, Pas-de-Calais 173
Tournières, Calvados 166
Tournon-sur-Rhône, Ardèche 211
Tourrettes-sur-Loup, Alpes-Maritimes 211
Tours, Indre-et-Loire 147
Touzac, Lot 121
Tranche-sur-Mer, la, Vendée 147
Trébeurden, Côtes-D'Armor 166
Trégunc, Finistère 166
Trélévern, Côtes-D'Armor 166
Tréport, le, Seine-Maritime 166
Trept, Isère 91
Trévou-Tréguignec, Côtes-D'Armor 166
Trinité-sur-Mer, la, Morbihan 166
Trizac, Cantal 182
Troche, Corrèze 148
Trogues, Indre-et-Loire 148
Turballe, la, Loire-Atlantique 148
Turckheim, Haut-Rhin 95
Ucel, Ardèche 212
Uchizy, Saône-et-Loire 100
Ur, Pyrénées-Orientales 212
Urbès, Haut-Rhin 95
Urçay, Allier 182
Urrugne, Pyrénées-Atlantiques 121
Urt, Pyrénées-Atlantiques 121
Uzès, Gard 212
Vagney, Vosges 95
Vailly-sur-Aisne, Aisne 173
Vaison-la-Romaine, Vaucluse 212
Val-des-Prés, Marne 100
Valenáay, Indre 148
Valence, Drôme 212
Valeuil, Dordogne 121
Vallabrègues, Gard 212
Vallerauge, Gard 212
Vallon-Pont-D'ARC, Ardèche 212
Valras-Plage, Hérault 213
Vandenesse-En-Auxois, Côte-D'Or 100
Varennes-sur-Allier, Allier 182
Varennes-sur-Loire, Maine-et-Loire 148
Varilhes, Ariège 121
Vauvert, Gard 213
Vayrac, Lot 121
Vedène, Vaucluse 213
Veillon, le, Vendée 148
Velles, Indre 148
Venarey-les-Laumes, Côte-D'Or 100
Vence, Alpes-Maritimes 214
Vendays-Montalivet, Gironde 122
Vendôme, Loir-et-Cher 148
Vercheny, Drôme 214
Verdon-sur-Mer, le, Gironde 122
Verdun, Meuse 95
Véreilles, Hérault 214
Vergt-de-Biron, Dordogne 122
Vermenton, Yonne 100
Verneuil-sur-Seine, Yvelines 173
Vernioz, Isère 91
Verrières-En-Forez, Loire 182
Versailles, Yvelines 173
Veules-les-Roses, Seine-Maritime 167
Veyrines-de-Domme, Dordogne 122
Vézac, Dordogne 122
Vias, Hérault 214
Vic-la-Gardiole, Hérault 215
Vic-sur-Cère, Cantal 182
Vieille-Brioude, Haute-Loire 183
Vielle-St-Girons, Landes 122
Vieux-Boucau-les-Bains, Landes 122
Vigan, le, Gard 215
Vigan, le, Lot 122
Villard-de-Lans, Isere 91
Villars-Colmars, Alpes-de-Haute-Provence 215
Villars-les-Dombes, Ain 91
Villefort, Lozère 183

Villefranche-de-Panat, Aveyron 183
Villefranche-de-Rouergue, Aveyron 183
Villefranche-du-Queyran, Lot-et-Garonne 122
Villemoustaussou, Aude 215
Villenave-D'Ornon, Gironde 122
Villeneuve-de-Berg, Ardéche 215
Villeneuve-de-la-Raho, Pyrénées-Orientales 215
Villeneuve-Lès-Avignon, Gard 215
Villeneuve-les-Genêts, Yonne 100
Villeneuve-Loubet-Plage, Alpes-Maritimes 216
Villennes-sur-Seine, Yvelines 173
Villeréal, Lot-et-Garonne 122
Villerouge-la-Crémade, Aude 216
Villers-Hélon, Aisne 173
Villers-Lès-Nancy, Meurthe-et-Moselle 95
Villers-sur-Authie, Somme 173
Villers-sur-Mer, Calvados 167
Villes-sur-Auzon, Vaucluse 216
Villiers-le-Morhier, Eure-et-Loir 148
Vincelles, Yonne 100
Vineuil, Loir-et-Cher 148
Vironchaux, Somme 173
Vitrac, Dordogne 122
Vitrolles, Bouches-du-Rhône 216
Viviers, Ardèche 217
Vogüé, Ardèche 217
Voiron, Isère 91
Volonne, Alpes-de-Haute-Provence 217
Wacquinghen, Pas-de-Calais 173
Wasselonne, Bas-Rhin 95
Wattwiller, Haut-Rhin 95
Wihr-Au-Val, Haut-Rhin 95
Xonrupt/longemer, Vosges 95
Yssingeaux, Haute-Loire 183

GERMANY

Aach Bei Oberstaufen, Bayern 222
Abtsgmünd, Baden-Württemberg 230
Achern, Baden-Württemberg 230
Aitrang, Bayern 222
Alpirsbach, Baden-Württemberg 230
Alt Schwerin, Meklenburg-Vorpommern 236
Altenau, Niedersachsen 249
Altensteig, Baden-Württemberg 230
Altneudorf, Baden-Württemberg 230
Arlaching, Bayern 222
Asbacherhütte, Rheinland-Pfalz 239
Attendorn, Nordrhein-Westfalen 239
Augsburg, Bayern 222
Bacharach, Rheinland-Pfalz 239
Badenweiler, Baden-Württemberg 230
Balhorn, Hessen 239
Bamberg, Bayern 222
Barntrup, Nordrhein-Westfalen 239
Berchtesgaden, Bayern 222
Bergen, Bayern 222
Berlin 236
Bernkastel-Kues, Rheinland-Pfalz 239
Birkenfeld, Rheinland-Pfalz 239
Bleckede, Niedersachsen 249
Bodenwerder, Niedersachsen 250
Bodstedt, Mecklenburg-Vorpommern 237
Bömighausen, Hessen 239
Bothel, Niedersachsen 250
Braunfels, Hessen 240
Braunlage, Niedersachsen 250
Breisig, Bad, Rheinland-Pfalz 240
Bremen, Bremen 250
Brietlingen-Reihersee, Niedersachsen 250
Brunnen Forggensee, Bayern 222
Büchen, Schleswig-Holstein 250
Buchhorn Bei Öhringen, Baden-Württemberg 230
Bühl, Baden-Württemberg 230
Bullay, Rheinland-Pfalz 240
Burg (Island of Fehmarn), Schleswig-Holstein 250
Burgwedel, Niedersachsen 250
Caputh, Brandenburg 237
Chieming, Bayern 222
Clausthal-Zellerfeld, Niedersachsen 250
Cochem, Rheinland-Pfalz 240
Colditz, Sachsen 237
Cologne see Köln 240
Creglingen, Baden-Württemberg 230
Dahn, Rheinland-Pfalz 240
Dahrenhorst, Niedersachsen 250
Dausenau, Rheinland-Pfalz 240
Detern, Niedersachsen 250
Diemelsee-Heringhausen, Nordrhein-Westfalen 240
Diessen, Bayern 222
Diez, Rheinland-Pfalz 240
Dingelsdorf, Baden-Württemberg 231
Dinkelsbühl, Bayern 222
Donaueschingen, Baden-Württemberg 231
Dorsel an Der Ahr, Rheinland-Pfalz 240
Dortmund, Nordrhein-Westfalen 240
Dorum, Schleswig-Holstein 251
Dreieich-Offenthal, Hessen 240
Dresden, Sachsen 237
Drolshagen, Nordrhein-Westfalen 241
Dülmen, Nordrhein-Westfalen 241
Dürkheim, Bad, Rheinland-Pfalz 241
Dürrheim, Bad, Baden-Württemberg 231
Düsseldorf, Nordrhein-Westfalen 241
Egestorf, Niedersachsen 251
Eimke, Niedersachsen 251
Elisabeth Sophienkoog, 251
Ellwangen-Jagst, Baden-Württemberg 231
Ems, Bad, Rheinland-Pfalz 241
Endorf, Bad, Bayern 222
Erlangen, Bayern 223
Erpfingen, Baden-Württemberg 231
Escherndorf, Bayern 223
Eschwege, Hessen 241
Esens-Bensersiel, Niedersachsen 251
Essen, Nordrhein-Westfalen 241
Estenfeld, Bayern 223
Ettenheim, Baden-Württemberg 231
Eutin-Fissau, Schleswig-Holstein 251
Falkenberg, Brandenburg 237
Fallingbostel, Niedersachsen 251
Fehmarn (Island of), 251
Fehmarnsund, Schleswig-Holstein 251
Feilnbach, Bad, Bayern 223
Fichtelberg, Bayern 223
Finsterau, Bayern 223
Freest, Mecklenburg-Vorpommern 237
Freiburg Im Breisgau, Baden-Württemberg 231
Freudenstadt, Baden-Württemberg 231
Frickenhausen, Bayern 223
Fürth Im Odenwald, Hessen 241
Fürth Im Wald, Bayern 223
Füssen, Bayern 223
Füssing, Bad, Bayern 223
Gaden, Bayern 223
Gammelsbach, Hessen 241
Gandersheim, Bad, Niedersachsen 251
Garmisch-Partenkirchen, Bayern 224
Gartow, Niedersachsen 251
Geisenheim, Hessen 241
Gemünden Am Main, Bayern 224
Gemünden-Hofstetten, Bayern 224
Georgenthal, Thüringen 237
Gerbach, Rheinland-Pfalz 241
Gifhorn, Niedersachsen 251
Gillenfeld, Rheinland-Pfalz 241
Glücksburg-Holnis, Schleswig-Holstein 251
Gottsdorf, Bayern 224
Griesbach, Bad, Bayern 224
Gross-Leuthen, Brandenburg 237
Gross-Quassow, Mecklenburg-Vorpommern 238
Grube, Schleswig-Holstein 252
Grünberg, Hessen 242
Grundmühle Bei Quentel, Hessen 242
Guldental, Rheinland-Pfalz 242
Haddeby, Schleswig-Holstein 252
Hademstorf, Niedersachsen 252
Hahnenklee, Niedersachsen 252
Haldern, Nordrhein-Westfalen 242
Hallwangen, Baden-Württemberg 231
Hameln, Niedersachsen 252
Hannover, Niedersachsen 252

Hardegsen, Niedersachsen 252
Haslach, Bayern 224
Hassendorf, Niedersachsen 252
Hatten, Niedersachsen 252
Hattorf, Niedersachsen 252
Hausbay, Rheinland-Pfalz 242
Hausen, Baden-Württemberg 231
Heidelberg, Baden-Württemberg 231
Heidenburg, Rheinland-Pfalz 242
Heikendorf, Schleswig-Holstein 252
Heimbach, Nordrhein-Westfalen 242
Heimertshausen, Hessen 242
Hellenthal, Nordrhein-Westfalen 242
Helmstedt, Niedersachsen 252
Hemeln, Niedersachsen 253
Herbolzheim,
Baden-Württemberg 231
Heringen, Hessen 242
Hermannsburg, Niedersachsen 253
Hersbruck, Bayern 224
Hirschhorn Am Neckar, Hessen 242
Höfen an Der Enz,
Baden-Württemberg 232
Hofgeismar, Hessen 242
Hofheim, Bayern 224
Hohegeiss, Niedersachsen 253
Hohenwarth, Bayern 224
Holle, Niedersachsen 253
Honnef, Bad,
Nordrhein-Westfalen 242
Horb, Baden-Württemberg 232
Horn-Bad Meinberg,
Nordrhein-Westfalen 243
Idstein, Hessen 243
Ingenheim, Rheinland-Pfalz 243
Ingolstadt, Bayern 224
Irrel, Rheinland-Pfalz 243
Isny, Baden-Württemberg 232
Issigau, Bayern 224
Joditz, Bayern 224
Kalletal-Varenholz,
Nordrhein-Westfalen 243
Kamenz, Sachsen 238
Karlsruhe, Baden-Württemberg 232
Kehl, Baden-Württemberg 232
Kelbra, Thüringen 238
Kell, Rheinland-Pfalz 243
Kipfenberg, Bayern 224
Kirchberg, Baden-Württemberg 232
Kirchheim, Hessen 243
Kirchzarten, Baden-Württemberg 232
Kirchzell, Bayern 225
Kirn, Rheinland-Pfalz 243
Kissingen, Bad, Bayern 225
Kitzingen, Bayern 225
Kleinmachnow, Brandenburg 238
Kleinröhrsdorf, Sachsen 238
Kleinsaubernitz, Sachsen 238
Kleinwaabs, Schleswig-Holstein 253
Klingenbrunn, Bayern 225
Klint-Bei-Hechthausen,
Niedersachsen 253
Koblenz (Coblence),
Rheinland-Pfalz 243
Köln (Cologne),
Nordrhein-Westfalen 243
Könen, Rheinland-Pfalz 243
Königsdorf, Bayern 225
Königssee, Bayern 225
Königstein, Sachsen 238
Königstein Im Taunus, Hessen 243
Kressbronn, Baden-Württemberg 232
Kröv, Rheinland-Pfalz 243
Krun, Bayern 225
Kühnhausen, Bayern 225
Lackenhäuser, Bayern 225
Ladbergen, Nordrhein-Westfalen 243
Lahnstein, Rheinland-Pfalz 243
Laichingen, Baden-Württemberg 232
Langholz Über Eckernförde,
Schleswig-Holstein 253
Langlau, Bayern 225
Lassan, Meklenburg-Vorpommern 238
Lauterberg, Bad, Niedersachsen 253
Lauterburg, Baden-Württemberg 233
Lechbruck, Bayern 225
Lehnin, Brandenburg 238
Leiwen, Rheinland-Pfalz 244
Lemgo, Nordrhein-Westfalen 244
Lengfurt, Bayern 225
Lenzkirch, Baden-Württemberg 233
Liblar, Nordrhein-Westfalen 244
Liebelsberg, Baden-Württemberg 233
Liebenzell, Bad,
Baden-Württemberg 233
Lindau Im Bodensee, Bayern 226
Lindenfels, Hessen 244
Lingerhahn, Rheinland-Pfalz 244
Loose, Schleswig-Holstein 253
Lorch, Hessen 244
Lörrach, Baden-Württemberg 233
Losheim, Saarland 244
Ludwigshafen Am Bodensee,
Baden-Württemberg 233
Mainz-Kostheim, Hessen 244
Malente-Gremsmühlen,
Schleswig-Holstein 253
Mannheim, Baden-Württemberg 233
Marburg an Der Lahn, Hessen 244
Markdorf, Baden-Württemberg 233
Meerbusch, Nordrhein-Westfalen 244
Mehlem, Nordrhein-Westfalen 244
Meinhard, Hessen 244
Melbeck, Niedersachsen 253
Memmingen, Bayern 226
Mergentheim, Bad,
Baden-Württemberg 233
Meschede, Nordrhein-Westfalen 245
Mesenich, Rheinland-Pfalz 245
Michelstadt, Hessen 245
Mittelhof, Rheinland-Pfalz 245
Mittenwald, Bayern 226
Monschau, Nordrhein-Westfalen 245
Montabaur, Rheinland-Pfalz 245
Mörfelden-Walldorf, Hessen 245
Mörslingen, Bayern 226
Mörtelstein, Baden-Württemberg 233
Mühlberg, Thüringen 238
Mühlhausen Bei Augsburg, Bayern 226
Mülheim, Rheinland-Pfalz 245
Mülheim an Der Ruhr,
Nordrhein-Westfalen 245
Müllenbach, Rheinland-Pfalz 245
München (Munich), Bayern 226
Münstertal, Baden-Württemberg 233
Murrhardt, Baden-Württemberg 233
Neckargemünd,
Baden-Württemberg 234
Neckarzimmern,
Baden-Württemberg 234
Nehren, Rheinland-Pfalz 245
Neubäu, Bayern 226
Neuenburg, Baden-Württemberg 234
Neukirchen Vorm Wald, Bayern 226
Neustadt, Bayern 227
Neustadt, Schleswig-Holstein 253
Niedereisenhausen, Hessen 245
Niederkrüchten,
Nordrhein-Westfalen 245
Niesky, Sachsen 238
Niewisch, Brandenburg 238
Nordstrand, Island of,
Schleswig-Holstein 251, 253
Northeim, Niedersachsen 253
Nürnberg (Nuremberg), Bayern 227
Nussdorf, Baden-Württemberg 234
Oberammergau, Bayern 227
Obersgegen, Rheinland-Pfalz 246
Oberstdorf, Bayern 227
Oberweis, Rheinland-Pfalz 246
Oberwössen, Bayern 227
Oehe-Draecht, Schleswig-Holstein 254
Olpe, Nordrhein-Westfalen 246
Osnabrück, Niedersachsen 254
Osterode, Niedersachsen 254
Ostrhauderfehn, Niedersachsen 254
Östringen, Baden-Württemberg 234
Otterndorf, Niedersachsen 254
Passau, Bayern 227
Pforzheim, Baden-Württemberg 234
Pfraundorf, Bayern 227
Piding, Bayern 227
Pielenhofen, Bayern 227
Plön, Schleswig-Holstein 254
Plötzky, Sachsen 238
Porta Westfalica,
Nordrhein-Westfalen 246
Potsdam, Brandenburg 239
Pottenstein, Bayern 227
Prien Am Chiemsee, Bayern 227

Prüm, Rheinland-Pfalz 246
Pyrmont, Bad, Niedersachsen 254
Reichenberg, Sachsen 239
Reinsfeld, Rheinland-Pfalz 246
Rheinmünster, Baden-Württemberg 234
Rieste, Niedersachsen 254
Rinteln, Niedersachsen 254
Rosenberg, Baden-Württemberg 234
Rosshaupten, Bayern 228
Rothemann, Hessen 246
Rothenburg Ob Der Tauber, Bayern 228
Rottenbuch, Bayern 228
Rüdesheim, Hessen 246
Ruhpolding, Bayern 228
Saarburg, Rheinland-Pfalz 246
Saarlouis, Saarland 246
Schachen, Hessen 247
Schalkenmehren, Rheinland-Pfalz 247
Schapbach, Baden-Württemberg 234
Schechen, Bayern 228
Schiltach, Baden-Württemberg 234
Schleiden, Nordrhein-Westfalen 247
Schlüchtern, Hessen 247
Schobüll, Schleswig-Holstein 254
Schömberg, Baden-Württemberg 234
Schönau Am Königssee, Bayern 228
Schönenberg, Saarland 247
Schotten, Hessen 247
Schussenried, Bad, Baden-Württemberg 235
Schwäbisch Gmünd, Baden-Württemberg 235
Schwäbisch Hall, Baden-Württemberg 235
Seck, Rheinland-Pfalz 247
Seefeld, Bayern 228
Senheim, Rheinland-Pfalz 247
Sensweiler Mühle, Rheinland-Pfalz 247
Solingen, Nordrhein-Westfalen 248
Sommerach Am Main, Bayern 228
Sonthofen, Bayern 229
St Andreasberg, Niedersachsen 254
St Goar, Rheinland-Pfalz 247
St Goarshausen, Rheinland-Pfalz 247
St Peter, Baden-Württemberg 234
Stadtkyll, Rheinland-Pfalz 248
Stadtsteinach, Bayern 229
Staufen, Baden-Württemberg 235
Steinach, Baden-Württemberg 235
Steinen, Rheinland-Pfalz 248
Stelle, Niedersachsen 254
Stukenbrock, Nordrhein-Westfalen 248
Stuttgart, Baden-Württemberg 235
Suderburg, Niedersachsen 255
Suhrendorf, Mecklenburg-Vorpommern 239
Tann, Hessen 248
Tarmstedt, Niedersachsen 255
Tellingstedt, Schleswig-Holstein 255
Tettenhausen, Bayern 229
Tinnum (Island of Sylt), Schleswig-Holstein 255
Titisee-Neustadt, Baden-Württemberg 235
Tittmoning, Bayern 229
Todtnau, Baden-Württemberg 235
Tönning, Schleswig-Holstein 255
Trausnitz, Bayern 229
Treis-Karden, Rheinland-Pfalz 248
Trendelburg, Hessen 248
Trier, Rheinland-Pfalz 248
Trippstadt, Rheinland-Pfalz 248
Tübingen, Baden-Württemberg 235
Tüchersfeld, Bayern 229
Überlingen, Baden-Württemberg 236
Uhldingen, Baden-Württemberg 236
Uslar, Niedersachsen 255
Utscheid, Rheinland-Pfalz 248
Velburg, Bayern 229
Viechtach, Bayern 229
Vinkrath Bei Grefrath, Nordrhein-Westfalen 248
Vlotho, Nordrhein-Westfalen 248
Waging, Bayern 229
Waldkirch, Baden-Württemberg 236
Waldshut, Baden-Württemberg 236
Walkenried, Niedersachsen 255
Waltenhofen, Bayern 229
Warburg, Nordrhein-Westfalen 248
Wasserfall, Nordrhein-Westfalen 249
Waxweiler, Rheinland-Pfalz 249
Weener, Niedersachsen 255
Weilburg, Hessen 249
Weissach, Bayern 229
Weissenstadt, Bayern 229
Wemding, Bayern 230
Wertach, Bayern 230
Wertheim, Baden-Württemberg 236
Wietzendorf, Niedersachsen 255
Wildbad Im Schwarzwald, Baden-Württemberg 236
Wilsum, Niedersachsen 255
Wingst, Niedersachsen 255
Winkl Bei Bischofswiesen, Bayern 230
Winsen-Aller, Niedersachsen 255
Winterberg, Nordrhein-Westfalen 249
Wissel, Nordrhein-Westfalen 249
Wittenborn, Schleswig-Holstein 256
Witzenhausen, Hessen 249
Wolfstein, Rheinland-Pfalz 249
Wulfen (Island of Fehmarn), Schleswig-Holstein 256
Zerf, Rheinland-Pfalz 249
Zinnowitz, Mecklenburg-Vorpommern 239
Zwesten, Hessen 249
Zwiesel, Bayern 230

ITALY

Aglientu, Sassari 295
Alba Adriatica, Teramo 283
Albenga, Savona 277
Albinia, Grosseto 277
Anfo, Brescia 260
Angera, Varese 260
Arbatax, Nuoro 295
Arona, Novara 260
Arsie, Belluno 269
Arvier, Aosta 260
Asiago, Vicenza 269
Assisi, Perugia 284
Aurisina, Trieste 269
Avola, Siracusa 296
Baia Domizia, Caserta 291
Barberino Val D'Elsa, Firenze 277
Bardolino, Verona 269
Barrea, L'Aquila 284
Bastia Mondovi, Cuneo 260
Battipaglia, Salerno 291
Baveno, Novara 260
Bellagio, Como 260
Bellaria, Forli 284
Bevagna, Perugia 284
Bibbona, Marina di, Livorno 277
Bibione, Venezia 269
Bogliasco, Genova 278
Bologna, Bologna 284
Bolsena, Viterbo 289
Bolzano-Bozen, Bolzano 260
Bordighera, Imperia 278
Borghetto, Perugia 284
Bottai, Firenze 278
Bracciano, Roma 290
Bréccia, Como 260
Brentonico, Trento 261
Brenzone, Verona 269
Bressanone-Brixen, Bolzano 261
Briatico, Catanzaro 291
Ca'Noghera, Venezia 269
Cágliari, 295
Calasetta, Cagliari 295
Calceranica, Trento 261
Calenzano, Firenze 278
Camerota, Marina di, Salerno 291
Campitello di Fassa, Trento 261
Canazei, Trento 261
Cannigione di Arzachena, Sassari 295
Cannobio, Novara 261
Caorle, Venezia 272
Capalbio, Grosseto 278
Capannole, Arezzo 278
Capo Vaticano, Catanzaro 291
Carovigno, Brindisi 291
Casal Borsetti, Ravenna 284
Casale Marittimo, Pisa 278
Cassone, Verona 272
Castagneto Carducci, Livorno 278

Castel Del Piano, Grosseto 279
Castel di Tusa, Messina 296
Castelletto di Brenzone, Verona 272
Castelletto Ticino, Novara 261
Castiglione Del Lago, Perugia 284
Castiglione Della Pescaia, Grosseto 279
Catánia, Catánia 296
Cavallino, Venezia 272
Cefalú, Palermo 296
Ceriale, Savona 279
Cervia, Ravenna 284
Cervo, Imperia 279
Cesenatico, Forli 284
Chioggia, Venezia 272
Chioggia Sottomarina, Venezia 273
Chiusa-Klausen, Bolzano 261
Cirú Marina, Catanzaro 292
Cisano, Verona 273
Citta di Castello, Perugia 284
Colfosco, Bolzano 262
Colombare, Brescia 262
Corigliano Cálabro, Cosenza 292
Cortina D'Ampezzo, Belluno 273
Cupra Marittima, Ascoli Piceno 285
Cutigliano, Pistoia 279
Dante, Lido di, Ravenna 285
Desenzano Del Garda, Brescia 262
Deiva Marina, La Spezia 279
Dimaro, Trento 262
Domaso, Como 262
Duino-Aurisina, Trieste 273
Eboli, Salerno 292
Edolo, Brescia 262
Elba, Isola D', Livorno 279
Eraclea Mare, Venezia 273
Estensi, Lido Degli, Ferrara 285
Fano, Pesaro & Urbino 285
Feriolo, Novara 263
Ferrara, Ferrara 285
Fiano Romano, Roma 290
Fiésole, Firenze 280
Figline Valdarno, Firenze 280
Finale di Pollina, Palermo 296
Fiorenzuola di Focara,
Pesaro & Urbino 285
Firenze (Florence), Firenze 280
Florence See Firenze 280
Fondachello, Catania 296
Fondotoce, Novara 263
Formia, Latina 290
Fucine di Ossana, Trento 263
Fúrnari Marina, Messina 297
Fusina Venezia, Venezia 273
Gallipoli, Lecce 292
Gatteo Mare, Forli 285
Gemona Del Friúli, Udine 273
Germignaga, Varese 263
Giovinazzo, Bari 292
Giulianova Lido, Teramo 285
Grado, Gorizia 274
Grosseto, Marina di, Grosseto 280
Guardavalle, Marina di, Catanzaro 292
Gubbio, Perugia 285
Idro, Brescia 263
Iseo, Brescia 263
Jésolo, Lido di, Venezia 274
Kaltern, Bolzano 264
Lacona, Livorno 279
Laives-Leifers, Bolzano 264
Latsch, Bolzano 264
Láura, Salerno 292
Lazise, Verona 274
Lecco, Como 264
Leporano, Marina di, Taranto 292
Lerici, La Spezia 281
Levico Terme, Trento 264
Lignano Sabbiadoro, Udine 274
Lillaz, Aosta 264
Limite, Firenze 281
Limone Piemonte, Cuneo 264
Limone Sul Garda, Brescia 264
Lotzorai, Nuoro 295
Maccagno, Varese 264
Mácchia, Foggia 292
Malcesine, Verona 274
Malga Ciapela, Belluno 274
Manerba Del Garda, Brescia 265
Manfredonia, Foggia 292
Marcelli di Numana, Ancona 286
Marghera, Venezia 274
Marone, Brescia 265
Marotta, Pesaro & Urbino 286
Martiniscuro, Teramo 286
Masarè, Belluno 274
Massa Lubrense, Napoli 292
Massa, Marina di, Massa Carrara 281
Mattinata, Foggia 292
Menfi, Agrigento 297
Mestre, Venezia 274
Metaponto, Lido di, Matera 293
Milano Marittima, Ravenna 286
Minturno, Marina di, Latina 290
Molina di Ledro, Trento 265
Molveno, Trento 265
Monéglia, Genova 281
Moniga Del Garda, Brescia 265
Montalto di Castro,
Marina di, Viterbo 290
Monte di Fo, Firenze 281
Montecatini Terme, Pistoia 281
Montegrotto Terme, Padova 276
Montenero, Marina di,
Campobasso 286
Monteriggioni, Siena 281
Montescudáio, Livorno 281
Monticello Amiata, Grosseto 281
Narni, Terni 286
Naturno-Naturns, Bolzano 265
Nazioni, Lido Delle, Ferrara 286
Nicolosi, Catania 297
Nicótera Marina, Catanzaro 293
Nisporto, 280
Novate Mezzola, Sondrio 265
Oliveri, Messina 297
Oriago, Venezia 276
Orta San Giulio, Novara 265
Ortano, 280
Ősola Delle Fémmine, Palermo 297
Otranto, Lecce 293
Ottone, 280
Pacengo, Verona 276
Pachino, 297
Padenghe, Brescia 265
Palafavera, Belluno 276
Palazzolo Acreide, Siracusa 297
Palmi, Reggio di Calabria 293
Parma, Parma 286
Passignano, Perugia 286
Pegli, Genova 281
Peio, Trento 266
Pera di Fassa, Trento 266
Pérgine, Trento 266
Perugia, Perugia 286
Peschici, Foggia 293
Peschiera Del Garda, Verona 276
Pettenasco, Novara 266
Pieve di Manerba, Brescia 266
Pievepelago, Modena 286
Pinarella, Ravenna 287
Pineto, Teramo 287
Pisa, Pisa 281
Pisogne, Brescia 266
Pizzo, Catanzaro 293
Pompei, Napoli 293
Pomposa, Ferrara 287
Ponte Tresa, Varese 266
Populónia, Livorno 282
Porlezza, Como 266
Porto Azzurro, 280
Porto Rotondo, Sassari 295
Porto Sant'Elpídio, Ascoli Piceno 287
Porto Santa Margherita, Venezia 276
Portoferraio, 280
Pozza di Fassa, Trento 266
Pozzuoli, Napoli 293
Práia A Mare, Cosenza 293
Preci, Perugia 287
Punta Braccetto, Ragusa 297
Punta Marina, Ravenna 287
Punta Sabbioni, Venezia 276
Ragusa, Marina di, Ragusa 297
Rasun, Bolzano 267
Ravenna, Marina di, Ravenna 287
Riccione, Forli 287
Riotorto, Livorno 282
Riva Del Garda, Trento 267
Rivoltella, Brescia 267
Rodi Garganico, Foggia 293
Roma (Rome), Roma 290
Roseto Degli Abruzzi, Teramo 288

Rosolina Mare, Rovigo 276
Rossano Scalo, Cosenza 293
S Arcangelo Sul Trasimeno, Perugia 288
Salsomaggiore Terme, Parma 288
Salto di Fondi, Latina 291
San Antonio di Mavignola, Trento 267
San Baronto, Firenze 282
San Felice Del Benaco, Brescia 267
San Gimignano, Siena 282
San Marino, 288
San Martino di Castrozza, Trento 268
San Menáio, Foggia 294
San Piero A Sieve, Firenze 282
San Piero In Bagno, Forli 288
San Pietro di Corteno Golgi, Brescia 268
San Teodoro, Nuoro 296
San Vigilio di Marebbe, Bolzano 268
San Vincenzo, Livorno 282
Sant' Alessio Siculo, Messina 297
Sant' Antonio di Barcellona, Messina 297
Santa Cesárea Terme, Lecce 294
Santa Lucia, Nuoro 296
Santa Maria di Castellabate, Salerno 294
Sardegna (Sardinia), 295
Sarre, Aosta 268
Sarteano, Siena 282
Sarzana, La Spezia 282
Sasso Marconi, Bologna 288
Scacchi, Lido Degli, Ferrara 289
Seccagrande, Agrigento 297
Senigallia, Ancona 289
Sestri Levante, Genova 282
Sexten, Bolzano 268
Sicilia (Sicily), 296
Siena, Siena 282
Sorico, Como 268
Sorrento, Napoli 294
Spina, Lido di, Ferrara 289
Spoleto, Perugia 289
Stella San Giovanni, Savona 283
Terracina, Latina 291
Teulada, Cagliari 296
Torbole, Trento 268
Torino di Sangro Marina, Chieti 289
Torre Daniele, Torino 269
Torre Del Lago Puccini, Lucca 283
Torre Rinalda, Lecce 294
Torre Salinas, Cagliari 296
Toscolano Maderno, Brescia 269
Treporti, Venezia 276
Troghi, Firenze 283
Ugento, Lecce 294
Vada, Livorno 283
Valledoria, Sassari 296
Vallicella di Monzuno, Bologna 289
Valnontey, Aosta 269
Vasto, Chieti 289
Viareggio, Lucca 283
Vicenza, Vicenza 277
Vico Equense, Napoli 294
Vieste, Foggia 295
Viverone, Vercelli 269
Vols, Bolzano 269
Zinola, Savona 283
Zocca, Modena 289
Zoldo Alto, Belluno 277

LUXEMBOURG

Berdorf 300
Boulaide 300
Clervaux 300
Consdorf 300
Diekirch 300
Dillingen 300
Echternach 300
Enscherange 300
Esch-sur-Alzette 300
Heiderscheid 300
Ingledorf 301
Kockelscheuer 301
Larochette 301
Maulusmühle 301
Mersch 301
Mondorf-les-Bains 301
Nommern 301
Obereisenbach 301
Rosport 301
Steinfort 301
Vianden 301
Weiler-la-Tour 301

THE NETHERLANDS

Aalsmeer, Noord-Holland 305
Afferden, Limburg 311
Alkmaar, Noord-Holland 306
Amen, Drenthe 304
Amsterdam, Noord-Holland 306
Andijk, Noord-Holland 306
Annen, Drenthe 304
Appeltern, Gelderland 306
Arcen, Limburg 312
Arnemuiden, Zeeland 312
Arnhem, Gelderland 306
Assen, Drenthe 304
Baarland, Zeeland 312
Baarle Nassau, Noord-Brabant 312
Baarlo, Limburg 312
Babberich, Gelderland 306
Barendrecht, Zuid-Holland 312
Beekbergen, Gelderland 307
Berg En Terblijt, Limburg 312
Bergeyk, Noord-Brabant 312
Bergum, Friesland 304
Berkhout, Noord-Holland 307
Bilthoven, Utrecht 307
Blokzijl, Overijssel 307
Borger, Drenthe 304
Bosschenhoofd, Noord-Brabant 312
Boxtel, Noord-Brabant 312
Breskens, Zeeland 312
Brielle, Zuid-Holland 312
Broekhuizenvorst, Limburg 313
Brouwershaven, Zeeland 313
Burgh-Haamstede, Zeeland 313
Buurse, Overijssel 307
Callantsoog, Noord-Holland 307
Dalfsen, Overijssel 307
Delft, Zuid-Holland 313
Denekamp, Overijssel 307
Diepenheim, Overijssel 307
Diever, Drenthe 304
Doesburg, Gelderland 307
Doetinchem, Gelderland 307
Doorn, Utrecht 307
Dronten, Gelderland 308
Dwingeloo, Drenthe 304
Echt, Limburg 313
Edam, Noord-Holland 308
Eerbeek, Gelderland 308
Eersel, Noord-Brabant 313
Egmond Aan Zee, Noord-Holland 308
Enschede, Overijssel 308
Epe, Gelderland 308
Ermelo, Gelderland 308
Franeker, Friesland 304
's-Gravenzande, Zuid-Holland 313
Groede, Zeeland 313
Groet, Noord-Holland 308
Groningen, Groningen 304
Groote Keeten, Noord-Holland 308
Haag, Den (The Hague), Zuid-Holland 313
Haaksbergen, Overijssel 308
Halfweg, Noord-Holland 308
Harkstede, Groningen 304
Harlingen, Friesland 304
Hattem, Gelderland 308
Hee (Island of Terschelling), Friesland 304
Heiloo, Noord-Holland 309
Helder, Den, Noord-Holland 309
Hellevoetsluis, Zuid-Holland 313
Hengelo, Gelderland 309
Hengelo, Overijssel 309
Hengstdijk, Zeeland 313
Herpen, Noord-Brabant 313
Heumen, Gelderland 309
Hilvarenbeek, Noord-Brabant 313
Hindeloopen, Friesland 304
Hoek, Zeeland 313
Hoek Van Holland, Zuid-Holland 314
Hoenderloo, Gelderland 309
Hoeven, Noord-Brabant 314
Hoogerheide, Noord-Brabant 314
Hoorn, Den (Island of Texel), Noord-Holland 309

Island of Terschelling) Friesland 305
Kamperland, Zeeland 314
Katwijk Aan Zee, Zuid-Holland 314
Kesteren, Gelderland 309
Koog, de (Island of Texel), Noord-Holland 309
Kootwijk, Gelderland 310
Kortgene, Zeeland 314
Koudekerke, Zeeland 314
Koudum, Friesland 305
Laag-Soeren, Gelderland 310
Lage Mierde, Noord-Brabant 314
Landgraaf, Limburg 314
Lathum, Gelderland 310
Lauwersoog, Groningen 305
Luttenberg, Overijssel 310
Luyksgestel, Noord-Brabant 314
Maarn, Utrecht 310
Maasbree, Limburg 314
Maastricht, Limburg 314
Makkum, Friesland 305
Markelo, Overijssel 310
Middelburg, Zeeland 315
Mierlo, Noord-Brabant 315
Mijnden, Utrecht 310
Neede, Gelderland 310
Nieuwvliet, Zeeland 315
Noord Scharwoude, Noord-Holland 310
Noordwijk Aan Zee, Zuid-Holland 315
Nunspeet, Gelderland 310
Oisterwijk, Noord-Brabant 315
Onnen, Groningen 305
Oosterhout, Noord-Brabant 315
Oostkapelle, Zeeland 315
Oostvoorne, Zuid-Holland 315
Opende, Friesland 305
Ouddorp, Zuid-Holland 315
Plasmolen, Limburg 316
Putten, Gelderland 310
Renesse, Zeeland 316
Retranchement, Zeeland 316
Reutum, Overijssel 310
Rhenen, Utrecht 310
Rijnsburg, Zuid-Holland 316
Rockanje, Zuid-Holland 316
Roermond, Limburg 316
Roosendaal, Noord-Brabant 316
Ruinen, Drenthe 305
Ruurlo, Gelderland 310
Sevenum, Limburg 316
Sluis, Zeeland 316
's-Gravenzande, Zuid-Holland 313
Soest, Utrecht 311
Sondel, Friesland 305
St Anthonis, Noord-Brabant 316
St Maartenszee, Noord-Holland 311
St Oedenrode, Noord-Brabant 316
Steenwijk, Overijssel 311
Termunterzijl, Groningen 305
Terschelling (Island of), 305
Texel (Island of), 311
Uitdam, Noord-Holland 311
Urk, Flevoland 311
Utrecht, Utrecht 311
Valkenburg, Limburg 316
Venray, Limburg 317
Vogelenzang, Noord-Holland 311
Vrouwenpolder, Zeeland 317
Wageningen, Gelderland 311
Wassenaar, Zuid-Holland 317
Wedde, Groningen 305
Weert, Limburg 317
Well, Limburg 317
Wemeldinge, Zeeland 317
West Terschelling 305
Westkapelle, Zeeland 317
Wezep, Gelderland 311
Wijdenes, Noord-Holland 311
Winterswijk, Gelderland 311
Zoutelande, Zeeland 317

PORTUGAL

Abrantes, Ribatejo 322
Albufeira, Algarve 321
Alenquer, Estremadura 323
Alvito, Baixo Alentejo 321
Arganil, Beira Litoral 323
Beja, Baixo Alentejo 321
Caldas Da Rainha, Estremadura 323
Caminha, Minho 322
Campo Do Geres, Minho 322
Casfreires, Beira Litoral 323
Coja, Beira Litoral 323
Costa Da Caparica, Estremadura 323
Évora, Alto Alentejo 324
Évora de Alcobaça, Estremadura 324
Figueira Da Foz, Beira Litoral 324
Gouveia, Beira Litoral 324
Guarda, Beira Alta 324
Guincho, Estremadura 324
Louriçal, Beira Litoral 324
Luso, Beira Litoral 324
Matosinhos, Douro Litoral 322
Mondim de Basto, Minho 322
Montargil, Alto Alentejo 324
Nazaré, Estremadura 324
Olhão, Argarve 321
Palheiros de Mira, Beira Litoral 324
Penacova, Beira Litoral 325
Peniche, Estremadura 325
Portalegre, Alto Alentejo 325
Portimão, Algarve 321
Póvoa de Varzim, Douro Litoral 322
Praia Da Luz, Algarve 321
Quarteira, Algarve 321
Sagres, Algarve 321
Salvaterra de Magos, Ribatejo 325
Santo Andre, Baixo Alentejo 322
São Jacinto, Beira Litoral 325
São Pedro de Moel, Estremadura 325
Sines, Baixo Alentejo 322
Viana Do Castelo, Minho 322
Vila Do Bispo, Algarve 322
Vila Nova de Gaia, Douro Litoral 322
Vila Nova de Milfontes, Baixo Alentejo 322
Vila Real, Tras-Os-Montes Alto Douro 322
Viseu, Beira Alta 325

SPAIN

Adra, Almeria 356
Aguilas, Murcia 356
Ajo-Bareyo, Cantabria 351
Alba de Tormes, Salamanca 340
Albarracin, Teruel 340
Alcazares, los, Murcia 356
Alcoceber, Castellón 342
Alfaz Del Pi, Alicante 342
Almayate, Málaga 356
Altea, Alicante 342
Ametlla de Mar, l', Tarragona 342
Andorra 359
Aranda de Duero, Burgos 353
Aranjuez, Madrid 340
Baiona, Pontevedra 355
Baños de Fortuna, Murcia 356
Bareyo, Cantabria 351
Barreiros, Lugo 351
Begur, Girona 330
Bellver de Cerdanya, Lleida 353
Benicarló, Castellón 342
Benicasim, Castellón 342
Benidorm, Alicante 342
Benisa, Alicante 343
Bergondo, La Coruña 351
Biescas, Huesca 353
Blanes, Girona 330
Bolnuevo, Murcia 356
Bonansa, Huesca 353
Bordeta, la, Lleida 353
Bossost, Lleida 354
Cabo de Gata, Almeria 356
Cabrera, la, Madrid 340
Cadavedo, Asturias 351
Calatayud, Zaragoza 354
Calella de la Costa, Barcelona 330
Cambrils, Tarragona 343
Campello, Alicante 343
Carchuna, Granada 356
Carlota, la, Cordoba 356
Castell D'Aro, Girona 330
Castelló D'Empuries, Girona 330
Castillo de Baños, Granada 357
Castro-Urdiales, Cantabria 351
Cóbreces, Cantabria 351
Comillas, Cantabria 351
Conil de la Frontera, Cádiz 357

Cubelles, Barcelona 331
Cubillas de Santa Marta, Valladolid 355
Cudillero, Asturias 352
Cuenca, Cuenca 340
Cunit, Tarragona 343
Daimus, Valencia 346
Escala, l', Girona 331
Escorial, El, Madrid 340
Espot, Lleida 354
Estartit, l', Girona 331
Estella, Navarra 354
Estepona, Malága 357
Foz, Lugo 352
Franca, la, Asturias 352
Fuente de Piedra, Malága 357
Fuente de San Esteban, la, Salamanca 340
Gallardos, los, Almeria 357
Gargantilla de Lozoya, Madrid 340
Getafe, Madrid 340
Granada, Granada 357
Guardamar Del Segura, Alicante 346
Guardiola de Bergueda, Barcelona 331
Guijarrosa, la, Cordoba 357
Guils de Cerdanya, Girona 331
Guingueta, la, Lleida 354
Hospitalet de l'Infant, l', Tarragona 346
Huesca, Huesca 354
Isla Cristina, Huelva 357
Isla Plana, Murcia 357
Islares, Cantabria 352
Jaca, Huesca 354
Jaraco, Valencia 346
Labuerda, Huesca 354
Laredo, Cantabria 352
Llanes, Asturias 352
Lloret de Mar, Girona 333
Luarca, Asturias 352
Madrid, Madrid 340
Malgrat de Mar, Barcelona 333
Malpartida de Plasencia, Cáceres 341
Manga Del Mar Menor, la, Murcia 357
Marbella, Málaga 357
Marina, la, Alicante 346
Masnou, El, Barcelona 333
Mazagón, Huelva 358
Mendigorria, Navarra 354
Mérida, Badajoz 341
Miramar Playa, Valencia 346
Miranda Del Castañar, Salamanca 341
Mojácar, Almeria 358
Mont-Roig Del Camp, Tarragona 346
Moratalla, Murcia 358
Motrico (Mutriku), Guipúzcoa 352
Motril, Granada 358
Nájera, La Rioja 354
Navajas, Castellón 346
Navalafuente, Madrid 341
Nigrán, Pontevedra 355
Noja, Cantabria 352
Nuevalos, Zaragoza 354
Oliva, Valencia 346
Oricain, Navarra 354
Orio, Guipúzcoa 352
Oropesa Del Mar, Castellón 348
Otura, Granada 358
Palafrugell, Girona 333
Palamós, Girona 333
Pals, Girona 334
Pancorbo, Burgos 354
Pechón, Cantabria 352
Peligros, Granada 358
Peñiscola, Castellón 348
Perlora-Candas, Asturias 352
Pineda de Mar, Barcelona 334
Platja D'Aro, la, Girona 334
Portonovo, Pontevedra 355
Puebla de Castro, la, Huesca 355
Puebla de Farnals, Valencia 348
Puerto de Santa María, El, Cádiz 358
Puigcerdà, Girona 335
Reinante, Lugo 353
Ribera de Cardós, Lleida 355
Ripoll, Girona 335
Ronda, Málaga 358
Roquetas-de-Mar, Almeria 358
Salamanca, Salamanca 341
Saldes, Barcelona 335
Salou, Tarragona 348
San Sebastián (Donostia), Guipúzcoa 353
San Vicente Do Mar, Pontevedra 355
Sant Antoni de Calonge, Girona 335
Sant Cebriá de Vallalta, Barcelona 335
Sant Feliu de Guixols, Girona 335
Sant Julià de Lúria, Andorra 359
Sant Pere Pescador, Girona 337
Santa Cristina D'Aro, Girona 335
Santa Elena, Jaén 358
Santa Marina de Valdeon, Léon 355
Santa Marta de Tormes, Salamanca 342
Santa Oliva, Tarragona 350
Santa Susana, Barcelona 335
Santiago de Compostela, La Coruña 353
Santillana Del Mar, Cantabria 353
Santo Domingo de la Calzada, La Rioja 355
Segovia, Segovia 342
Sevilla (Seville), Sevilla 358
Simancas, Valladolid 355
Sitges, Barcelona 337
Solsona, Lleida 355
Tamarit, Tarragona 350
Taradell, Barcelona 337
Tarifa, Cádiz 358
Tarragona, Tarragona 350
Tiermas, Zaragoza 355
Toledo, Toledo 342
Tordesillas, Valladolid 356
Torla, Huesca 355
Torre Del Mar, Málaga 359
Torreblanca, Castellón 351
Torroella de Montgri, Girona 337
Tossa de Mar, Girona 337
Valdemaqueda, Madrid 342
Valdoviño, La Coruña 353
Valencia, Valencia 351
Valencia de Don Juan, Léon 356
Vallromanes, Barcelona 339
Vejer de la Frontera, Cádiz 359
Vendrell, El, Tarragona 351
Vilallonga de Ter, Girona 339
Vilanova de Prades, Tarragona 351
Vilanova I la Geltrú, Barcelona 339
Villamayor, Salamanca 342
Villamejil, Léon 356
Villoslada de Cameros, La Rioja 355
Vinaroz, Castellón 351
Viveiro, Lugo 353
Zarauz (Zarautz), Guipúzcoa 353

SWITZERLAND

Acquacalda, Ticino 369
Aeschi, Bern 364
Agarn, Valais 370
Agno, Ticino 369
Aigle, Vaud 370
Altdorf, Uri 364
Altnau, Thurgau 363
Andeer, Graubünden 368
Appenzell, Appenzell 363
Arolla, Valais 370
Arosa, Graubünden 368
Ballens, Vaud 370
Bern (Berne), Bern 364
Bourg-St-Pierre, Valais 370
Bouveret, le, Valais 370
Brenzikofen, Bern 364
Brunnen, Schwyz 364
Bullet, Vaud 370
Château-D'Oex, Vaud 370
Châtel-St-Denis, Fribourg 371
Chessel, Vaud 371
Chur (Coire), Graubünden 368
Churwalden, Graubünden 368
Colombier, Neuchâtel 364
Cudrefin, Vaud 371
Cugnasco, Ticino 369
Düdingen, Fribourg 371
Erlach, Bern 364
Eschenz, Thurgau 363
Euthal, Schwyz 365
Evolène, Valais 371
Flüelen, Uri 365
Forel, Vaud 371
Fouly, la, Valais 371

Frutigen, Bern 365
Gampelen, Bern 365
Genève (Geneva), Genève 371
Giswil, Obwalden 365
Goldau, Schwyz 365
Goldingen, St-Gallen 363
Gordevio, Ticino 369
Grandson, Vaud 371
Grindelwald, Bern 365
Gstaad, Bern 365
Gumefens, Fribourg 371
Innertkirchen, Bern 365
Interlaken, Bern 365
Kandersteg, Bern 366
Krummenau, St-Gallen 363
Künten, Aargau 363
Landeron, le, Neuchâtel 366
Läufelfingen, Basel 363
Lausanne, Vaud 371
Lauterbrunnen, Bern 366
Lenz, Graubünden 368
Leutswil Bei Bischoffzell, Thurgau 363
Leysin, Vaud 371
Lignières, Neuchâtel 367
Locarno, Ticino 369
Locle, le, Neuchâtel 367
Luzern (Lucerne), Luzern 367
Mammern, Thurgau 363
Meiringen, Bern 367
Möhlin, Aargau 363
Molinazzo di Monteggio, Ticino 370
Morgins, Valais 371
Mosen, Luzern 367
Müstair, Graubünden 368
Nottwil, Luzern 367
Ottenbach, Zürich 364
Payerne, Vaud 372
Pontresina, Graubünden 369
Poschiavo, Graubünden 369
Prêles, Bern 367
Raron, Valais 372
Reckingen, Valais 372
Reinach, Basel 363
Ried-Brig, Valais 372
Saanen, Bern 367
Saas-Grund, Valais 372
Sachseln, Obwalden 368
Salgesch, Valais 372
Samedan, Graubünden 369
Schönengrund, Appenzell 364
Sembrancher, Valais 372
Sempach, Luzern 368
Sierre (Siders), Valais 372
Sorens, Fribourg 372
Splügen, Graubünden 369
Stechelberg, Bern 368
Sursee, Luzern 368
Susch, Graubünden 369
Susten, Valais 372
Tenero, Ticino 370
Thusis, Graubünden 369
Tschierv, Graubünden 369
Ulrichen, Valais 372
Vallorbe, Vaud 372
Vers-l'Église, Vaud 372
Vétroz, Valais 373
Vitznau, Luzern 368
Wagenhausen, Schaffhausen 364
Walenstadt, St-Gallen 364
Wildberg, Zürich 364
Wilderswil, Bern 368
Winterthur, Zürich 364
Yvonand, Vaud 373
Zernez, Graubünden 369
Zug, Zug 368
Zurzach, Aargau 363

PICTURE CREDITS

Front cover images are held in the Automobile Association's own library (AA World Travel Library) with contributions from the following:

Steve Day Front & Back t, Terry Harris Back b.

The following photographs are held in the Automobile Association's own photo library (AA World Travel Library) and were taken by the following photographers:

Adrian Baker 21t, 57; Peter Baker 30, 31b, 35, 37, 54; Michelle Chaplow 6, 17; Steve Day 355; Terry Harris 2, 8, 16, 33; Caroline Jones 9; Max Jourdan 3, 10t, 28, 32; Paul Kenward 11; Alex Kouprianoff 10b, 21b, 34, 72; Simon McBride 27; Anna Mockford & Nick Bonetti 15, 36t, 312; Clive Sawyer 18t, 18b, 22, 24, 25, 26, 29, 31t, 36b, 81, 252, 319; Barrie Smith 13; Tony Souter 215; Rick Strange 4, 12, 20r, 23; Doug Traverso 214; Wyn Voysey 14; Jon Wyand 20l.

COUNTRY MAP SECTION

1 AUSTRIA

2 BELGIUM

3 FRANCE-NORTH

4 FRANCE-SOUTH

5 GERMANY

6 GERMANY-DETAIL

7 NETHERLANDS

8 ITALY

9 SPAIN & PORTUGAL

10 SWITZERLAND

AUSTRIA

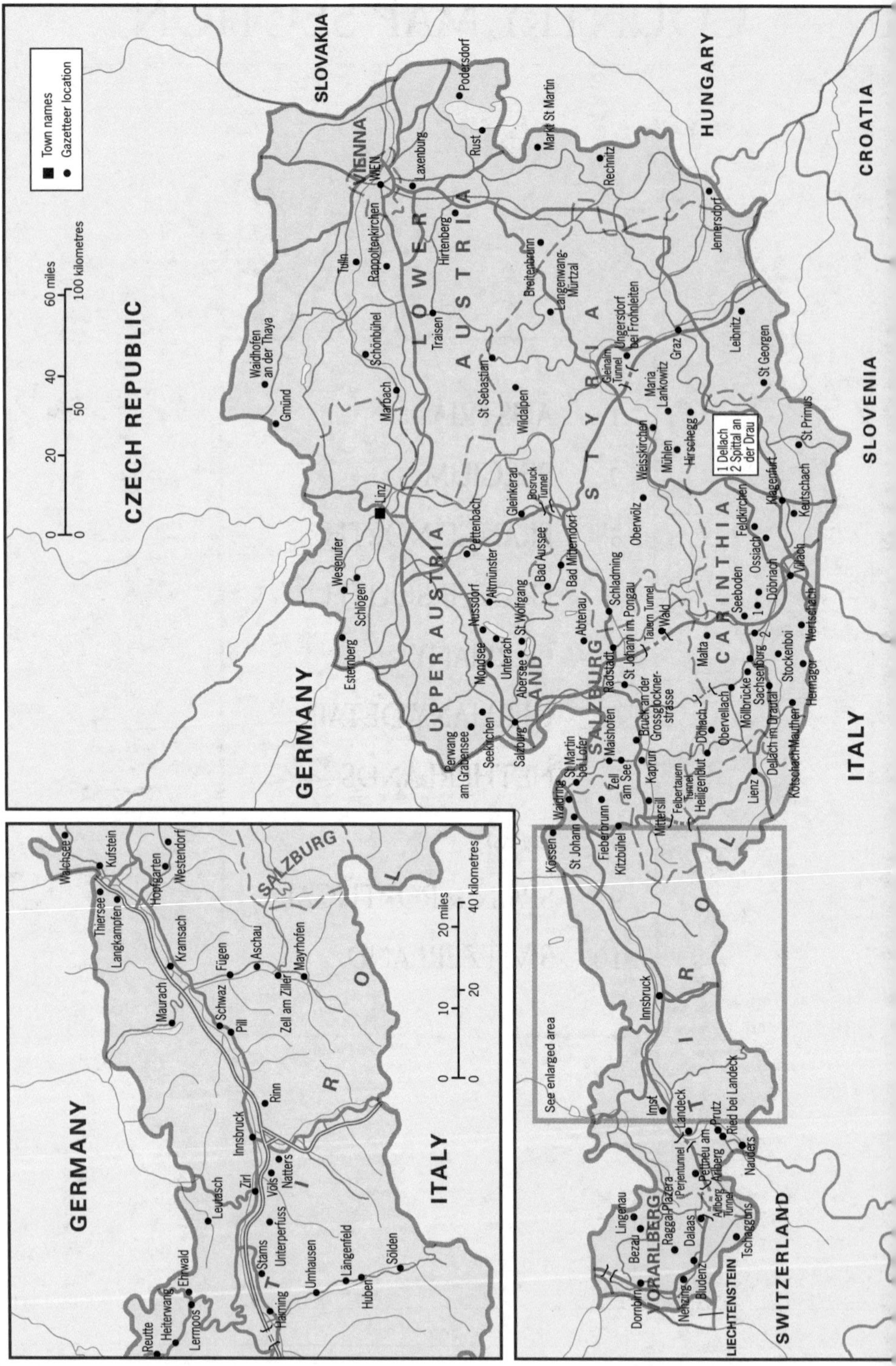
Town names
Gazetteer location
0 20 40 60 miles
0 50 100 kilometres
CZECH REPUBLIC
SLOVAKIA
HUNGARY
CROATIA
SLOVENIA
ITALY
SWITZERLAND
LIECHTENSTEIN
GERMANY
LOWER AUSTRIA
UPPER AUSTRIA
STYRIA
CARINTHIA
SALZBURG LAND
TIROL
VORARLBERG
VIENNA
WIEN
Linz
Podersdorf
Markt St Martin
Rust
Laxenburg
Rechnitz
Hirtenberg
Jennersdorf
Tulln
Rappoltenkirchen
Breitenbrunn
Langenwang-Mürztal
Waidhofen an der Thaya
Gmünd
Schönbühel
Traisen
Marbach
St Sebastian
Wildalpen
Ungersdorf bei Frohnleiten
Gleinalm Tunnel
Graz
Leibnitz
St Georgen
Maria Lankowitz
Hirschegg
Weisskirchen
Mühlen
St Primus
1 Dellach
2 Spittal an der Drau
Gleinkerau
Bosruck Tunnel
Pettenbach
Altmünster
Nussdorf
Bad Aussee
Bad Mitterndorf
Oberwölz
Wesenufer
Schlögen
Eferding
Klagenfurt
Keutschach
Feldkirchen
Ossiach
Döbriach
Villach
Seeboden
Wertschach
Schladming
Abtenau
St Wolfgang
Unterach
Mondsee
Abersee
Tauern Tunnel
Wald
St Johann im Pongau
Radstadt
Malta
Stockenboi
Sachsenburg
Möllbrücke
Obervellach
Dollach
Hermagor
Dellach im Drautal
Kötschach-Mauthen
Lienz
Bruck an der Grossglockner-strasse
Perwang am Grabensee
Seekirchen
Salzburg
Maishofen
Zell am See
Kaprun
Heiligenblut
Felbertauern Tunnel
Mittersill
St Martin bei Lofer
Waidring
Fieberbrunn
Kitzbühel
Kössen
St Johann
See enlarged area
Innsbruck
Imst
Landeck
Prutz
Ried bei Landeck
Nauders
Perjentunnel
Pettneu am Arlberg
Arlberg Tunnel
Tschagguns
Raggal-Plazera
Lingenau
Bezau
Dalaas
Dornbirn
Nenzing
Bludenz
Walchsee
Kufstein
Thiersee
Langkampfen
Hopfgarten
Westendorf
Kramsach
Fügen
Aschau
Mayrhofen
Zell am Ziller
Maurach
Schwaz
Pill
Rinn
Natters
Völs
Zirl
Leutasch
Unterperfuss
Stams
Haiming
Umhausen
Längenfeld
Huben
Sölden
Ehrwald
Lermoos
Heiterwang
Reutte
0 10 20 miles
0 20 40 kilometres

BELGIUM & LUXEMBOURG

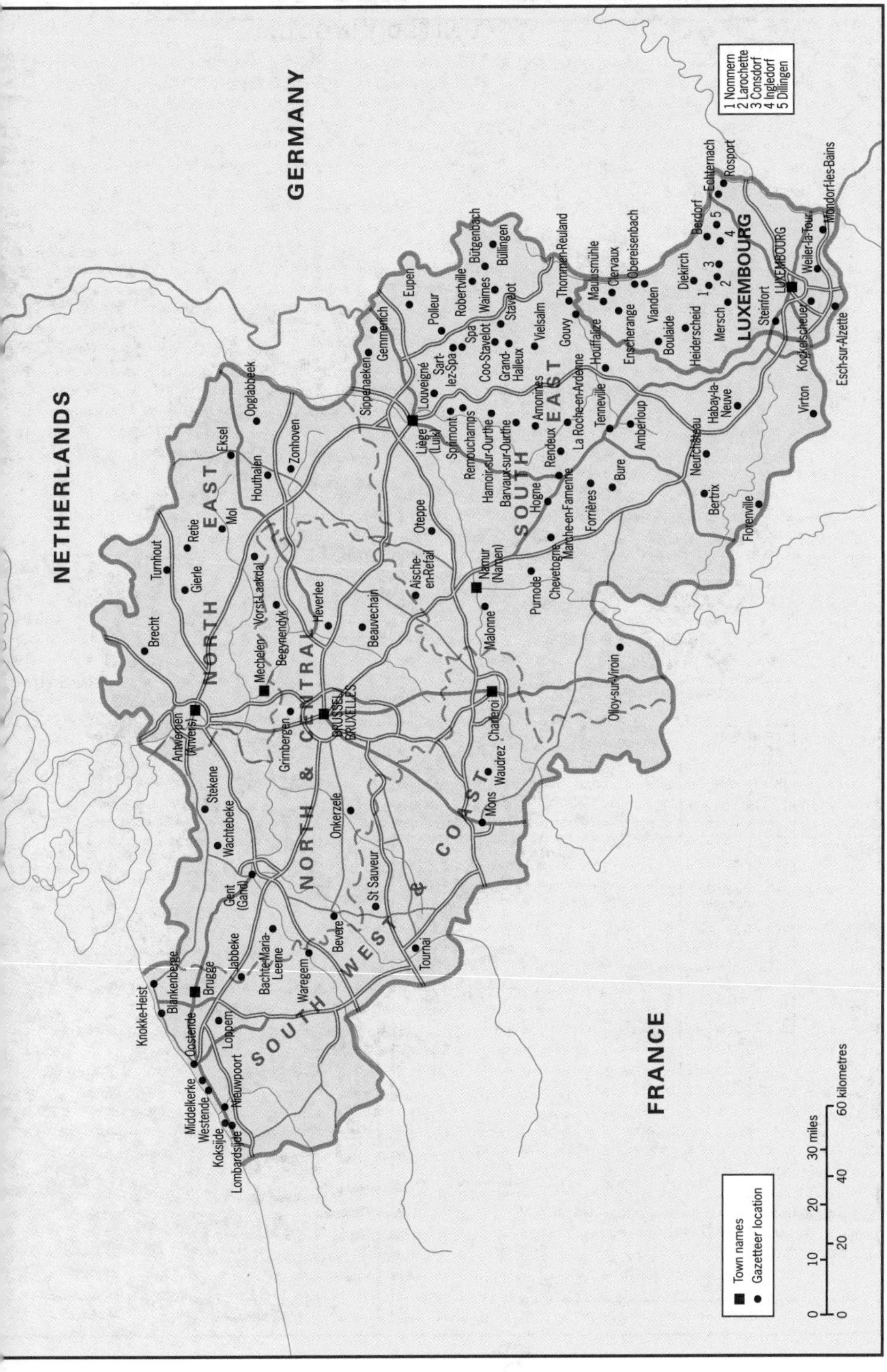

FRANCE

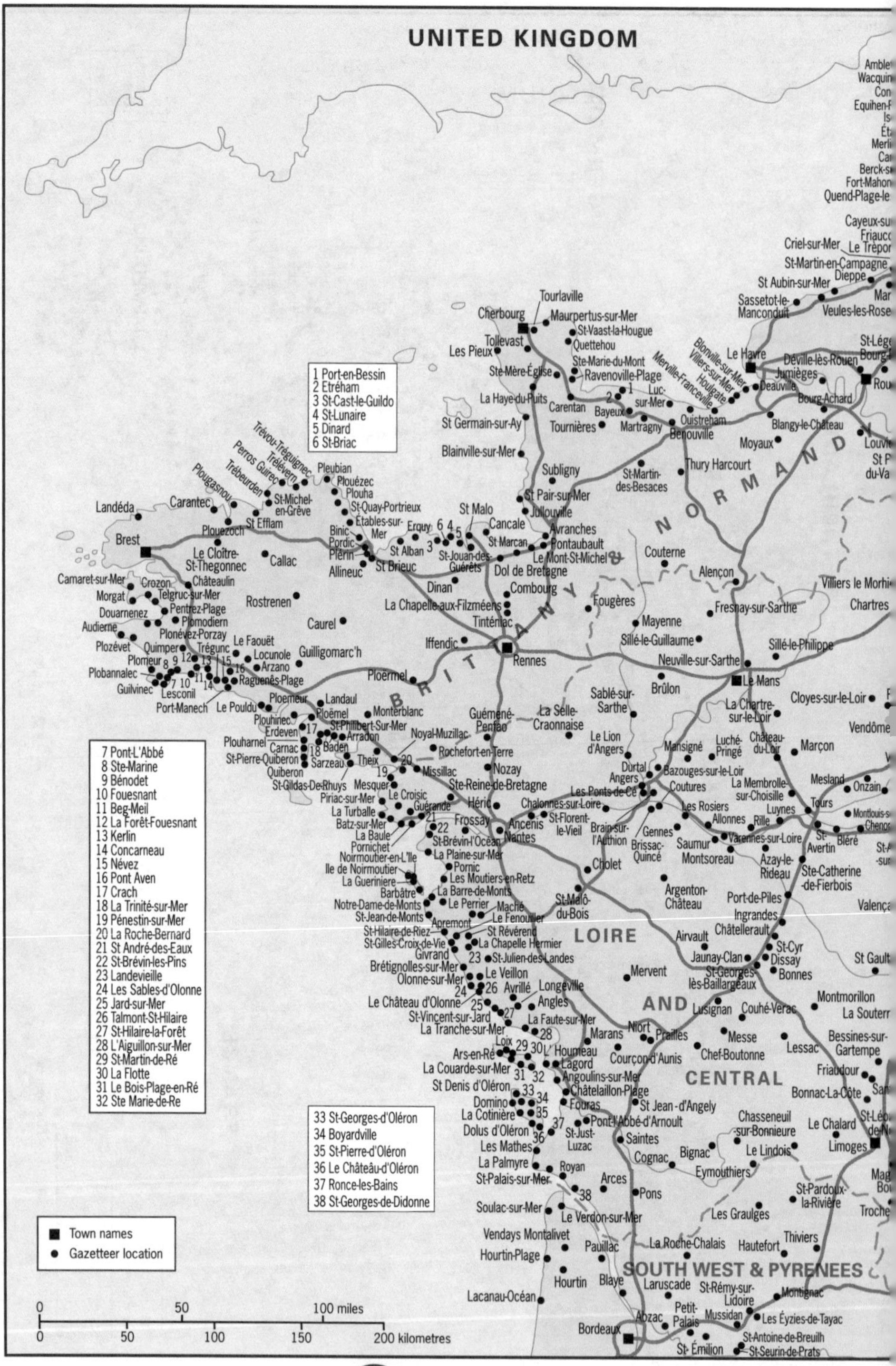

UNITED KINGDOM
1 Port-en-Bessin
2 Etréham
3 St-Cast-le-Guildo
4 St-Lunaire
5 Dinard
6 St-Briac
7 Pont-L'Abbé
8 Ste-Marine
9 Bénodet
10 Fouesnant
11 Beg-Meil
12 La Forêt-Fouesnant
13 Kerlin
14 Concarneau
15 Névez
16 Pont Aven
17 Crach
18 La Trinité-sur-Mer
19 Pénestin-sur-Mer
20 La Roche-Bernard
21 St André-des-Eaux
22 St-Brévin-les-Pins
23 Landevieille
24 Les Sables-d'Olonne
25 Jard-sur-Mer
26 Talmont-St-Hilaire
27 St-Hilaire-la-Forêt
28 L'Aiguillon-sur-Mer
29 St-Martin-de-Ré
30 La Flotte
31 Le Bois-Plage-en-Ré
32 Ste Marie-de-Re
33 St-Georges-d'Oléron
34 Boyardville
35 St-Pierre-d'Oléron
36 Le Château-d'Oléron
37 Ronce-les-Bains
38 St-Georges-de-Didonne
Town names
Gazetteer location
0 50 100 miles
0 50 100 150 200 kilometres
NORMANDY
BRITTANY
LOIRE
AND
CENTRAL
SOUTH WEST & PYRENEES
Tourlaville
Cherbourg
Maurpertus-sur-Mer
St-Vaast-la-Hougue
Quettehou
Tollevast
Les Pieux
Ste-Mère-Église
Ste-Marie-du-Mont
Ravenoville-Plage
La Haye-du-Puits
Carentan
Bayeux
Luc-sur-Mer
St Germain-sur-Ay
Tournières
Martragny
Ouistreham
Benouville
Merville-Franceville
Houlgate
Villers-sur-Mer
Blonville-sur-Mer
Deauville
Le Havre
Blainville-sur-Mer
Sublighy
St-Martin-des-Besaces
Thury Harcourt
Moyaux
Blangy-le-Château
Bourg-Achard
Jumièges
Déville-lès-Rouen
Sassetot-le-Mauconduit
St Aubin-sur-Mer
Dieppe
St-Martin-en-Campagne
Criel-sur-Mer
Le Trepor
Veules-les-Roses
Fort-Mahon
Quend-Plage-le
St Pair-sur-Mer
Jullouville
Avranches
Pontaubault
Le Mont-St-Michel
St Malo
Cancale
St Marcan
St-Jouan-des-Guérets
Dol de Bretagne
Dinan
Combourg
La Chapelle-aux-Filzméens
Tinténiac
Couterne
Alençon
Fougères
Mayenne
Sillé-le-Guillaume
Fresnay-sur-Sarthe
Villiers le Morhier
Chartres
Sillé-le-Philippe
Neuville-sur-Sarthe
Le Mans
Brûlon
Rennes
Iffendic
Ploërmel
Landéda
Carantec
Plougasnou
Trébeurden
Perros Guirec
Trélévern
Trévou-Tréguignec
Pleubian
Plouézec
Plouha
St-Quay-Portrieux
St-Michel-en-Grève
St Efflam
Plouezoch
Brest
Le Cloître-St-Thegonnec
Callac
Étables-sur-Mer
Binic
Pordic
Plérin
Erquy
St Alban
St Brieuc
Allineuc
Camaret-sur-Mer
Crozon
Châteaulin
Morgat
Telgruc-sur-Mer
Douarnenez
Pentrez-Plage
Plomodiern
Audierne
Plonévez-Porzay
Plozévet
Quimper
Trégunc
Le Faouët
Locunole
Arzano
Guilligomarc'h
Rostrenen
Caurel
Plomeur
Plobannalec
Guilvinec
Lesconil
Port-Manech
Le Pouldu
Raguenès-Plage
Ploemeur
Landaul
Ploëmel
Monterblanc
Plouhinec
Erdeven
St-Philibert-Sur-Mer
Arradon
Plouharnel
Carnac
Baden
St-Pierre-Quiberon
Sarzeau
Theix
Quiberon
St-Gildas-De-Rhuys
Noyal-Muzillac
Rochefort-en-Terre
Missillac
Guémené-Penfao
La Selle-Craonnaise
Sablé-sur-Sarthe
Le Lion d'Angers
Nozay
Mesquer
Piriac-sur-Mer
Le Croisic
Guérande
La Turballe
Batz-sur-Mer
La Baule
Pornichet
Ste-Reine-de-Bretagne
Héric
Frossay
Ancenis
Nantes
St-Brévin-l'Océan
La Plaine-sur-Mer
Pornic
Noirmoutier-en-L'Ile
Ile de Noirmoutier
La Gueriniere
Les Moutiers-en-Retz
Barbâtre
La Barre-de-Monts
Notre-Dame-de-Monts
Le Perrier
St-Jean-de-Monts
Machè
Le Fenouiller
Apremont
St-Hilaire-de-Riez
St Révérend
St-Gilles-Croix-de-Vie
La Chapelle Hermier
Givrand
St-Julien-des-Landes
Brétignolles-sur-Mer
Le Veillon
Olonne-sur-Mer
Avrillé
Longeville
Angles
Le Château d'Olonne
St-Vincent-sur-Jard
La Tranche-sur-Mer
La Faute-sur-Mer
Loix
Ars-en-Ré
La Couarde-sur-Mer
St Denis d'Oléron
Domino
La Cotinière
Dolus d'Oléron
Les Mathes
La Palmyre
St-Palais-sur-Mer
Royan
Soulac-sur-Mer
Le Verdon-sur-Mer
Vendays Montalivet
Hourtin-Plage
Hourtin
Lacanau-Océan
Pauillac
Blaye
Bordeaux
Durtal
Angers
Mansigné
Luché-Pringé
Château-du-Loir
La Chartre-sur-le-Loir
Bazouges-sur-le-Loir
Les Ponts-de-Cé
Coutures
Chalonnes-sur-Loire
St-Florent-le-Vieil
Brain-sur-l'Authion
Gennes
Brissac-Quincé
Les Rosiers
Allonnes
Saumur
Montsoreau
Varennes-sur-Loire
Cholet
St-Malô-du-Bois
Argenton-Château
Airvault
Mervent
Marans
Niort
Prailles
L' Houmeau
Lagord
Angoulins-sur-Mer
Châtelaillon-Plage
Fouras
Courçon-d'Aunis
St Jean-d'Angely
Pont-l'Abbé-d'Arnoult
St-Just-Luzac
Saintes
Cognac
Arces
Pons
Lusignan
Couhé-Vérac
Messe
Chef-Boutonne
Lessac
Jaunay-Clan
St-Georges-lès-Baillargeaux
Dissay
St-Cyr
Bonnes
Châtellerault
Ingrandes
Port-de-Piles
Azay-le-Rideau
Ste-Catherine-de-Fierbois
Avertin
Bléré
Tours
Luynes
Rille
La Membrolle-sur-Choisille
Mesland
Onzain
Marçon
Cloyes-sur-le-Loir
Vendôme
St Gaultier
Montmorillon
La Souterraine
Bessines-sur-Gartempe
Friaudour
Bonnac-La-Côte
Chasseneuil-sur-Bonnieure
Le Chalard
Limoges
Le Lindois
Bignac
Eymouthiers
St-Pardoux-la-Rivière
Les Graulges
La Roche-Chalais
Hautefort
Thiviers
Laruscade
St-Rémy-sur-Lidoire
Montignac
Petit-Palais
Abzac
Mussidan
Les Eyzies-de-Tayac
St-Antoine-de-Breuilh
St-Seurin-de-Prats
St-Émilion

4

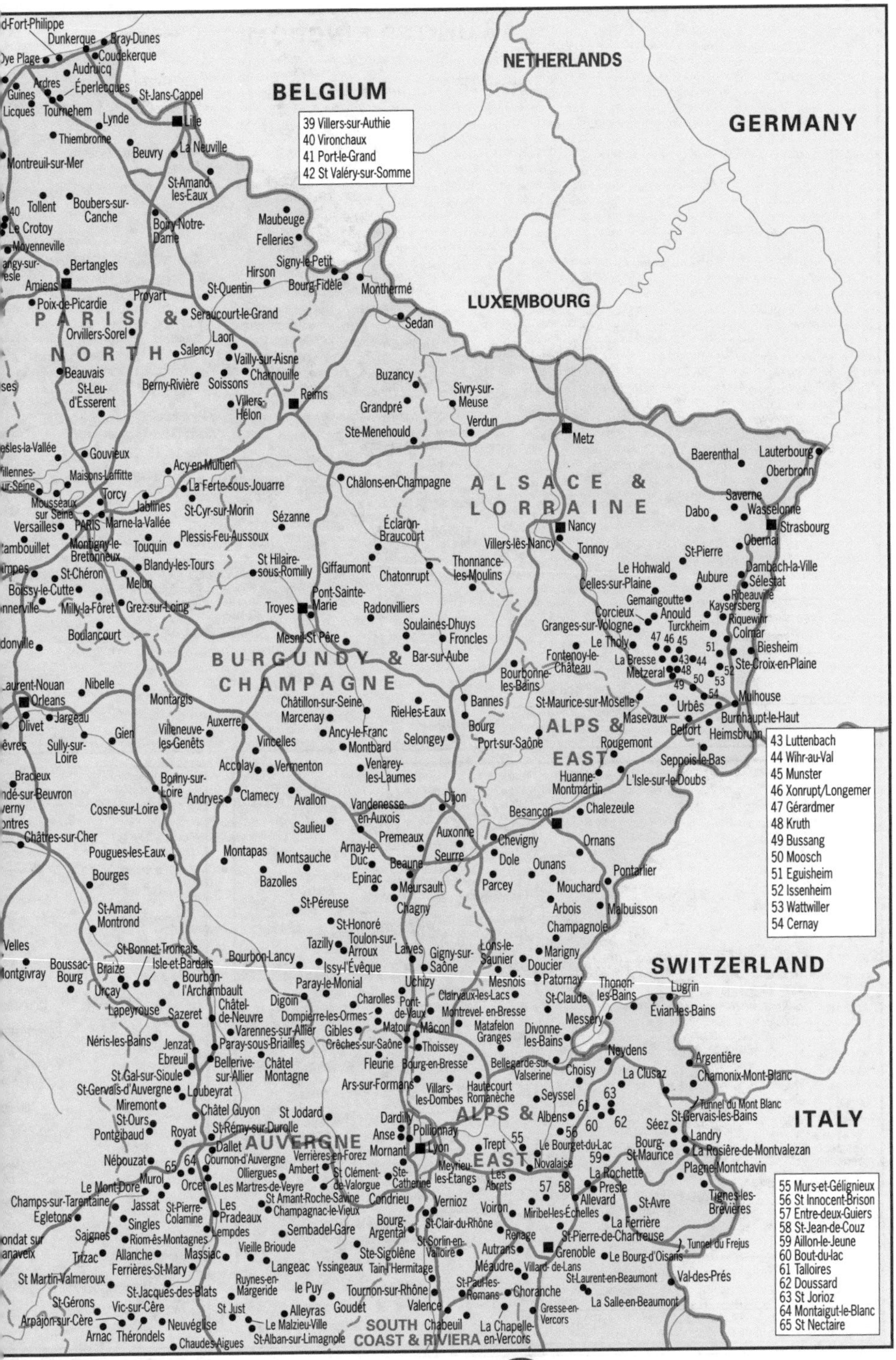
BELGIUM
NETHERLANDS
GERMANY
LUXEMBOURG
SWITZERLAND
ITALY
PARIS & NORTH
ALSACE & LORRAINE
BURGUNDY & CHAMPAGNE
ALPS & EAST
AUVERGNE
SOUTH COAST & RIVIERA
39 Villers-sur-Authie
40 Vironchaux
41 Port-le-Grand
42 St Valéry-sur-Somme
43 Luttenbach
44 Wihr-au-Val
45 Munster
46 Xonrupt/Longemer
47 Gérardmer
48 Kruth
49 Bussang
50 Moosch
51 Eguisheim
52 Issenheim
53 Wattwiller
54 Cernay
55 Murs-et-Gélignieux
56 St Innocent-Brison
57 Entre-deux-Guiers
58 St-Jean-de-Couz
59 Aillon-le-Jeune
60 Bout-du-lac
61 Talloires
62 Doussard
63 St Jorioz
64 Montaigut-le-Blanc
65 St Nectaire
Dunkerque
Bray-Dunes
Coudekerque
Audruicq
Ardres
Guines
Éperlecques
St-Jans-Cappel
Licques
Tournehem
Lynde
Lille
Thiembronne
Beuvry
La Neuville
Montreuil-sur-Mer
St-Amand-les-Eaux
Tollent
Boubers-sur-Canche
Le Crotoy
Moyenneville
Boiry-Notre-Dame
Maubeuge
Felleries
Bertangles
Amiens
Hirson
Signy-le-Petit
Bourg-Fidèle
Monthermé
St-Quentin
Poix-de-Picardie
Proyart
Seraucourt-le-Grand
Orvillers-Sorel
Sedan
Laon
Salency
Vailly-sur-Aisne
Charnouille
Beauvais
Berny-Rivière
Soissons
St-Leu-d'Esserent
Villers-Hélon
Reims
Buzancy
Grandpré
Sivry-sur-Meuse
Verdun
Ste-Menehould
Metz
Gouvieux
Acy-en-Multien
Maisons-Laffitte
La Ferte-sous-Jouarre
Châlons-en-Champagne
Baerenthal
Lauterbourg
Oberbronn
Torcy
Saverne
Wasselonne
Dabo
Strasbourg
Jablines
St-Cyr-sur-Morin
Sézanne
Versailles
PARIS
Marne-la-Vallée
Plessis-Feu-Aussoux
Éclaron-Braucourt
Nancy
Villers-lès-Nancy
Tonnoy
Obernai
Montigny-le-Bretonneux
Touquin
St-Pierre
St-Chéron
Blandy-les-Tours
St Hilaire-sous-Romilly
Giffaumont
Chatonrupt
Thonnance-les-Moulins
Le Hohwald
Dambach-la-Ville
Sélestat
Aubure
Melun
Boissy-le-Cutte
Pont-Sainte-Marie
Celles-sur-Plaine
Ribeauvillé
Kaysersberg
Riquewihr
Colmar
Milly-la-Fôret
Grez-sur-Loing
Troyes
Radonvilliers
Gemaingoutte
Anould
Corcieux
Turckheim
Granges-sur-Vologne
Soulaines-Dhuys
Froncles
Boulancourt
Mesnil-St Père
Bar-sur-Aube
Le Tholy
Fontenoy-le-Château
Biesheim
La Bresse
Metzeral
Ste-Croix-en-Plaine
Bourbonne-les-Bains
Nibelle
Orleans
Montargis
Châtillon-sur-Seine
Marcenay
Riel-les-Eaux
Bannes
St-Maurice-sur-Moselle
Urbès
Mulhouse
Jargeau
Olivet
Masevaux
Burnhaupt-le-Haut
Auxerre
Belfort
Heimsbrunn
Gien
Villeneuve-les-Genêts
Ancy-le-Franc
Bourg
Sully-sur-Loire
Vincelles
Montbard
Selongey
Port-sur-Saône
Rougemont
Seppois-le-Bas
Bracieux
Accolay
Vermenton
Venarey-les-Laumes
Huanne-Montmartin
L'Isle-sur-le-Doubs
Bonny-sur-Loire
Andryes
Clamecy
Avallon
Dijon
Cosne-sur-Loire
Vandenesse-en-Auxois
Besançon
Chalezeule
Châtres-sur-Cher
Saulieu
Premeaux
Auxonne
Chevigny
Ornans
Montapas
Montsauche
Arnay-le-Duc
Seurre
Dole
Ounans
Pougues-les-Eaux
Beaune
Pontarlier
Bourges
Bazolles
Epinac
Meursault
Parcey
Mouchard
St-Péreuse
Chagny
Arbois
Malbuisson
St-Amand-Montrond
St-Honoré
Champagnole
Tazilly
Toulon-sur-Arroux
Laives
Gigny-sur-Saône
Lons-le-Saunier
Marigny
Doucier
St-Bonnet-Troncais
Isle-et-Bardais
Bourbon-Lancy
Issy-l'Évêque
Boussac-Bourg
Braize
Urçay
Bourbon-l'Archambault
Paray-le-Monial
Uchizy
Mesnois
Patornay
Thonon-les-Bains
Lugrin
Évian-les-Bains
Lapeyrouse
Sazeret
Châtel-de-Neuvre
Digoin
Charolles
Pont-de-Vaux
Clairvaux-les-Lacs
St-Claude
Dompierre-les-Ormes
Matour
Mâcon
Montrevel-en-Bresse
Matafelon Granges
Divonne-les-Bains
Messery
Néris-les-Bains
Jenzat
Varennes-sur-Allier
Gibles
Thoissey
Ebreuil
Paray-sous-Briailles
Crêches-sur-Saône
Neydens
Argentière
Bellerive-sur-Allier
Châtel Montagne
Fleurie
Bourg-en-Bresse
Bellegarde-sur-Valserine
Choisy
La Clusaz
Chamonix-Mont-Blanc
St Gal-sur-Sioule
St-Gervais-d'Auvergne
Loubeyrat
Ars-sur-Formans
Villars-les-Dombes
Hautecourt Romanèche
Seyssel
Miremont
Châtel Guyon
St Jodard
Tunnel du Mont Blanc
St-Ours
Albens
St-Gervais-les-Bains
Pontgibaud
Royat
St-Rémy-sur-Durolle
Dardilly
Anse
Pollionnay
Séez
Landry
Dallet
Lyon
Trept
Le Bourget-du-Lac
Bourg-St-Maurice
La Rosière-de-Montvalezan
Nébouzat
Cournon-d'Auvergne
Verrières-en-Forez
Mornant
Novalaise
Plagne-Montchavin
Le Mont-Dore
Murol
Orcet
Olliergues
Ambert
St Clément-de-Valorgue
Ste-Catherine
Meyrieu-les-Étangs
Les Abrets
La Rochette
Les Martres-de-Veyre
Presle
Champs-sur-Tarentaine
Jassat
St-Pierre-Colamine
Les Pradeaux
St Amant-Roche-Savine
Champagnac-le-Vieux
Condrieu
Vernioz
Voiron
Miribel-les-Échelles
Allevard
St-Avre
Tignes-les-Brevières
Egletons
Singles
La Ferrière
Saignes
Riom-ès-Montagnes
Lempdes
Sembadel-Gare
Bourg-Argental
St-Clair-du-Rhône
Renage
St-Pierre-de-Chartreuse
Trizac
Allanche
Massiac
Vieille Brioude
Ste-Sigolène
St-Sorlin-en-Valloire
Autrans
Grenoble
Le Bourg-d'Oisans
Tunnel du Frejus
Ferrières-St-Mary
Langeac
Yssingeaux
Tain-l'Hermitage
Méaudre
Villard-de-Lans
St Martin-Valmeroux
St-Jacques-des-Blats
Ruynes-en-Margeride
le Puy
Tournon-sur-Rhône
St-Paul-les-Romans
Choranche
St-Laurent-en-Beaumont
Val-des-Prés
St-Gérons
Vic-sur-Cère
St Just
Alleyras
Goudet
Valence
Gresse-en-Vercors
La Salle-en-Beaumont
Arpajon-sur-Cère
Neuvéglise
Le Malzieu-Ville
Chabeuil
La Chapelle-en-Vercors
Arnac
Thérondels
Chaudes-Aigues
St-Alban-sur-Limagnole

FRANCE

3

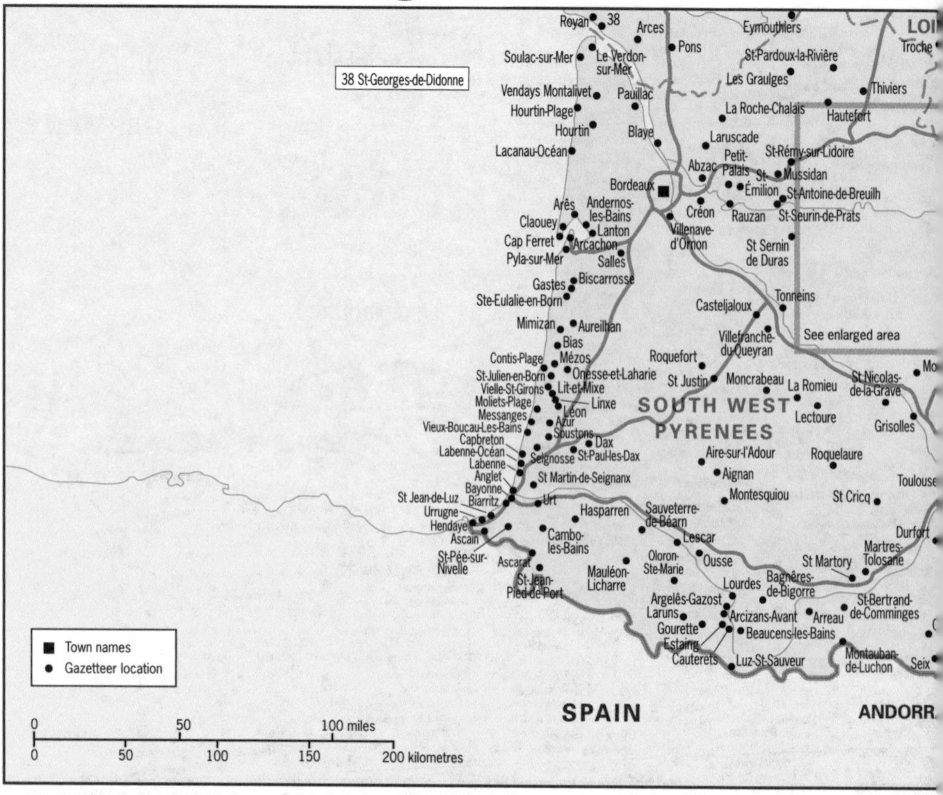
38 St-Georges-de-Didonne
Royan
38
Arces
Pons
Soulac-sur-Mer
Le Verdon-sur-Mer
Eymouthiers
St-Pardoux-la-Rivière
Les Graulges
Thiviers
Vendays Montalivet
Pauillac
Hourtin-Plage
Hourtin
Blaye
Lacanau-Océan
La Roche-Chalais
Hautefort
Laruscade
Petit-Palais
St-Rémy-sur-Lidoire
Abzac
St-Émilion
Mussidan
St-Antoine-de-Breuilh
Bordeaux
Arès
Andernos-les-Bains
Créon
Rauzan
St-Seurin-de-Prats
Claouey
Lanton
Villenave-d'Ornon
St Sernin de Duras
Cap Ferret
Arcachon
Pyla-sur-Mer
Salles
Biscarrosse
Gastes
Ste-Eulalie-en-Born
Tonneins
Casteljaloux
Mimizan
Aureilhan
Bias
Villefranche-du-Queyran
See enlarged area
Contis-Plage
Mézos
Roquefort
St-Julien-en-Born
Onesse-et-Laharie
St Justin
Moncrabeau
La Romieu
St Nicolas-de-la-Grave
Vielle-St-Girons
Lit-et-Mixe
Moliets-Plage
Linxe
Léon
SOUTH WEST
PYRENEES
Lectoure
Messanges
Azur
Vieux-Boucau-Les-Bains
Soustons
Grisolles
Capbreton
Dax
Labenne-Océan
Seignosse
St-Paul-les-Dax
Aire-sur-l'Adour
Roquelaure
Labenne
Anglet
St Martin-de-Seignanx
Aignan
Toulouse
Bayonne
St Jean-de-Luz
Biarritz
Urt
Montesquiou
St Cricq
Urrugne
Hendaye
Hasparren
Sauveterre-de-Béarn
Ascain
Cambo-les-Bains
Lescar
Durfort
St-Pée-sur-Nivelle
Oloron-Ste-Marie
Ousse
Martres-Tolosane
Ascarat
St Martory
Mauléon-Licharre
Bagnères-de-Bigorre
St-Jean-Pied-de-Port
Lourdes
Argelès-Gazost
St-Bertrand-de-Comminges
Laruns
Arcizans-Avant
Arreau
Gourette
Beaucens-les-Bains
Estaing
Montauban-de-Luchon
Cauterets
Luz-St-Sauveur
Seix
Town names
Gazetteer location
SPAIN
ANDORR
0
50
100 miles
0
50
100
150
200 kilometres

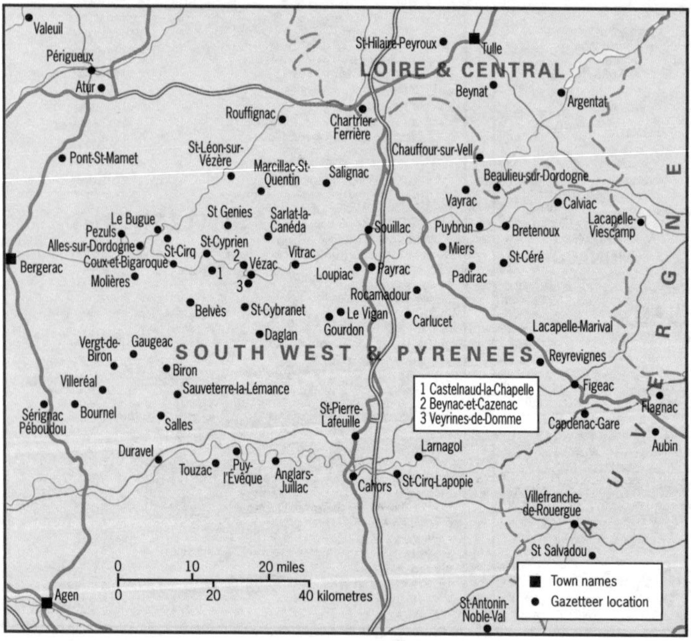
Valeuil
Périgueux
St-Hilaire-Peyroux
Tulle
Atur
LOIRE & CENTRAL
Beynat
Argentat
Rouffignac
Chartrier-Ferrière
Pont-St-Mamet
St-Léon-sur-Vézère
Chauffour-sur-Vell
Marcillac-St-Quentin
Salignac
Beaulieu-sur-Dordogne
Vayrac
Calviac
St Genies
Sarlat-la-Canéda
Le Bugue
Souillac
Puybrun
Bretenoux
Lacapelle-Viescamp
Pezuls
Alles-sur-Dordogne
St-Cirq
St-Cyprien
Miers
Coux-et-Bigaroque
Vitrac
St-Céré
Bergerac
2
Vézac
1
Loupiac
Payrac
Molières
3
Padirac
Rocamadour
Belvès
St-Cybranet
Le Vigan
Carlucet
Gourdon
Daglan
Lacapelle-Marival
Vergt-de-Biron
Gaugeac
SOUTH WEST & PYRENEES
Reyrevignes
Biron
Villeréal
Sauveterre-la-Lémance
1 Castelnaud-la-Chapelle
2 Beynac-et-Cazenac
3 Veyrines-de-Domme
Figeac
Sérignac Péboudou
Bournel
St-Pierre-Lafeuille
Flagnac
Salles
Capdenac-Gare
Aubin
Duravel
Larnagol
Touzac
Puy-l'Évêque
Anglars-Juillac
Cahors
St-Cirq-Lapopie
AUVERGNE
Villefranche-de-Rouergue
St Salvadou
0
10
20 miles
0
20
40 kilometres
Agen
Town names
Gazetteer location
St-Antonin-Noble-Val

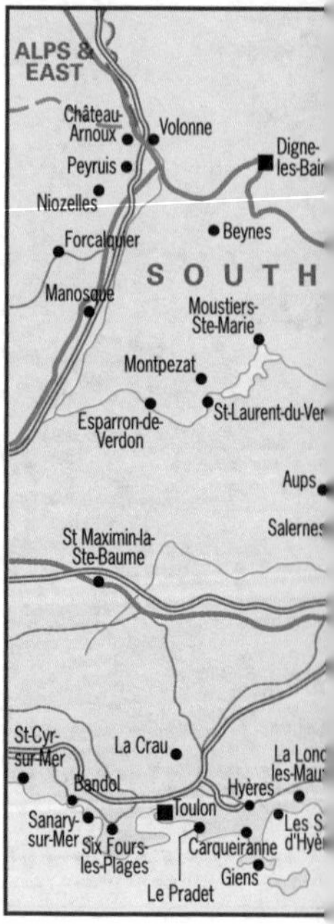
ALPS & EAST
Château-Arnoux
Volonne
Peyruis
Digne-les-Bai
Niozelles
Forcalquier
Beynes
SOUTH
Manosque
Moustiers-Ste-Marie
Montpezat
Esparron-de-Verdon
St-Laurent-du-Ver
Aups
Salernes
St Maximin-la-Ste-Baume
St-Cyr-sur-Mer
La Crau
La Lond les-Mau
Bandol
Hyères
Toulon
Sanary-sur-Mer
Six Fours-les-Plages
Carqueiranne
Les S d'Hyè
Giens
Le Pradet

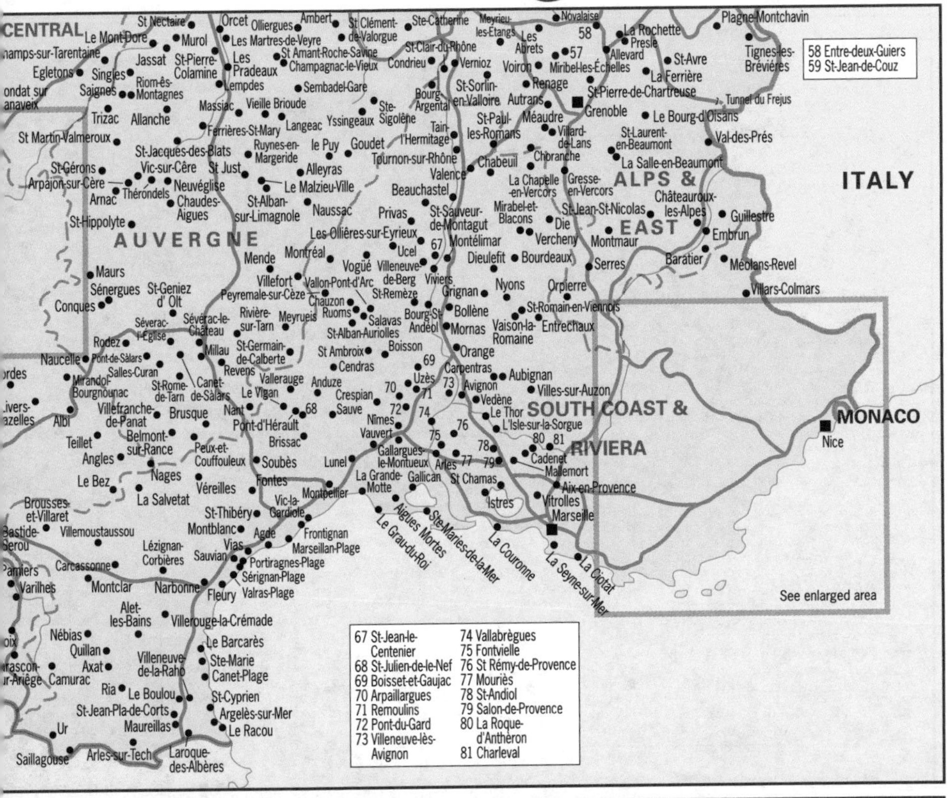
CENTRAL
Le Mont-Dore
Murol
St Nectaire
Orcet
Olliergues
Ambert
St Clément-de-Valorgue
Ste-Catherine
Meyrieu-les-Etangs
Novalaise
58
La Rochette
Presle
Plagne-Montchavin
Tignes-les-Brévières
Champs-sur-Tarentaine
Jassat
St-Pierre-Colamine
Les Martres-de-Veyre
Les Pradeaux
St Amant-Roche-Savine
Champagnac-le-Vieux
St-Clair-du-Rhône
Condrieu
Vernioz
Les Abrets
57
Voiron
Miribel-les-Echelles
Allevard
St-Avre
La Ferrière
Egletons
Singles
Riom-ès-Montagnes
Saignes
Lempdes
Sembadel-Gare
St-Sorlin-en-Valloire
Renage
Bourg-Argental
St-Pierre-de-Chartreuse
Tunnel du Frejus
Condat sur Trizac
Allanche
Massiac
Vieille Brioude
Ste-Sigolène
Autrans
Grenoble
Le Bourg-d'Oisans
St Martin-Valmeroux
Ferrières-St-Mary
Langeac
Yssingeaux
St-Paul-les-Romans
Méaudre
Villard-de-Lans
St-Laurent-en-Beaumont
Val-des-Prés
St-Jacques-des-Blats
Ruynes-en-Margeride
le Puy
Goudet
Tain-l'Hermitage
Tournon-sur-Rhône
Chabeuil
Choranche
La Salle-en-Beaumont
St-Gérons
Vic-sur-Cère
St Just
Alleyras
Valence
Arpajon-sur-Cère
Thérondels
Neuvéglise
Le Malzieu-Ville
Beauchastel
La Chapelle-en-Vercors
Gresse-en-Vercors
ALPS &
ITALY
Arnac
Chaudes-Aigues
St-Alban-sur-Limagnole
Naussac
Privas
St-Sauveur-de-Montagut
Mirabel-et-Blacons
St-Jean-St-Nicolas
Châteauroux-les-Alpes
Guillestre
St-Hippolyte
Les Ollières-sur-Eyrieux
Die
EAST
Embrun
AUVERGNE
Mende
Montréal
Ucel
67
Montélimar
Vercheny
Montmaur
Maurs
Vogüé
Villeneuve-de-Berg
Dieulefit
Bourdeaux
Serres
Baratier
Méolans-Revel
Sénergues
St-Geniez d'Olt
Villefort
Vallon-Pont-d'Arc
Viviers
Grignan
Nyons
Orpierre
Villars-Colmars
Conques
Peyremale-sur-Cèze
Chauzon
St-Remèze
Bollène
St-Romain-en-Viennois
Sévérac-l'Eglise
Sévérac-le-Château
Rivière-sur-Tarn
Meyrueis
Ruoms
Salavas
Bourg-St-Andéol
Mornas
Vaison-la-Romaine
Entrechaux
Rodez
St-Alban-Auriolles
Millau
St-Germain-de-Calberte
St Ambroix
Boisson
Orange
Naucelle
Pont-de-Salars
Salles-Curan
Revens
Cendras
69
Carpentras
Aubignan
Mirandol-Bourgnounac
St-Rome-de-Tarn
Canet-de-Salars
Vallerauge
Anduze
Uzès
73
Avignon
Villes-sur-Auzon
Albi
Le Vigan
Crespian
70
71
Vedène
Villefranche-de-Panat
Brusque
Nant
68
Sauve
72
Le Thor
SOUTH COAST &
MONACO
Nîmes
74
L'Isle-sur-la-Sorgue
Nice
Teillet
Belmont-sur-Rance
Pont-d'Hérault
Vauvert
75
76
80
81
RIVIERA
Angles
Peux-et-Couffouleux
Brissac
Soubès
Lunel
Gallargues-le-Montueux
Arles
77
78
79
Cadenet
Mallemort
Le Bez
Nages
Fontès
La Grande-Motte
Gallican
St Chamas
Aix-en-Provence
Véreilles
Montpellier
Istres
Vitrolles
La Salvetat
Brousses-et-Villaret
Vic-la-Gardiole
St-Thibéry
Marseille
Bastide-Sérou
Villemoustaussou
Montblanc
Agde
Frontignan
Marseillan-Plage
Aigues Mortes
Ste-Maries-de-la-Mer
La Couronne
La Ciotat
La Seyne-sur-Mer
Le Grau-du-Roi
Lézignan-Corbières
Vias
Sauvian
Portiragnes-Plage
Carcassonne
Pamiers
Varilhes
Montclar
Narbonne
Sérignan-Plage
Valras-Plage
Fleury
See enlarged area
Alet-les-Bains
Villerouge-la-Crémade
Nébias
Le Barcarès
Quillan
Axat
Villeneuve-de-la-Raho
Ste-Marie
Canet-Plage
Tarascon-sur-Ariège
Camurac
Ria
Le Boulou
St-Cyprien
St-Jean-Pla-de-Corts
Argelès-sur-Mer
Maureillas
Le Racou
Ur
Saillagouse
Arles-sur-Tech
Laroque-des-Albères
58 Entre-deux-Guiers
59 St-Jean-de-Couz
67 St-Jean-le-Centenier
68 St-Julien-de-le-Nef
69 Boisset-et-Gaujac
70 Arpaillargues
71 Remoulins
72 Pont-du-Gard
73 Villeneuve-lès-Avignon
74 Vallabrègues
75 Fontvielle
76 St Rémy-de-Provence
77 Mouriès
78 St-Andiol
79 Salon-de-Provence
80 La Roque-d'Anthéron
81 Charleval

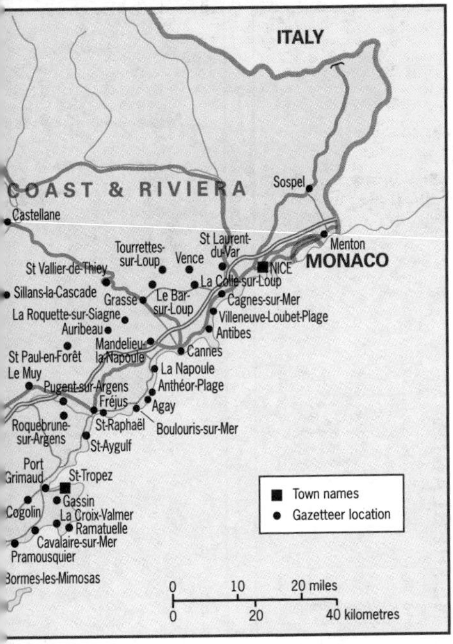
ITALY
COAST & RIVIERA
Sospel
Castellane
St Laurent-du-Var
Menton
Tourrettes-sur-Loup
Vence
NICE
MONACO
St Vallier-de-Thiey
La Colle-sur-Loup
Sillans-la-Cascade
Grasse
Le Bar-sur-Loup
Cagnes-sur-Mer
La Roquette-sur-Siagne
Villeneuve-Loubet-Plage
Auribeau
Antibes
Mandelieu-la-Napoule
Cannes
St Paul-en-Forêt
La Napoule
Le Muy
Anthéor-Plage
Pugent-sur-Argens
Fréjus
Agay
Roquebrune-sur-Argens
St-Raphaël
Boulouris-sur-Mer
St-Aygulf
Port Grimaud
St-Tropez
Gassin
Cogolin
La Croix-Valmer
Ramatuelle
Cavalaire-sur-Mer
Pramousquier
Bormes-les-Mimosas
Town names
Gazetteer location
0 10 20 miles
0 20 40 kilometres

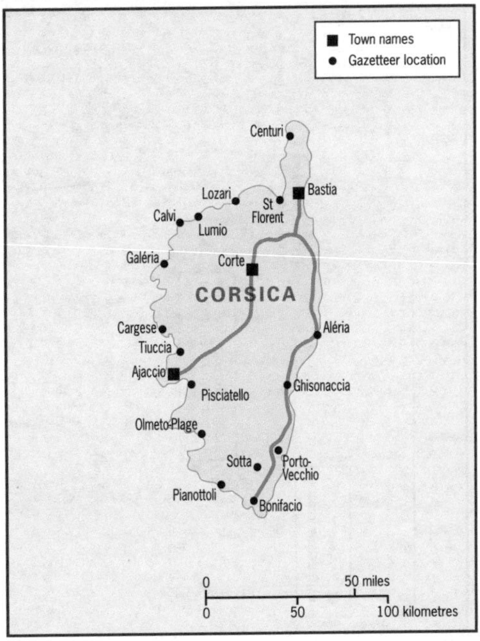
Town names
Gazetteer location
Centuri
Lozari
St Florent
Bastia
Calvi
Lumio
Galéria
Corte
CORSICA
Cargese
Aléria
Tiuccia
Ajaccio
Ghisonaccia
Pisciatello
Olmeto-Plage
Sotta
Porto-Vecchio
Pianottoli
Bonifacio
0 50 miles
0 50 100 kilometres

GERMANY

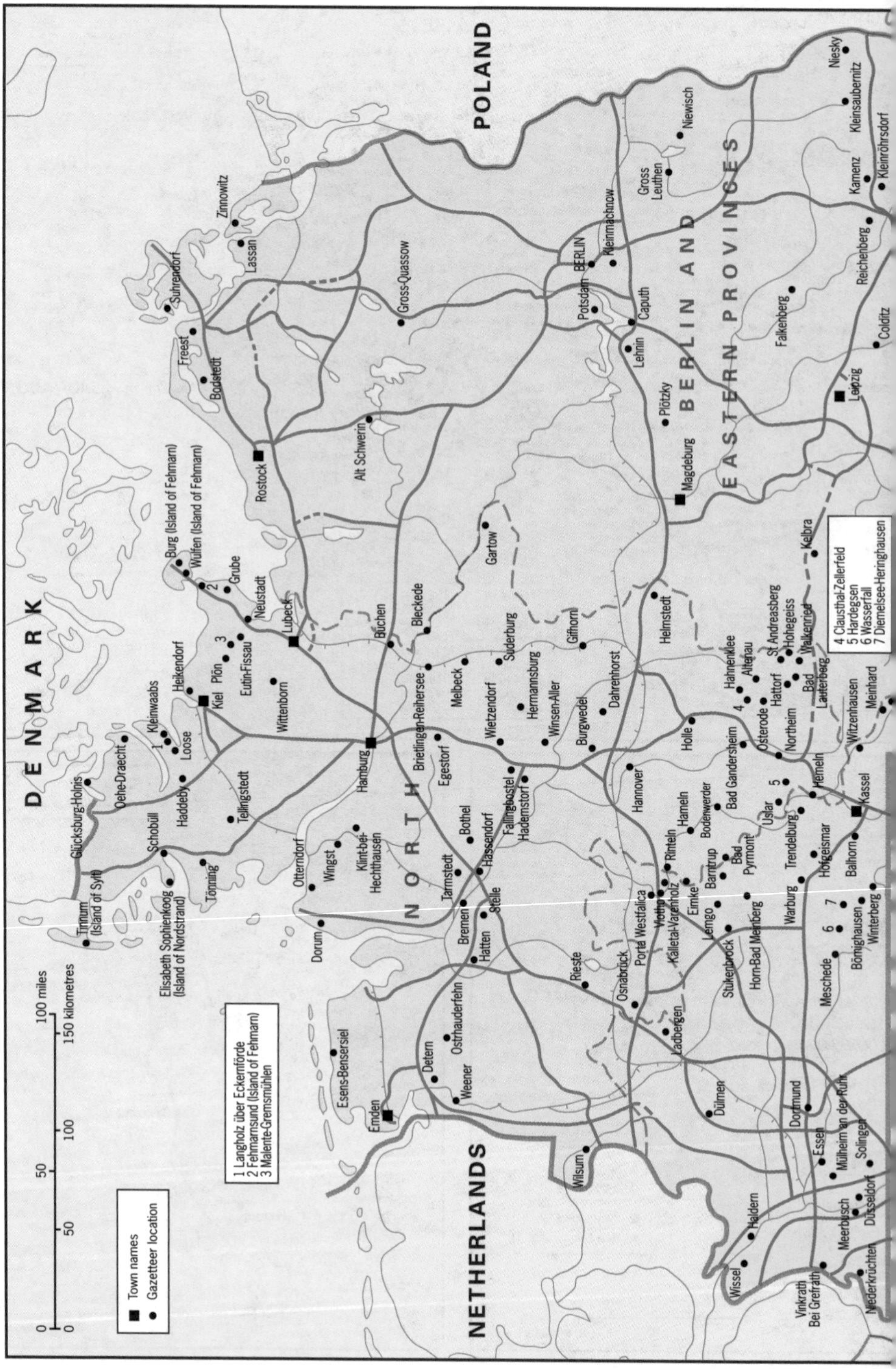
DENMARK
POLAND
NETHERLANDS
NORTH
BERLIN AND
EASTERN PROVINCES
Town names
Gazetteer location
0
50
100 miles
0
50
100
150 kilometres
1 Langholz über Eckernförde
2 Fehmarnsund (Island of Fehmarn)
3 Malente-Gremsmühlen
4 Clausthal-Zellerfeld
5 Hardegsen
6 Wasserfall
7 Diemelsee-Heringhausen
Tinnum (Island of Sylt)
Glücksburg-Holnis
Oehe-Draecht
Kleinwaabs
Loose
Schobüll
Elisabeth Sophienkoog (Island of Nordstrand)
Tönning
Haddeby
Tellingstedt
Heikendorf
Kiel
Plön
Eutin-Fissau
Wittenborn
Burg (Island of Fehmarn)
Wulfen (Island of Fehmarn)
Grube
Neustadt
Lübeck
Rostock
Bodstedt
Freest
Suhrendorf
Lassan
Zinnowitz
Alt Schwerin
Gross-Quassow
Otterndorf
Dorum
Wingst
Klint-bei-Hechthausen
Hamburg
Büchen
Bleckede
Brietlingen-Reiherseee
Egestorf
Melbeck
Wietzendorf
Suderburg
Hermannsburg
Gartow
Gifhorn
Dahrenhorst
Winsen-Aller
Burgwedel
Fallingbostel
Hademstorf
Bothel
Hassendorf
Tarmstedt
Bremen
Stelle
Hatten
Esens-Bensersiel
Emden
Detern
Ostrhauderfehn
Weener
Rieste
Osnabrück
Porta Westfalica
Vlotho
Kalletal-Varenholz
Rinteln
Hameln
Bodenwerder
Eimke
Barntrup
Bad Pyrmont
Lemgo
Stukenbrock
Horn-Bad Meinberg
Hannover
Holle
Bad Gandersheim
Uslar
Osterode
Hattorf
Northeim
Hahnenklee
Altenau
St Andreasberg
Hohegeiss
Walkenried
Bad Lauterberg
Hemeln
Witzenhausen
Kassel
Trendelburg
Hofgeismar
Warburg
Balhorn
Winterberg
Bömighausen
Meschede
Ladbergen
Wilsum
Dülmen
Dortmund
Essen
Mülheim an der Ruhr
Solingen
Düsseldorf
Meerbusch
Haldern
Wissel
Vinkrath Bei Grefrath
Niederkrüchten
Helmstedt
Magdeburg
Plötzky
Lehnin
Caputh
Potsdam
BERLIN
Kleinmachnow
Gross Leuthen
Niewisch
Kelbra
Leipzig
Falkenberg
Colditz
Reichenberg
Kamenz
Kleinröhrsdorf
Kleinsaubernitz
Niesky
Meinhard

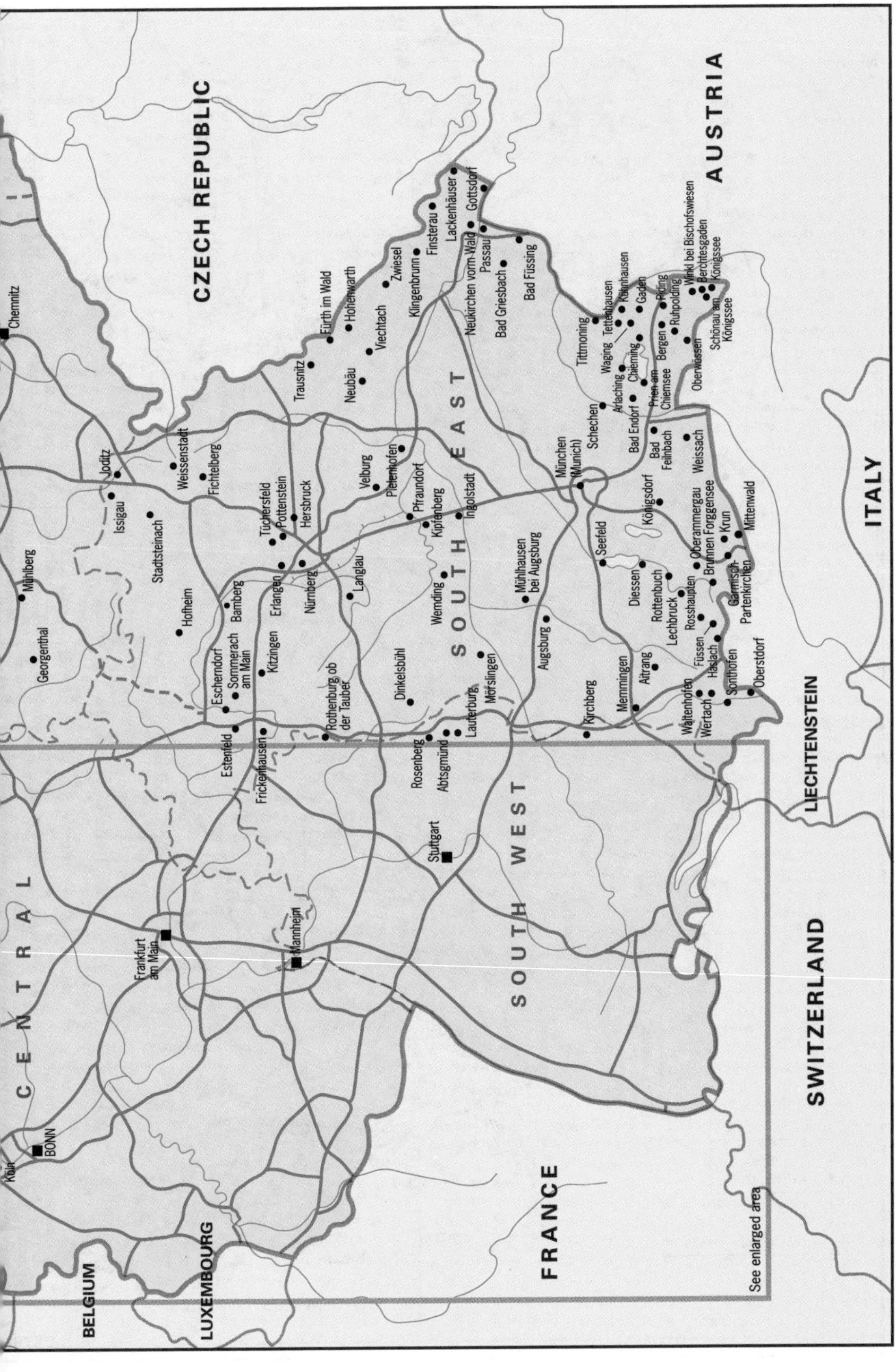
CZECH REPUBLIC
AUSTRIA
ITALY
LIECHTENSTEIN
SWITZERLAND
FRANCE
LUXEMBOURG
BELGIUM
CENTRAL
SOUTH EAST
SOUTH WEST
Chemnitz
Mühlberg
Georgenthal
Köln
BONN
Frankfurt am Main
Mannheim
Stuttgart
Joditz
Issigau
Stadtsteinach
Weissenstadt
Fichtelberg
Hofheim
Bamberg
Escherndorf
Sommerach am Main
Kitzingen
Estenfeld
Frickenhausen
Tüchersfeld
Pottenstein
Hersbruck
Erlangen
Nürnberg
Langlau
Rothenburg ob der Tauber
Dinkelsbühl
Rosenberg
Abtsgmünd
Lauterburg
Mörslingen
Wemding
Kipfenberg
Pfraundorf
Ingolstadt
Velburg
Pielenhofen
Trausnitz
Neubäu
Fürth im Wald
Hohenwarth
Viechtach
Zwiesel
Klingenbrunn
Finsterau
Lackenhäuser
Gottsdorf
Neukirchen vorm Wald
Passau
Bad Griesbach
Bad Füssing
München (Munich)
Mühlhausen bei Augsburg
Augsburg
Kirchberg
Memmingen
Aitrang
Seefeld
Diessen
Rottenbuch
Lechbruck
Rosshaupten
Füssen
Haslach
Waltenhofen
Wertach
Sonthofen
Oberstdorf
Königsdorf
Oberammergau
Brunnen Forggensee
Krun
Mittenwald
Garmisch-Partenkirchen
Bad Feilnbach
Weissach
Schechen
Bad Endorf
Arlaching
Prien am Chiemsee
Chieming
Waging
Tittmoning
Tettenhausen
Kühnhausen
Gaden
Bergen
Ruhpolding
Piding
Oberwössen
Winkl bei Bischofswiesen
Berchtesgaden
Königssee
Schönau am Königssee
See enlarged area

GERMANY

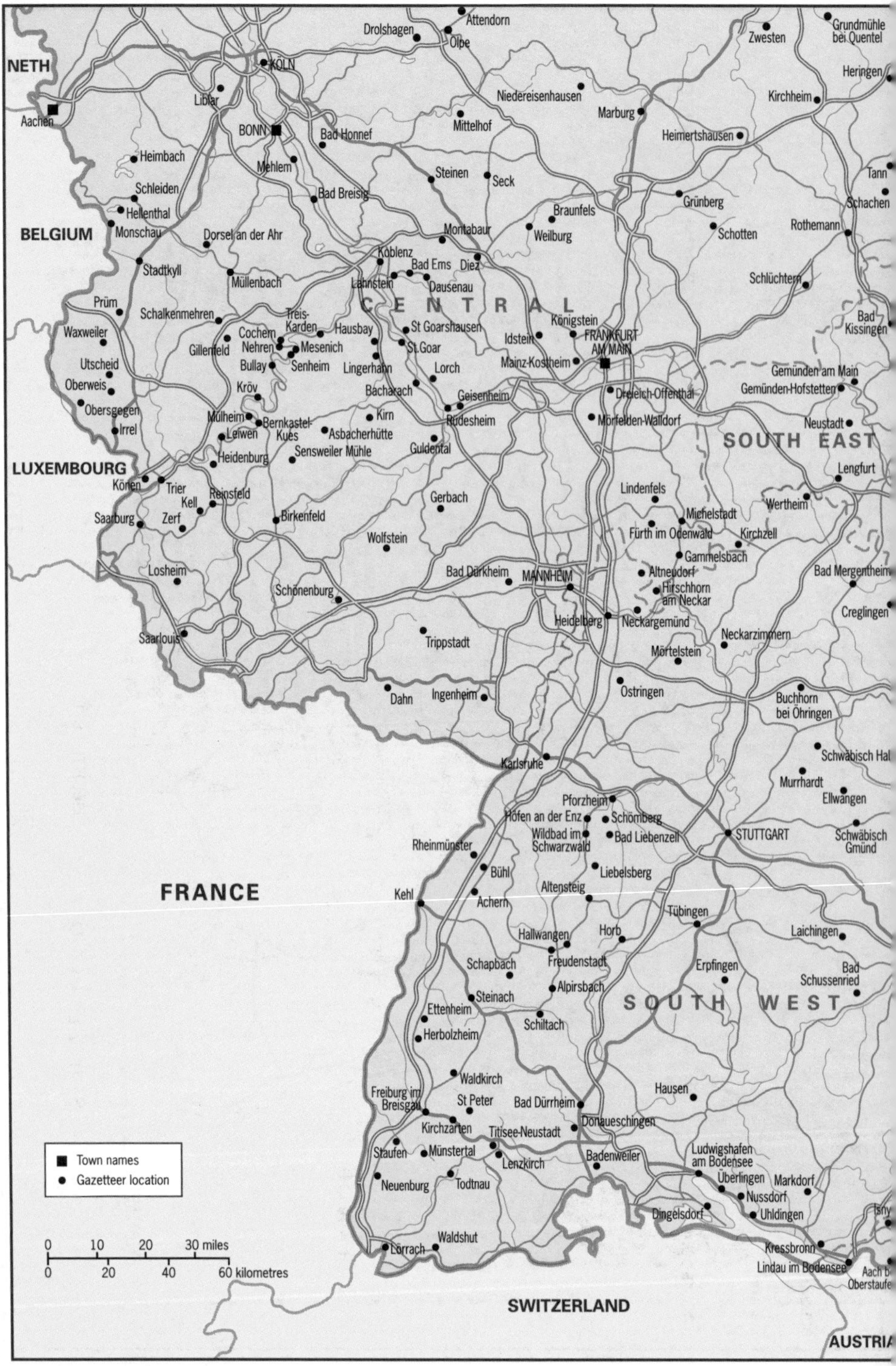

NETH
BELGIUM
LUXEMBOURG
FRANCE
SWITZERLAND
AUSTRI
CENTRAL
SOUTH EAST
SOUTH WEST
Attendorn
Drolshagen
Olpe
KÖLN
Liblar
Aachen
BONN
Bad Honnef
Mittelhof
Niedereisenhausen
Marburg
Zwesten
Grundmühle bei Quentel
Heringen
Kirchheim
Heimertshausen
Tann
Schachen
Rothemann
Heimbach
Mehlem
Steinen
Seck
Schleiden
Bad Breisig
Grünberg
Hellenthal
Braunfels
Schotten
Monschau
Dorsel an der Ahr
Montabaur
Weilburg
Stadtkyll
Koblenz
Bad Ems
Diez
Müllenbach
Lahnstein
Dausenau
Schlüchtern
Prüm
Schalkenmehren
Treis-Karden
Hausbay
St Goarshausen
Königstein
Idstein
FRANKFURT AM MAIN
Bad Kissingen
Waxweiler
Cochem
Gillenfeld
Nehren
Mesenich
St.Goar
Utscheid
Bullay
Senheim
Lingerhahn
Lorch
Mainz-Kostheim
Gemünden am Main
Oberweis
Kröv
Bacharach
Gemünden-Hofstetten
Obersgegen
Geisenheim
Dreieich-Offenthal
Irrel
Mülheim
Bernkastel-Kues
Kirn
Rüdesheim
Mörfelden-Walldorf
Neustadt
Leiwen
Asbacherhütte
Heidenburg
Sensweiler Mühle
Guldental
Lengfurt
Könen
Trier
Reinsfeld
Kell
Lindenfels
Gerbach
Wertheim
Michelstadt
Saarburg
Zerf
Birkenfeld
Fürth im Odenwald
Kirchzell
Wolfstein
Gammelsbach
Losheim
Bad Dürkheim
MANNHEIM
Altneudorf
Bad Mergentheim
Schönenburg
Hirschhorn am Neckar
Creglingen
Heidelberg
Neckargemünd
Saarlouis
Trippstadt
Neckarzimmern
Mörtelstein
Ostringen
Dahn
Ingenheim
Buchhorn bei Öhringen
Karlsruhe
Schwäbisch Hal
Murrhardt
Ellwangen
Pforzheim
Höfen an der Enz
Schömberg
Wildbad im Schwarzwald
Bad Liebenzell
STUTTGART
Schwäbisch Gmünd
Rheinmünster
Bühl
Liebelsberg
Kehl
Achern
Altensteig
Tübingen
Laichingen
Hallwangen
Horb
Freudenstadt
Schapbach
Erpfingen
Bad Schussenried
Alpirsbach
Steinach
Ettenheim
Schiltach
Herbolzheim
Waldkirch
Hausen
Freiburg im Breisgau
St Peter
Bad Dürrheim
Kirchzarten
Titisee-Neustadt
Donaueschingen
Staufen
Münstertal
Lenzkirch
Badenweiler
Ludwigshafen am Bodensee
Überlingen
Markdorf
Neuenburg
Todtnau
Nussdorf
Dingelsdorf
Uhldingen
Isny
Waldshut
Lörrach
Kressbronn
Lindau im Bodensee
Aach b Oberstaufe
Town names
Gazetteer location
0
10
20
30 miles
0
20
40
60 kilometres

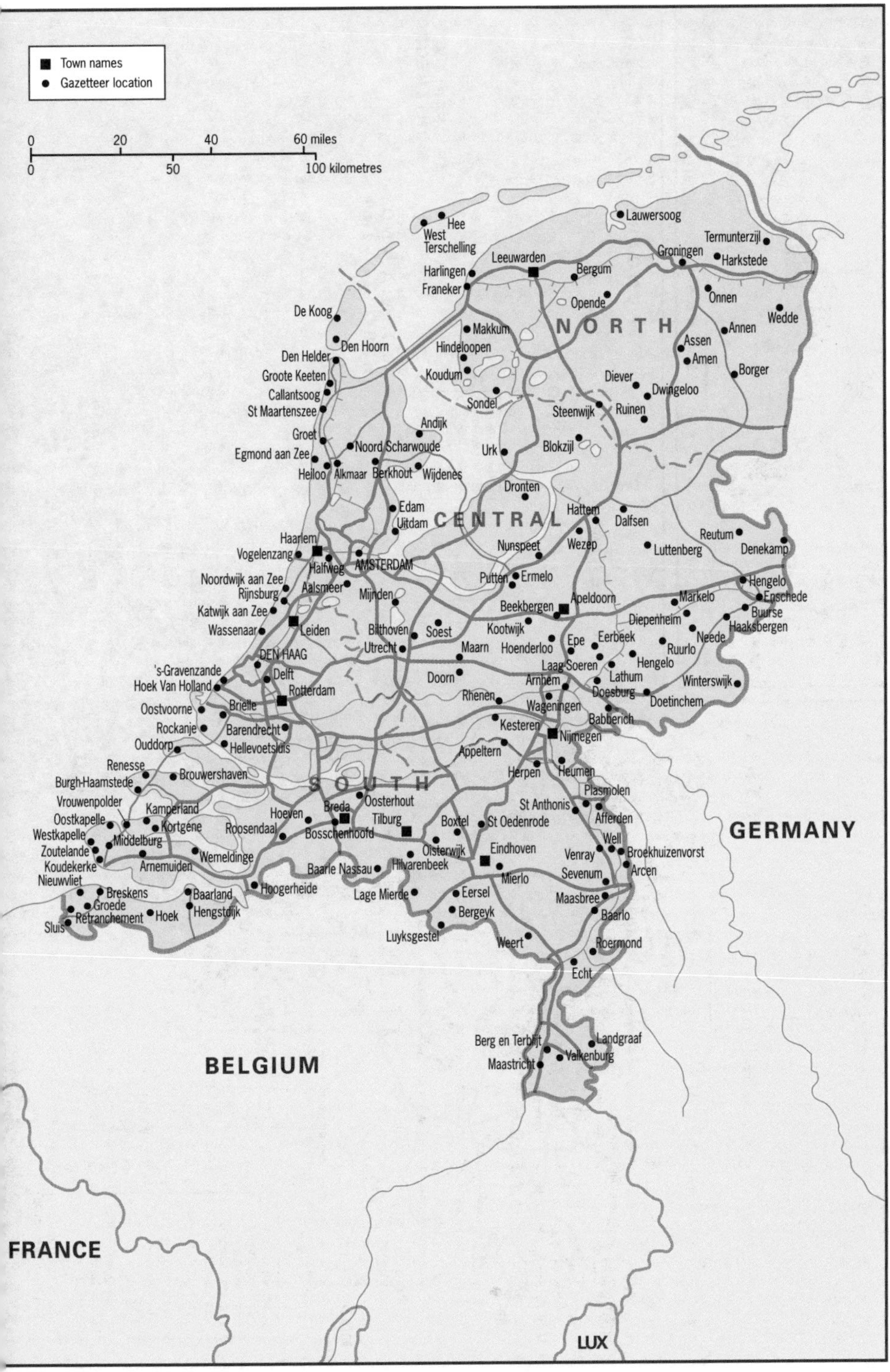
Town names
Gazetteer location
0
20
40
60 miles
0
50
100 kilometres
NORTH
CENTRAL
SOUTH
GERMANY
BELGIUM
FRANCE
LUX
Hee
West Terschelling
Lauwersoog
Termunterzijl
Groningen
Harkstede
Leeuwarden
Bergum
Harlingen
Franeker
Opende
Onnen
Wedde
De Koog
Makkum
Annen
Den Hoorn
Assen
Den Helder
Hindeloopen
Amen
Groote Keeten
Koudum
Diever
Borger
Callantsoog
Dwingeloo
Sondel
St Maartenszee
Steenwijk
Ruinen
Andijk
Groet
Noord Scharwoude
Urk
Blokzijl
Egmond aan Zee
Heiloo
Alkmaar
Berkhout
Wijdenes
Dronten
Edam
Hattem
Dalfsen
Uitdam
Reutum
Haarlem
Nunspeet
Wezep
Luttenberg
Denekamp
Vogelenzang
Halfweg
AMSTERDAM
Noordwijk aan Zee
Putten
Ermelo
Hengelo
Rijnsburg
Aalsmeer
Mijnden
Markelo
Enschede
Katwijk aan Zee
Beekbergen
Apeldoorn
Buurse
Leiden
Bilthoven
Kootwijk
Diepenheim
Haaksbergen
Wassenaar
Soest
Neede
DEN HAAG
Utrecht
Maarn
Hoenderloo
Epe
Eerbeek
Ruurlo
Delft
Hengelo
's-Gravenzande
Laag-Soeren
Hoek Van Holland
Doorn
Arnhem
Lathum
Winterswijk
Rotterdam
Rhenen
Doesburg
Doetinchem
Oostvoorne
Brielle
Wageningen
Babberich
Rockanje
Barendrecht
Kesteren
Nijmegen
Ouddorp
Hellevoetsluis
Appeltern
Renesse
Herpen
Heumen
Burgh-Haamstede
Brouwershaven
Plasmolen
Vrouwenpolder
Oosterhout
St Anthonis
Kamperland
Breda
Afferden
Oostkapelle
Hoeven
Tilburg
Boxtel
St Oedenrode
Westkapelle
Kortgene
Roosendaal
Bosschenhoofd
Well
Zoutelande
Middelburg
Oisterwijk
Eindhoven
Venray
Broekhuizenvorst
Koudekerke
Wemeldinge
Arnemuiden
Baarle Nassau
Hilvarenbeek
Arcen
Nieuwvliet
Mierlo
Sevenum
Hoogerheide
Breskens
Baarland
Lage Mierde
Eersel
Maasbree
Groede
Hengstdijk
Bergeyk
Baarlo
Retranchement
Hoek
Sluis
Luyksgestel
Weert
Roermond
Echt
Berg en Terblijt
Landgraaf
Valkenburg
Maastricht

ITALY

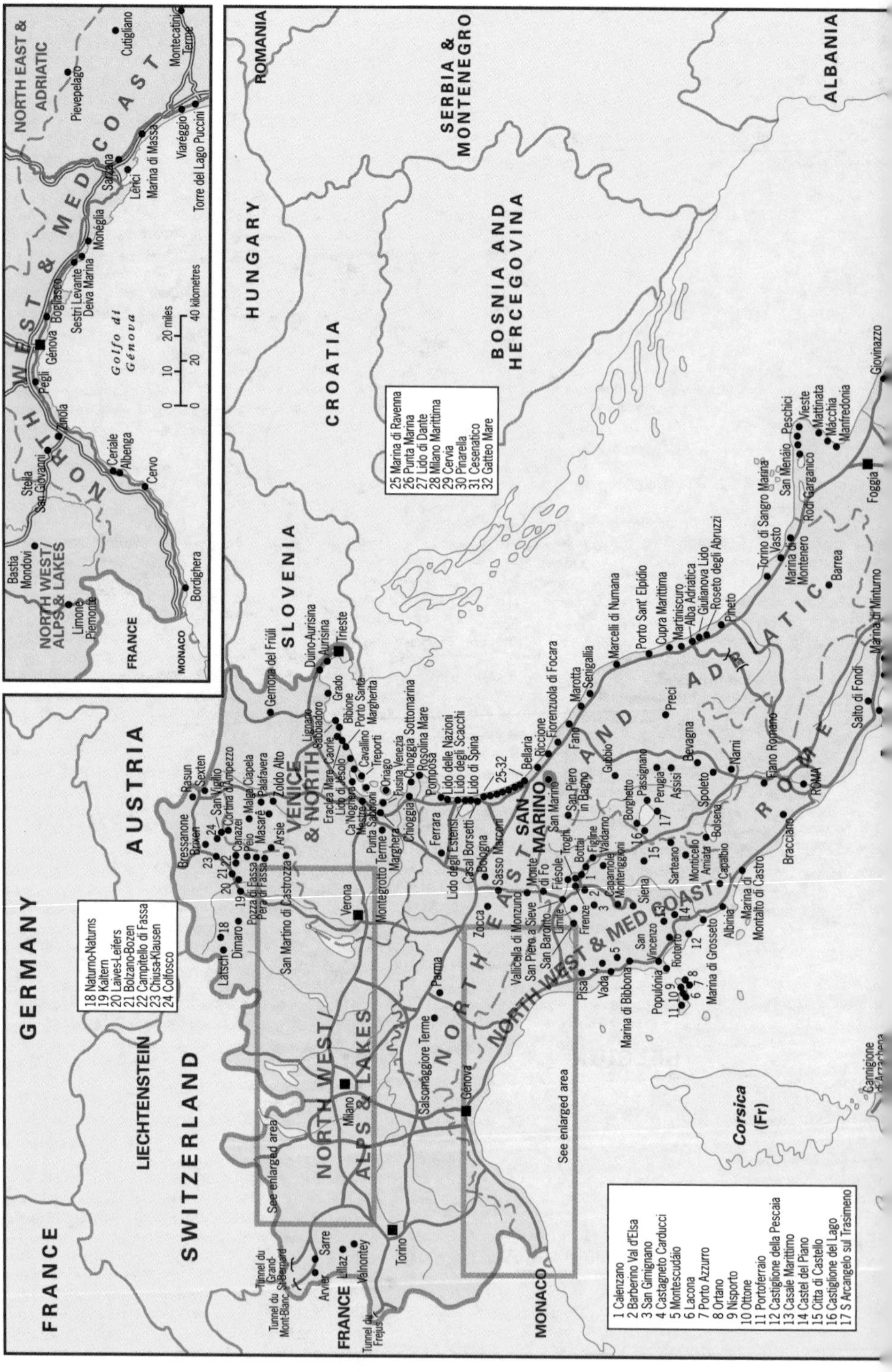

NORTH EAST & ADRIATIC
NORTH WEST & MED COAST
NORTH WEST/ ALPS & LAKES
FRANCE
MONACO
Golfo di Génova
0 10 20 miles
0 20 40 kilometres
Génova
Pegli
Zinola
Bogliasco
Sestri Levante
Deiva Marina
Monéglia
Sarzana
Lerici
Marina di Massa
Viaréggio
Torre del Lago Puccini
Montecatini Terme
Cutigliano
Pievepelago
Stella San Giovanni
Ceriale
Albenga
Cervo
Bordighera
Bastia Mondovì
Limone Piemonte
GERMANY
AUSTRIA
LIECHTENSTEIN
SWITZERLAND
FRANCE
SLOVENIA
HUNGARY
CROATIA
ROMANIA
SERBIA & MONTENEGRO
BOSNIA AND HERCEGOVINA
ALBANIA
Corsica (Fr)
See enlarged area
VENICE & NORTH
NORTH WEST/ ALPS & LAKES
NORTH EAST
NORTH WEST & MED COAST
SAN MARINO
AND ADRIATIC
ROME
ROMA
Milano
Torino
Génova
Verona
Trieste
Foggia
18 Naturno-Naturns
19 Kaltern
20 Laives-Leifers
21 Bolzano-Bozen
22 Campitello di Fassa
23 Chiusa-Klausen
24 Colfosco
25 Marina di Ravenna
26 Punta Marina
27 Lido di Dante
28 Milano Marittima
29 Cervia
30 Pinarella
31 Cesenatico
32 Gatteo Mare
1 Calenzano
2 Barberino Val d'Elsa
3 San Gimignano
4 Castagneto Carducci
5 Montescudáio
6 Lacona
7 Porto Azzurro
8 Ortano
9 Nisporto
10 Ottone
11 Portoferraio
12 Castiglione della Pescaia
13 Casale Marittimo
14 Castel del Piano
15 Città di Castello
16 Castiglione del Lago
17 S Arcangelo sul Trasimeno

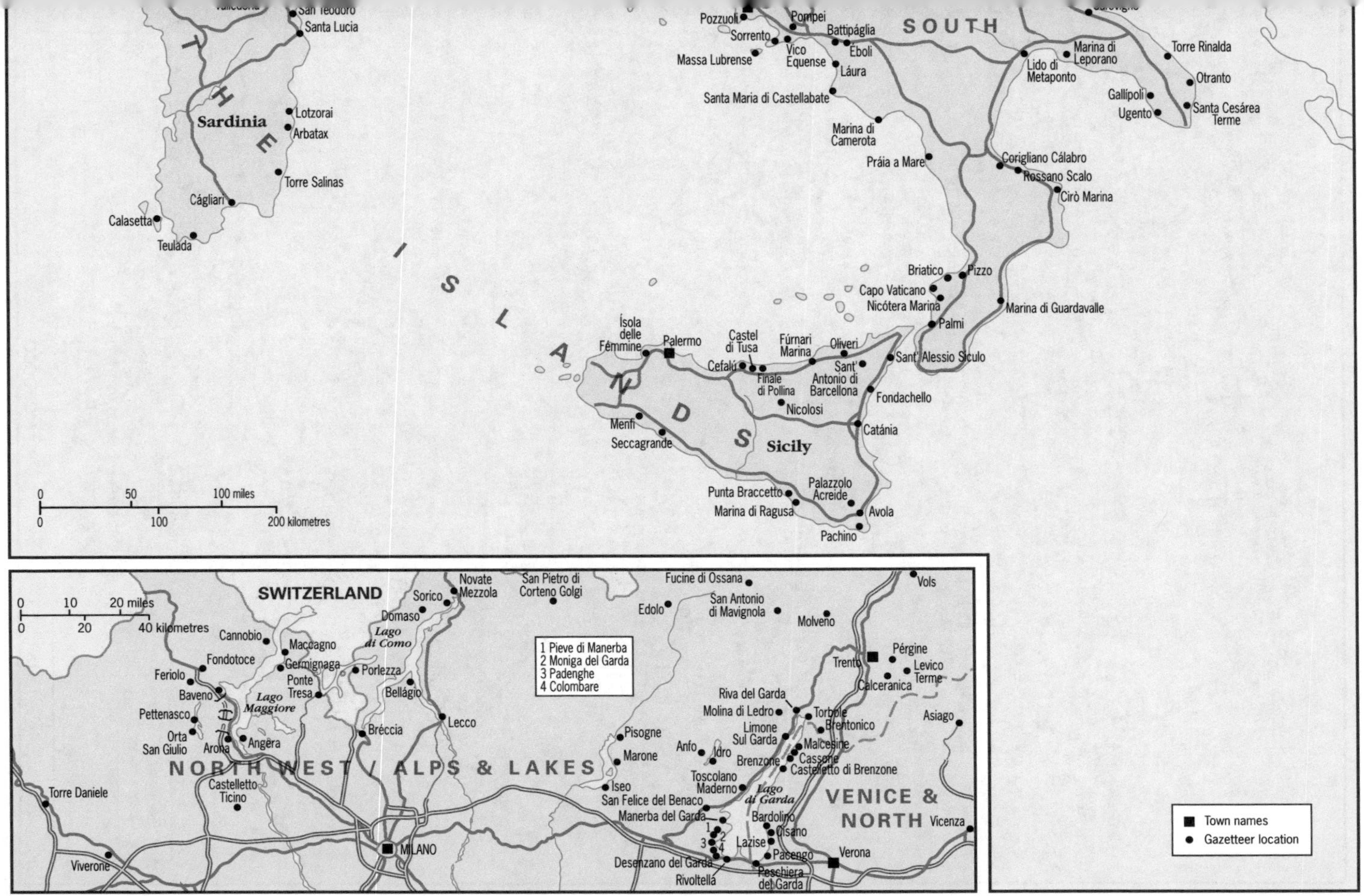
SOUTH
THE ISLANDS
Sardinia
Santa Lucia
Lotzorai
Arbatax
Torre Salinas
Cágliari
Calasetta
Teulada
Pozzuoli
Pompei
Sorrento
Massa Lubrense
Vico Equense
Battipáglia
Eboli
Láura
Santa Maria di Castellabate
Marina di Camerota
Práia a Mare
Lido di Metaponto
Marina di Leporano
Torre Rinalda
Otranto
Gallípoli
Ugento
Santa Cesárea Terme
Corigliano Cálabro
Rossano Scalo
Cirò Marina
Briatico
Pizzo
Capo Vaticano
Nicótera Marina
Palmi
Marina di Guardavalle
Sant' Alessio Siculo
Ísola delle Fémmine
Palermo
Castel di Tusa
Cefalù
Finale di Pollina
Fúrnari Marina
Oliveri
Sant' Antonio di Barcellona
Fondachello
Nicolosi
Catánia
Menfi
Seccagrande
Sicily
Punta Braccetto
Marina di Ragusa
Palazzolo Acreide
Avola
Pachino
0 50 100 miles
0 100 200 kilometres
SWITZERLAND
0 10 20 miles
0 20 40 kilometres
Cannobio
Maccagno
Germignaga
Fondotoce
Feriolo
Baveno
Pettenasco
Orta San Giulio
Arona
Angera
Lago Maggiore
Ponte Tresa
Porlezza
Lago di Como
Domaso
Sorico
Novate Mezzola
Bellágio
Bréccia
Lecco
San Pietro di Corteno Golgi
1 Pieve di Manerba
2 Moniga del Garda
3 Padenghe
4 Colombare
Fucine di Ossana
San Antonio di Mavignola
Edolo
Molveno
Vols
Pérgine
Trento
Levico Terme
Calceranica
Riva del Garda
Molina di Ledro
Torbole
Brentonico
Asiago
Limone Sul Garda
Malcesine
Cassone
Castelletto di Brenzone
Anfo
Idro
Brenzone
Pisogne
Marone
Iseo
Toscolano Maderno
Lago di Garda
San Felice del Benaco
Manerba del Garda
Bardolino
Cisano
Lazise
Pacengo
Desenzano del Garda
Rivoltella
Peschiera del Garda
Verona
Vicenza
VENICE & NORTH
NORTH WEST / ALPS & LAKES
Castelletto Ticino
Torre Daniele
Viverone
MILANO
Town names
Gazetteer location

SPAIN AND PORTUGAL

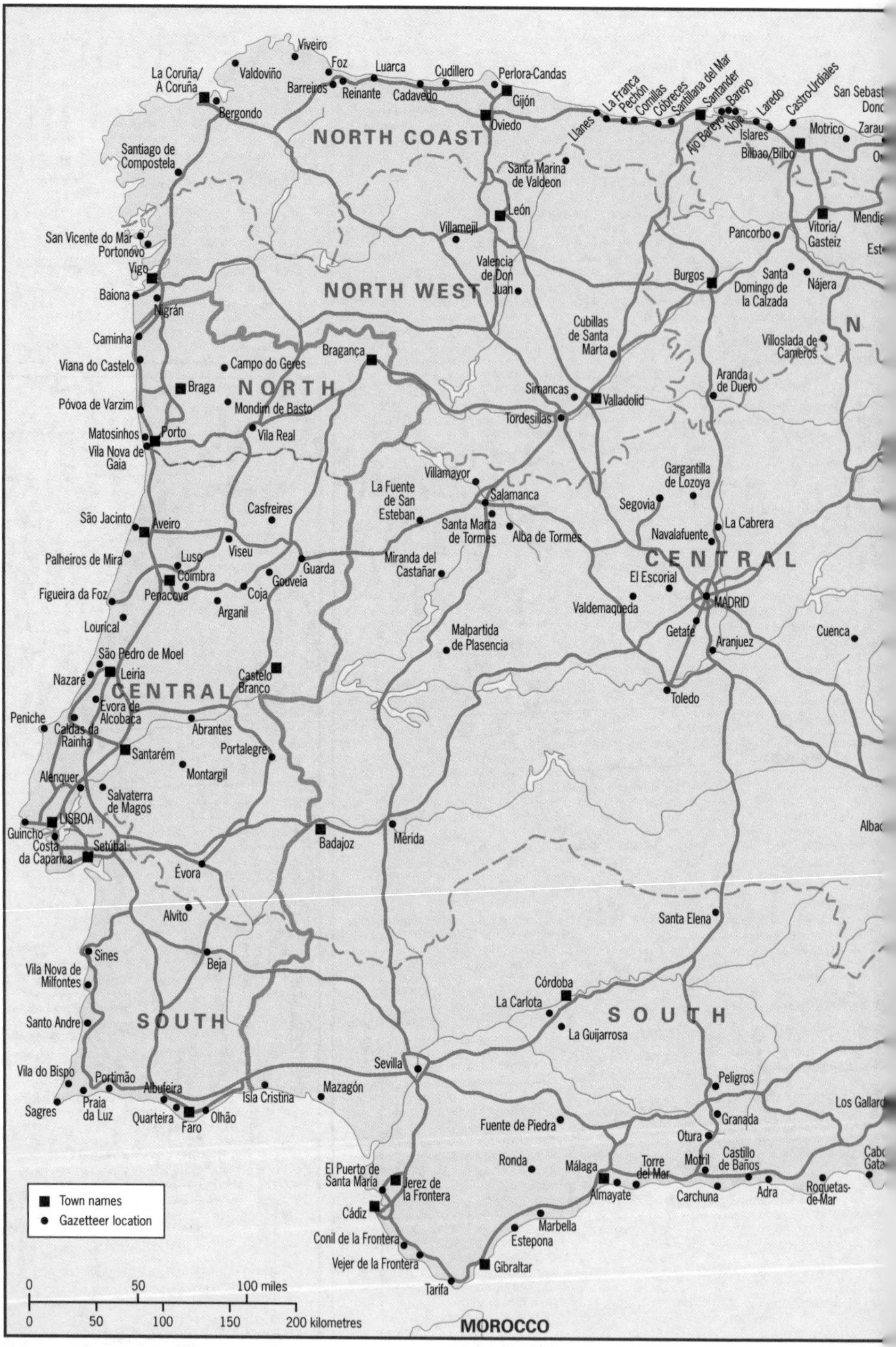

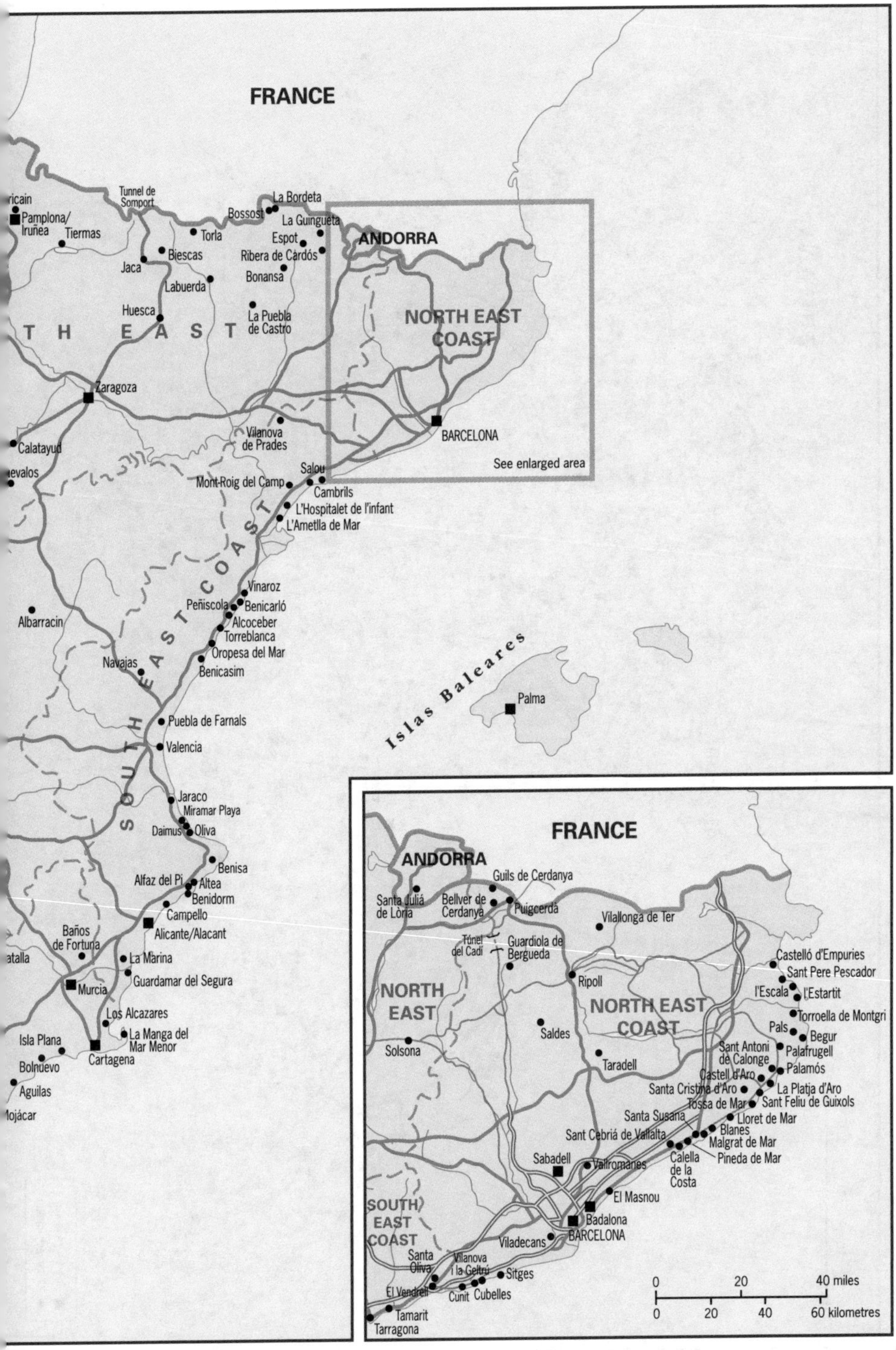

FRANCE
ricain
Pamplona/ Iruñea
Tiermas
Tunnel de Somport
Torla
Biescas
Jaca
Labuerda
Huesca
La Bordeta
Bossost
La Guingueta
Espot
Ribera de Cardós
Bonansa
La Puebla de Castro
ANDORRA
NORTH EAST COAST
T H E A S T
Zaragoza
Calatayud
evalos
Vilanova de Prades
BARCELONA
See enlarged area
Salou
Mont-Roig del Camp
Cambrils
L'Hospitalet de l'infant
L'Ametlla de Mar
Vinaroz
Peñiscola
Benicarló
Alcoceber
Torreblanca
Oropesa del Mar
Benicasim
Albarracin
Navajas
SOUTH EAST COAST
Islas Baleares
Palma
Puebla de Farnals
Valencia
Jaraco
Miramar Playa
Daimus
Oliva
Benisa
Alfaz del Pi
Altea
Benidorm
Campello
Alicante/Alacant
Baños de Fortuna
atalla
La Marina
Murcia
Guardamar del Segura
Los Alcazares
La Manga del Mar Menor
Isla Plana
Cartagena
Bolnuevo
Aguilas
ojácar
FRANCE
ANDORRA
Guils de Cerdanya
Santa Julià de Lòria
Bellver de Cerdanya
Puigcerdà
Vilallonga de Ter
Túnel del Cadí
Guardiola de Bergueda
Castelló d'Empuries
Sant Pere Pescador
Ripoll
l'Escala
l'Estartit
NORTH EAST
NORTH EAST COAST
Torroella de Montgri
Pals
Begur
Saldes
Solsona
Sant Antoni de Calonge
Palafrugell
Taradell
Palamós
Castell d'Aro
Santa Cristina d'Aro
La Platja d'Aro
Tossa de Mar
Sant Feliu de Guixols
Santa Susana
Lloret de Mar
Sant Cebriá de Vallalta
Blanes
Malgrat de Mar
Calella de la Costa
Pineda de Mar
Sabadell
Vallromanes
El Masnou
SOUTH EAST COAST
Badalona
BARCELONA
Viladecans
Santa Oliva
Vilanova i la Geltrú
Sitges
El Vendrell
Cunit
Cubelles
Tamarit
Tarragona
0 20 40 miles
0 20 40 60 kilometres

SWITZERLAND

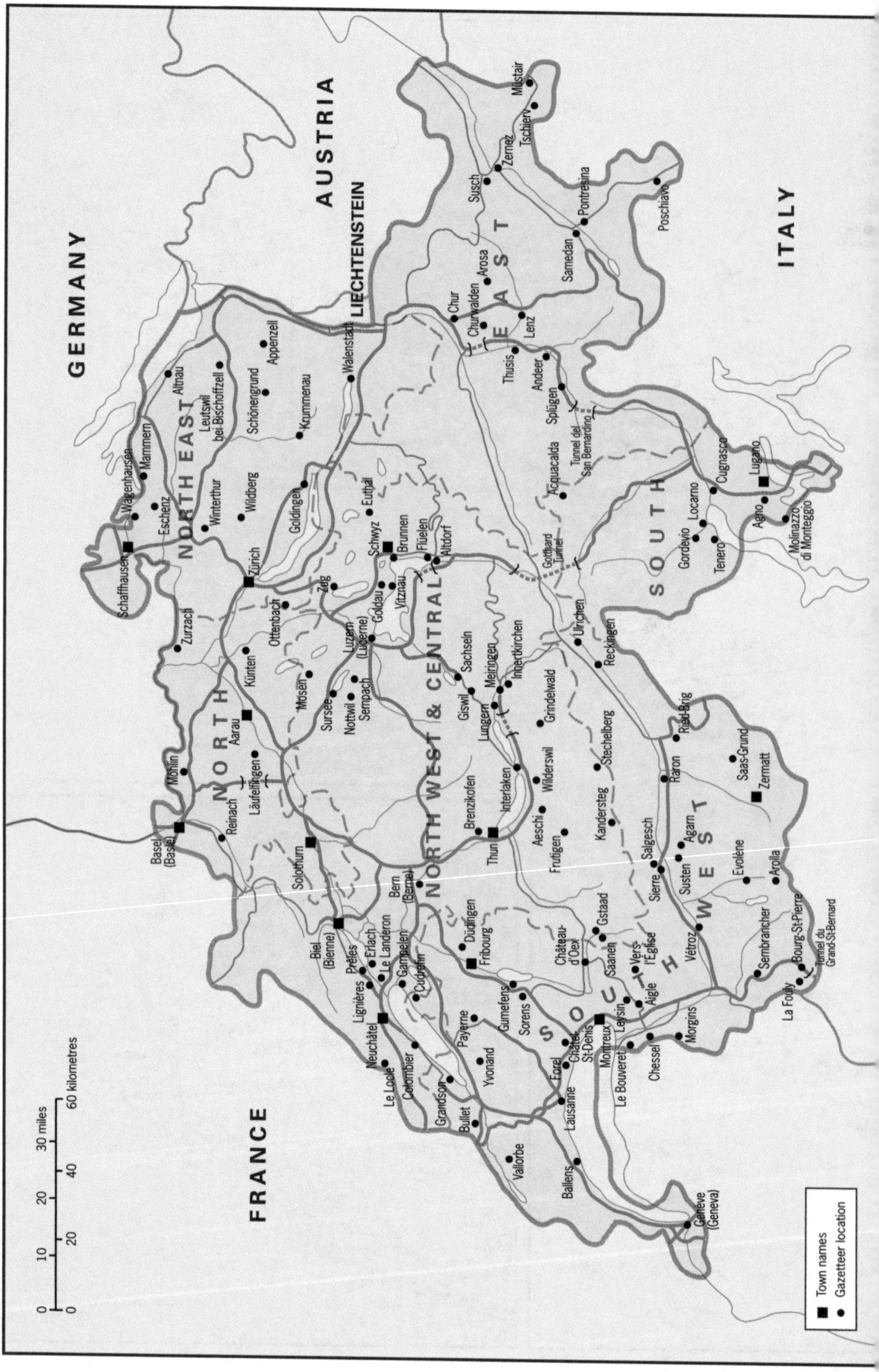

Reader's Report Form

Please send this form to:
Editor, Caravan & Camping Europe
AA Lifestyle Guides,
Fanum House,
Basingstoke RG21 4EA

or fax 01256 491647
or email lifestyleguides@theAA.com

Please use this form to recommend any caravan and camping park where you have stayed, whether it is included in the guide or not. You can also help us to improve the guide by completing the short questionnaire on the reverse.

The AA does not undertake to arbitrate between guide readers and campsites, or to obtain compensation or engage in correspondence.

Date:

Your name (block capitals)

Your address (block capitals)

....

....

....

....

email address:

Name of park:

Comments

....

....

....

....

....

....

....

(please attach a separate sheet if necessary)

Please tick here if you DO NOT wish to receive details of AA offers or products ☐

PTO

How often do you visit a caravan park or camp site?

Once a year ☐ Twice a year ☐ 3 times a year ☐ More than 3 times ☐

How long do you generally stay at a park or site?

1 night ☐ Up to 1 week ☐ 1 week ☐ 2 weeks ☐ Over 2 weeks ☐

Do you have a: tent ☐ caravan ☐ motorhome ☐

Which of the following is most important when choosing a site?

☐ Location
☐ Toilet/Washing facilities
☐ Personal Recommendation
☐ Leisure facilities
☐ Other

Do you prefer self-contained, cubicled washrooms with WC, shower and washhand basin to open-plan separate facilities?

Yes ☐ No ☐ Don't Mind ☐

Do you buy any other camping guides? If so, which ones?

....

Have you read the introductory pages and features in this guide? ....

Do you use the location atlas in this guide? ....

Which of the following most influences your choice of park from this guide?

Gazetteer entry information and description ☐

Photograph ☐ Advertisement ☐

Do you have any suggestions to improve the guide?

....

....

....

....

....

Thank you for completing this form